MW00573388

J.C. BOOKS

SELECTED WORKS OF JOSEPH E. STIGLITZ

SELECTED WORKS OF JOSEPH E. STIGLITZ

VOLUME I:
INFORMATION AND ECONOMIC ANALYSIS

JOSEPH E. STIGLITZ

OXFORD
UNIVERSITY PRESS

OXFORD
UNIVERSITY PRESS

Great Clarendon Street, Oxford ox2 6DP

Oxford University Press is a department of the University of Oxford.
It furthers the University's objective of excellence in research, scholarship,
and education by publishing worldwide in

Oxford New York

Auckland Cape Town Dar es Salaam Hong Kong Karachi
Kuala Lumpur Madrid Melbourne Mexico City Nairobi
New Delhi Shanghai Taipei Toronto

With offices in

Argentina Austria Brazil Chile Czech Republic France Greece
Guatemala Hungary Italy Japan Poland Portugal Singapore
South Korea Switzerland Thailand Turkey Ukraine Vietnam

Oxford is a registered trade mark of Oxford University Press
in the UK and in certain other countries

Published in the United States
by Oxford University Press Inc., New York

First published 2009

British Library Cataloguing in Publication Data

Data available

Library of Congress Cataloging in Publication Data

Data available

Typeset by SPI Publisher Services, Pondicherry, India
Printed in Great Britain
on acid-free paper by
Antony Rowe

ISBN 978–0–19–953370–1

1 3 5 7 9 10 8 6 4 2

CONTENTS

PART V. WELFARE ECONOMICS OF INFORMATION

PART VI. INFORMATION AND MACRO ECONOMICS

Preface to *The Selected Works of Joseph E. Stiglitz*

These six volumes bring together my major scientific papers in economics, written over the past almost 40 years. While these papers have spanned a wide range of topics and fields, there is a unifying theme behind a large proportion: the standard economic model (the neoclassical model, based on rational, fully informed households maximizing their utility and rational, fully informed firms maximizing their market value interacting in perfectly competitive markets) is badly flawed, so badly flawed as to provide little understanding of what actually happens in a market economy and little guidance about what policies will increase economic efficiency and societal well being.

A large fraction of the papers focus on a particular assumption—that of perfect information, or more precisely, on the assumptions that (a) all individuals have the same information; and (b) nothing that occurs within the economy has any effect on the information (beliefs) of market participants. Of course, no economist could seriously believe in either assumption; but they had been at the center of economic analyses for more than 200 years, taken so much for granted that they were not typically even noted as assumptions.[1] It was not that economists were so foolish as to believe that these assumptions provided an accurate description of the world; but rather, they did not have the tools with which they could analyze a market economy with imperfect information—or at least not analyze it with any mathematical rigor. So they formulated precise models with perfect information—and they then made a leap of faith, that a world in which information was not too imperfect would look not too different from the world of perfect information. The papers presented here show that that faith was misplaced—even a little bit of imperfect information can have large consequences. Indeed, none of the most basic propositions of economics proved robust.

There were other assumptions in the neoclassical framework that I call into question in the papers collected here: the existence of a complete set of markets (such that individuals could buy insurance, for instance, against any risk), perfect capital markets (such that any individual could borrow as much as s/he wanted at the risk-adjusted market rate of interest), perfect competition (such that all firms faced a horizontal demand curve for their products), and a fixed technology (just as nothing the firm did affected information, so firms could not invest in research that would affect technology) were all assumptions of the standard Walrasian model. (The failure

---

[1] For instance, in Gerard Debreu's classic formulation of the competitive equilibrium model, he listed ten assumptions. The information assumptions were not on the list (Debreu 1959).

of many of these assumptions can, in turn, be related to the failure of the underlying assumption about perfect information.)[2] Again, it was not that any economist really believed these assumptions; many advocates of the market even praised the capitalist system for its innovativeness; it was simply that they didn't know how to construct general models in which, for instance, technology was endogenous; and they hoped that the central results of the Walrasian model would still be valid even if these assumptions were lifted, and replaced with alternatives providing a more apt description of the market economy.

Questioning the information assumptions led to questioning even the *mathematics* of the old paradigm. No principle was more ingrained than the "law of diminishing returns," reflected in the assumption of convexity that underlay most of the standard proofs of existence and efficiency of the market equilibrium.[3] Of course, enormous efforts were made in showing the existence of equilibrium, under weaker *mathematical* structures; but the underlying problems were with the *economic* structures—and no degree of mathematical generalization would solve those problems. Moreover, there was a link: non-convexities were *inherent* in problems of information and changing knowledge. I was concerned with the underlying economics: If, for instance, non-convexities were pervasive, how could we have confidence in competition? Even small search costs could lead to large market power.

I and others working in this new field of "information economics" showed that the assumptions underlying the neoclassical paradigm were not assumptions of convenience: they were essential to the results of the analysis, such as that the market economy was efficient, or that the equilibrium was described by demand equaling supply, or by the law of one price, with price equaling marginal cost. Nor were they problems that would be resolved by deeper mathematics. Indeed deeper analysis cast further doubts on the Arrow-Debreu Walrasian edifice—for instance, if the *results* depended on there being *today* a complete set of securities, for all states of nature, for all contingencies, extending infinitely far into the future, what if there are contingencies that have not yet been conceived of? Innovation creates new possibilities, some of which may not yet even have been thought of. How can there exist securities for these?[4] Not only was it *assumed* that technology was unchanging, but the framework itself could only embrace limited forms of innovation.

---

[2] Some of these failures could, of course, be related to other problems as well: high transactions costs might also contribute to the absence of certain markets.

[3] Indeed, Paul Samuelson's great contribution in his *Foundations of Economic Analysis* (Samuelson 1947) was to present a unifying framework for the analysis of firms and households; that unifying framework was "maximization subject to constraints"; assumptions about convexity were central.

[4] One could not, for instance, have an insurance market against the risk of an atomic energy plant blowing up prior to the development of the idea of atomic energy. The Arrow-Debreu model assumed that all markets (for all contingencies) existed at time zero.

THE NEW PARADIGM

I was concerned not just with destroying the old edifice, but also with constructing an alternative, a New Paradigm, a new way of thinking about the economy.[5, 6] The papers in these *Selected Works* present the outline of this New Paradigm. In this introductory essay, I want to put this entire enterprise in perspective, to explain why economics was ripe for a paradigm shift, to relate the work presented in this volume to other ongoing work, and to suggest directions for future work.

This alternative paradigm provided a new theory of the firm (including a theory of corporate governance, finance, and organization), a new theory of labor, capital, and product markets, and a new theory of the behavior of the entire economy (macro economics, both in the short run and in the long.) Each level of the analysis was based on work done at the other levels. They were all interwoven. For instance, information imperfections explained credit and equity rationing, and were key to understanding how capital markets worked. But credit and equity rationing was central to the analysis of the theory of the firm. And the theory of the firm, based on credit and equity rationing, was a key building block in the macro economic model, affecting both economic fluctuations and growth.

The New Paradigm unified macro economics and micro economics, and did so in a way that not only explained the consequences of market imperfections, like wage and price rigidities and the absence of risk markets for both the behavior of firms and macro economic aggregates; but also explained the existence and persistence of these and other imperfections of labor, capital, and product markets. Most importantly, the New Paradigm explained the existence and persistence of unemployment. As it answered these questions, it also began to help define the appropriate role for government, how and when collective action could lead to welfare improvements.

Of course, in the old paradigm, there were often discussions about *information*, including claims about the informational efficiency of the price system: consumers did not have to know anything about technology or scarcity; firms did not have to know about the preferences of particular individuals; and, marvelously, the price system provided firms with all the information they needed to know about what to produce and how to produce it and households with all the information they need to know to make the "right" consumption decisions. But the models only evaluated the ability of the price system to solve a once-and-for-all-time problem; it did not assess how well it could solve real-time problems, with new disturbances, new changes in preferences

---

[5] I should make clear that this work rests firmly on the shoulders of many others, cited here, in my Nobel lecture, and in the other papers collected here. I should, perhaps, mention in particular Ken Arrow, who, as he was providing the culminating formalization of the old paradigm, realized its limitations, and began a research agenda into the consequences of imperfect information. I benefited enormously from a small class that he taught as a visitor in my second year as a graduate student at MIT and from a class that Robert M. Solow taught, based on Arrow's *Jahnsson* lectures on risk, which included brief discussions of adverse selection and moral hazard (Arrow 1965).

[6] See also my Nobel lecture, a shortened version of which is reprinted here as Chapter 2.

or technologies. And, equally importantly, it addressed only one set of information problems, those concerned with *scarcity*, balancing demand and supply, not with the far richer and more complicated set of problems concerning, for instance, the quality of workers, jobs, products, investment opportunities, etc.

In the old paradigm, households were simple automata maximizing utility subject to budget constraints; and firms were simple automata maximizing profits, taking technology and prices as given. The New Paradigm made economics into a much richer subject. If, for instance, actions conveyed information, and individuals and firms knew that, then actions would be affected by the beliefs about what information was being conveyed. Individuals' decisions about how much education to get, how much insurance to purchase, or what goods to buy would be determined not just by prices and income, but by beliefs about how those actions might affect others' beliefs and their own opportunity sets.

In the old paradigm, too, little attention was paid to what went on inside the firm, partly because it made little difference. Knowing the production function and factor and goods prices, one could predict outputs and inputs. In the New Paradigm, the insides of the black box of the firm became something that could and should be explained and understood.

The assumptions of the old theory fit together—with perfect information, fixed technologies, and universal diminishing returns, there was every reason to believe that markets would be competitive. The arguments for why market equilibrium would have to be described by zero profits and demand equaling supply were compelling. And the conclusions concerning market efficiency (in the absence of externalities or the other limited number of market failures) followed naturally. So too for the New Paradigm: with imperfect information and innovation, competition was naturally limited; with pervasive problems of moral hazard and adverse selection, there were externality-like effects of actions by individuals and firms on others. Externalities were pervasive—not just limited to problems of the environment.

The Theory of Capitalism and the Market Economy

While the center of my work has been on *economics of information*, that does not really indicate what I view to be either its major contribution, or its major thrust. My major concern has always been understanding how the economic *system* worked. By the time I had finished my graduate studies, I had realized that the model of the economic system that was being taught—and that was at the center of policy analyses—was *not* the model of a modern capitalist economy. It was little more than a fancy version of a primitive agriculture exchange/production economy, slightly updated to include manufacturing—so long as there were sufficient diminishing returns. There was but a short distance between Smith and Ricardo and Walras, and between Walras and Samuelson. And I also realized that the major lacuna was *not* imperfections of competition (monopoly capitalism, monopolistic competition, oligopoly),[7] which represented slight (but nonetheless economically important) perturbations in the central ideas.

Ironically, the neoclassical economists tried to deny the relevance of "capitalism," saying it made no difference whether capital hired labor or labor hired capital. And that was true in the kinds of models that they constructed. But the question was, in the real world, did it make a difference? In the real world, was it just a happenstance that one typically saw capital hiring labor, rather than vice versa, an institutional detail of little substantive concern? In the New Paradigm, who made decisions mattered, and thus who controlled the firm mattered.[8] In the Old Paradigm, there was no theory of take-overs, because no matter who "owned" the firm, the decisions would be the same. By contrast, constructing a theory of take-overs was an important component of the New Paradigm.[9]

Modern Capitalism

Modern capitalism differs in many respects from a primitive market economy. The most obvious is that the basic unit of production is not peasants working their own land or the land of their landlords, or a single proprietor engaged in trading or production. Much of the production occurs in large scale enterprises; but even medium sized enterprises can employ dozens of individuals. Production within firms and the allocation of resources is typically not regulated by markets, though, of course, market prices have an important bearing on their resource utilization. In that sense, the modern market economy is not fully a market economy. It is a *decentralized* economy, with one of the central questions being what activities occur *within* firms.

Large enterprises face a problem that small ones do not: how to organize themselves, including how to organize the process of decision making, for instance, hierarchically, where every decision has to be approved up a chain of command, or polyarchically, with large numbers of independent decision makers.

Primitive agriculture involves a limited set of investment decisions—labor is invested at planting in the spring, with the fruits borne in the harvest the following

---

[7] As many critics of the market economy earlier in the twentieth century had suggested (see Robinson 1933 and Sweezy 1968).

[8] The difference is highlighted by contrasting the fundamental economic questions as posed by Samuelson's classic principles of *Economics*, textbook, first published in 1948, and my own *Principles*, first published 44 years later. Samuelson focused on what was produced, how it was produced, and for whom it was produced. To this list, I added a fourth question: who makes these decisions?

[9] Thus, one of my earliest papers (first presented at a conference in Hakone, Japan, in 1970) was concerned with take-overs (Stiglitz 1972c). In later work with Sanford Grossman, I explored whether value maximization would lead either to the maximization of shareholder or more societal welfare, and whether shareholders would agree on *any* set of actions. See Grossman and Stiglitz (1977, 1980b).

fall. Modern capitalism involves long term investments, sometimes in the billions of dollars, clearly beyond the resources of most individuals.

Firms can *finance* some of this investment with their retained earnings; but much of it must be financed through funds raised from outside investors. Finance thus becomes one of the central issues of modern capitalism. But as important as finance is, sometimes it seems that it is given excessive importance. At the very least, it is important to recognize the distinction between *finance* and the real economy. This becomes particularly clear in discussions of macro economics (Part IV). What is good for finance (Wall Street) may not be good for the real sector (Main Street). One of the challenges in the analysis of modern capitalism is understanding the relationship between finance and the real sector.

The modern capitalist system is based on long term investments, and this is where one of the *market failures* discussed earlier has a particular bearing: there are not markets for goods and services extending far into the future. Firms must make investments today, but can only guess what will be the prices (demand) for the goods that these investments will produce years from now. How individuals and firms make these guesses—how they formulate their *expectations*—is thus crucial.[10]

A theory of modern capitalism is, accordingly, different from the traditional Walraisan (Arrow-Debreu) competitive equilibrium model in a large number of ways. That model was highly influenced by developments in nineteenth century physics, with a focus on notions of *equilibrium*. My work on information economics began as a struggle to understand the limitations of that model which has so shaped thinking about economic processes for more than a century, by at first working within that *equilibrium* framework; but the eventual goal was always to construct an alternative framework.[11]

In the following paragraphs, I describe several key insights that the New Paradigm has made to the understanding of modern capitalism.

Incentives

Some have said that economics is the science of incentives. Yet, in spite of its centrality, prior to the development of the New Paradigm economists had not really analyzed deeply the problem of incentives. In the standard model, workers did not have to be motivated to do a good job: they got paid if they did the job contracted for, and not otherwise.

In this respect, the Old Paradigm had even failed to provide a good theory of the primitive agriculture economy. It argued that institutions did not matter, that

---

[10] At one time, it was hoped that the basic results of the competitive equilibrium model with a full set of Arrow-Debreu securities would extend, e.g. to competitive economies with more limited risk markets, at least if there is rational expectations. Unfortunately, that has turned out not to be the case (see, for instance, Chapter 23 below; Stiglitz 1982b; and Newbery and Stiglitz 1982).

[11] I made this clear even in the earliest survey paper of my work in the economics of information, reprinted here as Chapter 1, where I pointed the way towards evolutionary economics, towards models influenced more by modern biology than classical physics. Though there have been important advances in this area, it has not progressed as much as I would have hoped.

one could describe and explain the behavior of the economy by simply focusing on *supply and demand*. Yet, throughout the world, hundreds of millions of people were paid through sharecropping contracts. With peasants receiving 50 percent (and in some cases even less) of their output, incentives were obviously attenuated. This seemingly inefficient system was both persistent and pervasive. One of my earliest papers (Stiglitz 1974e) explained these contractual arrangements.[12] Economic theory could help explain the institutions that existed, and these institutional arrangements mattered.

As I wrote the paper, it became clear that the theory I was developing was actually a general theory of incentives, relevant not only to a primitive agriculture economy, but also to modern corporations. Just as landlords rely on workers to farm their land, employers have to delegate to their workers (shareholders to those who manage their firms) responsibility for taking actions; employers typically do not even have the information required to know what the employees should do. They want to motivate the employees to act in their interest. A single framework, that came to be called that of principal–agent, could describe all of these relationships.[13,14]

In recent years, many corporate "reforms" have focused on improving managerial incentives; but they have picked up more of the vocabulary of modern incentive analysis than the substance. As I explain in the papers in Part II, many of the prevalent forms of incentive pay are inefficient, providing little effective incentives. They are designed more to make it difficult for shareholders to assess the magnitude of managerial compensation; and they are more a testimony of the problems of corporate governance—to be discussed shortly—than to the efficiency of American style corporate capitalism.[15]

[12] The failure of the Old Paradigm to explain even a primitive agriculture economy was more widespread. It did not explain the nature of credit, labor, or product markets in developing countries, including their interlinkages. One of the important applications of the New Paradigm has been developing a general theory of rural organization. See, in particular, the papers in Volume VI of the the *Selected Works*.

[13] I first formulated this general incentive problem, while working in Kenya in 1969, in the context of the problem of sharecropping—the landlords who wished their risk-averse tenants to work hard. At the end of the paper, I explained how this model was a general model of incentives, and in particular, could help analyze the problem of modern corporations. The paper was eventually published five years later, and is reprinted here, in slightly abridged form, in Part III, Chapter 13. Meanwhile, Stephen Ross developed a similar analysis, creating the vocabulary that is still used (see Ross 1973). Contemporaneously, Mirrlees realized that his optimal tax problem (1971) could be reformulated as an optimal incentive problem.

[14] Of course, many economists outside of the mainstream neoclassical tradition had discussed extensively the problems that arise from the separation of ownership and control within corporations, following upon the work of Berle and Means (1932). Marris (1964), Baumol (1959), and Galbraith (1967) developed theories of *managerial capitalism*. These theories were glibly dismissed as not being rooted in economic theory. Sometimes, it was argued that if a manager did not maximize stock market value, it would be taken over: someone could buy it at its current market price, change the firm's action, and make a capital gain. But these assertions were made before the theory of take-overs was developed, which highlighted the difficulties of take-overs. Part of my own contribution was to show that these critiques of managerial capitalism were at least partially unfair: with imperfect information, managers could pursue actions which did not maximize shareholder value. See Stiglitz (1972c), Edlin and Stiglitz (1995), Grossman and Hart (1980, 1996).

[15] The difficulties in ascertaining the magnitude of compensation, let alone the effectiveness of the incentive structures, are themselves aspects of the economics of information. The chapters in Volume II

xvi   SELECTED WORKS OF JOSEPH E. STIGLITZ VOL I

Corporate Governance

Marshall, who had done so much to create the old paradigm's theory of the firm, understood the limitations of the old paradigm (Marshall 1897). The firm had a single owner. There was no problem of incentivizing him/her: s/he wished to maximize his/her income or wealth, and that meant s/he took those actions which maximized the firms profit or market value. Modern capitalism had required the agglomeration of huge amounts of capital, beyond the capacity of any single individual. Joint stock companies developed, and these seemingly were different from the owner managed firm of Marshall. How could one ensure that managers acted in the interests of shareholders?

Indeed, by the first part of the twentieth century, some acute observers[16] were noting the important implications of the separation between ownership and control. There needed to be a new theory of the firm (dealing with finance, management, and organization)[17]—it was not just that the old theory viewed the firm as a black box (as we noted earlier), but probably provided wrong behavioral predictions, at least in certain critical situations.[18] In this new theory of the firm, managers did not always act in the interests of shareholders (Edlin and Stiglitz 1995), or of stakeholders more generally; firms did not necessarily maximize share market value (Grossman and Stiglitz 1977, 1980b); and value maximization was not in general consistent with welfare maximization (Stiglitz 1972b, 1982b). Some had hoped that in spite of all of these complexities and market imperfections, the threat of take-over would act as an effective discipline device: firms that did not maximize their value would be taken over; those engineering the take-over would reap large capital gains as a reward for their efforts. But as I and others looked at both the theory and evidence on take-overs, it became clear that these hopes were not justified.[19]

It was clear that corporate governance—the rules and regulations, the institutional design and arrangements—were of central importance in understanding the behavior

---

will make clear the disparity between the prevalent forms of compensation and optimal compensation schemes. In *Roaring Nineties* (2003c), I provide a popular account of the forms that this corporate deception took, the consequences, and the political battles to reduce its scope.

[16] Marshall (1897); Berle and Means (1933).

[17] The new information paradigm provided part of the intellectual underpinnings of these and other topics (like accounting and that part of human relations focusing on compensation) that have long been the staple of business schools. See, in particular, Parts II, III, and IV, and Stiglitz and Wolfson (—).

[18] Many economists wave their hands, suggesting that even though managers' interests may differ from those of shareholders, nonetheless companies act *as if* they maximize profits and market value. The deeper question is: why should that be so, if we believe individuals act rationally, and managers' compensation is not designed so that they should take actions which maximize firm market value? These are questions which are pursued in Part III. Some blithely assumed that if firms did not maximize their market value, they would be taken over. Of course, in a world with perfect information/perfect markets, that might be true; but in a world with perfect information, as we have noted, the problems with which we have been concerned would themselves not have arisen. To even a casual observer of markets, it seemed clear that the take-over mechanism often did not work well. This was part of the motivation for the research on take-overs that I began in the late 1960s, which (together with the work of others, especially Grossman and Hart 1980) demonstrated why that was so (see footnote 14).

[19] Jensen and Meckling (1976); and the references cited in footnote 14.

of firms.[20] If there was any doubt about the importance of these issues, they should have been removed by the scandals that rocked American accounting firms, banks, and many of its largest corporations during the nineties, and the vast asset stripping that marked the transition from Communism to the market in Russia, the Czech Republic and elsewhere (Stiglitz 2000e; Hoff and Stiglitz 2005).

Finance

In the old theory, finance too was simple: there was some kind of (ex ante) homogeneous capital, which could be used for production; it was an input, like any other input. There was a supply and demand, and market equilibrium balanced the two. Capital was nothing more than seed that was harvested but not consumed, ready to be planted the next year. Equilibrium in the capital market was just a balancing out of the demand for seed by farmers who wanted to plant more than they had saved, and supply by those who wanted to plant less than they had saved.

Economists spent little time worrying about the different forms of finance—debt versus equity. These were institutional details, to be left to their business school colleagues. When modern neoclassical tools were used to study corporate finance, Modigliani and Miller (1958) came up with the startling result that corporate finance simply did not matter; it made no difference whether firms financed themselves with debt or equity, whether they paid dividends or not. Modigliani and Miller argued that finance was important—it was part of economics, not just a subject taught in business schools. But they too viewed financial markets simply as a repackaging of risks.[21] And little had been lost as a result of economists ignoring the subject.

It was ironic that after economists had long ignored finance, the first important result was that they had been right to ignore it all along: finance did not matter. While I subsequently showed that, within the *old* paradigm, these results were far more general than Modigliani and Miller had envisioned,[22] it was clear that something was missing: surely, if finance did not matter, what were all those corporate finance specialists in Wall Street doing for a living?

The New Paradigm provided the answer: it saw financial markets as the "brain" of the economy, allocating scarce capital: information was central to its functioning. And, in the New Paradigm, corporate finance *did* matter. How firms raise capital—whether through debt or equity—can, for instance, convey information.

---

[20] As I already hinted, the corporate governance problem can be viewed as one manifestation of the general "principal–agent" incentive problem discussed in the previous sub-section. See Chapter 17 below for an articulation of the corporate governance problem in these terms. For a more extensive modern review, see Jensen (2000).

[21] More generally, before the work described here, financial markets were viewed as doing little more than financial intermediation, which included not just packaging risks, but transferring risks, and converting short term liabilities into long term loans. These intermediation services are, of course, still important.

[22] See Stiglitz (1969b, 1974f). (I also showed that the assumption of no-bankruptcy which they had employed was far from innocuous.)

Innovation

If the nineteenth century and early twentieth were marked by a shift from agriculture to manufacturing, the late twentieth century has been marked by a shift to innovation. Innovation has been systemized. While by definition new ideas are different from old (or previously known) knowledge, the processes by which new ideas and knowledge is created can be routinized. The large research labs of the major manufacturing firms succeeded in doing this in the mid-twentieth century. But by the end of the twentieth century, we had developed a broader research system, with institutions and markets supporting innovation, such as venture capital to finance innovation, and research universities with their attached research parks. In the advanced industrial countries, like the United States, manufacturing—the production of widgets—employed only 11 percent of the population by the beginning of the New Millennium.

Just as these trends were beginning, at the start of the twentieth century, Knight (1921) and Schumpeter (1934) recognized that something key was left out of the Walrasian model—innovation, entrepreneurship, and risk taking. In the New Paradigm, these take on central importance. By contrast, in the old paradigm, innovation was either assumed away or treated as exogenous.

As I recognized early on,[23] the economics of innovation and the economics of information were intimately connected: innovation and screening were particular forms of information (knowledge), and some of the same problems and concepts (appropriability, externalities, the public goods nature of information, the fact that expenditures on research and information are fixed, sunk costs) were equally applicable to both. There was little reason that one should expect efficiency in innovation.

Innovation, especially when protected by intellectual property rights, resulted in at least temporary monopolies. Schumpeter (1942) argued that what later came to be called Schumpeterian competition—competition for new products and cheaper production processes—was at the heart of the market economy. This view of competition was markedly different from that which underlay the traditional competitive analysis. Schumpeter was right that the kind of competition captured in the standard competitive (Arrow-Debreu) model did not reflect the underlying true nature of competition in a market economy, but Schumpeter did not really analyze the innovation–competition process. This was one of the early tasks of the New Paradigm, and Schumpeter's conclusions were shown to be (in general) wrong:[24] Schumpeter believed that there would be a succession of monopolists; we showed that monopoly power could persist. Schumpeter believed that this competitive pressure led to high levels of innovation; we showed that an incumbent monopolist could simultaneously limit his own research expenditures (below an efficient level) and

---

[23] A point that I recognized early and explicitly, in my first review article of the newly developing field of economics of information in 1974 (vol. I, chap. 1). It was perhaps no accident that the most important early contributor to the modern theory of innovation, Ken Arrow, was almost contemporaneously making important contributions to the economics of information.

[24] See, in particular, Dasgupta and Stiglitz (1980a, b). Similar results were derived by Gilbert and Newbery (1982).

deter entry from potential competitors.[25] (These are topics we explore in greater detail in later volumes).

There were, in fact, many links between the economics of information and innovation.[26] Schumpeter was aware, for instance, of capital constraints that might impede innovation. The papers presented in Volume I help explain why these capital constraints are so important, especially in an area like R&D.

Innovation can affect the cost and availability of information of relevance to monitoring (Braverman and Stiglitz 1986b). This is true not just for innovations in technologies which are explicitly viewed as information technologies. For instance, the assembly line monitored the work effort of each individual—the consequences of any one sloughing off could easily be detected. Just-in-time inventory management was hailed for the reduced cost of capital; but its real contribution may have been as a monitoring mechanism. The rough stones of production problems were often covered by the deep water; lower inventories brought the problems into the open.[27]

Thus, long before the so-called modern endogenous growth theory made its appearance in Chicago (Romer 1986), not only were the micro foundations of innovation being analyzed,[28] but students of Samuelson, Arrow, Solow and Uzawa[29] and others were using these ideas to help develop macro economic models where not only the rate of innovation, but its direction, was determined by market forces. In the New Paradigm, not only was information endogenous, but so was technology.

But while the New Paradigm made enormous progress in the economics of innovation, I confess that there has been only limited progress in fully understanding what makes for an innovative economy. We understand better the economic conditions that are favorable to innovation—how, for instance, patent races or intellectual property can affect expenditures on research or the direction of research, and therefore the pace of technological change. We understand better the difficulties of collateralizing research and the importance played by a new form of finance, venture capital. But there are many other attributes of a society that can have an effect on the level of

---

[25] See, in particular Fudenberg et al. (1983); Stiglitz (1988d), and Dasgupta and Stiglitz (1988b).

[26] One aspect of this has often been stressed in discussions of the "new economy": the lowering of search costs which increases the degree of competition in the economy. However, as useful as the Internet is in providing price comparisons for homogeneous commodities, its value in the many areas where products (labor) are heterogeneous is far more limited.

[27] Such changes in technology of course affect the entire nature of the workplace; the loss of discretion may lead to alienation and a loss of productivity. These social dimensions are typically omitted from the formal economic analysis, but there is evidence that they can often play a central role. See Stiglitz (2000c, 2001d, 2002a).

[28] See, in particular, Arrow's classic papers (1962a, b). In Stiglitz 1987a (originally presented in 1978), I developed the idea of knowledge as a public good. This was further elaborated on in Stiglitz (1999b).

[29] Uzawa gathered a large group of students from across the country to study these questions in the summer of 1965 at the University of Chicago. My own contributions in this area include Atkinson and Stiglitz (1969), Stiglitz (1987g, 1990b, 1992, 1994a, b, 2006), Sah and Stiglitz (1987a), Fudenberg et al. (1983), and Greenwald et al. (1990) and Greenwald and Stiglitz (2006) as well as the previously cited papers. See also Shell (1966, 1967) and Nordhaus (1969). Indeed, there was a large and robust literature in the 1960s and 1970s on the theory of endogenous innovation. See, in addition to the works already cited, Samuelson (1965), Uzawa (1965), Phelps and Drandakis (1966), Kennedy (1964), and Weizacker (1966). See Volume III for a fuller discussion of the differences in perspectives.

innovativeness: Russia showed that even a Communist government could organize well defined large scale engineering fetes, like putting a man on the moon. In Russia, too, certain branches of basic science (like mathematics) flourished and developed. But innovation across a wide spectrum requires questioning of old models and assumptions; it is fundamentally anti-authority. Karl Popper (1945) has referred to the *open society*, and an open society may be the society which is most conducive to innovation. Authoritarian societies cannot be open; but not all democracies are truly open, and some may create environments that are not conducive to the advancement of science. The most important ingredient for an innovative economy is creativity; and while, almost by definition, the creative process cannot be routinized, there may be conditions that are more conducive to innovation. We can learn to learn (Stiglitz 1987f). Learning how we learn, and more broadly what societies can do to promote the pace of innovation is, I believe, one of the major challenges lying ahead. (This is perhaps particularly relevant for developing countries, whose major challenge is closing the knowledge gap that separates them from advanced industrial countries. As I argue in Volume VI, too much attention has been paid to increasing the efficiency of markets and the stock of capital—though both are admittedly important—and too little attention to understanding what kinds of policies will enhance the pace at which the knowledge is transmitted and absorbed.)[30]

The analysis of these questions requires, of course, going well beyond the standard paradigm in more fundamental ways. (See the discussion below.) As I wrote in my All Souls Inaugural Lecture[31] (as well as in subsequent work),[32] it seemed to me that there is something deeper in the difference between an *innovative* and a *bureaucratic* economy that these formals models were not capturing, and as I have spent time in Washington enmeshed in bureaucracy, my conviction has been reinforced. There are different "rules of the game," and the characteristics that make for success in one environment may make for failure in another. The challenges to the *system* posed by constant innovation may impair the survival of bureaucratic procedures; but bureaucracies may be able to stifle innovative impulses. It seemed to me possible (as I showed in my 1995b paper) that different economies could evolve into different equilibria— one in which bureaucratic rules and characteristics flourished, and another in which more innovative characteristics dominated. Clearly, these models just touched the surface of a complex subject: there is, in these areas, a rich future research agenda.

Entrepreneurship and Risk-Taking

The remarkable property of the Arrow-Debreu model of the competitive market is that it simply ignored so much of what gives a capitalist economy its vitality. There was no scope for gathering information, for innovation, or for risk taking and entrepreneurship. Markets for risk worked perfectly—so one could buy insurance against any possible risk. There was no role for outsmarting the market—for figuring

---

[30] This has been the subject of my 2006 paper with Bruce Greenwald, where we argue that broad based industrial protection may promote development. See Greenwald and Stiglitz (2006).

[31] See Volume II.   [32] Sah and Stiglitz 1989a, b; Stiglitz 1995b.

out future trends in technology and tastes. There were a complete set of prices that provided all the information required to know what should be produced and how it should be produced.

Much of my earlier work was conducted within the prevailing paradigm of the day, the Arrow-Debreu competitive equilibrium model; it was devoted to trying to understand why a full set of markets didn't exist, and what happened when there was not a full set of markets. The New Paradigm went a long way in explaining the absence of these markets, and describing their consequence.[33] Sometimes, firms were driven by fear—fear of bankruptcy, or the threat of take-overs.[34]

Just as I expressed a dissatisfaction with what we have been able to accomplish in understanding the innovativeness process, so too here: we have done a better job in explaining the failures of the standard paradigm than in understanding what makes for successful entrepreneurship, and for much the same reason. We have developed tools that enable us to understand risk averse and risk loving behavior. Entrepreneurship entails taking risks, but there is a difference between entrepreneurship, seeing new trends and seizing new opportunities, and mad gambling (though skeptics might claim that the difference can be seen ex post: successful gambles are credited with foresight; unsuccessful are labeled as reckless). And even if, in a certain sense, entrepreneurs are reckless—that they undertake risks which no one with even a moderate degree of risk aversion would undertake—they may still contribute to the dynamism of the economy. For the evolution of the economy requires experiments—a constant flow of experiments from which the most successful survive. Entrepreneurs provide that flow of experiments. They often do not get paid the full social value of their contribution, for successful experiments can often be imitated.[35] The most important ideas cannot be patented, and even when patented, the holders of the patent garner for themselves only a fraction of the social benefits. Reckless entrepreneurship—entrepreneurs who so love risk that their *private* return may be negative—may thus have a positive social return, and societies which encourage this kind of entrepreneurship may flourish.

Expectations

Earlier, we noted that the absence of a complete set of markets extending infinitely far into the future and covering all contingencies forced entrepreneurs to form expectations about future prices. But an aspect of the modern economy which makes

[33] As we already noted, it meant that managers might not maximize market value; and that even if they did, in general, stock market value maximization did not lead to economic efficiency.

[34] See Greenwald and Stiglitz (1990a) and our other joint papers in Volumes III and IV. See also Stiglitz (1972b). One of my earliest papers explored the implications of bankruptcy for the Modigliani-Miller Theorem (see Stiglitz 1969b). Curiously, as important as bankruptcy and takeovers were in modern capitalist economies, economic theory had largely bypassed these concepts, assuming presumably that they made little difference for the behavior of the firm. This, as I showed even in my earliest enquiry, was not true.

[35] The same thing is true in terms of discovering who is a good entrepreneur. This is one of the central points in Emran and Stiglitz (2006).

the task of forming expectations particularly difficult is the high pace of innovation and change. In a simple agriculture economy, where the weather is the same year after year, and there are no changes in technology, one might be able to describe the probability distribution of prices; given the probability distribution of prices for different crops, farmers make particular decisions about how to allocate their land, how much effort to exert in each crop, how much to invest in fertilizer, etc. With an unchanging world, they make the same decisions year after year, and given the variability of weather, these decisions generate the price distributions. A rational expectations equilibrium—where farmers predicated their decisions on price distributions which in fact conform to the realized distributions—might in such a context seem reasonable.[36] With somewhat better educated farmers, they might even figure out more complex dynamic processes: the willingness to undertake risks might be affected by their wealth, and hence the pattern of crops being planted, and accordingly, the price distributions which emerge at the end of the season might themselves be dependent on wealth at the beginning of the period.

With more complicated production processes, analyzing dynamic rational expectations equilibria become themselves more complicated. Some crops are perennials (trees), and so one has to form expectations about prices over a large number of years, and with investment decisions each period depending, for instance, on particularities of each period (the weather, wealth inherited that period), the price distribution in any period becomes dependent on a potentially long history. And this is even more so in a world in which the behavior of individuals (families) cannot be perfectly aggregated, where, for instance, the distribution of wealth matters (not just mean wealth) for aggregate behavior.[37]

Of course, if we had a stationary world, even if individuals could not perform the complicated calculations required for optimization in such a rational expectations equilibrium, they might learn: individuals or families that somehow acted more rationally (in this sense) might prosper, and one might imagine that the world eventually acted *as if* there were a rational expectations equilibrium.

But the world is not stationary, and it is changing in complicated ways which question the relevance of the whole exercise. Take perhaps the single most important set of decisions that individuals make, how much to save for their retirement or where to invest it. We have a well defined theory of how individuals make choices among different kinds of lettuces. They do not know their preferences a priori, but find out about them through experience. They try romaine and red leaf lettuce; they quickly ascertain their preferences, and adjust their consumption patterns to reflect relative prices.

[36] Climate change brought on as a result of the increase of greenhouse gases in the atmosphere has shown that even that may not be true.

[37] If, for instance, there are imperfect risk markets, then poorer farmers will want to plant more in "safe" crops, richer farmers in riskier crops. But if the amount planted in any crop is not linear in wealth, then the distribution of wealth will matter. Many of the simple examples explored in the literature assume that utility functions take on a form which generates these linear relationships, but the empirical evidence is overwhelming: though they simplify the calculations, they do not provide a good description of risk taking behavior (see Volume III).

But in making decisions about consumption now versus consumption 30 years from now, in retirement, individuals cannot go through such a period of experimentation. Except if one believes in reincarnation (with memories going across lives), one cannot try consuming a little less now, a little more 30 years from now, and saying, "Yes, that was far better than what I had originally done." One takes risks. One sees the outcome of those risks. But one does not see the whole probability distribution of outcomes; nor does one ever see fully the "inputs." One may see other people who took risks which turned out against them. But they obviously did not face exactly the same risks as those confronting the current generation.

Moreover, the public context—the provision of social security—has changed dramatically, so that what might have been reasonable savings and investment decisions 25 years ago may not be today. There are continuing risks of changes in these public programs, and there is no easy way of assessing these risks.[38]

Rational expectations have played an important role in the development of modern economics. Some have taken these models more seriously than they should—as if they are good descriptions of the world, rather the "benchmark" models that help us understand the real world, by focusing our attention on ways in which the world differs from these benchmarks. Though rational expectations models help us think through rigorously certain benchmark cases, they miss out much of the dynamics, and complexities, of modern capitalism. The fact that, in general, rational expectations equilibrium are *not* Pareto efficient[39] is important, because it tells us that even under these most favorable circumstances, when the world is so static that they could in principle formulate rational expectations, the market equilibrium is in general not efficient. In the real world, the presumption of inefficiency may be even stronger.[40]

The New Paradigm, Institutions, and the Distribution of Income

In the Old Paradigm institutions don't matter. What matters are the underlying economic forces. One society might be characterized by sharecropping, another by a plantation system, and another by farmers who work their own land. But it is the supply of labor relative to land which determines the income of workers and the rents to land; the institutions are just a façade, and the job of the economist is to see beneath the surface, to the underlying economics. Since institutions don't matter, the Old

---

[38] I explored the implications of this in a note "Retirement Savings—Games That Asset Managers, Distributors and Investors Play" (2005).

[39] See, in particular, Chapter 23 and Volume III and the references cited there.

[40] There is another set of problems discussed more extensively below: rational expectations models have been wrongly used (or abused), with particular conclusions (like the inefficacy of government policy) being attributed to the rational expectations assumption, when the results are a consequence of *other* assumptions in the model; as we explain, rational expectations may actually enhance the efficacy of government interventions.

Paradigm put no effort into understanding why they changed over time, or why they differed from one society to another.

By the same token, the distribution of wealth mattered little. An economy in which workers owned their own land was little different from that in which workers were landless—though obviously, landless workers would be poorer, since they wouldn't enjoy the benefits of land rents. Issues of distribution and efficiency could be neatly separated: any distribution of well being that was desired could be achieved through the market mechanism—all one had to do was to undertake the appropriate initial wealth redistributions.

By contrast, in the New Paradigm institutions mattered. Some of my earliest work in the economics of information was motivated by an attempt to explain the institution of sharecropping.[41] And it soon became clear that not only did institutions matter, so did wealth distribution. For instance, a disparity between labor and land ownership gave rise to agency problems—the landlord had to worry about motivating his/her workers, or whether his/her tenant would be able to pay the rent. (Of course, there had been an old institutionalist school which had stressed the importance of institutions, but it was too atheoretical; it was dismissed by the neoclassicals as simply ignoring the underlying economics.) Roughly contemporaneous with the work here, some economic historians, including Douglas North,[42] revived an interest in institutions. Curiously, by that time, a quarter century after I had written my paper on sharecropping, the World Bank was arguing that the development of institutions was at the *center* of economic development.[43]

Interest in institutions grew as the limitations in markets became recognized. In some of the earlier work on institutions, it seemed almost as if institutions were created to fill the gaps created by market failures. Arnott and I showed (Chapter 24), however, that non-market institutions could actually make matters worse; dysfunctional non-market institutions could crowd out market institutions. Later work tended also to emphasize the role of institutions in preserving inequalities of income and wealth, sometimes at the expense of economic efficiency.[44]

In short, it has become increasingly clear that the neoclassical model, whatever it was a model of, was not a model of modern capitalism. While the New Paradigm began by questioning the information assumptions underlying the old paradigm, it quickly went beyond that, to provide the beginnings of a theory of capitalism, a theory that addresses issues of corporate governance, finance, and organization, which helps explain its success in promoting innovation, as well as its limitations in ensuring that resources are fully employed. The New Paradigm has also begun to provide the

[41] See Chapter 13.

[42] North received the Nobel Prize for his work in the role institutions play in economic growth (see North 1990).

[43] See, for instance, the *World Development Report 2001* and Stiglitz (2001a) It was not always clear, however, what was meant by good institutions, and even more importantly, how to create them.

[44] See Arnott and Stiglitz (1991a) and Stiglitz (2000d).

foundations of our understanding of the role that institutions play in the economy. The New Paradigm is clearly a work in the process of being created; but already it has provided enormous insights into the workings of the modern capitalist system.

Since debates over economic policy are so closely linked to views about how the economy functions, there were clear policy consequences of a shift in Paradigm. Thomas Kuhn (1970) describes the resistance to a paradigm shift. In this case, in addition to the normal "intellectual" resistance, there was another: a resistance to the policy implications.

Ripe for a Paradigm Shift

Thomas Kuhn and others have written not only about the resistance to a paradigm shift, but also about the circumstances that are conducive to a shift. There are both internal and external forces.

The timing of my research was fortunate—or prescient: my work on the economics of information and innovation began long before the term "information economy" became commonplace.[45] But with information, innovation, and finance increasingly seen as the center of the economy, an economic theory that ignored finance, had nothing to say about innovation, and assumed perfect information could not have remained as the dominant paradigm. It was inevitable that there would have to be a New Paradigm. What is remarkable is the ability of the old paradigm to survive.

Part of the reason is that neoclassical theory had provided a coherent theory of the firm (and household behavior), of labor, capital, and product markets, and of the behavior of the macro economy. The pieces not only fit together beautifully, they had a similar mathematical structure. While it was *coherent*, it was not credible. At each level, there were strong predictions, many of which were clearly wrong. Under the assumptions of neoclassical theory, there was never unemployment. And as neo-classical theory developed further, its deficiencies became increasingly apparent. As we have already noted, Modigliani and Miller showed that corporate finance did not matter. Solow (1956) had constructed a growth model in which the *logic* predicted the convergence in incomes of the developed and developing countries, and Samuelson (1948) had constructed a simple trade model which predicted the equalization of factor prices. If they described forces that were at play, there were also strong forces, not described as well, which were preventing the convergence in incomes per capita or of wages. Equally or more troubling, the past 50 years has uncovered a host of "paradoxes" that could only be reconciled with the standard theory by a stretch of

---

[45] Though Fritz Machlup had called attention to the importance of this part of the economy (see Machlup 1962).

Ptolemaic constructions.[46] It was obvious that neoclassical theory was leaving out some things that were of first order importance.

For me, and for many others, the failure of the standard competitive model to deal with the fundamental problems confronting the economy, such as persistent unemployment, other than as seemingly ad hoc "rigidities," was deeply disturbing. If that explanation were correct, the prescription followed: make labor markets more flexible. And while many employers and conservatives were attracted to the idea that the "solution" to the problem of unemployment was lower real wages, I was unconvinced. A clear undertone in Keynes' writing is that this might make matters even worse.[47]

Obviously, the assumptions underlying the model—perfect information, perfect competition, perfect rationality—were unpersuasive. But if, somehow, with all of these "unrealistic" assumptions, the model provided a good description of the economy, all would have been forgiven. The problem was, I have just noted, that the predictions of the model were *not* even vaguely in accord with the world. Of course, there were heroic attempts to salvage the theory. "Perhaps the theory would have been true, were it not for government intervention." Or "perhaps those who thought they were involuntarily unemployed were really voluntarily unemployed—after all, there was surely some job that they could have gotten." "Yes, the economy may not be fully efficient, but the deviations are small and can be ignored." But the fact of the matter is that the deviations are pervasive and large[48] and touch on the functioning of each of the markets. Corporate finance *does* matter, many borrowers do face credit rationing, and individuals cannot buy insurance against many of the most important risks which they face. Economies do face problems of unemployment, even in the absence of (enforced) minimum wage legislation and even in countries without strong labor protections and unions.[49] And all of this does make a difference for the well being of individuals and the functioning of markets.

For much of the profession, however, the motivation for a New Paradigm came not so much from these huge disparities between the predictions of the model and reality, but from internal forces, from the drive for internal coherence and completeness.

---

[46] For instance, in Stiglitz (1973d) I explained why firms should never pay dividends (the "dividend paradox"), and in Stiglitz (1982e, 1987c) I presented a number of other tax paradoxes. As editor of the *Journal of Economic Perspectives*, I ran a regular column on paradoxes, focusing in particular on those in financial markets. See, e.g. Thaler (1990) and Rabin and Thaler (2001). Equally striking is how hard it is to confirm empirically some of the most widely accepted propositions. For instance, standard economic theory argues that raising the minimum wage should result in an increase in unemployment. Card and Krueger (1994) argue otherwise. While their work has been the subject of extensive controversy, what is clear from the entire debate is that the large negative effects that are predicted by the standard theory do not emerge from the data.

[47] Moreover, in most economies there are some sectors in which unions are weak and in which government is unable to enforce minimum wages, and yet unemployment persists.

[48] Thus, attempts by defenders of the neoclassical model, such as Lucas (1987), suggesting that the loss of welfare is small depend on a host of assumptions, such as that there is no credit rationing; that each person has an equiproportionate reduction in employment (rather than, as in fact the case, a few individuals facing large constraints on their sales of labor services—unemployment.)

[49] Indeed, as Latin America stripped away much of its labor protections, unemployment actually increased.

There is a drive within any discipline for internal consistency, for general theories that explain a multiplicity of phenomena, as opposed to specific theories designed to address particular problems.

The State of Economic Theory in the Middle of the Twentieth Century

Let me say a few words then about the state of economic theory in the 1950s and 1960s. The mainstream consisted of two bodies of work: competitive equilibrium theory and macro economics.[50] The Walrasian theory of the economy—equilibrium determined in competitive markets at the point where demand equaled supply—was being finely honed; Arrow and Debreu and others were proving the existence of equilibrium and establishing the conditions under which the market was efficient. This rigorous body of analysis played a critical role in the development of the New Paradigm, as I shall shortly explain. Simultaneously, Samuelson and Solow and the MIT school were using simplified versions of the general equilibrium model to enhance understanding of how the economy functions, explaining, for instance, how with free trade factor prices would be equalized.

The world had emerged from the Great Depression, and, fortunately, the worries about the global economy sinking into another depression after World War II proved unfounded. The Great Depression had shaken confidence in the market economy, but Keynes' prescriptions about how to restore the economy to full employment were by then well accepted, as was Samuelson's neoclassical synthesis—the belief that once the economy was restored to full employment, the neoclassical model, with all of its implications for economic efficiency, could then be safely relied upon.

Macro economics describing the overall behavior of the aggregate variables of the economy was not based on the "rigorous" foundations that had marked developments in micro economics. The two branches were compartmentalized. One branch "predicted" that the problems on which the other branch focused could not occur.

There "had" to be a revolution which reconciled the two, either by changing macro economics to make it consistent with micro economics, or vice versa. One major strand took the first course; I, and others (most notably Edmund Phelps),[51] focusing on market information took the second—though in the end, having developed a

---

[50] I should, perhaps, note that the mainstream here refers to that in the United States. At this time, Marxian economics still held sway in large parts of academia elsewhere in the world. At Cambridge, Robinson, Kaldor, and others were trying to build a broader set of models based on Keynesian economics. They rejected the neoclassical synthesis. At the time, except in isolated research centers at various parts of the world, little attention was paid to the ideas of Schumpeter, Knight, and Hayek. They neither were discussed in the standard principles textbooks, nor made more than a brief appearance in graduate courses. As the discussion below will make clear, the New Paradigm both rediscovered them and re-examined their conclusions, trying to clarify the ways in which the underlying assumptions differed from that of the more standard analyses.

[51] See Phelps (1970), which identified the important role of imperfections in labor markets (see also, in particular, the paper by Mortenson 1970) and product markets (see, in particular, the Phelps-Winter

new micro economics, it became clear that the macro economics too needed to be changed, for reasons which I shall explain below.

Mathematical models made an important contribution in setting the stage for a paradigm shift: increasing the precision of the assumptions and their implications made it possible to identify the role of each assumption and their full implications, and it was this that eventually made a new paradigm both possible and essential. The work of Arrow and Debreu laying out rigorously the foundations of modern competitive analysis played a particularly important role; by identifying the conditions that had to be satisfied if the market economy were to be efficient, it laid out an agenda exploring the consequences of each of the market failures that might arise, when those assumptions were not satisfied.

Some of the assumptions had long been recognized—the importance of externalities and competition—but others, in particular, the importance of the need for a complete set of risk and future markets, had not been fully grasped. It gave rise to an obvious research program: were there weaker assumptions under which the central results of the competitive (neoclassic paradigm) would still hold? In each of the cases, there were a few additional contexts in which standard results could be obtained— but they were so restrictive as to be uninteresting, and simply reinforced a view of the limitations of the standard model.

After Arrow and Debreu's work, there followed, for instance, a set of papers exploring the dynamic inefficiency and instability of economies without future markets extending infinitely far into the future.[52] It was obvious that such markets did not exist; but it was not obvious how badly wrong matters could go if they did not. The new presumption was that the economy was likely not to be dynamically efficient, nor to converge smoothly to a steady state equilibrium. Indeed, it was easy to construct simple models where, even with rational expectations, the economy "wobbled" along, an almost infinity of paths, neither settling down to a steady state equilibrium nor diverging in an explosive manner.[53] The fact that the standard neoclassical results still held, if the economy consisted of a single individual living infinitely long, even in the absence of futures market extending infinitely far into the future, was hardly reassuring.

Another set of papers explored the behavior of the economy when there was not a full set of risk markets. They showed it was not even clear what firms should or do

---

1970 paper, which Bruce Greenwald and I subsequently reformulated in terms of our New Theory of the Firm (see Greenwald and Stiglitz 2003)).

[52] Hahn (1960); Shell and Stiglitz (1967); Shell et al. (1969); Stiglitz (1973b).

[53] See Stiglitz (1973b). The possibility of multiple dynamic equilibria was a major theme in the growth literature of the 1960s. The later literature did not resolve the matter, but rather ignored it, by using representative agent models in which, by assumption, distributional issues simply do not arise. But the problems of multiplicity were, in fact, far worse than we realized in the 1960s, especially when account is taken of the absence of risk markets (see the important literature on "sunspot equilibria," Cass and Shell 1983). The existence of multiplicity of equilibria is a theme to which I return repeatedly. For instance, in Stiglitz and Greenwald (2003), we showed that there could be an equilibrium in which interest rates are low and bankruptcy probabilities low, and another in which interest rates are high and bankruptcy probabilities are high. Hoff and Stiglitz (2000) provide a general discussion of the structure of dynamic models with multiple equilibria. I should emphasize that what I have been concerned with is not a theoretical nicety, that is just the *possibility* of a multiplicity of equilibria, but the fact that with plausible parameters and structures, the economy is quite likely to be characterized by a multiplicity of equilibria.

maximize, and even under the restrictive circumstances in which one could define clearly what value maximization might mean, value maximization did not in general lead to economic efficiency.[54]

Soon, it became clear how important the absence of risk markets was to some of the most cherished beliefs of economists: with David Newbery, I was able to show that free trade, rather than making everyone better off, could actually make everyone worse off (Newbery and Stiglitz 1984). Capital market liberalization, rather than stabilizing the economy, could lead to more volatility (Stiglitz 2004).

But the absence of a full set of futures and risk markets raised, in many ways, deeper problems: why did these markets not exist? Neoclassical theory had no way of beginning to answer this question.[55]

It soon became clear to me, however, that there was a more profound problem with the standard paradigm, one which earlier work on the foundations of competitive equilibrium analysis had not fully realized: the underlying information assumptions. In the years immediately following Arrow and Debreu's work, there were some attempts to extend the Arrow-Debreu framework into domains where information was imperfect, by such important scholars as Radner (1968), Marschak (1971), and Hurwicz (1960). Debreu, for instance, had assumed that all participants in the economy had the same information sets, in other words, they could ascertain whether a particular state of nature had occurred. But what would happen if there were some states observable to some, but not to others? This obviously restricted the set of feasible contracts; it went a little way, but only a little way, in explaining the absence of risk markets.

Other work, on the Theory of Teams,[56] highlighted how organizations could function where different members of the team had different information, though they shared the same objectives.

But for all of these advances, the competitive general equilibrium approach found it difficult to develop into a new paradigm; the models were so complex that the simple insights which could form the basis of a revolution, of a paradigm shift, largely eluded them.

This work, as well as much of the work emanating out of the MIT school then rising to its ascendancy suffered from another problem. The thrust of the research was to show that the results of Arrow and Debreu, including the fundamental theorem of welfare economics, were *more* robust than the assumptions that they had employed might have led one to believe. They sought, as we noted, to find conditions under

---

[54] Diamond (1967), building on the work of Modigliani and Miller (1958), had shown that if the only decision facing firms was the scale of production—the probability distribution of returns was fixed and unalterable—then there was a sense in which one could show that stock market value maximization leads to (constrained) Pareto efficiency. But an essential assumption in his analysis was that there was only a single commodity in the economy. If there were two commodities, then even under the highly restrictive assumptions postulated by Diamond, the market was not efficient. See Stiglitz (1982b). More general analyses of the behavior of the firm and the efficiency of the markets were provided by Stiglitz (1982c); Grossman and Stiglitz (1980a); and Greenwald and Stiglitz (1986a).

[55] One approach taken was to assume that transactions costs prevented the existence of certain markets; but such an explanation was unpersuasive, given the value associated with the transfer of risk relative to the costs of running a market.

[56] Marschak (1960) and Marschak and Radner (1972).

which, even when there were problems of moral hazard or incentives or an incomplete set of insurance markets, the market could be efficient; they succeeded in obtaining such results—if there were, for instance, a single good produced.[57]

My reaction was the opposite: I became convinced that Arrow and Debreu had essentially found that singular set of assumptions under which the market economy was efficient. It was a remarkable achievement—but more in telling us about the limits of the market than in its strength. It seemed a mistake to focus one's research on finding the minor generalizations in which the standard results held. Anyone who understood the role that the assumptions played in the proofs of the efficiency of the market economy understood that the search for a major extension was likely to be fruitless; and that has proven to be the case. Indeed, one didn't need to go very far: with two commodities, the inefficiency of the stock market, the insurance market, or the sharecropping economy could easily be established.[58] Once one understood more fully the mathematical structure of economies with imperfect information and limited risk markets, it became almost obvious that the market economy was inefficient; for instance, in the moral hazard model, actions by individuals (in the care they undertook to avoid an accident) had, even in a competitive market, externality-like effects on others, as the premia charged had to change commensurately.

Part of my conviction was based on the study of *second best economics*, pioneered by James Meade (1955) and Lipsey and Lancaster (1957). They had shown that when there were two or more market failures, remedying one quite likely could lead to a worsening of welfare. Problems of imperfect information or incomplete markets could be viewed as "market failures." Eliminating one source of information im-perfection, or doing something about one consequence (like wage or price rigidity) might well constitute a lowering of general welfare. Research over the succeeding three decades showed that there was much to this intuition. For instance, no proposition in economics has been more of the hallmark of the well trained or indoctrinated economist than the belief in free trade; a transaction which is mutually freely engaged in must make both sides better off. The logic extended, in somewhat modified form, to changes in trade regimes: while free trade might not make everyone better off, the winners could more than compensate the losers. But the analysis was predicated on *first best economics*. If there were imperfect risk markets, then trade liberalization might expose countries to more risk; the response to the increased risk was to pro-duce less of the high risk high return goods; and *everyone could be worse off*. Free trade, rather than being a Pareto improvement, led, as I noted above, to a Pareto inferior equilibrium (Newbery and Stiglitz 1984). Of course, a naïve response would be: retain the faith in free trade, simply address the market failure of incomplete insurance markets. But that's where the New Paradigm comes in in a powerful way: the incompleteness of insurance markets may be an inherent consequence of the

---

[57] For instance, Diamond (1967) showed that the stock market was efficient, if there was a single commodity (and if some other stringent conditions, like the absence of bankruptcy, were also satisfied).

[58] See Newbery and Stiglitz (1982), Stiglitz (1982b). The two papers setting forth the general mathematical structure—making it clear why competitive markets *had* to be inefficient, were Greenwald and Stiglitz (1986) and Arnott et al. [1994]. For a broader discussion of this work, see the introductory essay to Volume III.

existence of costly, imperfect, and asymmetric information, problems which cannot simply be wished away. The problem is *endogenous*.

The Problem of Completeness and Coherence

The fact that the standard theory could not explain the absence of key markets was an example of the incompleteness of the previous paradigm—one of the reasons that it was inevitable that a new paradigm eventually be created.

Ronald Coase had attacked another lacuna. While neoclassical economics praised the role of markets and prices, in fact, most transactions occurred within firms (and much occurred within households), and internally few firms resorted to market mechanisms. Clearly, there were limitations to the market mechanism. Coase argued that transactions costs were the key, and used that idea to explain the boundary between firms and markets (1937).

Following Coase's work, transactions costs became the favored explanation for any *seeming* deviation between neoclassical theory and what was observed; and once transactions costs were incorporated, it was asserted, the standard paradigm could reign once again. Stigler (1967), for instance, argued that observed imperfections in capital markets could be explained by transactions costs. Of course, transactions costs were real, and in some contexts they were important. There were, however, two deeper questions: could they account for the deviations between what was observed and predicted? And was it true that, once account was taken of transactions costs, the *properties* of the system remained essentially unchanged? That is, transactions costs might explain why some markets didn't exist, and why resource allocations internal to the firm did not use markets; but that did not mean that all the standard properties of the neoclassical model—from market clearing to efficiency (taking into account these real costs)—were still valid. Unfortunately, this gambit directed at saving the neoclassical paradigm simply didn't work. Even small transactions costs could lead to large levels of monopoly power[59] and market inefficiency (Greenwald and Stiglitz 1986a). But the main thrust of the New Paradigm was that the behavior of the economy was, in many ways, *qualitatively* different. In equilibrium there could exist credit rationing or unemployment.

The Information Economy, Information Economics, and Statistical Inference

As the discussion of the new economy and the information economy[60] moved center stage, it was hard *not* to discuss innovation, but, as we have noted, the standard

---

[59] Diamond (1971); Stiglitz (1988d).

[60] The term 'new economy' arose in the mid-1990s to describe the quickly evolving economy, in which services, and especially those related to information (the Internet, the dot com revolution, and telecommunications) were of increasing importance. These sectors differed in many ways from manufacturing: returns to scale were far more important (indeed, almost all costs were fixed and sunk), as were network externalities. The new economy was sometimes described as the weightless economy (because it was based not on material goods, but on ideas) or the knowledge economy (see, for instance Stiglitz 1999d).

models had little to say about the subject. These developments played an important role in drawing attention to the New Paradigm but had less to do with the development of the field itself.

What did make a difference for me (and I suspect for many other researchers in the field) was the development of the modern statistical theory of inference.[61] How did people come to believe what they believed?[62] Once one realized that beliefs were affected by behavior, it became clear that behavior would be affected by how individuals believed beliefs would be affected by what they did, one of the key insights of the New Paradigm.

Imperfect Competition and Non-convexities

In many ways, Paul Samuelson's *Foundations of Economic Analysis* (1947) defined neoclassical economics as of the middle of the twentieth century. One of Samuelson's great contributions in the *Foundations* was to argue that economic problems could be reduced to constrained maximization problems. (More accurately, the problems of households and firms could be so reduced. The fact that the *Nash equilibrium* of the economy as a whole was not efficient meant that in general, the behavior of the economic system as a whole could not be reduced to the solution of a maximization problem, or at least not one that was of much interest.)

Essential to the neoclassical paradigm, as Samuelson pointed out so clearly, was the assumption of convexity—notions of diminishing returns which had played a central role in standard economics up to that time. But as we noted, one of the aspects of the shift to the *New Paradigm* was the recognition of the pervasiveness of non-convexities. One could not simply wave one's hands and ignore them

Of course, the most immediate consequence was to complicate the mathematics. Proofs of the existence of equilibrium relied heavily on convexity, as did the second fundamental theorem of welfare economics (asserting that every Pareto Optimal allocation could be achieved by market mechanisms, given some lump sum redistribution.)

But behind the mathematics were some fundamental economic issues, and the resolution of these economic and mathematical issues, and the construction of equilibrium models in which non-convexities played an essential role, represented one of the achievements of the New Paradigm. Most notably, with Avinash Dixit, I constructed a general equilibrium model of monopolistic competition; increasing returns meant there were sufficiently few firms that each faced a downward sloping demand curve, yet the demand by consumers for diversity meant that there were still

---

[61] I am particularly indebted to my statistics teacher at MIT, Harold Freeman, who approached statistics and econometrics from a probabilistic perspective. The theory of subjective probability had been developed not long before, by Savage (1954) and the influence of Blackwell can be seen especially in my joint work with Roy Radner, reprinted in this volume, Chapter 22.

[62] I also owe a debt to my Amherst College education, where much of our attention was centered on epistemological questions.

large numbers of firms. (One could use the model to assess how well the market did in trading off diversity versus fixed costs.)[63] This paper has become a central ingredient of recent models in growth theory (Romer 1986), international finance (Obstfeld and Rogoff 1995), and international trade (Krugman 1998).

There were several reasons that increasing returns presented such a challenge. Think first about the problem of economic efficiency. If a firm has increasing returns to scale, then clearly it is better to have fewer firms, and most importantly, to have one firm rather than two or more firms producing a given commodity. That means there will be a monopoly in each industry. Having a monopoly in an industry means that one cannot assume price taking behavior (a central hypothesis in the neoclassical model), but it does not mean that one has unlimited market power: there always exist substitutes. The model of monopolistic competition was predicated on the belief that there were large numbers of substitutes, enough that the firm's behavior had no significant effect on any particular firm—there were no *strategic* interactions. (The analysis of markets with strategic interactions is obviously more complicated, and is discussed at greater length in Volume III.) The fact that consumers preferred diversity limited the benefits that accrued from the returns to scale. This is, in fact, the central issue in the construction of models with increasing returns at the firm level: what are the "factors" that offset the economies of scale, the sources of diseconomies of scale. That there were such factors underlay Marshallian economics, with its familiar U-shaped cost curve; in traditional discussions, it was managerial diseconomies of scale.

Information and the increasing importance of R&D changed the importance attached to the economies of scale. They also redirected attention to understanding the sources of diseconomies of scale. It was not just problems arising from span of control, although that remained important. In Dixit-Stiglitz (1977), it was the desire for product diversity; in Stiglitz (1986d) and in Arnott and Stiglitz (1981) it was transportation costs; in Stiglitz (1974g) and Arnott and Stiglitz (1979) it was, in part, the costs of congestion; and in Sah and Stiglitz (1985c) it was human fallibility—and the diversity of views that came from having many decision makers. Capital constraints (arising, for instance, from agency costs/information problems) also limited firm size.[64] A balancing of the costs and benefits led to an equilibrium in which there was more than one firm—but that, of course, did not necessarily mean that the way the market balanced the advantages and disadvantages of size was optimal.[65]

---

[63] In a series of papers, I explored the robustness of the results. See, for instance Stiglitz (1986) and Stiglitz (2003). For a more extensive discussion of the issues, see Volume III.

[64] The constraints/costs of agglomeration are related. Investors wanted to diversify their risk because of human fallibility.

[65] In Volume III, we discuss a view that became popular for a while as it was recognized that increasing returns would limit the number of firms: under "contestability theory" all that was required to ensure efficiency was potential competition, not actual competition. In Stiglitz (1988d) I explained why even small sunk costs would mean that potential competition would not suffice; and indeed demonstrated the curious result that the stronger ex post competition (after entry), the weaker potential competition was in ensuring efficiency.

In these models, there was increasing returns *in some dimensions*; but the overall economy might or might not exhibit increasing returns. Aggregate increasing returns presented a more fundamental problem—a fact that was evident to everyone working in growth theory in the 1950s and 1960s. What would limit the rate of growth, if, in some sense, the economy became more efficient as it became larger and larger? (Again, there might be some balancing, with diseconomies of scale from fixed land just offsetting economies of scale, but, except in special parameterizations, this seemed like a knife edge.) And what determined the distribution of income? With aggregate constant returns to scale, each factor could get paid the value of its marginal product, and the total product would be exhausted. With increasing returns, total product would be more than exhausted, as marginal products exceeded average products. Once again, there was room for a theory of capitalism, where entrepreneurs hired labor, paid them their marginal product, and received for themselves the residual; monopoly power arising from say control of technology (patents) or limitations on access to capital markets (arising from imperfect information) limited entry competition. (There was another way out: the increasing returns could arise simply from externalities, so that firm-level production functions continued to have constant returns to scale. No one, of course, captured these external benefits, but at least there was no problem of distribution. But this too seemed a knife edge case of little interest; for a slight re-organization in production would internalize what had been an externality, and returns to scale would appear at the level of the firm. More generally, whatever the spillovers that existed across firms and gave rise to increasing returns could clearly exist within a firm.) We explore these issues at greater length in Volumes III and IV.[66]

The neoclassical theory had provided a simple theory of distribution of income—it was not power or politics, but simply the demand and supply of different factors. And by emphasizing the costs of redistribution (adverse incentive effects), it even provided a word of caution to those who would interfere with market mechanisms. The New Paradigm raised questions about these explanations of the determinants of

---

[66] Increasing returns and non-convexities more generally had another set of effects: they introduced a new source of randomness into the economy. Equilibrium may require randomization—in game theory (see next section), the use of mixed strategies. In some cases, randomization is Pareto optimal: If there is not enough food available to support everyone, it is better to randomly choose a subset of people to receive subsistence than to treat everyone the same; and this principle holds more generally. In Chapter 1, I explained (long before mixed strategies became standard tools among game theorists) how randomization could characterize the equilibrium in models with imperfect information, where if only one firm screened the same workers, they would use their differential information to obtain information rents in excess of the costs of screening; but if more than one firm screened the same workers, they would totally bid away rents, and so the firm would be unable to recover their investment in screening. For the general theory, see Dasgupta and Maskin (1986). Arnott and Stiglitz (1988b) showed the desirability of random taxation. (Most of the analyses of optimal taxation simply look for the optimal non-random tax structure; but the non-convexities which are pervasive in these models means that in general, randomization is desirable (see Stiglitz 2002b)). By the same token, non-convexities are, of course, pervasive in agency models, presenting difficult problems in the design of optimal compensation schemes. While these have not been well studied, I did analyze a predecessor problem: the non-convexity associated with efficiency wage models, where workers who are paid more are more productive because of nutrition. See Stiglitz (1976b) and Dasgupta and Ray (1987).

income distribution, and about the consequences of attempts at redistribution, which I discuss at greater length in the introduction to Part I.

The Political and Social Context

I have argued that the time was ripe for a shift in paradigm: advances in neoclassical economics had made clear its limitations, and changes in the economy made the deficiencies in the model—as a model of a modern market economy—increasingly evident. Advances in analytic tools (such as those provided by the theory of statistical inference) meant that some of the seemingly intractable problems posed by information and innovation (such as the non-convexities just discussed) could be addressed.

The revolution in economics, however, cannot be fully separated from what was going on elsewhere in society. This is not the occasion for a historical treatise on the subject. Suffice it to say that the 1960s was a period of a more general breakdown in authority. A system of discrimination, of Jim Crow, of segregation, that had survived in America for a hundred years after the end of slavery finally began to crumble. That in the midst of these titanic shifts, a distinguished American economist, later to win the Nobel Prize (Becker 1971), could argue that discrimination *could not persist* simply because it would not be profitable suggested that something was wrong. If the *logic* of economics was correct, then it was the assumptions that went into that logic that were at fault.

The *logic* of economics contributed to its own undermining in other ways. I and like-minded colleagues, like George Akerlof, were worried about the failure of convergence, the continuing disparities between the developed and less developed countries, the persistence of unemployment and discrimination;[67] we didn't want models that told us these problems could not exist, or that they would go away. We wanted models that told us what to do about these problems. We doubted our elders who told us to continue to toil in the old paradigm in the hopes that some revision might provide us with the requisite insights. A New Paradigm was needed.

THE OLD PARADIGM AND THE NEW

Many of these *Selected Works*, however, are not contributions to the New Paradigm, but to the Old. It was important to understand the strengths and limitations of the Old Paradigm to understand fully why a new one was needed—or to know how to construct it (perhaps, much as the creators of modern art first demonstrated their

---

[67] Indeed, one of the earliest applications of the New Paradigm was to the economics of discrimination. See Stiglitz (1973a, 1974h) and Rothschild and Stiglitz (1982).

mastery of classical techniques).[68] Moreover, the New Paradigm did not mean that the Old Paradigm was irrelevant: there were still important domains where the implications of the standard assumptions had to be more fully explored. Since Tobin and Markowitz's important work in portfolio analysis, economists had focused attention on the importance of risk; yet no one had defined precisely what it meant for one situation to be riskier than another (see Volume III). The rising oil prices brought to the fore the key issue of the intertemporal allocation of scarce depletable resources, a subject also explored in Volume III. In spite of Ramsey's path breaking work (1927), there had in subsequent decades been remarkably little progress in the analysis of the design of optimal tax structures, a subject taken up in Part V. One could, in addition, begin to understand some of the limitations of markets—the consequences, for instance, of imperfections of risk markets or wage and price rigidities—even before one had a fully articulated explanation of these failures, of the kind that the new theory of information provided (see Volumes III and IV).

Still, the most important contribution of these *Selected Works* is the critique of the Old Paradigm and the construction of a new. The central tenets of the old paradigm were easy to state: (a) equilibrium in competitive markets (with rational profit maximizing firms with a fixed technology and utility maximizing households with well defined preferences) was determined by demand equaling supply; (b) in competitive equilibrium profits are driven to zero, prices to marginal cost; (c) there is a single price in the market; (d) equilibrium exists and is Pareto efficient, that is, no one can be made better off without making anyone else worse off; (e) capital markets are efficient—prices transmit all information from the informed to everyone else; (f) efficiency requires decentralization (through the price system); and (g) finance does not matter.

With imperfect information, every one of these conclusions is not, in general, correct (as the papers in this volume demonstrate.) Equilibrium may be characterized by unemployment—yet firms do not lower wages; or by credit rationing—yet lenders do not raise interest rates. Prices are systematically above marginal costs; the differences—rents—are necessary to ensure firms have an incentive to maintain their quality reputation. Markets are often characterized by a price distribution. And, in equilibrium, prices cannot fully convey information—if they did, no one would have an incentive to gather information. There is an equilibrium amount of disequilibrium. Finance does matter, and not just because of the risk of bankruptcy with excessive debt. Actions convey information, and if the original owners try to sell too large of a share of their firm, others will think that the market has overvalued its shares—and the price will fall.

While it is easy to describe simply the critique of the Old Paradigm, it is not so simple to describe market equilibrium under the New Paradigm, precisely because what matters is not just scarcity: what matters, for instance, is how actions convey information, and while there are some general principles (described below), the

---

[68] For instance, I showed (Stiglitz 1969b) the argument that finance was irrelevant was far more general than that originally presented by Modigliani and Miller—before going on to show that when information was imperfect, finance *was* relevant.

particular actions which convey particular information are very situation specific. The articles collected here and subsequent research has, for instance, provided the basis of the design of incentive contracts in labor markets, of a theory of rural organization in developing countries, and of the analysis of optimal financial structures in capital markets.

The New Paradigm also cast a new light on several of the most important concepts in economics: when can the economy be efficiently decentralized? What is the nature and role of competition? The notion embedded in the Arrow-Debreu model not only does not capture what most individuals intuitively mean by competition; but it also does not accurately reflect the role competition plays in the capitalist system.

Macro Economics

One of the most important contributions of the New Paradigm (still I believe insufficiently appreciated) is in providing new foundations for macro economics. Seventy-five years ago, Keynes argued that (a) the economy may be persistently below full employment—even if there are market forces restoring the economy to full employment, they operate slowly; (b) monetary policy may be ineffective in restoring the economy to full employment; but (c) fiscal policy—cutting taxes and increasing expenditures—may be able to stimulate the economy. His policy stance was directly the opposite of much of the conventional wisdom of the time; as the economy slowed down and tax revenues shrunk, deficits increased; conservatives urged governments to cut back on expenditures and raise taxes. Keynes' recipes worked, and, in the many instances in which countries followed the opposite tack (often at the urging of the IMF), the alternative usually failed miserably. Nonetheless, the lack of micro foundations for Keynes' macro economic analyses—combined with the shift in attention in the 1970s from the problem of unemployment to that of inflation—led much of the macro economics profession to go in another direction: a macro economics based on the discredited micro foundations of the Old Paradigm. But micro foundations which assume markets clear—that there is no unemployment—obviously cannot be used as a basis of a macro economic analysis of economic fluctuations involving intermittent periods of underutilization of resources. This is true whether there are rational expectations or not, whether there is imperfect information or not.[69]

As Volume IV makes clear, the New Paradigm not only provides rigorous foundations for traditional Keynesian analysis—explaining, for instance, wage and price rigidities—but provides a broader understanding of macro economic fluctuations and the role of fiscal and monetary policies. It argues that a range of policies and institutions affects not only the extent to which the economy faces shocks, but the extent to which those shocks are amplified and their effects persist. It identifies the

---

[69] Thus, some of the important work in the "alternative" branch of macro economics did recognize information imperfections, and such imperfections even played an important role in explaining how money could have real effects; still, the exploration of the consequences of information imperfections was limited. See in particular, the Phelps-Lucas "islands model," Phelps (1969), Lucas (1972, 1973).

xxxviii SELECTED WORKS OF JOSEPH E. STIGLITZ VOL I

circumstances under which either monetary or fiscal policy may be ineffective. It reinforces, qualifies, and enriches Keynes' conclusions: it helps explain, for instance, why market forces do not quickly restore the economy to full employment, showing that even when wages and prices are flexible, redistributions generated as part of the adjustment process can have a depressing effect on the economy. It helps explain the relative role played by various market imperfections,[70] and the role, for instance, of monetary versus real rigidities.[71] It identifies more fully the important channels/mechanisms through which policies work, some of which were given short shrift in earlier analyses (partially because in the simplistic conventional models with a representative agent and perfect markets, they were irrelevant): the role of finance constraints (credit and equity rationing), balance sheet effects and redistributions. Supply side effects (including through the supply of finance) turn out to be as or even more important than traditional Keynesian demand side effects, especially for small open economies. By the same token, new foundations are provided for monetary policy. With credit increasingly relied upon as the basis of transactions, the traditional analysis based on the transactions demand for money seemed increasingly irrelevant. We analyze how monetary policy—including not only standard open market operations and reserve requirements, but also regulatory policies, like capital adequacy standards—affect the demand and supply for *credit*, and how that affects macro economic equilibrium.[72] Moreover, we explore more carefully the role of expectations— and in particular the part played by rational expectations in, for instance, the consequences of economic policy. Some have contended that with rational expectations, given policy will be ineffective: if increases in the money supply are anticipated and expected, prices will increase in tandem, and there will be no increases in the real money supply; if government spends more, individuals will anticipate the extra taxes that will be required to repay the resulting debt.[73] Expectations—whether rational

[70] As I explain in Volume IV, product market rigidities and imperfections (and consequent changes in markups over the business cycle) may help explain many aspects of the business cycle, but they cannot explain why wages do not fall to clear the labor market (i.e. they cannot explain unemployment).

[71] Keynes himself seems confused about the role of money (nominal) price and wage rigidities. Much of the discussion seems to suggest that if wages fell more rapidly, workers' demand for consumption would fall, and the problem of the insufficiency of aggregate demand would be aggravated. Yet, in the strand of Keynes that was picked up by Hicks (1936)—and which became central to the interpretation that was prevalent within the economics profession—money wage and price rigidities were central. Later Hicks largely recanted on his earlier formulation, developing models which emphasized real balance effects, akin in many ways to some of the ideas presented in Volume IV (Hicks 1988, 1989). (Our ideas, as we note below, are also closely akin to those developed by Irving Fisher (1933), who was concerned with the adverse effects of deflation on debtors. It is curious that though Fisher's work was published before that of Keynes (1932 and 1933), Keynes makes no reference to it.) We suspect that the reason that the money wage/price rigidity model has dominated is that it is easy to analyze the consequences in the context of the standard competitive equilibrium model. Dynamics add an extra layer of complexity.

[72] Although the papers included in Volume IV lay out many of the key ingredients to this reformulation of monetary theory, the most systematic analysis is contained in Greenwald and Stiglitz (2003).

[73] On the ineffectiveness of monetary policy with rational expectations, see Sargent and Wallace (1975); on the ineffectiveness of increases in government expenditures, see Barro (1974) (whose results were anticipated by several years by an unpublished MIT seminar paper by Robert Hall; I substantially extended these results to show—under these highly unrealistic neoclassical assumptions—the inefficacy of government financial policies more generally (see Stiglitz 1983a, 1988c).)

or not—can play an important role in the dynamics of adjustment; but I explain why they cannot, by themselves, explain the lack of efficacy of government policy, in general, even though in particular models, government policy may be ineffective. Indeed, in work with Peter Neary, we showed that with rational expectations, government fiscal policy was even more effective than in standard models; multipliers were actually increased (Neary and Stiglitz 1983).

In short, Keynesian-like results were obtained but in a framework that was distinctly different from that of Keynes; and not only were rigorous micro foundations provided, but there were new insights both into the dynamics of adjustment and economic policy.

While the New Paradigm has become widely accepted among micro economists, much of modern macro economics continues to be based on old fashioned competitive equilibrium analysis. The very dichotomy that motivated anti-Keynesian developments, like new classical theory, the disparity between macro economics and micro economic foundations, has been re-opened, but it is the "new" macro economics which has fallen behind. Indeed, the popular representative agent models even eliminated all possibilities of information asymmetries and any distributional effects. Over time, as the inadequacies of these models to deal with the real world problems on which they were supposed to shed light became evident, various ad hoc complications have been introduced, e.g. concerning wage rigidities. These models have served as a basis for complex analyses, such as the design of optimal monetary policy, but the confidence in the results should be circumscribed by the limitations of the underlying models. While these modifications of the representative agent models are a step in the right direction, efforts would be better directed at developing a better understanding of the underlying macro economic forces. These subjects are pursued in greater depth in Volume IV.

Market Efficiency: The Greatest Challenge Posed by the New Paradigm

Perhaps no result in economics is of greater importance than the "invisible hand theorem" of Adam Smith: in the competitive market economy, individuals and firms in the pursuit of their self-interest are led, as if by an invisible hand, to economic efficiency. This "theorem" provides the foundations of our belief in the free market economy. The sense in which Smith's conjecture was true—and the conditions under which it was valid—have occupied economic theorists for more than two centuries. It was not until 175 years after Smith's 1776 *Wealth of Nations* that Arrow and Debreu[74] established the *fundamental theorems of welfare economics*, showing that (under highly restrictive conditions) competitive markets lead to *Pareto efficiency*, in other words, no one can be made better off without making someone else worse off.

---

[74] Arrow (1951); Debreu (1959).

The assessment of the overall efficiency of the economy is an extraordinarily difficult one, because it involves the performance of the entire *system*, not just the pieces. It was easy to provide a new theory of the firm, or even a new theory of financial markets, and to show that these new theories provided predictions that were more in accord with what was observed, or provided explanations for phenomena about which the neoclassical theory had little to say. Each firm could itself be efficient, each household perfectly rational, yet the system as a whole could still be inefficient. The beauty of Smith's argument and the power of Arrow and Debreu's analysis was that they attempted to address the efficiency of the system as a whole. Of course, if firms are wasting money, if there are massive inefficiencies (of the kind seen during the bubble in the American economy in the later 1990s,)[75] then there is a strong presumption that the market economy *as a system* is not efficient. The central thrust of the results presented in these volumes is that the inefficiencies are pervasive. The market economy is not, in general, efficient. The reason that the invisible hand so often seems invisible is that it's not there.

The most general articulation of this result is in my paper with Bruce Greenwald (Chapter 23). We showed that, in general, whenever information is imperfect or markets incomplete (that is, always)—the economy is not Pareto efficient, *even taking into account the imperfections of information and, the costs of obtaining information and creating markets;*[76] there is a role for government, a far more important role than that associated with the much more limited sets of market failures that had previously been identified, such as arose when competition was limited, or there were externalities, such as associated with pollution. The presumption had changed: while before, the presumption was that the market economy was efficient, now the presumption was that markets were not Pareto efficient, even taking into account the costs of operating markets and gathering information. There were always government interventions which could improve the performance of the economy.

We showed that when information was imperfect, actions of one agent (firm, household) gave rise to "externality like" effects on others; but unlike the traditional theory, where pecuniary externalities did not matter, these did. The risks which individuals undertake affects, for instance, the insurance premia charged, affecting all other insured. The "externalities" to which information imperfections give rise were fundamentally different from environmental externalities. Coase had argued that individuals could get together to internalize the externalities, suggesting that government intervention was not necessary (Coase 1960). Of course, he ignored transactions costs and the problems of preference revelation: bargaining outcomes with imperfect information would itself be inefficient (Farrell 1987). But the externality-like effects to which information imperfections give rise could not so "easily" be resolved.

---

[75] See Stiglitz (2003c); for a historical account showing that this was no isolated incident, see Kindleberger (1978).

[76] We referred to this as "constrained Pareto inefficiency," to remind readers that we had not ignored these important constraints. The paper showed that there were always government interventions which could make some people better off without making anyone else worse off.

While the Greenwald-Stiglitz paper completely undermined the standard argument for the efficiency of the market economy; the analysis of innovation (described earlier and in Volume III) weakened it further. While no one had argued formally for the efficiency of the market in innovation, clearly the belief that the market economy spurred innovation provided one of the bases of confidence in it. Our attack was fundamental: for we argued that knowledge was a public good, and that therefore there was a strong argument that it should be publicly provided. The patent system might provide incentives for innovation, but at a huge cost—not just the creation of monopoly power, which interfered with the efficient allocation of resources, but an inefficiency in the utilization of knowledge itself. The monopoly power not only could persist (contrary to Schumpeter's assertion), but abuses of monopoly power could actually deter innovation. These were not just theoretical niceties: Microsoft seemed to provide a real-life example in an industry that was central to the new economy that was emerging at the end of the twentieth century. If there was an argument for the role of the market economy in spurring innovation, it was clearly different from and more nuanced than that which had been traditionally presented.[77]

Not surprisingly, for those who saw economic analysis as providing the intellectual underpinnings of their faith (or their advocacy) of the market economy, these results were highly disturbing. To be sure, I did not disagree that some individuals had done very well under current arrangements. Bill Gates has little to complain about. But that does not speak to the overall efficiency—or social justice—of the system as a whole.

It is clear who won the great debate between capitalism and socialism. Capitalism *had* to win, because market economies were more efficient and more dynamic. Central planning could not work. One had to decentralize; and markets seemingly provided the basis of efficient decentralization. But what happened in the transition from communism to the market turned out to be a great disappointment: the reforms led to huge decreases in GDP, in the case of Russia, by some 40 percent, in the case of some others, by 70 percent, accompanied by enormous lowering of living standards and increases in poverty. The decreases were more than just a "transition recession." The contrast with what happened in China and Vietnam—which saw enormous increases in GDP and reductions in poverty—is striking.

I had argued in *Whither Socialism?* (1994e) that if the Arrow-Debreu model had been "right," then there is a good chance that one particular variant of socialism—market socialism—would have succeeded. As I argue in the papers in Volume VI, these "experiments" in the transition from communism to the market provide further evidence against that model, and attest to the importance of issues like corporate governance stressed by the New Paradigm.

There was a battle of ideas that corresponded to this battle of economic systems. The New Paradigm had shown that Adam Smith was wrong. It also showed that, in general, when there were information failures, market based decentralization did not lead to economic efficiency; in some cases where the information failures were

---

[77] See Volume III. The argument of Sah and Stiglitz for the advantages of polyarchy over hierarchy constitutes part of that broader argument.

particularly important, it provided the rationale for of "economic integration," (e.g. between land, labor, and capital markets, as in the rural sectors of many developing economies).[78] The Arrow-Debreu model did not explain the success of the market economy—nor the failures, the periodic recessions, the persistent unemployment, or the scandals that rocked the American economy in the 1990s; nor did it explain the failures and successes of the transition from Communism to a market economy. The New Paradigm provided insights into all of these phenomena.

The implications of these results are, of course, profound, and have occupied a large fraction of my attention during the past four decades—both as a theorist and as a policymaker.

The Third Way

I noted earlier that the New Paradigm provided a basis of a new institutional economics and among the most important institutions to be studied was government. The New Paradigm provided, at the same time, both a model of the mixed (government and private) economy of the late twentieth century and a rationale for why that was the best way of organizing the economy. It provided an explanation for why markets by themselves did not lead to economic efficiency and why some form of collective action was required.

In the political language that emerged in the last decade of the twentieth century, it provided the intellectual underpinnings for the "third way," a blend of market and government;[79] but it did more than this: it provided guidance as to the specific roles that each should undertake. The neoclassical model, on the other hand, was a model of a laissez faire economy; and it provided a rationale of policies that often were referred to as neoliberalism, arguing for a minimal role of government, including the elimination of barriers to trade and of economic regulations. If the neoclassical model provided a good description of the economy, then there would be a strong case for neoliberal policies. Thus, as the papers in Volume VI bring home forcefully, debates over policies became intricately linked to debates over *models*.[80]

Response

Sometimes intellectual forces move in sync with forces of society going around them; sometimes there are strong cross-currents. As we noted, while information economics preceded the "information economy," clearly the two reinforced each other. But the move to the right in American and British politics, under Reagan and Thatcher,

[78] This phenomenon, which had long been noticed, but not well explained, was called market interlinkage. It played a central role in the general theory of rural organization, see Bravermann and Stiglitz (1982) and Hoff Braverman, and Stiglitz (1993).

[79] This blend is more complicated than just saying that certain sectors should be assigned to the market, others to the government. In some sectors, for instance, there is an important role for both: government may be both a regulator, a provider of certain kinds of credit, and a guarantor of others. It may subsidize some types of credit, but tax others.

[80] Though as I suggest there, given that the models were so obviously untenable, something more was at issue

occurred just as the intellectual foundations for the belief in free and unfettered markets were being undermined, and the need for government intervention was being put on solid foundations. Privatizations were being advocated just as it was being discovered how restrictive were the conditions under which privatization would lead to efficiency (Sappington and Stiglitz 1987). The international financial institutions (IMF and the World Bank) were pushing the Washington consensus, just as, as academics, we were understanding better why neoliberal policies were not likely to work.[81]

These cross-currents were especially noteworthy, given the success they were having within academia, with a large fraction of PhD theses being written on the various applications of information economics, or other topics, like game theory, questioning the assumptions underlying the competitive model.

I did not, of course, expect an immediate surrender from policymakers. In any subject, the acceptance of a new paradigm is often slow, even when the problems of the old are widely recognized. Those who have invested their reputations and have accumulated skills in the old paradigm loathe seeing all of that go by the wayside. Keynes had remarked how "practical" men are often the slaves of theories of a bygone era.[82] He should have gone on to explain that it was partly because the theories underlying their mindset are so ingrained, and implicit rather than explicit, it was hard for them to think critically about these policies. The policy stances become almost a matter of religion.

But in economics, the problems run deeper; it is not just a matter of intellectual obstinacy—for the paradigm serves particular interests, and these interests have strengthened the incentives for maintaining the old paradigm. As I noted, some have done well under the status quo, and can only lose by a change in thinking.

But I must confess to being slightly disappointed with the quality of the intellectual response. Over the past four decades, the theories underlying the New Paradigm have proven remarkably robust. Not surprisingly, for instance, no one has provided an effective criticism to the fundamental Greenwald-Stiglitz results on the inefficiency of competitive economies when information is imperfect or markets incomplete—that is, always.

Hence, the debate has shifted to two other grounds. One is to move the debate from theory to practice—how empirically significant are these market failures? Largely theoretical work cannot, of course, quantify the losses. Unfortunately, economists have not developed the tools to provide even good ranges of the overall losses in welfare. But certainly, the costs of events like the Great Depression or the booms and busts which have marked capitalist economies since their conception are enormous. The argument that the information efficiencies are small was often simply faith-based:[83] those who believed in the market economy *had* to believe that. It was,

---

[81]   I discuss this anomaly at greater length in the first keynote address I gave as Chief Economist of the World Bank in 1997 (Stiglitz 1998d).

[82]   "Practical men, who believe themselves to be quite exempt from intellectual influences, are usually the slaves of some defunct economist" Keynes (1936).

[83]   In other cases, perfect market assumptions—the existence of perfect capital markets—were used to show that other market imperfections (unemployment) would not have much welfare consequence.

however, partly based on the belief that information in a modern market economy is *relatively* good, and nature abhors discontinuities—if the economy is fully efficient with perfect information, then it will be relatively efficient if there is only a limited amount of information imperfection (and if there are large amounts, there will be strong incentives to acquire information; therefore the size of the information gaps will have to be limited.) But the research program of the New Paradigm was designed to undermine this style of reasoning—for we showed that even a small amount of information imperfections could have very large effects on the nature of the equilibrium; there were large and important discontinuities. Diamond (1971) showed that even small search costs could lead to monopoly pricing. Rothschild and Stiglitz (1976) showed that even small differences in the ability of individuals or their accident probabilities could lead to the non-existence of equilibrium.

This led to a second response: while markets are inefficient, so is government. We had shown only that there were potential interventions of government that could improve the economy. The old theory did not have to have a theory of government, since it argued that no government, no matter how good, could improve upon the performance of the economy. Since government was not needed, it could only make matters worse. It is noteworthy that this defense of free market economics is based not on economic analysis, but on political analysis—and often remarkably unsophisticated political analysis.

But having shown that markets did not necessarily work well, there was still a burden to show that governments could improve matters. Some critics of government intervention naïvely suggested that, after all, government faces information problems just as markets do. But this criticism is not valid. The theories developed in these *Selected Works* and, more generally, within the New Paradigm define particular interventions which the government could undertake which could and would make everyone better off, or which could or would increase societal well being more broadly. We showed that the constraints and information facing government are markedly different from that facing the private sector; and that the objectives being pursued differ too.

Theory by itself cannot settle the matter, though one can use theoretical analysis to assess some of the theoretical criticisms of government waste (such as those associated with rent dissipation)[84] and some of the arguments for privatization (which rest on as weak micro foundations as do the corresponding models arguing for the efficiency of the market economy). As Nobel economist Herbert Simon—founder of modern organization theory and an astute student of firm behavior—put it (1991):

Most producers are employees, not owners of firms...Viewed from the vantage point of classical [economic] theory, they have no reason to maximize the profits of the firms, except to the extent that they can be controlled by owners...Moreover, there is no difference, in this respect, among profit—making firms, non-profit organizations, and bureaucratic organizations. All have exactly the same problem of inducing their employees to work toward the organizational goals. There is no reason, *a priori*, why it should be easier (or harder) to

---

[84] Which typically assume perfect competition in the market for rents (see, e.g. Krueger 1974).

produce this motivation in organizations aimed at maximizing profits than in organizations with different goals. *The conclusion that organizations motivated by profits will be more efficient than other organizations does not follow in an organizational economy from the neoclassical assumptions. If it is empirically true, other axioms will have to be introduced to account for it* (emphasis added).

If theory cannot settle these matters, what about empirical analyses? Empirical analyses are suggestive, but not surprisingly those with different prejudices read history differently. Certainly, governments have played a large role in the developing countries that have done the best.[85] These issues are discussed more thoroughly in Volumes III, V, and VI.

While free market advocates were right to emphasize the importance of political processes (which might inhibit the ability of the government to improve upon the market's resource allocation), regretfully, much of those developments in political theory (which supported the conservative position) rested on some of the same faulty hypotheses that underlay neoclassical economics. Just as economists began to question "rational actors with full information operating in perfectly competitive markets" models, political scientists began using that model to explore the implications for political equilibrium. The results of these analyses may be as questionable as those more narrowly within the economics domain.[86]

Understanding better political processes—including the consequences of information imperfections, and the interlinkages between economics and politics—is one of the important tasks ahead. Interestingly, popular discourse has recently focused on precisely these topics: there is considerable discussion, for instance, of the importance of *transparency*, i.e. of good information about what the government is doing. My more recent work has begun exploring not only the incentives for secrecy (lack of disclosure), its consequences, as well as the consequences of creating asymmetries of information between government and citizens (rights to privacy) (Stiglitz 2001d), I have also explored how economic policies can help create—or undermine—the demand for a rule of law, with long term implications for the evolution of society.[87] Karla Hoff and I have, for instance, attempted to analyze the transition from communism to the market economy from this perspective: economic policies affect the demand for the rule of law, just as the absence (or presence) of the rule of law affects economic behavior.[88] There is a rich research agenda ahead, and the outcome of this research will, I am confident, provide us with better guidance on the circumstances in which government intervention will improve societal well being—and the forms of government intervention that are most likely to succeed.

[85] See, for instance, the World Bank's (1993) study of the East Miracle countries (of which I was one of the principal authors), and Stiglitz (1996).

[86] Thus, the results on rent dissipation by Krueger (1974) depend on fully contestable "political markets," but in both economics and in politics, small sunk costs can undermine contestability. See Stiglitz (1988d).

[87] See Volume VI, and in particular Hoff and Stiglitz (2004, 2005, 2008).

[88] See Hoff and Stiglitz (2008).

I cannot help but wonder what role did politics and ideology play in the research strategies which attempted to sweep aside market imperfections and second best considerations, and which attempted to show that the result that markets were efficient was robust; it seemed that these researchers wanted to believe that the economy was efficient, and their research *had* to be directed at repairing that edifice.[89] Was it ideology and politics that led so many of these researchers, when it became clear that the presumption that markets were efficient could not be defended, to argue simply that whatever market imperfections existed, the government could not be relied on to correct them?

There is an important corollary of economists' reluctance to abandon their faith in markets: economists have been slow to revise their policy prescriptions; policy advice today by pro-market economists is remarkably similar to what it was a quarter century ago. I believe that markets have been at the center of the most successful economies, but still, I believe that it is foolish to ignore the many instances in which they fail to lead to economic efficiency. Indeed, doing so is likely to lead to failures which will undermine democratic confidence in markets. Just as Keynes can be credited with saving capitalism—by explaining that the market economy can lead to persistent unemployment and what can be done to restore the economy to full employment—so too for the New Paradigm: by identifying a wider set of market failures (including, for instance, those associated with corporate governance), it can lead to a stronger, more stable and resilient market economy. The market economy is too important to be left to the ideological advocates of free markets.

Social Justice and the Distribution of Income

Adam Smith's invisible hand only said that markets would lead to an efficient allocation of resources; no one, in defending the market economy, ever claimed that it would lead to a distribution of income consistent with principles of social justice. What neoclassical economics did argue, however, was that issues of efficiency and equity could be separated from each other, which meant that economists could devote themselves to efficiency. To those who were dissatisfied with the distribution of income that resulted from market forces, they could say: that is a political problem; if there is a political consensus behind a different distribution of well being, "all" one has to do is engage in lump sum redistributions, through which any Pareto efficient outcome can be achieved. The New Paradigm explained why issues of distribution and efficiency could not be separated. For instance, agency problems arose from the separation of land ownership from those who provided the labor required to work the land.

---

[89] I sometimes wonder, what would have happened if my research had led to the opposite result: that I had been able to establish, under quite general conditions, that the market equilibrium was efficient. My concerns with social equality and justice would still have left me with the conviction that there was an important role for government, but the nature of that role, and the kinds of actions required, would have been much circumscribed.

Moreover, the lack of information on the part of government meant that lump sum redistributions were not, in general, feasible; governments in fact rely on income and other taxes which are distortionary. The New Paradigm explained why and provided the basis of a new, more general theory of taxation, called the Pareto Efficient Tax Structures (Volume V), which maximized the well being of one group (given that of all others), subject to the constraints on the information and instruments available to the government. Mirrlees' (1971) theory of optimal income taxation could be viewed as a special application of this theory—identifying the Pareto efficient tax structure which maximized a utilitarian social welfare function.[90]

Given the distortionary nature of income taxation, the problem of changing the distribution of income becomes a much more complex matter: there are advantages of "improving" the ex ante distribution of income (e.g. through increasing the supply of factors which are complementary, say, to unskilled labor or by improving the skills of unskilled labor (Stiglitz 1998b)) and distributional consequences of government expenditures become important.[91]

Finally, in the standard theory, factors simply got paid the value of their marginal product. Perhaps this was one of the reasons that so little attention was paid to the distribution of income. One could only change the after tax distribution of income by changing factor ownership, by changing relative factor supplies (which led to changes in relative factor prices), and by engaging in redistributions. (One of my earliest papers tried to explain the distribution of factor ownership (1969a).) But in a world of imperfect competition and imperfect information, there were other determinants of the distribution of income. *Information* about the relative abilities of individuals could lead to more inequality (see Chapter 3 below). Imperfect information could also lead to discrimination—using race or gender, for instance, as a basis of making inferences about ability when ability itself was not directly observable.[92] But even in the absence of imperfect information, discrimination could persist—one of the important applications of game theory (see below).[93] Asymmetries in liberalization—leading to capital being more mobile than labor—could lead to a weakening of

[90] Mirrlees' work also assumed that the only tax was a tax on income; there were no taxes, for instance on commodities or on wages (presumably because wage rates were unobservable).

[91] Thus, contrary to Musgrave (1959), it is not possible to separate out the "allocative" branch of government from the distributive one.

[92] See Stiglitz (1973a, 1974h) and Rothschild and Stiglitz (1982) (Chapter 6, this volume). For other early discussions of statistical discrimination and information and discrimination, see Arrow (1973) and Phelps (1972).

[93] As I noted earlier, Becker (1971) had tried to argue that in competitive markets, the scope for discrimination was limited, because discrimination would lead to lower wages, and anyone not sharing the "taste" for discrimination would thereby have an incentive to hire the discriminated-against individual. His analysis was deeply flawed, in the way standard competitive theory was flawed: the results which were so counter to what could be seen so transparently should have itself signaled that something was wrong with the underlying theory. Instead, it was used to support policies of ignoring discrimination which was both pervasive and persistent. Perhaps even more important than the imperfect information theories were those employing game theory showing how those that did not discriminate could themselves be "punished," so that a discriminatory equilibrium could be sustained. See Akerlof [1980] and Abreu [1986].

workers' bargaining power and an increase in the burden of taxation on labor (see Volume VI).

In neoclassical theory, the distribution of income was determined by impartial forces; and defenders of the status quo warned that there were high costs to interfering with those forces. Raising minimum wages would simply lead to unemployment; re-distributive taxes would lead reductions in factor supplies (savings and work.) There was almost a moral overtone to the existing distribution of income: higher income individuals were those who worked harder and saved more. In the New Paradigm, managers might receive higher incomes because they had used their powers to en-hance asymmetries of information, limiting the scope for takeovers (Edlin and Stiglitz 1995). It was hard to reconcile the huge levels of executive compensation that suddenly appeared in the late 1980s and 1990s with any "marginal productivity theory;" rather they reflected the abuses of the *Roaring 90s*[94]—in which CEO's awarded themselves stock options and failed to disclose accurate information about the firm's future prospects and the dilution resulting from the options.

The intertwining of politics and the distribution of income was evident: politics had, for instance, stopped the passage of regulations that would have forced meaning-ful disclosure of information about the costs of stock options; and politics had pushed for asymmetric liberalization, with capital flows being far more liberalized than labor flows. Many of the new fortunes depended on intellectual property rights; had they been defined differently, the distribution of wealth would have been different; and certain corporate interests pushed to strengthening intellectual property rights in ways which would enhance their wealth further.

By the same token, in models of statistical discrimination, affirmative action can be an effective way of eliminating discrimination at little or no cost to the economy. So too, the education system, by engaging in excessive screening, may result in excessive inequality: by changing the design of the education system, there can be an increase both in efficiency and equality (see Chapter 3, this volume).

The New Paradigm put new perspectives on achieving economic efficiency; but it also provided new perspectives on attaining social justice.

RESEARCH STRATEGY

From a Narrow Attack to a Broad Agenda

My attack on the conventional paradigm was extraordinarily narrow—I took all the assumptions of the standard model, including that of rationality, and focused my attention on debunking only one assumption, that of perfect information. Surely, I thought, no one would defend that assumption (though many of my colleagues

[94] Discussed more fully in Stiglitz [2003c].

would defend to the end the hypothesis of rationality, simply on the grounds that economics would be groundless without it).[95] If the standard paradigm was shown not to be robust against these mild and realistic changes in assumptions—if the standard results no longer held—then, it seemed to be, support for the conventional paradigm would have to wither away. I wanted to narrow the debate—no one could deny that information was imperfect and markets incomplete. I wanted to show the proponents of the market economy that their conclusions were wrong *using their own models*, but varying only the assumption of information, in ways to which they could not object.

After decades of exploration, the New Paradigm has shown itself to be remarkably robust. In the early days, some worried that we had opened up a Pandora's box. It was, in fact, a curious stance: yes, there is only one way in which information is *perfect*, and so the assumption of perfect information had narrowed the analysis enormously. It was a precise, but wrong, assumption. What should have been viewed as a criticism of the neoclassical model was raised to a virtue.

Actually, the *general competitive theory* yielded few concrete predictions. Virtually any set of demand functions could be shown to be consistent with rational, utility maximizing behavior. It was only when additional assumptions, like the existence of a representative agent (assuming away all distribution effects) that stronger predictions could be obtained. With equally stringent (and implausible) assumptions, models of the New Paradigm can also give equally clear predictions. The problem is more with social conventions than with analytics: the assumption of the representative agent has come to be accepted *as a working model*, even though it leaves out much that is important, and clearly cannot be relied on to provide an accurate description of the economy as a whole. It *assumes*, for instance, that the distribution of income has no effects. Within the New Paradigm, there are fewer working hypotheses that have received such general acceptance. And without these, there is always a worry that any results lack generality, depending on the particular assumptions made in the analysis. Economists feel more comfortable working with generally accepted assumptions that are known to be wrong (such as the assumption of perfection information) *and* critical, than they are working with assumptions that might be right, at least within a certain domain, but have not yet come to be generally accepted.[96, 97]

[95] Once the issue of *endogenous* information is introduced, there is a seeming limit to rationality. We can say we "rationally" balance (expected) costs and benefits of gathering information only if we have information about what those costs and benefits are. But how are we to have that information? Are we to make a rational calculation about gathering information about the costs of acquiring information? But how are we to make a rational calculation about *that*. There is an infinite regress (see Winter 1964).

[96] This stance has come to look increasingly peculiar, as economists have moved away from working with general functions (with weak restrictions like concavity) to particular parameterizations. Modern economic theory is rife with examples. The cash-in-advance model has enjoyed enormous popularity in monetary theory, even as the fraction of transactions that require cash in advance (and cannot be facilitated by credit) diminishes. Menu cost theory has been used to explain price rigidities, even though costs of adjusting quantities may be an order of magnitude greater, and even though not adjusting prices imposes, as a result, much higher adjustments in quantities.

[97] In the attempt to minimize the significance of these developments in economic theory, some have suggested that the results in the economics of information (and the broader agenda described below) are

The basic themes we identified early on (such as moral hazard and adverse selection) have remained at the center of the discussion, though they have been amplified and extended in many directions, and put on far more rigorous groundings, as we discuss briefly in the introductions to Parts I and II.

While tactically, the strategy of working within the neoclassical framework—altering only the assumption about information—may have made sense, I must confess a certain degree of dissatisfaction with having kept so much of the edifice of the Old Paradigm; and I felt this particularly as my work on development economics proceeded. Underlying development is a transformation of society[98]—changing preferences and institutions as well as changing technology. But the standard theory was based on fixed preferences and rational behavior.

Behavioral Economics, Endogenous Preferences, and Rationality

Behavioral economics has identified numerous areas where there are systematic deviations from rationality, and there is even somewhat of a superstructure within which these deviations from rationality are coming to be understood.[99] Still, the questions remain: how robust and general are the results? How profoundly do they affect the behavior of the economic system? While our thinking on particular problems has changed, how have they affected how we think about the performance of the economic system as a whole? To some, the field has some of the feeling of the economics of information in its early days.

Some of the behaviors uncovered by behavior economics can be viewed as simply responses to imperfect and limited information, and to that extent, this agenda is simply a (more realistic) expansion of the agenda I began. I asked, how do individuals *rationally* respond to imperfect information. Behavioral economics asks, how do individuals actually respond. It shows, for instance, that individuals may put too much or too little weight on low probability events, or that their beliefs can easily be "anchored" (Tversky and Kahnemann 1974).

The standard paradigm also began with the assumption that individuals not only have well defined beliefs but also well defined preferences. But individuals often do not know fully the consequences of their actions, and do not even really know what they like or dislike. As I discussed earlier in this preface, when it comes to

simply wrinkles in a well established theory. After all, the models have almost all of the same assumptions. (As I noted, that was deliberate: I wanted to make clear the critical role of the informational assumptions.) But that is like dismissing a revolution in architecture, simply because the building is made of bricks, mortar, wood, and concrete. The ingredients, the tools, are the same. What matters is how they are put together. With every one of the central conclusions of the standard paradigm having been questioned, it is hard to see these results as just a "wrinkle" in established doctrines.

[98] See, in particular, my Prebisch lecture (Stiglitz 1998c). Earlier, I had investigated the implications of the rationality hypothesis in development in Stiglitz (1989i).

[99] See Akerlof (2001); Tversky and Kahneman (1974); and Kahneman (2002).

key decisions—like savings—it is hard to see how individuals can learn about the consequences of mistaken decisions.

There are further difficulties as individuals themselves change with the experiences they confront over their lifetime.[100] It is a commonplace that experiences shape us. But the hypothesis of well defined preferences suggests the contrary. If experiences do shape us, then our choices today affect our preferences tomorrow. Knowing this affects our choices today. These are more than theoretical niceties. Development entails changes in perceptions and beliefs—a recognition, for instance, that change is possible. Describing and understanding these changes—and the forces that resist them—is part of the core of development economics; a theory based on given, fixed, well defined preferences can be of only limited usefulness in understanding these changes.

The Social Determination of Preferences and Behavior

Individuals do not live in isolation; their values (preferences) and beliefs (say, about the likelihood of various events) are affected by those of others.[101] This is seen most dramatically in the fads that come and go; but is evidenced too by choices in food and clothing. The belief in the neoclassical paradigm is also a case in point: few who say that they believe in the efficiency of markets have studied the underlying proofs of Arrow and Debreu, few understand the limitations, the role of the assumptions that are employed to establish the fundamental theorems of welfare economics. Their beliefs are at least supported by the fact that others, who they trust, believe these propositions. Few ask, how do we *know* what we believe? To be a skeptic about everything is impossible. Few of us can confirm the experiments in physics that underlay our beliefs about the forces of nature. In most areas of the physical sciences, there is sufficient consensus that this is hardly troubling. The problem is that in the social sciences, beliefs are held with a conviction beyond that which is warranted. To be sure, the fundamental theorems of welfare economics and the

---

[100] There is, of course, a large philosophical literature on the meaning of identity.

[101] Moreover, the billions of dollars spent on advertising is testimony to the belief that choices can be shaped; and while some advertisers mainly provide information, much of the expenditures on advertising is directed at shaping preferences. Just as the existence of the huge corporate financial industry provides evidence against the neoclassical theory of finance (in which capital structure does not matter), the existence of the huge advertising industry provides evidence against the postulate of well defined preferences. (Alternatively, firms irrationally believe they can shape preferences; they are simply wasting money.)

Of course, in a world with imperfect information, in which different individuals get different "signals" (have different information), it is rational to base one's behavior partly on observations of others' behavior. Several important literatures have explored these interdependencies in beliefs—in particular, the theory of auctions (where failure to take into account differences in information can lead to the winners' curse—where those who bid most aggressively because they have obtained the strongest "positive" signals concerning the value of the asset systematically find that they have overbid; see Kagel and Levin (1986) and herding theory (see, e.g. Brunnermeier (2001) and Chamley (2004).

But many of the instances where behavior of individuals is affected by that of others cannot be explained simply in these terms; and such "contagion" can have enormous consequences, for instance in the spread of crisis (as in the global financial crises of 1997–98.)

Greenwald-Stiglitz theorem on the inefficiency of the economies with imperfect information and incomplete markets are *theorems*—they have withstood the test of time, and the conclusions follow logically from the assumptions. The problem is going from models to the real world; we can make precise statements about the consequences of policies in a precisely formulated model; but it is a leap of faith that those have much bearing on the real world. Yet we make those leaps of faith every day. Sometimes, what gives us confidence is that the predictions come true. But often, the world is so complex, with so many things going on, that there is ample scope for explaining any discrepancy between predictions and what happens. In the end, what gives most people confidence in their beliefs is that they are held by others who they respect. This explains, in part, why it is so difficult to get a shift in paradigm; and it also explains why, in two different societies, there can be different belief systems, each held with strong conviction.

Multiple Equilibria, Hysteresis, and Social Innovation

In fact, in many of the models of the New Paradigm, there are multiple equilibria. The economy could have ended up in configuration A—and that would have been self-sustaining; or in configuration B. They are both "rational expectations" equilibria. In each, the behavior of each is rational, given their beliefs about how others will behave, and their beliefs about others' behavior is based on their belief about others' beliefs.

Indeed, the most important part of the environment in which we live is the behavior of others. Darwin recognized this as he visited seemingly similar islands in the Galapagos with marked different species. They appeared to have markedly different equilibria. So too, as we look around at economies in different parts of the world, they have markedly different institutional arrangements (Hoff and Stiglitz 2000). The standard mortgage in the UK is very different from the standard mortgage in the US, and there are no differences in preferences (or technology) which can explain the differences.[102]

The Old Paradigm often pretended that it could predict the equilibrium of the economy, so long as it knew the (well defined) preferences and technology. In the New Paradigm, these do not suffice. But the New Paradigm helps explain why social changes in institutional (contractual) arrangements are so difficult to bring about: given the imperfect and asymmetric information about the structure of the economy, there is always a suspicion that people proposing what they suggest is a Pareto improvement are really just proposing an alteration to garner for themselves greater income, and it is difficult to write contracts that ensure that that is not the case (Stiglitz 1992c). (While we have made considerable progress in recent decades in developing a theory of *technological progress*, we have had much less success in an area of equal or greater importance, the development of a theory of social progress or social innovation.)

---

[102]   Indeed, it can be argued that the British variable rate mortgage form in which payments are fixed, but the maturity of the loan is variable is distinctly superior to the American form in which payments can vary markedly. Yet the British form has made few inroads into the American market.

Sometimes, we may not be able to say much about why the economy is in the particular equilibrium it is in. Sometimes, we can trace it to "history." History matters. Once a belief system develops, it can be sustained.

Social context matters in another important way. We care not only about outcomes, but also about processes. It makes a difference, for instance, whether we *choose* what we consume, or if it is given to us. In the standard neoclassical formulation, this should not matter at all; all that matters is *what* we consume. And we care about *fairness*, how we are treated relative to others. An economic system is to be evaluated not just on outcomes but on how those outcomes are arrived at. (This is, in part, I think, too a consequence of imperfect information: We care about fairness, but we may be less sure of what a fair outcome is, e.g. taking into account differences in circumstances and contributions, than what a fair process is.)

The Rationality of the Belief in Rationality

Earlier, I described some of the predictions of the neoclassical theory that seemed hard to reconcile with standard (neoclassical) theory. My research strategy, focusing on imperfections of information, provided an explanation of many phenomena (like unemployment and credit rationing) which were inconsistent with the standard theory. Still, there were some phenomena—including some of the "paradoxes" noted earlier—that remain hard to explain even within the New Paradigm. For instance, in Stiglitz (1973d), I noted that firms could distribute funds from corporations to shareholders much more efficiently (i.e. with less of a tax burden) by buying back shares. This "imperfection" (and the others to which I called attention elsewhere)[103] was not trivial: it appeared that corporations were unnecessarily giving the government billions and billions of dollars every year. Tax paradoxes were of particular importance because, while it might be difficult for us to second guess decisions by GM (were they really making the decisions that maximized value? One might suspect if, after spending say US$100 billion, one ends up with a firm worth US$20 billion, something is wrong with the decision), we can all ascertain the "tax technology." And, given the "tax technology," it appeared that firms were not maximizing market value. Though over the subsequent years and decades, economists worked hard to provide explanations (e.g. concerning signaling (Bhattacharya 1979)), I found most of these explanations unpersuasive: one could convey the same information through share repurchases that one could convey through dividends.[104] Still, it appeared that the market was in an inefficient "social" equilibrium. Many market participants

---

[103] See footnote 46 above.

[104] There is only one minor difference: firms cannot make a commitment on share repurchases, without running the risk that the IRS would treat the share repurchase as a dividend. Firms can make a verbal commitment on dividends, and changes in dividends are often treated as important signals. Still, using dividends is an extremely costly signaling/commitment device, and it is hard to believe that there are not less costly ways of conveying whatever information/commitments are made through dividends. Indeed, the fact that dividends as a fraction of distributions from the corporate sector to the household sector has declined so markedly *after* discussions of the dividend paradox is consistent with this perspective.

looked to dividends as a measure of the strength of a firm, and so long as that was the case, it made sense for firms to issue dividends. By the same token, in the 1990s, it became common for firms to pay senior management with stock options. The "story" that these provided high powered incentives essential for motivating managers was generally accepted. The reality—that one could design better incentive systems, with higher marginal returns to effort with less bearing of risk and preferable tax treatment—was ignored.[105] It seems clear though that these *beliefs*, whether grounded in sound theory or economic reality or not, had an enormous effect on behavior. (And it was also clear that that economic reality was sufficiently complex that seemingly intelligent individuals could persist in these beliefs.)[106]

These are all aspects of economic behavior (many, as we have suggested, closely related to information imperfections) that remain to be developed and incorporated into the New Paradigm.

Relationship Between the New Paradigm and Game Theory

Game theory has provided one of the most important advances in tools available to economists. It is particularly important in the analysis of small group interactions, such as in oligopolistic markets, where each firm has to worry about how its actions may affect the behavior and beliefs of others. In traditional competitive analysis, each player was assumed to be so small as to have no effect on anyone else.

I began my work in the economics of information trying to keep as close to the standard competitive paradigm as possible. But even with the smallest of perturbations in the information assumptions, it became clear that the behavior of even a smaller player could have large results. In Rothschild and Stiglitz (1976), for instance, a new entrant offering a new contract could upset an apparent equilibrium.

Moreover, costly information (costly search) means that while there may be many players in the economy, individuals interact only with a limited number. There is imperfect competition. (For instance, the typical borrower may have access to only one or two banks as a source of funds, even if there are many banks in the world.)

The New Paradigm has thus provided a fertile field in which game theory can show its prowess, and many of the more recent developments in the economics of information have employed game theory. Still, it needs to be emphasized, game theory is a tool; what matters are the assumptions (about behavior, about information,

---

[105] See Chapter 18 below; Nalebuff and Stiglitz (1983b); and Stiglitz (1987c).

[106] Worse still, as I found out when I came to serve in the White House and at the World Bank, such beliefs provided the argumentation behind many policies. I say "provided the argumentation for these policy beliefs" because the real drive for the policy positions may well have been the interests they served. The analysis, for instance, of the problems posed by the standard accounting practices concerning stock options was clear; still, those who benefited, and those who reflected the interests of those who benefited, developed self-serving arguments. I never was persuaded that the analytic skills of those who took these positions was so limited that they actually believed those arguments; rather, it seemed that they knew the conclusion, and they were willing to grasp at any argument that would do.

etc.) and in most of the papers in these *Selected Works,* that is where I have put the emphasis.

THE ORGANIZATION OF THE
SELECTED WORKS

Let me say a word about the overall organization of the *Selected Works*. There is an overall arching theme to the six volumes—the creation of a new paradigm in economics, one which recognizes the central role that imperfections and asymmetries of information play in the economy, how it affects, for example, the existence of markets and their performance, the nature of competition, the roles that prices play, the existence of price dispersions, the ability of the macro economy to respond to shocks, the persistence and pervasiveness of fluctuations in the level of economic activity and its rate of growth, with periodic episodes of underemployment of economic resources. The first two volumes focus on the economics of information, but later volumes take up related issues, such as the bases for technological progress.

The New Paradigm helps define a new way of thinking about the overall organization of the economy—the role of markets and government, the role of other institutions, like banks, and specific markets, like securities markets, and the internal organization of firms. It helps us think about concrete policy issues, like the design of tax structures, privatization, and regulation, with how to deal with long standing problems, like inequality, discrimination, growth and development, and unemployment, and with new problems, such as the transition of the former Communist countries to the market. Thus, much of the last four volumes are the working out, more fully, of the implications of the New Information Paradigm. It is hoped that the *Selected Works* will make clear why a New Paradigm was so badly needed, how far the New Paradigm has gone in addressing the deficiencies of the Old, and the large tasks that remain ahead.

Volume I presents the foundational articles on the economics of information, including the classic papers that describe market equilibrium with adverse selection (where the characteristics of items being traded in the market are not known, but where the mix may change as prices or other terms of the contract change) and moral hazard (where behavior is not perfectly observable and can be altered by prices or other terms of the contract.)

While I have been highly critical of the relevance of the standard competitive paradigm and the policy conclusions that have been drawn from it, I have also argued that the Arrow-Debreu model *underestimates* the importance of competition in the economy (a) because it underestimates the *information* provided by competition, which provides the basis for the design of better incentive structures (Chapter 15; and

Nalebuff and Stiglitz 1983b); (b) because it underestimates the value of the diversity of judgments provided by decentralization, given human fallibility;[107] and (c) because it placed no emphasis on the incentives for innovation (a subject to which we turn in Parts III and IV).

The papers in this volume too show the role of prices in conveying information—a role which is markedly different from that portrayed by the standard competitive equilibrium model. Some have argued, in addition, that stock markets are *efficient*, in the sense that all relevant information is reflected in prices, so that all relevant information is conveyed from the informed to the uninformed through prices. I show that, simply as a matter of economic logic, this cannot be true. Together with the discussions in *Volume II*, they help understand the important, but limited, role that stock markets play in a modern market economy.

Volume II considers how the general theory affects the behavior of every major market—capital, labor, and product markets. It develops, for instance, a general theory of compensation, explains why markets are typically characterized by price and wage distributions, and explains some of the limitations on competition that arise from information imperfections.

The papers analyze what the New Paradigm has to say about the organization and behavior of firms. This new theory of the firm, developed further in *Volume III*, provides the micro foundations for the macro economic analysis of *Volume IV*.

The new information paradigm puts, for instance, a new perspective on the old issues of corporate governance and corporate finance. *Volume III* broadens out the discussion into other areas of micro economics, and includes work that intellectually pre-dates the work on the economics of information: what do we mean by risk, when can we say one situation is riskier than another; how does risk affect behavior, especially firm behavior, and how do economies with imperfect risk markets behave? Of course, the work in Volumes I and II on imperfect information help explain why risk markets are so often imperfect. We explore the objectives of firms when beliefs of different stakeholders differ, and the behavior of firms more generally in the absence of a complete set of risk markets (Arrow- Debreu securities.)

To my mind, the most important results of *Volume III* are those that deal with the efficiency of the competitive economy in the presence of risk; and with innovation and technical progress. The first set of papers show that in the absence of perfect risk markets, the market equilibrium is not Pareto efficient, and a new chapter written for this volume sets the debate on the efficiency of the market economy into context.

Joseph Schumpeter had, in his work, emphasized the importance of dynamic competition. But his work predated the development of analytic approaches to the study of innovation. Volume III contains the papers in which I began the exploration of more general equilibrium models with innovation and began to put Schumpeterian competition on firmer grounds. One may think of these papers as providing (part of) the intellectual underpinnings to the analysis of the new economy (variously called the information economy or the innovation economy).

---

[107] See, e.g. Sah (1991), Sah and Stiglitz (1985c, 1986, 1988a, b); and Stiglitz (1989c, 1991d).

One of the important tasks undertaken here deals with the rear guard attempt to shore up the competitive model, by showing that even when there are important returns to scale (as there are whenever innovation is important), what matters is not actual competition, but potential competition. Some argue that long as the market is contestable, then even if there is only one firm, it will be efficient. We explain why this conclusion is wrong—if there are even arbitrarily sunk costs associated with entry or exit, then markets will not be contestable. Dominant firms, like Microsoft, can maintain their dominance for an extended period of time, and in doing so can suppress the level of innovation. I am pleased to say that this work has played a role in thinking about anti-trust policy in the new economy.

One of the most important advances in micro economic theory of the 1930s was the development of the theory of monopolistic competition, by Edward Chamberlain (1933). There were many markets in which there were enough firms that none worried about the impact of its behavior on others—there were no strategic interactions— yet few enough that (given the extent of product differentiation) all faced downward sloping demand curves. In spite of the potential importance of this theory, it re- mained on the sidelines, until Avinash Dixit and I provided rigorous foundations, which have subsequently found extensive applications, e.g. in international trade, growth theory, and international finance.

Macro economics is concerned with the movements in aggregate variables, like output and employment. A central task of economics over the past century has been to explain the persistent economic fluctuations and extended periods of unemploy- ment, and to reconcile these observations with standard competitive analysis, in which there is no unemployment. Keynes overthrew neoclassical analysis, showing that there could be persistent unemployment, and that government actions could improve matters. But 35 years after Keynes, his analysis came under attack on several grounds. Standard Keynesian analysis was based on the hypothesis of wage rigidities, but wages and prices do adjust, and the first part of *Volume IV* explores some of the consequences of different hypotheses concerning adjustment processes.

The major portion of *Volume IV* is to build a new macro economics based on solid micro foundations—not the perfect markets, perfect information, perfect com- petition micro foundations which led to models in which the central problems of macro economics made no appearance, but the imperfect information, imperfect competition, and incomplete markets view that was developed in Volumes I to III. These models go a long way to creating a New Paradigm for macro economics and monetary policy, a set of models that is far better at explaining actual observed fluctuations, and far better able to develop policies that help the economy deal more effectively with the shocks it confronts. The models are sometimes referred to as new Keynesian models,[108] and while they provide what we believe to be a new and better

[108] The term "new Keynesian models" has been used in a variety of ways. Some of the new Keynesian models simply focus on explaining wage and price rigidities, implicitly assuming that such rigidities are the main, if not only, deviation with the standard competitive model. We argue, to the contrary, that capital market imperfections are equally, if not more, important for understanding macro economic behavior.

explanation of wage and price rigidities, they also emphasize the problems posed by capital market imperfections—with incomplete indexing, wages and price flexibility too can give rise to serious problems.[109]

Volume V turns to the economics of the public sector—both the organization of the public sector, taxation, and expenditure. Given the fundamental results of the previous volumes, that markets by themselves do not lead to efficient outcomes—or socially acceptable distributions of income—it is not surprising that the organization and financing of collective action has been one of my fundamental concerns. Much of this work too is based on the economics of information, in two senses. First, the standard analysis of the incidence of taxation is based on a competitive equilibrium model; but just as macro economics cannot be based on *wrong* micro foundations, so too it is a mistake to make judgments concerning the incidence of taxes on models of the economy that are wrong, which ignore, for instance, the possibilities of credit rationing, unemployment, or the problems posed by corporate governance (the managers typically make the decisions, and they may well not maximize stock holder market value). While the papers presented here make some progress in some of the areas, I have been disappointed by the extent to which tax and expenditure analysis remains confined within the standard competitive paradigm.[110]

More fundamentally, I introduce the concept of Pareto efficient taxation, the set of taxes such that no group can be made better off without making some group worse off, subject to the information constraints facing the government. These information constraints may be different in a developing country than in a developed country; accordingly the Pareto efficient set of taxes may differ. I show, for instance, that the design and reliance on indirect taxes should differ markedly in economies in which there is a good income tax system; or that excessive reliance on value added tax is not desirable in most developing countries with a large, untaxed informal sector.

One of the most important questions is the *level* at which public goods and services should be provided—local, national, or global; and the role of competition among communities in ensuring the efficient provision of public services. While some of the earlier papers presented here develop the general theory of local public goods, some of the later papers introduce, and develop, the concept of global public goods, which has taken on such importance as globalization has proceeded.

The *Selected Works* concludes in *Volume VI* with a discussion of development, transition from Communism to the market economy, the problems of global financial instability, and of globalization. My work on development began almost 40 years ago in Nairobi—and, as I explain in my Nobel lecture,[111] had an enormous influence on shaping my ideas on the economics of information.[112] Developing countries provided

---

[109] The theories presented here can be thought of as putting new theoretical groundings under Robertson's Loanable Funds theories of interest rate determination (1940) and Fisher's debt deflation models (1933).

[110] See my (2002b) public finance retrospective.   [111] And in Stiglitz (2002c).

[112] For instance, the fundamental work on incentives was based on the theory of sharecropping; the work on efficiency wages grew out of the observation that the productivity of workers in developing countries depends on their wage; and the theory of screening was developed in part in response to a

a natural setting in which to examine the consequences of incomplete markets and imperfect information, and my earlier work focused on the enhanced role for government action in development that this entailed.

In the past 15 years, I have been actively involved in major policy debates, both within the United States, as Chairman of President Clinton's Council of Economic Advisers, and in the international community, particularly from my position as the Chief Economist of the World Bank. Some saw this work as disjointed from my earlier theoretical work. I hope the papers produced here will show that this is simply not true. The policy positions I took were based on the economic models of the New Paradigm, which in many cases came to quite different conclusions about strategies for development, the management of crises, and policies for transitioning from Communism to a market economy. The policies that were pushed by the Washington based institutions, the so called Washington Consensus policies, were largely based on the Old Paradigm, and though there were many reasons for the failures of these policies, there is, I believe, overwhelming evidence that among those were deficiencies in the Old Paradigm that the work on the New Paradigm had made abundantly clear. Where strategies and policies based on the New Paradigm have been tried, the outcomes have been far more favorable.

Why This Work?

In these days of the Internet and online access to papers on demand, one has to ask, what is the function of a collection such as this? There are several parts to the answer, which help clarify how the papers included have been selected and organized: the first is the belief that the whole is greater than the sum of the parts. I have attempted to construct a New Paradigm, a new way of thinking, about economics and about the economy, one in which imperfections of information play a central role. My work has, of course, been built on foundations provided by others and a shift in the paradigm of the magnitude that we have seen requires the work of dozens, even hundreds of scholars. As I have extended the work into almost every sub-field of economics— from organization theory and accounting at the micro-micro level, to the theory of the firm, corporate governance, corporate finance, and industrial organization, to the function and conduct of labor, capital and product markets, to public policy issues like public finance and welfare, and to macro and monetary policy—there is a certain unity of thought that can only really be noted by seeing the papers together.

Economic science, like many of the other sciences, has advanced largely by breaking up big problems into smaller parts. The unit of publication has been the short article, taking on one little piece of a broader problem or another. Much work, particularly

request by the Kenyan government for views concerning the optimal level of investment in higher education.

of graduate students, is generated by taking one of these pieces, and adding on to it, modifying it, or qualifying its results. But what matters most is the entire picture.

My style of research was not well suited for the way the profession as a whole was proceeding. I wanted to grapple with a question head on—why were wages in developing countries rigid, what was the role of corporate finance? These were big questions that could not be answered in a 25-page paper. I tended to write massive tomes, papers of 100 to 200 pages, exploring the problems from different angles. The journals were distinctly uninterested in these explorations, where one model provides a critique or a complement for another. To survive, I had to adapt my publications strategy: the larger paper was divided into many smaller papers, published and revised over many subsequent years.[113] Some things inevitably fell into the cracks, but most importantly, the unity of thinking that had motivated the entire process was lost. This collection allows me, for the first time, to bring together the disparate pieces.

I have, no doubt, written too much. But my writing was motivated in part by an unquenchable thirst for a better understanding of how the economy functions, for finding policies that would improve growth and reduce inequality—to help create a better society. I discovered early on that only by thinking through the problems through concrete models and writing down in detail the analysis could I have some confidence in the conclusions. I also believe very strongly that knowledge must be public, that while I may achieve a certain satisfaction from knowing that I had found an answer, only by testing the ideas with others, through discussion and debate, could I be aware of hidden assumptions, slips in the reasoning, or other approaches from which the questions could be attacked.

There is another important reason for a collection such as this. Often, papers written decades ago seem antiquated. Styles of modeling and even language evolve. The questions which motivated us then are often lost on the students of today. Students today are often forced to rediscover for themselves what we knew so long ago. While there is nothing wrong with this rediscovery process—students really do not understand a result unless they recreate it on their own—the consequence is that the profession often gets carried away with wasteful fads and fashions—and because the policy advice of economists often is taken seriously, what is at stake is more than a waste of the researchers' time.

At the beginning of each volume, and at critical points within each volume, I try to put into context what I was doing—the state of thinking of the time, what motivated me and other researchers, what were the questions we successfully answered, and what was left unresolved as we moved on to other topics. And from the current vantage point, I attempt to look back at what has happened since. What questions have remained unresolved? Where is more research needed? How has the thinking been incorporated—or not incorporated—both into the work of the discipline and into policy?

---

[113] For instance, my long paper on efficiency wages written in Nairobi in 1969 was published in approximately five sections between 1974 and 1992. My paper on corporate finance was presented at a meeting in Hakone, Japan in 1969, and was published in at least four sections between 1972 and 1976.

Modern technology has allowed me to keep my *Selected Works* to a manageable length, by providing online the full text of several papers which have had to be edited down here. Also, about a third of my papers have not been included in these six volumes. While I may have my (and the profession, as evidenced by citations, seems to have its) favorites each paper was written for a distinctive reason, as I tried to puzzle out one problem or another, and three decades later I still feel reluctant to relegate any of them to a second class citizenship. In the introductory material I refer briefly to many of them.[114]

This is a long work, and I hope that the reader will be convinced, by the time the journey is over, that it was a road worth taking. In spite of its length, it is a work that is just begun. This, in the end, is the major motivation for this collection: hoping to guide future students into directions that will enhance our understanding of the economy, and lead to policies that will enhance the well being of our society.

---

[114] You may find these and other of my articles at www.josephstiglitz.com

ACKNOWLEDGMENTS

It is commonplace to observe that each advance in our understanding of economics is only possible because we stand on the shoulders of giants that have gone before us. In my case, this is unusually true. My theses advisers at MIT included two of the great economists of the twentieth century, Paul Samuelson and Robert Solow. Other teachers included Nobel Laureates Kenneth Arrow and Franco Modigliani. I owe a debt too to E. Cary Brown who first introduced me to public finance, to Evsey Domar (father of the Harrod-Domar model), Robert Bishop (from whom I learned the intricacies of the Marshallian model, perhaps the last generation of the twentieth century to be so exposed to the doctrines of the nineteenth), and Charles Kindleberger, who taught me international trade.

But even before going to MIT, I had benefited from the marvelous education provided by Amherst College, and not just from my economics professors (Ralph Beals, Arnold Collery, and James Nelson). In history courses, I first came to understand the consequences of colonialism and imperialism, the early encounters between the West and the East, an introduction to globalization before that word became fashionable. In other courses, I came to appreciate the intellectual and social developments of the nineteenth century that had given rise to theories of socialism and liberalism. My physics and mathematics courses gave me the tools so necessary to address the complex economic problems to which I would later turn. Most importantly, Amherst instilled in me the spirit of the Enlightenment, the questioning of assumptions and authority, a commitment to liberal values, and the intellectual frame of mind that is so strongly reflected in the papers collected here.

I left MIT after two years, to go to Cambridge, UK, at the time the other major center of research in economics, where the influence of Keynes and the conflicts he had inspired still lingered. Here, I had the good fortune to be supervised by both Frank Hahn and Joan Robinson, to discuss issues of income distribution with James Meade (whose comments on my theory of income distribution (1969a) were particularly invaluable) and David Champernowne, and debate issues of innovation and macro economics with the likes of Nicholas Kaldor and Richard Goodwin. A brief interlude at the University of Chicago working with Hirofumi Uzawa (which led to our jointly edited book on theories of economic growth)[1] was also extremely influential. Equally important at both MIT and Cambridge were my fellow graduate students and the young assistant professors who became life long friends, and in many

---

[1] Uzawa and Stiglitz (1969).

cases co-authors as well—George Akerlof, James Mirrlees, Peter Diamond, Karl Shell, Eytan Sheshinski, Partha Dasgupta, Geoff Heal, Tony Atkinson, David Newbery, Mrinal Datta-Chaudhuri, Robert Hall, William Nordhaus, Miguel Sidrauski, and a host of others.

I have been lucky: as I moved from MIT to Yale, Kenya, and then onto Stanford, Oxford, Princeton, the Council of Economic Advisers, the World Bank, and finally Columbia, at each place there were intellectual companions that became friends; students that became co-authors; an atmosphere that encouraged debate and discussion—and the resources necessary to make all of this possible were provided. It would be too long to list all of those from whom I have learned and benefited so much, but I do want to single out my co-authors—already some 102-strong and growing, who, in addition to those already listed, include those who worked closely with me in developing various aspects of the New Information Paradigm (Michael Rothschild, Richard Arnott, Andrew Weiss, Carl Shapiro, Barry Nalebuff, Steve Salop, Raaj Sah, Sandy Grossman, Karla Hoff, Dwight Jaffee, Roy Radner, Andrés Rodríguez, Thomas Hellman, Kevin Murdoch, Aaron Edlin, Mark Gersovitz, Arthur Hosios, and Patrick Rey) as well as those who worked with me on a host of other issues: Philippe Aghion, Costas Azariadis, Kaushik Basu, Stefano Battiston, David Bevan, Amar Bhattacharya, Linda Bilmes, Alan Blinder, Charles Blitzer, Robin Boadway, Michael Boskin, Avishay Braverman, Dagobert L. Brito, William A. Brock, Gerard Caprio, David Cass, Andrew Charlton, Karen Clay, Paul A. David, Domenico Delli Gatti, Avinash Dixit, William Easterly, Jonathan Eaton, David Ellerman, M. Shahe Emran, Giovanni Ferri, Ricardo Ffrench-Davis, Drew Fudenberg, Jason Furman, Garance Genicot, Ian Gale, Mauro Gallegati, Richard Gilbert, Sergio Godoy, Jose Goldemberg, Bruce Greenwald, Jonathan H. Hamilton, Robert Holzmann, Patrick Honohan, Macartan Humphreys, Athar Hussain, Roumeen Islam, Ravi Kanbur, Meir Kohn, Anton Korinek, Lawrence J. Lau, Daniel Lederman, Jeffrey Leitzinger, Alec Levinson, Gerald M. Meier, Marcus Miller, Deepak Nayyar, Peter Neary, Jose Ontario Ocampo, Peter Orszag, Guillermo Perry, Boris Pleskovic, Yingyi Qian, Jeffrey Sachs, Michael Salinger, David Sappington, Shari Spiegel, Steven M. Slutsky, Lyn Squire, Nicholas Stern, Jean Tirole, Marilou Uy, Scott J. Wallsten, Carl Walsh, Mark Wolfson, Michael Woodford, Jungyoll Yun, and Shahid Yusuf.

I would be remiss too if I did not mention James Tobin, Bill Brainard, and Gus Ranis—who taught me so much while I was teaching at Yale; and the short interlude from 1969 to 1971 in Kenya, where I not only first became acquainted first hand with the problems of development, but which was a major center of development thinking, with the likes of Gary Fields, John Harris and Michael Todaro. It was there that I made the friendship with David Bevan and Nick Stern (later to be my successor as Chief Economist of the World Bank).

I owe an especial thanks to my colleagues at Columbia University, too numerous to name, but I should single out Ned Phelps and Bruce Greenwald. I began my collaboration with Bruce in the late 1970s, when he was working at Bell Labs, at that time one of the great scientific research centers in the world, and for which I was a consultant. Over the succeeding almost three decades, we have written a book and more than 20 articles together, and taught students from Berkeley, Columbia, and London Business School in a joint course on globalization and markets, and became thoroughly intertwined in our thinking.

An undertaking of this magnitude could not have been accomplished without the assistance of many research assistants working on this project over many years, including Stephan Litschig, Lumi Stevens, Giselle Guzman, and Mo Ji (who was responsible for preparing a Chinese version of *Selected Works*). Jill Blackford was responsible for the overall management of the project at Columbia, and Sara Caro shepherded the book through Oxford University Press. To all of these I owe an immense debt.

INTRODUCTION
TO VOLUME I

ECONOMICS OF INFORMATION

THIS volume and the next collect together the major papers I have written on the economics of information. When I began my research, more than 35 years ago, there was no field called "the economics of information;" no one talked of "the information economy." Today, these ideas touch on every branch of economics—and increasingly, have entered into other social sciences as well. And today, we all talk about the economy as the "information economy."

The papers collected here developing this new branch of economics were in many ways prescient. As classic papers often do, they speak to current concerns, partly because of the influence they have had in shaping modern thinking. New issues— moral hazard, corporate governance, the design of efficient compensation schemes, bankruptcy, accounting—are raised here and in the following volume, sometimes for the first time in modern economics (though in many cases I am able to trace back historical antecedents who foreshadowed the new insights, but were limited by the lack of modern mathematical tools).[1]

This Part sets forth the basic concepts underlying the economics of information, while Part II applies and extends these concepts in a number of different settings, in labor, capital, and product markets. In this introductory essay to Volume I, I want to put the work into context and provide a guide to what follows. This introduction is divided into four parts. In the first, I take up several of the central themes of economics that the New Paradigm helped highlight—in each, it helped change perspectives on the functioning of the economy. In the second, I take up two of the methodological innovations that underlie the New Paradigm. In the third, I describe the organization

---

[1] See, for instance, the quotations at the beginning of Chapter 12, "The Causes and Consequences of the Dependence of Quality on Prices," 1987.

of Volume I and the major results presented. And in the fourth, I turn to Part I of this volume, the two *Perspectives* written over the past three decades, using them to reflect upon the historical development of the New Paradigm.

CENTRAL THEMES

Modern science breaks up big problems into more manageable pieces, each focusing on a narrow set of issues, and I approached the problem of developing a new economics of information by asking (a) what were the key "gaps" in information—it was clear that the problems confronting firms and households were not just those of scarcity; (b) what were the incentives for obtaining information, i.e. what were the consequences of *not* having the information; (c) what were the key mechanisms by which individuals obtained (extracted) information; (d) how did they appropriate the returns from getting information; (e) what did market equilibrium look like with imperfect information; and (f) how efficient were markets, in obtaining, transmitting, and using information, and in allocating resources when information was imperfect (which it always was).

Consider, for instance, the central problem of appropriation of returns. Information was like a public good: there was no marginal cost of an additional individual having information, once discovered. If there were no costs of transmission, that would imply that it should be freely disseminated. "Knowledge is power," but that aphorism really refers to differential information: without information asymmetries, how could one appropriate any returns? It was clear, from the onset, that there was a fundamental tension: if the economy were efficient in the utilization (transmission) of knowledge, then there would be little incentive to gather information. If information remained "private," then there would be incentives to garner information, but not only was information not being efficiently used, but there was also scope for monopoly power. In short, as I began my research into the economics of information, I realized that I was entering a subject of enormous complexity, with inescapable conflicts between static and dynamic efficiency. It also became clear that what had been treated almost as assumptions—that competitive markets always clear, that in equilibrium profits were zero—would have to be re-examined: if true, they were *results* that had to be proved under the new assumptions of imperfect and incomplete information. In many cases, what had simply been taken as obvious assumptions, almost truisms, turned out not to be true.

In this introduction, I want to focus on the implications of the New Paradigm for several of the central themes of modern economics. The standard competitive paradigm focuses on the role—and efficiency—of the price system in conveying information about scarcity, on the importance of competition, and on the role of decentralization. These discussions were part of the broader analysis of the efficiency of the market economy. The New Paradigm put fresh perspectives on each of these themes.

The Role of the Price System

In what was the standard model before the advent of information economics, with the only information problem being scarcity, only prices conveyed information, and they only conveyed information about scarcity. Prices equilibrated demand and supply; a sudden decrease, say, in the supply of oil results in an increase in the price, providing the "signal" for consumers to use less oil. No consumer has to know what other consumers are doing, or even the amount by which supply has decreased; yet overall, consumption is reduced by the requisite amount. But for the economy to function, or to function well, we need to have information about the characteristics of workers, firms, products, those who buy insurance, etc. Standard theory began with the assumption of markets on which homogenous products were being traded. But how did buyers know that the products were all the same? People did not buy and sell Platonic ideals but actual products. Moreover, there were incentives to disguise and to cheat—to try to pass oneself for a higher grade person or product, or to do less work than promised. It seemed to me that a large fraction of real economic activity was directed at these processes of *sorting* and trying to *be sorted*, and of providing *incentives* and *enforcing contracts*—all subjects which had no role in the conventional paradigm.

Though economists used the *language* of incentives, their models really did not analyze the design of incentive systems. Individuals either did the work which was contracted for and got paid, or they did not. There was no issue of trying to motivate workers to work harder or more carefully. Implicitly, it was assumed that one could costlessly observe whether the individuals had done the contracted for work. The essential insight of the New Paradigm[2] was that it was costly—and in some cases impossible—to observe what the individual actually did on a continual basis. In some cases, one could observe the consequences—say the output—but output was affected by variables other than the worker's efforts (like the weather), and typically, output was the result of the efforts of many individuals, with the impact of each being impossible to sort out.

It is here that the conventional paradigm went so far wrong: prices played a larger role in conveying information than just information about scarcity; sometimes they were used as part of the basis of sorting and providing incentives. It would have been nice if the different roles played by prices could have been kept distinct. The standard theory would have continued to have been applicable; the analysis would have been enriched by adding a new dimension. But unfortunately, the roles in conveying information about scarcity and about quality were hopelessly intermingled. Because

---

[2] In Chapter 13 "Incentives and Risk Sharing in Sharecropping," 1974.

of the role in conveying information about quality, prices sometimes became less effective in conveying information about scarcity.

But while the standard paradigm *underestimated* the role of prices, it simultaneously overestimated their roles as well: prices were only part of the information-bases of the economy.[3] In the standard model, prices were essentially a sufficient statistic: they conveyed *all* the relevant information about scarcity. In reality, a host of other things conveyed information and affected behavior. Firms in their production decisions look not only at prices but inventories; investors look at what others in the market are doing (subjecting the market to herd behavior[4]). Investors in developing countries may want to have quantitative information (irrelevant in the standard competitive analysis) concerning total risk exposure.[5]

At the same time, the standard model also overestimated the ability of the price system to convey information. Indeed, a view that became popular in the latter half of the twentieth century held that prices convey perfectly information from the informed to the uninformed, a result referred to as the efficient markets hypothesis.[6] This result was important because it meant that not everyone had to be well informed—and it was apparent that many were not. So long as enough were well informed, the market worked well. Because of their ability to aggregate and convey information, prices conveyed all the relevant information, not only about aggregate scarcity, but, for instance, to investors, about what to invest in.[7]

To me, these results seemed nonsense, and I attacked them at both a theoretical and practical level. Theoretically, with Sandy Grossman, I explained that if markets were perfectly efficient, no one would have an incentive to gather information (Chapter 25): the market would only gather costless information. There was a trade-off between market incentives to gather information and its ability to convey (aggregate and transmit) information. While we showed that there was an equilibrium level of disequilibrium, there was no reason to believe that the way the market solved the problem balanced the trade-offs optimally.

Moreover, the signal extraction problem is extraordinarily complex, so that it should come as no surprise that markets may not efficiently aggregate information; that is, for instance, futures markets, based on disparate individual's behavior reflecting their own information, may not provide a good summary predictor of future spot prices (see Chapter 19).

Indeed, as Salop and I showed (Chapter 20[8] below), not only do markets fail to efficiently "arbitrage" out exogenous noise (disturbances to the economy), but

---

[3] When scarcity was the only problem, under the idealized conditions of the standard model, prices conveyed *all* of the relevant information, so that there was no need for firms to look at other signals.

[4] See Brunnermeier (2001) and Chamley (2004).

[5] In the 1997–98 global financial crisis, the US Treasury and the IMF called for more transparency—including the disclosure of total amounts of short term and long term capital flows. Evidently, while both espoused belief in the competitive market model, neither believed that prices conveyed all the relevant information.

[6] See, for instance, Fama (1970).   [7] This role of prices was called its "price discovery role."

[8] See also Salop and Stiglitz (1982).

markets also sometimes even created noise. Firms might randomize prices in order to extract more consumer surplus from individuals.

The 1990s provided ample evidence that firms (and their CEOs) often successfully manipulated information (often with the support of their accountants). The result was massive misallocation of resources. While the purpose of accounting standards is to provide information about firms on a comparable basis,[9] firms and their accountants often have incentives to provide distorted information, and when that happens, prices will not reflect "realities," and whatever reliance firms place on prices in guiding investment allocations, it may lead to resource misallocations (Stiglitz 2003c). (In practice, of course, as we have already noticed, firms rely only to a limited extent on prices in making their investment decisions: just because dentists in Peoria become enthusiastic about the possibility of steel and the stock price of steel companies goes up, managers of steel companies are not likely to invest more in steel. Rather, they rely more on their own detailed analysis of the market for steel, including developments in technology and changes in demand.[10])

The Meaning of Competition

These papers are about the organization of economic activity—how different organizational forms (firms, markets, and governments, each organized differently) can affect the overall functioning of the economy. My goal was to understand the performance of the *system as a whole*. Thus, the analysis of the theory of the firm, as interesting as it might be in its own right, was really just a building block in this greater structure. I was interested in how the parts interacted to form the whole, and I was interested in trying to create a coherent picture.

At an intuitive level, economists have long recognized the importance of competition. Competition provides the incentives necessary for efficiency. It spurs innovation, finding products that meet the needs and preferences of consumers better. It provides the dynamism to a market economy. While there are many ingredients that go into making a market economy work, clearly competition is one of the most important. Indeed, in the early days of the transition from Communism to a market economy, there arose a debate about the *relative* importance of competition and private property.[11] Clearly, both are ultimately needed. But some focused on the importance of rapid privatization—paying little concern to whether in the process competition was undermined as the result of the creation of monopolies or

---

[9] See Stiglitz and Wolfson (1988) and Greenwald and Stiglitz (1992).

[10] Simplistic investment models had investment depend only on stock market prices. (Empirically, Tobin's q theory has not fared well. See, for example, Summers (1981)). The recent debate about the irrationality of markets—including the prevalence and persistence of anomalies has supported the "rationality" of this kind of behavior. See the discussion in the Preface and in Volume II of *Selected Works*.

[11] The debate was often conducted in a somewhat naïve way, without understanding the complexity of property rights (as they are defined in modern capitalist economies), which carry with themselves, for instance, both obligations and restrictions.

oligopolies. Others focused on competition—paying little attention to whether the units competing were publicly owned or privately owned. To a large extent, Russia and the former Soviet Union took the first route; China (with its reliance in township and village enterprises, especially in the early stages of its transition to the market economy, in the 1980s), the second. The enormous success of China and the failures of Russia are consistent with the view of the key role that competition plays (Stiglitz 1980b).

But these intuitive notions of competition differ from that reflected in the standard competitive model (Stiglitz 1992g). Here, competition means that firms are so small that they have no effect on prices. Each firm is a price taker—faces a horizontal demand curve for its goods. The efficiency of the competitive price system depended on firms and households being price takers.

Once imperfections of information were brought to the fore, hypotheses about firms facing horizontal demand curves become implausible—models of monopolistic or oligopolistic competition are naturally more relevant than are models of perfect competition. A firm can garner an entire market for itself by lowering its price only if others know that it has lowered its prices; if it raises its prices, it still may not lose some customers, because the cost of finding another supplier may be too large. Thus, with costly search, firms naturally face downward sloping demand curves and upward sloping labor supply curves. Even small search costs can lead to monopoly prices.[12]

This is only one of several links between imperfect information and imperfections of competition.[13] Another link is also obvious: the cost of obtaining information is a fixed cost (and as Chapter 19 shows, there are fundamental non-concavities associated with information). There is at least a region of increasing returns to scale. In the context of some kinds of "information"—R&D—this region can be so large that the number of viable firms in the market is limited, so that competition is limited.[14] Changes in the economy—the increasing role of innovation—have heightened these concerns. But these fixed costs play a critical role even in ordinary markets The fixed costs of finding out whether a potential borrower is a good risk result in a limited number of suppliers of funds to any potential lender.[15]

But the possibilities of asymmetries of information can actually completely undermine the competitiveness of certain markets. Akerlof in the *Theory of Lemons* (1970) showed that asymmetric information in the used car market made that market thinner than it otherwise would have been. But while markets might be thinner, they

[12] See, e.g. Diamond (1971); Stiglitz (1985c, published version of 1974c); and Stiglitz (1987b).
[13] A subject explored briefly in my inaugural lecture as Drummond Professor of Economics at All Souls College, Oxford, given in June 1978 (Chapter 2, Volume II).
[14] The argument is even stronger: as I point out in Stiglitz (1987i) if there are *any* fixed, sunk costs (and research expenditures are always sunk) and competition is intense (e.g. Bertrand competition), then in equilibrium, competition ex ante will be limited, and potential competition will not suffice to ensure competitive markets, contrary to the assertion of contestability theory (see Baumol et al. 1982). See Part III of *Selected Works* and Dasgupta and Stiglitz (1988b).
[15] See Jaffee and Stiglitz (1990). As I point out in "The Theory of 'Screening'..." (Chapter 3) and "Information and Economic Analysis..." (Chapter 1), strong competition implies that, with fixed costs, there will only be one lender. The relationship between the strength of ex post competition (after firms have entered the market) and ex ante competition (before entry) is discussed at greater length in Volume III, *Selected Works*.

were still competitive—in his model, everyone was still a price taker. However, in real market situations, asymmetries of information may effectively eliminate competition. This was brought home to me forcefully at the time of my original work on the theory of screening in some consulting work I was doing for the Department of Interior on the design of oil lease auctions. Exploration on a lease gave the firm doing the exploration asymmetric information about the value of that and neighboring leases. Others would not bid as vigorously, knowing that they were in a lose–lose situation: they only would win if they bid more than the informed bidder, who knew how much oil there really was. The asymmetric information had significantly weakened competition and lowered the price that the government could get. In some cases, no firm would bid against the informed bidder.[16]

As Greenwald subsequently showed, these asymmetries—and their consequences for competition—were pervasive in all markets (Greenwald 1986). A worker's current employer knows more about him/her than others, and so a firm attempting to recruit a worker away may worry that they will only be successful if they offer too high a wage—a wage that the existing employer won't match.

The implication was clear: labor mobility was much more limited than the standard model had postulated, giving employers enormous market power. Of course, workers and employers know this (or at least, if they are rational, they *should* realize this), and this affects bidding for the worker at his/her first job. But even if, as a result, employer rents are bid away, market equilibrium is still markedly different from what it would be with perfect labor mobility in each period.

The presence of intertemporal linkages undermines the force of competition further, for instance, in Stiglitz and Weiss (1983b) it is shown that one can design better contractual arrangements extending over many periods rather than period by period. Punishments in later periods can be used to enhance incentives in earlier periods.[17] Such long term commitments, while they enhance incentive efficiency, can significantly restrict the scope for competition.

Rothschild and Stiglitz (Chapter 4, this volume) provide a further argument for long term contracts, but such contracts undermine competition in the short term. Over time, more information (e.g. about an individual's type, such as his/her likelihood of having a health problem) becomes revealed; once such information becomes available, one cannot buy insurance against the risk (in a sense, it no longer is a risk, it is a "known"). One can only buy insurance against, say, some disease hidden behind a veil of ignorance, a veil which is gradually removed as individuals move through their life. But again, if an individual has bought lifetime health or accident insurance, then the force of competition in the market is reduced: even if his/her insurance company provides terrible service, s/he cannot switch.

---

[16] When firms ignored this, they discovered that when they won the bid, they lost money. This phenomenon is known as the "winner's curse." See Wilson (1969); Capen et al. (1971); Leitzinger and Stiglitz (1984); and Stiglitz (1975a). Of course, even without asymmetric information, the fixed costs of finding out about the characteristics of each tract of land (the amount of oil and the cost of extraction) contributes to the limited number of bidders on each tract when the government puts them up for leasing.

[17] See the discussion below.

The theory of incentives showed that the force of competition may be so diminished that in equilibrium, there would be profits. Standard competitive theory argued that competition had to drive prices down to marginal cost. But if firms are to have an incentive to produce high quality products (or workers are to have an incentive not to shirk), they have to receive some surplus, a price in excess of marginal cost. Firms that survived had developed a reputation, and it was not easy for newcomers to displace them, even by undercutting: potential customers would worry that, at the low price, firms had every incentive not to produce a high quality good. Only if customers knew that the firm had to invest huge amounts—had a large incentive to establish a reputation—would it be credible that the firm was providing a high quality good; but this meant that information itself created a huge entry barrier. Moreover, if prices convey information about quality, a firm attempting to recruit customers by lowering prices may be misunderstood: customers may only think that the firm is offering a lower quality product. Indeed, as Chapters 10–12 below point out, competition may be so attenuated that a market equilibrium with unemployment or credit rationing may persist: workers who accepted lower wages are simply taken to be lower quality workers, more likely to shirk or quit; or borrowers who accepted higher interest rates to get loans are simply taken to be higher risk borrowers.

The various "forces" by which information imperfections reduce competition interact: asymmetries of information lead to thin markets, fixed costs to markets with a limited number of firms; and the two together make it even less likely that markets will be highly competitive.

While the New Paradigm thus questioned the assumptions that underlay the *standard* theory of competition—and the understandings it provided for why competition was important—it also provided insights into why competition was so important. Economists had always talked about the importance of competition in providing incentives, but in the standard theory, competition was not needed. One could just as well have provided incentives through compensation schemes.[18] The reason that competition is so important is that the information required to design good incentive schemes is lacking. We do not know how hard a task is—except by comparison.

Thus, the New Paradigm provided a new rationale for competition: it allowed the design of more effective (more efficient) incentive structures. Competition, in effect, bases compensation on *relative* performance—and under a variety of circumstances can lead to increased efficiency, *even taking into account unnecessary duplication,* as might arise in the case of duplicative research (See Chapter 14).[19]

---

[18] Indeed, the design of optimal compensation schemes is one of the contributions to information economics, taken up in Chapter 13 and 14 and elaborated on in Volume II. With perfect information, the difficulty of each task was known—and therefore the effort and appropriate compensation for obtaining any given desired result. (Stiglitz 1988d).

[19] I will return to the theme of competition in later volumes, especially in Volume III. Large fixed costs, as we have noted, give rise to a limited number of firms. Some argued not to worry: what matters is potential competition. But I showed that potential competition will not suffice to drive down profits to zero or to ensure economic efficiency, whenever there are *any* sunk costs. Of course, R&D expenditures are sunk, and I show that Schumpeterian competition—competition among firms to provide new

Decentralization

The decentralizability of the market economy is one of its most praised features; it means that there is no need for a central planner to aggregate all of the relevant information, say about scarcity, consumer preferences, or technology. All of the coordination can be done by the price system. Each individual and household can act on their own.

Of course, the decentralization of the market has always been exaggerated; much production occurs *within* firms, and few firms rely on decentralization. Almost all use some degree of command and control, with only limited coordination through prices.[20]

One of Coase's major contributions was to attempt to define the boundaries of firms through transactions costs (Coase 1937). But, of course, Coase looked at the problem from a partial equilibrium perspective, not from the perspective of the system as a whole, and he did not show that the organizational structure which emerged, from the perspective of the system as a whole, had any efficiency properties.

Greenwald and Stiglitz (Chapter 23) showed that the competitive economy was not in general efficient. But their analysis raised questions concerning the decentralizability of the economy; for they showed that problems of inefficiency could be looked at through the lens of externalities: actions by one firm had effects on others that they did not take into account. If smokers smoke more, then insurance rates will rise, but each smoker ignores the consequences. If peasants work harder (as a result of better incentives provided by landlords), then the likelihood that loans will be repaid is increased. *There are important interlinkages across markets; decentralization is not, in general, efficient.*[21] Of course, one has to compare the advantages of integration with the limitations presented by diseconomies of scope.

Just as the notion of competition embedded in the standard competitive (Arrow-Debreu) framework did not accurately reflect the role that competition plays in a market economy, so too for discussions concerning decentralization. In principle, a centralized firm could do everything that a decentralized firm could do—but it could do more. It could have various parts interact through prices, or through more complicated non-linear price relationships, or it could have them more fully integrated. When circumstances changed, it could change the degree of internal decentralization. But in practice, this misses some of the essential aspects of decentralization and centralization. It is difficult if not impossible for the central headquarters (CEO) of a firm not to take some degree in responsibility for all of its parts; it cannot fully

---

products—may be less effective than Schumpeter and his followers thought. Of course, some argued again that this shouldn't give rise to concern: some degree of monopoly is not only desirable but even necessary to finance innovation. But I also demonstrate the enervating effect of monopoly on innovation. In Volume V, I also discuss the (limited) ability of Tiebout (1956) competition—competition among communities—to ensure efficiency in the supply of local public goods (see Stiglitz 1977c, 1983c).

[20] The point is, of course, more general: firms look not just at prices, but also at what is happening to their inventories. They gather enormous amounts of data about what is happening to aggregate demand and to the composition of demand.

[21] This was a point taken up directly in Braverman and Stiglitz (1982).

decentralize. It cannot commit itself not to intervene; and maintaining residual rates of control (to intervene) affects behavior both of the central headquarters and the decentralized unit.

Decentralization is, most importantly, about how decisions get made, and in Chapter 15, I analyze the circumstances in which decentralized decision making is superior to centralized decision making.

The Efficiency of the Market

In my view, the most important question to be posed of any organizational system is its efficiency, and the most far reaching implication of the New Paradigm was casting doubt on the efficiency of the competitive market economy.

Samuelson had tried to show that households and firms could be described as if they were solving well defined maximization problems; simple versions of the fundamental theorem of welfare economics, establishing the efficiency of the market economy, proceeded analogously. The market economy could be described as maximizing the weighted average of the utilities of different individuals (subject to resource availability and technology constraints), for some set of weights. Heuristically, in the case of symmetry, if each individual in the market economy takes that action, a_i which maximizes his/her welfare, subject to others taking their optimal action, then this Nash equilibrium (depicted in Figure I.1), coincides with the coordinated equilibria where they all choose their $\{a_i\}$ together.

In effect, Greenwald and I showed that this picture was fundamentally wrong. Figure I.2 provided a more accurate depiction. There, $\{a_i^*\}$ is the equilibrium, since if everyone else chooses a_i^*, it pays the remaining market participant to choose a_i^*. The true optimum, a^{**}, is not sustainable as a Nash equilibrium.

Our results were extremely powerful, for they showed that there were, in principle, simple (typically price) interventions in the market economy which could lead to a Pareto improvement. Indeed, small distortions (which by themselves would have a second order welfare cost) which (in the case where $a^* < a^{**}$) induce individuals to increase a_i^* slightly can have first order effects on welfare. The thrust of all of the work in the New Paradigm was that one should not limit oneself just to price interventions; and within this broader range of interventions, the possibilities for welfare enhancement are increased further.

The papers in Volume I and the subsequent volumes provide a systematic account of the market failures associated with imperfect and costly information. There were, in general, marked differences between private and social incentives to acquire information. For instance, too little information may be acquired (e.g. as a result of problems of appropriating returns) or too much (some of the returns are "rents," gains in income by one individual at the expense of others), or more generally too much expenditure on the acquisition of some kinds of information, too little on others. The information that is acquired is not used efficiently (sharing information might improve economic efficiency—knowledge is a public good—but would lower rents; there are incentives not to disclose all relevant information). There are incentives

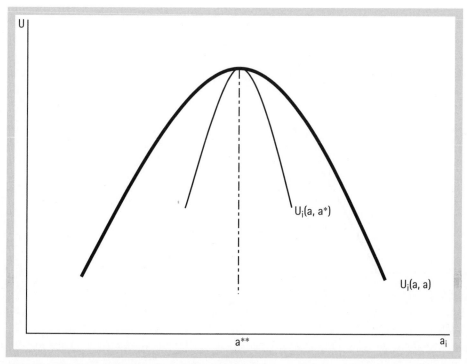

Fig. I.1. Nash equilibrium is socially optimal

Notes: U i(a_i, a_{-i}) is the ith individual's utility when s/he undertakes action a_i and all others undertake action a_{-i}. The thick curve depicts the utility levels, where all individuals act together (that is, $a_i = a_{-i}$). The coordinated equilibrium occurs where all individuals choose a^{**}. The thin curve depicts the ith individual's utility when all others choose the utility level $a_{-i} = a^*$. A Nash equilibrium occurs when the optimum for a_i is a^*. Because the two curves are tangent at $a_i = a^*$, the Nash equilibrium is Pareto optimal, labeled a^{**}.

to create information asymmetries, which impede efficiency. Whether endogenous or exogenous, information imperfections give rise to market power, which in turn gives rise to market distortions. With imperfect information, there are externality like effects from actions (in insurance markets, as individuals undertake riskier actions, the premia of all insured increase). And because imperfect information gives rise to distortions in one market, second best considerations are pervasive: distortions in other markets may help undo the effects. These market imperfections play out differently in different markets: the feasible and optimal interventions may according differ markedly.

METHODOLOGICAL INNOVATIONS

The models presented here represent a style of analysis that has now become everyday but was in its infancy then. At the time, there was a well formulated general

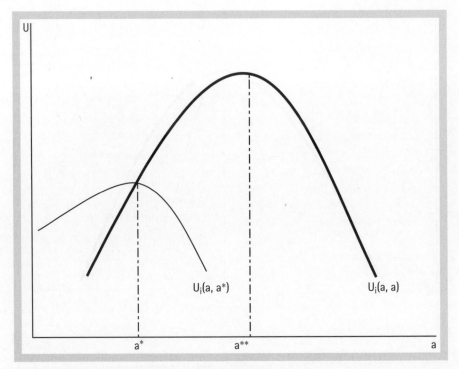

Fig. I.2. Nash equilibrium not socially optimal

Note: The Nash equilibrium occurs at a level of $a^* < a^{**}$.

equilibrium model, some standard partial equilibrium models, and a few simplified reductions of the general equilibrium model (e.g. the model underlying Samuelson's factor price equalization theorem).

Toy Models—The Risks of Over- and Undersimplification

At MIT in the late 1950s and 1960s, a new style emerged. They were sometimes called toy models—simple enough to see what was going on, but complete enough to incorporate all of the (then viewed as) important general equilibrium interactions. Some of these earlier models were simple tweakings of the standard general equilibrium models—what would happen, for instance, if the assumption of a complete set of Arrow-Debreu Securities were replaced with competitive markets for firms with well defined risk classes? I do not mean to denigrate these papers, for even trying to figure out what was meant by a competitive market equilibrium was no easy task. But the more adventurous of these models, like Akerlof's "Theory of Lemons," broke new ground in asking questions which, at first blush, seemed not to have even been asked before (Akerlof 1970). The paper was received with rejection after rejection—referees questioned whether it was even economics. (Of course, it eventually became recognized that his paper was a formalization of the theory of adverse incentives, which had long been a subject within the insurance literature, and on which Ken Arrow (1965) had written shortly before.)

The style had one major disadvantage: each paper stood on its own. It was hard to see the relationship between Akerlof's "Theory of Lemons," the Rothschild-Stiglitz "Equilibrium in Competitive Insurance Markets" (Chapter 5), Stiglitz's, "The Theory of 'Screening'," (Chapter 3), the Shapiro-Stiglitz theories of unemployment (Chapter 11) or the Stiglitz-Weiss theories of credit rationing (Chapter 10). Were these all special cases of a more general theory? In a sense, the answer to that question is, yes: there is a general framework, within which all of these lie. But in certain circumstances, some actions are admissible or some information may be observable, which may not be the case in other circumstances. In the discussion below, we hope to clarify these differences.

The style had a second problem: if the model was *too* simple, the information "problem" could be resolved, in one way or another. Full information (and sometimes with it, the efficiency properties of the market) could be restored. If there were as many goods as states of nature, it was conceivable that the relative prices of the goods would convey full information about the state of nature—even if not everyone could directly observe the state of nature. (That was why Sandy Grossman and I, in our papers (1976, 1980, Chapters 19 and 21), developed models with a continuum of states of nature, but a finite number of commodities, models of such complexity that relative prices could not then possibly be fully revealing.) A careful balancing was required—sufficient complexity that the "real" information problem could not trivially be solved (within the model); but sufficient simplicity that one could see what was going on.

Thus, the chapters presented in this volume typically look at one information problem at a time—there may be a moral hazard or an adverse selection problem, but not both.[22] There may be a moral hazard problem on one side of the market but not on the other. There may be problems in the labor market or the capital market, but not both.

There was, in addition, a natural progression, which led from simpler to more complex models. Once it can be shown that imperfections of information undermine the existence of risk markets and lead to what may be called equity rationing, it is natural to focus on *risk averse* rather than risk neutral firms (see Volumes III and IV).

Once it is realized that the interests of managers of firms do not necessarily coincide with those of the shareholders, then issues of corporate governance have to come to the fore; and once that happens, one has to look at all the checks and balances on firms—including banks. Financial institutions not only provide capital, they become part of the corporate governance structure. My concern has been that the piecemeal approach so prevalent in economics in recent years—so necessary as part of the normal advancement of the science—risks losing sight of these interconnections.

---

[22] See, however, Stiglitz and Weiss (1986). In Hellman and Stiglitz (2000) we explore a model which there is simultaneously credit and equity rationing.

For a while, securities markets may free ride off the information services provided by banks; but the problem of acquiring information and appropriating returns to information cannot be ignored, and while securities markets may do a better job in divesting risk, they may be less adept at basing the provision of credit in the short run on relevant information.[23]

The difficulty is that real world complexities arise from the *interactions* both of different institutions and different information problems. Consider the Shapiro-Stiglitz efficiency wage model (Chapter 11), where the existence of unemployment provides the discipline required to prevent individuals from shirking. There is another, far less costly, method of doing so: simply require individuals to post bonds, which they forfeit if they shirk. But individuals cannot post bonds if they do not have any capital; and if they buy the bond from a third party, they simply shift the moral hazard problem elsewhere: it is not resolved. Moreover, even if individuals had the wealth to post a bond, if it cannot easily be ascertained whether the individual has shirked, then the firm may have an incentive to claim that the individual has shirked, when in fact s/he has not. (This is what I have called the "double moral hazard" problem.)

Or consider the problem of moral hazard in credit markets. With larger collateral requirements, the adverse incentive problem might be mitigated (Bester 1985). But larger collateral requirements might preclude from the market those with limited amounts of capital—and there would be a resulting adverse selection problem. Market efficiency cannot so easily be restored.[24]

There is still one more danger of the "toy models:" most of these models involved some degree of parameterization. Many used specific utility functions, production functions, contractual forms, etc. It was important to know to what extent the results were the result of these parameterizations. For instance, a key question, particularly in macro economics, concerns aggregation: does the distribution of income matter? A long standing result is that if all demand functions are linear (and everyone has the same marginal propensity to consume particular goods), *obviously* the distribution of income does not matter. But linearity is an extremely strong hypothesis, questionable empirically, and derivable only from highly restrictive utility and production functions. By the same token, the standard parameterizations, employing homotheticity or constant absolute risk aversion, give special—and highly implausible—results; yet these models tend to be the ones for which it is most easy to obtain closed form solutions.

That is why, in much of the research program in which I have been engaged, I have tried to find the most general *tractable* functions, and to explore the sensitivity of results to alternative parameterizations (engaging in thought experiments in a world in which real world experiments were not feasible). I have been concerned that with greater reliance on computer simulations, there has been a tendency to use much more tightly specified parameterizations; and experiments within those

---

[23] See Stiglitz (1992a) where I discuss the risk of one part of the economic system (securities markets) attempting to free ride off of the information provided by other parts of the economic system (banks).

[24] See Stiglitz and Weiss (1983b).

parameterizations might not really yield as much insight as one would have hoped. For instance, precise aggregation may be possible so long as the relevant functions are linear; experimenting with particular parameterizations *within* the class of linear functions may yield no insights in the sensitivity of aggregate behavior to the distribution of income.

The Theory of Contracts

A second methodological innovation concerned the theory of contracts. In the real world, contracts are important. But in the traditional world of economics, they are intrinsically uninteresting. Individuals contract to provide certain work of certain quality for certain compensation, and they get paid if and only if they perform that work. The contract is nothing more than the price system. But as I began my work on sharecropping and in competitive equilibrium insurance markets (Chapters 5 and 13), contracts moved to the center of the analysis. What firms offer is contracts—insurance contracts with a certain co-payment and certain deductibility, land contracts with a certain amount of land with a certain share of crops. There is an equilibrium in *contracts*, not in prices. The demand and supply for each type of contract has to be balanced; and there can be no room for a new contract to replace existing contracts. Since then, the theory of contracts has become a major subject of economic research.[25]

THE ORGANIZATION OF VOLUME I

Volume I is divided into five parts. It begins with several *review essays* in Part I, presented in chronological order. Part IIA develops the general *theory of screening*—how and why markets differentiate among objects (people) that otherwise might be treated the same, the differences between the private and social payoffs, and the resulting implications for economic efficiency—and inequality. This discussion of the general theory is followed by one of the most important bases of differentiation—where individual actions reveal information (*the theory of self-selection*) in Part IIB. The final section, Part IIC, shows how this theory can naturally lead to *credit rationing and unemployment*.

Part III focuses on *incentives and organization*. A key concept in the economics of information (some might say it is the key concept in all of economics) is *incentives*. When the actions of individuals cannot be observed directly, individuals' compensation can only depend on what is observable. This simple observation provides

[25] See, e.g. Hart and Holmstrom (1987); Hart (1995); Salanie (1997); and Dewatripont and Bolton (2005).

the basis of the general theory of incentives, applied here first in the context of sharecropping, but with the obvious implications to rewarding corporate managers noted.

Just as insurance provided the simple framework for analyzing screening/self-selection within a competitive equilibrium model, so too did it provide a framework for analyzing incentive effects—referred to more specifically in this context as *moral hazard* effects. With Richard Arnott, I provided a remarkably simple diagrammatic analysis (Chapter 16), which showed that there was an underlying unity of mathematical structure between moral hazard (incentive) problems and screening (self-selection) problems.

Another essential insight was to see the link between incentives and information. The organization of the economy—including the nature of competition—may affect the information providing the basis on which compensation may be paid, an idea explored in Chapter 14.

The basic unit of organization in the modern economy is the corporation. Corporations are different than firms that are run by a single proprietor. The interests of managers, shareholders, and other stakeholders all differ. Majority shareholders interests may differ from minority shareholders, equity owners from lenders. In general, there will not be unanimity among these stakeholders concerning what the firm should do (Grossman and Stiglitz 1980b). While we postpone until Volume III the construction of the General Theory of the Firm, the New Paradigm, for the first time, put a clear theoretical structure around the issue of *corporate governance*, focusing on the managerial discretion provided by imperfect information as well as the free rider/collective action problem when all members of a class (shareholders, bondholders) benefit from actions by any one within the class to enhance their returns or reduce their risk (Chapter 17).

The previous two sections discussed two of the principle ways of overcoming information asymmetries—by direct examination of the characteristics and behavior (screening and monitoring) and by self-selection and incentive compatibility constraints, designing contractual structures such that individuals reveal who they are by their choices or such that individuals have an incentive to make the choices (take the actions) that we (the lender, the insurer, the employer) want them to make. Typically, we think of monitoring as hierarchical—bosses supervise their workers. But an individual's peers (co-workers) may be more effective in monitoring; they can see more easily whether the individual is shirking or not.

The same principle holds for other markets, and in Chapter 18, we introduce the basic theory of peer monitoring in the context of rural credit markets. The paper provides the intellectual foundations for the micro credit schemes which have since then spread around the world, enabling access to credit by millions who previously could not obtain access.[26]

---

[26] In 2006, Mohammed Yunus received the Nobel Peace prize, in recognition of the important role that micro credit has played in alleviating poverty.

Finally, the organization of the economy matters because of *human fallibility*—in effect, the organization of the economy affects how information (or misinformation) is "aggregated up" and acted upon. One form of organization may be better at preventing bad projects from being adopted but suffer from the affliction of too often rejecting good projects (Chapter 15).

Part IV deals with the role of *prices in conveying information*. It includes the classic papers, Chapters 19 and 21, with Grossman, showing the *logical* impossibility of informationally efficient markets, demonstrating that when information is costly, there must exist an equilibrium amount of disequilibrium. We investigate here, too, how well futures markets perform in predicting future prices.

Part IV also deals with another problem: how markets can create noise, which gives firms a greater ability to exploit consumers. Those who wished to minimize the consequences of imperfect information used to argue that so long as *enough* individuals are well informed, they will fully arbitrage the market, eliminating the exogenous disturbances coming from elsewhere. This part explains why that hypothesis is not true.

Of course, it has been long recognized that the value of information can differ markedly from its cost or price. Earlier work had established the intellectual framework within which the value of information could be calculated; Chapter 22 with Radner established a remarkable property—that the value was always non-concave in the value of information; there was, as a result, a natural discontinuity in the demand for information.

For me, Part V of this volume is perhaps the most important, for it is here that we can use the results of the previous parts to assess the critical question: what can we say about the *efficiency of the market economy* when markets are incomplete and information is imperfect—as they always are. The classic Greenwald-Stiglitz paper, Chapter 23, showed that market failures associated with imperfect information and incomplete markets were pervasive. There was no longer a *presumption* that markets were efficient, especially in contexts in which information problems were important (as in financial, labor, and insurance markets). The burden of proof had shifted.

Adam Smith's invisible hand theorem had grabbed the imagination of economists for 200 years. It was a remarkable result—almost too good to be true. But in terms of the loss of "welfare," the real concerns with the market economy were the periodic episodes of high unemployment and a significant shortfall between the economy's actual and potential output. Those who retained their faith in the market economy thought of these as aberrations, that could either be ignored or addressed—but in ways which left the overall edifice standing. More likely than not, it was government that was at the root of the problem, through the imposition of minimum wage laws or its tolerance of unions, leading to uncompetitive labor markets. The prevalent form of Keynesian economics contributed to this misunderstanding, by repeatedly referring to wage rigidities as the source of market failure—with the obvious implication that if wages could be made more flexible, the efficiency of the economy would be restored. The New Paradigm showed, however, that wage rigidities can arise *endogenously*, having nothing to do with government intervention or union monopolization. But in Part VI, we show that the problem of economic fluctuations is far deeper than just a matter of wage and price rigidities.[27] Information imperfections can lead to capital market imperfections, and these capital market imperfections result in the impacts of shocks being amplified and persisting.

THE PERSPECTIVES

Part I contains my earliest and my most recent "perspectives" on the economics of information. A review of these provides some historical perspectives on the evolution of the New Paradigm. The first was presented to the Association of University Teachers of Economics in 1974, when I was just five years into my research program. The final review, my Nobel lecture was delivered 27 years later.[28]

As I reread my first presentation of *Information and Economic Analysis*, in 1974, three things strike me.

Early Progress

The first was how far we had already gone by 1974 in understanding the basic analytics of the economics of information, in particular the theory of screening and signaling. To be sure, the following three decades were to develop a myriad examples and applications. But most of the *principles* had already been developed. We understood much about the structure of the equilibria, the motivations for sorting, and the mechanisms. And indeed, a surprisingly large fraction of the basic results, too, had been derived.

When I began my work on screening and incentives, it was not immediately obvious—were there other important branches to the Economics of Information, or were the simple models that we were developing special cases of more general models that would eventually be developed? The subsequent three decades and more have provided at least a tentative answer: it seems that we identified the central issues. The models today are, to be sure, mathematically more sophisticated

---

[27] In Volume IV, other explanations based on imperfect information and incomplete markets are developed.

[28] In between, I wrote three other review articles, reprinted in Volume II. The second was delivered a decade later, before the same audience. By that time most of the "destructive" work attacking the conventional paradigm had been completed, and I had begun the task of constructing a New Paradigm. My inaugural lecture as the Drummond Professor at All Souls College focused on one particular issue—the implications of imperfect information for competition. The fourth review was written in 2000 as part of a series of papers summarizing the achievements of twentieth century economics.

and complex; and interrelationships between problems of adverse selection and incentives have been explored. But the ideas themselves have proven remarkably robust.

The Structure of Equilibria

In my 1975f paper,[29] I had already distinguished between the two kinds of equilibria: pooling equilibria, in which individuals (firms, products) that were different were treated as if they were the same; and separating equilibria, where different groups were fully differentiated,[30] and had shown that more information was not necessarily better—there could be multiple equilibria, in which the pooling equilibria Pareto dominated the separating equilibrium.

In showing that the market equilibrium was not Pareto efficient, I had uncovered the key role that the assumptions about information played in demonstrating the efficiency of the market economy. The proofs had required that, if information was not perfect, then at least it could not be altered by any of the actions of any of the agents in the economy. I had identified what is perhaps the Achille's heel in the standard presumption of the efficiency in the market economy.[31]

The Efficiency of Markets—Divergence Between Private and Public Incentives for Gathering Information

In this first study, I had asked, what were the incentives for differentiation, and who paid for it—the individual or the firm? A monopolist's motive was simply to increase his/her profits, by extracting more of the consumer surplus; a perfectly discriminating monopolist (not relying on self-selection mechanisms) would be efficient (except for the expenditures in information which allowed perfect discrimination, which were simply redistributive.) But there were large distortions arising from imperfect discrimination and discrimination based on self-selection mechanisms.

Competitors also attempted to differentiate to increase profits, but they faced far different constraints. The social returns (related to increased efficiency) differed from private returns (which were more related to gathering rents.) The more able individuals would want to be identified as more able, so their wages would be increased; firms, on the other hand, were looking for workers (securities, assets) that were underpriced. In these contexts, any gains in profit from improved information were at the expense

---

[29] The paper was written five years earlier, when I was in Kenya, in response to a question posed to me by the Kenyan government. See the discussion in Chapter 2.

[30] Of course, there were also mixtures, "partially" pooling equilibria, in which some groups were pooled together, others separated.

[31] We also noted that *formally* one could see the reason for the lack of efficiency of the market as due to a classic market failure—the presence of a pecuniary externality, but unlike standard pecuniary externalities, which have no adverse welfare consequences, these did. This idea was to elaborate with far more rigor and generality in my joint work with Bruce Greenwald, also contained in this volume (Chapter 23).

of others.[32] Of course, matters were more complicated, since the less able individuals did not have an incentive to have that information revealed; but one had to approach the problem of information revelation from a general equilibrium perspective—and when one did that, one could show that everyone except the least able had an incentive for information about his/her ability to be revealed.[33]

The Theory of Screening was written when I was visiting the Institute for Development Studies in Nairobi in the summer of 1969, at the request of the government, as it attempted to determine how much to invest in education. To answer that question, one had to analyze carefully the relationship between private and social returns to screening. Those who were getting jobs as a result of higher education did so more because of the credential than the human capital that they had acquired; the human capital model on which economists had long focused seemed to have overestimated the return to education.

While much of the expenditure on information (e.g. in capital markets[34]) was dissipative—the gains of the winners were at the expense of the losers—this is not always the case; there were, for instance, significant social returns to education from allowing a better matching of individuals with tasks; ignorance could be viewed as a tax—or more accurately, a tax on the more able, a subsidy on the less able—and like any such tax, there was a dead weight loss. This theme, the difference between the *social* and *private* returns to information is one which occurs repeatedly throughout the chapters of these volumes.

Among the disturbing aspects of the new theory were two results to which these early studies called attention: while expenditures on information did not increase overall economic efficiency, they could result in greater inequality. There had long been a presumption that (a) the more information the better; and (b) there was a trade-off between equality and efficiency. We showed that in the simplest of models, neither result held.

The Problem of Appropriability and the Public Goods Nature of Information

Another related theme (contributing to the divergence between social and private returns to the acquisition and dissemination of information), repeated through these volumes, is that of *appropriability*—the person investing in the education might not be able to appropriate the returns (even when there are social returns.) If two employers simultaneously discover that an individual is "more able" and underpaid, they will bid for his/her services; s/he will garner the return. Others may infer that, when an individual is promoted to a senior position, his/her employer has

---

[32] Hirschleifer had independently made this point in his important paper (Hirschleifer 1971).
[33] I referred to this as the Walras law of screening.
[34] See, e.g. Stiglitz (1982c) and Stiglitz (1989k).

concluded s/he has strong managerial abilities, and they may be tempted to recruit him/her away.

Moreover, knowledge (information) is like a *public good*—the use of knowledge by one person does not detract from what the other person knows (though it may detract from the economic returns s/he can get); and it is often difficult to stop others from enjoying the benefits of the knowledge, or to appropriate for oneself all of the returns.

These are two of the key ways in which the *Economics of Information* and the *Economics of Innovation* (Volume III) are linked together. And it implies that there will be underinvestment in information (knowledge) acquisition and, when information (knowledge) is acquired, there will be incentives to restrict dissemination.

Self-selection

When I returned from Nairobi, where I wrote the "Basic Theory of Screening," I began working with Michael Rothschild on a second important question—the mechanisms for differentiation; in my earlier study, I had assumed that individuals were differentiated by examination; the idea we had was a simpler one, that people's behavior revealed information about their characteristics, information which was of value to other participants in the market. Of course, one reason that individuals differed in their behavior, for instance, in insurance markets was that those who were more likely to have an accident—and knew it—would want insurance more; they would be less willing to accept large deductibles. In "Monopoly, Non-linear Pricing, and Imperfect Information" (Chapter 7 below), I showed how a monopolist could design insurance contracts (or choices in product markets) to maximize profit; choices in effect revealed information, e.g. about who valued the insurance (good) more. That turned out to be relatively easy conceptually (though slightly complex mathematically). But it provided, for the first time, a rigorous and coherent basis for the theory of monopoly (see the introduction to Part IIB). The more difficult question was the analysis of the *competitive* equilibrium, which we provided in our 1976 paper (reproduced here as Chapter 5).

Further Steps in the Destruction of the Existing Paradigm

By the time I left Nairobi in 1971, I had already shown how the new Information Paradigm was leading to the repeal of long standing "laws" of economics—the efficiency wage theory showed that firms might not lower wages even when there was excess supply of labor; market equilibria could be characterized by persistent wage and price distributions; competitive-like equilibrium could be characterized by the persistence of profits and price in excess of marginal costs. I was, by then, convinced that I was engaged in the construction of a New Paradigm, though I was not yet sure what shape it would take.

Lost Insights

The second thing that struck me as I re-read the first review, now three decades old, was how some of the insights that we had gleaned and puzzles that had been posed—and even some of the insights that we had had—seemed to have become lost in the succeeding quarter century. In the Preface, I have discussed two of these: the close links between the theory of innovation and the economics of information; and the pervasiveness of non-convexities. Here, I call attention to three other issues.

Asymmetric and Imperfect Information

In awarding me the Nobel Prize, the committee noted in particular my work on the theory of screening, and the Prize was shared with Michael Spence, for his work on signaling, and with George Akerlof, for his work on adverse selection. Overall, the prize was on how markets with asymmetric information work. This has led many to think that the theory of *imperfect* information and the theory of *asymmetric* information were one and the same. Obviously, when information is asymmetric—when some people know something that others do not—information is imperfect; but the theory of asymmetric information focuses on only one narrow set of issues within the more general theory.

While the theory of asymmetric information focuses on situations where employees know their abilities more than the employers or the insured more than the insurance company, in practice, that may not be the case. Insurance companies with their vast databases may be in a far better position to predict losses that particular individuals might be expected to have than the individuals themselves. Still, the general theory of screening says that the insurance company has an incentive to identify who the low risk individuals are, and that it can do so either by providing examinations or by looking at systematic ways in which those with low risk behave differently from those with high risk—differences in behavioral responses. The theory of self-selection could still be employed, even if the differences in behavior were not based on differences in beliefs about accident probabilities.

In short, my work had laid out the incentives and mechanisms for screening and being screened, for identifying differences (and for being identified as different). More able or less risky individuals would want to be identified—if they knew that they were more able or less risky. But firms would have an incentive to screen and sort even if individuals did not have differential information. The theory of screening (and the economics of information) was more general than the theory of asymmetric information. And, when there were information asymmetries, it encompassed behavior by both sides of the market, both the informed and the uninformed. And it embraced both mechanisms for sorting, both as a result of behavior and of direct examination.

Moreover, most of the literature began with *innate* differences and existing *asymmetries* of information. One of the questions with which I have been concerned is *endogenous* differences and asymmetries of information. Those who screen individuals and find an "underpriced" worker have an incentive to hide that information (Waldman 1984). Managers wishing to entrench themselves (so as to extract more rents from their roles of managers) may deliberately set out of enhance information asymmetries between themselves and outsiders (Edlin and Stiglitz 1995). Even whether or not individuals know about their own abilities can be viewed as endogenous (see Stiglitz 1984a).

Screening and Signaling Equilibria

Within the common parlance, there have been two major branches to the theory of asymmetric information: signaling and screening equilibria. The relationship between the two has not always been clear, nor has the explanation of some of the seeming differences in results. For instance, in the Rothschild-Stiglitz screening analysis, there is often a problem of existence; in the Spence signaling analysis, there is sometimes a problem of multiplicity of equilibria. Some of these differences have to do with differences in the game-theoretic specification; and there has been less discussion than there should have been about what formulation makes more sense.[35] Some of the problem arose from Spence's failure to have a full specification of the market equilibrium. (We postpone to the introduction of Part IIC a fuller discussion of these issues.)

Existence of Competitive Equilibria

In what I view to be one of our major contributions, Michael Rothschild and I showed that *using the natural intuitive notion of competition—the firm assumes that its actions do not have an effect on the behavior of others, and certainly on the market equilibrium*—there was no competitive equilibrium.

The results were striking in that they showed how non-robust the standard competitive model was to slight perturbations in assumptions; for the problem of non-existence arose particularly strongly when the differences between the groups were slight. In that case, the cost of pooling (see above for the definition) was less than the cost of separating. This had a strong and rather easily derived implication: when there is a continuum of market participants, e.g. individuals purchasing insurance with different probabilities of having an accident, then *there cannot exist a fully separating equilibrium*; those most likely to have an accident would be willing to buy a pooling contract that would "break" the separating equilibrium. To be sure, the *mathematics* defining a separating equilibrium still held; one could show what the separating equilibrium would look like, *if it existed*. Our definition of equilibrium required, however, that there not exist an insurance contract which would be purchased by a set of individuals (given the set of existing contracts) and make a profit. While models with

---

[35] See for example, Arrow (1973a); Spence (1973); and Rothschild and Stiglitz (1976).

a continuum of individuals often looked more general, and more mathematically sophisticated, typically no equilibrium existed, at least as we had defined, a fact that was too often ignored.

One response was to look for a different definition, and in the years following the publication of our paper, there were a number of such attempts.[36] To our knowledge, no one succeeded with a definition that accorded with what seemed to us as the basic notion of competitive, atomistic markets: that firms were able to ignore the consequences of their actions for the behavior of market participants and the market equilibrium. If a single firm offering an alternative pooling contract realized that it would unravel the existing equilibrium, and so contracts currently available would no longer be available, then that market was not atomistically competitive, in the way the term is usually used.[37]

The approach I preferred was to face the problem of competition head on: to realize that even in markets with many participants competition is not perfect; firms face downward sloping demand curves. We should be constructing models of monopolistic competition, and of oligopolistic interactions within large markets. This is a direction which, unfortunately, there has been far too little work. (See Chapter 6 for a brief discussion.)

Unresolved Issues

I have already hinted at several of the major issues on which further research on the foundations of the New Paradigm would be valuable, such as a more complete analysis of market equilibria in which multiple information problems (adverse selection and moral hazard, double moral hazard[38]) problems arise.

Adjustment

There are three more topics, however, to which I wish to draw attention. Traditional economics had never been very good in describing the process of *adjustment* to equilibrium; adjustment models were typically ad hoc—outside the "maximizing" framework which, through Samuelson, had become the centerpiece of mid-twentieth

---

[36] Riley (1975, 1979 and 2001).

[37] In the Introduction to Part IIB, and in the postscript to Chapter 9 (published here for the first time), I propose an atomistic equilibrium concept—entailing firms offering multiple contracts, with profits on one subsidizing losses on another, and with the loss making contract offered in fixed proportions to the profit making contract. Such an equilibrium exists (that is, if every insurance company offers a particular set of contracts, in a particular ratio, it does not pay any firm to alter its offerings or any new firm to offer any new contract or set of contracts, or the same contracts in different proportions) and is (constrained) Pareto efficient.

[38] That is, situations where two agents interact, and both can cheat on the other. (The employee may shirk, and the employer may fire the worker, forcing him/her to forfeit the bond, even if s/he has not shirked.)

century economics. Adjustments in contracts, with the multiplicity of dimensions, posed an even more difficult problem, especially as the adjustment process itself was hampered by problems of information asymmetries. Imperfect information made it more difficult to identify and design Pareto improvements, even when such might exist; moves to change the equilibrium might convey information which would adversely affect the party initiating the move; and new contracts put forward by better informed individuals, in a position perhaps to design a Pareto improvement, would be looked at askance—was it really a Pareto improvement, or simply an attempt to shift rents towards themselves? Thus, it seemed even more likely that inefficient contractual equilibria could exist *and persist* than that inefficient price equilibria could.[39]

Evolution

Our work showed that there was no presumption for the efficiency of market *equilibria;* but the notion that the evolution of the economy—given all of the uncertainties— had any teleology or optimality properties seemed even more absurd. Of course, in a world with known technology (including known changes in technology) one can describe the dynamics of a firm or even the economy, through simple differential equations. But the really interesting issues of economic dynamics—how the economy responds to a new technology like the Internet or to new market innovations like the creation of derivatives, or how these innovations come about—cannot really be addressed within an equilibrium framework. (How can one have rational expectations about the implications of these events, when there have not been previous events that are of the same nature?[40])

Evolutionary frameworks provide a still relatively underdeveloped alternative approach. In my 1974 review, I emphasized the desirability of taking this approach— and suggested how the New Information Paradigm (with its emphasis, for instance, on capital market imperfections) might suggest limitations on the efficiency of such processes. Firms whose long run prospects might be quite strong cannot borrow today against those future prospects; and firms better adapted to today's niches may outcompete them. I regret that I have had a chance to explore these topics only briefly.[41]

---

[39] See Stiglitz (1992c).

[40] Indeed, one of the issues in dispute is often what other previous occurrences (or innovations) are similar to the one in question. Simple statistical models in which there are "shocks" to, say, aggregate supply curves do not really capture what is at issue.

[41] Namely, in Stiglitz (1994e); Sah and Stiglitz (1991); and in my Osaka lecture, Stiglitz (1992i). Hoff and Stiglitz (2005) can be viewed as a contribution to the evolutionary literature. It describes in particular the likelihood that a country will move from a no-rule-of-law regime to a rule of law regime. It also shows how particular policies and decisions (e.g. concerning monetary policy or the timing of privatization) affects the evolution. Not only is there the possibility of an inefficient transition, but the economy may get stuck in an inefficient equilibrium.

CONCLUDING REMARKS

This volume sets forth the basic ideas of the New Information Paradigm. The richness of the New Information Paradigm is illustrated not only in the papers selected for this volume, but in those of the succeeding volumes. It has provided a framework for thinking about a host of issues, touching on the gamut of human interactions. It has, accordingly, had enormous influence not only on economics, but on the other social sciences as well. Some critics had worried that by moving away from the perfect information paradigm, one was opening up a Pandora's box: there were an infinity of ways in which information could be imperfect. There was a kind of precision in the assumption of perfect information; and such critics seemed to prefer that precision— even if it was clearly wrong. The conventions of the standard competitive equilibrium model were well established, and there was a certain comfort in working within those conventions. How did one know which was the "right" model of imperfect information? How did one know that the results were robust? (The results presented in this volume (as well as other work in the New Paradigm) had, of course, shown that the perfect information model was not robust.)

One of the reasons that the New Paradigm has proven so fruitful and so successful is precisely that there are so many forms that information imperfections can take. This meant that there was not a mechanistic formula that could be applied from one problem to another. Both the formulation of models and their analysis required insight and often deep and complicated analysis. But the New Paradigm provided a new way of thinking, a common structure, within which a myriad of problems could be approached. The basic concepts presented in this volume have remained the bedrock on which much of the ensuing superstructure has been built. It is these concepts that have proven robust.—at least for the time being. But inevitably, if history is our guide, this New Paradigm will be replaced by another.

PART I

PERSPECTIVES ON INFORMATION ANALYSIS

CHAPTER 1

....

INFORMATION
AND ECONOMIC
ANALYSIS*

....

UNDERLYING this paper are three important observations:

1. A large fraction of economic activity is concerned not with the production of commodities but with the 'production' and transmission of 'information' in its broadest sense. Clearly, the primary object of the research and development sectors of the economy is the production of information (knowledge) and a primary object of the education sector and of the publishing and communications industry is the transmission of information. One of the main functions of middlemen, including insurance brokers, stockbrokers, and marketing specialists, is to obtain information about the qualities of different commodities and about the prices being charged by different sellers. One of the important functions of managers is to obtain information about employees, to assign them to jobs for which they are suited. Indeed, a careful look at various jobs would show that a large fraction entail some significant proportion of the time of the individual being spent on the production and dissemination of information.

2. The production and dissemination of information is different in a number of fundamental ways from the production of ordinary commodities. One simply cannot transfer the tools and modes of thinking that have been developed for the latter into

* I am indebted to G. Akerlof, P. Diamond, A. Dixit, M. Farrell, F.H. Hahn, M. Rothschild, M. Spence, N. Stern and C. von Weizacker for helpful conversations on the topics discussed in this paper. This work was supported by National Science Foundation Grant GS-40104 at the Institute for Mathematical Studies in the Social Sciences, Stanford University. This article is reprinted from Parkin & Nobay: Current Economic Problems. Proceedings of the Association of University Teachers of Economics Annual Conference: Manchester 1974 and was originally presented at that meeting. © Cambridge University Press, 1975. Reprinted with permission of Cambridge University Press.

the analysis of the production of information. (This is not to say, however that there is no carry over.)

It is the failure to recognise this difference which largely accounts for the failure of earlier attempts to develop a meaningful 'economics of information'. For instance, the conventional approach would entail an analysis of the cost of producing a given 'quantity' of information. But how is one to measure the 'quantity' of information? The Shannon measure of the amount of information which has proved useful in other branches of science does not appear to be particularly appropriate for economic analysis.[1] In the approach developed below we will find it unnecessary to talk of a 'quantity of information'.

3. But I would argue further that imperfect information necessitates serious modification of the conventional analysis of the production and exchange of commodities. Indeed, even what we mean by a 'commodity' is dependent upon our 'information structure'. There are a number of phenomena with which the conventional theory finds difficulty coping e.g., the existence of different prices for different commodities, tie in sales, quantity discounts in excess of the differences in transaction costs—for which the theory which we are about to develop does provide considerable insight. Somewhat loosely, what I am arguing is that it is not as if there is a 'commodity' sector for which the conventional theory is applicable and an 'information sector' for which a new theory is required; the production of goods and information are so intertwined that an attempt to construct a theory of 'information' immediately leads to a reconstruction of at least a part of the conventional theory.

We shall be able to go only a little way in the direction of constructing an 'economics of information'. At this point I can make no claims for having a general theory; indeed I have some doubts about the usefulness that such a general theory might have. What has been done so far is to examine the problem of 'information' in detail in a number of fairly specific institutional settings. From this analysis, some fairly general conclusions do emerge, and it is these general conclusions on which I wish to focus.

There are two kinds of 'information' which I shall discuss; one is associated with what we call 'research and development', the other with 'screening'. Since the meaning of the former is fairly clear, let me begin my discussion with the economics of screening. Later, I hope to show that these two 'kinds' of information can be viewed as 'polar cases', while most other kinds of information can be thought of as mixtures of these two.

The discussions of sections 1.1 through 1.6 attempt to present, integrate, and extend slightly the results of a recent series of papers on the economics of screening. Proofs of most of the propositions will be omitted. The remainder of the paper is an attempt to interpret these results, to present some conjectures, and to suggest further directions of research.

---

[1] See, for instance, K.J. Arrow (1972b).

1 The Economics of Screening

1.1 Definition of Screening and Examples

As long as there are differences among individuals, resources will be allocated to find out about the characteristics by which the individuals differ. Even if nothing else in the economy were changing, it would require an expenditure of resources to obtain information about each new individual.

More generally, *screening* is simply the process of *discrimination*, of distinguishing among 'things' which, in the absence of screening, would, for economic purposes, be treated the same, even though it may be known that they differ in perhaps some important ways. For instance, it may be known that some individuals are high ability, some low ability, but it requires some process to ascertain which individuals are which.

Anything which distinguishes two individuals may be used as a screening device: race, education, height, weight, etc. We would like to be able to say something about what actually turns out to be used as the basis for screening.

Among the 'screens' that are widely observed are the following:

(a) An egg sorter is a screening device which screens eggs according to size. Eggs are also sorted according to colour.
(b) Any grading system in a school 'screens' individuals according to performance in certain dimensions.
(c) If students who enroll in a university are different in some important economic way, from students who do not, then attendance at a university—even without graduating—may act as a screening device.
(d) Stockbrokers attempt to discriminate among different securities; they believe they can screen, i.e., that they are not just throwing darts at a dartboard.
(e) As individuals search different firms for their terms of employment including their non-pecuniary characteristics, they are 'screening' firms.

It is important to emphasise that the source of the 'lack of information' need not be innate, e.g., in the genetic differences of individuals; some of it is market induced, e.g., the differences in wages paid by firms. But even when it is 'innate', which characteristics are of 'value', i.e., which characteristics it is important to screen for, are determined by the nature of the technology and the structure of the market, as we shall show below.

1.2 Screening Mechanisms

Examination

Let us consider first in somewhat more detail the mechanisms by which screening is performed. Assume we are interested in the performance of an individual in a particular situation. His performance is determined by a set of characteristics. Some of these characteristics may be observed at essentially zero cost (say the sex, weight, or height of an individual). Other characteristics may be observed at a cost, which may be sufficiently low that it is feasible to observe the characteristic. Still others may be unobservable or are observable only at prohibitively high cost. Moreover, the observations may be—indeed, in general will be—made with errors. There may also exist characteristics which are observable which are correlated with the unobserved characteristics of interest. Of necessity, so long as not *all* the relevant characteristics are observed with perfect accuracy, the categories into which individuals are placed will not be 'perfect predictors'.

The systems of screening I have discussed so far are basically direct *examination* systems. (The search models are special cases of systems of 'screening by examination'.)

Of the examples given above, the egg sorter is probably the best illustration of this. There is clearly a cost involved in this method of screening; in the case of the egg sorter, there is the capital cost, the cost of operating the sorter, and the cost in terms of broken eggs as the eggs pass through the sorter.

There is an obvious parallel between egg sorters and the educational system. There are, however, two important differences: we are willing to talk about the 'expected' return from egg sorting, without worrying about what happens to any single egg. The fact that some get broken, some get misclassified does not upset us. In educational systems, we may, however, worry about what happens to the individual. Moreover, no matter what kind of examination system we devise, the egg cannot respond, whereas the concern of many educators is that sorting 'distorts' behaviour.

Self-Selection Mechanism

This brings us to our second method of obtaining information about individuals and that is to look at the individual's behaviour. Indeed, since it often is his behaviour under particular situations which we are interested in predicting, it is not surprising that we use his behaviour in other situations as a method of obtaining information about his behaviour in the situations of interest. We are saying, in effect, that whatever the characteristics are that determine behaviour in situation A they are related to (correlated with) the characteristics that determine behaviour in situation B. This presents two interesting problems:

1. The fact that the individual's actions in situation B affects how he is 'categorised' ('judged') and therefore affects his future opportunity set affects his actions in situation B; that is, what we observe as the individual's action in situation B if we are using that as a source of 'information' about the individual is different from what we would have observed as the individual's behaviour had he not known we were observing him.

There are innumerable examples of this. Present performance on a job conveys 'information' about the individual's ability to the manager, which may then result in a promotion. It is not that those who perform better in the present job are *necessarily* more able to perform the next job than those who do not do so well; it is rather that *on average*, those who perform better are more able, and thus performance on the present job acts as a screening device. The incentives for working in many jobs—apart from the information conveyed—may be minimal; the individual works 'harder' than he would in the absence of the information effect.

Similarly, quitting 'conveys information' to the employer. Again, it is not that those who have a high quit experience are necessarily poorer employees; they are only on average—partly because of the difficulty in discriminating between 'true quits' and 'discharges'. Thus, even if, in the absence of the 'information effect' an individual would have quit his job, he may stay on the job because of the effect that quitting has on how the market values him.

Similarly, because the grade completed by an individual conveys information about the individual's ability individuals may be induced to stay in school longer than they otherwise would.

2. The fact that it is individuals' actions (choices) which can be the basis of a 'screen' has a second important implication: there is no reason that firms need to rely on the observed behaviour of the individual in the form of essentially uncontrolled experiments. One of the most revealing 'actions' an individual takes are the choices he makes ('You can tell a man by the wife he takes'). The firm can confront the individual with a 'structured' set of choices, and from that structure infer charac-teristics of the individual. For instance, consider an insurance company insuring a group of individuals, some of which are known to have a higher probability of having an accident than others (for simplicity, assume that if an accident occurs, the loss will be the same). Individuals may also differ with respect to their degree of risk aversion. If the insurance company offers two policies, differing say in deductability or coinsurance clauses, it is likely that the accident rate among one group will differ from that of the other group. A firm will attempt to expand its business in the policy with higher profitability, contract its business in the other policy (possibly by lowering the premium in one case, raising the premium in the other). There are a variety of other 'choices' which the insurance company might use to sort out individuals: whether they take the guarantee renewability feature, whether they come into the insurance broker's office, or whether he has to 'find' the customer, whether they pay premiums on an annual, quarterly, or monthly basis, etc. Any such choice provides the insurance company a basis for discriminating among customers.

Similarly, a firm can give individuals a choice of job contracts and from the choice infer much about the individuals. Individuals who are more likely to move will be less willing to accept low wages now in return for high wages in the future. Individuals who are very confident of their ability and believe that this ability will be recognised may be willing to accept low wages now for the promise (if the individual is in fact able) of a higher wage in the future. If, on average, individuals who believe they are more able or less likely to move are in fact more able or less likely to move, then average abilities, turnover rates, etc. will differ among those who choose different contracts.

Individuals who purchase different quantities of a service are likely to differ in their price elasticity; or the quantity of electricity on sumed use may convey information about his price elasticity.

One important reason that individuals may make different choices which played a role in several of our examples is associated with differential information. Individuals *know* their different accident probabilities, or at least their judgments are correlated with 'reality'. One of the reasons that more able individuals may stay in school longer is that they *know* their probability of success is higher. However, this 'conveying' of information from one side of the market to the other is not an essential part of the process. That is, asymmetrics of information on the part of buyers and sellers are likely to generate attempts by one side to find out information from the other through the mechanism of revealed choices, or what has been called elsewhere self-selection processes. There is little difference though, between this case and that where the differences in choices are generated by some other characteristic and where, say, the buyer of insurance is ignorant of his probabilities of having an accident.

The costs of 'operating' such self-selection devices are not as apparent as those for operating direct examination schemes, and we shall return to this question later.

So far, all we have done is to show the alternative mechanisms by which screening is done, and suggested in doing so that screening may have important effects on behaviour. To carry the analysis further, we need next to enquire into what are the economic motivations for screening.

1.3 Motivations for Screening: Monopoly

For a monopolist the motivation is clear: it introduces the possibility of his acting as a discriminating monopolist and thus increasing his profits. Let us return to our earlier example of an insurance company insuring for an accident of a given size. Assume there are only two groups in the population, which have identical degrees of risk aversion, but differ only with respect to the probability of an accident. Then a monopolist will always offer a choice of contracts which will perfectly discriminate between the two groups. The high risk individual will purchase effectively complete insurance, the low risk individual will either purchase no insurance at all, or will purchase a policy with a large deductibility clause. Or assume that the individuals had the same probability of an accident, but different degrees of risk aversion. Again, the insurance company will always offer a set of contracts which completely discriminates between the two groups; the high risk aversion group again buys effectively complete insurance; the low risk aversion group buys either a policy with a large deductibility clause or no insurance at all. By contrast, with perfect information, a monopolist would offer complete insurance to every individual at terms which leave him only slightly better off than he would have been in the absence of insurance. Thus, the inability to screen costlessly has resulted in a gain to the high risk/high risk aversion individuals at the expense of the monopolist.

The point of this is that a monopolist differs from a competitor not only in the prices he charges, but in the set of insurance policies he offers. The presence of imperfect information has significantly altered the behaviour of the monopolist.

Other examples may easily be found. But perhaps the most striking—whether it is important in practice is another thing—is that discussed by Salop (1977). He shows that it might pay a monopolist to vary randomly the price it charges for the same commodity at different stores. Individuals for whom search is cheaper, e.g. because they have a low wage, search more and thus obtain the commodity at a lower price. The random price enables the firm to discriminate between high wage and low wage individuals. If the price elasticity decreases with an increase in the wage, it may thus be optimal to randomise prices. Conversely, if the price elasticity increases with an increase in the wage, and on average individuals with higher wages buy more of the commodity and face lower interest rates, quantity discounts are likely to be optimal.

1.4 Screening in Competitive Markets: Motivation

For competitors, the matter is more difficult. Let us continue with our insurance example to see what insights it might provide us. In a competitive insurance market, if insurance companies were risk neutral, the premiums that any 'group' of individuals pay must be equal to the mean benefits which they receive from the insurance company, i.e. there will be zero profit. Those who are high risk are being subsidised by the low risk individuals. Thus, there is an obvious incentive for the lowest risk individuals to have themselves identified; for if they can be so identified, their premiums will go down.

This explains the incentive for the lowest risk individual. What about the incentives for other individuals? Certainly the highest risk individual has no incentive to be screened. But if the lowest risk individual is screened off, then, since all the remaining individuals will be pooled together (without screening) there is an incentive for the lowest risk individuals of this group to have themselves screened; the process continues until all except the highest risk individuals have been screened. But if all but one of the groups have been screened, then the last group has, in effect, been screened. (This is the Walras law of screening.)

But there is also an incentive on the part of the insurance company. For if it can ascertain which individuals are 'high risk' and which individuals are 'low risk', it need only 'accept' the good risks; and if other firms are failing to 'discriminate' between the high and the low risk individuals, then it will be able to make a profit on these 'good risks'. These arguments suggest that, provided costs of screening are not too high, competitive equilibrium (if it exists) must entail some screening.

In the context of capital markets, there is a further reason why no no-screening equilibrium is viable: the temptation to offer an essentially worthless security on the market would be irresistible.[2] A minimal amount of screening to eliminate such securities seems essential.[3]

1.5 Screening in Competitive Markets: Existence of Equilibrium and Appropriability of Returns

So far we have established that, *provided the 'screening costs' are sufficiently low, there cannot exist an equilibrium with no screening.* But closer enquiry reveals that there cannot exist a *competitive* equilibrium with screening, provided screening costs are positive, if individuals do not know what their own risks are and if they are risk averse.

There are two problems both of which are aspects of the classic problem of appropriating returns to information.[4] First, at the point we left the above analysis there was only a single firm doing research into who was a good risk, who was a bad risk. That firm had, as it were, a monopoly over the 'information' about the risk of a particular individual. Assume now that there are two (or more) firms which conduct the research into the qualities of a particular individual. The research acts as a fixed cost; having done the research, the terms at which they will accept the individual depend simply on the probabilities of his having an accident, and do not depend on the amount of resources required to obtain the information. The competitors will bid against each other for the 'business' of the good risk; the competition will continue until the individual obtains a policy which (in expected value terms) just breaks even. But then, of course, the insurance company is making a loss, since it expended resources to 'screen' the individuals. What has happened is that the 'low risk' individual captures the return from screening in a competitive market.

There is an alternative reason that firms may not be able to capture the returns from screening. Assume that a company rejects some applicants and accepts others in screening by examination. If there is any sense in the firm's acceptance policy, the individuals whom it rejects are higher risk individuals than those it accepts. Thus, the acceptance–rejection of an individual by one firm conveys information to other firms (and to the insured individual). But these other firms obtain the information without having to expend resources on research. (The firm may attempt to avoid the 'sharing' of information in this way by insisting on the individual paying the fee in advance, which is returned if the application is rejected; but, as we shall show below,

---

[2] The prevention of the sale of such securities is clearly a public good, and not surprisingly, our legal system makes some attempt to deal with this problem (fraud). But although obvious fraud is prevented, more subtle methods of taking advantage of the imperfection of information are not.

[3] Actually, so long as there is a disutility to effort a similar argument applies to labour services; for with absolutely no screening, every one would have an incentive to completely shirk work. Again, at least a minimal amount of screening is essential.

[4] Note that if the individual is informed of his own ability, then he captures all returns to his providing that information—there is no appropriability problem.

a risk averse person who is uncertain of his risks will never apply to such a firm, since rejection will convey information to other firms. The insurance company which screens must seek out customers; i.e. many insurance firms use their salesmen as 'screening devices'; the firm uses whatever bases it can to guess who the good risks are and approaches them with a 'better premium'—the others are rejected only by implication. Still, 'acceptance' by such a firm does convey information.)

What we have now shown is that if there is to be screening in a competitive market, the costs must be borne by the individuals being screened. Will they be willing to bear this cost? That depends on whether they know their own risks and their degree of risk aversion. If they had perfect knowledge of their own risks, as we showed earlier it would pay the lowest risk individual to be screened (provided screening costs are sufficiently low). But if he is risk averse and is not perfectly certain (say at an extreme, he thinks his probability of being a low risk is equal to the proportion of low risk individuals in the population) then screening simply increases the variance of his income and lowers the mean (if he bears the costs): he will never be willing to pay for it. Since we established earlier that in competitive equilibrium, there must be screening, and we have now established that no one will be willing to undertake the cost of screening, it appears as if there may be no competitive equilibrium. We shall return later to an interpretation of exactly what this means.

Let me pause for a few minutes to reinterpret the analysis in terms of another example. Consider differences in ability; what we have suggested is that if individuals are not screened, there is an incentive for firms to ascertain who are the more able; but that in a competitive market, the more able will capture their own ability rents; that is firms will compete for the more able until their wage reflects their marginal productivity, once that is discovered. And even if only one firm were to do research the nature of the 'appointment' made by the firm conveys information to other firms, so that it is difficult for the firm to capture the returns to doing research.[5] But likewise, if individuals do not know their own abilities, they will not be willing to pay for the screening.

There are numerous other examples of the difficulty of appropriating returns from screening information. For instance, an attempt to take over an 'underpriced' firm is likely immediately to raise the value of the firm.

In any of these situations, if firms believe that were they to expend resources on screening, they would not be able to appropriate the returns, then, assuming there is no problem of cheating or shirking, there may exist an equilibrium with no screening. But it is important to emphasise that this equilibrium construct is markedly different from that employed in the usual analysis: as we established earlier, if no one is screening, and if everyone assumes (as we usually do in competitive analysis) that his behaviour has no affect on the behaviour of other individuals, then it pays any firm to do screening.

---

[5] There are, of course, other kinds of information about individuals which are of relevance to one firm alone. Such information I have called 'specific information' to distinguish it from the information discussed so far, which is 'of general value'.

1.6 Screening in Competitive Economies: Self-selection

The foregoing analysis assumed individuals have no knowledge of their risks or ability, and the problems arose because, in competitive markets, it is the individuals who are being screened who obtain the returns to screening, but they are unwilling to pay for the screening.

We now turn to the case where individuals do know their own abilities or their own accident probabilities. This generates a new set of problems. In this case self-selection mechanisms are likely to be brought into use; in the case of insurance, we suggested earlier that the choice among insurance contracts would convey information to the insurance company; just as the choice among educational programmes and job contracts would convey information to the employer about the individual's ability.

The following seems to be the most natural definition of a competitive equilibrium in this context: a competitive equilibrium is a set of 'contracts' such that there exists no other contract or contracts which any insurance firm might offer that would be purchased by a subset of the population and make an (expected) profit. It turns out that such a competitive equilibrium may not exist. There are two rather different reasons for this, the first of which is, in some sense, more fundamental than the other, and is best illustrated by the case with only two groups in the population differing only in the probability of an accident. Clearly, an equilibrium were it to exist will consist of only a single contract, purchased by both groups, or two contracts, in which case the 'market' reveals completely the information about the riskiness of the individual. But it can be shown that there can never be an equilibrium where the two groups are pooled together: there would always exist then a policy which would be preferred by the low risk individual to the 'pooling contract' and not preferred by the high risk individuals and which at the same time would make a profit. Thus, if an equilibrium exists, it must consist of each group purchasing a different policy; in particular, it can be shown that the high risk individuals obtain complete insurance and the low risk individuals obtain insurance with a large deductibility clause (similar to the monopoly case, except the terms of the contract differ). But there is a cost to the low risk individuals in being 'identified': they only obtain partial insurance. And thus there *may* exist another contract which will be purchased by both high and low risk individuals which will make a profit.

Indeed, if there is a continuum of individuals of differing probabilities, there never exists an equilibrium in the insurance market.

I have not been entirely successful in coming up with an intuitive explanation of this non-existence. It is related to the fact that the information conveyed by the individual's choice of a particular contract depends on the set of contracts which are available. Thus, in providing a new contract, an insurance firm generates an informational externality which he does not take into account. In particular, he ignores the fact that the viability of the other contracts which are offered, and which allow him to make a profit by offering his contract and having self-selection work to ensure that those who purchase it are low risk individuals, is destroyed when he offers the new contract.

Note that when an equilibrium does exist, it looks much different from the usual competitive model: now the price one pays depends on the quantity one purchases, since that conveys information, i.e. in this context, the cost per $1,000 of insurance is a function of the number of units of insurance purchased.

Note, too, when an equilibrium does exist, the high risk individuals exert a strong negative externality on the low risk individuals: the high risk individuals are no better off than they would have been in isolation, but the low risk individuals are made worse off by the presence of high risk individuals.

The contrast with conventional 'reasoning' concerning the 'robustness' of the competitive model should be noted: we normally suggest that a little bit of imperfect information does not make 'much difference' (this obviously involves considerable hand waving, but if the model is to have any 'credibility' this hand waving must be done). It turns out that in this analysis an equilibrium will never exist when there is just a little bit of imperfect information, i.e. the probabilities of accidents of the two groups differ only a little or there are only a few of the high risk individuals.

The same kind of analysis can be applied to the education market. The number of years one goes to school 'conveys' information in the same way as the amount of insurance one purchases. The cost of this information process is that the high ability individuals attend school longer than they would in the absence of the low ability individuals.

Probably the first clearly articulated example of this kind of process was that of George Akerlof; he suggested that the speed of an assembly line might also sort individuals according to their ability; in order to get themselves identified the more able 'work harder' than they otherwise would have. For this process, he provides the apt title of the 'rat race'.

The second source of difficulty with existence is best seen when there also exists an examination process by which individuals can be screened. If the individual knows his own risks in principle, the firm need do no screening. It asks individuals to tell it what their abilities are, and announces that it will randomly test for honesty by examination. If the individual has been dishonest, he is fined. By increasing the fine, one can get complete sorting with only a small number of examinations. On the other hand, the limit—where no exams are given and fines are infinitely large—does not sort at all. In this case, however, there is, I think, a meaningful quasi-equilibrium. In effect what we have done here is to use the threat of screening by examination to introduce a type of screening by self-selection. (In practice, individuals often accept low wages until they have 'proved' themselves. The difference between the low wage he receives now and what he could have received elsewhere acts as a fine should he not prove himself out.)

1.7 Interpretation of Non-existence

What are we to make of the results reported above, that there may not exist a competitive equilibrium when there is imperfect information? How would we recognise a problem of 'non-existence' in the real world? Is the kind of problem we are discussing limited to a few specialised markets, like insurance, or is it more pervasive?

Of course, some of the markets for which the analysis seems to be particularly appropriate—for instance markets for education—clearly are not competitive: most education is provided publicly. In other markets, e.g. insurance, there is a large element of government regulation; perhaps in the absence of this regulation, the problems associated with non-existence of equilibrium would be more apparent.

But I believe that screening is an important aspect of many other economic activities, in particular of labour markets, capital markets, and indeed, in all contractual relations. For almost all contracts entail a promise by one party to perform some task (say deliver some product) in the future; and although there may be sanctions against non-performance, performance is never certain and the resulting costs may be large. Moreover, no contract has clauses to take care of all contingencies. Thus, most businessmen put a high value in 'knowing with whom they are dealing'.

The matter may be put another way. One of the essential elements in the conventional theory of perfect competition is that of anonymity: a ton of steel is the same no matter who sells it or who buys it; transactions occur in markets in which there is no need to know the name of either the buyer or seller. In economies with the kind of imperfect information we have been discussing, 'names' are essential: working for GM is different from working for Xerox (even as an unskilled worker, such as a janitor); a Travelers insurance policy for the same nominal amount is different from that provided by Prudential. A contract to deliver a certain amount of steel by Bethlehem may be different from a similar contract by US Steel. A loan of $100,000 to individual A is different from a loan to individual B. This absence of anonymity thus introduces an essential element of imperfect competition, the importance of which clearly may vary from market to market. What I am suggesting, however, is that in situations where screening is important, a monopolistically competitive model rather than a purely competitive model of the conventional sort may be more appropriate.

The construction of models in which there does exist an equilibrium—although not a purely competitive one—in the presence of the kinds of imperfect information we have been discussing is a task which remains to be done. What I would like to do is to sketch the outlines of three rather different modifications in our analysis which *might* lead, when appropriately developed, to such a model.

A Partial Screening Model

Consider the problem of screening individuals according to ability in the labour market. Assume that only a fraction of all firms screen everyone. Then a fraction of the individuals will be screened by no firms, a fraction will be screened by only one firm, and a fraction will be screened by several. Those individuals who are screened only by one firm receive the same wage as those who are not screened at all. But those who are above the average of those working for firms who do no screening who are screened by two or more firms receive their true marginal productivity. Thus, on a fraction of its employees, the firm which screens is able to appropriate the returns to screening (because of its 'monopoly position').[6] In equilibrium, the fraction of firms screening (of individuals being screened) is determined so as to make the profitability of the screening firms the same as that of the no screening firms. (This model does reflect one characteristic of labour markets that is sometimes commented upon: individuals who appear to be of roughly comparable ability receive very different wages, simply depending on the 'luck' of being screened by two or more firms.)

Imperfect Information on Both Sides of Market

Most of our analysis has focussed on imperfections of information on one side of the market only. But in fact there are imperfections on both sides. In the insurance market, not only does the insurance company not know the accident probability of the individual buying the insurance, but also the individual buying the insurance may not know several important characteristics of the insurance company: how quickly it settles claims, what it accepts as proof of loss, how generous it is in interpreting various provisions of the insurance contract, etc. This seriously effects the response to a new company offering a new contract. Purchase of the new contract is limited to those who (a) find out about it (b) have sufficiently low risk aversion to be willing to undertake the 'gamble' of a new company or (c) have sufficient time to investigate its characteristics in detail, and who prefer this contract to their present contract. Imperfections of information of this sort do not necessarily affect the non-viability of the pooling equilibrium; but it does make an equilibrium in which two separate contracts are offered more likely. For although there might exist a contract which, if both groups were equally well informed, risk averse, etc. would be preferred by both risk groups, and make a profit, in the absence of perfect information by buyers, it might be purchased by a differentially higher proportion of high risk individuals and make a loss.

Labour markets provide perhaps a better illustration of how imperfect information by workers 'stabilises' the market. Different firms have different non-pecuniary characteristics, many of which do not really become apparent until after the individual goes to work for the firm (e.g. the personality of many of his colleagues). This means that the 'effective wage' on any new job is uncertain. If an individual is risk averse, in order to induce him to change jobs, the expected value of his 'effective wage'

---

[6] This does not completely solve the appropriability problem, since other firms can use the fact that a 'screening firm' has hired an individual as evidence that he must be 'above average'. There are two ways that firms might be able to ameliorate these problems: (a) By making it difficult for other firms to tell the extent to which it is screening and the characteristics it is screening for; for instance, it may screen for characteristics which are specifically useful to the firm more than for characteristics which are of more general use; it may screen only a fraction of its employees, etc. (b) By introducing devices to reduce labour turnover, e.g. vested pensions.

in the new job must be sufficiently higher than his effective wage in the old job to compensate him for undertaking this risk.

Competitive Capital Markets with Borrowing Limitations

In the capital market, a further limitation is imposed by the limited resources available to any individual. Assume an individual does research into the 'true value' of a given security, and discovers that it is underpriced. He should borrow enough to buy all the stock of the firm. But assume each individual can borrow only a limited amount. Then it is possible that several individuals could obtain the information simultaneously, and still the price of the security would be relatively unaffected. It seems as if what we would normally consider a market imperfection—the limitations on borrowing—enables an equilibrium in a competitive capital market to be established. What still needs to be explained is why individuals can only borrow a limited amount. There are, of course, numerous explanations; it is perhaps worth noting that our theory can account for this limitation as well; for the lender, like the stock speculator, is investing in a risky asset; the 'riskiness' of the loan depends on the size of the loan. The greater the size of the loan, the greater the necessity for the lender to 'screen' the security. In the absence of such screening, the lender would require a higher nominal interest rate the more he loaned. On the other hand, if screening is undertaken when loans become large, again large loans will have to be more expensive to pay for the cost of screening. Moreover, if the lender has to scrutinise the asset, and it really is as good as the borrower believes it to be, there is no reason that the lender should use his resources to lend rather than to invest in the security directly.

1.8 Extension to the Analysis

There are three extensions of the analysis which I wish to take up very briefly.

(a) There are other methods of sorting for ability besides those discussed so far, and one of the most interesting and important involves a combination of self-selection and examination processes: assume individuals do not have knowledge of their own abilities; we divide the population into two groups. The proportion of high ability individuals in the first group is p_1 and in the second group is p_2, $p_1 > p_2$. Individuals know which group they belong to, and their subjective probability of being of high ability is equal to the objective proportions in their group. In that case, the high fine system described earlier for the case where individuals had perfect knowledge of their abilities will not work. It turns out that, if an equilibrium exists, it will entail everybody of group one being screened, those who are identified as more able receiving a wage less than their true marginal product but still greater than that received by those who do not submit to the examination or who submit and fail, and those who submit and fail receive a lower income than those who do not submit to the examination. Thus, there are two costs borne by members of the first group in order to 'select themselves out': a cost in direct examination and a cost of risk absorption.

Now if the group can identify itself by some other criterion, e.g. race or religion, then neither of those costs need to be borne; this provides a strong economic incentive for discrimination.

(b) So far, our analysis has implicitly assumed that the individuals engaged in the given transaction (hiring labour, selling insurance) are those involved in the 'production' of information, and that the two occur roughly simultaneously. In the case of individual abilities, there is a considerable amount of information produced by educational institutions. This is both because the efficient running of educational institutions requires some sorting, knowledge about individuals' abilities is an inevitable by-product of the attempting to transmit knowledge to individuals, and one of the main functions of educational institutions is to sort out individuals according to their comparative advantages. But this separation of the 'purchase' of information from the actual transaction produces further problems. We can then easily obtain multiple equilibria in the economy, one of which is unambiguously Pareto Inferior to the other. For instance, assume there were only two ability groups. The costs of screening may be such that, when there is no screening, it does not pay the high ability individuals to get themselves screened, but when there is complete screening, it does pay them to be certified that they are more able (that is the more able don't mind being labeled 'average', but if all those who are not labeled 'high ability' are implicitly labeled 'low ability' it does pay to be labeled 'high ability'). There are thus two equilibria, and it can be shown that everybody is better off in the no screening equilibrium than in the screening equilibrium.

(This obviously could not happen if the screening and production processes were integrated. For then individuals would all go to firms which did no screening. But there are good reasons why at least part of the screening process must be separated from production: complete integration would require individuals at birth being committed to one firm.)

Further problems with screening equilibria have been noted: if there are alternative bases on which screening may be done, there may exist equilibria involving use of one or another 'screens'; again one of the equilibria may be Pareto Superior to the other.

(c) Another assumption which we have made so far that may seem objectionable is that the screening, when it is done, is perfectly accurate. Let us consider what happens if, alternatively we can choose the degree of accuracy where more accurate screening costs more money. For simplicity, assume the higher ability individuals are risk neutral. It can be shown that expected income of the higher ability individuals is a convex function of the accuracy of screening. If, as we might naturally assume, the costs are also a convex function, then we can easily describe the equilibrium level of screening. However, a small change in the cost function (as a result of, say, some change in factor prices) may result in a discrete change in the level of screening (say from fairly accurate screening to zero screening). Hence, the demand functions for factors in the screening industry is discontinuous, and this provides a further reason for the possible non-existence of equilibrium. Moreover, since the amount of information supplied is discontinuous, demand functions for labour (and the supply of labour by individuals) will be discontinuous.

1.9 Welfare Economics of Screening

So far we have little explicit to say about the welfare economics of screening, in particular on what are the 'social returns' to screening, and whether there will be too little or too much screening.

In some sense, the question hardly calls for discussion: can one imagine an efficient allocation of resources without knowing the characteristics of different machines, i.e. treating all capital goods as identical? Yet the ethical beliefs about equality of individuals have sometimes become confused with economic beliefs about identicalness of individuals, at least for economic purposes; so perhaps we should briefly remind ourselves of a few of the ways in which, for instance, knowledge about individual's abilities may yield returns. These may be divided into roughly two categories:

Trade-offs

In the absence of information, individuals receive a wage which differs from their true marginal product. Imperfect information acts just like a wage tax on the more able, a wage subsidy on the less able. Like all taxes, the 'information tax' is distortionary in its effect on the consumption–leisure decision, on the decision of trading-off pecuniary and non-pecuniary returns, etc.

Matching

Individuals differ in the comparative skills with which they can perform different tasks and the ease with which they learn different skills. From the theory of comparative advantage, we know that there are returns to assigning each to the job where he has a comparative advantage, but this requires screening individuals for their comparative advantage.

Even with a given occupation, there are further 'matching problems'. The performance of an individual may for instance depend on the characteristics of the individuals with whom he works.

The private returns to screening (say in the labour market) are the ability rents which the able individual is thereby able to capture. These bear no direct relation to these social returns, and as a result, there may be either too much or too little expenditure on screening (see Stiglitz, 1975f).

1.10 Bibliographic Notes on the Economics of Screening

The basic outlines of the theory of screening were developed in a series of papers, largely independently written, in the early 70s. Akerlof (1976)[7] examined screening in a variety of contexts within the labour market, and provided the model referred to earlier as the 'rat race'. Gary Fields (1973), working in 1970–1 at the Institute for Development Studies in Nairobi, recognized the importance of screening both for

---

[7] The basic ideas were developed and presented in seminars as early as 1970.

the demand for education and the private returns to it, and developed an equilibrium model of the education market.

There were three aspects of his model which limited its applicability to other situations where screening might be important: first, he assumed (as is conventional in models of LDCs) that wages were rigid. Secondly, although education served as a basis for allocating jobs, the screening the education system itself was doing played an inessential role in the analysis. Thirdly, the equilibration of the 'supply' of education to the demand occurred through political processes, but an explicit model of political decision was not provided.

Screening in educational markets where wages were competitively determined was analysed by Arrow (1973a), Spence (1973, 1974a), and Stiglitz (1971a, 1972a, 1974b, 1975f), and Rothschild and Stiglitz (1976).

Spence in his highly insightful work focussed on what we have referred to above as self-selection mechanisms where individuals are reasonably well informed of their own abilities. The actions which individuals take which affect how they are judged he refers to as *signals*. Although in the Spence work (unlike Fields) wages are competitively determined, there is an incomplete theory of the determination of the 'supply of education' (the equilibrium level of screening). An analysis of the determination of the equilibrium level of screening in private, public and mixed public–private school systems is provided in Stiglitz (1974b, 1975f).

It is not surprising, of course, that the difficulties of competitive economies discussed above were not noticed in education markets, since these are, as we commented earlier, hardly competitive. But in the context of labour markets (e.g. screening for ability), capital markets, and insurance markets these problems could hardly be avoided.

Salop and Salop (1976) discussed screening of individuals according to their turnover rates, and Stiglitz (1971b) showed how concepts of screening he had earlier developed for labour markets (1971a) could be applied to the capital market (see also Stiglitz, 1982c).[8] These two papers provided the first suggestion of the the difficulties that screening might present for competitive equilibrium analysis.

These were more fully articulated in the paper by Rothschild and Stiglitz (1976). They were also able to show that the formal analysis they developed there for the insurance market could be immediately applied to the analysis of the competitive education market and of competitive labour markets (in particular, to Akerlof's analysis of the rat race).

---

[8] My own interest in the economics of screening owes much to several conversations with George Akerlof when we were graduate students together at MIT in 1965–6. He suggested that one might view education as an 'egg sorter'. Discussions with Fields while I was in Nairobi in the summer of 1971 rekindled my interest. The similarity between the basic formulation I employed (see Stiglitz 1975f) and that independently arrived at by Spence (1974a) is striking. I subsequently recognized that the basic ideas of screening could be used to resolve some of the difficulties of information in the capital market; my conversations with C. von Weizacker over the years on these matters have been particularly helpful. Finally, I should acknowledge a debt to my students, in particular Steve Salop, who not only listened patiently through early and unfinished versions of my papers, but who pointed out a number of weaknesses in the early analyses.

The analysis of screening by monopolists is contained in the papers by Salop (1977), Spence (1974a), and Stiglitz (1977a). The welfare economics of screening is discussed in Spence (1974b) and Stiglitz (1975f). Two important antecedents of the Theory of Screening should be noted. The first is Akerlof's seminal paper on the 'market for "lemons"'. The other is the literature on the economics of discrimination (Arrow, 1972a; Phelps, 1972; Stiglitz, 1973c, 1974h).

2 Basic Research

Let me now turn to the second kind of 'information', which is generated by what might be called fundamental research. Although I find it difficult to come up with a simple definition, the distinction between this and the earlier 'screening information' should be clear; screening information consists of putting objects into one of a set of pre-assigned categories; it is, in this sense, essentially a repetitive process. On the other hand, one of the objects of fundamental research is to discover and develop new 'categories', new concepts.

Moreover, screening, as we have modeled it, is a process in which there is no learning, which is a basic element of all 'fundamental' research. Finally, as Popper has emphasised, in a basic sense, the 'output' of fundamental research is unpredictable.

Many of the problems associated with this kind of information are similar to those in the economics of screening; e.g. the problem associated with appropriability and the inherent non-convexity associated with 'information'. But there are several other difficulties, associated with absence of futures and risk markets, which have to date been inadequately explored. I shall do little more here than list and comment on some of the problems. Since this is an area in which little work has been done, my remarks must be somewhat more speculative than those made in the first part of this paper.

The fact that the outcome of 'fundamental research' cannot be predicted throws serious doubt on the applicability of that fundamental construct of the modern attempt to extend conventional competitive analysis to inter-temporal and risk situations: the Arrow–Debreu or contingent-claim securities. For how can there be securities for classes of events before those events are conceived of? How, to take an absurd case, could there have been an Arrow–Debreu security for 'an atomic disaster' before the possibility of an atomic bomb was conceived.

It is natural in this context to consider the economy as evolving in a stochastic manner with the characteristics of the stochastic process (e.g. the rate of technical change, the regularity with which inefficient firms are eliminated, etc.) depending on the 'organisation' of the economy.[9] This 'evolutionary' view immediately suggests

---

[9] The organisation of the economy is itself subject to evolutionary forces. See Winter (1964) both for an excellent discussion of the basic issues and an attempt to formalise some of these ideas.

certain analogies to Darwinism and Social Darwinism, and in particular, to the concepts of 'natural selection' and 'survival of the fittest'.

The application of these concepts to economics has lead to the suggestion that even if firms do not consciously maximise profits, it is the maximisers who are 'fittest' and thus who will survive: the eventual evolution of the economy is as if firms were consciously profit maximising. Although the process of natural selection may have to be tempered, there is a suggestion that this process does have some optimality properties.

Winter (1964) and Farrell (1970) in their highly original and insightful papers, have shown that the presumption that natural selection will eliminate non-profit maximising firms is dubious.[10] As Winter has put it (Winter, 1964, p. 265).

To sum up, the importance of information costs to the selection argument lies in the fact that, when information is costly, the types of closely calculated behavior that economists generally impute to firms may be less viable than unsophisticated behavior which simply happens to be well adapted to the conditions that actually exist. A firm that is prepared to respond to unprecedented situations in approximately the fashion that economists predict is probably a firm that is overspending on decision making in the precedented situations. Even if a firm can hold its own, however, it clearly has no *advantage* in viability over less sophisticated but well adapted firms—until the unprecedented occurs. At that point, however, the response of the economy as a whole will not be accurately predicted by a theory which assumes that all firms are sophisticated.

It should also be pointed out that the presumption of optimality of evolutionary processes is also dubious: the process of evolution—both biological and economic—suffers from two limitations, myopia and imperfect futures markets. This means that the outcomes of evolutionary processes may not be optimal from the point of view of a longer horizon. Let me first illustrate this by considering the survival of a species which has two important characteristics, A_1 and A_2. A_2 may be such that, given the present environment, the species does not survive, but, were it able to survive, A_1 is a characteristic which, in the kind of environment which will eventually evolve, may be very 'successful'. There are, so to speak, imperfect biological capital markets; the species cannot borrow from its future prosperity to finance its present (temporary) impoverished state.

Moreover, the random element in the evolutionary process means that two islands in isolation starting off together, will evolve in quite different directions; the eventual evolutionary states may be such that, when they are brought into contact, one 'dominates' the other.

In what sense then has 'survival of the fittest' led to 'optimal evolution'? The consequences of myopia and imperfect capital markets for the evolution of the economy are similar. At any moment, there are innumerable commodities that might be produced but are not; innumerable processes for the producing of commodities that might be tried, but are not. We can think of 'technical progress' as a sequence of inventions,

---

[10] The argument may be put in a somewhat different way: if survival means avoidance of bankruptcy, or profits falling below some critical level, then a policy which minimises that may clearly be different from a policy which maximises the expected profits.

discoveries, enabling us better to attain one of the basic 'objectives' of food, shelter, etc. In this sense, we can reduce all inventions, both what are conventionally called process and product inventions, to process inventions. We cannot 'predict' how the 'costs' of meeting these basic needs will be reduced, but we may be able to describe the sequence of cost reductions in terms of a stochastic process. And we may be able to evaluate alternative evolutionary paths in terms of the 'costs' they generate for meeting these basic needs.

Let me emphasise that this does not really resolve the problem of comparing alternative evolutionary paths, for tastes may also be selected out along evolutionary paths, generating problems essentially like those raised by endogenous preferences. Nor does this representation of technical change fully capture the virtues, the richness, of the evolutionary process. That is, I suspect, one loses something by assuming that the new commodities being produced are simply better at doing the same kinds of things that the older commodities do. One could, of course, develop some measure of the 'variety' of commodities, but there is more to it than that.

Recognising the limitations of the approach, it is still probably worthwhile to proceed to see what kinds of insights this approach might yield.

Assume for instance, that some firm, some individual, tries to produce a 'new' commodity (use a new process) and is successful. Assume it 'replaces' some other commodity or process, say B. Successive inventions or discoveries are likely to be more 'clustered' around this commodity or process which has been replaced (see Atkinson–Stiglitz (1969)). Let us compare this economy with one in which A, the given commodity, is not discovered and B continues to be used. This economy will have, initially, a lower level of utility (income); but it may be that the long run prospects of innovation with B—provided one continues to 'work with it'—are greater than for A; then in the long run, the B economy may have a higher level of income (utility) than the A economy. Clearly, if the A economy 'knew this' and there were perfect capital markets, depending on the rate of interest, the A economy would not discard the B process. But capital markets are imperfect and there is, in general, no method by which, today, we can know what the eventual evolutionary outcome of a particular set of decisions will be; the point of the example is to illustrate the dangers inherent in making welfare economic statements concerning 'competitive' market forces in an evolutionary context.

Let me give another example, which may be couched in the more familiar static equilibrium analysis of economics. Assume we have four commodities, and two types of individuals. There are fixed costs associated with establishing a market, and for simplicity, assume each market can trade in only two commodities. So there are a total of six possible markets. Assume the fixed costs are borne equally by all participants in the market. Define an equilibrium as a set of 'open' markets and a set of trades, such that given the set of 'open markets' all open markets clear and, given the *after* trade vector of commodities of the individuals, it does not pay to open a new market. There may be multiple equilibria of this sort, in some of which everyone is better off than in others. These equilibria differ in the set of markets which are open.

If we think of the economy initially as being in a 'pre-market' situation, and then someone 'discovering' that everyone could be made better off if we open market AB, we can view the set of markets which are actually opened as having evolved. Different evolutionary paths lead to different equilibria. There is nothing to guarantee the 'optimality' of the path which will evolve out of a competitive process.

The recent experiences with coalfields provide another interesting example. Without government intervention, competitive forces would have led to more extensive reductions in the coalfields in the 1950s or 1960s than actually occurred. Yet, as it turns out, with soaring oil prices this would probably have been a mistake.

What are we to make then of those who extol the 'dynamic efficiency of the competitive system'? Is this simply a reflection of ideology, or can we give it some content? Those who make such statements base it on the actual observation of alternative systems and on *a priori* arguments concerning the incentives involved in the different systems. The experiences of the Soviet Union make clear what was perhaps not so clear in Schumpeter's day: that a centralised socialist economy can direct resources to research and development no less so than a competitive economy, and with some successs (e.g., Sputnik).

It may be possible to compare one particular economic system, with its incentive structure, with another particular economic system. One could, for instance, specify a particular stochastic process as describing the outcome of allocations to research. One could then trace out the development of the economy under the different incentive structures on the different realisations of the stochastic process. One might then compare the performance of the economy on these different realisations. All we actually observe is a particular realisation of the stochastic process; the fact that one incentive structure worked better in this particular realisation is hardly evidence that it is a better incentive structure.

The intuition behind the merit of the competitive process is that it selects out for *adaptability*, the ability to respond to changes, and in the long run it is adaptability which counts. Bureaucratic structures may be adaptable, but there is no necessity for them to be. A ministry of steel *could* respond to a change in the underlying technology by imitating how a competitive market would respond; but it could also lay down an administrative ruling that the change in technology is to be suppressed.

Indeed, since the magnitude of the stresses imposed on the various parts of 'system' are determined by the system, there may be 'survival value' in basically stagnant systems. That is, the stability of a system may depend on its adaptability relative to the need of adapting which it engenders. Bureaucratic systems may have less adaptability, but may so reduce the incentives for innovation, originality, etc. that the necessity for adapting is also reduced.[11]

One of the reasons it may be difficult to make clear judgments concerning the virtues of one economic structure relative to another is that the 'speed of evolution' may be small; differences in 'evolutionary forces' may show up only in time spans that are greater than those in which we have become accustomed to thinking. Long range planning is often taken to involve planning in excess of ten to fifteen years; we tend to evaluate policies with respect to their effects on this and possibly the next generation;

---

[11] These remarks correspond to Winter's observation that 'the viability of an organization form cannot in general be determined without reference to the entire *system* of organization forms in the economy' (Winter, 1964, p. 260).

yet in discussing evolutionary forces, one can hardly confine oneself to such a narrow viewpoint.

The use of the standard competitive equilibrium theory for making welfare judgments is a reflection of—and perhaps a contributing factor in—the prevalent extreme myopic view in judging economic performance.

3 Screening and 'Pure Research' as Polar Cases

I suggested in my earlier remarks that 'pure research' and 'screening' can be viewed as polar cases; that most other kinds of information could be viewed as a 'mixture' of the two. Let me elaborate briefly on this. Assume we wish to know whether it will rain tomorrow. This is an example of what may be 'called' predictive information. Assume we had a complete model of the pattern of weather determination, and assume it had a Markovian structure. Then by fully knowing the relevant characteristics today (screening 'today') we could perfectly predict the kind of day tomorrow will be. But so long as we do not have a 'complete model'—and there may be reasons for arguing we are never likely to—then the prediction will entail two elements missing from pure screening information: a *judgment* whether an event for which the 'model' does not work well is occurring and *research* into better predictors.

4 Methodological Implications

I also suggested earlier that one of the reasons that the 'economics of information' is such a fascinating and important question is that it has strong implications for current economic methodology. I have drawn attention to several of these implications; let me conclude by making some further methodological observations.

It has become almost conventional to begin papers with some criticism of the 'conventional' approach to economics, to be followed, if one is an analytically trained economist, by a conventional model within the conventional framework; if not, one follows the 'criticism' by a 'call' for a fundamental rethinking of our approach to economic problems, and leaves the matter at that. Such criticisms are all the more celebrated when they come from a theorist who has contributed, at least, in his youth, to the development of the 'conventional wisdom'. These criticisms are taken as an admission of the sterility of theoretical economists—as many non-theorists have claimed all along. My observations of these criticisms is that they can be, roughly, placed into three categories: the first, probably the most strident, comes from those no longer actively engaged in research; they sense the subject has passed them by, and they seem to resent this. One often detects a slight feeling of paranoia, a sense that they have been insufficiently appreciated, perhaps a regret at having been chosen to spend a lifetime on a set of problems which, though important, are not central to their current political concerns.

A second kind of criticism comes from those who have never contributed to the subject; they sense that they have passed the subject by, and blame the subject for that.

The other kind of criticism comes from those who are actively engaged in research, who believe that the tools, techniques and ways of thinking of the analytically trained economist have much to contribute towards our understanding of economic processes. The criticism is part of the ongoing scientific dialogue, attempting to define what are the most important areas towards which research should be directed. It is in this sense of 'criticism' that the following remarks are to be taken.

Conventional economic theory has been constructed on the basis of a set of assumptions and related concepts which 'fit together' neatly. This 'fitting together' is more than a question of simple logical consistency; it is a certain kind of empirical plausibility. That is, in a world in which 'most' of the conventional assumptions obtain, one might 'expect' that the other assumptions obtain (although they need not).

Consider, for instance, the assumptions of perfect competition, perfect information, and convexity of technology and the concept of equilibrium. The assumptions of perfect information and convexity of technology make the assumption of perfect competition more plausible; in the absence of perfect information, firms are likely to have at least some short-run monopoly power over their customers; if they raise prices, customers leave only gradually, not in the 'rush' that they would in a world with perfect information. With returns to scale, there may well be sufficiently few firms that it is not reasonable for firms to act as price takers. In turn, the assumption of convexity makes the assumption of perfect information more 'plausible'. If a firm or an individual would like to know 'what would happen if ...' then it can experiment, on an infinitesimally small scale, and find out.

And out of these assumptions, a certain world-view of how the economy operates has developed. We think of the economy as being at least approximately in equilibrium at each moment; this equilibrium has certain welfare properties; except for certain problems, e.g. increasing returns industries, externalities, public goods, and correcting the income distribution, government intervention is not required. For some markets, for some problems, this view of the economy may be a good first approximation, e.g. for an analysis of the incidence of certain taxes.[12] Recent discussions of the implications of exhaustible natural resources have, I think, been rather insightful.[13]

[12] On the other hand, it is probably not particularly useful as a framework to analyze the effects of the selective employment tax, whose introduction was partly justified on the basis of a 'model' assuming increasing returns in manufacturing and monopolistic competition in the retail sector.

[13] See, for instance, the symposium on natural resources in the *Review of Economic Studies*, 1974.

There are, of course, numerous attempts to extend the model, to make it more realistic, to accommodate the model better to 'reality'. Usually they take the form of altering one assumption at a time. What our analysis has shown is that the introduction of a little bit of 'imperfect information' alters the analysis in fundamental ways; the theory does not appear to be sufficiently robust to withstand modifications of a kind which any acceptable theory ought to be able to withstand.

An alternative theory would focus on imperfect information, non-convexities, and imperfect competition not as minor footnotes to the 'normal case' but as essential to understanding the workings of the economy. These assumptions 'hang together' neatly, and lend empirical plausibility to each other, in much the same way that we described the corresponding assumptions of the purely competitive model did.

Consider, for instance, a technology with the conventional U-shaped cost curves, representing, say, some fixed cost in constructing a plant. Conventional discussions dismiss this type of non-convexity as unimportant; provided the level of output at the minimum cost level is small relative to market output, the market will be 'approximately' in equilibrium. Certainly, this limited amount of increasing returns is not likely to affect the validity of the competitive assumption. But assume that this is a product which has not been produced; the firm does not know what the demand curve for it is. Because there are large costs involved in the experimentation, no firm may undertake the experiment of finding out, even if, were the experiment to be undertaken, it would be successful and all individuals might be better off. Thus, the presence of non-convexity makes it more natural that states of 'imperfect information' persist.

In turn, our earlier discussion suggested that imperfect information was likely to be associated with imperfect competition. The world-views which emerge from the alternative approaches to the economy presented in this paper are markedly different from the conventional approaches which I described above. Views of competition, equilibrium and optimality need to be reassessed.

Although I know I have not gone very far in this paper towards accomplishing this task, what I hope I have done is to communicate some of the perspective which the economics of information brings to these questions and to share some of the excitement that I feel as at last we begin to explore systematically an area, the potential importance of which has long been felt but whose full implications we are only now beginning to grasp.

....

CHAPTER 2

INFORMATION
AND THE CHANGE
IN THE PARADIGM
IN ECONOMICS*

....

THE research for which George Akerlof, Michael Spence, and I are being recognized is part of a larger research program which today embraces a great number of researchers around the world. In this article, I want to set the particular work which was cited within this broader agenda, and that agenda within the still broader perspective of the history of economic thought. I hope to show that information economics represents a fundamental change in the prevailing paradigm within economics.

Information economics has already had a profound effect on how we think about economic policy and is likely to have an even greater influence in the future. Many of the major policy debates over the past two decades have centered around the related issues of the efficiency of the market economy and the appropriate relationship between the market and the government. The argument of Adam Smith (1776) that free markets lead to efficient outcomes, "as if by an invisible hand," has played a central role in these debates: It suggested that we could, by and large, rely on markets *without government intervention* (or, at most, with a limited role for government). The set of ideas that I will present here undermined Smith's theory and the view of the role of government that rested on it. They have suggested that the reason that the hand may be invisible is that it is simply not there—or at least that if it is there, it is palsied.

* This article is a revised version of the lecture Joseph E. Stiglitz delivered in Stockholm, Sweden on December 8, 2001, when he received the Bank of Sweden Prize in Economic Sciences in Memory of Alfred Nobel. The article is copyright © The Nobel Foundation 2001 and is published here with the permission of the Nobel Foundation. Reprinted with permission from the *American Economic Review*, 92(3) (June), 2002.

When I began the study of economics some 41 years ago, I was struck by the incongruity between the models that I was taught and the world that I had seen growing up in Gary, Indiana. Founded in 1906 by U.S. Steel, and named after its Chairman of the Board, Gary has declined to but a shadow of its former self. But even in its heyday, it was marred by poverty, periods of high unemployment, and massive racial discrimination. Yet the economic theories we were taught paid little attention to poverty, said that all markets cleared—including the labor market, so that unemployment must be nothing more than a phantasm—and claimed that the profit motive ensured that there could not be economic discrimination (Gary Becker, 1971). As a graduate student, I was determined to try to create models with assumptions— and conclusions—closer to those that accorded with the world I saw, with all of its imperfections.

My first visits to the developing world in 1967, and a more extensive stay in Kenya in 1969, made an indelible impression on me. Models of perfect markets, as badly flawed as they might seem for Europe or America, seemed truly inappropriate for these countries. While many of the key assumptions that went into the competitive equilibrium model seemed not to fit these economies well, I was particularly struck by the imperfections of information, the absence of markets, and the pervasiveness and persistence of seemingly dysfunctional institutions, such as sharecropping. I had seen cyclical unemployment—sometimes quite large—and the hardship it brought as I grew up, but I had not seen the massive unemployment that characterized African cities, unemployment that could not be explained either by unions or minimum wage laws (which, even when they existed, were regularly circumvented). Again, there was a massive discrepancy between the models we had been taught and what I saw.

In contrast, the ideas and models I will discuss here have proved useful not only in addressing broad philosophical questions, such as the appropriate role of the state, but also in analyzing concrete policy issues. For example, I believe that some of the huge mistakes which have been made in policy in the last decade, in for instance the management of the East Asian crisis or the transition of the former communist countries to the market, might have been avoided had there been a better understanding of issues—such as financial structure, bankruptcy, and corporate governance—to which the new information economics has called attention. And the so-called "Washington consensus"[1] policies, which have predominated in the policy advice of the international financial institutions over the past quarter century, have been based on market fundamentalist policies which ignored the information-theoretic concerns; this explains, at least partly, their widespread failures. Information affects decision making in every context—not just inside firms and households. More recently, as I discuss below, I have turned my attention to some aspects of what might be called the *political economy* of information: the role of information in political processes and collective decision-making. There are asymmetries of information between those governing and those governed, and just as participants in markets strive to overcome

---

[1] See John Williamson (1990) for a description and Stiglitz (1998a, 1998d) for a critique.

asymmetries of information, we need to look for ways by which the asymmetries of information in political processes can be limited and their consequences mitigated.

I THE HISTORICAL SETTING

I do not want here to review in detail the models that were constructed exploring the role of information; in recent years, there has been a number of survey articles and interpretive essays, even several books in this area.[2] I do want to highlight some of the dramatic impacts that information economics has had on how economics is approached today, how it has provided explanations for phenomena that were previously unexplained, how it has altered our views about how the economy functions, and, perhaps most importantly, how it has led to a rethinking of the appropriate role for government in our society. In describing the ideas, I want to trace out some of their origins. To a large extent, these ideas evolved from attempts to answer specific policy questions or to explain specific phenomena to which the standard theory provided an inadequate explanation. But any discipline has a life of its own, a prevailing paradigm, with assumptions and conventions. Much of the work was motivated by an attempt to explore the limits of that paradigm—to see how the standard models could embrace problems of information imperfections (which turned out to be not very well).

For more than 100 years, formal modeling in economics had focused on models in which information was assumed to be perfect. Of course, everyone recognized that information was in fact imperfect, but the hope, following Marshall's dictum "*Natura non facit saltum*," was that economies in which information was not too imperfect would look very much like economies in which information was perfect. One of the main results of our research was to show that this was not true; that even a small amount of information imperfection could have a profound effect on the nature of the equilibrium.

The creators of the neoclassical model, the reigning economic paradigm of the twentieth century, ignored the warnings of nineteenth-century and still earlier masters about how information concerns might alter their analyses—perhaps because they could not see how to embrace them in their seemingly precise models, perhaps because doing so would have led to uncomfortable conclusions about the efficiency of markets. For instance, Smith, in anticipating later discussions of adverse selection, wrote that as firms raise interest rates, the best borrowers drop out of the

---

[2] Review articles include Stiglitz (1975c, 1985d, 1987a, 1988b, 1992b, 2000b) and John G. Riley (2001). Book-length references include, among others, Drew Fudenberg and Jean Tirole (1991), Jack Hirshleifer and Riley (1992), and Oliver D. Hart (1995).

market.[3] If lenders knew perfectly the risks associated with each borrower, this would matter little; each borrower would be charged an appropriate risk premium. It is because lenders do not know the default probabilities of borrowers perfectly that this process of adverse selection has such important consequences.

I have already noted that *something* was wrong—indeed seriously wrong—with the competitive equilibrium models which represented the prevailing paradigm when we went to graduate school. The paradigm seemed to say that unemployment did not exist, and that issues of efficiency and equity could be neatly separated, so that economists could set aside problems of inequality and poverty as they went about their business of designing more efficient economic systems. But beyond these questionable conclusions there were also a host of empirical puzzles—facts that were hard to reconcile with the standard theory, institutional arrangements left unexplained. In microeconomics, there were public finance puzzles, such as why firms appear not to take actions which minimize their tax liabilities; security market paradoxes,[4] such as why asset prices are so volatile (Robert J. Shiller, 2000) and why equity plays such a limited role in the financing of new investment (Colin Mayer, 1990); and other important behavioral questions, such as why firms respond to risks in ways markedly different from those predicted by the theory. In macro-economics, the cyclical movements of many of the key aggregate variables proved difficult to reconcile with the standard theory. For example, if labor-supply curves are highly inelastic, as most evidence suggests is the case (especially for primary workers), then falls in employment during cyclical downturns should be accompanied by large declines in the real consumption wage. This does not appear to happen. And if the perfect market assumptions were even approximately satisfied, the distress caused by cyclical movements in the economy would be much less than seems to be the case.[5]

There were, to be sure, some Ptolemaic attempts to defend and elaborate on the old model. Some authors, like George J. Stigler (1961), Nobel laureate in 1982, while recognizing the importance of information, argued that once the real costs of information were taken into account, the standard results of economics would still hold. Information was just a transactions cost. In the approach of many Chicago School economists, information economics was like any other branch of applied economics; one simply analyzed the special factors determining the demand for and supply of information, just as one might analyze the factors affecting the market for wheat. For the more mathematically inclined, information could be incorporated into production functions by inserting an I for the input "information," where I itself

---

[3]   "If the legal rate ... was fixed so high ... the greater part of the money which was to be lent, would be lent to prodigals and profectors, who alone would be willing to give this higher interest. Sober people, who will give for the use of money no more than a part of what they are likely to make by the use of it, would not venture into the competition" (Smith, 1776). See also Jean-Charles-Leonard Simonde de Sismondi (1815), John S. Mill (1848), and Alfred Marshall (1890), as cited in Stiglitz (1987a).

[4]   There was so many of these that the *Journal of Economic Perspectives* ran a regular column with each issue highlighting these paradoxes. For a discussion of other paradoxes, see Stiglitz (1973d, 1982e, 1989f).

[5]   Robert E. Lucas, Jr. (1987), who won the Nobel Prize in 1995, uses the perfect markets model with a representative agent to try to argue that these cyclical fluctuations in fact have a relatively small welfare costs.

could be produced by inputs, like labor. Our analysis showed that this approach was wrong, as were the conclusions derived from it.

Practical economists who could not ignore the bouts of unemployment which had plagued capitalism since its inception talked of the "neo-classical synthesis": If Keynesian interventions were used to ensure that the economy remained at full employment, the story went, the standard neoclassical propositions would once again be true. But while the neoclassical synthesis (Paul A. Samuelson [1947], Nobel laureate in 1970) had enormous intellectual influence, by the 1970's and 1980's it had come under attack from two sides. One side attacked the underpinnings of Keynesian economics, its microfoundations. Why would rational actors fail to achieve a full employment equilibrium in the way that John Maynard Keynes (1936) had suggested? This form of the argument effectively denied the existence of the phenomena that Keynes was attempting to explain. Worse still, from this perspective some saw the unemployment that did exist as largely reflecting an interference (e.g., by government in setting minimum wages, or by trade unions using their monopoly power to set too-high wages) with the free workings of the market. The implication was that unemployment would be eliminated if markets were made more *flexible*, that is, if unions and government interventions were eliminated. Even if wages fell by a third in the Great Depression, they should have, in this view, fallen even more.

There was however an alternative perspective (articulated more fully in Bruce C. Greenwald and Stiglitz, 1987b, 1988a) which asked why we shouldn't believe that massive unemployment was just the tip of an iceberg of more pervasive market inefficiencies that are harder to detect. If markets seemed to function *so* badly some of the time, they must be underperforming in more subtle ways much of the time. The economics of information bolstered this view. Indeed, given the nature of the debt contracts, falling prices in the Depression led to bankruptcy and economic disruptions, actually exacerbating the economic downturn. Had there been more wage and price flexibility, matters might have been even worse.

In a later section, I shall explain how it was not just the discrepancies between the standard competitive model and its predictions which led to its being questioned, but the model's lack of robustness—even slight departures from the underlying assumption of perfect information had large consequences. But before turning to those issues, it may be useful to describe some of the specific questions which underlay the beginnings of my research program in this area.

II SOME MOTIVATING IDEAS

A Education as a Screening Device

Key to my thinking on these issues was the time between 1969 and 1971 I spent at the Institute for Development Studies at the University of Nairobi with the support of the Rockefeller Foundation. The newly independent Kenyan government was asking questions that had not been raised by its former colonial masters, as it attempted to forge policies which would promote its growth and development. For example, how much should the government invest in education? It was clear that a better education got people better jobs—the credential put one at the head of the job queue. Gary S. Fields, a young scholar working at the Institute of Development Studies there, developed a simple model (published in 1972) suggesting, however, that the private returns to education—the enhanced probability of getting a good job—might differ from the social return. Indeed, it was possible that as more people got educated, the private returns got higher (it was even more necessary to get the credential) even though the social return to education might decline. From this perspective, education was performing a markedly different function than it did in the traditional economics literature, where it simply added to human capital and improved productivity.[6] This analysis had important implications for Kenya's decision about how much to invest in higher education. The problem with Fields' work was that it did not provide a full *equilibrium* analysis: wages were fixed, rather than competitively determined.

This omission led me to ask what the market equilibrium would look like if wages were set equal to mean marginal products *conditional on the information that was available* (Stiglitz, 1975f). And this in turn forced me to ask: what were the *incentives* and *mechanisms* for employers and employees to acquire or transmit information? Within a group of otherwise similar job applicants (who therefore face the same wage), the employer has an incentive to identify who is the most able, to find some way of *sorting* or *screening* among them, *if he could keep that information private*. But often he cannot; and if others find out about a worker's true ability, the wage will be bid up, and the employer will be unable to appropriate the return to the information. At the very beginning of this research program we had thus identified one of the key issues in information economics: the difficulty of *appropriating* the returns to creating information.

On the other hand, if the employee knew his own ability (that is, if there were *asymmetries of information* between the employee and the employer), then a different set of incentives were at play. Someone who knows his abilities are above average has an incentive to convince his potential employer of that, but a worker at the bottom of the ability distribution has an equally strong incentive to keep the information private. Here was a second principle that was to be explored in subsequent years: there are incentives on the part of individuals for information not to be revealed, for secrecy, or, in modern parlance, for a lack of transparency. This raised questions: How did the forces for secrecy and for information disclosure get balanced? What was the equilibrium that emerged? I will postpone until the next section a description of that equilibrium.

---

[6] See, e.g., Theodore W. Schultz (1960), who won the Nobel Prize in 1979, and Jacob Mincer (1974). At the time, there was other ongoing work criticizing the human-capital formulation, which focused on the role of education in socialization and providing credentials; see, for example, Samuel Bowles and Herbert Gintis (1976).

B Efficiency Wage Theory

That summer in Kenya I began three other research projects related to information imperfections. At the time I was working in Kenya, there was heavy urban unemployment. My colleagues at the Institute for Development Studies, Michael Todaro and John Harris, had formulated a simple model of labor migration from the rural to the urban sector which accounted for the unemployment.[7] High urban wages attracted workers, who were willing to risk unemployment for the chance at those higher wages. Here was a simple, general equilibrium model of unemployment, but again there was one missing piece: an explanation of high urban wages, well in excess of the legal minimum wage. It did not seem as if either government or unions were *forcing* employers to pay these high wages. One needed an equilibrium theory of wage determination. I recalled discussions I had once had in Cambridge with Harvey Leibenstein, who had postulated that in very poor countries, because of nutrition, higher wages led to higher productivity (Leibenstein, 1957b). The key insight was that imperfections in information and contracting might also rationalize a dependence of productivity on wages.[8] In that case, firms might find it profitable to pay a higher wage than the minimum necessary to hire labor; such wages I referred to as *efficiency wages*. With efficiency wages, unemployment could exist in equilibrium. I explored four explanations for why productivity might depend on wages (other than through nutrition). The simplest was that lower wages lead to higher turnover, and therefore higher turnover costs for the firm.[9] It was not until some years later that we were able to explain more fully—based on limitations of information—why it was that firms have to bear these turnover costs (Richard J. Arnott and Stiglitz, 1985; Arnott et al., 1988).

Another explanation for efficiency wages was related to the work I was beginning on asymmetric information. Any manager will tell you that paying higher wages attracts better workers—this is just an application of the general notion of adverse selection, which played a central role in earlier insurance literature (Kenneth J. Arrow, 1965). Firms in a market do not passively have to accept the "market wage." Even in competitive markets, firms could, if they wanted, offer higher wages than others; indeed, it might pay a firm to offer a higher wage, to attract more able workers. Again,

---

[7] See Michael P. Todaro (1969) and John R. Harris and Todaro (1970). I developed these ideas further in Stiglitz (1969b).

[8] Others were independently coming to the same insight, in particular, Edmund S. Phelps (1968). Phelps and Sidney G. Winter (1970) also realized that the same issues applied to product markets, in their theory of customer markets.

[9] In Nairobi, in 1969, I wrote a long, comprehensive analysis of efficiency wages, entitled "Alternative Theories of Wage Determination and Unemployment in LDC's." Given the custom of writing relatively short papers, focusing on one issue at a time, rather than publishing the paper as a whole, I had to break the paper down into several parts. Each of these had a long gestation period. The labor turnover paper was published as Stiglitz (1974a); the adverse selection model as Stiglitz (1982a, 1992j [a revision of a 1976 unpublished paper]). I elaborated on the nutritional efficiency wage theory in Stiglitz (1976b). Various versions of these ideas have subsequently been elaborated on in a large number of papers, including Andrew W. Weiss (1980), Stiglitz (1982g, 1986b, 1987a, 1987j), Akerlof and Yellen (1986), Andrés Rodríguez and Stiglitz (1991a, b), Raaj K. Sah and Stiglitz (1992), Barry J. Nalebuff et al. (1993), and Patrick Rey and Stiglitz (1996).

the efficiency wage theory explained the existence of unemployment *in equilibrium*. It was thus clear that the notion that underlay much of traditional competitive equilibrium analysis—that markets *had* to clear—was simply not true if information were imperfect.

The formulation of the efficiency wage theory that has received the most attention over the years, however, has focused on problems of *incentives*. Many firms claim that paying high wages induces their workers to work harder. The problem that Carl Shapiro and I (1984) faced was to try to make sense of this claim. If all workers are identical, then if it benefited one firm to pay a high wage, it would likewise benefit all firms. But if a worker was fired for shirking, and there were full employment, he could immediately get another job at the same wage. The high wage would thus provide no incentive. Only if there were unemployment would the worker pay a price for shirking. We showed that *in equilibrium* there *had* to be unemployment: unemployment was the discipline device that forced workers to work hard (see Rey and Stiglitz [1996] for an alternative general-equilibrium formulation). The model had strong policy implications, some of which I shall describe below. Our work illustrated the use of highly simplified models to help clarify thinking about quite complicated matters. In practice, of course, workers are not identical, so problems of adverse selection become intertwined with those of incentives. For example, being fired usually does convey information—there is typically a stigma.

There was a fourth version of the efficiency wage, where productivity was related to *morale* effects, perceptions about how *fairly* they were being treated. While I briefly discussed this version in my earlier work (see in particular Stiglitz, 1974h), it was not until almost 20 years later that the idea was fully developed in the important work of Akerlof and Yellen (1990).

C Sharecropping and the General Theory of Incentives

This work on the economics of incentives in labor markets was closely related to the third research project that I began in Kenya. In traditional economic theory, while considerable lip service was paid to incentives, there was little serious attention to issues of incentives, motivation, and monitoring. With perfect information, individuals are paid to perform a particular service. If they perform the service they receive the contracted amount; and if not, they do not. With *imperfect* information, firms have to motivate and monitor, rewarding workers for observed good performance and punishing them for bad. My interest in these issues was first aroused by thinking about sharecropping, a common form of land tenancy in developing countries. Under sharecropping, the worker surrenders half (sometimes two-thirds) of the produce to the landlord in return for the use of his land. At first blush, this seemed a highly inefficient arrangement, equivalent to a 50-percent tax on workers' labor. But what were the alternatives? The worker could rent the land. He would have full incentives but then he would have to bear all the risk of fluctuations in output; and beside, he often did not have the requisite capital to pay the rent ahead of time and access to credit was limited (for reasons to be explained below). He could work as wage labor, but then the landlord would have to monitor him, to ensure that he worked. Sharecropping represented a compromise between balancing concerns about risk sharing and incentives. The underlying information problem was that the input of the worker could not be observed, but only his output, which was not perfectly correlated with his input. The sharecropping contract could be thought of as a combination of a rental contract *plus* an insurance contract, in which the landlord "rebates" part of the rent if crops turn out badly. There is not full insurance (which would be equivalent to a wage contract) because such insurance would attenuate all incentives. The adverse effect of insurance on incentives to avoid the insured-against contingency is referred to as *moral hazard*.[10]

In Stiglitz (1974e) I analyzed the equilibrium sharecropping contract. In that paper, I recognized the similarity of the incentive problems I explored to those facing modern corporations, e.g., in providing incentives to their managers—a type of problem later to be called the *principal-agent problem* (Stephen A. Ross, 1973). There followed a large literature on optimal and equilibrium incentive schemes, in labor, capital, and insurance markets.[11] An important principle was that contracts had to be based on *observables*, whether they be inputs, processes, or outcomes. Many of the results obtained earlier in the work on adverse selection had their parallel in this area of "adverse incentives." For instance, Arnott and I (1988b, 1990) analyzed equilibria which entail partial insurance as a way of mitigating the adverse incentive effects (just as partial insurance characterized equilibrium with adverse selection).

D Equilibrium Wage and Price Distributions

A fourth strand of my research looked at the issue of wage differentials from a different perspective. My earlier work had suggested that firms that faced higher turnover might pay higher wages to mitigate the problem. But one of the reasons that individuals quit is to obtain a higher-paying job, so the turnover rate in turn depends on the wage distribution. The challenge was to formulate an *equilibrium* model that incorporated both of these observations, that is, where the wage distribution *itself* which motivated the search was *explained* as part of the equilibrium.

More generally, efficiency wage theory said that firms might pay a higher wage than necessary to obtain workers; but the level of the efficiency wage might vary across firms. For example, firms with higher turnover costs, or for which worker

[10] This term, like adverse selection, originates in the insurance literature. Insurance firms recognized that the greater the insurance coverage, the less incentive there was for the insured to take care; if a property was insured for more than 100 percent of its value, there was even an incentive to have an accident (a fire). Not taking appropriate care was thought to be "immoral"; hence the name. Arrow's work in moral hazard (Arrow, 1963, 1965) was among the most important precursors, as it was in the economics of adverse selection.

[11] For a classic reference see Hart and Bengt Holmström (1987). In addition, see Stiglitz (1975b, 1982c), Kevin J. Murphy (1985), Michael C. Jensen and Murphy (1990), Joseph G. Haubrich (1994), and Brian J. Hall and Jeffrey B. Liebman (1998).

inefficiency could lead to large losses of capital, or for which monitoring was more difficult, might find it desirable to pay higher wages. The implication was that similar labor might receive quite different compensation in different jobs. The distribution of wages might not, in general, be explicable solely in terms of differences in abilities.

I was to return to these four themes repeatedly in my research over the following three decades.

III FROM THE COMPETITIVE PARADIGM TO THE INFORMATION PARADIGM

In the previous section, I described how the disparities between the models economists used and the world that I saw, especially in Kenya, had motivated a search for an alternative paradigm. But there was another motivation, driven more by the internal logic and structure of the competitive model itself.

The competitive model virtually made economics a branch of engineering (no aspersions on that noble profession intended), and the participants in the economy better or worse engineers. Each was solving a maximization problem, with full information: households maximizing utility subject to budget constraints, firms maximizing profits (market value), and the two interacting in competitive product, labor, and capital markets. One of the peculiar implications was that there never were disagreements about what the firm should do. Alternative management teams would presumably come up with the same solution to the maximization problems. Another peculiar implication was for the meaning of risk: When a firm said that a project was risky, that (should have) meant that it was highly correlated with the business cycle, not that it had a high chance of failure (Stiglitz, 1989f). I have already described some of the other peculiar implications of the model: the fact that there was no unemployment or credit rationing, that it focused on only a limited subset of the information problems facing society, that it seemed not to address issues such as incentives and motivation.

But much of the research in the profession was directed not at these big gaps, but at seemingly more technical issues—at the mathematical structures. The underlying *mathematics* required assumptions of convexity and continuity, and with these assumptions one could prove the existence of equilibrium and its (Pareto) efficiency (see Gerard Debreu, 1959; Arrow, 1964). The standard proofs of these fundamental theorems of welfare economics did not even list in their enumerated assumptions those concerning information: the perfect information assumption was so ingrained it did not have to be explicitly stated. The *economic* assumptions to which the proofs of efficiency called attention concerned the absence of externalities and public goods. The market failures approach to the economics of the public sector (Francis M. Bator,

1958) discussed alternative approaches by which these market failures could be corrected, but these market failures were highly circumscribed by assumption.

There was, moreover, a curious disjunction between the language economists used to explain markets and the models they constructed. They talked about the information efficiency of the market economy, though they focused on a single information problem, that of scarcity. But there are a myriad of other information problems faced by consumers and firms every day, concerning, for instance, the prices and qualities of the various objects that are for sale in the market, the quality and efforts of the workers they hire, or the potential returns to investment projects. In the standard paradigm, the competitive general-equilibrium model (for which Kenneth J. Arrow and Gerard Debreu received Nobel Prizes in 1972 and 1983, respectively), there were no shocks, no unanticipated events: At the beginning of time, the full equilibrium was solved, and everything from then on was an unfolding over time of what had been planned in each of the contingencies. In the real world, the critical question was: how, and how well, do markets handle fundamental problems of information?

There were other aspects of the standard paradigm that seemed hard to accept. It argued that institutions did not matter—markets could see through them, and equilibrium was simply determined by the laws of supply and demand. It said that the distribution of wealth did not matter, so long as there were well-defined property rights (Ronald H. Coase [1960], who won the Nobel Prize in 1991). And it said that (by and large) history did not matter—knowing preferences and technology and initial endowments, one could describe the time path of the economy.

Work on the economics of information began by questioning each of these underlying premises. Consider, to begin with, the convexity assumptions which corresponded to long-standing principles of diminishing returns. With imperfect information (and the costs of acquiring it) these assumptions were no longer plausible. It was not just that the cost of acquiring information could be viewed as fixed costs.[12] My work with Roy Radner (Radner and Stiglitz, 1984) showed that there was a *fundamental nonconcavity in the value of information*, that is, under quite general conditions, it never paid to buy just a little bit of information. Arnott and Stiglitz (1988b) showed that such problems were pervasive in even the simplest of moral hazard problems (where individuals had a choice of alternative actions, e.g. the amount of risk to undertake). While we had not repealed the law of diminishing returns, we had shown its domain to be more limited than had previously been realized.

Michael Rothschild and I (1976) showed that under natural formulations of what might be meant by a competitive market with imperfect information, equilibrium

---

[12] In the natural "spaces," indifference curves and isoprofit curves were ill behaved. The nonconvexities which naturally arose implied, in turn, that equilibrium might be characterized by randomization (Stiglitz, 1975c), or that Pareto-efficient tax and optimal tax policies might be characterized by randomization (see Stiglitz [1982h], Arnott and Stiglitz [1988b], and Dagobert L. Brito et al. [1995]). Even small fixed costs (of search, of finding out about characteristics of different investments, of obtaining information about relevant technology) imply that markets will not be *perfectly* competitive; they will be better described by models of *monopolistic competition* (see Avinash K. Dixit and Stiglitz [1977], Steven Salop [1977], and Stiglitz [1979a, b, 1989e]), though the basis of imperfect competition was markedly different from that originally envisioned by Edward H. Chamberlin (1933).

often did not exist[13]—even when there was an arbitrarily small amount of information imperfection.[14] While subsequent research has looked for alternative definitions of equilibrium (e.g., Riley, 1979), we remain unconvinced; most of these alternatives violate the natural meaning of "competition," that each participant in the market is so small that he believes that he will have no effect on the behavior of others (Rothschild and Stiglitz, 1997).

The new information paradigm went further in undermining the foundations of competitive equilibrium analysis, the basic "laws" of economics. For example, we have shown how, when prices affect "quality"—either because of incentive or selection effects—equilibrium may be characterized by demand not equaling supply; firms will not pay lower wages to workers, even when they can obtain such workers, because doing so will raise their labor costs. Contrary to the law of one price, we have shown that the market will be characterized by wage and price distributions, even when there is no exogenous source of "noise" in the economy, and even when all firms and workers are (otherwise) identical. Contrary to standard competitive results, we have shown that in equilibrium, firms may charge a price in excess of the marginal costs, or workers may be paid a wage in excess of their reservation wage, so that the incentive to maintain a reputation is maintained (see also Benjamin Klein and Keith B. Leffler, 1981; Shapiro, 1983). Contrary to the efficient markets hypothesis (Eugene F. Fama, 1970), which holds that stock prices convey all the relevant information from the informed to the uninformed, Sanford J. Grossman and I (1976, 1980a) showed that, when information is costly to collect, stock prices necessarily aggregate information imperfectly (to induce people to gather information, there must be an "equilibrium amount of disequilibrium"). Each of these cornerstones of the competitive paradigm was rejected, or was shown to hold only under much more restrictive conditions.

The most fundamental reason that markets with imperfect information differ from those in which information is complete is that, with imperfect information, market actions or choices convey information. Market participants know this and respond accordingly. For example, firms provide guarantees not only because they are better able to absorb the risk of product failure but to convey information about their confidence in their products. A person takes an insurance policy with a large deductible to convey to the insurer his belief that the likelihood of his having an accident is low. Information may also be concealed: A firm may not assign an employee to a highly

---

[13] Nonconvexities naturally give rise to discontinuities, and discontinuities to problems of existence, but the nonexistence problem that Rothschild and I had uncovered was of a different, and more fundamental nature. The problem was in part that a single action of an individual—a choice of one insurance policy over another—discretely changed beliefs, e.g., about his type; and that a slight change in the actions of, say an insurance firm—making available a new insurance policy—could lead to discrete changes in actions, and thereby beliefs. Partha Dasgupta and Eric Maskin (1986a, 1986b) have explored mixed strategy equilibria in game-theoretic formulations, but these seem less convincing than the imperfect competition resolutions of the existence problems described below. I explored other problems of nonexistence in the context of moral hazard problems in work with Richard Arnott (1987, 1991b).

[14] This had a particularly inconvenient implication: when there was a continuum of types, such as in the A. Michael Spence (1973, 1974b) models, a full equilibrium never existed.

visible job, because it knows that the assignment will be interpreted as an indication that the employee is good, making it more likely that a rival will try to hire the person away.

One of the early insights (Akerlof, 1970) was that, with imperfect information, markets may be thin or absent. The absence of particular markets, e.g., for risk, has profound implications for how *other* markets function. The fact that workers and firms cannot buy insurance against many of the risks which they face affects labor and capital markets; it leads, for instance, to labor contracts in which the employer provides *some* insurance. But the design of these more complicated, but still imperfect and incomplete, contracts affects the efficiency, and overall performance, of the economy.

Perhaps most importantly, under the standard paradigm, markets are Pareto efficient, except when one of a limited number of market failures occurs. Under the imperfect information paradigm, markets are almost never Pareto efficient.

While information economics thus undermined these long-standing principles of economics, it also provided explanations for many phenomena that had long been unexplained. Before turning to these applications, I want to present a somewhat a more systematic account of the *principles* of the economics of information.

A Some Problems in Constructing an Alternative Paradigm

The fact that information is imperfect was, of course, well recognized by all economists. The reason that models with imperfect information were not developed earlier was that it was not obvious how to do so: While there is a single way in which information is perfect, there are an infinite number of ways in which information can be imperfect. One of the keys to success was formulating simple models in which the set of relevant information could be fully specified—and so the precise ways in which information was imperfect could also be fully specified. But there was a danger in this methodology, as useful as it was: In these overly simplistic models, full revelation of information was sometimes possible. In the real world, of course, this never happens, which is why in some of the later work (e.g., Grossman and Stiglitz, 1976, 1980a), we worked with models with an infinite number of states. Similarly there may well be ways of fully resolving incentive problems in simple models, which collapse when models are made more realistic, for example by combining selection and incentive problems (Stiglitz and Weiss, 1986).

Perhaps the hardest problem in building the new paradigm was modeling equilibrium. It was important to think about both sides of the market—employers and employees, insurance company and the insured, lender and borrower. Each had to be modeled as "rational," in some sense, making inferences on the basis of available information and behaving accordingly. I wanted to model *competitive* behavior, where each actor in the economy was small, and believed he was small—and so his actions could not or would not affect the equilibrium (though others' inferences about himself might be affected). Finally, one had to think carefully about what was the feasible set of actions: what might each side do to extract or convey information to others.

As we shall see, the variety of results obtained (and much of the confusion in the early literature) arose partly from a failure to be as clear as one might have been about the assumptions. For instance, the standard adverse selection model had the quality of the good offered in the market (say of used cars, or riskiness of the insured) depending on price. The car buyer (the seller of insurance) knows the *statistical* relationship between price and quality, and this affects his demand. The market equilibrium is the price at which demand equals supply. But that is an equilibrium if and only if there is no way by which the seller of a good car can convey that information to the buyer—so that he can earn a quality premium—and if there is no way by which the buyer can sort out good cars from bad cars. Typically, there are such ways, and it is the attempt to elicit that information which has profound effects on how markets function. To develop a new paradigm, we had to break out from long-established premises, to ask what should be taken as assumptions and what should be derived from the analysis. Market clearing could not be taken as an assumption; neither could the premise that a firm sells a good at a particular price to all comers. One could not *begin* the analysis even by assuming that in competitive equilibrium there would be zero profits. In the standard theory, if there were positive profits, a firm might enter, bidding away existing customers. In the new theory, the attempt to bid away new customers by slightly lowering prices might lead to marked changes in their behavior or in the mix of customers, in such a way that the profits of the new entrant actually became negative. One had to rethink all the conclusions from first premises.

We made progress in our analyses because we began with highly simplified models of particular markets, that allowed us to think through carefully each of the assumptions and conclusions. From the analysis of particular markets (whether the insurance market, the education market, the labor market, or the land tenancy/sharecropping market), we attempted to identify general principles, to explore how these principles operated in each of the other markets. In doing so, we identified particular features, particular informational assumptions, which seemed to be more relevant in one market or another. The nature of competition in the labor market is different from that in the insurance market or the capital market, though these markets have much in common. This interplay, between looking at the ways in which such markets are similar and dissimilar, proved to be a fruitful research strategy.[15]

---

[15] Some earlier work, especially in general-equilibrium theory, by Leonid Hurwicz (1960, 1972), Jacob Marschak and Radner (1972), and Radner (1972), among others, had recognized the importance of problems of information, and had even identified some of the ways that limited information affected the nature of the market equilibrium (e.g., one could only have contracts that were contingent on states of nature that were observable by both sides to the contract). But the attempt to modify the abstract theory of general equilibrium to incorporate problems of information imperfections proved, in the end, less fruitful than the alternative approach of beginning with highly simplified, quite concrete models. Arrow (1963, 1965, 1973a, 1974a, 1978), while a key figure within the general-equilibrium approach, was one of the first to identify the importance of adverse selection and moral hazard effects.

B Sources of Information Asymmetries

Information imperfections are pervasive in the economy. Much of the research I describe here focuses on *asymmetries* of information, exploring the implications of the fact that different people know different things. Workers know more about their own abilities than the firm does; the person buying insurance knows more about his health, e.g., whether he smokes and drinks immoderately, than the insurance firm. Similarly, the owner of a car knows more about the car than potential buyers; the owner of a firm knows more about the firm that a potential investor; the borrower knows more about the riskiness of his project than the lender does; and so on.

An essential feature of a decentralized market economy is that different people know different things, and in that sense, economists had long been thinking about markets with information asymmetries. But the earlier literature had neither thought about how these were created, or what their consequences might be. While such information asymmetries inevitably arise, the extent to which they do so and their consequences depend on how the market is structured, and the recognition that they will arise affects market behavior. For instance, even if an individual has no more information about his ability than potential employers, the moment he goes to work for a specific employer, an information asymmetry has been created—the employer may now know more about the individual's ability than others do. A consequence is that the "used labor" market may not work well. Other employers will be reserved in bidding for the worker's services, knowing that they will succeed in luring him away from his current employer only if they bid too much. This impediment to labor mobility gives market power to the first employer, which he will be tempted to exercise. But then, because a worker knows he will tend to be locked into a job, he will be more risk averse in accepting an offer. The terms of the initial contract thus have to be designed to reflect the diminution of the worker's bargaining power that occurs the moment he accepts a job.

To take another example, it is natural that in the process of oil exploration, a company may obtain information relevant to the likelihood that there will be oil in a neighboring tract—an informational externality (see Stiglitz, 1975a; Jeffrey J. Leitzinger and Stiglitz, 1984). The existence of this asymmetric information affects the nature of the bidding for oil rights on the neighboring tract. Bidding when there is known to be asymmetries of information will be markedly different from that where such asymmetries do not exist (Robert B. Wilson, 1977). Those who are uninformed will presume that they will win only if they bid too much—information asymmetries exacerbate the problem of the "winner's curse" (Wilson, 1969; Edward Capen et al., 1971). The government (or other owners of large tracts to be developed) should take this into account in its leasing strategy. And the bidders in the initial leases too will take this into account: part of the value of winning in the initial auction is the information rent that will accrue in later rounds.

While early work in the economics of information dealt with how markets overcame problems of information asymmetries, later work turned to how actors in markets *create* information problems, for example in an attempt to exploit market power. An example is managers of firms who attempt to entrench themselves, and reduce competition in the market for managers, by taking actions to increase information asymmetry (Andrei Shleifer and Robert W. Vishny, 1989; Aaron S. Edlin and Stiglitz, 1995). This is an example of the general problem of corporate governance, to which I will return later. Similarly, the presence of information imperfections give rise to market power in product markets. Firms can exploit this market power through "sales" and other ways of differentiating among individuals who have different search costs (Salop, 1977; Salop and Stiglitz, 1977, 1982; Stiglitz, 1979a). The price dispersions which exist in the market are *created* by the market—they are not just the failure of markets to arbitrage fully price differences caused by shocks that affect different markets differently.

C Overcoming Information Asymmetries

I now want to discuss briefly the ways by which information asymmetries are dealt with, how they can be (partially) overcome.

1. *Incentives for Gathering and Disclosing Information.*—There are two key issues: what are the *incentives* for obtaining information, and what are the *mechanisms*. My brief discussion of the analysis of education as a screening device suggested the fundamental incentive: More able individuals (lower risk individuals, firms with better products) will receive a higher wage (will have to pay a lower premium, will receive a higher price for their products) if they can establish that they are more productive (lower risk, higher quality).

We noted earlier that while some individuals have an incentive to disclose information, some have an incentive not to have the information disclosed. Was it possible that in market equilibrium, only *some* of the information would be revealed? One of the early important results was that, if the more able can costlessly establish that they are more able, then the market will be fully revealing, even though those who are below average would prefer that no information be revealed. In the simplest models, I described a process of unraveling: If the most able could establish his ability, he would; but then all but the most able would be grouped together, receiving the mean marginal product of that group; and the most able of that group would have an incentive to reveal his ability. And so on down the line, until there was full revelation. (I jokingly referred to this as "Walras' Law of Sorting"—if all but one group sorts itself out from the others, then the last group is also identified.)

What happens if those who are more able cannot credibly convince potential employers of their ability? The other side of the market has an incentive too to gather information. An employer that can find a worker that is better than is recognized by others will have found a bargain, because the worker's wage will be determined by what others think of him. The problem, as we noted, is that if what the employer knows becomes known to others, the worker's wage will be bid up, and the employer will be unable to appropriate the returns on his investment in information acquisition.

The fact that competition makes it difficult for the screener to appropriate the returns from screening has an important implication: In markets where, for one reason or another, the more able cannot fully convey their attributes, investment in screening requires *imperfect competition in screening*. The economy, in effect, has to choose between two different imperfections: imperfections of information or imperfections of competition. Of course, in the end, there will be both forms of imperfection, and no particular reason that these imperfections will be "balanced" optimally (Stiglitz, 1975c; Dwight Jaffee and Stiglitz, 1990). This is but one of many examples of the *interplay* between market imperfections. Earlier, for instance, we discussed the incentive problems associated with sharecropping, which arise when workers do not own the land that they till. This problem could be overcome if individuals could borrow to buy their land. But capital market imperfections—limitations on the ability to borrow, which themselves arise from information imperfections—explain why this "solution" does not work.

There is another important consequence: if markets were fully informationally efficient—that is, if information disseminated instantaneously and perfectly throughout the economy—then no one would have any incentive to gather information, so long as there was any cost of doing so. Hence markets cannot be fully informationally efficient (Grossman and Stiglitz, 1976, 1980a).

2. *Mechanisms for Eliminating or Reducing Information Asymmetries.*—In simple models where (for example) individuals know their own abilities there might seem an easy way to resolve the problem of information asymmetry: Let each person tell his true characteristic. Unfortunately, individuals do not necessarily have the incentive to tell the truth. Talk is cheap. Other methods must be used to convey information credibly.

The simplest way by which that could be done was an exam. Models of competitive equilibrium (Arrow, 1973a; Stiglitz, 1974a) with exams make two general points. First, in equilibrium *the gains of the more able were largely at the expense of the less able*. Establishing that an individual is of higher ability provides that person with higher wages, but simultaneously establishes that others are of lower ability. Hence the private returns to expenditures on educational screening exceed the social returns. It was clear that there were important *externalities* associated with information, a theme which was to recur in later work. Second, and a more striking result, there could exist multiple equilibria—one in which information was fully revealed (the market identified the high and low ability people) and another in which it was not (called a pooling equilibrium). The pooling equilibrium Pareto-dominated the equilibrium with full revelation. This work, done some 30 years ago, established two results of great policy import, which remarkably have not been fully absorbed into policy discussions even today. First, markets do not provide appropriate incentives for information disclosure. There is, in principle, a role for government. And second, expenditures on information may be too great (see also Hirshleifer, 1971).

3. *Conveying Information Through Actions.*——But much of the information firms glean about their employees, banks about their borrowers, or insurance companies about their borrowers, or insurance companies about their insured, comes not from examinations but from making inferences based on their *behavior*. This is a common-place in life—but it was not in our economic models. As I have already noted, the early discussions of adverse selection in insurance markets recognized that as an insurance company raised its premiums, those who were least likely to have an accident might decide not to purchase the insurance; the willingness to purchase insurance at a particular price conveyed information to the insurance company. George Akerlof recognized that this phenomenon is far more general: the owner's willingness to sell a used car, for instance, conveyed information about the car's quality.

Bruce C. Greenwald (1980, 1986) took these ideas one important step further, show-ing how adverse selection applied to labor and capital markets (see also Greenwald et al., 1984; Stewart C. Myers and Nicholas S. Majluf, 1984). For example, the will-ingness of insiders in a firm to sell stock at a particular price conveys information about their view of what the stock is really worth. Akerlof's insight that the result of these information asymmetries was that markets would be thin or absent helped explain why labor and capital markets often did not function well. It provided part of the explanation for why firms raised so little of their funds through equity (Mayer, 1990). Stigler was wrong: imperfect information was not just like a transactions cost.

There is a much richer set of actions which convey information beyond those on which traditional adverse selection models have focused. An insurance company wants to attract healthy applicants. It might realize that by locating itself on the fifth floor of a walk-up building, only those with a strong heart would apply. The willingness or ability to walk up five floors conveys information. More subtly, it might recognize that how far up it needs to locate itself, if it only wants to get healthy applicants, depends on other elements of its strategy, such as the premium charged. Or the company may decide to throw in a membership in a health club, but charge a higher premium. Those who value a health club—because they will use it—willingly pay the higher premium. But these individuals are likely to be healthier.

There are a host of other actions which convey information. The quality of the guarantee offered by a firm can convey information about the quality of the product; only firms that believe that their product is reliable will be willing to offer a good guarantee. The guarantee is desirable not just because it reduces risk, but because it conveys information. The number of years of schooling may convey information about the ability of an individual. More able individuals may go to school longer, in which case the increase in wages associated with an increase in schooling may not be a consequence of the human capital that has been added, but rather simply be a result of the sorting that occurs. The size of the deductible that an individual chooses in an insurance policy may convey information about his view about the likelihood of an accident or the size of the accidents he anticipates—*on average*, those who are less likely to have an accident may be more willing to accept high deductibles. The willingness of an entrepreneur to hold large fractions of his wealth in a firm (or to retain large fractions of the shares of the firm) conveys information about his beliefs in the firm's future performance. If a firm promotes an individual to a particular job, it may convey information about the firm's assessment of his ability.

The fact that these actions may convey information affects behavior. In some cases, the action will be designed to obfuscate, to limit information disclosure. The firm that knows that others are looking at who it promotes, and will compete more vigorously for those workers, may affect the willingness of the firm to promote some individuals or assign them to particular jobs (Michael Waldman, 1984). In others, the action will be designed to convey information in a credible way to alter beliefs. The fact that customers will treat a firm that issues a better guarantee as if its product is better— and therefore be willing to pay a higher price—may affect the guarantee that the firm is willing to issue. Knowing that selling his shares will convey a negative signal concerning his views of the future prospects of his firm, an entrepreneur may retain more of the shares of the firm; he will be less diversified than he otherwise would have been (and accordingly, he may act in a more risk-averse manner).

A simple lesson emerges: Some individuals wish to convey information; some individuals wish not to have information conveyed (either because such information might lead others to think less well of them, or because conveying information may interfere with their ability to appropriate rents). In either case, the fact that actions convey information leads people to alter their behavior, and changes how markets function. This is why information imperfections have such profound effects.

Once one recognizes that actions convey information, two results follow. First, in making decisions about what to do, individuals will not only think about what they like (as in traditional economics) but how it will affect others' beliefs about them. If I choose to go to school longer, it may lead others to believe that I am more able. I may therefore decide to stay in school longer, not because I value what is being taught, but because I value how it changes others' beliefs concerning my ability. This means, of course, that we have to rethink completely firm and household decision-making.

Secondly, we noted earlier that individuals have an incentive to "lie"—the less able to say that they are more able. Similarly, if it becomes recognized that those who walk up to the fifth floor to apply for insurance are more healthy, then I might be willing to do so even if I am not so healthy, simply to fool the insurance company. Recognizing this, one needs to look for ways by which information is conveyed *in equilibrium*. The critical insight in how that could occur was provided in a paper I wrote with Michael Rothschild (1976). If those who were more able, less risk prone, or more creditworthy *acted* in some observable way (had different preferences) than those who were less able, less risk prone, or less creditworthy, then it might be possible to design a set of *choices,* which would result in those with different characteristics in effect *identifying* themselves through their *self-selection.* The particular mechanism which we explored in our insurance model illustrates how self-selection mechanisms work. People who know they are less likely to have an accident will be more willing to accept an insurance policy with a high deductible, so that an insurance company that offered two policies, one at a high premium and no deductible, one with a low premium and high deductible, would be able to sort out who were high risk and who low. It is an easy matter to construct choices which thus *separate* people into classes.

It was clear that information was conveyed because the actions were costly, and more costly for some than others. The attempt to convey information had to *distort* behavior. Our analysis also made it clear that it was not just information asymmetries, but information imperfections more generally, that were relevant. Even if those buying insurance did not know their accident probabilities (or know them with greater accuracy than the insurance company), so long as those with higher accident probabilities *on average* differed in some way reflected in their preferences and actions, self-selection mechanisms could and would be employed to sort.

Yet another set of issues arise from the fact that actions may not be costlessly observable. The employer would like to know how hard his worker is working; the lender would like to know the actions which borrower will undertake. These asymmetries of information about *actions* are as important as the earlier discussed asymmetries. Just as in the adverse selection model, the seller of insurance may try to overcome the problems posed by information asymmetries by *examination*, so too in the moral hazard or adverse incentive model, he may try to *monitor* the actions of the insured. But examinations and monitoring are costly, and while they yield some information, typically there remains a high level of residual information imperfection. One response to this problem is to try to induce desired behavior through the setting of contract terms. For example, borrowers' risk-taking behavior may be affected by the interest rate charged by the lender (Stiglitz and Weiss, 1981).

D Consequences for Market Equilibrium

The law of supply and demand had long been treated as a fundamental principle of economics. But there is in fact no law that requires the insurance firm to sell to all who apply at the announced premium, or the lender to lend to all who apply at the announced interest rate, or the employer to employ all those who apply at the posted wage. With perfect information and perfect competition, any firm that charged a price higher than the others would lose all of its customers; and at the going price, one faced a perfectly elastic supply of customers. In adverse selection and incentive models, what mattered was not just the supply of customers or employees or borrowers, but their "quality"—the riskiness of the insured or the borrower, the returns on the investment, the productivity of the worker.

Since "quality" may increase with price, it may be profitable (for example) to pay a higher wage than the "market-clearing" wage, whether the dependence on quality arises from adverse selection or adverse incentive effects (or, in the labor market, because of morale or nutritional effects). The consequence, as we have noted, is that market equilibrium may be characterized by demand not equaling supply in the traditional sense. In credit market equilibrium, the supply of loans may be rationed (William R. Keeton, 1979; Jonathan Eaton and Mark Gersovitz, 1981a; Stiglitz and Weiss, 1981). Or, in the labor market, the wage rate may be higher than that at which the demand for labor equals the supply (an efficiency wage), leading to unemployment.[16]

Analyzing the choices which arise in *full* equilibrium, taking into account fully not only the knowledge that the firms have, say, about their customers but also the knowledge that customers have about how firms will make inferences about them from their behavior, and taking into account the fact that the inferences that a firm might make depends not only on what that firm does, but also on what other firms do, turned out, however, to be a difficult task. The easiest situation to analyze was that of a monopolist (Stiglitz, 1977a). The monopolist could construct a set of choices that would *differentiate* among different types of individuals, and analyze whether it was profit maximizing for him to do so fully, or to (partially) "pool"—that is, offer a set of contracts such that several types might choose the same one. This work laid the foundations of a *general theory of price discrimination*. Under standard theories of monopoly, with perfect information, firms would have an incentive to price discriminate perfectly (extracting the full consumer surplus from each). If they did this, then monopoly would in fact be nondistortionary. Yet most models assumed no price discrimination (that is, the monopolist-offered the same price to all customers), without explaining why they did not discriminate. The new work showed how, given limited information, firms could price discriminate, but could do so only imperfectly. Subsequent work by a variety of authors (such as William J. Adams and Yellen, 1976; Salop, 1977) explored ways by which a monopolist might find out relevant characteristics of his customers. Information economics thus provided the first coherent theory of monopoly.

The reason that analyzing monopoly was easy is that the monopolist could structure the entire choice set facing his customers. The hard question is to describe the full competitive equilibrium, e.g., a set of insurance contracts such that no one can offer an alternative set that would be profitable. Each firm could control the choices that it offered, but not the choices offered by others; and the decisions made by customers depended on the entire set of choices available. In our 1976 paper, Rothschild and I succeeded in analyzing this case.

Three striking results emerged from this analysis. The first I have already mentioned: Under plausible conditions, given the natural definition of equilibrium, equilibrium might not exist. There were two possible forms of equilibria: *pooling equilibria*, in which the market is not able to distinguish among the types, and *separating equilibria*, in which it is. The different groups "separate out" by taking different actions. We showed in our context that there never could be a pooling equilibrium— if there were a single contract that everyone bought, there was another contract that another firm could offer which would "break" the pooling equilibrium. On the other

---

[16] Constructing *equilibrium models* with these effects is more difficult than might seem to be the case at first, since each agent's behavior depends on opportunities elsewhere, i.e., the behavior of others. For example, the workers that a firm attracts at a particular wage depend on the wage offers of other firms. Shapiro and Stiglitz (1984), Rodríguez and Stiglitz (1991a, b), and Rey and Stiglitz (1996), represent attempts to come to terms with these general-equilibrium problems.

hand, there might not exist a separating equilibrium either, if the cost of separation was too great. Any putative separating equilibrium could be broken by a profitable pooling contract, a contract which would be bought by both low risk and high risk types.[17]

Second, even small amounts of imperfections of information can change the standard results concerning the existence and characterization of equilibrium. Equilibrium, for instance, never exists when the two types are very similar to each other. As we have seen, the competitive equilibrium model is simply not robust.

Third, we now can see how the fact that actions convey information affects equilibrium. In perfect information models, individuals would fully divest themselves of the risks which they face, and accordingly would act in a risk neutral manner. We explained why insurance markets would not work well—why most risk averse individuals would buy only partial insurance. The result was important not only for the insights it provided into the workings of insurance markets, but because there are important elements of insurance in many transactions and markets. The relationship between the landlord and his tenant, or the employer and his employee, contains an insurance component.

In short, the general principle that actions convey information applies in many contexts. Further, limitations on the ability to divest oneself of risk are important in explaining a host of contractual relationships.

E Sorting, Screening, and Signaling

In equilibrium, both buyers and sellers, employers and employees, insurance company and insured, and lender and creditor are aware of the informational consequences of their actions. In the case where, say, the insurance company or employer takes the initiative in sorting out applicants, self-selection is an alternative to examinations as a sorting device. In the case where the insured, or the employee, takes the initiative to identify himself as a more attractive contractual partner, then it is conventional to say he is *signaling* (Spence, 1973). But of course, in equilibrium both sides are aware of the consequences of alternative actions, and the differences between signaling and self-selection screening models lie in the technicalities of game theory, and in particular whether the informed or uninformed player moves first.[18]

---

[17] Of course, insurance markets do exist in the real world. I suspect that a major limitation of the applicability of Rothschild-Stiglitz (1976) is the assumption of perfect competition. Factors such as search costs and uncertainty about how easy it is to get a company to pay a claim make the assumption of perfect competition less plausible. Self-selection is still relevant, but some version of monopolistic competition may be more relevant than the model of perfect competition.

[18] See, in particular, Stiglitz and Weiss (1983a, 1994) and Shiro Yabushita (1983). As we point out, in the real world, who moves first ought to be viewed as an endogenous variable. In such a context, it appears that the screening equilibria are more robust than the signaling equilibrium. Assume, for instance, that there were some signaling equilibrium that differed from the screening equilibrium, e.g., there were a pooling equilibrium, sustained because of the out-of-equilibrium beliefs of firms. Then such an equilibrium could be broken by a prior or later move of firms.

Still, some of the seeming differences between signaling and screening models arise because of a failure to specify a *full* equilibrium. There might be many separating contracts, but a unique separating equilibrium. We argued that if one considered any other set of separating contracts, then (say, in the insurance market) a firm could come in and offer an alternative set of contracts and make a profit. Then the original set of separating contracts could not have been an equilibrium. The same is true in, say, the education signaling model. There are many educational systems which "separate"—that is, the more able choose to go to school longer, and the wages at each level of education correspond to the productivity of those who go to school for that length of time. But all except one are not *full equilibria*. Assume, for instance, there were two types of individuals, of low ability and of high ability. Then if the low-ability person has, say, 12 years of schooling, then any education system in which the high-ability person went to school sufficiently long—say, more than 14 years—might separate. But the low-ability types would recognize that if they went to school for 11 years, they would still be treated as having low ability. The unique equilibrium level of education for the low-ability person is that which maximizes his net income (taking into account the productivity gains and costs of education). The unique equilibrium level of education for the high-ability type is the lowest level of education such that the low-ability type does not have the incentive to mimic the high-ability person's educational attainment.

The education system, of course, was particularly infelicitous for studying *market* equilibrium. The structure of the education system is largely a matter of public choice, not of market processes. Different countries have chosen markedly different systems. The minimum level of education is typically not a matter of choice, but set by the government. Within educational systems, examinations play as important a role as self-selection or signaling, though *given* a certain standard of testing, there is a process of self-selection involved in deciding whether to stay in school, or to try to pass the examination. For the same reason, the problems of existence which arise in the insurance market are not relevant in the education market—the "competitive" supply side of the market is simply absent. But when the signaling concepts are translated into contexts in which there is a robust competitive market, the problems of existence cannot be so easily ignored. In particular, when there is a continuum of types, as in the Spence (1973) model, there never exists a screening equilibrium.

F Equilibrium Contracts

The work with Rothschild was related to earlier work that I had done on incentives (such as the work on sharecropping) in that both lines of work entailed an "equilibrium in contracts." The contracts that had characterized economic relations in the standard competitive model were extraordinarily simple: I will pay you a certain amount if you do such and such. If you did not perform as promised, the pay was not given. But with perfect information, individuals simply would not sign contracts that they did not intend to fulfill. Insurance contracts were similarly simple: A payment occurred if and only if particular specified events occurred.

The work on sharecropping and on equilibrium with competitive insurance markets showed that with imperfect information, a far richer set of contracts would be employed and thus began a large literature on the theory of contracting. In the simple sharecropping contracts of Stiglitz (1974e), the contracts involved shares, fixed payments, and plot sizes. More generally, optimal payment structures related payments to *observables*, such as inputs, processes, or outputs.[19] Further, because what goes on in one market affects other parts of the economy, the credit, labor, and land markets are *interlinked;* one could not decentralize in the way hypothesized by the standard perfect information model (Avishay Braverman and Stiglitz, 1982, 1986a, b, 1989).

These basic principles were subsequently applied in a variety of other market contexts. The most obvious was the design of labor contracts (Stiglitz, 1975b). Payments to workers can depend not only on output, but on *relative* performance, which may convey more relevant information than absolute performance. For example, the fact that a particular company's stock goes up when all other companies' stock goes up may say very little about the performance of the manager. Nalebuff and Stiglitz (1983a, b) analyzed the design of these relative performance compensation schemes (contests).

Credit markets too are characterized by complicated equilibrium contracts. Lenders may specify not only an interest rate, but also impose other conditions (collateral requirements, equity requirements) which would have both incentive and selection effects.[20] Indeed, the simultaneous presence of both selection and incentive effects is important in credit markets. In the absence of the former, it might be possible to increase the collateral requirement *and* raise interest rates, still ensuring that the borrower undertook the safe project.

As another application, "contracting"—including provisions that help information be conveyed and risks be shared—have been shown to play an important role in explaining macroeconomic rigidities. (See, for instance, Costas Azariadis and Stiglitz (1983), the papers of the symposium in the 1983 *Quarterly Journal of Economics,* the survey article by Sherwin Rosen (1985), Arnott et al. (1988), and Lars Werin and Hans Wijkander (1992)). Moreover, problems of asymmetries of information can help explain the perpetuation of seemingly inefficient contracts (Stiglitz, 1992c).

---

[19] In Stiglitz (1974e) the contracts were highly linear. In principle, generalizing payment structures to nonlinear functions was simple. Though even here, there were subtleties, e.g., whether individuals exerted their efforts before they knew the realization of the state of nature, and whether there were bounds on the penalties that could be imposed, in the event of bad outcomes (James A. Mirrlees [1975c]; Stiglitz [1975b]; Mirrlees [1976]). The literature has not fully resolved the reason that contracts are often much simpler than the theory would have predicted (e.g., payments are linear functions of output), and do not adjust to changes in circumstances (see, e.g., Franklin Allen, 1985; Douglas Gale, 1991). (When resale is possible and unobservable, equilibrium contracts will be linear—another illustration of low subtleties in informat structures affect equilibrium.)

[20] See, for instance, Stiglitz and Weiss (1983b, 1986, 1987a). Even with these additional instruments there could still be nonmarket-clearing equilibria.

G Equilibrium Wage and Price Distributions

One of the most obvious differences between the predictions of the model with perfect information and what we see in everyday life is the conclusion that the same good sells for the same price everywhere. In reality, we all spend a considerable amount of time shopping for good buys. The differences in prices represent more than just differences in quality or service. There are *real* price differences. Since Stigler's classic paper (1961), there has been a large literature exploring optimal search behavior. However Stigler, and most of the search literature, took the price or wage distribution as given. They did not ask how the distribution might arise and whether, given the search costs, it could be sustained.

As I began to analyze these models, I found that there could be a nondegenerate equilibrium wage or price distribution even if all agents were identical, e.g., faced the same search costs. Early on, it had become clear that even small search costs could make a large difference to the behavior of product and labor markets. Peter A. Diamond (1971) had independently made this point in a highly influential paper, which serves to illustrate powerfully the lack of robustness of the competitive equilibrium theory. Assume for example, as in the standard theory, that all firms were charging the competitive price, but there is an epsilon cost of searching, of going to another store. Then any firm which charged half an epsilon more would lose no customers and thus would choose to increase its price. Similarly, it would pay all other firms to increase their prices. But at the higher price, it would again pay each to increase price, and so on until the price charged at every firm is the monopoly price, even though search costs are small. This showed convincingly that the competitive price was not the equilibrium. But in some cases, not even the monopoly price was an equilibrium. In general, Salop and Stiglitz (1977, 1982, 1987) and Stiglitz (1979b, 1985c, 1987b, 1989b) showed that in situations where there were even small search costs, markets might be characterized by a price distribution. The standard wisdom that said that not everyone had to be informed to ensure that the market acted perfectly competitive was simply not, in general, true (see Stiglitz, 1989b, for a survey).

IV EFFICIENCY OF THE MARKET EQUILIBRIUM AND THE ROLE OF THE STATE

The fundamental theorems of neoclassical welfare economics state that competitive economies will lead, as if by an invisible hand, to a (Pareto-) efficient allocation of resources, and that every Pareto-efficient resource allocation can be achieved through a competitive mechanism, provided only that the appropriate lumpsum redistributions are undertaken. These theorems provide both the rationale for the reliance on free markets, and for the belief that issues of distribution can be separated from issues of efficiency, allowing the economist the freedom to push for reforms which increase efficiency, regardless of their seeming impact on distribution. (If society does not like the distributional consequences of a policy, it should simply redistribute income.)

The economics of information showed that neither of these theorems was particularly relevant to real economies. To be sure, economists over the preceding three decades had identified important market failures—such as the externalities associated with pollution—which required government intervention. But the scope for market failures was limited, and thus the arenas in which government intervention was required were correspondingly limited.

Early work, already referred to, had laid the foundations for the idea that economies with information imperfections would not be Pareto efficient, *even taking into account the costs of obtaining information*. There were interventions in the market that could make all parties better off. We had shown, for instance, that incentives for the disclosure and acquisition of information were far from perfect. On the one hand, imperfect appropriability meant that there might be insufficient incentives to gather information; but on the other, the fact that much of the gains were "rents," gains by some at the expense of others, suggested that there might be excessive expenditures on information. A traditional argument for unfettered capital markets was that there are strong incentives to gather information; discovering that some stock was more valuable than others thought would be rewarded by a capital gain. This price discovery function of capital markets was often advertised as one of its strengths. But while the individual who discovered the information a nanosecond before anyone else might be better off, was society as a whole better off? If having the information a nanosecond earlier did not lead to a change in real decisions (e.g., concerning investment), then it was largely redistributive, with the gains of those obtaining the information occurring at the expense of others (Stiglitz, 1989b).

There are potentially other inefficiencies associated with information acquisition. Information can have adverse effects on volatility (Stiglitz, 1989k). And information can lead to the destruction of markets, in ways which lead to adverse effects on welfare. For example, individuals may sometimes have incentives to create information asymmetries in insurance markets, which leads to the destruction of those markets and a lowering of overall welfare. Welfare might be increased if the acquisition of this kind of information could be proscribed. Recently, such issues have become sources of real policy concern in the arena of genetic testing. Even when information is available, there are issues concerning its use, with the use of certain kinds of information having either a discriminatory intent or effect, in circumstances in which such direct discrimination itself would be prohibited.[21]

While it was perhaps not surprising that markets might not provide appropriate incentives for the acquisition and dissemination of information, the market failures associated with imperfect information may be far more profound. The intuition can

---

[21] See, e.g., Rothschild and Stiglitz (1982, 1997). For models of statistical discrimination and some of their implications, see Arrow (1972a), Phelps (1972), and Stiglitz (1973a, 1974h). See also Stiglitz (1984a).

be seen most simply in the case of models with moral hazard. There, the premium charged is associated with the *average* risk and, therefore, the average care, taken by seemingly similar individuals. The moral hazard problem arises because the level of care cannot be observed. Each individual ignores the effect of his actions on the premium; but when they all take less care, the premium increases. The lack of care by each exerts a negative externality on others. The essential insight of Greenwald and Stiglitz (1986a)[22] was to recognize that such externality-like effects are pervasive whenever information is imperfect or markets incomplete—that is always—and as a result, markets are essentially never constrained Pareto efficient. In short, market failures are pervasive. Arnott et al. (1994) provide a simple exposition of this point using the standard self-selection and incentive compatibility constraints.

An important implication is that efficient allocations cannot in general be decentralized via competitive markets. The notion that one could decentralize decision-making to obtain (Pareto-) efficient resource allocation is one of the fundamental ideas in economics. Greenwald and Stiglitz (1986a) showed that that was not possible in general. A simple example illustrates what is at issue. An insurance company cannot monitor the extent of smoking, which has an adverse effect on health. The government cannot monitor smoking any better than the insurance company, but it can impose taxes, not only on cigarettes, but also on other commodities which are complements to smoking (and subsidies on substitutes which have less adverse effects). See Arnott and Stiglitz (1991a) and Stiglitz (1989g, 1998c).

A related result from the new information economics is that issues of efficiency and equity cannot easily be delinked. For example, with imperfect information, a key source of market failure is *agency problems,* such as those which arise when the owner of land is different from the person working the land. The extent of agency problems depends on the distribution of wealth, as we noted earlier in our discussion of sharecropping. Moreover, the notion that one could separate out issues of equity and efficiency also rested on the ability to engage in lump sum redistributions. But as Mirrlees (1971) had pointed out, with imperfect information, this was not possible; all redistributive taxation must be distortionary. But this fact implies that interventions in the market which change the before-tax distribution of income could be desirable, because they lessened the burden on redistributive taxation (Stiglitz, 1998b). Again, the conclusion: The second welfare theorem, effectively asserting the ability to separate issues of distribution and efficiency, was not true.

In effect, the Arrow-Debreu model had identified the *single set* of assumptions under which markets were efficient. There had to be perfect information; more accurately, information could not be *endogenous,* it could not change either as a result

---

[22] Greenwald and Stiglitz (1986a) focus on models with adverse selection and incentive problems. Greenwald and Stiglitz (1988e) showed that similar results hold in the context of search and other models with imperfect information. Earlier work, with Shapiro (1984) had shown, in the context of a specific model, that equilibria in an economy with an agency or principal-agent problem were not (constrained) Pareto efficient. Later work, with Arnott (1990), explored in more detail the market failures that arise with moral hazard. Earlier work had shown that with imperfect risk markets, themselves explicable by imperfections of information, market equilibrium was Pareto inefficient. See David M. G. Newbery and Stiglitz (1982, 1984) and Stiglitz (1972b, 1981, 1982b).

of the actions of any individual or firm or through investments in information. But in the world we live in, a model which assumes that information is *fixed* seems irrelevant.

As the theoretical case that markets in which information is imperfect were not efficient became increasingly clear, several new arguments were put forward against government intervention. One we have already dealt with: that the government too faces informational imperfections. Our analysis had shown that the incentives and constraints facing government differed from those facing the private sector, so that even when government faced exactly the same *informational* constraints, welfare could be improved (Stiglitz, 1989g).

There was another rear-guard argument, which ultimately holds up no better. It is that market failures—absent or imperfect markets—give rise to nonmarket institutions. For example, the absence of death insurance gave rise to burial societies. Families provide insurance to their members against a host of risks for which they either cannot buy insurance, or for which the insurance premium is viewed as too high. But in what I call the *functionalist fallacy,* it is easy to go from the observation that an institution arises to fulfill a function to the conclusion that actually, *in equilibrium,* it serves that function. Those who succumbed to this fallacy seemed to argue that there was no need for government intervention because these nonmarket institutions would "solve" the market failure, or at least do as well as any government. Richard Arnott and I (1991a) showed that, to the contrary, nonmarket institutions could actually make matters worse. Insurance provided by the family could crowd out market insurance, for example. Insurance companies would recognize that the insured would take less risk because they had obtained insurance from others, and accordingly cut back on the amount of insurance that they offered. But since the nonmarket (family) institutions did a poor job of divesting risk, welfare could be decreased.

The Arnott-Stiglitz analysis reemphasized the basic point made at the end of the last subsection: it was only under very special circumstances that markets could be shown to be efficient. Why then should we expect an equilibrium involving nonmarket institutions and markets to be efficient?

V FURTHER APPLICATIONS OF THE NEW PARADIGM

Of all the market failures, the extended periods of underutilization of resources—especially human resources—is of the greatest moment. The consequences of unemployment are exacerbated in turn by capital market imperfections, which imply that even if the future prospects of an unemployed individual are good, he cannot borrow enough to sustain his standard of living.

We referred earlier to the dissatisfaction with traditional Keynesian explanations, in particular, the lack of microfoundations. This dissatisfaction gave rise to two schools of thought. One sought to use the old perfect market paradigm, relying heavily on representative agent models. While information was not perfect, expectations were rational. But the representative agent model, by construction, ruled out the information asymmetries which are at the heart of macroeconomic problems. If one begins with a model that *assumes* that markets clear, it is hard to see how one can get much insight into unemployment (the failure of the labor market to clear).

The construction of a macroeconomic model which embraces the consequences of imperfections of information in labor, product, and capital markets has become one of my major preoccupations over the past 15 years. Given the complexity of *each* of these markets, creating a general-equilibrium model—simple enough to be taught to graduate students or used by policy makers—has not proven to be an easy task. At the heart of that model lies a new theory of the firm, for which the theory of asymmetric information provides the foundations. The modern theory of the firm in turn rests on three pillars, the theory of corporate finance, the theory of corporate governance, and the theory of organizational design.

A Theory of the Firm

Under the older, perfect information theory (Franco Modigliani and Merton H. Miller, 1958, 1961; see also Stiglitz, 1969b, 1974f, 1988e), it made no difference whether firms raised capital by debt or equity, in the absence of tax distortions. But information is at the core of finance. The information required to implement equity contracts is greater than for debt contracts (Robert J. Townsend, 1979; Greenwald and Stiglitz, 1992). Most importantly, the willingness to hold (or to sell) shares conveys information (Hayne E. Leland and David H. Pyle, 1977; Ross, 1977; Stiglitz, 1982c; Greenwald et al., 1984; Myers and Majluf, 1984; Thomas F. Hellman and Stiglitz, 2000; for empirical verification see, e.g., Paul Asquith and David W. Mullins, Jr., 1986), so that how firms raise capital does make a difference. In practice, firms rely heavily on debt (as opposed to equity) finance (Mayer, 1990), and bankruptcy, resulting from the failure to meet debt obligations, matters. Both because of the cost of bankruptcies and limitations in the design of managerial incentive schemes, firms act in a risk-averse manner—with risk being more than just correlation with the business cycle (Greenwald and Stiglitz, 1990a; Stiglitz, 1989f). Moreover, because of the potential for credit rationing, not only does the firm's net worth matter, but so does its asset structure, including its liquidity.[23]

While there are many implications of the theory of the risk-averse firm facing credit rationing, some of which are elaborated upon in the next section, one example should suffice to highlight the importance of these ideas. In traditional neoclassical

[23] The very concept of liquidity—and the distinction between lack of liquidity and insolvency—rests on information asymmetries. If there were perfect information, any firm that was solvent would be able to obtain finance, and thus would not face a liquidity problem.

investment theory, investment depends on the real interest rate and the firm's perception of expected returns. The firm's cash flow or its net worth should make no difference. The earliest econometric studies of investment, by Edwin Kuh and John R. Meyer (1957), suggested however that this was not the case. Nevertheless these variables were excluded from econometric analyses of investment for two decades following the work of Robert E. Hall and Dale W. Jorgenson (1967). It was not until work on asymmetric information had restored theoretical respectability to the notion that finance mattered that it became acceptable to introduce financial variables into investment regressions. When that was done, it was shown that—especially for small and medium-sized enterprises—these variables are crucial. (For a survey of the vast empirical literature see R. Glenn Hubbard, 1998.)

In the traditional theory, firms simply maximized the expected present discounted value of profits (which equaled market value); with perfect information, how that was to be done was simply an engineering problem. Disagreements about what the firm should do were of little moment. In that context, *corporate governance*—how firm decisions were made—mattered little as well. But again, in reality, corporate governance matters a great deal. There *are* disagreements about what the firm should do—partly motivated by differences in judgments, partly motivated by differences in objectives (Stiglitz, 1972c; Grossman and Stiglitz, 1977, 1980b). Managers can take actions which advance their interests at the expense of that of shareholders, and majority shareholders can advance their interests at the expense of minority shareholders. The owners not only could not monitor their workers and managers, because of asymmetries of information, they typically did not even know what these people who were supposed to be acting on their behalf *should* do. That there were important consequences for the theory of the firm of the separation of ownership and control had earlier been noted by Adolph A. Berle and Gardiner C. Means (1932), but it was not until information economics that we had a coherent way of thinking about the implications (Jensen and Willima H. Meckling, 1976; Stiglitz, 1985a).

Some who still held to the view that firms would maximize their market value argued that (the threat of) takeovers would ensure competition in the market for managers and hence ensure stock market value maximization. If the firm were not maximizing its stock market value, then it would pay someone to buy the firm, and change its actions so that its value would increase. Early on in this debate, I raised questions on theoretical grounds about the efficacy of the takeover mechanism (Stiglitz, 1972c). The most forceful set of arguments were subsequently put forward by Grossman and Hart (1980), who observed that any small shareholder who believed that the takeover would subsequently increase market value would not be willing to sell his shares. The subsequent work by Shleifer and Vishny (1989) and Edlin and Stiglitz (1995), referred to earlier, showed how existing managers could take actions to reduce the effectiveness of competition for management, i.e., the threat of takeovers, by increasing asymmetries of information.

So far, we have discussed two of the three pillars of the modern theory of the firm: corporate finance and corporate governance. The third is *organizational design*. In a world with perfect information, organizational design too is of little moment. In practice, it is of central concern to businesses. For example, as we have already discussed, an organizational design that has alternative units performing comparable tasks can enable a firm to glean information on the basis of which better incentive systems can be based (Nalebuff and Stiglitz, 1983a, b). But there is another important aspect of organization design. Even if individuals are well intentioned, with limited information, mistakes get made. To err is human. Raaj K. Sah and I, in a series of papers (1985f, 1986, 1988a, b, 1991) explored the consequences of alternative organizational design and decision-making structures for organizational mistakes: for instance, whether good projects get rejected or bad projects get accepted. We suggested that, in a variety of circumstances, decentralized polyarchical organizational structures have distinct advantages (see also Sah, 1991; Stiglitz, 1989c). These papers are just beginning to spawn a body of research; see, for example, Bauke Visser (1998), Amar Bhidá (2001), and Michael Christensen and Thorbjorn Knudsen (2002).

B Macroeconomics

With these new understandings of the theory of the firm, we can return to the important area of *macroeconomics*. The central macroeconomic issue is unemployment. The models I described earlier explained why unemployment could exist *in equilibrium*. But much of macroeconomics is concerned with *dynamics*, with explaining why sometimes the economy seems to amplify rather than absorb shocks, and why the effects of shocks may long persist. In joint work with Bruce Greenwald and Andy Weiss, I have shown how theories of asymmetric information can help provide explanations of these phenomena. (For an early survey, see Greenwald and Stiglitz [1987b, 1988a, 1993b] and Stiglitz [1988b, 1992b].) The imperfections of capital markets—the phenomena of credit and equity rationing which arise because of information asymmetries—are key. They lead to risk-averse behavior of firms and to households and firms being affected by cash flow constraints.

Standard interpretations of Keynesian economics emphasized the importance of wage and price rigidities, but without a convincing explanation of how those rigidities arise. For instance, some theories had shown the importance of costs of adjustment of prices (Akerlof and Yellen, 1985; N. Gregory Mankiw, 1985). Still at issue, though, is why firms tend to adjust quantities rather than prices, even though the costs of adjusting quantities seem greater than those of prices. The Greenwald-Stiglitz theory of adjustment (1989b) provided an explanation based on capital market imperfections arising from information imperfections. In brief, it argued that the risks created by informational imperfections are generally greater for price and wage adjustments than from quantity adjustments. Risk-averse firms would make smaller adjustments to those variables for which the consequences of adjustment were more uncertain.

But even though wages and prices were not perfectly flexible, neither were they perfectly rigid, and indeed in the Great Depression, they fell by a considerable amount. There had been large fluctuations in earlier periods, and in other countries, in which there had been a high degree of wage and price flexibility. Greenwald and I (1987a, b,

1988a, c, d, 1989b, 1990b, 1993a, b, 1995) argued that other market failures, in particular, the imperfections of capital markets and incompleteness in contracting, were needed to explain key observed macroeconomic phenomena. In debt contracts, which are typically not indexed for changes in prices, whenever prices fell below the level expected (or in variable interest rate contracts, whenever real interest rates rose above the level expected) there were transfers from debtors to creditors. In these circumstances, excessive downward price flexibility (not just price rigidities) could give rise to problems; Irving Fisher (1933) and Stiglitz (1999h) emphasize the consequences of differences in the speed of adjustment of different prices. These (and other) redistributive changes had large real effects, and could not be insured against because of imperfections in capital markets. Large shocks could lead to bankruptcy, and with bankruptcy (especially when it results in firm liquidation) there was a loss of organizational and informational capital.[24] Even if such large changes could be forestalled, until there was a resolution, the firm's access to credit would be impaired, and for good reason. Moreover, without "clear owners" those in control would in general not have incentives to maximize the firm's value.

Even when the shocks were not large enough to lead to bankruptcy, they had impacts on firms' ability and willingness to take risks. Since all production is risky, shocks affect aggregate supply, as well as the demand for investment. Because firm net worth would only be restored over time, the effects of a shock persisted. By the same token, there were hysteresis effects associated with policy: An increase in interest rates which depleted firm net worth had impacts even after the interest rates were reduced. Firms that were bankrupted with high interest rates do not become "unbankrupt" when interest rates decline. If firms were credit rationed, then reductions in liquidity could have particularly marked effects (Stiglitz and Weiss, 1992). Every aspect of macroeconomic behavior is affected: The theories helped explain, for instance, the seemingly anomalous cyclical behavior of inventories (the procyclical movements in inventories, counter to the idea of production smoothing, result from cash constraints and the resulting high shadow price of money in recessions); or of pricing (in recessions, when the "shadow price" of capital is high, firms do not find it profitable to invest in acquiring new customers by cutting prices). In short, our analysis emphasized the supply-side effects of shocks, the interrelationships between supply and demand side effects, and the importance of *finance* in propagating fluctuations.

Earlier, I described how the information paradigm explained credit rationing. A second important strand in our macroeconomic research explored the link between credit rationing and macroeconomic activity (Alan S. Blinder and Stiglitz, 1983), explained the role of banks as risk-averse firms, as information institutions involved in screening and monitoring, in determining the supply of credit (Greenwald and Stiglitz, 1990b, 1991, 2003; Stiglitz and Weiss, 1990), described the macroeconomic

---

[24] In traditional economic theories bankruptcy played little role, partly because control (who made decisions) did not matter, and so the change in control that was consequent to bankruptcy was of little moment, partly because with perfect information, there would be little reason for lenders to lend to someone, rather than extending funds through equity (especially if there were significant probabilities of, and costs to, bankruptcy). For an insightful discussion about control rights see Hart (1995).

impacts of changes in financial regulations, and analyzed the implications for monetary policy under a variety of regimes, including dollarization (Stiglitz, 2001b). These
differed in many respects from the traditional theories, such as those based on the
transactions demand for money, the microfoundations of which were increasingly
being discredited as money became increasingly interest bearing (the interest rate was
not the opportunity cost of holding money) and as credit, not money, was increasingly being used for transactions. We also explained the importance of credit linkages
(e.g., not only between banks and firms but among firms themselves) and their role
in transmitting shocks throughout the economy. A large body of empirical work
has subsequently verified the importance of credit constraints for macroeconomic
activity, especially investment; see Kuh and Meyer (1957), Charles W. Calomiris and
Hubbard (1990), and Hubbard (1990).

C Growth and Development[25]

While most of the macroeconomic analysis focused on exploring the implications
of imperfections of credit markets for cyclical fluctuations, another strand of our
research program focused on growth. The importance of capital markets for growth
had long been recognized; without capital markets firms have to rely on retained
earnings. But how firms raise capital is important for their growth. In particular, "equity rationing"—especially important in developing countries, where informational
problems are even greater—impedes firms' willingness to invest and undertake risks,
and thus slows growth. Changes in economic policy which enable firms to bear more
risk (e.g., by reducing the size of macroeconomic fluctuations, or which enhance
firms' equity base, by suppressing interest rates, which result in firm's having larger
profits) enhance economic growth. Conversely, policies, such as those associated with
IMF interventions, in which interest rates are raised to very high levels, discourage the
use of debt, forcing firms to rely more heavily on retained earnings.

The most challenging problems for growth lie in economic development. Typically,
market failures are more prevalent in less developed countries, and these market
failures are often associated with information problems—the very problems that
inspired much of the research described in this paper (see Stiglitz, 1985b, 1986a, 1988a,
1989d, i, 1991b, 1997a; Braverman et al., 1993). While these perspectives help explain
the failures of policies based on *assuming* perfect or well-functioning markets, they
also direct attention to policies which might remedy or reduce the consequences of
informational imperfections (World Bank, 1999b).

One of the most important determinants of the pace of growth is the acquisition
of knowledge. For developed countries, this requires investment in research; for less
developed countries, efforts at closing the knowledge gap between themselves and

---

[25] For discussions of growth, see Greenwald et al. (1990) and Stiglitz (1990b, 1992e, 1994a, b). The
somewhat separate topic of development is analyzed in Stiglitz (1985b, 1986a, 1988a, 1989a, d, i, 1991b,
1993d, 1995b, 1996, 1997a, b, 1998c, 1999c, e, 2000d, 2001a, c), Sah and Stiglitz (1989a, b), Karla Hoff and
Stiglitz (1990, 1998, 2001), Nicholas Stern and Stiglitz (1997), and Stiglitz and Shahid Yusuf (2000).

more developed countries. Knowledge is, of course, a particular *form* of information, and many of the issues that are central to the economics of information are also key to understanding research—such as the problems of appropriability, the fixed costs associated with investments in research (which give rise to imperfections in competition), and the public good nature of information. It was thus natural that I turned to explore the implications in a series of papers that looked at both equilibrium in the research industry and the consequences for economic growth.[26] While it is not possible to summarize briefly the results, one conclusion does stand out: Market economies in which research and innovation play an important role are not well described by the standard competitive model, and the market equilibrium, without government intervention, is not in general efficient.

D Theory of Taxation[27]

One of the functions of government is to redistribute income. Even if it did not actively wish to redistribute, the government has to raise revenues to finance public goods, and there is a concern that the revenue be raised in an equitable manner, e.g., that those who are more able to contribute do so. But government has a problem of identifying these individuals, just as (for example) a monopolist may find it difficult to identify those who are willing to pay more for its product. Importantly, the self-selection mechanisms for information revelation that Rothschild and I had explored in our competitive insurance model or that I had explored in my paper on discriminating monopoly can be applied here. (The problem of the government, maximizing social "profit," i.e., welfare, subject to the information constraints, is closely analogous to that of the monopolist, maximizing private profit subject to information constraints. For this reason, Mirrlees' (1971) paper on optimal taxation, though not couched in information-theoretic terms, was an important precursor to the work described here.)

The critical question for the design of a tax system thus becomes *what is observable*. In older theories, in which information was perfect, lump-sum taxes and redistributions made sense. If ability is not directly observable, the government had to rely on other observables—like income—to make inferences; but, as in all such models, market participants, as they recognize that inferences are being made, alter their behavior. In Mirrlees (1971) only income was assumed observable. But in different circumstances, either more or less information might be available. It might be possible to observe hours worked, in which case wages would be observable. It might be

---

[26] There were, of course, several precursors to what has come to be called endogenous growth theory. See in particular, the collection of essays in Karl Shell (1967) and Anthony B. Atkinson and Stiglitz (1969). For later work, see, in particular, Dasgupta and Stiglitz (1980a, b, 1981, 1988), Dasgupta et al. (1982), and Stiglitz (1987c, f, 1990b).

[27] The discussion of this section draws upon Mirrlees (1971, 1975a), Atkinson and Stiglitz (1976), Stiglitz (1982f, 1987d). Arnott and Stiglitz (1986), and Brito et al. (1990, 1991, 1995).

possible to observe the quantity of each good purchased by any particular individual or it might be possible to observe only the aggregate quantity of goods produced.

For each information structure, there is a *Pareto-efficient tax structure*, that is, a tax structure such that no group can be made better off without making some other group worse off. The choice among such tax structures depends on the social welfare function, including attitudes towards inequality.[28] While this is not the occasion to provide a complete description of the results, two are worth noting: What had been thought of as optimal commodity tax structures (Frank P. Ramsey, 1927) were shown to be part of a Pareto-efficient tax system only under highly restricted conditions, e.g., that there was no income tax (see Atkinson and Stiglitz, 1976; Sah and Stiglitz, 1992; Stiglitz, 1998b). On the other hand, it was shown that in a central benchmark case, it was not optimal to tax interest income.

E Theory of Regulation and Privatization

The government faces the problems posed by information asymmetries in regulation as well as in taxation. Over the past quarter century, a huge literature has developed making use of self-selection mechanisms (see, for example, David E. M. Sappington and Stiglitz [1987a]; Jean-Jacques Laffont and Tirole [1993]), allowing far better and more effective systems of regulation than had existed in the past. An example of a sector in which government regulation is of particular importance is banking; we noted earlier that information problems are at the heart of credit markets, and it is thus not surprising that market failures be more pervasive, and the role of the government more important in those markets (Stiglitz, 1994j). Regulatory design needs to take into account explicitly the limitations in information (see, e.g., Hellman et al., 2000; Patrick Honahan and Stiglitz, 2001; Stiglitz, 2001e; Greenwald and Stiglitz, 2003).

The 1980's saw a strong movement towards privatizing state enterprises, even in areas in which there was a natural monopoly, in which case government ownership would be replaced with government regulation. While it was apparent that there were frequently problems with government ownership, the theories of imperfect information also made it clear that even the best designed regulatory systems would work imperfectly. This naturally raised the question of under what circumstances we could be sure that privatization would enhance economic welfare. As Herbert A. Simon (1991), winner of the 1978 Nobel Prize, had emphasized, both public and private sectors face information and incentive problems; there was no compelling theoretical argument for why large private organizations would solve these incentive problems

---

[28] In that sense, Mirrlees' work confounded the two stages of the analysis. He described the point along the Pareto frontier that would be chosen by a government with a utilitarian social welfare function. Some of the critical properties, e.g., the zero marginal tax rate at the top, were, however, characteristics of *any* Pareto-efficient tax structure, though that particular property was not *robust*—that is, it depended strongly on his assumption that relative wages between individuals of different abilities were fixed (see Stiglitz, 2002b).

better than public organizations. In work with Sappington (1987b), I showed that the conditions under which privatization would necessarily be welfare enhancing were extremely restrictive, closely akin to those under which competitive markets would yield Pareto efficient outcomes (see Stiglitz [1991f, 1994e] for an elaboration and applications).

VI SOME POLICY DEBATES

The perspectives provided by the new information paradigm not only shaped theoretical approaches to policy, but in innumerable concrete issues also led to markedly different policy stances from those wedded to the old paradigm.

Perhaps most noted were the controversies concerning development strategies, where the *Washington consensus* policies, based on market fundamentalism—the simplistic view of competitive markets with perfect information, inappropriate even for developed countries, but particularly inappropriate for developing countries—had prevailed since the early 1980's within the international economic institutions. Elsewhere, I have documented the failures of these policies in development (Stiglitz, 1999e), as well as in managing the transition from communism to a market economy (see, for instance, Athar Hussein et al., 2000; Stiglitz [2000g, 2001f]) and in crisis management and prevention (Stiglitz, 2000a). Ideas matter, and it is not surprising that policies based on models that depart as far from reality as those underlying the Washington consensus so often led to failure.

This point was brought home perhaps most forcefully by the management of the East Asia crisis which began in Thailand on July 2, 1997. While I have written extensively on the many dimensions of the failed responses (Jason Furman and Stiglitz, 1998; Stiglitz, 1999f), here I want to note the close link between these failures and the theories put forward here. Our work had emphasized the importance of maintaining the credit supply and the risks of (especially poorly managed) bankruptcy. Poorly designed policies could lead to an unnecessarily large reduction in credit availability and unnecessarily large increases in bankruptcy, both leading to large adverse effects on aggregate supply, exacerbating the economic downturn. But this is precisely what the IMF did: by raising interest rates to extremely high levels in countries where firms were already highly leveraged, it forced massive bankruptcy, and the economies were thus plunged into deep recession. Capital was not attracted to the country, but rather fled. Thus, the policies even failed in their stated purpose, which was to stabilize the exchange rate. There were strong hysteresis effects associated with these policies: when the interest rates were subsequently lowered, firms that had been forced into bankruptcy did not become "unbankrupt," and the firms that had seen their net worth depleted did not see an immediate restoration. There were alternative policies available, debt standstills followed by corporate financial restructurings, for example; while these might not have avoided a downturn, they would have made it shorter and more shallow. Malaysia, whose economic policies conformed much more closely to those that our theories would have suggested, not only recovered more quickly, but was left with less of a legacy of debt to impair its future growth, than was neighboring Thailand, which conformed more closely to the IMF's recommendation. (For discussions of bankruptcy reform motivated by these experiences see Marcus Miller and Stiglitz, 1999; Stiglitz, 2000f.)

On another front, the *transition from communism to a market economy* represents one of the most important economic experiments of all time, and the failure (so far) in Russia, and the successes in China, shed considerable light on many of the issues which I have been discussing. The full dimension of Russia's failure is hard to fathom. Communism, with its central planning (requiring more information gathering, processing, and dissemination capacity than could be managed with *any* technology), its lack of incentives, and its system rife with distortions, was viewed as highly inefficient. The movement to a market, it was assumed, would bring enormous increases in incomes. Instead, incomes plummeted, a decline confirmed not only by GDP statistics and household surveys, but also by social indicators. The numbers in poverty soared, from 2 percent to upwards of 40 percent, depending on the measure used. While there were many dimensions to these failures, one stands out: the privatization strategy, which paid little attention to the issues of corporate governance which we stressed earlier. Empirical work (Stiglitz, 2001f) confirms that countries that privatized rapidly but lacked "good" corporate governance did not grow more rapidly. Rather than providing a basis for wealth creation, privatization led to asset stripping and wealth destruction (Hussein et al., 2000; Stiglitz, 2000g).

VII BEYOND INFORMATION ECONOMICS

We have seen how the competitive paradigm that dominated economic thinking for two centuries was not robust, did not explain key economic phenomena, and led to misguided policy prescriptions. The research over the past 30 years on information economics that I have just described has focused, however, on only one aspect of my dissatisfaction with that paradigm. It is not easy to change views of the world, and it seemed to me the most effective way of attacking the paradigm was to keep within the standard framework as much as possible. I only varied one assumption— the assumption concerning perfect information—and in ways which seemed to me highly plausible.

There were other deficiencies in the theory, some of which were closely connected. The standard theory assumed that technology and preferences were fixed. But changes in technology, R & D, are at the heart of capitalism. The new information economics—extended to incorporate changes in knowledge—at last began to address systematically these foundations of a market economy.

As I thought about the problems of development, I similarly became increasingly convinced of the inappropriateness of the assumption of fixed preferences, and of the importance of embedding economic analysis in a broader social and political context. I have criticized the Washington consensus development strategies partly on the grounds that they perceived of development as nothing more than increasing the stock of capital and reducing economic distortions. But development represents a far more fundamental transformation of society, including a change in "preferences" and attitudes, an acceptance of change, and an abandonment of many traditional ways of thinking (Stiglitz, 1995b, 1998e). This perspective has strong policy implications. For instance, some policies are more conducive to effecting a development transformation. Many of the policies of the IMF—including the manner in which in interacted with governments, basing loans on conditionality—were counterproductive. A fundamental change in development strategy occurred at the World Bank in the years I was there, one which embraced this more comprehensive approach to development. By contrast, policies which have ignored social consequences have frequently been disastrous. The IMF policies in Indonesia, including the elimination of food and fuel subsidies for the very poor as the country was plunging into depression, predictably led to riots. The economic consequences are still being felt.

In some ways, as I developed these perspectives, I was returning to a theme I had raised 30 years ago, during my work on the efficiency wage theory in Kenya. In that work I had suggested psychological factors—morale, reflecting a sense that one is receiving a fair wage—could affect efforts, an alternative, and in some cases more persuasive reason for the efficiency wage theory. It is curious how economists have almost studiously ignored factors, which are not only the center of day-to-day life, but even of business school education. Surely, such attention would not be given to such matters, to issues of corporate culture and intrinsic rewards, unless they were of some considerable importance. And if such issues are of importance within a firm, they are equally important within a society.

Finally, I have become convinced that the dynamics of change may not be well described by equilibrium models that have long been at the center of economic analysis. Information economics has alerted us to the fact that history matters; there are important hysteresis effects. Random events—the Black Plague, to take an extreme example—have consequences that are irreversible. Dynamics may be better described by evolutionary processes and models, than by equilibrium processes. And while it may be difficult to describe fully these evolutionary processes, this much is already clear: there is no reason to believe that they are, in any general sense, "optimal." (I discussed these issues briefly in Atkinson and Stiglitz (1969) Stiglitz [1975c, 1992i, 1994e] and Sah and Stiglitz [1991]; some of the problems are associated with capital market imperfections.)

Many of the same themes that emerged from our simpler work in information economics applied here. For instance, in the information-theoretic models discussed above we showed that multiple equilibria (some of which Pareto-dominated others) could easily arise. So, too, here (Stiglitz, 1995b). This in turn has several important consequences, beyond the observation already made that history matters. First, it means that one cannot simply predict where the economy will be by knowing preferences, technology, and initial endowments. There can a high level of indeterminacy (see, e.g., Stiglitz, 1973b). Second, as in Darwinian ecological models, the major determinant of one's environment is the behavior of others, and their behavior may in turn depend on their beliefs about others' behavior (Hoff and Stiglitz, 2001). Third, government intervention can sometimes move the economy from one equilibrium to another; and having done that, continued intervention might not be required.

VIII The Political Economy of Information

Information affects political processes as well as economic ones. First, we have already noted the distributive consequences of information disclosures. Not surprisingly, then, the "information rules of the game," both for the economy and for political processes, can become a subject of intense political debate. The United States and the IMF argued strongly that lack of transparency was at the root of the 1997 financial crisis, and said that the East Asian countries had to become more transparent. The attention to quantitative data on capital flows and loans by the IMF and the U.S. Treasury could be taken as conceding the inappropriateness of the competitive paradigm (in which *prices* convey all the relevant information); but the more appropriate way of viewing the debate was *political*, a point which became clear when it was noted that partial disclosures could be of only limited value. Indeed, they could possibly be counterproductive, as capital would be induced to move through channels involving less disclosure, channels like off-shore banking centers, which were also less well regulated. When demands for transparency went beyond East Asia to Western hedge funds and offshore banking centers, suddenly the advocates of more transparency became less enthralled, and began praising the advantages of partial secrecy in enhancing incentives to gather information. The United States and the Treasury then opposed the OECD initiative to combat money laundering through greater transparency of offshore banking centers—these institutions served particular *political and economic interests*—until it became clear that terrorists might be using them to help finance their operations. At that point, the balance of American interests changed, and the Treasury changed its position.

Political processes inevitably entail asymmetries of information (for a more extensive discussion, see Patrick D. Moynihan, 1998; Stiglitz, 2003a): our political leaders are *supposed* to know more about threats to defense, about our economic situation, etc., than ordinary citizens. There has been a delegation of responsibility for day-to-day decision-making, just as there is within a firm. The problem is to provide incentives for those so entrusted to act on behalf of those who they are supposed to be serving—the standard principal-agent problem. Democracy—contestability in political processes—provides a check on abuses of the powers that come from delegation just as it does in economic processes; but just as we recognize that the takeover mechanism provides an imperfect check on management, so too we should recognize that the electoral process provides an imperfect check on politicians. As in the theory of the firm where the current management has an incentive to *increase* asymmetries of information in order to enhance market power, so too in public life. And as disclosure requirements—greater transparency—can affect the effectiveness of the takeover mechanism and the overall quality of corporate governance, so too these factors can affect political contestability and the quality of public governance.

In the context of political processes, where "exit" options are limited, one needs to be particularly concerned about abuses. If a firm is mismanaged—if the managers attempt to enrich themselves at the expense of shareholders and customers and entrench themselves against competition, the damage is limited—customers, at least, can switch. But in political processes, switching is not so easy. If all individuals were as selfish as economists have traditionally modeled them, matters would indeed be bleak, for—as I have put it elsewhere—ensuring the public good is itself a public good. But there is a wealth of evidence that the economists' traditional model of the individual is too narrow—and that indeed intrinsic rewards, e.g., of public service, can be even more effective than extrinsic rewards, e.g., monetary compensation (which is not to say that compensation is not of some importance). This public spiritedness (even if blended with a modicum of self-interest) is manifested in a variety of civil society organizations, through which individuals voluntarily work together to advance their perception of the collective interests.

There are strong incentives on the part of those in government to reduce transparency. More transparency reduces their scope for action—it not only exposes mistakes, but also corruption (as the expression goes, "sunshine is the strongest antiseptic"). Government officials may try to enhance their power by trying to advance specious arguments for secrecy, and then saying, in effect, to justify their otherwise inexplicable or self-serving behavior, "trust me . . . if you only knew what I knew."

There is a further rationale for secrecy, from the point of view of politicians: Secrecy is an artificially created scarcity of information, and like most artificially created scarcities, it gives rise to rents, rents which in some countries are appropriated through outright corruption (selling information). In other contexts these rents become part of a "gift exchange," as when reporters trade "puff pieces" and distorted coverage in exchange for privileged access to information. I was in the unfortunate position of watching this process work, and work quite effectively. Without unbiased information, the effectiveness of the check that can be provided by the citizenry is limited; without good information, the contestability of the political processes can be undermined.

One of the lessons of the economics of information is that these problems cannot be fully resolved, but that laws and institutions can decidedly improve matters.

Right-to-know laws, for example, which require increased transparency, have been part of governance in Sweden for 200 years; they have become an important if imperfect check on government abuses in the United States over the past quarter century. In the past five years, there has become a growing international acceptance of such laws; Thailand has gone so far as to include such laws in its new constitution. Regrettably, these principles of transparency have yet to be endorsed by the international economic institutions.

IX Concluding Remarks

In this article I have traced the replacement of one paradigm with another. The deficiencies of the neoclassical paradigm—the failed predictions, the phenomena that were left unexplained—made it inevitable that it would be challenged. One might ask, though, how can we explain the persistence of this paradigm for so long? Despite its deficiencies, the competitive paradigm did provide insights into many economic phenomena. There are some markets in which the issues which we have discussed are not important—the market for wheat or corn—though even there, pervasive government interventions make the reigning competitive paradigm of limited relevance. The underlying forces of demand and supply are still important, though in the new paradigm, they become only part of the analysis; they are not the whole analysis. But one cannot ignore the possibility that the survival of the paradigm was partly because the belief in that paradigm, and the policy prescriptions that were derived from it, has served certain interests.

As a social scientist, I have tried to follow the analysis, wherever it might lead. My colleagues and I know that our ideas can be used or abused—or ignored. Understanding the complex forces that shape our economy is of value in its own right; there is an innate curiosity about how this system works. But, as Shakespeare said, "All the world's a stage, and all the men and women merely players." Each of us in our own way, if only as a voter, is an actor in this grand drama. And what we do is affected by our perceptions of how this complex system works.

I entered economics with the hope that it might enable me to do something about unemployment, poverty, and discrimination. As an economic researcher, I have been lucky enough to hit upon some ideas that I think do enhance our understanding of these phenomena. As an educator, I have had the opportunity to reduce some of the asymmetries of information, especially concerning what the new information paradigm and other developments in modern economic science have to say about these phenomena, and to have had some first-rate students who, themselves, have pushed the research agenda forward.

As an individual, I have however not been content just to let others translate these ideas into practice. I have had the good fortune to be able to do so myself, as a public servant both in the American government and at the World Bank. We have the good fortune to live in democracies, in which individuals can fight for their perception of what a better world might be like. We as academics have the good fortune to be further protected by our academic freedom. With freedom comes responsibility: the responsibility to use that freedom to do what we can to ensure that the world of the future be one in which there is not only greater economic prosperity, but also more social justice.

PART IIA

··

THE GENERAL THEORY OF SCREENING

··

Introduction to Part IIA

In the general introduction, we presented the basic insights of the general theory of screening. In the years after developing the basic theory, the general theory was elaborated in several directions, and gave rise to several controversies, to which I want to call attention.

We noted in the Introduction to this volume that there are market distortions both in the *level* of expenditures on information, and in the kind of information that is acquired. A firm might not have an incentive to disclose information that would suggest its shares or products are suitable to some, but not to others, for such information will not necessarily enhance profits, even though such information would be socially very valuable. Stiglitz (1982b) provides an illustration of this kind of matching in security markets, and Arnott and Stiglitz (1985) provide an illustration in the labor market. A derivative implication is that markets do not, in general, provide appropriate incentives for voluntary disclosure of relevant information.[1] There may be a role for government in forcing disclosure.

The theory of screening had been developed in response to a concrete policy question posed to me by the Kenyan government—how much should be invested in education.[2] In standard human capital theory, there was no discrepancy between social and private returns to education; here the discrepancy was marked. It soon became clear that there was a myriad of questions for which the new theory was relevant: problems of screening arose in virtually all markets, including capital and product markets.

In the basic theory, I had assumed that the characteristics of relevance could be directly observed. But what happens if that is not the case? If there are characteristics that are correlated with the characteristics of interests, then these will be used as the basis of screening—and it is easy to generate out of this a general theory of statistical discrimination.[3] So long as there is any information in "race," it will be used as a basis of differentiation. In later work (Stiglitz 1973c, 1974h), I showed that this could give rise to multiple equilibria—differential treatment led to differential incentives to obtain (unobservable) skills, and to the persistence of discriminatory equilibria, to which affirmative action programs could bring an end.

In Chapter 6, written on the 25th anniversary of our classic paper, Rothschild and I consider an example of increasing public policy relevance: the existence of

---

[1] There are some special models where that may be the case (see, e.g. Grossman 1981).

[2] What was relevant was not just the disparity between social and private returns, but the magnitude of the marginal social returns, because imperfections in capital markets meant that most individuals could not afford to invest much in the education of their children, even if there were large private returns.

[3] See also Phelps (1972).

genetic testing which will identify an individual as having an increased risk for certain diseases. Such information can destroy insurance markets, if insurance cannot be provided prior to the testing. More information may not be welfare improving.

As we noted in the introduction to the volume, much of the literature was predicated on the assumption of the existence of information asymmetries. In the general *theory of screening*, I had also considered the case—quite relevant in practice—where individuals might not know their own characteristics. The question was whether firms would invest money to find out who is a productive worker (or for an insurance firm, who is a low risk individual). I argued that there was a problem of appropriability—for instance, if more than one firm identified an individual as more able, then they would compete for the individual, bidding up his/her wage to his/her marginal productivity. The individual, not the firms, would appropriate the returns on the investment in information.[4] (This illustrates the more general point, made in the Preface, that the economics of information, or even the theory of screening, encompasses more than situations with information asymmetries.)

More generally, asymmetries are often *endogenous*. For instance, in Stiglitz (1984a), I consider a situation where individuals initially do not know whether they are more able or less able. It turns out that in equilibrium, they may all expend money to find out their types—and (as in the Rothschild-Stiglitz (1982) analysis) the resulting equilibrium *may* be Pareto inferior to one where such information could not be acquired. It is the ability to create information asymmetries which gives rise to a problem. (In later Parts, we will consider situations where managers deliberately create such information asymmetries in order to enhance their market power, since information asymmetries reduce the effectiveness of competition in the market place.)

There are other important examples of endogenously created information asymmetries: when a worker goes to work for an employer, the employer may quickly come to know more about that employee's abilities than others (and perhaps even more than the individual him/herself.) This information asymmetry has important implications for the nature of competition.[5]

---

[4] In Chapter 1 of this volume, I showed how there could nonetheless be an equilibrium with *some* investment in screening by firms.

[5] See, in particular, Stiglitz (1978b).

CHAPTER 3

THE THEORY OF "SCREENING," EDUCATION, AND THE DISTRIBUTION OF INCOME*

ONE of the most important kinds of information concerns the *qualities* of a factor or a commodity. We know that there are important differences among individuals, among bonds, among equities, among brands of automobiles. The identification of these qualities we call *screening*, and devices that sort our *commodities* (individuals) according to their qualities we call *screening devices* (for example, egg sorters).

This paper focuses on the labelling of individuals, on the economic costs and benefits of labelling, the institutions that provide it, and the determination of the equilibrium amount of screening under various institutional arrangements.

* Reprinted with Permission from the *American Economic* Review, 65(3) (June), 1975.

The research described in this paper was conducted in part while I was a Research Fellow at the Institute for Development Studies, University of Nairobi, 1969–71 under a grant from the Rockefeller Foundation. Financial support from the Ford and National Science Foundation is also gratefully acknowledged. I am indebted to Gary Fields, Michael Rothschild, Michael Spence, and to participants at seminars at Yale, Pennsylvania, Chicago, Queens, Wesleyan, and Princeton at which earlier versions of this paper were presented, for helpful conversations and comments.

The idea that education serves as a screening device and that as a result the allocation of resources to education may not be optimal is, of course, an old one. (See, for instance, Hull and Peters (1970) and Young (1958).) More recently, Thurow (1972), Fields (1973), Akerlof (1973), Spence (1973), and Arrow (1973a) have discussed education as a screening device. The first two papers assume a disequilibrium in the labor market (i.e., wages of any group of individuals need not equal the mean marginal product of

Economists have traditionally argued that because of the problem of appropriability in a market context, too few resources will be allocated to obtaining "information." This is not the case with the information provided by screening processes: individuals who can be labelled as "more productive" are able thereby to obtain a higher wage, partly, however, at the expense of others. Thus, by its very nature, screening information has important effects on the distribution of income.

The basic argument of this paper is that economies with imperfect information with respect to qualities of individuals differ in fundamental ways from economies with perfect information. There may be, for instance, multiple equilibria in which one of the equilibria is Pareto inferior to another; the Pareto inferior equilibrium may involve either too much or too little screening, or it may entail the wrong kind of screening. On the other hand, there may be situations where there exists no equilibrium.

The paper is divided into two parts. In Section I, I develop, partly by means of a number of examples, the central aspects of the theory of screening. Section II is devoted to an analysis of the implications of screening for the allocation of resources to education.

I The Theory of Screening

A The Benefits and Costs of Screening: Private Returns

We begin with the simplest possible example involving screening. All our later examples (and the examples of George Akerlof (1973), Kenneth Arrow (1973a), Michael Spence (1973), J. K. Salop and S. C. Salop (1976), and Michael Rothschild and the author (1976)) can be thought of as elaborations—on the screening mechanism, the production technology, etc.—of this example.

Consider a population in which individuals can be described (at least for economic purposes) by a single characteristic, which we denote by θ, and which is proportional to the individual's productivity p:

$$p = m\theta$$

the group); none of the papers, with the exception of Fields, appears to contain a completely articulated theory of the equilibrium of the system (the "supply" of education), and without a theory of the determination of the screening mechanism, it is difficult to make welfare economic evaluations of the system. For a more extensive discussion of this point, see Rothschild and Stiglitz (1976). Several of the results are closely related to those obtained independently by Akerlof (1973), Spence (1973), and Arrow (1973a). As we show below, the presumption that these papers attempt to establish, that there is too much screening, is not necessarily valid. Various aspects of the theory of screening have recently been the subject of extensive discussion in other areas besides those of the capital market and education referred to earlier: in insurance markets (Rothschild and Stiglitz (1976)), in labor markets (Salop and Salop (1976)), in discrimination (Arrow (1972a), Phelps (1972), Stiglitz (1973c, 1974h)), and in product markets (Salop (1977). See also Akerlof (1970) seminal work on the theory of lemons.

(That is, an individual of type θ_2 can do in an hour what a worker of type θ_1 can do in θ_1/θ_2 hours.) The variable p can be interpreted as the individual's marginal product. We choose our units so that $m = 1$. The fraction of the population that is of type θ is given by $h(\theta)$.

Assume that the individual knows his ability but the market does not, and in the absence of any information treats all individuals identically. Firms are risk neutral, and act competitively. Assume moreover that the individual is assigned to an assembly line, and on that assembly line it is impossible to tell the productivity of any single individual without prohibitively costly examination. The output per man of the assembly line is proportional to the average value of θ for those working on the assembly line, and there are no other factors of production.

Under these assumptions, a worker will receive a wage equal to the mean value of those with whom he is grouped. If individuals with higher θ can be identified, they will receive a higher wage. They thus have an economic incentive to be identified.

Consider a case where there are only two groups, denoted by θ_1 and θ_2, $\theta_1 > \theta_2$, and which we refer to as the more able and less able, respectively. Assume there is a screening process which screens perfectly[1] and which costs c per individual screened, where

$$\theta_1 - \theta_2 > c > \theta_1 - \bar{\theta} \tag{1}$$

$$\bar{\theta} = \theta_1 h(\theta_1) + \theta_2(1 - h(\theta_1)) = \text{average value of } \theta \tag{2}$$

First we consider a case where the supply of labor by each individual is inelastic, so that with perfect knowledge, the first group would receive an income of θ_1 and the second an income of θ_2. These are best thought to be lifetime incomes, i.e., present discounted values of wage streams.

We now establish that there are two equilibria:

(a) *The no-screening equilibrium.* Since no differentiation is made among individuals, they will all receive the same income, equal to the mean productivity of the population, $\bar{\theta}$. To see that this is an equilibrium observe that it does not pay any individual, in particular, it does not pay the more able individual, to be screened. For with screening, he would obtain a gross income of θ_1, from which we must subtract the cost of screening to obtain net income, $\theta_1 - c$, and by (1), this is less than the income he would have received in the absence of screening, $\bar{\theta}$.

(b) *The full-screening equilibrium.* The individuals of type θ_1 receive a gross income of θ_1, a net income of $\theta_1 - c$ (after paying for screening costs); individuals of type θ_2 receive an income of θ_2. Since these individuals know that they are the less able, they do not pay for any screening. Clearly, it pays individuals of type 1 to pay for screening: By our assumptions, all individuals who are not screened are "lumped" together and receive the same wage, so an individual of type 1 who is not screened

---

[1] Implicitly, we assume that the technology of screening is such that if less than c is spent, there is no screening. i.e., labels are assigned randomly.

would have received an income of θ_2, which by (1) is less than his net income with screening.

This simple example illustrates four propositions concerning economies with screening:

1) *There may be multiple equilibria.*[2]
2) *Some of the equilibria are unambiguously Pareto inferior to other equilibria.* Note that in the full-screening equilibrium, both groups have lower net incomes than in the no-screening equilibrium: the first group has an income of $\theta_1 - c$, which by (1) is less than $\bar{\theta}$; the second group an income of θ_2 which is obviously less than $\bar{\theta}$.
3) In both equilibria, *the presence of the less able individuals lowers the net income of the more able*; in the absence of the second group the first group would have received a wage of θ_1; in the full-screening equilibrium, net income is $\theta_1 - c$, in the no-screening equilibrium it is $\bar{\theta}$. *Conversely, the presence of the more able may increase the income of the less able* (in the no-screening equilibrium, they receive an income of $\bar{\theta}$ rather than an income of θ_2), *but need not* (as in the full-screening equilibrium).
4) *If one of the functions of education is to screen individuals*, as we shall argue later, *social returns* (ignoring distributional effects) *differ from private returns*. The gross social return, in this example, is zero (since the only effects of screening are distributional), the net returns are negative (since there is a cost). But the private rate of return (in the screening equilibrium) to screening, for the more able, is clearly positive:

$$\frac{\theta_1 - \theta_2}{c} - 1$$

Many screening equilibria have the characteristic that some individuals are better off than they would be in the absence of screening, some individuals are worse off, but total net national output is lower. One might be inclined to conclude that such a screening equilibrium is not Pareto optimal, but one must be careful. Assume instead of (1),

$$\theta_1 - \bar{\theta} > c \tag{1'}$$

Then there would not exist a no-screening equilibrium, but the losses from screening to group 2 exceed the gains to group 1. Clearly, if we forbade screening, we could compensate the upper group and divide the costs of screening among the population to make everyone better off. Such an argument misses, however, the essential nature of screening: neither the government nor the private producing sector knows who are the more able without screening; hence, in this example, even though with

---

[2] The multiplicity of equilibria noted here is different from the kind observed by Spence, which arises from an incomplete specification of the equilibrium conditions (or, alternatively, from a different notion of equilibrium than that employed here). (See Rothschild and the author 1976.)

screening net national output is lower than without it, the screening equilibrium is Pareto optimal in the sense that the redistributions which would be required to make "someone better off without making anyone worse off" than they were in the screening equilibrium, are not feasible in the absence of the screening itself.

On the other hand, since the screening does lower net national output and increases the inequality of income, *under any quasi-concave* (equality preferring) *social welfare function the screening equilibrium just described is socially undesirable* (see Anthony Atkinson (1970), Rothschild and the author (1973)).

These examples illuminate the nature of the private returns to screening: the individual's capturing of his "ability rents" which in the absence of screening he shares with others. It has several special characteristics which are essential for the results: (i) The more able are better in every relevant sense than the less able. Since there is an unambiguous ranking of abilities, we call such screening *hierarchical*. (ii) Labor is inelastically supplied and there are no increases in production from sorting individuals. (iii) Individuals have perfect information about their own abilities. (iv) There is no method of on-the-job screening. (v) The screening is perfectly accurate. (vi) The information acquired is "general" information. General information is information about characteristics of an individual which affect his productivity in a wide variety of jobs; specific information concerns characteristics which affect his productivity in a specific firm, for example, his ability to operate a particular machine. (The distinction corresponds to Gary Becker's distinction between general and specific training. These are clearly polar cases; as with training, there is a continuum of degrees of specificity/generality of information.) In subsequent sections I shall show the results are dependent on these characteristics.

In the remainder of this section I consider the private returns to the acquisition of general hierarchical screening information by an individual who is fully informed of his own abilities. I shall argue that in a private economy, as a first approximation, the benefits of such information would accrue to and the costs of information would be borne by the individual as opposed to the firm.

To see this, consider an economy in which individuals did not provide information about themselves. The wage in competitive equilibrium would be equal to the mean marginal product of the workers, and all workers would receive the same wage. Now assume that some firm did research which detected which workers (or groups of workers) were more productive. If it were able to keep that information secret, it would be able to earn, as a return to obtaining that information, the difference between the marginal productivity of these workers and the average of the population as a whole. Thus, it would pay firms to do research to obtain this information, provided, of course, that the costs of obtaining the information were sufficiently low. If the information were to become *public*, however, the worker would receive the benefits of the information: other firms would bid for his service, until his wage rose to his marginal productivity.

There are thus two conflicts of interest: the worker wishes to have all such information public, the firm private; and to the extent that some of the return is captured

by the worker, the firm will not allocate as much resources to obtaining information about the quality of the individual as the more able individuals would have
liked.

We have so far established that the most able individuals have an economic interest
in providing information about their capabilities. But the gain of the more productive
workers may be at least partially at the expense of the less productive workers. It may
be in the interests of the poorer workers for the information about who is the best
worker not to be known. I shall now argue that if information were relatively costless,
in a competitive economy everyone except the poorest (least capable) individual
would have an economic interest in providing such information. For, assume the
most able is able to provide information certifying to his abilities. The market would
then, in equilibrium, pay the remaining workers their (now lower) mean marginal
productivity. It would clearly pay, then, for the most able person of this group to
have his ability certified. And the analysis proceeds, until information about the
capabilities of all individuals except for the least capable is provided: but if we have
sorted out all except for the least capable, we have also sorted out the least capable.
This may be called the Walras Law of screening information.

Our basic argument can be summarized as follows: *since individuals are able to
capture the returns to general information about their skills themselves, they are willing
to spend resources to provide this information*—indeed, this is the only way they can
fully capture their "ability rents"; and in a competitive economy, firms that allocate
resources to obtaining general screening information about individuals will be unable
to appropriate (most of) the returns.

There are some conditions under which even the most able may not be willing to
pay for "general screening." (a) If there are self-employment opportunities where they
can realize the same returns that they would have realized had they been accurately
screened, any "underrated" individual would be self-employed. For most individuals,
this is not a relevant possibility. (b) If individuals are perfectly certain of their ability,
and if it is possible for their ability to be costlessly observed "on the job" then the individual would offer to absorb all the risk involved in hiring and training costs. There
are obviously instances of this sort, individuals who persuade the employer to hire
them at low wages until they can "prove themselves." But for many jobs, ascertaining
abilities (productivities) on the job may be relatively costly; most individuals are not
perfectly certain of their abilities, and the screening is far from perfectly accurate.
(c) If individuals are very risk averse and not perfectly certain of their abilities, then
they may prefer to be treated simply as average rather than to undertake the chance
of being screened and labelled below average. Indeed, in the examples given above,
screening increases the variance of the individual's income and reduces the mean
(since there is a cost to screening) and so, in such a situation, a "completely uninformed" individual, that is, one who took as the subjective probability distribution
of his abilities the distribution of abilities in the population, would never screen.
But even if there is a social return to screening, uninformed individuals may not
undertake it (see Section ID below).

B The Social Benefits from Screening

The examples of the previous section explicitly assumed that there was no social return to screening; i.e., screening did not increase output, it just redistributed it. Here we discuss the two major categories of social returns.

1. *Tradeoffs.* In the absence of information, individuals receive a wage which differs from their true marginal product. Imperfect information acts just like a wage tax on the more able, a wage subsidy on the less able. Like all taxes, the "information wage tax" is distortionary in its effect on the consumption-leisure decision. If screening costs are small enough, so long as labor is elastically supplied, everyone can be made better off as a result of screening (provided we have the appropriate tax instruments). (Often, however, the requisite redistributive taxes may not exist; in that case, some of the gains of the more able may be at the expense of the less able.)

Similarly, in choosing a job, an individual must trade off nonpecuniary returns with monetary returns, and if his wage does not correspond to his marginal productivity, he will not make the socially correct decision.

2. *Matching.* Even in the absence of nonpecuniary differences among firms, there is a "matching problem" in the individual's choice of jobs. It is widely recognized that individuals differ in the comparative skills with which they can perform different tasks (jobs) and the ease with which they learn different skills. If the typist has a comparative advantage in plumbing and the plumber a comparative advantage in typing, we can have both more typing and more plumbing if they "switch" jobs.

Educators often talk of the importance of matching an "educational program" to the needs and abilities of our students. The efficiency losses in attempting to train a less able individual to be an engineer are obvious; other kinds of education mismatching while not as obvious may in the aggregate be quite important.

Even within a given occupation, there are further matching problems. In many economic activities, individuals act together. What is easy to observe is the net output of the group, but this in turn is a complicated function of the different qualities of the individuals of the group. In the previous section, for instance, we considered an assembly line, the speed (output) of which depended simply on the average of the "productivities" of the individuals working on the line. It would perhaps have been more accurate to assume that it is a weighted average, with the individuals who are below average slowing the line down by more than those who are above average speed it up. In that case, total output would be greater if we had two assembly lines, one with slow workers, the other with fast workers, than if the workers were randomly mixed together. Although this example is based on the assumption that there are returns to group homogeneity, the argument that there exist social returns only requires that output depend in part on how individuals of different characteristics are grouped together.

A similar argument can be made with respect to man-machine interactions. Assume that there are different kinds of machines for producing a given level of output. There is a large training cost associated with the operation of each machine; training for one machine does not equip one for operating another. Each machine is optimally designed for an individual of a given ability (value of θ). Clearly there are social returns to knowing the individual's ability (θ). (If there were no training costs, we could quickly observe the output of the machine with any individual, and infer his ability from this.)

C Is There Too Little Screening?

The previous two sections should make it clear that there is no clear correspondence between social and private returns to screening; in the absence of screening individuals are "grouped" together and so may either be subsidized by or be subsidizing other members of the group. Individuals capture the direct increase in their own productivity as a result of screening; but if, as a result of screening, individuals can be "better organized" (for example, by using more homogeneous assembly lines) then there is a kind of externality provided by the availability of information. Moreover, screening eliminates the subsidy which the individual will have been receiving (or extending to others with whom he is grouped). This is a private cost (return) which is not social. As a result of these two factors, there may be too little or too much screening. The following two examples illustrate important situations in which there is too little screening.

1. *Job-Matching Screening: Screening for Comparative Advantage.* Assume a type 1 worker has a productivity of θ_{1s} when assigned to a skilled job but a productivity of θ_{1u} when assigned to an unskilled job. Type 2 workers have a zero productivity on the skilled job. We assume that type 2 workers are actually more productive at the unskilled job than the type 1 workers:

$$\theta_{1s} > \theta_2 > \theta_{1u} \tag{3a}$$

The productivity differentials are such, however, that with no screening, all workers are assigned to unskilled jobs. Let $\bar{\theta}_u$ be the mean wage with no screening in the unskilled jobs,

$$\bar{\theta}_u = h(\theta_1)\theta_{1u} + h(\theta_2)\theta_2$$

Then

$$\bar{\theta}_u > h(\theta_1)\theta_{1s} \tag{3b}$$

If screening costs are such that

$$\max(\theta_{1s} - \bar{\theta}_u, \theta_2 - \bar{\theta}_u) < c < \theta_{1s} - \theta_{1u} \tag{3c}$$

then equilibrium entails no screening; for if an individual of type 1 is screened, his net income is $\theta_{1s} - c$ which is less than his income on the unskilled job, and if an individual of type 2 is screened his net income is $\theta_2 - c < \bar{\theta}$ (again by (3c)). On the other hand, if

$$\max(\theta_2 - \bar{\theta}_u, \theta_{1s} - \theta_2) < c < \theta_{1s} - \bar{\theta}_u < \theta_{1s} - \theta_{1u} \tag{3d}$$

then equilibrium entails a fraction γ of type 1 individuals being screened, where

$$\frac{\theta_2 h(\theta_2) + (1 - \gamma)\theta_{1u}h(\theta_1)}{h(\theta_2) + (1 - \gamma)h(\theta_1)} = \theta_{1s} - c \tag{4}$$

It is clear that $0 < \gamma < 1$ (at $\gamma = 0$, the right-hand side of (4) exceeds the left-hand side; at $\gamma = 1$, the left-hand side of (4) exceeds the right-hand side). In both cases, net national income maximization entails $\gamma = 1$. Using (3c) and (3d) one can show that by having a subsidy for screening so the cost of screening is lowered to $\theta_{1s} - \theta_2$, financed by a lump sum tax, everyone can be made better off. *If type 1 workers are less productive in unskilled jobs than type 2 workers, there is too little screening.* The reason for this is that in the alternative occupation, the potentially skilled workers are in effect subsidized by the unskilled.

These results do not depend on the lack of complementarity between the two kinds of jobs. For instance, if

$$Q = F(\theta_{1s\gamma}, \theta_2 + (1 - \gamma)\theta_{1u})$$

where Q is output and F is a constant return to scale production function, maximization of Q may entail less than full screening but the equilibrium level of screening will still be smaller than the optimal level.

2. *Information Externalities: Returns to Homogeneity.* Assume that the output per worker of the assembly line is of the form

$$\bar{\theta} - \beta\sigma^2 \tag{5}$$

where σ^2 is the variance of abilities on the assembly line. Moreover, assume that there is a fixed, large number of individuals working on the assembly line. Equation (5) embodies the notion that homogeneous work forces work more efficiently. Let σ_θ^2 be the expected variance on the assembly line drawn from an unscreened population, and assume

$$\theta_1 - \bar{\theta} < \theta_1 - \theta_2 < c < \theta_1 - \bar{\theta} + \beta\sigma_\theta^2 \tag{6}$$

Then the (unique) equilibrium involves no screening: with no screening, everyone receives $\bar{\theta} - \beta\sigma_\theta^2$. If a single individual were to buy screening, his income would be (approximately) $\theta_1 - \beta\sigma_\theta^2 - c$ (since the degree of heterogeneity of the labor force would be unaffected, we assume that the costs of heterogeneity are allocated uniformly over all individuals) which by (6) is less than $\bar{\theta} - \beta\sigma_\theta^2$. On the other hand, with full screening everyone is better off: the lower group receives $\theta_2 > \bar{\theta} - \beta\sigma_\theta^2$ (again by (6)) and the upper group receives $\theta_1 - c > \bar{\theta} - \beta\sigma_\theta^2$. *Although Pareto optimality requires full screening, the market equilibrium entails no screening.* To see that the full-screening situation cannot be sustained by a competitive market (assuming individuals have to pay for their own screening), observe that with full screening the net income of the first group is $\theta_1 - c < \theta_2$, the net income of the lower group.

One might have thought that if $c < \beta\sigma_\theta^2$, it would pay firms to screen their workers if they do not screen themselves, since they would then obtain an average output of $\bar{\theta}$ rather than $\bar{\theta} - \beta\sigma_\theta^2$. But if the information about the outcome of screening could not be kept secret (for example, if the two types of assembly lines are different), then type 1 individuals would all be bid away, and so screening would be unprofitable. We assume the firm is aware of this and therefore would do no screening.

D Uninformed Individuals

There is another reason besides the two presented in the previous section why there may not be screening even when it might be possible for everyone to be better off with screening: individuals are uninformed about their abilities and are risk averse. Assume, for instance, that labor is elastically supplied. Then it is possible to show that with the appropriate set of taxes, if the costs of screening are sufficiently small, everyone can be made better off both *ex ante* (expected utility before screening) and *ex post* than in the no-screening equilibrium, but if individuals are sufficiently risk averse, the only equilibrium will entail no screening. The source of "market failure" here is different from those discussed earlier: now the problem is the unobtainability of "ability" insurance, presumably largely because of difficulties with moral hazard.

In such a situation, there is still an incentive for the firm to obtain information about individuals; for if the firm can find individuals whose market wage is below their marginal productivity it can capture the difference between the two, if it can keep the information sècret. If, as is often the case, this information cannot easily be kept secret, for example, if individuals of different abilities are assigned to different jobs (kinds of machines), then it would not pay any firm to do screening even if the firm were risk neutral. For other firms would bid away the more productive workers. The firm doing the research would not be able to capture the returns.

There is another problem in competitive economies with uninformed individuals: if two competing firms "discover" that a given individual's marginal product is greater than his wage, then they compete against each other; the individual's wage is bid up until it equals his marginal product, and neither firm is able to capture the returns from doing the research. For a more extended discussion of this point, see the author (1975c).

E On-the-Job Screening

The previous analysis assumed that the screening and production activities were completely separated and there was no on-the-job screening. This is important for two reasons. First, with binding contracts (for the firm not to fire the unproductive, for the productive individuals not to quit), the equilibrium will always be Pareto optimal. For if it were not, any firm, by integrating the screening and production processes could make a pure profit: in effect there is nothing the government could do in these circumstances that an intelligent entrepreneur could not do. In fact, even though there is some on-the-job screening, considerable screening does occur in the educational system, and as long as that is the case, the problems we have detailed above remain. Secondly, on-the-job screening is likely to screen for somewhat different characteristics than, say, educational screening; the return to on-the-job screening is likely to depend on the amount of educational screening and conversely. In the absence of coordination of screening and production, *the equilibrium screening may well be Pareto inefficient*, as the following example illustrates.

Assume individuals are characterized by two characteristics, θ and ϕ, and their productivity is a function of θ and ϕ. (θ may be viewed as a characteristic screened for by the education system, ϕ is a characteristic screened for on the job.) For simplicity, we let $p = p(\theta, \phi) = \theta\phi$. We consider a population with four groups $(\theta_1\phi_1)$, $(\theta_2\phi_1)$, $(\theta_1\phi_2)$, $(\theta_2\phi_2)$, with $\phi_1 > \phi_2$, $\theta_1 > \theta_2$. Let $h(\theta_i, \theta_j)$ be the proportion of the population with characteristics θ_i and ϕ_j. Define

$$\bar{\theta}(\phi_i) \equiv \frac{\theta_1 h(\theta_1, \phi_i) + \theta_2 h(\theta_2, \phi_i)}{h(\theta_1, \phi_i) + h(\theta_2, \phi_i)}$$

and similarly define $\bar{\phi}(\theta_i)$. Let

$$\max[\phi_i(\theta_1 - \bar{\theta}(\phi_i)), \theta_i(\phi_1 - \bar{\phi}(\theta_i))] < c_\theta < c_\phi < \theta_1\phi_1 - \sum_i\sum_j \theta_i\phi_j h(\theta_i, \phi_j) \quad (7)$$

where c_θ and c_ϕ represent the costs of screening for θ and ϕ, respectively. Costs are assumed to be such that it always pays to screen for one and only one characteristic. It immediately follows from (7) that there may be two equilibria, one in which θ is to be used as the "screen," the other in which ϕ is used. When ϕ is being used as a screening device, it does not pay to use θ, and when θ is used, it does not pay to use ϕ. Clearly national income is higher if θ is used rather than ϕ. Indeed, it is even possible to construct examples[3] in which everyone is worse off in the latter equilibrium rather than the former! *An attempt to eliminate educational screening may just shift the focus of screening, and make everyone worse off.*

F Accurate Screening and Fines

Another important implication of the possibility of on-the-job screening at any finite cost is that if it is perfectly accurate and individuals are perfectly informed, *the market*

---

[3] Let $\theta_1 = \phi_1 = 2$, $\theta_2 = \phi_2 = 1$; $h(\theta_1, \phi_1) = h(\theta_2, \phi_1) = 1/3$, $h(\theta_1, \phi_2) = h(\theta_2, \phi_2) = 1/6$. Let Y_{ij} be gross income of someone with characteristics (θ_i, ϕ_j). Then with screening for θ: $Y_{11} = Y_{12} = 10/3$, $Y_{21} = Y_{22} = 5/3$; with screening for ϕ: $Y_{11} = Y_{21} = 3$, $Y_{12} = Y_{22} = 3/2$. If $c_\theta - 1/3 \le c_\phi$, $c_\theta \le 11/6$, and $c_\phi \ge 4/3$, all individuals are better off under θ screening than under ϕ screening. For these to be equilibria, we require in addition, $1 \le c_\theta \le 5/3$, and $c_\phi < 3/2$. With the further restriction that $c_\theta + c_\phi > 9/4$, it can be shown that there are no other equilibria.

equilibrium will be characterized by full screening without spending any resources on screening. The individual agrees to pay the firm a large fine if it turns out he has overstated his ability. The firm announces it will undertake screening of individuals on an assembly line if the output of that assembly line differs from what it should be, given the ability levels which the individuals have declared. Clearly, for a sufficiently high fine, only individuals of ability level θ_1 will declare themselves to be of ability θ_1, and hence no screening need actually be undertaken.

This type of screening often occurs, although in a slightly modified form. Individuals accept low wages while they prove themselves; the low wages today are compensated for by high wages later if they do prove themselves. If they do not, the difference between the low wages and what they could have obtained elsewhere acts as a fine (see Section IIB below and Salop and Salop 1976). Lack of knowledge about one's own abilities and imperfectly accurate screening, combined with risk aversion, places a limit on the efficacy of this kind of screening; if screening is to occur, there will have to be some expenditures for examination. (See the author (1975c).)

G Nonexistence of Equilibrium

We have exhibited examples of too much screening, too little screening, the wrong kind of screening, and multiple equilibria. But another striking aspect of screening models is that *there may be no competitive equilibrium* where individuals take the action of others as well as the wages paid to an individual of any label as given.

The simplest example involves a slight modification of the one given in Section IE. For simplicity we present only a numerical version: Let $p(\theta_1, \phi_1) = 4$, $p(\theta_2, \phi_2) = 2$, $p(\theta_2, \phi_1) = p(\theta_1, \phi_2) = 0$, $h(\theta_i, \phi_j) = \frac{1}{4}$, all i, j; let $c_\phi = c_\theta = 1.5$. Clearly, there exists no no-screening equilibrium ($4 - 1.5 > 1.5$).

Let us consider alternative possible screenings. Assume $(\theta_1\phi_1)$ screens for θ only. It then pays $(\theta_1\phi_2)$ to screen for θ_1. But this cannot be an equilibrium, for it then pays $(\theta_1\phi_1)$ to screen for ϕ as well. (His net income would then be 1.) But if $(\theta_1\phi_1)$ screens for both θ and ϕ, it does not pay $(\theta_1\phi_2)$ to screen for θ. But if $(\theta_1\phi_2)$ does not screen, it does not pay $(\theta_1\phi_1)$ to screen for both θ and ϕ. Other possibilities (for example, $(\theta_1\phi_1)$ screening for ϕ, partial screening, etc.) may be checked, to see that there in fact exists no equilibrium. (This is similar to the result of Rothschild and the author (1973a).)

II SCREENING AND EDUCATION

Section I established some general characteristics of screening equilibria. We now focus in more detail on screening in educational institutions. Educational institutions are not the only institutions which do screening in our economy. Employment agencies and the College Entrance Examination Board both screen; there is considerable on-the-job screening; how an individual dresses, his accent, his socioeconomic background, his race or ethnic group may all provide bases for screening. The fact that there are other bases for screening does not detract from the importance of educational screening; indeed the screening done by educational institutions provides the primary determinant of one's initial job opportunities and hence of what screening can occur subseqeuntly. In this section we enquire into why educational institutions are important for screening (Section IIA), the mechanisms used for screening (Section IIB), and the implications this has for the structure of the educational system (Sections IIc–e).

A Why Educational Institutions?

Educational institutions provide information about individuals' abilities for a number of reasons: (a) The efficient allocation of scarce educational resources requires the identification of different individuals' abilities, i.e., some individuals would gain little from a Ph.D. program in economics, but would clearly benefit greatly from a course in automobile mechanics, and conversely for other individuals. (b) Most educators would argue that even within a given educational level there are returns from recognizing that some individuals learn certain skills faster than others. (c) Part of the social marginal product of educational institutions is finding each individual's comparative advantage (as educators are wont to say, "helping the individual find out about himself") and information about absolute advantages is almost an inevitable by-product of obtaining information about comparative advantages. (d) In the interchange between teacher and student which is common to many (but not all) educational processes, the teacher obtains a great deal of information about his student. The fact that there are a large number of teachers making those "observations," makes the information more valuable than the judgment of a single individual (for example, an employer).

In short, it is hard to imagine an educational system which did not obtain some information about individuals. Not all educational *processes* involve screening; that is, large lectures may impart a great deal of information, but the teacher need never ascertain how much of the information the student has absorbed. Some students have even argued that screening diverts them from "real" education to the acquisition of the particular skills and pieces of information which will be tested. Our analysis is predicated on the fact that for the reasons mentioned above, all educational *systems* do some screening.

B The Provision of Screening Information: The Screening Mechanisms

As discussions of grading systems make clear, there is, however, an important difference between obtaining information and making it public. There are several mechanisms by which such information about the individual's capabilities become public:

1) If the education system does any sorting for its own purposes (as it must), the groups into which an individual has been sorted will convey some information to the firm about the individual.

2) Another mechanism is performance tests: individuals have been confronted with roughly similar learning experiences (say geometry). Some individuals "learn" geometry better than others: this fact may be ascertained by a "grade" from the teacher, or by "standardized" objective examination. Failure to pass a course in college, or failure to pass a grade in elementary and secondary schools, conveys a great deal of information, which adversely affects the wages received by those individuals. As long as the school system does any grading, if only on a pass-fail basis, it is providing some information; and even when it does not do the grading itself, others can do the grading for it (Graduate Record Examination, etc.).

3) A great deal of information is provided, however, by *self-selection*:[4] a self-selection mechanism works as follows. Consider any characteristic of an individual about which the individual has more information than the firm. (We do not require that the individual have perfect information, only that on average he be better informed than the firm.) Some individuals have "more" of the given characteristic than others, for example, more brains, more mechanical ability, a higher turnover rate. We construct two (or more) reward-penalty structures such that on average individuals with more of the given characteristics will do better under one reward-penalty structure than under the other, and conversely. If individuals are asked to choose among these reward-penalty structures, and if they are rational, they will sort *themselves* out into those who have more of the characteristic and those who have less. (The better the information of the individuals and the greater the differential rewards, the better the sorting will be.)

Assume that wages are a function of the number of grades completed, and the length of time to complete a grade is a function of the individual's ability. Then if the two functions have the appropriate shape, individuals with lesser ability will quit at a lower grade level than persons with a higher ability. Grade completed is a complete surrogate for ability (see Spence 1973).

Alternatively, assume we have a hierarchy of schools, from those for the most able to those for the least able. Assume that the schools only use a pass-fail system. Assume that the schools for the more able are more expensive. If individuals had perfect information about their capabilities (and ignoring motivation, emotional, and other problems) then in fact no one need ever fail. Students would apply to the school of the appropriate ability.

---

[4] This is related to Akerlof's theory of lemons (1970). Akerlof argues that the used car market is a self-selection mechanism in which the worst cars become traded. Self-selection mechanisms provide what Spence has called "signals" to the market.

It should be noted that all these self-selection devices are based on *performance tests*; that is, although the employer is using information from self-selection, self-selection only works because of the performance tests. If there were no *possibility* of failures, everyone would attempt to go to the best school (and then screening would have to be done by admissions committees) and everyone would pass on from grade to grade at the same rate.[5]

C The Structuring of Educational Systems

Although we have argued that an educational system inevitably provides some information about the capabilities of individuals, there are a number of characteristics of the school system which determine how much and what kind of information is provided either by performance test or by self-selection. The school system can decide on the fineness or coarseness of screening. The structure of payments for education and the differences in "levels of education" provided by different schools are also important determinants of the effectiveness of self-screening.

Earlier, we noted that the reason that the school system is the major screening institution in our society is that this information is a natural by-product of its principal activity of providing knowledge (skills) and guiding individuals into the right occupations. In most of the ensuing analysis, we shall employ a stronger hypothesis: the more educational institutions perform their principal functions, the more screening that is produced as a by-product.[6] The more accurately it is able to place individuals into the right "slots," i.e., ascertain their comparative abilities, the more accurately it must ascertain the individuals' absolute abilities. The more knowledge it attempts to impart, the more it is able to "separate the men from the boys." At the extreme, if it tried to teach nothing, there would be no basis for performance testing, and there would similarly be no basis on which the self-screening mechanisms could be based.

There is thus the possibility that in imparting more skills to the abler students, we will simultaneously increase the inequality of income. This has made the organization of the educational system, and the method by which the levels of screening and skill acquisition are determined, an intensely political question.

Many of the social issues involving education arise because of differences in the wealth of parents. It is important, however, to observe that this parental distributional question can at least partly be separated from the questions of educational organization on which we are focusing. Thus the government could provide its support

---

[5] This is, of course, not true of other self-selection mechanisms, e.g., those discussed by Salop and Salop (1976). The absence of performance tests plays a crucial role in the economics of self-selection devices discussed by Akerlof (1973), and Rothschild and the author (1973).

[6] That is, for most of the analysis we shall assume that they are joint products, and that the mix between screening and "skill formation" is technologically determined. We could generalize the model to allow for the determination of this mix. In this paper we will not enquire in detail how the skill acquisition and screening take place (e.g. the nature of the grading system). We shall employ a general formulation which is consistent with a number of alternative microstructures.

for education in the form of vouchers, allowing individuals to use these in private schools. Even if there were no inequality in parental ability to pay for education, there would be, as we have argued above, important distributional consequences to alternative methods of organizing the educational system. To isolate our attention on these, we shall assume in the subsequent discussion that an individual's attitude towards education is determined completely by the own private monetary returns.[7]

D The Comprehensive School Systems with Majority Voting and Fairly Accurate Screening

In this section, we shall show that *with majority voting a comprehensive school system will under reasonable assumptions allocate too many or too few resources to education (screening), relative to the amount which would maximize net national output depending on whether individuals are informed or uninformed about their abilities.*

The model is a slight extension of that presented in Section 1. Individuals are described by a single characteristic θ; the distribution of θ over the population is given by $h(\theta)$. We let λ denote the "intensity" of education.[8] More intensive education (a) costs more, (b) screens better, and (c) increases the productivity of the group educated, either because of skill acquisition or better matching of individuals and jobs.

The Productivity Effect

Let $p(\theta, \lambda)$ be the productivity of an individual of ability θ who has received an education of intensity λ. For simplicity, we shall let p take on the special form (upon appropriate choice of units)[9]

$$p(\theta, \lambda) = m(\lambda)\theta, \quad m' \geq 0, \quad m'' \leq 0 \tag{8}$$

---

[7] This would be the case for instance even without government redistribution if (a) there were a perfect capital market, (b) education were not a consumption good, and (c) there were no tax distortions in the allocation of capital between human and physical capital.

[8] Throughout the discussion we make the extreme assumption that all information about individuals' abilities is obtained through the educational system, and hence the individuals' wages are determined by the label imposed by the schools. Obviously, there is some information obtained on the job. The qualitative results of our analysis will, however, be unaffected so long as (a) firms cannot obtain information on the job instantaneously, and/or (b) there are any fixed costs of hiring and training. Intensity can be thought of as either "length" (number of years of schooling) or "quality" within a program of fixed length.

[9] It should be noted that the model may be considerably generalized without affecting its qualitative properties. In particular, the restriction embodied in equation (8) may be dropped, and an additional kind of education which increases skills without screening may be introduced. See the author (1972a).

Screening

The educational system places labels on individuals; it gives a point estimate of the individual's ability. Let $e(\theta, \hat{\theta}, \lambda)$ be the probability that an individual of type θ be labelled $\hat{\theta}$, in an educational system of intensity λ. As λ increases, the probability of error decreases, i.e.,

$$\left. \frac{\partial e(\theta, \hat{\theta}, \lambda)}{\partial \lambda} \right|_{\hat{\theta}=\theta} \geq 0 \tag{9}$$

Costs of Education

Finally, we assume that the cost of education per pupil $c(\lambda)$ is an increasing function of λ and that the marginal cost also increases with λ.

$$c' > 0 \quad \text{and} \quad c'' > 0 \tag{10}$$

In a comprehensive educational system all schools have the same value of λ. The model includes as special cases the traditional model of pure skill acquisition $(\partial e/\partial \lambda = 0)$ and the pure screening model $(m' = 0)$.

Wage Determination

Workers whose ability is estimated to be $\hat{\theta}$ receive a wage equal to their mean marginal product

$$w(\hat{\theta}) = m(\lambda) \int \theta e(\theta, \hat{\theta}, \lambda) h(\theta) d\theta \div \int e(\theta, \hat{\theta}, \lambda) h(\theta) d\theta \tag{11}$$

The expected wage which a person whose true ability is θ will receive is then given by

$$W(\theta) = \int w(\hat{\theta}) e(\theta, \hat{\theta}, \lambda) d\hat{\theta} \tag{12}$$

We shall consider the special case of a fairly accurate grading system in which $e(\theta, \hat{\theta}, \lambda)$ takes on the form

$$e(\theta, \hat{\theta}, \lambda) = f(\theta - \hat{\theta}, \lambda) = f(\epsilon, \lambda) \tag{13}$$

where $\epsilon = \theta - \hat{\theta}$ is the error. We thus assume that the distribution of error is independent of the value of θ. Moreover, we assume $E\epsilon = 0$ and $E\epsilon^2 = g(\lambda)$, $g'(\lambda) \leq 0$. Thus from (11)

$$w(\hat{\theta}) = m(\lambda)\hat{\theta} + \frac{m(\lambda)\int \epsilon f(\epsilon, \lambda)h(\hat{\theta} + \epsilon)d\epsilon}{\int f(\epsilon, \lambda)h(\hat{\theta} + \epsilon)d\epsilon} \simeq m(\lambda)\left[\frac{h'(\hat{\theta})g}{h(\hat{\theta})} + \hat{\theta}\right] \quad (14)$$

$$W(\theta) \simeq m(\lambda)\int \left[\hat{\theta} + \frac{h'(\hat{\theta})}{h(\hat{\theta})}g\right] f(\theta - \hat{\theta}, \lambda)d\hat{\theta}$$

$$= \int \left[m(\lambda)(\theta - \epsilon) + m(\lambda)\frac{h'(\theta - \epsilon)}{h(\theta - \epsilon)}g\right] f(\epsilon, \lambda)d\epsilon$$

$$\simeq m(\lambda)\left[\theta + \frac{h'(\theta)}{h(\theta)}g\right] \gtrless m(\lambda)\theta \text{ as } h' \gtrless 0 \quad (15)$$

Thus in an unimodal distribution, individuals below the mode get more than they would under perfect screening, individuals above the mode get less than they would. The reason for this is that individuals are being averaged with some individuals who are better than they are, but have been underrated, and some who are worse, but who are overrated; if there are more who are worse (within a given range of error) than who are better, the individual will receive less than his true marginal productivity (on average).

Output Maximizing Educational Intensity

If we wish to maximize national output less educational expenditures, i.e.,

$$\max\left\{m(\lambda)\int \theta h(\theta)d\theta - c(\lambda)\right\} \quad (16)$$

we set

$$c'(\lambda) = \bar{\theta}m'(\lambda) \quad (17)$$

where $\bar{\theta}$ is the mean level of ability in the economy. The solution to (17) we shall call the "optimal level of education," bearing in mind that we are using the term in a very restricted sense.

Majority Voting

We now come to the choice of an educational intensity (and the associated degree of screening) in a majority voting political system. We assume the educational system is paid for by proportional wage taxes. Then if τ is the tax rate,

$$\tau m(\lambda)\bar{\theta} = c(\lambda) \tag{18}$$

and the net expected wage of someone at ability θ (using (15) and (18)) is

$$W(\theta)(1-\tau) \simeq m(\lambda)\left[\theta + \frac{h'}{h}g\right]\left(1 - \frac{c(\lambda)}{m(\lambda)\bar{\theta}}\right)$$

$$= \left(\theta + \frac{h'}{h}g\right)\left(m(\lambda) - \frac{c(\lambda)}{\bar{\theta}}\right) \tag{19}$$

Taking the derivative of (19), we can see how varying educational intensity affects different groups

$$\frac{dW(1-\tau)}{d\lambda} = \frac{W}{m}\left(m' - \frac{c'}{\bar{\theta}}\right) + (1-\tau)m\frac{h'}{h}g'$$

This depends on both θ and λ. Consider the optimal level of education. Note then that the first term drops out, and we are left with only the second term: individuals above the mode will want more than the optimal level of education, individuals below the mode will want less. It is possible to show that if c'', $g'' \geq 0$, and $m'' < 0$, preferences will be single peaked. Thus, the majority decision will be determined on the basis of the median value of h'/h. It is clear that if the mode lies below the median as it does for the income distribution, there will be an excess of investment in education over the optimum amount.

Indeed, it is easy to establish that not only is output lower, but the coefficient of variation in after tax expected wage income is greater, as illustrated in Figure 1.

It is worth noting at this point a major difference between fairly accurate screening systems and those which, for low values of λ, are very inaccurate. Take as an extreme case a system in which with "no information" and no education everyone receives the average value of the marginal product, as discussed earlier. Assume education only screens and that the distribution of abilities is lognormal. With no screening, the median receives the average, with perfect screening, he receives the median. As screening increases, his gross income initially declines. The cost of education increases with screening. Thus, there are two "peaks" to his net income, and accordingly there may not exist a majority voting equilibrium.[10] (See Figure 2.)

The above analysis assumed that everyone knew perfectly his own ability. The other polar case is where at least a majority of individuals are completely uninformed as to their abilities, i.e., their subjective probability distribution of their abilities is identical to the frequency distribution of abilities in the population. It is clear then that the median voter will vote for a level of education which is below that which maximizes net national output.

---

[10] I am indebted to John Chant for discussions on these points.

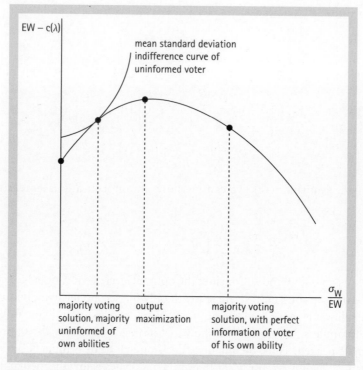

Fig. 1.

E Noncomprehensive School Systems[11]

Although there is an institutional and analytical simplicity to a comprehensive school system, it is easy to establish that in general net national output is not as high as in a system in which different individuals receive a different education. Indeed, if by greater ability we mean in part the ability to learn more easily, then it is more efficient (if our objective is maximizing net national output) to spend more resources on the more able.[12] This will be a characteristic of most noncomprehensive school systems. The allocation, however, will differ between a governmentally organized system attempting to maximize net national output, a private educational system, and a mixed public-private system. A full analysis would take us beyond the scope of this paper, but what we wish to do here is to characterize the major reasons that the equilibrium in pure private as well as mixed public-private systems does not maximize net national income.

For simplicity, it is best to return to the special case of Section IA, where there are only two ability groups in the population. The school system will consist of two

[11] For a more extensive discussion of the issues discussed here as well as the development of a formal model, the reader is referred to the author (1972a, 1974b).
[12] Although the precise quantitative relationship clearly depends on the specific technological assumption embedded in equation (8) so long as some are able to learn more quickly and easily than others, the result remains valid.

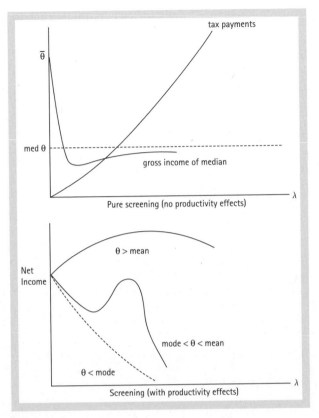

Fig. 2.

schools, one run for the more able, one for the less able. In the mixed public-private school system, the school for the more able is private, for the less able, public. Private schools charge a tuition equal to per pupil expenditure; public schools raise revenue by general proportional taxation. We assume that the less able are in the majority. Each school system will have some of both kinds of individuals, the upper school will contain some individuals of lower ability who are attempting the "gamble" of being able to pass through the system and hence be grouped with the more able, and those of lower ability who overestimate their ability. Conversely for the lower school.

We shall now argue that there is some presumption for excessive expenditure even in a private school system. Consider the three effects of an increase in educational expenditure in the upper school. First, there is the direct productivity effect. Since the upper school focuses its attention on those who will "succeed," it spends more on this account than a government-run school which is also concerned with those who do not succeed in the upper school. Secondly, there is the direct screening effect, which, as we argued above, is simply redistributive in character, and again leads to "too much" spending on education. Thirdly, there is the "self-selection effect." By increasing educational expenditure and the quality of screening, the upper school discourages those of lower ability from attempting to go to the upper school. There is some social return to this, since the amount of education which is optimal for the less able is less than that which is optimal for the more able. The private return, however, is derived not from the increased "efficiency" of the educational system, but from the ability of the more able to capture more of their "ability rents." The private return to self-selection may be more or less than the social return. Thus, only if the social return to self-selection exceeds the private return by just the right amount to compensate for the excess of the private productivity and direct screening returns over the social returns will the level of expenditure be at the output maximizing level; normally we would expect there to be too much expenditure in the upper school.

A similar analysis applies to the lower school. It is obviously not in interests of those of lower ability to have extensive screening. Although the social return to self-selection is positive, the private return to those of lower ability is negative. By increasing the level of educational expenditures they are, however, able to attract those of higher ability who are less sure of their abilities and more risk averse.

This again leads to some presumption of excess spending even in the lower school. When the lower school is publicly financed, there is a further incentive for excess spending, since now the costs for the lower school are borne by the population as a whole.

F Concluding Comments

In recent years economists have shown an increasing awareness of "market failures" and have increasingly called upon government intervention to correct these failures. But to turn over an allocation process to the public sector is to make it subject to "political laws" which may be no less forceful—and even less efficient—than the "economic laws" which previously governed the allocation process. The fact that these political laws are less well understood, perhaps more amorphous, than the corresponding economic laws is not an excuse for relying on the mythical "benevolent despot" who plays the central role in most economists' models of the public sector.

The educational sector provides an important point of comparison between the two allocation processes. If, as we have suggested, education provides information as well as skills, then it is providing a "commodity" for which it is well known that the market "fails"; we have shown how social returns differ from private returns and have examined in detail the market allocation of resources to education as well as the structure of the educational system which would emerge from a simplified political process in a highly idealized setting. Some important results emerge. Screening has productivity returns, but tends to increase inequality. There will thus be a tradeoff between efficiency and distributional considerations; but beyond a certain point, further increases in educational expenditure may both increase inequality and decrease net national income. We noted a tendency for all the school systems examined—public, private, and mixed—to operate at these levels even when all citizens are simply concerned with their own income maximization. One of the reasons for this—found in all of the systems—is that some of the returns to higher levels of education (those returns derived from the increased accuracy of labelling individuals' abilities), are private but not social returns; we argued that if abilities are distributed skewly to the right, for the median voter these private returns were positive. A further reason, in publicly supported systems, is (with proportion or progressive taxation and skewed income distributions) that the median voter pays for less than his proportionate share in marginal costs. As a result, the tendency for excessive spending on education may be greater in the publicly financed schools.

On the other hand, it should be emphasized, that whether there is "too much" or "too little" screening in a competitive economy depends on a number of assumptions concerning the screening technology, how well-informed individuals are concerning their own abilities, the nature of the production process, and whether screening is primarily hierarchical or "job-matching."

Finally, we note that attempts to curtail educational screening may simply shift the focus of screening (for example, to on-the-job screening), with the possibility of a lowering of net national output without any commensurate gain in equality.

CHAPTER 4

A MODEL OF EMPLOYMENT OUTCOMES ILLUSTRATING THE EFFECT OF THE STRUCTURE OF INFORMATION ON THE LEVEL AND DISTRIBUTION OF INCOME*

We present a model of how employers use information about workers to make salary and job placement decisions when they have imperfect information about workers' ability. Job placement decisions are important because workers are more productive if they work at jobs appropriate to their ability.

* This paper was written with Michael Rothschild and extends work which originally appeared in Diamond and Rothschild (1978). We are grateful to A.S. Goldberger and G. Werden for helpful discussions and to the National Science Foundation for research support. Reprinted with permission from Elsevier.

1 INTRODUCTION

This paper presents a model of the way in which employers use information about workers to make salary and job placement decisions when they have imperfect information about workers' ability. In the model, job placement decisions are important because workers are more productive if they work at jobs appropriate to their ability. A skilled worker who works at an unskilled job produces less than he would if he worked at a skilled job [this is eq. (1) below]. Equivalently—at least in our model—an unskilled worker is more productive at an unskilled job than a skilled worker [this is eq. (1′) below]. This model generalizes and synthesizes previous theoretical work, in particular that of Aigner and Cain (1977).

Our model distinguishes between the direct contribution of a characteristic or credential to productivity and its indirect effect through the information that it conveys. It also emphasizes the trade-off between efficiency and equity: the more information is used the more smoothly the production process runs and the more output (as measured by average wages) there is. However, as information usage increases so does the dispersion of income.

Our model is relevant for analysis of such anti-discrimination legislation as Title VII of the 1964 Civil Rights Act. Courts and government agencies have often interpreted this legislation as requiring employers to demonstrate that criteria on which hiring decisions are based have a direct effect on productivity.[1] We conclude that there is no good economic reason to distinguish between the direct and indirect effects mentioned above—in fact, a cost minimizing employer may be unable to distinguish between direct and indirect effects. The important question, for research and for policy, is how the structure of information is determined.

2 THE MODEL

Our model is

$$Q(A, S) = \alpha + \beta A - \delta(A - S)^2, \tag{1}$$

where $Q(A, S)$ is the output of an employee with ability A who is placed in job level S.[2] The interpretation of (1) is that employees work best when they work at a job

---

[1] The legislative history of Title VII is not without controversy; our view [as expressed in Rothschild and Werden (1982)] is that Congress intended only to prohibit discriminatory behavior on the part of employers. Title VII was explicitly not supposed to interfere with or remedy competitive (but racially and sexually neutral) market processes which produce employment outcomes which are not racially and sexually neutral.

[2] Tinbergen (1959) uses a similar specification as part of a model explaining the distribution of income.

requiring skills commensurate with their ability. Employers determine S on the basis of their estimates of A.

It might be argued that a specification

$$Q(A, S') = a' + \beta' S' - \gamma' (A - S')^2 \tag{1'}$$

is more plausible than (1). In this story S' is the speed of the assembly line on which a worker is placed and $(A - S')^2$ is a measure of the number of items which the worker spoils because he is forced to work at the wrong speed. It is easy to check that (1) and (1') are equivalent if $a' = a - \beta^2/4\gamma^2$; $S' = S + \beta/2\gamma$; $\beta' = \beta$ and $\gamma' = \gamma$. Formula (1) emphasizes the importance of finding the right job for a man; (1') stresses the need to find the right man for a job. They are equivalent ways of looking at the same phenomenon. Since (1) leads to more transparent formulae than (1'), we use it.

The ability A of (1) is a random variable; we suppose it is determined by a worker's characteristics—a random vector $X \in R^n$. In this model A is a linear function of X so that

$$A(X) = a'X = \sum_{i=1}^{n} a_i X_i. \tag{2}$$

We further assume that the characteristics X are distributed among the population of workers according to a multivariate normal distribution function so that

$$X \sim N(0, \Sigma), \tag{3}$$

where 0 is a vector of n zeroes and Σ is an n-by-n variance–covariance matrix. The assumption that $EX = 0$ is a harmless normalization as non-zero means are easily absorbed in the constant term, a. Assumptions (2) and (3) imply that ability is a normal random variable with mean zero and variance $V(A) = a'\Sigma a$.

3 THE STRUCTURE OF INFORMATION AND THE DETERMINATION OF EMPLOYMENT OUTCOMES

The characteristics which determine ability are partitioned into two classes, observable and unobservable. That is, $X = (Y, Z)$, where variables in Y are observable and can be used by employers in determining wages and jobs for employees. The partition of characteristics into the observable and unobservable reflects both facts of nature and legal or social conventions. Some characteristics may be unobservable because they are really unobservable. The model is general enough to include in the variable X virtually any random influence. Other characteristics may be unobservable because it is too costly to observe them. For example, x_i might be a potential test score on an exam which is costly to give. Still others might be unobservable because the law makes it illegal for employers to use them in employment decisions. Suppose, for example, that x_i is age.

From the point of view of an employer, a worker with observable characteristics Y has ability which is a random variable A. Under our assumptions $A|Y$ is normal with mean $E(A|Y)$ and variance $V(A|Y)$. The conditional mean of A given Y, $E(A|Y)$, is a function of Y,

$$E(A|Y) = a'E(X|Y) = a'_y Y + a'_z \Sigma_{zy} \Sigma_{yy} Y, \tag{4}$$

where the subscripts y and z represent the obvious partition of the vector a and the matrix Σ. Our assumption of normality, however, implies that the conditional variance of ability $V(A|Y)$ is a constant independent of Y. The variance of ability *is* a function of the partition of X into observable and non-observable variables, but for a given partition it is a constant independent of Y.

If employers are risk neutral they will place employees in jobs which maximize expected output. It is clear from (1) that this implies that $S(Y) = E(A|Y)$, where $S(Y)$ is the job assignment of a worker with observed characteristics Y. Thus, worker output is

$$Q(A, S|Y) = \alpha + \beta A - \gamma(A - E(A|Y))^2.$$

If there is competition, workers will be paid their expected output so that

$$W(Y) = E[Q(A, S|Y)] = \alpha + \beta E(A|Y) - \gamma V(A|Y). \tag{5}$$

4 THE VALUE OF CHARACTERISTICS

We now examine two implications of (5). First we look at its implications for the value of observed characteristics. Eq. (5) is a linear in Y. It is of the form

$$W(Y) = \text{constant} + \sum_{j=1}^{J} d_j y_j,$$

where J is the number of observable variables. The coefficient d_j is the value of the characteristic j. From (4) we know that d_j can be broken up into two parts

$$d_j = \beta(a_j + f_j), \tag{6}$$

where a_j is the direct effect of characteristic j on productivity and f_j is the indirect information which y_j provides about the unobserved characteristics (the Z's) which influence productivity. It is worth noting that there is no particular reason to suppose that a_j and f_j (or even a_j and d_j) are of the same sign. This suggests that requiring employers to validate that those characteristics which are used for screening and placement have a direct effect on productivity is a burdensome requirement which a competitive but not discriminating firm could not meet. The cost minimizing firm has no reason to draw the distinction between direct and indirect effects; indeed, once the structure of information is given, the firm cannot decompose d_j as in (6).

5 THE DISTRIBUTION OF (WAGE) INCOME

The second implication of the wage determination formula (5) concerns the relationship between the mean and variance of wages. It is clear that in this model, the more characteristics which are observable, the higher average output will be as more information implies less misclassification. It also seems likely that the more characteristics there are, the greater the dispersion of income. This suggests that our model implies an association between the mean and the variance of income. As we shall see, this is correct. For a given partition, mean income is

$$E[W] = a + \beta EE(A|Y) - \gamma V(A|Y) = a - \gamma V(A|Y) \tag{7}$$

[since $EE(A|Y) = EA = 0$].

For the same partition, the variance of wage income is

$$V(W) = \beta^2 VE(A|Y).$$

But,

$$V(A) = VE(A|Y) + EV(A|Y) = VE(A|Y) + V(A|Y), \text{ so}$$

$$V(W) = \beta^2[V(A) - V(A|Y)] \quad \text{or} \quad V(A|Y) = V(A) - (1/\beta^2)V(W).$$

Substitute into (7) to obtain

$$E(W) = (a - \gamma V(A)) + (\gamma/\beta^2)V(W).$$

This equation, which holds for all partitions, demonstrates that there is a linear relationship between the mean and the variance of the distribution of wage income.

THEORY OF SELF-SELECTION

Introduction to Part IIB

In the general theory of screening, I focused on the social and private returns to obtaining information which differentiated among individuals. The analysis focused on differentiation through costly examination.[1] But there is another important way that firms can find out about their workers (insurance firms about the characteristics of insurees, lenders about characteristics of borrowers), and that is through observing their behavior.

While my paper with Rothschild on competitive markets (Chapter 5) was published before my paper on monopoly and self-selection, the latter paper (Chapter 7) intellectually pre-dated the former. The problem of the monopolist was far simpler than that of analyzing competitive equilibrium. The monopolist wants to extract as much profit out of his/her customers as possible. In a world of perfect information s/he would act as a perfectly discriminating monopolist, extracting the entire consumer surplus. And in the standard formulations, there would be no inefficiency.

The standard models are, in that sense, unsatisfactory—for they assume perfect information, but they do not allow the monopolist to use that information. Chapter 8 here provides, for the first time, the foundations of a true theory of monopoly; monopoly is distortionary, as its critics claim, but it is only as a monopolist tries to extract information from his/her customers that inefficiencies in the economy are introduced.

The paper here focuses on how s/he can use complicated (non-linear) insurance contracts to ascertain who is more risk averse or more risk prone. It was based on the remarkably simple idea that the monopolist can structure a set of policies so that individuals' choices reveal information about themselves. A monopolist can structure the choices to be fully revealing, that is, so that each type buys a different policy. There is, of course, a social cost: to force individuals to reveal who they are, the firm offers partial insurance contracts, with more favorable terms, so that the less risky are induced to buy incomplete insurance. But there is also a private cost: the partial insurance policies are less desirable, and hence the firm can obtain less profit from them. It turns out that the firm may decide not to differentiate completely.[2]

A number of students and colleagues were able to show how more sophisticated contracts could be used for partial discrimination—tying in sales, random pricing,

---

[1] Though some of the discussion simply focused on disclosure—presumably with "fraud" penalties for those who misreported their characteristics.

[2] The monopoly equilibrium entailed, in the vocabulary of screening, partial separation/partial pooling.

non-linear pricing functions.[3] It also became clear that the structure of the optimum depended heavily on what was observable. If, for instance, a monopolist could not monitor resales, then s/he was restricted to a linear schedule (a single price, plus a fixed fee—the case of the standard theory.) It is curious how, a quarter century later, textbooks continue to focus on the old (and largely intellectually incoherent)[4] theory of monopoly.

The general theory of a monopolist trying to identify the characteristics of different "agents" has had enormous applications. One contemporaneous theory was that of Mirrlees—how government can use tax systems to differentiate among individuals of different types, when those types are not directly observable.[5] Just as the structure of monopoly prices depended on what was observable, so too in the case of taxation. If an individual's total consumption bundle could be observed, in general it would be desirable to impose both non-linear income and commodity taxes; though in a critical case, it turned out that *only* an income tax was desirable.[6] A second application entails the design of regulatory systems, when the regulated has more information about, say, the relevant technology, than the regulator.[7]

In competitive markets, however, no single firm controls the set of contracts that are available. The essential idea of Rothschild and Stiglitz was that individual's choices (and the information revealed by those choices) were based on the set of contracts available on the market—part of the market equilibrium itself. A competitive equilibrium was a set of insurance contracts, all of which at least broke even, such that no one had an incentive to offer an alternative contract. The set of Pareto efficient contracts could be easily enough described; and as in the general *Theory of Screening* (1975f), Pareto efficiency[8] might entail a pooling equilibrium (where individuals of different types buy the same policy). When it entailed a separating equilibrium (where each type purchased a different policy), that equilibrium could be sustained by a competitive market; but when it entailed a pooling equilibrium, it could not be. (This formulation oversimplifies—for it assumes only one commodity. When there is more than one commodity, the market equilibrium is not Pareto efficient; see Chapter 23 below.)

In Rothschild-Stiglitz (1976), the benefit (to the low risk individual) of separation is that the subsidy to the high risk individual is avoided. If there are relatively few high risk individuals (or if the high risk individuals differ little from the low risk individuals), the benefit is small. On the other hand, the cost is that the low risk individual obtains only partial insurance; and the "best" separating contract does not

---

[3] Adams and Yellen (1976); Salop and Stiglitz (1982); and Katz (1984).

[4] It makes sense only if transactions costs are low and the monopolist cannot monitor resale. In that case, the monopolist has to charge a single price.

[5] Mirrlees (1971). Mirrlees himself did not articulate the problem in information theoretic terms.

[6] See Atkinson and Stiglitz (1976); Mirrlees (1976); and Stiglitz (1998b). Ramsey's (1927) analysis of optimal commodity taxation thus presumed implicitly that there was no income taxation.

[7] See Sappington and Stiglitz (1987a). The literature on this topic has become huge (see, e.g. Laffont and Tirole 1993).

[8] When each firm was restricted to offering only one contract. The more general case is discussed below, and in Chapter 9.

depend on the numbers of each type. Hence, when there are few enough high risk individuals, the costs exceed the benefits, and a competitive equilibrium never exists.

Given this intuition, it is not surprising that if there exists a continuum of individuals, Pareto optimality always entails at least some pooling—those with the highest risk get pooled together.[9] This means that if there is a continuum of types of individuals, there never exists a competitive equilibrium (in the natural sense of Rothschild-Stiglitz).

Subsequent work (never published) showed that the nature of Pareto efficient and market equilibrium in the Rothschild-Stiglitz model could differ from standard models in still other ways:

1. Equilibrium could be characterized by positive profits (if the high risk individuals are less risk averse than low risk individuals.)[10] The self-selection equilibrium is the contract which maximizes the expected utility of the low risk individual subject to (a) the high risk individual does not purchase the policy; and (b) the policy at least breaks even. In the absence of the "single crossing property," the second constraint may not be binding, in other words, the equilibrium involves positive profits. Any firm attempting to bid away the profit, by lowering the premium or the deductible will find itself inundated with high risk individuals and losing money. (See Figure IIB.1.)

2. Pareto optimality may entail the low risk individuals subsidizing the high risk individuals. We explained before how the pooling equilibrium may be preferred to the separating equilibrium, *where the high risk individual buys the full insurance policy which just breaks even*. But the low risk individuals are still better off if they subsidize the high risk individual.

3. If insurance companies can announce a strategy of selling two policies, a zero deductible and a high deductible, in fixed proportions, then the Pareto efficient set of policies (with one policy cross subsidizing the other) can constitute a Nash equilibrium. There exists, of course, a policy which would be preferred by the low risk individuals and not by the high risk individuals (to those they purchase in equilibrium) and which, were it bought only by the low risk individuals, would make a profit. But if any firm tried to "cream skim" by selling such a policy, it would find that there would be "floating" on the market a high risk individual, for whom the given policy would be preferable to no-insurance. And when both the high risk and low risk individuals purchase the policy, the policy makes a loss. Hence, no firm would attempt to cream skim.

While the theories of screening and signaling have played a prominent role in the development of economic theory over the past 35 years, since they were first formulated, the ideas have simultaneously come to play an important role in policy

---

[9] The result is not quite obvious: with a continuum of individuals, the benefit of separating from those with almost the same accident probabilities goes to zero as the differences go to zero, but so do the costs of separating; one can use L'Hopital's rule to show that the benefits of separating go to zero faster than the costs. See also Riley (1979).

[10] In this case, the so-called single crossing property, such that the indifference curves of one type are always steeper than those of the other, is not satisfied.

debates. In the US, for instance, some of the complexities of the failed attempt by President Clinton to reform the healthcare system arose from an attempt to prevent cream skimming; and the Democratic criticism of Republican reform initiatives, focusing on private medical accounts financed through tax deductible contributions, is that they would exacerbate the problems of the uninsured: more healthy, wealthy people would be induced to self-insure and drop out of the insurance pool; because the mix of those left behind would be worse, premia would rise, and hence more firms would drop or reduce coverage of workers, and more workers without employer funded insurance would decide that health insurance was not affordable.

Chapter 8 extends the theoretical work in another direction. Individuals' behavior (choices) is affected not just by the choice of contracts but by market conditions. In my early work on efficiency wages, I had noted that higher wages may lead to higher productivity, either because of lower turnover, improved incentives, higher quality of labor force, or improved morale. While these various versions were explored in a series of papers,[11] I remained concerned about the *general equilibrium*. Individual's behavior (turnover, incentives) were affected not just by what his/her employer did, but also by what other firms did. By the same token, the workers I could recruit depended not just on my wages, but on the wages paid by others.

Shapiro and Stiglitz (Chapter 11 below) constructed a general equilibrium *incentives* model, but some years earlier (1976c), I had constructed a general equilibrium *adverse incentive* model (not published until 1992j, reprinted here as Chapter 8). Whether a high productivity individual would apply to my firm would depend on the wage I offered *and his/her chance of getting the job*, which depended on the length of the queue (the firm specific unemployment rate). But the length of the queue depended on the hiring and wage decisions of *all* of the other firms. To analyze the market equilibrium, one had to analyze the wage and hiring decisions of all the firms simultaneously, a task which that paper successfully accomplished. Of course, equilibrium was characterized by unemployment, and of course the level of unemployment was not efficient. The paper reinforced four general conclusions, which subsequent research would further substantiate: (a) wages did more than just convey information about supply and demand—together with other *endogenous* variables, they conveyed information about quality of workers; (b) in competitive market equilibrium—with no imposed outside wage rigidities—there might necessarily be unemployment; (c) it is not just wages that convey information—here so too does the length of queues; and (d) the market equilibrium is, in general, not efficient.

In this model, there were no strategic interactions. In general, the characteristics of those workers a firm can hire if it raises its wages depend on how its competitors respond. If they match the job offer, the firm will not be able to get a better pool of

---

[11] The original paper, "Alternative Theories of Wage Determination and Unemployment in L.D.C.'s" was written in 1969 while I was visiting the Institute for Development Studies at the University of Nairobi. That paper was subsequently published (substantially revised) in several parts: Stiglitz (1974a) focused on the labor turnover model; Stiglitz (1982a) on the adverse selection model; the "morale" model was discussed in Stiglitz (1973c and 1974h); and the much revised "incentives" version appeared as Shapiro and Stiglitz (1984).

applicants. If they do not, it may. The same thing of course applies to credit markets. A lender that lowers the interest rate it charges may be able to attract a better pool of applicants, so long as its competitor does not respond. Developing models with such strategic interactions remains an important lacuna in the literature.

I should say a word about the interactions between screening and self-selection models. In a world with *perfect* and *costless* screening by examination, there would be no room for self-selection. But screening is never perfect, and *conditional on the observables (including the results of any examination)* there is still considerable scope for self-selection processes to work.[12]

There is a second form of interaction: subjecting one-self to an examination can be a very revealing self-selection mechanism. Those who fail the test pay a price. In fact, much of life takes this form. Individuals who are confident about themselves take a job with low wages but also with a strongly upward sloping wage profile. They are, in effect, saying that they are willing to subject themselves to the market test; they believe that they will survive.

The final paper in this section (Chapter 9) addresses the fundamental question of the relationship between signaling and screening models. Both, of course, focus on sorting—differentiating among individuals (firms, buyers of insurance, workers, borrowers) who are different, but who, in the absence of information, would be treated the same. The theory of screening argues that it may be in the interests of the more able workers (less risky purchasers of insurance) to be identified, and in the interests of firms to identify more able workers (lower risk insurees). The theory of *signaling*[13] emphasizes the former; screening the latter. It might seem that in equilibrium it makes little difference: in either case, better workers are identified (as are low risk insurees). In a *separating* equilibrium, the more able (less risky) individuals are separated from the less able (more risky), and it would thus seem that the two theories are really equivalent. But the signaling and screening models *seem* to yield some different results. While in standard screening models (such as Rothschild-Stiglitz, Chapter 5) equilibrium might not exist, and if it did, it would entail full separation and would be unique and Pareto optimal; but in Spence (1973) it seemed possible that there were multiple signaling equilibria. Consider a model with two groups of individuals, identical in preferences, but different only in the probability of an accident. Any set of insurance contracts with the property that low risk individuals prefer the high deductible policy and high risk prefer the low deductible could be a signaling equilibrium in a game in which the insured move first by announcing the contract that they are willing to buy—with the appropriate assumptions about the consequences of out of equilibrium behavior, in other words, what happens if some individual announces s/he wants to buy another policy, not one of the two. If the insurance firm believes that individual is of some third type, with much higher accident probability, then it would want to sell the policy to the individual only at

---

[12] And indeed, if differences among types get narrowed, as we have noted, problems of non-existence are enhanced.

[13] As the paper notes, the term signaling has come to be associated with Spence's (1973) model, where more able individuals signal their greater ability by going to school longer.

a premium that would make the individual far worse off than the one s/he chose in equilibrium. Chapter 9 argues, while it is true that, if one imposes no restrictions on, for instance, inferences made for out of equilibrium moves, there can be multiple equilibria, one should in fact focus one's attention on plausible inferences, and if that is done, the set of equilibria in signaling and screening models coincide in a wide range of cases.

Chapter 9 models the difference between signaling and screening equilibria as a difference between whether the informed or the uninformed move first. In the screening equilibrium, the uninformed (the insurance company) offers a set of contracts to the informed. In the signaling equilibrium, the informed takes an action first—choosing a level of education or announcing it wants an insurance policy with a given level of deductibility. But Chapter 9 argues that most of the differences in the results are not due to these differences in the structure of the model, but to implausible assumptions made in some versions of the signaling model about inferences concerning out-of-equilibrium moves.

To see this most clearly, consider the education context studied by Spence. In the context of a model with two types, he asserted (in a world in which education *only* screened, i.e. provided no skills) that there was an infinity of equilibria. For each level of education chosen by the low ability, there was a (minimum) level of education of the high ability such that the low ability would prefer the low level—with the low wage. If θ_i is the productivity of type i, $\theta_1 < \theta_2$ and $c_i e$ is the cost of education level e, then any pair $\{e_1, e_2 \geq e_1 + (\theta_2 - \theta_1)/c_1\}$ is an equilibrium, since it pays the low ability individual to choose the low level of education, signaling his/her ability. But if some low ability individual were to chose $e < e_1$, then the *worst* the firm could think is that the individual is of type 1, and the minimum rational wage to offer is thus θ_1, and thus the individual would be unambiguously better off. The only possible equilibrium is $\{0, e_2 = (\theta_2 - \theta_1)/c_1\}$.

The same reasoning applies in the insurance market. If the insurance firms know the statistical information about the economy, for example that there are only two groups, with specified accident probabilities, but the only information problem is whether any particular individual is of a particular type, then there is a unique "plausible" equilibrium. For if the high risk individual announces s/he wants, say, a policy with a zero deductible, but which generates positive profits, clearly some insurance firm will offer to sell the policy, for the worst that the insurance firm can think of him/her is that s/he is a high risk individual. Hence, in equilibrium, the high risk individual must offer to purchase that policy which makes zero profits and has a zero deductible. But if this is the policy offered by the high risk individuals, and a low risk individual offers to buy a policy which would *not* be purchased by the high risk individual, but still breaks even (if the individual is in fact a low risk individual), then it is plausible that any insurance firm will infer that the person offering this policy is in fact a low risk person, and accordingly, it will offer to sell that policy. In short, the only plausible equilibrium *given reasonable inferences about out of equilibrium behavior* is the same as that which emerged in the screening model, in which insurance firms move first, offering a set of contracts.

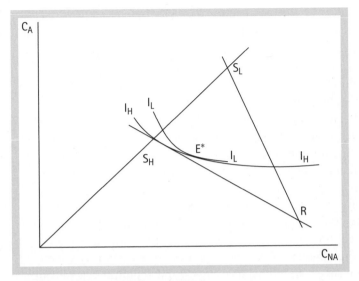

Fig. IIB.1. Positive profit equilibrium

Notes: The vertical axis gives consumption in the state of nature with an accident (C_A), the horizontal axis in the state of nature without accident (C_{NA}). R is the "endowment" the initial condition without insurance, S_L is consumption for the low risk individual with the actuarially fair full insurance policy; S_H is the similar point for the high risk individual. $I_H I_H$ is the high risk individual's indifference curve through S_H. The best policy, from the low risk individual's perspective, is the policy which maximizes the low risk individual's utility subject to (a) breaking even (being on or below the line $R S_L$); and (b) not being purchased by the high risk individuals, i.e. lying on or below $I_H I_H$. The Contract E^*, which lies strictly below $R S_L$, is the optimum contract—it generates positive profits.

The same results hold if there is a continuum of types (the case investigated by Spence). Contrary to Spence, there is at most one fully separating signaling equilibrium. Those with lower accident probabilities buy larger deductibles. Given the deductible chosen by the highest risk individuals, d_o, there is a premium/deductible schedule, $p = p(d; d_o)$ such that (a) only one type buys each policy; and (b) each policy breaks even, given the type which buys it. Spence argued that there was an infinity of separating equilibria, one for each d_o. But consider what happens if the highest risk individual announces s/he wishes to buy a policy with $d < d_o$, paying the actuarial fair premium for the worst type. The *worst* inference is that s/he is of that type, and clearly, any (risk neutral) insurance firm would be willing to sell the policy at that price. It pays all individuals of this type to offer such a policy, and accordingly, the only sustainable equilibrium is that in which $d_o = 0$.

In "Sorting out the Differences between Screening and Signaling Models," we consider more generally "rational" responses to out of equilibrium moves, in other words, those that make sense given the knowledge of the properties of the economy (market) of the participants. Spence focused on the job market, where individuals were using education to signal their abilities; and he did not consider either how firms might respond to out of equilibrium moves (choices of education) by workers, or how education systems might respond to the existence of a clearly inefficient school system. Given that education is typically provided publicly, it was perhaps not unreasonable to ignore the competitive response of providers of schooling, and there was perhaps no scope for "out of equilibrium" moves; but this simply suggests that the education market was perhaps not well chosen for understanding the role of screening/sorting/signaling in a market economy.

While the multiplicity of equilibria to which Spence called attention was artificial, a consequence of what may be viewed as a failure to fully specify the model (or, alternatively, an unpersuasive specification of the consequences of out of equilibria moves), multiplicity of equilibria may indeed arise in screening models (as we saw in Chapter 3).

While focusing on "optimal response equilibria" narrows the set of equilibria down,[14] the question of whether an equilibrium exists at all turns out to be more complicated; as Chapter 9 points out, it depends on the plausibility of certain further restrictions on the set of plausible responses to out of equilibrium moves, on assumptions about shapes of indifference curves, and about the sets of contracts that firms can offer. (If, for instance, firms can offer more than one contract, the answer may be different than if they can offer only one contract.) The results can be summarized as follows for optimal response equilibria:

1. If the separating equilibrium (without cross subsidies) is Pareto optimal, then it is both a signaling and a screening equilibrium. The Rothschild-Stiglitz and Spence equilibria coincide.

2. If the separating equilibrium is not Pareto optimal (and if there are a continuum of types, it will not in general be Pareto optimal), if the single crossing property is satisfied, and if each firm can offer only one contract, then there exists no Rothschild-Stiglitz screening equilibrium; but depending on assumptions made about beliefs about out of equilibrium moves, there may exist a pooling signaling equilibrium,[15] a partially pooling/separating signaling equilibria, or a fully separating signaling equilibrium (see Figure IIB.2a).

3. If the separating equilibrium is not Pareto optimal, if the single crossing property is not satisfied, and if each firm can offer only one contract, then there exists a positive profits Rothschild-Stiglitz screening equilibrium (where the low risk individual's contract has positive profits); that equilibrium can also be a signaling equilibrium, where customers call off a {deductible, premium} contract. But if, as in the education model, individuals can only signal an education level, then the wage must adjust to the competitive level, so there cannot exist a positive profit equilibrium; depending on assumptions made about beliefs about out of equilibrium moves, there may exist a pooling equilibrium and a (Pareto dominated) separating equilibrium.

---

[14] There is, of course, a problem where there is no worst type, or where there is an infinitesimal probability that the individual is of a very, very high risk (low ability) type.

[15] The Wilson (1977) equilibrium, the pooling equilibrium which maximizes the utility of the low risk (high ability) individual.

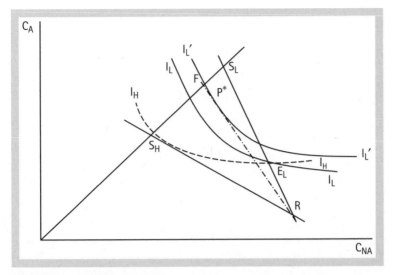

Fig. IIB.2a. Pooling contract

Notes: The pooling contract, P^*, Pareto dominates the potential separating equilibrium (the pair of contracts $\{S_H, E_L\}$ where E_L is the intersection of the zero profit line RS_L and the high risk individual's indifference curve through S_H). P^* is the best contract from the low risk individual's perspective that breaks even when everyone buys it (RF). The pooling contract cannot, however, be sustained in the standard Rothschild-Stiglitz analysis as shown in Figure IIB.2b.

4. If the Pareto optimal equilibrium involves cross subsidization,[16] if each firm can offer two contracts, rationing the supply of one (the loss making) conditional on the sales of the other (the profit making contract), then the Pareto optimal allocation can be supported by a Rothschild-Stiglitz equilibrium (see Figure IIB.2c).

These problems about inferences concerning out of equilibrium moves may, in fact, be somewhat artificial: in the real world, observations are made with noise, and with sufficient dispersion it is possible that *in equilibrium every possible action is observed*. There is, in this sense, no out of equilibrium move. Then, there are a set of types associated with each observed action, and, in particular, an average type. An individual taking any action can then infer the probability distribution of observed actions, and the rational inferences about his/her type that follows. (In a sense, the artificiality that arises about inferences from out of equilibrium behavior is replaced by the arbitrarily specified "noise" associated with observations.)

So far, we have looked at the differences between screening and signaling models in the context of well specified game theoretic models in which the key difference is who moves first, the informed or the uninformed. In real life, there is no rule maker who specifies that, say, the informed player should move first. Sometimes, there is a natural

---

[16] In both of the previous cases (where the single crossing property is not satisfied, and the single contract separating equilibrium involves positive profits, and where there does not exist a Rothschild Stiglitz single contract equilibrium, because the pooling contract can upset the separating equilibrium), Pareto optimality entails cross-subsidization.

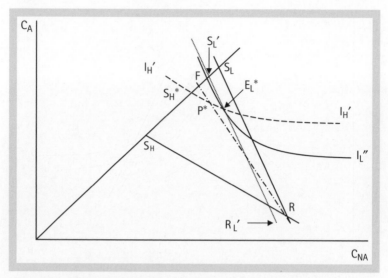

Fig. IIB.2b. Separating equilibrium breaks pooling contract

Notes: There is a separating equilibrium if firms can issue two types of contracts in a fixed proportion N_H / N_L. A pair of contracts, $\{S_H{}^*, E_L{}^*\}$ which left the high risk individuals on the same indifference curve as P^* but provided complete insurance would entail a lower subsidy to the high risk individuals than the contract P^* and would make low risk individuals better off. $E_L{}^*$ is defined as the intersection of the indifference curve $I_H{}' \; I_H{}'$, the high risk individual's indifference curve through $S_H{}^*$, and the "break-even locus for the low risk individuals." This is the locus of contracts for the low risk individuals which, in conjunction with the losses on the high risk contracts, breaks even for the firm as a whole. Taking into account the subsidy that is provided to the high risk individuals and given that the ratio of sales of contract $S_H{}^*$ to sales of the contract $E_L{}^*$ is equal to N_H / N_L in equilibrium, we draw this locus as $R_L{}' \; S_L{}'$, parallel to $R S_L$ but shifted down by the amount of the subsidy. By further subsidizing the high risk individuals, the low risk individuals may be able to do even better as illustrated in Figure IIB.2c.

order to moves: people decide on their education levels before they enter the job market. Ordinary buyers of insurance do not make offers to insurance companies; the insurance companies offer a set of policies. In the first context, the model where the informed move first seems natural; in the second, the model where the uninformed move first seems more appropriate (though in both cases, one can raise questions about whether individuals are really more informed than firms). But large buyers of insurance may approach insurance companies with a proposal, one which signals that they are low risk. If the signaling equilibrium which emerged in such a market involved pooling, then it would make sense for some insurance firm to make an offer that would attract the good risks. The order of moves should be determined endogenously, as part of a meta game. When that is done, Chapter 8 argues, that in those instances where the signaling equilibrium differs from the screening equilibrium,[17] the signaling results are not robust: in a meta game, there would be an incentive for a prior move by the uninformed.

Game theory has been useful in helping us think rigorously about equilibria. But too often, there are a multiplicity of equilibrium concepts, and a multiplicity of

---

[17] And in particular, does not maximize the welfare of the low risk (high ability) individuals

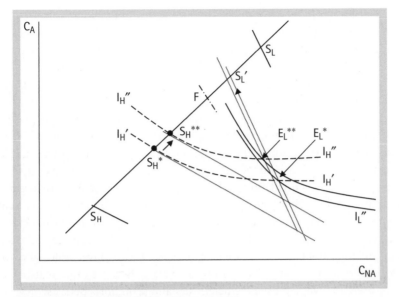

Fig. IIB.2c. Optimal subsidy, focused plot

Notes: The Pareto efficient set of contracts is $\{S_H{}^{**}, E_L{}^{**}\}$, where $E_L{}^{**}$ is at the intersection of the high risk individual's indifference curve through $S_H{}^{**}$ and the "modified" break-even curve for the low risk types (the break-even locus which has been shifted further down to finance the subsidies to the high risk individual).

equilibria within some of the familiar concepts. Standard game theory has little to say about reasonable out of equilibrium inferences, or about what are reasonable "structures" for games (where both moves and players may be endogenous), and these appear to be crucial in determining what are sustainable as equilibria. The analysis of this paper (and this introduction) suggests that introducing a little economics into the analysis may go a long way into narrowing the set of equilibria.[18]

At the same time, this broad discussion of equilibria in screening/signaling models may in fact provide us insight into the persistence of seemingly anomalous behavior. For instance, in my 1973 paper on taxation (Stiglitz 1973d), I explained that there were

[18] Similar results hold in models with a continuum of types, generating a continuum of, say, contracts. In this context, an individual of a given type offering a contract currently being offered by another type will be inferred to be of that type, so long as the set of contracts satisfy the self-selection constraints. The only problem of "out of equilibrium" inferences arises at the end points, e.g. if in the putative equilibrium, the highest risk individual offers a contract with a positive deductibility, all individuals of that type could offer a zero profit, zero deductible policy which would make themselves better off. Clearly, such a policy would be accepted by an insurance company, and hence the only plausible equilibria entail the highest risk individual offering a zero deductible policy. In this case, there is a possible difference in the set of screening and signaling equilibria. A central result of Rothschild-Stiglitz is that there is no competitive equilibria in this model, which translates (in this context) into no screening equilibrium. The signaling equilibrium just described cannot be sustained as a screening equilibrium, because some insurance firm would offer a "pooling" policy which would be purchased by high risk (but not just the highest risk) individuals and make a profit. But, as Rothschild and Stiglitz explain, this pooling contract cannot be part of a screening equilibrium, because it would pay some insurance firm to offer a contract which would only be purchased by the lowest risk individuals (of the "pooled" group).

ways of distributing money from the corporate sector to the household sector which resulted in lower levels of taxation than paying dividends. Some have suggested that dividends act as a signal; but the analysis of my 1973 paper makes clear that firms could just as effectively signal by buying back shares—with a far lower tax burden. But the spirit of signaling theory is that inefficient signals may persist, especially in contexts where market participants are ill-informed; they may not understand that the same information could just as effectively be conveyed by share buybacks. They may not know how to interpret these share buybacks; they have come to believe that dividends signal firms earnings and prospects, and to believe that firms understand this; a firm which replaces a dividend with a share buyback is treated just like any other firm that cuts its dividends; and the punishment it receives provides a strong lesson to any who deviate from the equilibrium. Of course, owners of closely held firms who are not planning to sell their shares in the near future may not care about the market's response; and they have an incentive to buy back shares and distribute firms to the household sector in other tax-preferred ways. Over time, since writing my 1973 paper, an increasing share of profits have thus come to be redistributed in these tax-preferred ways; yet the inefficient signaling equilibria persists.

CHAPTER 5

....

EQUILIBRIUM IN COMPETITIVE INSURANCE MARKETS: AN ESSAY ON THE ECONOMICS OF IMPERFECT INFORMATION*

....

INTRODUCTION

....

ECONOMIC theorists traditionally banish discussions of information to footnotes. Serious consideration of costs of communication, imperfect knowledge, and the like would, it is believed, complicate without informing. This paper, which analyzes competitive markets in which the characteristics of the commodities exchanged are

* Written with Michael Rothschild. This work was supported by National Science Foundation Grants SOC 74-22182 at the Institute for Mathematical Studies in the Social Sciences, Stanford University and SOC 73-05510 at Princeton University. The authors are indebted to Steve Salop, Frank Hahn, and Charles Wilson for helpful comments, and to the participants in the seminars at the several universities at which these ideas were presented. © 1976 by the President and Fellows of Harvard College. Published by John Wiley & Sons, Inc. Reprinted with permission from *The Quarterly Journal of Economics*, 90(4), pp. 629–49. This paper was part of a Symposium on the economics of information

not fully known to at least one of the parties to the transaction, suggests that this comforting myth is false. Some of the most important conclusions of economic theory are not robust to considerations of imperfect information.

We are able to show that not only may a competitive equilibrium not exist, but when equilibria do exist, they may have strange properties. In the insurance market, upon which we focus much of our discussion, sales offers, at least those that survive the competitive process, do not specify a price at which customers can buy all the insurance they want, but instead consist of both a price and a quantity—a particular amount of insurance that the individual can buy at that price. Furthermore, if individuals were willing or able to reveal their information, everybody could be made better off. By their very being, high-risk individuals cause an externality: the low-risk individuals are worse off than they would be in the absence of the high-risk individuals. However, the high-risk individuals are no better off than they would be in the absence of the low-risk individuals.

These points are made in the next section by analysis of a simple model of a competitive insurance market. We believe that the lessons gleaned from our highly stylized model are of general interest, and attempt to establish this by showing in Section II that our model is robust and by hinting (space constraints prevent more) in the conclusion that our analysis applies to many other situations.

I THE BASIC MODEL

Most of our argument can be made by analysis of a very simple example. Consider an individual who will have an income of size W if he is lucky enough to avoid accident. In the event an accident occurs, his income will be only $W - d$. The individual can insure himself against this accident by paying to an insurance company a premium α_1, in return for which he will be paid $\hat{\alpha}_2$ if an accident occurs. Without insurance his income in the two states, "accident," "no accident," was $(W, W - d)$; with insurance it is now $(W - \alpha_1, W - d + \alpha_2)$, where $\alpha_2 = \hat{\alpha}_2 - \alpha_1$. The vector $\alpha = (\alpha_1, \alpha_2)$ completely describes the insurance contact.[1]

[1] Actual insurance contracts are more complicated because a single contract will offer coverage against many potential losses. A formal generalization of the scheme above to cover this case is straightforward. Suppose that an individual will, in the absence of insurance, have an income of W_i if state i occurs. An insurance contract is simply an n-tuple $(\alpha_1, \ldots, \alpha_n)$ whose i-th coordinate describes the net payment of the individual to the insurance company if state i occurs. We confine our discussion to the simple case mentioned in the text, although it could be trivially extended to this more complicated case.

Many insurance contracts are not as complicated as the n-tuples described above—Blue Cross schedules listing maximum payments for specific illnesses and operations are an isolated example—but are instead resolvable into a fixed premium and a payment schedule that is in general a simple function of the size of the loss such as $F(L) = \text{Max}[0, c(L - D)]$, where $c \times 100\%$ is the co-insurance rate and D is the deductible. With such a contract when a loss occurs, determining its size is often a serious

I.1 Demand for Insurance Contracts

On an insurance market, insurance contracts (the a's) are traded. To describe how the market works, it is necessary to describe the supply and demand functions of the participants in the market. There are only two kinds of participants, individuals who buy insurance and companies that sell it. Determining individual demand for insurance contracts is straightforward. An individual purchases an insurance contract so as to alter his pattern of income across states of nature. Let W_1 denote his income if there is no accident and W_2 his income if an accident occurs; the expected utility theorem states that under relatively mild assumptions his preferences for income in these two states of nature are described by a function of the form,

$$\hat{V}(p, W_1, W_2) = (1 - p)U(W_1) + pU(W_2), \tag{1}$$

where $U(\ )$ represents the utility of money income[2] and p the probability of an accident. Individual demands may be derived from (1). A contract a is worth $V(p, a) = \hat{V}(p, W - a_1, W - d + a_2)$. From all the contracts the individual is offered, he chooses the one that maximizes $V(p, a)$. Since he always has the option of buying no insurance, an individual will purchase a contract a only if $V(p, a) \geq V(p, 0) = \hat{V}(p, W, W - d)$. We assume that persons are identical in all respects save their probability of having an accident and that they are risk averse ($U'' < 0$); thus $V(p, a)$ is quasi-concave.

I.2 Supply of Insurance Contracts

It is less straightforward to describe how insurance companies decide which contracts they should offer for sale and to which people. The return from an insurance contract is a random variable. We assume that companies are risk-neutral, that they are concerned only with expected profits, so that contract a when sold to an individual who has a probability of incurring an accident of p, is worth

$$\pi(p, a) = (1 - p)a_1 - pa_2 = a_1 - p(a_1 + a_2). \tag{2}$$

Even if firms are not expected profit maximizers, on a well-organized competitive market they are likely to behave as if they maximized (2).[3]

problem. In other words, finding out exactly what state of the world has occurred is not always easy. We ignore these problems. A large literature analyzes optimal insurance contracts. See, for example, Arrow (1971) and Borch (1968).

   [2] We assume that preferences are not state-dependent.
   [3] Since the theory of the firm behavior under uncertainty is one of the more unsettled areas of economic theory, we cannot look to it for the sort of support of any assumption we might make, which the large body of literature devoted to the expected utility theorem provides for equation (1) above. Nonetheless, two arguments (and the absence of a remotely as attractive distinguishable alternative) justify (2): the first is the rather vaguely supported but widely held proposition that companies owned by stockholders who themselves hold diversified portfolios ought to maximize their expected profits; management that does not follow this policy will be displaced. The second supposes that insurance companies are held by a large number of small share holders each of whom receives a small share of the

Insurance companies have financial resources such that they are willing and able to sell any number of contracts that they think will make an expected profit.[4] The market is competitive in that there is free entry. Together these assumptions guarantee that any contract that is demanded and that is expected to be profitable will be supplied.

I.3 Information about Accident Probabilities

We have not so far discussed how customers and companies come to know or estimate the parameter p, which plays such a crucial role in the valuation formulae (1) and (2). We make the bald assumption that individuals know their accident probabilities, while companies do not. Since insurance purchasers are identical in all respects save their propensity to have accidents, the force of this assumption is that companies cannot discriminate among their potential customers on the basis of their characteristics. This assumption is defended and modified in subsection II.1.

A firm may use its customers' market behavior to make inferences about their accident probabilities. Other things equal, those with high accident probabilities will demand more insurance than those who are less accident-prone. Although possibly accurate, this is not a profitable way of finding out about customer characteristics. Insurance companies want to know their customers' characteristics in order to decide on what terms they should offer to let them buy insurance. Information that accrues after purchase may be used only to lock the barn after the horse has been stolen.

It is often possible to force customers to make market choices in such a way that they both reveal their characteristics and make the choices the firm would have wanted them to make had their characteristics been publicly known. In their contribution to this symposium, Salop and Salop call a market device with these characteristics a *self-selection mechanism*. Analysis of the functioning of self-selection mechanisms on competitive markets is a major focus of this paper.

firm's profits. If the risks insured against are independent or otherwise diversifiable, then the law of large numbers guarantees that each shareholder's return will be approximately constant and any individual insurance contract contributes to his profits only through its expected value. In this case stockholders' interests will be well served if, and only if, management maximizes expected profits.

A variant of the second argument is obtained by considering the case in which shareholders and policyholders are the same people, or in more familiar terms, when the insurance company is a mutual company. In this case the insurance company is just a mechanism for risk pooling. Under conditions where diversification is possible, each contract's contribution to the company's dividend (or loss) is proportional to its expected value.

[4] The same kinds of arguments used to justify (2)—in particular the appeal to the law of large numbers—can be used to justify this assumption. Weaker conditions than independence will suffice. See Revesz (1960), p. 190, for a theorem that states roughly that, if insurance contracts can be arranged in space so that even though contracts that are close to one another are not independent, those that are far apart are approximately independent, then the average return from all contracts is equal to its expected value with probability one. Thus, an insurance company that holds a large number of health policies should be risk-neutral, even though the fact that propinquity carries illness implies that not all insured risks are independent. Some risks that cannot be diversified; i.e., the risk of nuclear war (or of a flood or a plague) cannot be spread by appeal to the law of large numbers. Our model applies to diversifiable risks. This class of risks is considerably larger than the independent ones.

I.4 Definition of Equilibrium

We assume that customers can buy only one insurance contract. This is an objectionable assumption. It implies, in effect, that the seller of insurance specifies both the prices and quantities of insurance purchased. In most competitive markets, sellers determine only price and have no control over the amount their customers buy. Nonetheless, we believe that what we call price and quantity competition is more appropriate for our model of the insurance market than traditional price competition. We defend this proposition at length in subsection II.2 below.

Equilibrium in a competitive insurance market is a set of contracts such that, when customers choose contracts to maximize expected utility, (i) no contracts in the equilibrium set makes negative expected profits; and (ii) there is no contract outside the equilibrium set that, if offered, will make a nonnegative profit. This notion of equilibrium is of the Cournot-Nash type; each firm assumes that the contracts its competitors offer are independent of its own actions.

I.5 Equilibrium with Identical Customers

Only when customers have different accident probabilities will insurance companies have imperfect information. We examine this case below. To illustrate our, mainly graphical, procedure, we first analyze the equilibrium of a competitive insurance market with identical customers.[5]

In Figure I the horizontal and vertical axes represent income in the states: no accident, accident, respectively. The point E with coordinates $(\hat{W}_1, \hat{W}_2)$ is the typical customer's uninsured state. Indifference curves are level sets of the function of equation (1). Purchasing the insurance policy $\alpha = (\alpha_1, \alpha_2)$ moves the individual from E to the point $(\hat{W}_1 - \alpha_1, \hat{W}_2 + \alpha_2)$.

Free entry and perfect competition will ensure that policies bought in competitive equilibrium make zero expected profits, so that if α is purchased,

$$\alpha_1(1 - p) - \alpha_2 p = 0. \tag{3}$$

The set of all policies that break even is given analytically by (3) and diagrammatically by the line EF in Figure I, which is sometimes referred to as the fair-odds line. The equilibrium policy α^* maximizes the individual's (expected) utility and just breaks even. Purchasing α^* locates the customer at the tangency of the indifference curve with the fair-odds line. α^* satisfies the two conditions of equilibrium: (i) it breaks even; (ii) selling any contract preferred to it will bring insurance companies expected losses.

Since customers are risk-averse, the point α^* is located at the intersection of the 45°-line (representing equal income in both states of nature) and the fair-odds line.

---

[5] The analysis is identical if individuals have different p's, but companies know the accident probabilities of their customers. The market splits into several submarkets—one for each different p represented. Each submarket has the equilibrium described here.

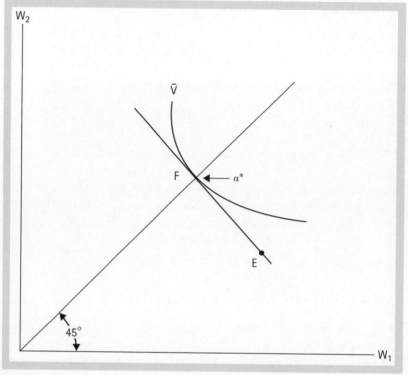

Fig. I.

In equilibrium each customer buys complete insurance at actuarial odds. To see this, observe that the slope of the fair-odds line is equal to the ratio of the probability of not having an accident to the probability of having an accident $((1 - p)/p)$, while the slope of the indifference curve (the marginal rate of substitution between income in the state no accident to income in the state accident) is $[U'(W_1)(1 - p)]/[U'(W_2)p]$, which, when income in the two states is equal, is $(1 - p)/p$, independent of U.

I.6 Imperfect Information: Equilibrium with Two Classes of Customers

Suppose that the market consists of two kinds of customers: low-risk individuals with accident probability p^L, and high-risk individuals with accident probability $p^H > p^L$. The fraction of high-risk customers is λ, so the average accident probability is $\bar{p} = \lambda p^H + (1 - \lambda)p^L$. This market can have only two kinds of equilibria: *pooling equilibria* in which both groups buy the same contract, and *separating equilibria* in which different types purchase different contracts.

A simple argument establishes that *there cannot be a pooling equilibrium*. The point E in Figure II is again the initial endowment of all customers. Suppose that α is a

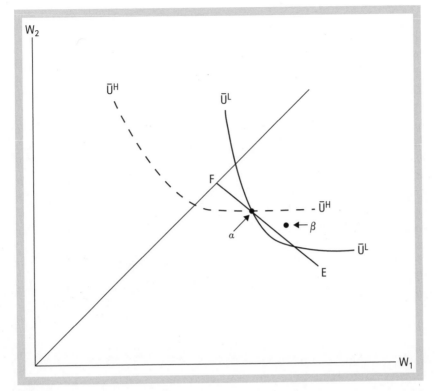

Fig. II.

pooling equilibrium and consider $\pi(\bar{p}, \alpha)$. If $\pi(\bar{p}, \alpha) < 0$, then firms offering α lose money, contradicting the definition of equilibrium. If $\pi(\bar{p}, \alpha) > 0$, then there is a contract that offers slightly more consumption in each state of nature, which still will make a profit when all individuals buy it. All will prefer this contract to α, so α cannot be an equilibrium. Thus, $\pi(\bar{p}, \alpha) = 0$, and α lies on the market odds line EF (with slope $(1 - \bar{p})/\bar{p}$).

It follows from (1) that at α the slope of the high-risk indifference curve through α, $\bar{U}^H$, is $(p^L/1 - p^L)(1 - p^H/p^H)$ times the slope of $\bar{U}^L$, the low-risk indifference curve through α. In this figure $\bar{U}^H$ is a broken line, and $\bar{U}^L$ a solid line. The curves intersect at α; thus there is a contract, β in Figure II, near α, which low-risk types prefer to α. The high risk prefer α to β. Since β is near α, it makes a profit when the less risky buy it, $(\pi(p^L, \beta) \simeq \pi(p^L, \alpha) > \pi(\bar{p}, \alpha) = 0)$. The existence of β contradicts the second part of the definition of equilibrium; α cannot be an equilibrium.

If there is an equilibrium, each type must purchase a separate contract. Arguments, which are, we hope, by now familiar, demonstrate that each contract in the equilibrium set makes zero profits. In Figure III the low-risk contract lies on line EL (with slope $(1 - p^L)/p^L$), and the high-risk contract on line EH (with slope $(1 - p^H)/p^H$). As was shown in the previous subsection, the contract on EH most preferred by high-risk customers gives complete insurance.

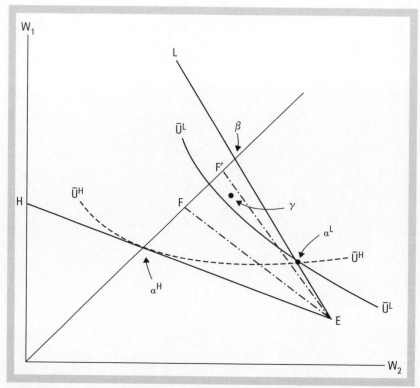

Fig. III.

This is a^H in Figure III; it must be part of any equilibrium. Low-risk customers would, of all contracts on EL, most prefer contract β which, like a^H, provides complete insurance. However, β offers more consumption in each state than a^H, and high-risk types will prefer it to a^H. If β and a^H are marketed, both high- and low-risk types will purchase β. The nature of imperfect information in this model is that insurance companies are unable to distinguish among their customers. All who demand β must be sold β. Profits will be negative; (a^H, β) is not an equilibrium set of contracts.

An equilibrium contract for low-risk types must not be more attractive to high-risk types than a^H; it must lie on the southeast side of U^H, the high-risk indifference curve through a^H. We leave it to the reader to demonstrate that of all such contracts, the one that low-risk types most prefer is a^L, the contract at the intersection of EL and U^H in Figure III. This establishes that *the set (a^H, a^L) is the only possible equilibrium for a market with low- and high-risk customers.*[6] However, (a^H, a^L) may not be an equilibrium. Consider the contract γ in Figure III. It lies above U^L, the low-risk indifference curve through a^L and also above U^H. If γ is offered, both low- and high-risk types will purchase it in preference to either a^H or a^L. If it makes a profit when both groups buy it, γ will upset the potential equilibrium of (a^H, a^L). γ's profitability

---

[6] This largely heuristic argument can be made completely rigorous. See Wilson (1976).

depends on the composition of the market. If there are sufficiently many high-risk people that *EF* represents market odds, then γ will lose money. If market odds are given by *EF'* (as they will be if there are relatively few high-risk insurance customers), then γ will make a profit. Since (a^H, a^L) is the only possible equilibrium, in this case the competitive insurance market will have no equilibrium.

This establishes that *a competitive insurance market may have no equilibrium.*

We have not found a simple intuitive explanation for this nonexistence; but the following observations, prompted by Frank Hahn's note (1973), may be suggestive. The information that is revealed by an individual's choice of an insurance contract depends on all the other insurance policies offered; there is thus a fundamental informational externality that each company, when deciding on which contract it will offer, fails to take into account. Given any set of contracts that breaks even, a firm may enter the market using the informational structure implicit in the availability of that set of contracts to make a profit; at the same time it forces the original contracts to make a loss. But as in any Nash equilibrium, the firm fails to take account of the consequences of its actions, and in particular, the fact that when those policies are no longer offered, the informational structure will have changed and it can no longer make a profit.

We can characterize the conditions under which an equilibrium does not exist. An equilibrium will not exist if the costs to the low-risk individual of pooling are low (because there are relatively few of the high-risk individuals who have to be subsidized, or because the subsidy per individual is low, i.e., when the probabilities of the two groups are not too different), or if their costs of separating are high. The costs of separating arise from the individual's inability to obtain complete insurance. Thus, the costs of separating are related to the individuals' attitudes toward risk. Certain polar cases make these propositions clear. If $p^L = 0$, it never pays the low-risk individuals to pool, and by continuity, for sufficiently small p^L it does not pay to pool. Similarly, if individuals are risk-neutral, it never pays to pool; if they are infinitely risk averse with utility functions

$$\bar{V}(p, W_1, W_2) = \text{Min}(W_1, W_2), \tag{1'}$$

it always pays to pool.

I.7 Welfare Economics of Equilibrium

One of the interesting properties of the equilibrium is that the presence of the high-risk individuals exerts a negative externality on the low-risk individuals. The externality is completely dissipative; there are losses to the low-risk individuals, but the high-risk individuals are no better off than they would be in isolation.

If only the high-risk individuals would admit to their having high accident probabilities, all individuals would be made better off without anyone being worse off.

The separating equilibrium we have described may not be Pareto optimal even relative to the information that is available. As we show in subsection II.3 below, there may exist a pair of policies that break even together and that make both groups better off.

II ROBUSTNESS

The analysis of Section I had three principal conclusions: First, competition on markets with imperfect information is more complex than in standard models. Perfect competitors may limit the quantities their customers can buy, not from any desire to exploit monopoly power, but simply in order to improve their information. Second, equilibrium may not exist. Finally, competitive equilibria are not Pareto optimal. It is natural to ask whether these conclusions (particularly the first, which was an assumption rather than a result of the analysis) can be laid to the special and possibly strained assumptions of our model. We think not. Our conclusions (or ones very like) must follow from a serious attempt to comprehend the workings of competition with imperfect and asymmetric information. We have analyzed the effect of changing our model in many ways. The results were always essentially the same.

Our attempts to establish robustness took two tacks. First, we showed that our results did not depend on the simple technical specifications of the model. This was tedious, and we have excised most of the details from the present version. The reader interested in analysis of the effects (distinctly minor) of changing our assumptions that individuals are alike in all respects save their accident probabilities, that there are only two kinds of customers, and that the insurance market lasts but a single period, is referred to earlier versions of this paper.[7] An assessment of the importance of the assumption that individuals know their accident probabilities, while insurance companies do not (which raises more interesting issues), is given in subsection II.1 below.

Another approach to the question of robustness is the subject of the next three subsections. In them we question the behavioral assumptions and the equilibrium concepts used in Section I.

---

[7] See Rothschild and Stiglitz (1975). One curious result of these investigations should be mentioned. In other areas of economic theory where existence of equilibrium has been a problem, smoothing things by introducing a continuum of individuals of different types can insure existence. Not so here. If there is a continuous distribution of accident probabilities (but customers are otherwise identical), then equilibrium never exists. There is an intuitive explanation for this striking result. We argued above that, if accident probabilities were close together, then equilibrium would not exist. When there is a continuum of probabilities, there always are individuals with close probabilities with whom it pays to "pool." For a proof of this result, which is not elementary, see Riley (1979).

II.1 Information Assumptions

Suppose that there are two groups of customers and that not all individuals within each group have the same accident probability. The average accident probability of one group is greater than that of the other; individuals within each group know the mean accident probability for members of their group, but do not know their own accident probabilities. As before, the insurance company cannot tell directly the accident probability of any particular individual, or even the group to which he belongs. For example, suppose that some persons occasionally drink too much, while the others almost never drink. Insurance firms cannot discover who drinks and who does not. Individuals know that drinking affects accident probabilities, but it affects different people differently. Each individual does not know how it will affect him.

In such a situation the expected utility theorem states that individuals make (and behave according to) estimates of their accident probabilities; if these estimates are unbiased in the sense that the average accident probability of those who estimate their accident probability to be p actually is p, then the analysis goes through as before.

Unbiasedness seems a reasonable assumption (what is a more attractive alternative?). However, not even this low level of correctness of beliefs is required for our conclusions. Suppose, for example, that individuals differ both with respect to their accident probabilities and to their risk aversion, but they all assume that their own accident probabilities are $\bar{p}$. If low-risk individuals are less risk-averse on average, then there will not exist a pooling equilibrium; there may exist no equilibrium at all; and if there does exist an equilibrium, it will entail partial insurance for both groups. Figure IV shows that there will not exist a pooling equilibrium. If there were a pooling equilibrium, it would clearly be with complete insurance at the market odds, since both groups' indifference curves have the slope of the market odds line there. If the low-risk individuals are less risk-averse, then the two indifference curves are tangent at F, but elsewhere the high-risk individuals' indifference curve lies above the low-risk individuals' indifference curve. Thus, any policy in the shaded area between the two curves will be purchased by the low-risk individuals in preference to the pooling contract at F.

Other such cases can be analyzed, but we trust that the general principle is clear. Our pathological conclusions do not require that people have particularly good information about their accident probabilities. They will occur under a wide variety of circumstances, including the appealing case of unbiasedness. Neither insurance firms nor their customers have to be perfectly informed about the differences in risk properties that exist among individuals: What is required is that individuals with different risk properties differ in some characteristic that can be linked with the purchase of insurance and that, somehow, insurance firms discover this link.

II.2 Price Competition Versus Quantity Competition

One can imagine our model of the insurance market operating in two distinct modes. The first, price competition, is familiar to all students of competitive markets.

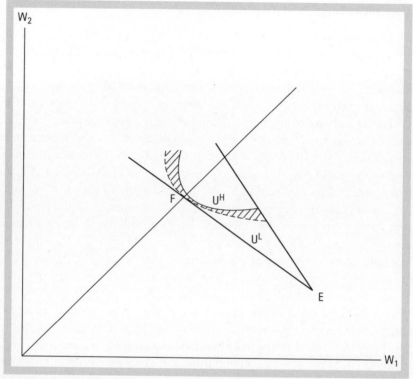

Fig. IV.

Associated with any insurance contract α is a number $q(\alpha) = \alpha_1/\alpha_2$, which, since it is the cost per unit coverage, is called the price of insurance. Under price competition, insurance firms establish a price of insurance and allow their customers to buy as much or as little insurance as they want at that price. Thus, if contract α is available from a company, so are the contracts 2α and $(1/2)\alpha$; the former pays twice as much benefits (and costs twice as much in premiums) as α; the latter is half as expensive and provides half as much coverage.

Opposed to price competition is what we call price and quantity competition. In this regime companies may offer a number of different contracts, say $\alpha^1, \alpha^2, \ldots, \alpha^n$. Individuals may buy at most one contract. They are not allowed to buy arbitrary multiples of contracts offered, but must instead settle for one of the contracts explicitly put up for sale. A particular contract specifies both a price and a quantity of insurance. Under price and quantity competition it is conceivable that insurance contracts with different prices of insurance will exist in equilibrium; people who want more insurance may be willing to pay a higher price for it (accept less favorable odds) than those who make do with shallower coverage. Under price competition customers will buy insurance only at the lowest price quoted in the market.

The argument of Section I depends heavily on our assumption that price and quantity competition, and not simply price competition, characterizes the competitive insurance market. This assumption is defended here. The argument is basically quite simple. Price competition is a special case of price and quantity competition. Nothing in the definition of price and quantity competition prevents firms from offering for sale a set of contracts with the same price of insurance. Since the argument above characterized all equilibria under price and quantity competition, it also characterized all equilibria when some firms set prices and others set prices and quantities. Thus, it must be that price competition cannot compete with price and quantity competition.[8]

This argument hinges on one crucial assumption: regardless of the form of competition, customers purchase but a single insurance contract or equivalently that the total amount of insurance purchased by any one customer is known to all companies that sell to him. We think that this is an accurate description of procedures on at least some insurance markets. Many insurance policies specify either that they are not in force if there is another policy or that they insure against only the first, say, $1,000 of losses suffered. That is, instead of being a simple bet for or against the occurrence of a particular event, an insurance policy is a commitment on the part of the company to restore at least partially the losses brought about by the occurrence of that event. The person who buys two $1,000 accident insurance policies does not have $2,000 worth of protection. If an accident occurs, all he gets from his second policy is the privilege of watching his companies squabble over the division of the $1,000 payment. There is no point in buying more than one policy.

Why should insurance markets operate in this way? One simple and obvious explanation is moral hazard. Because the insured can often bring about, or at least make more likely, the event being insured against, insurance companies want to limit the amount of insurance their customers buy. Companies want to see that their customers do not purchase so much insurance that they have an interest in an accident occurring. Thus, companies will want to monitor the purchases of their customers. Issuing contracts of the sort described above is the obvious way to do so.

A subtler explanation for this practice is provided by our argument that price and quantity competition can dominate price competition. If the market is in equilibrium under price competition, a firm can offer a contract, specifying price and quantity, that will attract the low-risk customers away from the companies offering contracts specifying price alone. Left with only high-risk customers, these firms will lose money. This competitive gambit will successfully upset the price competition equilibria if the entering firm can be assured that those who buy its contracts hold no other insurance. Offering insurance that pays off only for losses not otherwise insured is a way to guarantee this.

---

[8] We leave to the reader a detailed proof. A sketch follows. Suppose that there are two groups in the population. If the price of insurance is q, high- and low-risk customers will buy $a^H(q)$ and $a^L(q)$, respectively. It is easy to figure out what total insurance company profits, $P(q)$, are. The equilibrium price q^* is the smallest q such that $P(q) = 0$. Since $P(q)$ is continuous in q and it is easy to find q such that $P(q) > 0$ and $P(q) < 0$, such a q^* exists. To show that price competition will not survive, it is only necessary to show that $(a^H(q^*), a^L(q^*))$ is not an equilibrium set of contracts as defined in subsection I.4 above.

It is sometimes suggested that the term "competitive" can be applied only to markets where there is a single price of a commodity and each firm is a price taker. This seems an unnecessarily restrictive use of the term competitive. The basic idea underlying competitive markets involves free entry and noncollusive behavior among the participants in the market. In some economic environments price taking without quantity restrictions is a natural result of such markets. In the situations described in this paper, this is not so.

II.3 Restrictions on Firm Behavior and Optimal Subsidies

An important simplification of the analysis of Section I was the assumption that each insurance company issued but a single contract. We once thought this constraint would not affect the nature of equilibrium. We argued that in equilibrium firms must make nonnegative profits. Suppose that a firm offers two contracts, one of which makes an expected profit of say, $S, per contract sold, the other an expected loss of $L per contract. The firm can make nonnegative expected profits if the ratio of the profitable to the unprofitable contracts sold is at least μ, where $\mu = L/S$. However, the firm can clearly make more profits if it sells only the contracts on which it makes a profit. It and its competitors have no reason to offer the losing contracts, and in competitive equilibrium, they will not be offered. Since only contracts that make nonnegative profits will be offered, it does not matter, given our assumptions about entry, that firms are assumed to issue only a single contract. If there is a contract that could make a profit, a firm will offer it.

This argument is not correct. The possibility of offering more than one contract is important to firms, and to the nature and existence of equilibrium. Firms that offer several contracts are not dependent on the policies offered by other firms for the information generated by the choices of individuals. By offering a menu of policies, insurance firms may be able to obtain information about the accident probabilities of particular individuals. Furthermore, although there may not be an equilibrium in which the profits from one contract subsidize the losses of another contract, it does not follow that such a pair of contracts cannot break what would otherwise be an equilibrium.

Such a case is illustrated in Figure V. EF is again the market odds line. A separating equilibrium exists $(\bar{a}^H, \bar{a}^L)$. Suppose that a firm offered the two contracts, $a^{H\prime}$ and $a^{L\prime}$; $a^{H\prime}$ makes a loss, $a^{L\prime}$ makes a profit. High-risk types prefer $a^{H\prime}$ to $\bar{a}^H$, and low-risk types prefer $a^{L\prime}$ to $\bar{a}^L$. These two contracts, if offered by a single firm together, do not make losses. The profits from $a^{L\prime}$ subsidize the losses of $a^{H\prime}$. Thus, $(a^{H\prime}, a^{L\prime})$ upsets the equilibrium $(\bar{a}^H, \bar{a}^L)$.

This example points up another possible inefficiency of separating equilibria. Consider the problem of choosing two contracts (a^H, a^L) such that a^L maximizes the utility of the low-risk individual subject to the constraints that (a) the high-risk individual prefers a^H to a^L and (b) the pair of contracts a^H and a^L break even when bought by high- and low-risk types, respectively, in the ratio λ to $(1 - \lambda)$. This is a

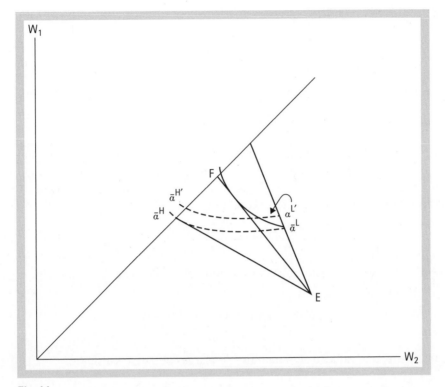

Fig. V.

kind of optimal subsidy problem. If the separating equilibrium, when it exists, does not solve this problem, it is inefficient. Figure V shows that the separating equilibrium can be inefficient in this sense. We now show that if there are enough high-risk people, then the separating equilibrium can be efficient.

The optimal subsidy problem always has a solution (a^{H*}, a^{L*}). The optimal high-risk contract a^{H*} will always entail complete insurance so that $V(p^H, a^{H*}) = U(W - p^H d + a)$, where a is the per capita subsidy of the high risk by the low risk. This subsidy decreases income for each low-risk person by γa (where $\gamma = \lambda/(1 - \lambda)$) in each state. Net of this charge a^{L*} breaks even when low-risk individuals buy it. Thus, $a^{L*} = (a_1 + \gamma a, a_2 - \gamma a)$, where $a_1 = a_2 p^L/(1 - p^L)$.

To find the optimal contract, one solves the following problem: Choose a and a_2 to maximize

$$U(X)(1 - p^L) + U(Z)p^L,$$

subject to

$$U(Y) \geq U(X)(1 - p^H) + U(Z)p^H$$

$$a \geq 0,$$

where

$$X = W_0 - \gamma a - a_2 p^L / (1 - p^L),$$
$$Y = W_0 - p^H d + a,$$

and

$$Z = W_0 - d - \gamma a + a_2.$$

The solution to this problem can be analyzed by standard Kuhn-Tucker techniques. If the constraint $a \geq 0$ is binding at the optimum, then the solution involves no subsidy to the high-risk persons; (a^{H*}, a^{L*}) is the separating equilibrium. It is straightforward but tedious to show that a sufficient condition for this is that

$$\frac{(p^H - p^L)\gamma}{p^L(1 - p)^L} > \frac{U'(Y)[U'(Z) - U'(X)]}{U'(X)U'(Z)} \tag{4}$$

where X, Y, and Z are determined by the optimal a^*, a_2^*. The right-hand side of (4) is always less than

$$\frac{U'(W_0 - d)[U'(W_0 - d) - U'(W_0)]}{U'(W_0)^2}$$

so that there exist values of γ (and thus of λ) large enough to satisfy (4).

II.4 Alternative Equilibrium Concepts

There are a number of other concepts of equilibrium that we might have employed. These concepts differ with respect to assumptions concerning the behavior of the firms in the market. In our model the firm assumes that its actions do not affect the market—the set of policies offered by other firms was independent of its own offering.

In this subsection we consider several other equilibrium concepts, implying either less or more rationality in the market. We could, for instance, call any set of policies that just break even given the set of individuals who purchase them an *informationally consistent equilibrium*. This assumes that the forces for the creation of new contracts are relatively weak (in the absence of profits). Thus, in Figure III, a^H and any contract along the line *EL* below a^L is a set of informationally consistent separating equilibrium contracts; any single contract along the line *EF* is an informationally consistent pooling equilibrium contract. This is the notion of equilibrium that Spence (1973) has employed in most of his work. The longer the lags in the system, the greater the difficulty of competing by offering different contracts, the more stable is an informationally consistent equilibrium. Thus, while this seems to us a reasonable equilibrium concept for the models of educational signaling on which Spence focused, it is less compelling when applied to insurance or credit markets (see Jaffee and Russell's contribution to this symposium (Jaffee and Russell, 1976)).

A *local* equilibrium is a set of contracts such that there do not exist any contracts in the vicinity of the equilibrium contracts that will be chosen and make a positive profit. If we rule out the subsidies of the last subsection, then the set of separating contracts, which maximizes the welfare of low-risk individuals, is a local equilibrium.

The notion that firms experiment with contracts similar to those already on the market motivates the idea of a local equilibrium. Even if firms have little knowledge about the shape of utility functions, and about the proportions of population in different accident probabilities, one would expect that competition would lead to small perturbations around the equilibrium. A stable equilibrium requires that such perturbations not lead to firms making large profits, as would be the case with some perturbations around a pooling point.

These two concepts of equilibrium imply that firms act less rationally than we assumed they did in Section I. It is possible that firms exhibit a greater degree of rationality; that is, firms ought not to take the set of contracts offered by other firms as given, but ought to assume that other firms will act as they do, or at least will respond in some way to the new contract offered by the firm. Hence, in those cases where in our definition there was no equilibrium, because for any set of contracts there is a contract that will break even and be chosen by a subset of the population, given that the contracts offered by the other firms remain unchanged, those contracts that break the equilibrium may not break even if the other firms also change their contracts. The peculiar provision of many insurance contracts, that the effective premium is not determined until the *end* of the period (when the individual obtains what is called a dividend), is perhaps a reflection of the uncertainty associated with who will purchase the policy, which in turn is associated with the uncertainty about what contracts other insurance firms will offer.

Wilson (1976) introduced and analyzed one such nonmyopic equilibrium concept. A Wilson equilibrium is a set of contracts such that, when customers choose among them so as to maximize profits, (a) all contracts make nonnegative profits and (b) there does not exist a new contract (or set of contracts), which, if offered, makes positive profits even when all contracts that lose money as a result of this entry are withdrawn. In the simple model of Section I, such equilibria always exist. Comparing this definition with the one of subsection 1.4 above makes it clear that, when it exists, our separating equilibrium is also a Wilson equilibrium. When this does not exist, the Wilson equilibrium is the pooling contract that maximizes the utility of the low-risk customers. This is β in Figure VI. β dominates the separating pair (a^L, a^H). Consider a contract like γ, which the low risk prefer to β. Under our definition of equilibrium it upsets β. Under Wilson's it does not. When the low risk desert β for γ, it loses money and is withdrawn. Then the high risk also buy γ. When both groups buy γ, it loses money. Thus, γ does not successfully compete against β.

Although this equilibrium concept is appealing, it is not without its difficulties. It seems a peculiar halfway house; firms respond to competitive entry by dropping policies, but not by adding new policies. Furthermore, although counterexamples are very complicated to construct, it appears that a Wilson equilibrium may not exist if groups differ in their attitudes towards risk. Finally, in the absence of collusion

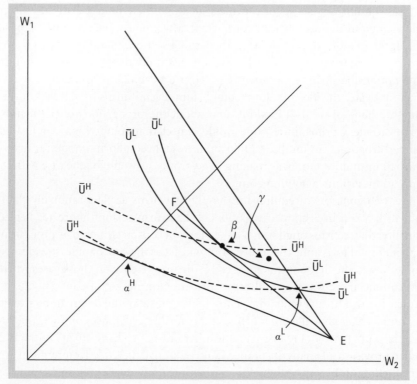

Fig. VI.

or regulation, in a competitive insurance market, it is hard to see how or why any single firm should take into account the consequences of its offering a new policy. On balance, it seems to us that nonmyopic equilibrium concepts are more appropriate for models of monopoly (or oligopoly) than for models of competition.

III CONCLUSION

We began this research with the hope of showing that even a small amount of imperfect information could have a significant effect on competitive markets. Our results were more striking than we had hoped: the single price equilibrium of conventional competitive analysis was shown to be no longer viable; market equilibrium, when it existed, consisted of contracts which specified both prices and quantities; the high-risk (low ability, etc.) individuals exerted a dissipative externality on the low-risk (high ability) individuals; the structure of the equilibrium as well as its existence depended on a number of assumptions that, with perfect information, were inconsequential; and finally, and in some ways most disturbing, under quite plausible conditions equilibrium did not exist.

Our analysis, and our conclusions, extend beyond the simple insurance market described above. The models of educational screening and signaling studied by, among others, Arrow (1973a), Riley (1975), Spence (1973, 1974b), and Stiglitz (1971b, 1972a, 1974b, 1975f), are obvious examples. The other papers in this symposium describe models that can be profitably studied using our techniques and our concepts.[9] Models in which communities choose the level of public goods and individuals choose among communities on the basis of the menu of public goods and taxes that the different communities offer, provide a less obvious but, we think, important case.[10]

Do these theoretical speculations tell us anything about the real world? In the absence of empirical work it is hard to say. The market on which we focused most of our analysis, that for insurance, is probably not competitive; whether our model may partially explain this fact is almost impossible to say. But there are other markets, particularly financial and labor markets, which appear to be competitive and in which imperfect and asymmetric information play an important role. We suspect that many of the peculiar institutions of these markets arise as responses to the difficulties that they, or any competitive market, have in handling problems of information. Establishing (or refuting) this conjecture seems to provide a rich agenda for future research.

---

[9] See Spence (1976b), Akerlof (1976), Salop and Salop (1976), and Jaffee and Russell (1976).

[10] See F. Westhoff's dissertation (1974), and Stiglitz (1974g). A more complete discussion of these is in our earlier working paper referred to in footnote 7 above. Salop and Salop (1972) demonstrated, in an early draft of their symposium paper, that contingent loan plans for repayment of tuition, and their possible defects, can be analyzed along these lines.

CHAPTER 6

COMPETITION AND INSURANCE TWENTY YEARS LATER*

WE are honoured to address the European Group of Risk and Insurance Economists and will take the opportunity to make some reflections on the rather uneasy relationship between insurance and competition.

Economists generally prescribe competition as a solution for markets that do not work well. Competition allocates resources efficiently and encourages innovation and attention to what customers want. Insurance markets differ from most other markets because in insurance markets competition can destroy the market rather than make it work better.

One of the dimensions along which insurance companies compete is underwriting—trying to ensure that the risks covered are "good" risks or that if a high risk is insured, the premium charged is at least commensurate with the potential cost. The resulting partitioning of risk limits the amount of insurance that potential insurance customers can buy. In the extreme case, such competitive behaviour will destroy the insurance market altogether. A simple model illustrates.

* Written with Michael Rothschild. Eighth Geneva Risk Economics Lecture of The Geneva Association, Hanover, 1996. This lecture was originally published in *The Geneva Papers on Risk and Insurance Theory*, 22: 73–79 (1997). We are grateful for helpful discussions with David Bradford, Martin Hellwig, and Philip Kitcher. Reprinted with permission from Geneva Association.

1 A MODEL OF UNDERWRITING

Suppose that a group of individuals have income $Z = W + \tilde{\eta}$, where $\tilde{\eta}$ is an insurable risk and $E[\tilde{\eta}] = 0$. If there is actuarially fair insurance, risk-averse individuals will purchase insurance against $\tilde{\eta}$ and have income W. Suppose that the risk $\tilde{\eta}$ can be decomposed so that $\tilde{\eta} = \tilde{\epsilon} + \tilde{\delta}$ where $E[\tilde{\delta}|\tilde{\epsilon}] = 0$. As a concrete example suppose that $\tilde{\eta}$ represents the risk of getting breast cancer (normalized to have zero mean and converted into monetary units). Then $\tilde{\epsilon}$ can take one of two values depending on whether the person in question has the breast cancer gene, $BrCa_1$. If the gene is present, $\tilde{\epsilon} < 0$; if it is not, $\tilde{\epsilon} > 0$. Here $\tilde{\delta}$ represents the (monetized) risk of incurring breast cancer conditional on one's genetic makeup; clearly, $\tilde{\delta}$ may be dependent on $\tilde{\epsilon}$. If insurance companies know ϵ, they will offer policies conditional on $\tilde{\epsilon}$.

This is a general way of modelling underwriting. When the insurance market divides up risk classes into smaller groups, it is partitioning $\tilde{\eta}$ into the sum $\tilde{\epsilon} + \tilde{\delta}$ and offering to insure only the conditional risks $(\tilde{\delta}|\tilde{\epsilon})$ instead of the unconditional risk $\tilde{\eta}$. In the extreme case, $\sigma^2(\tilde{\epsilon}) = \sigma^2(\tilde{\eta})$, and no insurance is available.

2 WELFARE IMPLICATIONS

Underwriting decreases expected utility for risk-averse individuals who do not know their $\tilde{\epsilon}$. Prior to underwriting, those who bought insurance received a certain income of W. After underwriting, they get the random variable $W + \tilde{\epsilon}$. Since $\sigma^2(\tilde{\epsilon}) > 0$, risk averters prefer the situation before underwriting.

Arguably this analysis is misleading. Individuals may know what their $\tilde{\epsilon}$ is. Those with a good value (those without $BrCa_1$) will be happy not to be pooled with those who had a bad value. This logic drove our previous analysis of the interaction of competition and adverse selection, and we shall return to this point.

The cogency of this argument depends on what one considers the initial situation. Consider a woman who does not know whether she has $BrCa_1$ but does know that the insurance company will test her before it decides what policy to offer her. For this woman, underwriting clearly decreases expected utility.

The same logic applies if we try to evaluate the distribution of income in a society with and without underwriting. Any concave social welfare function will prefer the distribution of income in a society without underwriting to the distribution of income in a society with underwriting. To see this, imagine yourself behind a Rawlsian veil of ignorance; ask whether you would prefer to be born in a society with underwriting or a society without underwriting. If you are risk-averse, you will choose the society without underwriting. This argument assumes that obtaining information about risks is free. Taking account of the fact that underwriting uses real resources strengthens our conclusion. In many cases risk-averse insurance customers would not get the information that is required to decompose the risk $\tilde{\eta}$ into $\tilde{\epsilon} + \tilde{\delta}$. Competing insurance companies will get this information. Thus, competition works to limit the scope of what insurance will do. In this sense there is a fundamental tension between competition and insurance. One of the natural methods that insurance companies use to compete (underwriting) destroys or considerably limits what insurance markets can do.

Recent and projected developments in genetics[1] make the concern about the underwriting of some interest for policy. We are fast accumulating genetic information that will permit tight predictions of future health status. Huntington's Disease is a striking example. Huntington's is a fatal degenerative disease whose symptoms become apparent in young adulthood; Woody Gutherie died of Huntington's. A single dominant gene controls Huntington's Disease. Genetic tests now predict with essentially complete accuracy whether someone will get this fatal degenerative disease. This will make it impossible to insure against Huntington's. It would make sense for insurance companies to exclude Huntington's from general coverage and write riders covering Huntington's only to those willing to get tested. However, testing would reveal whether someone would get the disease so there would be no insurance. Adding to the poignancy of this example is the fact that many at risk for Huntington's have decided not to get tested. They have decided they would rather not know whether they will eventually succumb.[2]

Huntington's is a dramatic but not a singular example. Many common diseases (including breast cancer, asthma, and diabetes) have a genetic base. We soon will have the ability to predict, with much more accuracy than now, who will get many diseases. If this information is available, insurance companies will want to use it for underwriting. The consequence will be a decrease in the risks that people can insure themselves against.

3 ADVERSE SELECTION

The knowledge that modern genetics will soon be able to provide about people's future health status is dramatic. We now stand behind a Rawlsian veil that is about to

[1] See Kitcher (1996) for a good general introduction to these issues.
[2] The standard decision theory approach to the value of information assumes that information *per se* can have no value. Information is valuable if and only if you can use it to make better decisions than you would in its absence. In this theory the value of information is never negative. Within this framework it is not possible to comprehend people actively not wanting information. Yet this does happen. Letting people avoid unwanted information is an important policy problem that developments in genetics will require us to confront. Economists guided by standard decision theory have little to offer to the study of this and similar problems.

be lifted. Policymakers in the United States are trying to grapple with an appropriate response to this coming change. The major policy response in the United States has been to try to prevent insurance companies from using genetic information. This is the recommendation of the prominent group of scientists who work on ELSI (the Ethical, Legal and Social Implications of the Human Genome Project) (see Hudson et al., 1995, p. 391). The Kennedy-Kassebaum bill that just became law in the United States prohibits insurance companies from denying coverage on the basis of pre-existing conditions. Most analysts interpret genetic status as a prime example of a pre-existing condition. Again many analysts expect that this legislation will be followed by legislation that sharply limits the price differences that insurance companies can charge customers on the basis of pre-existing conditions. This, you all understand, has the potential of creating a serious problem of adverse selection.

Adverse selection occurs (in insurance markets)[3] when an insurance customer has more information about his or her health than the insurance company does (or can) use.[4] If insurance companies are prohibited from using information about the genetic traits of their customers then a situation in which customers have more information than insurance companies has been created. Adverse selection actually requires only that individuals with different risk profiles behave differently in some way which the insurance company can exploit. Differences in information do give rise to such behavioural differences.

Our earlier article studied the desultory consequences of mixing insurance and adverse selection. We review some of that argument here. Before doing so, we think it important to make two points. The first is that even though the maximizing behaviour of consumers has some unfortunate consequences, it has beneficial consequences as well. Indeed, most sensible plans to reduce or control the increase of health costs in the United States rely heavily on the assumption that many consumers want to control the amount they spend on healthcare.[5]

The second is that we believe that the evidence is now good that adverse selection is an important phenomenon. We quote from a leading student of healthcare in the United States (Cutler, 1996, p. 30):

---

[3] The phenomenon is, of course, much more general. Insurance markets are not the only contexts in which one party to a contract has information about the likely profitability of the contract that other parties do not (or cannot) use. The literature is replete with examples and analyses of adverse selection in labour, education, product, and other markets.

[4] Laws sometimes prohibit insurance companies from acting on information they may have. In the United States insurance companies cannot offer different contracts to men and women even though their actuarial risks are quite different.

[5] Cutler (1996) argues convincingly that the major driver of medical costs is "the over provision of technologically intensive care". He also presents evidence that most expensive technology does not lead to a lasting improvement of health. Typically, the effects of new procedures on mortality disappear after a year. Cutler uses the example of treatment after a heart attack (where angioplasty is now routine) to illustrate. The best and most expensive treatments (for example, angioplasty or open-heart surgery after a heart attack) prolong life—but not for more than a year. (A representative study looks at survival rates from heart attacks as a function of distance from a hospital that can do a new and expensive catheterization procedure; life expectancy for a few months after the attack is negatively correlated with distance; life expectancy for a year after the attack is only slightly related.) Arguably this is not a situation that consumers want. If they knew what they spent on healthcare bought them, they might spend less.

"Almost all health insurance systems where individuals are allowed choice of insurance have experienced adverse selection. Medicare enrollees who choose managed care...are healthier than...[those] who do not. The Federal Employees Health Benefits Program...has adverse selection between more and less generous policies. The spread in premiums between more and less generous policies is 68 percent greater than benefits alone would dictate...And almost every large firm that has encouraged employee choice has found the cost of the most generous policies increases sufficiently rapidly that these policies are no longer viable (often termed a 'death spiral')."

Adverse selection leads insurance customers to pick and choose among different contracts. Our original article analysed some of the difficulties that arise when companies recognize that consumers with different health risks have different preferences over insurance policies. When companies use this information to compete, there are important consequences. Customers with different health risks will choose different policies. Assume, as we do unless we explicitly state otherwise, that consumers differ only in their health risks. Then, competition ensures that the only possible equilibrium is one in which all the purchasers of an insurance policy have the same risks and one in which each insurance contract breaks even.[6] Competition *separates rather than pools risks* and thus eliminates cross-subsidies among policies.

In our article we noted two further desultory consequences of mixing adverse selection and competition. The first was an observation about social welfare. Consider a *simple* world as one with no moral hazard (the actions of the insured do not influence the probability that he or she will become ill) in which risk-averse consumers purchase insurance contracts from risk-neutral providers of insurance.[7] Elementary arguments imply that in such a simple world with only one class of customers (remember that consumers differ *only* in their riskiness), the best (socially optimal) insurance contract is the one that provides complete insurance at actuarially fair odds.

Now consider a simple world with several classes of customers. Since competition separates, each risk class will purchase a contract that breaks even when only people of that risk class buy it. Call such a set of contracts a *simple separating set of contracts*. Notice that

The set of separating contracts which provides complete insurance to each class of consumers Pareto dominates any other simple separating set of contracts.

The Pareto dominating set of simple separating contracts is a competitive equilibrium when the risk class to which each consumer belongs is publicly observable. (Suppose each person's odds of getting ill were stamped on his or her forehead.) Competitive, risk-neutral companies will not enter into contracts with negative expected value. Insurance companies will refuse to sell to high-risk consumers policies that break even only when purchased by people with low risks.

---

[6] We make the usual assumption that in competition firms make zero profits.

[7] This assumption can of course be justified in a general equilibrium model of a large economy in which consumers own shares of insurance companies.

Now consider what happens when no information about consumers' risk status is available except what insurance companies can glean from their behaviour. To insurance companies all potential customers are the same. We showed in our earlier article that firms respond to this dilemma by selling a set of separating contracts. But the set of separating contracts cannot provide complete insurance, for then all customers would attempt to buy the contract that broke even when only those with the lowest risk bought it. But this contract will lose money when everyone buys it and thus cannot possibly be an equilibrium.

It is clear which simple separating set of contracts *can* be an equilibrium. Consider first those with the highest risk. Let them buy the contract—which we denote a_H—that offers complete insurance at their odds. Now consider the group with the next-highest risk. They will prefer the contract that offers complete insurance at their odds to a_H. Among the contracts that break even when the second-highest risk group buys them, consider those that the second-highest risk group finds equal in value to a_H. Select the one of these contracts that maximizes the utility of the second-highest group and call it a_{H-1}. Let the second-highest risk group buy a_{H-1}. Continue in this way finding break-even contracts that group k finds equal in value to those bought by group $k + 1$, and find the contracts most preferred by group $k + 1$. The sets of contracts $\{a_H, a_{H-1}, \ldots, a_1\}$ is the only possible equilibrium with competition and adverse selection.

Note that $\{a_H, a_{H-1}, \ldots, a_1\}$ is Pareto dominated by a simple separating set of contracts that provide complete insurance. This welfare-dominant set of contracts would be an equilibrium were there complete information. We thus see that a possible consequence of prohibiting insurance companies from using genetic information is to move from the simple separating set of contracts—that would be an equilibrium were genetic information public—to $\{a_H, a_{H-1}, \ldots, a_1\}$.

Our second observation concerned the existence of equilibrium. We established that the only possible equilibrium was the set of contracts $\{a_H, a_{H-1}, \ldots, a_1\}$. It is easy, however, to find examples in which $\{a_H, a_{H-1}, \ldots, a_1\}$ cannot be an equilibrium. Consider the contract β that offers complete insurance and breaks even when every potential consumer buys it. Those with lowest risk might prefer β to a_n because β offers them more insurance albeit at worse odds than a_n. So might all other groups. Then if a company offered β (or even a contract that offered complete insurance at slightly less favourable odds than β), all consumers would prefer this contract to the set $\{a_H, a_{H-1}, \ldots, a_1\}$. This shows that $\{a_H, a_{H-1}, \ldots, a_1\}$ may not be an equilibrium; since it was the only possible equilibrium, we concluded that in an insurance market where competition worked through adverse selection, equilibrium might not exist.

Since we wrote our article much hard and good work has been devoted to the question of the existence of equilibrium. Some work has established that the problem is more pervasive than we had indicated. We noted that equilibrium would not exist when there were relatively few high-risk individuals. Then for the low risk the gains from distinguishing themselves from the common pool (being able to buy insurance at slightly better odds) are low relative to the costs of separation (purchasing partial insurance). Riley (1979) established that this kind of argument could be extended to show that equilibrium (of the sort we defined) would not exist in a simple world where agents differed continuously in their riskiness.

Other work has taken issue with the concept of equilibrium that we proposed. We defined equilibrium as a Nash equilibrium in insurance contracts. A set of contracts $\{a_H, a_{H-1}, \ldots, a_1\}$ was an equilibrium only if (1) when these contracts were offered and consumers selected from the set to maximize expected utility, each contract made non-negative profits and (2) there did not exist another contract β such that when the set of contracts $\{a_1, a_2, \ldots, a_n, \beta\}$ was offered to consumers and consumers choose contracts to maximize expected utility, β made positive profits.

This seemed to us, in our context, the most natural sort of equilibrium concept. Work since our article has focused on other concepts. We do not present a survey of this work here. Much work that has followed has used (and developed) concepts of game theory to make precise the nature of the game played between insurance companies and customers and focused on the exact sequence of moves that each side (insurers and customers) make. Other work has stressed the calculation of entrants into the markets. As Wilson (1977) pointed out, equilibrium will exist if firms that offer new contracts on the insurance market consider properly what might happen when these contracts drive other contracts out of the market. Others have considered various kinds of mixed strategy equilibria and shown that they exist. We admire the ingenuity, energy, and technical difficulty of this work, but we persist in our belief that the equilibrium concept we originally proposed is the natural one. We doubt that mixed strategies, reaction equilibria, or even carefully staged games play much role in real insurance markets. In addition, many of the proposed equilibrium concepts seem inappropriate for analysing a market where the usual assumptions about atomistic competition would seem to describe consumers. Does it make sense for a small firm to worry that its actions will bring about a collapse of the entire market? We leave it to others to judge whether this reaction reflects wisdom or the incipient senility that comes with age and a concern for practical policy.

What then are we to make of our non-existence result? To us it is an indication that competition does not mix easily with adverse selection and that competitive markets with adverse selection are often unstable. Since the competitive outcome, when it exists, is not a lovely one, this does not strike us as a cause for alarm.

4 CONCLUSION

An important problem, both for theory and policy, is to devise ways of providing health insurance that use the power of competition to bring about efficiencies without severely limiting people's ability to insure against ill fortune. As our ability to predict health outcomes improves, this issue becomes more salient. It would be wrong to imply that better knowledge of the genetic basis of disease can bring only disaster. If used properly, better information can make insurance markets work better.

Up to this point we have assumed that individuals can do nothing to affect their health status. In particular, we have assumed that genetic information is, in the sense of decision theory, information of no value. This is clearly false. Indeed, much of the more mundane promise of the genetic revolution lies precisely in the possibility of alerting some of us of the need to take particular kinds of care. Those with a predisposition to high blood pressure and heart attacks have more reason to moderate their consumption of fats than those without such a predisposition. While risk segmentation in general leads to a diminution of welfare, the threat of risk segmentation can lead people to take efficient care.

Similarly, it is possible that science will provide policymakers and insurance companies with good enough objective information about a consumer's health status that risk adjustment can work. Suppose the objective probability of a consumer contracting a given illness were public knowledge. Then risk adjustment would allow markets to operate competitively and provide complete insurance. Insurance companies would compete to sell policies offering complete insurance. The government would reimburse insurance companies for their expected costs, which would be determined by the (publicly known) health propensities of their customers. Such risk adjustment would remove any incentives for companies to try to use their prospective customers' behaviour to reveal their health status. To date, policymakers have not had enough good information about health status to make risk adjustment practical. It may be that the revolution in genetics will provide insurers and regulators with enough information to make real risk adjustment possible. If this is so, it will truly be a beneficial revolution.

CHAPTER 7

MONOPOLY, NON-LINEAR PRICING AND IMPERFECT INFORMATION: THE INSURANCE MARKET*

INTRODUCTION

IT is well known that, when it is possible, a monopolist can increase his profits by engaging in price discrimination. For price discrimination to be feasible and desirable two conditions need to be satisfied:

(a) the firm must be able to identify two or more groups with different demand functions;

(b) it must not be possible for an "arbitrageur" to equalize the price.

* Reprinted with permission from *The Review of Economic Studies*, 44(3), pp. 407–30, Blackwell publishing. In this chapter, notes are displayed as endnotes, beginning on page 191. The author is indebted to the National Science Foundation for financial support and to J. Mirrlees, K. Roberts, S. Salop and M. Spence for helpful discussions. This paper is part of a Symposium on the economics of information, which included Salop (1977), Grossman (1977b), Green (1977), Butters (1977), Salop and Stiglitz (1977), Wilson (1977), Bradford and Kelejian (1977), Grossman, Kihlstrom, and Mirman (1977), Heal (1977), and Spence (1977a).

Conventional theory has focused on discrimination between two localities (countries) for which the elasticity of demand differs and for which transport costs are sufficiently large to prevent price equalization.

The conventional theory of monopoly has, however, been unnecessarily restrictive in at least two important respects.

(i) First, it assumes the monopolist will charge customers an amount proportional to the quantity consumed (what I shall refer to as a linear price schedule). In fact, such a policy is almost never profit maximizing; i.e. non-linear price schedules, when feasible, are almost always desirable. For instance, if all individuals were identical the firm should charge a fixed fee—equal to the value of the consumer surplus the individual would have enjoyed had a linear price system with price equal marginal cost been employed—plus marginal cost. Not only does this increase profits but it also implies that there is no inefficiency associated with the monopoly. The monopolist introduces inefficiencies because he cannot use a non-linear price schedule, e.g. because of secondary resale markets (which are not likely to be important for many commodities) or because individuals differ and he is unable as a result to act as a perfectly discriminating monopolist. Charging any fixed fee greater than the minimum consumer surplus enjoyed by a consumer would lead to some potential customers not consuming. The firm thus has a trade-off between the number of customers and the profits per customer; and this provides the firm with an incentive to use more complicated non-linear price schedules.

(ii) Secondly, it assumes that the firm has a much more limited ability both to differentiate and discriminate among customers than is, in fact, the case. Location is not the only potential basis of differentiation. The quantity consumed of a commodity often is correlated with the consumer surplus; thus, the quantity consumed may be a basis for discriminating. Other bases may be found: the choice of an insurance contract among a set of available insurance contracts may serve to differentiate customers who differ—either in attitudes towards risk or in the risks they face. These are all examples of what I have called elsewhere *screening devices*—a screening device is any mechanism used to differentiate among individuals—and indeed all of these are examples of the particular kind of screening device called self-selection mechanisms where the action of the individual (e.g. his choice of insurance policy) is the basis of differentiation. The trade-offs involved in the design of the screening mechanism by the monopolist are complicated and provide the basic subject of of this paper.

Most of this paper is devoted to investigating in detail the behaviour of a monopolist in an insurance market. This example is chosen because the behaviour of the competitive analogue market with imperfect information has been analysed in detail, and thus we are able to provide a detailed comparison both of the analytical structure of the problem and of the behaviour of the markets. In both cases individuals are confronted with a choice of insurance contracts, and it is the choices made which provide information to the insurance company. In the competitive market there is no overall planning of the kinds of contracts offered to ensure that the information revealed (say, about the relative probabilities of an accident) are "efficiently" revealed. There was a cost in obtaining the information in that individuals with low probabilities of having an accident obtain only partial insurance. A contract was offered if, given the other contracts being offered, it could make a profit. The consequences for the profits of the other contracts were ignored.

A monopolist, on the other hand, must decide on the whole set of contracts which he makes available. He must worry not only about the information the additional contract provides and about its profitability, but also about the effect of the new contract on the profitability of old contracts; in addition, he is aware that the information provided by a new contract depends on the set of contracts already available.

As a result, as we shall see in our analyses of the insurance market, competitive and monopoly equilibrium differ in far more fundamental ways than the classical argument that the monopolist charges too high a price suggests:

(a) the whole set of contracts which are available will differ in the two equilibria;
(b) the basis for discrimination differs: in competition only differences in risk (e.g. accident probabilities) motivate the attempt to differentiate; in monopoly, anything which gives rise to a difference in demand curves—differences in risk aversion as well as differences in risk—provides a basis of differentiation.

But before turning to a detailed analysis of the insurance market we consider a more general problem of monopoly and price discrimination for which, in some special cases, results may be directly borrowed from a closely related literature: the theory of optimal taxation. (See Mirrlees 1971.)

Both the problem of the monopolist and the optimal taxation problem can be viewed as screening problems. The monopolist would like to distinguish among individuals in order to charge them a different price; in the optimal tax problem the government would like to distinguish among individuals in order to tax them according to their "ability to pay". If it had perfect information it would levy a lump sum tax on their "earning ability"; in fact, it cannot observe that directly. Hence income earned serves as a screening device. There are other possible screening devices. If there are large differences among individuals with respect to their attitudes to the leisure–consumption trade-off then the income tax may not be as good a *screening device* as perhaps a housing tax, just as in the insurance model, if attitudes towards risk differ greatly the policy purchased may not serve as a very good screening device (i.e. the accident probabilities for individuals who purchase different policies may not differ markedly). For a more extended discussion of taxation and screening, see Atkinson and Stiglitz (1976).

In this paper we focus only on a limited set of potential screening devices for the monopolist, the quantity of various commodities purchased.

But even this restricted analysis provides an explanation of a number of phenomena observed in non-competitive markets: quantity discounts, tie-in sales, commodity bundling, etc. (See also Adams and Yellen 1976, and Spence 1977.) The paper by Salop (1977) in this symposium provides another example of an ingenious screening device.

1 A General Monopoly-Price Discrimination Problem

1.1 A General Formulation

Consider a firm which has a monopoly over a set of commodities. There is a cost associated with producing a total quantity of the goods, $X_1, \ldots, X_m$, given by $C(X_1, \ldots, X_m)$. The jth individual has a utility function defined over his consumption of the m commodities $(x_1^j, \ldots, x_m^j) = \underline{x}^j$, and his expenditure on other goods, which we shall denote by x_0^j. Different individuals differ in a systematic and continuous way (say in income); thus, we write the utility of an individual of type θ as:

$$U^j = U^j(x_0^j, \ldots, x_m^j; \theta).$$

The problem of the monopolist is to find a *revenue function* $R(x_1, \ldots, x_m)$ giving the payment which a consumer who purchases a vector of goods $x_1, \ldots, x_m$ from the firm must pay the firm, which maximizes firm profits. For any particular revenue function the jth consumer maximizes his utility.

$$\max U^j(x_0^j, x_1^j, \ldots, x_m^j; \theta) \tag{1.1}$$

subject to his budget constraint

$$R(\underline{x}^j) + x_0^j = W_0^j(\theta), \tag{1.2}$$

where W_0^j represents total available wealth.

The solution to this yields a vector of consumption for the θ type individual $\underline{x}^j(\theta; R)$, which is written to remind us of the dependence of the consumption vector on the payments function R. Total profits of the firm are then

$$\pi = \int R(\underline{x}^j(\theta; R)dF(\theta)) - C\left(\int \underline{x}^j(\theta; R)dF(\theta)\right) \tag{1.3}$$

where $F(\theta)$ is the distribution of individuals according to the parameter θ.

1.2 Special Cases

This general formulation includes several special cases which have been dealt with elsewhere in the literature.

(*a*) Conventional monopoly theory has focused on the case where R is separable and linear, i.e.

$$R(\underline{x}^j) = \sum_i p_i x_i^j$$

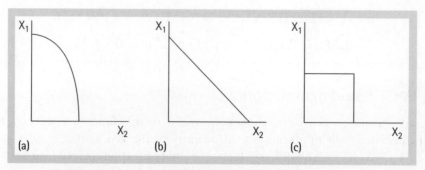

Fig. 1. (a) Bundles purchasable for a dollar; (b) No tie-in sales or bundling; (c) Strict bundling

(b) Commodity discounts would be consistent with

$$R(\underline{x}^j) = \sum_i r_i(x_i^j)$$

with $r_i'' < 0$.

(c) Tie-in sales and bundling are associated with non-separable payment functions. If the number of units of a tied bundle which are consumed by a particular individual is not observable

$$R(\underline{x}^j) = x_1^j r\left(\frac{x_2^j}{x_1^j}, \frac{x_3^j}{x_1^j}, \dots, \frac{x_m^j}{x_1^j}\right).$$

Consider the case of two commodities. If separate purchases are not observable, i.e. there is no way that a monopolist can prevent a customer from mixing two bundles, then the function R is restricted to functions which are quasi-convex, as depicted in Figure 1 (a). If tie-in sales or bundling is not desirable then $R(x_1, x_2) = \overline{R}$ defines a straight line as depicted in Figure 1 (b). Strict bundling—the availability of only a package $(\hat{x}_1, \hat{x}_2)$ is illustrated in Figure 1 (c).

1.3 Analogy to Optimal Tax Problem

It should be obvious that the problem of the monopolist is exactly analogous to the general optimal taxation problem formulated by Atkinson and Stiglitz (1976). There, the government had to find a tax function $T(x_1, \dots, x_m) = T(\underline{x})$ which maximized social welfare subject to the government's attaining the desired level of revenues. For simplicity, let the competitive prices of all commodities be constant and normalized at unity. Then the consumer maximizes his utility subject to the budget constraint

$$T(\underline{x}^j) + \sum_{i=0}^{m} x_i^j = W_0^j,$$

yielding a vector of consumption of $\underline{x}^j(\theta; T)$. Total revenues of the government are then $T(\underline{x}^j(\theta; T))$. Consider the problem of maximizing a weighted average of consumers' welfare (say, as represented by a utilitarian social welfare function) and government revenues,

$$\max \lambda \int T(x^j(\theta))dF + (1-\lambda) \int U^j(x^j(\theta); \theta)dF.$$

It is immediate that the monopolist's problem is the special case of this with $\lambda = 1$, whereas in the government's problem the value of λ depends on the magnitude of the revenue which the government must raise.

1.4 Some Properties of the Optimal Payments Function

Making use of (1.2) and our assumption of constant unit costs (normalized at unity) we rewrite (1.3) to read:

$$\max \int \left\{ W_0^j(\theta) - \sum_{i=0}^{m} x_i^j(\theta) \right\} dF(\theta). \tag{1.4}$$

In addition we assume that U is thrice differentiable and there are no inferior goods. Let U^j be our state variable and $x_1^j, \ldots, x_m^j$ our control variables;

$$\frac{dU^j}{d\theta} = \frac{\partial U^j}{\partial \theta} + U_0^j \frac{\partial W_0^j}{\partial \theta}. \tag{1.5}$$

Then our Hamiltonian can be written as

$$H = \left\{ W_0^j(\theta) - \sum_{i=0}^{m} x_i^j(\theta) \right\} f(\theta) + \mu \left[\frac{\partial U^j}{\partial \theta} + U_0^j \frac{\partial W^j}{\partial \theta} \right], \tag{1.6}$$

where $f(\theta)$ is the density function of θ. Then,

$$\frac{\partial H}{\partial x_i^j} = f(\theta) \left(\frac{U_i^j}{U_0^j} - 1 \right) + \mu \left\{ \frac{\partial^2 U^j}{\partial \theta \partial x_i^j} + U_{0i}^j \frac{\partial W^j}{\partial \theta} - \frac{U_i^j}{U_0^j} \left[\frac{\partial^2 U^j}{\partial \theta \partial x_0^j} + U_{00}^j \frac{\partial W^j}{\partial \theta} \right] \right\} = 0. \tag{1.7}$$

The first-order conditions for utility maximization imply that

$$R_i \equiv \frac{\partial R}{\partial x_i} = \frac{U_i^j}{U_0^j}. \tag{1.8}$$

Substituting (1.8) into (1.7) and using the differential equation for $\mu(\theta)$:

$$-\frac{d\mu(\theta)}{d\theta} = -\frac{f(\theta)}{U_0^j} + \frac{\mu}{U_0^j} \left(\frac{\partial^2 U^j}{\partial \theta \partial x_0^j} + U_{00}^j \frac{\partial W^j}{\partial \theta} \right) \tag{1.9}$$

and the boundary value conditions we can solve in principle for the optimal payments function.

Here we focus on some special cases:

Individuals differ only in wealth. Without loss of generality we let $\partial W^j / \partial \theta = 1$. Then

$$-\left(\frac{R_i - 1}{R_i}\right) = -\frac{\mu}{f}\left(U_{00}^j - \frac{U_0^j}{U_i^j}U_{0i}^j\right).\tag{1.10}$$

Note that

$$\frac{(R_i - 1)/R_i}{(R_k - 1)/R_k} = \frac{U_{00}^j - \frac{U_{0i}^j U_0^j}{U_i^j}}{U_{00}^j - \frac{U_0^j U_0^j}{U^j}},\tag{1.11}$$

the relative mark-up over marginal costs between any two commodities sold by the monopolist depends only on properties of the utility function, not on the density distribution of the population (f).

Letting $\mathrm{MRS}_{0i} = U_0/U_i$, the marginal rate of substitution between good 0 and good i, (1.11) can be re-written as (where, on taking the partial derivatives, it is understood that $x_1, \ldots, x_m$ are kept constant)

$$\frac{R_i - 1}{R_k - 1} = \frac{\partial \mathrm{MRS}_{0i}/\partial W_0}{\partial \mathrm{MRS}_{0k}/\partial W_0};\tag{1.11'}$$

the relative mark-up depends on how the marginal rate of substitution is affected (relatively) by a change in wealth (or x_0).

Next consider the still further specialization of constant marginal utility of income. Then it is optimal to charge price equal to marginal cost; all of the monopoly power is exercised by having a fixed fee to purchase from the monopolist. (This is not surprising, since then all individuals who purchase from the firm purchase the same amount.)

More generally we have under fairly weak conditions that the poorest and richest individuals are charged, at the margin, marginal cost: $R_i(\underline{x}(\underline{\theta})) = R_i(\underline{x}(\infty)) = 1$, when when $\underline{x}(\underline{\theta})$ and $\underline{x}(\infty)$ stand for the consumption vector of the poorest individual who purchases the commodity and the richest individual, respectively.[1] Thus, for small purchases there must be quantity premia; for large purchases quantity discounts. If repeated purchases are unobservable, there cannot be quantity premia and hence the price schedule will entail a fixed charge, a constant price up to a point and quantity discounts beyond that.

Individuals differ in marginal utilities of income. For simplicity we assume the monopolist produces a single good, x_1. We assume the utility function takes on the special form

$$U = z(x_1) + \theta x_0 = z(x_1) + \theta(W_0 - R(x_1))$$

and W_0 is the same for everyone, but θ, the marginal utility of income, differs. For each individual, however, θ is a constant. Then (1.7) to (1.9) become:

$$z' = \theta R' \tag{1.8'}$$

$$\frac{R' - 1}{R'} = \frac{\mu}{f} \tag{1.7'}$$

$$-\frac{d\mu}{d\theta} = \frac{-f + \mu}{\theta}. \tag{1.9'}$$

Then the firm should charge a fixed fee and a constant price per unit if, and only if, μ/f is a constant, i.e.

$$\frac{1}{\mu}\frac{d\mu}{d\theta} = \frac{f}{\mu\theta} - \frac{1}{\theta} = \frac{f'}{f}$$

i.e.

$$\frac{\theta f'}{f} = \left(\frac{f}{\mu} - 1\right)$$

or

$$f = a\theta^\gamma.$$

We assume

$$0 \leqq \theta \leqq \left(\frac{1+\gamma}{a}\right)^{1-\gamma}.$$

Hence

$$\frac{R' - 1}{R'} = \frac{1}{1 + \gamma}$$

The fixed entry fee, c, is chosen to maximize profits. For the marginal entrant, $\bar{\theta}$,

$$U(x^*(\bar{\theta})) + \bar{\theta}(W_0 - c - R'x^*) = z(0) + \bar{\theta}W_0.$$

Profits are:

$$\int_0^{\bar{\theta}} \{(R' - 1)x^* + c\} f(\theta) d\theta$$

so profits are maximized when

$$1 - \frac{x^*(\bar{\theta})}{R(x^*(\bar{\theta}))} = \frac{1}{1 + \gamma}.$$

Individuals differ in tastes. We further specialize the model by assuming that (a) purchases and sales cannot be monitored, and (b) the monopolist controls two commodities, x_1 and x_2, which are required in fixed proportions by each individual, but the individuals differ in the proportions required. Assumption (a) implied that the revenue function must be of the form

$$R(x_1, x_2) = x_1 R(1, x_2/x_1) + c(x) = x_1 r(x) + c(x),$$

where $x \equiv x_2/x_1$ and $c(x)$ is the fixed charge for buying bundle x.

We shall further simplify by assuming that the fixed charge is arbitrarily set to zero $(c(x) \equiv 0)$. This considerably simplifies the analysis and yields results that are more easily interpretable. With that restriction, $r'' \geq 0$, for if $r'' < 0$ over some interval $\underline{x} \leq x \leq \overline{x}$, then any bundle in the interval can be purchased more cheaply by buying, say, bundles $\underline{x}$ and $\overline{x}$, and mixing. The second assumption implies that we can write the θ individual's utility as

$$U = U(\min(\theta x_1, x_2), W - R(x_1, x_2), \theta) = U(x_1(\min(\theta, x), W - x_1 r(x), \theta).$$

The first-order conditions give $x = \theta$ and $U_0/U_1 = r(x)/\theta$, from which we can calculate the demand curve

$$x_1(\theta) = D(r(\theta), \theta).$$

The profits of the firm are then (under the earlier normalization that it costs one unit of our numeraire to produce one unit of x_1 and one to produce one unit of x_2)

$$\int_0^\infty D(r(\theta), \theta)(r(\theta) - (1 + \theta))dF(\theta)$$

subject to the constraint that

$$r' \geq 0, \quad r'' \geq 0.$$

Ignoring the constraint we obtain

$$\frac{r - (1 + \theta)}{r} = \frac{1}{\eta(\theta)} \quad \text{or} \quad r = \frac{\eta(1 + \theta)}{\eta - 1},$$

where $\eta(\theta) = -D_r r/D$, the elasticity of demand; the mark-up over marginal cost $(1 + \theta)$ is inversely proportional to the demand elasticity.

In Figure 2 we have plotted $\eta(\theta)(1 + \theta)/(\eta(\theta) - 1)$.

In Figure 2 (a), it is an increasing convex function, so the curve plotted satisfies the constraint and gives the optimal $r(x)$ function. In Figure 2 (b), there is an interval over which the function is concave; the optimal $r(x)$ function then consists of a strictly convex portion joined to a linear portion as in the figure.

2 THE INSURANCE MARKET

The remainder of this paper is devoted to examining monopoly with imperfect information in a specific market: the market for accident insurance. This market is chosen

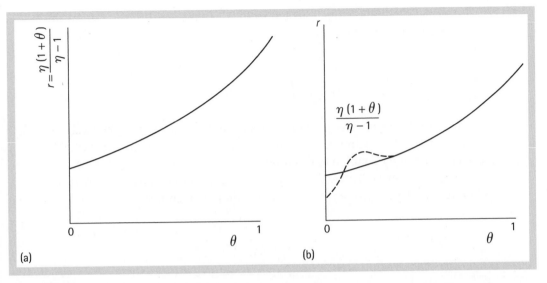

Fig. 2.

for two reasons: (i) since the corresponding competitive market has been analysed, we can make precise comparisons between monopoly and competition with imperfect information; (ii) there are, for this market, natural parameterizations describing how individuals differ from one another.

The basic model is the same as that presented for the competitive economy in Rothschild–Stiglitz (1976), where there is a more detailed discussion of the assumptions of the model. All individuals are assumed to be identical, except with respect to the probability of having an accident. They have an initial endowment of W_0; the loss, if an accident occurs, is d, and the probability of an accident is p. Their expected utility in the absence of insurance is thus

$$\mathcal{W} = U(W_0 - d)p + U(W_0)(1 - p). \tag{2.1}$$

An insurance policy pays an amount, β, in the event of an accident; in turn, individuals must pay the insurance firm an amount α, if there is no accident. (This does not quite correspond to the conventional characterization of an insurance policy, which entails a premium paid in all states of nature and a receipt from the firm only in the state of nature "accident", i.e. in the conventional terminology, α would be the premium and $\alpha + \beta$ the benefit.) Thus the individual's expected utility with an insurance policy (α, β) is

$$U(W_0 - d + \beta)p + U(W_0 - \alpha)(1 - p) \equiv V(\alpha, \beta; p). \tag{2.2}$$

The individual chooses from the available set of insurance policies that policy which maximizes his expected utility V. Let $\{a(p), \beta(p)\}$ denote the policy chosen by an individual of type p. The insurance company's expected profit on that policy is clearly

$$\pi(p) = (1 - p)a(p) - \beta(p)p. \tag{2.3}$$

Let $F(p)$ be the distribution function of individuals in the population. For simplicity, let us normalize the size of the population at unity. Then the expected profits of the insurance company are just

$$\bar{\pi} = \int \pi(p) dF(p). \tag{2.4}$$

We assume that the insurance company is risk neutral and hence it wishes to choose a set of contracts to maximize expected profits. We are concerned here with the characterization of the solution to this problem.

In the next section we analyse the solution for the two-group case; in the following section we consider the case where there is a continuum of groups.

3   TWO GROUPS DIFFERING ONLY IN PROBABILITY OF ACCIDENT

The advantage of considering the case where there are only two groups in the population, differing only in the probability of having an accident, is that we can neatly characterize the solution diagrammatically. For each individual, there are only two states of nature, "Accident" and "No Accident". Wealth in the former state is $W_0 - d$, in the latter, W_0. The point E in Figure 3 (a) (and subsequent diagrams) represents this initial "endowment". As we noted earlier, an insurance contract may then be viewed as a promise by the individual to pay an amount α to the firm if he has no accident, in return for a promise by the insurance to pay β if he does have an accident. Thus, with insurance contract $\{\alpha, \beta\}$ the individual's wealth in the state of nature "no accident" is $W_0 - \alpha$, and in the state of nature "accident" is $W_0 - d + \beta$. Thus, any point to the north-west of E (below the 45° line) represents the wealth of the individual after having purchased some insurance contract with $\alpha > 0$, $\beta > 0$.[2] For instance, the point C_H corresponds to a contract with benefit α_H and premium β_H. For simplicity, we shall sometimes refer to the point C_H as "the contract C_H" rather than as the wealth generated by the contract $\{\alpha_H, \beta_H\}$.

Variables pertaining to the high-risk individuals will be denoted by the subscript H, for the low-risk individuals by the subscript L.

The set of contracts which just breaks even (on average) for the high-risk individuals is given by

$$\alpha_H(1 - p_H) - \beta_H p_H = 0$$

and is depicted in Figure 3 (a) by the line EF_H. The point F_H represents the expected wealth of the high-risk individual, i.e. $W_0 - p_H d$. Similarly, the set of contracts with

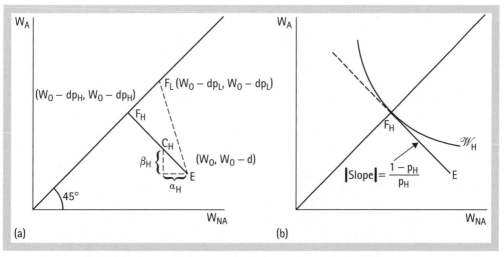

Fig. 3. Basic diagrams

a given level of expected profits, $\bar{\pi}_H$, is given by

$$a_H(1 - p_H) - p_H\beta_H - \bar{\pi}_H = 0,$$

i.e. lines parallel to EF_H. Clearly, lines above EF_H represent higher benefits for the same premium, so expected profits are negative, and conversely for lines below EF_H.

The corresponding line for the low-risk individual is denoted by EF_L. F_L clearly lies above F_H, since the expected wealth of the low-risk individual, $W_0 - p_L d$, is greater than that of the high-risk individual.

Finally, in Figure 3 (b) we have drawn the indifference curves of the individuals. There are two critical aspects of these indifference curves. First, observe that the marginal rate of substitution (the slope of the indifference curve) along the 45° line is just equal to the ratio of the probability of not having an accident to that of having an accident,

$$-\left.\frac{\partial W_A}{\partial W_{NA}}\right|_{\mathscr{W}} = \frac{U'(W_{NA})(1 - p)}{U'(W_A)p} = \frac{(1 - p)}{p}$$

when $W_{NA} = W_A$ (where W_A is wealth in state of nature "accident", W_{NA} is wealth in state of nature "no accident"), which in turn is the same as the slope of the constant profits curve for the group of individuals with those accident probabilities. Secondly note that so long as everyone has the same degree of risk aversion, the absolute value of the slope of the high-risk individual's indifference curve through any point is less than that of the low-risk individual's indifference curve through the same point:

$$\frac{U'(W_{NA})(1 - p_H)}{U'(W_A)p_H} < \frac{U'(W_{NA})(1 - p_L)}{U'(W_A)p_L}.$$

For purposes of comparison, it may be useful to recall the equilibrium for (a) competition with perfect information about accident probabilities, (b) competition with imperfect information and (c) monopoly with perfect information.

Competition with perfect information leads to each individual paying his own "actuarial odds" (since we have assumed that the insurance companies are risk neutral) and obtaining complete insurance. Indeed, for this solution to emerge, we do not require that the individual know his own probabilities of having an accident, only that the insurance firm can, somehow, ascertain those probabilities. Thus, in Figure 4 (a) the points C_H and C_L denote the equilibrium contracts; the point on the zero profit line for the respective groups which maximizes expected utility occurs along the 45° line; at that point the indifference curve and the zero profit line have the same slope.

In competitive markets with imperfect information, if an equilibrium existed, it always entailed there being a separate contract for each of the two groups; there was never any "pooling". The high-risk group obtained complete insurance, the low-risk group partial insurance. But both groups purchased some insurance. Figure 4 (b) depicts the equilibrium for this case. The high-risk individual is at exactly the same point he was with perfect information. The low-risk individual, however, purchases the "best" contract which breaks even and which will not, at the same time, be purchased by the high-risk individual, given that he has the option of buying the contract C_H. The low-risk individuals avoid "subsidizing" the high-risk individuals (as they would if they purchased the same insurance contract) but only at the "price" of purchasing only partial insurance. Since the high-risk individuals *know* that they are high risk, it is far more important for them to obtain "complete coverage" than it is for the low-risk individuals. This enables a "separation" of the market according to risk groups.

Finally, in monopolistic markets with perfect information, the monopolist offers the contract to each individual which maximizes his expected profit. This is the contract with complete insurance at terms which leave the individual "just indifferent" between purchasing the policy and having no insurance, i.e. the monopolist is able to extract all the consumer surplus involved in the reduction of risk. (This is easy to see, since the set of contracts which the individual will purchase (rather than have no insurance) is given by the points which lie above the indifference curve through E. The iso-expected profits lines are parallel, say, for the high-risk individuals, to EF_H. Again, the indifference curve is tangent to an iso-expected profit line at the 45° line.) Figure 4 (c) depicts the solution with the two contracts C_H and C_L.

The characterization of the monopolistic equilibrium with imperfect information is somewhat more difficult. We shall show that, as in the other three cases analysed, the same contract will never be purchased by both high- and low-risk individuals, i.e. again there never exists a pooling equilibrium. But now the low-risk individual may not purchase any insurance at all; the high-risk individual, however, always purchases complete insurance. This analysis provides an explanation for the fact that low-risk individuals often would like to buy partial insurance at "favourable terms" but are unable to do so; the reason is that at any set of terms which they would

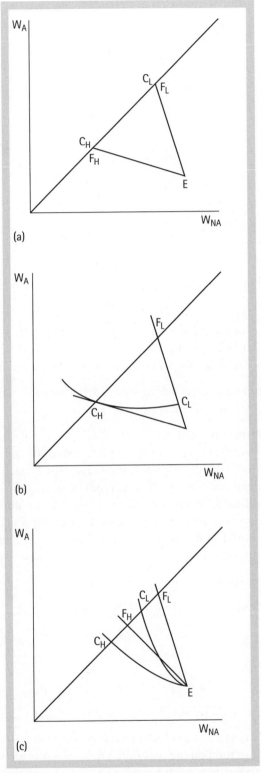

Fig. 4. (a) Competitive equilibrium: perfect information; (b) Competitive equilibrium: imperfect information; (c) Monopoly: perfect information

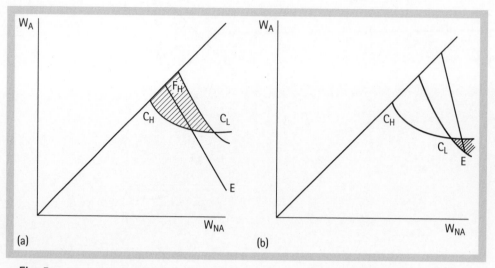

Fig. 5.

find favourable, the high-risk individuals will switch to the partial insurance and the profits of the firm will be lowered.

More formally, we establish the following properties of the equilibrium:

Property 1. *The optimal contract for the high-risk individual is complete insurance, if the high- and low-risk individuals buy separate insurance.*

Proof. The solution may be seen very easily diagrammatically in Figure 5. We are constrained to choosing contracts which are preferred to the contract purchased by the low-risk group (C_L) by the high-risk individuals, but which are not preferred by the low-risk individuals. The set of such points is shaded in Figure 5 (a). Since the slope of the indifference curve is equal to $(1 - p)/p$, the slope of the "constant profits" line, at the 45° line, but elsewhere it is flatter, clearly profits are maximized by the contract which is at the intersection of the 45° line and the high-risk individuals' indifference curve through C_L.

For separation, we require

$$U(W_0 - d + \beta_H)p_H + U(W_0 - \alpha_H)(1 - p_H)$$
$$\geqq U(W_0 - d + \beta_L)p_H + U(W_0 - \alpha_L)(1 - p_H) \tag{3.1a}$$

and

$$U(W_0 - d + \beta_L)p_L + U(W_0 - \alpha_L)(1 - p_L)$$
$$\geqq U(W_0 - d + \beta_H)p_L + U(W_0 - \alpha_H)(1 - p_L). \tag{3.1b}$$

(3.1) says that each type of individual prefers his contract to the other contract. Clearly, profit maximization on the part of the monopolist must entail (3.1) holding with equality. Otherwise, there exists a contract $\{\alpha'_H, \beta'_H\}$ such that

$$\alpha'_H(1 - p_H) - \beta'_H p_H > \alpha_H(1 - p_H) - \beta_H p_H$$

and (recalling the definition of V from (2.2))

$$V(a_L, \beta_L, p_H) \leqq V(a'_H, \beta'_H, p_H) \leqq V(a_H, \beta_H, p_H)$$
$$\leqq V(a_H, \beta_H, p_L) \leqq V(a_L, \beta_L, p_L).$$

The choice of contract of the low-risk individual will be unaffected as we change contracts, so long as (3.1) holds; and so long as it holds with inequality, we can increase the premium (a_H), without changing the benefits, and hence increase the profits. There is one minor technicality: how do we know as we increase the premiums that the high-risk group will continue to buy insurance? Because it is easy to establish that if

$$V(0, 0, p_L) < V(a_L, \beta_L, p_L)$$

then

$$V(0, 0, p_H) < V(a_L, \beta_L, p_H)(\leqq V(a_H, \beta_H, p_H)).$$

Profits may be written

$$\pi = [a_H(1 - p_H) - \beta_H p_H]N_H + [a_L(1 - p_L) - \beta_L p_L]N_L, \tag{3.2}$$

where N_L is the number of low-risk individuals, N_H the number of high-risk individuals.

Hence, if we maximize profits subject to (3.1) we obtain

$$\frac{d\pi}{d\beta_H} = \left[(1 - p_H) \frac{U'(W_0 - d + \beta_H)p_H}{U'(W_0 - a_H)(1 - p_H)} - p_H \right] N_H = 0, \tag{3.3}$$

when $a_H = d - \beta_H$.

Thus, we must have complete insurance for the high-risk individual (just as we did in the competitive market).

Property 2. *If the low-risk individual buys insurance which is different from that of the high-risk individual his level of utility is "essentially" the same as it would have been had he not purchased any insurance.*

Proof. We assume the contract for the high-risk individual, C_H, is given. Following Property 1, it must lie along the 45° line. Thus, the set of contracts which the monopolist can choose and which "separate" the groups are the points below the high-risk individual's indifference curve through C_H and above the low-risk individual's indifference curve through E (the no insurance point). Again using the fact that the indifference curves are flatter than the line of constant profits, profits are maximized at C_L, the intersection of the two indifference curves (Figure 5 (b)).

Property 3. *High-risk and low-risk individuals never purchase the same policy.*

Proof. To show this, we show that there exists a pair of policies one of which will be purchased by each group, which will increase profits.

In Figure 6, we have labelled a "pooling contract", i.e. one which is purchased by both groups, by C_P. Assume C_P does not entail complete insurance. There are two

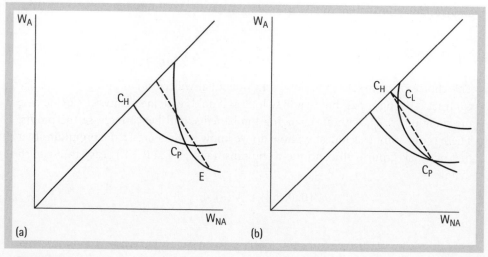

Fig. 6.

possibilities. At C_P, the high-risk individuals are in effect being subsidized, or the firm is making a profit even on the high-risk individuals. In the latter case, consider the pair of contracts, such that C_H involves complete insurance and the high-risk individual is indifferent between C_H and C_P, and $C_L = C_P$. Using the fact noted above that the slope of the low-risk individual's indifference curve through any point is greater than that of the high-risk individual's, it is clear that profits on the high-risk individual are increased, and on the low-risk individuals unchanged.

In the former case, we show that the implicit subsidy from the low-risk to the high-risk individuals is "inefficient". The value of the subsidy (the negative profit on the contracts purchased by high-risk individuals) is constant along a line through C_P which has a slope of $1 - p_H/p_H$ (Figure 6 (b)). Thus, let the firm offer the contract C_H, involving complete insurance, with an equal effective subsidy, and the contract C_L, the intersection of low risk individual's indifference curve through C_P and the high risk individual's indifference curve through C_H (see Property 2). Clearly, profits on C_L exceed those on C_P purchased by low-risk individuals.

This establishes that if there is a pooling contract, it must provide complete insurance. But direct calculation establishes that the best pooling contract cannot involve complete insurance: clearly, if there is a single policy purchased by both groups

$$V(0, 0, p_H) \leqq V(\alpha, \beta, p_H) \tag{3.4a}$$

$$V(0, 0, p_L) \leqq V(\alpha, \beta, p_L). \tag{3.4b}$$

If (3.4b) is satisfied (3.4a) is. Moreover, profit maximization entails (3.4b) holding with equality. (Otherwise we could increase premiums without changing benefits and the policy would still be purchased.) Thus we must maximize

$$\overline{\pi} = \alpha(1 - \overline{p}) - \beta\overline{p} \tag{3.5}$$

subject to

$$U(W_0 - d)p_L + U(W_0)(1 - p_L) = U(W_0 - d + \beta)p_L + U(W_0 - a)(1 - p_L),$$

i.e.

$$\frac{d\bar{\pi}}{d\beta} = \frac{(1 - \bar{p})p_L U'(W_0 - d + \beta)}{(1 - p_L)U'(W_0 - a)} - \bar{p} = 0, \tag{3.6}$$

whence

$$\frac{U'(W_0 - d + \beta)}{U'(W_0 - a)} = \frac{\bar{p}/(1 - \bar{p})}{p_L/(1 - p_L)} > 1.$$

There remains then only one problem for the monopolist: what policy to offer the high-risk individual, i.e. he will offer complete insurance, but he may offer any contract between that which just induces the high-risk individual to purchase insurance (in which case the low-risk individual clearly will purchase no insurance) and that where the low-risk individual is just indifferent to buying no insurance and the given policy. Obviously, if almost all the individuals in the population are high risk, then the first gives the maximum profit; if all the individuals in the population are low risk, the second gives the maximum profit. What is more interesting, however, is

Property 4. *There exists a critical (finite) ratio of high- to low-risk individuals, such that if the actual ratio exceeds the critical ratio, low-risk individuals purchase no insurance.*

In the full text, the proof is given, and it is shown that the magnitude of the critical ratio depends on the magnitude of the differences in their accident probabilities, the size of the accident, and the degree of risk aversion.

4 CONTINUUM OF INDIVIDUALS

More interesting from an analytical point of view is the case where there is a continuum of individuals. We let $F(p)$ be the distribution function of individuals by their accident probability. Let p and $\bar{p}$ be the minimum and maximum accident probabilities respectively. We assume F is differentiable; f will denote the density function. We assume f is continuous. In a competitive market, we established that there was never an equilibrium. The behaviour of the monopolist is a fairly complex problem, but we can use many of the results of the previous section to give us some insights into its solution.

The "policy" set can be described by a function $\beta = \beta(a)$ giving the maximum benefit available for any given premium. Clearly, these will be the only policies purchased. Thus, if

$$a_1 > a_2,$$
$$\beta(a_1) > \beta(a_2). \tag{4.1}$$

Table I. Comparison of equilibria

	Competition		Monopoly	
	Perfect information	Imperfect information	Perfect information	Imperfect information
High risk	Complete insurance at actuarial odds	Complete insurance at actuarial odds	Complete insurance at terms which make individual indifferent to buying no insurance	Complete insurance, at terms which range from those which make high-risk individual indifferent to buying insurance to terms which make low-risk individual indifferent to buying insurance. Firms may make loss on contract
Low risk	Complete insurance at actuarial odds	Partial insurance at actuarial odds	Complete insurance at terms which make individual indifferent to buying no insurance	Partial or no insurance; terms always such as to make individual indifferent to buying no insurance

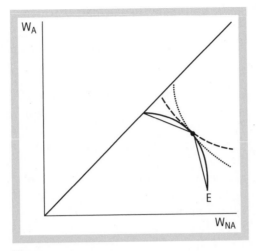

Fig. 7.

Let $a(p)$ denote the policy purchased by individuals with accident probability p. It is clear that if

$$p_1 > p_2,$$ (4.2)

$$a(p_1) \geqq a(p_2).$$

It can also be shown that the policy function is a continuous function but it may not be differentiable. The points of non-differentiability are of some economic interest, for they are "pooling contracts", i.e. contracts which are purchased by individuals with differing probabilities of having an accident (see Figure 7).

When β is a differentiable function of a,

$$\frac{d\beta}{da} = \frac{U'(W - a)(1 - p)}{U'(W - d + \beta)p} \equiv \lambda(a, \beta, p)$$ (4.3)

λ is the marginal rate of substitution of an individual with accident probability p, of income in state of nature "accident" for income in state of nature "no accident". In this section, where there is no ambiguity, we shall write just W for W_0.

On the other hand, if at some $\{\hat{a}, \beta(\hat{a})\}\beta$ is not differentiable, but $d\beta^+/da$ and $d\beta^- da$ exist and $d\beta^+/da < d\beta^-/da$, then all individuals with

$$p^{**} < p < p^*,$$

where

$$\lambda(\hat{a}, \hat{\beta}, p^{**}) = (\partial\beta/\partial a)^+ \quad \text{and} \quad \lambda(\hat{a}, \hat{\beta}, p^*) = (d\beta/da)^-$$

purchase the policy $\{\hat{a}, \beta\}$.[3]

It immediately follows that for any piecewise differentiable policy function $\beta(a)$,

$$\frac{d\beta}{dp} = \lambda(a, \beta, p)\frac{da}{dp}$$ (4.4)

(where it is understood that at points of non-differentiability we take, say, the left hand derivative).

Thus, we wish to choose $\{a(p), \beta(p)\}$ functions, satisfying (4.4) to

$$\max \int \pi(p) f(p) dp. \tag{4.5}$$

We analyse the problem using Pontryagin's technique. We form the Hamiltonian

$$H \equiv (a(1-p) - \beta p) f + u \frac{da}{dp} + v\lambda \frac{da}{dp}$$

where a, β are state variables, and da/dp is the control variable. Thus

$$\frac{da}{dp} = \left\{ \substack{\infty \\ \text{indeterminate} \\ 0} \right\} \quad \text{as} \quad u + v\lambda \gtreqless 0. \tag{4.6}$$

We obtain the auxiliary equations

$$\frac{du}{dp} \equiv -\frac{\partial H}{\partial a} = -(1-p) f - v\lambda_a \frac{da}{dp} \tag{4.7}$$

$$\frac{dv}{dp} = -\frac{\partial H}{\partial \beta} = pf - v\lambda_\beta \frac{da}{dp}. \tag{4.8}$$

Our "strategy" for analysing the solution to this problem is

(i) If we can find a set of functions $\{a(p), \beta(p), u(p), v(p)\}$ satisfying the equation

$$\frac{d\beta}{da} = \lambda(a(p), \beta(p), p) \tag{4.9}$$

and the equations (4.7) and (4.8), such that

$$u(p) + v(p)\lambda(a(p), \beta(p), p) = 0$$

for all p and, letting $\bar{p}$ denote the lowest p actually purchasing insurance, if

$$u(\bar{p}) = v(\bar{p}) = u(\hat{p}) + \lambda v(\hat{p}) = 0, \tag{4.10a}$$

(the familiar transversality condition) and (to ensure that the policies offered will be purchased),

$$V(a(\hat{p}), \beta(\hat{p}), \hat{p}) \geqq V(0, 0, \hat{p}) \tag{4.10b}$$

then $\{a(p), \beta(p)\}$ gives the optimal set of policies. This is a solution which entails *complete separation*, i.e. every group buys a different policy.

(ii) It turns out, however, that there will not always exist such a solution. We then find a solution of the form

$$u(p) + v(p)\lambda(a(p), \beta(p), p) \leqq 0, \frac{da}{dp} \geqq 0 \tag{4.11}$$

$$\{u(p) + v(p)\lambda(a(p), \beta(p), p)\} \frac{da}{dp} = 0 \tag{4.12}$$

if

$$u(p) + v(p)\lambda(\alpha(p), \beta(p), p) = 0, \frac{d\beta}{d\alpha} = \lambda \qquad (4.13)$$

if

$$u(p) + v(p)\lambda(p) < 0 \quad \text{for} \quad p^{**} < p < p^{*}$$

$$\{\alpha(p), \beta(p)\} \quad \text{same for} \quad p^{**} < p < p^{*}$$

and

$$\left(\frac{d\beta}{d\alpha}\right)^{+} < \lambda(\alpha(p), \beta(p), p) < \left(\frac{d\beta}{d\alpha}\right)^{-}$$

for which the functions satisfy (4.7) and (4.8) and the boundary values (4.10).

(4.11) says that $u + v\lambda$ is non-positive and $d\alpha/dp$ is non-negative. (4.12) says further that either $u + v\lambda = 0$ or $d\alpha/dp = 0$. (4.13) says that when $u + v\lambda = 0$, $d\beta/d\alpha = \lambda$, the marginal rate of substitution of the individual who purchases the policy; when $u + v\lambda < 0$, over an interval, all individuals in that interval purchase the same policy, and their marginal rates of substitution are bracketed by the left- and right-hand derivatives of $\beta(\alpha)$ at that "policy".

Thus, whether equilibrium entails complete separation or some "pooling" (i.e. some policy bought by individuals with different accident probabilities) depends on whether $u + v\lambda$ can be constant at zero for an interval of p. There follows in the full text an analysis of what this entails. The results are summarized in points (1) to (4) from the original text, and the additional point (5).

(1) The monopolist will always offer a continuum of contracts, provided individuals are unambiguously risk averse. It is shown in the full text that if α is a linear function of β and there is constant absolute risk aversion ($-U''/U'$ is constant), then the density function will be of the form

$$\ln f = \ln c - \ln \left\{ p^{(1+2m)/(1+m)} (1 - p)^{(2+m)(1+m)} \right\}$$

where $m = (1 - p_{\max})/p_{\max}$. More generally, knowing the utility function and the contract curve, one can solve back for the density function which will support that contract curve.

(2) The premium may be either a convex or concave function of the benefits. Only in special cases will it be linear.

(3) Whereas, in competitive markets, equilibrium was characterized by different individuals purchasing different contracts (i.e. no pooling of risks), with monopoly the same policy may be purchased by individuals of different risks. A sufficient condition for "separation" at p, i.e. every type of individual with accident probability "near" p purchasing a different contract, is that the density of function at p satisfy

$$\frac{f'}{f} > \frac{3p - 2}{p(1 - p)}.$$

(4) There may be a set of individuals (those with the lowest accident probabilities) who do not purchase any insurance.

(5) There is never pooling among the most high risk individuals if $h' > 0$, where $h(p) \equiv (1 - p)p^2 f$, but there may be otherwise. If there is pooling, α is not a differentiable function of β.

5 Two Groups Different in Attitudes Towards Risk

In a competitive economy, if individuals differed only in attitudes towards risk then risk neutral competitive insurance firms would offer complete insurance and would pay no attention to the degree of risk aversion of a particular individual. Thus, the absence of information about attitudes towards risk of particular individuals is of no importance. For a monopolist, this information is, however, valuable. If the monopolist knew which individuals were highly risk averse and which were only mildly risk averse, it would act as a discriminating monopolist, offering each complete insurance, but at different terms.

On the other hand, if it does not know who is highly risk averse and who is not, it can obtain this information by offering the individual a choice from among a set of contracts. But since it obtains a smaller profit from partial insurance than from complete insurance, it must trade off the gains from the ability to discriminate against the loss in profits from selling only partial insurance to the not very risk averse. Thus, in the case with two groups, the optimal set of policies sold may either entail a single contract, purchased only by the very risk averse, a single contract purchased by everyone, or two contracts.

By exactly the same kinds of arguments that we used earlier, we can establish

Property 5. *The high risk aversion group obtains complete insurance.*

Property 6. *If the low risk aversion group purchases insurance, it purchases a policy which leaves it at approximately the same level of expected utility as it had without insurance.*

More precisely, let $\{a_L, \beta_L\}$ and $\{a_H, \beta_H\}$ denote the policies purchased by the low risk aversion and high risk aversion groups respectively. Then

$$a_H = d - \beta_H \tag{5.1}$$

$$V(0, 0, R_L) = V(a_L, \beta_L, R_L) \geqq V(a_H, \beta_H, R_L) \tag{5.2}$$

$$V(a_H, \beta_H, R_H) = V(a_L, \beta_L, R_H), \tag{5.3}$$

where $V(a, \beta, R_H)$ is the expected utility of the high risk aversion individual who obtains policy $\{a, \beta\}$; similarly for $V(a, \beta, R_L)$.

In short, we have established

Property 7. *There is a critical ratio of highly risk averse to low risk aversion individuals, such that if the ratio in the population exceeds the critical ratio, only the highly risk averse purchase policies. There is another critical ratio, such that if the ratio in the population is less than this, there is only one policy, purchased by both groups (entailing complete insurance). In between two policies are offered, complete insurance for the high risk averse, partial insurance for the less risk averse.*

In the full text, Property 7, with the critical ratios, is derived.

6 CONCLUDING COMMENTS

This paper has attempted to show that the scope for at least partial discrimination by a monopolist among his customers is much greater than has previously been thought. The attempt to discriminate among his customers leads the monopolist to engage in practices restricting the set of insurance contracts he sells, using non-linear price schedules, bundling and tie-in sales, random prices (see Salop 1977), which would otherwise be difficult to explain. Some of these practices, such as the use of non-linear pricing, would occur in some circumstances in competitive markets, e.g. in insurance markets, under imperfect information; most of them, however, would not. Thus monopoly and competition differ in far more significant ways than just simply the price charged. Whether these practices may occur in market structures other than the polar ones analysed here is a question which will be pursued elsewhere.

NOTES

1. This follows from the fact that

$$\lim_{\theta \to 0} \frac{\mu(\theta)}{f(\theta)} = \lim_{\theta \to \infty} \frac{\mu(\theta)}{f(\theta)} = 0.$$

The problem in establishing this arises because, by the transversality condition (provided $\underline{x}$ is positive)

$$\lim_{\theta \to 0} \mu(\theta) = \lim_{\theta \to \infty} \mu(\theta) = 0,$$

while for distributions without finite support

$$\lim_{\theta \to 0} f(\theta) = \lim_{\theta \to \infty} f(\theta) = 0.$$

Hence we use L'Hopital's rule to establish

$$\lim \frac{\mu}{f} = \begin{cases} \lim \dfrac{f - \mu U_{00}/U_0}{f'} = 0 & \text{if } f' > 0 \text{ and } U_{00}/U_0 \text{ is bounded} \\[2em] \lim \dfrac{\partial^{n-1} f/\partial \theta^{n-1}}{\partial^n f/\partial \theta^n} = 0 & \text{if } \partial^n f/\partial \theta^n \text{ is the first non-zero derivative.} \end{cases}$$

(1.7)–(1.9) were derived on the hypothesis that all individuals consume all commodities. If this is not true the equations have to be modified. In particular it is possible that $R_i(0) > 1$.

In some other problems, for certain distributions without a finite support, $\lim_{x \to \infty} R_t(\underline{x}) > 1$, as the next example illustrates.

2. Points above the 45° line represent in effect more than 100 per cent insurance: after buying the insurance policy, the individual is actually better off in the state of nature "accident" than he is in the state of nature "no accident". Although such contracts are clearly conceivable, they will not be observed in monopolistic or competitive markets, and so we shall ignore them. The points to the north-east of E represent a negative premium with a positive benefit, to the south-east a negative benefit with a negative premium, and to the south-west of E a positive premium with a negative benefit.

3. That is, the individual maximizes $U(W - a)(1 - p) + U(W - d + \beta)p$ so if $d\beta/da$ exists,

$$-U'(1 - p) + U'p\frac{d\beta}{da} = 0.$$

If $(d\beta/da)^+$ and $(d\beta/da)^-$ exist, then clearly there exists an interval $p^{**} < p < p^*$ such that

$$-U'(1 - p) + pU'\left(\frac{d\beta}{da}\right)^+ < 0$$

$$-U'(1 - p) + pU'\left(\frac{d\beta}{da}\right)^- > 0$$

i.e. all individuals in the interval buy the same policy.

CHAPTER 8

PRICES AND QUEUES AS SCREENING DEVICES IN COMPETITIVE MARKETS*

1 INTRODUCTION

THIS paper is concerned with the analysis of competitive equilibrium in markets where there is imperfect information. The commodities being sold on the market differ with respect to some important qualities, and these qualities cannot be directly observed. However, the mix of the qualities offered on the market is a function of the price. Thus, in such markets, prices play more than just the role of Lagrange multipliers which they play in conventional economic analysis; they provide information about what is being sold. The consequences of this for the meaning of equilibrium, for the existence of equilibrium, and for its optimality are profound, and it is the purpose of this paper to explore these implications by means of a well-developed example.

The phenomenon with which I am concerned has been noted for a long time; there is a small literature on "judging quality by price," but this literature has never

* Reprinted with permission from *economic Analysis of Markets and Games: essays in Harour of Frank Hahu*, P. Dasgupta et al, eds., Cambridge: MIT Press, 1992, pp 128–166. First printed in *IMSSS Technical Report No.* 212, Stanford University, August 1976.

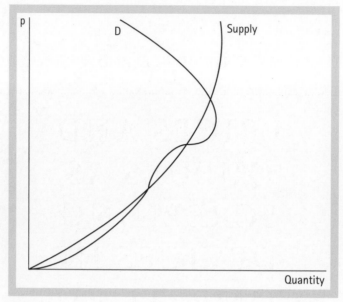

Fig. 1.

been integrated with the rest of economics. Akerlof (1970) discussed the subject, with the apt title "the market for lemons." But his discussion has led to some confusion between the phenomenon of thin markets and the non-existence of equilibrium, and although he intuited correctly that these markets when they exist lacked the conventional optimality properties, he failed to demonstrate this.

The phenomenon appears, in a slightly different guise, under the rubric of adverse selection in the insurance literature; there it has been observed that the mix of policyholders with respect to their riskiness depends on the premium charged.[1]

The particular example I shall develop is that of the labor market. But before I present the model in detail, it may be useful to describe the the results of my analysis in an intuitive way. Assume that the sellers of a commodity know the quality of the commodity they are selling. The buyer knows that sellers of low-quality commodities have a greater incentive to sell their commodities than sellers of high-quality commodities; moreover, as the price is lowered, individuals with high quality commodities prefer not to trade rather than to sell. Hence, as the price is lowered, the average quality is lowered. Demanders, in equilibrium, come to know this; whether the demand for the commodity is increased or decreased as the price is lowered depends on whether, in a rough sense, quality is reduced more or less than proportionately to price. Thus, demand curves may have (depending on the distribution of sellers of different qualities) any peculiar shape, and there may be multiple equilibria, as depicted in figure 1.

Indeed, among the equilibria may be a zero-price equilibrium; at that price, the quality of the goods offered is so low that there is a zero demand (only individuals with worthless commodities would offer them for sale). But note that the zero price-zero trade equilibrium is Pareto inferior to any equilibrium with a positive price. Individuals trade with one another only when they are better off, at least in an

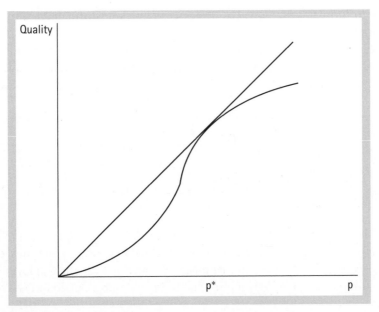

Fig. 2.

expected-utility sense; and it has been assumed that individuals do correctly foresee the composition of qualities sold on the market.

More fundamentally, the conventional notion of equilibrium as necessarily entailing supply equal to demand must be questioned. Conventional analysis argues that if supply exceeds demand, prices will fall, as suppliers attempt to underbid each other (conversely in cases of excess demand). But here, as the price changes, the mix of the qualities being offered on the market changes; in a sense, we can say that there is a different (quality) commodity offered at every price. Competitive behavior in this context entails firms (buyers) taking the wage-quality (price-quality) function as given, and choosing the wage-quality (price-quality) function the quality (or mix of qualities) which they most prefer. Figure 2 depicts such a perceived quality-price function. Individuals choose the price that minimizes *price-per-unit quality* (e.g., with labor, the wage per *effective* laborer). But note that at p^* demand may not equal supply. If supply exceeds demand, suppliers will not "underbid," because as they lower their price they are judged to belong to a mix that has a lower average quality. It would thus appear that market equilibrium may in fact entail demand not equaling supply.

When there is an excess supply of labor, queues will form for jobs; these queues will serve as screening devices, differentiating individuals according to their characteristics. This paper develops an equilibrium theory of queues and assesses its welfare properties.

The main thrust of my analysis is to confirm the results, obtained in other contexts, showing that the analysis of markets in which there is imperfect information is qualitatively different from that of conventional economic analysis:

1. Competitive equilibrium may not entail market clearing.
2. Competitive equilibria are not Pareto optimal. (A number of different sources of inefficiency are noted below.)

3. Pareto optimality may entail some degree of unemployment, but less than in the market solution.

4. Both the market and optimal allocations may entail wage distributions (i.e., different plants paying different wages), although the observable characteristics of individuals applying at the different plants are identical. Both may also entail discrimination.

2 The Basic Model

Assume that there are two types of individuals and there are two types of jobs: each individual can be self-employed or can work in "manufacturing." The ith group has an effective productivity of A_i in manufacturing and $\gamma_i A_i$ in self-employment; i.e., those in group 1 can do in $1/A_1$ hours what those in group 2 can do in $1/A_2$ hours.

Assume that

$$A_1 > A_2;$$

i.e., in manufacturing, group 1 is more productive.[2] Group 1 has a comparative advantage in manufacturing (self-employment) if $\gamma_1 < (>)\gamma_2$.

We assume constant returns to scale in self-employment,[3] and we choose our units so that $\gamma_i A_i$ represents the wages which an individual of type i can earn in self-employment. Thus, $\gamma_i A_i$ is the reservation wage for workers of type i; i.e., below $\gamma_i A_i$ a worker of type i will not supply any labor to the market. For simplicity, we assume that each worker supplies a unit of labor, so that we can use the terms *wage rates* and *incomes* interchangeably.

Because individuals of different productivities have different reservation wages, the mix of individuals offering their services on the labor market will differ as the wage increases. Let $A(w)$ represent the mean productivity of those offering their services at wage w.[4] We call this the wage-productivity curve.

Assume that firms know that some individuals are more productive than other individuals, but there is no method by which they can ascertain which individual is the more productive. They find out, after hiring, that some workers are good and some are bad. They observe that by varying the wage they can vary the relative proportions of good and bad workers, but they still cannot predict which individual is going to be good and which is going to be bad.[5]

We can easily derive the wage-quality relationship, $A(w)$.

(i) If $\gamma_1 A_1 > A_2 \gamma_2$, type 1 has absolute advantage in self-employment (see figures 3a and 3b):

$$A(w) = \begin{cases} A_2, & A_2\gamma_2 < w < A_1\gamma_1 \\ \bar{A}, & w > A_1\gamma_1. \end{cases} \qquad (2.1a)$$

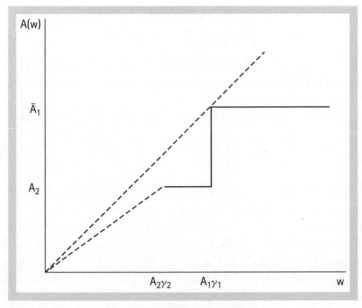

Fig. 3a. $A_1\gamma_1 > A_2\gamma_2$: $A_1\gamma_1$ efficiency wage

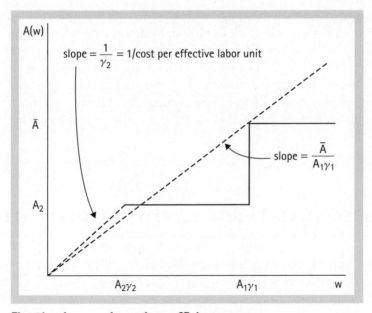

Fig. 3b. $A_1\gamma_1 > A_2\gamma_2$: $A_2\gamma_2$ efficiency wage

where

$$\bar{A} = \lambda A_1 + (1 - \lambda)A_2$$

represents the mean productivity of the population as a whole, where λ is the proportion of the population that is of type 1. If we let $\bar{L}$ be the total (potential) supply of labor and $\overline{L}_i$ be the total (potential) supply of laborers of type i, we have

$$\overline{L}_1 = \lambda \overline{L}, \quad \overline{L}_2 = (1 - \lambda)\overline{L}.$$

The wage that maximizes $A(w)/w$ is called the efficiency wage. $A(w)/w$ is given by the slope of a line from the origin to the wage productivity curve. In figure 3a $A_1\gamma_1$ is the efficiency wage; in figure 3b $A_2\gamma_2$ is.

(ii) If $A_1\gamma_1 < A_2\gamma_2$, type 1 has absolute disadvantage in self-employment:

$$A(w) = \begin{cases} A_1, & A_1\gamma_1 < w < A_2\gamma_2 \\ \overline{A}, & w > A_2\gamma_2 \end{cases} \tag{2.1b}$$

In this case it is clear that $A_1\gamma_1$ is always the efficiency wage. The interesting case is that where $A_1\gamma_1 > A_2\gamma_2$, and $\gamma_1 < \gamma_2$, and we focus on that.

Two caveats concerning (2.1) should be noted: First, these quality-wage relationships obtain if there is only a single "manufacturing" firm; otherwise, the wage-quality relationship facing any single firm may depend on the wage policies of other firms. Second, the wage that is relevant is the "expected wage"[6]; as will be noted below, in equilibrium there may be excess supply of laborers, and hence the probability of not being employed may have to be taken into account. We shall return to both of these matters later.

We proceed in our analysis as follows: First, we derive, for purposes of comparison, the market equilibrium with full information. Next, we describe a rather simple case, where there is a single firm in the "employed" sector. We then compare this semi-monopsony solution (it is not complete monopsony, since individuals all have the opportunity for self-employment) with the corresponding behavior when the single firm in the employed sector is government-controlled. Finally, with these results as background, we turn to the case where there are a large number of firms in the "employed" sector.

3 THE FULL-INFORMATION EQUILIBRIUM

Each labor unit obtains its marginal product. Hence, if the aggregate production function in manufacturing is

$$Q = F(E), \tag{3.1}$$

where E = effective labor, we obtain a demand function for effective units of labor as depicted in figure 4.

$$E^d = F'^{-1}(\omega),$$

where ω is the wage *per effective labor unit*. The supply of effective labor units is as follows:

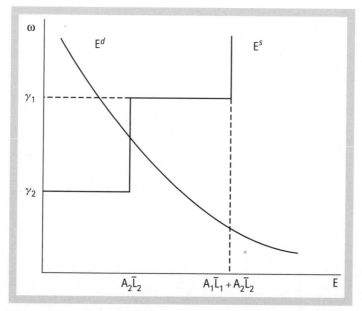

Fig. 4. Demand and supply of labor, full information $\gamma_1 > \gamma_2$

If $\gamma_1 > \gamma_2$ (figure 4),

$$E^s(\omega) = \begin{cases} 0, & \omega < \gamma_2 \\ A_2\overline{L}_2, & \gamma_2 < \omega < \gamma_1 \\ A_1\overline{L}_1 + A_2\overline{L}_2, & \omega > \gamma_1. \end{cases} \quad (3.2)$$

Equilibrium is determined in the conventional way, where

$$E^d(\omega) = E^s(\omega).$$

Clearly, those workers with a comparative advantage in manufacturing work in that sector.

4 The Semi-Monopsony Case—Single Wage

Now assume that there is a single firm, which pays a single wage. If at the wage it offers there is excess supply, individuals who do not obtain employment may work at their self-employment occupations. We assume there is no cost of applying for a job. Thus, the quality-wage relationship is exactly as described in equation 2.1.

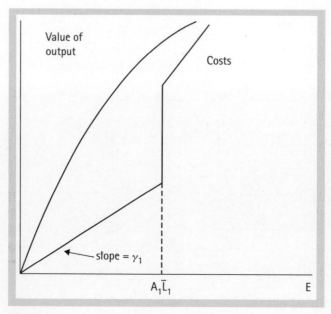

Fig. 5.

Perfect Information

The perfect-information solution to this case is simple, and is illustrated in figure 5. The total cost curve for efficiency units is derived from the supply curves (as depicted in figure 4). At $A_1\overline{L}_1$ there is a discontinuity (given our assumption of a single wage, here interpreted as a wage per efficiency unit in manufacturing); below this point the slope of the curve is γ_1, above it, γ_2, assuming "1" has a comparative advantage in manufacturing. (The other case is straightforward.) The total revenue curve is drawn in figure 5. The firm chooses the point at which profits are maximized. In figure 5 this is at the point of discontinuity, in which only those with a comparative advantage in manufacturing are hired, and at their reservation wage. But if the slope of the revenue curve at A_1L_1 is less than γ_1, then not all type 1 are hired, and if it is greater than γ_2 then some of type 2 are hired.

Imperfect Information

We now consider the behavior of the firm that knows that different individuals differ in their abilities, and knows that it cannot distinguish between the more and the less productive, but knows that the average productivity of those applying for a job will depend on the wage offered.

The firm wishes to maximize its profits, i.e.

$$\max F(A(w)L) - wL, \qquad (4.1a)$$

subject to the constraint

$$L \le L(w), \tag{4.1b}$$

where $A(w)$ denotes the dependence of the average quality of labor on the wage and where $L(w)$ is the maximum supply of labor at the given wage.

If $A_1\gamma_1 > A_2\gamma_2$,

$$L(w) = \begin{cases} 0, & w < A_2\gamma_2 \\ \overline{L}_2, & A_2\gamma_2 < w < A_1\gamma_1 \\ \overline{L}_1 + \overline{L}_2, & w > A_1\gamma_1. \end{cases} \tag{4.2}$$

If the constraint (4.1b) is not binding, we can think of the equilibrium as a (modified) competitive one; i.e., the firm can hire all the laborers it wants at the wage it *chooses* to pay.

It is easy to show that the firm will pay either a wage of $A_2\gamma_2$ or a wage of $A_1\gamma_1$.

Its decision will depend both on the wage-quality trade-off and on the supply function. If $A(w)$ were differentiable and the supply constraint were not binding, then the firm would set

$$A(w)F' = w \tag{4.3a}$$

and

$$A'F' = 1. \tag{4.3b}$$

Dividing (4.3b) by (4.3a), we obtain

$$A' = \frac{A}{w}. \tag{4.4}$$

The solution to (4.4) is known as the *efficiency wage* (see Liebenstein 1957 and Stiglitz 1976). It is the wage that minimizes wage costs per effective laborer:

$$\min \left\{ \frac{w}{A(w)} \right\}. \tag{4.5}$$

Thus, the two conditions are that the wage cost per effective unit of labor be minimized and that the marginal product equal the wage per effective labor unit.

In our example, the efficiency wage is found simply by comparing (when $A_1\gamma_1 > A_2\gamma_2$)

$$\frac{A_1\gamma_1}{\overline{A}} \text{ and } \frac{A_2\gamma_2}{A_2},$$

which depends critically on the relative proportions of the population in the two groups. Let w^e denote the efficiency wage. Then

$$w^e = \begin{cases} A_1\gamma_1 \\ A_2\gamma_2 \end{cases} \text{ as } \lambda \gtrless \lambda^* \equiv \frac{A_1\gamma_1 - A_2\gamma_2}{\gamma_2(A_1 - A_2)}. \tag{4.6}$$

Note that if $\gamma_1 > \gamma_2$, $\lambda^* > 1$, so $\lambda < \lambda^*$ and $w^e = A_2\gamma_2$. *If the type of labor that has an absolute advantage in manufacturing has a comparative advantage in self-employment, the efficiency wage is the reservation wage of the less productive group. Similarly, if the type of labor that has an absolute advantage in manufacturing has an absolute disadvantage in self-employment, then the efficiency wage is the reservation wage of the group that is more productive in manufacturing.*

The firm pays the efficiency wage if the labor constraint is not binding. Note that if the efficiency wage exceeds the minimum reservation wage, i.e.,

$$w^e > \min(A_1\gamma_1, A_2\gamma_2),$$

then, if the labor constraint is not binding, we have an equilibrium with an excess supply of laborers. There are individuals (all the individuals with a low reservation wage) who are not obtaining employment at the going wage and would be willing to work for less. In our model, the labor constraint is *not* binding if

$$F'(A(w^e)L(w^e)) < \frac{w^e}{A(w^e)}; \tag{4.7}$$

i.e., if $A_2\gamma_2 < A_1\gamma_2$ and $\lambda < \lambda^*$,

$$F'(A_2\overline{L}_2) < \gamma_2;$$

if $A_2\gamma_2 < A_1\gamma_1$ and $\lambda > \lambda^*$,

$$F'(\overline{A}\,\overline{L}) < \frac{A_1\gamma_1}{\overline{A}}.$$

When the labor constraint is binding, the firm sets

$$F'(A'L + AL') = L + wL'$$

or

$$AF' = \frac{w(1 + \eta^s)}{(A'w/A) + \eta^s}, \tag{4.8}$$

where η^s is the elasticity of labor supply,

$$\eta^s = \frac{L'w}{L}.$$

The marginal product exceeds the wage (that is why the labor-supply constraint is binding), and the wage exceeds the efficiency wage (i.e., $A' < A/w$). Equation 4.8 differs from the conventional formula for monopsony in that the firm takes into account the increased productivity resulting from an increase in the wage. This leads the firm to pay a higher wage than it would in the conventional monopsony case (where $\eta^s AF'/1 + \eta^s = w$).

In our particular example, the firm simply compares the profits it obtains by paying a low wage and hiring all the available labor at that wage against those it earns by paying the efficiency wage and hiring the optimal number of laborers at that wage,

$$F'(\overline{A}L) = \frac{w^e}{\overline{A}}.$$

In the 1976 version of the paper I provided an explicit analysis of that comparison, identifying conditions under which job rationing would occur.

5 COMPARISON OF SEMI-MONOPSONY CASES WITH PARETO OPTIMALITY

It is important in making welfare statements that we make the appropriate comparisons. That is, we should not compare a full-information equilibrium with a partial-information equilibrium. In this context, with imperfect information whenever $A_1\gamma_1 > A_2\gamma_2$ and $\gamma_1 < \gamma_2$ the manufacturing firm hires at least some of those with a comparative disadvantage in manufacturing employment, and this clearly is not optimal in the case of full information.

The appropriate comparison requires an analysis of the behavior of a government, faced with the same information constraints, and that of the market. Greenwald and Stiglitz (1986a) provide a general result showing that when information is imperfect and markets are incomplete market equilibrium is not constrained Pareto efficient—that is, there exist government policies that respect these market imperfections and yet can make some individuals better off without making anyone else worse off. Greenwald and Stiglitz (1988e) show how this argument can be extended to a version of the efficiency-wage model. Here, to develop our intuition about the nature of the market's inefficiency, we compare the behavior of the market with that of a government interested in maximizing national output. (It will be apparent that most of the differences identified below arise neither from the special notion of the social-welfare function implicit in this formulation nor from the assumption of a semi-monopsony in the market analysis.[7] These market failures arise, in perhaps modified form, in the competitive model described below.)

Formally, the problem of the government is to choose w and L so as to

$$\max F(A(w)L) - B(w)L \quad \text{s.t. } L \leq L(w), \tag{5.1}$$

where

$B \equiv A\gamma$ = productivity in self-employment

and

$B(w) \equiv$ mean opportunity cost of labor hired at wage w.

The market solution differs from the information-constrained optimal allocation because, with imperfect information, mean opportunity cost will in general differ from the wage,

$$B(w) \neq w.$$

In terms of our example, if

$$w = A_1\gamma_1 \quad \text{and} \quad A_1\gamma_1 > A_2\gamma_2, \tag{5.2}$$

then

$$B(w) = \lambda\gamma_1 A_1 + (1-\lambda)\gamma_2 A_2 = A_1\gamma_1 - (1-\lambda)(A_1\gamma_1 - A_2\gamma_2)$$

$$= A_2\gamma_2 + \lambda(A_1\gamma_1 - A_2\gamma_2) < w.$$

The market may differ from the informationally constrained optimal allocation in two respects: the wage paid and the numbers of laborers hired.

If the labor constraint is not binding, the government will choose w so that

$$\frac{A'}{A} = \frac{B'}{B},$$

i.e. to maximize $\ln(A/B)$ rather than $\ln(A/w)$, and hire labor to the point where

$$AF' = B.$$

Thus, in our example, the government efficiency wage, w_g^e, is equal to the reservation wage of the group with a comparative advantage in manufacturing[8]; i.e.,

$$w_g^e = \left\{ \begin{array}{c} \gamma_1 A_1 \\ \gamma_2 A_2 \end{array} \quad \text{as } \gamma_1 \lessgtr \gamma_2 \right\}.$$

Thus, if $\gamma_1 > \gamma_2$ or if $\gamma_1 < \gamma_2 A_2/A_1$,

$$w_g^e = w^e,$$

but if $\gamma_2 A_2/A_1 < \gamma_1 < \gamma_2$

$$w_g^e = A_1\gamma_1 \text{ always}$$

while

$$w^e = A_1\gamma_1 \text{ if and only if } \lambda > \lambda^*.$$

The private firm pays too *low* a wage if $\lambda < \lambda^*$. Even when it pays the correct wage, when $\gamma_2 A_2/A_1 < \gamma_1 < \gamma_2$ it hires too few laborers, since $B(w) < w$ then. When $\gamma_2 A_2/A_1 < \gamma_1 < \gamma_2$ and $\lambda < \lambda^*$, output in manufacturing is greater under government control. But employment may be smaller or larger, depending on the elasticity of demand for labor in manufacturing.

Finally, the conditions under which the firm operates with a labor constraint will differ.

In the 1976 version of the paper, I provided an explicit analysis of the differing conditions under which the labor constraint will be binding, i.e., in which there will be "involuntary" unemployment.

6 MULTIPLE-WAGE POLICY

There is no reason, however, that the single manufacturing firm needs to pay all individuals the same wage. It can use a multiple-wage (or, in our example, a two-wage) policy to sort individuals.

The objective in sorting out individuals is to act as a discriminating monopsonist; individuals differ in their reservation wages. The firm would like to act as a perfectly discriminating monopsonist, paying each individual only his reservation wage. It does not know which individuals have low reservation wages and which high, but by offering multiple wages it partially discriminates. Assume that an individual can apply for only one job (in the manufacturing sector); if he does not succeed in obtaining employment there, he returns to self-employment.

Assume the firm has two plants but can freely shift machines between them. At one plant it pays a wage w_H; at the other, a wage w_L, with $w_H > w_L$. At the first plant the firm hires N_H workers; at the second, N_L workers. Workers have to decide to which plant to apply. We assume that they allocate themselves to the plant with the higher expected wage; i.e., they are risk-neutral. (The analysis may be easily modified if they are risk-averse.)

We focus here on the case where type 1 has an absolute advantage in self-employment.[9] The most interesting case is that where $A_2\gamma_2$ is the efficiency wage but the firm wishes to hire more laborers than $\overline{L}_2$. We can show that the manufacturing firm maximizes its profits by paying at the high-wage plant a wage of $A_1\gamma_1$—so type 1 workers apply to the high-wage plant—and a wage in the low-wage plant which is just high enough to attract all the low-wage workers. All the type 1 workers apply to the high-wage plant, so the probability of getting a job is

$$p_H = \frac{N_H}{\overline{L}_1}.$$

The low-wage plant must pay a wage at least high enough to induce the low-productivity workers to apply there rather than at the high-wage plant:

$$w_L \geq \frac{A_1\gamma_1 N_H}{\overline{L}_1} + \left(1 - \frac{N_H}{\overline{L}_1}\right) A_2\gamma_2.$$

The total efficiency units purchased, if the firm hires N_H workers at the high-wage plant, is

$$E = A_1 N_H + A_2\overline{L}_2,$$

and the total cost is

$$C = w_L \overline{L}_2 + N_H A_1 \gamma_1.$$

Note that the marginal cost of increasing efficiency units is greater than it would be with perfect information; in the region where the low wage has to be increased to stop type 2 individuals from applying to the high-wage plant, it is[10]

$$\left(\overline{L}_2 (A_1 \gamma_1 - A_2 \gamma_2) / A_1 \overline{L}_1 \right) + \gamma_1.$$

It is less expensive to increase efficiency units by using queues at the high-wage firm as a screening device, and keeping wage differentials such that they act as a perfect screening device, than in any other way.

(Though it may thus be desirable to use a wage distribution as part of a screening mechanism, it is not always desirable to do so. See the 1976 version of the paper for a fuller discussion.)

Similar arguments hold if $A_1 \gamma_1 < A_2 \gamma_2$; two wages are paid when the demand for labor exceeds the supply of type 1 laborers.

The results of this section could have been derived more formally from the solution to the following problem: Assume that the firm consists of a large number of identical plants, each of whose production function we denote by $F()$. Let β denote the fraction paying a low wage. Then the firm maximizes

$$\max_{\{\beta, N_H, N_L, w_L\}} Y \equiv \beta F \left(\frac{N_L}{\beta} A_2 \right) - N_L w_L$$

$$+ (1 - \beta) F \left(\frac{N_H}{1 - \beta} \frac{A_1 \overline{L}_1 + A_2 L_2^A(w_H)}{\overline{L}_1 + L_2^A(w_H)} \right) - N_H A_1 \gamma_1$$

$$\text{s.t. } N_L \leq L_2^A(w_L), \quad N_H \leq \overline{L}_1 + L_2^A(w_H)$$

where $L_2^A(w_H)$ is the number of type 2 workers applying to the high-wage firm and $L_2^A(w_L)$ is the number applying to the low-wage firm.

7 OPTIMAL MULTIPLE-WAGE POLICY

A government-controlled manufacturing sector would also generally pay multiple wage rates; but the objective of the government is different. If it is indifferent as to distribution, it simply maximizes as follows:

$$\max_{\{\beta, N_H, N_L, w_H, w_L\}} Y^G \equiv \beta F \left(\frac{N_L A_2}{\beta} \right) - N_L \gamma_2 A_2 + (1 - \beta) F \left(\frac{N_H}{1 - \beta} \overline{A}_H \right)$$

$$- N_H \{ A_1 \gamma_1 \rho + A_2 \gamma_2 (1 - \rho) \}$$

(where ρ is the fraction of type 1 individuals in the high-wage manufacturing jobs, and $\overline{A}_H$ is the average ability in the high-wage firm) subject to the same constraints as before. As in section 5, the difference between the market allocation and the optimal allocation is attributed to the difference between the marginal cost of labor and the opportunity cost of labor $(A_1\gamma_1\rho + A_2\gamma_2(1 - \rho))$ in the high-wage firm, $A_2\gamma_2$ in the low).

There is another important difference: While the objective of the private manufacturer in introducing differential wages is to act as a discriminating monopsonist, paying, on average, a lower wage to those with a lower reservation wage (and in this sense, the wage distribution is analogous to that discussed by Salop (1977)), from the social point of view the objective of introducing differential wages is to enable the hiring in manufacturing of a larger proportion of those who have a comparative advantage in manufacturing. That is, in the absence of wage discrimination, the manufacturing sector hires only those with an absolute disadvantage in self-employment, or it hires the two groups in the proportions in which they occur in the population.

It is thus easy to show that it is socially optimal for the firm to pay different wages in different plants if and only if the labor that has an absolute disadvantage in self-employment also has a comparative disadvantage in self-employment; by using discriminatory wage policies, the firm can increase the proportion of this group that it hires.

Thus, while both semi-monopsony and optimality may entail wage distributions, the conditions under which the wage distributions arise differ.

8 Discrimination

If there are two groups in the population, and if the groups differ slightly, so that the minimum cost per efficiency unit purchased at the "social efficiency wage" is less for one group than for the other, there will be both hiring and wage discrimination (i.e., members of the two groups will receive different wages; it is possible that members of only one of the two groups will be hired). Whether discrimination exists, and its nature, may differ between the market and the social optimum, however.

9 The Competitive Solution

I have postponed the treatment of the competitive solution, because it is the most difficult; the distribution of abilities facing any single firm is a function of the actions taken by the other firms.

Earlier I stressed that the nature of the market equilibrium depends on whether firms, recognizing the dependence of quality on price (that is, productivity on wages), set their wages so as to minimize wage cost per efficiency unit. It turns out that the market equilibrium also depends critically on whether workers can apply, costlessly, to all firms simultaneously. If they cannot, then firms may be able to take actions that affect the quality of the applicant pool.

Unlimited Applications

In the case where workers can apply to all firms simultaneously, and all hiring decisions are made simultaneously, each firm will pay the efficiency wage so long as, at the efficiency wage, the total demand for labor is less than the supply; that is, if $A(w)$ is the average productivity of those applying at wage w, then w^c (the competitive wage) is the wage that minimizes $w/A(w)$, i.e.,

$$A'(w) = A(w)/w,$$

provided (in the obvious notation)

$$L^s(w^c) \geq L^d(w^c).$$

In our two-group model, with $A_2\gamma_2 < A_1\gamma_1$,

$$w^c = \begin{cases} A_2\gamma_2 & \text{if } 1/\gamma_2 > \overline{A}/A_1\gamma_1 \\ A_1\gamma_1 & \text{if } 1/\gamma_2 < \overline{A}/A_1\gamma_1. \end{cases}$$

Only One Application Allowed

To investigate the effects of costly and/or limited application, we consider here the special case where individuals can apply to only one firm, but that application is costless.[11] The results reported here are, however, general.

We first establish that there cannot exist a "pooling" equilibrium, in which all firms pay the efficiency wage. For if all firms did that, it would pay some firm to deviate by paying a slightly higher wage. If it did so, it would wind up with a longer queue. The longer queue would serve to detract all low-productivity applicants, and since the firm could thus get only high-productivity applicants its profits would be increased.

More formally, if individuals are risk-neutral, they will apply to the job that maximizes their expected income. If p^j is the probability of getting a job at firm j, and w^j is that firm's wage, then an individual of type i's expected income is[12]

$$p^j w^j + (1 - p^j)A_i\gamma_i \equiv V^i(w^j, p^j),$$

where

$$p^j = N^j/j\text{th firm applicants},$$

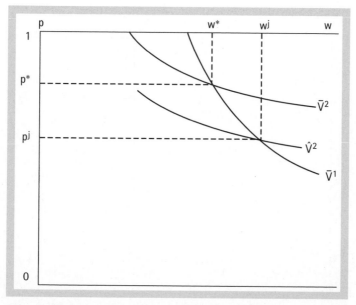

Fig. 6. There cannot exist a pooling equilibrium. As a firm increases its wage, the queue increases along $\overline{V}^1$. At all points on $\overline{V}^1$, with $w > w^*$, $\hat{V}^2 < \overline{V}^2$: only type 1 applies

where N^j is the number of jobs in the jth firm. Assuming that the costs of applying to all firms are the same, individuals will, in equilibrium, sort themselves among firms so as to equate the expected incomes of all firms among which they apply (and expected income at firms at which they do not apply is lower):

$$V^i(w^j, p^j) = \overline{V}^i \text{ for all } j \text{ for which type } i\text{'s apply,}$$

$$V(w^j, p^j) < \overline{V}^i \text{ for all } j \text{ for which type } i\text{'s do not apply.}$$

One small firm believes it has no effect on the level of expected income that workers of any type can obtain. It takes, in other words, $\overline{V}^i$ as given. As the firm changes its wage, queue length adjusts so as to keep the expected income of those applying the same. Figure 6 shows the indifference curves of types 1 and 2 through the putative pooling equilibrium, $\{w^*, p^*\}$. Here

$$\frac{dp}{dw} = -\frac{p^*}{w^* - A_i \gamma_i}; \tag{9.1}$$

thus, the indifference curve of the more productive workers is always steeper, as depicted in figure 6.[13] This means that any firm that raises its wage will find that as it does so, its queue length is lengthened, but as it is lengthened, eventually, all the type 2 workers stop applying, and in "equilibrium" only type 1 individuals apply. The equilibrium queue length is given by (for $w > w^*$)

$$V^1(w^*, p^*) = V^1(w^j, p^j), \tag{9.2}$$

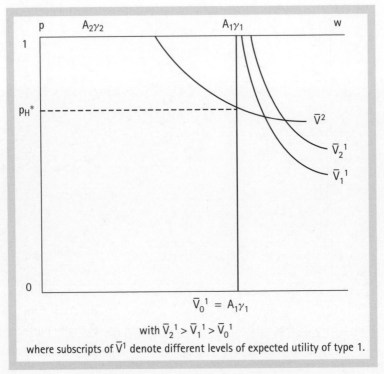

with $\bar{V}_2^{\,1} > \bar{V}_1^{\,1} > \bar{V}_0^{\,1}$

where subscripts of $\bar{V}^1$ denote different levels of expected utility of type 1.

Fig. 7. Separating equilibrium with $w_L = \gamma_1 A_2$ and $w_H = \gamma_1 A_1$

and, since at the resulting $\{w^j, p^j\}$

$$V^2(w^*, p^*) > V^2(w^j, p^j) \equiv \hat{V}$$

(see figure 7), no individual of type 2 applies. Since there is a discrete change in the quality mix with a marginal change in the wage, any firm deviating must discretely increase its profits. Thus, there cannot exist a pooling equilibrium; there must be separation.

For future reference, note that in the special case being considered here, where individuals are risk-neutral and there are no costs of applying, the limiting "indifference curve" as V^1 approaches $A_1\gamma_1$ is a vertical straight line, as in figure 7.

We focus here on the case where type 2 has a comparative advantage in manufacturing, i.e.,[14] $1/\gamma_1 < 1/\gamma_2$.

The separating market equilibrium always has the following characteristics: (i) If more than one wage is paid, costs per efficiency unit are the same at both firms; if only one wage is paid, costs per efficiency unit are higher at any wage at which the other type could be obtained. (ii) There is separation; i.e., only members of one type apply to each firm. (iii) The wage equals the value of the marginal product of labor.

In the case at hand, the equilibrium is described as follows.[15] For a single wage (only type 2 hired):

(a) $w = A_2\gamma_2$ if $A_2 F'(A_2\bar{L}_2) \leq A_2\gamma_2$: only some of type 2 hired;
(b) $A_2\gamma_2 \leq w \leq A_2\gamma_1$ if $A_2\gamma_1 \geq A_2 F'(A_2\bar{L}_2) \geq A_2\gamma_2$: all of type 2 hired.

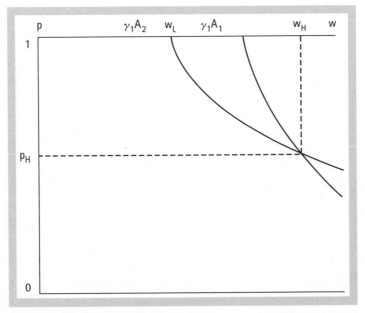

Fig. 8. Separating equilibrium with $w_L > \gamma_1 A_2$ and $w_H > \gamma_1 A_1$

For a wage distribution:

(a) $w_L = A_2\gamma_1$, $w_H = A_1\gamma_1$, if $F'(A_2\overline{L}_2) > \gamma_1$ and $F'(A_2\overline{L}_2 + p_H^*\overline{L}_1 A_1) \le \gamma_1$, where p_H^* is such that $V^2(w_H, p_H) = V^2(w_L, 1)$. All of type 2 hired. N_H type 1 hired, where $f'(A_2\overline{L}_2 + N_H A_1) = \gamma_1$; the size of the queue is given by $p_H = N_H/\overline{L}_1$. All type 2 hired weakly prefer to apply to the low-wage jobs. See figure 11.

(b) If $F'(A_2\overline{L}_2 + p_H^*\overline{L}_1 A_1) > \gamma_1$, then the equilibrium will have $A_2\gamma_1 < w_L < w_H$; $w_H > A_1\gamma_1$; $p_H > 0$. See figure 8. More precisely, the equilibrium is described by the following three equations:

$$\frac{A_2}{w_L} = \frac{A_1}{w_H} \quad \text{(equal cost per effective laborer)},$$

$$w_L = w_H\left(\frac{N_H}{\overline{L}_1}\right) + A_2\gamma_2\left(1 - \frac{N_H}{\overline{L}_1}\right) \quad \text{(self-selection condition)},$$

$$N_H A_1 + A_2\overline{L}_2 = F'^{-1}\left(\frac{w_L}{A_2}\right) \quad \text{(demand-for-labor equation)},$$

where N_H is the number of individuals hired at the high wage.

Figure 9 provides an explicit calculation of the equilibrium (w_L^*, N_H^*) for this case.[16] w_H can be obtained from the equal cost per effective laborer condition.

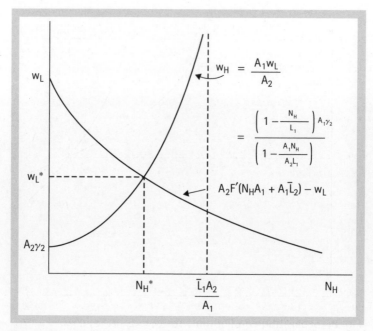

Fig. 9.

The Wage-Taking Adervse Selection Model

For the sake of completeness, we mention the one final possible equilibrium configuration, where firms fail to recognize their ability to set wages. They act as wage-takers, and the equilibrium is the intersection of the demand and supply curves for labor, where firms, in determining their demand, do recognize the dependence of productivity on wages. For the case where there are no application costs, the demand and supply for labor curves appear as in figure 10. There is a discrete increase in supply when wages rise to type 1's reservation wage; at the same point, there is a discrete *increase* in demand, since at that point there is a discrete increase in productivity. In the figure, there are multiple equilibria.

10 CONSTRAINED PARETO EFFICIENCY OF COMPETITIVE MARKET EQUILIBRIUM

The preceding section described a number of different competitive equilibrium configurations. Most of these are not constrained Pareto efficient; that is, the government, faced with the same information constraints, can make some individuals better off without making anyone else worse off.

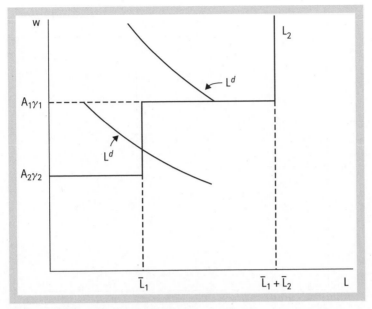

Fig. 10. Wage-taking competitive equilibrium—two-group case

The government can be thought of as facing two problems: whether to attempt to "screen" (i.e., offer a wage distribution that induces self-selection) and, if it does try to screen, what is the optimal wage-hiring policy.

No Screening Equilibria

In the above analysis, no screening equilibria arose in two cases: that where individuals could apply costlessly to as many jobs as they wished, and that where firms acted as wage takers.

In both cases, firms hire workers up to the wage that equals the (average) value of the marginal product of labor. We noticed earlier that the market solution does not maximize net national product; for it fails to recognize that the wage, on average, exceeds the opportunity cost of labor.

Restricted Applications

If the government could impose a restriction that individuals could apply to only one firm, it might be able to induce a constrained Pareto improvement. Figure 11 shows the "pooling equilibrium" and a low-productivity worker's indifference curve through the pooling equilibrium (assuming he can apply to only one job). If the government hires a low-productivity worker at $\hat{w}_L$ (the wage that makes him just indifferent), it will improve the mix of applicants at the "pooling" equilibrium. If the government adjusts the number hired at that equilibrium, to leave p^* unchanged, all workers will be indifferent. Under certain circumstances, this perturbation will increase profits; the low-productivity worker is willing to accept a low wage, to

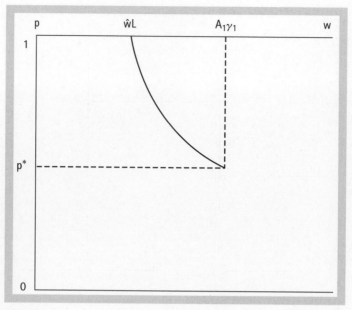

Fig. 11.

eliminate his risk of not getting hired, and the quality mix of the applicants at the high-wage firm is increased.

Wage-Taking Equilibrium

The wage-taking market equilibrium may also not be constrained Pareto efficient. As was noted, there may be multiple equilibria. The low-wage equilibrium may be Pareto dominated by the high-wage equilibrium. In the low-wage equilibrium, the low-productivity workers are just indifferent to getting a job in manufacturing and self-employment; in the high wage equilibrium, all of the low-productivity workers who do get jobs are unambiguously better off. Moreover, if $A_1\gamma_1$ is the efficiency wage, profits are higher at the high-wage equilibrium, because costs per efficiency unit are lower.

Screening Equilibria

In the case of screening, constrained Pareto optimality entails

$$\max V^2(w_L, p_L)$$

$$\text{s.t. } V^1(w_H, p_H) \geq \overline{V}^1,$$

$$\pi \geq \overline{\pi},$$

$$\pi + w_L p_L \overline{L}_2 + p_H \overline{L}_1 \leq \beta F\left(\frac{A_2 \overline{L}_2 p_L}{\beta}\right) + (1-\beta)F\left(\frac{p_H \overline{L}_1}{1-\beta}\right),$$

$$V^2(w_L, p_L) \leq V^2(w_H, p_H),$$

where π denotes total profits for firms.

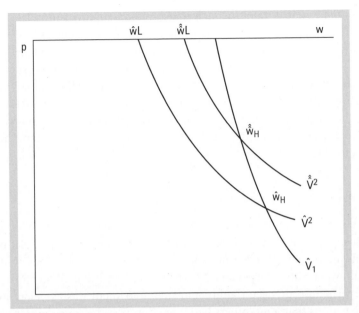

Fig. 12. Raising w_L lowers the "separating" high wage

Note that the problem we have formulated is the general problem of constrained Pareto optimality (Greenwald and Stiglitz 1986a), which is somewhat more general than the problem of maximizing net national output analyzed earlier.

A major difference between the market solution and constrained Pareto optimality is that the former requires the cost per efficiency unit to be the same at all firms; the government can tax, say, high-wage firms to subsidize low-wage firms. Moreover, the government recognizes that policies undertaken by one (group of) firm(s) has effects on other firms: if the low-wage firms increase their wages, it lowers the wage that the high-wage firms must pay to still be able to obtain just high-productivity workers. (See figure 12.)

Thus, it is possible to show that there are conditions under which we (i) tax the high-wage firms; (ii) use the proceeds to finance a subsidy to the low-wage firms; (iii) adjust the wage and hiring policy at the high-wage firms so that there is, in equilibrium, "separation" and still leave high-productivity individuals on their reservation indifference curve; and (iv) still have money left over to increase profits. The low-productivity workers are better off; the high-productivity workers remain on their reservation indifference curves, and are thus unaffected; and there are profits left over, which can be used to make everyone better off.[17]

11 Concluding Remarks

The results of this paper may be looked at in two ways. As a positive theory, the interaction of wages, quality, and queues that has been explored here may provide at least part of the explanation of the high wages and unemployment in less-developed countries; it may provide part of the explanation of why laborers with seemingly similar skills are paid different wages; it may provide part of the explanation of why in parts of a recession firms do not lower wages in response to excess supply; and it may provide part of the explanation of both wage and hiring discrimination.

Alternatively, the analysis of this paper may be viewed as a criticism of the standard economic theory in which perfect information is assumed. Conventional notions of equilibrium are shown to be inappropriate, and conventional optimality results are shown not to obtain.

Postscript

I am sometimes asked why was I so tardy getting this paper published. There are two reasons. One was that I continued to look for alternative formulations, both simpler and more general; I did not succeed in doing so, at least before my attention was drawn to other problems.[18,19] The second was that I was not convinced that *this* explanation of wage rigidity and unemployment was as persuasive as the other explanations that I and others had offered in what became the fast-expanding literature on efficiency wages.[20] The model formulated in the last sections of the paper suggests that unemployment will be concentrated among the more able, as they seek to prove that they have a higher fallback wage. There may be important instances of this—Harley Street doctors and many US surgeons work short work weeks, shorter than seems plausible on the basis of standard income effects. And interpreting information-theoretic models is often tricky; the theory makes predictions about relative unemployment among groups of individuals who are otherwise observationally equivalent. It does not compare unemployment rates among doctors and blue-collar workers—these are not observationally equivalent—but rather among doctors, or among plumbers. How much of total unemployment could be attributed to this still remains problematic.

This paper represents an attempt to formulate an *equilibrium* theory of unemployment. I have increasingly come to the view that to explain cyclical unemployment one needs to focus on models of adjustment. The question is, what will happen to the quality of a firm's labor force, and therefore to its long-run profits, if, in response to some disturbance, it lowers its wages, rather than laying off a particular fraction of its workers? The kinds of "adverse selection" effects upon which I have focused here may take on first-order importance in that context.[21]

Acknowledgments

This work was supported by the National Science Foundation and the Hoover Institution. I have benefited greatly from conversations with Andy Weiss; he has dealt with some of the same issues in the context of imperfectly competitive economies (1976). His recently published book (1990) provides an excellent description of a wide range of efficiency wage models.

Notes

1. Although in our discussions we assume that the seller knows what he is selling but the buyer does not know what he is buying, this is not essential for our analysis; the seller may also be uninformed, and much of what we have to say still remains valid (so long as sellers of different qualities of commodities differ in their supply responses).

2. In later analysis, it will be clear that what is of importance is whether type 1 or 2 has a comparative advantage in manufacturing, i.e. whether

$$\frac{1}{\gamma_1} = \frac{A_1}{A_1 \gamma_1} > \text{ or } < \frac{1}{\gamma_2} = \frac{A_2}{A_2 \gamma_2}.$$

The actual value of γ makes no difference, since production in manufacturing will be governed by a production function described below (equation 3.1), which will transform units of labor power in manufacturing into units of manufacturing goods. If we choose units so $Q = E$, where Q is output in manufacturing and E is effective labor, and so the price of manufacturing output is the same as self-employment output, then it is natural to assume that $\gamma_1 < 1$ (productivity of type 1 is greater in manufacturing than in the rural sector) but $\gamma_2 > 1$ (productivity of type 2 workers is greater in self-employment than in manufacturing).

3. And that the relative price of the output of self-employment to that of manufacturing is constant (and normalized at unity).

4. Later it will be noted that, in general, we should write $A_j(w_1, \ldots, w_n, L_1, \ldots, L_n)$. The mean ability of those offering themselves to the jth firm is a function of the wages and hiring of all firms. When we simply write $A(w)$, we are implicitly assuming that all firms in the manufacturing sector are paying the same wage, and that quality does not depend on the amount of hiring. $A(w)$ then represents the mean quality of those offering themselves for employment in the urban sector. Alternatively, we assume there is a single manufacturing firm. These matters are elaborated on below.

5. The obvious objections may be raised to these informational assumptions: First, if the firm cannot observe productivity, why do individuals work at all? The answer to this is that firms can identify abilities and productivities within a range; that is, there may be individuals who are much more productive and individuals who are much less productive, but these have been screened off. Moreover, after they have hired and trained the individual, they may be able to observe both ability and effort and thus can enforce contracts requiring a stipulated level of effort. But then, it might be asked, why do not the more able "guarantee" that they are more able? They presumably would, if they were perfectly certain of their abilities, or, if uncertain, they were risk-neutral. But if individuals are risk-averse and there is even a slight degree of uncertainty about their own abilities, individuals will be unwilling to provide complete insurance; and so long as they do not provide complete insurance, firms will be concerned with the

mix of individuals they hire. The particular model developed here can be thought of as the polar case of infinitely risk-averse individuals facing infinitesimally small risks, i.e., an infinitesimally small fraction of individuals of type actually have productivity A_2; all individuals have a utility function of the form $U = \min\{w\}$, the minimum income in any state of nature. But then any payment scheme depending on the actual performance will not act as a screening device, since for both groups min $\{w\}$ is the same.

6. Or, more generally, we need to specify both the wage and the number of individuals hired (from which we can derive the length of the queue).

7. In some instances, where there is *not* unemployment, the semi-monopsonist hires fewer workers than is efficient, with this restriction in employment arising from its noncompetitive position.

8. That is, if $A_2\gamma_2 < A_1\gamma_1$, at $w = A_2\gamma_2$,

$$\frac{B}{A} = \frac{A_2\gamma_2}{A_2}$$

while at $w = A_1\gamma_1$

$$\frac{B}{A} = \frac{\lambda A_1\gamma_1 + (1-\lambda)A_2\gamma_2}{\lambda A_1 + (1-\lambda)A_2}.$$

The latter exceeds the former if $\gamma_1 > \gamma_2$, and conversely.

9. See the 1976 version of the paper for other cases, as well as details substantiating the argument below.

10. Note that so long as

$$w_L > A_1\gamma_1 \frac{N_H}{L_1} + A_2\gamma_2 \left(1 - \frac{N_H}{L_1}\right)$$

the marginal cost of hiring additional efficiency units is just $A_1/A_1\gamma_1$.

If, instead of increasing w_L, the firm had simply allowed some of the low-productivity workers to apply to the high-wage firm, applications would have continued until

$$w_L = \frac{w_H N_H}{\overline{L}_1 + \hat{L}_2} + A_2\gamma_2 \left(1 - \frac{N_H}{\overline{L}_1 + \hat{L}_2}\right),$$

where $\hat{L}_2$ is the number of type 2 individuals applying to the high-wage firm.

Now, hiring an additional worker at the high-wage firm has a deleterious effect on quality, and reduces the number of applicants at the low-wage firm.

The equations

$$E = N_H \left(\frac{A_1\overline{L}_1 + A_2\hat{L}_2}{\overline{L}_1 + \hat{L}_2}\right) + A_2(\overline{L}_2 - \hat{L}_2)$$

and

$$C = \left(\frac{\overline{L}_2 - \hat{L}_2}{\overline{L}_1 + \hat{L}_2} + 1\right) w_H N_H + A_2\gamma_2(\overline{L}_2 - \hat{L}_2)\left(1 - \frac{N_H}{\overline{L}_1 + \hat{L}_2}\right)$$

where we have made use of the expression for w_L, can be thought of as defining isocost and iso-efficiency unit curves for $N_L = \overline{L}_2 - \hat{L}_2$ and N_H:

$$\left.\frac{dN_H}{d\hat{L}_2}\right|_c = \frac{N_H}{\overline{L}_1 + \hat{L}_2} - \frac{A_2\gamma_2(N^H - (\overline{L}_1 + \hat{L}_2))}{(\overline{L}_2 - \hat{L}_2)(A_1\gamma_1 - A_2\gamma_2) + (\overline{L}_1 + \hat{L}_2)A_1\gamma_1}$$

$$\left.\frac{dN_H}{d\hat{L}_2}\right|_E = \frac{N_H}{\overline{L}_1 + \hat{L}_2}\left(\frac{(A_1 - A_2)\overline{L}_1 + A_2(\overline{L}_1 + \hat{L}_2)^2/N_H}{A_1\overline{L}_1 + A_2\hat{L}_2}\right),$$

from which it is apparent that there will be a corner solution, with $\hat{L}_2 = 0$ under the assumed conditions.

11. In effect, the second application can be thought of as having a prohibitively high application cost.

12. More generally, if there were a cost of c_i for a type i to apply to a job, individuals of type i's expected utility from applying to firm j would be given by

$$EU^1 \equiv p^j u^i(w^j) + (1 - p^j)u^i(A_i\gamma_i) - c_i \equiv V^i(w^j, p^j).$$

13. This result is true with risk-averse individuals and with application costs, so long as type 2 individuals are risk-averse than type 1 individuals.

14. More general cases, when there is risk aversion and costs to applying, may be handled similarly.

15. In the special case of risk neutrality and no costs of application, if $\gamma_1 < \gamma_2$, then there may either exist no equilibrium, or it may be characterized by a single wage, $w = A_2\gamma_2$ (e.g., if $F'(A_2\overline{L}_2) < \gamma_2$ and if $A_2\gamma_2$ is the efficiency wage) or by a two-wage distribution (w_L, w_H), with

$$V^2(w_L, 1) = V^2(w_H, p_H),$$

$$w_L/A_2 = w_H/A_1,$$

$$A_2 F'(L_2A_2 + p_H\overline{L}_1A_1) = w_L.$$

The conditions under which each at these may occur are spelled out in Rodriguez 1991.

16. The equilibrium just described may be given a slightly different interpretation. Assume that firms enter a market sequentially. Once workers have accepted a job, they are committed. In deciding to accept a job, they must look at the opportunities they are forgoing. The opportunity cost of accepting a job is thus *endogenous*—the inability to accept a higher-wage job, should it come along. In competitive equilibrium, (i) wages must be such that it pays workers to accept a job, rather than to turn down the job, in the hopes that a better opportunity will show up; and (ii) all firms must face the same wage costs per efficiency unit obtained.

As Guasch and Weiss (1980a) note, later entrants appear to have a marked advantage over earlier entrants. Earlier entrants hire lower-productivity workers (those with "low" reservation wages); this shifts the wage-productivity curve, seeming to imply that later entrants would pay higher wages and face lower costs per efficiency unit. This is the advantage of being late. But this cannot be a competitive equilibrium; and it ignores the reaction of workers who, anticipating higher wage offers in the future, will alter their reservation wages.

Assume that there are two rounds to wage offers. In the first round, firms make an offer of w_L; in the second round they offer w_H, where w_L and w_H are as described earlier. Note that if the low-wage workers correctly anticipate the future wages and hiring probabilities, they will all apply for and accept the low-wage offers; and when they do this, the cost per efficiency unit at the low-wage-early-entrant firms is identical to that at the high-wage-later-entrant firms. There is no disadvantage to being late. Wages and probabilities of getting a job are acting as screening devices among what would otherwise appear to be observationally equivalent workers.

These results are generalized by Nalebuff and Stiglitz (1982, 1985), who also address whether job commitments will arise endogenously as part of an equilibrium.

17. This is seen most clearly in the case of constant-returns-to-scale production functions, for which $\pi = 0$, and in the separating equilibrium, for suitable choice of units, $w_L = A_2$ and $w_H = A_1$. Accordingly, under our assumptions of risk neutrality and no application costs, all the high-ability individuals apply to the high-wage firms, so $p_H = N_H/\overline{L}_1$, where N_H is the number hired at the high-wage firms and where p_H is restricted, so that the self-selection condition is satisfied. Total profits is given by

$$\pi = (A_1 - w_H)p_H\overline{L}_1 + (A_2 - w_L)\overline{L}_2.$$

If w_H is increased, then to keep type I's on the same indifference curve

$$\frac{dp_H}{dw_H} = -\frac{p_H}{w_H - A_1\gamma_1}.$$

If w_H is lowered and p_H increased, the separating wage $\hat{w}_L$ is increased:

$$\frac{d\hat{w}_L}{dw_H} = p_H + (w_H - A_2\gamma_2)\frac{dp_H}{dw_H}$$

$$= \frac{A_1\gamma_1 - A_2\gamma_2}{w_H - A_1\gamma_1}p_H.$$

Hence, total profits are increased when w_H is reduced if

$$p_H\overline{L}_1 - p_H\overline{L}_2\frac{A_1\gamma_1 - A_2\gamma_2}{w_H - A_1\gamma_1}$$

$$= \frac{p_H\overline{L}}{w_H - A_1\gamma_1}[\lambda w_H + (1 - \lambda)(A_2\gamma_2 - A_1\gamma_1)] > 0.$$

See Rodriguez 1991 for a more general result.

18. Barry Nalebuff and I (1982, 1985) did manage to formulate some *less* simple but more general models, which were partly focused on the "advantages of being late" that Guasch and Weiss discussed (1980a).

19. A few further bibliographic remarks are in order. The most widely cited paper explaining wage rigidities in terms of adverse selection is perhaps Weiss (1980), but in that paper Weiss does not formulate a competitive equilibrium market of the labor market, which I have attempted to do here. Further results are reported in Weiss (1990). A more rigorous analysis of Akerlof's model is contained in Wilson (1980).

In Stiglitz (1987a); I explain in greater detail the differences between this model, the standard Arrow-Debreu model, and the Akerlof lemons model. Greenwald (1986) provides perhaps the best articulation of the Akerlof lemons model in the context of labor markets.

The use of unemployment (or more generally, the failure to engage in a transaction) as a screening device has subsequently been explored more thoroughly, e.g. in the bargaining literature. See Myerson (1985) and Farrell (1987).

20. For a survey, see Yellen (1984) or Stiglitz (1987a).

21. Bruce Greenwald and I (1988e) have attempted to model this adjustment process formally, showing why firms would choose not to lower wages even in the face of an excess supply of labor. See also Arnott, Hosios, and Stiglitz (1988).

CHAPTER 9

SORTING OUT THE DIFFERENCES BETWEEN SCREENING AND SIGNALING MODELS

INTRODUCTION, 2007

WHEN I reread this paper in preparing the *Selected Works*, I was struck by how, in some ways, the literature on screening and signaling had progressed so little since our work several decades ago—in spite of the fact that screening and signaling models have entered into the toolkits of economists in every field. Spence, in his work on signaling, had concluded that there was infinity of equilibria; Rothschild and I, that there might not be any equilibria. It was clear that we were analyzing the same problem; were the differences in results due to differences in details of model specification, due to the fact that in Spence's model the informed agent moves first, whereas in Rothschild-Stiglitz, the uninformed moves first? And which is the *natural* economic specification?

As I note in the Introduction to this volume, Spence's results on the multiplicity of equilibria come from what may be viewed as a misspecification, or an incomplete specification. Most simply put, if the least able individual reduces his education level, then he will still be classified as the least able—or, that is the worst that could happen to him. Hence, in an "optimum" response equilibrium—where each individual thinks how markets will respond "rationally" to out of equilibrium moves—the least able will choose the level of education which maximizes his/her utility (when education has no effect on productivity, that means a zero level of education.) That provides the boundary condition for the signaling differential equation, so there is a unique equilibrium.

Nonetheless, since in signaling equilibria, the informed agent must think about how the market might punish out of equilibrium moves, it seems conceivable that the set of equilibria will be *richer* than when the uninformed move first. But that intuition runs into another problem: positive profit equilibria. In the signaling equilibrium, competition will ensure that each market participant pays the actuarial value of his insurance, gets a wage corresponding to his expected productivity, etc. Profits are driven to zero. But it is easy to see that there may be positive profit equilibrium when the uninformed move first.

Consider the Rothschild-Stiglitz insurance market, where the separating equilibrium is easily described: the high risk individual gets perfect insurance at his/her actuarial odds. Let $U_H(a, \beta)$ be his/her expected utility, a function of the premium, a, and the benefit net of the premium, β, and let p_H be the probability of an accident for the high risk individual. Actuarially fair insurance requires that:

$$(1 - p_H)a_H = p_H\beta_H$$

and complete insurance implies that:

$$d - a_H = \beta_H$$

where d is the loss in the event of an accident.

Then the separating contract, $\{a_L, \beta_L\}$ is that contract which maximizes utility subject to the non-profit constraint and the self-selection constraint:

$$\max U_L(a_L, \beta_L)$$
s.t.
$$(1 - p_L)a_L \geq p_L\beta_L \qquad\qquad (A.1)$$
$$U_H(a, \beta) \geq U_H(a_L, \beta_L) \qquad\qquad (A.2)$$

When the so-called single crossing property is satisfied (indifference curves for one group are always steeper than those of the other), then the solution occurs at the *intersection* of the two constraints. When the single crossing property is not satisfied—which it will not be if, for instance, the low risk individuals are more risk averse than the high risk individuals—then the solution to the maximization problem may occur when (A.2) is binding, but not (A.1), that is, *equilibrium may entail positive profits*. If the firms selling insurance policies to the low risk individuals lower their premium slightly, in an attempt to get more of these highly profitable customers, they discover that they are inundated by high risk individuals. The policy goes discontinuously from making a profit to making a loss. And that is why positive profit equilibrium can be sustained. In short, while in the paper, we provide a set of conditions which rule out positive profit equilibrium, there is no intrinsic reason why these assumptions will be satisfied.

SINGLE CONTRACT EQUILIBRIA
AND PARETO EFFICIENCY

This paper, like much of the literature, focuses on situations where each firm offers a single contract, which can be problematic. Rothschild and Stiglitz showed that there might not be a competitive equilibrium (in the natural definition). That there is a problem can be seen in a slightly different way. If we ask what set of break-even contracts maximizes the well being of the low risk individuals (high ability individuals, in the education ability model), subject to the non-profit constraint for both types of contracts *together* and to the self-selection constraint, i.e.

$$\max U_L(\alpha_L, \beta_L)$$
$$\text{s.t.}$$
$$N_L[(1 - p_L)\beta_L - p_L\alpha_L] + N_H[(1 - p_H)\beta_H - p_H\alpha_H] \geq 0 \qquad \text{(A.3)}$$
$$U_H(\alpha, \beta) \geq U_H(\alpha_L, \beta_L), \qquad \text{(A.4)}$$

where N_L is the number of L risk individuals, N_H the number of high risk individuals, then the solution may entail losses on the high risk contracts, made up by profits on the low risk contracts. (The conditions under which this is so are the same as the conditions under which an equilibrium in which each firm issues a single contract does not exist.) Obviously, if firms only issue one contract, this cannot be sustained: no one will issue the loss making contracts.

A similar problem arises in the case of the positive profit contracts discussed in the previous subsection, for these contracts too are not (constrained) Pareto efficient. If some of the profits are spent to subsidize the high risk individuals, their indifference curve shifts up, and the maximum utility attainable by the low risk individual shifts up in tandem. Pareto optimality requires there to be subsidies paid by the high risk out of the profits on the low risk, so that in total, there are no net profits. But this equilibrium too cannot be sustained if each insurance firm offers only one contract.

But there is no a priori reason to restrict insurance firms to issuing a single contract. And clearly, the government can sustain the Pareto optimal allocation.

There is, however, a problem: if a firm issues both a profit making and a loss making contract, another firm could always enter, offering only the profitable contract; its profits would be higher. And as a result of the skimming off of the positive profit contracts, the two contract firm(s) will be making losses and will shut down. But then the contract that was offered to the low risk individuals will attract both high and low risk individuals. It will no longer be profitable.

There is a way around this problem: the two contract firm can insist that it issue contracts in a fixed ratio, N_L / N_H. Then, if a new entrant tries to skim off a low risk individual, the high risk individuals will find that they cannot get insurance, and the new entrant will find that s/he faces an applicant pool that reflects the riskiness of the population as a whole. He/she cannot free ride off of the "selection" of the two contract firm.

It is perfectly rational for the two contract firm to act in this way; and there is a natural sense in which this constitutes a competitive equilibrium. But it differs from an ordinary competitive equilibrium: there are quantity constraints. Firms do not stand willing to sell as much insurance of a given contract as they can.

These equilibria, involving cross subsidies, cannot be sustained as part of a signaling (informed individuals move first) equilibrium. This is a second sense in which the set of equilibria with uninformed moves first may be richer than the set of equilibria in which the informed party moves first.

Out of Equilibrium Moves: Further Discussion

We have shown how the assumption that there is a "optimal response" narrows the set of equilibria; it is natural to ask, can we reduce the range of equilibria still further, by asking who might have an incentive to deviate from the equilibrium in the observed way? Thus Cho and Kreps (1987) suggest that a pooling equilibrium could not be sustained because the high ability would deviate (e.g. by obtaining a higher level of education). There is a sufficiently high level of education that even if the employer took the signal as conveying that the individual was of high ability, the low ability individual would be worse off *than s/he is in the pooling equilibrium*, but the high ability individual would be better off. (That there always exists such a level of education is the point, of course, of the Rothschild-Stiglitz analysis.) Employers would infer that clearly the low ability would have no incentive to deviate in this way. Hence, the employer would infer that this is a high ability individual. Accordingly, the pooling equilibrium could not be sustained.

The Cho-Kreps analysis provides a game–theoretic interpretation of the Rothschild-Stiglitz result, but there is a fundamental difference. Rothschild-Stiglitz was concerned with competitive markets, where each individual and insurance firm was so small and insignificant that s/he believed his/her actions would have no impact on the market equilibrium. Thus, any small insurance company announcing that it would offer a policy with a high deductibility would assume it would not affect the policies offered by others, and hence it would be able to attract only the good risks; similarly, any employer announcing that it would hire individuals with a high level of education would be able to attract only the high ability workers. But, of course, if it pays one small insurance firm to do so, it pays many of them—so many that the equilibrium is in fact destroyed. This dilemma is at the heart of the non-existence result of Rothschild-Stiglitz: though each believes that they will not destroy the equilibrium, in fact they do.

The Cho-Kreps analysis operates in the much more elusive arena of beliefs: if workers believe that the firm will infer that those who make an out of equilibrium move are of higher ability, then it is, of course, rational for all more able to make such a move. But if it is rational for all of those who are more able to make such a move, what inference would an employer make about someone who does not make such a move? Clearly, s/he must infer that s/he is of less ability. And if the firm makes that inference, then the wage that would be offered would not be the wage previously hypothesized (corresponding to the *average* ability), but the far lower wage in which the employer assumed the individual was low ability. But if the low ability worker reasoned this way, then it would pay for him/her to obtain the higher level of education. S/he realizes his/her choice is not between getting the pooling equilibrium and the high ability {wage, education} contract, but between the low ability {wage, education} contract and the high ability contract. Only if there is a very high level of education will the low ability individual prefer not to imitate; but at that level of education, the high ability individual is actually better off in the pooling equilibrium. (That was why the separating set of contracts was not a Rothschild-Stiglitz equilibrium.) But if both the more and less able obtained the higher level of education, then we are again in a pooling equilibrium; the wage offered would again correspond to that of the average ability.

Reasoning this way, it is clear that if there exists a pooling equilibrium, it will be the one which maximizes the utility of the high ability (low risk) type.[1] But if there are relatively few low ability individuals, there may be no way that the high ability individuals (low risk individuals) can simultaneously signal that they are high ability—which won't be at the same time imitated by the low ability.[2] In short, I find the Cho-Kreps "intuitive criterion" (as they refer to it) not only unintuitive: I find it unpersuasive. It seems to me that there are, in fact, a richer set of equilibria that can be plausibly sustained than Cho and Kreps suggests.

On the other hand, even though the full separating equilibrium is not Pareto efficient (within the set of contracts that allow cross subsidization), it is sustainable as a signaling (Nash) equilibrium. Returning to the insurance model, there are rational inferences about the type that offers each policy for $d \leq d_{max}$, where d_{max} is the policy

---

[1] In the literature, this has come to be called the Wilson equilibrium (see Wilson 1977).

[2] Formally, assume $w_1(E)$ is the break even wage for high ability workers ($w_2(E)$ for low ability workers), and w_p be the break even wage with pooling. Let $U^i(E, w)$ be the utility function of type i. Let $\{w_p(E^*), E^*\} \max U^1(E, w_p(E))\} \equiv U^{1*}$. Type 2 knows that, if it is identified, the best it can do is U^{2*}, where U^{2*} is utility at the solution to max $U^2(E, w_2(E))$. There may be no E satisfying the constraints $U^2(E, w_1(E)) \leq U^{2*}$ and $U^1(E, w_1(E)) \geq U^{1*}$.

purchased by the lowest risk individual. All of the out of equilibrium moves which might be accepted by an insurance company—offering to purchase a policy with a larger deductible than d_{max} or a higher premium for a given deductible—entail individuals being worse off than the choices made in equilibrium.

But there may be partially separating equilibria that are also sustainable as signaling equilibrium. Consider, for instance, the Pareto efficient equilibrium which entails pooling of the highest risk individuals, and separation of lower risk individuals. Again, all of the out of equilibrium offers which might be accepted by an insurance company entail individuals being worse off than the choices made in equilibrium.[3]

TIMING

To the extent that the set of equilibria in screening and signaling models are identical, then it makes little difference whether the informed or the uninformed party moves first. There are many situations where institutional details matter little, for instance, whether we impose a social security tax on workers or employers. But, as we have seen, there are some instances—potentially important instances—where the set of equilibria differ; and then it is natural to ask, which is economically relevant?

In some cases, there seems to be a prevalent market structure which provides an answer to this question. For instance, for the most part, insurance companies lay out a menu of insurance contracts. The insured chooses among those being offered. In this context, the Rothschild-Stiglitz assumption of the uninformed moving first was the natural assumption. Still, there are cases where someone with a given risk approaches a set of insurance companies and asks for a bid. S/he may (will) try to signal positive information about him/herself through the way s/he structures his/her request. In these cases, the signaling models might seem more relevant.

At the other extreme, individuals typically decide on a level of education *before* they have a set of job (wage) offers conditional on education. It would seem that in this context, the signaling model would appear more relevant (putting aside the fact that decisions concerning the structure of the education system, including the nature of the filters, are typically largely determined politically, and surely not by market forces alone). But individuals make their education decisions on the basis of their perceptions of the relationship between wages and education, which firms have previously set. If firms have set that relationship on the basis of their beliefs about

---

[3] To my knowledge, the full set of equilibria when there is a continuum of individuals has not been described. The equilibrium may consist of a set of pooling contracts, each of which breaks even, and such that the lowest risk individual in each contract is indifferent between buying that contract and buying the contract with the next highest deductible. Such a set of contracts satisfies the self-selection and zero-profit constraints (the only constraints that are relevant for the Spence signaling equilibrium).

the abilities of those who previously had chosen different levels of education, then experiences of the signaling equilibrium in one period affect behavior in subsequent periods (by confirming that the beliefs about how firms will interpret these signals are in fact correct)—and again, the signaling concept would appear to be more relevant. If firms have set that relationship on the basis of their beliefs about how individuals in the future will make choices, then the screening equilibrium would appear to be more relevant. Since, in practice, the signaling and screening equilibria are often identical, there is no way of easily differentiating between the two concepts.

The signaling model seems more relevant in the labor/education market, since the individual chooses his/her education well before knowing who his/her employer(s) will be. Even if a particular employer laid out a fully articulated education/wage menu, the individual would not want to rest his/her educational decision on the assumption that s/he was going to work for that particular firm. (Of course, in equilibrium, all firms lay out the same education/wage menu.)

In practice, too, firms often engage in screening; and individuals in signaling. Firms may encourage their workers to get advanced training, with increasing compensation, knowing that this is a way of screening among individuals. They may offer different kinds of compensation packages, knowing that this too will screen among employees. At the same time, in smaller firms, workers may come to their employers with an "offer"—e.g. an advanced degree, in the hopes that their employer, or possibly some other employer, will pay a higher wage. In doing so, they may be trying to send a signal concerning their ability, their commitment to their firm, or some other attribute of concern to their employer.

In short, *both* screening and signaling are integral parts of most economic relations, and it is perhaps fortunate that, in many cases, little rides on the question of who moves first. But since there are these instances where there are differences, one would like to know, in those situations where it is at least conceivable that either the uninformed or informed move first, which will prevail? The modeler poses a particular order of moves on the players, but nature does not necessarily do so. If, for instance, it is assumed that the informed move first, then, observing (or reasoning about) the equilibrium, the uninformed could pre-empt the first move of the informed, moving before the informed. One can embed a particular game in a larger game. The equilibrium in this meta game would presumably have the characteristic that no one would want to change the order of moves.

Consider, for instance, the equilibrium in which the informed move first; and assume that the equilibrium which emerged was different from the screening equilibrium (in a situation where the screening equilibrium is Pareto efficient). Then, prior to the informed being able to move, the uninformed would have an incentive to lay out a set of choices—the choices that constitute the screening equilibrium. The informed could, of course, simply ignore those choices; they could go ahead and make the signals that they otherwise would have. The low risk individuals might offer to buy an insurance contract with a high level of deductibility or coinsurance. But since the set of offers already on the table Pareto dominates the signals (and the rationally expected responses to those signals) that individuals would have given, it would be irrational for them to ignore the set of offers. Thus, it would appear that in meta games in which firms (the uninformed) have the option of pre-empting an inefficient signaling equilibrium, they would have an incentive to do so: the inefficient Spence signaling equilibria cannot be sustained.

Consider, by contrast, a positive profit screening equilibrium, where the insurance firm is, say, making a profit off of the low risk individual. It might seem natural that the low risk individual would want to signal the fact that s/he is low risk—and thereby capture the profit which accrues to the insurance firm. S/he could do so by offering to buy a policy with a large deductible. But the high risk individuals, knowing that the low risk individual will attract a favorable premium (if it were to work as an effective signal) will imitate; and, as they do so, the advantages that they thought would emerge from signaling disappear. Thus, they will not have an incentive to pre-empt the screening equilibrium.[4]

As we noted, this screening equilibrium cannot be sustained if firms can cross subsidize by issuing two contracts. Again, it might seem that the high ability individuals could pre-empt this equilibrium by signaling, thereby avoiding the subsidy. But they should reason: if they do, the equilibrium that emerges will be the Pareto inferior equilibrium with no cross subsidies. The low risk individual would reason that the only possible signaling equilibrium (or the best of the possible signaling equilibrium) is that which "separates," *given* that the high risk individual gets no subsidy, and that would make him/her worse off than if he simply accepts the screening equilibrium. Might a low risk individual reason: "I am sufficiently small that what I do has no effect on what others do and on the market equilibrium. The market will know that if I offer to buy an insurance policy with a high deductible, I could not be a high risk individual." But such expectations are not truly rational or consistent; for a high risk individual, reasoning the same way, would actually be better off signaling by offering to buy a high deductible (assuming that the market believes that only the low risk individual would buy the policy). In short, there is no reason to believe that only the low risk individual will offer the signal; and if that is the case, then the signal will not convey the desired information. (By construction, there is no deductible such that, if the market believed that it was only the low risk individuals which purchased the insurance, the equilibrium price would be such that the high risk individual would not want to imitate the signal.)

In short, it appears that in those situations where the screening equilibrium is *not* a signaling equilibrium, the screening equilibrium is *robust*: even if individuals could signal prior to the uninformed moving, they would not do so.

The literature on screening and signaling has, unfortunately, been dominated by a detailed analysis of models satisfying the single crossing property (so the positive

---

[4] Actually, matters are somewhat more complicated. It is conceivable that the optimum pooling equilibrium is preferable to the positive profit screening equilibrium; in which case, the pooling equilibrium could be sustained as a signaling equilibrium. But it could not be sustained as part of an equilibrium in a meta game; for so long as the indifference curves are not tangent at this point, there exists a contract that could break this equilibrium (as in the standard Rothschild-Stiglitz model).

profit equilibrium described earlier cannot arise) and in which firms issue only one contract (so the issue of cross subsidies does not arise). As we have seen, it is easy to construct models in which the single crossing property naturally is not satisfied, and in which market equilibria without cross subsidies are not Pareto efficient. It is in these domains particularly that the set of equilibria of signaling and screening models is likely to differ.

....

SORTING OUT THE DIFFERENCES BETWEEN SIGNALING AND SCREENING MODELS*

....

In recent years a good deal of interest has focused on markets with asymmetric information in which some of the participants have information that the other participants seek to acquire. Often information can be inferred from the actions taken by the informed participants. The uninformed may try to induce the informed to take actions that convey information and the choices of the informed are influenced by the information conveyed by those choices. The informed may also try to shape the views of themselves held by the uninformed. Of course, actions also directly affect the payoffs of both the informed and uninformed. In general the actions taken and the information transmitted is likely to be sensitive to details of the economic environment. We shall focus on one aspect of the economic environment: whether informed agents move before or after uninformed agents.[1]

In models of markets with asymmetric information the equilibrium outcomes are sensitive to assumptions about how participants react to previous moves. It seems reasonable to assume that individuals react optimally; however, the definition of an

---

* Written with Andrew Weiss. This paper was first written in June 1981. We revised it slightly in 1990 to take into account recent developments in the literature and circulated it as NBER Technical Working Paper No. 93. We were surprised to find that the points we made at that time are not totally irrelevant to the ongoing debate on these issues. The postscript and various footnotes comment briefly on some issues that have arisen since we wrote this paper.

[1] Throughout this paper we restrict our analysis to competitive environments. Clearly, equilibrium outcomes in non–competitive environments will differ markedly from those in competitive environments.

optimal reaction is likely to depend on the economic context of the problem being analyzed. We shall specify below what we mean by optimal reactions: clearly optimal reactions can depend on the beliefs of the people going second concerning who made a particular move.

In much applied research on markets with asymmetric information the informed move first. These models include the Stiglitz [1982c] and Bhattacharya [1980] models in which (informed) firms issue dividends that convey information about the true profitability of the company to investors who are uninformed; the Milgrom and Roberts [1982] and Salop [1979b] models in which firms know their cost functions and choose a price which signals their production costs to potential entrants, who are uninformed; and the Weiss [1983] model of education in which individuals, who know their own abilities, choose a level of schooling which signals their productivity. All of these models share the characteristic that the informed participants move first, choosing a price, education level or dividend policy, and the uninformed then respond. The actions that the informed agents take may or may not fully reveal their private information. Typically these models generate a multiplicity of equilibria including some in which all the informed choose the same action (pooling equilibria) and some in which they each choose different actions (separating equilibria). Consequently models of this sort can be used to explain why individuals go to school, even if schooling is unproductive, or why firms pay dividends, despite the adverse tax effects of that practice.[2]

On the other hand, in some models unreasonable equilibria emerge that seem due to peculiarities of the model or the definition of equilibrium employed rather than the underlying structure of the markets. For example, suppose that firms believe that if anyone chooses other than 8 years of education that person has zero productivity, then equilibrium will be characterized by all individuals choosing 8 years of education. These beliefs are unreasonable. Or suppose investors believe that any company choosing a dividend pay out rate below 5% of net asset value is in imminent danger of bankruptcy and value the stock accordingly, then one equilibrium is characterized by all solvent firms paying a 5% dividend.

Parallel to the treatment of markets in which informed agents move first—make choices to which the uninformed respond—have been analyses of markets in which the uninformed participants move first. Early treatments of this problem were by Stiglitz [1975f] Riley [1975, 1979], Rothschild and Stiglitz [1976] and Wilson [1977].[3] In the Stiglitz and Riley papers uninformed firms offer wage contracts—a wage

---

[2] The literature arguing that dividends are paid because they provide a signal concerning the firm's net worth is, however, not completely persuasive. Presumably, buying back shares would provide an equally effective signal, at much lower cost. On the other hand, we show below that there may exist signalling equilibria which are far from Pareto efficient. Perhaps the dividend signalling equilibrium is a dramatic example of this.

[3] The order of moves in the Spence model [1973, 1974b] is somewhat ambiguous. Spence [1976] interprets Spence [1973] as the informed agents choosing education levels before firms make wage offers. One could also view the original Spence model as a simultaneous move game.

conditional on an education level—and informed individuals react to those wage contracts by choosing the education level that maximizes their utility. In the Rothschild-Stiglitz-Wilson papers uninformed insurance companies offer contracts and customers choose their most desirable contract given their probability of an accident and their risk preferences.[4]

We refer to models in which the informed move first as signaling models—the more desirable informed agents signal who they are.[5] We refer to models in which the uninformed move first as screening models—contracts are designed to screen the more desirable agents from the less desirable ones. One quality shared by signaling and screening models is that they generate surprising and often counterintuitive results. In signaling models there are often multiple (optimal reaction) equilibria, some of which seem implausible; in screening models a pure strategy equilibrium often does not exist.[6] That is, there is no set of contracts offered by all the uninformed agents that would not induce at least one uninformed participant to offer a contract different from the one assigned him. Thus it would appear that the set of outcomes when the uninformed move first is a subset of the set of outcomes when the informed move first (a claim along these lines was made in Spence [1976] in the context of active and passive responses to signals). This conjecture turns out not to be strictly correct. In particular when the uninformed move first (sequential) equilibrium outcomes may be characterized by some contracts generating positive profits and others generating losses for the uninformed. These outcomes cannot arise when the informed move first. Only when the parameter values of the problem are such that these contracts are not offered in equilibrium, are we able to prove an inclusion relationship.

In the screening literature the equilibrium notions customarily used implicitly impose optimal reactions by the informed agents to any contracts that are offered (whether in equilibrium or not). The signalling literature faces a more difficult problem: informed agents (who move first) must make an inference about how the uninformed agents will respond to any action (including any out-of-equilibrium action) they take. What are the "optimal" responses of uninformed agents depends on the inferences they draw, and it is not always clear what those inferences will, or "should", be when there are heterogeneous agents. This is particularly true for "out of equilibrium" actions; for the theory predicts that no rational agent will take those actions. Consequently, in the signaling literature the optimal reaction assumption is not always imposed (for example, it is not present in Spence's signaling models).

---

[4] Bhattacharya [1980], Weiss [1980], Gausch and Weiss [1980b, 1982], and Salop and Salop [1976], Lazear and Rosen [1981] and Nalebuff and Stiglitz [1983b] among others have modeled labor markets where uninformed firms first offer wage contracts and individuals then apply to the firm offering the most advantageous contract given their characteristics.

[5] Since we first circulated this paper this terminology has become commonplace. Spence [1976] refers to a model in which the informed move first as a passive response model.

[6] See Rothschild-Stiglitz [1976], Guasch and Weiss [1980b, 1982], Bhattacharya [1980] and Riley [1979] for examples of models in which equilibria fail to exist.

In this paper we define optimal reaction equilibria for both screening and signaling models. For screening models the optimal reaction equilibria are subgame perfect or Stackelberg equilibria with the uninformed as leaders and the informed as followers. (They can also be described as two stage games in which the uninformed move first.)

For signaling models, optimal reaction equilibria are roughly equivalent to sequential equilibria appropriately modified to allow for continuous action spaces. Following Kreps-Wilson [1982a] we implicitly assume that all uninformed agents have the same beliefs and that they react optimally given these beliefs (and the strategies of all agents) to the observed actions. Beliefs assign to each action a probability distribution of agents taking it, and have the following properties:

(a) the equilibrium combination of strategies and beliefs cannot contradict one another: if the equilibrium strategy combination calls for only player i to choose action a then uninformed agents seeing action a must believe that it was chosen by player i;

(b) if out of equilibrium actions were to be observed, uninformed agents could not believe that those actions were taken by agents that are not present in the economy or by agents for whom they are not feasible;

(c) beliefs cannot be contradicted by the observed distribution of actions. For instance, suppose there are two equal sized groups I_1 and I_2 of informed individuals. Members of groups I_1 have single feasible action a_1. Then the only inference consistent with the observation that precisely half the informed chose a_1 is that actions other than a_1 were taken only by members of group I_2.

As we shall see in the examples in section 2, assumption c is quite strong. However it is necessary if beliefs are to satisfy Bayes Rule. These restrictions on beliefs motivate the restrictions we place on strategies when we formally define optimal reaction equilibria. As one might expect, in many models there will be several optimal reaction equilibria. On the other hand, the optimal reaction restrictions eliminate some of the least reasonable Nash equilibria in the same way they are eliminated by imposing sub-game perfection or sequentiality.[7]

The principal result of this paper is that if we restrict ourselves to economies in which the only contracts realized in equilibrium are ones that break even, then the set of outcomes of the optimal reaction equilibria when the uninformed move first are a subset of the optimal reaction equilibria when the informed move first. But the restrictions needed to eliminate positive profit contracts are surprisingly strong.

This result can best be understood by considering reasonable reactions to out-of-equilibrium moves in each game. When the uninformed move first, the optimal reactions of the informed to out-of-equilibrium moves are dictated solely by the preferences of the informed agents. When the informed move first, however, the

---

[7] In many game theoretic formulations of general signaling games stronger restrictions on beliefs are imposed such as the Cho and Kreps intuitive criterion, or Divinity or Universal Divinity in Banks and Sobel. There is some controversy over whether these stronger restrictions are not too strong. We have chosen to make weak assumptions about beliefs and allow the reader to draw upon the particular features of the market(s) that interest him to justify stronger restrictions on beliefs.

optimal reactions of the uninformed to out-of-equilibrium moves depend on their beliefs about which agent(s) took those moves as well as on their preferences. Hence, there is more leeway for "bad" reactions to out-of-equilibrium moves when the informed move first than when the uninformed move first.

In an optimal reaction equilibrium when the uninformed move first unreasonable reactions are precluded. The informed *always* choose their most desirable contracts from the set of contracts being offered; and the uninformed know this. Hence the uninformed have no uncertainty about the matching of informed agents to actions in response to any set of contracts. Profit maximizing behavior by the informed *precisely* determines the actions that would be chosen in response to all price schedules, including those not offered in equilibrium.

When the informed move first it is possible for the uninformed to believe that if an out-of-equilibrium action were chosen, that it was chosen by the least desirable informed agent. These pessimistic beliefs could deter informed agents from departing from their assigned actions. Consequently by allowing for pessimistic beliefs, outcomes that are precluded in the optimal reaction equilibria when the uninformed move first may be sustained as equilibria when the informed move first. Since pessimistic beliefs hurt informed agents taking the action to which those beliefs apply, we consider those beliefs as punishing the agents taking the associated out-of-equilibrium action, and thus enforcing the equilibrium.

I A GENERAL MODEL

In this section we describe the general class of markets with which we are concerned. Because the structure of the model depends on the order in which moves occur, we postpone our discussion of the strategies of players in each game (informed moving first, uninformed moving first and simultaneous moves) until after we have described the preferences and available actions and information of the participants. We will allow agents to only pursue pure strategies.

There are finite sets I and K of informed and uninformed agents respectively. Sets I and K each have at least 2 members. Informed and uninformed agents trade with one another, and the terms of trade can be predicated on the action taken by an informed agent.

Each informed agent i chooses an action $a \in A_i$, where all A_i are compact sets in R^n. We define A as $\cup A_i$. Action a has cost $c(a, \{i\}) \in R^1$ for agent i. We refer to all informed agents with the same feasible set A_i and same $c(a, \{i\})$ functions as being the same type. Each informed agent makes one transaction (e.g. chooses a level of education and works for a single firm).

There are constant returns to scale in transactions for uninformed agents, so the number of trades an agent makes does not directly affect his net payoff per transaction. Each uninformed agent k chooses a price p for each action $a \epsilon A$.[8] The price p is the monetary transfer from the uninformed to the informed, and may be negative. Uninformed agents are uninformed only about the identity of the informed. If an action is feasible for more than one informed agent, uninformed agents cannot discriminate among agents choosing that action.

We allow uninformed agents to be either buyers or sellers—so that prices refer either to the prices they pay as buyers or the prices they receive as sellers. (When the uninformed are sellers p is typically negative.) In sorting models of the education-employment market, uninformed firms are buyers of labor services. The action is an education level chosen by individuals, and the price is the wage that a firm offers to pay workers with a given education level. The reader will find it helpful to keep the education example in mind throughout most of this paper. In the Rothschild-Stiglitz and Wilson models of the insurance market, uninformed insurance companies are sellers of insurances. The action is the amount of insurance customers demand, and the price is the cost of insurance for a customer demanding a given amount of coverage, and $-c(a, \{i\})$ is the value individual i places on "a" units of insurance coverage.

The expected value to an uninformed agent from a trade with an informed agent randomly selected (with equal probability) from the set J choosing action a is $\theta(a, J)$. In the education example $\theta(a, \{i\})$ is the expected value of the labor input of individual i with "a" years of education." The expected payoff of this trade for an uninformed agent offering price (wage) p for that action is $\theta(a, J) - p$. The uninformed are buyers: p is the wage and $\theta(a, J) - p$ is the firm's expected profit per worker hired with education level "a" and paid wage p. When the uninformed are sellers, $\theta(a, J)$ is generally negative and refers to the cost of providing the good (or service) to a buyer that is randomly selected from set J. However, we would again emphasize that the paper can be most easily followed by keeping in mind the education example in which the uninformed are firms hiring workers, the actions are education levels chosen by workers, and the prices are the wages paid by firms to workers.

To ensure that there always exists a "best" action or set of actions for informed agents, so that payoffs are defined for all combinations of prices, we impose the technical restriction that any price schedule offered by an uninformed agent must be upper semicontinuous.

The preferences of agents are to maximize their expected payoffs.[9] This implies that informed agents always trade with the uninformed agent offering the highest price for their selected actions. The payoff for informed agent i choosing action $\hat{a}$ when p is the highest price offered for action $\hat{a}$ is $p - c(\hat{a}, i)$. In the education employment example this is the worker's wage net of his cost of education. We adopt the following tie-breaking rules: if k uninformed agents are offering the maximum price (wage)

[8] This is a restriction on the strategy space of uninformed agents. For instance, it rules out strategies in which the uninformed agent fixes the ratio of the numbers of trades he is willing to engage in at different prices.
[9] These are simplifying assumptions. Our results are valid for a more general class of preferences $v(a, i, p)$ as would be required in the insurance example.

for action (education) $\hat{a}$, an informed agent choosing action $\hat{a}$ trades with each of them with probability $1/k$. If the net payoffs for contracts offered in equilibrium are identical at two or more different actions, we assume that informed agents choose the action at which the profits of the uninformed are highest. Finally we assume that an agent participates in the market if and only if the expected payoff from participation is greater than or equal to zero.

There is common knowledge about the parameters, and distribution of agents in the economy. In particular, all agents know the elements of I, each A_i, and for $\forall a$ the values of $c(a, \{i\})$, and $\theta(a, \{i\})$.

Case 1: Uninformed Agents Move First

In this case the uninformed choose a price schedule, the informed then choose actions. Finally each informed agent automatically trades with the uninformed agent(s) whose contract yields the highest payoff to that informed agent (with ties broken as above). We shall not allow the uninformed agents to predicate the price schedule they offer upon the subsequently observed *distribution* of realized actions of the informed agents.[10] Thus the strategy of uninformed agent k is the price schedule $P_k : A \rightarrow R^1$. This specifies the price the kth agent offers to any informed agent choosing action a. The upper envelope of these price schedules is an upper semicontinuous function denoted by P; that is, $\forall a$, $P(a) = \max_k P_k(a)$. Since the informed agents undertaking action a always trade with the uninformed agent offering the highest price for the action, trades will only occur along the price locus P.

The strategies of informed agents are potentially more complicated: they observe all the prices offered before choosing an action (though only the upper envelope of those price schedules is relevant for their payoffs). Let Π denote the set of feasible combinations of price schedules and π be an element of Π. Then a strategy combination for informed agents is described by a function $f: I \times \Pi \rightarrow A$; $f(i, \pi)$ describes the action chosen by agent i when the combination of price schedules π obtains. $f^{-1}(a, \pi)$ denotes the set of informed agents choosing action a under f when π is the combination of price schedules being offered. For any set of price schedules π and strategy combination of informed agents, the set of actions a for which $f^{-1}(a, \pi)$ is non-empty is denoted by $\tilde{A}$.

Definition 1. *A Nash equilibrium when the uninformed move first is a combination of strategies $\{P_1^* .. P_m^*, f^*\}$ such that, given the strategies of all other players, no uninformed agent k could increase his expected payoff by offering a price schedule $\hat{P}_k \neq P_k^*$, and no informed agent i could increase his payoff by choosing an action $a \neq f^*(i, \pi^*)$, where $\pi^* = (P_1^* \ldots P_k^*)$.*

---

[10]   If the uninformed were able to make the price they offer for action a be a function of the distribution of actions taken by the informed, the distinction between the informed moving first and the uninformed moving first would be blurred. By precluding contingent contracts of that form we preserve the distinction between the informed moving first and the uninformed moving first.

This definition of equilibrium places no restrictions on the reactions of informed agents to combinations of price schedules other than π^*.

In the context of the education example, suppose $\forall_i : \theta(8, i) - c(8, i) > 0$. As noted earlier, one Nash equilibrium would be for (uninformed) firms to offer a wage equal to the average productivity of a randomly selected worker if all workers were to have 8 years of schooling, and a zero wage to any worker choosing other than 8 years of schooling and for all (informed) individuals to choose 8 years of education regardless of the wage offers of firms. Note that any individual choosing other then 8 years of education is worse off than if he had chosen 8 years of education, while no firm is better off by offering a positive wage for education levels other than 8 since no individual chooses education levels different from 8 years.

Clearly this equilibrium is unreasonable. Analyses of models of asymmetric information when the uninformed move first have eliminated equilibria of this sort by implicitly or explicitly imposing an optimal reaction assumption. Optimal reactions such as those generated in a Stackelberg or subgame perfect equilibrium of this game assume that whatever price schedules are offered, each informed agent must react by choosing the action that maximizes his expected payoff. The reasoning behind this restriction is that it is reasonable to expect the informed agents to choose actions which yield the maximum payoff for any price schedule. These reactions are anticipated by the uninformed agents before they offer contracts; hence, they determine responses to possible out-of-equilibrium moves. The uninformed is assumed then to choose a price schedule which maximizes his profits, given his beliefs about the actions of other firms and the responses of the informed agent.

Definition 2. $\{P_1^* \ldots, P_n^*, f^*\}$ *is an optimal reaction equilibrium when the uninformed move first (ORUF) if* $\{P_1^* \ldots, P_n^*, f^*\}$ *satisfy the conditions for a Nash equilibrium and* $\forall_i \epsilon I, \pi \epsilon \Pi, f^*(i, \pi) = a \epsilon \arg \max_{a \epsilon A_i}(P^*(a) - c(a, i))$. *If* $\arg \max_{a \epsilon A_i}(\bullet)$ *has more than one member, agent i chooses the action in that set which maximizes* $\theta(a, i) - P^*(a)$. *If several of those actions maximize* $\theta(a, i) - P^*(a)$ *they choose each with equal probability.*

The ORUF coincide with the sub-game perfect equilibria. The additional restrictions imposed by ORUF are particularly compelling since they only eliminate equilibria which use dominated strategies.

Case 2. Informed Agents Move First

In this case the informed first choose actions. The uninformed then offer price schedules. Finally, each informed agent automatically trades with the uninformed agent whose contract gives the highest payoff to the informed. For example, individuals first go to school, firms then offer wages conditional on years of education, and, finally, each individual goes to work for the firm offering the highest wage given the selected level of education. Since the informed choose their actions before the uninformed choose price schedules, the actions of the informed agents cannot depend on the price schedules of the uninformed. For this game we shall let ψ denote a strategy combination for the informed agents; $\psi : I \to A$. Thus $\psi(I)$ describes an action chosen by agent i, and $\psi^{-1}(a)$ denotes the set of agents choosing action a. The set of actions for which $\psi(I)$ is non-empty is denoted by $\tilde{A}$. (The use of the same notation as in case 1 eases the exposition.) On the other hand the uninformed agents choose price schedules after having observed the distribution of realized actions of the informed agents. Let T denote the set of observable distributions of the actions of the informed agents; $t \in T$, is a particular observed distribution of actions.

Turning now to the strategies of the uninformed agents, let ρ_k denote the price offered by agent k to any informed agent choosing action "a" when the distribution of actions is t, so that $\rho_k : A \times T \to R^1$. That is, for each $t \in T$, agent k may choose a different upper semi-continuous price schedule. Note that a price may be offered for actions which were not chosen; those prices are irrelevant for the equilibrium payoffs but do affect whether a strategy combination is an equilibrium.

Definition 3. *A Nash equilibrium when the informed move first is a combination of strategies $\{\rho_1^* \ldots \rho_m^*, \psi^*\}$ such that, given the strategies of all other agents, no uninformed agent k could increase his expected payoff by offering a price schedule $\hat{\rho}_k \neq \rho_k$ and no informed agent i could increase his payoff by choosing action $\hat{a} \in A_i$ such that $a \neq \psi$ (i).*

As in the previous game the Nash definition allows for unreasonable equilibria. We shall now apply the logic behind the Kreps-Wilson notion of a sequential equilibrium to define an optimal reaction equilibrium for this game.[11] We consider reasonable restrictions on $\rho(.)$, the maximum price offered by the uninformed agents in response to different actions. The motivation for the restrictions we impose is:

a) All the uninformed agents have the same beliefs about the probability distribution of agents choosing an out-of-equilibrium action, if such an action were observed;

b) these beliefs are consistent with the feasible action spaces of each informed agent and the observed distribution of actions, t.

Definition 4. *An optimal reaction equilibrium when the informed agents move first (ORIF) is a Nash equilibrium with the additional property that $\forall a \epsilon \tilde{A}$, $t \in T$, $\rho(a, t) \geq \min_{\tilde{I}_{a,t} \subset I} \theta(a, \tilde{I}_{a,t})$ where $\tilde{I}_{a,t}$ is any non-empty subset of the informed agents for whom action a is feasible, and $\tilde{I}_{a,t}$ choosing a is consistent with having observed t.*

In the context of the education example, the definition of ORIF precludes the highest wage offers made for out-of-equilibrium education levels being below the value of the lowest labor input that any worker could possibly achieve at that education level.

In the special case where A is discrete, the outcomes of the set of ORIF coincide with the outcomes of sequential equilibria. (Sequential equilibrium is not defined when A is continuous.) Our definition avoids both the additional notation required

---

[11] When the informed move first there are no proper subgames. Consequently subgame perfection does not reduce the set of Nash equilibria.

by beliefs in Kreps-Wilson and the complexity inherent in applying their concept to games with continuous action spaces.[12]

II SOME EXAMPLES

We can most readily show how the ordering in which players move affects the trades realized as optimal reaction, or Nash, equilibria through a series of simple examples. These examples are intended to serve as pedagogical tools to illustrate some problems that have arisen in analyses of markets with asymmetric information. Since the point of these examples is purely illustrative, we shall not describe the outcomes for every definition of equilibrium and ordering of moves. To ease the notation and shorten the exposition, when no confusion would result, we shall use the notation $p_k(a)$ and $p(a)$ to describe price offers that are independent of the observed combinations of actions. (When the notation $p(a)$ is used for a game in which the informed move first, the reader should assume that all uninformed agents are offering the same price schedule, and the strategies of the uninformed agents are such that prices are independent of the observed distribution of actions.) This section can be skipped without loss of continuity.

Example 1
The first example illustrates cases in which there are Nash equilibrium of both the signaling and screening models that are clearly unreasonable. There are two types of informed agents I_1 and I_2. A type I_1 agent can only choose action a_1. A type I_2 agent can choose either action a_1 or a_2. All actions are costless. The expected value to an uninformed agent of trading with a randomly selected type i agent choosing action j is denoted by θ_{ji}. The expected value to an uninformed agent of trading with a randomly selected individual choosing action a_1 when that action is chosen by the entire population is $\bar{\theta}_1$.

Suppose $0 < \theta_{12} < \bar{\theta}_1 < \theta_{11} < \theta_{22}$. Thus the uninformed value trade with a type 2 informed agent choosing action a_2 more highly than with a type 1 informed agent choosing action a_1. They also value a trade with a type 2 agent choosing action a_2 more than if that agent chose action a_1. One characterization of the moves in a Nash equilibrium, regardless of who moves first, is for both informed types to choose action a_1, and for the uninformed to offer prices $p(a_1) = \bar{\theta}_1$ and $p(a_2) = 0$.

---

[12] The restrictions we have imposed on the strategies of the uninformed in the ORIF equilibria are quite weak, yet, as we shall see, they are not sufficient to generate the subset relationship ORUF ⊂ ORIF conjectured by Spence. Cho and Kreps impose stronger restrictions in a somewhat different signaling game and show that given their restrictions the outcome when the informed move first coincides with the outcome when the uninformed move first (if the latter exists).

The strategies of the agents in each game are to make these moves regardless of any observation of the moves of other agents. An uninformed agent offering $P_k(a_1) > \bar{\theta}_1$ would generate losses, $P_k(a_1) < \bar{\theta}_1$ would not attract any informed agents, $P_k(a_2) \neq 0$ would also not attract any informed agents—recall that the definition of Nash equilibrium holds the strategies of all other agents fixed, and all informed agents are choosing action a_1 regardless of the observed prices. Similarly no informed agent gains from deviating from action a_1 given the equilibrium contracts offered by the uninformed. Although the strategy choices of the uninformed satisfy the criteria for a Nash equilibrium they seem unreasonable. Only type 2 agents can choose action a_2; one would imagine that in equilibrium they would choose that action and be appropriately rewarded. A more reasonable combination of moves that is also sustained as a Nash equilibrium, regardless of which agents move first, is for the type 1 informed agents to choose action 1, type 2 to choose action 2 (again these choices are made independently of observed prices) and for uninformed agents to offer prices $p(a_1) = \theta_{11}$, $p(a_2) = \theta_{22}$.

When the uninformed move first, there is also a positive profit (albeit also unreasonable) Nash equilibrium for this example.

$$\pi^* \begin{cases} \forall k, P_k^*(a_1) = \theta_{11} \\ \forall k, P_k^*(a_2) = \bar{\theta} \text{ where } \theta_{11} < \bar{\theta} < \theta_{22} \end{cases}$$
$$f^*(I_1, \pi^*) = a_1$$
$$f^*(I_2, \pi^*) = a_2$$
$$f^*(I_2, \pi) = a_1, \text{ for } \pi \neq \pi^*$$

where I_1 denotes a type 1 agent, and I_2 denotes a type 2 agent. In this Nash equilibrium the contracts offered to agents choosing action a_1 break even, the contracts offered to agents choosing action a_2 make positive profits. Any contract offering a higher price than $\bar{\theta}$ for action a_2 would precipitate a move by the type 2 agents *away* from a_2 to a_1. This irrational response by the informed agents would decrease the expected payoff of the uninformed agent deviating from that equilibrium. (Recall that irrational responses to out-of-equilibrium moves are permitted by the definition of a Nash Equilibrium.)

Let us now consider the case where the informed move first and the uninformed react optimally (ORIF). The only ORIF equilibrium is

All agents of type 1 choose a_1
All agents of type 2 choose a_2

$$\forall k \in K, t \in T, \begin{cases} \rho_k(a_1, t) = \theta_{11} \\ \rho_k(a_2, t) = \theta_{22} \end{cases}$$

Both types choosing a_1 is not an equilibrium because the informed know that profit maximizing behavior by the uninformed will cause them to offer $\rho(a_2, t) = \theta_{22}$ if action a_2 is observed (this is the optimal reaction which is consistent with profit maximizing behavior by the uninformed agents).

Similarly if the uninformed agents move first, the only optimal reaction equilibrium is the separating one, $P(a_1) = \theta_{11}$, $P(a_2) = \theta_{22}$. An uninformed agent knows that if uninformed agents offer the pooling contract $P(a_1) = \bar{\theta}_1$, then a contract $P_k(a_2) = \theta_{22} - \epsilon$, with $0 < \epsilon < \theta_{22} - \bar{\theta}_1$ will attract only type 2 agents and earn positive profits. Thus, in this example, the realized actions and payoffs in the optimal reaction equilibrium are the same regardless of who moves first.

Example 2

We shall now modify example 1 to show that both ORIF and ORUF equilibria may fail to maximize output. We now assume action a_2 is available to type 1 as well as to type 2, and let the expected value of a trade with type 1 choosing a_2 be θ_{21}.
   Suppose that

$$0 < \theta_{21} < \theta_{12} < \bar{\theta}_1 < \bar{\theta}_2 < \theta_{11} < \theta_{22}.$$

If the informed agents move first there are several combinations of moves characterizing optimal reaction equilibria (ORIF) in this example.

(i) Both types choose a_1 and $\forall t \in T$,

$$\rho(a_1, t) = \bar{\theta}_1$$
$$\rho(a_2, t) = \theta_{21}$$

Implicitly, the uninformed expect that if action 2 is chosen it is chosen by type 1.

(ii) Both types choose action a_2, and $\forall t \in T$,

$$\rho(a_2, t) = \bar{\theta}_2$$
$$\rho(a_1, t) = \theta_{12}$$

In this case the uninformed expect that if action a_1 is chosen, it is chosen by type 2. Both of these pooling equilibria are sustained by pessimistic beliefs by the uninformed.

(iii) If we were to change our assumption on how informed agents choose actions in cases of indifference there is a third category of ORIF equilibria. Those equilibria are characterized by action a_1 and a_2 being chosen by the informed agents in proportions such that the value of a trade with a randomly selected agent choosing either action is identical. For instance, one ORIF equilibrium has all type 1 agents choosing a_2 and the proportion of type 2 agents choosing action a_2 being such that the values of a trade with a randomly selected agent choosing action a_2 is $\tilde{\theta}_2 = \theta_{12}$. The uninformed then offer $P(a_1) = P(a_2) = \theta_{12}$.

We have not restricted the expectations of the uninformed except that (a) given their expectations the strategies of the informed must be consistent with those expectations, and (b) the expectations must be feasible.
   In each of these ORIF equilibria, resources are being misallocated. Agent i does not necessarily choose the action which maximizes $\theta(a, \{i\})$. Indeed, none of the ORIF equilibria described thus far maximize output. Output is maximized if type 1 choose a_1 and type 2 choose a_2. Those choices will only emerge as an ORIF equilibrium

if the self-selection constraint is violated—in particular type 1 would prefer the contract received by type 2 to their own contract. Because of our assumptions that the distribution of realized actions is observed by the uninformed before they choose price schedules, and that there is a finite number of informed agents it is possible to construct such an equilibrium. We propose these equilibria as curiosities. They depend on the action chosen by a single individual affecting the distribution of prices paid by the informed.

Suppose there are ℓ type 2 agents. Let $\hat{\theta}_2$ denote the belief the uninformed agents have about the expected value of a trade with an agent choosing action a_2 if the number of agents choosing a_2 differs from ℓ. Then if $\hat{\theta}_2 < \theta_{11}$ there is an output maximizing ORIF equilibrium:

Type 1 chooses a_1.
Type 2 chooses a_2.
For t such that ℓ agents choose a_2, $\rho(a_2, t) = \theta_{22}$ and $\rho(a_1, t) = \theta_{11}$.
For t such that m $\neq \ell$ agents choose a_2, $\rho(a_2, t) = \hat{\theta}_2$ and $\rho(a_1, t) \leq \theta_{11}$.

One motivation for these strategies is that the uninformed believe that if they observe m $\neq \ell$ agents choosing action a_2 then the proportion of type 1 agents choosing a_2 is sufficiently large that the expected productivity of an agent randomly selected from among those choosing a_2 is $\hat{\theta}_2$.

This ORIF equilibrium violates the self selection constraint usually imposed in models with asymmetric information. Type 1 agents are choosing action a_1 although, holding the contracts fixed, they would do better if they chose action a_2. However, if any type 1 agent were to switch to action a_2 the distribution of actions observed by the uninformed would change causing them to revise their beliefs in such a way as to make the type 1 agent regret having switched to action a_2.

If the uninformed move first there is only one optimal reaction equilibrium in which each contract breaks even: the uninformed agents offer $P(a_2) = \bar{\theta}_2$ and $P(a_1) < \bar{\theta}_2$, and both types of informed agents choose action a_2. Note that in this ORUF equilibrium type 1 agents are choosing the action which *minimizes* $\theta(a, I_1)$. Resources are being misallocated. Because actions are costless there cannot be an ORUF equilibrium where the two types of agents choose different actions. Thus the output maximizing actions cannot be outcomes of an ORUF equilibrium.

Thus far neither of our examples have dealt with what is often considered the quintessential problem in the analysis of market with imperfect information— nonexistence of equilibrium. To discuss that problem we need to expand the action space of the informed agents.

Example 3

This example illustrates the Spence model of the education market. The informed agents are individuals and the action they choose is an education level. The uninformed are firms offering a wage level. The standard result that equilibrium may not exist in this market only applies to ORUF equilibria. Spence's original specification of multiple equilibria in this market can be formally justified if we consider ORIF or Nash equilibria—regardless of the ordering of moves. To be precise, suppose the set of actions available to the informed agents is the open interval $A = (0, \bar{a})$ and actions are costly, where cost to a type i individual of action a is $c_i a$ and $c_1 > c_2$. We simplify the exposition by following Spence in assuming that actions do not affect the value of a trade with a given type. The value of a transaction with type i is denoted θ_i, the expected value of a transaction involving a randomly chosen individual from the population is $\bar{\theta}$ and $\theta_1 < \bar{\theta} < \theta_2$, and $\theta_2 - c_1 \bar{a} < 0$. In this example there are again many Nash equilibrium outcomes regardless of the ordering of moves. For instance all informed individuals choosing the same action $\hat{a} \in A$ and the uninformed offering prices

$$p(\hat{a}) = \bar{\theta}$$
$$\text{and for } a \neq \hat{a}, \; p(a) = 0$$

is a Nash equilibrium for any $\hat{a} \in A$ (and $t \in T$ for the case when the informed move first). There is also a Nash equilibrium characterized by type 1 choosing $a = a^*$, $0 \leq a^* \leq \bar{a} - (\theta_2 - \theta_1)/c_1$, type 2 choosing $\tilde{a} = \frac{\theta_2 - \theta_1 + c_1 a^*}{c_1}$, and the uninformed choosing prices $p(\tilde{a}) = \theta_2$, $p(a^*) = \theta_1$, and $p(a) = 0$ for $a \neq (a^*, \tilde{a})$. A type 1 is no better off choosing $a \neq a^*$, a type 2 is worse off choosing $a \neq \tilde{a}$, and no uninformed participant can be made better off, given the strategies of the other participants, by offering contracts other than those specified.

Let us now consider the optimal reaction equilibria when the informed agents move first (ORIF). The set of optimal reaction equilibria where both types choose the same action $\hat{a}$ (pooling equilibria) are characterized by for $\forall t \in T, \hat{a} \in A, \rho(\hat{a}, t) = \bar{\theta}$

$$\text{and } a \neq \hat{a}, \theta_1 \leq \rho(a, t) \leq \bar{\theta} - \max\{c_i(\hat{a} - a)\}$$

There is also a separating equilibria. Type 1 chooses $a^* = 0$ and type 2 $\tilde{a} = \frac{\theta_2 - \theta_1}{c_1}$. In this example, the restriction imposed by the optimal reaction condition eliminates all but one of the separating Nash equilibria when the informed agents move first. Assume type 1 choose $a_1^* > 0$, and type 2 choose $\tilde{a}_2 = \frac{\theta_2 - \theta_1}{c_1} + a^*$. This separates, but the rational response to any out of equilibrium move of $a \leq a_2^*$ is $p \geq \theta_2$. Hence the putative equilibrium with $a_1^* > 0$ could not be sustained.

On the other hand in this example there may not exist an ORUF equilibrium. First, we know there cannot be a pooling equilibrium where both types choose the same action. The proof is by contradiction; a pooling equilibrium where both types choose action $\hat{a}$ would be characterized by $p(\hat{a}) = \bar{\theta}$.

Let some uninformed agent k offer a contract $p_k(\tilde{a}) = \tilde{\theta}, \theta_2 > \tilde{\theta} > \bar{\theta}$ and $\tilde{a} > \hat{a}$, such that

$$c_1[\tilde{a} - \hat{a}] > \tilde{\theta} - \bar{\theta} > c_2[\tilde{a} - \hat{a}]$$

This contract attracts only type 2 individuals and makes positive profits. Notice that for this example generic nonexistence of a pooling optimal reaction equilibrium when the uninformed move first depends on the set of actions available to the informed being an open set. To break the pooling equilibrium in our example it is necessary that there exist some $\tilde{a} > \hat{a}$. If A were a closed set $[0, \bar{a}]$, and if further assumptions were made concerning θ_2 and $c_1 \bar{a}$, an ORUF equilibrium could be characterized by all informed agents choosing action $\bar{a}$. (In that case a competitor cannot break the equilibrium by offering a contract contingent on an action greater than $\bar{a}$, since those actions are not feasible.)

(These boundary problems could also be avoided by assuming that $\theta_2 - c_1 \bar{a} < 0$. Then an individual rationality constraint precludes an ORUF pooling equilibrium at $\bar{a}$.)

An optimal reaction equilibrium in which each type of informed agent chooses a different action (sorting) does not exist if, for all actions $a \in A$ satisfying

$$\theta_2 - ac_1 \leq \theta_1$$

(a necessary condition for type 1 to be dissuaded from choosing the same action chosen by type 2) it is the case that

$$\theta_2 - ac_2 < \bar{\theta}.$$

In that case for an equilibrium contract to only attract type 2, it must require an action so large that if an alternate contract $P_k(0) - \bar{\theta} - \epsilon$ were offered, ϵ could be made sufficiently small that it would attract both types and make positive profits.

Example 4

In the full text of the original paper, we present an example of an ORUF that is characterized by some contracts generating positive profits and others generating losses.

III A PARTIAL ORDERING OF EQUILIBRIA

Before proceeding we need to introduce some additional notation. Defining an outcome as a mapping of individuals to action-price pairs, let θ_U, θ_I denote the sets of outcomes in ORUF and ORIF equilibria respectively.

Lemma 1. *In both the optimal reaction and the Nash equilibria when the informed move first, all contracts generate zero profits.*

This result is trivial. The uninformed observe the action of the informed and compete with one another driving their profits to zero.

Because of the possibility of nonzero profit contracts when the uninformed move first, it is not true for all economies that $\theta_U \subset \theta_I$. However, if we impose the following restrictions on $c(a, i)$ and $\theta(a, i)$ we can eliminate ORUF equilibria in which some contracts generate non-zero profits.

A1. $\forall i \in I$, A_i is convex, $\theta(a, i)$ is continuous in A_i, and $c(\cdot, i)$ is continuously differentiable,

A2.   For any pair of contracts $\{\hat{a}, \hat{p}\}$, $\{\bar{a}, \bar{p}\}$ such that there is a type i that is indifferent between those contracts, then no type $j \neq i$ can also be indifferent between that same pair of contracts. (Note that this assumption is analogous to the usual assumption that indifference curves satisfy a single crossing property in a one dimensional action space.)

A3.   If B denotes the union of the boundaries of A_i, then for $\forall a \in B, \forall i \in I$,
$$\theta(a, i) - c(a, i) < 0.$$

Assumption A3 ensures that the equilibrium contract will lie in the interior of the action space of all agents. If a contract were on the boundary of the feasible set of actions of some agent then, notwithstanding A1 and A2, it might not be possible to attract that agent while repelling other agents who either are also choosing that contract or who are indifferent between that contract and the contract they are choosing in equilibrium.

Lemma 2. *If A1, A2, A3 hold then each contract in an ORUF equilibrium generates zero profits.*

Proof. If $\forall a \in \tilde{A}$, $P(a) > \theta(a, f^{-1}(a, \pi))$, then firms generate losses and would be better off offering prices that did not elicit any trades. Thus $\exists a \in \tilde{A}$, such that $P(a) \leq \theta(a, f^{-1}(a, \pi))$. (Recall that $\tilde{A}$ is the set of realized actions when the uninformed move first.)

Consider $a \in \tilde{A}$ such that $P(a) < \theta(a, f^{-1}(a, \pi))$. Then, given the preferences of the informed and uninformed agents, that contract makes positive profits and hence is offered by every uninformed agent. For any $a \in \tilde{A}$ such that $P(a) > \theta(a, f^{-1}(a, \pi))$ that contract is only offered by one uninformed agent: If two or more uninformed agents were offering the same money losing contract, one of those agents could increase its profits by lowering its price, so that no informed agents would purchase its contract, without affecting the distribution of actions chosen by the informed agents.

Thus, if some contracts make positive profits and others make losses, we would find all the positive profit contracts being offered by all the uninformed agents and each negative profit contract being offered by a single uninformed agent. The negative profit contract would offer the highest price consistent with preventing informed agents taking it from switching to another contract—the only reason negative profit contracts are offered is because of their sorting effects. Because uninformed agents can choose to offer prices which do not result in trades we know that in equilibrium all uninformed agents make non-negative profits. Assume some uninformed agents make positive profits equal to π^*. Consider an uninformed agent k whose profits are less than or equal to the average for the uninformed. That uninformed agent could perturb the equilibrium price schedule by offering a price schedule $\hat{P}(a) - P(a) + \epsilon(a)$, where $\epsilon(a)$ is everywhere positive but arbitrarily close to zero; the $\epsilon(a)$ function is chosen so that no informed agent chooses a different action from those induced by $P(a)$. (Our assumption that informed agents are risk neutral is sufficient to ensure the existence of such a function.) That contract enables the uninformed agent to capture the entire market and earn profits that are arbitrarily close to the average profits times the number of uninformed agents, which, of course, exceeds the average profits. Since we have chosen agent k such that its original profits were no greater than the average, this deviation is profitable for agent k. Therefore, an ORUF equilibrium cannot be characterized by any uninformed agent making positive profits.

Thus the only possibility left to consider is that each uninformed agent offers a combination of contracts some of which lose money while others make money. Each combination breaks even. The positive profit contracts are offered by all the uninformed agents. Each loss generating contract is offered by only one uninformed agent. Informed agents choosing money losing contracts are indifferent between that contract and at least one positive profit contract. Consider a contract $\{\hat{p}, \hat{a}\}$ that generates positive profits. (From A3, $\hat{a}$ lies on the interior of every set A_i.) Let S denote the set of types of agents who are indifferent between $\{\hat{p}, \hat{a}\}$ and the contract they are choosing, which could be $(\hat{p}, \hat{a})$. Let j denote the type of agent with the steepest indifference curve in the two dimensional surface $A^k \times P$ through $\{\hat{p}, \hat{a}\}$, where A^k is the kth dimension of the action space. From A2 there is only one such type, and j's indifference surface through $(\hat{p}, \hat{a})$ does not pass through a contract chosen by some type $i \in J$, $i \neq j$.

Suppose j is choosing $\{\hat{p}, \hat{a}\}$ and trade with that type is profitable. Then from A1, A2, A3, and the previous assumption that there is a finite number of types of agents, a contract can be offered in the neighborhood of $\{\hat{p}, \hat{a}\}$ that attracts only type j, and all of them. From A2 and the existence of several uninformed agents offering contract $\{\hat{p}, \hat{a}\}$, this new contract enables the uninformed agent offering it to make positive profits. Suppose j is choosing $\{\hat{p}, \hat{a}\}$ and trade with j is unprofitable for the uninformed. Then from A1, A2, A3, one of the uninformed could offer a price schedule with the following two properties: One of the contracts, $\{p^*, a^*\}$, lies in the neighborhood of $\{\hat{p}, \hat{a}\}$ and is preferred to $\{\hat{p}, \hat{a}\}$ by every type in S except j and type j prefers $\{\hat{p}, \hat{a}\}$ to $\{p^*, a^*\}$; and for every action $a \neq \hat{a}$ chosen by an informed agent, the new price schedule induces those agents to choose the same actions by offering a price that is slightly higher than that offered in the initial equilibrium. Thus the deviating firm attracts every type except j at an arbitrarily small change in prices and in the actions chosen by any agent. Since there is a discrete number of type j agents, each of whom generated losses, and since aggregate trade with the informed broke even, the new price schedule would make positive profits. It would approximate the profits and losses from all trades in the neighborhood of the old trades except those at $\{p^*, a^*\}$ and would make discretely greater profits at $\{p^*, a^*\}$ than at $\{\hat{p}, \hat{a}\}$. Finally, if j is choosing $\{\hat{p}, \hat{a}\}$ and trade with j breaks even, then consider the type of informed agents whose indifference curves through $\{\hat{p}, \hat{a}\}$ in $A^k \times P$ space has the second steepest slope, and proceed as before. If trade with that type

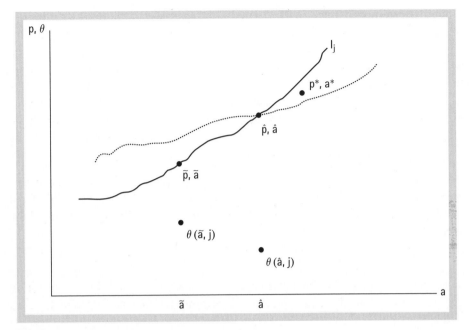

Fig. 1.

also breaks even, continue until reaching a type with which trade generates non-zero profits.

Now suppose j chooses $\{\check{p}, \tilde{a}\} \neq \{\hat{p}, \hat{a}\}$ and causes losses on contract $\{\check{p}, \tilde{a}\}$ for the uninformed agent offering that contract. There is a contract $\{p^*, a^*\}$ in the neighborhood of $\{\hat{p}, \hat{a}\}$ that all informed agents in S except type j prefer to contract $\{\hat{p}, \hat{a}\}$ and type j prefers $\{\hat{p}, \hat{a}\}$ to this new contract. Any uninformed agent not offering $\{\check{p}, \tilde{a}\}$ could now offer this new contract and contracts in the neighborhood of all the old contracts except $\{\check{p}, \tilde{a}\}$ so that all informed types continue to choose contracts in the neighborhood of their previous contracts. From A1 and the equilibrium condition that each uninformed agent breaks even, this new set of contracts generates positive profits. The new set of contracts approximates the sum of the profits and losses from all trades except those at contract $\{\check{p}, \tilde{a}\}$. Since trades at $\{\check{p}, \tilde{a}\}$ generated losses and the set of all previous trades generates zero profits, by omitting only trades with type j the new set of contracts generates positive profits.

Therefore, an equilibrium could not exist in which there are positive profit contracts because a new contract (or set of contracts) could be offered that generates positive profits for the agent offering that contract(s).

Theorem 1. *Given A1, A2, A3, $\theta_U \subset \theta_I$.*

Proof. From Lemmatta 1 and 2, regardless of the ordering of moves in an optimal reaction equilibrium, $\forall a \in \tilde{A}$, the highest price being offered is equal to the expected value of a trade with a randomly selected agent choosing that action, and no informed agent will wish to deviate to a different contract within $\tilde{A}$. All outcomes with these properties can be generated by Nash equilibria regardless of the order of moves in the game.[13] The maximum price offered for action $a \notin \tilde{A}$ could be arbitrarily low in a Nash equilibrium of either game, thus sustaining any combination of moves with the two properties cited above. The outcome in θ_I has the additional restriction that deviations to $\hat{a} \notin \tilde{A}$ are awarded contracts $p(\hat{a}) \geq \min_{i \in I} \theta(\hat{a}, (i))$. Thus there is some bound on the penalty for departing the actions specified in ORIF that is not imposed on the penalties in a Nash equilibrium. This lower bound precludes some combination of plays which are supported in a Nash equilibrium from being supported as an ORIF equilibrium, but not conversely.

The penalties for deviations from actions specified in ORUF do not merely have a lower bound; they are precisely determined. If a price schedule $\hat{P}(a) \neq P(a)$ is offered that induces some action $a \notin \tilde{A}$, that action is chosen by all agents (and only those agents) for whom

$$\hat{P}(a) - c(a, i) > P(f(i, \pi)) - c(f(i, \pi), i).$$

Since these reactions are known by all agents, in the ORUF equilibrium competition among the uninformed agents completely determines the contract offered for $a \notin \tilde{A}$: $\forall a \epsilon A; P(a) = \theta(a, f^{-1}(a, \pi))$.

Since $\theta(a, f^{-1}(a, \pi)) > \min_{i \in I} \theta(a, i)$, threats in the ORUF to punish out-of-equilibrium behavior are less onerous than in an ORIF equilibrium. Since equilibrium outcomes are supported by these more onerous threats, $\theta_U \subset \theta_I$.

IV REMARKS

1. Because the agents moving second could have strategies which depended on the observed distribution of moves of the agents moving first, Nash equilibria in these models may have some peculiar properties. In particular, if the uninformed move first, choosing price schedules before the informed choose actions, the strategies of the informed agents could enforce a positive profit Nash equilibrium.[14] The possibility of unreasonable positive profit Nash equilibria when the uninformed move first seems to be a basic feature of these models. If the informed move second, for them to choose the action which maximizes their expected pay off they must know

---

[13] There are also combinations of moves without these properties which are Nash equilibria—see examples 1 and 2.

[14] The converse is not true. When the informed move first, competition among the uninformed will result in their earning zero profits. This is because while peculiar strategies of the uninformed could force the informed to choose almost any actions, once those actions are chosen the uninformed will bid for the informed by offering prices that break even. There is no opportunity for either the informed or uninformed to use strategies that penalize high (or low) prices. We have assumed that after the informed choose their actions, they must trade with the firm(s) offering the highest price for their action.

the upper envelope of the price schedules of all agents. Hence the actions chosen by each informed agent is a function of this upper envelope. However, that condition would allow the informed agents to change their actions in such a way as to penalize an uninformed agent for *raising* his price(s), thus enforcing a positive profit Nash equilibrium when the uninformed move first. Obviously strategies of this form make little sense.

2. The reader should also note that our definition of ORIF equilibrium is consistent with the Kreps-Wilson definition of sequential equilibrium in allowing extremely pessimistic beliefs about which agents took out-of-equilibrium actions. In Weiss (1983) more stringent restrictions were placed on the beliefs of the uninformed agents when faced with out of equilibrium actions. That paper defined a Robust Expectations Equilibrium (REE). It assumed that all agents with the same equilibrium strategy (and for whom the out-of-equilibrium action was feasible) are equally likely to have chosen a particular out-of-equilibrium action. Because the Weiss (1983) results are similar to ours, we suspect that $\theta_U \subset \theta_I$ holds for a broad class of definitions of equilibrium.

3. Many recent macro-economic models have been concerned with the effect of exogenous shocks on the equilibrium of an economy. If the exogenous shocks were observed by the informed but not by the uninformed, then, even if the uninformed moved first, optimal reactions would not necessarily be sufficient to enable the uninformed to know which informed agents would choose which contracts. The uninformed might not be able to offer contracts that separate the informed agents, if the preferences of the informed were affected by these exogenous shocks that are unknown to the uninformed.

V Postscript[15]

Since this paper was written in 1981 there has been considerable research done on game theoretic models of markets with asymmetric information. In this postscript we shall try to connect the approach we took with current research on models with asymmetric information and comment on the direction we think research in this field should be headed

Most research on the nature of equilibria in markets with informational asymmetries has focused on what we have called signaling games (Rosenthal and Weiss [1984], Wilson [1980] and Dasgupta and Maskin [1986] are exceptions). That research has been directed toward constructing new definitions of equilibrium that eliminate unreasonable Nash equilibria of the sort presented in the examples in section 2 of this paper, and more particularly, find a unique equilibrium. For instance Cho and Kreps

[15] Written in 1990.

show that by imposing the "intuitive criterion" on a particular formulation of the Spence signaling game there is a unique equilibrium outcome of the signaling game: the Pareto efficient separating equilibrium. Similarly Noldeke and van Damme obtain uniqueness in a different formulation of the Spence signaling game by imposing their "plausibility" criterion.

We think the quest for a single "correct" equilibrium notion that will predict the precise outcome for any signaling game is unlikely to be useful for understanding real economic problems. Details of the economic structure of the market being analyzed and the entire history of all relevant interactions are likely to have important effects on behavior in almost any interesting economic setting.

One reason for this is that, as we have seen, the nature of the equilibrium depends on inferences that participants make about out-of-equilibrium moves and the consequence actions which those moves give rise to. These inferences will be sensitive to the economic context in which the out-of-equilibrium move occurs, and the history of past interactions. The standard theory assumes that participants are rational, know that other participants are rational, know all the payoffs, and do not make mistakes. One inference that could be drawn from observing an action which a theory says should never occur is that some aspect of the theory is wrong. Which aspect of the theory is thought to be wrong will depend on the precise nature of the out-of-equilibrium move, and the economic context in which it took place. Since these inferences could favor the deviator, there will be situations in which it will be in the strategic interest of one participant to make what would appear, in the standard theory, to be an out-of-equilibrium move (though from a different perspective, a move which is fully rational). For instance, it may be in the interest of one participant to be thought of as someone who frequently makes mistakes.

One way to address these issues is to formulate a model in which there are no out-of-equilibrium events. All feasible observations occur with some probability, either because of a rich heterogeneity in the types of participants, or because of a variety of kinds of errors.[16] With the latter approach the results may be highly dependent on the particular nature of errors introduced. Thus there may be no general theory (although there may be a general approach), since the sources and nature of errors in one market context may differ markedly from those in another. In general, participants will have a subjective probability distribution over the reasons for out-of-equilibrium moves.

There is a second reason that institutional and historical considerations will almost inevitably be drawn into a relevant analysis of equilibria. One of the lessons we have learned in the past decade is that the nature of the equilibrium of a game is highly dependent on the precise specification of the game. A slight reformulation of the standard Rothschild-Stiglitz insurance model can yield the quite different solution discussed by Wilson. Standard game theoretic models have participants forming beliefs and making inferences in an introspective manner; their reasoning is based

---

[16] Myerson (1979) focuses on mistakes in the evaluation of payoffs. Weiss (1983) and Simon (1987) focus on unintended actions.

on asking, what would a rational individual do in such a situation? But to make those inferences, two things are required: (a) each participant must know (or believe) that the other participants have precisely the same (correct) understanding of the rules of the game; and (b) there must be common knowledge of rationality, that is, each participant must not only believe that his opponent is rational, but that his opponent believes that he is rational, and that his opponent believes that he believes that his opponent is rational ... Neither of these assumptions are reasonable, and it is certainly not reasonable to assume that all participants have confidence in the reasonableness of these assumptions.

Not being able to precisely model all the relevant details of any market interaction, and not trusting their judgments about the appropriateness of particular models, individuals tend to rely heavily on past experience to make inferences and judgments about their best course of action.

There are still other reasons that an historical-institutional approach is required. In many models, there are multiple equilibrium. There is no way, by introspection alone, that individuals can figure out what it is that their opponents are likely to do. History provides a natural coordinating mechanism for the choice of equilibria; unfortunately, history does not necessarily choose Pareto efficient equilibria.

Of course, even after we acknowledge the importance of history in selecting an outcome in the current period, questions remain as to how the past outcomes came about, under what conditions will a particular outcome persist, will future outcomes be near or far from those in the recent past, and how will the outcomes change over time. For instance will outcomes cycle? All of these questions are, of course, closely interconnected.

In the end, the strongest argument for an historical-institutional approach, is this: economics is a behavioral science; it is concerned with explaining a particular aspect of social behavior. In most contexts, individuals rely heavily on past experience to make inferences and judgments; they seldom rely exclusively, or even mainly, on introspective analysis. The question of why this is so remains a legitimate subject for enquiry.

It is perhaps worth noting that not only are our views supported by general observations of behavior, both of firms and individuals, but our views have also been widely confirmed by experimental evidence. Even in the simplest finitely repeated prisoner dilemma games, the predictions of standard game theory are not borne out. The persistence of—what appears from one perspective to be—unreasonable outcomes may be due to past learning or enculturation that teaches the players to value a particular process as opposed to payoff. For instance, if players are taught that cooperation is good, irrespective of the payoffs, then players might even cooperate in a one-shot prisoner's dilemma game.

Clearly whether or not a particular past interaction is relevant is a subjective decision of the participants in the market. It will be difficult for researchers to reach a consensus concerning which aspects of the past are relevant. However, because judging relevance is difficult does not imply that the entire history of past interactions is irrelevant. In particular, we would argue that the choices the uninformed made in response to actions chosen by a previous cohort of informed players will affect the actions the current cohort of informed players choose. (Note while we are very sympathetic to the forward induction arguments made by Kohlberg and Mertens on the importance of a particular player's past actions as signals of that player's future actions, we are making a different point.)

The points we have just made may be illustrated by the employment-education relationship which has motivated much of the literature on signaling models—including our own analysis. Currently, the standard treatment of that problem has become to consider a single informed agent whose type is randomly chosen from some distribution. The informed agent then chooses an education level (action) and the key question addressed by most research in this field is how firms react to out-of-equilibrium education levels (actions).

In practice, however, many individuals simultaneously choose whether or not to continue in school. In making these decisions they observe the wages offered to current and past school leavers at different education levels. Thus although not a repeated game, since both the players and the state variables change over time, informed and uninformed agents will infer from the outcomes of the previous period what payoffs they are likely to receive in the next period.[17]

It does not strike us as a fruitful exercise to see what the outcomes of a particular game would be the first time it, or any similar, game were played. It seems to be a better operating assumption to think that history is always relevant and that there is never a first period. Consequently we would argue that ahistoric models (including our own) are seriously flawed, and that in trying to explain equilibrium outcomes researchers must not only take into account strategic considerations of the participants, but also the history of past play of this and similar games and any other relevant experiences of the participants. Indeed history (broadly defined to include learned notions of fairness) may even enforce what appear to the analyst to be unreasonable equilibria.

Similarly, the inferences drawn from out-of-equilibrium moves are likely to depend critically on the context. For instance if an equilibrium analysis suggests that no one should drop out of school within one week of graduation from high school nor should anyone pursue less than one year of junior college, the inferences that potential employers are likely to draw about a person who dropped out just prior to graduation are likely to be different from the inferences drawn about a person who went to college for one week. The latter is likely to have discovered he didn't like that college or college in general, the former is unlikely to have discovered one week prior to graduation that he so disliked high school that he didn't want to continue for the last week and graduate. In the case of the college dropout the unanticipated move can best be explained by misperceptions of one's own tastes. In the case of the high school

---

[17] Not only is there considerable experimental literature showing that equilibrium outcomes tend to persist, even if they are Pareto inefficient, but looking across countries it is hard to account for some of the variations in patterns of education in other than historical terms.

dropout the unanticipated move may be best explained by irrational behavior or by some exogenous event.[18]

We have emphasized the difficulties of making judgments about the appropriateness of particular equilibrium concepts in the abstract; one must analyze behavior within particular contexts. Individuals are seldom in the single-play, one period context envisaged in some standard formulations. This may explain why, when we place them in experimental situations corresponding precisely to those theoretical models, they so frequently behave in ways which are not consistent with the "theory." They extend to these highly stylized and unrealistic situations modes of behavior that were adapted to the more complex, dynamic environments in which they live.

Recent attempts to develop more dynamic models seem to us to represent one of the more fruitful lines of on-going research. While we have noted one aspect of this—the development of historic models, in which individuals use past experience to formulate their expectations—there are three others to which we would like to call attention.

First, in this paper, we have contrasted models in which the informed move first with those in which the uninformed move first. But the question of who moves first should not be exogenously imposed. We not only need to know which of these assumptions is more appropriate in various market contexts, but why.

Second, even in simple (one shot, no repeated play) markets, there may be complex dynamics. Elsewhere (Stiglitz-Weiss, 1987c), we have provided one detailed example, in the context of the credit market, which we have analyzed as a four move game. Banks announce a set of policies; borrowers make applications; banks decide which of the applications to accept; and finally borrowers decide which of the loan offers they wish to accept. Equilibria in these multi-move (but single transaction period) games may be markedly different from those analyzed in the simpler games discussed in this paper. Deciding on the appropriate order of moves when transaction periods overlap is likely to affect the results of any analysis and is likely to require a detailed understanding of the market being analyzed.

Third, many of the actions involved in signalling and screening games take place over an extended period of time. They involve, as we have already noted, sequential decision making. And there may or may not be reversibility. Consider models in which firm's issuance of equity is used as a signal. If owners choose not to issue equity, it indicates that they believe that returns are high, and accordingly, potential buyers will pay more for their shares. But the original owners are, in general, not committed to retaining their ownership shares forever. Having sold some of their shares at a high price (because purchasers believed that they were going to retain their shares), they may subsequently sell more of their shares, at admittedly a lower price. Implicitly, earlier theories assumed that the original owners could make a commitment not to sell their shares in the future. In the absence of such a commitment, market

---

[18] In the high school attended by one of the authors a student changed schools just prior to graduation because two of his fellow students, with whom he was not on friendly terms, were observed carrying guns.

equilibrium is markedly different from that characterized by the earlier models. (See Gale and Stiglitz (1986).)

Similarly, in the education market, individuals make decisions about whether to go to school for one more year on a year to year basis. The dynamic equilibrium may entail pooling, in contrast to the standard model, where individuals at birth commit themselves to a level of schooling.

The (partial) reversibility of some actions also introduces some inherent asymmetries into the choices of agents. An individual that drops out of school after 9th grade can later choose to resume her education. A college graduate cannot later choose to have had only 11 years of education. With imperfect capital markets consumption today precludes investing tomorrow, but saving today leaves open the option of saving or consuming tomorrow.

To sum up, we think that future research in the economics of information should have one or several of the following features:

1. It should be explicitly dynamic with stochastic state variables.
2. History should be allowed to affect the equilibrium outcomes.
3. Responses to out-of-equilibrium moves should depend on the institutional features of the market (including past interactions) and the nature of the particular out-of-equilibrium move.

THEORY OF ADVERSE SELECTION, EFFICIENCY WAGES, AND CREDIT RATIONING

INTRODUCTION TO PART IIC

The general theory of screening recognized that individuals differed. So far, we have discussed two ways in which differences can be identified—examination and self-selection.

The long standing theory of adverse selection recognized a particular, and particularly simple, form of self-selection—those willing to buy insurance at a given premium were, on average, more risky than those who were not. Quality depended on price. Chapter 12 explores the general structure of these models—where interest rates affect the risk of default in credit markets, where wages affect the productivity of the labor market, and where the price of used cars affects the quality of cars being offered.

In these markets, participants are assumed to have rational expectations: buyers of used cars, for instance, know the average quality of the car being offered at each price, and since quality falls as price falls, their demand for cars may fall as price falls. In the standard adverse selection model, formulated in Akerlof's classic Theory of Lemon's paper (1970), demand curves may be backward bending (since the lower price signals a lower quality, the "effective price" is actually high), and it is easy to show that there may exist multiple equilibria, or an equilibrium in which there is no trade (see Figure IIC.1).

But there was something very peculiar about these adverse selection models—for while market participants knew that there was a relationship between quality and price, they remained completely passive, refusing even to attempt to exploit that information. In my work on efficiency wages, I realized that by raising the wages, they could obtain a higher quality labor force, and they would have an incentive to do so, *even if there was excess supply of labor, so that they could obtain a worker at a lower wage*. The same thing held in credit and other markets.

As early as my 1969 work on efficiency wages, I had realized the closer parallel between incentive and selection models; and this was made clearer in the 1981 paper on credit rationing with Weiss. Raising the interest rate discouraged low risk borrowers and encouraged borrowers who had a choice of investment projects to undertake the riskier projects. In either case, the riskiness of the pool of credit applicants was increased.

And just as unemployment served as a *screening device* in my *Prices and Queues* paper (Chapter 8), so too could unemployment serve as an *incentive device*—as Shapiro and I established in our 1984 paper. The penalty for being caught shirking was being fired, but if there was no unemployment, a worker could immediately get another job. With unemployment, there is a penalty, and it is this penalty that deters shirking. This was established within a simple, but general, equilibrium framework.

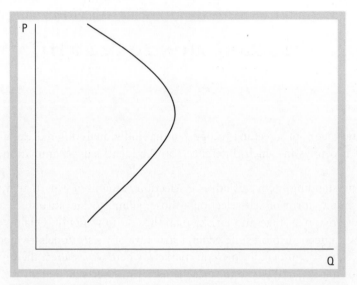

Fig. IIC.1. Demand curve for a good, when quality depends on price

The striking result here was that we showed that equilibrium *had* to be characterized by unemployment. Later, in work with Patrick Rey (1996), we explored the consequences of other penalties, and we reset the incentives problem in a more conventional incentive compatibility framework. A striking result is that "sand in the wheels" may improve the performance of the economy. If it is costly for workers to move from firm to firm, then there may be less need for reliance on unemployment as a discipline device. Calls for more labor market flexibility may be counterproductive.

More generally, we showed that the market equilibrium may not be Pareto efficient,[1] but that the nature of the inefficiencies depends, at least in part, on the distribution of income and wealth. If individuals have enough wealth to post a bond,[2] then that can reduce the amount of unemployment required to induce workers not to shirk. Workers, of course, value security, and so may be willing to accept lower wages in return for more job security. In assessing the optimality of these market driven contracts, the focus has to be on externalities. When all firms provide more security (e.g. higher penalties for discharging a worker), labor turnover will be lower, and, for any level of unemployment, the penalty of being fired is increased. This means, in turn, that the equilibrium unemployment rate is reduced.[3]

The model has had enormous influence on the development of modern macro economics, and yet I have remained surprised at how little the basic framework has

---

[1] These externalities are pervasive in labor markets, and can take on a number of different forms. In Stiglitz (1974a), Arnott and Stiglitz (1985), and Arnott et al. (1988), we explore further the externalities associated with labor turnover.

[2] And if there is no "double moral hazard problem," where the firm declares a worker as having shirked, in order to receive payment on the bond.

[3] Formally, the no-shirking constraint shifts down—the wage which a firm has to pay to induce individuals not to shirk is lowered.

been developed, both to enrich the model and to address key policy issues. There are obvious extensions (some of which we began to explore): what happens, for instance, if expenditures on supervision are endogenous? If there are several types of workers (i.e., a model in which there are both adverse selection and incentive problems)? What implications are there for the incidence of taxation?[4] The conclusions are markedly different from the standard competitive analysis, on which so much of incidence analysis has been based. Should government intervene with job security provisions that employers and employees voluntarily arrive at? Should it subsidize or tax these arrangements? What happens in more dynamic settings—how does, for instance, an anticipated increase in productivity affect the equilibrium wage today? These intertemporal linkages are interesting, important, and markedly different than in the standard general equilibrium models.

[4] See, e.g. Stiglitz (1999g).

CHAPTER 10

CREDIT RATIONING IN MARKETS WITH IMPERFECT INFORMATION*

WHY is credit rationed? Perhaps the most basic tenet of economics is that market equilibrium entails supply equalling demand; that if demand should exceed supply, prices will rise, decreasing demand and/or increasing supply until demand and supply are equated at the new equilibrium price. So if prices do their job, rationing should not exist. However, credit rationing and unemployment do in fact exist. They seem to imply an excess demand for loanable funds or an excess supply of workers.

One method of "explaining" these conditions associates them with short- or long-term disequilibrium. In the short term they are viewed as *temporary disequilibrium* phenomena; that is, the economy has incurred an exogenous shock, and for reasons not fully explained, there is some stickiness in the prices of labor or capital (wages and interest rates) so that there is a transitional period during which rationing of jobs or credit occurs. On the other hand, long-term unemployment (above some "natural rate") or credit rationing is explained by governmental constraints such as usury laws or minimum wage legislation.[1]

* Written with Andrew Weiss. We would like to thank Bruce Greenwald, Henry Landau, Rob Porter, and Andy Postlewaite for fruitful comments and suggestions. Financial support from the National Science Foundation is gratefully acknowledged. An earlier version of this paper was presented at the spring 1977 meetings of the Mathematics in the Social Sciences Board in Squam Lake, New Hampshire. Reprinted with permission from the *American Economic Review*, 71(3) (June), 1981.

[1] Indeed, even if markets were not competitive one would not expect to find rationing; profit maximization would, for instance, lead a monopolistic bank to raise the interest rate it charges on loans to the point where excess demand for loans was eliminated.

The object of this paper is to show that in *equilibrium* a loan market may be characterized by credit rationing. Banks making loans are concerned about the interest rate they receive on the loan, and the riskiness of the loan. However, the interest rate a bank charges may itself affect the riskiness of the pool of loans by either: 1) sorting potential borrowers (the adverse selection effect); or 2) affecting the actions of borrowers (the incentive effect). Both effects derive directly from the residual imperfect information which is present in loan markets after banks have evaluated loan applications. When the price (interest rate) affects the nature of the transaction, it may not also clear the market.

The adverse selection aspect of interest rates is a consequence of different borrowers having different probabilities of repaying their loan. The expected return to the bank obviously depends on the probability of repayment, so the bank would like to be able to identify borrowers who are more likely to repay. It is difficult to identify "good borrowers," and to do so requires the bank to use a variety of *screening devices*. The interest rate which an individual is willing to pay may act as one such screening device: those who are willing to pay high interest rates may, on average, be worse risks; they are willing to borrow at high interest rates because they perceive their probability of repaying the loan to be low. As the interest rate rises, the average "riskiness" of those who borrow increases, possibly lowering the bank's profits.

Similarly, as the interest rate and other terms of the contract change, the behavior of the borrower is likely to change. For instance, raising the interest rate decreases the return on projects which succeed. We will show that higher interest rates induce firms to undertake projects with lower probabilities of success but higher payoffs when successful.

In a world with perfect and costless information, the bank would stipulate precisely all the actions which the borrower could undertake (which might affect the return to the loan). However, the bank is not able to directly control all the actions of the borrower; therefore, it will formulate the terms of the loan contract in a manner designed to induce the borrower to take actions which are in the interest of the bank, as well as to attract low-risk borrowers.

For both these reasons, the expected return by the bank may increase less rapidly than the interest rate; and, beyond a point, may actually decrease, as depicted in Figure 1. The interest rate at which the expected return to the bank is maximized, we refer to as the "bank-optimal" rate, $\hat{r}^*$.

Both the demand for loans and the supply of funds are functions of the interest rate (the latter being determined by the expected return at $\hat{r}^*$). Clearly, it is conceivable that at $\hat{r}^*$ the demand for funds exceeds the supply of funds. Traditional analysis would argue that, in the presence of an excess demand for loans, unsatisfied borrowers would offer to pay a higher interest rate to the bank, bidding up the interest rate until demand equals supply. But although supply does not equal demand at $\hat{r}^*$, it is the equilibrium interest rate! The bank would not lend to an individual who offered to pay more than $\hat{r}^*$. In the bank's judgment, such a loan is likely to be a worse risk than the average loan at interest rate $\hat{r}^*$, and the expected return to a loan at an interest rate above $\hat{r}^*$ is actually lower than the expected return to the loans the bank is presently

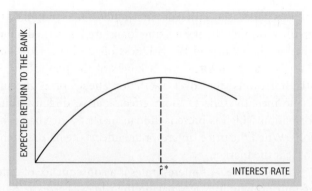

Fig. 1. There Exists an Interest Rate which Maximizes
the Expected Return to the Bank

making. Hence, there are no competitive forces leading supply to equal demand, and credit is rationed.

But the interest rate is not the only term of the contract which is important. The amount of the loan, and the amount of collateral or equity the bank demands of loan applicants, will also affect both the behavior of borrowers and the distribution of borrowers. In Section III, we show that increasing the collateral requirements of lenders (beyond some point) may decrease the returns to the bank, by either decreasing the average degree of risk aversion of the pool of borrowers; or in a multiperiod model inducing individual investors to undertake riskier projects.

Consequently, it may not be profitable to raise the interest rate or collateral requirements when a bank has an excess demand for credit; instead, banks deny loans to borrowers who are observationally indistinguishable from those who receive loans.[2]

It is not our argument that credit rationing will always characterize capital markets, but rather that it may occur under not implausible assumptions concerning borrower and lender behavior.

This paper thus provides the first theoretical justification of true credit rationing. Previous studies have sought to explain why each individual faces an upward sloping interest rate schedule. The explanations offered are (a) the probability of default for any particular borrower increases as the amount borrowed increases (see Stiglitz (1971b), (1972c); Marshall Freimer and Myron Gordon (1965); Dwight Jaffee (1971); George Stigler 1967), or (b) the mix of borrowers changes adversely (see Jaffee and Thomas Russell (1976)). In these circumstances we would not expect loans of different size to pay the same interest rate, any more than we would expect two borrowers, one of whom has a reputation for prudence and the other a reputation as a bad credit risk, to be able to borrow at the same interest rate.

We reserve the term credit rationing for circumstances in which either (a) among loan applicants who appear to be identical some receive a loan and others do not, and the rejected applicants would not receive a loan even if they offered to pay a higher

---

[2] After this paper was completed, our attention was drawn to W. Keeton's book (1979). In chapter 3 he develops an incentive argument for credit rationing.

interest rate; or (b) there are identifiable groups of individuals in the population who, with a given supply of credit, are unable to obtain loans at any interest rate, even though with a larger supply of credit, they would.[3]

In our construction of an equilibrium model with credit rationing, we describe a market equilibrium in which there are many banks and many potential borrowers. Both borrowers and banks seek to maximize profits, the former through their choice of a project, the latter through the interest rate they charge borrowers and the collateral they require of borrowers (the interest rate received by depositors is determined by the zero-profit condition). Obviously, we are not discussing a "price-taking" equilibrium. Our equilibrium notion is competitive in that banks compete; one means by which they compete is by their choice of a price (interest rate) which maximizes their profits. The reader should notice that in the model presented below there are interest rates at which the demand for loanable funds equals the supply of loanable funds. However, these are not, in general, equilibrium interest rates. If, at those interest rates, banks could increase their profits by lowering the interest rate charged borrowers, they would do so.

Although these results are presented in the context of credit markets, we show in Section V that they are applicable to a wide class of principal-agent problems (including those describing the landlord-tenant or employer-employee relationship).

I INTEREST RATE AS A SCREENING DEVICE

In this section we focus on the role of interest rates as screening devices for distinguishing between good and bad risks. We assume that the bank has identified a group of projects; for each project θ there is a probability distribution of (gross) returns R. We assume for the moment that this distribution cannot be altered by the borrower.

Different firms have different probability distribution of returns. We initially assume that the bank is able to distinguish projects with different mean returns, so we will at first confine ourselves to the decision problem of a bank facing projects having the same mean return. However, the bank cannot ascertain the riskiness of a project. For simplicity, we write the distribution of returns[4] as $F(R, \theta)$ and the density function as $f(R, \theta)$, and we assume that greater θ corresponds to greater risk in the sense of mean preserving spreads[5] (see Rothschild-Stiglitz 1970), i.e., for

---

[3] There is another form of rationing which is the subject of our 1980 paper: banks make the provision of credit in later periods contingent on performance in earlier period; banks may then refuse to lend even when these later period projects stochastically dominate earlier projects which are financed.

[4] These are subjective probability distributions; the perceptions on the part of the bank may differ from those of the firm.

[5] Michael Rothschild and Stiglitz (1970) show that conditions (1) and (2) imply that project 2 has a greater variance than project 1, although the converse is not true. That is, the mean preserving spread criterion for measuring risk is stronger than the increasing variance criterion. They also show that (1)

$\theta_1 > \theta_2$, if

$$\int_0^\infty R f(R, \theta_1) dR = \int_0^\infty R f(R, \theta_2) dR \tag{1}$$

then for $y \geqslant 0$,

$$\int_0^y F(R, \theta_1) dR \geqslant \int_0^y F(R, \theta_2) dR \tag{2}$$

If the individual borrows the amount B, and the interst rate is $\hat{r}$, then we say the individual defaults on his loan if the return R plus the collateral C is insufficient to pay back the promised amount,[6] i.e., if

$$C + R \leqslant B(1 + \hat{r}) \tag{3}$$

Thus the net return to the borrower $\pi(R, \hat{r})$ can be written as

$$\pi(R, \hat{r}) = max(R - (1 + \hat{r})B; -C) \tag{4a}$$

The return to the bank can be written as

$$\rho(R, \hat{r}) = min(R + C; B(1 + \hat{r})) \tag{4b}$$

that is, the borrower must pay back either the promised amount or the maximum he can pay back $(R + C)$.

For simplicity, we shall assume that the borrower has a given amount of equity (which he cannot increase), that borrowers and lenders are risk neutral, that the supply of loanable funds available to a bank is unaffected by the interest rate it charges borrowers, that the cost of the project is fixed, and unless the individual can borrow the difference between his equity and the cost of the project, the project will not be undertaken, that is, projects are not divisible. For notational simplicity, we assume the amount borrowed for each project is identical, so that the distribution functions describing the number of loan applications are identical to those describing the monetary value of loan applications. (In a more general model, we would make the amount borrowed by each individual a function of the terms of the contract; the quality mix could change not only as a result of a change in the mix of applicants, but also because of a change in the relative size of applications of different groups.)

We shall now prove that the interest rate acts as a screening device; more precisely we establish

---

and (2) can be interpreted equally well as: given two projects with equal means, every risk averter prefers project 1 to project 2.

[6] This is not the only possible definition. A firm might be said to be in default if $R < B(1 + \hat{r})$. Nothing critical depends on the precise definition. We assume, however, that if the firm defaults, the bank has first claim on $R + C$. The analysis may easily be generalized to include bankruptcy costs. However, to simplify the analysis, we usually shall ignore these costs. Throughout this section we assume that the project is the sole project undertaken by the firm (individual) and that there is limited liability. The equilibrium extent of liability is derived in Section III.

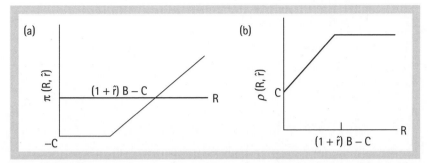

Fig. 2. (a) Firm Profits are a Convex Function of the Return on the Project; (b) The Return to the Bank is a Concave Function of the Return on the Project

Theorem 1. *For a given interest rate* $\hat{r}$, *there is a critical value* $\hat{\theta}$ *such that a firm borrows from the bank if and only if* $\theta > \hat{\theta}$.

This follows immediately upon observing that profits are a convex function of R, as in Figure 2a. Hence expected profits increase with risk.

The value of $\hat{\theta}$ for which expected profits are zero satisfies

$$\Pi(\hat{r}, \hat{\theta}) \equiv \int_0^\infty max[R - (\hat{r} + 1)B; -C]dF(R, \hat{\theta}) = 0 \qquad (5)$$

Our argument that the adverse selection of interest rates could cause the returns to the bank to decrease with increasing interest rates hinged on the conjecture that as the interest rate increased, the mix of applicants became worse; or

Theorem 2. *As the interest rate increases, the critical value of* θ, *below which individuals do not apply for loans, increases.*

This follows immediately upon differentiating (5):

$$\frac{d\hat{\theta}}{d\hat{r}} = \frac{B \int_{(1+\hat{r})B-C}^\infty dF(R, \hat{\theta})}{\partial \Pi / \partial \hat{\theta}} > 0 \qquad (6)$$

For each θ, expected profits are decreased; hence using Theorem 1, the result is immediate.

We next show:

Theorem 3. *The expected return on a loan to a bank is a decreasing function of the riskiness of the loan.*

Proof. From (4b) we see that $\rho(R, \hat{r})$ is a concave function of R, hence the result is immediate. The concavity of $\rho(R, \hat{r})$ is illustrated in Figure 2b.

Theorems 2 and 3 imply that, in addition to the usual direct effect of increases in the interest rate increasing a bank's return, there is an indirect, adverse-selection effect acting in the opposite direction. We now show that this adverse-selection effect *may* outweigh the direct effect.

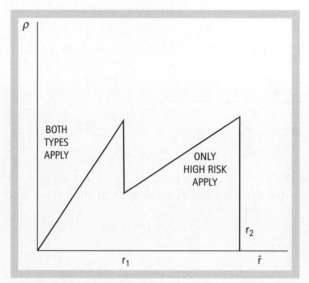

Fig. 3. Optimal Interest Rate r_1

To see this most simply, assume there are two groups; the "safe" group will borrow only at interest rates below r_1, the "risky" group below r_2, and $r_1 < r_2$. When the interest rate is raised slightly above r_1, the mix of applicants changes dramatically: all low risk applicants withdraw. (See Figure 3.) By the same argument we can establish

Theorem 4. *If there are a discrete number of potential borrowers (or types of borrowers) each with a different θ, $\bar\rho(\hat r)$ will not be a monotonic function of $\hat r$, since as each successive group drops out of the market, there is a discrete fall in $\bar\rho$ (where $\bar\rho(\hat r)$ is the mean return to the bank from the set of applicants at the interest rate $\hat r$).*

Other conditions for nonmonotonicity of $\bar\rho(\hat r)$ will be established later. Theorems 5 and 6 show why nonmonotonicity is so important:

Theorem 5. *Whenever $\bar\rho(\hat r)$ has an interior mode, there exist supply functions of funds such that competitive equilibrium entails credit rationing.*

This will be the case whenever the "Walrasian equilibrium" interest rate—the one at which demand for funds equals supply—is such that there exists a lower interest rate for which $\bar\rho$, the return to the bank, is higher.

In Figure 4 we illustrate a credit rationing equilibrium. Because demand for funds depends on $\hat r$, the interest rate charged by banks, while the supply of funds depends on ρ, the mean return on loans, we cannot use a conventional demand/supply curve diagram. The demand for loans is a decreasing function of the interest rate charged borrowers; this relation L^D is drawn in the upper right quadrant. The nonmonotonic relation between the interest charged borrowers, and the expected return to the bank per dollar loaned $\bar\rho$ is drawn in the lower right quadrant. In the lower left quadrant we depict the relation between $\bar\rho$ and the supply of loanable funds L^S. (We have drawn L^S as if it were an increasing function of $\bar\rho$. This is not necessary for our analysis.) If banks are free to compete for depositors, then $\bar\rho$ will be the interest rate received by

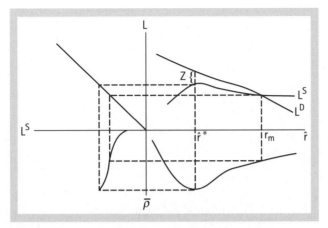

Fig. 4. Determination of the Market Equilibrium

depositors. In the upper right quadrant we plot L^S as a function of $\hat{r}$, through the impact of $\hat{r}$ on the return on each loan, and hence on the interest rate $\bar{\rho}$ banks can offer to attract loanable funds.

A credit rationing equilibrium exists given the relations drawn in Figure 4; the demand for loanable funds at $\hat{r}^*$ exceeds the supply of loanable funds at $\hat{r}^*$ and any individual bank increasing its interest rate beyond $\hat{r}^*$ would lower its return per dollar loaned. The excess demand for funds is measured by Z. Notice that there is an interest rate r_m at which the demand for loanable funds equals the supply of loanable funds; however, r_m is not an equilibrium interest rate. A bank could increase its profits by charging $\hat{r}^*$ rather than r_m: at the lower interest rate it would attract at least all the borrowers it attracted at r_m and would make larger profits from each loan (or dollar loaned).

Figure 4 can also be used to illustrate an important comparative statics property of our market equilibrium:

Corollary 1. *As the supply of funds increases, the excess demand for funds decreases, but the interest rate charged remains unchanged, so long as there is any credit rationing.*

Eventually, of course, Z will be reduced to zero; further increases in the supply of funds then reduce the market rate of interest.

Figure 5 illustrates a $\bar{\rho}(\hat{r})$ function with multiple modes. The nature of the equilibrium for such cases is described by Theorem 6.

Theorem 6. *If the $\bar{\rho}(r)$ function has several modes, market equilibrium could either be characterized by a single interest rate at or below the market-clearing level, or by two interest rates, with an excess demand for credit at the lower one.*

Proof. Denote the lowest Walrasian equilibrium interest rate by r_m and denote by $\hat{r}$ the interest rate which maximizes $\rho(r)$. If $\hat{r} < r_m$, the analysis for Theorem 5 is unaffected by the multiplicity of modes. There will be credit rationing at interest rate $\hat{r}$. The rationed borrowers will not be able to obtain credit by offering to pay a higher interest rate.

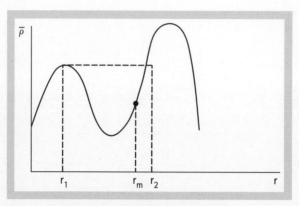

Fig. 5. A Two-Interest Rate Equilibrium

On the other hand, if $\hat{\hat{r}} > r_m$, then loans may be made at two interest rates, denoted by r_1 and r_2. r_1 is the interest rate which maximizes $\rho(r)$ conditional on $r \leqslant r_m$; r_2 is the lowest interest rate greater than r_m such that $\rho(r_2) = \rho(r_1)$. From the definition of r_m, and the downward slope of the loan demand function, there will be an excess demand for loanable funds at r_1 (unless $r_1 = r_m$, in which case there is no credit rationing). Some rejected borrowers (with reservation interest rates greater than or equal to r_2) will apply for loans at the higher interest rate. Since there would be an excess supply of loanable funds at r_2 if no loans were made at r_1, and an aggregate excess demand for funds if no loans were made at r_2, there exists a distribution of loanable funds available to borrowers at r_1, and r_2 such that all applicants who are rejected at interest rate r_1 and who apply for loans at r_2 will get credit at the higher interest rate. Similarly, all the funds available at $\rho(r_1)$ will be loaned at either r_1 or r_2. (There is, of course, an excess demand for loanable funds at r_1 since every borrower who eventually borrows at r_2 will have first applied for credit at r_1.) There is clearly no incentive for small deviations from r_1, which is a local maximum of $\rho(r)$. A bank lending at an interest rate r_3 such that $\rho(r_3) < \rho(r_1)$ would not be able to obtain credit. Thus, no bank would switch to a loan offer between r_1 and r_2. A bank offering an interest rate r_4 such that $\rho(r_4) > \rho(r_1)$ would not be able to attract any borrowers since by definition $r_4 > r_2$, and there is no excess demand at interest rate r_2.

A Alternative Sufficient Conditions for Credit Rationing

Theorem 4 provided a sufficient condition for adverse selection to lead to a non-monotonic $\bar{\rho}(\hat{r})$ function. In the remainder of this section, we investigate other circumstances under which for some levels of supply of funds there will be credit rationing.

1 Continuum of Projects

Let $G(\theta)$ be the distribution of projects by riskiness θ, and $\rho(\theta, r)$ be the expected return to the bank of a loan of risk θ and interest rate r. The mean return to the bank which lends at the interest rate $\hat{r}$ is simply

$$\tilde{\rho}(\hat{r}) = \frac{\int_{\hat{\theta}(\hat{r})}^{\infty} \rho(\theta, \hat{r}) dG(\theta)}{1 - G(\hat{\theta})} \tag{7}$$

From Theorem 5 we know that $d\bar{\rho}(\hat{r})/d\hat{r} < 0$ for some value of $\hat{r}$ is a sufficient condition for credit rationing. Let $\rho(\hat{\theta}, \hat{r}) = \hat{\rho}$ so that

$$\frac{d\bar{\rho}}{d\hat{r}} = -\frac{g(\hat{\theta})}{[1 - G(\hat{\theta})]}(\hat{\rho} - \bar{\rho})\frac{d\hat{\theta}}{d\hat{r}} + \frac{\int_{\hat{\theta}}^{\infty}[1 - F((1+\hat{r})B - C, \theta)]dG(\theta)}{1 - G(\hat{\theta})} \tag{8}$$

From Theorems 1 and 3, the first term is negative (representing the change in the mix of applicants), while the second term (the increase in returns, holding the applicant pool fixed, from raising the interest charges) is positive. The first term is large, in absolute value, if there is a large difference between the mean return on loans made at interest rate $\hat{r}$ and the return to the bank from the project making zero returns to the firm at interest rate $\hat{r}$ (its "safest" loan). It is also large if $(g(\hat{\theta})/[1 - G(\hat{\theta})])(d\hat{\theta}/d\hat{r})$ is large, that is, a small change in the nominal interest rate induces a large change in the applicant pool.

2 Two Outcome Projects

Here we consider the simplest kinds of projects (from an analytical point of view), those which either succeed and yield a return R, or fail and yield a return D. We normalize to let $B = 1$. All the projects have the same unsuccessful value (which could be the value of the plant and equipment) while R ranges between S and K (where $K > S$). We also assume that projects have been screened so that all projects within a loan category have the same expected yield, T, and there is no collateral required, that is, $C = 0$, and if $p(R)$ represents the probability that a project with a successful return of R succeeds, then

$$p(R)R + [1 - p(R)]D = T \tag{9}$$

In addition, the bank suffers a cost of X per dollar loaned upon loans that default, which could be interpreted as the difference between the value of plant and equipment to the firm and the value of the plant and equipment to the bank. Again the density of project values is denoted by $g(R)$, the distribution function by $G(R)$.

Therefore, the expected return per dollar lent at an interest rate $\hat{r}$, if we let $J = \hat{r} + 1$, is (since individuals will borrow if and only if $R > J$):

$$\rho(J) = \frac{1}{\int_J^K g(R)dR}\left[J\int_J^K p(R)g(R)dR \right.$$

$$\left. + \int_J^K [1 - p(R)][D - X]g(R)dR \right] \tag{10}$$

Using l'Hopital's rule and (1), we can establish sufficient conditions for $\lim_{J \to K}(\partial \rho(J)/\partial J) < 0$ (and hence for the nonmonotonicity of ρ).[7]

(a) if $\lim_{R \to K} g(R) \neq 0, \infty$ then a sufficient condition is $X > K - D$, or equivalently, $\lim_{R \to K} p(R) + p'(R)X < 0$

(b) if $g(K) = 0$, $g'(K) \neq 0, \infty$ then a sufficient condition is $2X > K - D$, or equivalently, $\lim_{R \to K} p(R) + 2p'(R)X < 0$

(c) if $g(K) = 0$, $g'(K) = 0$, $g''(K) \neq 0$, then a sufficient condition is $3X > K - K - D$, or equivalently, $\lim_{R \to K} p(R) + 3p'(R)X < 0$

Condition (a) implies that if, as $1 + \hat{r} \to K$, the probability of an increase in the interest rate being repaid is outweighed by the deadweight loss of riskier loans, the bank will maximize its return per dollar loaned at an interest rate below the maximum rate at which it can loan funds ($K - 1$). The conditions for an interior bank optimal interest rate are significantly less stringent when $g(K) = 0$.

3 Differences in Attitudes Towards Risk

Some loan applicants are clearly more risk averse than others. These differences will be reflected in project choices, and thus affect the bank-optimal interest rate. High interest rates may make projects with low mean returns—the projects undertaken by risk averse individuals—infeasible, but leave relatively unaffected the risky projects. The mean return to the bank, however, is lower on the riskier projects than on the safe projects. In the following example, it is systematic differences in risk aversion which results in there being an optimal interest rate.

Assume a fraction λ of the population is infinitely risk averse; each such individual undertakes the best perfectly safe project which is available to him. Within that group,

---

[7] The proofs of these propositions are slightly complicated. Consider 1. Since $p(R) = T - D/R - D$, the expected profit per dollar loaned may be rewritten as

$$\rho(J) = [J - D + X][T - D]\frac{\int_J^K \frac{g(R)}{R-D}dR}{\int_J^K g(R)dR} + D - X$$

Differentiating, and collecting terms

$$\frac{1}{T-D}\frac{\partial \rho}{\partial J} = \frac{\int_J^K \frac{g(R)}{R-D}dR}{\int_J^K g(R)dR} + [J - D + X]\left[\frac{\frac{-g(J)}{J-D}\int_J^K g(R)dR + g(J)\int_J^K \frac{g(R)}{R-D}dR}{\left[\int_J^K g(R)dR\right]^2}\right]$$

Using l'Hopital's rule and the assumption that $g(K) \neq 0, \infty$

$$\lim_{J \to K}\left(\frac{1}{T-D}\frac{\partial \rho}{\partial J}\right) = \left(\frac{1}{K-D} - \frac{K-D+X}{2(K-D)^2}\right);$$

or

$$sign\left(\lim_{J \to K}\frac{1}{T-D}\frac{\partial \rho}{\partial J}\right) = sign(K - D - X)$$

Conditions 2 and 3 follow in a similar manner.

the distribution of returns is $G(R)$ where $G(K) = 1$. The other group is risk neutral. For simplicity we shall assume that they all face the same risky project with probability of success p and a return, if successful, of $R^* > K$; if not their return is zero. Letting $\hat{R} = (1 + \hat{r})B$ the (expected) return to the bank is

$$\bar{p}(\hat{r}) = \frac{\left\{\lambda\left(1 - G(\hat{R})\right) + (1 - \lambda)p\right\}}{\lambda\left(1 - G(\hat{R})\right) + (1 - \lambda)}(1 + \hat{r})$$

$$= \left[1 - \frac{(1 - p)(1 - \lambda)}{\lambda\left(1 - G(\hat{R})\right) + (1 - \lambda)}\right]\frac{\hat{R}}{B} \qquad (11)$$

Hence for $R < K$, the upper bound on returns from the safe project

$$\frac{dln\bar{p}}{dln(1 + \hat{r})} = 1 - \frac{(1 - \lambda)(1 - p)\lambda g(\hat{R})\hat{R}}{\left(1 - \lambda G(\hat{R})\right)\left(\lambda\left(1 - G(\hat{R})\right) + p(1 - \lambda)\right)} \qquad (12)$$

A sufficient condition for the existence of an interior bank optimal interest rate is again that $lim_{R \to K}\,\partial\bar{p}/\partial\hat{r} < 0$, or from (12), $\lambda/1 - \lambda\,lim_{R \to K}g(R)\hat{R} > p/1 - p$. The greater is the riskiness of the risky project (the lower is p), the more likely is an interior bank optimal interest rate. Similarly, the higher is the relative proportion of the risk averse individuals affected by increases in the interest rate to risk neutral borrowers, the more important is the self-selection effect, and the more likely is an interior bank optimal interest rate.

II INTEREST RATE AS AN INCENTIVE MECHANISM

A Sufficient Conditions

The second way in which the interest rate affects the bank's expected return from a loan is by changing the behavior of the borrower. The interests of the lender and the borrower do not coincide. The borrower is only concerned with returns on the investment when the firm does not go bankrupt; the lender is concerned with the actions of the firm only to the extent that they affect the probability of bankruptcy, and the returns in those states of nature in which the firm *does* go bankrupt. Because of this, and because the behavior of a borrower cannot be perfectly and costlessly monitored by the lender, banks will take into account the effect of the interest rate on the behavior of borrowers.

In this section, we show that increasing the rate of interest increases the relative attractiveness of riskier projects, for which the return to the bank may be lower. Hence, raising the rate of interest may lead borrowers to take actions which are contrary to the interests of the lender, providing another incentive for banks to ration credit rather than raise the interest rate when there is an excess demand for loanable funds.

We return to the general model presented above, but now we assume that each firm has a choice of projects. Consider any two projects, denoted by superscripts j and k. We first establish:

Theorem 7. *If, at a given nominal interest rate r, a risk-neutral firm is indifferent between two projects, an increase in the interest rate results in the firm preferring the project with the higher probability of bankruptcy.*

Proof. The expected return to the ith project is given by

$$\pi^i = E\left[\max\left(R^i - (1+\hat{r})B, -C\right)\right] \tag{13}$$

so

$$\frac{d\pi^i}{d\hat{r}} = -B(1 - F_i((1+\hat{r})B - C)) \tag{14}$$

Thus, if at some $\hat{r}$, $\pi^j = \pi^k$, the increase in $\hat{r}$ lowers the expected return to the borrower from the project with the higher probability of paying back the loan by more than it lowers the expected return from the project with the lower probability of the loan being repaid.

On the other hand, if the firm is indifferent between two projects with the same mean, we know from Theorem 2 that the bank prefers to lend to the safer project. Hence raising the interest rate above $\hat{r}$ could so increase the riskiness of loans as to lower the expected return to the bank.

Theorem 8. *The expected return to the bank is lowered by an increase in the interest rate at $\hat{r}$ if, at $\hat{r}$, the firm is indifferent between two projects j and k with distributions $F_j(R)$ and $F_k(R)$, j having a higher probability of bankruptcy than k, and there exists a distribution $F_l(R)$ such that*

(a) *$F_j(R)$ represents a mean preserving spread of the distribution $F_l(R)$, and*
(b) *$F_k(R)$ satisfies a first-order dominance relation with $F_l(R)$; i.e., $F_l(R) > F_k(R)$ for all R.*

Proof. Since j has a higher probability of bankruptcy than does k, from Theorem 7 and the initial indifference of borrowers between j and k, an increase in the interest rate $\hat{r}$ leads firms to prefer project j to k. Because of (a) and Theorem 3, the return to the bank on a project whose return is distributed as $F_l(R)$ is higher than on project j, and because of (b) the return to the bank on project k is higher than the return on a project distributed as $F_l(R)$.

B An Example

To illustrate the implications of Theorem 8, assume all firms are identical, and have a choice of two projects, yielding, if successful, returns R^a and R^b, respectively (and nothing otherwise) where $R^a > R^b$, and with probabilities of success of p^a and p^b, $p^a < p^b$. For simplicity assume that $C = 0$. If the firm is indifferent between the projects at interest rate $\hat{r}$, then

$$[R^a - (1 + \hat{r})B] \, p^a = \left[R^b - (1 + \hat{r})B\right] p^b \tag{15}$$

i.e.,

$$B(1 + \hat{r}) = \frac{p^b R^b - p^a R^a}{p^b - p^a} \equiv (1 + \hat{r}^*)B \tag{16}$$

Thus, the expected return to the bank as a function of r appears as in Figure 6.

For interest rates below $\hat{r}^*$, firms choose the safe project, while for interest rates between $\hat{r}^*$ and $(R^a/B) - 1$, firms choose the risky project. The maximum interest rate the bank could charge and still induce investments in project b is $\hat{r}^*$. The highest interest rate which attracts borrowers is $(R^a/B) - 1$, which would induce investment only in project a. Therefore the maximum expected return to a bank occurs when the bank charges an interest rate $\hat{r}^*$ if and only if

$$p^a R^a < \frac{p^b(p^b R^b - p^a R^a)}{p^b - p^a}$$

Whenever $p^b R^b > p^a R^a$, $1 + \hat{r}^* > 0$, and ρ is not monotonic in $\hat{r}$, so there may be credit rationing.

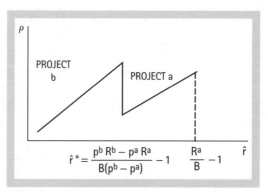

Fig. 6. At Interest Rates Above $\hat{r}^*$, the Risky Project is Undertaken and the Return to the Bank is Lowered

III THE THEORY OF COLLATERAL AND LIMITED LIABILITY

An obvious objection to the analysis presented thus far is: When there is an excess demand for funds, would not the bank increase its collateral requirements (increasing the liability of the borrower in the event that the project fails); reducing the demand for funds, reducing the risk of default (or losses to the bank in the event of default) and increasing the return to the bank?

This objection will not in general hold. In this section we will discuss various reasons why banks will not decrease the debt-equity ratio of borrowers (increasing collateral requirements)[8] as a means of allocating credit.

A clear case in which reductions in the debt-equity ratio of borrowers are not optimal for the bank is when smaller projects have a higher probability of "failure," and all potential borrowers have the same amount of equity. In those circumstances, increasing the collateral requirements (or the required proportion of equity finance) of loans will imply financing smaller projects. If projects either succeed or fail, and yield a zero return when they fail, then the increase in the collateral requirement of loans will increase the riskiness of those loans.

Another obvious case where increasing collateral requirements may increase the riskiness of loans is if potential borrowers have different equity, and all projects require the same investment. Wealthy borrowers may be those who, in the past, have succeeded at risky endeavors. In that case they are likely to be less risk averse than the more conservative individuals who have in the past invested in relatively safe securities, and are consequently less able to furnish large amounts of collateral.

In both these examples collateral requirements have adverse selection effects. However, we will present a stronger result. We will show that even if there are no increasing returns to scale in production and all individuals have the same utility function, the sorting effect of collateral requirements can still lead to an interior bank-optimal level of collateral requirements similar to the interior bank-optimal interest rate derived in Sections I and II. In particular, since wealthier individuals are likely to be less risk averse, we would expect that those who could put up the most capital would also be willing to take the greatest risk. We show that this latter effect is sufficiently strong that increasing collateral requirements will, under plausible conditions, lower the bank's return.

To see this most clearly, we assume all borrowers are risk averse with the same utility function $U(W)$, $U' > 0$, $U'' < 0$. Individuals differ, however, with respect to their initial wealth, W_0. Each "entrepreneur" has a set of projects which he can undertake; each project has a probability of success $p(R)$, where R is the return if successful. If the project is unsuccessful, the return is zero; $p'(R) < 0$. Each individual has an alternative safe investment opportunity yielding the return ρ^*. The bank cannot observe either the individual's wealth or the project undertaken. It offers the same contract, defined by C, the amount of collateral, and $\hat{r}$, the interest rate, to all customers. The analysis proceeds as earlier; we first establish:

Theorem 9. *The contract $\{C, \hat{r}\}$ acts as a screening mechanism: there exist two critical values of W_0, $\hat{W}_0$, and $\check{W}_0$, such that if there is decreasing absolute risk aversion all individuals with wealth $\hat{W}_0 < W_0 < \check{W}_0$ apply for loans.*

Proof. As before, we normalize so that all projects cost a dollar. If the individual does not borrow, he either does not undertake the project, obtaining a utility of $U(W_0\rho^*)$, or he finances it all himself, obtaining an expected utility of (assuming $W_0 \geqslant 1$)

$$\max_R \{U((W_0 - 1)\rho^* + R)p(R) + U((W_0 - 1)\rho^*)(1 - p(R))\} \equiv \hat{V}(W_0) \quad (17)$$

Define

$$V_0(W_0) = \max[U(W_0\rho^*), \hat{V}(W_0)] \quad (18)$$

We note that

$$\frac{dU(W_0\rho^*)}{dW_0} = U'\rho^* \quad (19)$$

$$\frac{d\hat{V}(W_0)}{dW_0} = [U_1'p + U_2'(1 - p)]\rho^* \quad (20)$$

(where the subscript 1 refers to the state "success" and the subscript 2 to the state "failure"). We can establish that if there is decreasing absolute risk aversion,[9]

$$\frac{dU(W_0\rho^*)}{dW_0} < \frac{d\hat{V}(W_0)}{dW_0}$$

Hence, there exists a critical value of W_0, $\hat{W}_0$, such that if $W_0 > \hat{W}_0$ individuals who do not borrow undertake the project.

For the rest of the analysis we confine ourselves to the case of decreasing absolute risk aversion and wealth less than $\hat{W}_0$.

If the individual borrows, he attains a utility level[10]

$$\left\{\max_R U(W_0\rho^* - (1 + \hat{r}) + R)p + U((W_0 - C)\rho^*)(1 - p)\right\} \equiv V_B(W_0) \quad (21)$$

---

[9] To prove this, we define $\hat{W}_0$ as the wealth where undertaking the risky project is a mean-utility preserving spread (compare Peter Diamond-Stiglitz (1974)) of the safe project. But writing $U'(W(U))$, where $W(U)$ is the value of terminal wealth corresponding to utility level U,

$$\frac{dU'}{dU} = \frac{U''}{U'} = -A; \quad \frac{d^2U'}{dU^2} = -\frac{A'}{U'} \gtreqless 0 \quad \text{as} \quad A' \lesseqgtr 0$$

Hence with decreasing absolute risk aversion, U' is a convex function of U and therefore EU' for the risky investment exceeds $U'(\rho^* W_0)$.

[10] In this formulation, the collateral earns a return ρ^*.

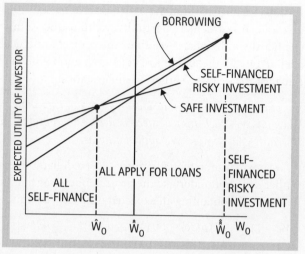

Fig. 7. Collateral Serves as a Screening Device

The individual borrows if and only if

$$V_B(W_0) \geqslant V_0(W_0) \tag{22}$$

But

$$\frac{dV_B}{dW_0} = (U_1' p + U_2'(1-p))\rho^* \tag{23}$$

Clearly, only those with $W_0 > C$ can borrow. We assume there exists a value of $W_0 > 0$, denoted $\hat{W}_0$, such that $V_B(\hat{W}_0) = U(\rho^*\hat{W}_0)$. (This will be true for some values of ρ^*.) By the same kind of argument used earlier, it is clear that at $\hat{W}_0$, borrowing with collateral is a mean-utility preserving spread of terminal wealth in comparison to not borrowing and not undertaking the project. Thus using (20) and (23), $dV_B/dW_0 > dV_0(W_0)/dW_0$ at $\hat{W}_0$. Hence, for $\hat{W}_0 < W_0 < \overset{\ast}{W}_0$ all individuals apply for loans, as depicted in Figure 7. Thus, restricting ourselves to $W_0 < \overset{\ast}{W}_0$, we have established that if there is any borrowing, it is the wealthiest in that interval who borrow. (The restriction $W_0 < \overset{\ast}{W}_0$ is weaker than the restriction that the scale of projects exceeds the wealth of any individual.)

Next, we show:

Theorem 10. *If there is decreasing absolute risk aversion, wealthier individuals undertake riskier projects: $dR/dW_0 > 0$.*

Proof. From (21), we obtain the first-order condition for the choice of R:

$$U_1' p + (U_1 - U_2)p' = 0 \tag{24}$$

so, using the second-order conditions for a maximum, and (24),

$$\frac{dR}{dW_0} \gtrless 0 \text{ as } \frac{U_1'' p + (U_1' - U_2')p'}{U_1' p} = -A_1 - \frac{(U_1' - U_2')}{U_1 - U_2} \gtrless 0 \tag{25}$$

But

$$\lim_{W_1 \to W_2} -\frac{U_1' - U_2'}{U_1 - U_2} = -\frac{U_1''}{U_1'} = A_1$$

implying that, if $W_1 = W_2$, $dR/dW_0 = 0$. However,

$$\left.\frac{\partial\left(-A_1 - \frac{U_1'-U_2'}{U_1-U_2}\right)}{\partial W_1}\right|_{A_1 = -\frac{U_2'-U_1'}{U_1-U_2}} = -A_1' - \frac{U_1''}{U_1 - U_2} + \frac{U_1' - U_2'}{U_1 - U_2}\frac{U_1'}{U_1 - U_2}$$

$$= -A_1' \gtrless 0 \text{ as } A_1' \lessgtr 0$$

Hence $dR/dW_0 > 0$ if $A' < 0$.

Next we show

Theorem 11. *Collateral increases the bank's return from any given borrower:*

$$dp/dC > 0$$

Proof. This follows directly from the first-order condition (24):

$$sign\frac{dR}{dC} = sign\ U_2'\rho^* p' < 0$$

and thus $dp/dC > 0$. But

Theorem 12. *There is an adverse selection effect from increasing the collateral requirement, i.e., both the average and the marginal borrower who borrows is riskier,*[11] $d\hat{W}_0/dC > 0$.

Proof. This follows immediately upon differentiation of (21)

$$dV_B/dC = -U_2'\rho^*(1 - p) < 0$$

It is easy to show now that this adverse selection effect *may* more than offset the positive direct effect. Assume there are two groups; for low wealth levels, increasing C has no adverse selection effect, so returns are unambiguously increased; but there is a critical level of C such that requiring further investments select against the low wealth-low risk individuals, and the bank's return is lowered.[12] (See Figure 8.)

This simple example has demonstrated[13] that although collateral may have beneficial incentive effects, it may also have countervailing adverse selection effects.

[11] At a sufficiently high collateral, the wealthy individual will not borrow at all.
[12] If we had not imposed the restriction $W_0 < \hat{W}_0$, then there may exist a value of W_0, $\hat{\hat{W}}_0 > \hat{W}_0$, such that for $W_0 > \hat{\hat{W}}_0$, individuals self-finance. It is easy to show that $\partial\hat{W}_0/\partial C < 0$, so there is a countervailing positive selection effect. However if the density distribution of wealth is decreasing fast enough, then the adverse selection effect outweighs the positive selection effect.
[13] It also shows that the results of earlier sections can be extended to the risk averse entrepreneur.

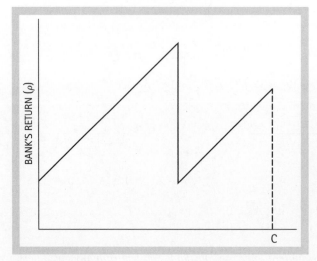

Fig. 8. Increasing Collateral Requirement Lowers Bank's Returns

A Adverse Incentive Effects

Although in the model presented above, increasing collateral has a beneficial incentive effect, this is not necessarily the case. The bank has limited control over the actions of the borrowers, as we noted earlier. Thus, the response of the borrower to the increase in lending may be to take actions which, in certain contingencies, will require the bank to lend more in the future. (This argument seems implicit in many discussions of the importance of adequate initial funding for projects.) Consider, for instance, the following simplified multiperiod model. In the first period, θ occurs with probability p_1; if it does, the return to the project (realized the second period) is R_1. If it does not, either an additional amount M must be invested, or the project fails completely (has a zero return). If the bank charges an interest rate $r_2 \leqslant \hat{r}_2$ on these additional funds, they will invest them in "safe" ways; if $r_2 > \hat{r}_2$ those funds will be invested in risky ways. Following the analysis in Section II, we assume that the risk differences are sufficiently strong that the bank charges $\hat{r}_2$ for additional funds. Assume that there is also a set of projects (actions) which the firm can undertake in the first period, but among which the bank cannot discriminate. The individual has an equity of a dollar, which he cannot raise further, so the effect of a decrease in the loan is to affect the actions which the individual takes, that is, it affects the parameters of the projects, R_1, R_2, and M, where M is the amount of second-period financing needed if the project fails in the first period. For simplicity, we take R_2 as given, and let L be the size of the first-period loan. Thus the expected return to the firm is simply (if the additional loan M is made when needed)

$$p_1 \left(R_1 - (1 + \hat{r}_1)^2 L \right) + \hat{p} \left(R_2 - \left[(1 + \hat{r}_1)^2 L + (1 + \hat{r}_2) M \right] \right)$$

where $\hat{p} = p_2(1 - p_1), (1 + \hat{r}_1)^2$ is the amount paid back (per dollar borrowed) at the end of the second period on the initial loan and $\hat{r}_2$ is the interest on the additional loan M; thus the firm chooses R_1 so that

$$p_1 = \hat{p}(1 + \hat{r}_2)\frac{dM}{dR_1}$$

Assume that the opportunity cost of capital to the bank per period is ρ^*. Then its net expected return to the loan is

$$p_1(1 + \hat{r}_1)^2 L + \hat{p}\left[(1 + \hat{r}_1)^2 L + (1 + \hat{r}_2)M\right] - \rho^*[\rho^* L + (1 - p_1)M]$$

We can show that under certain circumstances, it will pay the bank to extend the line of credit M. Thus, although the bank controls L, it does not control directly the total (expected value) of its loans per customer, $L + (1 - p_1)M$.

But more to the point is the fact that the expected return to the bank may not be monotonically decreasing in the size of the first-period loans. For instance, under the hypothesis that $\hat{r}_1$ and $\hat{r}_2$ are optimally chosen and at the optimum $\rho^* > p_2(1 + \hat{r}_2)$, the return to the bank is a decreasing function of M/L. Thus, if the optimal response of the firm to a decrease in L is an increase in M (or a decrease in M so long as the percentage decrease in M is less than the percentage decrease in L), a decrease in L actually lowers the bank's profits.[14]

IV OBSERVATIONALLY DISTINGUISHABLE BORROWERS

Thus far we have confined ourselves to situations where all borrowers appear to be identical. Let us now extend the analysis to the case where there are n observationally distinguishable groups each with an interior bank optimal interest rate denoted by r_i^*.[15] The function $\rho_i(r_i)$ denote the gross return to a bank charging a type i borrower interest r_i. We can order the groups so that for $i > j$, $max\ \rho_i(\hat{r}_i) > max\ \rho_j(\hat{r}_j)$.

Theorem 13. *For $i > j$, type j borrowers will only receive loans if credit is not rationed to type i borrowers.*

Proof. Assume not. Since the maximum return on the loan to j is less than that to i, the bank could clearly increase its return by substituting a loan to i for a loan to j; hence the original situation could not have been profit maximizing.

We now show

---

[14] For instance, if some of the initial investment is for "back-up" systems in case of various kinds of failure, if the reduction in initial funding leads to a reduction in investment in these back-up systems, when a failure does occur, large amounts of additional funding may be required.

[15] The analysis in this section parallels Weiss (1980) in which it was demonstrated that market equilibrium could result in the exclusion of some groups of workers from the labor market.

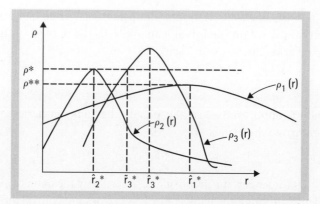

Fig. 9. If Groups Differ, there will Exist Red Lining

Theorem 14. *The equilibrium interest rates are such that for all i, j receiving loans,*
$\rho_i(\hat{r}_i) = \rho_j(\hat{r}_j)$.

Proof. Again the proof is by contradiction. Let us assume that $\rho_i(\hat{r}_i) > \rho_j(\hat{r}_j)$; then a bank lending to type j borrowers would prefer to bid type i borrowers away from other banks. If ρ^* is the equilibrium return to the banks per dollar loaned, equal to the cost of loanable funds if banks compete freely for borrowers, then for all i, j receiving loans $\rho_i(r_i) = \rho_j(r_j) = \rho^*$. These results are illustrated for three types of borrowers in Figure 9.

If banks have a cost of loanable funds ρ^* then no type 1 borrower will obtain a loan; all type 3 borrowers wishing to borrow at interest rate $\tilde{r}_3$ (which is less than $\hat{r}_3^*$, the rate which maximizes the bank's return) will obtain loans—competition for those borrowers drives their interest rate down; while some, but not necessarily all, type 2 borrowers receive a loan at $\hat{r}_2^*$. If the interest rate were to fall to ρ^{**}, then all types 2 and 3 would receive loans; and some (but not all) type 1 borrowers would be extended credit.

Groups such as type 1 which are excluded from the credit market may be termed "redlined" since there is no interest rate at which they would get loans if the cost of funds is above ρ^{**}. It is possible that the investments of type 1 borrowers are especially risky so that, although $\rho_1(\hat{r}_1^*) < \rho_3(\hat{r}_3^*)$, the total expected return to type 1 investments (the return to the bank plus the return to the borrower) exceeds the expected return to type 3 investments. It may also be true that type 1 loans are unprofitable to the bank because they find it difficult to filter out risky type 1 investments. In that case it is possible that the return to the bank to an investment by a type 1 borrower would be greater than the return to a type 3 investment if the bank could exercise the same control (judgment) over each group of investors.

Another reason for $\rho_1(\hat{r}_1^*) < \rho_3(\hat{r}_3^*)$ may be that type 1 investors have a broader range of available projects. They can invest in all the projects available to type 3 borrowers, but can also invest in high-risk projects unavailable to type 3. Either because of the convexity of the profit function of borrowers, or because riskier investments have higher expected returns type 1 borrowers will choose to invest in these risky projects.

Thus, *there is no presumption that the market equilibrium allocates credit to those for whom the expected return on their investments is highest.*

V Debt vs. Equity Finance, Another View of the Principal-Agent Problem

Although we have phrased this paper in the context of credit markets, the analysis could apply equally well to any one of a number of principal-agent problems. For example, in agriculture the bank (principal) corresponds to the landlord and the borrower (agent) to the tenant while the loan contract corresponds to a rental agreement. The return function for the landlord and tenant appears in Figures 10a and 10b. The central concern in those principal-agent problems is how to provide the proper incentives for the agent. In general, revenue sharing arrangements such as equity finance, or sharecropping are inefficient. Under those schemes the managers of a firm or the tenant will equate their marginal disutility of effort with their share of their marginal product rather than with their total marginal product. Therefore, too little effort will be forthcoming from agents.

Fixed-fee contracts (for example, rental agreements in agriculture, loan contracts in credit markets) have the disadvantage that they impose a heavy risk on the agent, and thus if agents are risk averse, they may not be desirable. But it has long been thought that they have a significant advantage in not distorting incentives and thus if the agent is risk neutral, fixed-fee contracts will be employed.[16] These discussions have not considered the possibility that the agent will fail to pay the fixed fee. In the particular context of the bank-borrower relationship, the assumption that the loan will always be repaid (with interest) seems most peculiar. A borrower can repay the loan in all states of nature only if the risky project's returns plus the value of the equilibrium level of collateral exceeds the safe rate of interest in all states of nature.

The consequences of this are important. Since the agent can by his actions affect the probability of bankruptcy, fixed-fee contracts do not eliminate the incentive problem.

Moreover, they do not necessarily lead to optimal resource allocations. For example, in the two-project case discussed above (Section II, Part B), if expected returns to the safe project exceed that to the risky ($p^s R^s > p^r R^r$) but the highest rate which the bank can charge consistent with the safe project being chosen (r^*) is too low (i.e., $p^s(1 + r^*) > p^r R^r$) then the bank chooses an interest rate which causes all its loans to be for risky projects, although the expected total (social) returns on these projects are less than on the safe projects. In this case a usury law forbidding interest rates in excess

---

[16] See, for instance, Stiglitz (1974e). For a recent formalization of the principal-agent problem, see Steven Shavell (1979b).

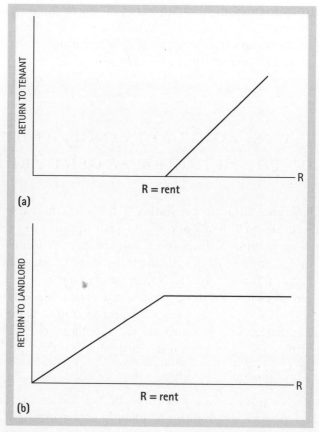

Fig. 10.

of r^* will increase net national output. Our 1980 paper and Janusz Ordover and Weiss show that government interventions of various forms lead to Pareto improvements in the allocation of credit.

Because neither equity finance nor debt finance lead to efficient resource allocations, we would not expect to see the exclusive use of either method of financing (even with risk-neutral agents and principals). Similarly, in agriculture, we would not expect to see the exclusive use of rental or sharecropping tenancy arrangements. In general, where feasible, the payoff will be a non-linear function of output (profits). The terms of these contracts will depend on the risk preferences of the principal and agent, the extent to which their actions (both the level of effort and riskiness of outcomes) can affect the probability of bankruptcy, and actions can be specified within the contract or controlled directly by the principal.

One possible criticism of this paper is that the single period analysis presented above artificially limits the strategy space of lenders. In a multiperiod context, for instance, banks could reward "good" borrowers by offering to lend to them at lower interest rates, and this would induce firms to undertake safer projects (just as in the labor market, the promise of promotion and pay increases is an important part of the incentive and sorting structure of firms, see Stiglitz 1975b, J. L. Guasch and Weiss, 1980b, 1981). In our 1980 paper, we analyze the nature of equilibrium contracts in a dynamic context. We show that such contingency contracts may characterize the dynamic equilibrium. Indeed, we establish that the bank may want to use quantity constraints—the availability of credit—as an additional incentive device; thus, in the dynamic context there is a further argument for the existence of rationing in a competitive economy. (See Stiglitz and Weiss, 1983b)

Even after introducing all of these additional instruments (collateral, equity, non-linear payment schedules, contingency contracts) there may exist a contract which is optimal from the point of view of the principal; he will not respond, then, to an excess supply of agents by altering the terms of that contract; and there may then be rationing of the form discussed in this paper, that is, an excess demand for loans at the "competitive" contract.

VI CONCLUSIONS

We have presented a model of credit rationing in which among observationally identical borrowers some receive loans and others do not. Potential borrowers who are denied loans would not be able to borrow even if they indicated a willingness to pay more than the market interest rate, or to put up more collateral than is demanded of recipients of loans. Increasing interest rates or increasing collateral requirements could increase the riskiness of the bank's loan portfolio, either by discouraging safer investors, or by inducing borrowers to invest in riskier projects, and therefore could decrease the bank's profits. Hence neither instrument will necessarily be used to equate the supply of loanable funds with the demand for loanable funds. Under those circumstances credit restrictions take the form of limiting the number of loans the bank will make, rather than limiting the size of each loan, or making the interest rate charged an increasing function of the magnitude of the loan, as in most previous discussions of credit rationing.

Note that in a rationing equilibrium, to the extent that monetary policy succeeds in shifting the supply of funds, it will affect the level of investment, not through the interest rate mechanism, but rather through the availability of credit. Although this is a "monetarist" result, it should be apparent that the mechanism is different from that usually put forth in the monetarist literature.

Although we have focused on analyzing the existence of excess demand equilibria in credit markets, imperfect information can lead to excess supply equilibria as well. We will sketch an outline of an argument here (a fuller discussion of the issue and of the macro-economic implications of this paper will appear in future work by the authors in conjunction with Bruce Greenwald).[17] Let us assume that banks make

---

[17] A similar argument to that presented here appears in Greenwald (1979) in the context of labor markets.

higher expected returns on some of their borrowers than on others: they know who their most credit worthy customers are, but competing banks do not. If a bank tries to attract the customers of its competitors by offering a lower interest rate, it will find that its offer is countered by an equally low interest rate when the customer being competed for is a "good" credit risk, and will not be matched if the borrower is not a profitable customer of the bank. Consequently, banks will seldom seek to steal the customers of their competitors, since they will only succeed in attracting the least profitable of those customers (introducing some noise in the system enables the development of an equilibrium). A bank with an excess supply of loanable funds must assess the profitability of the loans a lower interest rate would attract. In equilibrium each bank may have an excess supply of loanable funds, but no bank will lower its interest rate.

The reason we have been able to model excess demand and excess supply equilibria in credit markets is that the interest rate directly affects the quality of the loan in a manner which matters to the bank. Other models in which prices are set competitively and non-market-clearing equilibria exist share the property that the expected quality of a commodity is a function of its price (see Weiss, 1976, 1980, or Stiglitz 1976b, c, 1992; for the labor market, and C. Wilson 1980 for the used car market).

In any of these models in which, for instance, the wage affects the quality of labor, if there is an excess supply of workers at the wage which minimizes labor costs, there is not necessarily an inducement for firms to lower wages.

The Law of Supply and Demand is not in fact a law, nor should it be viewed as an assumption needed for competitive analysis. It is rather a result generated by the underlying assumptions that prices have neither sorting nor incentive effects. The usual result of economic theorizing, that prices clear markets, is model specific and is not a general property of markets—unemployment and credit rationing are not phantasms.

C H A P T E R 11

EQUILIBRIUM UNEMPLOYMENT AS A WORKER DISCIPLINE DEVICE*

INVOLUNTARY unemployment appears to be a persistent feature of many modern labor markets. The presence of such unemployment raises the question of why wages do not fall to clear labor markets. In this paper we show how the information structure of employer-employee relationships, in particular the inability of employers to costlessly observe workers' on-the-job effort, can explain involuntary unemployment[1] as an equilibrium phenomenon. Indeed, we show that imperfect monitoring necessitates unemployment in equilibrium.

The intuition behind our result is simple. Under the conventional competitive paradigm, in which all workers receive the market wage and there is no unemployment, the worst that can happen to a worker who shirks on the job is that he is fired. Since he can immediately be rehired, however, he pays no penalty for his misdemeanor. With imperfect monitoring and full employment, therefore, workers will choose to shirk.

To induce its workers not to shirk, the firm attempts to pay more than the "going wage"; then, if a worker is caught shirking and is fired, he will pay a penalty. If it pays one firm to raise its wage, however, it will pay all firms to raise their wages. When they all raise their wages, the incentive not to shirk again disappears. But as all firms

* Written with Carl Shapiro. We thank Peter Diamond, Gene Grossman, Ed Lazear, Steve Salop, and Mike Veall for helpful comments. Financial support from the National Science Foundation is appreciated. Reprinted with permission from *The American Economic Review*, 74(3) (June), 1984.

[1] By involuntary unemployment we mean a situation where an unemployed worker is willing to work for less than the wage received by an equally skilled employed worker, yet no job offers are forthcoming.

raise their wages, their demand for labor decreases, and unemployment results. With unemployment, even if all firms pay the same wages, a worker has an incentive not to shirk. For, if he is fired, an individual will not immediately obtain another job. The equilibrium unemployment rate must be sufficiently large that it pays workers to work rather than to take the risk of being caught shirking.

The idea that the threat of firing a worker is a method of discipline is not novel. Guillermo Calvo (1981) studied a static model which involves equilibrium unemployment.[2] No previous studies have treated general market equilibrium with dynamics, however, or studied the welfare properties of such unemployment equilibria. One key contribution of this paper is that the punishment associated with being fired is endogenous, as it depends on the equilibrium rate of unemployment. Our analysis thus goes beyond studies of information and incentives within organizations (such as Armen Alchian and Harold Demsetz, 1972, and the more recent and growing literature on worker-firm relations as a principal-agent problem) to inquire about the equilibrium conditions in markets with these informational features.

The paper closest in spirit to ours is Steven Salop (1979a) in which firms reduce turnover costs when they raise wages; here the savings from higher wages are on monitoring costs (or, at the same level of monitoring, from increased output due to increased effort). As in the Salop paper, the unemployment in this paper is definitely involuntary, and not of the standard search theory type (Peter Diamond, 1981, for example). Workers have perfect information about all job opportunities in our model, and unemployed workers strictly prefer to work at wages less than the prevailing market wage (rather than to remain unemployed); there are no vacancies.

The theory we develop has several important implications. First, we show that unemployment benefits (and other welfare benefits) increase the equilibrium unemployment rate, but for a reason quite different from that commonly put forth (i.e., that individuals will have insufficient incentives to search for jobs). In our model, the existence of unemployment benefits reduces the "penalty" associated with being fired. Therefore, to induce workers not to shirk, firms must pay higher wages. These higher wages reduce the demand for labor.

Second, the model explains why wages adjust slowly in the face of aggregate shocks. A decrease in the demand for labor will ultimately cause a lower wage and a higher level of unemployment. In the transition, however, the wage decrease will match the growth in the unemployment pool, which may be a sluggish process.

Third, we show that the market equilibrium which emerges is not, in general, Pareto optimal, where we have taken explicitly into account the costs associated with monitoring. There exist, in other words, interventions in the market that make everyone better off. In particular, we show that there are circumstances in which wage subsidies are desirable. There are also circumstances where the government should intervene in the market by supplying unemployment insurance, even if all firms (rationally) do not. A (small) turnover tax is desirable, because high turnover

[2] In his 1979 paper, Calvo surveyed a variety of models of unemployment, including his hierarchical firm model (also with Stanislaw Wellisz, 1979). There are a number of important differences between that work and this paper, including the specification of the monitoring technology.

increases the flow of job vacancies, and hence the flow out of the unemployment pool, making the threat of firing less severe.

Additionally, our theory provides predictions about the characteristics of labor markets which cause the natural rate (i.e., equilibrium level) of unemployment to be relatively high: high rates of labor turnover, high monitoring costs, high discount rates for workers, significant possibilities for workers to vary their effort inputs, or high costs to employers (such as broken machinery) from shirking.

Finally, our theory shows how wage distributions (for identical workers) can persist in equilibrium. Firms which find shirking particularly costly will offer higher wages than other firms do. The dual role wages play by allocating labor and providing incentives for employee effort allows wage dispersion to persist.

Although we have focused our analysis on the labor market, it should be clear that a similar analysis could apply to other markets (for example, product or credit markets) as well. This paper can be viewed as an analysis of a simplified general equilibrium model of an economy in which there are important principal-agent (incentive) problems, and in which the equilibrium entails *quantity constraints* (job rationing). As in all such problems, it is important to identify what is observable, and, based on what is observable, what are the set of feasible contractual arrangements between the parties to the contract. Under certain circumstances, for instance, workers might issue performance bonds and this might alleviate the problems with which we are concerned in this paper. In Section III we discuss the role of alternative incentive devices.

In the highly simplified model upon which we focus here, all workers are identical, all firms are identical, and thus, in equilibrium, all pay the same wage. The assumption that all workers are the same is important, because it implies that being fired carries no stigma (the next potential employer knows that the worker is no more immoral than any other worker; he only infers that the firm for which the worker worked must have paid a wage sufficiently low that it paid the worker to shirk). We have made this assumption because we wished to construct the simplest possible model focussing simply on incentive effects, in which adverse selection considerations play no role. In a sequel, we hope to explore the important interactions between the two fundamental information problems of adverse selection and moral hazard.[3]

The assumption that all firms are the same is not critical for the existence of equilibrium unemployment. Firm heterogeneity will, however, lead to a wage distribution. If the damage that a particular firm incurs as a result of a worker not performing up to standard is larger, the firm will have an incentive to pay the worker a higher wage. Similarly, if the cost of monitoring (detecting shirking) for a firm is large, that firm will also pay a higher wage. Thus, even though workers are all identical, workers for different firms will receive different wages. There is considerable evidence that, in fact, different firms do pay different wages to workers who appear to be quite

---

[3] Other studies have focused on quantity constraints (rationing) with adverse-selection problems. See Stiglitz (1976c), Charles Wilson (1980), Andrew Weiss (1980), and Stiglitz and Weiss (1981).

similar (for example, more capital intensive firms pay higher wages). The theory we develop here may provide part of the explanation of this phenomenon.

In Section I, we present the basic model in which workers are risk neutral. Quit rates and monitoring intensities are exogenous. A welfare analysis of the unemployment equilibrium is provided. In Section II, we comment on extensions of the analysis to situations where monitoring intensities and quit rates are endogenous, and where workers are risk averse. Section III compares the role of unemployment as an incentive device with other methods of enforcing discipline on the labor force.

I THE BASIC MODEL

In this section we formulate a simple model which captures the incentive role of unemployment as described above. Extensions and modifications of this basic model are considered in subsequent sections.

A Workers

There are a fixed number, N, of identical workers, all of whom dislike putting forth effort, but enjoy consuming goods. We write an individual's instantaneous utility function as $U(w, e)$, where w is the wage received and e is the level of effort on the job. For simplicity, we shall assume the utility function is separable; initially, we shall also assume that workers are risk neutral. With suitable normalizations, we can therefore rewrite utility as $U = w - e$. Again, for simplicity, we assume that workers can provide either minimal effort ($e = 0$), or some fixed positive level of $e > 0$.[4] When a worker is unemployed, he receives unemployment benefits of $\overline{w}$ (and $e = 0$).

Each worker is in one of two states at any point in time: employed or unemployed. There is a probability b per unit time that a worker will be separated from his job due to relocation, etc., which will be taken as exogenous. Exogenous separations cause a worker to enter the unemployment pool. Workers maximize the expected present discounted value of utility with a discount rate $r > 0$.[5] The model is set in continuous time.

---

[4] Including effort as a continuous variable would not change the qualitative results.

[5] That is, we assume individuals are infinitely lived, and have a pure rate of time preference of r. They maximize

$$W = E \int_0^\infty u(w(t), e(t)) \exp(-rt)dt,$$

where we have implicitly assumed that individuals can neither borrow nor lend. Allowing an exponential death rate would not alter the structure of the model; neither would borrowing in the risk-neutral case.

B The Effort Decision of a Worker

The only choice workers make is the selection of an effort level, which is a discrete choice by assumption. If a worker performs at the customary level of effort for his job, that is, if he does not shirk, he receives a wage of w and will retain his job until exogenous factors cause a separation to occur. If he shirks, there is some probability q (discussed below), per unit time, that he will be caught.[6] If he is caught shirking he will be fired,[7] and forced to enter the unemployment pool. The probability per unit time of acquiring a job while in the unemployment pool (which we call the job acquisition rate, an endogenous variable calculated below) determines the expected length of the unemployment spell he must face. While unemployed he receives unemployment compensation of $\overline{w}$ (also discussed below).

The worker selects an effort level to maximize his discounted utility stream. This involves comparison of the utility from shirking with the utility from not shirking, to which we now turn. We define V_E^S as the expected lifetime utility of an employed shirker, V_E^N as the expected lifetime utility of an employed nonshirker, and V_u as the expected lifetime utility of an unemployed individual. The fundamental asset equation for a shirker is given by

$$r V_E^S = w + (b + q)\left(V_u - V_E^S\right),$$ (1)

while for a nonshirker, it is

$$r V_E^N = w - e + b\left(V_u - V_E^N\right).$$ (2)

Each of these equations is of the form "interest rate times asset value equals flow benefits (dividends) plus expected capital gains (or losses)."[8] Equations (1) and (2) can be solved for V_E^S and V_E^N:

$$V_E^S = \frac{w + (b + q)V_u}{r + b + q};$$ (3)

$$V_E^N = \frac{(w - e) + b V_u}{r + b}.$$ (4)

---

[6] For now we take q as exogenous; later it will be endogenous. The assumption of a Poisson detection technology, like a number of the other assumptions employed in the analysis, is made to ensure that the model has a simple stationary structure.

[7] This will be firm's optimal policy in equilibrium.

[8] A derivation follows: taking V_u as given and looking at a short time interval $[0, t]$ we have

$$V_E = wt + (1 - rt)[bt V_u + (1 - bt)V_E],$$

since there is probability bt of leaving the job during the interval $[0, t]$ and since $e^{-rt} \approx 1 - rt$. Solving for V_E, we have

$$V_E = [wt + (1 - rt)bt V_u]/[(1 - (1 - rt)(1 - bt)].$$

Taking limits as $t \to 0$ gives (1). Equation (2) can be derived similarly.

The worker will choose not to shirk if and only if $V_E^N \geq V_E^S$. We call this the *no-shirking condition* (NSC), which, using (3) and (4), can be written as

$$w \geq rV_u + (r + b + q)e/q \equiv \hat{w}. \tag{5}$$

Alternatively, the NSC also takes the form $q(V_E^S - V_u) \geq e$. This highlights the basic implication of the NSC: unless there is a penalty associated with being unemployed, everyone will shirk. In other words, if an individual could immediately obtain employment after being fired, $V_u = V_E^S$, and the NSC could never be satisfied.

Equation (5) has several natural implications. If the firm pays a sufficiently high wage, then the workers will not shirk. The critical wage, $\hat{w}$, is higher

(a) the higher the required effort (e),
(b) the higher the expected utility associated with being unemployed (V_u),
(c) the lower the probability of being detected shirking (q),
(d) the higher the rate of interest (i.e., the relatively more weight is attached to the short-run gains from shirking (until one is caught) compared to the losses incurred when one is eventually caught),
(e) the higher the exogenous quit rate b (if one is going to have to leave the firm anyway, one might as well cheat on the firm).

C Employers

There are M identical firms, $i = 1, \ldots, M$. Each firm has a production function $Q_i = f(L_i)$, generating an aggregate production function of $Q = F(L)$.[9] Here L_i is firm i's effective labor force; we assume a worker contributes one unit of effective labor if he does not shirk. Otherwise he contributes nothing (this is merely for simplicity). Therefore firms compete in offering wage packages, subject to the constraint that their workers choose not to shirk. We assume that $F'(N) > e$, that is, full employment is efficient.

The monitoring technology (q) is exogenous. Monitoring choices by employers are analyzed in the following section. We assume that other factors (for example, exogenous noise or the absence of employee specific output measures) prevent monitoring of effort via observing output.

---

[9] That is,

$$F(L) \equiv \max_{\{L_i\}} \sum f_i(L_i)$$

such that $\sum L_i = L$. This assumes that in market equilibrium, labor is efficiently allocated, as it will be in the basic model of this section. The modifications required for more general cases, when different firms face different critical no-shirking wages, $\hat{w}_i$, or have different technologies, are straightforward.

A firm's wage package consists of a wage, w, and a level of unemployment benefits, $\overline{w}$.[10] Each firm finds it optimal to fire shirkers, since the only other punishment, a wage reduction, would simply induce the disciplined worker to shirk again.

It is not difficult to establish that all firms offer the smallest unemployment benefits allowed (say, by law).[11] This follows directly from the NSC, equation (5). An individual firm has no incentive to set $\overline{w}$ any higher than necessary. An increase in $\overline{w}$ raises V_u and hence requires a higher w to meet the NSC. Therefore, increases in $\overline{w}$ cost the firm both directly (higher unemployment benefits) and indirectly (higher wages). Since the firm has no difficulty attracting labor (in equilibrium), it sets $\overline{w}$ as small as possible. Hence we can interpret $\overline{w}$ in what follows as the minimum legal level, which is offered consistently by all firms.

Having offered the minimum allowable $\overline{w}$, an individual firm pays wages sufficient to induce employee effort, that is, $w = \hat{w}$ to meet the NSC. The firm's labor demand is given by equating the marginal product of labor to the cost of hiring an additional employee. This cost consists of wages and future unemployment benefits. For $\overline{w} = 0$,[12] the labor demand is given simply by $f'(L_i) = \hat{w}$, with aggregate labor demand of $F'(L) = \hat{w}$.

D Market Equilibrium

We now turn to the determination of the equilibrium wage and employment levels. Let us first indicate heuristically the factors which determine the equilibrium wage level.

If wages are very high, workers will value their jobs for two reasons: (a) the high wages themselves, and (b) the correspondingly low level of employment (due to low demand for labor at high wages) which implies long spells of unemployment in the event of losing one's job. In such a situation employers will find they can reduce wages without tempting workers to shirk.

Conversely, if the wage is quite low, workers will be tempted to shirk for two reasons: (a) low wages imply that working is only moderately preferred to unemployment, and (b) high employment levels (at low wages there is a large demand for labor) imply unemployment spells due to being fired will be brief. In such a situation firms will raise their wages to satisfy the NSC.

Equilibrium occurs when each firm, taking as given the wages and employment levels at other firms, finds it optimal to offer the going wage rather than a different

---

[10] More complex employment contracts, for example, wages rising with seniority, are discussed in Section III. With our assumptions of stationarity and identical workers, employers cannot improve on the simple employment provisions considered here.

[11] We are implicitly assuming that the firm cannot offer $\overline{w}$ only to workers who quit. This is so because the firm can always fire a worker who wishes to quit, and it would be optimal for the firm to do so.

[12] For $\overline{w} > 0$ the expected cost of a worker is the wage cost for the expected employment period of $1/b$, followed by $\overline{w}$ for the expected period of unemployment, $1/a$. This generates labor demand given by

$$f'(L_i) = w + \overline{w}b/(a+r).$$

wage. The key market variable which determines individual firm behavior is V_u, the expected utility of an unemployed worker. We turn now to the calculation of the equilibrium V_u.[13]

The asset equation for V_u, analogous to (1) and (2), is given by

$$r V_u = \overline{w} + a(V_E - V_u), \tag{6}$$

where a is the job acquisition rate and V_E is the expected utility of an employed worker (which equals V_E^N in equilibrium). We can now solve (4) and (6) simultaneously for V_E and V_u to yield

$$r V_E = \frac{(w - e)(a + r) + \overline{w} b}{a + b + r}; \tag{7}$$

$$r V_u = \frac{(w - e)a + \overline{w}(b + r)}{a + b + r}. \tag{8}$$

Substituting the expression for V_u (i.e., (8)) into the NSC (5) yields the *aggregate NSC*

$$w \geq \overline{w} + e + e(a + b + r)/q. \tag{9}$$

Notice that the critical wage for nonshirking is greater: (a) the smaller the detection probability q; (b) the larger the effort e; (c) the higher the quit rate b; (d) the higher the interest rate r; (e) the higher the unemployment benefit ($\overline{w}$); and (f) the higher the flows out of unemployment a.

We commented above on the first four properties; the last two are also unsurprising. If the unemployment benefit is high, the expected utility of an unemployed individual is high, and therefore the punishment associated with being unemployed is low. To induce individuals not to shirk, a higher wage must be paid. If a is the probability of obtaining a job per unit of time, $1/a$ is the expected duration of being unemployed. The longer the duration, the greater the punishment associated with being unemployed, and hence the smaller the wage that is required to induce nonshirking.

The rate a itself can be related to more fundamental parameters of the model, in a steady-state equilibrium. In steady state the flow *into* the unemployment pool is bL where L is aggregate employment. The flow *out* is $a(N - L)$ (per unit time) where N is the total labor supply. These must be equal, so $bL = a(N - L)$, or

$$a = bL/(N - L). \tag{10}$$

Substituting for a into (9), the aggregate NSC, we have

$$w \geq e + \overline{w} + \frac{e}{q}\left(\frac{bN}{(N - L)} + r\right) \tag{11}$$

$$= e + \overline{w} + (e/q)(b/u + r) \equiv \hat{w},$$

---

[13] We have already shown that all firms offer the same employment benefits $\overline{w}$, so V_u is indeed a single number, i.e., an unemployed person's utility is independent of his previous employer.

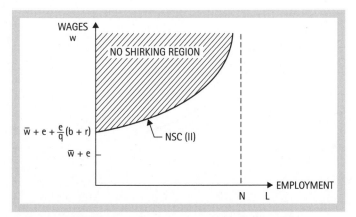

Fig. 1. The Aggregate No-Shirking Constraint

where $u = (N - L)/N$, the unemployment rate. This constraint, the aggregate *NSC*, is graphed in Figure 1. It is immediately evident that *no shirking is inconsistent with full employment*. If $L = N$, $a = +\infty$, so any shirking worker would immediately be rehired. Knowing this, workers will choose to shirk.

The equilibrium wage and employment level are now easy to identify. Each (small) firm, taking the aggregate job acquisition rate a as given, finds that it must offer at least the wage $\hat{w}$. The firm's demand for labor then determines how many workers are hired at the wage. Equilibrium occurs where the aggregate demand for labor intersects the aggregate *NSC*. For $\overline{w} = 0$, equilibrium occurs when

$$F'(L) = e + (e/q)(bN/(N - L) + r).$$

The equilibrium is depicted in Figure 2.[14] It is important to understand the forces which cause E to be an equilibrium. From the firm's point of view, there is no point in raising wages since workers are providing effort and the firm can get all the labor it wants at w^*. Lowering wages, on the other hand, would induce shirking and be a losing idea.[15]

From the worker's point of view, *unemployment is involuntary*: those without jobs would be happy to work at w^* or lower, but cannot make a credible promise not to shirk at such wages.

Notice that the type of unemployment we have characterized here is very different from search unemployment. Here, all workers and all firms are identical. There is perfect information about job availability. There is a different information problem: firms are assumed (quite reasonably, in our view) not to be able to monitor the activities of their employees costlessly and perfectly.

---

[14] Aggregate labor demand is $F'(L)$ only when $\overline{w} = 0$ (see fn. 12).
[15] We have assumed that output is zero when an individual shirks, but we need only assume that a shirker's output is sufficiently low that hiring shirking workers is unprofitable.

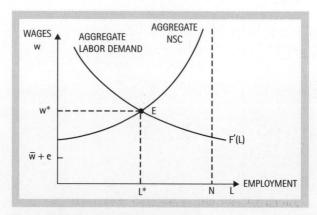

Fig. 2. Equilibrium Unemployment

E Simple Comparative Statics

The effect of changing various parameters of the problem may easily be determined. As noted above, increasing the quit rate b, or decreasing the monitoring intensity q, decreases incentives to exert effort. Therefore, these changes require an increase in the wage necessary (at each level of employment) to induce individuals to work, that is, they shift the *NSC* curve upwards (see Figure 3). On the other hand, they leave the demand curve for labor unchanged, and hence the equilibrium level of unemployment and the equilibrium wage are both increased. Increases in unemployment benefits have the same impact on the *NSC* curve, but they also reduce labor demand as workers become more expensive, so they cause unemployment to rise for two reasons.

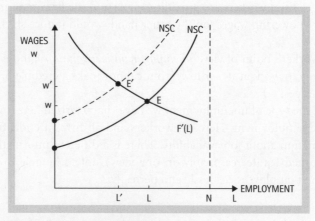

Fig. 3. Comparative Statics

Note: A decrease in the monitoring intensity q, or an increase in the quit rate b, leads to higher wages and more unemployment.

Inward shifts in the labor demand schedule create more unemployment. Due to the *NSC*, wages cannot fall enough to compensate for the decreased labor demand. The transition to the higher unemployment equilibrium will not be immediate: wage decreases by individual firms will only become attractive as the unemployment pool grows. This provides an explanation of wage sluggishness.

F Welfare Analysis

In this section we study the welfare properties of the unemployment equilibrium. We demonstrate that the equilibrium is not in general Pareto optimal, when information costs are explicitly accounted for.

We begin with the case where the owners of the firms are the same individuals as the workers, and ownership is equally distributed among N workers. The central planning problem is to maximize the expected utility of the representative worker subject to the *NSC* and the resource constraint:

$$\max_{w,\overline{w},L}(w - e)L + \overline{w}(N - L) \qquad (12)$$

subject to

$$w \geq e + \overline{w} + (e/q)((bN/(N - L)) + r) \quad (NSC)$$

subject to

$$wL + \overline{w}(N - L) \leq F(L) \quad (\text{Feasibility})$$

subject to $\overline{w} \geq 0$.

Since workers are risk neutral it is easy to check[16] that the optimum involves $\overline{w}$ at the minimum allowable level, which is assumed to be 0. The reason is that increases in $\overline{w}$ tighten the *NSC*, so all payments should be made in the form of w rather $\overline{w}$.

Setting $\overline{w} = 0$, the problem simplifies to

$$\max_{w,L}(w - e)L \qquad (12')$$

---

[16] Formally,

$$\mathcal{L} = (w - e)L + \overline{w}(N - L) + \lambda[w - e - \overline{w} - (e/q)(bN/(N - l) + r)]$$
$$+ \mu[F(L) - wL - \overline{w}(N - L)].$$

Differentiating with respect of w and $\overline{w}$ yields

$$\mathcal{L}_w = L + \lambda - \mu L \leq 0 \text{ and } = 0 \text{ if } w > 0.$$

$$\mathcal{L}_{\overline{w}} = (N - L) - \lambda - \mu(N - L) \leq 0 \text{ and } = 0 \text{ if } \overline{w} > 0.$$

We know $w > 0$ by the *NSC*, so $\mathcal{L}_w = 0$, i.e., $L(1 - \mu) + \lambda = 0$. Therefore, since $\lambda > 0, \mu > 1$. But then $\mathcal{L}_{\overline{w}} = (N - L)(1 - \mu) - \lambda < 0$. This implies that $\overline{w} = 0$.

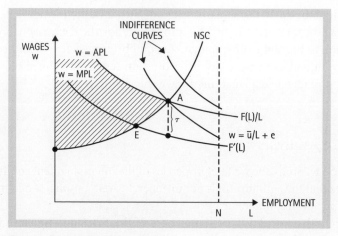

Fig. 4. Social Optimum at *A*

subject to

$$w \geq e + (e/q)((bN/(N - L)) + r);$$

and

$$wL \leq F(L).$$

The set of points which satisfy the constraints is shaded in Figure 4. Iso-utility curves are rectangular hyperbolas. So long as $F'(L) > e$, these are steeper than the average product locus, so the optimum occurs at point A where the *NSC* intersects the curve $w = F(L)/L$, that is, where wages equal the average product of labor. In contrast, the market equilibrium occurs at E where the marginal product of labor curve, $w = F'(L)$, intersects the *NSC* (Figure 2). Observe that in the case of constant returns to scale, $F'(L)L = F(L)$, so the equilibrium is optimal.

Wages should be subsidized, using whatever (pure) profits can be taxed away. An equivalent way to view the social optimum is a tax on unemployment to reduce shirking incentives; the wealth constraint on the unemployed requires that $\overline{w} \geq 0$, or equivalently that profits after taxes be nonnegative.[17] The optimum can be achieved by taxing away all profits and financing a wage subsidy of τ, shown in Figure 4. *The "natural" unemployment rate is too high.*

In the case where the workers and the owners are distinct individuals, the tax policy described above would reduce profits, increase wages, and increase employment levels. While it would increase aggregate output (net of effort costs), such a tax policy would *not* constitute a Pareto improvement, since profits would fall. For this reason, the equilibrium is Pareto optimal in this case, even though it fails to maximize net national product. We thus have the unusual result that the Pareto optimality of

---

[17] The constraint $\overline{w} \geq 0$ can be rewritten, using the resource constraint, as $F(L) - wL \geq 0$, i.e., $\pi \geq 0$.

the equilibrium depends upon the distribution of wealth. The standard separation between efficiency and income distribution does not carry over to this model.

It should not be surprising that the equilibrium level of unemployment is in general inefficient. Each firm tends to employ too few workers, since it sees the private cost of an additional worker as w, while the social cost is only e, which is lower. On the other hand, when a firm hires one more worker, it fails to take account of the effect this has on V_u (by reducing the size of the unemployment pool). This effect, a negative externality imposed by one firm on others as it raises its level of employment, tends to lead to overemployment. In the simple model presented so far, the former effect dominates, and the natural level of unemployment is too high. This will not be true in more general models, however, as we shall see below.

II EXTENSIONS

In this section we describe how the results derived above are modified or extended when we relax some of the simplifying assumptions. We discuss three extensions in turn: endogenous monitoring, risk aversion, and endogenous turnover. Detailed derivations of the claims made below are available in our earlier working paper.

A Endogenous Monitoring

When employees can select the monitoring intensity q, they can trade off stricter monitoring (at a cost) with higher wages as methods of worker discipline. In general, firms' monitoring intensities will not be optimal, due to the externalities between firms described above. In general, it is not possible to ascertain whether the equilibrium entails too much or too little employment. In the case of constant returns to scale ($F(L) = L$), however (which led to efficiency with exogenous monitoring), the competitive equilibrium involves too much monitoring and too much employment.

The result is not as unintuitive as it first seems: each firm believes that the only instrument at its control for reducing shirking is to increase monitoring. There is, however, a second instrument: by reducing employment, workers are induced not to shirk. This enables society to save resources on monitoring (supervision). These gains more than offset the loss from the reduced employment.

It is straightforward to see how this policy may be implemented. If firms can be induced to reduce their monitoring, welfare will be increased. Hence a tax on monitoring, with the proceeds distributed, say, as a lump sum transfer to firms, will leave the no-shirking constraint/national-resource constraint unaffected, but will reduce monitoring.

B Risk Aversion

With risk neutrality, the optimum and the market both involve $\overline{w} = 0$. Clearly $\overline{w} = 0$ cannot be optimal if workers are highly risk averse and may be separated from their jobs for exogenous reasons. Yet the market always provides $\overline{w} = 0$ (or the legal minimum). The proof above that $\overline{w} = 0$ carries over to the case of risk-averse workers.

When equilibrium involves unemployment, firms have no difficulty attracting workers and hence offer $\overline{w} = 0$, since $\overline{w} > 0$ merely reduces the penalty of being fired. When *other* firms offer $\overline{w} = 0$, this argument is only strengthened: unemployed workers are even easier to attract. It is striking that the market provides no unemployment benefits even when workers are highly risk averse. Clearly the social optimum involves $\overline{w} > 0$ if risk aversion is great enough. This may provide a justification for mandatory minimum benefit levels.

C Endogenous Turnover

In general a firm's employment package will influence the turnover rate it experiences among its employees. Since the turnover rate b affects the rate of hiring out of the unemployment pool, and hence V_u, it affects other firms' no-shirking constraints. Because of this externality, firms' choices of employment packages will not in general be optimal. This type of externality is similar to search externalities in which, for example, one searcher's expected utility depends on the number or mix of searchers remaining in the market. In the current model, policies which discourage labor turnover are attractive as they make unemployment more costly to shirkers.

III ALTERNATIVE METHODS FOR THE ENFORCEMENT OF DISCIPLINE

This paper has explored a particular mechanism for the enforcement of discipline: individuals who are detected shirking are fired, and in equilibrium the level of unemployment is sufficiently large that this threat serves as an effective deterrent to shirking. The question naturally arises whether there are alternative, less costly, or more effective discipline mechanisms.

A Performance Bonds

The most direct mechanism by which discipline might be enforced is through the posting by workers of performance bonds. Under this arrangement the worker would forfeit the bond if the firm detected him shirking. One problem with this solution is that workers may not have the wealth to post bond.[18] A more fundamental problem with this mechanism is that the firm would have an incentive to *claim* that the worker shirked so that it could appropriate the bond. Assuming, quite realistically, that third parties cannot easily observe workers' effort (indeed, it is usually more costly for outsiders to observe worker inputs than for the employer to do so), there is no simple way to discipline the *firm* from this type of opportunism.

Having recognized this basic point, it is easy to see that a number of other plausible solutions face the same difficulty. For example, consider an employment package which rewards effort by raising wages over time for workers who have not been found shirking. This is in fact equivalent to giving the worker a level wage stream, but taking back part of his earlier payments as a bond, which is returned to him later. Therefore, by the above argument, the firm will have an incentive to fire the worker when he is about to enter the "payoff" period in which he recovers his bond. This is the equivalent to the firm's simply appropriating the bond. It is optimal for the firm to replace expensive senior workers by inexpensive junior ones.[19]

Clearly the firm's reputation as an honest employer can partially solve this problem; the employer is implicitly penalized for firing a worker if this renders him less attractive to prospective employees. Yet this reputation mechanism may not work especially well, since prospective employees often do not know the employer's record, and previous dismissals may have been legitimate (it is not possible for prospective employees to distinguish legitimate from unfair earlier dismissals, if they are aware of them at all). If the reputation mechanism is less than perfect, it will be augmented by the unemployment mechanism.

B Other Costs of Dismissal

Unemployment in the model above serves the role of imposing costs on dismissed workers. If other costs of dismissal are sufficiently high, workers may have an incentive to exert effort even under conditions of full employment. Examples of such costs are search costs, moving expenses, loss of job-specific human capital, etc. In

---

[18] This is especially true if detection is difficult (low q) so that an effective bond must be quite large. Even if workers could borrow to post the bond, so long as bankruptcy is possible, the incentives for avoiding defaulting on the bond are not different from the incentives to avoid being caught shirking by the firm in the absence of a bond. Note once again the importance of the wealth distribution in determining the nature of the equilibrium. If all individuals inherit a large amount of wealth, then they could post bonds.

[19] In competitive equilibrium, the average (discounted) value of the wage must be equal to the average (discounted) value of the marginal product of the worker. If there is a bonus for not shirking, *initially* the wage must be below the value of the marginal product. It is as if the worker were posting a bond (the difference between his marginal product and the wage), and as such this scheme is susceptible to precisely the same objections raised against posting performance bondings. The employer has an incentive to appropriate the bond. Since workers know this, this is not a viable incentive scheme. For a fine study in which firms' reputations are assumed to function so as to make this scheme viable, see Edward Lazear (1981).

markets where these costs are substantial, the role of equilibrium unemployment is substantially diminished. The effect we have identified above will still be present, however, when effort levels are continuous variables: each firm will still find that employee effort is increasing with wages, so wages will be bid up somewhat above their full-employment level. The theory predicts that involuntary (as well as frictional) unemployment rates will be higher for classes of workers who have lower job switching costs.

C Heterogeneous Workers

The strongest assumption we have made is that of identical workers. This assumption ruled out the possibility that firing a worker would carry any stigma. Such a stigma could serve as a discipline device, even with full employment.[20] In reality, of course, employers *do* make wage offers which are contingent on employment history. Such policies make sense when firms face problems of adverse selection.

We recognize that workers' concern about protecting their reputations as effective, diligent workers may provide an effective incentive for a disciplined labor force.[21] Shapiro's earlier (1983) analysis of reputation in product markets showed, however, that for reputations to be an effective incentive device, there must be a cost to the loss of reputation. It is our conjecture that, under plausible conditions, even when reputations are important, equilibrium will entail some use of unemployment as a discipline device for the labor force, at least for lower-quality workers. An important line of research is the study of labor markets in which adverse selection as well as moral hazard problems are present. In this context, our model should provide a useful complement to the more common studies of adverse selection in labor markets.

IV Conclusions

This paper has explored the role of unemployment, or job rationing, as an incentive device. We have argued that when it is costly to monitor individuals, competitive equilibrium will be characterized by unemployment, but that the natural rate of unemployment so engendered will not in general be optimal. We have identified several forces at work, some which tend to make the market equilibrium unemployment rate too high, and others which tend to make it too small. Each firm fails to take

[20] See Bruce Greenwald (1979) for a simple model in which those who are in the "used labor market" are in fact a lower quality than those in the "new" labor market.
[21] This suggests once again that our results may be most significant in labor markets for lower-quality workers: in such markets employment histories are utilized less and workers already labeled as below average in quality have less to lose from being labeled as such.

into account the consequences of its actions on the level of monitoring and wages which other firms must undertake in order to avoid shirking by workers. Although these externalities are much like pecuniary externalities, they are important, even in economies with a large number of firms.[22] As a result, we have argued that there is scope for government interventions, both with respect to unemployment benefits and taxes or subsidies on monitoring and labor turnover, which can (if appropriately designed) lead to Pareto improvements.

The type of unemployment studied here is not the only or even the most important source of unemployment in practice. We believe it is, however, a significant factor in the observed level of unemployment, especially in lower-paid, lower-skilled, blue-collar occupations. It may well be more important than frictional or search unemployment in many labor markets.

[22] For a more general discussion of pecuniary, or more general market mediated externalities, with applications to economies with important adverse selection and moral hazard problems, see Greenwald and Stiglitz (1986a).

CHAPTER 12

THE CAUSES AND CONSEQUENCES OF THE DEPENDENCE OF QUALITY ON PRICE*

If the legal rate ... was fixed so high ..., the greater part of the money which was to be lent, would be lent to prodigals and profectors, who alone would be willing to give this higher interest. Sober people, who will give for the use of money no more than a part of what they are likely to make by the use of it, would not venture into the competition. ... Adam Smith, Wealth of Nations, *1776.*

A plentiful subsistence increases the bodily strength of the laborer and the comfortable hope of bettering his condition and ending his days perhaps in ease and plenty animates him to exert that strength to the utmost. Adam Smith, Wealth of Nations, *1776.*

Low wages are by no means identical with cheap labour. From a purely quantitative point of view the efficiency of labour decreases with a wage which is physiologically insufficient ... the present-day average Silesian mows, when he exerts himself to the full, little more than two-thirds as much land as the

* I am greatly indebted to my several coauthors, with whom I have worked on the analysis of the causes and consequences of the dependence of quality on price: Carl Shapiro, Barry Nalebuff, Andy Weiss, and Bruce Greenwald. I am also indebted to helpful conversations with George Akerlof, Janet Yellen, Franklin Allen, Bill Rogerson, Mark Gersovitz, Jonathan Eaton, Partha Dasgupta, among others. Larry Summers and Gary Fields provided helpful comments on an earlier draft.

The opening quotations were supplied by Michael Perelman, Gavin Wright (second and fourth quotation), Graciela Chichilnisky, and Franklin Allen.

Gavin Wright has drawn my attention to the fact that there was a large literature in the eighteenth and nineteenth centuries arguing for a link between wages and productivity. For instance, he cites the former *better paid and nourished Pomeranian or Mecklenburger, and the Pole, the further East he comes from, accomplishes progressively less than the German. Low wages fail even from a purely business point of view wherever it is a question of producing goods which require any sort of skilled labour, or the use of expensive machinery which is easily damaged, or in general wherever any greater amount of sharp attention of initiative is required. Here low wages do not pay, and their effect is the opposite of what was intended.* Max Weber, The Protestant Ethic and the Spirit of Capitalism *(Scribner, New York, 1925, p. 61).*

... highly paid labour is generally efficient and therefore not dear labour; a fact which though it is more full of hope for the future of the human race than any other that is known us, will be found to exercise a very complicating influence on the theory of distribution. Alfred Marshall, Principles of Economics, *1920.*

... the landlord who attempted to exact more than his neighbour ... would render himself so odious, he would be so sure of not obtaining a metayer who was an honest man, that the contract of all the metayers may be considered as identical, at least in each province, and never gives rise to any competition among peasants in search of employment, or any offer to cultivate the soil on cheaper terms than one another. J. C. L. Simonde de Sismondi, Political Economy, *1814, cited in* John Stuart Mill, Principles of Political Economy, *1848.*

CONVENTIONAL competitive economic theory begins with the hypothesis of price-taking firms and consumers, buying and selling homogeneous commodities at well-defined marketplaces. In many situations, these assumptions are implausible: in insurance markets, firms know that some risks are greater than others (some individuals' life expectancy is greater than others'; some individuals are more likely to have an automobile accident than others), but cannot tell precisely who is the greater risk, even within fairly narrowly defined risk categories. In labor markets, firms know that some workers are better than others, but at the time they hire and train the worker, they cannot tell precisely who will turn out to be the more productive. In product markets, consumers know that some commodities are more durable than others, but at the time of purchase, they cannot ascertain precisely which are more durable. In

U.S. Secretary of State Thomas F. Bayard's "Introductory Letter" to Jacob Schoenhof (in *The Economy of High Wages* New York, 1893) as saying, "The facts you have adduced and your deductions irresistibly establish the proposition that low wages do not mean cheap production, and that the best instructed and best paid labor proves itself to be the most productive. ..." Similarly, Thomas Brassey, Jr., is quoted by John H. Habbakuk (*American and British Technology in the Nineteenth Century,* 1962) as saying, "The cheap labour at the command of our competitors seems to exercise the same enervating influence as the delights of Caphua on the soldiers of Hannibal" (*Work and Wages,* 1872, p. 142).

Some of this earlier literature is reviewed by Gregory Clark, in "Productivity Growth without Technical Change: European Agriculture before 1850" (1986), and by A. W. Coats, in "Changing Attitudes to Labour in the Mid-eighteenth Century," *Economic History Review* (August 1958, 2(11), pp. 35–51). Coats traces the idea that high wages lead to high productivity back to Jacob Vanderlint, in *Money Answers All Things* (London, 1734).

Financial support from the Hoover Institution and the National Science Foundation is gratefully acknowledged.

capital markets, banks know that the probability of bankruptcy differs across loans, but cannot tell precisely which loans are better.

This heterogeneity has important consequences, some of which have long been recognized. There are strong incentives to sort, to distinguish the high risk from the low risk, the more able from the less able. This sorting can be done on the basis of observable characteristics (say, sex or age) or the (inferences made from) actions undertaken by individuals, e.g., the job for which the individual applies (George Akerlof 1976), the wage structure chosen by the individual (Joanne Salop and Steven Salop 1976), or the quantity of insurance purchased (Michael Rothschild and Joseph Stiglitz 1976). In these models, the choices made convey information; individuals know this, and this affects their actions.

Willingness to trade may itself serve as a sorting device. In insurance markets, firms have recognized that as the price of insurance increases, the mix of applicants changes *adversely*. Akerlof (1970) has shown how such adverse selection effects may also arise in other markets, including the market for used cars (see Charles Wilson 1979, 1980). His analysis has subsequently been applied to the labor market (Bruce Greenwald 1986) and to capital markets (Greenwald, Stiglitz, and Andrew Weiss 1984; Stewart Myers and Nicholas S. Majluf 1984). In each of these instances, the uninformed party (the seller of insurance, the used car buyer, etc.) forms rational expectations concerning the quality mix of what is being offered on the market; the price serves as a signal or as a screening device. The fact that an employee is willing to work for $1 an hour suggests that she knows of no better offers; others who have looked at her have evidently decided that she is worth no more than $1 an hour.

Insurance firms have also long recognized that the terms at which they write insurance contracts may affect the actions undertaken by individuals; that is, the likelihood of the insured against an event occurring is an *endogenous* variable, which the insurance firm can hope to affect. The fact that individuals can undertake un-observable actions that affect the likelihood of an accident is referred to as the *moral hazard* problem. The term has come to be used to describe a wide range of incentive problems. In particular, employers know that the incentives workers have to work hard may be affected by the wage paid; and the incentives borrowers have to undertake risky projects may be affected by the interest rate charged on the bank's loan. Thus, the characteristics of what is being traded again depend on the price at which the trade is consummated, though now because of *incentive* effects rather than *selection* effects.

These are instances in which price serves a function in addition to that usually as-cribed to it in economic theory: It conveys information and affects behavior. Quality depends on price. Of course, in standard economic theory, higher-quality items will sell at higher prices: Prices depend on quality. But here, beliefs about quality, about what it is that is being traded, depend (rationally) on price.[1]

---

[1] Some 40 years ago, Tibor Scitovsky (1945) wrote a brief but important paper discussing the consequences of the habit of judging quality by price. Another antecedent of the recent literature is Alvin Klevorick and Roger Alcaly (1970), who explore the implications for the traditional theory of consumers' behavior.

This dependence of beliefs about quality on price has some fundamental implications. Firstly, demand curves, may under quite plausible conditions, not be downward sloping. When the price of some security is higher, uninformed buyers may infer that the expected return is higher, and their demand may increase (Jerry Green 1973; Sanford Grossman and Stiglitz 1976, 1980a). An increase in the wage may so increase the productivity of the workers that the demand for labor may actually increase. A decrease in the price of used cars results in a decrease in the average quality of those being offered and this may decrease demand (Akerlof 1970). In each of these instances, one can think of the change in the price as having two effects: a movement along a fixed-information demand curve, and a shift in the demand curve from the change in information (beliefs).

Secondly, one may not be able to separate out neatly the analysis of demand and supply. Individuals' demands are based on inferences they are making from prices, and these inferences are critically dependent on the nature of the supply responses. Thus, any alteration, say, in the probability distribution of supply characteristics will, in general, lead to an alteration in the demand functions.

Thirdly, markets may be thin. At the equilibrium price of insurance, some risk averse individuals choose not to purchase insurance, even though with perfect information, they would have. The marginal person buying insurance is, in effect, subsidizing other purchasers; he is not obtaining actuarially fair insurance, as he would in a (risk neutral) competitive market with full information.[2]

These models, while departing from the traditional paradigm in denying the validity of the hypothesis of homogeneous markets, retain the assumption of price-taking firms and consumers. In many situations, firms are not price or wage takers. Banks do not simply take the interest rate that they charge on loans as given.

This paper is concerned with situations where firms not only recognize the dependence of quality on price (of productivity on wages, of default probability on the interest rate charged), but also attempt to use what control they have over price (wages, interest rates) to increase their profits. The recognition of this possibility has important implications for economic theory.

This paper is divided into four parts. In Part I, we discuss the most important implications of the dependence of quality on price for competitive equilibrium theory—the repeal of the law of supply and demand (Part I.1), the repeal of the law of the single price (Part I.2), the existence of discriminatory equilibria (Part I.3), the comparative static consequences (Part I.4), and the inefficiency of market equilibria (Part I.5). Part II discusses alternative explanations for the dependence of quality on price in labor, capital, and product markets. Part III explains more precisely how these models

---

[2] Akerlof (1970) investigated a case where equilibrium entailed no trade. As the price of cars decreased, supply decreased and demand decreased (the deterioration in car quality was so great that the quality-adjusted price actually increased): Intersection occurred only at zero trade. But this is a special case which arises primarily because of the limited incentives to trade in his model. The effect he noted in the used car market is the same as had long been recognized in insurance markets. As the price of insurance increases, the adverse selection effect implies that the mix of applicants changes adversely; thus the premium required for the insurance firms to break even must increase. Nonetheless, there may exist insurance markets in which trade occurs.

differ from standard competitive models and from other models with imperfect information. Finally, Part IV discusses some of the more important applications of the theory, including those in macroeconomics (Part IV.1) and in development economics (Part IV.2).

I The Fundamental Implications of the Dependence of Quality on Price

1 Repeal of the Law of Supply and Demand

No law in economics has such standing as the "Law of Supply and Demand." There is an old joke about being able to teach a parrot to be an economist—and a good economist at that—simply by teaching it to repeat the words "demand and supply." The law holds that competitive market equilibrium is characterized by demand equaling supply. It asserts that the way to analyze changes in market equilibrium is to isolate the changes in the demand function and in the supply function.

When quality depends on price, market equilibrium *may* be characterized by demand not equaling supply.[3]

Consider the labor market. Assume there is an excess supply of labor. The conventional story is that in the face of excess supply, unemployed workers go to potential employers and offer their services at lower wages. The wage is bid down. As the wage decreases, the demand for labor increases and the supply decreases. This process continues until the wage is bid down to the level where supply equals demand.

If, however, the firm believes that the workers who offer their services at a lower wage are less productive, then—if they are sufficiently less productive—it will not hire the lower-wage workers, for the cost per effective unit of labor service will actually be higher with the lower-wage worker.

Thus, in Figure 1 we have depicted the cost per effective unit of labor service as initially falling as the wage is increased. There is a wage, w^*, at which wage costs per effective unit of labor service are minimized. This is referred to as the *efficiency wage*. For this section, we assume the same costs per efficiency unit schedule faces all firms and characterizes all workers. (In the following sections we shall consider the consequences of differing costs per efficiency unit schedules.)

If, at the efficiency wage, there is an excess supply of laborers, no firm has an incentive to lower its wage, or to hire a worker who offers his services at a lower wage, for to do so simply increases labor costs. Thus, when at w^*, the supply of labor equals or exceeds the demand, w^* is the equilibrium wage.

[3] And as we have already noted, because the inferences that can be drawn from observing a given price—and hence the demand at a given price—depend on the nature of supply, it may not be possible in some cases to isolate demand and supply disturbances.

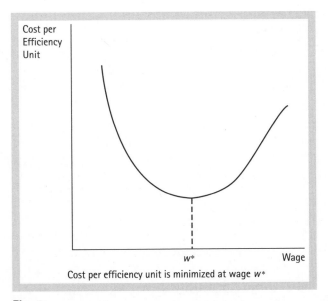

Cost per efficiency unit is minimized at wage w^*

Fig. 1.

This curve, giving the relationship between the cost per effective unit of labor and the wage rate, is derived from the more fundamental *wage productivity curve*, giving the productivity of the representative worker hired at a particular wage. The curve depicted in Figure 2 shows λ, the productivity of the worker, increasing with the wage; the essential feature of this productivity curve is that there is initially a region of increasing returns, where an increase in the wage leads to a more than proportionate increase in the productivity. Many of our results depend critically on the existence of some region for which this is true; in the models that we investigate in detail, we establish that this is in fact the case.

In Figure 2, the cost per efficiency unit (cost per effective unit of labor) is given by the (inverse of the) slope of a line through the origin to a point on the wage productivity curve. Because the slope is increasing as we increase the wage from 0 to w^*, the cost per effective unit of labor is decreasing. Beyond w^* the slope decreases and hence the cost per effective unit of labor increases. It is clear, then, that the wage-productivity curve generates a cost per effective unit of labor curve of the form depicted in Figure 1.

The existence of wage-productivity relationship has long been recognized, as the quotations at the beginning of this article indicate. The more recent revival of interest may be attributed to Harvey Leibenstein (1957a) who discussed it in the context of less developed countries and the subsequent developments by James Mirrlees (1975a) and Stiglitz (1976b). There, however, the relationship is based on nutritional considerations.[4] Near subsistence, workers are not very productive; increases in wages

---

[4] For discussions of the validity of this relationship, see Christopher Bliss and Nicholas Stern (1978, 1981). See also P. H. Prasad (1970), G. B. Rodgers (1975), and Dasgupta and Ray (1986b).

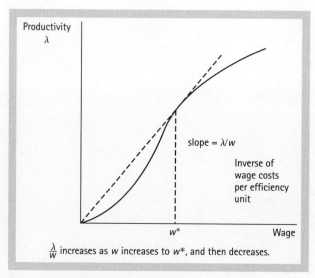

Productivity λ

slope = λ/w

Inverse of
wage costs
per efficiency
unit

w^* Wage

$\frac{\lambda}{w}$ increases as w increases to w^*, and then decreases.

Fig. 2. Wage Productivity Curve

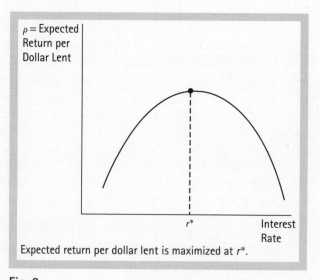

ρ = Expected
Return per
Dollar Lent

r^* Interest
Rate

Expected return per dollar lent is maximized at r^*.

Fig. 3.

may lead to marked increases in efficiency. Though our analysis focuses on alternative explanations of the relationship, the consequences are very similar.

Exactly the same analysis applies to the capital market (Stiglitz and Weiss 1981). Assume that as the bank increases the interest rate, the "quality" of those who apply decreases; that is, those who apply have, on average, a higher probability of defaulting, of not repaying their loans. The safest borrowers are unwilling to borrow at high interest rates. Then, the expected return on a loan, ρ, may actually decrease as the interest rate, r, increases, as depicted in Figure 3; r^* is the efficiency interest rate. If,

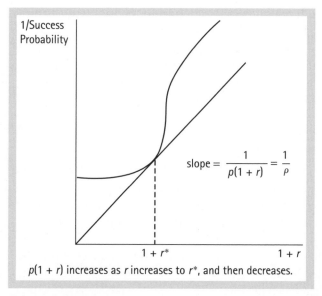

Fig. 4. Default Curve

at r^*, there is an excess demand for loans (credit is rationed), r^* is still an equilibrium. The bank will refuse to lend to anyone offering to borrow at a higher interest rate; its expected return would be lower than what it obtains by lending at r^*.

The curve in Figure 3 may be derived from the default curve. The probability of a default is postulated to increase with the rate of interest charged. Let p = probability that the loan is repaid; we assume, for simplicity, that when the loan is not repaid the lender receives nothing. Thus, the expected return to a lender is

$$\rho = p(1+r).$$

In Figure 4, we have plotted $1/p$ as a function of $1 + r$. Thus, the slope of any line from the origin to the default curve is $1/(1 + r)p$. The bank wishes to maximize $p(1 + r)$, i.e., find the point on the default curve with the lowest slope; this is clearly just the point of tangency of a line through the origin with the default curve. Note that the slope decreases as r increases up to $1 + r^*$ (i.e., ρ increases) and decreases thereafter (i.e., ρ decreases), just as depicted in Figure 3. (We postpone until later a justification for the shape of the default curve.)

Again, the conventional story for why there cannot be credit rationing in equilibrium is that those who are willing to borrow at the given interest but denied credit go to the bank and offer it a higher interest rate; this bids up the interest rate. As the interest rate is bid up, the supply of credit is increased and demand decreases. The process continues until equilibrium is reached at the point where the demand for loans equals the supply; there is no credit rationing. But now, the bank realizes that if it charges a higher interest rate, the probability of default increases; and it may increase so much that the expected return to the bank actually decreases. Thus, no bank will ever charge an interest rate above r^*.[5, 6]

In each of these cases, the story is the same: Because quality (labor efficiency, bankruptcy probability) changes as the price (wage, interest rate) changes, excess supply or demand may persist without any tendency for price (wages, interest rates) to move to correct the market imbalance.

General Formulation

In each of the instances described above, an individual (firm) sets the terms of the contract with another individual or firm to maximize its utility (profits), subject to offering terms that make the contract acceptable; under the circumstances described, the optimal contract will be such that the constraint on acceptability is not binding. That is, if $U[p, x, q(p, x)]$ is the utility of the buyer, paying a price p, and offering nonprice terms[7] of the contract x, where $q(p, x)$ represents a description of the (expected value of the) quality of the object (service) being purchased, a function of p and x, then the individual chooses p and x to

$$\operatorname*{Max}_{(p,x)} U \tag{1}$$

subject to the constraint of being able to obtain the item, i.e., if $V[p, x, q(p, x)]$ is the (expected) utility of an individual (firm) selling an item of quality q and V^* represents the reservation utility level,[8] then

$$V[p, x, q(p, x)] \geq V^*. \tag{2}$$

In a variety of circumstances, the solution to this problem may entail the constraint (2) not being binding, at least for some potential sellers.[9] When that happens, market equilibrium will be characterized by demand not equaling supply.[10]

---

[5] A cartoon appeared in several newspapers in the early eighties, when interest rates were soaring, in which a banker is seen leaning over his desk, asking the loan applicant, "What kind of person would be willing to borrow at the interest rates we charge?"

[6] Note too that in the circumstances with which we have just been concerned, where quality depends on price, the quantity demanded at any price depends on the quality supplied: Thus, for instance, a change in the mix of loan applicants will affect the supply of loans available at any interest rate; a change in the mix of job applicants will affect the demand for labor at any wage.

[7] Nonprice terms in credit markets include collateral requirements, specifications of circumstances under which credit is terminated, etc.

[8] The reservation utility level also may vary across sellers.

[9] In the incentive (moral hazard) versions, q is a result of an action taken by the individual; the action taken is a function of the terms of the contract. In the selection version, q is the average quality of those offering goods (services) at the price p and x; the constraint (2) is to be read as saying that at least one item is offered for sale at the given terms. In general, in adverse selection models, the constraint (2) is binding for only some individuals offering to sell the commodity.

[10] It is worth noting that while (2) may be viewed, from the perspective of the buyer, as what has come to be called the "individual rationality constraint," V^* is in general itself endogenously determined (it represents the individual's best alternative opportunity); and in the adverse selection models, (2) also can be viewed as a self-selection constraint, differentiating between those for whom the job (loan) is acceptable and those for whom it is not.

2 Repeal of the Law of the Single Price

The law of supply and demand is of course, only one of the fundamental "laws" of conventional economics. Another central aspect of the traditional paradigm is codified in the "Law of the Single Price." This law holds that all objects with the same observable characteristics should sell at the same price. When there is a relationship between quality and price, the price itself becomes a relevant characteristic; market equilibrium may be characterized by a price distribution (or a wage distribution, or a distribution of interest rates) for objects that cannot be distinguished (before purchase) other than by price.

It has been widely observed that some firms have a high-wage policy; others pursue a low-wage policy. It is important to bear in mind that the differences we are concerned with here are not differences in whether the firm hires those with more education or less education, those with more work experience or those with less work experience. Rather, we are comparing the wages paid by firms for workers with a *given* set of observable qualifications.

There are several reasons that economies in which productivity depends on wages (or more generally quality on prices) may be characterized by a wage (price) distribution.

Differences in Firms

If the wage-productivity relationship differs across firms the efficiency wage may differ. More generally, firms where net productivity is more sensitive to wages (with higher turnover costs, higher monitoring costs, or where shirking workers can do more damage) will find it desirable to pay higher wages for workers of identical characteristics (Steven Salop 1973). This is consistent with the observation that more capital intensive firms tend to pay higher wages, because the "damage" a worker can do in such jobs may be higher. If monitoring costs are higher in firms employing large numbers of workers, one might expect to see such firms paying higher wages (other things being constant).

Wage Distributions When Costs per Effective Unit Are Not Monotonic

Wage (price, or interest rate) distributions also arise when costs per effective unit are not monotone, as we suggested that they might not be.

Assume, in particular, that the reason that productivity increases with wage is nutritional;[11] though productivity always increases with wage, it may increase more or less than proportionately. When it increases more than proportionately, labor costs per efficiency unit decline with wage increases. Thus, if over some ranges, say, for very

---

[11] We choose this example because in more general models, with adverse selection or incentive effects, the productivity of a worker at one firm depends on the wages paid at other firms and on the unemployment rate. We wish to avoid these complications in this simple exposition.

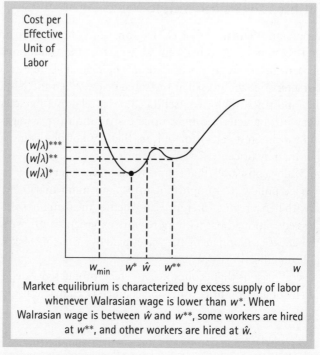

Market equilibrium is characterized by excess supply of labor whenever Walrasian wage is lower than w^*. When Walrasian wage is between $\hat{w}$ and w^{**}, some workers are hired at w^{**}, and other workers are hired at $\hat{w}$.

Fig. 5. Wage Distribution

low wages and for an intermediate range of wages, productivity increases more than proportionately with wages, one would obtain a curve describing wage per efficiency unit as in Figure 5.

We define the Walrasian wage, $\bar{w}$, as that wage at which demand for labor equals the supply. However, the Walrasian wage is not the equilibrium wage whenever there exists a wage higher than the Walrasian wage with a lower cost per efficiency unit. For it would pay any firm to increase its wage. Assume, in Figure 5, that the Walrasian equilibrium occurred at some wage between $\hat{w}$ and w^{**}. One might be tempted to suggest that w^{**}, the wage greater than the Walrasian wage at which costs per efficiency unit are minimized, is the market equilibrium; but at w^{**}, there is unemployment; and by lowering their wage enough (to any wage between $\hat{w}$ and w^*), workers can be hired with a cost per efficiency unit that is lower than at w^{**}. The equilibrium now entails full employment with a wage distribution; some workers are hired at w^{**} and others at $\hat{w}$. Costs per efficiency unit are exactly the same. If all workers were paid a wage of $\hat{w}$, there would be (by assumption) an excess demand for labor; that is why $\hat{w}$ is not an equilibrium. If all workers were paid w^{**}, there would be an excess supply of laborers. There is a particular proportion of workers hired at $\hat{w}$ and w^{**} at which demand is equal to supply for the low-wage jobs, though there is excess supply of labor at the high-wage firms.

Similar arguments apply to other markets.

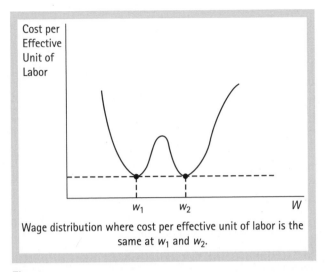

Wage distribution where cost per effective unit of labor is the same at w_1 and w_2.

Fig. 6.

Wage Distributions When Costs per Effective Unit Are Minimized at Several Different Wages

The previous subsection considered a situation where the cost per effective unit was not monotonic. Equilibrium wage distributions also arise when the curve describing the cost per effective unit of labor, depicted earlier, has several peaks, and all of the peaks generate exactly the same level of costs per effective unit of labor, as illustrated in Figure 6. Such a configuration would seem to be an anomaly. Even if there is no reason that the productivity curve has a single peak, why should the peaks occur at the same level? One can show that this may, in fact, occur quite easily. The curve that we have depicted is the curve facing a particular firm, *given* the wages paid by all other firms. Stiglitz (1974c, 1985c) shows, in the context of the labor-turnover model, that there is a wage distribution (and in fact many such distributions) with the property that the productivity curve has many peaks, each of which yields exactly the same cost per effective unit of labor. The reason for this is that the turnover costs facing any firm are a function of the fraction of firms paying a higher wage, which itself is an endogenous variable. The low-wage firm faces a higher turnover. The fraction of high-wage firms is such that the total labor costs—wages plus turnover costs—are the same at low-wage firms and high-wage firms (see also Phillip Dybvig and Gerald Jaynes 1980).

Similar results can be obtained in the context of selection models. If different individuals have different costs associated with queuing, or with not selling their commodity (their labor), then high-wage firms may find that they face a longer queue and a higher quality of applicants. In these models, high-wage labor looks (in terms of observable characteristics) the same as low-wage labor, but in fact it is more productive with differences in productivity corresponding (in equilibrium) precisely to

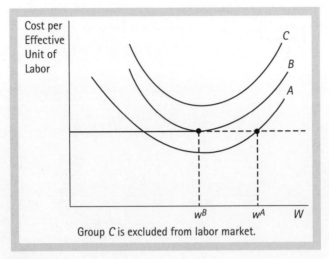

Group C is excluded from labor market.

Fig. 7.

differences in wages. Wages together with queues are acting as self-selection devices.[12]
(See Barry Nalebuff and Stiglitz 1982 and Stiglitz 1976c.)

3 Discrimination

It has long been noted that, in the absence of perfect information, there may be statistical discrimination: Members of a group will be paid the mean marginal product
of the group, or will be charged an interest rate corresponding to the mean default
probability of their group or charged an insurance premium corresponding to the
mean probability of accident, illness, or death of their group. But the traditional
theory of statistical discrimination (see, e.g., Dennis Aigner and Glen Cain 1977 or
Rothschild and Stiglitz 1982) has not provided an explanation of job discrimination
or red lining—the differential access to certain jobs or credit of certain groups. The
theories we are concerned with here do this.

Assume that in the labor market there are a number of different identifiable groups,
each with its own "cost per effective unit of labor" curve, as depicted in Figure 7.
Then, equilibrium will be characterized by all groups hired having the same cost per
effective labor unit; those with lower costs per effective labor service at any wage are
paid a higher wage. (There is, thus, wage discrimination.) But there are some groups,
such as Group C in Figure 7, for whom the cost per labor service, at the optimum
wage, and hence at any wage, exceeds that of the market equilibrium; such workers
will not be hired. "Discrimination" takes the form not of paying the workers in group
C a lower wage, but of refusing to hire them.

---

[12] Note, however, that the length of queue is not chosen by the firm, but is an endogenous property of
the equilibrium. In this respect, these models differ in an important way from those in which the terms
of the contract are determined either by the uninformed agent or the informed agent.

While all of those in category A will be hired, and none of those in category C, in general only some of those in category B will be hired. *Other apparently identical workers will not be employed.*

When productivity depends on the unemployment rate, there may be large differences in equilibrium in group specific unemployment rates as well as wage rates.[13]

The theory not only predicts that some groups may be rationed out of the market, but also suggests that the brunt of changes in the demand for labor (aggregate demand) will be felt by some groups in increased job rationing. Moreover, some versions of the theory predict which groups will be rationed out of the market. In particular, in the incentive version of the model (Carl Shapiro and Stiglitz 1984), the wage that must be paid to a worker to induce him not to shirk depends on the cost of being fired. This cost is likely to be lower for part-time workers, for those close to retirement, and for secondary participants in the labor force (e.g., low-wage workers with high-income spouses).

Exactly the same phenomenon can occur in credit markets. The practice of denying credit to certain categories of potential borrowers is called red-lining. (Some of those in category B, where the maximal expected return is equal to ρ^*, receive loans, while others do not.)

4 Comparative Statics

With "normally" shaped demand and supply curves, an increase in supply (that is, a shift in the supply curve such that at every price a greater quantity of the good is supplied) leads to an equilibrium with a lower price and a greater quantity traded. Similarly, a decrease in demand (that is, a shift in the demand curve such that at every price a smaller quantity of the good is demanded) leads to an equilibrium with a lower price and a lower quantity traded. Now, in the class of models being examined in this paper, the major effect of such a shift may be a change in the magnitude of rationing, with little effect on prices. Thus, in the labor market, when there is an equilibrium with excess supply of labor, a small increase in the demand for labor has no effect on the wage rate, but increases employment. An increase in the supply of credit available may have no effect on interest rates, but may simply lead to more loans (less credit rationing) at the old interest rates (Figure 8).

In markets where there are many groups in the population, a decrease in the demand for labor may result in some groups being completely excluded from the market, with only a slight lowering of the wage of those remaining. This is distinctly

---

[13] If the productivity of group λ_i is a function of its wage w_i and its unemployment rate, U_i then in equilibrium, for all groups hired (for which $0 < U, < 1$)

$$\lambda_i(w_i, U_i)/w_i$$

is the same, and

$$\partial\lambda_i(w_i, U_i)/\partial w_i = \lambda_i(w_i, U_i)/w_i.$$

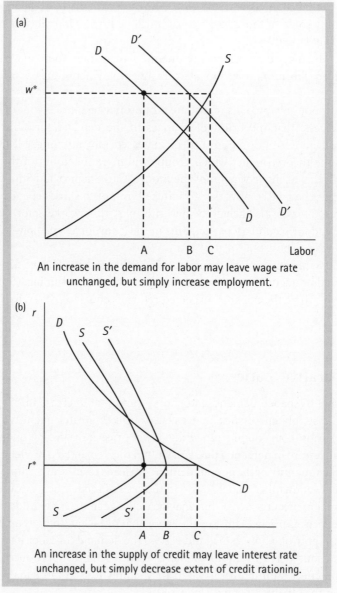

(a)

An increase in the demand for labor may leave wage rate
unchanged, but simply increase employment.

(b)

An increase in the supply of credit may leave interest rate
unchanged, but simply decrease extent of credit rationing.

Fig. 8.

different from the conventional models, in which the wage for all workers would
be reduced, and no group of workers would be excluded (though some groups of
workers may decide to drop out of the labor market) (Figure 9a).

Similarly, in markets with credit rationing, a decrease in the supply of available
credit may result in some groups being excluded from the credit market, with

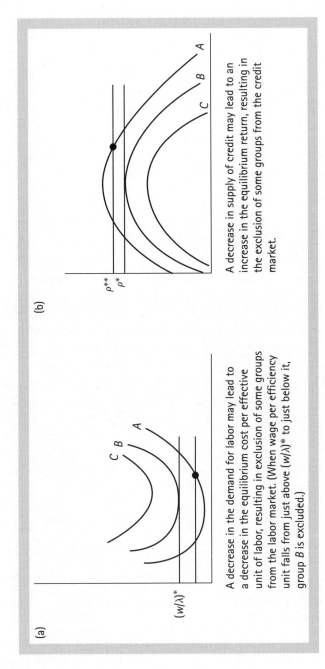

(a)

(b)

A decrease in the demand for labor may lead to a decrease in the equilibrium cost per effective unit of labor, resulting in exclusion of some groups from the labor market. (When wage per efficiency unit falls from just above $(w/\lambda)^*$ to just below it, group B is excluded.)

A decrease in supply of credit may lead to an increase in the equilibrium return, resulting in the exclusion of some groups from the credit market.

Fig. 9.

relatively small increases in the interest rates charged to those who are not excluded (Figure 9b).[14]

Shifts in the Productivity Curves. The other important source of changes in the equilibrium comes from changes in the productivity (or return) curves. In the labor market, a change in technology may result in a change in the efficiency wage, as depicted in Figure 10a. If the efficiency wage increases markedly, but the cost per effective unit of labor decreases only slightly, as in Figure 10b, then the new equilibrium may be characterized by a lower level of employment and a higher wage.

Similarly, if banks' expectations of defaults increase, then the expected return, at any interest rate, will decrease. This will normally result in a decrease in the supply of credit; the effect on the extent of credit rationing will depend on how the changed expectations affect the demand for credit. But there are no clear implications for the interest rate charged by the bank; it may either increase or decrease.[15]

5 Implications for Welfare Economics

One of the crowning achievements of competitive equilibrium theory during the past half century has been the proof of the fundamental theorem of welfare economics—providing a precise statement of the meaning of Adam Smith's invisible hand conjecture.

An implicit assumption in the standard proofs of the Fundamental Theorem of Welfare Economics is that there is perfect information.[16] Obviously, economies with perfect information are likely to function better than economies with imperfect information:[17] That is an irrelevant comparison. The relevant question is, in a market characterized by incomplete information, are there interventions that can attain a Pareto improvement? Is the market, in other words, constrained Pareto efficient, taking into account the imperfections of information and costs of obtaining more information?

Greenwald and Stiglitz (1986a) have shown that competitive economies with incomplete markets and/or imperfect information are essentially never constrained Pareto efficient. These authors develop a general framework within which a variety of informational imperfections can be analyzed. They limit themselves to tax and

---

[14] Indeed, in some circumstances a decrease in supply may actually lead to a decrease in the weighted mean interest rate charged. See Stiglitz and Weiss (1986a, 1986b).

[15] In the simple models presented here, only one group in the population is rationed; those above the critical cutoff level receive all the credit they wish, or can sell all the labor they wish, while others are completely excluded from the market. But it is easy to construct models in which rationing is extended to many groups. See Barry Nalebuff and Stiglitz (1982) and Stiglitz and Weiss (1986, 1987b, c).

[16] The analyses can be extended to situations where there is uncertainty, provided there is a complete set of risk markets, and provided that the nature of the commodity being traded (the quality of labor, the probability of bankruptcy, etc.) does not change as prices (wages, interest rates) change. It is the latter which concerns us here.

[17] This section focuses on the welfare economics of the imperfect information models. For a discussion of the welfare economics of the nutrition-based efficiency wage models, see Partha Dasgupta and Debraj Ray (1986a).

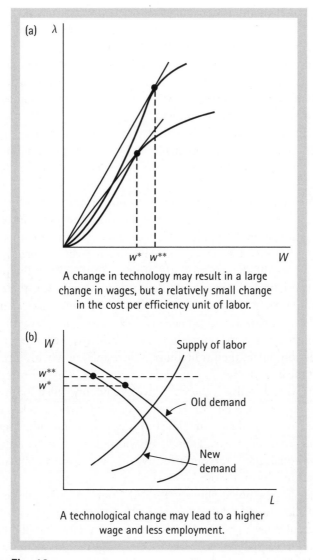

(a)

A change in technology may result in a large change in wages, but a relatively small change in the cost per efficiency unit of labor.

(b)

A technological change may lead to a higher wage and less employment.

Fig. 10.

subsidy interventions. They apply their analysis to one of the models that are the subject of discussion in this paper, namely, the Akerlof adverse selection model, where the quality offered is a function of the price but markets clear. In the context of the labor market, they show that a welfare improvement can be attained by subsidizing commodities whose consumption increases the mean quality of labor sold on the market and by taxing commodities whose consumption decreases the mean quality. The mean quality of labor offered on the market resembles the mean quality of air: There is an important externality in each individual's decision.

Their earlier paper was limited to economies with market clearing. In a sequel (Greenwald and Stiglitz 1986b, 1988e), they identify the inefficiencies that arise in economies in which quality is dependent on prices and markets do not clear. There are inefficiencies both in setting wages (interest rates) and determining the level of employment (the number of loans of different types).

A direct consequence of the Fundamental Theorem of Welfare Economics is the decentralizability of efficient resource allocations; and a direct consequence of the failure of the Fundamental Theorem—of the externalities we have noted—is that the scope for decentralization may be limited.[18]

Some rationing may be consistent with Pareto efficiency. Assume the government has no more information about the quality of workers or potential borrowers than do firms (or banks). It has to allocate workers to different jobs. It has to allocate capital among different firms. The wage at which workers are willing to work or the interest rate at which firms are willing to borrow conveys information to the government, just as it does to the employer or the bank, and it will, in general, wish to use this information, even though to use it necessitates rationing—unemployment or credit rationing. But the objectives of the government, what it wishes to glean from the information, are different from those of firms and banks in the private market equilibrium. The latter are simply concerned with maximizing their own profits. Thus, in choosing a wage, the government would be concerned with ascertaining that those with a comparative advantage in a job get assigned to that job; the firm is simply concerned with cost per efficiency unit. (Similarly, the bank is not concerned with how its actions affect the profitability of investors, only with how it affects the profitability of the bank.)

Private firms will not only set the wage incorrectly; they will also hire an incorrect number of workers. Because all workers whose opportunity cost is less than the wage offer themselves for work, the mean opportunity cost of an individual randomly hired by a firm is less than the wage. Thus firms will not hire workers up to the point where the wage equals the mean opportunity costs, as a government concerned with maximizing national income would.

The inefficiencies we noted above are not the only inefficiencies associated with private market allocations and there may be other grounds for government intervention. Taxes and subsidies may affect the consumption vector of individuals, and thus indirectly the effort exerted by the worker (or the wage required to induce the worker not to shirk). Such taxes and subsidies may thus be welfare enhancing (Arnott and Stiglitz 1985).

Shapiro and Stiglitz (1984) point out a variety of other inefficiencies that arise in their model where high wages are used to reduce shirking. These relate to the intensity of monitoring and policies that affect quits and shirking. For instance, if workers are very risk averse, unemployment insurance may be desirable even though in their model private firms will never supply unemployment insurance; if there is an

---

[18] One should perhaps distinguish between two situations: that where the decentralized allocation *without* government intervention is inefficient, but government intervention, in the form of taxes and subsidies, can induce a decentralized efficient allocation; and those where even with this form of intervention, a decentralized allocation, cannot attain certain Pareto efficient allocations. Both problems may arise here.

excess supply of labor, firms can obtain the desired labor force at the going wage; any increases in unemployment compensation simply increase the wage that a firm must pay to induce workers not to shirk.[19]

These models also have some more basic implications for how we think about the welfare properties of market economies. One of the important consequences of the Fundamental Theorem of Welfare Economics was that it enabled a neat separation of efficiency and equity issues. In particular, whether the economy is or is not Pareto efficient did not depend on the distribution of wealth. In the models under examination, this is not true, for two reasons. First, the inefficiencies with which we have been concerned arise because of the asymmetric information between two parties to a transaction—between landlord and worker, or between worker and capitalist. But whether these transactions arise is, at least partly, determined by the distribution of wealth. For instance, sharecropping arises largely because of the concentration of wealth. Secondly, the distribution of ownership of factors determines whether it is, in fact, feasible to design Pareto improvements. In the Shapiro-Stiglitz model, for instance, national income can be increased by taxing capital and subsidizing wages; if wealth were equally distributed, the losses individuals would suffer qua capitalists would be more than offset by the gains that would be received qua workers. But if there are two distinct groups in the population, capitalists and workers, there may be no way of improving the welfare of the workers without simultaneously hurting the capitalists—the market equilibrium, while not maximizing net national product, is Pareto efficient (see Shapiro and Stiglitz 1984; Dasgupta and Ray 1986).

II Explanations for the Dependence of Quality on Price

In the introduction, we described two broad classes of models giving rise to a dependence of quality on price based on incentive and selection effects. In the preceding sections, we showed that if the dependence of quality on price took on particular forms (e.g., the cost per effective unit had an interior minimum) then there might exist an equilibrium in which demand did not equal supply, or in which there might be, in equilibrium, a price (wage, interest rate) distribution. We now consider in more detail not only why quality may depend on price in certain situations, but why the dependence should take on a form that may give rise to nonmarket-clearing equilibria and/or wage/price/interest rate distributions.

---

[19] This assumes that the firm cannot treat quits and fires differentially. There are good reasons for this: If quits are treated preferentially, a worker who knows he is about to be fired will quit. For a more extended discussion, see Shapiro and Stiglitz (1985a).

The analysis is divided into three sections, describing selection models, incentive models, and nutritional models.

1 Selection Models

Labor Market

The reasons for the presence of adverse selection in the labor market are clear (Stiglitz 1976b; Weiss 1976, 1980; Greenwald 1979, 1986). One of the inferences I can make from the fact that a worker is willing to work for me for 50 cents an hour is that he does not have (know of) a better offer elsewhere.[20] If other firms are screening workers, keeping high-productivity workers and letting go of low-productivity workers, or adjusting their wages to reflect their lower productivity, the fact that no other firm has offered the worker a wage in excess of 50 cents an hour conveys a considerable amount of information. (Obviously, the inferences I make depend on a number of details of the surrounding circumstances; if the worker is a newly arrived worker to the United States, the fact that he is willing to accept a job at 50 cents an hour is more likely to reflect his limited opportunities for search and his lack of knowledge of the job market; if a job has a number of extremely attractive nonpecuniary advantages, the inferences I make should take that into account.)

More productive workers are likely to have better wage offers from other firms, but even if they are self-employed, they are likely to have a higher reservation of wage (that is, if those who are more able in one production task are more able, on average, in other production tasks as well).

In the simplest formulation of the adverse selection-labor model, a worker whose reservation wage is v has a productivity of $a(v)$; if all workers whose reservation wage v is less than or equal to w apply for a job with wage w,[21] then mean productivity of the applicants is

$$\sum a(v) f(v)/F(v)$$

where $F(v)$ is the distribution function of the population by reservation wages, and $f(v)$ the density function. It is clear that if $a' > 0$, then mean productivity will increase with w. To see that it may have the shape depicted in Figure 1, consider a two group model; low-productivity individuals with productivity a_1 have a reservation wage of v_1 while high-productivity individuals with productivity a_2, have a reservation wage of v_2. $\bar{a}$ is the mean productivity; obviously, at high wages, when

---

[20] Unless a worker's productivity is completely firm-specific, then no information is conveyed to one firm by another firm's refusal to hire him.

[21] More generally, the reservation wage of an individual will depend on his fallback (self-employment) income and the probability that he will obtain a higher wage, and this depends on the probability distribution of abilities and wage offers in the population, on the nature of the search technology, and on the costs of quitting a job once it has been accepted. See Nalebuff and Stiglitz (1982). Schlicht (1986) argues for a link between reservation wage and productivity based on the shorter expected duration of holding a job by less competent individuals.

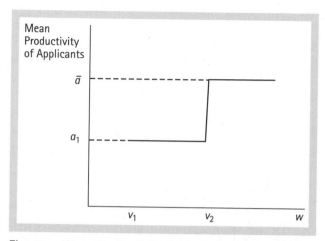

Fig. 11a. Wage Productivity Curve in Two Group Model

everyone is willing to work, $a = \bar{a}$. The resulting productivity curve is depicted in Figure 11a.

A variant of this model arises when there are job-specific skills and positive search costs; the larger the applicant pool, the higher the expected productivity, simply because the firm can find a larger number of individuals that fit in well with the needs of the firm.

Capital Market

The intuitive reasons for the presence of adverse selection in the capital market follow along parallel lines to those in the labor market (Stiglitz and Weiss 1981). The fact that an individual is willing to borrow from a bank at a 25 percent interest rate implies that he has found no one else willing to lend to him at lower interest rate, and this fact conveys considerable information. Moreover, even if the individual had not been turned down by other banks, those who are undertaking very risky projects, with little prospect of repaying the loan, are likely to be less concerned about the interest rate they have promised to pay (when they do not default) than those who are undertaking safe projects and will always repay.

More formally, Stiglitz and Weiss (1981) consider a set of projects that the bank has identified as "similar." They all yield the same mean return, and require the same amount of bank finance. They show (a) the riskier projects[22] yield a lower return to the bank; (b) at any interest rate charged by the bank, firms with riskier projects apply, those with safer projects do not; and (c) as the bank increases the interest rate charged there is an adverse selection effect, with firms with the best projects (the least risky, i.e., those yielding the bank the highest expected return) no longer applying.[23] They

---

[22] A project is said to be riskier than another if its return is a mean preserving spread of that of the other.

[23] The first result is a direct consequence of the concavity of the payoff function of the bank (in the absence of collateral, this is max $[R, (1+r)B]$, where R is the return to the project, $(1+r)B$ the

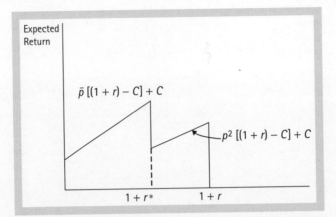

Fig. 11b. Expected Return as Function of Interest Rate Change: Two Group Model

show that the adverse selection effect may outweigh the direct gain from an increase in the interest rate. This may be seen most easily in the case where there are only two kinds of firms; each project costs B dollars, and is entirely bank financed. The firm is required to put up c dollars worth of collateral per dollar loaned, which it forfeits in the event of a default. The projects of type i firm yield a return of R^i if successful, and nothing otherwise; the probability of success is p^i. The expected return to the bank per dollar loaned from a loan to a firm of type i is just $p^i(1+r) + (1-p^i)c$, where r is the interest rate charged. Thus, if $p^1 > p^2$, *one* is the safe project and yields a higher return to the bank, provided $c < (1+r)$, which it always would be (otherwise, the bank faces no risk).

The expected return to a firm of type i is $p^i[R^i - B(1+r)B] - cB(1-p^i)$. It follows then that if the two projects have the same mean return, the riskier project yields the higher return to the firm. The safe firms no longer apply when

$$p^1[R^1 - (1+r)B] - cB(1-p^1) = 0.$$

Thus, for interest rates below $[p^1R^1 - cB(1-p^1)]/p^1B - 1 = r^*$, both types of firm apply; for higher interest rates, only the risky firms apply. Even if at r^* there is an excess demand for funds, banks may not raise the interest rate (see Figure 11b).

2 Incentive Effects

We are concerned here with the variety of circumstances under which the quality of the product (the likelihood of bankruptcy, the productivity of a worker) is affected by actions of the seller (borrower, worker), and those actions are affected by the price

amount the firm has promised to repay); the second result is a direct consequence of the convexity of the payoff function of the borrower ($\min[R - (1+r)B, 0]$ in the absence of collateral); the third result is an immediate consequence of the second.

(interest rate, wage). Two broad categories of models will be discussed, depending on whether there is or is not a long-term relationship. The latter are of particular interest; bad performance is (in these models) often punished by a termination of the relationship. For the threat of termination to be an effective incentive, the terms of the contract (relationship) must be such as to make that contract strictly better than that of the next best opportunity; e.g., price must be in excess of marginal cost or the wage paid must be higher than the minimum wage required to recruit the worker.

We now describe in greater detail the effects of wages, prices, or interest rates on economic incentives.

Capital Markets

An increase in the interest rate charged on a loan may induce the borrower to undertake greater risks, lowering the expected return to the lender (William R. Keeton 1980; Stiglitz and Weiss 1981). This may be seen most simply in the case where the firm has two projects that it can undertake, each of which costs B. As before, project i has a return, if successful, of R^i, and the probability of success is p^i; if unsuccessful, the project yields no return. For simplicity, we ignore collateral. Then, the expected return to the firm of undertaking project i when the interest rate is r is

$$p^i[R^i - (1+r)B].$$

As Figure 12 illustrates, the safe project 1 has a higher expected return to the firm for $r \leq r^*$, where

$$(1+r^*)B = (p^1 R^1 - p^2 R^2)/(p^1 - p^2).$$

Thus, the bank will not raise the interest rate above r^*, even if there is an excess demand for funds at r^*, because to do so would induce firms to undertake the risky project, lowering the bank's return.

This is an example of what has come to be called a *principal agent* problem.[24] The principal (here the bank) can exert only indirect control over the actions of the agent (the firm) and, he does so through the design of the payoff schedule. Changing the nominal price (here the interest rate) may have adverse (in terms of the interests of the principal) effects on the actions undertaken by the agent.

The discussion so far has focused on a single period model. Stiglitz and Weiss (1983b) have extended the analysis to a multi (two) period model. They establish that the threat of *terminating* the credit relationship may have beneficial incentive effects and that terminations are a better incentive device than threats to charge higher interest rates (pay lower wages).

Their analysis is similar to the explanation of why the expected return may decrease with the rate of interest charged provided by the models of Jonathan Eaton and Mark

---

[24] A vast literature has developed on the principal agent problem since the early papers by Steve Ross (1973), Mirrlees (1974), and Stiglitz (1974e). We make note of only those papers that are directly relevant to the subject of this review, the dependence of quality on price.

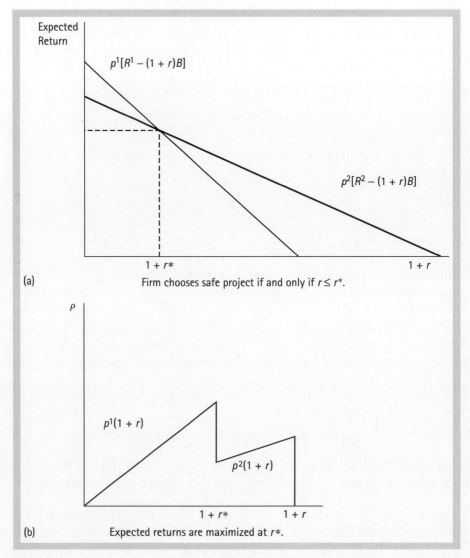

Fig. 12.

Gersovitz (1980, 1981a, 1981b), Eaton (1985), and Franklin Allen (1980a, 1981, 1983). They are concerned with situations where contracts are not enforceable. We might say that there are implicit contracts, which have to be designed to be self-enforcing. The terms of the contract determine whether, and under what circumstances, it will pay a borrower to refuse to repay a loan (for a sovereign to repudiate his debt).[25]

---

[25] In the Stiglitz and Weiss (1983b) analysis, contracts are explicit, but enforceable only if it is in the interests of at least one party to the contract to do so. In the papers discussed in this paragraph, there is no legal enforcement mechanism. "Moral hazard" issues arise both in the compliance with the contract, and in the actions borrowers take which affect the likelihood they will wish to comply.

In these models, it is again the threat of termination of the relationship that induces the borrower to repay the loan. (In the Eaton-Gersovitz model, access to international capital markets enables the country to smooth out income variability.) For any given amount loaned, the higher the rate of interest charged, the more likely it is that the loan will be repudiated.[26]

Labor Markets

There are several different explanations for why the wage might affect the productivity of workers and the profitability of the firm.

(a) Shirking

(Walter J. Wessels 1979, 1985; Guillermo Calvo 1979; Calvo and Phelps 1977; Calvo and Stanislaw Wellisz 1979; Shapiro and Stiglitz 1984; Samuel Bowles 1985;[27] Stiglitz and Weiss 1983b; Steve Stoft 1982.) If there were no unemployment and if all firms paid the market-clearing wage, then the threat of being fired would not lead individuals to reduce their shirking: they would know that they could costlessly obtain another job. But if the firm pays wages in excess of that of other firms, or if there is unemployment (so that a fired worker must spend a period in the unemployment pool before he again obtains a job) then workers have an incentive not to shirk; there is a real cost to being fired.[28] One of the immediate consequences, then, of costly monitoring is that equilibrium must be characterized by unemployment and/or wage dispersion.

It also implies that the productivity of the worker hired by the ith firm, λ_i, is a function of the wage it pays, the wage paid by all other firms, w_{-i}, and the unemployment rate, U:

$$\lambda_i = \lambda_i(w_i, w_{-i}, U).$$

In the simplest version of the shirking model, workers either work or shirk; there is a critical wage below which the worker shirks. This critical wage is an increasing function of the employment level or of the wage differential between this firm and other firms. In the case where all firms pay the same wages, the so-called no-shirking constraint, giving the minimum wage below which shirking occurs, is depicted in

[26] Repudiation could always be avoided if the repayments could be made state dependent, and if all states were perfectly observable and verifiable by both parties. For a more general discussion, see Eaton, Gersovitz, and Stiglitz (1986).

[27] There is a large "radical" literature emphasizing the effect of the employment relationship on worker productivity. Other contributions to this literature include Herbert Gintis and Tsuneo Ishikawa (1985), Tom Weisskopf, Bowles, and David Gordon (1983), Gerry Oster (1980), and Geoff Hodgson (1982). The distinction between this literature and the nonradical literature is not always readily apparent. For instance, the Bowles (1985) and Shapiro and Stiglitz (1984) models appear to be essentially identical; some of the interpretations given to the model, and the lessons drawn, differ.

[28] These models are thus long-term models. The "punishment" is provided "publicly" by the period of unemployment (rather than privately, through reduced wages or other means). Stiglitz and Weiss (1983) provide conditions showing that termination is in fact the optimal punishment.

These models are constructed with identical individuals so there is no reputation effect associated with being fired. In any case, it is often hard to distinguish among voluntary and involuntary termination, in which case, the reputation effect of separations may be minimal (Shapiro and Stiglitz 1985a).

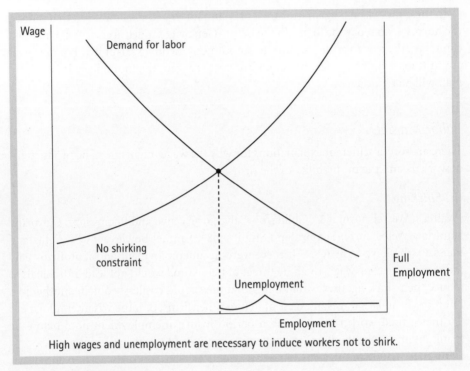

High wages and unemployment are necessary to induce workers not to shirk.

Fig. 13a. Shirking Model

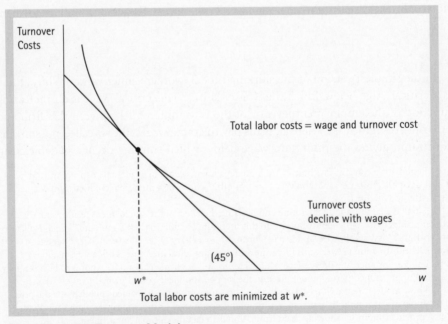

Total labor costs are minimized at w^*.

Fig. 13b. Labor Turnover Model

Figure 13a. The demand for labor, given that workers do not shirk, is a decreasing function of the wage. Equilibrium, at the intersection of the demand curve and the no-shirking constraint, always entails unemployment.

(b) Labor turnover

(John Pencavel 1972; Wessels 1979; Stiglitz 1974c, 1974a, 1985c; Robert Hall 1975; Salop 1973, 1979; Dybvig and Jaynes 1980; Ekkehart Schlicht 1978.) A second important way that workers' behavior affects the productivity of firms is through labor turnover.[29] In most jobs, there are costs to hiring and training that are specific to the firm. So long as individuals do not pay their full costs at the moment they are hired (recouping them later in the form of higher wages)[30] then the greater the quit rate, the greater the firm's expenditures on training and hiring costs. Increasing the wage rate (relative to wages paid by other firms) will, in general, lead to a reduction in the quit rate; there is a wage that minimizes total labor costs of the firm (Figure 13b). Moreover, the greater the unemployment rate, the less likely it is that the worker will find a better job. Because the effect of higher quit rates is to decrease the "net" productivity (net of turnover costs), we obtain a productivity wage relationship of the above form.

(c) Morale effects

(James E. Annable 1977, 1980, 1988; Stiglitz 1973a, 1974h; Pencavel 1977; Akerlof 1984; Whiteside 1974.) Employers often allege that paying higher wage results in higher productivity, and not simply because of the greater penalty associated with being fired. A worker who believes he is being treated more than fairly may not only get more job satisfaction from his job, but also may put out more for his employer. And notions of fairness are closely related to how one *perceives* others of similar ability being treated. Thus, we can postulate that an individual's efforts depend not only on his own wage, but on the wage of others in his reference group, $\hat{w}$, the monitoring intensity, m, and the cost of being fired (the unemployment rate):[31]

$$e_i = e(w_i, \hat{w}, m, U).$$

The formal analysis of this model follows closely along the lines of that of the shirking model.[32] (It may, in fact, be possible to derive at least some variants of this morale

---

[29] The importance of this had, of course, long been recognized by labor economists. See Sumner Slichter (1919).

[30] Richard Arnott and Stiglitz (1985) and Shapiro and Stiglitz (1985a) provide explanations for why individuals do not bear the full costs of training; these have to do with worker risk aversion, incomplete insurance, and imperfect capital markets (though these market imperfections in turn, can be related to information imperfections).

[31] These effects have, of course, long been discussed by labor economists. For an early formalization of the notion of interdependence, see Dan Hamermesh (1975).

[32] The observation that it is individuals' perceptions of whether they are being treated fairly that affects behavior has one important consequence. The productivity curve of a group that believes it is being treated unfairly will (if our argument is correct) lie below that of groups of identical abilities that do not believe they are being treated unfairly. Such individuals either will not be hired, or will be hired at lower wages than someone of the *same* ability (let alone someone of the ability that they believe that they

model from a standard utility maximizing model, in which utility depends not only on effort and wages, but on relative wages.[33] Obviously, quit rates too will depend on morale effects: Individuals may spend more resources searching for a better job if they believe that they are being unfairly treated on their present job.)

Product Markets

(Joseph Farrell 1979, 1980; Shapiro 1983; Dybvig and Chester Spatt 1983; Allen 1984; Ben Klein and Keith B. Leffler 1981.) In the product market, incentive effects similar to those described earlier arise: Buyers often cannot ascertain the quality of a commodity before they purchase it. Earlier, we noted that the penalty associated with a worker caught shirking and who is thereupon fired depended on the wage relative to the wage paid by other firms and the cost of getting another job (which depends, in part, on the unemployment rate). Similarly, the penalty a customer levies on a firm that has cheated him is to terminate the relationship; and the penalty associated with this depends on how high the price is relative to the production costs (the profit the firm attains from the relationship) and how hard it is to recruit another, similar customer.

The essential insights are provided by the following simple model. Assume that the cost of production for a high-quality commodity is c^h, for a low-quality commodity is c^l, and the price is p. Assume that when a customer observes a bad quality commodity, he infers that the seller will always continue to sell a bad quality. The bad quality commodity is worth nothing to the customer, so if he believes that the commodity is bad, he will terminate the relationship. Then, the value to the firm of continuing to produce good-quality commodities is

$$(1 + r)(p - c^h)Q/r$$

where Q is the quantity sold, r the rate of interest. The value of cheating and producing a bad quality commodity is

$$(p - c^l)Q.$$

Thus, for it to be worthwhile for the firm to produce good-quality commodities,

$$(1 + r)(p - c^h)/r > p - c^l$$

or

$$p > (1 + r)c^h - rc^l = p^*.$$

have). The fact that they are hired at lower wages reconfirms their belief they are not being treated fairly. The employer who pays the lower wage does not believe he is discriminating, only that he is paying wages that are in accord with productivity, which depends both on (statistical projections of) ability and effort.

[33] Akerlof (1980, 1982) and Schlicht (1981a, 1981b) develop alternative theories of the employer-employee relationship in which psychological and sociological considerations lead to a dependence of productivity on wages. Akerlof (1984) describes some experiments in which different workers are assigned identical jobs and paid identical wages, but believe that they are either being under- or overpaid. These perceptions affect productivity.

Accordingly, any individual who saw a firm attempting to sell a commodity for less than p^* would infer that that commodity was a low-quality commodity.[34]

3 Nutritional Models

This paper focuses on the dependence of quality on price arising from imperfect information (adverse selection, moral hazard). But, as we noted, in one of the earliest sets of efficiency-wage models the quality of labor depended on the wage for nutritional reasons. How are these nutritional models related to the information models?

If the output of workers were perfectly observable, then presumably all workers would be paid on a piece rate basis. In equilibrium, some workers would be employed (at the efficiency wage), and other identical workers would be unemployed. Assume that workers get zero disutility from work, up to 40 hours per week, and infinite disutility thereafter (there is no disutility associated with effort up to a critical level λ, and infinite disutility thereafter) and that the output per unit time with the maximum effort level e is a function of nutrition. Then the number of labor units supplied will be a function of the wage rate. There is no way of obtaining any labor at a cost per efficiency unit of less than $w^*/\lambda(w^*)$. At wages in excess of w^* effective labor supply increases, as depicted in Figure 14. Although, by assumption at w^*, each worker supplies either zero effective labor units or $\lambda(w^*)$, all workers strictly prefer to supply the latter; at w^* there is an excess supply of labor.

Although nutritional models can give rise to unemployment even if workers are paid on a piece rate basis, they obviously can also give rise to unemployment when piece rates are not feasible; thus, in the example given above, there are no incentive problems, whether workers are paid on a piece rate basis or not.[35]

Thus, the nutritional efficiency-wage models, while differing in fundamental ways from the informational efficiency-wage models in their microfoundations, yield similar conclusions: They generate similar reduced form relationships between productivity and the wage paid by the firm, wages paid by other firms, and the unemployment rate. It is worth noting, however, that in one polar form of the efficiency-wage model, where individuals do not share any of their income with others, productivity depends

---

[34] These beliefs are "rational"; given the beliefs of the individual, it would not pay the firm to produce a high-quality commodity, if it ever produced a low-quality commodity; and given that the firm indeed produces a low-quality commodity, the beliefs of individuals are consistent with firm behavior. More formally, the equilibrium can be shown to be a perfect equilibrium. See Dybvig and Spatt (1983).

This is a "reputation" model based solely on incentive considerations. Other reputation models entail a mixture of incentive and adverse selection effects. There are good producers and bad producers. When a buyer purchases a commodity that turns out to be a low-quality commodity, then he infers that the seller must be a low-quality seller. It is their concern about being so labeled that induces good producers to produce high-quality commodities. One does not necessarily need many "bad" firms to induce good behavior on the part of the good firms, as David Kreps and Robert Wilson (1982a) show in a rather different context.

[35] It is straightforward to construct models that incorporate both incentive and nutritional effects.

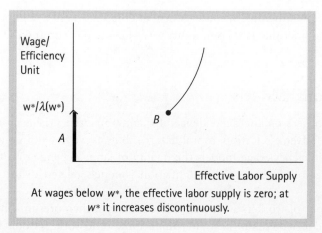

At wages below *w**, the effective labor supply is zero; at
w* it increases discontinuously.

Fig. 14.

only on the absolute value of the wage paid by the firm; accordingly the equilibrium wage will be independent of the unemployment rate. (This stands in contrast with several versions of the informational efficiency-wage model, where relative wages and the unemployment rate are the primary determinants of productivity.)

III THE IMPLICATIONS OF THE DEPENDENCE OF QUALITY ON PRICE FOR ECONOMIC THEORY

1 Differences Between Economies in Which the Law of Supply and Demand Is Repealed and Those Where It Still Holds

It is useful to clarify the differences between the assumptions in our analysis and those that are (often implicit) in the traditional competitive paradigm, e.g., of the model of Arrow and Debreu. Arrow and Debreu assume that each employer has perfect information concerning the quality of his labor, that each buyer of a commodity has perfect information concerning the quality of the commodities which he purchases, and that each lender has perfect information concerning the characteristics of those to whom he lends. Thus, when they speak of a market for a commodity, they have in mind a market for a collection of objects, all of which are identical, at least in all relevant aspects. The person buying a commodity or hiring on the market is completely indifferent about which commodity he obtains; the firm hiring a worker is indifferent about which worker he obtains, and no additional information would change his indifference.

This assumption of a competitive market for homogeneous commodities is neither plausible nor innocuous. Markets in which commodities are completely homogeneous—with respect to location and the date as well as other characteristics—are almost inherently sufficiently thin so that the postulate of perfect competition is inapplicable. Markets that are sufficiently "thick" to be competitive are almost always nonhomogeneous. Consider the market for labor. If we define a submarket, say, J. E. Stiglitz's labor, then it may be homogeneous, but hardly competitive; if we take a broader definition of the market, say, those with PhDs in economics, it may be fairly competitive, but it is hardly homogeneous.

The problems with which we are concerned are central in capital markets and insurance markets. Both markets are essentially intertemporal: In the capital market, the lender lends the borrower money today, in return for a promise to repay $\$(1 + r)$ next period, provided the borrower can; in the insurance market, the insurer agrees today to pay the insured a given amount next period if a particular event occurs. The lender cares about the likelihood that the borrower will default; the insurer cares about the likelihood that the insured against event will occur. Borrowers (the insured) differ, but lenders (insurers) cannot tell who is more likely to default (to have an accident).

Moreover, the probability of default (of an accident) can be affected by the actions of the borrower (insured).

The Arrow-Debreu model does not actually require perfect information. What it does require is that the nature of the "commodity" be fixed (i.e., that the average quality of labor be unaffected by prices or wages and that average default (accident) probability be unaffected by the terms of the loan (insurance policy)). There can be neither adverse selection or moral hazard effects; that is, if all individuals (commodities) are not identical, at least the mix of types is fixed *and* any actions which they might take that affect their productivity (or default, or accident, probabilities) are observable.

Many economic relationships involve an element of insurance and/or loan. This is the case, for instance, with most employment and rental arrangements.

There is one set of circumstances under which a firm does not care about the characteristics of those it hires. If the firm can perfectly and costlessly monitor the *actions*[36] of its employees, and pay the employee for the services performed, and there are no fixed costs associated with hiring a worker, then the firm is unconcerned whether the worker is a low-ability worker pulling out three medium sized weeds a day, or a high-productivity worker pulling out three hundred a day. It pays a fixed price per medium sized weed pulled out.

In fact, relatively few workers are paid even partially on a piece rate basis (which is not to say that performance goes unrewarded, either in terms of promotions or

---

[36] Where "actions" are sufficiently precisely specified to imply a particular outcome in a particular situation, regardless of who performed the action.

salary). The literature on compensation schemes details a number of reasons for this, all of which attest to the importance of the informational concerns that are the center of our analysis (Stiglitz 1975b) but are completely ignored in the traditional competitive paradigm.[37]

Because most workers are not paid a piece rate equal to the value of their marginal product, and because there are costs associated with hiring workers, some of which are borne by the firm, firms are concerned both about the quality of the workers they hire, their productivity on the job, and their turnover rate.[38] The wage affects all of these variables. And so long as that is the case, the possibilities with which we have been concerned here—that equilibrium will be characterized by an excess supply of labor, and/or by a wage distribution—are real possibilities.[39]

It should be noted that most of the issues with which we have been concerned here would arise so long as individuals are not paid on a piece rate, regardless of the reason. Similarly, if the firm must pay a uniform wage to all workers, even though it knows which workers are more productive, it will worry about the adverse selection effects of lowering wages.

The conventional models assume not only that there is not imperfect information concerning what is being bought, but also, in trades which occur over time, that there are no *enforcement* problems. In fact, of course, there are important enforcement

[37] The monitoring required by piece rate systems is costly; for it to be effective, there can be little variation in the quality of what is produced, or it needs to be easy to write a contract that specifies the relationship between quality and price, and then to observe and verify the quality of what is produced.

Moreover, as technology changes, the piece rate needs to change; but this is often a contentious process. If, of course, there were no costs of labor mobility (no costs of hiring workers and no costs to the worker of moving to another firm) then if the firm offered too low a piece rate, resulting in an income below the worker's opportunity cost, then the worker would simply quit; exit would replace voice, to use Albert Hirschman's insightful terminology. But labor mobility is costly, and thus workers and firms are concerned about how the piece rate is set; it determines the division of the "*ex post* surplus"—given that the workers are working for the firm, the difference between the worker's income and his opportunity cost; and the difference between the profits of the firm from the current employees and what the profits would be if the employer had to replace them.

[38] To the extent that firms bear these turnover costs or pay workers not solely on the basis of their actions, firms can be thought of as providing insurance.

[39] There is one other situation where moral hazard problems do not arise in labor markets: When workers are risk neutral (so there is no need for an insurance component in the relationship), then they can rent the machines on which they work (rent the land); because they receive all the residual, they will have "correct incentives"; and because what the capitalist (landlord) receives is independent of the action of the worker, he is indifferent to the actions they undertake. But even this is not correct if the worker cannot pay the rent ahead of time; then there is some probability that he will fail to pay the promised rent, and the likelihood of this is, in general, a function of the actions he undertakes: There is still a moral hazard problem. When rents are paid *ex post*, then it is as if the owner lent the money to the renter (see Johnson 1950; Stiglitz and Weiss 1981). Moreover, if how the worker uses the machine affects its future productivity and if it is difficult to verify whether the deterioration in the machine is due to misuse, there is a further moral hazard problem limiting the extent of rental markets. The contractual arrangements between the parties will try to limit these moral hazard problems, by stipulating restrictions on the use of the rented property. Thus, a landowner may stipulate what crops are to be planted, and he may impose restrictions on grazing. These moral hazard problems can be avoided by selling the machine; but this increases the risk of the worker; and it is even less likely that he will have the resources to pay for the purchase than to rent.

problems, arising both from the incompleteness of contracts and from the costs of enforcing the contract terms that are explicit.[40]

The nutritional efficiency wage models can give rise to unemployment even without informational problems, as we have already noted. These models differ from the conventional Arrow-Debreu model in two technical respects, which turn out to be important: There is a nonconvexity associated with the productivity wage relationship, and in equilibrium individuals are on the boundary of their feasible set.[41]

2 Alternative Equilibrium Concepts

In Section I we argued that when quality depends on price, equilibrium may be characterized by markets not clearing. In traditional economic theory, equilibrium is defined as market clearing. Clearly, different notions of equilibrium are being employed. Indeed, even within the literature recognizing the dependence of quality on price, more than one equilibrium notion has been employed, with contrasting results. In this section, we review and contrast several of the more important equilibrium concepts that have been used.

Walrasian Versus Rationing Equilibria

In models where quality depends on price, there may exist a market-clearing price, for instance, a wage at which demand equals supply. We referred to this as the Walrasian equilibrium, but this may *not* be a market equilibrium. Whenever in the labor market there is a region where cost per effective labor unit decreases with an increase in the wage, or in the capital market there is a region where the expected return decreases with an increase in the interest rate, there *may* exist an equilibrium with excess supply of labor or excess demand for capital. Indeed, there always exists some level of demand for labor or supply of funds for which this is true.[42]

---

[40] These enforcement problems are, of course, central both in international lending, in implicit contract theory, in sharecropping markets, and in product markets.

[41] Thus what appears to be a technical assumption in Gerard Debreu's *Theory of Value* becomes of central importance in this analysis. Loosely speaking, to prove the existence of a market-clearing equilibrium, one must show that the supply correspondences are continuous, and to do this one must show that the budget sets are continuous functions of prices. To recast the nutritional efficiency-wage model in standard terms, we let $w\#$ denote the wage per efficiency unit. While at $w\# = w^*/\lambda^*$, the individual supplies λ^* efficiency units of labor, and at higher wages, the individual can supply, say, up to $\lambda(w)$ units of labor, at lower values of $w\#$ the feasible set shrinks to zero.

Note that with nonconvex preferences, an equilibrium exists with a continuum of individuals, but a market-clearing equilibrium does not exist in the efficiency-wage model. Moreover, while with standard nonconvexities those who supply labor and those who do not have the same level of utility, this is not true in our model. For a more extended discussion, see Dasgupta and Ray (1986a).

[42] The demand curve is derived as follows. Assume the firm's production function is $Q = F[\lambda(w)L]$. It chooses w and L to maximize $Q - wL$ where we have chosen output as the numeraire. From the first-order conditions, $\lambda/\lambda' = w$ meaning that the wage is chosen to minimize labor costs per unit of

It is important to emphasize that we are not arguing here that equilibrium is *never* characterized by the equality of demand and supply, only that it may not be.[43]

The Walrasian wage (*interest rate*) is the market equilibrium if and only if there exists no higher wage (*lower interest rate*) at which costs per efficiency unit (*expected returns*) are lower (*higher*).[44]

The Choice of Appropriate Equilibrium Concepts

Our analysis thus differs from the standard Arrow-Debreu model not only in its informational assumptions, but also in its definition of equilibrium. Traditional theory has taken the equality of supply and demand to be part of the definition of equilibrium. This, I think, is wrong.

Equilibrium is defined, loosely, as a state where no economic agents have an incentive to change their behavior. Whether a particular configuration of the economy is an equilibrium depends, then, on agents' perceptions of the consequences of changes in their behavior. If employers believed that at a lower wage they would obtain exactly the same quality of laborers as they obtained at a higher wage, then clearly, if a worker offered to work for a wage lower than that of existing workers, the firm would hire him (assuming there were no further repercussions of what might be viewed by other workers as antisocial behavior).[45] Under these circumstances, equilibrium would be characterized by demand equaling supply.

The fact that under these circumstances equilibrium is characterized by demand equaling supply is thus a theorem (admittedly trivial) to be proven; the equality of demand and supply should not be taken as a definition of equilibrium, but rather as a consequence following from more primitive behavioral postulates. What we have established in this paper is that, under plausible behavioral postulates, equilibrium may not be characterized by demand equaling supply. At the same time, it should be emphasized that our economy is competitive in the conventional sense in which that word is used: We are concerned with atomistic equilibria, in which

---

effective labor (the efficiency wage). Employment is chosen so that, at the efficiency wage, the real wage equals the value of the marginal product of labor: $w = F'(w)\lambda$.

[43] In paticular, if the Walrasian wage exceeds the efficiency wage, the market equilibrium is the Walrasian wage, and the law of supply and demand holds. Any firm that attempted to lower the wage to the efficiency wage would not be able to obtain any labor.

[44] In this example, the cost per effective unit of labor curve has taken on a simple shape: At wages below w^*, cost per effective labor unit is decreasing, and at wages greater than w^*, it is increasing. There is no intrinsic reason why the cost per effective unit of labor curve should take on such a simple shape as we have already noted (see Figure 5). Then, there will be an excess supply of labor if the Walrasian wage is below w^* or between $\hat{w}$ and w^{**}. It always pays the firms to pay the wage in excess of the Walrasian wage, which minimizes cost per effective unit of labor. Thus, for Walrasian wages in the interval between $\hat{w}$ and w^{**} it pays the firm to increase the wage to w^{**}. (In these circumstances, equilibrium may be characterized by a wage distribution, as we noted earlier.)

[45] These repercussions have been at the center of recent literature focusing on the distinction between insiders and outsiders. See Assar Lindbeck and Dennis Snower (1984a).

all agents are small relative to the market though in spite of this they are not price takers.[46]

Passive Versus Active Sellers and Buyers

While the models presented here differ from the conventional competitive paradigm both in informational assumptions and in the equilibrium concept, these models differ from Akerlof's analysis of adverse selection only with respect to the equilibrium concept. In Akerlof's model, as in the traditional perfect information model, however, both buyers and sellers act completely passively. For instance, although firms know the statistical relationship between the wage paid and the productivity of the workers they hire, they do not try to use this knowledge to increase their profits, e.g., by setting wages at other than a market-clearing level. We would argue that there is, in most situations, no persuasive reason to limit uninformed agents to the passive role that conventional theory has assigned to them.

Nonprice Rationing

A number of writers have argued that when, in the capital market, interest rates cannot fall, there are other methods by which markets can be made to clear; similarly, in labor markets, when wages cannot fall, there are other methods by which markets can be made to clear. In markets with imperfect information, contractual arrangements involve more than a single term; and it must be shown that none of these can adjust in a way as to restore market clearing. There may be adverse selection and incentive effects from changes in each of the contract terms.

In the capital market, emphasis has been placed on the role of collateral. Increasing collateral does induce firms to undertake less risky projects, but may have adverse selection effects (Stiglitz and Weiss 1981; Hildegard Wette 1983; Gerhard E. Clemenz 1984, 1985; ChangHo Yoon 1984, 1985). Several authors (e.g., Helmut Bester 1985) have constructed models in which, if banks can design contracts with varying interest rates and collateral, there will be no credit rationing.

It is important to recall that our contention has been not that equilibrium would always be characterized by credit rationing, but that it may be, under plausible conditions. Indeed, it is easy to construct examples in which equilibrium is not characterized by credit rationing. Bester (1985) and David Besanko and Anjan Thakor (1984) provide examples with the peculiar property in that bankers can obtain, through offering a set of contracts, perfect information concerning their borrowers. By contrast, Stiglitz and Weiss (1986, 1987c) argue that as long as there is a residual of imperfect information there may be scope for credit rationing.[47]

---

[46] The concept of equilibrium employed by Dasgupta and Ray (1986a) in their analysis of the nutritional efficiency wage model corresponds to a quasiequilibrium in Debreu (1959) and to the concept of a compensated equilibrium in Kenneth Arrow and Frank Hahn (1971).

[47] They constructed a simple model in which they combine incentive and selection effects; there are two groups in the population, and each group has two activities (a safe and a risky project). Even though

In the Stiglitz-Weiss models, each borrower borrows the same amount. Another term of the contract that can adjust is the amount lent. Under certain circumstances, reducing the amount lent reduces the risk faced by the bank. Thus, adjustments in the loan size can eliminate credit rationing (H. Milde and John Riley 1988). Again, the issue is not whether one can construct examples in which rationing does not occur, but rather, are there alternative, plausible structures under which it does. In a multiperiod context, Stiglitz and Weiss (1981) have shown that reducing the size of the loan may have an adverse effect on the risks undertaken by the borrower; they undertake projects that in effect, "force" the lender to ante up more money in subsequent periods, if they are to recover their initial loans (see also Martin Hellwig 1977).

In the labor market, discussions have focused on the role of bonding and "job" purchases. That is, a worker could put down a sum of money that he surrenders in the event of being caught shirking. Bonding, it is argued, can alleviate the incentive problems. B. Curtis Eaton and William White (1982), Shapiro and Stiglitz (1984, 1985a), Edward Lazear (1982), and Stoft (1985) have argued against this on several grounds: Firstly, they note that with young individuals having limited capital there is, at least for these workers, incomplete bonding, so that firms are, in fact, concerned with the relationship between wages and productivity. (Though they could borrow to put up the bond, this simply shifts who bears the risk that the worker fails to perform, from the firm to the lender. Though nonvested pensions can be viewed as a form of bonding, it takes individuals a number of years to accumulate enough within their pension fund to serve as a sufficiently effective bond to eliminate the need for firms to be concerned with whether their workers shirk.) Secondly, they note the "double moral hazard" problem, the incentive of the firm to declare that the worker has shirked when he has not. This may be alleviated by making the bond forfeiture go to a third party: again, the empirical relevance may be questioned; moreover such arrangements are sensitive to complicity by two of the parties against the third.[48] Thirdly, they note that many individuals may not have funds to post a bond; to borrow the funds would entail all the adverse effects noted earlier in our discussion of capital markets; and to restrict applicants to those who could finance the bond themselves would have the adverse selection effects noted earlier in connection with collateral.

---

the bank is able to sort individuals perfectly, it cannot raise interest rates, because to do so would induce greater risk taking. Hence, they show that there may be credit rationing at one or both credit contracts. Credit rationing may also arise if individuals differ in more than one dimension, e.g., with respect to risk aversion and wealth.

[48] These problems would also be ameliorated if firms could establish a reputation.

Another mechanism for providing incentives for workers that does not suffer from the "double moral hazard" problem are contests (Lazear and Sherwin Rosen 1981; Green and Nancy Stokey 1983; Nalebuff and Stiglitz 1983b; Sudipto Bhattacharya 1983). They do impose some risk for workers, and workers have to believe that the contests are fairly administered, and that they are evenly matched with their competitors. Intrafirm contests may also have deleterious morale effects.

Similar problems arise with job purchases (or, what is equivalent, in the context of labor turnover, with requiring individuals to pay for their full costs of training).[49]

Advocates of the efficiency wage models claim, in the end, that the central point is that firms do care about quit rates, they do care about the incentives of their workers, and they do use wage policies to affect the net profitability of their employees.

3 Other Imperfect Information Models

The last two decades have seen a burgeoning in imperfect information models. It is worth noting the relationships between the models that are the center of discussion here and some of these other models.

Prices Versus Quantities

Earlier literature (Rothschild and Stiglitz 1976; Akerlof 1976; Michael Spence 1974a) stressed the role of *quantities* in conveying information; the literature this paper is concerned with stresses the role of prices in conveying information.

The quantity of education obtained by an individual conveys information because it is more costly for a less able individual to acquire education than for a more able individual. But it is no more costly for a less able individual to announce that he is willing to work only at a higher wage than a more able individual. How then can workers (informed sellers) use prices to convey information about themselves? There must be some cost to announcing a higher reservation price: The price is the lower probability of being employed (or selling one's commodity). Stiglitz (1976c) and Nalebuff and Stiglitz (1982) have constructed models in which higher-quality workers are willing to face a higher probability of not obtaining a job because their fallback wage is higher. (Wilson [1979, 1980] has constructed a similar model for the product market.)[50] Thus, if there are two types of workers, whose reduced form utility function can be represented by $U_i = U_i(w, g)$, where g is the probability of obtaining a job, then equilibrium may be characterized by both groups obtaining wages commensurate with their abilities (though employers cannot observe them directly), but with the high-ability individuals having a probability g^* just large enough to induce the low-ability not to apply, i.e., letting superscript 1 denote the

---

[49] Some of the "problems" with job purchases explain why the price for jobs would be low (e.g., workers' risk aversion, limitations on workers' access to the capital market), but not why the market for jobs does not clear.

[50] Similarly the probability of consummating a deal may serve as a self-selection device within a bargaining model.

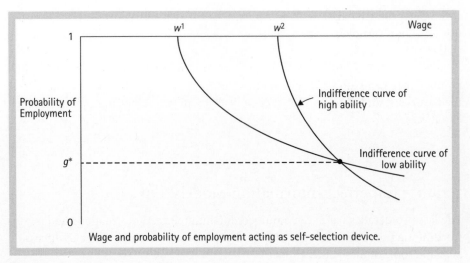

Fig. 15.

low-ability workers

$$U^1(w^1, 1) = U^1(w^2, g^*)$$

(See Figure 15).[51, 52]

In the simple models analyzing the dependence of quality on price, quantity variables are not observable. (There is no variable, like education, to reveal the individual's true ability.) But all that is required for wages/prices/interest rates to play

[51] Technically this analysis should be contrasted with that of Rothschild and Stiglitz (1976), where each firm (uninformed agent) sets the price and quantity; here firms set only the price; the unemployment rate is determined as part of the equilibrium. This is also true of the Stiglitz-Weiss (1986) model of the capital market.

Some questions have been raised about the relevance of this particular model for the description of labor markets; it may have more to do with the number of hours worked by a Harley Street doctor than it does with unemployment among the low skilled. It is important to note, however, that in this model "unemployment" does not have the same interpretation that it does in the national income statistics: It means that the individual is not employed by others. For the low skilled, this may indeed correspond to unemployment; for the high skilled, it may correspond to self-employment.

[52] This model has been extended by Nalebuff and Stiglitz (1982) to the case where individuals can apply for several jobs. In that case, the nature of the equilibrium depends critically on whether contracts are binding—whether once a job has been accepted, the worker can quit when he is offered a better job. If contracts are binding, the opportunity cost of accepting a low-wage job is the foregone possibility of a high-wage job, the likelihood of which depends on both the job offers of different firms and the behavior of other individuals (how high they set their reservation wages). They show that there exists a particular wage distribution, such that when all workers rationally set their reservation wages, the cost-per-efficiency unit of the firm is the same for all firms. (In their equilibrium, while the quality of those who apply at each wage are, in fact, different, it is only the wage-cum-unemployment rate that distinguishes them: in all other respects the workers look the same. Moreover, at each wage, except the lowest, there is an excess supply of applicants.)

By contrast, if the first firm to enter the market had simply hired at what it thought was the efficiency wage, because it would have hired only lower-ability workers, those with reservation wages below the efficiency wage, the "new" efficiency-wage schedule facing the later entrant would lie above the old one, for $w > w^*$, and hence there would be an advantage to being late. See Lewis Guasch and Weiss (1980a).

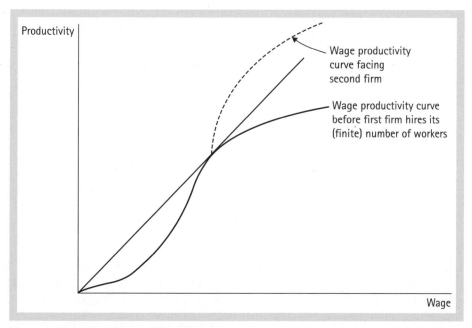

Fig. 16. The Advantages of Being Late

a role in conveying quality information given whatever variables that are observable is that there remains some residual uncertainty of either the adverse selection or moral hazard sort.[53]

Information Revealing Prices in the Capital Market

There is a closely related literature to that discussed here, where prices also convey information. In capital markets, the price at which a security sells may convey information concerning the expected return of the security (or the likelihood of the occurrence of various states). (See Green 1973; Grossman and Stiglitz 1976, 1980a; Margaret Bray 1981; Roy Radner 1979.) In structure, these models are most like the Akerlof "Lemons" (1970) model, in which both sellers and buyers act nonstrategically: They take prices, and the information conveyed by the price, as given. They differ in that, while there is only one seller (and usually only one buyer) of any particular automobile, or any particular person's labor services, there are many potential buyers

[53] Thus, models in which there are only limited sources of imperfect information may be very misleading. For instance, if individuals differ only in one dimension, then education may serve to sort individuals perfectly: There will be no residual imperfect information, and hence no need to lower wages to improve the mix of laborers. But if individuals differ in several dimensions, then education alone will not suffice to provide complete information. Similarly, in the capital market, if borrowers differ only in one dimension, and there is no moral hazard problem, there may exist a fully revealing self-selection equilibrium, and there will be, as a consequence, no role for credit rationing. But if borrowers differ in several dimensions and/or there are moral hazard problems, there may exist credit rationing. Though self-selection devices may reveal some information, they will not be perfectly revealing.

and sellers of any particular security. (Indeed, in the absence of transactions costs, with risk aversion and imperfectly correlated securities, virtually everyone is a buyer or seller.) Thus, while the price of a car sold at an auction reflects the valuation placed on it by those who value it most highly, in a security market, those who believe that a security is overpriced will sell it short, and their beliefs are, accordingly, reflected in the market equilibrium price.

IV APPLICATIONS

1 Implications for Macroeconomics

These models have direct and important implications for macroeconomics.[54]

This section is divided into four subsections, dealing respectively with labor markets, capital markets, product markets, and the relationship of these theories to other recently advanced theories.

Labor Markets

The fact that these theories have yielded competitive market equilibrium in which wages do not fall in the face of unemployment, in which there is an equilibrium level unemployment, immediately suggests the possibility that these theories may provide an important part of the explanation of involuntary unemployment. What I wish to do here is to explain why some economists find these models more persuasive than at least several of the competing theories, and to present what appear to be at the present time the major issues, both the criticism and the defenses, pointing to certain unsettled controversies.

(a) The Pattern and Form of Unemployment

A theory purporting to explain cyclical fluctuations in unemployment should not only show that it can generate unemployment, but also explain the pattern and form of unemployment. This efficiency-wage theories do.[55] Less productive workers— those for whom the minimum wage per efficiency unit is below some critical level—cannot get jobs, though they might at higher levels of effective demand. (These

---

[54] It is important to emphasize that although we believe that these models provide an important part of the microfoundations for macroeconomics, they do not provide the whole story: Other models (many of them also based on considerations of imperfect information) are required.

This section owes much to the comments of Bruce Greenwald and Larry Summers.

[55] This should be contrasted with the standard implicit contract theories (e.g., Costas Azariadis 1983; Grossman and Oliver Hart 1981b; for recent surveys, see Azariadis and Stiglitz 1983; and Hart 1983) which, at best, provide an explanation of work sharing (see Stiglitz 1986b). Arnott, Arthur Hosios, and Stiglitz (1983) incorporate some aspects of efficiency-wage theory in their analysis of labor contracts with costly labor mobility.

may include young workers, part-time workers, or others for whom the total surplus from work is small, so that the no-shirking wage, at any unemployment level, is high.)

Moreover, there is no work sharing, with the associated income reductions, for this would simply reduce the quality (productivity) of the labor force. In the incentive efficiency-wage model, it is the total surplus (the amount by which the value of wage payments exceeds the foregone leisure) that determines whether workers shirk; in the turnover model, it is the total surplus (relative to that offered by other firms) that determines whether a worker quits; in the selection models, it is again the total surplus that determines the individual's choice of one job over another. Work sharing reduces the surplus available to any individual, and thus adversely affects the effort (quality, labor turnover). See, for example, Arnott, Hosios, and Stiglitz (1983) or Michael Hoel and Bent Vale (1986).

(b) Criticisms

Critics have raised several objections, concerning both the quantitative significance of the efficiency-wage effects and the consistency of the theory with certain observed macroeconomic phenomena.

1. Can efficiency wage theory explain involuntary unemployment? Perhaps the most widely cited criticism is that, unless efficiency wage considerations are important in all sectors, the theory cannot explain unemployment; that is, if there is some sector (such as agriculture) where workers can be paid on a piece rate basis, and the piece rate is flexible, then that sector should absorb all workers laid off from those sectors where efficiency-wage considerations are important. Thus, efficiency-wage theory might be able to explain wage differentials (the secondary labor market), but not unemployment. (Note that this objection can be raised against implicit contract theory explanations of unemployment as well.)[56]

Several of the efficiency-wage models have attempted to incorporate a flexible wage sector. In Stiglitz (1974a), for instance, the agricultural sector has flexible wages, while efficiency-wage considerations are important in the industrial sector. Individuals must choose in which sector to locate (mobility between the sectors is not costless and instantaneous). Unemployment in the urban sector is such as to equilibrate expected income (of the marginal migrant) in that sector to that in the rural sector.[57]

---

[56] Including theories of staggered contracts (Taylor 1980), which need to explain why labor is not absorbed into those sectors whose contracts are up for negotiation.

[57] John Harris and Michael Todaro (1970) have developed a similar analysis to explain urban unemployment in LDCs. The major difference between the Harris-Todaro model and the Stiglitz model is that in the former, the wage is exogenous and in the latter—as in all the work under examination here—it is endogenous. Robert Hall (1975) has used a similar model to explain differences in unemployment rates in different urban areas.

Jeremy Bulow and Larry Summers (1985) assume that individuals can search for a (high-wage) job only while unemployed, and thus even if individuals could have obtained a low-wage job, they choose not to do so.[58]

Greenwald has provided several alternative explanations for why individuals may not accept a low-wage job, based on information theoretic considerations: Accepting a low-wage job may convey information about the individual's ability; with high-ability individual's expecting to get a "good" job sooner than a low-ability individual, an individual who readily accepts a low-wage job signals that he thinks of himself as low-ability, and this signal will lower his future wages.[59] Moreover, accepting a job creates an information asymmetry—the firm's new employer will know more about the individual's ability than other prospective employers. Just as Akerlof showed that these information asymmetries lead to thin markets for used cars, Greenwald has shown that they result in thin markets for "used labor."[60] Finally, he has attempted to relate unemployment to capital market imperfections, which themselves can be explained by information theoretic concerns. There are, in general, some training costs that firms must bear when they hire a worker; moreover, hiring a worker represents a risky investment. With imperfect capital markets, firms cannot divest themselves of this risk; as a result, the implicit cost of capital may be very high in a recession, and hence it is possible that in a recession, firms are willing to hire workers only if the lifetime wages are lower than they would be if the worker were hired in a later period, when the risks faced by the firm are less.

Critics might say at this juncture, "Aha, so unemployment is really voluntary." We think little is gained from a semantic debate over whether unemployment is, in this sense, voluntary or involuntary. What is critical is (a) in the market equilibrium, some individuals, with a given set of characteristics, have a distinctly higher level of (expected) utility than other similar individuals; (b) the equilibrium has, for one reason or another, some individuals in the unemployment pool who, under other circumstances, would be working; and (c) the market equilibrium is not (constrained) Pareto efficient.

2. Are there alternative mechanisms for ensuring quality? A second criticism is that if these efficiency-wage considerations were really important, alternative mechanisms would be found that would not be anywhere near as socially costly as the

---

[58] Similarly, Arnott, Hosios and Stiglitz (1985) assume that the costs of search for the unemployed and the employed may be different and show that optimal contracts may entail some individuals being laid off even if it means a finite probability of being unemployed for a period.

[59] As is often the case, there may be another equilibrium in which accepting a low-wage job does not signal one's ability: When there are significant transactions costs, it is more plausible that the acceptance of a low-wage job will serve as a signal. Alternatively, the argument to be given next serves to explain why accepting a job would lower one's lifetime wage prospects quite apart from signaling considerations: Signaling considerations would then serve to strengthen the magnitude of the effect of the acceptance of a low-wage job on lifetime income.

[60] This result depends, in part, on the firm's not being able to commit itself to paying higher wages in the future. Those commitments themselves are, at best conditional on the firm's surviving. Thus, a worker who accepts a low wage now from a firm in bad financial straits with the promise of a high wage in the future takes, in effect, an equity position in the firm. The reasons why workers may not be willing to do so have been set forth in Greenwald, Stiglitz and Weiss (1984).

unemployment to which it gives rise. There are several answers to this objection: Firstly, the fact of the matter is that firms are concerned about the quality of their labor force and their rates of turnover. Secondly, we have already detailed some reasons why at least some of the proposed alternatives that would eliminate unemployment (credit rationing) may be ineffective. Some of these arguments may hold with more force for some groups of workers or for some industries than for others. Thus, consider the argument that bonding is not employed because workers have insufficient capital. This argument seems more applicable to young workers and to low-wage (unskilled) workers than to older workers, and therefore might suggest that the effort-efficiency wage model is more relevant for these workers than for other groups of laborers.[61]

Finally, we note that because of the presence of the important externalities discussed in Part 1.5., the private costs of pursuing, say, high-wage policies (leading to unemployment) and of not employing alternative strategies of sorting and providing incentives may be much less than the social costs. This has been stressed by Akerlof and Janet Yellen (1985).[62] In particular, if firms are risk averse[63] then they may not revise their wages or may not change other policies even in the presence of some disturbance to the economy which leads to an excess supply of labor, even if were they to do so would be welfare enhancing.

3. Can efficiency wage theory explain nominal as well as real wage rigidities? Although the criticism that these models provide an explanation of real-wage rigidities, not of nominal-wage rigidities, is valid against most versions of the efficiency-wage models—as it is against most versions of implicit contract theory (where, in principle, contracts should be indexed)—it is worth nothing that the labor-turnover efficiency-wage model is also consistent with money-wage rigidities: The turnover rate facing any firm depends on the wages set by other firms; if each firm believes that other firms will leave the wages unchanged in nominal terms, it pays it to leave its wage unchanged in nominal terms. The Akerlof (1984) morale model is also consistent with nominal-wage rigidities.

4. Can efficiency wage theory explain rationing among several groups? Simpler versions of the efficiency-wage theory yielded rationing for only one group in the population. For all other groups, either no one was hired or there was full employment. But with more general specifications, with productivity depending on (each group's) unemployment rate then in equilibrium, there may be unemployment among several groups. And even if there were a continuum of groups, with only one

---

[61] This argument was put forward by Robert Hall in his discussion of Yellen's survey of efficiency-wage models at the San Francisco meetings of the American Economic Association, December 1984.

[62] This is in fact a general property of economies that are not (constrained) Pareto efficient. There then exist large classes of perturbations to the economy that effect pareto improvements. If the firm sets its wage in a privately optimal way, there exist some pertubations of this wage that have a second order effect on the profits of the firm but have a first order effect on the welfare of other agents in the economy. See Greenwald and Stiglitz (1986a).

[63] Again, the fact that firms behave in a risk averse manner can be explained in terms of certain capital market imperfections which, in turn, can be related to imperfect information.

group rationed, the discontinuity in utility (between similar groups) would remain. It is this discontinuity—with similar individuals being treated discretely differently—which is so much at odds with standard competitive theory.

5. Can efficiency wage theory explain wage and employment dynamics? The final criticism[64] is that while the efficiency-wage theory may provide an explanation of the "natural unemployment rate," it does not provide an explanation of cyclical movements in real wages.

The criticism that the efficiency-wage theories have yet to provide a dynamic theory is, for the most part, valid: The models constructed to date have been static. At a heuristic level, these models do provide an explanation for why when there is a sudden shift in, say, the demand for labor, it is not quickly reflected in a change in the wage, but rather is reflected in a decrease in employment; the new equilibrium may entail unemployment, but even if in the long run equilibrium entails full employment of labor, the adjustment process may entail unemployment as part of the transition.

The intuitive reason for this is easy to see. Under a variety of conditions, the quality of the workers obtained (or their productivity on the job) depends on the wage paid by the given firm relative to that of other firms. Thus, if the different firms in the economy do not simultaneously adjust their wages, given the high wages of other firms, it will not pay any single firm to lower its wage very much.[65]

Our analysis of dynamics stands in marked contrast to the standard kind of dynamics, which simply assumes slowness in the adjustment of wages and prices, and thus derives the transitional unemployment as a consequence of the ad hoc dynamic adjustment assumptions.

Consider, for instance, the staggered wage contract model (Taylor 1980). The *assumption* of nonsynchronous long-term contracts explains why wages at any particular firm do not fall instantaneously in the face of a decrease in the demand for labor, and why average wages fall only gradually. But in the absence of some kind of efficiency-wage story, staggered contracts cannot explain the persistence, even for a short while, of unemployment: At the first instance at which a contract comes up for renewal, the wage should fall to the market-clearing level.

Moreover, the explanation of the process by which wages change is markedly different from the conventional story. We have argued that in general the quality of the labor force (its productivity) depends on the unemployment rate as well as the wage. At higher unemployment levels, the efficiency wage may be lower. For a

[64] This list of criticisms is not meant to be exhaustive. Another objection is that these models require not only that productivity increase with wages, but also that there be a range of wages over which increases in wages lead to more than proportionate increases in productivity. This objection has been dealt with where we showed how several simple models exhibiting these properties can be constructed. It then becomes an empirical question whether in practice the wage-productivity relationship has the required shape. Unfortunately, there is insufficient empirical evidence to date to provide a convincing answer.

[65] The analysis is somewhat more subtle than this suggests: Each firm's wage is dependent not only on other firms' wages, but also on the unemployment rate; nevertheless, in at least some versions of the efficiency-wage model, the unemployment effect is dominated by the wage effect, and wages do not fall, or fall only slowly in the face of a downward shift in the demand curve for labor.

variety of reasons, firms may be slow to fire workers, and thus the unemployment rate increases only slowly in response to a decrease in the "long-run" demand for workers. In such circumstances, the fall in the wage rate can be viewed both as a consequence of the increased unemployment and as mitigating the extent to which unemployment increases. But in this theory the wage does not fall because of the "pressure" of excess supply directly on the labor market, but only because of the indirect effect, through the effect on the efficiency wage.

Fixed Price Models and Efficiency Wage Theories

One of the reasons for interest in the efficiency-wage theories is that they provide an explanation of wage and price rigidities, which play such a central role in the fixed wage-price models that have enjoyed such popularity during the past decade. Though the two approaches are, to that extent complementary,[66] the efficiency-wage models can also be seen as providing a critique of the fixed-wage models, or at least of the relevance of those models for policy purposes. Though wages do not fall to a market-clearing level, government policies can affect the level of wages and thus the equilibrium level of employment. (In contrast, the fixed-wage price models simply assume that wages and prices will remain unchanged.)

2 Implications for Development Economics

We noted earlier that much of the recent interest in the unemployment consequences of the dependence of productivity on wages originated in the development literature, where the relationship was attributed to nutritional considerations. Since then a large literature has explored a variety of other causes and consequences of the wage-productivity nexus within LDCs.[67]

Mirrlees (1975) and Stiglitz (1976b) showed that wage-productivity relations of the form depicted in Figure 2 would give rise, even within utilitarian families (maximizing the sum of the utility of the members of the family) to inequality in consumption; some members would receive a low consumption level, others a high consumption level; those with a low consumption level would have a low productivity. What they consumed would exceed their marginal product, but be less than their marginal product plus a pro rata share of the rents. Conversely for the high consumers. Indeed, even if the family is Rawlsian (maximizes the welfare of the worst off individual) there may be consumption inequality.

Because productivity depends on consumption, individuals with landholdings will be more productive than landless workers, and will, accordingly, receive higher wages. Dasgupta and Ray (1986a, 1987) have explored the implications of inequality in land ownership for wages and output. In particular, they note that the very poor, those

[66] For an explicit attempt to integrate the two approaches, see Karl Moene (1985).

[67] In this section, we focus our discussion on the consequences of the nutritional-wage productivity nexus for LDCs. For a discussion of alternative explanations, see Stiglitz (1982a, 1974a).

with very small landholdings, may be completely excluded from the market because their minimum wage costs per efficiency unit is too high. In their model, whether the economy is in an unemployment regime or a full employment regime will depend on the aggregate land supply (relative to the labor supply), in effect, on whether the Walrasian wage is below or above the efficiency wage; it may also depend on the distribution of land. A land reform may thus have a significant effect on national output.

The dependence of productivity on wages in the urban sector results in urban wages being set at levels in excess of the rural wage. This, by the familiar Harris-Todaro migration mechanism (Todaro 1968, 1969; Harris and Todaro 1970) and its generalizations (Stiglitz 1974a; Gary Fields 1975; Raaj Sah and Stiglitz 1987, 1985c), results in urban unemployment. As noted earlier (Part 1.5 above) the wage and employment levels set by private firms do not maximize national income (and are not Pareto efficient). On the other hand, even if the government could directly control the urban wage, it would not set it at the rural wage: Some level of unemployment is optimal. Moreover, policy prescriptions to reduce the real wage indirectly, through increasing the prices of commodities, are, at best, misguided. For private firms would respond, say, to an increase in the price of food by increasing the wage. Indeed, if productivity is more sensitive to the consumption of food than to the consumption of other commodities, government should subsidize the consumption of food.[68] In this context, specific and ad valorem wage subsidies have distinctly different effects on wage setting and employment policies. Because there are two objectives that the government wishes to achieve (the correct wage level and the correct urban employment level), it requires two instruments; the two forms of wage subsidies/taxes provide the requisite instruments.

The wage-productivity nexus also has important implications for the determination of the shadow wage of labor (particularly in the context of models with Harris-Todaro and related migration mechanisms). The opportunity cost of labor is not zero (in spite of the presence of unemployment) or even the rural wage. In some central cases, the shadow wage is the urban wage, independent of attitudes toward future generations; in other cases, it lies between the urban wage and the rural wage (see Stiglitz 1987j).

3 Further Applications

The dependence of quality on price has a large number of other implications, one of which we briefly note here.

---

[68] Firms would, in such circumstances, find it in their interests to subsidize the consumption of food; but unless the subsidy is provided for on-premise consumption, workers could resell the subsidized food, and the firm would thus not directly gain from the food subsidy.

For an analysis of optimal taxation and subsidies in the presence of productivity effects, see Sah and Stiglitz (1987).

Technological Change and Competitive Entry

The fact that a lower price is associated with lower quality has important implications for technological change. Normally, we argue that if a firm develops a cheaper way of making a mousetrap it will be able to undercut its rivals, and thus to capture the whole market for itself. When prices convey information, the firm may not be able to undercut its rivals; lowering the price may simply lead potential customers to believe that it is selling a lower-quality mousetrap. (Farrell 1984, 1986, has discussed the entry barriers that arise in these models.)

Concluding Remarks

The observation that quality may depend on price (productivity on wages; default probability on interest rates) has provided a rich mine for economic theorists: A simple modification of the basic assumptions results in a profound alteration of many of the basic conclusions of the standard paradigm. The Law of Supply and Demand has been repealed. The Law of the Single Price has been repealed. The Fundamental Theorem of Welfare Economics has been shown not to be valid.

More than that, the theories that we describe here provide the basis of progress toward a unification of macroeconomics and microeconomics. They provide an explanation of unemployment and credit rationing, derived from basic microeconomic principles. It is a theory in which the extensive idleness that periodically confronts society's resources, human and capital, is seen as but the most obvious example of market failures that prevasively and persistently distort the allocation of resources.

Several caveats should, however, be borne in mind. Firstly, the repeal of the Law of Supply and Demand (and the Law of the Single Price) is a selective repeal: We have not contended that equilibrium is never described by the equality of demand and supply, only that it need not be, and will not be in some important circumstances.

Secondly, though the basic outlines of the general theory appear now to be well established, there remain several important extensions and developments. The models presented here are, for the most part, static; it is imperative to develop an explicitly dynamic model if these theories are to provide part of the foundations of a theory explaining cyclical fluctuations in employment. Moreover, on several occasions we contrasted efficiency-wage theory with implicit contract theory, arguing that efficiency-wage theory provides a far better explanation of unemployment than does implicit contract theory. In fact, individuals do have long-term implicit contract relationships with their employers; these relationships are affected in fundamental ways by efficiency-wage considerations. The integration of implicit contract theory and efficiency-wage theory thus is a second important topic for a research agenda.[69]

---

[69] See Arnott, Hosios, and Stiglitz (1983) for one such attempt.

We have also noted that the problems with which we have been concerned are mitigated, but not eliminated, by monitoring and bonding (among other instruments that may be available to the firm). The limitations on monitoring and bonding have, however, received only limited theoretical scrutiny. Finally, we have, for the most part, analyzed incentive models and selection models in isolation from each other.[70] We have noted, however, that there may be important interactions between the two, and these require further study.

Thirdly, we have focused our attention on the burgeoning theoretical literature (but have made no pretense of being even complete within the scope of the topics covered). There is a need for extensive empirical testing.[71] We hope, in fact, that this survey will spur continuation of efforts in that direction.

This paper has, however, attempted to show how similar ideas have found application in the analysis of labor, capital, and product markets. These models provide an explanation of several phenomena within these markets that cannot be easily explained within the more conventional paradigm.

[70] An exception is the Stiglitz and Weiss (1986) study.

[71] There have, however, been numerous studies addressing particular aspects of the theories described in this paper. For an early investigation of the price-quality relationship, see Gabor and Granger (1966). For a recent examination of the empirical evidence on whether the labor market clears, see Thomas Kniesner and Arthur Goldsmith (1985). For a recent discussion of the relationship between productivity and wages, see, for example, James Medoff and Katharine Abraham (1981). Macroeconomic analyses of the relationship between unemployment and productivity include James Rebitzer (1987) and Weisskopf, Bowles, and Gordon (1983).

There is a growing literature attempting to test the credit-rationing models. See, for instance, Charles Calomiris and R. Glenn Hubbard (1985), Leonard Nakamura (1985), and P. Kugler (1985).

PART III

THEORY OF INCENTIVES AND ECONOMIC ORGANIZATION

Introduction to Part III

As we noted in the Introduction to this volume, the problem of incentives *is* an information problem. It is remarkable how economists have long tried to discuss incentives, without explicitly discussing the economics of information. I shall have much more to say about the general theory of incentives in Volume II, where I elaborate at greater length on these topics. For now, I want to briefly discuss the origins and key issues raised by these papers.

I noted in the Preface to the *Selected Works* how some of the simplistic models had helped bring to the fore the deficiencies in the standard paradigm—corporate finance did not matter, discrimination could not exist. Cheung's discussion of sharecropping (1968), long criticized as an inefficient system of land tenancy, provided another example. Sharecropping was viewed as inefficient because the worker received only 50 percent (or so) of his/her crop. It was as if s/he confronted a 50 percent tax rate. Cheung argued—not to worry. With perfect information, the landlord would specify how much labor the worker would have to work; the "complete" contract would therefore be totally non-distorting.

The problem was that Cheung ignored the very reason for sharecropping. If it was costless to monitor workers, they would have been hired on a wage contract; landlords were far better able to absorb the risk of output and price fluctuations. But wage contracts required heavy investments in monitoring, and it was easier to monitor output than input. One could make an inference—an imperfect inference—about output from input. The optimal sharecropping contract balanced the cost of forcing the worker to bear risk with the benefit of improved incentives. A full rent contract had the tenant bearing all of the risk but with perfect incentives (ignoring problems of default). This was a simple insight, and my paper embedded this in a simple general equilibrium model, in which markets for land and labor simultaneously cleared through *contract* equilibrium.[1]

I concluded the paper by pointing out that these results had far more general applications, for example to the modern theory of the firm, paralleling the contemporaneous work of Steve Ross on principals and agents. (In my model, the landlord was the principal, the tenant the agent.)[2] A quite similar analysis applies to the design of labor incentive contracts: workers can get paid a high piece rate (wages heavily dependent on performance), which provides high powered incentives, but

---

[1] The paper was thus the first paper to begin the formal analysis of contracts, and contract equilibrium.

[2] Ross's paper (1973) was published shortly before mine, though mine was written a half-decade before publication. Ross's model was partial equilibrium. The principle agent vocabulary which he introduced has proven to be very useful.

also imposes high risk on workers. The optimal contract reflects a balancing of risk and incentives (Stiglitz 1975b).

I had limited myself to simple, linear contracts—though sharecropping contracts are in fact typically linear.[3] The subsequent literature has considered more complex settings and more complex contracts. Here, I want to call attention to three issues.[4]

The first is that one may be able to provide better incentives (for any given level of risk) by using *contests*, basing pay on relative performance. Consider a situation where a task might be easier or harder for all market participants, but where the employer could not ascertain which was the case. A fixed reward structure would overpay workers in one case and underpay them in another. When pay depends on relative performance, when the task is easier, output (for any given level of effort) will be high for all. In some cases (see Chapter 15), we showed that one could obtain perfect incentives with no risk. In other cases, we showed that the best incentive systems entailed punishing the worst performer—paying everyone else the same (Nalebuff and Stiglitz 1983b). The fear of being the worst individual can provide strong incentives, but, if there are large numbers of individuals competing, with each in an equal position, then the penalty is faced relatively seldom.

In fact, while firms frequently defend executive pay based on stock options as important in providing strong incentives, the analysis questions these arguments; for stock options impose high risk, with rewards largely contingent on overall movements of the stock markets, which depend on interest rates and other factors largely out of the control of the executives. In the 1990s, executives were paid handsomely for the run up of the stock market—having little to do with the efforts of the executives. Basing pay on relative performance would provide strong incentives with much lower risk: it would provide a far better estimate of the contribution of the executives; but relatively few companies employ such schemes.[5]

Secondly, there are many things that an employer can do to enhance the efforts of his workers or that a landlord can do to enhance the efforts of his tenant. By providing subsidized lunches at work, the employer makes it less likely that the worker will eat off-site; and this may mean that s/he is less likely to take a long lunch hour. An employer may restrict an employee from having a second job, which will

[3] Indeed, typically they entail just a fixed fraction of output—there is no fixed payment from or to the landlord. Though there are some special utility functions in which linear contracts are optimal, in general, optimal contracts are not linear. If farmers can trade output with each other (without landlords observing these trades) then there will have to be a single sharecropping rate (within the trading community) (see Allen 1985).

[4] Part II, including the introductory essay, explores these issues in greater detail.

[5] There are other grounds for doubting the validity of these self-serving arguments. A closer look at the relationship between compensation and performance shows that compensation is not closely related to performance; when stocks perform poorly—as they did in 2000 and 2001—the firm simply changes the form of compensation or resets the terms of the options. Moreover, there are ways of rewarding managers with just as strong incentives but lower overall tax burden. Finally, it is unpersuasive that a manager receiving, say, US$5 million a year is holding back on his/her effort simply because his/her pay does not increase with the firm's performance; and it is questionable whether a firm would really want managers who announced that they would only "give their all" under these circumstances. For a more extensive discussion of these issues, see Part II and Stiglitz (1987c, 2003c).

leave him/her with less energy to devote to his/her primary employer. A landlord that subsidizes fertilizer or better seeds may increase the marginal returns to effort, thereby inducing the tenant to work harder.[6] This helps explain the interlinkage of land and credit markets in developing countries. By the same token, there are intertemporal linkages—the threat of punishment in a later period can help induce better behavior in earlier periods. And these interlinkages limit both the extent of efficient decentralizability of the economy and the scope of competition.[7]

Thirdly, there are costs to sharecropping and similar compensation schemes— individuals are forced to bear risks, and if individuals are risk averse, this lowers their welfare. The extent of reliance on these output measures depends on the extent to which inputs (effort) can be (accurately) measured; but it is costly to measure inputs. Often, peers can do a better job of monitoring (at less cost) than bosses. And this implies that it may be desirable to organize production where *peer monitoring* plays a central role. For instance, when pay is based on team performance, then each member of the team has an incentive to ensure that other members of the team work hard. By contrast, standard economic theory has argued against team rewards, since in standard theory, each individual has an incentive to free ride on the efforts of others. (Of course, there have to be ways by which members of the team can discipline those who try to free ride, e.g. through social sanctions or by reporting shirking to the boss.)

Peer monitoring plays a central role in one of the most successful social innovations of recent years: the micro credit schemes, first initiated by the Grameen Bank in Bangladesh, but which have since spread around the world. Chapter 15 was written shortly after the Grameen scheme had begun and long before it drew the attention which it since has deservedly received. I sought to provide the theoretical foundations, explaining their remarkable success in achieving high repayment rates.

Given the high costs both of monitoring and of incentive schemes, it is natural that there are attempts to reduce those costs. One of the important sets of innovations has been those that reduce monitoring costs. The assembly line meant that it was easy to detect any worker who did not keep up the specified pace of work. One of the benefits of just-in-time production was that the consequences of problems in production could be more easily observed and corrected. (As it was sometimes put, lowering the level of water in a stream exposed the rough stones (Braverman and Stiglitz 1986b).)

In many contexts, emphasis is placed on processes: it may be easier to observe production processes than to measure accurately either inputs or outputs. And it may be that by specifying processes one can indirectly control (imperfectly) inputs. For instance, part of the reason that some of the seeds of the green revolution may have been so successful is that they may have had less tolerance to a failure to weed; because the marginal return to weeding was accordingly higher, workers were induced

---

[6] These ideas are explored in a series of papers with Braverman (1982, 1986a, b) and in the collection of papers in Braverman et al. (1993). The implications of intertemporal linkages are explored in Stiglitz and Weiss (1983). Arnott and I explored interlinkages in moral hazard and insurance in Arnott and Stiglitz (1986, 1990).

[7] See the discussion in Chapter 3, above.

to weed more thoroughly. The level of inputs of labor may thereby have increased; some of the increased output is really attributable to this increased (unobservable) input.[8]

Just as insurance provided the natural setting in which to examine selection problems, so too in the area of incentives. The effect of insurance on incentives to avoid accidents has long been noted and is referred to as "moral hazard." Of course, if insurance firms could monitor what individuals did, they would relate premia with actions, and individuals would have appropriate incentives to avoid accidents, since they would balance out the marginal benefit with the marginal cost. But effort is not observable, and insurance firms induce effort by providing incomplete insurance, so the individual has some incentive to avoid the accident. (With full insurance, there is no incentive to engage in accident avoidance.) There is a trade-off: the less complete their insurance, the more incentives individuals have to avoid accidents, but the greater the risk they have to bear. "The Basic Analytics of Moral Hazard" shows the formal similarity between screening models and moral hazard models and describes the competitive market equilibrium. Most striking, even in the simplest formulation, we show that all the basic functions (the indifference curves, the iso-profit curves) in the natural space of benefits and premia exhibit non-convexities. As a result, there may be discontinuities in behavior and in equilibrium, and there may be positive profits. Because analogous incentive problems arise in all markets, the convexity assumptions which play such an important role in standard economics no longer seem plausible. (The full implications of this have yet to be adequately explored.)[9]

The remaining two papers of the section deal with incentives and decision making in organizations. In "Credit Markets and the Control of Capital," I use the tools of information economics to address the classical problem of corporate governance— indeed, for the first time to put the issue on sound theoretical foundations. The paper sets the issue as a combination of a multiple principal/agent problem and a freerider (public good) problem. Imperfect information leads to the delegation of decision making to managers. (Hence the separation of ownership and control.) At the same time, imperfect information makes it impossible for owners to know whether the manager has taken actions that are in his/her best interests. In modern corporations, there are many stakeholders. Creditors, suppliers of equity, and other stakeholders of the firm all wish the manager to take actions which advance their interests (and not just his/her own interests). The interests of these different groups do not perfectly coincide. Bond holders want the firm to engage in safe activities so that it can repay what is owned. Equity owners receive the residual returns, so they are more willing

---

[8] In judicial proceedings, there is a great deal of concern about procedural justice, partly because it is easier to ascertain that the procedures have been conducted in a fair way than it is to ascertain that a particular decision is fair; the assumption is that if the proceedings are fair, it is more likely that outcomes will be fair. By the same token, in bureaucracies, where both inputs and outputs are hard to observe, there is greater reliance on ensuring that procedures are followed.

[9] For instance, it implies that random taxation may be optimal (see Arnott and Stiglitz 1988b). See also Stiglitz (2002b).

for the firm to undertake risks which increase expected returns sufficiently. Legally, decision making resides in the shareholders; but in modern corporations shareholders are diverse. With no shareholder having more than a small fraction of the shares, none has much of an incentive to monitor; any gains benefit all shareholders. This is the public good nature of good management. Good corporate governance involves a combination of monitoring and incentives: designing incentives such that managers act in the interests of the various stakeholders, and monitoring to assess whether he has done so. Banks, because they bear less risk, can take a larger stake in a given firm, and hence face less strongly the freerider problems confronting equity. They also have an important instrument not available (or not so easily available) to others: they can withdraw their credit, forcing the firm into a crisis (bankruptcy).[10] Equity owners that do no like the actions of the firm cannot withdraw their capital; they can only sell it to others. They can try to change management, but this is a difficult and slow process. We argue, accordingly, that banks, while they do not have residual rights of control, actually often play a more active role in control than shareholders.

At the time I wrote this piece, I had hoped that there was enough coincidence of interests between shareholders and banks that banks could play an important role in ensuring that managers work in the interests of suppliers of capital, in general: neither, for instance, wanted the firm to undertake large risks which would significantly increase the probability of bankruptcy. But in circumscribing the behavior of managers (not, for instance, to take risks which endanger the risk of repayment), they do not necessarily ensure that managers act in the interests of (especially minority) shareholders; managers may still be able to grab for themselves a significant fraction of the residual. Indeed, in *the Roaring 90s* (2003c), I showed how banks had often colluded with management against the interests of shareholders.[11]

Accounting is an important part of monitoring, and the economics of information provided, in a sense, the intellectual foundations of the modern discipline of accounting. Indeed, without the development of good accounting, it is arguable that modern capitalism, with diverse ownership, could not have evolved (see Greenwald and Stiglitz 1992). But information systems are designed for particular purposes. An information system can provide information to tax collectors, to investors, or to managers; a firm might want true information about how profitable each of its various activities are, but may want to exaggerate reported profits to entice investors and minimize reported profits to reduce tax liabilities (Stiglitz and Wolfson 1988). A firm might, accordingly, like to have three systems of accounts, but both securities regulators and tax authorities frown on firms keeping multiple accounts. One of the

---

[10] This is one of the reasons that lending is short term, even in situations where long term contracts might be better from the perspective of risk sharing. See Rey and Stiglitz (1993). More broadly, banks have a comparative advantage over securities markets, in terms of their ability to monitor (see Stiglitz 1992a).

[11] Some argued that in spite of these limitations, the threat of take-overs would ensure that managers maximized shareholder value, acting in accordance with the interests of all shareholders. In Stiglitz (1972c) I began a research program showing that that was not the case.

financial "innovations" of the 1970s and 1980s was that firms found ways, within the law, to manipulate accounts to show lower taxable profits; one of the "achievements" of the 1980s and 1990s was firms extended these techniques to manipulate accounts to show higher profits to investors—and with executive compensation often tied to stock price, and stock price often closely linked to reported profits, many firms had strong incentives to implement such schemes. In some cases, they found ways of doing so without unduly increasing tax liabilities; but in other cases, higher taxation was simply one of the prices one had to pay to pump up reported profits and compensation.

The experiences of the 1990s showed convincingly that the problem of corporate governance, of inducing managers to act in the interests of shareholders, had not yet been solved.[12] Several of the papers in later volumes[13] not only address the manifestations of these problems, but also describe the incentives of (and opportunities for) managers to increase asymmetries of information.

In "Human Fallibility and Economic Organization" I explore the implications of information imperfections for the design of decision making in organizations, a topic also explored in greater depth in Volume II. The general problem is how to aggregate the knowledge and beliefs of different individuals—when they have different knowledge and beliefs. In Part IV, I explore how the price system "aggregates" information. But inside organizations, decisions typically get made by voting. Sometimes differences in views reflect differences in preferences; but often they simply reflect differences in judgments, and it is this case that we explore here and in Volume II. Some think that a project will be successful, others do not. We do not explore the reason for these differences—it may reflect differences in their past experiences or differences in the information they have about the particular project; nor do we explore whether there is a way of reaching consensus through an exchange of underlying information. Here, we simply take the view that each individual has a certain probability of being right. We show that the structuring of organizational decision making depends on the relative cost of the two types of errors: accepting a bad project or rejecting a good project. If there is a high cost of the former, then hierarchical decision making is preferable; if the cost of the latter is high, more decentralized (what we call polyarchical decision making) is desirable. This paper opened up an important line of research, discussed more fully in Volume II.

---

[12] Other seemingly anomalous aspects of corporate behavior—the failure to use "efficient" compensation schemes—reflect too failures in corporate governance (see, e.g. Stiglitz 1982e, 1987c).

[13] See, in particular, Stiglitz (1972c, 2000b) and Edlin and Stiglitz (1995).

CHAPTER 13

INCENTIVES AND RISK SHARING IN SHARECROPPING*

AT least from the time of Ricardo, economists have begun their investigations of how competitive markets work, how wages, rents and prices are determined, by a detailed examination of agriculture. Even today, agriculture is taken as the paradigm—and perhaps almost the only important example—of a truly competitive market (or at least this was the case until the widespread government intervention in this market). For a number of years I have been concerned with how competitive markets handle risk taking, and how risk affects real resource allocation. Risks in agriculture are clearly tremendously important, yet remarkably the traditional theoretical literature has avoided explicit treatment[1] of risk sharing in agricultural environments. The consequences of this are important. First, it makes suspect the traditional conclusions regarding sharecropping. Is it really true that sharecropping results in too low a supply of labour, because workers equate their share of output times the (value of the) marginal productivity of labour to the marginal disutility of work, whereas Pareto optimality requires the (value of the) marginal productivity of labour be equal to

* Reprinted with permission from *Review of Economic Studies*, 41(2) (April), 1974, pp. 219–255, Blackwell Publishing. The research described in this paper was supported under grants from the National Science Foundation and from the Ford Foundation. The author is indebted to G. Heal, D. Newbery and G. Hughes for helpful comments.

[1] With a few exceptions. See, in particular, the important work of Cheung (1969a) and the extensive bibliography he provides. His conclusions closely parallel those reached by this study. His analytic approach is, however, markedly different. Since his study, two further important papers have appeared: that of Rao, which provides empirical support of some of the hypotheses advanced here, and that of Bardhan and Srinivasan, which does not explicitly treat uncertainty.

Because of Cheung's excellent discussion of it, I shall omit any further references to the literature.

the marginal disutility of work? Or is it true, as Wicksell asserted, that there is no distinction between landlords hiring labour or labour renting land? Second, it leaves unanswered many of the important economic questions. How is the equilibrium share determined? Why have some economies (in the past or at present) used one distribution system, other economies used others?

Our object is to formulate a simple general equilibrium model of a competitive agricultural economy. Other general equilibrium models of competitive economies with uncertainty have been formulated by Arrow (1964) and Debreu (1959), Diamond (1967), and Stiglitz (1972b). Each of these has its serious limitations in describing the workings of the modern capitalist economy. (See Stiglitz (1971b).) The model is of interest not only for extending our understanding of these simple economies but also in gaining some insight into the far more complex phenomena of shareholding in modern corporations. Our focus is on the risk sharing and incentive properties of alternative distribution systems.

The analysis is divided into two parts. In the first, the amount of labour (effort) supplied by an individual is given, and the analysis focuses on the risk sharing aspects of sharecropping. Among the major qualitative propositions are the following.

(a) If workers and landlords can both "mix contracts" (i.e. workers can work for several different landlords and landlords hire workers on several different "contracts") then the economy is productively efficient (the land-labour ratio is the same on every plot of land); if not, the economy may not be productively efficient.

(b) In the former case, there is, in our model, a linear relationship between the fixed payment a worker receives (his "wages") and his share. We can thus identify a "price of risk absorption". We show that whenever there is a pure sharecropping contract, and workers and landlords can mix contracts, the pure sharecropping contract can be dispensed with, in the sense that all the risk-sharing opportunities could be provided by combining pure wage and pure rental contracts.

(c) The mean marginal product of a labourer is greater or less than his mean income as the worker pays a rent or receives a wage (in addition to some share in the total output). Thus the landlord's income can be thought of as a payment for "rent of land" plus a payment for absorbing some of the labourers' proportionate share of risk. In the case of pure sharecropping (i.e. no fixed payments to or from workers), the mean marginal product is equal to the mean income.

(d) There will be (in our model) a pure wage (rental) system if and only if all landlords (workers) are risk neutral.

(e) If workers cannot mix contracts, more risk averse landlords may have a smaller number of workers per acre than less risk averse landlords (so the economy may not be productively efficient). If there are systematic relations between size of farm (wealth of landlord) and the landlord's degree of risk aversion, as one might expect, then there would be a systematic relation between size of farm and output per acre.

The derivation of further qualitative properties requires the assumptions of a "representative" landlord and a "representative" worker.

(f) The worker pays some fixed rent to the landlord (in addition to a share of the return) or receives a fixed wage (in addition to a "share" of the return) as the worker is less or more risk averse than the landlord. An increase in the variance of the output of the farm increases (decreases) the share of the crop paid to the landlord as well as the share of mean income received on average by the landlord if the landlord is less (more) risk averse than the worker.

In the second part of the paper, the supply of labour (effort) is assumed to be variable. If effort can easily (costlessly) be observed, and quantified, then the level of effort is specified in the contract. It is shown then that, contrary to the classical proposition, there is not an undersupply of labour (effort) as a result of a sharecropping system.

On the other hand, if effort (labour supply) cannot be easily observed, then sharecropping has an important *positive* incentive effect. If the landlord were risk neutral, and if there were no incentive effects (as in the models of Part I), he would absorb all the risk. Here, on the contrary, the worker still receives a share of the output. The more responsive the individual is to incentive effects the greater the incentive share (and the greater the risk he must absorb). On the other hand, whether the worker receives more or less on average than his mean marginal product depends solely on whether the elasticity of substitution between land and labour is greater or less than unity.

Although we have not developed a normative framework within which to evaluate the competitive "incentive" system we are able to establish the following: (a) in comparing a wage system with a sharecropping system, there is no presumption in a general equilibrium model that sharecropping reduces effort (labour) from what it would have been under a wage system with enforceable contracts; (b) the economy will not be "productively efficient"; there will be differences in output per acre arising because of differences in the efficacy of incentives among different individuals.

The presence of a third factor (capital) considerably complicates the analysis; we are able to show, however, that in general the capital will be entirely provided either by the landlord or the worker; in the former case, we argue that there is a greater return to closer supervision, and because of the non-convexity associated with supervision, a greater likelihood of using a wage system. This part of the paper closes with some speculative remarks about alternative incentive schemes.

PART I RISK SHARING WITH INELASTIC LABOUR SUPPLY

1 The Basic Model

The economy consists of two groups of individuals, landlords (who own the land, but do no work) and workers, who own no land.

On each farm, output, Q, is a stochastic constant returns to scale function of land, T, and labour, L:

$$Q = g(\theta)F(L, T), \tag{1.1}$$

where θ is the "state of nature". (1.1) has two strong implications: (*a*) "risk" is independent of inputs, e.g. rainfall affects the crop output the same way, regardless of what techniques are used to generate that output; (*b*) the returns to different farms (labourers) are perfectly correlated. Much of the literature on the economics of uncertainty has focused on the role of diversification. Risk sharing can, however, be treated as an important economic phenomenon quite apart from risk diversification; the particular assumption that we have made is chosen with that in mind.[2]

Because F is homogeneous of degree one, we have

$$Q/T = g(\theta)F(L/T, 1) \equiv g(\theta)f(l), \tag{1.2}$$

where

$$l = L/T \quad \text{and} \quad Eg(\theta) \equiv 1$$
$$\sigma_g^2 \equiv E(g - 1)^2 > 0.$$

We assume, moreover, that f is an increasing, concave function of l

$$f' > 0, \ f'' < 0. \tag{1.3}$$

Our primary concern in this section is the determination of the equilibrium distribution of income. We limit ourselves to linear distribution systems, i.e. if Y_w is the income of a worker and Y_r the income of the landlords (rentiers) then

$$Y_w = \frac{aQ}{L} + \beta \tag{1.4a}$$

$$Y_r = (1 - a)Q - \beta L, \tag{1.4b}$$

---

[2] Since some of the variations in output are due to events which affect particular individuals (a particular worker becoming sick at harvest time) or particular pieces of land (a small creek floods, destroying the crop) there are advantages to be had from risk diversification by the landlord, in hiring more individuals, and for the worker, by working on several different plots of land. The implications of risk diversification are discussed briefly in Part II, Section 3.

where

$$0 \lneqq a \lneqq 1.$$

Three special cases should be noted

$\beta = 0$ the pure sharecropping system

$a = 0$ the wage system: landlords hire labour at a fixed fee

$a = 1$ workers rent land at a fixed fee.

There is no reason to expect on *a priori* grounds that the economy will be in one of these polar cases. Note that if $\beta < 0$, the worker pays the landlord a fixed fee for the use of the land, and the landlord is entitled, in addition, to a given percentage of the crop. $\beta > 0$ is the case where the worker receives a basic wage plus "incentive pay".

Our problem then is the competitive determination of a and β, which determine the distribution of income as well as the distribution of risk taking.

The process for the determination of the equilibrium levels of a and β is, in some ways, fundamentally different from that discussed in the usual competitive models. For there we have a single price, say the wage, for allocating a single factor, labour, and another price, rent, for allocating the other factor, land. Here we have two "prices", "a fixed fee" and "a share" for allocating land and labour, *and risk*, and they are intertwined in a most complex way.

Moreover, the fixed fee and the share do not by themselves determine the value of a contract, since if $a > 0$ the worker must know how much land he will be allowed to work, and if $a < 1$, the landlord must know how much "labour" his labourers will supply. In the usual competitive analysis, *physical data*, such as the amount of land the worker is to work, plays no role in the decision making of the individual; only the price data of the wage he will receive per hour is of relevance.

In the corresponding competitive model without uncertainty there is, in effect, only one equilibrium condition: at the announced wage, all firms hire workers up to the point where the wage, w, is just equal to the value of the marginal product. This generates a demand curve for labour, L^d, and equilibrium requires demand equal supply.

Here, we must have the demand for labourers under *each* kind of contract (each specification of a and β) equal to the supply of labourers for that contract. Most of our analysis focuses on the contracts which will actually be made. For a contract to be signed, three conditions must be satisfied.

Equilibrium condition (a)

Workers choice among existing contracts. Of the set of contracts available in the economy, there exists none which the individual worker prefers to the one which he has.[3]

---

[3] For simplicity, we have expressed the condition for the case when each worker signs a contract with only one landlord. When he can sign several contracts, i.e. allocates different fractions of his labour to different landlords with different contracts, we obtain:

Equilibrium condition (b)

Landlords choice among existing contracts. Of the set of contracts available in the economy, there exists no subset which the landlord prefers to the subset which he employs.[4]

The implicit assumption underlying these two equilibrium conditions is that there is a reasonable amount of "mobility" of agricultural labourers. For traditional agricultural environments, this is probably not a very good assumption. On the other hand, in such societies, variations, for instance, in attitudes towards risk may not be as important, so that essentially a "uniform" contract develops for all workers. In that case, equilibrium conditions (a) and (b) are of no concern. Moreover, in most such societies today workers have a choice between working for a wage and working on their farm, with the resulting "risk" in the income stream. Different individuals allocate their time between these alternative "contracts" differently.

Equilibrium condition (c)

Determination of available contracts. Of the set of utility equivalent contracts— the set of contracts which give the worker the same level of (expected) utility—the contract(s) signed must be the most preferred by the landlord.[5]

We explicitly assume here that the kinds of contracts offered are not determined by tradition, but are determined by economic forces.

The remainder of this section is devoted to the elucidation of these conditions and their implications.

1.1 Choice of Preferred Contract from Given Set of Contracts

All individuals are assumed to be expected utility maximizers. We shall denote the utility function of workers by U_w and of landlords (rentiers) by U_r. Workers are risk averse ($U_w'' < 0$). In Part I we assume that landlords are risk averse ($U_r'' < 0$), and that the supply of labour by a worker is inelastic. Each worker has one "unit" of labour.

Let us first look at the problem from the point of view of the workers. Income in any state of nature from a contract which has share a, fixed payment β per worker, and assigns to the worker an amount of land such that the labour-land ratio is l, is

---

Equilibrium Condition (a'). Of the set of contracts available in the economy, there exists no (feasible) subset which the worker prefers to the subset which he has.

The conditions in which equilibrium condition (a') is more "reasonable" than (a) are discussed below.

[4] Again, if the landlord had to sign the same contract with all his workers, we would have:

Equilibrium Condition (b'). Of the set of available contracts, there exists none which the landlord prefers to the one which he employs.

[5] Given the other contracts he has signed. Provided both landlord and workers can mix contracts, the analysis could have been conducted completely symmetrically, in terms of workers hiring land. The formal symmetry breaks down later.

given by

$$Y_w(\theta) = ag(\theta)\frac{f(l)}{l} + \beta \tag{1.5}$$

$$= g(\theta)x + \beta,$$

where

$$x \equiv \frac{af(l)}{l}. \tag{1.6}$$

(1.5) has the important implication that the income stream can be characterized by two parameters x and β, alone.[6] It is easy to see that for all θ, Y_w increases with x and β. Thus all individuals prefer, at any given β, more "x" to less "x" and at any given x more "β" to less "β". Denote the function giving the maximum value of β attainable for any given value of x in the set of available contracts by

$$\beta = \beta(x). \tag{1.7}$$

Then the worker maximizes

$$\max_{\{x\}} EU_w[Y_w(\theta)] = EU_w[xg(\theta) + \beta(x)]$$

or, if β is differentiable,

$$\frac{EU'_w g}{EU'_w} = -\beta'. \tag{1.8}$$

Diagrammatically, we can see the nature of the solution if we write

$$EU_w[Y_w(\theta)] = V_w(x, \beta). \tag{1.9}$$

Since U is a concave function of Y, and Y a linear function of x and β, $V(x, \beta)$ is a concave function, the indifference curves of which look as in Figure (1.1a). The set of possible contracts is also drawn in Figure (1.1a). The nature of this set is one of the objects of this study. Note that if the function $\beta(x)$ is convex and if the worker can supply fractions of his labour to different landlords, then he can attain any point on the line defined by $\max_{\{\gamma_i\}} \sum \gamma_i \beta(x_i)$ s.t. $\sum \gamma_i = 1, \gamma_i \geq 0$ as in Figure (1.1b).

Thus, if the worker is allowed to work for more than one landlord, the contracts along the line ABC will never be signed by risk averse workers. Only the contracts A and C will be observed.

A perfectly symmetric analysis applies to the landowner. His income, $Y_r(\theta)$, if he signs a contract with share α, fixed payment β, and assigns l workers to a unit of land is,

$$Y_r(\theta) = [(1-\alpha)g(\theta)f(l) - \beta l]T, \tag{1.10}$$

---

[6] That is, the worker is indifferent among contracts with the same value of β and x; there can be a higher value of l if at the same time α is increased to keep x constant.

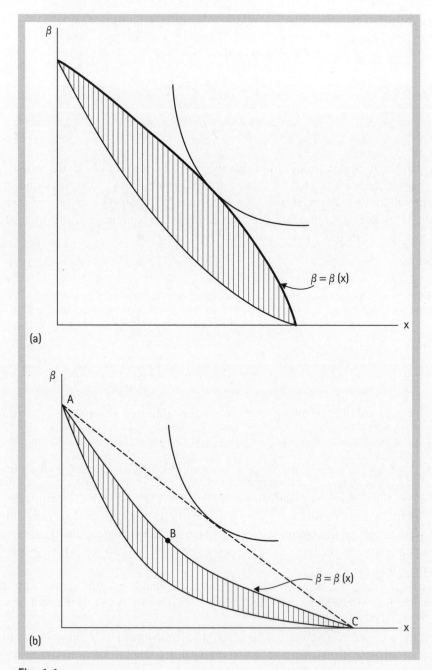

Fig. 1.1.

where T is the total land ownership of the landlord. This may be rewritten

$$Y_r(\theta) = \left[\left(\frac{f(l)}{l} - x\right) g(\theta) - \beta\right] lT. \tag{1.10'}$$

His income depends not only on β and x, but also on l.[7] The landlord must choose not only a contract, (β, x), but also the number of such contracts (labourers per acre). Let $\hat{\beta}(x)$ = the minimum value of β associated with any x. He wishes to maximize

$$\max_{\{l,x\}} EU_r[Y_r(\theta)] = EU_r\left[\left(\left(\frac{f(l)}{l} - x\right) g - \hat{\beta}(x)\right) lT\right]. \tag{1.11}$$

Again, if $\hat{\beta}$ is differentiable, he obtains as first order conditions[8]

$$\frac{EU'_r g}{EU'_r} = -\beta' \tag{1.12a}$$

$$EU'_r f - lf'(l)g = EU'_r Y_r(\theta). \tag{1.12b}$$

It is not so easy to depict diagrammatically the solution to (1.11), for there are three variables involved. But let us assume that we have somehow chosen l. Then we can write

$$EU_r[Y_r(\theta)] = V_r(x, \beta; l),$$

where V_r is now a *convex* function of x and β. Since utility decreases with x and β, the only contracts which will be signed are those which, at any value of x, minimize β. Since workers sign only contracts which, at any value of x, maximize β, the set of contracts actually signed must lie along a line, i.e. $\beta(x) \equiv \hat{\beta}(x)$. Moreover, by exactly the same argument as before, if landlords can mix the kinds of contracts they sign, if $\beta(x)$ is a convex function, such as we have depicted in Figure (1.2b), they can attain any point on the line AC. Hence the only contracts they will sign are A and C.

Proposition 1. *The set of contracts actually observed must lie along a line defined by $\beta = \beta(x)$. If labour and landlords can both mix contracts, the set of contracts that are observed must lie along a straight line, i.e.*

$$\beta = -ax + b. \tag{1.13}$$

If workers can mix contracts but landlords cannot, β is a concave function of x; if landlords mix contracts but workers do not, β is a convex function of x.

Proposition 1 has the following immediate

---

[7] Although this makes the analysis appear slightly asymmetrical, note that we could have defined an alternative (but somewhat less natural) set of variables symmetric to x and β for the landlord. (l obviously is important to the worker, but its effects are subsumed in "x".)

[8] We shall return later to a detailed interpretation of these first-order conditions.

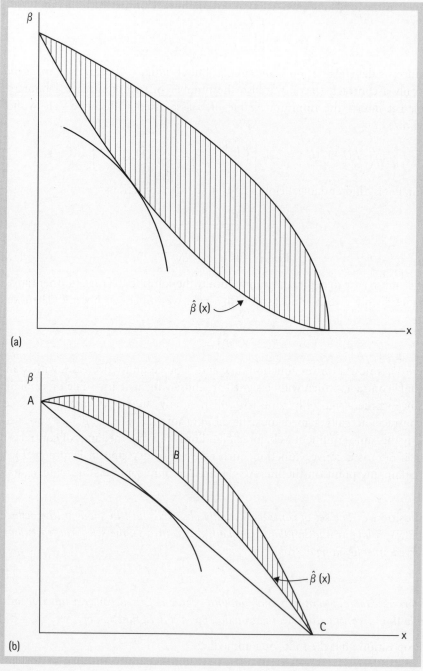

Fig. 1.2.

Corollary. *There is a linear relationship in the contracts signed between the mean and standard deviation (of workers' income).*

Defining

$$\mu_w \equiv EY_w = x + \beta \tag{1.14}$$

$$\sigma_{\gamma_w} = x\sigma_g,$$

(1.13) can be rewritten

$$\mu_w = p\sigma_{\gamma_w} + b, \tag{1.15}$$

where

$$p = \frac{1-a}{\sigma_g}.$$

Note that nowhere in the analysis have we made the usual assumptions required for mean variance analysis to be applicable. p is like a price of "risk" and indeed we shall show later that if workers and landlords treat it as such, the economy will possess the usual optimality properties associated with the price system.

The assumption that landlords can sign different kinds of contracts with different labourers seems a reasonable one; the other assumption required for the validity of these results, that workers can work half their time with one landlord, half with another, is somewhat more suspect, particularly in more traditional agricultural environments. The difficulty is that there is nothing in the assumptions made so far which would seem to warrant a requirement that a worker work with only one landlord. (That is, under the assumptions of constant returns to scale, there is no difference between a worker selling half his time to a landlord to work on a half an acre, or selling all his time to a landlord to work on a whole acre.) The fixed costs of moving from one landlord to another, the difficulty of making sure that the labourer is really spending half his time with each of the two landlords, the suspicion that the worker will allocate more of his "effort" at certain crucial times to the contract with the greater incentive payoffs (greater x)[9]—all important considerations which we have omitted from our analysis—provide some explanation of why workers work only with one landlord.

1.2 Determination of Set of Available Contracts: Identical Individuals

We now turn to an examination of equilibrium condition (c), for a determination of the set of contracts that will be available in the economy.[10] The problem is seen most clearly in the case of the economy in which all landlords are identical and in which all

[9] See below, Part II, Section 4.
[10] The problem is somewhat analogous to the problem that arises in ordinary competitive analysis when fewer commodities can be produced than the total number of commodities; given the

workers are identical. In equilibrium, there will be only one contract observed. How are the competitive values of α and β determined simultaneously?

To answer this question, we introduce the concept of "utility equivalent contracts"—contracts which yield the same level of expected utility, U_w^j, to the jth worker:

$$EU^j \equiv W_w^j = EU_w^j \left[\alpha \frac{f(l)}{l} g(\theta) + \beta \right] = EU_w^j [xg + \beta]. \tag{1.16}$$

For a given value of W_w we can solve (1.16) for β as a function of x

$$\beta = h^j(x; W_w), \tag{1.17}$$

with[11]

$$-\frac{\partial h}{\partial x} = \frac{EU_w' g}{EU_w'} \lessgtr 1 \text{ as } U_w'' \lessgtr 0 \tag{1.17a}$$

$$-\frac{\partial^2 h}{\partial x^2} = \gtreqless 0 \quad \text{(by Schwartz's inequality)} \tag{1.17b}$$

and

$$\frac{\partial h}{\partial W_w} = \frac{1}{EU_w'} > 0. \tag{1.17c}$$

The difference between h^j and the function $\beta(x)$ introduced earlier should be clear. The latter is simply a description of the set of contracts available on the market; the former is a kind of "offer curve" of the individual. Indeed (1.17) is just an analytic representation of the (x, β) indifference curves given in Figure (1.1). While we argued that under certain conditions the former had to be linear, the latter is always a concave function. The offer curve will, of course, differ from individual to individual and for each individual, it will depend on his level of utility.

Assume that the landlord knew this function, i.e. individuals tradeoffs between "x" and fixed payments. Then, he would choose that particular contract which maximized his expected utility, i.e. choosing our units so the representative landlord has one unit of land, the landlord

$$\text{maximizes } EU_r[(1-\alpha)f(l)g - \beta l] = EU_r\left[\left(\left(\frac{f(l)}{l} - x\right)g - \beta\right)l\right] \tag{1.18}$$

subject to the constraint that he be able to obtain workers. If W is the level of utility that the representative worker can obtain elsewhere, he can obtain workers provided

commodities which are produced, the theory provides an explanation of the quantities that are produced and the prices they sell at. But how are the commodities that are actually produced determined?

11
$$EU_w'(g-1) = E[U_w' - U_w'(x+\beta)][g-1] + U_w' E(g-1)$$
$$= E[U_w' - U_w'(x+\beta)][g-1] < 0 \quad \text{if} \quad U_w'' < 0.$$

Where there is no ambiguity, we omit the superscript j and subscript w.

he offers them a contract yielding a level of expected utility at least equal to W.[12] Thus, we replace the simple price taking assumption of the usual competitive model by a "utility taking" assumption; the landlord maximizes (1.18) subject to (1.17) where he takes W_w as given. The landlord makes two decisions—a choice of contract (x, β) and a "density" decision, l.

The first order conditions are

$$\frac{\partial EU_r}{\partial x} = -EU'_r \left(g + \frac{\partial h}{\partial x} \right) l = 0 \tag{1.19a}$$

$$\frac{\partial EU_r}{\partial l} = EU'_r [(f' - x)g - \beta] = 0. \tag{1.19b}$$

These can be rewritten as (using (1.17a)

$$f' = \frac{-1}{(d \ln \beta)/dx)_U} + \frac{af}{l} = \overline{Y}_w - h \left(1 + \frac{1}{h'} \right) \tag{1.20a}$$

and

$$\frac{EU'_r g}{EU'_r} = \frac{EU'_w g}{EU'_w}. \tag{1.20b}$$

A mean-variance interpretation

The interpretation of the first-order conditions may be somewhat clearer in terms of mean-variance analysis. The mean and standard deviation of the landlord's income are given by

$$\overline{Y}_r \equiv (1 - a)f - lh \tag{1.21}$$

$$\sigma_{Y_r} \equiv ((1 - a)f)\sigma_g,$$

and (using (1.17a) and (1.15))

$$\frac{\partial \overline{Y}_r}{\partial a} = -f(1 + h') \leqq 0 \qquad \frac{\partial \overline{Y}_r}{\partial l} = f' - \overline{Y}_w + \frac{a}{l}(1 + h')(f - f'l)$$

$$\frac{\partial \sigma_{Y_r}}{\partial a} = -f\sigma_g < 0 \qquad \frac{\partial \sigma_{Y_r}}{\partial l} = (1 - a)f'\sigma_g > 0.$$

If workers are risk neutral, $1 + h' = 0$, hence increasing a leaves the mean unchanged but reduces the variance. Thus, a is set at unity, and l is chosen to maximize $\overline{Y}_r$ (since σ_{Y_r} is identically zero), i.e. $f' = \overline{Y}_w$, workers receive on average their mean marginal product. Similarly, if landlords are risk neutral, they choose a to maximize $\overline{Y}_r$, so $a = 0$, and again, l is chosen so that $f' = \overline{Y}_w$. More generally, however, landlords will stop short of maximizing expected output, because as expected output increases, so does standard deviation. If a is given, the choice of l is depicted in Figure (1.3). Increasing l increases σ_{Y_r}, and, up to a point, increases $\overline{Y}_r$ as well.

[12] Clearly, he will not offer them a higher level of utility since that will not be maximizing his own utility. Thus he must offer them exactly W.

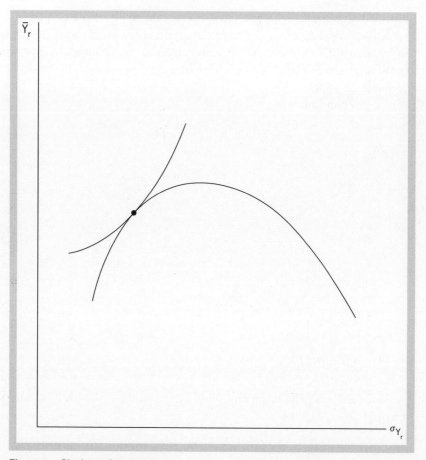

Fig. 1.3. Choice of *l* given *α*

If *l* is given, the mean and standard deviation of total output is given: the standard deviation of the workers' income plus the standard deviation of the capitalists' income equals the total standard deviation,[13] and the mean income of the workers plus the mean income of the landlords equals the total mean income; thus we can represent the set of possible allocations by means of a standard Edgeworth box. This is done in Figures (1.4*a*) and (1.4*b*). Our only question is how is mean and standard deviation divided between the two groups? To the landlord, the utility level of the workers is given, and so he faces the following possibilities: he can give his workers a wage of $w = h(0; W)$ and absorb all the risk himself, or by increasing the share, he can increase the mean he gives the workers but decrease the standard deviation along the indifference curve WW.

Obviously, the landlord chooses a point where his indifference curve is tangent to that of the workers. If this point of tangency occurs along the diagonal (Figure (1.4*b*)), it means that there is a pure sharecropping system, i.e. mean and standard deviation

[13] Throughout this and the next section, we assume that the both groups have no other sources of income.

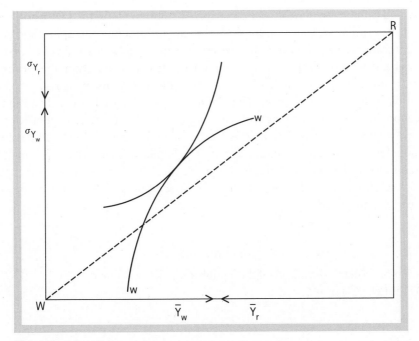

Fig. 1.4a. $\beta < 0$

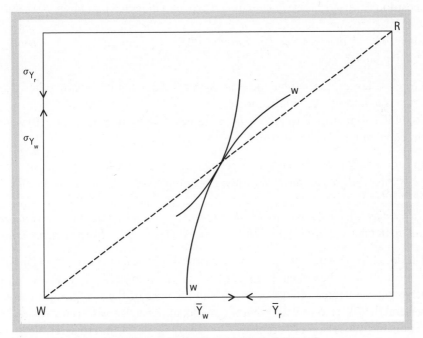

Fig. 1.4b. Pure sharecropping. Choice of $\{\alpha, \beta\}$ (given l)

are shared proportionately; if we have a corner solution along the lower horizontal axis, it means that we have a pure wage system, and if along the upper horizontal axis, it means we have a pure rental system. Let us say that one individual is more risk averse than another if, at any value of the coefficient of variation, the increment in mean income required to compensate him for an increment in risk (standard deviation of income) is greater. (This definition clearly parallels the definition, in conventional production theory, of one sector being more capital intensive than another.) Then it immediately follows that the equilibrium contract will be above, on, or below the diagonal in Figure (1.4), as the landlord is less risk averse than, has the same risk aversion as, or is more risk averse than the representative worker (that is, β is greater than, equal to, or less than zero as landlords are less, equally, or more risk averse than workers).

Further implications of first-order conditions

To see in more detail the nature of the equilibrium, first we note that if $U_w'' < 0$, $U_r'' < 0$, $EU_r'g/EU_r' \lesseqgtr 1$ as $\alpha \lesseqgtr 1$, and

$$EU_w'g/EU_w' \lesseqgtr 1$$

as $\alpha \gtreqless 0$, so that if both groups are risk averse, we will never have a pure wage or rental system. We have thus established

Proposition 2. *A pure wage or pure rental system will occur if and only if workers or landlords are risk neutral. The risk neutral group absorbs all the risk, and the whole economy acts as if there were no uncertainty with factors on average receiving their mean marginal products.*

The existence of pure rental and wage systems requires introducing other factors not yet taken into account in the model.

Secondly, from (1.17a), we have $-h' < 1$ unless[14] $U_w'' = 0$ or $\alpha = 0$ or $g(\theta)$ is identically equal to 1. Hence from (1.20a) we obtain

Proposition 3. *If both workers and landlords are risk averse, then if workers receive a share plus a fixed fee contract, they are hired to the point where their mean marginal product is less than their average income, and by symmetry if landlords receive a share plus a fixed fee, then labourers are hired to a point where their mean marginal product is greater than their average income. The amount $-h(1 + 1/h')$ is like a "risk premium".*

The difficult question is the determination of whether $\beta \gtreqless 0$, i.e. whether labourers take more or less than their proportionate share of the risk. The answer clearly depends on the degrees of risk aversion and incomes of the two groups; there are no general theorems to be had. What we can do, however, is to ascertain, on the basis of reasonable values of the "parameters" the likely sign of β, and to determine how β changes with certain changes in the economy.

---

[14] From the previous paragraph, we know that $\alpha \neq 0$ unless $U_r'' \equiv 0$,

We assume both groups have constant elasticity utility functions,

$$U_w = \frac{Y^{-\eta_w}}{\eta_w}, \qquad U_r = \frac{Y^{-\eta_r}}{\eta_r},$$

where $\eta_w + 1$ and $\eta_r + 1$ are the Arrow-Pratt measures of relative risk aversion.
We can establish

$$\beta \gtreqless 0 \quad \text{as} \quad \eta_w \gtreqless \eta_r.$$

Proposition 4. *The group which is relatively risk averse assumes less than its proportion of the risk. The proof is presented in the appendix of the original paper.*

Determination of α and β for small variances

Explicit expressions for the equilibrium values of the relevant variables can be derived if we assume the variance of g is small.

Defining $\gamma \equiv \frac{f'l}{f}$, $\eta_i \equiv \frac{w_i'' y_i}{u_i'}$, the measure of relative risk aversion, it can be shown that

$$\alpha = \alpha^* - \frac{\gamma(1-\gamma)}{\eta_w \eta_r} \frac{\sigma_g^2 \left(\frac{1}{\eta_r} - \frac{1}{\eta_w} \right)}{\left(\frac{\gamma}{\eta_w} + \frac{1-\gamma}{\eta_r} \right)^4} \tag{1.22}$$

$$\frac{\beta}{f/l} = \gamma - \alpha^* - \frac{\gamma(1-\gamma) \left(\frac{1}{\eta_r} - \frac{1}{\eta_w} \right)}{\left(\frac{\gamma}{\eta_w} + \frac{1-\gamma}{\eta_r} \right)^2} \left(1 - \frac{\eta_w \eta_r}{(\eta_w(1-\gamma) + \gamma\eta_r)^2} \right) \sigma_g^2.$$

Thus, if $\eta_w = 2$, $\eta_r = \frac{1}{2}$, $\gamma = \frac{2}{3}$, and $\sigma_g^2 = \frac{1}{2}$, $\alpha^* = \frac{1}{3}$, $S_w \approx \frac{1}{2}$, $\alpha \approx \frac{1}{6}$ (see original paper).

Comparative statics

We now analyse the effect of changes in risk, in labour/land ratios, and of technical progress on the equilibrium of the system. In addition to the assumptions made in the previous analysis of small variance, we now assume constant relative risk aversion. We focus our remarks on the case where $\eta_w > \eta_r$ (so $\beta > 0$); the other case follows symmetrically.

(a) Changes in Risk (σ_g^2)

Proposition 5a. *An increase in risk lowers (raises) α, lowers (raises) S_w and may raise or lower β if $\beta > (<)0$. β is lowered (raised) when $\gamma \leq (\geq)\frac{1}{2}$ and $\beta > (<)0$.*

(b) Effects of Changes in the Labour/Land Ratio

For simplicity, we focus on the effects on (a^*, β^*), the limiting value of the distribution parameters. Straightforward calculations establish

$$\frac{da^*}{dl} = \frac{\eta_w \eta_r \gamma'}{(\eta_w(1-\gamma) + \eta_r\gamma)^2} \gtreqless 0 \text{ as } m \gtreqless 1$$

where m = elasticity of substitution = $-f'(f - lf')/flf''$.

The percentage of worker's income received as fixed payments $\beta/\overline{Y}_w$, is given by

$$\frac{\overline{Y}_w}{\beta} \approx 1 + \frac{\eta_r}{(1-\gamma)(\eta_w - \eta_r)} = \frac{(1-\gamma)\eta_w + \gamma\eta_r}{(1-\gamma)(\eta_w - \eta_r)}$$

so

$$\frac{d(\overline{Y}_w/\beta)}{dl} = -\frac{\eta_r\gamma'}{(\eta_w - \eta_r)(1-\gamma)^2} \gtreqless 0 \quad \text{as} \quad \beta(m-1) \lesseqgtr 0.$$

The actual change in β is more complicated, because when l increases, $\overline{Y}_w$ falls, so even if $\beta/\overline{Y}_w$ increases, β may actually fall: ($\sim$ denotes "is of the same sign as")

$$\frac{d\beta}{dl} \sim \gamma^2\eta_r - (1-\gamma)^2\eta_w - m\gamma\eta_r$$

$$\sim \frac{-(1-\gamma)}{m} - (1 - 1/m)\frac{\gamma\eta_r}{\gamma\eta_r + (1-\gamma)\eta_w}.$$

Note that $d\beta/dl < 0$ if $m \geq 1$; but that if m is sufficiently small, even though total mean wage payments are decreasing, the fixed part is increasing. Alternatively, if $\gamma \leq \frac{1}{2}$ and $\eta_w > \eta_r$, then regardless of the value of m, $d\beta/dl < 0$. We thus have

Proposition 5b. *If the variance is small, an increase in the labour-land ratio increases (decreases) a, increases (decreases) the proportion of workers' income received in the form of fixed payments, and increases (decreases) the share of (mean) national income received by workers if the elasticity of substitution is greater (less) than unity.*

That is, as the workers become relatively better (worse) off, even though the degree of relative risk aversion is constant, the workers absorb proportionately more (less) of the risk although at the same time the proportion of their income received in fixed payments also increases (decreases).

(c) Technical Change

Consider the more general production function

$$Q = F(\lambda(\tau)L, \mu(\tau)T),$$

where λ is the rate of labour augmentation and μ is the rate of land augmentation. Then

$$\frac{da^*}{d\tau} \gtreqless 0 \quad \text{as} \quad (m-1)\left(\frac{\lambda'}{\lambda} - \frac{\mu'}{\mu}\right) \gtreqless 0 .$$

$$\frac{1}{\beta^*}\frac{d\beta^*}{\lambda} = \frac{\lambda'}{\lambda} \text{ for a Hicks neutral change(when } \lambda'/\lambda = \mu'/\mu)$$

$$= \frac{\lambda'}{\lambda} + \frac{1}{\beta^*}\frac{d\beta^*}{dl} \text{ for a Harrod neutral change}$$

$$\sim -\frac{d\beta^*}{dl} \text{ for a pure land augmenting invention.}$$

Proposition 5c. *a^* increases or decreases as technical change is land or labour saving in the Hicksian sense. β increases for a Hicks neutral change, but may increase or decrease in other cases.*

1.3 Diverse Individuals: Both Landlords and Workers Mix Contracts

Essentially all the results of the preceding sub-section can be extended in a straight-forward manner to the case where there are diverse individuals if both workers and landlords can mix contracts.

We argued in Section (1.1) that if both landlords and workers can "mix" contracts, the set of contracts (x, β) must lie along the straight line defined by (1.13). Although not all points on the line are available in the form of a single contract, by mixing contracts, the individual can get any point[15] along the line.

Thus the jth landlord (who owns T_j units of land)

$$\underset{\{x,l\}}{\text{maximizes }} EU_r^j[((f - xl)g - bl + axl)T^j]$$

so

$$EU_r^{j'}(-lg + al)T^j = 0 \qquad (1.23)$$

$$EU_r^{j'}[((f' - x)g - \beta)T^j] = 0$$

or

$$\frac{EU_r^{j'}g}{EU_r^{j'}} = a = \frac{\beta}{f' - x} \text{ for all } j \qquad (1.24)$$

or

$$f' = b/a \text{ for all } j. \qquad (1.25)$$

We have thus established

Proposition 6a. *The economy is productively efficient, i.e. all landlords use the same land/labour ratio.*

---

[15] If β_{max} is the "maximum" β available in a single contract and β_{min} the "minimum" β, then

$$\beta_{min} \leqq \beta \leqq \beta_{max}, \text{ and } (q - \beta_{max})/p < x < (q - \beta_{min})/p.$$

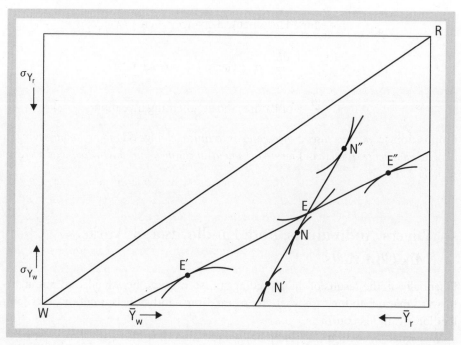

Fig. 1.5.

From (1.8), (1.13), and (1.24) we obtain

$$\frac{EU_w^{j'}g}{EU_w^{j'}} = a = \frac{EU_r^{j'}g}{EU_r^{j'}} \tag{1.26a}$$

$$f' = \overline{Y}_w - \beta \left(1 - \frac{EU_w^{j'}}{EU_w^{j'}g} \right). \tag{1.26b}$$

Equations (1.26) are identical to equations (1.20) and it is thus apparent that Propositions 2 and 3 apply here without modification.

The determination of the equilibrium values of b and a can be shown diagrammatically in Figure (1.5), using the Edgeworth-Bowley box introduced earlier. Since in equilibrium, the labour/land ratio must be the same on every farm, it must be the same as the aggregate labour/land ratio. This determines the mean and standard deviation of income. We assume there are two groups of equal size of labourers and one kind of landlord. Thus the point chosen by the landlord (E) must lie halfway between the points chosen by the two groups of workers (E' and E'').

A higher value of a would[16] decrease the landlord's demand for "risky" (from the workers' viewpoint) contracts, but decrease the supply of risky contracts by both groups of workers as illustrated in Figure (1.5). Hence, it is not an equilibrium.

If there are only a limited number of contracts (say because there are only two kinds of workers), differences in attitudes towards risk by landlords are reflected not in the contract they sign with any particular individual but in the mix of individuals

---

[16] From (1.25), given l we know b/a.

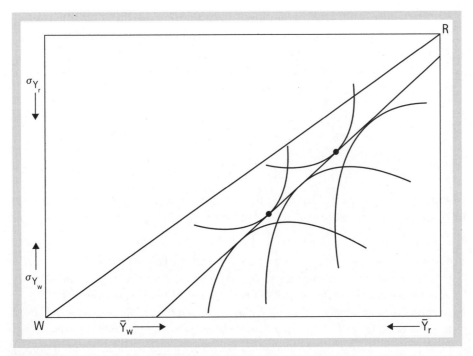

Fig. 1.6.

they have on the farm. This is illustrated in Figure (1.6). The large landlord can "mix" workers with different risk attitudes. Although under our assumptions there is no risk diversification from mixing, since the returns to each plot of land (each farmer) are perfectly correlated, this "mixing" allows, in effect, workers with different risk attitudes to "trade" risks with one another through the intermediation of the landlord.

Indeed, it is easy to establish

Proposition 6b. *If both landlords and workers can mix contracts, only two contracts are ever required. One of these is either the pure wage contract or the pure rental contract. If there is a pure sharecropping contract, it could have been dispensed with, i.e. all the relevant opportunities can be generated by mixing pure wage and pure rent contracts.*

These results follow upon observing that the slope of the diagonal is σg while the slope of the "contract line" $= \frac{\sigma \hat{g}}{1-a} > \sigma \hat{g}$ (using (1.15), (1.26) and (1.17a)). Thus the contract line must intersect either the bottom or the top of the Edgeworth-Bowley box, and if it crosses the diagonal, it must intersect both.

1.4 Diverse Individuals: Workers cannot mix Contracts

The more interesting—and perhaps realistic—case is where workers cannot mix contracts. Then, as we argued in Section 1, the set of contracts available to the landlord could be described by

$$\beta = \beta(x) \text{ with } \beta' < 0, \beta'' \gtreqqless 0.$$

The first order conditions for landlords' maximization can then be written as

$$\frac{EU_r^{j'} g}{EU_r^{j'}} = -\beta' = \frac{\beta}{f' - x}.$$

Thus

$$\frac{dl}{dx} = \frac{\beta \beta''}{\beta'^2 f''} \lessgtr 0 \text{ as } \beta \gtrless 0$$

$$\frac{dl}{d\alpha} = \frac{\frac{f}{l}\frac{dl}{dx}}{\frac{dl}{dx}\frac{x}{l}(1 - \gamma) + 1} \gtreqless 0 \text{ if } \beta \lesseqgtr 0,$$

where $\gamma = f'l/f$ = share of labour in the absence of uncertainty. If $\beta > 0$, $dl/d\alpha$ may be of either sign. Since less risk averse landlords choose contracts with a high β, and a lower x, we have established:

Proposition 7. *The presence of even a perfect rental market for land—in the absence of a perfect risk market—will not necessarily lead to productive efficiency for the economy. The more risk averse landlords who are less risk averse than their workers (so $\beta > 0$) have fewer workers per acre. The more risk averse landlords who are more risk averse than their workers (so $\beta < 0$) have more workers per acre, and their workers receive a larger share α. Note, however, that all landlords signing a particular contract $\{\beta, x\}$, employ the same land/labour ratio.*[17]

Proposition 7 may provide part of the explanation of the phenomenon, noted in a number of LDC's, that there are sizeable variations in output per acre on different farms,[18] and if, as we might expect, risk aversion is systematically related to the wealth of the landlord (the size of his farm), we would expect output per acre to vary systematically with the size of farm.

There is, in these circumstances, an incentive for the creation of a "stock market" for farms. If there were a "stock market", in which different landlords could buy shares in each others farms, in equilibrium the value of an acre would have to be the same regardless of the contract signed; hence the price of a "share" is the same regardless of the farm. We wish to know, will the introduction of this stock market result in production efficiency?

We are primarily interested in this question not for its implications for agricultural policy—with the exception of a few large American farms, shares in farms are not

---

[17] As long as there are only a finite number of types of individuals, $\beta(x)$ will be a piecewise linear function. The necessary modifications to the analysis are obvious.

[18] However, we should also expect to see these variations in output per acre to be systematically related to the kind of contracts signed. In practice, the variations of contracts in use at any point of time in a given economy probably have been much more limited than the variations in the contracts that have been employed over time. This may be either because, at any point of time, divergences in attitudes towards risk among landlords or among workers may be relatively small, or because preferences are of far less importance than the basic underlying technological considerations, or because the extreme assumptions of mobility which we employ were not satisfied in traditional societies. None the less, there is usually *some* range of choice (i.e. some sharecropping arrangement, a rental arrangement, or a wage arrangement).

generally traded, probably because of the high "costs of information" which we have not taken into account here—but for its possible relevance to the "shares market" in modern capitalist economies. There has been some controversy over whether a stock market (without the full set of Arrow-Debreu securities) will in general lead to the correct investment decisions being made.

In the particular model presented here, it can be established that

Proposition 8. *The economy will be productively efficient with a stock market—though workers cannot sell shares in their own "wage" income.*

Proposition 9. *If there exists a linear relationship between the workers' mean income from a contract and the standard deviation of the income from the contract, then the choice of techniques will be Pareto optimal.*

[In the full text, both of these propositions are proved. Subsequent research showed, however, that neither proposition was general. An economy with a stock market is not in general efficient, and, even with rational expectations, the choice of techniques is not in general optimal.]

PART II ELASTIC LABOUR SUPPLY

1 Introduction

In the traditional literature, sharecropping arrangements have been criticized in terms of their incentive effects on the supply of labour. In the previous analysis, we focused on the risk sharing aspects of sharecropping, and explicitly assumed that the labour supply was inelastic. On the other hand, there is a fundamental objection to the usual analyses of sharecropping: they fail to take account of the original motivations in using a sharecropping arrangement rather than a wage or rental system. Thus, if the motivation is risk sharing, as we have described it in the previous sections, then in general, the average income received by a worker will not be equal to his marginal product; an analysis of the "efficiency" of the sharecropping system must explicitly take into account the attitudes towards risk of the workers and landlords, and how this affects their behaviour. Clearly, a full analysis of a sharecropping economy must take into account both incentive and risk-sharing effects, and that we propose to do in the next two sections. In Section 2 we assume that contracts specify precisely the amount of labour to be provided and that they are enforceable without cost, while in Section 3, we examine the other polar case where the contract makes no specification concerning the labour to be supplied by the worker.

2 Enforceable Contracts

The landlord is interested in the amount of labour that will be supplied to any piece of land; he is not particularly interested in the number of labourers on a piece of land. Thus, contracts between landlords and their labourers will specify the amount of labour that a worker is to provide. (But this in itself is not sufficient to guarantee that the correct optimality conditions will be satisfied.)

Thus, there are two decisions for the worker to make: what kind of contract to sign, and how much labour to supply. A contract, recall, is specified by an assignment of labour per acre, l, a fixed fee, β, and a share, a. We assume labourers can "mix contracts", Hence, as we argued above, in equilibrium, labour (not however *labourers*) per acre is the same everywhere, and so can be taken as given by the worker; and we can take the fixed fee to be a linear function of the share

$$\beta = -a\frac{af(l)}{l} + b. \tag{2.1}$$

Thus a worker's maximization problem is to

$$\max_{\{a,L\}} V(L) + EU_w[(xg + \beta)L], \tag{2.2}$$

where L is the supply of labour by a labourer and where we have assumed for simplicity that workers have an additive utility function and $V' < 0$, $V'' < 0$. Substituting (2.1) into (2.2) we obtain

$$\max V(L) + EU_w\{(x(g - a) + b)L\}. \tag{2.2'}$$

The first-order conditions are thus

$$V' + EU'_w\left\{\frac{af(l)}{l}g + \beta\right\} = 0 \tag{2.3a}$$

$$EU'_w(g - a) = 0. \tag{2.3b}$$

The second condition is just another form of the familiar condition we have already discussed above [equation (1.8)]. Here our concern is with (2.3a). $a(f(l)/l)g + \beta$ is just the return per unit of labour. (2.3a) says that the marginal disutility of labour should be just equal to the expected marginal utility of the income received as a result.

To compare this with the optimal allocation, we consider a "command" economy in which the same risk sharing possibilities exist but in which the decision on the supply of labour is made centrally. Then, if all workers are identical and landlords are identical (the general case follows along identical lines, but is slightly more complicated notationally) we wish to

$$\max EU_r[(1 - a)f(L)g - \beta L] \tag{2.4}$$

where we have normalized the supply of land and of labourers at unity, subject to the constraint that

$$V(L) + EU_w[af(L)g + \beta L] = \bar{U} \tag{2.5}$$

where we have normalized the supply of land at unity. We then obtain as first order conditions

$$EU'_r g = vEU'_w g \tag{2.6a}$$

$$EU'_r = vEU'_w \tag{2.6b}$$

$$EU'_r[(1-a)f'g - \beta] + vEU'_w(af'g + \beta) + vV' = 0 \tag{2.6c}$$

where v is the Lagrange multiplier associated with the constraint (2.5).

Using (2.6a) and (2.6b), we can rewrite the condition (2.6c) as

$$V' + EU'_w gf' = 0.$$

This should be compared with (2.3a), which may be rewritten, using (1.29) and (2.3b), also to read

$$V' + EU'_w gf' = 0$$

i.e. the competitive supply of labour is optimal. The divergences between expected marginal products of labour and the marginal disutility of labour are just those which are "optimal" given the attitudes towards risk of the two groups. We have thus established

Proposition 10. *If labour is elastically supplied, and contracts are enforceable without cost, landlords will specify the amount of labour to be supplied by the sharecropper in the sharecropping contract and, if both landlords and workers can mix contracts, the equilibrium will be Pareto optimal.*

3 Incentive Effects

3.1 *The Basic Model*

It is curious that economists, in discussing the misallocation of resources resulting from a sharecropping arrangement, have focused on the *undersupply* of labour ("negative incentive") in the sharecropping system, while businessmen talk about the positive incentive effects of "sharing" arrangements (e.g. commissions) as one of their major advantages. The reason for the discrepancy lies in the economists' conventional simplifications of the production process. There is a "book of blueprints" (a recipe book), with a simple set of instructions on how to combine two homogeneous factors to produce the maximum output. There are no unexpected circumstances, no contingencies in the "field" to be taken account of, and no difficulty in ascertaining whether a given individual has followed the instructions in the book of blueprints.

The "contract" between the worker and the employer specifies that the worker will follow the appropriate page in the book for blueprints, and if he fails to do so, he receives no compensation. For some purposes, this is a useful simplification; for others—and in particular for the purpose of understanding the nature of the contract signed between landlord and worker—it is not.

To describe the input provided by a labourer, we must not only know the number of hours he works, but also what we shall loosely call, the "effort" of the individual. As difficult as it may be to ascertain the former (in an agricultural situation), it is even more difficult to ascertain the latter. "Effort" affects output in a number of ways: first, and most obvious, is the *pace* at which an individual works, say the number of weeds removed per hour. If this were the only consideration, we could simply measure labour supplied by the corresponding output (a piece-work system) and not by the hour. Secondly, there is the *thoroughness*; say the completeness with which a given acre is weeded. Two individuals may pick the same number of weeds per hour, but one picks the most obvious weeds in a two-acre plot, while the other picks all the weeds in a one-acre plot. The point of course is that there are different costs associated with picking different weeds, and that is one of the reasons that pay cannot be simply proportional to the number of weeds picked. But it is difficult except by very close supervision to ascertain the cost associated with each weed. Thirdly, there is the *efficiency* of the individual, which is equivalent to the individual equating the marginal cost of a weed picked on each plot of land.[19] This is even more difficult to ascertain than the thoroughness. Fourthly, there is the efficiency of decision making under uncertainty: if it rains right before harvest, will the farmer make the "correct" decision about revising plans about harvesting and carry those plans out. Presumably, if all the possible contingencies, e.g. all the possible sequences of rain, sun, and visitations by insects and disease were spelled out in the "book of blueprints" this would not be a factor. In fact, however, only a few of the possible contingencies can be simply described, and the appropriate courses of action to take specified. Finally, there is the *inventiveness* of the individual: as he picks weeds, he may develop more efficient and better ways of doing it. These "inventions" may be specific to the specific circumstances of the given farm, and therefore are not likely to be discussed except in very broad terms in any general treatment of weeding. This list of "qualities" associated with labour is not meant to be exhaustive. One of the very important considerations when a third factor, such as capital, is present, is the care which the worker takes of the capital supplied by the landlord.[20]

A contract, accordingly, may not only specify the hours of labour to be provided, but also something about the *effort* required of the individual, the degree of "control" over the day-to-day decisions that are to rest in his hands and the amount of supervision (direction) he will receive from managers. There is also an implicit or explicit penalty-rewards function. A piece-work wage and a commission

[19] Assuming the marginal benefit is constant, or equating the net marginal benefit of a weed picked on each piece of land, if the marginal benefit is not constant.

[20] In the absence of uncertainty, we could infer the level of input from the level of output; with uncertainty, this may not be possible. See Stiglitz 1971b.

for sales beyond a certain level are examples of rewards; being fired is an example of a penalty.

Contracts clearly vary in the preciseness with which the labour inputs (effort) required of the worker are specified, and in the extent and manner in which those terms are enforced. In this section we consider the polar case to that analysed in the previous one: there we implicitly assumed that the contract specified everything, here we assume that the contract specifies nothing concerning the amount (quality) of labour to be provided.[21] The reward to greater effort is thus provided by his share of the output (a). Both models are polar cases, but given the complexity of completely specifying (and enforcing) the labour inputs, as we have described them above, it may be argued that the model of this section is the better approximation to reality.

We assume the landlord is risk neutral, but that the worker is not.[22] Without incentive effects, the landlord would absorb all the risk; workers would all face a pure wage contract. We can show now, however, that there will still be some sharecropping (i.e. $a > 0$).

We return to our simpler model in which all individuals are identical. The worker's utility function is of the form,[23,24]

$$U = EU[Y_w] + V(e), \tag{3.1}$$

where $V' < 0$ is the marginal disutility from an increment in e, "effort" or "effective labour supply per individual". If this worker faces a contract (a, β, l) he chooses e to maximize U. Now l refers to the density of *workers*. An increase in e increases Q, so if $a > 0$, it increases Y_w. Assume that effort is "purely labour augmenting".[25] Then we have

$$Q = Tf(el) \tag{3.2}$$

and

$$Y_w = \frac{af(el)}{l}g + \beta \tag{3.3}$$

so, given a, l, and β, e is chosen so that

$$EU'_w af'(el)g + V' = 0. \tag{3.4}$$

A worker is indifferent among contracts that yield the same level of U when he has optimally chosen e. Thus, the set of utility equivalent contracts is given by

$$\overline{W} = \max_{\{e\}} EU\left[\frac{af(el)g}{l} + \beta\right] + V(e), \tag{3.5}$$

[21] Presumably because, even if there were specifications, the contract would not be enforceable because of prohibitive supervisory costs.

[22] Thus, in this section we can drop the subscript w on U_w without ambiguity.

[23] It should be clear that our analysis of incentive effects and "effort" is closely related to Leibenstein's important work on X-efficiency.

[24] "Effort" appears in this formulation exactly like "labour" in Section 2.

[25] Akerlof has argued that improvements in labour effort by reducing, for instance, damage to machines, is capital augmenting (Akerlof 1969).

which, as before, we can solve for β as a function of a and l:

$$\beta = h(a, l, \overline{W}) \tag{3.6}$$

$$\frac{\partial \beta}{\partial a} = -\frac{f}{l}\frac{EU'g}{EU'} < 0, \quad \frac{\partial \beta}{\partial l} = \frac{a(f - f'el)}{l^2}\frac{EU'g}{EU'} > 0. \tag{3.6a}$$

Different contracts, which are equivalent in utility terms to the worker, have different incentive effects: from (3.4) and (3.6) we obtain

$$\left(\frac{\partial \ln e}{\partial \ln l}\right)_W = -\frac{E\left\{U''af'g\left[\frac{a(f-f'el)}{l}\left(\frac{EU'g}{EU'} - g\right)\right] + U'af''elg\right\}}{E\left\{U''af'\frac{(af'el)}{l}g^2 + U'af''elg\right\} + V''} \tag{3.7a}$$

$$\left(\frac{\partial \ln e}{\partial \ln a}\right)_W = -\frac{E\left\{-U''af'g\left[\frac{af}{l}\left(\frac{EU'g}{EU'} - g\right)\right] + U'af'g\right\}}{E\left\{U''af'\frac{(af'el)}{l}g^2 + U'af''elg\right\} + V''e}. \tag{3.7b}$$

The landlord wishes to maximize,

$$\max_{\{a,l\}} (1 - a)f(el) - hl, \tag{3.8}$$

which yields the first-order conditions

$$-f - l\frac{\partial h}{\partial a} + (1 - a)f'l\left(\frac{\partial e}{\partial a}\right)_W = 0 \tag{3.9a}$$

$$\left(e + l\left(\frac{\partial e}{\partial l}\right)_W\right)(1 - a)f' - h - l\frac{\partial h}{\partial l} = 0. \tag{3.9b}$$

(3.9) may be rewritten as

$$a = \frac{\gamma\left(\frac{\partial \ln e}{\partial \ln a}\right)_W}{c + \gamma\left(\frac{\partial \ln e}{\partial \ln a}\right)_W}, \quad \frac{S_w - \gamma}{\gamma} = \frac{c\left(\left(\frac{\partial \ln e}{\partial \ln l}\right)_W + (1 - \gamma)\left(\frac{\partial \ln e}{\partial \ln a}\right)_W\right)}{c + \gamma\left(\frac{\partial \ln e}{\partial \ln a}\right)_w}, \tag{3.10}$$

where $c \equiv 1 - EU'g/EU' \geqq 0$, with equality only if $U'' = 0$ or $a = 0$. From (3.10) we can establish

Proposition 11. *If workers are risk averse, then $0 < a < 1$, and a is larger the greater is the responsiveness of effort to an increase in the share. a is smaller the more risk averse the individual. For a given response elasticity and degree of risk aversion, a is greater the greater is γ (the share of labour in the absence of uncertainty). If workers are risk neutral, $a = 1$.*

Proposition 12. *If workers are risk averse, they receive a mean income greater than, equal to or less than their mean marginal product as the elasticity of substitution is greater than, equal to, or less than unity. If workers are risk neutral, they receive on average their mean marginal product.*

This proof of Proposition 11 is straightforward;[26] proposition 12 follows from observing that

$$S_w - \gamma \gtreqless 0 \text{ as } - \frac{\left(\frac{\partial \ln e}{\partial \ln l}\right)_W}{\left(\frac{\partial \ln e}{\partial \ln a}\right)_W} \lesseqgtr (1 - \gamma)$$

and substituting (3.7) into the above.[27] As usual, $\beta \gtreqless 0$ as $S_w \gtreqless a$. We have not been able to find simple conditions for determining whether $S_w \gtreqless a$ except when the elasticity of substitution is unity. Then, from (3.10) $S_w = \gamma$; then

$$\beta \gtreqless 0 \text{ as } \left(\frac{\partial \ln e}{\partial \ln a}\right)_W \lesseqgtr \frac{c}{1 - \gamma}. \tag{3.11}$$

Earlier, we noted that if workers could not "mix" contracts, differences in attitudes towards risk would result in variations in output per acre. The economy would not be "productively efficient". Similar variations in output per acre arise because of differences in the efficacy of incentives among different individuals.

We first observe that the landlord must get the same rent from each piece of land, i.e.

$$(1 - a)f - \beta l = \bar{R} \quad \text{(a constant).} \tag{3.12}$$

Clearly,

$$f(el) = \frac{\bar{R}}{1 - S_w}. \tag{3.13}$$

Since S_w will differ with different labourers, because $(\partial \ln e/\partial \ln l)_W$, $(\partial \ln e/\partial \ln a)_W$, or c differ, unless $m = 1$ (so $S_w = \gamma$), $f(el)$ will differ.

We have thus shown

Proposition 13. *Output per acre will in general differ on different farms: the economy will not be productively efficient unless the production function has unitary elasticity of substitution.*

Other things being equal, an increase in uncertainty increases c and hence increases differences in S_w arising from differences in the strength of incentive effects. Other things being equal, the more risk averse, the greater c and hence the higher S_w and output per acre.[28]

A question of some interest in LDC's is whether output per acre is higher or lower on more densely populated land. Conventional analysis ignores the effect of effort, so argues the greater l, the greater el, the greater $f(el)$; e may, however, decrease with an increase in l, and if it decreases enough, el is reduced.

---

[26] At $a = 0$, $c = \left(\frac{\partial \ln e}{\partial \ln a}\right)_W = \left(\frac{\partial \ln e}{\partial \ln l}\right)_W = \frac{\partial h}{\partial l} = e = 0$. (3.9b) is satisfied only if $\beta = 0$.

[27] $\left(\frac{\partial \ln e}{\partial \ln a}\right)_W (1 - \gamma) + \left(\frac{\partial \ln e}{\partial \ln l}\right)_W \sim a\left(\frac{f'(f - f'el)}{f} + f''el\right)EU'g$.

[28] For m near unity. Otherwise, there may be large offsetting changes in γ.

3.2 *Comparison with Wage System*

We argued earlier that the conventional wisdom, that the sharecropping system results in too little supply of labour, errs in that it ignores the very reasons for introducing sharecropping. In Section 2 we showed that, when risk was taken into account, the supply of labour under sharecropping was in fact optimal with fully enforceable contracts. Here, we wish to make two further observations:

(1) It is not really meaningful—from a welfare point of view—to compare a situation where a particular kind of contract is enforceable at zero cost, with one in which it is not enforceable (or enforceable only at an infinite cost). By ignoring the costs of enforcing the contract, one is ignoring part of the essence of the problem.

(2) But even if we simply limit ourselves to comparing the allocation of resources, the conventional presumption does not appear to be correct. For it is a partial equilibrium analysis, and in going from one system to the other, the distribution of income as well as the sharing of risk will change. Since the switch to a wage system from a sharecropping system will in general change the individual's level of utility, the net result is a mixture of substitution and income effects.

We can compare this equilibrium with one where the contracts are enforceable (Section 2). Then $\alpha = 0$ (except in the case where there is no uncertainty when $\alpha = 1$ or $\alpha = 0$). We define β^* as the price of a unit of effort. The worker chooses e so that

$$V' + U'\beta^* = 0, \tag{3.4'}$$

while the landlord sets (if he is risk neutral)

$$lf' = \beta^*. \tag{3.9'}$$

Let superscripts s and w denote the variables for the sharecropping and wage systems respectively). There are two questions: (a) at $e = e^s$, is the increment in expected utility from additional effort greater or less under sharecropping than under the wage system, i.e. is

$$\alpha^s EU'\left[\frac{\alpha^s f(e^s l)g}{l} + \beta^s\right]g \gtrless U'[f'(e^s l)el^s]? \tag{3.14}$$

In the absence of uncertainty, the context in which these questions are usually investigated, the LHS of (3.14) always exceeds the RHS. That either inequality may hold may be seen by considering the Cobb-Douglas production function. By Proposition 12, $EY_w = f'e$, and hence by Jensen's inequality,

$$EU'Y_w \lessgtr f'elU'(f'el) \text{ as } \eta \lessgtr 1$$

and

$$f'eEU'g \gtrless EU'Y_w \text{ as } \beta \lessgtr 0.$$

It is clear that if $\eta < 1$, $\beta > 0$, the RHS of (3.14) exceeds the LHS. In other cases, the result is ambiguous.[29] (b) What is the effect of a change in e on

$$U'\beta^* + V'?$$

The conventional partial equilibrium analysis observes that by the second order condition

$$U''\beta^{*2} + V'' < 0,$$

but general equilibrium analysis takes into account the change in β^*; the general equilibrium effect depends on the sign of

$$V'' + U''f'^2l^2 + U''f''el^3f' + U'f''l^2 \sim -(1-\eta)\left(\frac{1}{d\ln e/d\ln\beta} + \frac{1-\gamma}{m}\right), \quad (3.15)$$

where m is the elasticity of substitution and $\eta = -U''\beta e/U'$.

We can thus establish that

Proposition 14. $e^w \gtrless e^s$ as

$$\left\{a^s EU'\left(\frac{a^s f(e^s l)}{l} + \beta^s\right)g - U'(f'(e^s l)e^s l)\right\}\left\{(\eta - 1)\left(\frac{1}{d\ln e/d\ln\beta} + \frac{1-\gamma}{m}\right)\right\} \lessgtr 0.$$

There appears to be no presumption that sharecropping reduces effort (labour) from what it would be under a wage system with enforceable contracts.

3.3 *Choices of Techniques*

Unlike the earlier economies analysed, where even though workers and landlords had different attitudes towards risk, if both landlords and workers could mix contracts the sharecropping system was able to equate their marginal rates of substitution (say between mean and standard deviation of income), here this is not true. In our example in the previous subsections, landlords were risk neutral, while workers still bore a large part of the risk. Thus, in questions of choice of technique and crops, there will appear to be conflict of interest between the landlord and workers. At any specified share contract, the landlord wants only to have the worker choose whatever technique or crop maximizes expected output; the worker is willing at the margin to sacrifice some mean output for a reduction in risk. Although some of the "conflict" can be avoided by careful stipulation within the contract (although both sides may feel "unhappy" in the sense that they could imagine a better "contract" presumably neither side would sign if there existed other individuals with whom they could sign a better contract) for many of the same reasons that it is difficult to enforce a contract

---

[29] E.g. if $\eta = 2$, $\left(\frac{\partial \ln e}{\partial \ln a}\right)_W = \frac{c}{1-\gamma}$, so $\beta = 0$, $a = \gamma$. Let

$$g = \begin{cases} \frac{1}{2} & \text{with probability } 0.5 \\ \frac{3}{2} & \text{with probability } 0.5 \end{cases}$$

Then the LHS exceeds the right as $\gamma \gtrless \frac{3}{4}$.

for a stated level of "effort", requirements on technique of production may be difficult to enforce without close (and costly) supervision.

One of the most important choices in technique involves the use of other factors of production, in particular, of capital.

If, as in Sections 1–2, there were no problems in contract enforcement, a contract would be specified by the amount of capital contributed by both the landlord and the worker. It can be shown

Proposition 15. *With completely enforceable contracts, if contracts can be mixed, and if there is a safe investment yielding a return of r, the mean marginal product of capital is just $r/(EU'g/EU')$, and will be the same for all farms. If workers' contracts cannot be mixed, then the more risk averse individuals will have a higher mean marginal product of capital.*[30]

The more interesting and difficult problems arise when there are "enforcement" problems. First, the operations that need to be specified in the contract are likely to be increased, and hence the need for supervision is increased. Did the machine break down because the worker did not treat it correctly? Secondly, in the absence of

---

[30] Let k_r be the capital per acre contributed by the landlord, k_w be the capital per acre contributed by worker. Then $\beta = \beta(a, l, k_w, k_r)$. The worker maximizes

$$EU_w\left[\frac{af(l, k_w + k_r)}{l}g + \beta + r\left(\frac{k}{l} - \frac{k_w}{l}\right)\right]$$

so

$$af_k\frac{EU'_w g}{EU'_w} \geqq r - \beta_{k_w}l \qquad (3.16a)$$

with equality always holding if workers can borrow;

$$af_k\frac{EU'_w g}{EU'_w} = -\beta_{k_r}l. \qquad (3.16b)$$

Similarly, for the landlord, we obtain

$$(1 - a)f_k\frac{EU'_r g}{EU'_r} = \beta_{k_w}l \qquad (3.16c)$$

$$(1 - a)f_k\frac{EU'_r g}{EU'_r} \geqq r + \beta_{k_r}l \qquad (3.16d)$$

with equality always holding if landlords can borrow. Assume $(3.16a)$ or $(3.16d)$ hold with equality. If

$$\frac{EU'_w g}{EU'_w} = \frac{EU'_r g}{EU'_r}$$

then

$$f_k\frac{EU'g}{EU'} = r.$$

Note also that if either $(3.16a)$ or $(3.16d)$ holds with equality, then they both must hold with equality.

close supervision, it is important to provide an incentive for the worker to use the capital goods supplied by the landlord appropriately. Thirdly, it is advantageous to the landlord (as long as he receives any share of the output) to have the worker supply as much of his own capital as possible, and conversely (for any given share-fixed fee contract) it is advantageous to the worker to have the landlord supply as much of the capital as possible.

We can use a simple modification of the model presented earlier to illustrate these points. The landlord, in deciding how much capital he should invest, needs to take account of the fact that, in general, the more capital he invests, the less his workers will invest; but the more capital he supplies, the higher the return to effort, and hence the greater effort he is likely to obtain from his workers. Thus, if he is risk neutral, he

$$\text{maximizes } (1 - a) f(el, k_w - k_r) - \beta(k_r, a, l)l + r(\bar{k} - k_r) \tag{3.17}$$

so that

$$f_k - r \leqq af_k - \left[(1 - a) f_{el} l \left(\frac{\partial e}{\partial k_r} \right)_w - \frac{\partial \beta}{\partial k_r} \right] \tag{3.17a}$$

$$e(1 - a) f_{el} \left(1 + \left(\frac{\partial \ln e}{\partial \ln l} \right)_w \right) - \beta - \frac{l \partial \beta}{\partial l} + (1 - a) f_k \left(\frac{\partial k_w}{\partial l} \right)_w = 0 \tag{3.17b}$$

$$-f - \frac{l \partial \beta}{\partial a} + (1 - a) \left[f_{el} l \left(\frac{\partial e}{\partial a} \right)_w + f_k \left(\frac{\partial k_w}{\partial a} \right)_w \right] = 0. \tag{3.17c}$$

$(3.17a)$ can be rewritten

$$f_k \leqq \frac{r - (1 - a) f_{el} l \left(\frac{\partial e}{\partial k_r} \right)_w}{1 - ac} \tag{3.18a}$$

with equality holding if the landlord does any investing. Similarly, if the worker does any investing

$$f_k = \frac{r}{a(1 - c)}. \tag{3.18b}$$

Hence we obtain

Proposition 16. *In contracts without supervision the capital is supplied by the worker or by the capitalist, depending on whether*

$$r + a(1 - c) f_{el} l \left(\frac{\partial e}{\partial k_r} \right)_w \lessgtr 0.$$

The case where $k_w = 0$ follows essentially along the lines developed earlier. On the other hand when $k_r = 0$, from $(3.17c)$ it is clear that a will be larger than in the cases analysed earlier: in addition to the incentive effect on effort, there is an incentive effect on the supply of capital, and the increased capital is likely to lead to a further increase in effort because it raises the marginal return to effort. It is still true however that $a < 1$.[31]

4 General Remarks on Incentive Schemes

In the previous section we analysed equilibrium in an economy with a particular incentive scheme, one in which there was no supervision at all of the individual. Such incentive schemes are particularly important in economies (processes) subject to great uncertainty: on the one hand, the uncertainty makes it difficult to ascertain whether a low output was a result of a low level of input by the worker or of "bad luck" on his particular plot of land (see Stiglitz 1971b); moreover, the multiplicity of contingencies would entail an impossible degree of complexity in the work contract were it to attempt to specify the action to be taken in each contingency. On the other hand, incentive schemes force the worker to bear a greater share of the risk than he otherwise would.

Most industrial processes—and many agricultural processes as well—rely on a fair amount of supervision in addition to, or as an alternative to, the incentive schemes sketched here. This is partly because, in production processes involving many individuals working together it may be difficult to separate out each individual's contribution but also partly because the same effort may be obtained without forcing the worker to bear as much risk.

Supervision would affect the analysis of the previous section in several ways. (a) There is probably an important element of fixed costs in supervision. That is, in the rental system, no supervision is required, but if $a < 1$, some supervision is required simply to ensure that the worker delivers the appropriate share of output. At $a = 0$, the landlord replaces incentive structures with direct supervision. If supervision costs look as in Figure (4.1) there is some inducement to use one of the "polar contracts"— a pure rent or pure wage system.[32] (b) The more supervision, the less effort (decision making) is required of the individual worker.

In most industrial processes, supervision serves an additional function: a higher degree of supervision results in a more accurate assessment of the individual's efforts; that is, supervision for the purpose of imposing rewards and penalties may be looked at as essentially a sampling of how the individual behaves under various circumstances; the larger the sample, the smaller the variance in the estimate of the worker's effort (the "quality" of his performance). Thus, considerations of equity require that a reward-penalty structure system with very high rewards and penalties have a higher degree of supervision than those with low rewards and penalties; employers,

[31] It should be emphasized that throughout our analysis we have been exploring the implications of first order conditions only. The problem described by (3.17) is not, however, in general a "nice concave" problem, so there may be local optima as well.

[32] The level of expenditure on supervision is in fact an endogenous variable, as we suggested earlier. To completely model the consequences of supervision would take us beyond the scope of this paper. Needless to say, the remarks in the last paragraph are meant only to be suggestive.

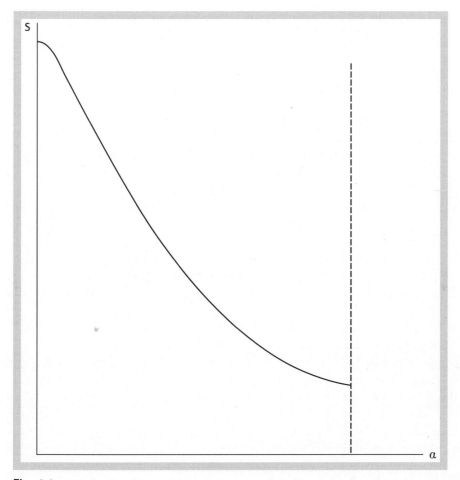

Fig. 4.1.

of course, are not likely to be directly concerned with equity; but the variability in income from the more random application of the penalty structure requires either a higher share or a higher fixed payment to induce the individual worker to accept a contract.

Many reward-penalty structures take the form of a fixed wage with a reward or penalty for a deviation from the "norm" or average performance. The deviations from the norm are more likely to be detected—and hence the incentives likely to be more effective—under close supervision.

A similar reward-penalty structure could be used in agriculture as an alternative to sharecropping. For instance, the following is a linear reward structure:

$$Y_w = \overline{Y}_w + \rho \left(\frac{f}{l} - \frac{\bar{f}}{l} \right) g,$$

where $\bar{f}/l$ is the average output per man. Since the average pay is just $\overline{Y}_w$, a risk neutral landlord will hire workers up to the point where

$$ef'(el) = \overline{Y}_w$$

(the bars denote averages taken over the population working for a given landlord), and workers supply effort up to the point where

$$\rho f'EU'g + V' = 0.$$

Increasing ρ has several effects. (a) If the level of effort of all other individuals were to remain constant, then it would increase the work effort of those near and below the mean but might decrease the work effort of those above the mean.[33] (b) An increase in average work effort results in all individuals working still harder; a decrease, in them all working still less hard. (c) If there is an increase in average work effort, it decreases the marginal productivity of the average worker if the elasticity of substitution is very low; thus "base pay" is reduced and the income effect again results in their working harder.[34] (d) if the base pay is fixed in the short run for some reason, it results in a decrease in the marginal product of the average worker and so workers will be "laid off".

This simple example illuminates a number of the statements one hears about incentive schemes (or about redistributive schemes more generally): Those who favour a high "ρ" argue that it is only "fair" that those who work harder—the others are, at least partially, just free riders—should get more pay, and point to the favourable effects on work effort of high "ρ". Those who oppose point out three things: (a) incentive schemes result in greater inequality; (b) they result in an important externality, commonly known as the rat race: the fact that others work harder "forces" all of them to work harder (i.e. an increase in mean work effort leads each utility maximizing individual to work harder). This is often couched in normative terms: observing the fact that there is an externality, it is alleged that individuals are lead to work *too hard*. I find it too difficult to evaluate such statements, since the normative reference allocation scheme against which this is being compared is not clear.[35] (c) Finally, observing the general equilibrium effects of either reduced wages per unit of effective effort or reduced employment, they point out that such schemes may not be in the interests of workers in general.

This raises the general problem of devising reward-penalty-supervisory structures which are "optimal", a question which we hope to pursue elsewhere.

5 Concluding Comments

We began the analysis of this paper with two objectives in mind. (a) Could we "explain" the change in the agricultural sector away from the use of sharecropping and

---

[33] I.e. the ambiguity arises because of the income effect.

[34] If the elasticity of substitution is not "very low", the opposite occurs.

[35] See for instance, Nalebuff and Stiglitz (1983a, 1983b) and Stiglitz (1980a)

to the use of the other two polar contracts: the wage system, primarily in the context of large farms and plantations, and the rental system (leasing-in land), primarily in smaller, family farms. (*b*) Could a model of sharecropping in agriculture shed any light on "shareholding" in the industrial sector.

It initially appeared to me curious that while earlier economies used sharing arrangements in the agricultural sector but not in the urban (artisan) sector, modern economies use sharing arrangements in the manufacturing sector, not in the agricultural sector. As I shall suggest in a moment, the two phenomena may be more closely related than at first seems to be the case.

In these concluding comments, I shall sketch, in a suggestive rather than definitive manner, the implications of our earlier analysis for these problems.

The End of Sharecropping

First, it appears from the results of Section 2, that the increase in wealth or a change in risk in agriculture cannot in themselves explain the change in the payments system; although they might have had an effect on the actual values of the parameters of the contract, there is no reason to believe that the differences in relative risk aversion between landlords and workers would have increased as a result of an increase in wealth to a sufficient extent to lead the economy near to one of the polar contracts, and even then it could only explain the use of a wage system.[36] And even as the risk goes to zero, the share goes to a limiting value that is not one of the polar (rental or wage) cases.

Secondly, the sharecropping system—in the absence of other methods of risk sharing—is not an inefficient system. It is not as if landlords and workers, anticipating the analysis of Marshall and other economists, discovered that it provided too little incentive to work and therefore they replaced an inefficient payments system with a more efficient one. Indeed, we argued that the labour supply in our simple model is identical to that which would result from a centrally controlled agricultural economy.

The sharecropping system may result in the economy not being *productively efficient*, i.e. the effective labour/land ratio may differ on different plots of land. But this does not demonstrate the inefficiency of the system as a whole given the relevant economic constraints. The sharecropping system is adopted because of its incentive effects (when direct supervision is costly or ineffective) and because of its risk-sharing features. Although the rental system has greater incentive effects, it forces the worker to bear all the risks, and although the wage system allows the landlord, if he is risk neutral, to absorb all the risk, it may force heavy supervision costs on him.

We come then to the following hypotheses concerning the elimination of the sharecropping system.

---

[36] Assuming that landlords are less risk averse than workers. Note that if there is decreasing relative risk aversion, this is what we would expect, since landlords have, in general, a larger income, than workers.

(a) The development of capital markets in which landlords and workers (to the extent that they had capital), could diversify their portfolio meant that the relative importance of sharecropping as a risk sharing arrangement declined.

(b) The increasing capital intensity of agriculture meant that either the landlord had to provide strong incentives (the rental system) or had to provide close supervision leading to the wage system. Since there is a natural nonconvexity associated with supervision, it was the larger farms which used the wage system. Similarly, since the rental system required the worker to provide the capital, it was the wealthier workers who became renters, the poorer workers becoming landless workers.

(c) The increase in the rate of technological change has much the same effect as the increased capital intensity of production. The landlord wants the best techniques to be used. Either he must provide a strong incentive to the worker to acquire these techniques or he must supervise the workers closely. Again technological change (information gathering) introduces another nonconvexity into the production process (i.e. the fixed costs of acquiring the information may be large relative to the variable cost of disseminating the information among the workers). This would imply that large farms might be technologically more advanced than smaller farms.[37]

---

[37] This model suggests in addition a possible interpretation to the enclosure movement. The essential question is, why did the landlords decide to capture rents from land which they previously had not been capturing? Two hypotheses have been put forward.

The first argues that until that time, the implicit rents were small, but increased land scarcity and technological advances made it more worthwhile for the landlord to capture these rents.

The second argues that there was an institutional change: the development of the market economy and the associated ideas of private ownership led landlords to take for themselves what until then had been viewed as public land.

In our view, the common land may be viewed as part of a complicated payments system. The rights to use the "common" land were part of this payments system, but in some sense all the land belonged to the landlord. Changes in technology and markets made it advantageous to change the payments system, including the "rights" to the common land. For instance, consider a situation where on some of the land crops were grown, providing the basis for survival. The inherent uncertainties in small-scale agriculture and the absence of appropriate insurance markets made a sharecropping system advantageous. For traditional crops grown by traditional methods, variations in effort may not have been significant, and so close supervision was not required. On the other hand, for other commodities, in particular for animal raising (which by its very nature is "capital intensive" (including cattle as "capital")) incentive effects were important. Thus the landlord gave the right to use the "common land" to the workers; this reduced the share and the fixed fee that workers otherwise would have had to have been paid. There was a potential cost to this particular method: since marginal cost pricing was not used in the allocation of the land, there was always the possibility of overgrazing. Whether or not this was a real cost depended on (a) the implicit terms of the contract, i.e. were the farmers allowed to graze as many cattle as cows or sheep as they wished, or was there any implicit understanding of the maximum "fair" number any single worker could have and (b) whether other constraints (the availability of capital with which to purchase cows or sheep) limited the amount of grazing.

The technological changes to which we referred earlier made it desirable for the landlord to change both the payments scheme and the land allocation among different uses. At the same time, if there were not implicit limits on the use of the common land, increased grazing reduced the value of the use of the common land as a means of payment.

This example is only meant to illustrate how incentives and risk sharing may lead to much more complicated contractual patterns than the simple ones discussed in the text. Whether our possible

The Corporation as a Form of Sharecropping

The relationship between sharecropping and joint stock companies may best be seen in terms of the early formation of such firms. There are two factors of production, "capital" and "entrepreneurship". The entrepreneur "hires" the capital (or the "capitalists" hire the entrepreneur) to work for him. The capital gets paid a fixed fee (bonds) and/or "a share"; the entrepreneur usually gets a share of the capital value of the firm as his payment (in addition often to a fixed fee). In a "closely held firm", we have then a simple theory of the optimal (or equilibrium) debt-equity ratio. It is a simple translation of our theory of the contract in agriculture.

There are, however, several important differences between the modern corporation and the simple agricultural economy. The first two differences arise out of the fact that shares of the firm are publicly marketed. In the simpler closely held corporation, there was no ambiguity about the objective of the firm. It was to maximize the utility of the worker (entrepreneur) (and the contract arrangements were such that it simultaneously maximized the utility of the landlord (the capitalist)). Now, we must consider the possibility of a new objective: maximizing the stockmarket value of the firm. Under certain very restricted conditions, again there is no conflict between this objective and maximizing the utility of the entrepreneur, and of the capitalists. But in general, in the absence of perfect insurance (futures) markets the objectives may not be congruent.[38]

Secondly, again because shares are publicly marketed, the entrepreneur can divest himself of his shares, and this may eliminate one of the major advantages of the sharing arrangements—its incentive effects. This in turn has two effects (a) it becomes necessary to devise more complicated incentive arrangements; and (b) because the entrepreneur has "inside information", he can take advantage of "bad news" as well as "good news" to make a profit. It is possible—at least in the short-run—for there to be perverse incentive effects.

Thirdly, because of the greater complexity of the operations of the modern corporation, it becomes much more difficult for the "capitalist" to supervise his worker ("the entrepreneur") to ascertain even whether he is doing a good job. This becomes all the more important because of the two difficulties we already noted: (a) the presence of conflicts of interest and (b) the difficulties in providing correct incentives.

Thus, it would appear that the main contribution of the model of risk sharing and incentives in agriculture may be more in extending our understanding of the operations of the closely held firm and the differences between it and the modern widely held corporation, than in its direct implications for the latter.

---

interpretation of the enclosure movement has any general validity depends on much more detailed empirical evidence.

[38] See, for instance, Stiglitz 1972b.

CHAPTER 14

INFORMATION, COMPETITION, AND MARKETS*

ONE of the dominant characteristics of modern capitalist economies is the important role played by competition: not the peculiar static form of pure price competition embodied in the Arrow-Debreu model, but rather a dynamic competition, more akin to the kind of competition represented by sports contests and other races (including patent races).

In recent years, there have been several attempts to explain why firms often base the pay of their workers and managers on relative performance. (See, for example, Edward Lazear and Sherwin Rosen, 1981.) Such compensation schemes become desirable when three conditions are satisfied: (a) The input (effort) of workers (managers) must not be directly observable, at least without cost. Thus firms must either expend resources to monitor inputs or devise reward structures in which compensation is a function of variables (such as output or profits) which are themselves functions of inputs but are less costly to observe. (b) The relationship between input and output must be stochastic, so that by observing output, one cannot perfectly infer what the input was. (c) Finally, the stochastic disturbances which affect the relationship between input and output of different workers (firms) must be correlated. By looking at the performance of one worker relative to that of others, one can make better inferences about his effort than one can make without using this information.

Not only can competition provide a basis of comparison, which enables the design of reward structures that can simultaneously provide a high level of incentives with relatively low level risk; but compensation schemes based on relative performance

* Written with Barry J. Nalebuff. We are indebted to Steve Salop, Sherwin Rosen, Ed Lazear, Felix Fitzroy, Joe Farrell, and Oliver Hart for helpful conversations. Financial support of the National Science Foundation is gratefully acknowledged. Reprinted with permission from the *American Economic Review*, 73(2) (May), 1983.

have the further advantage of automatically adjusting incentives to changes in the economic environment. (We refer to this as "built-in flexibility.") In a first best world, with perfect information concerning the nature of the technology (but where it is still costly to monitor individuals' activities), the compensation scheme would vary from time to time as the environment changed. Such changes in the compensation scheme are costly to implement and the information required to do so is seldom available. When a task is easier, the individual's rewards for performing the task should be reduced. If pay is based on *relative* performance, although all individuals perform better (when they exert the same level of effort), their compensation is automatically adjusted. Thus, teachers frequently grade on the curve and a significant fraction of the pay of successful salesmen often consists of bonuses based on relative performance.

I Competition and Compensation

To see more clearly exactly how competition can provide the basis of the design of a better compensation scheme, we consider a simple example. Assume the government wishes to develop a bomber. Neither the government nor the potential developers know how much it should cost to build the bomber. With a fixed-fee contract (where the amount received by the developer is independent of his costs), the contractor will require a large risk premium to compensate for the large risk he must bear. The government can reduce the risk by sharing in the costs; but to the extent that it does this, it also reduces the contractor's incentives to save on costs. There is an alternative contractual arrangement that may be superior. Assume there are a number of potential contractors of the same ability, so that the costs faced by one firm (at any particular level of effort) will be identical to those faced by another firm. Assume the government lets out two contracts; it promises to pay firm A a fixed amount *plus* whatever it costs firm B to produce the bomber; and conversely for firm B. Since their costs are perfectly correlated, this scheme eliminates all risk. At the same time, the scheme has perfect incentives: if firm A can, by exerting extra effort, reduce costs it gets to keep the savings. Having two separate firms provides us with information which simply would not be available otherwise. This information allows the implementation of a compensation scheme with lower risk and better incentives. There is a cost: the government has had to pay for duplicate research expenditure, but this may still be less expensive than the alternative.[1]

---

[1] With only two firms, there is the further danger of collusion. As the number of firms increases, the likelihood of collusion may decrease, but the excessive waste from duplication increases. In other contexts, however, such as natural monopolies with average cost curves only slightly declining, the loss in efficiency from having several competitors may be slight.

A General Theorems on the Optimality of Contests and Relative Performance Schemes

A natural question to raise at this point is, are there circumstances in which an appropriately designed contest or relative performance scheme can attain a first best allocation, that is, the same level of effort in every state as would obtain if information about the state were freely available and effort were costless to monitor, without the worker needing to bear any risk.

We consider a general structure in which the individual's output Q_i (assumed to be observable) is a function of a common random variable θ, his effort μ_i, and an idiosyncratic random variable ϵ_i; for simplicity, we assume a linear relationship of the form:[2]

$$Q_i = \mu_i \theta + \epsilon_i; E\epsilon_i = E\epsilon_i\epsilon_j = E\epsilon_j\theta = 0. \tag{1}$$

The worker observes θ before he decides on effort; but the manager-owner of the firm can neither observe θ, μ_i, nor ϵ_i; he can only observe the output of each of his workers. We now show that if the distribution of ϵ_i is compact (as a normalization, we assume it ranges from -1 to $+1$), then with only two workers, it is possible to design an incentive structure which attains the first best. (This result is stronger than that of the earlier example, since the technology of the two individuals is not perfectly correlated.)

We assume, for simplicity, that workers have additively separable utility functions of the form

$$U(Y) - V(\mu), \tag{2}$$

where Y is income. With perfect information, a first best allocation requires $Y = \overline{Y}$ (individuals obtain perfect insurance) and

$$\theta U(\overline{Y}) = V'(\mu). \tag{3}$$

(The marginal rate of substitution between leisure and goods equal the marginal rate of transformation.) The solution to (3) we refer to as the optimal level of effort, and denote by $\mu^*(\theta)$. Assume that after the individual has observed θ, but before he has allocated his effort (and, in particular, before the output has been produced), the individual is asked to announce a "goal." He is told if he comes within one unit of making his goal, he will have a given income; if he fails to come within a unit of meeting his goal, he receives minus infinity (or a suitably large punishment). The higher the goal he sets, the higher the income he will receive, provided he attains it. Finally, he is told that his pay will depend on the announcement of others as well; they observe, of course, exactly the same common random variable that he does. We now

---

[2] What is crucial about this specification is that the common random variable affects the marginal productivity of labor; as a result, in the first best allocation, effort will change from state to state. Since one of the issues with which we are concerned is the extent to which compensation schemes provide the appropriate incentives to change the level of effort in response to changes in circumstances, it is important that the model analyzed have this feature.

show that there exists a compensation structure of the form indicated which provides perfect incentives and eliminates all risk.

Consider the compensation scheme which pays the ith individual

$$Y^i = \frac{\phi(\hat{\theta}^i)}{U'(\overline{Y})} - \frac{\phi(\bar{\theta}^{-i})}{U'(\overline{Y})} + \overline{Y} \quad \text{if } Q_i \geq \mu^*(\hat{\theta}^i)\hat{\theta}^i - 1, \; -\infty \text{ otherwise;} \tag{4}$$

where $\hat{\theta}^i$ is the ith individual's announcement of θ, $\bar{\theta}^{-i}$ is the average of the announcements of other individuals. If each contestant tells the truth, the individual faces no risk, since $\phi(\hat{\theta}^i) = \phi(\bar{\theta}^{-i})$. Moreover, the individual will, if he announces θ, always make his target; he will choose his level of effort so that in the worst event ($\epsilon = -1$), he just makes it. The return to announcing a higher value of θ is then

$$U'(\overline{Y})\phi'/U'(\overline{Y}) - V'd\mu/d\hat{\theta}. \tag{5}$$

To guarantee meeting the quota,

$$\mu^*(\hat{\theta})\hat{\theta} = \mu\theta, \tag{6}$$

$$d\mu/d\hat{\theta} = (\hat{\theta}/\theta)(d\mu^*/d\hat{\theta}) + \mu^*(\hat{\theta})/\theta. \tag{7}$$

Hence if

$$\phi' = V'[d\mu^*/d\theta + \mu^*(\theta)/\theta], \tag{8}$$

equation (5) will equal zero when $\hat{\theta} = \theta$. By integrating (8), we obtain a ϕ function which, when used in the compensation scheme (4), provides perfect incentives and eliminates all risks.

Though the use of targets in conjunction with a relative performance scheme can, under some idealized conditions, provide the basis of an extremely effective compensation system, it has its limitations: if, for instance, individuals obtain information about their idiosyncratic random variable at different times, or if the support of the idiosyncratic random variable differs for different individuals or is not known by the employer. (If individuals know ϵ before the announcement occurs or if the announcement must be made before θ is known, the announcement conveys no information additional to that which is conveyed by observing Q.)

B Further Results on Contests

In our forthcoming article, we investigate the design of compensation schemes which do not employ announcements. We have shown how contests can be designed to provide the first best level of effort in every state of nature. In general, such contests do impose a greater risk on the individual than he would bear if monitoring effort were costless. There are two conditions under which contests may attain a first best outcome: (i) if the agents are risk neutral; or (ii) when there are a large number of contestants. Although generalized relative performance schemes include, as special cases, individualistic schemes (compensation schemes where pay depends only on the individual's own performance) and thus must be at least as good as such schemes, determining circumstances under which simple relative performance schemes (such as contests) do better than the simple kinds of individualistic schemes (such as piece rates) often found in practice is a far more difficult question. We show that contests will be preferred to (even nonlinear) individualistic schemes when the risk associated with the common environmental variable is large (relative to that of the idiosyncratic random variable). This is a theme to which we shall return later.

II Markets and Competition

Markets provide reward structures which have some of the properties of contests and relative performance schemes. The exact nature of the compensation scheme provided by the market for the owner-manager of a firm depends critically on the nature of the production technology and the market equilibrium. Consider, for instance, two firms engaged in cost reducing *R&D*. If the production technology is constant returns to scale, with marginal cost c, the profits of the ith firm will depend on his costs and those of his rival: $\pi_i(c_1, c_2)$. The profit function will differ markedly depending on whether the duopoly equilibrium is best described as a Nash-Cournot quantity setting equilibrium or as an Edgeworth-Bertrand price setting equilibrium. This is an example of a relative performance compensation scheme. But while our earlier study considered the *design* of a compensation scheme, here we are concerned with *describing* the consequences of the compensation scheme which is always *implicit* in the market equilibrium.

A Market Reward Structures Have the Property of Built-In Flexibility

If the cost functions facing different firms are correlated (there is a common environmental variable affecting all firms) when costs are low, price is low, and therefore profits will be less variable and rewards more commensurate with the difficulty of the task than in a noncompetitive environment. To see this, consider the following modification of the previous example: let the costs of production be

$$c_i = k - \theta\mu_i, \tag{9}$$

where μ_i is the (unobservable) level of managerial effort. There are a large number of firms, sufficiently large that they act as price takers. The "net" profit of the owner-manager $\hat{\pi}_i$ taking into account the utility cost of managerial effort, is[3]

$$\hat{\pi}_i = [P - k + \mu_i\theta - V(\mu_i)]Q_i = \pi_i - V(\mu_i)Q_i, \tag{10}$$

where Q_i is the output of the ith firm and P is the price of output. In competitive equilibrium

$$P = \underset{\{\mu_i\}}{Min} \{k - \mu_i\theta + V(\mu_i)\}; \tag{11}$$

and

$$\hat{\pi}_i = 0, \text{ for all producing firms.} \tag{12}$$

Thus, competition *forces* each of the competitors to expend the correct amount of effort at cost-reduction activities; and it does this in such a way as to eliminate all variability in net profits (they are identically zero).

An owner-manager monopolist would have the correct incentives for cost minimization, but would face considerable variability in his profits.

B The Consequences of the Separation of Ownership and Management

But markedly different results obtain in the comparative performance of managers who do not own all the resources which they manage. Assume that there is a competitive supply of managers. The equilibrium in the competitive market remains as described above. Since there is no risk, the optimal contract entails the manager receiving 100 percent of the profits at the margin. (Effectively, the identity of ownership and control is an endogenous characteristic of this economy.) But consider the problem of the monopolist attempting to hire a manager for his enterprise. He wishes to choose a contract which maximizes his own expected utility, subject to the constraint of being able to hire the manager. For simplicity, we assume the manager is risk averse, but the owner is risk neutral.[4] Then the optimal contract will entail some risk sharing by the original owner. (The interests of owner and manager do not coincide; the separation of the two is again an endogenous feature of this economy.) If we limit ourselves to simple linear contracts, then the pay of the manager will be of the form $\alpha\pi_i + \beta$, assuming that profits of the firm are observable, but the input of the manager is not. (β is a fixed fee, which may be either negative or positive, but plays no essential role in the subsequent analysis.) Three consequences follow immediately from the fact that it is optimal for $0 < \alpha < 1$.

1) Managers will not expend the efficient amount of resources on cost reduction; they will set $\alpha\theta = V'(\mu)$.

---

[3] In this formulation, the effort expended is proportional to the level of output; there are neither increasing nor decreasing returns to scale in managerial technology. This assumption is made to avoid the difficulties which arise in comparing economies in which the number of managers (as opposed to aggregate managerial effort) is relevant.

[4] All that is really required is that the manager be more risk averse than the original owner.

2) Managers will not adjust their effort to changes in circumstances as much as they would in the competitive regime; when it is easier to reduce costs, they effectively enjoy some of the benefits of the increased ease in greater leisure (to a greater extent than this would be true in a competitive economy): $d\mu/d\theta = a/V'' < 1/V''$. This phenomenon is sometimes referred to as managerial slack. The argument for why noncompetitive environments may experience managerial slack is perhaps even stronger than we have put it here. The owner of the firm may have knowledge about the "normal" state of nature; the contract thus may implicitly specify a normal level of effort, and a normal expected return. When the level of effort required to attain this "normal level" is greater, the managers have an incentive to present evidence to that effect; while if the level of effort required is less than this normal level, the managers have no incentive to present that information. The natural asymmetries of information give rise to an asymmetry in response to unusually good and unusually bad states.

3) Managers still have to bear some risk.

C Imperfect Competition

In the case of competitive economies, all the relevant information is embodied in the price; the owner of the firm does not have to base his manager's pay on the observed costs of his firm, say, relative to that of other firms. In the case of imperfectly competitive economies (for example, duopolies), the owner may wish to employ an incentive scheme which makes use of some of this detailed information, if it is available. Indeed, a slight modification of the first example given in this paper shows that it is possible with only two firms to design managerial incentive schemes in which the manager bears no risk yet has perfect incentives.

D Correlations Between Firms' Costs

The success of the relative performance schemes analyzed in the previous section was based on the fact that all firms faced identical cost functions. Assume that there are two firms, each of which has a choice of two technologies (or any linear combination of the two). If a firm devotes λ of its resource to technology i, its cost function per unit output will be $F(\lambda, \theta_1, \theta_2)$ (where θ_i are random variables). Define λ^* as the mixture which minimizes the expected costs, $EF_\lambda(\lambda^*, \theta_1, \theta_2) = 0$. Assume that the manager's pay depends on the difference between his costs and that of his rival. Clearly, if one firm imitates his rival, then costs are identical, and there is no risk. But if $\lambda \neq \lambda^*$, the manager can move λ towards λ^*, and decrease mean costs, and thus increase his pay. Though this increases his risk, for small deviations he acts in a risk neutral manner; thus *the Nash equilibrium entails an efficient choice of techniques and no risk.*

There are three important qualifications to this result. First, assume firms can only choose technique 1 or technique 2. The mean return with technique 2 is higher. If firm A chooses technique 1, the B manager's risk by choosing technique 2 may be so much higher that he isn't sufficiently compensated by the increased mean. Thus, there may be an equilibrium in which both firms choose technique 1, and an equilibrium in which both firms choose technique 2. One of these may Pareto dominate the other.

Second, if one firm has a comparative advantage in technique 1, and the other firm in technique 2, then each firm will not choose the technique which minimized its expected costs, but rather will choose a technique which is somewhere between the cost-minimizing technique and the technique chosen by the other firm.

Third, if there is idiosyncratic risk, then even when the two firms imitate each other, risk is not eliminated; still, if the two firms face the *same* stochastic technology, the only equilibrium is that where costs are minimized.

E The Anarchy of the Market Place: Excessive Competition

While the stories we have told here have pictured competition as reducing the risks faced by businessmen, businessmen often complain that unbridled competition forces them to bear an excessive amount of risk; they have, accordingly, often called upon the government to help regulate (stabilize) the market place. Some of these pleas are simply blatant attempts to cartelize the market, and to reap the monopoly rents which result. On the other hand, when the idiosyncratic risk is large, the variability in profits may be large.

In such situations, in our earlier studies of contests with risk-averse agents, relative performance schemes did not work well, since they imposed an excess amount of risk on the contestants. Similarly, in our earlier example of the development of the bomber, if the two researchers face different cost functions, then basing the compensation of one researcher on his performance relative to that of another imposes an additional source of risk. The market imposes similar risks on managers, even when the compensation scheme is not based directly on relative performance, but on profits; because profits will, to a large extent, reflect differences in the costs of the firm relative to its competitors (or differences in relative performance in some other dimension, such as quality or marketing). To attempt to alleviate these risks by making pay less dependent on performance is likely simultaneously to ameliorate incentives.

III CONCLUSIONS

This paper has attempted to delineate a central role that competition plays: it allows the development of compensation schemes where pay is based on relative performance. Such compensation schemes have risk sharing, incentive, and built-in flexibility properties which make them superior to the best (individualistic) schemes which can be designed which do not make use of such information. The reward structures provided in competitive markets are, implicitly, related to relative performance. This provides an additional reason that competitive economies perform better than monopolies, a reason which is quite distinct from the loss in consumer's surplus arising from the monopolist's reduction in output. In particular, we have formulated a model in which monopolies are less efficient and less adaptable, and there is more managerial slack than in competitive economies. (In spite of the widespread belief that monopolies are less efficient than competitive firms—including the intertemporal inefficiencies arising from inadequate allocation of resources to *R&D*—in traditional neoclassical models, there is no managerial slack and monopolies are perfectly efficient.) We have indicated that there are limits to the extent to which the market may reduce risks: in some cases, competition may effectively increase it. An examination of the full consequences of our observations, including an investigation of the constrained optimality of the economy and the implications of our analysis for policy, must await another occasion. What should be apparent is that the perspectives into the functions of competition in market economies arising from the approach taken here stand in market contrast to those provided by the traditional competitive paradigm.

....

CHAPTER 15

HUMAN
FALLIBILITY
AND ECONOMIC
ORGANIZATION*

....

DOCTRINES concerning what is a good way to organize a society have influenced human societies more deeply than any other set of doctrines. Specifically, beliefs that one way of organizing production and exchange is better than others have inspired a number of socioeconomic experiments leading to modern capitalist and socialist societies, with far reaching implications. Yet surprisingly, the central doctrines, though a source of continuing ideological debate, have been the subject of only limited scientific enquiry. The major proposition, the so-called Lange-Lerner-Taylor Theorem asserting the equivalence between competitive capitalist economies and decentralized socialist economies which make use of the price system, made a point in stressing that the issue of the ownership of the means of production might not be central in the comparison of economic systems. The theorem, however, was based on models both of capitalism and of market socialism in which the most important differences between the two systems were suppressed.

   This paper describes a research program attempting to delineate some of the critical differences among alternative forms of economic organization. We contend that central to an understanding of these differences is an understanding of differences in the organization of decision making; of who gathers what information, how it gets communicated and to whom, and how decisions get made, both concerning what actions to take and who should fill decision-making positions. This view should be contrasted with the traditional economic paradigm in which decision making plays no role: the manager, for instance, simply looks up in a book of blueprints what

* Written with Raaj Kumar Sah. This is a shortened version of our paper (1986).

the appropriate technique of production is for the given set of factor prices. In the conventional paradigm, moreover, mistakes are never made, either in gathering or transmitting information, or in making decisions, and indeed, there are no costs associated with these activities. By contrast, the view we take here is that "to err is human," and that different organizational systems differ not only in what kinds of errors individuals make in them, but also in how the systems "aggregate" errors. As a result, organizations differ systematically in the kinds of errors they make, and thus in their overall economic performance. Organizations also differ in the costs associated with information collection, with information communication and processing, and with decision making. Indeed, as we discuss below, perfect decision making can be achieved by arranging enough decision makers in an appropriate manner, no matter how fallible the decision makers are, provided their decisions are not purely random (or worse). What prevents perfect decision making is the cost.

We refer to the specification of the structure of information gathering, communication and decision making as an organization's *architecture*. The objective of our research program has been to construct stylized models of an economic organization within which the consequences of alternative organizational architectures can be examined.

Using these models, not only can we compare the performance of particular organizational forms but we can also ask, given a particular set of objectives and circumstances, what is the optimal structure (within a class of structures); for example, what is the optimal number of levels in a hierarchy. We have constructed both a positive and a normative theory. Thus our approach allows us to assess the validity of many of the traditional claims concerning the merits of alternative systems.

I THE BASIC MODEL

To illustrate the basic principles at issue, we present the simplest possible formulation. Consider an organization facing the problem of choosing among a large number of available projects that are of two types: good projects with an expected return of x_1 and bad projects with an expected return of $-x_2$. A fraction a of the projects are good. With perfect information, all good projects, and no bad projects, would be undertaken. A decision maker makes a judgment about whether the project is good or bad based on whatever information he has. We assume that the information available to one decision maker cannot be fully communicated to others. Here we represent a polar form of this "limited" communication such that individuals within any organization convey to one another only whether they judge a project to be good or bad, even though they might have more information at their disposal.

All decision making is imperfect; we assume that the probability that a decision maker judges a good project to be good is $p_1 < 1$, and that the probability that he judges a bad project to be good is $p_2 > 0$; the fact that there is some filtering is reflected in $p_2 < p_1$.

We consider two different organizations, each consisting of two individuals. In a *polyarchy*, each individual has the right to accept a project and projects rejected by one are evaluated by the other. Thus, the probability that a good project is accepted is p_1 (the probability of acceptance in the first evaluation) plus $(1 - p_1)$ (the probability of rejection in the first evaluation) times p_1, the probability of acceptance in the second review. The probability that a good project is accepted is thus: $f_1^P = p_1(2 - p_1)$. Similarly, the probability that a bad project is accepted is: $f_2^P = p_2(2 - p_2)$. The (expected value of the) output of the organization is $Y^P = ax_1 f_1^P - (1 - a)x_2 f_2^P$.

By contrast, in a *hierarchy*, for a project to be undertaken, it must be approved by both levels of hierarchy; the probability of this for a good project is $f_1^H = p_1^2$, and for a bad project it is $f_2^H = p_2^2$. The output of the hierarchical organization is $Y^H = ax_1 f_1^H - (1 - a)x_2 f_2^H$.

Two results immediately emerge: *polyarchical organizations accept more bad projectes* ($f_2^P > f_2^H$); while *hierarchical organizations reject more good projects* ($f_1^H < f_1^P$). The fact that the two systems make different kinds of errors suggests that there will be circumstances under which one or the other performs better. We can ascertain those conditions by comparing the net output of the two systems:

$$Y^P \gtrless Y^H \tag{1}$$

as

$$ax_1 p_1(1 - p_1) \gtrless (1 - a)x_2 p_2(1 - p_2).$$

Condition (1) has a natural interpretation. Assume that we conducted two tests of the project simultaneously; projects with both tests turning out positive should clearly be accepted, those with both tests turning out negative should be rejected (otherwise, there would be no reason to run the tests). The question arises what should we do in a split decision. The probability of a split decision for a good project is $2p_1(1 - p_1)$ and for a bad project it is $2p_2(1 - p_2)$. Thus, the expected value of projects with a split decision is $2[ax_1 p_1(1 - p_1) - (1 - a)x_2 p_2(1 - p_2)]$. We accept projects with split decisions if their expected value is positive, and reject them if this is negative. But this is precisely the condition (1); if a project would have been accepted with a split decision, there is no point in having a second review; polyarchy is preferable to hierarchy. On the other hand, if a project with a split decision would have been rejected, then the second review is of value: hierarchy is preferred to polyarchy. Second reviews are also of greater value, in this context, when the ratio of bad projects to good projects is larger and when the losses from bad projects relative to the gains from good projects are greater.

There is another interpretation of our result, which becomes clearest when $ax_1 = (1 - a)x_2$. Then the condition (1) is equivalent to the condition $p_2 \gtrless 1 - p_1$ where p_2 is the probability of accepting a bad project (Type II error), $1 - p_1$ is the probability of rejecting a good project (Type I error). In this central case, whether a polyarchy is better than a hierarchy depends on the relative likelihood of the decision maker making the two types of errors. (A more general formulation of this problem is examined in our 1986 paper.)

Committees: Another type of organizational architecture is a committee. Committees are collections of individuals with well defined rules for decision making (adoption of a project); for example, majority rule or complete unanimity. In a committee with n members which requires the approval of at least k members for adoption, the probability of acceptance of a project, for which the individual's probability of a favorable review is p, is $f^c(n, k, p) = \sum_{j=k}^{n} \binom{n}{j} p^j (1 - p)^{n-j}$.

There is a formal similarity between a polyarchy and a committee in which only one individual needs to approve a project for it to be undertaken, and between a hierarchy and a committee in which all individuals in the committee need to approve the project. In our 1984b paper, we have examined the optimal size and decision rules for committees, and show, for instance, that for fixed n, output is a single peaked function of k; and that, for the symmetric case ($\alpha x_1 = (1 - \alpha)x_2$), whether more or less than a majority consensus should be required depends simply on whether $p_2 \gtrless 1 - p_1$.

II Complex Organizations

It should be apparent that most organizations are not one of the pure forms (hierarchy, polyarchy, or committee) discussed above, but rather a mixture of organizational forms. We can build more complex organizations out of these basic building blocks. Consider, for instance, a polyarchy of hierarchies in which to be approved, a project must receive the approval of at least one of several decision units; but each decision unit is, itself, a hierarchy. This corresponds, rather loosely, to a market economy. If each unit has n hierarchical layers, and there are m such units in a polyarchy, the probability of a type i project being accepted is $f(n, m, p_i) = 1 - (1 - p_i^n)^m$. By an appropriate choice of n and m, we can ensure that $f(n, m, p_1) > p_1$ and $f(n, m, p_2) < p_2$; that is, the (n, m) polyarchy-hierarchy accepts more good projects and rejects more bad projects than a single decision maker. Moreover it rejects more bad projects than the simple polyarchy (for which $n = 1$) and accepts more good projects than a simple hierarchy (for which $m = 1$). We can construct a more complex organization in which the above polyarchy of hierarchies serves as a single unit, and a second level polyarchy of hierarchies is created using such units. With enough such levels to our complex organization, we obtain perfect screening. It is the cost of decision making that prevents perfect decision making. The cost of a multilevel organization rises rapidly with the number of levels, while there is diminishing returns to the increase in expected output. The balance between these two yields an optimal structure to the organization.

The intuition behind why, with enough layers, perfect screening can be obtained is simple. A hierarchy is successful in increasing the proportion of good to bad projects, but only at the expense of throwing out a lot of good projects. In a polyarchy, on the other hand, the stock of projects under consideration is "replenished." In fact, as the number of units in a polyarchy increases, the probability of a project, of any type, getting accepted goes to one. The sense of our result is that if we first filter the set of projects through a hierarchy, and then through a polyarchy, the set of approved projects is more "refined" than what could have been obtained by a single filter; repetition of such a procedure yields perfect selection.

We can use the analysis of complex organizations in the preceding section to prove other interesting results: for instance, if the organizational cost depends only on the number of managers, then *it is better to reorganize a very long hierarchy into two (or more) polyarchies*: and *it is better to rearrange a very large polyarchy as two (or more) polyarchic subunits within a hierarchy*. (See our 1985b and 1988a paper.)

III Selecting Managers: Towards Organizational Dynamics

Among the most important decisions made within any organization are those concerning who will fill what jobs. The fact that such attention is focused on this problem suggests that it makes a difference; individuals differ in their abilities to acquire, communicate, and process information. For each organizational architecture, there is an optimal assignment of individuals with different characteristics. More importantly, the performance of some organizational forms is more sensitive than others to how these assignments are made, and the errors in assignment are themselves functions of the organizational architecture.

The "rules" by which an organization chooses its successors give rise to stochastic processes, describing the assignments of individuals with different abilities to different positions within the organization. We can analyze, say, the steady state of these stochastic processes for various organizational architectures, and compare their relative performance. We illustrate here how this may be done.

Assume that there are two types of individuals, competent (C) and incompetent (I). Further, suppose that each person in a polyarchy chooses his own successor, whereas the higher level hierarch chooses his own successor as well as that of his subordinate. Clearly, there are four states of a system: (C, C), (C, I), (I, C), and (I, I). We can show $Pr(C, I)$ and $Pr(I, C)$ are larger in a polyarchy, whereas $Pr(C, C)$ and $Pr(I, I)$ are larger in a hierarchy. If the average output of the two systems were the same, any risk averse society would prefer a polyarchy. (For details, see our 1984c paper.)

Alternative economic organizations also differ in their ability to correct selection mistakes. We suspect, therefore, that a still stronger case for polyarchy can be made once (evolutionary) mechanisms for eliminating deficient organizations are introduced (for example, bankruptcies in a market system).

IV EXTENSIONS

The formulation presented here ignores three aspects of cost determination associated with organizational design: (a) time (the more levels to an organization, the greater the time required for decision making); (b) communication costs (not only the direct costs of communication, but also the errors which inevitably arise in the process of communication); and (c) the sequence of decision making (for instance, all individuals are assumed to review all projects in a committee, whereas the upper levels in a hierarchy review only those projects which have been sent up to them by lower levels). Since there are costs to review, the sequencing of the review process may have considerable effect on the resources spent on evaluation.

Elsewhere, we have explored these and other extensions of the basic analysis including (a) a more extensive treatment of the consequences of the use of Bayesian decision rules (though, given the information technology of our basic model, our analysis is Bayesian); (b) an analysis of the endogenous determination of the level of expenditures on information acquisition; (c) an analysis of the consequences of alternative organizational forms on the set of available projects (the mix of projects available to an organization itself is an endogenous variable, determined by the incentives provided to those who develop projects; this in turn is partly dependent on the likelihood of projects of different types being adopted, which differ markedly across organizational architectures); (d) an evaluation of alternative organizational forms faced with different problems, for example, choosing the best set of projects, rather than maximizing the expected profit; and (e) externalities. For instance, one organization's decision affects the productivity of projects undertaken by other organizations. Such interactions are important in certain circumstances, and they may strengthen the case for hierarchy.

V CONCLUDING REMARKS

The differences in the nature of the errors made by different organizational architectures, though important, are not the only differences among organizational forms.

We have not examined the widespread belief of a correspondence between economic architecture and political structures; for instance, the alleged correlation between hierarchies and authoritarianism. We have ignored some aspects of organizational comparisons which have already received extensive discussion in the literature. For example, the traditional models emphasize the computational advantages of decentralization (indeed, in some versions, the differences in organizational forms appear to be simply a comparison between alternative algorithms for solving a general equilibrium problem). The fact that the economy solves the problem in "real time" while the models solve for the equilibrium in pseudo time may mean that (at least as traditionally presented) this argument is of only limited relevance.

We have also ignored the problems of incentives, which have been so much at the center of recent discussions of organizational design. We believe these considerations are not only important, but also that the organizational structure may have a significant effect in determining the set of feasible incentives. For instance, when there is more than one decision unit, one can base rewards on relative performance; as the number of units increases, under certain circumstances, a first-best optimum can be achieved. (See Barry Nalebuff and Stiglitz, 1983a.) We would argue, however, that organizations may perform badly, not only because of misguided intentions, as stressed in the incentive literature, but also from human fallibility. We have been concerned with showing how even in the absence of incentive problems, individual errors are aggregated differently under different organizational forms, leading to systematic differences in organizational performance.

One argument that can be raised against our analysis is that a hierarchy can always decentralize itself, but the converse is not true; it thus appears, almost tautologically, that hierarchies dominate polyarchies. Within this perspective, the question we have addressed is, under what circumstances should a hierarchy organize itself polyarchically. But we would argue that this perspective is at best misleading: with the right to intervention within a hierarchical structure goes the obligation to intervene when appropriate circumstances arise, and the concomitant necessity to obtain information to effectuate those interventions. Only if there are hard and fast commitments not to intervene, will a hierarchy be equivalent to a polyarchy. The analysis of these issues must, however, await another occasion.

In this paper we couch most of our analysis in terms of a comparison between alternative economic systems; but our results can be applied at a number of different levels of economic analysis (at the level of a firm or an industry as well as for the economy as a whole). Moreover, our results have direct and obvious implications in the context of political decision making, both for the organization of micro decision making (the rules by which committees should operate, or the managerial processes by which public project selection should be conducted) and for the organization of the state. Indeed, we hope our analysis of self-perpetuating organizations, of the problem that all organizations face in selecting those who are to be in decision-making positions, and the comparative sensitivity of organizational performance to the nature of the selection process, will help put into perspective some longstanding fallacies in political theory concerning the virtues and vices of alternative political structures. Classical discussions of the design of State systems (see Karl Popper, 1950) have essentially ignored the problems arising from human fallibility in decision making. Plato, for example, while arguing for the superiority of aristocratic rule, never considered the problems that would arise in choosing the members of the aristocracy over time, or the consequences (by now all too familiar) of the failure to choose well.

In this paper our objective has not been to present definitive results on the comparison of economic systems. Rather, it has been to encourage a redirection of attention to what seems to us to be one of the most fundamental issues of economics, and to show how simple models can be constructed which provide considerable insights into some of the longstanding controversies concerning the relative merits of different economic systems.

CHAPTER 16

....

THE BASIC
ANALYTICS OF
MORAL HAZARD*

....

I Introduction

IN the standard (Arrow-Debreu) competitive treatment of risk, the states of nature, which occur with exogenous probabilities, are observable. Insurance contingent on the realized state entails lump-sum transfers across states and therefore has no incentive or substitution effects.

Moral hazard arises when neither the states of nature nor individuals' actions are observable to an insurer.[1] What is observable is whether a particular accident has occurred. Under these conditions, there is no mechanism by which the insurer can induce the insured to reveal either the state of nature or his level of precaution truthfully. Thus, the insured against events are accidents of varying degrees of severity, conditional on neither the state of nature nor the insured's actions. The provision of insurance against such events will generally affect the individual's incentives to take precautions[2]—i.e., have substitution effects. There is therefore a tradeoff between incentives and risk-bearing. This is the moral hazard problem.

Moral hazard is pervasive in the economy. It occurs whenever risk is present, individuals are risk averse, and "effort" is costly to monitor. And it arises not only

* Written with Richard Arnott. We would like to thank Seppo Honkapohja and two anonymous referees for useful comments, and the National Science Foundation, the Olin Foundation, and the Social Sciences and Humanities Research Council of Canada for financial support. Reprinted with permission from the *Scandinavian Journal of Economics*, 90(3) (September), 1988, pp. 383–413, Blackwell Publishing.

[1] This is the extreme form of moral hazard. Moral hazard problems arise, although they are diluted, when the states of nature and/or individuals' actions are imperfectly observable (observable with noise).

[2] The provision of insurance therefore affects the probabilities of the events. For this reason, we define moral hazard to arise when the provision of insurance affects the probabilities of the insured-against events.

in insurance markets, but also when insurance is provided by governments, through social institutions, or in principal-agent contracts.

The *basic analytics* of moral hazard are developed in this paper. The analysis focuses on the relationship between the insurance premium paid and the insurance benefits received in the event of an accident. We derive the properties of the indifference curves and of the feasibility set, the set of insurance contracts which at least break even. The central message of the paper is that even when the underlying functions, the expected utility function and the relationship between effort and the accident probability, are extremely well behaved, the indifference curves and feasibility sets are not—indifference curves need not be convex and feasibility sets never are; price- and income-consumption lines may be discontinuous; and effort is not in general a monotonic or continuous function of the parameters of the insurance policies provided or of the prices of goods.

These results are established in Part 1 of this paper, while some of their implications are discussed in Part 2. We show that our canonical model of an insurance market can be reinterpreted to provide a model of loans with bankruptcy or of work incentives. The properties that we uncover here have profound implications for the nature and existence of competitive equilibrium. We illustrate some of these.[3]

PART 1 BASIC ANALYTICS

II The Model

Throughout most of the paper we employ the simplest model in which moral hazard is present. Each individual in the economy engages in a single activity that has two possible outcomes, which we refer to as "accident" and "no accident".[4] The output of the economy is a consumption good which is the only good in the economy. An individual's level of output (his consumption or income in the absence of insurance) depends on whether or not an accident happens to him. The probability of an individual having an accident is a function of his accident-prevention effort,[5] and different individuals' accident probabilities are statistically independent. To isolate the phenomena arising from moral hazard (from those which would arise if there were adverse selection as well), we assume that individuals are identical. Alternatively, we

---

[3] Because of space limitations, we provide a thorough analysis of the nature and existence of competitive equilibrium in a companion paper; see Arnott and Stiglitz (1987).

[4] The two outcomes may instead be interpreted as "large damage conditional on an accident occurring" and "small damage conditional on an accident occurring."

[5] Our analysis is sufficiently general that effort may be interpreted variously as exertion, the time spent in accident-prevention activity, the nature (unpleasantness) of the accident prevention activity undertaken, and (for some utility functions) units of the consumption good used up in accident prevention.

could assume that insurers can observe all the relevant characteristics of the insured (except, of course, effort), and interpret our analysis as applying to a group with the same characteristics.

Because they are risk averse, individuals will want to insure against the accident. We assume that whoever provides the insurance can observe whether the accident has occurred, but neither the underlying states of nature nor individuals' effort levels— this is the informational asymmetry which gives rise to the moral hazard problem. Thus, insurance is provided against the accident. As more insurance is provided, the marginal *private* benefit to the individual of expending a given level of effort on accident prevention falls; as a result, he will tend to expend less effort which will increase the probability of his having an accident.

We denote by y_0 and y_1 consumption in the events no accident and accident, respectively. In the absence of insurance

$$y_0 = w \quad y_1 = w - d,$$

where w is the no-accident output and d the damage due to the accident, so that $w - d$ is the accident output. We characterize an insurance policy in terms of a net (of premium) payout or benefit α, which the individual receives in the event of accident, and a premium, β, which the individual pays if an accident does not occur.[6] Thus, with insurance

$$y_0 = w - \beta \quad \text{and} \quad y_1 = w - d + \alpha. \tag{1a,b}$$

The probability, p, that an accident happens to an individual is a function of his level of (accident-prevention) effort, e. At some points in the paper, we assume that the individual has a choice of only a discrete number of effort levels, each corresponding to a different accident-prevention activity or technique. In this case, effort need not be quantified. We denote by p^j the probability of accident when effort level j is chosen, and by $\bar{p}$ the probability of accident when nothing is done to prevent the accident.[7] We assume that $\bar{p} < 1$—with no effort an accident need not occur.

At other points in the paper, we assume that the individual has a choice over a continuum of effort levels. We assume that more effort always reduces the probability of accident and does so in a continuous manner, and we cardinalize effort in such a way that $e = 0$ with zero effort and $p(e)$ is strictly convex and analytic for $e > 0$. Thus, $p'(e) < 0$ and $p''(e) > 0$ for $e > 0$. For this case, too, we assume that $p(0) \equiv \bar{p} < 1$. We refer to $p(e)$ as the probability-of-accident function.

The individual's expected utility is

$$EU = (1 - p^j)U_0^j(y_0) + p^j U_1^j(y_1) \tag{2a}$$

[6] This corresponds to an insurance policy with β payable in both events, and a gross payout in the event of accident of $\alpha + \beta$.

[7] We allow the individual to mix activities on the assumption that

$$p = \sum_j \lambda^j p^j,$$

where λ^j is the proportion of "time" he devotes to accident-prevention activity j.

in the discrete effort levels case, where U_0^j is the individual's utility function with effort j if an accident does not occur, and U_1^j the corresponding utility function when an accident does occur. In the continuum of effort levels case, expected utility is

$$EU = (1 - p(e))U_0(y_0, e) + p(e)U_1(y_1, e). \qquad (2b)$$

We assume that $(\partial U_i/\partial y_i) > 0$ and $(\partial^2 U_i/\partial y_i^2) < 0$, $i = 0, 1$; i.e., in each event and for every effort level, there is positive but diminishing marginal utility of consumption. For the continuum of effort levels case, we assume additionally that $(\partial U_i/\partial e) < 0$ and $(\partial^2 U_i/\partial e^2) \le 0$,[8] but place no restrictions on $(\partial^2 U_i/\partial y_i \partial e)$.

In much of the subsequent analysis, it will prove insightful to focus on certain restricted classes of utility functions. Sometimes we treat expected utility functions of the form

$$EU = (1 - p^j)u_0(y_0) + p^j u_1(y_1) - e^j \qquad (2a')$$

in the discrete effort levels case, and

$$EU = (1 - p(e))u_0(y_0) + p(e)u_1(y_1) - e \qquad (2b')$$

in the continuum of effort levels case. We refer to these as *separable* expected utility functions. Note that to go from (2a) to (2a') and from (2b) to (2b') requires three assumptions: first, that utility in both events is strongly separable in consumption and effort; second, that the disutility of effort is event independent;[9] and third, that effort is measured by the disutility it causes. For part of the analysis, we go further and assume that the utility-of-consumption function is also *event independent*, that is $u_0(y) = u_1(y)$ for all y. The general theory requires, of course, neither the assumption of separability nor that of event-independence. Our objective is to show that even with these strong assumptions, the indifference curves and feasibility set will not be well behaved.

Unless specified otherwise, we assume separability. We consider some of the complications that arise with nonseparable utility in Sections V and VII.

III Ill-Behaved Consumers with Well-Behaved Utility Functions: The Peculiar Shape of Indifference Curves

Discrete Effort Levels

We define $V^j(\alpha, \beta)$ to be the expected utility as a function of α and β when effort level j is chosen in the discrete effort levels case, i.e., $V^j(\alpha, \beta) = (1 - p^j)U_0^j(w - \beta) + p^j U_1^j(w - d + \alpha) \equiv EU^j$. Let V_u^j be the indifference curve in $\alpha - \beta$ space along

---

[8] Since the cardinalization of e has been chosen so that $p(e)$ is convex, this assumption is restrictive.

[9] This and the previous assumptions are natural if our model is interpreted as static, since normally we think of effort as occurring prior to the realization of the event and prior to consumption. These two assumptions are less reasonable if our model is instead interpreted as describing a stationary state.

which expected utility is V_u with effort level j. From (2a'), with separability the slope of such an effort-fixed indifference curve at (α, β) is

$$\left.\frac{d\beta}{d\alpha}\right|_{V_u^j} = -\left(\frac{\partial EU^j/\partial\alpha}{\partial EU^j/\partial\beta}\right) = \frac{u_1'p^j}{u_0'(1-p^j)} \equiv s^j(\alpha, \beta) > 0, \tag{3}$$

where a' denotes a derivative and s^j is the marginal rate of substitution between α and β with effort level j. The slope is positive because α is a good and β is a bad. Let $A_0(\beta) \equiv -(u_0''/u_0')$ denote the (local) coefficient of absolute risk aversion in the no-accident event with premium β, and $A_1(\alpha) \equiv -(u_1''/u_1')$ denote the corresponding coefficient in the event of accident. Then the curvature of the effort-fixed indifference curve can be shown to be

$$\left.\frac{d^2\beta}{d\alpha^2}\right|_{V_u^j} = -s^j(A_1 + s^j A_0) < 0. \tag{4}$$

Thus, *effort-fixed indifference curves are strictly convex, reflecting the individual's aversion to risk.* Also since α is a good and β a bad, lower effort-fixed indifference curves are preferred.

We consider the case with two effort levels—high (H) and low (L). From (2a'), with the arbitrary insurance package $(\hat{\alpha}, \hat{\beta})$ and associated consumption levels $(\hat{y}_1, \hat{y}_0)$, the individual's expected utility is

$$V^H(\hat{y}_0, \hat{y}_1) = (1 - p^H)u_0(\hat{y}_0) + p^H u_1(\hat{y}_1) - e^H \tag{5a}$$

with high effort, and

$$V^L(\hat{y}_0, \hat{y}_1) = (1 - p^L)u_0(\hat{y}_0) + p^L u_1(\hat{y}_1) - e^L \tag{5b}$$

with low effort. From (3)

$$s^H(\hat{\alpha}, \hat{\beta}) = \frac{u_1'(\hat{y}_1)}{u_0'(\hat{y}_0)}\left(\frac{p^H}{1-p^H}\right) < \frac{u_1'(\hat{y}_1)}{u_0'(\hat{y}_0)}\left(\frac{p^L}{1-p^L}\right) = s^L(\hat{\alpha}, \hat{\beta}), \tag{6}$$

since $p^L > p^H$ (with higher effort, the probability of accident is lower). At any point in $\alpha - \beta$ space, the low-effort indifference curve is steeper than the high-effort indifference curve since with lower effort the probability of accident is higher, and therefore to maintain the same level of utility, the individual requires a smaller increase in payout to compensate for a given increase in premium.

Individuals choose the effort level to maximize their expected utility. From (5a) and (5b)

$$V^H(\hat{y}_0, \hat{y}_1) \gtreqless V^L(\hat{y}_0, \hat{y}_1)$$

$$\text{as } u_0(\hat{y}_0) - u_1(\hat{y}_1) \gtreqless \frac{e^H - e^L}{p^L - p^H} \equiv \gamma^{H,L}. \tag{7}$$

Along $\phi^{H,L}$, which we refer to as the *switching locus*, individuals are indifferent between the two effort levels; i.e. $\phi^{H,L}$ is the locus of (α, β) such that $u_0(\hat{y}_0) - u_1(\hat{y}_1) = \gamma^{H,L}$. Equation (7) implies that at low levels of insurance (below $\phi^{H,L}$) individuals

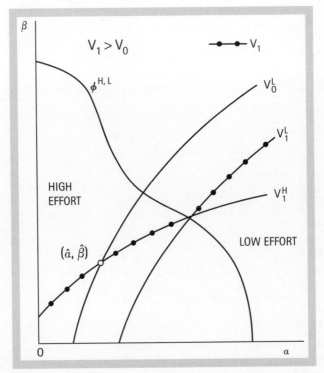

Fig. 1. Two activities, separable utility. Derivation of indifferences curves

choose high effort, while at high levels of insurance they choose low effort, which accords with intuition.[10]

We may now define an indifference curve with endogenous effort (hereafter simply indifference curve) corresponding to $V = V_u$ to be the locus of (α, β) such that $\max(V^H(\alpha, \beta), V^L(\alpha, \beta)) = V_u$. Since individuals choose high effort for (α, β) below $\phi^{H,L}$ and low effort for (α, β) above $\phi^{H,L}$, the indifference curve V_u coincides with V_u^H below $\phi^{H,L}$ and V_u^L above it. From Figure 1, this implies that *an indifference curve is the upper envelope of the corresponding effort-fixed indifference curves, and* furthermore that it *has an escalloped shape and is therefore not convex.*

The above argument generalizes straightforwardly to the case where there is an arbitrary number of discrete effort levels. Hence, *with separable utility, as more insurance is provided, the individual chooses successively lower levels of effort. Furthermore, indifference curves are not convex.*

Continuum of Effort Levels

Expected utility is a function of α, β, and e; i.e., $EU = EU(\alpha, \beta, e)$. We assume the individual chooses the level of effort taking α and β as fixed; thus,

$$e(\alpha, \beta) = \operatorname{argmax} EU(\alpha, \beta, e), \tag{8}$$

---

[10] We assume that high effort is chosen with zero insurance.

which we refer to as the effort supply function. Substitution of (8) into $EU(a, \beta, e)$ yields $V(a, \beta)$, which gives expected utility as a function of the benefit and premium. We now investigate the properties of the corresponding indifference curves.

Using the envelope theorem, it follows from (2b') that

$$\left.\frac{d\beta}{da}\right|_{\overline{V}} = s \quad \text{and} \quad \left.\frac{d^2\beta}{da^2}\right|_{\overline{V}} = \{-s(A_1 + s A_0)\} + \frac{rp'}{(1-p)^2}\left.\frac{de}{da}\right|_{\overline{V}} \qquad (9a,b)$$

where

$$s \equiv \frac{pu_1'}{(1-p)u_0'}$$

is the marginal rate of substitution between a and β and $r \equiv u_1'/u_0'$ is the ratio of marginal utilities. The expression in curly brackets in (9b) is negative, reflecting the observation made earlier that, with effort fixed, indifference curves would be strictly convex because of risk aversion. But increasing the amount of insurance decreases effort (we prove this shortly) and increases the probability of accident, which effect by itself causes indifferences curves to be concave; this is captured by the second term in (9b) which is positive

$$\left(p' < 0, r > 0, \left.\frac{de}{da}\right|_{\overline{V}} < 0\right).$$

Thus, there is one effect causing indifference curves to be convex, and another causing them to be concave. To ascertain which effect dominates requires evaluating

$$\left.\frac{de}{da}\right|_{\overline{V}}.$$

From (2b'), the first-order condition of the individual's maximization problem is

$$e\{(-u_0(y_0) + u_1(y_1))p'(e) - 1\} = 0. \qquad (10)$$

$(-u_0(y_0) + u_0(y_0))p'$ is the marginal private benefit of effort in utility terms, the decrease in the probability of accident times the gain in utility from not having an accident, while 1 is the marginal cost. Since $p''(e) > 0$, the second-order condition is satisfied at any local extremum. Furthermore, where effort is positive, differentiation of (10) yields,

$$\frac{\partial e}{\partial a} = -\frac{u_1'(p')^2}{p''} < 0 \quad \text{and} \quad \frac{\partial e}{\partial \beta} = -\frac{u_0'(p')^2}{p''} < 0. \qquad (11a,b)$$

These equations imply that at any (a, β) where the effort chosen by the individual is positive, *effort decreases as more insurance is provided until a point is reached beyond which effort is zero.* This result is shown in Figure 2.

Constant effort loci have slope and curvature

$$\left.\frac{d\beta}{da}\right|_{\bar{e}} = -r \quad \text{and} \quad \left.\frac{d^2\beta}{da^2}\right|_{\bar{e}} = r(A_1 - r A_0). \qquad (12a,b)$$

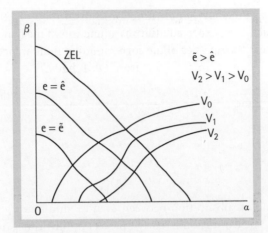

Fig. 2. Sample indifference curves with separable utility and a continuum of effort levels, and constant effort loci with separable utility

We now define the *zero effort line* (ZEL) to be the locus of (α, β) satisfying

$$(-u_0(y_0) + u_1(y_1)) \lim_{e \downarrow 0} p'(e) - 1 = 0. \tag{13}$$

Define $\mathscr{E}$ to be the set of (α, β) for which effort is positive. Then, using (9a) and (11a,b),

$$\left. \frac{de}{d\alpha} \right|_{\overline{V}} = \frac{\partial e}{\partial \alpha} + \frac{\partial e}{\partial \beta} \frac{d\beta}{d\alpha} \bigg|_{\overline{V}} = \begin{cases} -\dfrac{(p')^2}{p''} \dfrac{u_1'}{1-p} < 0 & \text{for } (\alpha, \beta) \in \mathscr{E} \\ 0 & \text{for } (\alpha, \beta) \notin \mathscr{E}. \end{cases} \tag{14}$$

And combining (14) and (9b) yields

$$\left. \frac{d^2\beta}{d\alpha^2} \right|_{\overline{V}} = \begin{cases} -s \left[(A_1 + s A_0) + \dfrac{u_1'(p')^3}{(1-p)^2 p p''} \right] & \text{for } (\alpha, \beta) \in \mathscr{E} \\ -s (A_1 + s A_0) & \text{for } (\alpha, \beta) \notin \mathscr{E}. \end{cases} \tag{15}$$

Equation (15) implies that *indifference curves are convex beyond the zero effort line, but below the zero effort line effort may fall off sufficiently fast as more insurance is provided that the indifference curves may not be convex.* More specifically, the indifference curve at a point (α, β) is more likely to be nonconvex, the less risk-averse are individuals (the smaller A_1 and A_0), the more responsive the probability of accident to effort, and the lower the curvature of the $p(e)$ function.

Most of the applied literature on moral hazard conducts the analysis on the assumption (explicit or implicit) that indifference curves are convex. We have shown that doing so is restrictive.

Sample indifference curves are also drawn in Figure 2. The slope discontinuity and subsequent nonconvexity in V_0 at the zero effort line occurs if

$$\lim_{e \downarrow 0} \frac{(p')^3}{p''} = -\infty. \tag{16}$$

This condition relates to the curvature of the probability of accident function as effort goes to zero. An example in which this condition holds is $p = \bar{p} - e^\epsilon$ for small e and $\epsilon < 1/2$, for which

$$\lim_{e \downarrow 0} \frac{(p')^3}{p''} = \lim_{e \downarrow 0} \frac{\epsilon^2}{\epsilon - 1} e^{2\epsilon - 1} = -\infty.$$

IV Price- and Income-Consumption Lines

The possible nonconvexity of indifference curves implies that income- and price-consumption lines may be discontinuous.

Two Effort Levels, Income-Consumption Line

We term

$$q \equiv \frac{\beta}{\alpha}$$

(the premium/benefit ratio) the "price" of insurance. Then an *income-consumption line* (IC) corresponding to price q is the locus of points of maximal utility on the family of (budget) lines $\beta = q(\alpha - \alpha_0)$ with $\beta \geq 0$ and $\alpha \geq 0$. An effort-fixed income-consumption line is defined analogously, but with effort fixed.

As in the previous section, to improve intuition, we first obtain the characteristics of the two effort-fixed income-consumption lines corresponding to slope q, and then determine how the corresponding income-consumption line is derived from the two effort-fixed income-consumption lines.[11] The high-effort income-consumption line, denoted by IC^H, is given by

$$\frac{(u_1')^H}{(u_0')^H} \left(\frac{p^H}{1 - p^H} \right) \equiv s^H = q, \tag{17}$$

and its slope by

$$\left. \frac{d\beta}{d\alpha} \right|_{IC^H} = -\frac{A_1^H}{A_0^H}. \tag{18}$$

The formula for the low-effort income-consumption line and its slope are analogous.

We now show that *income-consumption lines may be discontinuous*. We start with the situation shown in Figure 3, in which a line with slope q is tangent to the same

---

[11] To simplify exposition, we examine only those segments of income- and price-consumption lines for which $\alpha > 0$ and $\beta > 0$.

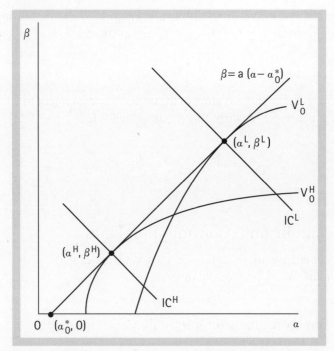

Fig. 3. Line tangent to same indifference curve at two points

indifference curve at two points and meets the a-axis at a_0^*. This is possible because the indifference curve has an escalloped shape. The lower tangency point corresponds to high effort, the higher one to low effort. Then we increase a_0, shifting the line of slope q to the right, and ascertain whether $V^H(a, \beta)$ or $V^L(a, \beta)$ increases faster along the respective effort-fixed income-consumption lines. Suppose, for the sake of argument, that V^H is increasing faster. Then in terms of Figure 3,

$$\left.\frac{dV^H}{da_0}\right|_{a_0^*}^{IC^H} > \left.\frac{dV^L}{da_0}\right|_{a_0^*}^{IC^L}.$$

Since

$$\left.V^H\right|_{a_0^*}^{IC^H} = \left.V^L\right|_{a_0^*}^{IC^L},$$

then

$$\left.V^H\right|_{a_0^*-\delta}^{IC^H} < \left.V^L\right|_{a_0^*-\delta}^{IC^L}$$

and

$$\left.V^H\right|_{a_0^*+\delta}^{IC^H} > \left.V^L\right|_{a_0^*+\delta}^{IC^L},$$

where δ is an arbitrarily small positive number. This implies that the point of maximal utility along the line $\beta = q(a - (a_0^* - \delta))$ is on IC^L, while the corresponding point along the line $\beta = q(a - (a_0^* + \delta))$ is on IC^H. Hence, in this case, the (effort-variable) income-consumption line jumps downwards at a_0^*, from (a^L, β^L) to (a^H, β^H), as a_0 increases.

It is straightforward to show that

$$\left.\frac{dV^j}{da_0}\right|_{IC^j} = \frac{\partial V^j}{\partial a} = p^j (u_1')^j. \tag{19}$$

To understand this result, we may decompose the effect of the increase in a_0. Prior to the increase, the individual was at (a^j, β^j). Then the initial effect of an increase in a_0 by da_0 is to change the individual's insurance purchases to $(a^j + da_0, \beta^j)$ which increases his utility by $(u_1')^j da_0$ with probability p^j, and hence his expected utility by $p^j (u_1')^j da_0$. The second effect results from movement from $(a^j + da_0, \beta^j)$ to some other point on the budget line $\beta = q(a - (a_0 + da_0))$. Since the budget line at (a^j, β^j) is tangent to the indifference curve there, by the envelope theorem the second effect has no first-order impact on utility. It follows from (19) that

$$\left.\frac{dV^H}{da_0}\right|_{IC^H} \mathrel{\substack{\geq \\ <}} \left.\frac{dV^L}{da_0}\right|_{IC^L} \Leftrightarrow p^H (u_1')^H \mathrel{\substack{\geq \\ <}} p^L (u_1')^L. \tag{20}$$

Since $p^H < p^L$, while $(u_1')^H > (u_1')^L$ along a budget line, then it appears that *the income-consumption line can jump either up or down at a point of discontinuity*. It can be shown that such is indeed the case.

Continuum of Effort Levels, Income-Consumption Line

Similar arguments show that with a continuum of effort levels, there may be discontinuities in the income-consumption line. Where D and D' are the lower and upper points of a discontinuity in the income-consumption line, the line jumps down if $p^D (u_1')^D > p^{D'} (u_1')^{D'}$ and up if the inequality is in the opposite direction. In addition, we can show that *there may be positively-sloped segments of the income-consumption line*. The slope of the income-consumption line (except at the points of discontinuity) is

$$\left.\frac{d\beta}{da}\right|_{IC} = -\left[A_1 + \frac{(p')^3 u_1'}{p'' p(1-p)}\right] \bigg/ \left[A_0 + \frac{(p')^3 u_0'}{p'' p(1-p)}\right], \tag{21}$$

which is positive if either the numerator or denominator is negative, but not both.

Price-Consumption Line

The *price-consumption line* (PC) is the locus of (a, β) of maximal utility on the family of lines $\beta = qa$ with $\beta \geq 0$ and $a \geq 0$ (i.e., rays emanating from the origin in the positive orthant). We derive the effort-fixed price-consumption lines and then obtain the price-consumption line with effort endogenous.

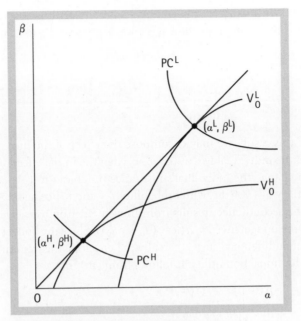

Fig. 4. Ray from origin tangent to same
indifference curve at two points

The price-consumption line with high effort denoted by PC^H, is the locus of points satisfying

$$\frac{(u_1')^H p^H}{(u_0')^H (1 - p^H)} = \frac{\beta}{\alpha}, \tag{22}$$

and its slope is

$$\left. \frac{d\beta}{d\alpha} \right|_{PC^H} = \frac{\beta}{\alpha} \left(\frac{1 - \alpha A_1^H}{1 + \beta A_0^H} \right), \tag{23}$$

from which we see that an effort-fixed *price-consumption line can be positively sloped*. The low-effort equations are analogous.

We now investigate points of discontinuity in the price-consumption line. Turn to Figure 4. We start off with a situation in which a ray from the origin with slope q_0 is tangent to the same indifference curve at two points, the lower one corresponding to high effort and the upper one to low effort. The price-consumption line jumps upwards at this price if

$$\left. \frac{dV^H}{dq} \right|_{q_0}^{PC^H} > \left. \frac{dV^L}{dq} \right|_{q_0}^{PC^L}$$

and downwards if the inequality is reversed. Proceeding as was done with income-consumption lines, we can show that the price-consumption line jumps upwards at a point of discontinuity if $(u_1')^H p^H \alpha^H < (u_1')^L p^L \alpha^L$, and downwards if the inequality is reversed. This inequality, too, can go in either direction. *Hence, the price-consumption line can be discontinuous and can jump either up or down at a point of discontinuity.*

Similar results hold for the continuum.[12]

We also note that the existence and properties of discontinuities in the price- and income-consumption lines depend on *global* rather than local properties of the utility and probability-of-accident functions. As a result, there appear to be no simple, primitive restrictions on these functions (except those which guarantee that indifference curves are everywhere convex) which guarantee that price- and/or income-consumption lines do not have discontinuities.

As shown later on, the possibility of discontinuities in the price- and income-consumption lines has important implications for the existence and properties of competitive equilibrium.

In Section III, we examined the properties of indifference curves when the expected utility function is separable. We now briefly consider some of the complications that arise when this assumption is relaxed.

V Nonseparable Utility Functions

The level of effort expended at accident avoidance may well affect the marginal rate of substitution between goods in the two events, accident and no accident. This is obviously the case where "effort" is an expenditure of money, so that $u_i(y, e) = u_i(y - e)$. This greatly complicates the analytics; we focus here on two interesting qualitative results which emerge—*effort may not be monotonic in the amount of insurance, and in the continuum of effort levels case effort, may not be a continuous function of the amount of insurance.*

Nonmonotonic Effort

The first result is seen mostly easily within the context of the discrete effort levels model. Here it is possible that $V_0^{e_1}$ and $V_0^{e_2}$ (defined as before, but now with nonseparable utility) intersect more than once, as shown in Figure 5. If this occurs, then the individual will employ one level of effort at both high and low amounts of insurance and the other level at intermediate amounts. The intuitive rationale for this is that as the (compensated) amount of insurance provided increases, the marginal cost (disutility) of effort may fall faster than the marginal benefit. The boundary lines in $\alpha - \beta$ space between different activities can have almost any shape.

---

[12] At interior points, the slope of the price-consumption line is given by

$$\left.\frac{d\beta}{d\alpha}\right|_{PC} = -\left[A_1 + \frac{(p')^3 u'_1}{p'' p(1 - p)} - \frac{1}{\alpha}\right] \bigg/ \left[A_0 + \frac{(p')^3 u'_0}{p'' p(1 - p)} + \frac{1}{\beta}\right].$$

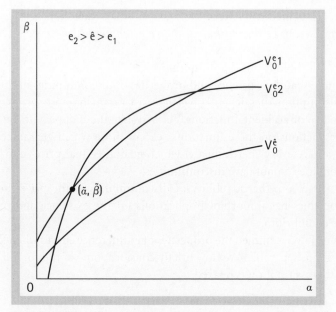

Fig. 5. With nonseparable utility and a continuum of effort levels, some effort levels may be dominated and effort may not be continuous

Discontinuous Effort

We now show that with a continuum of effort levels, but a non-separable utility function, effort may not be a continuous function of the amount of insurance, even though the underlying utility and probability-of-accident functions are "well behaved".

To see this, we write the first-order condition for effort (for an interior solution),

$$(-U_0 + U_1)p' = -\left(\frac{\partial U_0}{\partial e}(1 - p) + \frac{\partial U_1}{\partial e}p\right).$$

The LHS is the marginal benefit of effort, and the RHS the marginal cost. Since

$$\frac{\partial((-U_0 + U_1)p')}{\partial e} = \left(-\frac{\partial U_0}{\partial e} + \frac{\partial U_1}{\partial e}\right)p' + (-U_0 + U_1)p'',$$

the marginal benefit curve need not be downward-sloping. Increases in effort may increase the utility difference between the accident and no-accident events and hence increase the marginal return to further effort. Similarly, since

$$-\frac{\partial\left(\frac{\partial U_0}{\partial e}(1 - p) + \frac{\partial U_1}{\partial e}p\right)}{\partial e} = -\frac{\partial^2 U_0}{\partial e^2}(1 - p) - \frac{\partial^2 U_1}{\partial e^2}p + \left(\frac{\partial U_0}{\partial e} - \frac{\partial U_1}{\partial e}\right)p',$$

the marginal cost curve need not be upward sloping. If the *marginal* cost to effort is lower in the no-accident event, more effort makes the no-accident event more likely, and hence may lower the marginal cost of effort. Thus, at any (α, β) there may be multiple local optimal effort levels.

The possibility of multiple local optimal effort levels for a given (α, β) considerably complicates the analysis, since the effort level chosen by an individual may change discontinuously as α and β are altered.

A geometric interpretation of this discontinuity is also provided in Figure 5. Consider two fixed-effort indifference curves, corresponding to different levels of effort but the same level of utility, which intersect twice in (α, β) space. Consider $\hat{e}\epsilon(e_1, e_2)$. If at $(\tilde{\alpha}, \tilde{\beta})$, EU is convex in e, then $V_0^{e_1}(\tilde{\alpha}, \tilde{\beta}) = V_0^{e_2}(\tilde{\alpha}, \tilde{\beta}) > V^{\hat{e}}(\tilde{\alpha}, \tilde{\beta})$. At $(\tilde{\alpha}, \tilde{\beta})$, effort will switch discontinuously between e_1 and e_2. If, however, EU is concave in e at $(\tilde{\alpha}, \tilde{\beta})$, then there can be no such discontinuity.

VI Implications for Demand Functions

Quasi-concavity of indifference maps is important in conventional theory because without it, demand functions are discontinuous. The analysis of Section IV can be interpreted as establishing that if insurance firms offer individuals "linear" or price insurance contracts—a payment of α with premium αq—the demand for insurance (and hence effort) may be discontinuous in q. It is also easy to establish that the demand function for insurance may be discontinuous in other prices (e.g. the cost of automobile repairs) as well.

Furthermore, an increase in the price of insurance can lead to a discontinuous *increase* in insurance purchased (and a corresponding discontinuous decrease in effort) rather than the expected decrease.[13]

VII The Badly-Behaved Zero Profit Locus

In this section, we show that *with moral hazard the set of feasible contracts*, those at which profits are non-negative, which we term the feasibility set, *is never convex.* We focus our attention on the shape of the outer boundary of the set, which we refer to as the *resource constraint* or, where appropriate, the *zero profit locus* (*ZPL*). We again divide the analysis into two cases, one with two activities, the other with a continuum of effort levels.

Two Effort Levels, Separable Utility

When high effort is expended, the effort-fixed zero profit locus is

$$\beta(1 - p^H) - \alpha p^H = 0, \tag{24}$$

---

[13] With separable utility functions, insurance purchases decrease with the price of insurance and effort increases, except at points of discontinuity in the price-consumption line. This property does not extend to nonseparable utility functions. These results can be obtained straightforwardly from differentiation of the first-order conditions of the individual's effort choice problem.

which is a ray from the origin with slope

$$\frac{p^H}{1-p^H}.$$

Zero profits are made when the ratio of the premium to the net payout, which we have termed the price of insurance, equals the probability of accident divided by the probability of no accident. When low effort is expended, the corresponding effort-fixed zero profit locus is a ray from the origin with slope

$$\frac{p^L}{1-p^L}.$$

Since with low effort, the probability of accident is higher, a higher price must be charged for insurance to break even. The effort-fixed zero profit loci are shown in Figure 6.

We now derive the zero profit locus with effort endogenous. Define the feasibility set contingent on high effort to be the set of (a, β) for which expected profits are non-negative when high effort is expended, and denote it by $\mathscr{F}^H$. And let $\mathscr{H}$ be the set of (a, β) for which the individual chooses high effort; it was shown in Section III that this is the area below $\phi^{H.L.}$. Define $\mathscr{F}^L$ and $\mathscr{L}$ accordingly for low effort, and $\mathscr{F}$ to be the feasibility set with effort endogenous. A point (a, β) is in $\mathscr{F}$ if *either* it is in

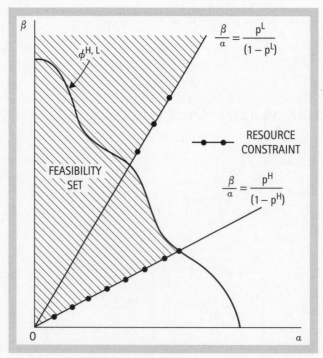

Fig. 6. The resource constraint and the feasibility set, two activities, separable utility

$\mathscr{F}^{\mathrm{H}}$ and the individual expends high effort there *or* it is in $\mathscr{F}^{\mathrm{L}}$ and the individual expends low effort there; i.e. $\mathscr{F} = (\mathscr{F}^{\mathrm{H}} \cap \mathscr{H}) \cup (\mathscr{F}^{\mathrm{F}} \cap \mathscr{L})$. The feasibility set with effort endogenous is shown by the cross-hatched area in Figure 6. The zero profit locus with effort endogenous is the boundary of $\mathscr{F}$. From the figure, it is clear that the feasibility set with effort endogenous is not convex.

Continuum of Effort Levels, Separable Utility

The zero profit locus is

$$\beta(1 - p(e)) - ap(e) = 0. \tag{25}$$

Its slope is given by

$$\left.\frac{d\beta}{da}\right|_{\mathrm{ZPL}} = \frac{p + (a + \beta)p'\frac{\partial e}{\partial a}}{(1 - p) - (a + \beta)p'\frac{\partial e}{\partial \beta}}. \tag{26}$$

Substituting (11a,b) into (26) gives

$$\left.\frac{d\beta}{da}\right|_{\mathrm{ZPL}} = \begin{cases} \left[p - \dfrac{(a + \beta)u_1'(p')^3}{p''} \right] \Big/ \left[(1 - p) + \dfrac{(a + \beta)u_0'(p')^3}{p''} \right] & \text{for } (a, \beta) \in \mathscr{E} \\[2ex] \bar{p}/(1 - \bar{p}) & \text{for } (a, \beta) \notin \mathscr{E}. \end{cases} \tag{26'}$$

Several properties of the zero profit locus for this case are generally worthy of note: (i) The zero profit locus is continuous. (ii) The curvature of the zero profit locus depends on third derivatives of the probability-of-accident function, restrictions on which have no persuasive economic justification. (iii) There are nonetheless restrictions on the feasible shape of the zero profit locus. First, beyond the zero effort line, the zero profit locus is $\beta(1 - \bar{p}) - a\bar{p} = 0$. Second, the zero profit locus includes the origin and has a slope $[p(e(0, 0))]/[1 - p(e(0, 0))]$ there.[14] Third, all points on the line segment joining a point on the zero profit locus and the origin must lie in the feasibility set.[15] Relatedly, at any point on a positively-sloped segment of the zero profit locus at which effort is positive, the ZPL is steeper than the ray joining the origin to that point.[16] And fourth, the zero profit locus can have an infinite slope and

[14] Furthermore, with separable and event-independent utility, the slope of the ZPL at the origin exceeds the slope of the indifference curve there; recall (9).

[15] Label the point on the ZPL (a_0, β_0) and a point on the line segment (a_1, β_1). Both have the same price of insurance, but since effort decreases as one moves out along the line segment, the probability of accident is higher at (a_0, β_0) than at (a_1, β_1). Since zero profits are made at (a_0, β_0), positive profits must be made at (a_1, β_1).

[16] The slope of the zero profit locus is given by (26'), that of a line joining the origin to the point (a, β) on the ZPL by $p(e(a, \beta))/(1 - p(e(a, \beta)))$.

backward-bending segments, but cannot have zero slope.[17] (iv) The feasibility set is never convex.[18]

Continuum of Effort Levels, Nonseparable Utility

We have seen that nonseparability of the expected utility function can cause effort to be discontinuous in the parameters of the insurance contract. This can result in the feasibility set not being connected, and in points on the boundary of the feasibility set having positive profits.

Part 2 Implications

In this part of the paper, we undertake two tasks: First, we show that the fact that both indifference curves and the feasibility set are "badly behaved" has strong implications for the existence and nature of equilibrium; and second, we illustrate that our analysis of insurance markets can be directly applied to other markets, including credit and labor markets.

VIII Existence and Properties of Equilibrium

A thorough analysis of the existence and properties of equilibrium turns out to be remarkably complex, even for the simplest case of separable, event-independent utility. A reasonably complete analysis is provided in Arnott and Stiglitz (1987). Here our aim is to use the geometric and analytic tools developed thus far in the paper to illuminate some of the issues involved. To simplify, we continue to assume separable utility.

The existence and properties of equilibrium are crucially dependent on what information is available to insurance firms. There are three items of information of concern to an insurance firm when insuring a client: (i) whether or not the accident

---

[17] Consider increasing β from some point on the ZPL, holding α fixed. This has an ambiguous effect on profits. The increase in β, with effort constant, increases profits. But the increase in β with α constant, lowers effort which effect by itself causes profits to fall. When the former effect dominates, the ZPL is positively-sloped; when the latter dominates it is negatively sloped; and when the two are offsetting, it is infinitely sloped.

Now consider increasing α, holding β constant. Both effects operate to decrease profits, which implies that the ZPL cannot have a zero slope.

[18] The slope of the ZPL beyond the zero effort line is $p(0)/(1 - p(0))$, while at the origin it is $p(e(0,0))/(1 - p(e)0,0))$, which is smaller. Hence, a necessary condition for the feasibility set to be convex is that β/α at the point of intersection of the ZPL and the ZEL be *strictly* less than $p(0)/(1 - p(0))$. But since the point is on the ZPL, $(\beta/\alpha) = (p(0))/(1 - p(0))$ there.

actually occurred; (ii) the effort undertaken by the client to prevent the accident; and (iii) if effort is not observable, the client's purchases of insurance from other firms.

In our analysis, we have assumed, and shall continue to assume, that firms cannot observe their clients' accident-prevention effort at all,[19] and can observe perfectly and without cost whether an accident occurred.

With respect to the other item of information, we treat only the two extremes: (i) where a firm can costlessly observe its clients' insurance purchases from other firms—we term this the "observable insurance purchases" case or simply the "observability" case; and (ii) where a firm cannot observe its clients' purchases from other firms, the "unobservable insurance purchases" or "unobservability" case. This information is relevant since in the former case the firm can ration its clients' purchases of insurance, whereas in the latter it cannot.

The existence and properties of equilibrium also depend on what insurance contracts are deemed admissible. The set of admissible contracts clearly depends on what is observable; if the quantity of insurance purchased at other firms is not observable, then admissible contracts cannot *directly* restrict the amount purchased at other firms. But there may be other restrictions on the set of admissible contracts which are motivated by other considerations: Should negative insurance[20] or random insurance[21] be allowed? Should *latent* policies—policies which are not purchased in equilibrium but serve to deter entry—be permitted? The nature of equilibrium turns out to depend critically on the answers to such questions. When the set of admissible contracts is expanded, not only may there be new equilibria, but also the newly-admissible contracts may upset the original equilibria (this occurs, for example, when the set of admissible contracts is expanded from price contracts to price and quantity contracts). It is our view that what contracts should be treated as admissible depends on context (and in particular, on transactions costs).[22]

Observability: Exclusive Contract Equilibrium

When it is feasible for firms to restrict the quantity of insurance (in particular, if the quantity of insurance which an individual buys is observable), equilibrium will be characterized by exclusive contracts, in which the individual will purchase all of his insurance from a single provider. The equilibrium is at the point of maximum utility on the feasibility set.

Figure 7 shows three possible exclusive contract equilibria for the two activities case—θ', θ'', θ'''. At θ'', the point of intersection of the high effort zero profit locus and the switching locus, the individual would like to purchase more insurance at the going price $(p^H/(1 - p^H))$ but were the firm to offer additional insurance, he would

---

[19] Holmström (1979) considers the case in which firms can observe their clients' effort with noise.

[20] Where the individual pays when an accident occurs and receives a payout when it does not.

[21] Arnott and Stiglitz (1988b) discuss random insurance with observability of insurance purchases.

[22] For instance, negative insurance requires verifying that an accident has not occurred, which may be far more costly than verifying that one has occurred; randomization may require verification that the firm is in fact randomizing according to the specified probabilities, again a task which is far harder than simply verifying that it pays a given amount in a given situation.

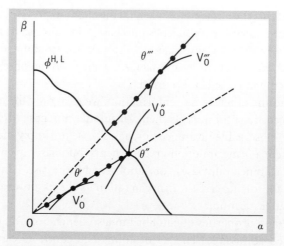

Fig. 7. Possible exclusive contract equilibria, two activities, separable utility

switch to a low level of effort, and the policy would make a loss. This result extends to the case where there is a continuum of effort levels. We showed in the previous section that at any point on a positively sloped segment of the ZPL at which effort is positive, the ZPL is steeper than the price line joining the origin to that point. This establishes that competitive equilibrium will normally entail rationing of insurance, when it is feasible, as well as positive effort and partial insurance (i.e., $u_0' < u_1'$).

Price Equilibrium

A second form of equilibrium, which is relevant with unobservability, is that where insurance firms simply offer price contracts, and do not restrict the quantity of insurance. Our earlier analysis can be used to derive several important results.

A zero profit price equilibrium, if it exists, must be at the intersection of the zero profit locus and the price-consumption line. Because the price-consumption line may jump across the zero profit locus (recall Section IV), a *zero profit price equilibrium may not exist.*

When the zero profit price equilibrium exists, the level of effort is zero with accidents which decrease or leave unchanged the marginal utility of income at each level of income. This follows from the fact that in a price equilibrium, individuals set the price, q, equal to their marginal rate of substitution:

$$q = u_0' p / (u_1'(1 - p)),$$

while from the zero profit condition

$$q = p/(1 - p).$$

Hence, $u_0' = u_1'$; i.e., there is full insurance at the zero profit price equilibrium. This implies that if accidents decrease or leave unchanged the utility of income, then

$$u_0 \leq u_1,$$

which in turn implies, from the first-order condition for effort, (10), that effort must be zero and that the equilibrium price is $q^* = (p(0))/(1 - p(0))$.

We now identify a set of sufficient conditions for the non-existence of a zero profit price equilibrium. Define the full insurance line (FIL) to be the locus of (a, β) for which $u_0' = u_1'$. From the above discussion it follows that if a zero profit price equilibrium exists, it lies at the point of intersection of the ZPL and the FIL; we label this point E. Now suppose that: (i) the expected utility function is event independent; (ii)

$$\lim_{e \downarrow 0} \frac{p'(e)^3}{p''(e)} = -\infty;$$

and (iii)

$$\lim_{e \downarrow 0} p'(e) = -\infty.$$

From (iii) and (13), it follows that the zero effort line is characterized by $u_0 = u_1$. Furthermore, with event-independent utility, the ZEL and FIL coincide and satisfy $a + \beta = d$. A necessary condition for E to be an equilibrium is that the indifference curves be convex near E. But we have already seen, that under condition (ii), indifference curves are nonconvex in the neighborhood of the zero effort line, and that E is on the zero effort line; see Figure 8.

Two further points should be noted. First, convexity of the indifference curves near E does not ensure the existence of a zero profit price equilibrium; to establish

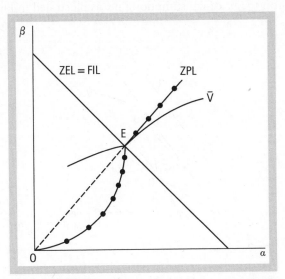

Fig. 8. Possible nonexistence of a zero profit price equilibrium

existence, a *global* analysis is required. Second, the nonexistence of a zero profit price equilibrium does not imply the nonexistence of a price equilibrium. In Arnott and Stiglitz (1987) we show that a price equilibrium always exists, but may entail zero insurance or positive profits.

Other Equilibrium Forms

The fact that an insurance firm cannot observe insurance purchases from *other* firms does not mean that equilibrium must be a price equilibrium. Since the insurance firm can observe its own sales of insurance to an individual, by insisting that the individual purchase a large quantity, it can attempt to discourage the individual from purchasing from other firms. We refer to equilibria in which firms offer only quantity contracts as Q-equilibria, and equilibria in which some firms offer price contracts and other quantity contracts as PQ-equilibria. In Arnott and Stiglitz (1987), we show that Q-equilibria and PQ-equilibria may not exist; that is, given any set of insurance contracts, each of which at least breaks even, there exists a new contract which if offered would be purchased and make a profit. (The entry of this new contract would, however, result in other firms making a loss.) The nonexistence of equilibrium hinges critically on the properties of the income-consumption lines.

To see this, assume that utility is separable and event-independent and consider the situation where there is a single incumbent firm in the market which offers a quantity policy. When can this be an equilibrium? If the incumbent's policy lies strictly inside the feasibility set, there exists a small, supplementary policy (possibly with negative insurance) which would be bought and be profitable. Thus, the incumbent's policy must lie on the ZPL. The incumbent's policy must also lie on the price-consumption line. Suppose, to the contrary, that the incumbent offers the policy G which lies on the ZPL but not on the price-consumption line, as illustrated in Figure 9. Then the

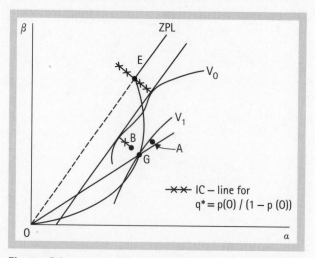

Fig. 9. G is upset by the supplementary contract GA. E is upset by B

supplementary policy GA will be purchased (since A is below the indifference curve through G); and if GA is small enough, it will make a profit, because the effort at A is only slightly lower than at G but the implicit price of policy GA is significantly higher than that of G. Since profits at A are negative, while the supplementary policy makes a profit, policy G makes a loss. Thus, if equilibrium exists with a single incumbent firm offering a quantity policy, the policy must lie at the point of intersection of the ZPL and the price-consumption line. If the price-consumption line does not intersect the ZPL, such an equilibrium does not exist. If the price-consumption line does intersect the ZPL, it does so at the point E,[23] and E may be a Q-equilibrium. A necessary condition for E to be a Q-equilibrium is that no part of the income-consumption line corresponding to the price $q^* = (p(0))/(1 - p(0))$ below (i.e., corresponding to a higher utility level) E lies in the interior of the feasibility set. This is illustrated in Figure 9. The contract B is preferred to E, and since B lies on the income-consumption line corresponding to price $q^* = (p(0))/(1 - p(0))$, the individual will prefer B to B plus E. Since also policy B by itself is profitable, it upsets E.

When we further modify the analysis to allow for latent policies, a much richer set of equilibria emerges; and the set of equilibria includes positive profit equilibria.

IX Applications

We have cast our presentation of the basic analytics of moral hazard in the context of an *explicit* insurance market. In this section, we wish to show that, with only a transformation of variables, the analysis can be employed to cast light on issues in the principal-agent literature. Although the basic framework of our analysis can be applied in many contexts, the appropriate equilibrium concept (the set of admissible contracts) may well differ, because what is easily observable in one market may not be so easily observable in another; e.g., while it may be possible to restrict insurance purchases from other firms, it may not be possible to restrict employment with other employers, or borrowing from other creditors. In the discussion below, we show how the model can be reinterpreted to investigate share cropping and credit contracts, but we do not consider the appropriate equilibrium concept for each of the markets.

First, consider the contract between a risk-neutral landlord and a risk-averse laborer in a competitive market; cf. e.g., Stiglitz (1974e). Should the laborer: (i) rent the land, thereby receiving output less rent; (ii) be paid a straight wage for farming the land; or (iii) share output with the landlord? The output from the land is a random variable and (in the sense of first-order stochastic dominance) increases with the laborer's effort. Moral hazard arises in the contract because the landlord is unable to observe the laborer's effort. Suppose, for purposes of exposition, that there are only two output levels, with the probability of the higher output level increasing in the laborer's effort. Let x^H and x^L denote the high and low outputs, respectively; R denote

---

[23] Recall that the point E is the point of intersection of the zero profit locus and the full insurance line, and that when the price-consumption line intersects the zero profit locus, it does so at E.

the landlord's required average return on the land; y^H and y^L denote the tenant's consumption in the high- and low-output events, respectively; and e denote the tenant's effort. Then with the transformation of variables $x^H - R \Leftrightarrow w$, $x^H - x^L \Leftrightarrow d$, $y^H \Leftrightarrow w - \beta$, $y^L \Leftrightarrow w - d + a$, the problem is identical to the one analyzed in the paper. The rental contract corresponds to no insurance, the wage contract to full insurance, and sharecropping to partial insurance. Our earlier result that, where exclusivity can be enforced, partial insurance is typical in equilibrium, corresponds to the result in the current context that, where the landlord can be sure that the worker will not obtain insurance against output variability from a third party, sharecropping will typically occur.

Second, consider the standard credit contract; cf. e.g., Stiglitz and Weiss (1981). The borrower obtains money from the lender and uses only this money to finance a project. The project is either successful, yielding return R, or unsuccessful, yielding a return of zero. Moral hazard occurs because the probability of success depends on the effort of the borrower, which is unobservable to the lender. The borrower starts with wealth W. We contrast the consequences of a limited liability loan, with collateral C and interest rate i, with an unlimited liability loan with rate of interest ρ. The limited liability loan increases consumption in the event that the project is unsuccessful, but because $i > \rho$, it reduces consumption in the event the project is successful. Thus, the limited liability loan is essentially an unlimited liability loan combined with insurance. With the transformation, $W + R - L(1 + \rho) \Leftrightarrow w$, $R \Leftrightarrow d$, $W + R - L(1 + i) \Leftrightarrow w - \beta$, $W - C \Leftrightarrow w - d + a$, the problem is identical to the insurance problem analyzed in the paper. In the insurance context, the exclusive contract equilibrium always (with separable, event-independent utility) entails positive insurance. The analogous result here is that a limited liability loan always dominates an unlimited liability loan. Another analogous result is that if the lender can enforce exclusivity (in this context, can ensure that the borrower does not obtain an additional loan, or additional insurance against the failure of the project, from a third party) the equilibrium contract will entail credit rationing, in the sense that at the implicit price of insurance

$$q = \frac{(i - \rho)L}{L(1 + \rho) - C},$$

the borrower would like to obtain a larger loan, but is unable to find a lender who will agree to this.

A similar analysis holds if instead of choosing an *effort* level, the borrower has a choice of the riskiness of the two projects, both of which require an investment L. One project has, say, a higher return if successful, but a lower probability of success. We assume that the magnitude of the return cannot be observed (otherwise, in those cases where the project was successful, the lender could infer what project the borrower had undertaken). If the borrower undertakes the safe(s) project, his expected utility is

$$U(W + R^s - L(1 + i))(1 - p^s) + U(W - C)p^s,$$

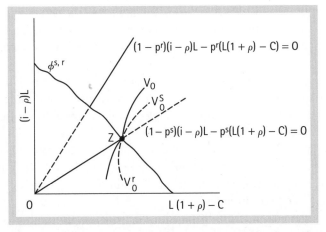

Fig. 10. Credit rationing with moral hazard when the lender cannot observe the riskiness of the project chosen by the borrower

while if the borrower undertakes the risky (r) project, his expected utility is

$$U(W + R^r - L(1 + i))(1 - p^r) + U(W - C)p^r,$$

where p is the probability of the project failing. The fixed-project indifference curves, shown in Figure 10, are well behaved. We can define the switching locus along which the individual switches from the safe to the risky project, $\phi^{s,r}$. Above the line (low collateral), the individual undertakes the risky project. The zero profit locus for the bank is that where the expected return to the loan $(1 - p)iL - p(L - C)$ is equal to the opportunity cost of funds, ρL. As drawn, the equilibrium, Z, will be characterized by rationing and an exclusive contract, where feasible. Since the implicit price of insurance is

$$q = \frac{(i - \rho)L}{L(1 + \rho) - C},$$

while the implicit quantity is $L(1 + \rho) - C$, rationing has several behavioral implications. Not only is the borrower unable to obtain as large a loan as he would like at the actuarially fair price, but he is also unable to obtain the equilibrium loan with less collateral. Furthermore, even though there is an excess demand for loanable funds, lenders will not respond by raising the interest rate, i, since doing so has adverse incentive effects.

X Concluding Comments

If one believes, as we do, that incentive/moral hazard problems are pervasive in our economy, then it is important to construct models exploring the existence and properties of market equilibrium taking these problems into account. It would be nice if we could simply assume that the relevant functions had the necessary mathematical properties to allow a convenient borrowing of concepts, methods, and results from standard competitive equilibrium analysis. Such, unfortunately, does not turn out to be the case.

The objective of this paper has been to develop the basic analytics of the economics of moral hazard. In spite of making standard convexity assumptions concerning the underlying utility functions and technology, we have established that insurance indifference curves are in general not convex and feasibility sets are never convex. Effort may change discontinuously as the parameters of the insurance contract are varied. And even when strong conditions are imposed on the forms of the underlying functions, price-consumption and income-consumption lines as well as demand curves may exhibit discontinuities.

We have suggested that these "perversities" have some profound implications for the existence and nature of equilibrium. For instance, equilibrium will be characterized by exclusive contracts entailing quantity rationing, when these are enforceable. When they are not, other contract forms will be seen. When only price contracts are offered, there may be no equilibrium with insurance in which firms make zero profits. And when each firm rations the quantity of insurance it sells, but cannot observe the quantities sold by other firms, no equilibrium may exist.

Though we have couched our analysis in terms of insurance markets, the results have a direct bearing on all markets in which uncertainty and incentive problems are both present; we illustrated this by showing how the model can be adapted to analyze labor and credit markets. The further investigation of the pervasive perversities which we have uncovered here, and their implications for equilibria under a variety of institutional settings, remain issues for future research.

APPENDIX: A BRIEF REVIEW OF THE EARLIER LITERATURE

It is unusual to have a literature review at the end of a paper. However, this paper is self-contained, and it is easier to explain here what contribution earlier papers made.

Pauly (1974) presented the basic two-outcomes moral hazard model. He assumed event-independent utility and convexity of indifference curves in $\alpha - \beta$ space. He identified and explained the exclusive contract equilibrium with observability and the zero profits price equilibrium with unobservability.

Helpman and Laffont (1975) broke new ground in recognizing the nonconvexities to which moral hazard can give rise. For the n-outcome case, they proved the existence of an exclusive contract equilibrium with observability, and of a zero profit price equilibrium with unobservability when indifference curves are convex in the analog to $\alpha - \beta$ space. They also presented an example demonstrating the non-existence of a zero profit price equilibrium with unobservability when indifference curves are non-convex. They did not, however, investigate the nonexistence problem further, or consider alternative equilibrium concepts.

Most of the subsequent literature has focussed on the principal-agent problem with a continuum of outcomes, on the assumptions of convex indifference curves and continuity of effort in the parameters of the insurance contract.

Stiglitz (1983b) provided an overview of the authors' preliminary work on moral hazard and introduced the analysis of price equilibria. Hellwig (1983) argued that in the case of unobservability of insurance purchases, there is a considerably larger set of candidate equilibria than the price equilibria; in particular, he considered Q-equilibria and some forms of PQ-equilibrium for the case of two discrete effort levels.

CHAPTER 17

CREDIT MARKETS AND THE CONTROL OF CAPITAL*

TRADITIONAL discussions of the role of capital markets have identified a number of distinct functions which they perform: they allocate scarce capital among competing users and uses,[1] and they provide signals to guide managers in making their investment decisions.[2] In this lecture, I wish to focus on a rather different function of the capital market: what I shall refer to as the *control of capital*.[3]

Conventional theory treats the typical firm in an anthropomorphic manner: it acts as a single, rational, individual doing what it is supposed to be doing, maximizing stock market value. That may have been well and good in those nostalgic bygone days of small firms, each run tightly by their owners who were single-mindedly pursuing their lust for wealth. But today a majority of production occurs in large corporations, in which no shareholder owns more than a small fraction of the shares, in which the separation of ownership and control that Frank Knight was so concerned with in his writings some sixty-five years ago has become a reality. Those who manage these corporations control enormous amounts of capital. If they perform their functions well, the economy, and the shareholders of the firms, will prosper. If they do not

* Financial support from the National Science Foundation is gratefully acknowledged. The author is indebted to Franklin Allen, Bruce Greenwald, Sandy Grossman, Oliver Hart, R. Gilbert, M. Spiegel, and A. Weiss for extensive discussions on the subject of this lecture. Reprinted with permission from *Journal of Money, Credit, and Banking*, 17(2) (May), 1985. Copyright © 1985 by the Ohio State University Press. The Money, Credit, and Banking Lecture was delivered on June 26, 1984, at the meetings of the Western Economic Association in Las Vegas.

[1] This is the role which I have, for instance, discussed extensively in Stiglitz (1982c). See also Stiglitz (1981).

[2] Tobin's q theory emphasizes this role of the stock market.

[3] This is not meant to be an exhaustive list of the functions performed by credit markets. Elsewhere, for instance, Grossman and I have emphasized the role of prices in conveying information from the uninformed to the informed and in aggregating information (see Grossman and Stiglitz 1976, 1980a).

perform their functions well, or if they divert the resources of the firm to their own personal use, both the economy and the shareholders will suffer. The question which I wish to address today is, what are the mechanisms in our society by which we ensure that those entrusted with the management of these resources do their job well? What are the institutions by which "control" is exerted over those who control capital? Are they effective? Could they be made more effective?

At the onset, it may be useful for me to present an overview of the argument which I shall present. In the first section, I shall review the traditional theory of the firm— the owner-managed firm. In this view, when the owner himself does not manage the firm, managers manage in the shareholders' interest; banks are like suppliers of pencils or toilet paper; each supplies a necessary ingredient in the production process of the firm, and there is no more reason to ascribe control to banks than to suppliers of these other inputs. There was a Populist view, common in the late nineteenth century, that banks were running the country; and there has been a continuing tradition in economics (particularly among institutional economists) that, even if banks do not run firms, managers do, in their own interests, and not necessarily in the interests of the shareholder. Modern theorists have, for the most part, dismissed this view: they have argued that there are mechanisms which ensure that managers who do not act in the interests of their shareholders get replaced. I would like to think of this as a triumph of theory over facts, which would bode well for theorists like myself; in fact, it appears to be more a triumph of ideology over theory and fact. The fact of the matter is that economic theory, taking into account costs of information, risk aversion, and the "public good" nature of management, is more consistent with what I shall loosely refer to as the Populist view than with what I shall call the nineteenth-century model of the firm.[4,5] Shareholders do not control the firm, and managers do not necessarily act in their interests.

Although I do not prove any theorems in this paper, I draw upon recent developments in the economics of information, particularly those developments which have focused on the problems of control (what have come to be called "principal-agent" problems), in which one individual attempts, through indirect control devices, to induce another to act in his own interests.[6] We argue that the problem at hand may most appropriately be viewed as a multiple-principal-agent problem, for which it is

---

[4] These attempts to encapsulate broad theories in single sentences will, no doubt, offend partisans of all these theories; any linking of these theories with particular periods will no doubt offend historians of economic thought. My only apology is that space limitations make some caricature of these opposing views necessary, and that in any case, the caricature serves the useful function of bringing out more clearly the particular views that I wish to stress.

[5] Thus, no particular novelty is claimed for the conclusions we reach; rather, the objective of this paper is to put what appears to be a currently unfashionable theory on firmer footing.

There has been a recent resurgence of interests in the problems discussed here, marked most notably by a recent conference at the Hoover Institution on Corporations and Private Property (the papers of which were published in the *Journal of Law and Economics*, 26(2), June 1983). The views of many of those papers are at variance with those presented here.

[6] For references and a fuller description of these theories, see below, section 2.

known that the Nash equilibrium is constrained Pareto inefficient.[7] Thus, the model of the firm that we present in section 2 represents an interpretation of this general multiple-principal-agent problem; in section 3 we examine the particular biases in resource allocations which it induces. In the fourth section, we suggest some reforms in our institutions which might alleviate some of the problems we have identified.

1 THE TRADITIONAL VIEW

In the model of primitive capitalism, with each firm controlled by a single owner, it is commonly argued that the issues with which we are concerned do not arise: because the owner-manager gets to keep the fruits of his labors and must bear the costs of any mistakes that he makes, he will have every incentive to exert the correct level of effort and to make the correct decisions. This view, however, is correct only if the probability of default of the firm is zero, an assumption which is as unrealistic for nineteenth-century firms as it is today. When a firm defaults, part of the costs of the mistakes of the firm that lead up to the default are borne not by the individual making the decision, but by his creditors. The recognition of this served as a serious impediment to the development of the limited liability firm.[8] The fact that the owner does not bear the full consequences of his actions has two important implications: the owner-manager has an incentive to undertake riskier actions than he otherwise would;[9] and the lender has an incentive to attempt to control, through one means or another, the actions of the borrower. We shall return later to the mechanisms by which lenders can exercise their control.

[7] The term "constrained Pareto inefficient" is used to remind the reader that in evaluating the efficiency of the economy, we have explicitly taken into account the costs of information. The remarkable part of the Fundamental Theorem of Welfare Economics is that it identifies the particular set of assumptions under which the competitive economy is Pareto efficient; if there are incomplete markets (as there are) or if there is imperfect information (as there is), then the economy is not, in general, constrained Pareto efficient (see Greenwald and Stiglitz 1986a). Though Greenwald and Stiglitz establish that there exists, in principle, interventions in the market (e.g., taxes and subsidies) that can make everyone better off, a legitimate question to ask is whether the interventions that would occur through the political process would indeed be Pareto improving. We take no position on this issue. In the last section, we do, however, suggest some reforms which might improve matters; but we do not necessarily argue that they should be implemented by legislation, though to the extent that legislation impedes their introduction, it may be desirable to alter it.

It is worth noting that the information problems with which we are concerned here also affect the structure of competition in other ways; for instance, they naturally lead to the use of long-term relationships (see Stiglitz and Weiss 1983b).

[8] For a discussion of this, see Allen (1980b).

[9] If the owner-manager were risk neutral, then his payoff function (under limited liability) is $\max[R - (1 + r)B, 0]$, where R is the return to the project, $(1 + r)B$ is the amount that the firm owes its lenders. (B is the debt; $1 + r$ is what is owed on the debt.) This is a convex function, and hence the owner-manager acts in a risk-loving manner. Even if the owner-manager is risk averse, he will act in a less risk averse manner (in the sense of Diamond and Stiglitz 1974) than he would have in the absence of limited liability (see Stiglitz and Weiss 1981).

As we have suggested, the nineteenth-century model of owner-managed firms is highly inappropriate for modern capitalist economies. Some managers are endowed with a sense of corporate responsibility: they maximize the stock market value of the firm because they believe that is what a good manager is supposed to do. They are individuals who are programmed to act in that manner; and the selection process of managers entails, in part, a search for individuals who are so programmed.[10] But an important part of standard economic doctrine is that individuals do what is in their own self-interest. Why is it in the self-interest of nonowner-managers to maximize, say, the stock market value of the firm?

Three arguments have been put forward—stockholder meetings, takeovers, and "voting with dollars." I shall now show why none of these is very effective as a control mechanism.

The Failure of Stockholder Meetings

The stockholder meeting is the forum by which, in a strictly formal legal sense, stockholders control the management; they can—and in principle should—replace any manager who fails to take those actions which maximize the stock market value of the firm. In practice, there is considerable evidence that such meetings are usually controlled by the management, and theoretical considerations suggest that this should be the case. Any shareholder views himself as having a negligible effect on the outcome. Since there is always some cost associated both with obtaining information to determine whether a manager is a good manager and with evaluating alternative management teams, in other words, to voting intelligently, and there is a negligible benefit, no rational shareholder should expend the resources required to vote intelligently. We have long recognized that the well functioning of the government is a public good, and that because it is a public good, there may be too little expenditure on resources to ensure that governments function well. But a publicly held corporation is like a (local) government.[11] Ensuring that it functions well is a public good for all those who own shares in the firm (or who are the firms' creditors).[12]

---

[10]   There is little doubt that much of human behavior is the result of some kind of conditioning and/or training. Most individuals when they vote do so because they believe it is their civic duty, not because they do a careful calculation of the expected costs and benefits of voting. Reward structures in most universities are such that they must rely almost completely on some vaguely defined sense of responsibility for individuals to carry out all the tasks that need to be performed in an efficient and effective manner. This is not to say that selfish (rational) considerations do not enter; only that one cannot explain behavior simply by relying on such considerations.

George Akerlof has suggested an insightful "rational" explanation for such seemingly irrational behavior. Parents like their children to appear to be honest and to have other similar virtues, because these virtues are rewarded in our society. Ideally, they might prefer that their children appear to be honest but really be dishonest, for by doing so they would be able both to obtain positions in which they have control of resources and to divert these resources to their own uses. Unfortunately, or fortunately, it is difficult to train children to appear to be honest, while they are actually being dishonest. Given this, the "second best" policy is to train one's children to be honest.

[11]   The analogy is discussed further in Stiglitz (1977c).

[12]   It has not yet become commonplace in our schools to indoctrinate children in the virtues of exercising their voting rights over shares in the way that it is conventional to instruct them on the virtues of voting in public elections.

What is surprising then is not that shareholder meetings generally fail to exercise effective control over management, but that there are instances in which shareholder meetings have had an effect.[13]

The Failure of Takeovers as a Control Device

Takeovers provide a second mechanism by which capital markets are alleged to ensure that errant managers get replaced. Assume the managers were not maximizing the market value of the firm. Any individual could come along, purchase the firm, change the policy to the value-maximizing policy, and reap the resulting movement in value as the return to his good management. There are at least four reasons why takeovers have not (and are not likely to be) an effective control mechanism.[14]

First, when it is observed that some firm is not performing well, it may be either because the management is not good, or because the assets of the firm are not what they appear to be.[15] The insiders (the managers of the firm) are likely to be more informed in this regard than are the outsiders. Thus, when those who have a controlling interest in the firm are willing to sell their shares,[16] it indicates that the individual or firm attempting the takeover has paid too much; if they refuse to sell, it indicates that the individual or firm attempting the takeover has paid too little: takeovers will only be successful when the firm taking over pays too much.[17]

---

[13] The fact that a risk-averse individual would be sufficiently widely diversified so that only a negligible fraction of his wealth would be tied up in any firm provides further justification for why a rational individual should not allocate resources to voting intelligently in shareholder meetings.

Conversely, if individuals have a significant fraction of their wealth tied up in a firm, and if at the same time they own a significant fraction of the shares of the firm, so that they may be able to affect the outcome, then it is rational for them to allocate resources to ensuring that the firm is well managed. But such individuals are frequently those involved in management, and thus do not provide any check on management. For an explanation (arising out of imperfect information concerning the characteristics of different firms) of why the original owners of firms do not become fully diversified and retain a significant fraction of the shares of the firm they established, see Stiglitz (1982c).

Note that to the extent that such individuals do have an incentive to exercise control, they have an incentive to exercise it in a way that promotes their own interests. Their interests will not coincide with those of small shareholders. (This will be true even if they could not divert resources to their own use, at the expense of other shareholders, i.e., the only differences may be those due to differences in attitudes towards risk.) See Grossman and Stiglitz (1977, 1980b).

[14] Not all of these may be relevant in any particular situation.

[15] That is, given the past mistakes of the firm, the firm may now be doing as well with what it has as anyone else could do.

[16] This assumes that those who are in a position to determine (or significantly affect) the outcome of a takeover bid have the interests of shareholders as a whole at heart; often they do not, as we shall argue below.

[17] Takeovers are like buying "used firms" just as secondary labor markets are like hiring "used labor." Akerlof's (1970) original insight into the thinness of used car markets applies here, just as it does to the used car market (see Stiglitz 1975c; Greenwald 1986). The argument applies, however, with even greater force to this market than to the labor or used car markets. There, trade might occur because individuals have different abilities that are specific to different firms or have different tastes for quality of used cars. Here, it is only differences in ability to manage the firm's assets that are relevant. (With rational expectations, differences in beliefs alone cannot give rise to trade (see Stiglitz 1982c). For an application of this general result to takeovers, see Grossman and Hart (1981a).) Without entering into the debate on

While the presence of asymmetric information gives rise to problems, so too may the inability to keep information secret. It is costly to ascertain which of the many firms in our economy are not very well managed and hence undervalued relative to their potential. Assume that some firm allocated resources to sift through a large set of firms to identify the most poorly managed one. It then made a takeover bid. This immediately provides a signal to other firms to evaluate whether the bid represents an underevaluation of the firm's true worth. If it does, they will then "bid" against the "discovery" firm; in equilibrium, the entry of these "secondary" bidders will drive their expected profits to zero; but this implies that the discovery firm, which has had to expand resources reviewing many firms that are not badly managed, has a negative expected profit.[18]

The third reason that takeover mechanisms are ineffective is related to the same "public good" argument that arose in our discussion of the inefficacy of stockholder meetings. If the takeover is successful, and if as a result the market value of a share is increased, those shareholders who have not sold out get a free ride; since each small shareholder believes that what he does will have no effect on the outcome (whether the takeover is or is not successful), it is in the interest of each to withhold his shares.[19] Only if he believes that the takeover will be successful and will result in a decline in the value of his shares will he have an incentive to sell.[20] Thus, whereas value-decreasing

---

the empirical literature assessing the effects of takeovers, let me simply assert that I have not found much convincing evidence that takeovers result in significant increases in the productivity of the firm taken over. It appears common for the firm taking over to have its market price fall if it is successful. If this is true, it suggests that the market perceives the "success" of the takeover as evidence that too high a price has been paid, and it provides further evidence that firms (here the firm taking over) are not controlled by their shareholders.

Even when there are some firms who have a reasonable idea about the value of a firm, there will be relatively few such firms, and some firms may have a better idea than others. Thus, the appropriate model is not the standard, fully competitive model, but a bidding model with a limited number of bidders and possibly asymmetric information.

[18] See Stiglitz (1975c). Firms will, in general, employ mixed strategies in making their takeover bids or in deciding whether they should evaluate a takeover bid to decide whether to compete.

[19] If there are well-developed option markets, presumably the individual could participate in any gain and at the same time sell his shares; these option markets have resulted in the creation of a class of securities that is formally equivalent to nonvoting shares.

[20] Note that this problem does not arise when there is a single shareholder. Then (ignoring the problem of asymmetric information discussed in the previous paragraph), one can think of the firm as continuously being on auction. It will be sold to the bidder who believes he or she can earn the highest return from the assets (and the rent will equal the difference between the value of those assets to him or her, and to the next highest bidder; with a large number of bidders and no significant differences in comparative advantages in management, this will be essentially zero). Although this argument explains why assets might be efficiently utilized in a "primitive capitalist economy," it does not work well for modern capitalism: no entrepreneur has sufficient capital to acquire all of the shares in any one of the major industrial firms; if he did succeed, he would probably not be able to be sufficiently widely diversified to act in a risk-neutral manner; and if he succeeded, he would have had to rely on considerable borrowings from financial institutions, which will impose important constraints on his behavior—a central theme of this lecture.

Grossman and Hart (1980b) have emphasized this explanation of the inefficacy of the takeover mechanism. They argue that, as a result, the only way that those taking over a firm can get compensated is through diverting the firm's resources to their own use. But if those who increase the efficiency of the

takeovers are easy (there is a rational expectations equilibrium in which all such takeovers are successful), value-enhancing takeovers are not.[21]

The fourth reason that takeover mechanisms are ineffective is that the current managers are often in a position to take strategic actions that deter takeovers.[22] Though the most dramatic of these have only recently come to public attention—golden parachutes, contingent sales of the firms assets, acquisitions that will result in antitrust violations if the takeover is successful—other actions, such as long term contracts with large penalties for breach of contract, restrict the scope of action of any firm attempting to take over another firm and thus make the takeover less attractive.[23]

Voting with Dollars

There is a third control mechanism that is often postulated: in analogy to the Tiebout (1956) model, in the theory of local public goods, where individuals vote with their feet, here individuals vote with their dollars. Firms that do not use resources efficiently will not be able to raise additional capital. There are, however, important limitations to this mechanism (as with the previous two): it is only effective to the extent that capital must be raised from the market; the managers of firms have considerable discretion over their cash flow. For some firms, with good investment opportunities (exceeding their cash flows), the "bribe" of future capital induces desirable behavior

---

firm can do so, so can those who fail to increase the efficiency of the firm: it is difficult for an outsider to assess whether the firm is or is not being managed efficiently.

[21] This analysis clearly depends on the rules confronting the firm attempting the takeover. Takeovers can be made easy if the firm taking over can offer to buy only 51 percent of the shares and can then take actions that dilute the interests of the minority shareholders. But as we note below, rules that make value-enhancing takeovers easier may also make value-decreasing takeovers easier, and may indeed result in the nonexistence of equilibrium. See Stiglitz (1972b).

[22] For a discussion of some of these devices, see Cary (1969).

[23] These are not the only problems with takeovers. The firm that is willing to bid the most in a takeover model is not necessarily the one that will use the resources most efficiently, but the one that is most effective in diverting the resources to its own use. Fraud laws do not stop this diversion, and indeed may put some firms (downstream or upstream suppliers or purchasers) at an advantage relative to other firms.

But what is at issue is more than just fraud or the diversion of the resources of the firm to the personal use of managers. Assume that there are three or more groups of individuals in the population with honest differences in opinion about how the resources may be best used. Then, type A individuals can buy out a majority of the shares from type B and change the production plan of the firm. Those who sell out—those among current owners who are most pessimistic concerning the firm's prospects—may be slightly better off; those who do not sell are worse off. This is true whether current market price goes up or down; type B individuals believed that, under the original production plan, their expected return was greater than from other assets (but there were sufficiently few of them that the marginal purchaser of shares was an individual of another type, say C). At the same time, once A controls the shares of the firm, type B individuals could buy out a majority of type A individuals. There is no equilibrium. Implicit in this analysis is an assumption of imperfect competition: individuals enjoy some "surplus" out of the ownership of the stock of a particular firm; the demand curve for the shares of the firm are downward sloping. There is considerable evidence in support of this "monopolistic competition" view of the stock market (see Stiglitz 1972b, 1974e, 1975e).

today. (And even then, what being "good" means need not correspond to "efficient utilization of resources.") But for other firms, with poor investment opportunities, the threat of the denial of access to future capital is not an effective control mechanism.

Note, moreover, that when firms do return to the market for additional capital, they almost invariably turn to banks. There are two reasons for this. The first (which is discussed in Greenwald, Stiglitz, and Weiss (1984)) is that resorting to the issue of equities often provides a signal concerning the "quality of the firm" and depresses the price of the shares. The second, which is the subject of this paper, is that raising capital through banks results in more effective control over capital than raising it through equity markets.[24]

Consequences of the Failure of Control Mechanisms

I have argued here that the standard "control mechanisms"—whether they were or were not effective in the days of primitive capitalism—are at best of only limited effectiveness in modern capitalist economies. Empirical evidence in support of my position is hard to come by: an essential part of the argument is the difficulty outsiders face in determining whether a firm is or is not efficiently managed. Still, there is both direct and indirect evidence in my support. First, the one aspect of technology that is "public" concerns taxes and tax-avoidance behavior. There is a considerable body of evidence supporting the view that a significant fraction of firms do not act in such a way as to minimize tax burdens (including both direct, i.e., corporate, taxation, and indirect taxation, the taxes shareholders and suppliers of credit must pay). (For a review of these tax "paradoxes," see Stiglitz (1982e).)[25] Second, the persistence, over an extended period of time, of closed-end mutual funds selling at a discount (implying that the managers had, at each moment, a strategy that would lead to an increase in market value), and the difficulties that the few takeovers which were attempted encountered, provides corroborating evidence. (This is similar to the resistance of many managers to "asset stripping takeovers," even when the value of the stripped assets is considerably more than the current value of the firm.) Third, the behavior of managers in many of the recent takeover wars seems more consistent with the view put forward here than with the standard view.[26]

[24] These are not the only alleged control mechanisms in a capitalist economy. For instance, there are evolutionary arguments which suggest that firms who manage their resources efficiently will survive, while those that do not will not. For some criticisms of this argument, see, for instance, Stiglitz (1975e, 1982e).

[25] It would be worth knowing whether the incidence of such seemingly anomalous behavior is greater among managerially controlled firms than among owner-managed firms.

[26] I realize, of course, that, to true believers in the religion of efficient markets and efficient firms, these arguments will not be completely persuasive. There may be Ptolemaic arguments by which each piece of evidence might be reconciled with what I have loosely termed "traditional" theory. My objective here is to present a simple, alternative theory that is consistent with the evidence and in which things are what they seem to be: behavior that appears to be inconsistent with value maximization is in fact inconsistent with it.

2 BANKS AND THE CONTROL OF CAPITAL

Our problem can now be simply put: how do we ensure that, in a capitalist economy, those entrusted with the management of its resources, the managers of our largest corporations, manage those resources efficiently.[27] I have argued that the traditional control mechanisms are not effective. The central thesis of this paper is that, to the extent that control is exercised, it is by banks, by lenders, and not by the owners of equity, in spite of the legal form that invests responsibility for control in the hands of the owners of equity. But before arguing this, and exploring its consequences, I need to explain at greater length what I mean by control.

Both the concept of control and its ambiguity are familiar to most of us from ordinary usage: we talk about losing control of our children, but then admit we never had it; we ask who runs (or controls) the university, but a single source of power appears to be elusive. In the present context, managers of the firm have "responsibility" for the management of certain assets; they can assign them to one use or to another. We say they control the disposition of those assets. But their control is not unfettered. They (the corporation which they manage) have received its resources (capital) from banks and from suppliers of equity. Each, in supplying capital, has imposed conditions on the manager, which circumscribe his actions, which limit his freedom.[28] The constraints which each can impose are markedly different. The equity owner cannot demand the return of his funds (he can try to persuade another individual to purchase his shares, but once he has turned over the capital to the manager, he cannot force the manager to give him back his money). He can exercise his vote in a shareholders meeting. The lender sets a term to the loan; at the end of the term, he can insist on his money back. If the manager fails to comply with his request, the lender has certain rights of intervention, defined both by the loan contract and by statutes. The lender has the right to intervene in other well-defined circumstances. The loan contract may, for instance, impose restrictions on additional loans, on what projects the firm may undertake, etc.[29] Note that the rights of the lender to get his

Note, however, that the argument that value-decreasing takeovers may be successful may provide a rationale for managerial resistance to takeovers, which is consistent with shareholder interests.

[27] As I have mentioned earlier, what is at stake is more than simple fraud; that, presumably, might be taken care of by direct legal remedies.

There is a view that managers make little differences to the performance of firms. The evidence usually cited is that changes in management do not have a significant effect on firm performance. This could be either because the selection process is sufficiently effective that good managers are replaced by good managers or because managers make no difference. (Alternatively, and probably more reasonably, though incompetent managers clearly can destroy a firm, within the range of those who appear to be good, the effect may be relatively small.)

[28] These are not the only sources of constraints on his action. The legal system imposed other constraints; buyers and sellers with whom the firm has contracts impose still further constraints.

[29] In some cases, the law restricts the set of interventions that may be stipulated in a loan contract; if the lender takes too active a position in management, he may lose the advantages that the law assigns to creditors.

money back are circumscribed. But they are undoubtedly less circumscribed than the rights of the equity owners to get their money back.

The terms of the contract are both explicit and implicit. Implicit contracts are enforced not through law but by other means: a borrower who fails to comply with the terms of the implicit contract may fail to have his loan renewed (and a lender who fails to renew a loan, all of the implicit terms of which have been complied with, may find it difficult to find willing borrowers).[30] Controllers control controlees not only directly, by imposing constraints on the set of actions which the controlled can undertake, but also indirectly, by designing reward structures which induce the controlled to take actions that are (more) in accord with those attempting to exercise control.

Thus, managers are partially controlled, directly and indirectly, through both explicit and implicit contracts and by both lenders and shareholders. The lenders exert control through both the formal terms of their contract and their refusal to renew a loan; shareholders exert control through both the voting process and their refusal to provide additional capital. Managerial incentives are affected by both the explicit pay schedule—the rewards provided by other firms who might hire them away, provided their behavior is appropriate—and the implicit punishments provided by other firms in their treatment of those who are dismissed by their firms (or whose firms go bankrupt). Both the rewards and punishments and the constraints, which determine the action of managers, are set not by a single individual, and not even by the firm's shareholders and lenders, but by the market as a whole.[31] No one controls the manager: a large number of individuals and institutions affect his behavior. While the earlier literature[32] attempted to view the manager as the agent of the supplier of credit (the "principal"), with the supplier of credit designing an efficient incentive contract for the agent,[33] a more appropriate model is a multiple-principal-agent model, in which each principal is only allowed to set certain of the terms of the

---

[30] As in labor contracts, it is not the case that explicit contracts are necessarily better than implicit contracts. The enforcement of explicit contracts requires not only that violations be observable, but that they be verifiable by a third party, the court; this is not so for implicit contracts. On the other hand, while one-period explicit contracts are enforceable, for implicit contracts to be enforceable requires long-term relationships.

[31] Thus, the threat of a lender to cut off credit would not have much force if the borrower could simply turn to other suppliers of credit. The threat of an employer to fire a worker would not have much force if the worker could simply turn to some other employer and obtain the same wage. Market equilibrium must be such that these threats are effective, that is, there is some cost to being fired or to having one's credit terminated by the bank that usually provides credit. For an analysis of equilibriums with this property, see Stiglitz and Weiss (1983b) and Shapiro and Stiglitz (1984).

[32] This view was first put forward in Stiglitz (1974e), where the analogy between the problem of the landlord, attempting to elicit effort from his workers, and the owner of capital, attempting to elicit effort from his manager, was drawn (see also Ross 1973). Since then, a huge literature on the principal-agent problem has developed, emphasizing not only the problem of eliciting the correct level of effort, but also the problem of ensuring that the manager undertakes the correct amount of risk.

[33] Although it should be emphasized that "efficient" in this sense is only a local concept, given the prices, etc. on the market, the principal cannot be made better off without making the agent worse off. The market equilibrium is not, however, in general Pareto efficient. See Arnott and Stiglitz (1990) and Greenwald and Stiglitz (1986a).

contract. These problems are, of course, ubiquitous in our economy, though they have received relatively little attention.

Let me give another example, where each of the principals has a natural set of controls. Consider a sharecropping economy, in which the tenant needs both capital and land to produce output. Assume that one individual owns the capital, the other land. Each writes a contract with the tenant specifying the compensation he is to receive for supplying his resource. The behavior of the individual is, of course, affected by the terms of both contracts. There is a kind of externality between the two contracts: an individual with a large outstanding loan may (in the presence of provisions for bonded labor) undertake less risk but supply more effort than he otherwise would have provided.[34] There is, as a result, an incentive for the internalization of these externalities; for the landlord, for instance, simultaneously to provide credit, or at least to force his tenant to disclose what credit contracts he has.[35] But for a variety of reasons, full internalization is frequently not possible.[36] In those cases, there will not be a single principal controlling the agent. This is the situation, I contend, with large joint stock firms. There is no single principal controlling the manager.

When there are several individuals exerting control, we are wont to ask, who exerts effective control, or who is most important in exerting control? The question, I think, is a meaningful one, but is hard to translate into quantitative terms: clearly agent A exerts more effective control than agent B if agent A can impose all the same constraints and rewards that agent B can, and then some. But usually, agent A can do some things that agent B cannot, and conversely. Equity owners can do some things that lenders cannot (they can vote at shareholder meetings), and lenders can do some things that equity owners cannot. This is not the occasion to attempt a precise definition (and it is hardly necessary for my purpose). I hope that the intuitive notions that I will present here will suffice for the moment.

In determining who exercises effective control, what is relevant is not only the *rights and means of intervention* but also the incentives: intervention is only desirable if it effects an improvement in behavior on the part of the agent (from the point of view of the "intervenor"). To ascertain this, the intervenor has to be informed about both the current course of action of the manager and the alternatives. But information is costly.

Here we obtain the basic dilemma: if the manager were to receive all of his resources from a single supplier, then that supplier would have an incentive to gather

[34] The externality is reciprocal: the terms of the tenancy contract affect the probability of default on the loan. For a more extensive discussion of these issues, see Braverman and Stiglitz (1982).

[35] For a more general discussion of these externalities in the context of principal-agent (moral hazard) problems, see Arnott and Stiglitz (1986). For an excellent discussion in terms of the multiple-principal-agent problem, see Bernheim and Whinston (1984).

[36] Limitations on information may make it impossible to enforce "exclusive" contracts. Alternatively, a single principal may not have control of all the resources required by the agent. Thus, the landlord may not have sufficient capital or the required bullocks. Presumably, he could obtain these resources from the same supplier that the tenant does; but this would simply introduce a new principal-agent problem.

A further limitation may be imposed by the fact that if the principal supplies all the resources required by the agent, the principal becomes too dependent, for his welfare, on the behavior of the agent: there is insufficient risk diversification.

information to ascertain that the manager acted in the interests of the supplier. But then the supplier would have to bear considerable risk; he might not be adequately diversified. On the other hand, it is not in the interests of any shareholder or small lender to devote much attention to the performance of a firm; for any gains that accrue to him as a result of his actions accrue to all similarly situated suppliers. There is the free-rider problem which we discussed earlier.

Thus, though both lenders and equity owners have certain rights to control managers, they do not individually have the incentives required to induce them to exercise those rights. The conclusion: managers are not effectively controlled.

If this were the end of the story, the prospects for large-scale capitalism would have indeed been dim. Given that managers could not be effectively controlled, no one would turn over to them the capital required for the development of modern industry. There are, however, three control mechanisms, which, though they work imperfectly, work sufficiently well that individuals are willing to turn over capital to others.

A Banks

The most important of these, I suspect, are banks (both the lending banks and the investment banks, which assist in the raising of capital). Banks frequently take large positions in a firm; the nature of the loan contract enables them to do this without undertaking undue risk. At the same time, the nature of the contract enables them to focus their attention on information gathering to a particular set of issues: those associated with the probability of default and the net worth of the firm in those low-return states. They need not concern themselves with either how good the best prospects of the firm are or what the probability is that the firm will make off like a bandit.

Since they are concerned with low-probability events, and since the managerial-incentives structure is such as to encourage managers to avoid those events, the payoff to banks exercising very effective control is limited.[37] We shall return to this later.

This argument says that the "public good of management" problem for lenders is resolved by having a single lender. This is not always the case: frequently there are syndicated loans, in which a single bank takes the "lead" position and undertakes responsibility for ensuring that the borrower is effectively controlled (from the perspective of the lender).[38] Here, the problem of public management as a public good is resolved by means of reputation: it is in the interest of each bank to ensure that the loans on which it acts as the lead banker are good, lest other banks refuse to participate in the loans it attempts to syndicate.[39]

---

[37] Collateral reduces the risk to the bank even further and, except for avoiding disastrous outcomes, also reduces the incentives for exercising close control.

[38] As usual, the problems of incentives and screening are hard to distinguish: the lead bank is also responsible for ascertaining the suitability of the borrower for the loan.

[39] The enforcement of cooperative equilibrium in multiperiod games has been the subject of extensive recent research. Though most of these studies have assumed no discounting, and therefore are

B *Concentrated equity ownership*

In the case of debt, the problem was resolved by having a single supplier (or having the several suppliers act cooperatively). In the case of a large, widely held firm, the number of shareholders is sufficiently large and there is sufficient anonymity about who the shareholders are that the same mechanism will not work. But if there are a few shareholders, each of whom has enough stake in the firm that his private incentives for controlling the manager are sufficiently great, then there will be a sufficiently large expenditure on information acquisition by these individuals that effective control will be exerted. (The small shareholders will continue to "free ride" on the efforts of the larger shareholders; the standard arguments suggest that as a result there will be an insufficient expenditure on resources for controlling managers, at least from the point of view of the shareholders as a class.) This has a cost: the limited diversification which these individuals can achieve. Moreover, the interests of these shareholders may well not coincide with the interests of the small shareholders.[40] Presumably, for individuals to be willing to undertake this limited risk diversification, they must be compensated, for example, by being allowed to divert some of the resources of the firm to their own use (such as high fees for being on the board of directors).[41]

of limited usefulness for our purposes, several recent studies have incorporated discounting. See, in particular, Abreu (1983).

As in the usual analysis, in a one-period model it would pay each bank to cheat: to syndicate a loan, but then to fail to expend the resources required to ensure that the lender used the funds properly. In a multiperiod context, this is not true. A bank that "lost its reputation" and could not syndicate its loans would have to bear greater risk. This "risk premium" can be viewed as the punishment for failing to exercise control. Note that the number of banks involved is sufficiently small so that each bank can assess the reputation of the other banks.

A similar reputation mechanism operates in the case of investment banks attempting to raise capital by means of bonds. Then, the bank agrees to act as "trustee" for the bondholders, exerting certain control. The argument does not carry over, however, to investment banks attempting to raise equity capital. After the equity is raised, the bank usually plays no role in ensuring that the firm's managers do what they should. The responsibility of the investment bank is limited to that of screening. (This is not quite true for venture capital and private placements.)

[40] The fact that a wealthier individual owns more shares of a firm does not necessarily imply that he has greater incentives for information acquisition and for exercising control: if the value of his time increases proportionately, then the cost of obtaining information rises with the return.

[41] If this were the only return extracted by such shareholders, it would be a small price to pay for the management of the public good. Unfortunately, apart from the other control mechanisms discussed here, there seems considerable discretion for the controlling shareholders and managers to cooperate in the diversion of resources from the common good of shareholders to their own benefit.

Note that there are other reasons for limited diversification: the original founder of a firm may wish to signal his confidence in the firm by retaining a considerable proportion of the shares (see Stiglitz 1982c). Firms that are controlled by the original founder represent a cross between the primitive capitalism discussed in section 1 and advanced capitalism under discussion here.

Just as the original founder of the firm may retain a significant fraction of shares in the firm to signal his confidence in the firm (and thus to increase the market value of the firm), so too has he an incentive to design the corporate charter in such a way as to provide "good incentives" to subsequent managers; presumably the market will reward him from doing so by increasing his current market value. Though there is obviously some truth in this argument, frequently when the corporate charter is drawn up, the founder has no intention of retiring; frequently, he has a contract with the firm which requires that he continue to provide certain services, for an extended period of time. Thus the present discounted value to designing contract terms that provide better incentives for some potential future manager, in ten,

C Managerial reputations

The third control mechanism is the concern of the manager for his good reputation. Others, both in his firm and outside, are judging his behavior. If he behaves "well" then he is apt to be promoted or to be bid away by some other firm. If he behaves in a way that is perceived to be "bad," at the very least his outside opportunities will be reduced; at the worst the firm will go bankrupt, the creditors will intervene, and he will be out of a job. He always risks the possibility of an internal coup d'état: underlings or outsiders attempting to convince the board of directors that they could do a better job.[42]

Managers are affected, of course, not only by their reputations, but also by their compensation schedule. Some have suggested this as an explanation, for instance, for stock options. Interestingly enough, a recent study by Larson (1984) of stock option incentive plans instituted over an extended period of time showed that firms with these plans did no better (in terms of stock market value) than the market as a whole. There are few firms with managerial-incentive plans which are even roughly in accord with what economic theory would predict.[43]

3 BIASES IN THE CONTROL MECHANISMS

Shareholders do not control the firm. We have posited here a set of alternative control mechanisms. Managers do respond to these controls. I wish to argue that,

twenty, or thirty years time is likely to be small; the founder is best advised to direct his attention to other problems.

[42] The fact that the board of directors often includes many individuals from management should not obscure the fact that the different managers and different members of the board have different incentives: they need not act as a team. It is obviously risky for the president of a firm to attempt to overthrow the CEO, but such palace revolutions are not that uncommon.

[43] A notable exception is the recently instituted executive compensation plan of TRW. Stock option plans reward the manager but not in terms of how his performance compares with others in comparable situations; such compensation depends on the performance of the stock market as a whole. Why should executives be forced to bear this risk? Doing so has one advantage in principle: managers should be more concerned with the correlation of the firm's return with the market. There is little evidence that this was an important consideration in the adoption of these plans or that it has been an important consequence of them. Indeed, if it were, contracts with managers should impose restrictions on their purchase of index options or other shares in the market. (Today, with futures markets, managers may be able to divest themselves of the market risk associated with being paid in options.)

The standard argument concerning the tax advantages are fallacious; indeed, quite the contrary, even if the pay were to be made dependent on the performance of the firm, it is advantageous to pay the bonus directly, rather than through stock options (see Stiglitz 1982e). (When I presented this argument recently to a conference in which a number of participants were responsible for designing the executive compensation programs for some large American firms, no countervailing argument was presented.)

It is interesting to note that when most stock option plans are instituted, the executive does not appear to bear more risk: they are introduced as supplements (allegedly at little cost to shareholders) to their salary structures. For a discussion of relative performance based incentive structures, see Nalebuff and Stiglitz (1983b).

as a result, firms do not maximize their stock market value;[44] whether there are other institutional arrangements which would ensure that capital would be more effectively utilized is a question to which I shall turn in the next section.

There are systematic biases associated with each of the control mechanisms described in the preceding section. Lenders are only concerned with the bottom part of the tail of the distribution of returns. Thus, they may require that the firm undertake projects with relatively little (bottom-tail) risk, even though the expected return is much lower. (Or, they may induce the firm to do the same thing through their indirect control devices, the control of the terms of the loan contract, the conditions under which they renew credit, the collateral which they require, or the interest rate which they charge.) In reducing the probability of default, they ensure that the manager does not abscond with the firm's funds, and thus provide a public good for all investors. But in other respects, the interests of banks and equity owners are antithetical. The bank, because it can withdraw funds, is in a position to exercise control: managers respond to the demands of their bankers.[45]

Managers' concern for their reputation, and their knowledge that judgments will frequently be made (implicitly) based on their relative performance, means that they may "follow the pack." If convention has it that the firm should pay dividends, then the managers instruct the firm to pay dividends, whether or not it is in the best interests of shareholders. Any manager of a large, publicly held firm who attempted to explain the dividend paradox to his shareholders would be considered flaky, and his future prospects diminished.[46] The firm's managers may ask the firm to pay them whatever convention dictates that managers of such firms get paid, regardless of the opportunity cost of the managers' time, and regardless of what it could obtain essentially similar managers for. Although the executives of the automobile industry were quick to claim their desserts for having brought the industry back to profitability (in spite of the significantly negative effects that these bonuses had on labor relations), they were not as quick to accept blame (and the commensurate pay reductions) when they led the industry to all-time losses.[47] Managers are (at best) temporary trustees of the firm's assets, and their reward structures are for the most part directed at current returns: few firms compensate their managers on the basis of the firm's

[44] This in itself does not mean that the economy is not constrained Pareto efficient; resources are not being used as effectively as they would be if information were costless, but this is a relatively uninteresting statement. It is, however, well known by now that whenever there are principal-agent (incentive) problems, the economy is not even constrained Pareto inefficient (see Arnott and Stiglitz 1986; Greenwald and Stiglitz 1986a).

[45] The term of the loan poses an interesting problem to the lender. On the one hand, short-term loans give the lender a right to his money back (or to intervene) at any date; but lenders cannot continuously monitor, and in the intervening periods borrowers may take actions that make it impossible to repay. They thus force the hand of the lender: he either renews the contract or takes the risk of getting what he can out of bankruptcy. It may be more efficient for the lender to commit himself to supplying funds over a certain extended period, effectively giving up some of his rights to intervention (see Stiglitz and Weiss 1981).

[46] Presumably, by the time the individual has reached this rung of the corporate ladder, any such tendencies have been identified and the individual barred from further progression.

[47] So long as the firm is making record profits, the lenders have no interest in restricting these payments; equity owners do, but for the reasons we have given above, they have no effective control.

performance ten or twenty years hence. Few, if any, require that the individual retain shares in the firm long after they have completed their term as chief executive. Yet the return on many long-term investments will not occur until some time in the future. Keynes, in the *General Theory*, expressed a concern that investors in the stock market were merely concerned with short-term gains, not the long-term returns. Today, increasingly, similar allegations are brought against the managers of many of America's largest enterprises: the heads of these enterprises are financial experts, not production experts. Their job is to allocate capital. And their perspective is not unlike that of the Keynesian investor: they wish to find underpriced assets, just before those assets are discovered by others, so that they can reap a short-term capital gain. Their behavior is not surprising: what incentive do they have to be concerned about the long-term prospects of the firm or the productivity of the economy?[48]

Small shareholders, since they cannot exercise control directly, must rely on the other control mechanisms. Large equity owners may have, as we have suggested, some incentives to exercise control, but their interests may well not coincide with those of the small shareholders. Similarly, though small shareholders may recognize that the interests of the lenders and those of small equity owners are not coincident, they know that the lenders' concern that the firm not abscond with the funds ensures some degree of safety for their investment; and that since managers in general have some stake in the outcome of the firm, their incentives will at least partially be coincident.

4 INSTITUTIONAL REFORM

Our arguments, if they are correct, suggest that the traditional view of how capitalist economies work is at best oversimplified and at worst simply wrong. Managers have considerable discretion: the control mechanisms work only imperfectly. Though the

[48] Their position should be contrasted with that of the owner-manager under primitive capitalism, whose dynastic ambitions included leaving his firm to his heirs. Such individuals were not concerned with what they might be able to sell their firm for on a day-to-day basis, but with the long-term prospects of the firm.

Evidence that managers are particularly concerned with the short-run prospects of the firm is provided by such so-called tax paradoxes as the extensive use of FIFO inventory accounting in inflationary times and the long lags in the shift to accelerated depreciation. The standard explanation of these phenomena is that managers were concerned that, were they to make these changes, the market would misinterpret the decline in accounting profits, and as a result the current market price would decline. This decline would occur despite the fact that the real (after tax) value of the firm should have increased. (If investors continued to behave naively on the basis of current reported profits, future values would eventually increase.)

Clearly, if the current market price accurately reflected the long-run prospects of the firm, there would be no discrepancy between maximizing current market valuation and long-run market valuation. In an economy in which there is an incomplete set of risk and futures markets, and investors are imperfectly informed concerning the activities of the firm, there is no reason to believe that the two will be perfectly congruent. The tax paradoxes described earlier provide illustrations of this.

earlier Berle-Means view that managers control firms and the March-Simon view that they simply satisfice may be incomplete, these views may provide a more accurate description of firm behavior than the other extreme view that firms maximize their stock market value. Managers face a variety of constraints and a variety of incentives, imposed by a variety of institutions. Managers of large corporations whose stock is widely held undoubtedly behave in ways which are markedly different from that of an owner-manager. We have identified a number of biases: lenders are more concerned with avoiding defaults than with maximizing returns, and managers are more concerned with short-run profitability than the long-run prospects of the firm.

The question arises, are there some institutional reforms which, if not ensuring complete efficiency, at least may improve matters?

Before putting forward some tentative suggestions, let me restate what I see to be the problems. First, the resources required by most large industrial enterprises are beyond the capabilities of any single individual; or even if one individual had the resources, he would have to bear more risk than he would like. What has evolved is a system in which there are two (or occasionally more) broadly defined classes of suppliers of capital. One class (equity) has a large number of participants; for each, the management of the firm represents a public good; because the effective exercise of control is costly, each individual is willing to be a free rider, and the consequence is that this class, which has nominal control, cannot effectively exercise it. The other class, lenders, has a small number of participants, and the institutional arrangements provide a mechanism by which the free-rider problems can be alleviated. Each of these classes has its own interests and its limited means of control. It is as if there is a multiple-principal/single-agent (or multiple-agent) problem, for which the Nash equilibrium (even ignoring the free-rider problems) is not efficient.

Our objective then is to find institutional arrangements that reduce the free-rider problem, that extend control to those for whom information is relatively costless, and that provide incentive structures such that those who are in a position to exercise control take into account the consequences for all the affected groups.

There are two tentative suggestions that I wish to put forward. Neither is without its problems. While I am not convinced that these reforms are desirable, I am convinced that there is considerable scope for institutional innovation in our economy: the malaise of our economy, as well as our theoretical analysis, suggests that we cannot rely on nineteenth-century ideology for our views of how the economy should be organized.

Both suggestions are based on the recognition of the importance of costs of monitoring: to have control effectively exercised, those exercising it must have a strong incentive for doing so. There are two institutions that have such incentives: banks and unions (as representatives of the workers).[49] One of the central problems with banks' exercise of their control function was their excessive concern for the lower tail of the distribution. This bias might be alleviated by allowing banks (or perhaps better, a

---

[49] If labor markets were perfectly competitive, and there were no costs associated with individuals changing jobs, then workers would have little interest in the prospects of their firms; but both assumptions are counterfactual.

related but independent subsidiary) to own equity shares in firms. Information could be shared between the bank and its equity subsidiary; and the bank, in exercising its control over the management, might be induced to look not only towards the bottom tail of the distribution of returns, but also towards the mean.[50]

The other major institution that is in a position to extend its powers of control is the unions. They have one advantage over virtually all other institutions: they (or their members) are intimately involved in the day-to-day functioning of the firm, and hence the costs of acquiring (certain kinds of) information concerning the firm are likely to be less than for others. They have a second advantage: they, like the banks, have a strong interest in the survival of the firm. The workers collectively may have the largest undiversified stake in the firm.[51] It has increasingly become recognized that the traditional adversarial role between management and workers is inappropriate: it is not a zero sum game. We have argued that workers (unions) have both the information base and the incentive to exercise surveillance and control. But will they do so only in their own narrow interests? The development of huge pension funds provides a vehicle by which a greater coincidence of interests can be achieved: if a significant fraction of the pension funds are invested in the firm, they will have an interest in ensuring that the managers take actions which are in the interests of shareholders as well. Employee stock ownership programs

---

[50] This proposal is not without its problems: the bank, knowing that its depositors are insured through the FDIC, might be willing to expose them to greater risks, in order to earn greater return on its equity subsidiary.

The recent episodes of large banks becoming overly committed to certain classes of correlated risks (oil and gas loans; loans to LDCs) raises questions concerning the ability of banks to perform the control functions that are under discussion here; it has been suggested that given the insurance provided by the FDIC (both explicit and implicit) these decisions may indeed have been the correct ones from the perspective of expected return to the owners of the bank, or in any case were natural consequences of the incentive structures facing loan officers.

Concerns about banks using their position to restrict competition are, I suspect, exaggerated, so long as the industries are subject to international competitive pressures and so long as the FTC and Justice Department maintain surveillance over anticompetitive practices. Moreover, what is at issue is not turning over all control to these banking institutions, only extending their roles to induce them to take the interests of shareholders more into account.

Throughout the discussion I have assumed that banks are concerned with avoiding defaults. Though banks should be concerned with this, I have frequently been asked in presentations of this talk if there is not a similar principal-agent problem facing banks. How do we know that the bank loan officers do not pursue some other policies? And if they do, are we not simply shifting the problem of control from one set of managers (those of the firms) to another set of managers (those of the banks)? In reply, I have two comments. First, I am not arguing that managers are completely uncontrolled, but rather that they have a large amount of discretion. At the same time, I believe that a change in the incentives structures (payoffs) to the bank will be reflected in the incentive structures facing its managers, at least to some extent. Second, I am not arguing here that these banks (bank managers) should be given more control, but that we should consider alternative institutional arrangements which will make it more likely that they take actions more in accord with the interests of shareholders.

[51] In the event of a bankruptcy, the loss to workers (the wages lost while they find alternative unemployment, and the return to specific training loss) may exceed the loss to the suppliers of capital. Moreover, these losses may represent, individually, a larger fraction of the wealth of workers than the corresponding losses are for the suppliers of capital.

may go even further in reducing the divergence of interests between workers and shareholders.[52]

There has long been a tradition that workers should work, and managers manage. This separation of functions may have been appropriate under primitive capitalism; but as we have argued, the problem of a modern joint stock company is not appropriately modeled as a single-principal/multiple-agent problem; rather it is a multiple-principal/multiple-agent problem, for which the Nash equilibrium is almost invariably inefficient. Each participant (or class of participants) pursuing his own interests, given the set of controls at his disposal, results in resource allocations that are not Pareto efficient. The actions of each group have important consequences for all other groups (there are important externalities). Moreover, we have repeatedly made note of the public good nature of good management: that it is not in the interests of any small member of the class of capital suppliers to devote resources to ensure that the interests of his class are pursued by the firms' managers. (And to the extent that actions which benefit the members of one class have spillovers onto members of other groups, each group's supply of "surveillance" services will be too small.)

Our problem is to design institutional structures that serve to internalize some of these externalities, that take advantage of those who are in the best position to obtain information and exercise control (surveillance), and that can ameliorate (although obviously not eliminate) some of the free-rider problems which are inherent in the maintenance of good management. The two proposals we have put forward here are aimed at those objectives: whether they go far enough or whether they would be accompanied by more than offsetting disadvantages remains to be seen.[53]

---

[52] This proposal too is not without its problems. To the extent that workers invest their saving (pensions) in the firm, they bear greater risks than they otherwise would.

Moreover, it is not always clear that unions act in the interests of their members. Unions can be viewed as an attempt to solve the problem of public good for workers, but as in any such institution, there is always the possibility of significant differences between the interests of the elected officials and those they are intended to serve.

[53] There are other reforms that, I think, might also improve matters. Managers might be encouraged to take a longer-run interest in the firm, for instance, by having part of their compensation based on the performance five, ten, or fifteen years into the future.

Tax laws that encourage shareholders to hold on to their shares for long periods of time, while they have a deleterious effect on liquidity, may encourage greater concern for the long-run profitability of the firm.

Attempts to restrict certain practices, where shareholder interest and manager interest seem most obviously in conflict (such as some golden parachutes) may have some salutary effect. But they are likely to provide only symptomatic relief—from the most obvious and publicly visible symptoms of the differences between managers' and shareholders' interests; the underlying problems will remain.

There are organizational forms by which large amounts of capital from a large number of individuals may be raised, but in which the problem of public good may be reduced: assume each firm were restricted to having at most ten shareholders. These firms would then invest in larger firms (but again, each of the larger firms would be limited to ten investors, where the investors are "firms" rather than individuals). At each stage, the number of investors is sufficiently small that the problem is greatly attenuated. This system has the disadvantage that there is now a "chain" of principal-agent relationships. The inefficiencies associated with such chains is a subject under current investigation.

At the very least, I hope my analysis has convinced you of the inappropriateness of the nineteenth-century model of owner-manager capitalism as a description of twentieth-century capitalism. There is no simple answer to the question of who controls the firm. But what is clear is that minority shareholders do not exercise control, that banks are in a better position to exercise some control over managers, and that to the extent that they do exercise control, there are important biases in the decisions made. Our system may work well, but I suspect that there is room for improvement: social innovations are no less important than technological innovations.[54]

[54] At the same time, it is important to bear in mind that the systems for control of capital which have evolved in other successful economies, such as Germany and Japan, are markedly different from that of the United States. It is worth inquiring whether the explanation for these differences is related to particular legal restrictions or to some other aspects of the economy, or whether it is simply a historical accident.

CHAPTER 18

PEER MONITORING AND CREDIT MARKETS*

A major problem for institutional lenders is ensuring that borrowers exercise prudence in the use of the funds so that the likelihood of repayment is enhanced. One partial solution is peer monitoring: having neighbors who are in a good position to monitor the borrower be required to pay a penalty if the borrower goes bankrupt. Peer monitoring is largely responsible for the successful financial performance of the Grameen Bank of Bangladesh and of similar group lending programs elsewhere. But peer monitoring has a cost. It transfers risk from the bank, which is in a better position to bear risk, to the cosigner. In a simple model of peer monitoring in a competitive credit market, this article demonstrates that the transfer of risk leads to an improvement in borrowers' welfare.

DIFFICULTIES in obtaining capital, and the high cost of capital when it can be obtained, may act as important impediments to improvements in productivity. Capital markets in the rural sector often appear to be underdeveloped. There are traditional moneylenders, but they are often reviled for charging usurious rates. The reason for these high rates remains a subject of controversy. There are widespread popular views that the rates are exploitative. These views implicitly assume that competition is limited. Local moneylenders make use of local knowledge, and this local knowledge may

  * This article is based on earlier work on the general theory of moral hazard (Arnott and Stiglitz 1985, 1986, 1988a) and on joint work with Richard Arnott on the general theory of peer monitoring (Arnott and Stiglitz 1991a). It also draws heavily upon earlier joint work with A. Weiss on the theory of credit markets (Stiglitz and Weiss 1981, 1983b, 1986, 1987b, 1987c). Financial support from the National Science Foundation, the Olin Foundation, and the Hoover Institution is gratefully acknowledged. I am greatly indebted to Richard Arnott and K. Hoff for helpful comments. © 1990 The International Bank for Reconstruction and Development / THE WORLD BANK.

  Reprinted from *World Bank Economic Review*, 4(3), September (1990), pp. 351–66 in a special issue on imperfect information and rural credit markets.

explain why competition is so limited. More recent views have questioned the extent of exploitation, suggesting that the high rates are a result of three factors: the high rates of default, the high correlations among defaults, and the high cost of screening loan applicants and pursuing delinquent borrowers.[1] Because of the importance of local information, moneylenders' loans are generally concentrated within a single geographical area; the inability to diversify means that the risks they must bear are large.

Both in the rates charged and the institutional arrangements by which loans are extended, traditional moneylending appears markedly different from modern banking institutions of the form found in more developed economies. As a result, many governments have encouraged formal banking institutions to go into the rural sector (see Siamwalla et al. 1990 and Bell 1990). These institutions would serve to increase both economic efficiency—by making credit more widely available—and equality, by lowering the interest rates which poor farmers have to pay. This, it was believed, would be true whether the high interest rates reflected exploitation as a result of limited competition, or whether they reflected compensation for the undiversified risks which local moneylenders had to bear. Presumably, these more efficient modern institutions would drive out the less efficient local moneylenders.

As it has turned out—as shown in Bell (1990) Siamwalla et al. (1990), and Aleem (1990)—the two groups have not only managed to coexist, but the local money-lenders seem able to continue to lend at high interest rates. Although the formal lending institutions often have suffered large losses, the local moneylenders have not only survived, in some cases they have actually thrived. Part of the reason for this is that the formal institutions have not made loans available to all farmers who would like them (or have not provided them with as much credit as they would like). But another part of the reason may be that the local moneylenders have one important advantage over the formal institutions: they have more detailed knowledge of the borrowers. They therefore can separate out high-risk and low-risk borrowers and charge them appropriate interest rates; and they can monitor the borrowers more effectively, making sure that the funds are used productively and thus lowering the default rate.[2] (See Aleem (1990) for the dramatic contrast in default rates.)

Of the banking institutions which have been set up to provide credit in the rural sector of developing countries, one institution, the Grameen Bank in Bangladesh, appears to be a model of success. It makes small loans—the average size is approximately seventy dollars. It makes about 475,000 loans a month. Its default rate is approximately 2 percent, in contrast to some other lenders, which have default rates of between 60 and 70 percent (Lurie 1988). There are a number of distinctive characteristics to the Grameen Bank, but the one I wish to focus on here is that the loans are made to self-formed groups of approximately five farmers, who are mutually

---

[1] See, for instance, Aleem (1990).
[2] The incentive (moral hazard) and selection problems are two of the central problems facing any credit market.

responsible for repaying the loans. Moreover, other members of the group cannot obtain credit until existing loans are repaid.[3]

Thus, the Grameen Bank is able to exploit the local knowledge of the members of the group. It has devised an incentive structure whereby others within the village do the monitoring for it. I call this *peer monitoring*. Elsewhere, Arnott and I (1987) have argued that peer monitoring may be an effective way of designing an incentive-monitoring system in the presence of costly information.[4]

Peer monitoring is not without its cost. The members of the borrowing groups in the Grameen Bank bear risks that, in the absence of the monitoring problem, could much better be absorbed by the bank. Indeed, in the case of borrowing groups, the interdependence among the members of the group is artificially created. They have been induced to bear more risks than they otherwise would.

This poses an analytical problem: are the gains from improved monitoring worth the costs of increased interdependence? This is the problem that this article sets out to model and answer. The article should be viewed as a first attempt at developing a general theory of peer monitoring. Thus the borrowing group consists of only two individuals. Moreover, the interdependence is limited—they have to pay only a limited amount in the event of default. But even this limited amount raises the risk that they must bear. I assume, moreover, that the information each member of the group has about each other is essentially costless; it is a by-product of living near each other. (In more general cases, the amount of monitoring will depend on the extent of interdependence, so that with only a little interdependence, one may obtain only limited monitoring.) Finally, I assume that the risks of default are independent. In practice, they are correlated. The existence of correlation would only strengthen the results of this analysis.

The article is divided into three sections. Section I presents the basic model, describing the equilibrium which would emerge in the absence of peer monitoring. Section II shows how peer monitoring works and explains why it will be adopted. Section III provides some concluding remarks.

I THE BASIC MODEL

I assume all individuals have two projects which they can undertake, a relatively safe project yielding, if successful, a return of $Y_S(L)$ when undertaken at scale L

---

[3] Peer monitoring through group loans also appears to be used in some African loan markets and in Thailand. (See Migot-Adholla et al. 1991 and Siamwalla et al 1990.)

[4] In labor markets workers frequently have much better information about whether peers are shirking than do managers. In insurance markets, family members have a much better idea about what precautions each is taking against some insured event than does the insurance firm. The principles of peer monitoring that are developed here thus have important implications and applications in a variety of settings.

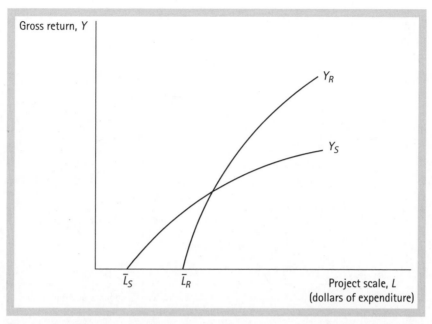

Fig. 1. Relationship between Gross Returns and Investment (Assuming Success) for Safe and Risky Projects

Note: $\overline{L}$ = fixed costs; R = risky project; S = safe project.

(measured in dollars of expenditure), and a relatively risky project yielding, if successful, a return of $Y_R(L)$. If a project fails, returns are zero. The probability of success for each project is p_S and p_R, with $p_S > p_R$. I assume that the return is an increasing function of scale, but that the fixed costs, $\overline{L}$, associated with the risky project are larger: $\overline{L}_R > \overline{L}_S$. Accordingly, in the relevant region, $Y'_R > Y'_S$, as depicted in figure 1.

Assume that, taking into account the probability of success, the safe project always yields a higher return than the risky project:

$$Y_S(L)p_S - (1+r)L > Y_R(L)p_R - (1+r)L \quad \forall L$$

where r is the rate of interest. An individual who invests his own funds, therefore, will always choose the safe project. An individual who invests borrowed funds and declares bankruptcy if the project fails, however, will discount the cost of funds to reflect the probability of bankruptcy.

In order to focus on the incentive problem, I assume all individuals are identical[5] and, for simplicity, that the level of effort required by the two projects at any given

---

[5] If villagers know each other's characteristics, then, in forming peer monitoring groups, there will be "assortative mating"; that is, the least likely to default will group together, the next most likely to default will group together, and so on, leaving the most likely to default to form a group. Thus the assumption that all members of the peer monitoring group are identical can really be viewed as one of the equilibrium conditions, which can be derived in a more general setting.

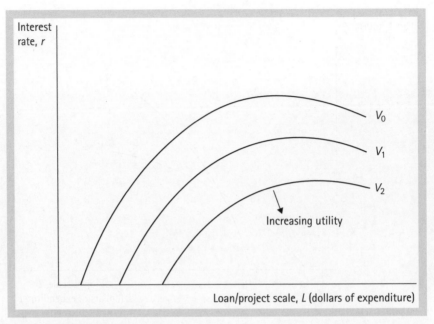

Fig. 2. Indifference Curves between Loan Size and Interest Rate Charged for a Single Project

Note: V_i = expected utility from project i, where $V_0 < V_1 < V_2$.

size is identical. Expected utility from undertaking project i is[6]

$$V_i(L, r) = U[Y_i(L) - (1 + r)L]p_i - v(e(L)) \tag{1}$$

where $U(Y)$ is the utility of income, $U' > 0, U'' < 0$, and the utility function is normalized so that $U(0) = 0$.[7],[8] The term $v(e(L))$ is the disutility of effort e; $v' > 0, v'' > 0$. It is assumed that the level of effort required goes up as project size increases: $e'(L) > 0$. The individual's indifference curve for a given project (risky or safe) is given in figure 2. This curve gives all the contracts (L, r) that yield the borrower the same utility.[9]

---

[6] I assume that either the individual has no source of income other than that from the project, or that whatever the income is, it is constant and cannot be garnished by the bank if the project fails.

[7] This normalization is a convenient one for the exposition of this article but is in no way essential and encounters difficulties, for instance, with constant absolute risk aversion utility functions.

[8] Implicit in this formulation is that the individual's investment in the project is equal to the amount that he can borrow, L. The results can be generalized to the case where the amount of his own funds that the individual is willing to invest depends on the amount that he can borrow.

[9] I assume that the lender can monitor the borrowing activity of the borrower, ensuring that he does not obtain funds elsewhere, though the lender cannot monitor other actions of the borrower. This assumption is not entirely satisfactory. While the lender can limit the size of the loan he extends, formal lenders often have difficulty enforcing restrictions on loans taken out with other lenders. Thus several of the case studies in this issue suggest that while information and other transaction costs imply that the borrower has a credit relationship with only one (or at the most, very few) informal lenders, borrowers frequently borrow from both formal and informal credit institutions.

The slope of the indifference curve if the individual undertakes project i is[10]

$$\frac{dr}{dL} = \frac{Y_i' - (1+r) - v'e'/U'p_i}{L} \qquad (2)$$

The "switch line" can be defined as those combinations of (L, r) for which the individual is indifferent between the two projects; that is:

$$V_S(L, r) = V_R(L, r). \qquad (3)$$

The switch line is negatively sloped under the plausible condition that, because returns to scale are more important for the risky project than for the safe, an increase in L, keeping r fixed, makes the risky project more attractive. In the relevant region $(L > \overline{L}_R)$,

$$\frac{\partial V_S}{\partial L} < \frac{\partial V_R}{\partial L}. \qquad (4)$$

Note that the indifference curve, letting the choice of project vary with the terms of the loan contract, is the escalloped shape shown in figure 3A. Above the switch line (at high levels of L) the individual undertakes the risky project.

To see that the switch line is downward-sloping, fix the loan size and note that utility decreases with increases in r by the amount $LU'p_i$. Since for the risky project U' is lower and p_i is lower, the decrease in utility for each increase in r is smaller for the risky project. Hence, starting from a value of (L, r) at which the borrower is indifferent between undertaking the safe or risky project, such as point E in figure 4, an increase in r causes the risky project to dominate the safe project. But it was assumed in equation 4 that an increase in L at a fixed r increases the expected utility from the risky project more than that from the safe project. Therefore, an increase in L must be accompanied by a fall in r to leave the borrower indifferent between the two projects, which proves that the switch line is negatively sloped.

The borrower is compensated for the extra risk associated with the risky project by a higher return when the project is successful, but the bank is not. The risky project has a lower probability of success and, hence, the bank has a lower chance of being repaid. Clearly, if the bank could directly control the actions of the borrower, it would specify that the borrower undertake the safe project. It cannot, and this is the basic problem with incentives in credit markets. By controlling the terms of the loan contract, the bank can induce the borrower to undertake the safe project. That is, the bank must offer a contract which lies on or below the switch line.

To analyze the market equilibrium one additional set of curves is needed—the zero-profit locus. The zero-profit locus can be constructed simply as follows. If the

A full analysis of market equilibrium in which formal institutions could not restrict the amount of outside loans would take us beyond the scope of this paper. (See Arnott and Stiglitz 1987 for an analysis of the analogous problem in the context of insurance markets with moral hazard.) Doing so, however, would strengthen the case for peer monitoring, because the inability to restrict outside loans will lower the level of expected utility attained by the borrower in formal credit markets without peer monitoring.

[10] The indifference curve for a given project is "well-behaved" in the relevant region where $Y_i' > (1+r)$ provided $Y_i'' < 0$ and $d^2(v'e')/dL^2 > 0$.

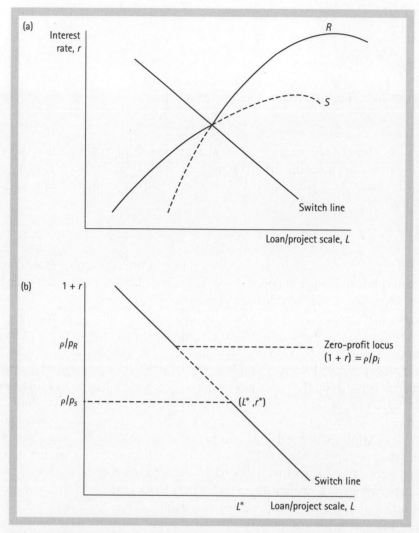

Fig. 3. Influence of Loan Size and Interest Rate in Selection of Safe and Risky Projects

Notes: (a) Because at larger loan sizes individuals undertake the risky project, the indifference curve—letting the technique employed vary with the contract—has an escalloped shape.
R = risky project; S = safe project.
(b) Market equilibrium occurs at the contract (L^*, r^*), where profits are zero. It is the largest loan size along the zero-profit locus for which individuals are willing to undertake the safe project. The variable ρ = cost of capital; p_i = probability of success of project i ($i = R$, S).

borrower undertakes the safe project, the expected return to the bank is $p_s(1 + r)$. If the cost of capital is ρ, then profits are zero provided $1 + r = \rho/p_s$. Similarly, if the borrower undertakes the risky project, expected profits are zero provided $1 + r = \rho/p_R$. The zero-profit locus is thus the peculiarly shaped dashed line in figure 3B.

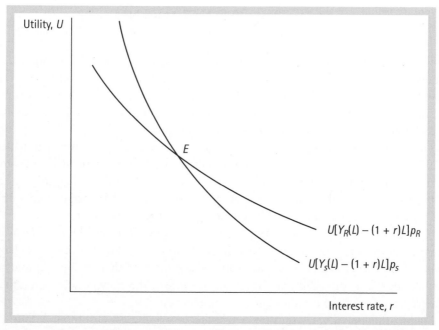

Fig. 4. Effect of Interest Rates on Utility in Selection of Risky or Safe Projects at a Given Loan Size

Note: L = loan/project size; p_i = probability of project success; R = risky project; S = safe project; Y = gross return.

The market equilibrium is that point on the zero-profit locus which maximizes the borrower's expected utility. (It is assumed that the borrower does not have alternative sources of credit or, equivalently, that the lender can monitor the total amount borrowed by any single individual.) In figure 3B, the equilibrium loan contract is (L^*, r^*). Clearly, the borrower would like to borrow more at the market rate of interest; and if the borrower could credibly commit himself to not undertaking the risky project, the lender would be willing to lend him a larger amount at that rate. But given that the borrower cannot commit himself, and that the lender cannot enforce such a promise, even were it made (and the borrower and lender both know that), the lender must limit his loan size to L^*.

This is only one of the two forms that credit rationing may take. It also may take the form that of a group of identical borrowers, some get loans and some don't. The usual argument for why this kind of credit rationing cannot occur is that those who have been rationed out of the market offer to pay higher interest rates. As they do so, the interest rate gets bid up, until demand for funds equals supply. But this argument does not work here, because lenders know that at any interest rate above the switch line, borrowers will undertake the risky project. Though the amount borrowers promise to pay is higher, the amount they actually pay (on average) is lower.[11]

---

[11] This argument is set forth in greater detail in Stiglitz and Weiss (1981). In the simple model presented here, lenders are indifferent to lending any size loan below the switch line, at a given interest

II Peer Monitoring

Now assume that every borrower has one (and only one) neighbor who is also a borrower. The success of their projects is independent. The two borrowers can monitor each other. The lender would like each to report if his neighbor is using the risky technique. He wants to create an environment in which it is in the interests of each to monitor the other and to report any cheating.

The following is a simple way of doing so. The lender offers a contract in which if his neighbor agrees to cosign—in a specific sense to be described below—the borrower can obtain a lower interest rate and additional funds. The cosigner agrees to pay qL dollars to the lender in the event that the loan he has cosigned goes into default—provided, of course, that he himself does not go into default.

Now, the cosigner's expected utility depends on whether his neighbor undertakes the risky or the safe project. Given their interdependence and the symmetry we have imposed on the problem, it is reasonable to assume that they cooperate; that is, they decide jointly on whether to undertake the safe or the risky project, and if they undertake the risky project, they agree not to report it.[12]

Making the individual cosign his neighbor's loan imposes on him an additional risk. Since the zero profit condition ensures that the interest rate will adjust to leave the expected return to the bank unchanged—taking into account the payment from the cosignee, the effect of the cosignatory provision is to induce a mean-preserving spread on the borrower's income at any given level of his loan L: if both borrowers are successful, utility is higher; but if one is successful and the other is not, the first borrower's utility is lower. To compensate him for undertaking this additional risk, the lender must provide a larger loan. The relationship between the minimum-size loan required to attain a given level of expected utility and the magnitude of the cosignee's payment rate, q, is depicted in figure 5. Equation A-5 in the appendix shows

rate. But if the model is modified slightly to allow p_i to increase slightly with loan size, then below the switch line the zero-profit locus is negatively sloped, and lowering the loan size below L^* actually lowers the expected return to the lender.

Other modifications to the model, to make it more realistic, provide further reasons why lenders will not wish to make small loans, to "underfund" projects. For instance, borrowers often have the discretion to take actions which put the lender in a position of choosing to ante up more money or risk the loss of everything previously lent. Borrowers thus can "force" lenders to lend them more. See Stiglitz and Weiss (1981) and Hellwig (1977).

[12] The interactions among the individuals which result in this being an equilibrium are not modeled in detail. It is easy to construct a game for which this is an equilibrium. For instance, assume that at any date at which one side reports that his neighbor has undertaken the risky project, the other side has time to report the same information. Then it would not pay either party to renege on the agreement not to report.

More generally, it is reasonable to assume that social sanctions would ensure that they behave cooperatively, when each's income depends not only on his own actions but also on those of his neighbor. There are natural information assumptions which assure that they cannot cheat on each other.

Throughout, it is assumed that if the borrower cheats on the contract by undertaking the risky project, the cosignee can "force" the reversal of the action; for example, the loan contract provides that in the event of such cheating, the loan is in default and the lender assumes control and gets all the returns.

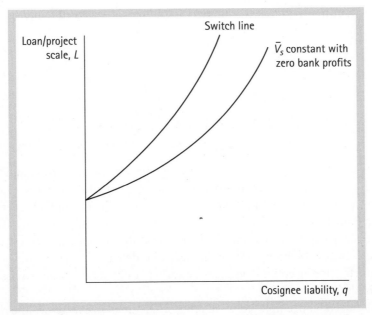

Fig. 5. Relationship between Loan Size and Cosignee's Liability at a Fixed Level of Expected Utility

Note: $\overline{V}_s$ = fixed level of utility from safe project (S). The switch line is the maximum loan size, for each q, which induces individuals to undertake the safe project.

that at $q = 0$, and given the bank's zero-profit condition

$$\left.\frac{dL}{dq}\right|_{\overline{V}_s} = 0 \tag{5}$$

This means that (at low levels of q) the risk burden imposed on the borrower by cosigning is exactly compensated by the reduction in the competitive interest rate charged.

The only remaining question is to ascertain what happens to the switch line. If the two parties act cooperatively, the switch line is now given by the equation

$$U[Y_s(L) - (1+r)L]p_s^2 + U[Y_s(L) - (1+r-q)L]p_s(1 - p_s)$$

$$= U[Y_R(L) - (1+r)L]p_R^2 + U[Y_R(L) - (1+r-q)L]p_R(1 - p_R) \tag{6}$$

Equation A-7 in the appendix shows that so long as the condition of equation 4 is satisfied and the interest rate adjusts as q increases to maintain zero profits for the lender, the maximum L at which the individual undertakes the safe project increases with q. That is,

$$\left.\frac{dL}{dq}\right|_{\text{switch line at } q=0} > 0. \tag{7}$$

As shown in figure 5, peer monitoring will be welfare-enhancing: for low levels of q, the increase in L which it allows (with borrowers undertaking the safe project) is greater than that required to compensate the individual for the increase in risk-bearing.

III Conclusions

This analysis of the value of peer monitoring suggests some of the ingredients in the design of successful peer monitoring systems. First, the members of the peer group must be provided with incentives to monitor the actions of their peers. In the Grameen Bank this is provided by the fact that members of the peer group are jointly liable for repayment of loans, and by the fact that they cannot gain access to credit until the debts of the group are discharged. The denial of access to further credit can be an effective incentive device, as the earlier study of Stiglitz and Weiss (1983b) emphasized.

The Grameen Bank employed small groups. The small size increased the risk from a single member's default but increased the incentives for peer monitoring. The gains from the latter exceeded the losses from the former. With large groups there is a free rider problem—each would prefer that others expend the energy required to monitor and incur the ill will that would result from reporting offenders who have misused the funds lent to them. Moreover, the costs to each as a result of a default by any member are sufficiently small that incentives to monitor—even apart from the free rider problem—would be minimal.

There are strong incentives for groups with similar risk characteristics to form. Because the group acts as a cooperative, if some individual is more prone to default than others, he is being subsidized. When groups are identical, there is no subsidy (at least in an ex ante sense). Of course, those with high risks of default would like to join groups with a low risk of default. The assortative grouping comes about as those with the lowest risk of default recognize their mutual interest in grouping together; then those with the lowest risk among the ones remaining group together; and the process continues until the individuals with the highest risk are forced to group together. Villagers have an informational advantage over formal credit institutions not only in monitoring but also in selection. By eliminating some of the cross-subsidization that occurs in credit markets with imperfect screening, peer selection with substantial cross-guarantees may enhance the effectiveness of rural credit markets, although, like peer monitoring, it increases the risks that borrowers have to bear. Having groups which are self-formed may thus be an important ingredient in the success of the Grameen Bank.[13]

---

[13] There still may be some cross-subsidization across groups if interest rates charged to different groups do not correspond to differences in group default rates. Successful peer monitoring, however, lowers group default rates to the point where this cross-subsidization may be relatively unimportant.

Provisions for cosigning have traditionally been viewed as a way of increasing the effective collateral behind a loan. This article has provided an alternative interpretation. Cosigning provides an incentive for the cosignee to monitor the actions of the person for whom he has cosigned the loan. Cosigning also increases risk. But in the kind of symmetric competitive equilibrium analyzed here, interest rates adjust to reflect the improved monitoring. It has been proven that at low levels of q, the gains from peer monitoring more than offset the loss in expected utility from the increased risk-bearing.

In developing countries the inability of those outside a village to monitor loans has posed a major impediment to the development of effective capital markets. Within the village, risks are sufficiently highly correlated and there are sufficiently few individuals with wealth that the lending market is both imperfectly competitive and carries with it high risk premia.

Although governments have recognized the existence of a problem, they have paid insufficient attention to its root causes. If informational problems are the barrier to the development of an effective capital market, then there is no reason to presume that governmental lending agencies will be in a superior position to address these problems. Indeed, the lack of incentives for government bureaucrats to monitor loans may exacerbate the problem. The experience of government losses in such programs (see, for instance, Sanderatne 1978, and Bell 1990) suggests that it may be foolish for government to go where the market has feared to tread.

But government may be able to use peer monitoring to offset its informational disadvantage. This article has illustrated a simple way by which such peer monitoring can be implemented, but there are alternative institutional arrangements that could work as well or better. For instance, government could lend to small lending cooperatives within a village, making each member of the cooperative collectively liable for the whole.

A question naturally arises at this juncture: if peer monitoring is so effective, why isn't it employed by private markets? In capital markets in developed countries, it may be extensively employed. As noted above, provisions for cosigning may be important not only for the increased effective collateral but also for the induced peer monitoring.

In developing countries a major impediment to the development of peer monitoring—as well as to the development of other institutions—comes from inadequate legal systems to enforce contracts. Government has one advantage over private lenders, a difference which is particularly important in developing countries, where the judicial system is at best slow, at worst ineffective. Government may have powers of enforcing contracts that private lenders might not have.

This suggests an alternative policy reform to more extensive government provision of credit: legal reforms giving lenders more security for the recovery of their loans. It may, however, be difficult to isolate legal reforms directed at making the credit markets more effective from a broader range of legal reforms. And there may be serious impediments to undertaking this broader range of legal reforms. Although legal reforms can facilitate the use of peer monitoring in private markets, even short of such fundamental reforms, well-designed government lending programs, taking advantage of the opportunities provided by peer monitoring, may, in these circumstances, be an effective second-best policy.

APPENDIX

....

No Peer Monitoring

To simplify the notation, let $\bar{r} \equiv 1 + r$, the principal and interest charged by the bank; $U_i \equiv U[Y_i(L) - \bar{r}L]$, the utility of a borrower who succeeds at project i; and $i = R, S$.[14]

Recall that $V_i(r, L) = U_i p_i$, the expected utility of a borrower who undertakes project i, and the switch line is the set of contractual terms (L, r) for a rationed borrower where

$$V_R = V_S \tag{A-1}$$

We assume in equation 4 in the text that in the relevant region $(L > \bar{L}_R)$, the benefit of an extra dollar of credit is greater for the risky than for the safe project:

$$U_R'(Y_R' - \bar{r})p_R = \frac{\partial V_R}{\partial L} > \frac{\partial V_S}{\partial L} = U_S'(Y_S' - \bar{r})p_s \tag{A-2}$$

Differentiating the switch line (A-1) completely yields

$$\left.\frac{dr}{dL}\right|_{\text{switch line}} = \frac{\left(\dfrac{\partial V_R}{\partial L} - \dfrac{\partial V_S}{\partial L}\right)}{L(U_R'p_R - U_S'p_S)} < 0$$

where the sign condition follows from equation A-2 and the fact that $p_R < p_S$ and $U_R' < U_S'$. Thus the switch line is downward-sloping, as illustrated in figure 3.

Peer Monitoring

With peer monitoring, the borrower faces in effect three states of the world: (1) both his own and his neighbor's projects succeed; (2) his own succeeds but his neighbor's fails; and (3) his own fails. Utility in the three states is

$$U_i \equiv U[Y_i(L) - \bar{r}L]$$

$$U_{iq} \equiv U[Y_i(L) - \bar{r}L - qL]$$

$$U(0) = 0$$

Expected utility in a symmetric equilibrium—where both the borrower and his neighbor choose the same project, R or S—is

$$\bar{V} = U_i p_i^2 + U_{iq} p_i(1 - p_i) = V_i(r, L, q) \tag{A-3}$$

---

[14] Throughout the appendix, the effort required to manage the project is ignored. Incorporating the effects of changes in effort induced by changes in loan size is straightforward.

Assuming that equilibrium is characterized by credit rationing, the bank chooses a contract (r, L, q) that ensures the individual will choose the safe project. The bank's zero-profit condition is

$$p_S(1+r) + p_S(1-p_S)q = \rho$$

so

$$\frac{dr}{dq} = -(1-p_S). \tag{A-4}$$

For any ρ equations A-3 and A-4 define a relationship between the borrower's loan limit and the copayment which keeps the borrower's expected utility unchanged and is consistent with the bank's zero-profit conditions. That relationship is characterized by

$$\frac{1}{L}\frac{dL}{dq}\bigg|_{\bar{v} \text{ and the bank's zero-profit condition}}$$

$$= \frac{-U_i' p_i^2(1-p_S) + U_{iq}' p_i p_S(1-p_i)}{U_i'(Y_i'-\bar{r})p_i^2 + U_{iq}'(Y_i'-\bar{r}-q)p_i(1-p_i)} = \frac{-M_i}{\partial V_i/\partial L} \tag{A-5}$$

$$= 0 \text{ if } q = 0 \quad \text{and} \quad p_i = p_S \tag{A-5'}$$

$$> 0 \text{ if } q = 0 \quad \text{and} \quad p_i = p_R \tag{A-5''}$$

where

$$M_i = \frac{\partial V_i}{\partial q} + \frac{\partial V_i}{\partial r}\frac{dr}{dq}.$$

Equation A-5' yields the result that in an equilibrium in which the borrower undertakes the safe project and banks earn zero profits, imposition of a low cosigner liability rate q at a fixed loan limit L leaves borrower utility unchanged. See the lower curve in figure 5.

It is useful to write the switch line (equation A-1 or equation 6 above) explicitly:

$$p_R^2 U_R + p_R(1-p_R)U_{Rq} = p_S^2 U_s + p_S(1-p_S)U_{Sq}. \tag{A-6}$$

Differentiating A-6 totally yields

$$\frac{dL}{dq}\bigg|_{\text{switch line}} = -\frac{M_R - M_S}{\partial V_R/\partial L - \partial V_S/\partial L}.$$

From the assumption stated as equation A-2, the denominator is positive. Using A-5' and A-5'', respectively, we have that at $q = 0$,

$$M_S = 0$$

$$M_R < 0$$

so

$$\frac{dL}{dq}\bigg|_{\text{switch line at } q=0} = \frac{-M_R}{\partial V_R/\partial L - \partial V_S/\partial L} > 0. \tag{A-7}$$

Equation A-7 shows that peer monitoring shifts up the switch line. It relaxes the constraint on (L, r) required to ensure that the borrower undertakes the safe project. Comparing A-5' and A-7 indicates that at low levels of q, the shift up in the switch line *exceeds* the shift needed to maintain the borrower at constant expected utility, as illustrated in figure 5. Peer monitoring will thus increase the borrower's welfare.

PART IV

INFORMATION AND PRICES

Introduction to Part IV

The first three papers (Chapters 19–21) in this section explore the role of prices in the economy. The first paper (Chapter 19) asks, when different individuals have disparate information and act upon it, how does the price system aggregate that information, and does it, in particular, provide good information about the behavior of the relevant economic aggregate? If each individual, for instance, knows something about his/her own (future) crop, do futures prices provide a good predictor of aggregate output? The answer is, in general, no. In some sense, the answer is not surprising: how could one expect a single number, the price, to summarize fully the relevant disparate information in the economy? Market participants might care not just about total future output but also about its variability. But the failure of the price system in the case explored here is, in a sense, more fundamental.[1] The problem arises because the demand (or supply) of futures depends on risk aversion; prices in futures markets might be high because very risk averse individuals have observed a very low output, or because slightly risk averse individuals have observed a moderately low output—but willing to take a large position on the basis of that information. In short, in general, it makes a difference who observes (or experiences) what. The paper raises an important question: are there other ways (a more elaborate set of markets, more complicated ways of eliciting information) which can provide the basis of extracting disparate information and aggregating it efficiently?

The next two papers (Chapters 20 and 21) address the closely related question of whether prices convey information from the informed to the uninformed. In these models, some individuals are informed, some uninformed. In "Bargains and Rip-Offs," (Chapter 20) some individuals know the prices charged by all stores. Of course, they will buy goods from only the low price stores. The question is, does this provide enough market discipline so that high price stores cannot exist? If so, those who do not search can, in effect, free-ride off the market discipline provided by those who do. The answer is not only can higher-priced stores exist—their sales may be lower, but the higher profits they get from their high price sales offsets the low sales—but that the market can create its own noise. It is not just that markets with search costs fail to fully arbitrage disturbances, leading to price dispersion, but that even without exogenous disturbances, the only possible equilibrium may entail price distributions. It pays some stores to exploit the high search cost individuals. This paper can be thought of as repealing one of the fundamental tenets of market economics—the law of one price.

---

[1] The problem just described might (if markets aggregate information well) be resolved by creating an options market, in which prices reflect information about variability.

Earlier work, by Stigler (1961), had analyzed search behavior in the presence of price distributions. But these studies had failed to ask, could these price distributions persist? Could they be part of a market equilibrium? This paper thus showed not only that they could, but that in some circumstances, the only equilibrium might be characterized by price dispersions. Subsequent work (in Volume II) explored more fully circumstances under which market equilibrium might be characterized by price and wage distributions, and in which search costs might give rise to demand curves facing firms that had peculiar shapes, in particular, that were kinked, so that changes in marginal cost led to no changes in prices or quantities (which is important in helping explain macroeconomic price rigidities.)[2]

The third paper (Chapter 21) takes on a central issue in financial markets—do prices fully convey information from the informed to the uninformed, as the efficient markets hypothesis had contended? Many market advocates had claimed so (Fama 1970) but, to me, this seemed a foolish claim on several grounds. Many of the arguments for efficient markets were based on the seeming randomness and unpredictability of stock market prices. If markets were fully efficient, this would, of course, be the case, because prices would only respond to new news, and by definition, new news is not predictable (if it were, it would not be new). But the randomness could also reflect markets' responding to random demands and supplies of uninformed agents. Surely, when the stock market crashed in October 1987, there was no new news that would have led people to so revise future beliefs that could account for wiping out a quarter of the value of the market. So too for many of the other major movements in markets. Today, the efficient markets hypothesis has far fewer adherents. The paper, "On the Impossibility of Informationally Efficient Markets," played, I think, a critical role in undermining belief in efficient markets,[3] by showing that if markets were fully efficient, it would not pay anyone to gather information; and if no one gathered information, then markets might be efficient—but only in transmitting costless information. We showed, by contrast, that there was an equilibrium level of disequilibrium—just enough noise in the price system that those who invested in information acquisition get compensated with higher returns.[4]

The final paper (Chapter 22) in this section focuses on a rather different question—the value of information. The value of information is related, of course, to how it enables individuals to make better decisions. The paper used standard statistical techniques to analyze the value of information and to establish a result, which even today remains controversial. We showed that there was a natural sense in which the value of information was never a concave function of the amount of information; that

[2] See, in particular, Stiglitz (1985c, 1987b, 1989b) and Salop and Stiglitz (1982). Other studies include Salop and Stiglitz (1987); Stiglitz (1979b).

[3] Our work provided a much needed theoretical refutation. The empirical evidence also helped—the persistence of a large number of stock market anomalies. See, for example, Siegel and Thaler (1997) and Rabin and Thaler (2001). Shiller's (2000) work showing that there was excess volatility in the market—beyond that which would seem consistent with efficient markets—also contributed to undermining confidence in the efficient markets hypothesis.

[4] Of course, there was no reason to believe that the equilibrium itself was efficient, e.g. that social welfare, appropriately defined, was maximized.

in a standard formulation, while ignorance might not be bliss, it was a local optimum. The result was of considerable importance, given the importance of concavity in establishing continuity of demand functions (in turn important in proving existence of equilibrium). The controversy relates to whether the assumptions employed, as natural as they might seem (given the kinds of normal distributions which economists typically use), are really reasonable.[5]

[5] See, for instance, Chade and Schlee (2002); Singh (1985); and Moscarini and Smith (2002).

CHAPTER 19

....

INFORMATION
AND
COMPETITIVE
PRICE SYSTEMS*

....

ALTHOUGH the price system is conventionally praised as an efficient way of transmitting the information required to arrive at a Pareto optimal allocation of resources, the context in which the price system is usually discussed is not one in which the informational efficiency of the price system can be properly evaluated. Questions of how the price system leads the economy to respond to a new situation, how it conveys information from informed individuals to uninformed individuals, and how it aggregates the different information of different individuals, are never directly attacked.

In a series of papers (Grossman 1977b, 1976, Grossman and Stiglitz 1980a, and Stiglitz 1971b, 1974d), we have attempted to remedy this deficiency. It is the object of this paper to draw attention to some of the more fundamental implications of our approach and to use it to assess the meaning and validity of the efficient market hypothesis. Although our discussion will accordingly focus on the capital market, the kind of analysis developed here is applicable to any competitive market subject to random shocks.

* Written with Sanford Grossman. This work was supported by National Science Foundation Grant SOC74-22182 at the Institute for Mathematical Studies in the Social Sciences (*IMSSS*), Stanford University. The authors are also indebted to the Dean Witter Foundation for financial support. Reprinted with permission from the *American Economic Review*, 66(2), May (1976), pp. 246–53.

I Prices and the Transfer
of Information

The basic idea behind our analysis[1] may be illustrated by the following example:

Assume there are two assets, one safe and one risky, and that the return to the risky security r, depends on a random variable η, which can be observed at a cost, and another, unobservable random variable ϵ:

$$r = \eta + \epsilon, \tag{1}$$

where η and ϵ are independent, normally distributed random variables. Knowing η reduces but does not eliminate the risk associated with the asset. The per capita demand, X_I, for the asset by those who are informed of η will depend both on the price of the asset and the value of η.

$$X_I = X_I(p, \eta). \tag{2}$$

We assume that $\partial X_I/\partial \eta > 0$ and $\partial X_I/\partial p < 0$. Equilibrium each period requires that demand equal supply:

$$\lambda X_I(p, \eta) + (1 - \lambda)X_U(p) = X^s, \tag{3}$$

where X_U is the per capita demand of the uninformed, X^s is the per capita supply and λ is the fraction of the individuals who are informed. Uninformed individuals observe only price, but from the price they may be able to infer η. For instance, if the stock of the resources were fixed, the uninformed individual can infer that a higher p is associated with a higher η, since an increase in η increases informed demand, and thus the price. Since there are no other stochastic elements in this model, there will be precisely one η corresponding to any p. Hence, the conditional distribution of r given p is the same as the conditional distribution of r given η. Thus, the price system conveys all the information from the informed individuals to the uninformed.

Now, let us introduce some further randomness; e.g., in the stock of the risky asset or in the demand functions of informed or uninformed individuals. Then the price may be high because η is high, but it may be high because the supply of the risky asset is low, or because informed individuals' demand functions have shifted upwards. Hence, corresponding to any p, there is a *distribution* of possible values of η. The price system conveys some information, but does not transmit all the information from the informed to the uninformed: on average, when the price is high, the return is high (i.e., η and price are correlated) but the price is a *noisy signal*; that is p and η do not contain the same information about r.

Assume that the source of randomness is the supply of the risky asset. (We shall use this example through the rest of the paper.) Then, from (3), the equilibrium price will depend on η and the stock of the risky asset, X^s; write $p = p(\eta, X^s)$. Solve for η

---

[1] See Grossman and Stiglitz (1980a) for proofs and a detailed analysis of the model described by equations (1)–(4).

as a function of (p, X^s) as, say, $\eta = t(p, X^s)$. Using (1):

$$r = t(p, X^s) + \epsilon. \tag{4}$$

The distribution of (X^s, ϵ) induces a distribution on r for a given p. Since the uninformed observe r and p, they come to learn the conditional distribution of r given p. When they observe a p, they use this distribution to determine the expected utility from purchasing a given amount of the risky asset; X_U is chosen to maximize expected utility. This is how the uninformed individual's demand function in (3) is derived. Finally for this to be an equilibrium, for all η and X^s, $p = p(\eta, X^s)$ must be a solution to (3). Such an equilibrium entails rational, self-fulfilling expectations.

This is a reasonable condition for longrun equilibrium. If this condition is not satisfied (and the stochastic process describing the returns is stationary),[2] then an individual will eventually observe that the frequency distribution of returns, conditional on the observable variables, is different from the subjective distribution, and accordingly, ought to revise his expectations.

As there are costs of obtaining information, the marginal individual who chooses to become informed must be indifferent to being informed or uninformed, i.e., the increment in expected utility from becoming informed is exactly offset by the cost of the information. In making this calculation, individuals assume that a change in their information (and hence in their demands) would have no effect on prices. This is an adaptation to this context of the conventional Nash equilibrium hypothesis of competitive equilibrium theory.

Since when no one is informed, the price system conveys no information, the value of information about η is likely to be high; when almost everyone is informed, the price system is very informative, so the value of knowing η precisely is low. Thus, provided the costs of information are positive but not too high, equilibrium entails a fraction, λ^*, of the population being informed—that λ which generates a price solution to (3) such that the marginal individual finds the expected utility to being informed equal to the expected utility of being uninformed.

Some striking features of the equilibrium which we have modeled should be noted. First, it provides a resolution of the following classical conundrum. If markets are perfectly arbitraged all the time, there are never any profits to be made from the activity of arbitrage. But then, how do arbitragers make money, particularly if there are costs associated with obtaining information about whether markets are already perfectly arbitraged? The conventional answer is that, when markets are not arbitraged, there are profits to be made, and so equilibrium *must* entail perfect arbitrage; the profits accrue in the process of responding to some unspecified disequilibrium. A particular example of this classical conundrum is presented by the efficient market hypothesis,

[2] One can argue that the limitation of our analysis to stationary stochastic processes is not a serious limitation; economic theory is concerned with identifying, describing, and explaining regularities in economic processes. Economic theory attempts to identify within a particular event those characteristics which it has in common with other events which have occurred. It is these regularities that are described by the stationary stochastic process.

which argues the prices on capital markets reflect all the relevant information instantaneously.

We resolve this paradox by arguing that there are constantly new shocks to the economy; although each of these shocks may have certain individual characteristics— the company president may be sick, a machine may break down—from the point of view of an analysis of market behavior, we are interested not in these individual characteristics, but in how these shocks affect market returns; and we postulate that we can describe the occurrence of these different shocks, in terms of their effects on returns, by a stationary stochastic process. The capital market must continually adjust to these shocks. We have formulated an equilibrium notion which explicitly takes account of the economy's response to these various shocks. Others have described this as a disequilibrium situation, but have been unable to say much about it.

In the structure we have developed, the market never fully adjusts. Prices never fully reflect all the information possessed by the informed individuals. Capital markets are not efficient, but the difference is just enough to provide the revenue required to compensate the informed for purchasing the information. The equilibrium fraction of informed traders λ^* is determined jointly with the informativeness of the price system in such a way as to generate a competitive return to arbitrage.

Perfect arbitrage has one important implication—not all traders need to be informed. The informed traders make prices reflect true values, and the uninformed can simply take advantage of these services provided by the informed. In our analysis this is not true. Indeed, it is only because prices do not accurately represent the true worth of the securities (i.e., the information of the informed is not fully conveyed through the price system, to the uninformed) that the informed are able to earn a return to compensate them for the costs associated with the acquisition of the information.

Those empirical tests of the weak version "efficient market hypothesis" which show there are no gains to be made from looking at current prices and the past performance of the security provide support for our model, which assumes uninformed traders have rational expectations. But contrary to strong versions of the efficient market hypothesis, prices do not fully reflect all available information, in particular, that of the informed; the informed do a better job in allocating their portfolio than the uninformed. "Efficient markets" theorists state that costless information is a *sufficient* condition for prices to fully reflect all available information (Eugene Fama, p. 387). They are not aware that it is a *necessary* condition as well. But this is a *reductio ad absurdum*, since prices are important only when information is costly. (See Friedrich A. Hayek 1945 and Grossman 1976.) Thus, an individual who throws darts at a dartboard to allocate his portfolio will not do as well as the informed individual;[3]

---

[3] It is still true that if individuals were all identical and purchased the "market basket" of securities, the uninformed would do as well as the informed. Here we assume that the kind of information to make that feasible is not available. If individuals differ in their attitudes towards risk, or in their information structures, even when such a strategy is feasible, it may not be optimal.

what can be decided by a toss of the coin is not the allocation of the portfolio but whether to be informed or uninformed.[4]

A second important characteristic of our analysis is that there is no proper separation between demand and supply. An increase in supply leads to a lowering of the price; since lower prices *on average* correspond to states in which returns are lower, the lowering of the price leads to a *lowering* of the evaluation of the risky security by the uninformed individuals, and hence of their demand. One cannot describe the equilibrium meaningfully in any period in terms of independently drawn demand and supply schedules, because the demand curves depend on the probability distribution of supply. This has the further consequence that an increase in price may actually increase demand; the presumption for a downward sloping demand curve is much weaker when individuals judge quality by price.

Still a third important and related observation is that prices, in our model, are serving two functions: not only are they being used to clear markets in the conventional way, but they convey information. In this sense, the models we have formulated are closely related to George Akerlof's lemons' model and to Akerlof (1973) and Stiglitz' (1975d) analysis of labor markets.

The discussion so far has focused on the decision of whether to be informed or uninformed. There is an alternative way of looking at this question, which may shed some light on an old question discussed by John M. Keynes (1936). He suggested that the stock market might be viewed as a beauty contest, where the participants are not concerned with judging who is the most beautiful woman, but with judging who the other judges will believe is the most beautiful woman. Keynes made these remarks with more than a hint of disapproval; our analysis suggests that this may be unwarranted. It may be more efficient for some individuals to obtain information from others—through the price system or by other mechanisms—rather than obtain it directly.

II PRICES AS AGGREGATORS

So far, we have discussed equilibrium in markets where prices convey information from the informed to the uninformed. In some market situations, different individuals have different information, and then the price system may serve to aggregate their information. That is, the demands for a risky security of an individual are affected by his information; total demand and accordingly equilibrium market prices thus depend on the information of all the individuals. In this sense the market price aggregates the various pieces of information.

---

[4] This is true only if no one has a comparative advantage in acquiring information.

A simple example may make this clearer. Assume there are a large number of isolated farmers. Each knows the size of his own crop, y_i. The size of the crop on any farm at any date is described by

$$y_i = a + \epsilon_i \tag{5}$$

where (ϵ_i, ϵ_j) are uncorrelated, a and ϵ_i are independent, normally distributed random variables with means $(\bar{a}, 0)$ and variances $(\sigma_\alpha^2, \sigma_\epsilon^2)$, respectively. Thus, if $Y \equiv \sum_1^n y_j$, then $E(Y|y_i)$ is just a linear function of y_i, i.e., $E(Y|y_i) = h_1 + nh_2 y_i$.[5] Assume that there is a linear demand curve for the crop, so

$$Y = a - bP_s \tag{6}$$

where P_s is the spot price next period. Then the subjective distribution of P_s is normal, with mean $(a - E[Y|y_i])/b$ and a variance which is independent of y_i, σ_p^2. Since individuals differ in their expectations, there is an incentive to set up a futures market. Assume all individuals have constant absolute risk aversion, k. Then their demand for "futures" Y_i^f is given by (where P_f is the futures price):[6]

$$Y_i^f = \left[\frac{\frac{a - E(Y|y_i)}{b} - P_f}{k\sigma_p^2} \right] + y_i \tag{7}$$

and the market equilibrium requires

$$0 = \sum Y_i^f = \frac{n}{k\sigma_p^2} \left\{ \frac{a - h_1 - h_2 Y}{b} - P_f \right\} + Y. \tag{8}$$

Using (6), we obtain the result that the futures price is a linear function of the spot price:

$$P_f = h_3 + h_4 P_s.$$

It is a perfect aggregator of the information collected by the different individuals, i.e.,

[5] $E[Y|y_i] = n[\gamma \bar{a} + (1 - \gamma)y_i] \equiv h_1 + h_2 y_i$

$$\text{where } \gamma \equiv \frac{\sigma_\epsilon^2 (n - 1)}{n(\sigma_\alpha^2 + \sigma_\epsilon^2)}.$$

[6] Profits are $\pi = (P_f - P_s) + P_s y_i$. Then under normality and constant absolute risk aversion k, the individual maximizes

$$Y_i^f (P_f - E[P_s|y_i]) + E(P_s|y_i)y_i - \frac{k}{2}(y_i - Y_i^f)^2 \sigma_p^2.$$

Solving for the optimal Y_i^f:

$$Y_i^f = y_i + \frac{E[P_s|y_i] - P_f}{k\sigma_p^2}.$$

by observing P_f, one can make a perfect prediction of the quantity available in the market and P_s.[7]

But there is a fundamental problem; if, as one would expect, individuals eventually come to realize that the futures price is a perfect predictor of the future spot price, then they will no longer base their demands on their own information, but rather base it solely on the market information. Since the futures price predicts the spot price perfectly (with zero variance) there is no need for hedging and there will be no trade. But without trade, there is no market; but without a market; their beliefs will differ. This paradox can be put another way. If the market aggregated their information perfectly, individuals' demands would not be based on their own information, but then, how would it be possible for markets to aggregate information perfectly?

So far, we have discussed some of the basic properties of our approach to equilibrium when information is costly. These models can also be used to address conventional questions related to existence, comparative statics, and welfare.

III Existence of Equilibrium Market Breakdown and Thinness

Both Akerlof (1970) and Grossman (1977b) argue that in markets where prices convey information between informed and uninformed traders, there is a possibility of market breakdown associated with a dwindling in the amount of trading. The example of the stock market presented above showed that this could indeed happen: if the price system were fully informative, there would be no differences in beliefs; and if there were no differences in beliefs, there would be no trade; but then it appears that it is prices in markets in which there are no trades which leads to uniformity of beliefs. Although this problem would be alleviated if prices did not perfectly convey information from the informed to the uninformed or if there were motivations for trade other than differences in information (e.g., differences in attitudes towards risk or in endowments), markets still might be thin, i.e., there would be a small volume of trade, and hence markets may be far from perfectly arbitraged.

Situations where markets might be thin or nonexistent need to be distinguished from those in which equilibrium does not exist. In the absence of noise, with costly information, an (Nash) equilibrium does not exist,[8] since when one is informed, every individual believes he can become informed, increase his expected utility and not affect the market price. However, when a positive fraction of the population

---

[7] If $1 \neq nh_2/bk\sigma_p{}^2$, then $h_4 \neq 0$.

[8] In the case where information is costless, an equilibrium exists; among the set of prices which might clear the market, there is a particular price function which clears it at zero trade and conveys all the relevant information, and this may be considered to be an equilibrium. There is no obvious mechanism for sustaining this particular set of prices, and this is a serious limitation.

becomes informed the price system is fully informative, so it does not pay anyone to purchase the information.[9]

IV WELFARE

The evaluation of the efficiency of the market in situations such as those analyzed in this paper is a subtle and difficult question. It is not obvious what the appropriate comparisons ought to be. Two alternative approaches might be delineated. In the *reformist* approach, we take as given the market structure, including the mechanisms for information transmittal. We ask simply, are there too many or too few informed individuals, or, is it desirable to have an information tax or subsidy? Although it is easy to show that the market solution is not, in general, efficient, it is difficult to ascertain whether there is too little or too much information acquisition. There are several effects, operating in different directions: some of the gains arising from *differential* information are private but not social returns, gains that some individuals make at the expense of others; on the other hand, since some information is conveyed by the price system, if that information is socially useful, those who purchase information generate a positive externality to those who do not. See Jerry R. Green (1973) and Stiglitz (1971b). Even if there were no differential information, the price distribution does depend on the state of information. To return to our example of Section I, since when everyone is fully informed, price varies with η and X^s, while when no one is informed, price varies only with X^s, it would not be surprising if information increases the variance of prices. Increased price variability is likely to lead to increased uncertainty about the value of one's endowments, and this is likely to lower expected utility. In one example we have analyzed in detail, where individuals have constant absolute risk aversion utility functions and randomly assigned endowments (all individuals having, however, the same endowment distribution), every one is better off if no one is informed than if all are informed.[10]

---

[9] There could not exist an equilibrium in which trade occurred even if an individual had a monopoly power over information. For then the uninformed individuals would observe that they would do better not trading with the monopolist than trading with him, and the information-monopolist would simply determine equilibrium market prices. (See Stiglitz 1974d.) Thus Jack Hirshleifer's classic analysis (1971) is not that of a competitive stock market with rational consumers. If his analysis refers to a market in which there is a monopolist in information, his results require irrationality on the part of other consumers in the market. If his analysis refers to a market in which the market for information-acquisition is competitive, then the results discussed in the text apply.

[10] This is a consequence of the unavailability of endowment insurance. This result has some important implications for a question which until now has not been satisfactorily resolved: Can there be destabilizing speculation? In this context, we interpret that to mean: Can the attempt to engage in intertemporal arbitrage lead to higher price variability which is associated with lower utility? The answer is yes, and indeed such attempts at intertemporal arbitrage can lower welfare. This occurs, in our constant absolute risk aversion example, because by the portfolio separation theorem, information has no allocative role.

Finally, if the return to holding an asset for a period is the dividend plus the capital gain, the increased variability in price of the risky asset makes the risky asset riskier; thus, while in general, information reduces the riskiness of a risky asset, this is at least partially offset by this general equilibrium effect.

More fundamental questions are raised by the choice of alternative approaches to information acquisition, e.g., a comparison between the decentralized process of the capital market and a centralized process. This, in some sense, was the central question of the Lange-Lerner-Taylor-Hayek debate.

Although this earlier debate was presumably about the informational efficiency of alternative organizational structures, models in which the systems had to adjust to new information were not formulated; rather it was argued that if the information were to be the same, the allocation would be the same, and thus, a comparison of alternative organizations came down to issues like a comparison of cost differentials arising from different patterns of information flows, or different speeds of convergence. Our analysis has suggested that a decentralized economy is likely to be characterized by individuals having *differential* information, that the separation in the earlier discussion of information and allocative questions is inappropriate, and that alternative informational structures will be characterized by different real allocations. In particular, Grossman (1976) formalized Hayek's contention that prices are aggregators of information. There it was proved that if prices are sufficient statistics, the competitive economy where traders have diverse information generates allocations that cannot be improved upon by a central planner with all the information. However such markets do not provide incentives for information acquisition for the reasons given earlier. Thus only markets with noise will exist in equilibrium and these markets will not produce prices which are perfect aggregators. In this case a central planner with all the information can improve on the competitive equilibrium. Thus in our view the Lange-Lerner-Taylor-Hayek debate comes down to the fundamental distinction between economies where: (1) prices and hence allocations are the outcome of a competitive arbitrage process which will, of necessity, be imperfect because of the costs of arbitrage as discussed in this paper, and (2) economies where prices and hence allocations are the outcome of a centralized allocative mechanism which will, of necessity, be imperfect because of the costs of monitoring bureaucrats.

Thus, although we cannot provide an answer to whether a centralized or decentralized organization is more efficient, without more knowledge of the costs of operating a centralized informational mechanism, what we have established is that the conventional formulations of this question are misleading if not incorrect.

....

CHAPTER 20

BARGAINS
AND RIPOFFS:
A MODEL OF
MONOPOLISTICALLY
COMPETITIVE
PRICE
DISPERSION*

....

INTRODUCTION

....

THIS paper analyses an economy in which agents differ in their ability and willingness to make economical decisions in the market-place. On the one hand there are economists, bargain-hunters and other price-conscious consumers who carefully and analytically gather the information required to make wise purchases. Other agents are less rational and calculating in their decisions. Most people do not understand even the simplest laws of probability; for example, an overwhelming majority will bet

* Written with Steven Salop. Reprinted with permission from the *Review of Economic Studies*, 44(3), October (1977), pp. 493–510.

The views expressed herein are those of the authors and do not necessarily represent the views of the Board of Governors of the Federal Reserve System. We are grateful to Avi Braverman, Andy Weiss, Larry Weiss and other participants at the IMSSS Conference at Stanford University and Steve Salant, Peter von zur Muehlen and Roger Waud at the Federal Reserve Board for helpful conversations. Stiglitz's work was supported by National Science Foundation Grant No. SOC74-22182 at the Institute for Mathematical Studies in the Social Sciences, Stanford University.

"heads" after a run of "tails" in a coin-flipping game. Many people do not calculate unit-prices in the supermarket. Disparity in incomes provides some further indirect evidence; because of differences in preference or ability, some agents perform much better than others in market decisions.

We explore this problem of heterogeneity of consumer rationality within a simple model of costly information-gathering. We assume that consumers differ in the "costs" of becoming perfectly informed. To make the model as simple and transparent as possible, the relevant information to gather and the flow of that information is highly unrealistic and oversimplified: only price information is gathered; consumers have "rational" though limited prior information; "perfect" information may be generated for some fixed cost. However, the model may be reinterpreted to include the more realistic cases of quality differentials and heterogenous commodity preferences and more complex information transmission such as sequential search, advertising and word-of-mouth.

The central implication of costly information-gathering is that the equilibrium will not occur at the perfectly competitive price. This is a fairly straightforward observation: Suppose every firm did charge the perfectly competitive price. Then some firm(s) could raise price slightly without losing any customers. Consumers would be unwilling to gather the extra information needed to switch stores or brands. Clearly there is a limit on the price increases at one store that consumers will tolerate without leaving. However, since the *relative* store prices determine the gains from a search, then as every store raises price slightly, the cycle of price rises by a few stores may occur again. Hence prices throughout the market continue to rise.

Akerlof's famous "Lemons Principle" (1970) asserted that prices will continue to rise (or quality fall) until the market is destroyed. Diamond (1971) realized that the prices may settle down at the pure monopoly price with each small firm acting as a complete monopolist over its usual customers. In our model, we show that the market will not be destroyed, for, when prices get high enough, some firm can lower its price substantially and induce search. At this point there are two possibilities; either prices may cycle forever, or they may settle down to some equilibrium configuration.

We show that if prices do settle down, they will settle at the monopoly price (or, as Braverman (1976) has pointed out, at a Chamberlinean monopolistically competitive price) or there may be permanent price dispersion in the range between the perfectly competitive and monopolistically competitive prices. The final spread of prices depends on the magnitude of information costs and degree of scale economies. For U-shaped average costs, higher-priced firms produce in the region of decreasing average costs; thus, there are too many small firms at equilibrium.

Moreover, the economy does not produce information efficiently. A "rational economic planner" could economize on information costs by eliminating the price dispersion; for with no price dispersion, there is no need for costly search. There is an informational externality at work between efficient and inefficient information-gatherers. Those agents who become informed give an external economy to the uninformed; the weight of their search keeps prices lower. In fact, if there are enough informed agents, the market price will settle down to the perfectly competitive price. On the other hand, by shopping at high-priced stores, the uninformed inflict an

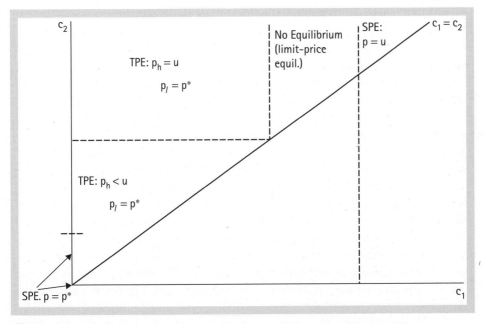

Fig. 1.

external diseconomy on the informed; these informed must gather costly information to obtain the lower price.

In this paper, a simplistic market with costly information-gathering for complete price-information will be studied. We will analyse an example in which there are only two groups of consumers by search costs. Four Nash equilibrium configurations can occur in this market:

(i) A Single-Price Equilibrium (SPE) at the Competitive Price, p^*.
(ii) A Single-Price Equilibrium at the Monopoly Price, u.
(iii) A Two-Price Equilibrium (TPE) in which the lower price, p_l, is the competitive price, and the higher price, p_h, is no greater than the monopoly price.
(iv) Non-existence of any Nash equilibrium.

Regions in which the four cases obtain are shown in Figure 1.

1 FORMAL MODEL

There are a large number, L, of consumers who form the potential market for a durable commodity. Each consumer has an identical inelastic demand curve for one and only one unit of the commodity. The maximum price a consumer will pay (the reservation price) is denoted by u^1; hence, u is the monopoly price. This assumption is made for simplicity; it has been generalized to downward sloping demand curves by Braverman (1976).

The most crucial assumptions of the model are those describing the consumers' degree of information and the corresponding information flows among consumers and firms. In the formal model here, the commodities sold at the different stores are known by consumers to be identical. However, consumers do not have perfect information regarding the price charged at each store in the market; this information must be generated at a cost. Suppose there are n stores selling the commodity at prices $\underline{p} = \{p_1, p_2, \ldots, p_n\}$ at locations $\underline{l} = \{l_1, l_2, \ldots, l_n\}$. The usual competitive model assumes that consumers are freely endowed with perfect information regarding the $\{\underline{p}, \underline{l}\}$ set. This model will move only one step from perfect information. We will assume that the consumer is freely endowed with the price vector $\underline{p}$; he knows the prices charged in the market. However, he does not know *a priori* the location vector $\underline{l}$ of these prices. That is, he knows what prices exist but he does not know which store charges which price. Clearly much of the information-gathering in markets attempts to discover locations, quality and other product characteristics as well as price. However, each of these variables affects the "effective" price a consumer pays per unit of a standard commodity bundle. The model could be generalized into a Lancasterian hedonic-price framework in which information increases a consumer's "net surplus".

We will assume that only *complete information* may be gathered: Consumer i may gather complete information regarding the $\underline{l}$-vector for a *fixed* cost c^i. Once $\underline{l}$ is known, he can then go costlessly to the minimum-price store and purchase the commodity there. This assumption could be thought of as follows: A newspaper exists that publishes full information; consumer i can purchase and process all the information in the newspaper for a cost c^i. Consumers differ in their information-gathering costs due to differences in analytic ability, the cost of time and preference for reading and processing information.

This complete information assumption is the central one in the model. It will be seen that it does generalize to include fixed-cost advertising. However, partial processing of information which generalizes to variable search costs (sequential search) and variable advertising costs lead to quite different results.[2] It is assumed that sequential sampling is quite costly and not economical for consumers to pursue.

Finally, we make the simplest assumption that there are only two groups of consumers distinguished by information-generating costs, a proportion, α, with cost c_1 and the rest, $(1 - \alpha)$, with higher cost c_2; this assumption is made for analytic convenience only, it is not crucial to any of the results obtained. For models with a continuous cost distribution, see Salop and Stiglitz (1975) and Braverman (1976).

The consumer has two decisions to make. He must decide whether to enter the market at all. He must also decide whether to buy the newspaper to obtain perfect information or purchase at a randomly selected store. We will first analyse the information-gathering decision.

If consumer i buys the newspaper at cost c^i, he will be able to purchase at the lowest available price, which we denote by $p^{\min}$. His total expenditure will be E_S^i where

$$E_S^i = p^{\min} + c^i. \tag{1}$$

Alternatively, he can purchase at a randomly selected store and on average pay a price equal to the mean price charged, $\bar{p}$. Thus, the total expected expenditure from the no-search strategy, E_N^i, is

$$E_N^i = \bar{p} = (1/n) \sum_{j=1}^{n} p_j. \tag{2}$$ [3]

Assuming the consumer is risk-neutral,[4] he will buy the newspaper if and only if

$$E_S^i < E_N^i,\text{[5]} \Leftrightarrow p^{\min} + c^i < \bar{p}. \tag{3}$$

Having decided on the optimal search strategy, a consumer will enter the market if and only if his total cost does not exceed his demand price, u, i.e. if and only if

$$u \geq \min[p^{\min} + c^i, \bar{p}]. \tag{4}$$

It is also true that no consumer will pay a price greater than u. Thus, a store charging a price greater than u will obtain no sales at all.

There are n firms selling the durable commodity. Every firm has identical technology characterized by a fixed cost T and variable costs $v(q)$ which depend on the quantity q produced. Marginal cost is assumed to be increasing ($v'(q) > 0$). Thus, the average cost (AC) curve is U-shaped.

Firms do not have the information problem facing consumers. Like consumers, they are assumed to know the prices charged by other firms; they need not know the actual locations of other firms. Furthermore, we assume they know costlessly the distribution of consumers' search costs and thus can perfectly predict how many consumers will search. This is the information that is necessary for each firm to know its expected demand curves. L is assumed large enough for the law of large numbers to assure that actual demand always equals expected demand. Thus, firms face no uncertainty or any critical shortage of information.

It is assumed that firms follow "Nash" price-setting behaviour *vis-à-vis* other firms. That is, a firm takes all other firms' prices as given in maximizing its profits. Formally, for firm j, we have

$$\max_{p} \pi^j(p|\underline{p}^{-j}), \quad \underline{p}^{-j} = \{p_1, p_2, \ldots, p_{j-1}, p_{j+1}, \ldots, p_n\}. \tag{5}$$

On the other hand, each firm follows a "Stackleberg" strategy *vis-à-vis* consumers. Rather than taking the consumer search *decisions* as given, it takes the consumer search *rule* as given and takes into consideration exactly how consumer search decisions will depend on the price it chooses. More precisely, the firm knows that an individual with cost c^i will search if

$$c^i < \bar{p} - p^{\min}. \tag{6}$$

Firm j calculates its effect on $\bar{p}$ and $p^{\min}$ in the following way.

$$\bar{p} = \frac{1}{n} p_j + \frac{1}{n} \sum_{i \neq j} p_i \tag{7}$$

$$p^{\min} = \min\left\{ p_j, \underline{p}^{-j} \right\}. \tag{8}$$

From these three equations and the distributions of consumers by information-gathering costs, we may calculate the demand curve for firm j given the prices of the other $(n-1)$ firms. We denote this demand curve by $D(p_j|\underline{p}^{-j})$. Note how the Nash and Stackleberg assumptions are contained in the demand curve. Firm j takes the other firms' prices $\underline{p}^{-j}$ as *given*. However, it considers how its price choice *induces* information-gathering by consumers.

Finally, we assume that entry occurs as long as profits are positive. This assumption assures that at equilibrium (if one exists), every firm makes identical zero profits. That is, denoting by $\hat{p}_j$ the price of firm j that comes from its profit-maximizing behaviour and by $\hat{\underline{p}}^{-j}$ the other firms' optimal prices, we have

$$\pi(\hat{p}_j|\hat{\underline{p}}^{-j}) = 0, \quad \text{for all} \quad j = 1, 2, \ldots, n. \tag{9}$$

This condition is used to compute the number of firms in equilibrium. It simply states that in equilibrium price equals average cost for each firm.[6,7] This is, of course, the monopolistic competition assumption.

Equilibrium

Given the assumptions just made, we may characterize the monopolistically competitive equilibrium in this market. An equilibrium is defined by a price vector $\underline{p}^* = \{p_1^*, p_2^*, \ldots, p_n^*\}$, a number n^* of firms in the market, and a percentage of consumers that gather information α^* that obey the following conditions:

(i) *Profit Maximization.* Each firm chooses a price to maximize its profits given the prices of the other firms and the search strategy of consumers summarized in its demand curve. For every firm j, we have

$$\max_p \pi(p_j|\underline{p}^{*-j}) = p_j D(p_j|\underline{p}^{*-j}) - v[D(p_j|\underline{p}^{*-j})] - T,$$

$$\text{for all } j = 1, 2, \ldots, n^*. \tag{10}$$

(ii) *Zero Profits.* Furthermore, the maximized value of profits for every firm j equals zero at equilibrium.

$$\pi(p_j^*|\overline{p}^{*-j}) = 0, \quad \text{for all } j = 1, 2, \ldots, n^*. \tag{11}$$

Thus, an equilibrium is characterized by n^* firms charging identical or different prices and each producing and selling just enough output to place them on the downward sloping portion of their common average cost curve, with enough firms so that every customer obtains one unit of the commodity. Note that the zero profit and profit-maximization conditions jointly imply that each firm's demand curve lies below the AC-curve at every point except the equilibrium price chosen.

(iii) *Search Equilibrium.* At equilibrium, consumers gather information optimally.

$$a^* = \begin{cases} 1 \text{ for } c_1 \leqq c_2 < \overline{p} - p^{\min} & (12) \\ \alpha \text{ for } c_1 < \overline{p} - p^{\min} \leqq c_2 & (13) \\ 0 \text{ for } \overline{p} - p^{\min} \leqq c_1 \leqq c_2. & (14) \end{cases}$$

2 OVERVIEW OF THE MODEL

Before turning to the technical details, it may be useful to summarize the argument in a more intuitive way. The basic TPE is pictured below: high-price, p_h, stores sell a smaller quantity, q_h, than do lower-priced, p_l, stores. Every store earns zero profits, $p = AC$. The TPE has the properties that: (a) the higher information-cost consumers $[(1 - a)L$ consumers with cost $c_2]$ *choose* to remain uninformed given the price dispersion in the market; they purchase randomly from the first store sampled, while (b) the lower information-cost consumers $[aL$ consumers with cost $c_1 < c_2]$ choose to become informed, and hence purchase from a p_l store. This property constrains the possible price dispersion in the market.

If a proportion, β, of the total stores, n, is low priced, and if consumers search optimally, it must be true that $c_1 < (1 - \beta)(p_h - p_l) \leqq c_2$, (where the expected gains from search are $(1 - \beta)(p_h - p_l)$, and costs are c_i for a type-i consumer).

Given that only the c_1's become informed, p_h stores sell only to unlucky uninformed consumers while p_l stores sell to informed consumers and lucky uninformed

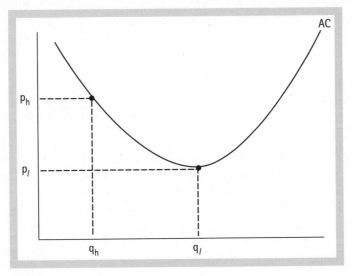

Fig. 2.

consumers. As there are $(1 - \beta)(1 - a)L$ unlucky c_2's and $(1 - \beta)n$ high-priced stores we have

$$q_h = (1 - a)\frac{L}{n}. \tag{15}$$

As each low-priced store gets a normal $(1/n)$th share of the $(1 - a)L$ uninformed c_2's and additionally the βn low-priced stores split the aL informed c_1's equally, we have

$$q_l = (1 - a)\frac{L}{n} + \frac{aL}{\beta n}. \tag{16}$$

Denoting the downward-sloping portion of the average cost curve by $AC = A(q)$, zero profits implies

$$p_h = A(q_h) \tag{17}$$

$$p_l = A(q_l). \tag{18}$$

The low price must equal the competitive price p^*. Otherwise, one low-priced store could shade its price slightly, obtain all the informed customers and even positive profits. Thus, we have

$$p_l = p^*. \tag{19}$$

Substituting, we have the equilibrium conditions

$$p^* = A\left[\left(\frac{a}{\beta} + (1 - a)\right)\frac{L}{n}\right]; \tag{20}$$

$$p^* + \frac{c_2}{1 - \beta} = A\left[(1 - a)\frac{L}{n}\right]. \tag{21}$$

This is the essence of the model. Complications arise from the possibility of corner solutions and non-existence of a TPE or any equilibrium.

3 DERIVATION OF EQUILIBRIA

We will now derive the equilibrium prices for this market. The methodology is as follows. A "potential" equilibrium satisfying the zero profit condition is proposed. We first check to see that the consumer search equilibrium condition is satisfied. Then, we examine the behaviour of a "deviant" firm to see whether its profit-maximization condition is satisfied at the "potential" equilibrium. If a "deviant" firm increases its profits by charging a different price, then the "potential" equilibrium is not an equilibrium. Only if the deviant prefers the equilibrium price is the potential equilibrium

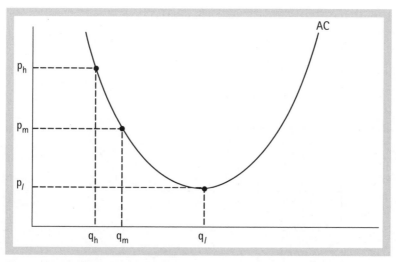

Fig. 3. Three-price equilibrium

an actual equilibrium. This is equivalent to assuming that firms experiment in their pricing decisions.

Lemma 1. *There are no Three-, Four-, ... -Price Equilibria. Only Single-Priced Equilibria* (SPE) *and Two-Price Equilibria* (TPE) *are possible.*

Proof. At these prices, suppose some consumers find it worth while to purchase complete information; these consumers pay the low price p_1. Of those consumers that do not search, every firm obtains an equal $(1/n)$th share. Since the p_m and p_h firms sell only to uninformed consumers, their sales are identical. Thus, the p_h firms must obtain higher revenue, breaking the zero profit condition.[8]

This lemma holds for all distributions of consumer search costs, for the consumers can always be split into an informed and an uninformed group. Incomplete information-gathering is necessary for equilibria with more than two prices.

Two-price and single-price equilibria are possible. We will first examine single-price equilibria and show that there may only be single-priced equilibria at the monopoly price u and at the competitive price p^*.

Single-Price Equilibria

Lemma 2. *There is no single-price equilibrium at any price p in the open interval $p \in (p^*, u)$.*

Proof. Consider a SPE at p in the open interval (p^*, u) obeying the zero profit condition as pictured below.

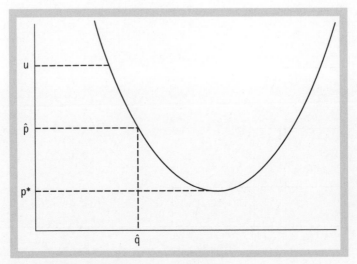

Fig. 4. Interior single–price equilibrium

Since there is no price dispersion, each of the n firms in production obtains equal sales, or $\hat{q} = L/n$. This defines the potential equilibrium number of firms. We will now show that it always pays a deviant to charge a price different from $\hat{p}$.

(a) *Local Price Rises.* Suppose a deviant raises his price slightly to $\hat{p} + \epsilon$. From (9), this raises the mean price to $\overline{p}' = \hat{p} + (\epsilon/n)$. The benefit of search becomes $b = \overline{p}' - p^{\min}$. Since $p^{\min} = \hat{p}$, we have a positive benefit or $b = (\epsilon/n)$. Consumer i will gather information if and only if $c_i \leq b$.

If $c_2 \geq c_1 > 0$, there exists some small $\epsilon > 0$ such that the deviant firm loses no customers; its demand curve is perfectly inelastic for some interval above $\hat{p}$. Thus, if it raises its price, its revenue rises. This breaks the profit-maximization equilibrium condition and thus the potential equilibrium. On the other hand, if $c_1 = 0$, even an ϵ-price change induces search and may make the deviant strategy unprofitable. However, in that case, price decreases will be profitable.

(b) *Local Price Decreases.* Suppose a deviant were to lower his price slightly to $\hat{p} - \epsilon$. From (9) and (10), both $\overline{p}$ and $p^{\min}$ fall. $p^{\min}$ falls by more. Thus, we have

$$b = \overline{p}' - p^{\min} = \frac{n-1}{n}\epsilon.$$

If $c_1 = 0$, those aL type 1 consumers will become informed and buy from the deviant. He will obtain a normal $(1/n)$th share of the $(1-a)L$ uninformed type 2's and all the aL informed type 1's. His sales jump from L/n to

$$q_d = (1-a)\frac{L}{n} + aL = \frac{L}{n} + aL\left(\frac{n-1}{n}\right).$$

Since his sales jump from this small price decrease, his profits become positive.[9] Once again, the profit-maximization condition is broken and the potential SPE is impossible.

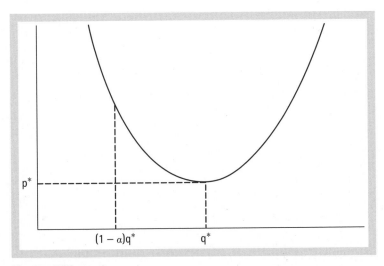

Fig. 5. SPE at p^*

At the monopoly price u,[10] the deviant strategy of raising price is not profitable; no consumer is willing to pay a price above u. Similarly, at the competitive price p^*, since $p^* = \min AC$, any price decreases must be unprofitable, regardless of the deviant's sales. As a result, there may be SPE's at u and p^*. We analyse the competitive price first.

Consider the potential SPE at the competitive price p^*. Zero profits implies that each firm must sell q^*, as pictured below. Since there is no dispersion, no search takes place at this equilibrium and the number of firms n^* is easily calculated from $q^* = L/n^*$. (Of course, we are assuming $u > p^*$. If $u < p^*$, no market can exist for this commodity.)

There are two cases in which p^* is a full equilibrium. If both groups can gather information costlessly ($c_1 = c_2 = 0$), then if a deviant raises price by $\epsilon > 0$, he loses all his customers. This is the conventional result that the purely competitive price obtains if consumers are perfectly informed. On the other hand, if both groups face costly search ($c_1, c_2 > 0$), the SPE at p^* cannot obtain.

Suppose the type 1's have perfect information ($c_1 = 0$), and the type 2's do not ($c_2 > 0$). If a deviant raises his price, he will lose all his type 1's and none of his type 2's. Since he will be earning a higher return on fewer sales, his profits may rise or fall. There is a limit on his price increase: if he chooses $p_d > u$, the type 2's will drop out of the market; if he chooses p_d such that type 2's find it worth while to gather information, he loses all his customers. If he charges p_d, the benefit of search is given by

$$b = \overline{p}' - p^{\min} = \frac{1}{n^*}(p_d - p^*).$$

He loses no type 2 customers if he chooses a p_d such that $c_2 \geq b$ and $p_d \leq u$; that is, if $p_d \leq \min[u, p^* + n^*c_2]$. Since the proportion of type 2's is $(1 - a)$ his sales will be

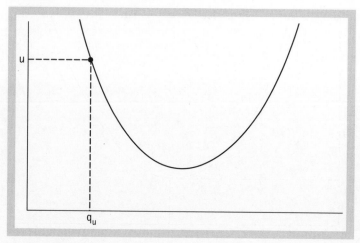

Fig. 6. SPE at u

$q_d = (1 - a)(L/n^*)$. Since $q^* = L/n^*$, we have $q_d = (1 - a)q^*$. This deviant strategy will be profitable if $A(q_d)$, the average cost of producing q_d, is less than the price p_d. Thus, the SPE is *not broken* if and only if

$$A[(1 - a)q^*] > \min(u, p^* + n^*c_2). \tag{22}$$

(22) will hold for small u and c_2, for steep AC curves, and most crucially, for large a. This formalizes a notion that has always been implicit in competitive theory: *Every consumer need not have perfect information. If there are enough perfectly informed consumers (a high enough), the weight of their potential search keeps the market competitive. The informed exert a positive pecuniary externality on the uninformed.* As we shall see subsequently, this externality remains even when there is a price dispersion at equilibrium.

We now analyse the conditions under which a SPE obtains at the monopoly price u. If there is a SPE at u, every firm produces a quantity q_u as shown in Figure 6.

As we argued previously, no firm will raise its price, for no consumer will pay more than u. If a deviant were to lower price to $p_d < u$, he lowers the minimum price more than he lowers the mean price. Since $\overline{p}' = ((n - 1)/n)u + (1/n)p_d$, and $p^{min'} = p_d$, the benefit of search rises to

$$b = \overline{p}' - p^{min'} = \frac{n - 1}{n}(u - p_d).$$

If $b \geq c_1$, the type 1's will search and the deviant's sales will jump to

$$q_d = (1 - a)\frac{L}{n} + aL = (1 - a)q_u + aL.$$

For large values of L,[11] this will be a profitable strategy if and only if

$$p_d \gtreqless p^*.$$

That is, a deviant firm can induce search by lowering price, but this will only lead to positive profits if the "search-inducing price", p_d, is above the competitive price. Setting $c_1 = b$, we have the condition that this SPE is a full equilibrium if and only if

$$p_d = u - (n/(n-1))c_1 < p^*$$

or

$$u - p^* < \frac{n}{n-1}c_1. \tag{23}$$

For $L \to \infty$, then $n \to \infty$ and we have

$$u - p^* \gtrsim c_1 \leqq c_2. \tag{24}$$

This condition makes intuitive sense. If the deviant lowers price to p^*, the gains from search are (approximately) $u - p^*$. If the cost, c_1, of informing the type 1's of its location outweighs the benefit, the deviant will not induce search.

Two-Price Equilibria (*TPE*)

For the (c_1, c_2) discussed above, a SPE will obtain. For all other values of (c_1, c_2) either a TPE or no Nash-equilibrium obtains. The interaction between the three equilibrium conditions is seen most clearly in the analysis of a TPE. We will adopt the following notation. An equilibrium will be defined by a number of firms, n, of which a proportion, β, charge a low price, p_l, and the rest, a proportion $(1 - \beta)$, charge a high price, p_h. A TPE with the property that $p_1 = p^*$ was pictured previously in Figure 2.

(i) *Search Equilibrium.* For a TPE to obtain, it must be true that only those lower cost consumers become informed. (If all or none of the consumers become informed, every firm will obtain identical sales.) From the search rule in (6), we have the necessary condition

$$c_1 < \overline{p} - p^{\min} \leqq c_2.$$

Substituting the definition of $\overline{p}$, $\overline{p} = \beta p_l + (1 - \beta)p_h$, we have

$$c_1 \leqq (1 - \beta)(p_h - p_l) \leqq c_2. \tag{25}$$

(ii) *Zero Profits.* Each of the n firms must earn zero profits. Given (25) the p_h firms sell only to uninformed consumers; the sales per firm-q_h is given by

$$q_h = (1 - a)\frac{L}{n}. \tag{26}$$

The p_l firms obtain an identical share of the uninformed and share the informed consumers among themselves. Thus βn firms split up aL informed consumers, and each gets $aL/\beta n$ of them. Each has sales given by

$$q_l = \left(1 - a + \frac{a}{\beta}\right)\frac{L}{n}.$$ (27)

These sales must yield zero profits:

$$p_h = A\left((1-a)\frac{L}{n}\right)$$ (28)

$$p_l = A\left(\left(1 - a + \frac{a}{\beta}\right)\frac{L}{n}\right),$$ (29)

where $A(q)$ is average costs.

(iii) *Maximum Profits.* As before, no deviant must be willing to break the TPE by charging a different price, either locally or globally. This consideration permits the following two Lemmas to be proved.

Lemma 3. $p_l = p^*$. *The low price is the competitive price.*

Proof. The proof of this proposition is straightforward. Consider a TPE in which $p_l > p^*$. If a deviant p_l firm were to shade its price slightly, it would obtain all the informed customers instead of only a proportion $(1/\beta n)$ of them. Its sales would jump and its profits would become positive. On the other hand, if $p_l = p^*$, then the deviant makes negative profits from price shading, regardless of the number of customers it obtains.

Lemma 4. $p_h = \min[u, p_l + (c_2/(1-\beta))]$. *Referring to (25), the high price is either the monopoly price or just high enough that the type 2's are indifferent between becoming informed and purchasing randomly.*

Proof. Suppose $p_h < p_l + (c_2/(1-\beta))$, that is, suppose $(1-\beta)(p_h - p_l) < c_2$. Then from (25), it is clear that the type 2 consumers prefer not to search. Thus, a deviant p_h firm could raise its price, lose no customers and increase its profits; this would break the TPE. Only if a deviant p_h firm loses its uninformed customers from price rises can the TPE obtain. This occurs only if small price rises induce them to exit from the market ($p_h = u$) or induce them to search, ($p_h = p^* + (c_2/1-\beta)$). Note that we follow the convention that if a consumer is indifferent between searching and purchasing randomly, he follows the latter strategy.

Substituting into (28) and (29) the results of Lemmas 3 and 4 for p_l and p_h, we summarize the TPE as follows:

$$A\left((1-a)\frac{L}{n}\right) = \min\left(u, p^* + \frac{c_2}{1-\beta}\right)$$ (30)

$$A\left(\left(1 - a + \frac{a}{\beta}\right)\frac{L}{n}\right) = p^*.$$ (31)

Further, since $p^* = A(q^*)$, we have

$$q^* = (1 - a - (a/\beta))(L/n).$$ (32)

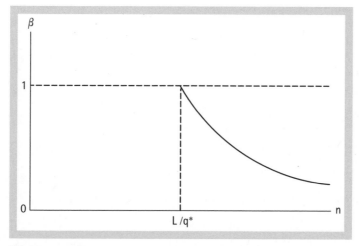

Fig. 7. $\pi_I = 0$

Equations (30) and (31) may be solved for the equilibrium values of β and n. Note we also have the implicit constraint $0 < \beta < 1$.

A solution to these equations is a full equilibrium only if no firm can earn positive profits from globally deviating by charging a different price, for Lemmas 3 and 4 were local conditions only, and global deviance must also be checked. We will now solve (30)–(31) for β, n, and then check on globally deviant behaviour. We will find that profitable global deviance sometimes breaks the equilibrium.

The clearest method of the solution is to diagramme equations (30)–(32). Equation (31) is illustrated in Figure 7. It is easy to show the curve is downward sloping, since $d\beta/dn = -(\beta^2/na)(1 - a + (a/\beta)) < 0$, where $(a/\beta) > a$ since $\beta < 1$.

From (31), when $\beta = 1$, $A(L/n) = p^*$. From (32), we have $p^* = A(q^*)$, and, when $\beta = 1$, $n = L/q^*$ where q^* is the minimum average cost quantity.

The diagram of equation (30) is more difficult. There are two regions, depending on whether u or $p^* + (c_2/(1 - \beta))$ is smaller. The boundary ($\hat{\beta}$) of these two regions may be positive or negative. Setting the two terms equal, we have

$$\hat{\beta} = 1 - \frac{c_2}{u - p^*}.$$

Setting $\hat{\beta} \gtreqless 0$, we have

$$\hat{\beta} \lesseqgtr 0 \Leftrightarrow c_2 \gtreqless u - p^*. \tag{33}$$

There are two β-regions to consider:

Region I ($\beta < 1 - c_2/(u - p^*)$). In this region, $p^* + (c_2/(1 - \beta))$ is smaller, and the $\beta - n$ curve is upward sloping, since $d\beta/dn = -(1 - \beta)^2 L(1 - a)A'/(c_2 n^2) > 0$. It is described by

$$p^* + \frac{c_2}{1 - \beta} = A\left((1 - a)\frac{L}{n}\right).$$

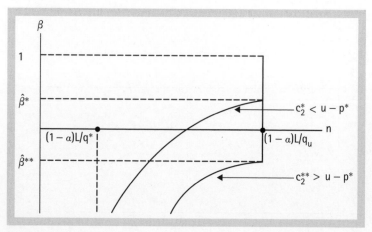

Fig. 8. $\pi_h = 0$

The curve is asymptotic (as $\beta \to -\infty$) to $n = (1 - a)(L/q^*)$, from (32).

Region II ($\beta \geq 1 - c_2/(u - p^*)$). In this region, u is the minimum, and the equation is described by

$$u = A\left((1 - a)\frac{L}{n}\right). \tag{34}$$

Defining the quantity on the average cost curve at u by q_u, we have

$$q_u = (1 - a)\frac{L}{n}, \tag{35}$$

which defines an n_u such that

$$n_u = (1 - a)\frac{L}{q_u}. \tag{36}$$

Equation (30) is shown in Figure 8 for two values of c_2. Possible TPE's occur where the curves cross. Noting that the minimum n in Figure 7 is L/q^* and maximum n in Figure 8 is $(1 - a)L/q_u$, then a necessary condition for a TPE arising from the interaction of the technology and the consumer distribution is given by

$$n_u = (1 - a)\frac{L}{q_u} > \frac{L}{q^*} \tag{37}$$

or rewriting

$$1 - a > \frac{q_u}{q^*}. \tag{38}$$

Thus, a TPE will not exist for large a or a steep average cost curve, $((q_u/q^*)$ large). The intuition behind this result is as follows. Suppose the market consists primarily of low cost consumers (large a). The high-price firms, which sell only to unlucky high-cost consumers, will have a small market. If the average cost curve is steep enough, there will not be enough high-cost consumers to support even one high-price firm.

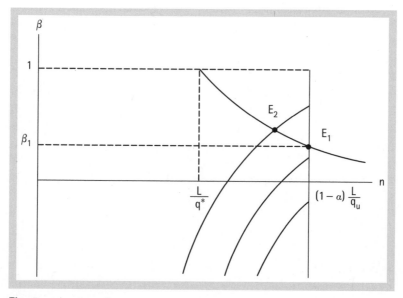

Fig. 9. $\pi_h = \pi_i = 0$

As we will discuss subsequently, if this necessary condition is not met, there will be either no equilibrium or a SPE at the monopoly price, depending on (c_1, c_2).

Assuming that this necessary condition is satisfied, a TPE exists as shown in Figure 9. If the equilibrium occurs at $n_u = (1-a)L/q_u$ (at a point like E_1), then the high price equals the monopoly price, u. If the equilibrium occurs at a point like E_2, the high price is below the monopoly price. Given the technology, which equilibrium occurs will depend on c_2. When $\hat{\beta} < 0$, we certainly have E_1, or

$$p_h = u \quad \text{for} \quad c_2 > u - p^*. \tag{39}$$

Intuitively, if c_2 is high enough, each high-price firm can raise its prices without inducing any c_2 customers to search. Thus, p_h will rise until the monopoly price is reached. (For $p > u$, c_2 customers will exit from the market. Thus, the rises in p_h stop at u.)

Referring to (30) and Figure 9, the TPE will occur at E_1, $(\beta = \beta_1)$, if

$$p^* + \frac{c_2}{1 - \beta_1} \gtreqqless u, \tag{40}$$

where β_1 is defined by (31) at $n_u = (1-a)\frac{L}{q_u}$ by

$$\left(1 - a + \frac{a}{\beta_1}\right)\frac{L}{n_u} = q^*. \tag{41}$$

Substituting from n_u, we have

$$\beta_1 = \frac{a}{1-a}\left(\frac{1}{\frac{q^*}{q_u} - 1}\right). \tag{42}$$

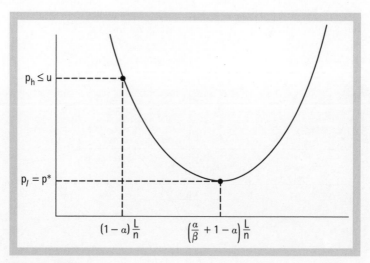

Fig. 10. TPE

If the necessary condition given by (38) holds, then $(q^*/q_u) - 1 > a/(1 - a)$. This defines a $\beta \in (0, 1)$, since $\beta_1 < 1$ follows from (42), and $\beta_1 > 0$ follows from $(q^*/q_u) > 0$. Substituting (42) into (40), we have

$$\beta = \beta_1, \ p_h = u \quad \text{for} \quad c_2 \geq (1 - \beta_1)(u - p^*). \tag{43}$$

Similarly, from Figure 9,

$$\beta > \beta_1, \ p_h < u, \quad \text{for} \quad c_2 < (1 - \beta_1)(u - p^*), \tag{44}$$

i.e. for smaller c_2, we have an equilibrium like E_2.

Substituting into (26) and (27), we may calculate the number of firms. We have

$$n = (1 - a)\frac{L}{q_h}. \tag{45}$$

We now confirm that these equations do define a full TPE. That is, we must show that in fact consumers are searching optimally, every firm is making zero profits, and every firm is maximizing profits.

(i) *Search Equilibrium.* From Lemmas 3 and 4, $c_2 \geq \bar{p} - p^{\min}$. Thus, c_2 consumers find it optimal to purchase randomly. At the $p_h < u$ TPE, since the c_2's are indifferent to search, then c_1 consumers do *prefer* to gather information, since $c_1 < c_2$. At the $p_h = u$ TPE, the necessary condition that the c_1 consumers do gather information is, of course, just opposite of the condition that the c_2 consumers do not search.

$$c_1 < (1 - \beta_1)(u - p^*) \tag{46a}$$
$$c_2 \geq (1 - \beta_1)(u - p^*). \tag{46b}$$

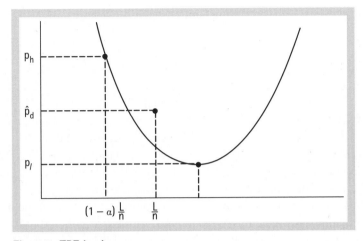

Fig. 11. TPE broken

(ii) *Zero Profits.* By setting price equal to average cost, the TPE was constructed to obey the zero profit conditions.

(iii) *Maximum Profits.* We now show that no potentially deviant p_l or p_h firm can increase its profits by charging a different price. We examine a p_l deviant first.

Suppose a p_l deviant raises his price to $p_d < p_h$. The mean price $\bar{p}$ will rise without affecting $p^{\min}$, raising the benefits of search. Since the c_1 consumers were already searching, their behaviour will not change. The c_2 consumers could be induced to search. If they do, they will purchase from the non-deviant p_l firms. The p_l deviant's sales will fall to that of a high price firm. Thus, p_l deviance is unprofitable.

Suppose a p_h deviant lowers his price to $p_d < p_h$. The mean price falls without affecting $p^{\min}$. This lowers the benefits from search. Since the c_2 consumers previously found it non-optimal to search, their behaviour is not affected. However, it is possible that the benefits fall enough to make search by the c_1 consumers non-optimal. If they begin purchasing randomly, the p_h deviant's sales rise from $(1 - a)L/n$ to $q_d = (L/n)$.

Thus, if the $\hat{p}_d$ which eliminates search is high enough for the deviant to cover his average costs, large p_h deviance will be profitable and the TPE will be broken. This situation is shown in Figure 11. The necessary condition for such "global" p_h deviance to be unprofitable is given by

$$\hat{p}_d < A\left(\frac{L}{n}\right), \tag{47}$$

where $\hat{p}$ is the price such that

$$\bar{p}' - p^{\min} = c_1, \tag{48}$$

where

$$\bar{p}' = \beta p^* + \left(1 - \beta - \frac{1}{n}\right) p_h + \frac{1}{n}\hat{p}_d. \tag{49}$$

Substituting (49) into (48) and using Lemmas 3 and 4, we have

$$\hat{p}_d = \begin{cases} p_h - n(c_2 - c_1) & \text{for} \quad p_h < u \\ p_h - n[(1 - \beta_1)(u - p^*) - c_1] & \text{for} \quad p_h = u. \end{cases} \tag{50}$$

For large values of L, n will be large and (47) will be satisfied. Intuitively, if there are many firms, a p_h deviant will have a very small effect on the average price; thus, it will be unable to stop the c_1 consumers from gathering information. Note that this condition assumed that only one firm deviated. If a significant number of p_h firms colluded in jointly lowering price, they could break the TPE more easily. This raises the possibility that duopoly may lead to lower prices than competition.

We have derived regions of (c_1, c_2) under which there are SPE, TPE and no equilibria. We summarized these regions in Figure 1. Under the assumption that $L \to \infty$, the regions do not overlap and the equilibrium (if it exists) is unique for all $c_2 \geq c_1 \geq 0$.[12]

If the technology is such that $\beta_1 \geq 1$ (i.e. $1 - \alpha \leq (q_u/q^*)$), there is a SPE at $p = u$ for $c_1, c_2 \geq u - p^*$ and no equilibrium for lower c_1, c_2.[13]

Non-existence of Equilibrium

For certain values of $(\alpha, q_u, q^*, c_1, c_2)$ we have shown that no equilibrium exists, because if some deviant changes his price substantially, he will earn positive profits. If firms engaged only in "local" price experiments, but not in "global" price experiments, the nonexistence region would not occur. Alternatively, if the deviant realizes that others will react to his deviance, then he may not break the equilibrium. With this in mind, a "limit price" equilibrium concept can be defined as follows. There exists some price p^L and associated quantity q^L for every firm such that (i) profits are zero, (ii) no deviant can break the equilibrium with price decreases and (iii) if any firm attempts to increase short-run profits by raising price, another deviant can lower its price discretely and capture all the c_1 consumers (and possibly the c_2 consumers as well). Thus, this limit price equilibrium is a reaction function equilibrium.

p^L is derived as follows for the case in which $c_1 = c_2 = c$.[14]

$$p^L = A(q^L). \quad \text{(zero profits)} \tag{51}$$

$$q^L = \frac{L}{n}. \quad \text{(equal market shares)} \tag{52}$$

$$\frac{n-1}{n}(p^L - p^*) = c. \quad \text{(search equilibrium)} \tag{53}$$

Equation (53) expresses the notion that if some deviant lowers price to p^*, he will just induce search. Rewriting, we have

$$p^L = p^* + \frac{n}{n-1}c, \tag{54}$$

where (51) and (52) define n. For large n, $n/(n-1) \cong 1$, and we have

$$p^L \cong p^* + c. \tag{55}$$

Note that p^L is not a "Nash" equilibrium with respect to deviant price increases. A single firm could raise price slightly without losing any customers. However, this would then induce another deviant to lower price. That is, if a firm acts in its *short-run* interest, it will destroy the equilibrium by allowing other firms drastically to cut prices to induce search. Prices may then begin to oscillate between the competitive price p^* and the limit price. The exact dynamics will depend on the dynamic learning process of consumers and firms. In general, prices may creep up slowly to slightly above the limit price, inducing a price war down to p^*, only to again begin the upward creep. The frequency and regularity of the cycle will depend on the adjustment speeds of price changes, entry, and the learning by consumers. In that smaller more competitive firms will be more likely to act in their short-run interests at the expense of the long-run, this leads to the notion that competitive markets will be more unstable than oligopolistic markets.

Conclusions

In this paper, we have analysed the industry equilibrium for an economy in which imperfectly informed consumers can only become perfectly informed at a cost. This assumption leads to a monopolistically competitive equilibrium and generally to price dispersion as well, even though the commodity produced by each firm is identical.

The price dispersion here is different from that analysed by Grossman and Stiglitz (1976) and Mortensen (1973), where costly information leads to incomplete market adjustments to exogenous shocks. Such markets are incompletely arbitraged. Furthermore, the price dispersion generated here is specifically associated with a market economy; a socialist economy with exactly the same information and production technology would require all stores to charge the same price.

This paper is one of a series dealing with the effects of costly information on market equilibrium. These studies differ with respect to the technology of information acquisition and the characteristics of consumers and producers. In the model examined here, consumers differ only in their costs of information acquisition. In Salop (1977) and Salop and Stiglitz (1982) individuals differ also in their demand functions. A further reason for price dispersion arises there. Firms attempt to act as discriminating monopolists. The costs of information allows them to exercise this kind of discrimination, which they would be unable to do in a competitive market with perfect information. Finally, in Salop and Stiglitz (1982), Butters (1977) and

Stiglitz (1974c), even when individuals are identical *ex ante* in both search costs and demand functions, price dispersion may occur.

Finally, one shortcoming with this model is that possible "indirect information" contained in the prices and market shares are ignored by consumers. Low-priced stores have larger market shares, since they sell to informed as well as uninformed buyers. If uninformed buyers observed the market shares of firms, then purchasing according to market shares would assure them the lower price. This is an example of the more general notion that in the presence of some informed consumers, uninformed consumers ought to "buy with the market"; price will reflect quality and market shares will reflect the overall "best buys".[15]

If there is no heterogeneity in preferences, advertising, or differential costs of production, this result is true in our model. However, in general there will be other "noise" in the market so that there is still a net benefit to becoming informed; Grossman and Stiglitz have shown that generally an equilibrium with price dispersion will still obtain.

Notes

1. u may be thought of as the marginal utility in dollar terms of the unit of the durable.
2. Cf. G. Butters (1977), P. von zur Muehlen (1976), Stiglitz (1974c) and Salop and Stiglitz (1982). The basic result on the existence of equilibrium with price distributions remains valid in these models.
3. Note that $\bar{p}$ is not weighted by sales of each store. It is not the mean price measured in the price dispersion literature. For a model in which consumers know market shares, see Smallwood and Conlisk (1979).
4. Risk aversion is effectively captured in c^i.
5. If $E_s^i = E_N^i$, the consumer is just indifferent. We follow the convention that indifferent consumers do not buy the newspaper. This assumption is not crucial. If the opposite convention were followed or it were assumed indifferent consumers flipped a coin, the equilibrium prices would change only by an arbitrarily small epsilon.
6. Its output is the lower of the two outputs which share a common AC. Thus, each firm's output is demand-constrained at equilibrium (it would like to sell more if it could) unless the firm charges the competitive price.
7. More precisely, we have, for a finite n^*,

$$\pi(\hat{p}_j|\hat{p}^{-j}) \geqq 0, \quad \text{for all} \quad j = 1, 2, \ldots, n^*$$
$$\pi(\hat{p}_j|\hat{p}^{-j}) \leqq 0, \quad \text{for all} \quad j = 1, 2, \ldots, n^* + 1.$$

8. If no consumers search, every firm has identical sales and the p_h firm has highest profits. If consumers all search, the p_m and p_h firms have no sales at all.
9. It is possible that q_d is so large that $p_d < AC(q_d)$. That is, the deviant is swamped with customers. This is a potential problem for any competitive model. Cf. Salop (1976).
10. With downward-sloping demand curves, this would be at the Chamberlinean monopolistically competitive price. See Braverman (1976).

11. We assume L is very large so as to not bias the case against perfect competition. Once again, we ignore the fact that the deviant will be swamped with customers.

12. For finite L, there are regions in which both a SPE at u and a TPE exist.

13. We effectively move the axes of Figure 1 over to $(1 - \beta_1)(u - p^*)$.

14. Note that if $c_1 = c_2$, a TPE must have the property that all consumers are just indifferent to search. If we follow the convention that indifference implies no search, then a TPE is impossible. On the other hand, if we assume that an indifferent consumer chooses to search with probability a, then a different TPE obtains for each a. For an example of such a model, see Stiglitz (1974c). Shilony (1977) derives a similar mixed strategy equilibrium.

15. This has been explored by Nelson (1970) and Smallwood and Conlisk (1979).

CHAPTER 21

....

ON THE
IMPOSSIBILITY OF
INFORMATIONALLY
EFFICIENT
MARKETS*

....

IF competitive equilibrium is defined as a situation in which prices are such that all arbitrage profits are eliminated, is it possible that a competitive economy always be in equilibrium? Clearly not, for then those who arbitrage make no (private) return from their (privately) costly activity. Hence the assumptions that all markets, including that for information, are always in equilibrium and always perfectly arbitraged are inconsistent when arbitrage is costly.

We propose here a model in which there is an equilibrium degree of disequilibrium: prices reflect the information of informed individuals (arbitrageurs) but only partially, so that those who expend resources to obtain information do receive compensation. How informative the price system is depends on the number of individuals who are informed; but the number of individuals who are informed is itself an endogenous variable in the model.

The model is the simplest one in which prices perform a well-articulated role in conveying information from the informed to the uninformed. When informed individuals observe information that the return to a security is going to be high, they bid its price up, and conversely when they observe information that the return is going to be low. Thus the price system makes publicly available the information obtained by

* Written with Sanford J. Grossman. Research support under National Science Foundation grants SOC76-18771 and SOC77-15980 is gratefully acknowledged. This is a revised version of a paper presented at the Econometric Society meetings, Winter 1975, at Dallas, Texas. Reprinted with permission from the *American Economic Review*, 70(3) June (1980), pp. 393–408.

informed individuals to the uniformed. In general, however, it does this imperfectly; this is perhaps lucky, for were it to do it perfectly, an equilibrium would not exist.

In the introduction, we shall discuss the general methodology and present some conjectures concerning certain properties of the equilibrium. The remaining analytic sections of the paper are devoted to analyzing in detail an important example of our general model, in which our conjectures concerning the nature of the equilibrium can be shown to be correct. We conclude with a discussion of the implications of our approach and results, with particular emphasis on the relationship of our results to the literature on "efficient capital markets."

I THE MODEL

Our model can be viewed as an extension of the noisy rational expectations model introduced by Robert Lucas (1972) and applied to the study of information flows between traders by Jerry Green (1973); Grossman (1975, 1976, 1978); and Richard Kihlstrom and Leonard Mirman (1975). There are two assets: a safe asset yielding a return R, and a risky asset, the return to which, u, varies randomly from period to period. The variable u consists of two parts,

$$u = \theta + \epsilon \tag{1}$$

where θ is observable at a cost c, and ϵ is unobservable.[1] Both θ and ϵ are random variables. There are two types of individuals, those who observe θ (informed traders), and those who observe only price (uninformed traders). In our simple model, all individuals are, *ex ante*, identical; whether they are informed or uninformed just depends on whether they have spent c to obtain information. Informed traders' demands will depend on θ and the price of the risky asset P. Uninformed traders' demands will depend only on P, but we shall assume that they have rational expectations; they learn the relationship between the distribution of return and the price, and use this in deriving their demand for the risky assets. If x denotes the supply of the risky asset, an equilibrium when a given percentage, λ, of traders are informed, is thus a price function $P_\lambda(\theta, x)$ such that, when demands are formulated in the way described, demand equals supply. We assume that uninformed traders do not observe x. Uninformed traders are prevented from learning θ via observations of $P_\lambda(\theta, x)$ because they cannot distinguish variations in price due to changes in the informed trader's information from variations in price due to changes in aggregate supply. Clearly, $P_\lambda(\theta, x)$ reveals some of the informed trader's information to the uninformed traders.

We can calculate the expected utility of the informed and the expected utility of the uninformed. If the former is greater than the latter (taking account of the cost

---

[1] An alternative interpretation is that θ is a "measurement" of u with error. The mathematics of this alternative interpretation differ slightly, but the results are identical.

of information), some individuals switch from being uninformed to being informed (and conversely). An overall equilibrium requires the two to have the same expected utility. As more individuals become informed, the expected utility of the informed falls relative to the uninformed for two reasons:

(a) The price system becomes more informative because variations in θ have a greater effect on aggregate demand and thus on price when more traders observe θ. Thus, more of the information of the informed is available to the uninformed. Moreover, the informed gain more from trade with the uninformed than do the uninformed. The informed, on average, buy securities when they are "underpriced" and sell them when they are "overpriced" (relative to what they would have been if information were equalized).[2] As the price system becomes more informative, the difference in their information—and hence the magnitude by which the informed can gain relative to the uninformed—is reduced.

(b) Even if the above effect did not occur, the increase in the ratio of informed to uninformed means that the relative gains of the informed, on a per capita basis, in trading with the uninformed will be smaller.

We summarize the above characterization of the equilibrium of the economy in the following two conjectures:

Conjecture 1: The more individuals who are informed, the more informative is the price system.

Conjecture 2: The more individuals who are informed, the lower the ratio of expected utility of the informed to the uninformed.

(Conjecture 1 obviously requires a definition of "more informative"; this is given in the next section and in fn. 7.)

The equilibrium number of informed and uninformed individuals in the economy will depend on a number of critical parameters: the cost of information, how informative the price system is (how much noise there is to interfere with the information conveyed by the price system), and how informative the information obtained by an informed individual is.

Conjecture 3: The higher the cost of information, the smaller will be the equilibrium percentage of individuals who are informed.

Conjecture 4: If the quality of the informed trader's information increases, the more their demands will vary with their information and thus the more prices will vary with θ. Hence, the price system becomes more informative. The equilibrium proportion of informed to uninformed may be either increased or decreased, because even though the value of being informed has increased due to the increased quality of θ, the value of being uninformed has also increased because the price system becomes more informative.

Conjecture 5: The greater the magnitude of noise, the less informative will the price system be, and hence the lower the expected utility of uninformed individuals. Hence,

---

[2] The framework described herein does not explicitly model the effect of variations in supply, i.e., x on commodity storage. The effect of futures markets and storage capabilities on the informativeness of the price system was studied by Grossman (1975, 1977b).

in equilibrium the greater the magnitude of noise, the larger the proportion of informed individuals.

Conjecture 6: In the limit, when there is no noise, prices convey all information, and there is no incentive to purchase information. Hence, the only possible equilibrium is one with no information. But if everyone is uninformed, it clearly pays some individual to become informed.[3] Thus, there does not exist a competitive equilibrium.[4]

Trade among individuals occurs either because tastes (risk aversions) differ, endowments differ, or beliefs differ. This paper focuses on the last of these three. An interesting feature of the equilibrium is that beliefs may be precisely identical in either one of two situations: when all individuals are informed or when all individuals are uninformed. This gives rise to:

Conjecture 7: That, other things being equal, markets will be thinner under those conditions in which the percentage of individuals who are informed (λ) is either near zero or near unity. For example, markets will be thin when there is very little noise in the system (so λ is near zero), or when costs of information are very low (so λ is near unity).

In the last few paragraphs, we have provided a number of conjectures describing the nature of the equilibrium when prices convey information. Unfortunately, we have not been able to obtain a general proof of any of these propositions. What we have been able to do is to analyze in detail an interesting example, entailing constant absolute risk-aversion utility functions and normally distributed random variables. In this example, the equilibrium price distribution can actually be calculated, and all of the conjectures provided above can be verified. The next sections are devoted to solving for the equilibrium in this particular example.[5]

II Constant Absolute Risk-Aversion Model

A The Securities

The ith trader is assumed to be endowed with stocks of two types of securities: $\overline{M}_i$, the riskless asset, and $\overline{X}_i$, a risky asset. Let P be the current price of risky assets and

---

[3] That is, with no one informed, an individual can only get information by paying c dollars, since no information is revealed by the price system. By paying c dollars an individual will be able to predict better than the market when it is optimal to hold the risky asset as opposed to the risk-free asset. Thus his expected utility will be higher than an uninformed person gross of information costs. Thus for c sufficiently low all uninformed people will desire to be informed.

[4] See Grossman (1975, 1977b) for a formal example of this phenomenon in futures markets. See Stiglitz (1971b, 1974d) for a general discussion of information and the possibility of nonexistence of equilibrium in capital markets.

[5] The informational equilibria discussed here may not, in general, exist. See Green (1977). Of course, for the utility function we choose equilibrium does exist.

set the price of risk free assets equal to unity. The ith trader's budget constraint is

$$PX_i + M_i = W_{0i} \equiv \overline{M}_i + P\overline{X}_i \tag{2}$$

Each unit of the risk free asset pays R "dollars" at the end of the period, while each unit of the risky asset pays u dollars. If at the end of the period, the ith trader holds a portfolio (M_i, X_i), his wealth will be

$$W_{1i} = RM_i + uX_i \tag{3}$$

B Individual's Utility Maximization

Each individual has a utility function $V_i(W_{1i})$. For simplicity, we assume all individuals have the same utility function and so drop the subscripts i. Moreover, we assume the utility function is exponential, i.e.,

$$V(W_{1i}) = -e^{-aW_{1i}}, \quad a > 0$$

where a is the coefficient of absolute risk aversion. Each trader desires to maximize expected utility, using whatever information is available to him, and to decide on what information to acquire on the basis of the consequences to his expected utility.

Assume that in equation (1) θ and ϵ have a multivariate normal distribution, with

$$E\epsilon = 0 \tag{4}$$

$$E\theta\epsilon = 0 \tag{5}$$

$$Var(u^*|\theta) = Var\,\epsilon^* \equiv \sigma_\epsilon^2 > 0 \tag{6}$$

since θ and ϵ are uncorrelated. Throughout this paper we will put a $*$ above a symbol to emphasize that it is a random variable. Since W_{1i} is a linear function of ϵ, for a given portfolio allocation, and a linear function of a normally distributed random variable is normally distributed, it follows that W_{1i} is normal conditional on θ. Then, using (2) and (3) the expected utility of the *informed* trader with information θ can be written

$$E(V(W_{1i}^*)|\theta) = -\exp\left(-a\left\{E\left[W_{1i}^*|\theta\right] - \frac{a}{2}Var\left[W_{1i}^*|\theta\right]\right\}\right)$$

$$= -\exp\left(-a\left[RW_{0i} + X_I\{E(u^*|\theta) - RP\} - \frac{a}{2}X_I^2 Var(u^*|\theta)\right]\right)$$

$$= -\exp\left(-a\left[RW_{0i} + X_I(\theta - RP) - \frac{a}{2}X_I^2\sigma_\epsilon^2\right]\right) \tag{7}$$

where X_I is an informed individual's demand for the risky security. Maximizing (7) with respect to X_I yields a demand function for risky assets:

$$X_I(P, \theta) = \frac{\theta - RP}{a\sigma_\epsilon^2} \tag{8}$$

The right-hand side of (8) shows the familiar result that with constant absolute risk aversion, a trader's demand does not depend on wealth; hence the subscript i is not on the left-hand side of (8).

We now derive the demand function for the uninformed. Let us assume the only source of "noise" is the per capita supply of the risky security x.

Let $P^*(\cdot)$ be some particular price function of (θ, x) such that u^* and P^* are jointly normally distributed. (We will prove that this exists below.)

Then, we can write for the uninformed individual

$$E(V(W_{1i}^*)|P^*) = -\exp\left[-a\left\{E\left[W_{1i}^*|P^*\right] - \frac{a}{2}Var\left[W_{1i}^*|P^*\right]\right\}\right]$$

$$= -\exp\left[-a\left\{RW_{0i} + X_U(E\left[u^*|P^*\right] - RP)\right.\right.$$

$$\left.\left. -\frac{a}{2}X_U^2 Var[u^*|P^*]\right\}\right] \tag{7'}$$

The demands of the uninformed will thus be a function of the price function P^* and the actual price P.

$$X_U(P; P^*) = \frac{E\left[u^*|P^*(\theta, x) = P\right] - RP}{a\,Var[u^*|P^*(\theta, x) = P]} \tag{8'}$$

C Equilibrium Price Distribution

If λ is some particular fraction of traders who decide to become informed, then define an equilibrium price system as a function of (θ, x), $P_\lambda(\theta, x)$, such that for all (θ, x) per capita demands for the risky assets equal supplies:

$$\lambda X_I(P_\lambda(\theta, x), \theta) + (1 - \lambda)X_U(P_\lambda(\theta, x); P_\lambda^*) = x \tag{9}$$

The function $P_\lambda(\theta, x)$ is a statistical equilibrium in the following sense. If over time uninformed traders observe many realizations of (u^*, P_λ^*), then they learn the joint distribution of (u^*, P_λ^*). After all learning about the joint distribution of (u^*, P_λ^*) ceases, all traders will make allocations and form expectations such that this joint distribution persists over time. This follows from (8), (8'), and (9), where the market clearing price that comes about is the one which takes into account the fact that uninformed traders have learned that it contains information.

We shall now prove that there exists an equilibrium price distribution such that P^* and u^* are jointly normal. Moreover, we shall be able to characterize the price distribution. We define

$$w_\lambda(\theta, x) = \theta - \frac{a\sigma_\epsilon^2}{\lambda}(x - Ex^*) \tag{10a}$$

for $\lambda > 0$, and define $w_0(\theta, x)$ as the number:

$$w_0(\theta, x) = x \quad \text{for all } (\theta, x) \tag{10b}$$

where w_λ is just the random variable θ, plus noise.[6] The magnitude of the noise is inversely proportional to the proportion of informed traders, but is proportional to the variance of ϵ. We shall prove that the equilibrium price is just a linear function of w_λ. Thus, if $\lambda > 0$, the price system conveys information about θ, but it does so imperfectly.

D Existence of Equilibrium and a Characterization Theorem

Theorem 1. *If $(\theta^*, \epsilon^*, x^*)$ has a nondegenerate joint normal distribution such that θ^*, ϵ^*, and x^* are mutually independent, then there exists a solution to (9) which has the form $P_\lambda(\theta, x) = a_1 + a_2 w_\lambda(\theta, x)$, where a_1 and a_2 are real numbers which may depend on λ, such that $a_2 > 0$. (If $\lambda = 0$, the price contains no information about θ.) The exact form of $P_\lambda(\theta, x)$ is given in equation (A10) in Appendix B. The proof of this theorem is also in Appendix B.*

The importance of Theorem 1 rests in the simple characterization of the information in the equilibrium price system: P_λ^* is informationally equivalent to w_λ^*. From (10) w_λ^* is a "mean-preserving spread" of θ; i.e., $E[w_\lambda^*|\theta] = \theta$ and

$$Var[w_\lambda^*|\theta] = \frac{a^2 \sigma_\epsilon^4}{\lambda^2} Var\, x^* \tag{11}$$

For each replication of the economy, θ is the information that uninformed traders would like to know. But the noise x^* prevents w_λ^* from revealing θ. How well-informed uninformed traders can become from observing P_λ^* (equivalently w_λ^*) is measured by $Var[w_\lambda^*|\theta]$. When $Var[w_\lambda^*|\theta]$ is zero, w_λ^* and θ are perfectly correlated. Hence when uninformed firms observe w_λ^*, this is equivalent to observing θ. On the other hand, when $Var[w_\lambda^*|\theta]$ is very large, there are "many" realizations of w_λ^* that are associated with a given θ. In this case the observation of a particular w_λ^* tells very little about the actual θ which generated it.[7]

From equation (11) it is clear that large noise (high $Var\, x^*$) leads to an imprecise price system. The other factor which determines the precision of the price system $(a^2 \sigma_\epsilon^4/\lambda^2)$ is more subtle. When a is small (the individual is not very risk averse) or σ_ϵ^2 is small (the information is very precise), an informed trader will have a demand for risky assets which is very responsive to changes in θ. Further, the larger λ is, the more responsive is the total demand of informed traders. Thus small $(a^2 \sigma_\epsilon^4/\lambda^2)$ means that the aggregate demand of informed traders is very responsive to θ. For a fixed amount of noise (i.e., fixed $Var\, x^*$) the larger are the movements in aggregate demand which are due to movements in θ, the more will price movements be due to movements in θ. That is, x^* becomes less important relative to θ in determining price movements. Therefore, for small $(a^2 \sigma_\epsilon^4/\lambda^2)$ uninformed traders are able to confidently know that

---

[6] If $y' = y + Z$, and $E[Z|y] = 0$, then y' is just y plus noise.

[7] Formally, w_λ^* is an experiment in the sense of Blackwell which gives information about θ. It is easy to show that, *ceteris paribus*, the smaller $Var(w_\lambda^*|\theta)$ the more "informative" (or sufficient) in the sense of Blackwell, is the experiment; see Grossman, Kihlstrom, and Mirman (1977, p. 539).

price is, for example, unusually high due to θ being high. In this way information from informed traders is transferred to uninformed traders.

E Equilibrium in the Information Market

What we have characterized so far is the equilibrium price distribution for given λ. We now define an *overall* equilibrium to be a pair (λ, P_λ^*) such that the expected utility of the informed is equal to that of the uninformed if $0 < \lambda < 1$; $\lambda = 0$ if the expected utility of the informed is less than that of the uninformed at P_0^*; $\lambda = 1$ if the expected utility of the informed is greater than the uninformed at P_1^*. Let

$$W_{Ii}^\lambda \equiv R(W_{0i} - c) + [u - RP_\lambda(\theta, x)]X_I(P_\lambda(\theta, x), \theta) \tag{12a}$$

$$W_{UI}^\lambda \equiv RW_{0i} + [u - RP_\lambda(\theta, x)]X_U(P_\lambda(\theta, x); P_\lambda^*) \tag{12b}$$

where c is the cost of observing a realization of θ^*. Equation (12a) gives the end of period wealth of a trader if he decides to become informed, while (12b) gives his wealth if he decides to be uninformed. Note that end of period wealth is random due to the randomness of W_{0i}, u, θ, and x.

In evaluating the expected utility of W_{Ii}^λ, we do not assume that a trader knows which realization of θ^* he gets to observe if he pays c dollars. A trader pays c dollars and then gets to observe some realization of θ^*. The overall expected utility of W_{Ii}^λ averages over all possible θ^*, ϵ^*, x^*, and W_{0i}. The variable W_{0i} is random for two reasons. First from (2) it depends on $P_\lambda(\theta, x)$, which is random as (θ, x) is random. Secondly, in what follows we will assume that $\overline{X}_i$ is random.

We will show below that $EV(W_{Ii}^\lambda)/EV(W_{Ui}^\lambda)$ is independent of i, but is a function of λ, a, c, and σ_ϵ^2. More precisely, in Appendix B we prove

Theorem 2. *Under the assumptions of Theorem 1, and if $\overline{X}_i$ is independent of (u^*, θ^*, x^*) then*

$$\frac{EV(W_{Ii}^\lambda)}{EV(W_{Ui}^\lambda)} = e^{ac}\sqrt{\frac{Var(u^*|\theta)}{Var(u^*|w_\lambda)}} \tag{13}$$

F Existence of Overall Equilibrium

Theorem 2 is useful, both in proving the uniqueness of overall equilibrium and in analyzing comparative statics. Overall equilibrium, it will be recalled, requires that for $0 < \lambda < 1$, $EV(W_{Ii}^\lambda)/EV(W_{Ui}^\lambda) = 1$. But from (13)

$$\frac{EV(W_{Ii}^\lambda)}{EV(W_{Ui}^\lambda)} = e^{ac}\sqrt{\frac{Var(u^*|\theta)}{Var(u^*|w_\lambda)}} \equiv \gamma(\lambda) \tag{14}$$

Hence overall equilibrium simply requires, for $0 < \lambda < 1$,

$$\gamma(\lambda) = 1 \tag{15}$$

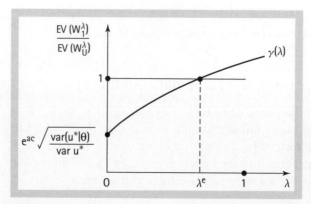

Fig. 1.

More precisely, we now prove

Theorem 3. *If* $0 \leqslant \lambda \leqslant 1, \gamma(\lambda) = 1,$ *and* P_λ^* *is given by* (A10) *in Appendix B, then* (λ, P_λ^*) *is an overall equilibrium. If* $\gamma(1) < 1,$ *then* $(1, P_1^*)$ *is an overall equilibrium. If* $\gamma(0) > 1,$ *then* $(0, P_0^*)$ *is an overall equilibrium. For all price equilibria* P_λ *which are monotone functions of* w_λ, *there exists a unique overall equilibrium* (λ, P_λ^*).

Proof. The first three sentences follow immediately from the definition of overall equilibrium given above equation (12), and Theorems 1 and 2. Uniqueness follows from the monotonicity of $\gamma(\cdot)$ which follows from (A11) and (14). The last two sentences in the statement of the theorem follow immediately.

In the process of proving Theorem 3, we have noted

Corollary 1. $\gamma(\lambda)$ *is a strictly monotone increasing function of* λ.

   This looks paradoxical; we expect the ratio of informed to uninformed expected utility to be a decreasing function of λ. But, *we have defined utility as negative.* Therefore as λ rises, the expected utility of informed traders does go down relative to uninformed traders.
   Note that the function $\gamma(0) = e^{ac}(Var(u^*|\theta)/Var\ u^*)^{1/2}$. Figure 1 illustrates the determination of the equilibrium λ. The figure assumes that $\gamma(0) < 1 < \gamma(1)$.

G   Characterization of Equilibrium

We wish to provide some further characterization of the equilibrium. Let us define

$$m = \left(\frac{a\sigma_\epsilon^2}{\lambda}\right)^2 \frac{\sigma_x^2}{\sigma_\theta^2} \tag{16a}$$

$$n = \frac{\sigma_\theta^2}{\sigma_\epsilon^2} \tag{16b}$$

Note that m is inversely related to the informativeness of the price system since the squared correlation coefficient between P_λ^* and θ^*, ρ_θ^2 is given by

$$\rho_\theta^2 = \frac{1}{1+m} \qquad (17)$$

Similarly, n is directly related to the quality of the informed trader's information because $n/(1+n)$ is the squared correlation coefficient between θ^* and u^*.

Equations (14) and (15) show that the cost of information c, determines the equilibrium ratio of information quality between informed and uninformed traders $(Var(u^*|\theta))/Var(u^*|w_\lambda)$. From (1), (A11) of Appendix A, and (16), this can be written as

$$\frac{Var(u^*|\theta)}{Var(u^*|w_\lambda)} = \frac{1+m}{1+m+nm} = \left(1 + \frac{nm}{1+m}\right)^{-1} \qquad (18)$$

Substituting (18) into (14) and using (15) we obtain, for $0 < \lambda < 1$, in equilibrium

$$m = \frac{e^{2ac} - 1}{1 + n - e^{2ac}} \qquad (19a)$$

or

$$1 - \rho_\theta^2 = \frac{e^{2ac} - 1}{n} \qquad (19b)$$

Note that (19) holds for $\gamma(0) < 1 < \gamma(1)$, since these conditions insure that the equilibrium λ is between zero and one. Equation (19b) shows that the equilibrium informativeness of the price system is determined completely by the cost of information c, the quality of the informed trader's information n, and the degree of risk aversion a.

H Comparative Statics

From equation (19b), we immediately obtain some basic comparative statics results:

1) An increase in the quality of information (n) increases the informativeness of the price system.

2) A decrease in the cost of information increases the informativeness of the price system.

3) A decrease in risk aversion leads informed individuals to take larger positions, and this increases the informativeness of the price system.

Further, all other changes in parameters, such that n, a, and c remain constant, do not change the equilibrium degree of informativeness of the price system; other changes lead only to particular changes in λ of a magnitude to exactly offset them. For example:

4) An increase in noise (σ_x^2) increases the proportion of informed traders. At any given λ, an increase in noise reduces the informativeness of the price system; but it increases the returns to information and leads more individuals to become informed;

the remarkable result obtained above establishes that *the two effects exactly offset each other* so that the equilibrium informativeness of the price system is unchanged. This can be illustrated diagrammatically if we note from (16a) that for a given λ, an increase in σ_x^2 raises m which from (18) lowers $(Var(u^*|\theta))/Var(u^*|w_\lambda)$. Thus from (14) a rise in σ_x^2 leads to a vertical downward shift of the $\gamma(\lambda)$ curve in Figure 1, and thus a higher value of λ^e.

5) Similarly an increase in σ_ϵ^2 for a constant n (equivalent to an increase in the variance of u since n is constant) leads to an increased proportion of individuals becoming informed—and indeed again just enough to offset the increased variance, so that the degree of *informativeness* of the price system remains unchanged. This can also be seen from Figure 1 if (16) is used to note that an increase in σ_ϵ^2 with n held constant by raising σ_θ^2 leads to an increase in m for a given λ. From (18) and (14) this leads to a vertical downward shift of the $\gamma(\lambda)$ curve and thus a higher value of λ^e.

6) It is more difficult to determine what happens if, say σ_θ^2 increases, keeping σ_u^2 constant (implying a fall in σ_ϵ^2), that is, *the information obtained is more informative.* This leads to an increase in n, which from (19b) implies that the equilibrium informativeness of the price system rises. From (16) it is clear that m and nm both fall when σ_θ^2 rises (keeping $\sigma_u^2 = \sigma_\theta^2 + \sigma_\epsilon^2$ constant). This implies that the $\gamma(\lambda)$ curve may shift up or down depending on the precise values of c, a, and n.[8] This ambiguity arises because an improvement in the precision of informed traders' information, with the cost of the information fixed, increases the benefit of being informed. However, some of the improved information is transmitted, via a more informative price system, to the uninformed; this increases the benefits of being uninformed. If n is small, both the price system m is not very informative *and* the marginal value of information to informed traders is high. Thus the *relative* benefits of being informed rises when n rises; implying that the equilibrium λ rises. Conversely when n is large the price system is very informative and the marginal value of information is low to informed traders so the relative benefits of being uninformed rises.

7) From (14) it is clear that an increase in the cost of information c shifts the $\gamma(\lambda)$ curve up and thus decreases the percentage of informed traders.

The above results are summarized in the following theorem.

Theorem 4. *For equilibrium λ such that $0 < \lambda < 1$:*

   A. *The equilibrium informativeness of the price system, ρ_θ^2, rises if n rises, c falls, or a falls.*

---

[8] From (14) and (18) it is clear that λ rises if and only if $Var(u^*|\theta) + Var(u^*|w_\lambda)$ falls due to the rise in σ_θ^2 for a given λ. This occurs if and only if $nm/(1 + m)$ rises. Using (16) to differentiate $nm/(1 + m)$ with respect to σ_ϵ^2 subject to the constraint that $d\sigma_u^2 = 0$ (i.e., $d\sigma_\theta^2 = -d\sigma_\epsilon^2$), we find that the sign of

$$\frac{d}{d\sigma_\theta^2}\left(\frac{nm}{1+m}\right) = sgn\left[m\left(\frac{n+1}{n}\right) - 1\right] = sgn\left[\left(\frac{\gamma}{n-\gamma}\right)\left(\frac{n+1}{n}\right) - 1\right]$$

where $\gamma \equiv e^{2ac} - 1$ and the last equality follows from equation (19a). Thus for n very large the derivative is negative so that λ falls due to an increase in the precision of the informed trader's information. Similarly if n is sufficiently small, the derivative is positive and thus λ rises.

B. *The equilibrium informativeness of the price system is unchanged if σ_x^2 changes, or if σ_u^2 changes with n fixed.*

C. *The equilibrium percentage of informed traders will rise if σ_x^2 rises, σ_u^2 rises for a fixed n, or c falls.*

D. *If $\bar{n}$ satisfies $(e^{2ac} - 1)/(\bar{n} - (e^{2ac} - 1)) = \bar{n}/(\bar{n} + 1)$, then $n(\lesseqgtr)\bar{n}$ implies that λ falls (rises) due to an increase in n.*

Proof. Parts A–C are proved in the above remarks. Part D is proved in footnote 8.

I Price Cannot Fully Reflect Costly Information

We now consider certain limiting cases, for $\gamma(0) \leqslant 1 \leqslant \gamma(1)$, and show that equilibrium does not exist if $c > 0$ and price is fully informative.

1) As the cost of information goes to zero, the price system becomes more informative, but at a positive value of c, say $\hat{c}$, all traders are informed. From (14) and (15) $\hat{c}$ satisfies

$$e^{a\hat{c}}\sqrt{\frac{Var(u^*|\theta)}{Var(u^*|w_1)}} = 1$$

2) From (19a) as the precision of the informed trader's information n goes to infinity, i.e., $\sigma_\epsilon^2 \to 0$ and $\sigma_\theta^2 \to \sigma_u^2$, σ_u^2 held fixed, the price system becomes perfectly informative. Moreover the percentage of informed traders goes to zero! This can be seen from (18) and (15). That is, as $\sigma_\epsilon^2 \to 0$, $nm/(1 + m)$ must stay constant for equilibrium to be maintained. But from (19b) and (17), m falls as σ_ϵ^2 goes to zero. Therefore nm must fall, but nm must not go to zero or else $nm/(1 + m)$ would not be constant. From (16) $nm = (a/\lambda)^2 \sigma_\epsilon^2 \sigma_x^2$, and thus λ must go to zero to prevent nm from going to zero as $\sigma_\epsilon^2 \to 0$.

3) From (16a) and (19a) it is clear that as noise σ_x^2 goes to zero, the percentage of informed traders goes to zero. Further, since (19a) implies that m does not change as σ_x^2 changes, the informativeness of the price system is unchanged as $\sigma_x^2 \to 0$.

Assume that c is small enough so that it is worthwhile for a trader to become informed when no other trader is informed. Then if $\sigma_x^2 = 0$ or $\sigma_\epsilon^2 = 0$, there exists no competitive equilibrium. To see this, note that equilibrium requires either that the ratio of expected utility of the informed to the uninformed be equal to unity, or that if the ratio is larger than unity, no one be informed. We shall show that when no one is informed, it is less than unity so that $\lambda = 0$ cannot be an equilibrium; but when $\lambda > 0$, it is greater than unity. That is, if $\sigma_x^2 = 0$ or $\sigma_\epsilon^2 = 0$, the ratio of expected utilities is not a continuous function of λ at $\lambda = 0$.

This follows immediately from observing that at $\lambda = 0$, $Var(u^*|w_0) = Var\, u^*$, and thus by (14)

$$\frac{EV(W_{Ii}^0)}{EV(W_{Ui}^0)} = e^{ac}\sqrt{\frac{\sigma_\epsilon^2}{\sigma_\epsilon^2 + \sigma_\theta^2}} = e^{ac}\sqrt{\frac{1}{1+n}} \tag{20}$$

while if $\lambda > 0$, by (18)

$$\frac{EV(W_{Ii}^\lambda)}{EV(W_{Ui}^\lambda)} = e^{ac}\sqrt{\frac{1}{1 + n\frac{m}{m+1}}}$$

But if $\sigma_x^2 = 0$ or $\sigma_\epsilon^2 = 0$, then $m = 0$, $nm = 0$ for $\lambda > 0$, and hence

$$\lim_{\lambda \to 0} \frac{EV(W_{Ii}^\lambda)}{EV(W_{Ui}^\lambda)} = e^{ac} \tag{21}$$

It immediately follows that

Theorem 5. (a) *If there is no noise* ($\sigma_x^2 = 0$), *an overall equilibrium does not exist if (and only if)* $e^{ac} < \sqrt{1+n}$. (b) *If information is perfect* ($\sigma_\epsilon^2 = 0$, $n = \infty$), *there never exists an equilibrium.*

Proof. (a) If $e^{ac} < \sqrt{1+n}$, then by (20) and (21), $\gamma(\lambda)$ is discontinuous at $\lambda = 0$; $\lambda = 0$ is not an equilibrium since by (20) $\gamma(0) < 1$; $\lambda > 0$ is not an equilibrium since by (21) $\gamma(\lambda) > 1$.

  (b) If $\sigma_\epsilon^2 = 0$ and $\sigma_\theta^2 = \sigma_u^2$ so that information is perfect, then for $\lambda > 0$, $nm = 0$ by (16) and hence $\gamma(\lambda) > 1$ by (21). From (20) $\gamma(0) = 0 < 1$.

If there is no noise and some traders become informed, then *all* their information is transmitted to the uninformed by the price system. Hence each informed trader acting as a price taker thinks the informativeness of the price system will be unchanged if he becomes uninformed, so $\lambda > 0$ is not an equilibrium. On the other hand, if no traders are informed, then each uninformed trader learns nothing from the price system, and thus he has a desire to become informed (if $e^{ac} < (1+n)^{1/2}$). Similarly if the informed traders get perfect information, then their demands are very sensitive to their information, so that the market-clearing price becomes very sensitive to their information and thus reveals θ to the uninformed. Hence all traders desire to be uninformed. But if all traders are uninformed, each trader can eliminate the risk of his portfolio by the purchase of information, so each trader desires to be informed.

In the next section we show that the non-existence of competitive equilibrium can be thought of as the breakdown of competitive markets due to lack of trade. That is, we will show that as σ_x^2 gets very small, trade goes to zero and markets serve no function. Thus competitive markets close for lack of trade "before" equilibrium ceases to exist at $\sigma_x^2 = 0$.

III ON THE THINNESS OF SPECULATIVE MARKETS

In general, trade takes place because traders differ in endowments, preferences, or beliefs. Grossman (1975, 1977b, 1978) has argued that differences in preferences are not a major factor in explaining the magnitude of trade in speculative markets. For this reason the model in Section II gave all traders the same risk preferences (note that none of the results in Section II are affected by letting traders have different coefficients of absolute risk aversion). In this section we assume that trade requires differences in endowments or beliefs and dispense with differences in risk preference as an explanatory variable.[9]

There is clearly some fixed cost in operating a competitive market. If traders have to bear this cost, then trade in the market must be beneficial. Suppose traders have the same endowments and beliefs. Competitive equilibrium will leave them with allocations which are identical with their initial endowments. Hence, if it is costly to enter such a competitive market, no trader would ever enter. We will show below that in an important class of situations, there is continuity in the amount of net trade. That is, when initial endowments are the same and peoples' beliefs differ *slightly*, then the competitive equilibrium allocation that an individual gets will be only *slightly* different from his initial endowment. Hence, there will only be a slight benefit to entering the competitive market. This could, for sufficiently high operating costs, be outweighed by the cost of entering the market.

The amount of trade occurring at any date is a random variable; a function of θ and x. It is easy to show that it is a normally distributed random variable. Since one of the primary determinants of the size of markets is differences in beliefs, one might have conjectured that markets will be thin, in some sense, if almost all traders are either informed or uninformed. This is not, however, obvious, since the amount of trade by any single trader may be a function of λ as well, and a few active traders can do the job of many small traders. In our model, there is a sense, however, in which our conjecture is correct.

---

[9] In the model described in Section II it was assumed that an individual's endowment $\overline{X}_i$ is independent of the market's per capita endowment x^*. This was done primarily so there would not be useful information in an individual's endowment about the total market endowment. Such information would be useful in equilibrium because an individual observes $P_\lambda(\theta, x)$. If due to observing $\overline{X}_i$, he knows something about x, then by observing $P_\lambda(\theta, x)$, $\overline{X}_i$ is valuable in making inferences about θ. To take this into account is possible, but would add undue complication to a model already overburdened with computations.

We first calculate the magnitude of trades as a function of the exogenous parameters, θ and x. Let $h \equiv \sigma_\epsilon^2$, $\bar{x} = Ex^*$, and $\bar{\theta} \equiv E\theta^*$. (The actual trades will depend on the distribution of random endowments across all of the traders, but these we shall net out.) Per capita net trade is[10]

$$X_I - x = (1 - \lambda)\left[\left(nm + \frac{ah}{\lambda}\right)(x - \bar{x}) + [(m+1)n - 1](\theta - \bar{\theta}) + \bar{x}nm\right]$$

$$\div [1 + m + \lambda nm] \tag{22}$$

Thus, the mean of total informed trade is

$$E\lambda(X_I - x) = \frac{(1 - \lambda)\lambda m \bar{x}}{1 + m + \lambda nm} \tag{23}$$

and its variance is

$$\sigma_\theta^2 (1 - \lambda)^2 \lambda^2 \left[[(m+1)n - 1]^2 + \left(nm + \frac{a\sigma_\epsilon^2}{\lambda}\right)^2 \frac{\sigma_x^2}{\sigma_\theta^2}\right] \div (1 + m + \lambda nm)^2 n^2 \tag{24}$$

In the last section we considered limiting values of the exogenous variables with the property that $\lambda \to 0$. The following theorem will show that the mean and variance of trade go to zero as $\lambda \to 0$. That is, the distribution of $\lambda(X_I - x)$ becomes degenerate at zero as $\lambda \to 0$. This is not trivial because as $\lambda \to 0$ due to $n \to \infty$ (very precise information), the informed trader's demand $X_I(P, \theta)$ goes to infinity at most prices because the risky asset becomes riskless with perfect information.

Theorem 6. (a) *For sufficiently large or small c, the mean and variance of trade is zero.* (b) *As the precision of informed traders' information n goes to infinity, the mean and variance of trade go to zero.*

Proof. (a) From remark 1) in Section II, Part I, $\lambda = 1$ if $c \leqslant \hat{c}$, which from (23) and (24) implies trade is degenerate at zero. From (14), for c sufficiently large, say

---

[10] Calculation of distribution of net trades

$$\frac{\lambda}{ah}(\theta - RP_\lambda) + \frac{(1 - \lambda)\left[(\bar{\theta} - RP_\lambda)(1 + m)n + \theta - \bar{\theta} - \frac{ah}{\lambda}(x - \bar{x})\right]}{ah(1 + m + nm)n} = x$$

or

$$\frac{(\theta - RP_\lambda)}{ah}\left(\lambda + \frac{(1 - \lambda)(1 + m)}{1 + m + nm}\right) = \left(\frac{\theta - RP_\lambda}{ah}\right)\left(\frac{1 + m + \lambda nm}{1 + m + nm}\right)$$

$$= x + \frac{(1 - \lambda)\left([(m+1)n - 1](\theta - \bar{\theta}) + \frac{ah}{\lambda}(x - \bar{x})\right)}{ah(1 + m + \lambda nm)n}$$

or

$$X_I = \frac{1 + m + nm}{1 + m + \lambda nm}\left[x + \frac{(1 - \lambda)\left([(m+1) - 1](\theta - \bar{\theta}) + \frac{ah}{\lambda}(x - \bar{x})\right)}{ah(1 + m + nm)n}\right]$$

$$X_I - x = \frac{(1 - \lambda)\left[\left(nm + \frac{ah}{\lambda}\right)(x - \bar{x}) + [(m+1) - 1](\theta - \bar{\theta}) + \bar{x}nm\right]}{(1 + m + \lambda nm)n}$$

c^0, $\gamma(0) = 1$, so the equilibrium $\lambda = 0$. As c goes to c^0 from below $\lambda \to 0$, and from (14), (15), and (18) $\lim_{c \uparrow c^0}(1 + nm/(1 + m))^{-1/2} = e^{-ac^0}$. Hence $\lim_{c \uparrow c^0}(nm/1 + m)$ is a finite positive number. Thus from (22) mean trade goes to zero as $c \uparrow c^0$. If the numerator and the denominator of (24) are divided by $(1 + m)^2$, then again using the fact that $m/1 + m$ has a finite limit gives the result that as $c \uparrow c^0$, $\lambda \to 0$, and variance of trade goes to zero.

(b) By (14), (15), and (18), $nm/(1 + m)$ is constant as $n \to \infty$. Further, from remark 2) of Section II, Part I, $\lambda \to 0$ as $n \to \infty$. Hence from (23) and (24), the mean and variance of trade go to zero.

(c) From remark 3) in Section II, Part I, m is constant and λ goes to zero as $\sigma_x^2 \to 0$. Therefore mean trade goes to zero. In (24), note that $(nm + a\sigma_\epsilon^2/\lambda)^2 \sigma_x^2/\sigma_\theta^2 = (nm\sigma_x/\sigma_\theta + (m)^{1/2})^2$ by (16a). Hence the variance of trade goes to zero as $\sigma_x^2 \to 0$.

Note further that $\lambda(X_I - x) + (1 - \lambda)(X_U - x) = 0$ implies that no trade will take place as $\lambda \to 1$. Thus, the result that competitive equilibrium is incompatible with informationally efficient markets should be interpreted as meaning that speculative markets where prices reveal a lot of information will be very thin because it will be composed of individuals with very similar beliefs.

IV ON THE POSSIBILITY
OF PERFECT MARKETS

In Section II we showed that the price system reveals the signal w_λ^* to traders, where

$$w_\lambda \equiv \theta - \frac{a\sigma_\epsilon^2}{\lambda}(x - Ex^*)$$

Thus, for given information of informed traders θ, the price system reveals a noisy version of θ. The noise is $(a\sigma_\epsilon^2/\lambda)(x - Ex^*)$. Uninformed traders learn θ to within a random variable with mean zero and variance $(a\sigma_\epsilon^2/\lambda)^2$ $Var\, x^*$, where σ_ϵ^2 is the precision of informed traders' information, $Var\, x^*$ is the amount of endowment uncertainty, λ the fraction of informed traders, and a is the degree of absolute risk aversion. Thus, in general the price system does not reveal all the information about "the true value" of the risky asset. (θ is the true value of the risky asset in that it reflects the best available information about the asset's worth.)

The only way informed traders can earn a return on their activity of information gathering, is if they can use their information to take positions in the market which are "better" than the positions of uninformed traders. "Efficient Markets" theorists have claimed that "at any time prices fully reflect all available information" (see Eugene Fama 1970, p. 383). If this were so then informed traders could not earn a return on their information.

We showed that when the efficient markets hypothesis is true and information is costly, competitive markets break down. This is because when $\sigma_\epsilon^2 = 0$ or $Var\,x^* = 0$, w_λ, and thus price, does reflect all the information. When this happens, each informed trader, because he is in a competitive market, feels that he could stop paying for information and do as well as a trader who pays nothing for information. But all informed traders feel this way. Hence having any positive fraction informed is not an equilibrium. Having no one informed is also not an equilibrium, because then each trader, taking the price as given, feels that there are profits to be made from becoming informed.

Efficient Markets theorists seem to be aware that costless information is a *sufficient* condition for prices to fully reflect all available information (see Fama 1970, p. 387); they are not aware that it is a *necessary* condition. But this is a *reducto ad absurdum*, since price systems and competitive markets are important only when information is costly (see Fredrick Hayek 1945, p. 452).

We are attempting to redefine the Efficient Markets notion, not destroy it. We have shown that when information is very inexpensive, or when informed traders get very precise information, then equilibrium exists and the market price will reveal most of the informed traders' information. However, it was argued in Section III that such markets are likely to be thin because traders have almost homogeneous beliefs.

There is a further conflict. As Grossman (1975a, 1977b) showed, whenever there are differences in beliefs that are not completely arbitraged, there is an incentive to create a market. (Grossman 1977b, analyzed a model of a storable commodity whose spot price did not reveal all information because of the presence of noise. Thus traders were left with differences in beliefs about the future price of the commodity. This led to the opening of a futures market. But then uninformed traders had two prices revealing information to them, implying the elimination of noise.) But, because differences in beliefs are themselves endogenous, arising out of expenditure on information and the informativeness of the price system, the creation of markets eliminates the differences of beliefs which gave rise to them, and thus causes those markets to disappear. If the creation of markets were costless, as is conventionally assumed in equilibrium analyses, equilibrium would never exist. For instance, in our model, were we to introduce an additional security, say a security which paid

$$z = \begin{cases} 1 & \text{if } u > E\theta^* \\ 0 & \text{if } u \leqslant E\theta^* \end{cases}$$

then the demand y for this security by the informed would depend on its price, say q on p and on θ, while the uninformed demand depends only on p and q:

$$\lambda y_I(q, p, \theta) + (1 - \lambda)y_u(q, p) = 0$$

is the condition that demand equals (supply is zero for a pure security). Under weak assumptions, q and p would convey all the information concerning θ. Thus, the market would be "noiseless" and no equilibrium could exist.

Thus, we could argue as soon as the assumptions of the conventional perfect capital markets model are modified to allow even a slight amount of information imperfection and a slight cost of information, the traditional theory becomes untenable. There *cannot* be as many securities as states of nature. For if there were, competitive equilibrium would not exist.

It is only because of costly transactions and the fact that this leads to there being a limited number of markets, that competitive equilibrium can be established.

We have argued that because information is costly, prices cannot perfectly reflect the information which is available, since if it did, those who spent resources to obtain it would receive no compensation. There is a fundamental conflict between the efficiency with which markets spread information and the incentives to acquire information. However, we have said nothing regarding the social benefits of information, nor whether it is socially optimal to have "informationally efficient markets." We hope to examine the welfare properties of the equilibrium allocations herein in future work.

Appendix A

Here we collect some facts on conditional expectations used in the text. If X^* and Y^* are jointly normally distributed then

$$E[X^*|Y^* = Y] = EX^* + \frac{Cov(X^*, Y^*)}{Var(Y^*)}\{Y - EY^*\} \tag{A1}$$

$$Var[X^*|Y^* = Y] = Var(X^*) - \frac{[Cov(X^*, Y^*)]^2}{Var(Y^*)} \tag{A2}$$

(See Paul Hoel 1962, p. 200.) From (A1) note that $E[X^*|Y^*]$ is a function of Y. If the expectation of both sides of (A1) is taken, we see that

$$E\left\{E[X^*|Y^* = Y]\right\} = EX^* \tag{A3}$$

Note that $Var[X^*|Y^* = Y]$ is not a function of Y, as $Var(X^*)$, $Cov(X^*, Y^*)$, and $Var(Y^*)$ are just parameters of the joint distribution of X^* and Y^*.

Two other relevant properties of conditional expectation are

$$E\{E[Y^*|F(X^*)]|X^*\} = E[Y^*|F(X^*)] \tag{A4}$$

$$E\{E[Y^*|X]|F(X^*)\} = E[Y^*|F(X^*)] \tag{A5}$$

where $F(\cdot)$ is a given function on the range of X^* (see Robert Ash 1972, p. 260).

Appendix B

Proof of Theorem 1:
  (a) Suppose $\lambda = 0$; then (9) becomes

$$X_U(P_0(\theta, x), P_0^*) = x \tag{A6}$$

Define

$$P_0(\theta, x) \equiv \frac{E\,\theta^* - ax\sigma_u^2}{R} \tag{A7}$$

where σ_u^2 is the variance of u. Note that $P_0(\theta^*, x^*)$ is uncorrelated with u^*, as x^* is uncorrelated with u^*. Hence

$$E[u^*|P_0^* = P_0(\theta, x)] = E u^* = E\,\theta^* \tag{A8}$$

and

$$Var[u^*|P_0^* = P_0(\theta, x)] = Var[u^*]$$

Substitution of (A8) in (8) yields

$$X_U(P_0^*, P_0(\theta, x)) = \frac{E\,\theta^* - R P_0(\theta, x)}{a\,Var\,u} \tag{A9}$$

Substitution of (A7) in the right-hand side of (A9) yields $X_U(P_0^*(\theta, x), P_0^*) = x$ which was to be shown.

   (b) Suppose $0 < \lambda \leqslant 1$. Let

$$P_\lambda(\theta, x) = \frac{\frac{\lambda}{a\sigma_\epsilon^2} + \frac{(1-\lambda)E[u^*|w_\lambda]}{a\,Var[u^*|w_\lambda]} - E x^*}{R\left[\frac{\lambda}{a\sigma_\epsilon^2} + \frac{(1-\lambda)}{a\,Var[u^*|w_\lambda]}\right]} \tag{A10}$$

Note that from equations (1), (10), (A1) and (A2):

$$E(u^*|w_\lambda) = E\,\theta^* + \frac{\sigma_\theta^2}{Var\,w_\lambda} \cdot (w_\lambda - E\,\theta^*) \tag{A11a}$$

$$Var(u^*|w_\lambda) = \sigma_\theta^2 + \sigma_\epsilon^2 - \frac{\sigma_\theta^2}{Var\,w_\lambda} \tag{A11b}$$

$$Var\,w_\lambda = \sigma_\theta^2 + \left(\frac{a\sigma_\epsilon^2}{\lambda}\right)^2 Var\,x^* \tag{A11c}$$

Since $P_\lambda(\theta, x)$ is a linear function of w_λ, it is immediate that $E(u^*|w_\lambda) \equiv E(u^*|P_\lambda)$, $Var(u^*|w_\lambda) = Var(u^*|P_\lambda)$, etc. To see thãt P_λ^* is an equilibrium, we must show that the following equation holds as an identity in (θ, x), for $P_\lambda(\cdot)$ defined by (A10):

$$\lambda \cdot \frac{\theta - R P_\lambda}{a\sigma_\epsilon^2} + (1 - \lambda)\frac{E[u^*|w_\lambda] - R P_\lambda}{a\,Var[u^*|w_\lambda]} = x \tag{A12}$$

It is immediate from (10) that (A12) holds as an identity in θ and x.

Proof of Theorem 2: (a) *Calculation of the expected utility of the informed.* Using the fact that W_{Ii}^λ is normally distributed conditional on $(\overline{X}_i, \theta, x)$

$$E\left[V\left(W_{Ii}^\lambda\right)|\overline{X}_i, \theta, x\right] = \exp\left[-a\left\{E\left[W_{Ii}^\lambda|\overline{X}_i, \theta, x\right] - \frac{a}{2}Var\left[W_{Ii}^\lambda|\overline{X}_i, \theta, x\right]\right\}\right] \tag{A13}$$

Using (8), (12), and the fact that (θ, x) determines a particular P,

$$E\left[W_{Ii}^\lambda|\overline{X}_i, \theta, x\right] = R(W_{0i} - c) + \frac{(E[u^*|\theta] - RP_\lambda)^2}{a\sigma_\epsilon^2} \tag{A14a}$$

$$Var\left[W_{Ii}^\lambda|\overline{X}_i, \theta, x\right] = \frac{(E[u^*|\theta] - RP_\lambda)^2}{a^2\sigma_\epsilon^2} \tag{A14b}$$

Substitution of (A14) into (A13) yields

$$E\left[V\left(W_{Ii}^\lambda\right)|\overline{X}_i, \theta, x\right] = -\exp\left[-aR(W_{0i} - c) - \frac{1}{2\sigma_\epsilon^2}(E[u^*|\theta] - RP_\lambda)^2\right] \tag{A15}$$

Note that, as $P_\lambda^*(\cdot) = P_\lambda(\theta, x)$,

$$E\left(E\left[V(W_{Ii}^\lambda)|\overline{X}_i, \theta, x\right]|P_\lambda, \overline{X}_i\right) = E\left[V\left(W_{Ii}^\lambda\right)|P_\lambda, \overline{X}_i\right] \tag{A16}$$

(see (A5)). Note that since W_{0i} is nonstochastic conditional on $(P_\lambda, \overline{X}_i)$, equation (A15) implies

$$E\left[V\left(W_{Ii}^\lambda\right)|P_\lambda, \overline{X}_i\right] = -\exp\left[-aR\left(W_{0i}^\lambda - c\right)\right].$$

$$E\left[\left\{\exp\left[-\frac{1}{2\sigma_\epsilon^2}(E[u|\theta] - RP_\lambda)^2\right]\right\}|P_\lambda, \overline{X}_i\right] \tag{A17}$$

Note that by Theorem 1, conditioning on w_λ^* is equivalent to conditioning on P_λ^*. Define

$$h_\lambda \equiv Var(E[u^*|\theta]|w_\lambda) = Var(\theta|w_\lambda), h_0 \equiv \sigma_\epsilon^2 \equiv h \tag{A18}$$

$$Z \equiv \frac{E[u^*|\theta] - RP_\lambda}{\sqrt{h_\lambda}} \tag{A19}$$

Using (3) and (A18), equation (A17) can be written as

$$E\left[V\left(W_{Ii}^\lambda\right)|P_\lambda, \overline{X}_i\right] = e^{ac}V(RW_{0i})E\left[\exp\left[-\frac{h_\lambda}{2\sigma_\epsilon^2}Z^2\right]|w_\lambda\right] \tag{A20}$$

since $\overline{X}_i$ and w_λ are independent. Conditional on w_λ, P_λ is nonstochastic and $E[u^*|\theta]$ is normal. Hence conditional on w_λ, $(Z^*)^2$ has a noncentral *chi*-square distribution (see C. Rao, p. 181). Then for $t > 0$ the moment generating function for $(Z^*)^2$ can be written

$$E[e^{-tZ^2}|w_\lambda] = \frac{1}{\sqrt{1 + 2t}}\exp\left[\frac{-(E[Z|w_\lambda])^2t}{1 + 2t}\right] \tag{A21}$$

Note that $E[u^*|\theta] = E[u^*|\theta, x]$. Hence

$$E\left[E[u^*|\theta]|w_\lambda\right] = E[u^*|w_\lambda] = E\theta^* + \frac{\sigma_\theta^2}{Var\,w_\lambda}(w_\lambda - E\theta^*) \tag{A22}$$

since w_λ is just a function of (θ, x). Therefore

$$E[Z^*|w_\lambda] = \frac{E[u^*|w_\lambda] - RP_\lambda}{\sqrt{h_\lambda}} \tag{A23}$$

Since $u = \theta + \epsilon$

$$Var(u^*|w_\lambda) = \sigma_\epsilon^2 + Var(\theta^*|w_\lambda) = \sigma_\epsilon^2 + h_\lambda \tag{A24}$$

The nondegeneracy assumptions on (x^*, ϵ^*, u^*) imply $h_\lambda > 0$. Set $t = (h_\lambda/2\sigma_\epsilon^2)$; and evaluate (A21) using (A23) and (A24):

$$E\left[\exp\left[-\frac{h_\lambda}{2\sigma_\epsilon^2}Z^2\right]|w_\lambda\right] = \sqrt{\frac{Var(u^*|\theta)}{Var(u^*|w_\lambda)}} \cdot \exp\left(\frac{-(E(u^*|w_\lambda) - RP_\lambda)^2}{2Var(u^*|w_\lambda)}\right) \tag{A25}$$

This permits the evaluation of (A20).

(b) *Calculation of expected utility of the uninformed.* Equations (8), (5), and the normality of W_{Ui}^λ conditional on w_λ can be used to show, by calculations parallel to (A13)–(A25), that

$$E\left[V(W_{Ui}^\lambda)|w_\lambda, \overline{X}_i\right] = V(RW_{0i})\exp\left(\frac{-(E(u^*|w_\lambda) - RP_\lambda)^2}{2Var(u^*|w_\lambda)}\right) \tag{A26}$$

Hence

$$E\left[V\left(W_{Ii}^\lambda\right)|w_\lambda, \overline{X}_i\right] - E\left[V\left(W_{Ui}^\lambda\right)|w_\lambda, \overline{X}_i\right] = \left[e^{ac}\sqrt{\frac{Var(u^*|\theta)}{Var(u^*|w_\lambda)}} - 1\right]$$

$$\times E\left[V\left(W_{Ui}^\lambda\right)|w_\lambda, \overline{X}_i\right] \tag{A27}$$

Taking expectations of both sides of (A27) yields:

$$E\left[V\left(W_{Ii}^\lambda\right)\right] - E\left[V\left(W_{Ui}^\lambda\right)\right] = \left[e^{ac}\sqrt{\frac{Var(u^*|\theta)}{Var(u^*|w_\lambda)}} - 1\right]EV\left(W_{Ui}^\lambda\right) \tag{A28}$$

Equation (13) follows immediately from (A28).

CHAPTER 22

A NONCONCAVITY IN THE VALUE OF INFORMATION*

1 INTRODUCTION

It is a truism of statistical decision theory that costless information is harmless, and if it is relevant to the decision problem at hand then it will have positive value.[1] In other words, as an input into economic decision-making, the productivity of information is non-negative, and is typically positive. Does information also obey the Law of Diminishing Returns? In particular, is the marginal productivity of information strictly positive, at least for small amounts?

The marginal productivity of information depends, of course, on the way the quantity of information is measured. We know that, in general, there is no way to measure the quantity of information (as a real number) so that, of two information structures, one is more valuable if and only if it has "more" information.[2] Nevertheless, for a particular decision problem there may be a family of available information structures indexed by a real parameter, in which larger values of the parameter correspond to more costly information, and in which a zero value of the parameter corresponds to a structure that is both costless and completely "noninformative" (in a sense to be defined below). In this context, we shall be able to talk meaningfully about a "small amount of information", i.e. the case in which the parameter is close to zero.

The net value of a particular information structure may be defined as the maximum expected utility that can be achieved using it (after subtracting the cost). The

* Written with Roy Radner. Research supported in part by the National Science Foundation. Reprinted with permission from *Baysian Models in Economic Theory*, edited by M. Boyer and R.E. Kihlstrom. © *Elsevier Science Publishers B. V., 1984.*

[1] See, for example, Marschak and Radner (1972, ch. 2).

[2] This is true, in particular, of the information measure commonly associated with the names of Shannon and Wiener; see, again, Marschak and Radner (1972, ch. 2).

object of this chapter is to show that, for an important class of decision problems, a small amount of information has a negative marginal net value whenever the marginal cost of information is strictly positive.[3] This result has some important implications. In particular, it implies: (1) if there is some amount of information that has positive net value, then value cannot be a concave function of the amount of information, i.e. there must be *increasing returns to information* over some range of the parameter; (2) the demand for information will not be a continuous function of its price; and (3) in economic activities where information is important, specialization may be common.

In section 2 we present the general theorem and its proof, while the remaining sections develop several applications of the general theorem: to consumer behavior (the optimal allocation of a portfolio); to problems of screening; and to a linear prediction problem.

Before presenting the proof, it may be worthwhile to present briefly the general context of the problem we are investigating. We consider a decision-maker facing a set of decisions. The outcome (payoff) depends on the decision as well as on the state of nature. There is a set of signals. Information provides the decision-maker with a basis for translating the signals into different actions. This basis is quantified in terms of the conditional probabilities of the signals given the states of nature. A completely noninformative information structure is one for which the conditional probability distribution of signals is the same for all states of nature. With a noninformative information structure, the decision-maker might just as well take the same action regardless of the signal received. A "small amount of information" leads to a small change in the conditional probabilities of signals given states. To prove our main result we shall require: (1) in the neighborhood of zero information these conditional probabilities vary smoothly (differentiably), and the corresponding optimal decisions vary continuously, with the amount of information; (2) the optimal decision for zero information is the same for all signals; and (3) utility is a continuous function.

2 THE BASIC THEOREM AND SOME COROLLARIES

We consider a family of decision problems, corresponding to a family of alternative information structures. Let S denote the set of alternative *states of the environment*, and Y the set of alternative *information signals*. S and Y are finite.

An *information structure* is a Markov matrix $((p_{sy}))$, where p_{sy} is the conditional probability of signal y given state s. The family of available information structures is

---

[3] A similar result holds if we define the net value of a particular information structure in terms of its dollar-equivalent value, in those problems in which such a dollar-equivalent is meaningful (see below, end of section 2).

indexed by a (real-valued) *parameter* θ. The index set, Θ, is taken to be an interval $[0, \theta_1]$, where θ_1 is strictly positive.

In response to an information signal, the decision-maker chooses an *action*; the set A of alternative actions is a subset of K-dimensional Euclidean space, IR^K. A *decision function* is a function, say $d = (d_y)$ from Y to A, where d_y denotes the action chosen in response to signal y.

There is a further *constraint* on action, determined by an inequality

$$g(a, \theta) \leqslant 0, \tag{1}$$

where g is a real-valued function defined on $A \times \Theta$. For each θ in Θ, let $\mathscr{A}(\theta)$ denote the set of actions in A that satisfy the constraint (1), and let $\mathscr{D}(\theta)$ denote the set of decision functions d that satisfy

$$g(d_y, \theta) \leqslant 0 \quad \text{all } y. \tag{2}$$

Call $\mathscr{D}(\theta)$ the set of admissible decision functions, given θ.

Given the state s, the action a, and the parameter θ, the *payoff* to the decision-maker is $u_s(a, \theta)$.

Let ϕ_s denote the prior probability of state s. The *expected value of a decision function* d, given θ, is:

$$U(d, \theta) \equiv \sum_{s,y} \phi_s \, p_{sy}(\theta) u_s(d_y, \theta). \tag{3}$$

The value of the information structure θ is

$$V(\theta) \equiv \sup\{U(d, \theta): d \quad \text{in} \quad \mathscr{D}(\theta)\}. \tag{4}$$

A decision function is *optimal for* θ if it is admissible for θ and its expected value achieves the supremum, $V(\theta)$. From (3) it is clear that, if d is a decision function that is optimal for θ, then for every y the decision d_y is an action that maximizes

$$\sum_s \phi_s \, p_{sy}(\theta) u_s(a, \theta)$$

subject to a in $\mathscr{A}(\theta)$.

We assume that among the available information structures there is one that is completely noninformative;[4] this one will be designated by $\theta = 0$. By the definition of "noninformative", $p_{sy}(0)$ is independent of s, for each y; we denote this common value by p_y^0. Thus,

$$p_{sy}(0) = p_y^0 \quad \text{all } y. \tag{5}$$

If d is optimal for $\theta = 0$, then for each y the decision d_y maximizes

$$\sum_s \phi_s \, p_{sy}(0) u_s(a, 0)$$

---

[4] For a systematic treatment of information structures and their comparison, see McGuire (1972).

on $\mathcal{A}(\theta)$; by the definition of noninformative information structure, (5), this last expression is equal to:

$$p_y^0 \sum_s \phi_s u_s(a, 0).$$

Hence, for $\theta = 0$, we may take the optimal action to be independent of the signal y, say a^0; i.e.

$$d_y = a^0 \quad \text{for all} \quad y. \tag{6}$$

We shall call a decision function *flat* if it results in the same action for all information signals y. In this terminology, we have just shown that for $\theta = 0$ there is an optimal decision function that is flat.

In the interpretation of the following theorem, the reader may have in mind the situation in which larger values of θ correspond to information structures that are more informative (in some sense), but also more "costly". The increased "cost" may be reflected in a lower payoff (u_s a decreasing function of θ), or a smaller constraint set (g an increasing function of θ), or both. However, for a strict interpretation of the theorem, there is no need to suppose that larger θ corresponds to more informative structures, but only that $\theta = 0$ corresponds to a noninformative structure.

We shall be concerned with a family of decision functions (one for each θ), which we can represent as a mapping D from Θ to the set of decision functions; thus, for every θ, $D(\theta)$ is an admissible decision function for θ. Since the set Y of signals is finite, each decision function may be thought of as a point in a Euclidean vector space of dimension equal to K times the number of signals in Y. Thus, a family D of decision functions is itself a function from Θ to this vector space.

Theorem. *If (i) for every s in S and y in Y, $p_{sy}(\cdot)$ is differentiable at $\theta = 0$, and (ii) for every s in S and a in A, $u_s(a, \cdot)$ is monotone nonincreasing and $g(a, \cdot)$ is monotone nondecreasing on Θ, and $u_s(\cdot, \cdot)$ is continuous on $A \times \Theta$, then for any family D of decision functions that is both flat and continuous at $\theta = 0$:*

$$\limsup_{\theta \to 0} \frac{U[D(\theta), \theta] - U[D(0), 0]}{\theta} \leq 0.$$

Proof. From (3):

$$U[D(\theta), \theta] - U[D(0), 0] = T_1(\theta) + T_2(\theta),$$

where

$$T_1(\theta) = \sum_{s,y} \phi_s p_{sy}(\theta) u_s[D_y(\theta), \theta] - \sum_{s,y} \phi_s p_{sy}(0) u_s[D_y(\theta), \theta],$$

$$T_2(\theta) = \sum_{s,y} \phi_s p_{sy}(0) u_s[D_y(\theta), \theta] - \sum_{s,y} \phi_s p_{sy}(0) u_s[D_y(0), 0].$$

Since $u_s(a, \cdot)$ is monotone nonincreasing on Θ,

$$u_s[D_y(\theta), \theta] \leq u_s[D_y(\theta), 0]. \tag{7}$$

Since $g(a, \cdot)$ is monotone nondecreasing, the decision function $D(\theta)$ is admissible for $\theta = 0$; but $D(0)$ is optimal for $\theta = 0$, so that

$$\sum_{s,y} \phi_s \, p_{sy}(0) u_s \, [D_y(\theta), 0] \leqslant \sum_{s,y} \phi_s \, p_{sy}(0) u_s \, [D_y(0), 0]. \tag{8}$$

Combining (7) and (8), we get:

$$T_2(\theta) \leqslant 0,$$

so that

$$\limsup_{\theta \to 0} \frac{T_2(\theta)}{\theta} \leqslant 0. \tag{9}$$

We may rewrite $T_1(\theta)$ as

$$T_1(\theta) = \sum_{s,y} \phi_s \, [p_{sy}(\theta) - p_{sy}(0)] u_s \, [D_y(\theta), \theta].$$

Since $D(0)$ is flat, there is an action, say a^0, such that $D_y(0) = a^0$ for all signals y. Also, D is continuous at 0, and $u_s (\cdot, \cdot)$ is continuous for each s. Therefore

$$\lim_{\theta \to 0} u_s \, [D_y(\theta), \theta] = u_s \, (a^0, 0),$$

and, since $p_{sy}(\cdot)$ is differentiable at 0,

$$\lim_{\theta \to 0} \frac{T_1(\theta)}{\theta} = \sum_{s,y} \phi_s \, p'_{sy}(0) u_s \, (a^0, 0)$$

$$= \sum_s \phi_s \, u_s \, (a^0, 0) \sum_y p'_{sy}(0).$$

For every s and θ:

$$\sum_y p_{sy}(\theta) = 1;$$

hence,

$$\sum_y p'_{sy}(0) = 0,$$

$$\lim_{\theta \to 0} \frac{T_1(\theta)}{\theta} = 0. \tag{10}$$

Therefore

$$\limsup_{\theta \to 0} \frac{T_1(\theta) + T_2(\theta)}{\theta} \leqslant 0,$$

which completes the proof.

A family D of decision functions is *optimal* if, for every θ, $D(\theta)$ is optimal for θ. The following corollary follows immediately from the theorem.

Corollary. *If hypotheses (i) and (ii) of the theorem are satisfied, and if there is an optimal family of decision functions that is both flat and continuous at $\theta = 0$, then*

$$\limsup_{\theta \to 0} \frac{V(\theta) - V(0)}{\theta} \leqslant 0. \tag{11}$$

To see that if the marginal cost of information is *strictly* positive, then the marginal net value of information (at $\theta = 0$) will be *strictly* negative, we consider a suitably specialized formulation. Suppose that: (i) the "gross" outcome of action a in state s is a real number (e.g. money), denoted by $w_s(a)$; (ii) the cost of information structure θ is $C(\theta)$; and (iii) the "utility" of the net outcome is $v_s[w_s(a) - C(\theta)]$. Thus, the pay off function $u_s(\cdot, \cdot)$ is given by:

$$u_s(a, \theta) = v_s[w_s(a) - C(\theta)]. \tag{12}$$

Assume that v_s and C have continuous and strictly positive derivatives, that $C(0) = 0$, and that w_s is continuous. Consider the function T_2 defined in the proof of the theorem. We may rewrite this function as:

$$T_2(\theta) = \sum_{s,y} \phi_s\, p_{sy}(0)\{u_s[D_y(\theta), \theta] - u_s[D_y(\theta), 0]$$

$$+ u_s[D_y(\theta), 0] - u_s[D_y(0), 0]\}. \tag{13}$$

Concentrating first on the first difference in the curly brackets of (13), and making use of the special formulation (12), we have:

$$u_s[D_y(\theta), \theta] - u_s[D_y(\theta), 0] = v_s[w_s(D_y[\theta]) - C(\theta)] - v_s[w_s(D[\theta])]$$

$$= -v'_s[w_s(D_y[\theta])]C(\theta) + 0(\theta), \tag{14}$$

where $0(\theta)/\theta$ converges to 0 as θ approaches 0. Hence,

$$\lim_{\theta \to 0} \frac{u_s[D_y(\theta), \theta] - u_s[D_y(\theta), 0]}{\theta} = -v'_s[w_s(D_y[0])]C'(0), \tag{15}$$

which is strictly negative. Combining (15) and (8) with (13) gives:

$$\limsup_{\theta \to 0} \frac{T_2(\theta)}{\theta} < 0,$$

which is a strengthening of (9). Hence, we can strengthen the conclusion of the theorem to:

$$\limsup_{\theta \to 0} \frac{U[D(\theta), \theta] - U[D(0), 0]}{\theta} < 0. \tag{16}$$

A corresponding analysis could be made to cover the case in which the effect of the cost of information is to restrict the set of admissible decisions, i.e. the case in which the constraint (2) is binding at $\theta = 0$ and the function $g(a, \cdot)$ is strictly increasing in θ, for every action a.

3 A LINEAR PREDICTION PROBLEM

Our first example does not quite fit theoretical framework in that the set S of states of the environment and the set Y of signals are both infinite. Nevertheless, the example provides a brief illustration of the basic result in a framework that is probably quite familiar to most readers.

Assume that y and s are normally distributed random variables with

$$\text{Corr}(y, s) = \rho. \tag{17}$$

We choose our units so that

$$\text{Var}(s) = \text{Var}(y) = 1, \tag{18}$$

and we choose our origins so that

$$Es = Ey = 0. \tag{19}$$

Let θ, the information structure, be represented by ρ, the correlation coefficient between s and y:

$$\theta \equiv \rho. \tag{20}$$

Let the gross payoff associated with taking some action a if state s occurs be:

$$-(a - s)^2,$$

and the net payoff be:

$$u(s, a, \theta) = -(a - s)^2 - C(\theta), \tag{21}$$

where $C(\theta)$ is the cost of obtaining the information structure θ. Assume that

$$C(0) = 0 \quad \text{and} \quad C'(0) > 0. \tag{22}$$

Thus, observing a variable that is uncorrelated with s is costless; observing any variable that is correlated with s has some cost.

The optimal decision rule, given θ, is the regression of s on y:

$$D_y(\theta) = E(s|y)$$
$$= \rho y. \tag{23}$$

Substituting (23) into (21), we immediately obtain the *value* of the information structure θ, i.e. the expected payoff using the optimal decision rule:

$$V(\theta) = \theta^2 - 1 - C(\theta), \tag{24}$$

so that

$$V'(\theta) = 2\theta - C'(\theta), \tag{25}$$

$$V'(0) = -C'(0) < 0. \tag{26}$$

If, instead of (20), we represent our information structure by

$$\theta = \rho^2, \tag{20'}$$

then, instead of (24), we obtain:

$$V(\theta) = \theta - 1 - \tilde{C}(\theta), \tag{24'}$$

where $\tilde{C}(\theta) \equiv C(\theta^{1/2})$. Thus,

$$V'(0) = 1 - \tilde{C}'(0), \tag{25'}$$

which could be positive. This appears to contradict our theorem. However, with this second representation of the "quantity" of information, condition (i) of the basic theorem, is violated. The conditional distribution of y given s is normal with mean ρs and variance $(1 - \rho^2)$; the corresponding conditional density is

$$p_{sy} = \frac{1}{[2\pi(1 - \rho^2)]^{1/2}} \exp\left(-\frac{(y - \rho s)^2}{2(1 - \rho^2)}\right).$$

One can verify that if $\theta = \rho^2$, then

$$\lim_{\theta \to 0} \frac{dp_{sy}}{d\theta} = +\infty,$$

so that p_{sy} would not be differentiable in θ at $\theta = 0$.

4 A Portfolio Model[5]

There are n securities, each of which has a price of one dollar, and n corresponding states. Security s pays r_s if state s occurs, and nothing otherwise. The investor has an initial wealth W, of which he allocates part to the purchase of information and the remainder to the purchase of securities. Let $C(\theta)$ denote the cost of information structure θ, and let

$$a_{ys}(\theta)[W - C(\theta)]$$

denote the remaining wealth allocated to the purchase of security s if signal y is observed; then the allocation proportions, $a_{ys}(\theta)$, must satisfy

$$\sum_s a_{ys}(\theta) = 1 \quad \text{all } y. \tag{27}$$

[5] Models like this one have been discussed frequently. See, for example, Arrow (1972b) and the references given there.

If signal y is observed and state s occurs, the payoff (return) from the purchase of securities will be:

$$r_s a_{ys}(\theta)[W - C(\theta)].$$

Assume that the investor's utility function is logarithmic. Then the expected utility associated with an information structure θ and allocation proportions $a_{ys}(\theta)$ is:

$$\sum_{s,y} \phi_s \, p_{sy}(\theta) \log\{r_s a_{ys}(\theta)[W - C(\theta)]\}, \tag{28}$$

where, as in section 2, ϕ_s is the prior probability of state s, and $p_{sy}(\theta)$ is the conditional probability of signal y given state s (for the information structure θ). The (unconditional) probability that signal y is observed is:

$$q_y(\theta) \equiv \sum \phi_s \, p_{sy}(\theta),$$

and the conditional ("posterior") probability of state s, given signal y, is:

$$\Pi_{ys}(\theta) \equiv \frac{\phi_s \, p_{sy}(\theta)}{q_y(\theta)}.$$

As in section 2, $\theta = 0$ denotes a noninformative information structure, so that

$$p_{sy}(0) = p_y^0 \quad \text{all } s,$$

$$q_y(0) = p_y^0, \quad \Pi_{ys}(0) = \phi_s. \tag{29}$$

With the foregoing notation, we can express the expected utility (28) as:

$$\sum_y q_y(\theta) \sum_s \Pi_{ys}(\theta) \log\{r_s a_{ys}(\theta)[W - C(\theta)]\}. \tag{30}$$

It is straightforward to verify that the optimal allocation proportions are equal to the corresponding conditional probabilities, i.e.

$$\hat{a}_{ys}(\theta) = \Pi_{ys}(\theta).$$

Therefore the net value of the information structure θ is:

$$V(\theta) = \sum_y q_y(\theta) \sum_s \Pi_{ys}(\theta) \log\{r_s \Pi_{sy}(\theta)[W - C(\theta)]\}. \tag{31}$$

The expression (31) for the value of θ can be rewritten in a way that relates it to the Shannon–Wiener measure of information:

$$V(\theta) = I(\theta) + f(\theta) + \log\{W - C(\theta)] + \sum_s \phi_s \log \phi_s, \tag{32}$$

where

$$I(\theta) = \sum_y q_y(\theta) \sum_s \Pi_{ys}(\theta) \log \Pi_{ys}(\theta) - \sum_s \phi_s \log \phi_s, \tag{33}$$

$$f = \sum_s \phi_s \log r_s. \tag{34}$$

Recall that the Shannon–Wiener measure of "uncertainty" in a probability distribution $P = (P_i)$ is defined as:

$$-\sum_i P_i \log P_i.$$

If signal y is observed, the conditional uncertainty about s is:

$$-\sum_s \Pi_{ys}(\theta) \log \Pi_{ys}(\theta).$$

Therefore $I(\theta)$ is the expected *reduction* in uncertainty about s associated with the information structure θ.

For example, consider the special case in which there are two states and two signals, with

$$p_{11} = p_{22} = 1/2 + \theta, \quad p_{12} = p_{21} = 1/2 - \theta,$$
$$\phi_1 = \phi_2 = 1/2, \quad 0 \leqslant \theta \leqslant 1/2.$$

Then

$$\Pi_{11}(\theta) = \Pi_{22}(\theta) = 1/2 + \theta, \Pi_{12}(\theta) = \Pi_{21}(\theta) = 1/2 - \theta,$$
$$I(\theta) = (1/2 + \theta) \log(1/2 + \theta) + (1/2 - \theta) \log(1/2 - \theta) + \log 2.$$

Here $I(\theta)$ varies from 0 ($\theta = 0$) to $\log 2$ ($\theta = 1/2$), the latter corresponding to "perfect information".

We return now to our more general formula (32), and calculate the marginal net value of information. First, we write $I(\theta)$ as

$$I(\theta) = \sum_{s,y} \phi_s\, p_{sy}(\theta) \log \Pi_{ys}(\theta) - \sum_s \phi_s \log \phi_s.$$

Differentiation with respect to θ yields:

$$I'(\theta) = \sum_{s,y} \left[\frac{\phi_s\, p_{sy}(\theta) \Pi'_{ys}(\theta)}{\Pi_{sy}(\theta)} + \phi_s\, p'_{sy}(\theta) \log \Pi_{ys}(\theta) \right]$$

$$= \sum_{s,y} \left[q_y(\theta) \Pi'_{ys}(\theta) + \phi_s\, p'_{sy}(\theta) \log \Pi_{ys}(\theta) \right]$$

$$= \sum_y q_y(\theta) \sum_s \Pi'_{ys}(\theta) + \sum_s \phi_s \sum_y p'_{sy}(\theta) \log \Pi_{ys}(\theta). \tag{35}$$

Since $\sum_s \Pi_{ys}(\theta) = 1$ for all y and θ, $\sum_s \Pi'_{ys}(\theta) = 0$, all s and θ. Similarly

$$\sum_y p'_{sy}(\theta) = 0, \quad \text{all } s \text{ and } \theta. \tag{36}$$

Therefore, letting $\theta = 0$, and using (29):

$$I'(0) = 0 + \sum_s \phi_s \log \phi_s \sum_y p'_{sy}(0)$$

$$= 0. \tag{37}$$

Since f is independent of θ, and $C(0) = 0$,

$$V'(0) = -\frac{C'(0)}{W}. \tag{38}$$

Thus, if the marginal cost of information is strictly positive, the marginal net value of information is negative at $\theta = 0$.

In the above analysis we calculated the value of information in terms of "utility units"; alternatively, we could have calculated the amount $\hat{V}(\theta)$ the investor would have been willing to give up to acquire the given information structure, i.e. $\hat{V}(\theta)$ is given by the solution of:

$$I(\theta) + f + \log[W - \hat{V}(\theta)] = I(0) + f + \log W,$$

or equivalently,

$$-\log \frac{W - \hat{V}(\theta)}{W} = [I(\theta) - I(0)]. \tag{39}$$

Differentiating (39) with respect to θ and solving for $\hat{V}'(\theta)$ one gets:

$$\hat{V}'(\theta) = [W - \hat{V}(\theta)]I'(\theta) \geqslant 0,$$

$$\hat{V}'(0) = [W - \hat{V}(0)]I'(0) = 0.$$

Thus, although the marginal "money value" of information is non-negative, it is zero at $\theta = 0$.

5 A General Screening Model[6]

A population consists of I types of individual, and each individual is to be assigned by a firm to one of J jobs. Let N_i denote the number of individuals in the population who are of type i (all $N_i > 0$). An examination θ is administered to each individual, and results in a "label" y for that individual ($y = 1, \ldots, I$); this label is the signal on the basis of which the individual is assigned to a job j. The decision rule, (d_y), relates the label of the individual to the job to which he is assigned. We represent this by the

---

[6] For a more extensive discussion of screening models, see Stiglitz (1975c).

matrix (d_{yj}), where

$$d_{yj} = \begin{cases} 1 & \text{if an individual of label } y \text{ is assigned to job } j, \text{ and} \\ 0 & \text{otherwise.} \end{cases} \qquad (40)$$

If an individual of type i is assigned to job j, the dollar value of his output is b_{ij}. Let $p_{iy}(\theta)$ denote the probability that an individual receives the label y, conditional on being of type i. Then, for a given decision rule, (d_{yj}), the expected value of output is:

$$Q(\theta) \equiv \sum_i N_i \sum_y p_{iy}(\theta) \sum_j d_{yj} b_{ij}. \qquad (41)$$

If the cost of the examination θ is $C(\theta)$, then the expected net profit to the firm is

$$Q(\theta) - C(\theta), \qquad (42)$$

and the firm's objective is to choose the examination θ and the decision rule (d_{yj}) so is to maximize this expected net profit.

Let $G(\theta)$ denote the maximum expected value of output, given θ, i.e. the maximum of (41) with respect to the decision rule (d_{yj}). If we write (41) as

$$Q(\theta) = \sum_y \sum_j d_{yj} \sum_i N_i p_{iy}(\theta) b_{ij}, \qquad (43)$$

it is easy to see that this maximum is attained by assigning each individual with label y to a job j for which

$$\sum_i N_i p_{iy}(\theta) b_{ij}$$

is maximum. Hence,

$$G(\theta) = \sum_y \max_j \sum_i N_i p_{iy}(\theta) b_{ij}, \qquad (44)$$

and the (expected) value of the examination θ is:

$$V(\theta) = G(\theta) - C(\theta). \qquad (45)$$

As we have formulated the screening problem, the decision variables are discrete, rather than continuous. However, if we allow "randomized" decisions, then we can reinterpret d_{yj} as the probability that a person with label y is assigned to job j. With this interpretation, (40) is replaced by:

$$\begin{cases} d_{yi} \geqslant 0 & \text{all } y \text{ and } j, \\ \sum_j d_{yj} = 1 & \text{all } y. \end{cases} \qquad (46)$$

Because of the linearity of $Q(\theta)$ in the variables (d_{yj}), any decision rule that was optimal for the first formulation is optimal for the second, and the formulae (44) and (45) are still valid for the value of the examination.

We now examine the conditions under which $G'(0) = 0$. There are two cases, according as the optimal assignment for $\theta = 0$ is or is not unique. Recall that for a noninformative examination ($\theta = 0$):

$$p_{iy}(0) = p_y^0 \quad \text{all } i. \tag{47}$$

Hence, for $\theta = 0$:

$$G(0) = \sum_y p_y^0 \max_j \sum_i N_i b_{ij}, \tag{48}$$

and each individual, regardless of label, should be assigned to a job j^0 for which $\sum_j N_i b_{ij}$ is at a maximum. (Of course, if $p_y^0 = 0$ for some label y, then all assignments for that label are optimal!) There are two cases.

Case I. j^0 *is unique, and* $p_y^0 > 0$ *for all y.*

In this case,

$$\sum_i N_i b_{ij^0} > \sum_i N_i b_{ij} \quad \text{all } j \neq j^0. \tag{49}$$

If $p_{ij}(\theta)$ is continuous in θ, then for all sufficiently small θ, say $0 \leqslant \theta \leqslant \theta_0$, and all y:

$$\sum_i N_i p_{iy}(\theta) b_{ij^0} > \sum_i N_i p_{iy}(\theta) b_{ij}, \quad j \neq j^0, \tag{50}$$

and so

$$G(\theta) = G(0), \quad 0 \leqslant \theta \leqslant \theta^0. \tag{51}$$

Hence,

$$G'(0) = 0, \tag{52}$$

and if $C'(0) > 0$, $V'(0) < 0$, so that *the net marginal value of the examination is negative for θ near zero.*

Case II. j^0 *is not unique, and/or* $p_y^0 = 0$ *for some y.*

To illustrate the implications of this case, we consider the special case of two types and two jobs ($I = J = 2$), with p_1^0 and p_2^0 both strictly positive. If j^0 is not unique, then

$$N_1 b_{11} + N_2 b_{21} = N_1 b_{12} + N_2 b_{22}. \tag{53}$$

For θ small but not zero, it will typically be true that, for both y:

$$N_1 p_{1y}(\theta) b_{11} + N_2 p_{2y}(\theta) b_{21} \neq N_1 p_{1y}(\theta) b_{12} + N_2 p_{2y}(\theta) b_{22}. \tag{54}$$

Without further loss of generality, we may suppose that the left-hand side of (54) is larger than the right-hand side for $y = 1$, and therefore the right-hand side is the larger for $y = 2$ (this last follows from (53) and the fact that

$$p_{i1}(\theta) + p_{i2}(\theta) = 1 \tag{55}$$

for each i). In other words, for θ small but not zero, individuals with label 1 should be assigned to job 1, and those with label 2 should be assigned to job 2. It follows that

$$G(\theta) = [N_1 p_{11}(\theta)b_{11} + N_2 p_{21}(\theta)b_{21}] + [N_1 p_{12}(\theta)b_{12} + N_2 p_{22}(\theta)b_{22}]$$

$$= N_1[p_{11}(\theta)b_{11} + p_{12}(\theta)b_{12}] + N_2[p_{21}(\theta)b_{21} + p_{22}(\theta)b_{22}],$$

and from this and (55) that

$$G'(\theta) = N_1 p'_{11}(\theta)(b_{11} - b_{12}) + N_2 p'_{22}(\theta)(b_{22} - b_{21}). \tag{56}$$

But, from (53):

$$N_1(b_{11} - b_{12}) = N_2(b_{22} - b_{21}), \tag{57}$$

so

$$G'(\theta) = [p'_{11}(\theta) + p'_{22}(\theta)]N_1(b_{11} - b_{12}). \tag{58}$$

We now show that $G'(0) > 0$ if $p'_{11}(0)$ and $p'_{22}(0)$ are not both zero, i.e. if the examination is informative for small θ. First we note that, by our convention that (for small θ) individuals with label 1 should be assigned to job 1:

$$N_1 p_{11}(\theta)b_{11} + N_2 p_{21}(\theta)b_{21} > N_1 p_{11}(\theta)b_{12} + N_2 p_{21}(\theta)b_{22},$$

$$p_{11}(\theta)N_1(b_{11} - b_{12}) > p_{21}(\theta)N_2(b_{22} - b_{21}),$$

so, using (53) again, and the fact that $N_1 > 0$:

$$[p_{11}(\theta) - p_{21}(\theta)][b_{11} - b_{12}] > 0. \tag{59}$$

Thus $[p_{11}(\theta) - p_{21}(\theta)]$ and $[b_{11} - b_{12}]$ are of the same sign. This has a natural interpretation. The conditional probabilities that an individual is of type 1 and type 2, respectively, given the label 1, are proportional to $p_{11}(\theta)$ and $p_{21}(\theta)$. If, conditional on the label 1, and individual is more likely to be of type 1 than of type 2 $[p_{11}(\theta) > p_{21}(\theta)]$, and if an individual of type 1 is more productive in job 1 than in job 2 $(b_{11} > b_{12})$, then an individual with label 1 should be assigned to job 1. The same assignment should be made if the individual is more likely to be of type 2 than of type 1 $[p_{11}(\theta) < p_{21}(\theta)]$, and is more productive in job 2 than in job 1 $(b_{11} < b_{12})$.

Suppose that $b_{11} > b_{12}$; then $p_{11}(\theta) > p_{21}(\theta)$, or

$$p_{11}(\theta) + p_{22}(\theta) - 1 > 0 \tag{60}$$

for θ small but > 0. However,

$$p_{11}(0) + p_{22}(0) - 1 = p_1^0 + p_2^0 - 1 = 0, \tag{61}$$

so that, comparing (60) with (61):

$$p'_{11}(0) + p'_{22}(0) \geqslant 0. \tag{62}$$

Therefore, from (58):

$$G'(0) \geqslant 0, \text{ and}$$

$$G'(0) > 0 \quad \text{if} \quad p'_{11}(0) \quad \text{and} \quad p'_{22}(0) \quad \text{are not both zero.} \tag{63}$$

The same conclusion follows, by similar reasoning, if $b_{11} < b_{12}$.

In summary, for case II, *the marginal net value of the examination at $\theta = 0$ will be positive if: (1) $p'_{11}(0)$ and $p'_{22}(0)$ are both zero, and (2) the marginal cost of the examination at $\theta = 0$ is not too large $[C'(0) < G'(0)]$.*

The situation just described in case II contradicts the conclusion of our main theorem. However, in this situation a family of optimal decision rules cannot be both flat and continuous at $\theta = 0$. If it is to be flat at $\theta = 0$, then it must assign all individuals to the same job. On the other hand, if either $p'_{11}(0)$ or $p'_{22}(0)$ are different from 0, then individuals with different labels should be assigned different jobs; so that if a family of optimal decision rules were flat at $\theta = 0$ it would be discontinuous there.

A Reformulation

We can easily reformulate our screening problem to conform to the postulates of our theorem. Assume there is a continuum of possible types of jobs. An individual of type i assigned to job a has a productivity of

$$K - (a - a_i)^2. \tag{64}$$

Thus, there is a social loss from misassigning individuals, which is an increasing function of the magnitude of the misassignment. It is easy to show that an optimal decision rule with an examination of accuracy θ must satisfy

$$D_y(\theta) = \frac{\sum_i N_i \, p_{iy}(\theta) a_i}{\sum_i N_i \, p_{iy}(\theta)} \equiv \bar{a}_y(\theta), \tag{65}$$

for all labels y with $\sum_i N_i \, p_{iy}(\theta) > 0$, where $D_y(\theta)$ is the optimal assignment of an individual with label y. Thus (given θ), the maximum expected value of output is:

$$G(\theta) = \sum_{i,y} N_i \, p_{iy}(\theta) [K - (\bar{a}_y(\theta) - a_i)^2]$$

$$= NK - \sum_{i,y} N_i \, p_{iy}(\theta) \left(a_i^2 - \bar{a}_y(\theta)^2 \right). \tag{66}$$

For $\theta = 0$, an optimal decision rule must satisfy:

$$D_y(0) = \frac{\sum_i N_i \, a_i}{\sum_i N_i} \equiv \bar{a} \tag{67}$$

for all labels y with $p_y^0 > 0$. In particular, there is a unique flat optimal decision rule for $\theta = 0$, namely $D_y(0) = \bar{a}$ for all y. On the other hand, if we let θ tend to 0 in (65) we get:

$$\lim_{\theta \to 0} D_y(\theta) = \begin{cases} \bar{a} & \text{if } p_y^0 > 0, \\ \dfrac{\sum_i N_i p_{iy}'(0) a_i}{\sum_i N_i p_{iy}'(0)} & \text{if } p_y^0 = 0, \end{cases} \tag{68}$$

for all labels y with $\sum_i N_i p_{iy}(\theta) > 0$ for θ near zero, provided the second line on the right-hand side of (68) is well defined. (The second line follows from l'Hôpital's Rule.) Comparing (67) and (68), we see that a family of optimal decision rules that is continuous at $\theta = 0$ need not be flat at $\theta = 0$, unless $p_y^0 > 0$ for every label y. The expression $\sum_i N_i p_{iy}(\theta)$ is the expected number of individuals who receive the label y (given the examination θ), and

$$\lim_{\theta \to 0} \sum_i N_i p_{iy}(0) = N p_y^0. \tag{69}$$

Thus, it is possible for the marginal net value of the examination to be positive only if there exists a label that does not appear ($p_v^0 = 0$) with the uninformative examination ($\theta = 0$), but does appear with positive frequency ($\sum_i N_i p_{iy}(\theta) > 0$) with an examination that is slightly informative ($\theta > 0$ but small). (This last is, of course, a necessary but not sufficient condition for $G'(0)$ to be strictly positive.)

Consider, for example, the special case of two types, with

$$N_1 = N_2,$$

$$p_{11}(\theta) = p_{22}(\theta) = 1/2 + \theta,$$

$$p_{12}(\theta) = p_{21}(\theta) = 1/2 - \theta, \quad 0 \leqslant \theta \leqslant 1/2. \tag{70}$$

Then the (unique) family of optimal decision rules is:

$$D_1(\theta) = \bar{a} + \theta(a_1 - a_2),$$

$$D_2(\theta) = \bar{a} + \theta(a_2 - a_1),$$

$$\bar{a} \equiv \frac{a_1 + a_2}{2}, \tag{71}$$

and the maximum expected value of output, given θ, is:

$$G(\theta) = NK - \left(\frac{N}{2}\right)\left(a_1^2 + a_2^2\right) + \left(\frac{N}{2}\right)\left(\bar{a}_1^2 + \bar{a}_2^2\right). \tag{72}$$

Hence, $G'(0) = 0$.

Similar considerations show that for "hierarchical" screening (as opposed to "job-matching" screening of the kind described above), if screening is undertaken at all it will be undertaken above some minimum level of quality (informativeness). We consider here only the special case just discussed, with two groups in the population. Now, however, productivity does not depend on job assignment. Rather, type 1 individuals are always more productive than type 2 individuals. Let a_1 and a_2 be their respective productivities. Assume $a_1 > a_2$. Each type of individual knows what type he is, but firms do not. Type 1 individuals are considering whether to attempt to persuade the government to subject all individuals to a screening system. (Assume, for instance, that there is one more type 1 individual than type 2.) If they get labeled i, they receive the mean marginal productivity of individuals labeled i. Thus, their expected income under a screening system of accuracy θ is:

$$[\bar{a} + \theta(a_1 - a_2)](1/2 + \theta) + [\bar{a} - \theta(a_1 - a_2)](1/2 - \theta),$$

so the increment in expected income is:

$$2\theta^2(a_1 - a_2).$$

It is immediately apparent that, even if the total costs of screening are borne uniformly over the population, there will be some minimal quality of screening before the more able wish to have it undertaken, i.e. letting

$$V(\theta) = \theta^2(a_1 - a_2) - C(\theta), \quad V'(0) = -C'(0) < 0.$$

The question naturally arises: How can we relate this result, which does not appear to arise from an optimization problem but rather from a description of market equilibrium, to our theorem?

Consider the problem of maximizing the expected income of the first group, subject to the constraints that

$$a_1(1/2 + \theta) + a_2(1/2 - \theta) < \bar{a} + 2\theta^2(a_1 - a_2)$$

and

$$a_1 + a_2 \leqslant \bar{a},$$

or

$$g(a, \theta) \equiv \theta(2a_1 - \bar{a}) - 2\theta^2(a_1 - a_2) \leqslant 0, \tag{73}$$

where a_y, the action, is the wage paid to a person with label y. The interpretation of the constraint is that the mean income of a person of type 1 must be less than or equal to his mean income were each label paid its marginal productivity. The constraint has the property that

$$g_\theta(a, \theta) = (2a_1 - \bar{a}) - 4\theta(a_1 - a_2),$$

which is zero at $a_1 = a_2$ and $\theta = 0$.

Thus, we maximize

$$a_1(1/2 + \theta) + a_2(1/2 - \theta) - C(\theta) \tag{74}$$

subject to (73).

The optimal decision rule is:

$$D_1(\theta) = \bar{a} + \frac{\theta(a_1 - a_2)}{2}, \quad D_2(\theta) = \bar{a} - \frac{\theta(a_1 - a_2)}{2}.$$

It is clear that with this formulation the theorem is applicable to our problem.

Table 3.1

Type	Label	
	1	2
1	$\lambda(1-\theta)+\theta$	$(1-\lambda)(1-\theta)$
2	$\lambda(1-\theta)$	$(1-\lambda)(1-\theta)+\theta$

Not every screening problem has a natural formulation which generates a decision function which is continuous and flat at $\theta = 0$. In particular, consider the problem of the optimal extraction of oil. There is some oil with zero extraction costs, and some with positive extraction costs of e. The stock of oil is to be consumed this period or next. There is a cost of ascertaining whether any particular well is a high or low extraction-cost well, $C(\theta)$, which is related to the quality of screening. With information structure θ, the probability that oil of type i is labelled j is as shown in table 3.1, where λ is the fraction of wells that are of type 1 (each well produces one unit of oil).

It is well known that it is optimal (with a positive interest rate) to extract the low extraction-cost oil first. Assume λ is sufficiently large that for all θ only oil of label 1 is extracted the first period; then the net value of resource savings for better θ is given by:

$$\frac{\partial V}{\partial \theta} = \frac{r Q_1}{1+r} e(1-\lambda) - C',$$

where Q_1 is the consumption of oil in the first period. It is clear that $\partial V/\partial \theta$ can be positive.

WELFARE ECONOMICS

INTRODUCTION TO PART V

In many ways, the papers in this section (Chapters 23 and 24) are the most important, for they provide the general refutation of Adam Smith's invisible hand theorem, the first fundamental theorem of welfare economics, arguing the Pareto efficiency of the market. We showed that whenever information is imperfect or markets incomplete—that is, essentially always—markets are not constrained Pareto efficient, taking into account the costs of information and of creating markets. Obviously, an economy with imperfect information might allocate resources less well than an economy with perfect information. Our result was far deeper: we showed that there were essentially always simple government interventions that could make some individuals better off without making anyone else worse off. The intuition behind our result was that whenever information was imperfect, actions generated externality-like effects: if individuals took, for instance, greater risks, it would drive up insurance premiums. In perfect markets, such pecuniary externalities are of no consequence, but when markets are imperfect, they are.

Both earlier and later work (some of which is contained in later volumes) have explored these issues in greater details in specific contexts, explaining, for instance, the inefficiencies in adverse selection and moral hazard models, or in search or efficiency wage models (or in economies with an incomplete set of securities).[1] The fact that the market equilibrium is inefficient has numerous policy collararies: free trade may not be desirable; in fact, we showed that it might lead everyone to be worse off (Newbery and Stiglitz 1984). Quotas might be superior to tariffs (Dasgupta and Stiglitz 1977). Capital market liberalization might be welfare reducing (Stiglitz 2004). The task of exploring the optimal interventions, however, has just begun. Greenwald-Stiglitz (1986), reprinted here as Chapter 23, showed, for instance, the existence of simple price interventions (corrective taxes), but there may be more effective non-linear price or non-price interventions.

The Greenwald-Stiglitz theorem not only constitutes the repeal of Adam Smith's invisible hand; it also has been referred to as the fundamental non-decentralizability theorem. One of the strengths of the price system is that it allowed a high level of decentralization. But our analysis showed how, for instance, prices in one market might affect the extent of moral hazard (and the welfare loss from self-selection constraints) in another. With insurance, individuals do not take full account of the

---

[1] See, in particular, Arnott and Stiglitz (1990) (on moral hazard); Greenwald and Stiglitz (1988e) on efficiency wages and search; and Stiglitz (1982b) on the efficiency of stock market equilibrium. Arnott, et al. (1994) provide an interpretation in terms of self-selection (incentive compatibility constraints); changes in price can have a first order effect on the extent to which such constraints bite, and therefore on welfare.

costs of their actions. People may smoke too much, knowing that someone else is picking up the hospital bills. But even if one can't directly control smoking, one can indirectly control it by taxing cigarettes (Arnott and Stiglitz 1986).

When it was discovered that, with imperfect information, markets often fail to produce efficient outcomes, there was a hope on the part of some that non-market institutions might fill the gap. Because of moral hazard, market equilibrium might be characterized by limited insurance, but families and other non-market institutions provide insurance. On the face of it, this seemed unlikely: the conditions under which markets resulted in efficiency were highly restrictive. Why would one expect these other institutions, without the sophisticated "signals" of prices, to do better? The results turned out to be more complex. In the case where families (the non-market institution explored) do not monitor care, the result we had expected turned out to be correct: the market knows that the family is providing non-market insurance, and that this results in the individual taking less care; and this in turn means that the insurance company further restricts the amount of insurance it provides. Non-market insurance displaces market insurance; but it is far better to diversify the risk over the entire economy, rather than just over the family. Hence, the non-market institution is dysfunctional; even though each family thinks that it is improving welfare as it fills the gap in market insurance, the general equilibrium is associated with a decrease in welfare.

But there is another situation. In Chapter 24, Arnott and I explained how peers may be able to do a better job of monitoring than others, which explained the success of peer monitoring based credit programs. Families provide an example of peer monitoring. But in that case, the markets may benefit from the peer monitoring driven by family-based insurance. Family based insurance not only partially fills the gap left by markets, but reduces the extent of moral hazard remaining within market-based insurance.[2]

---

[2] We have already discussed several other linkages in information across markets.

CHAPTER 23

EXTERNALITIES IN ECONOMIES WITH IMPERFECT INFORMATION AND INCOMPLETE MARKETS*

This paper presents a simple, general framework for analyzing externalities in economies with incomplete markets and imperfect information. By identifying the pecuniary effects of these externalities that net out, the paper simplifies the problem of determining when tax interventions are Pareto improving. The approach indicates that such tax interventions almost always exist and that equilibria in situations of imperfect information are rarely constrained Pareto optima. It can also lead to simple tests, based on readily observable indicators of the efficacy of particular tax policies in situations involving adverse selection, signaling, moral hazard, incomplete contingent claims markets, and queue rationing equilibria.

TRADITIONAL discussions of externalities have emphasized the distinction between technological externalities, in which the action of one individual or firm directly affects the utility or profit of another, and pecuniary externalities, in which one

* Written with Bruce Greenwald. Financial support of the National Science Foundation is gratefully acknowledged. Earlier versions of this paper were presented at seminars at Princeton, Harvard, Stanford, and LSE. We are indebted to participants at these seminars for helpful comments. We are also indebted to Larry Summers for detailed comments on an earlier draft. © 1986 by the President and Follows of Harvard College. Reprinted John Wiley & Sons, Inc. *The Quarterly Journal of Economics*, May 1986, with permission from 101(2), May 1986, pp. 229–264.

individual's or firm's actions affect another only through effects on prices. While the presence of technological externalities imply, in general, that a competitive equilibrium may not be Pareto efficient, pecuniary externalities by themselves are not a source of inefficiency. The fact that prices change has, of course important consequences: there are both distributional and allocational effects. But, the distribution effects "net" out: gains for example, by firms whose prices increase are precisely offset by losses e.g., to individuals who must pay higher prices. And, there are no welfare losses from the allocation effects as long as the price changes involved are small: if firms are maximizing profits and individuals are maximizing utility, both facing prices that correctly reflect opportunity costs, then standard envelope theorem arguments imply that changes in profits or utility induced by changes in allocations (resulting from any small change in prices) are negligible.

At the same time, pecuniary externalities have significant welfare consequences when there are distortions in the economy (e.g., from monopolies, technological externalities, or distorting taxes). An important determinant of the optimal tax on one commodity is for instance a calculation of its indirect effect on government revenue raised from other taxes.[1] It has not, however, been widely recognized that the distortions that arise in economies in which there is imperfect information and incomplete markets—for practical purposes, all economies—result in there being real welfare consequences of what would otherwise be viewed as purely pecuniary effects. As a result, economies in which there are incomplete markets and imperfect information are not, in general, constrained Pareto efficient. There exist government interventions (e.g., taxes and subsidies) that can make everyone better off. Moreover, the distortions that arise from imperfect information or incomplete markets often look analytically like externalities of the familiar technological sort, and viewing them in this way helps identify the welfare consequences of government interventions.

With these observations in mind, the objective of this paper is to develop a general methodology both for analyzing the impact of externalities and for calculating optimal corrective taxes in a general equilibrium context. The approach developed can be applied easily not only to conventional technological externalities but to the more subtle class of externalities associated with imperfect information and incomplete markets. We show how, in many cases, not only can it be demonstrated that there exist Pareto-improving government interventions, but also that the kind of intervention required can be simply related to certain parameters that, in principle, are observable.

The paper is divided into four parts. The first presents the model used and develops the general methodology. Section II applies this methodology to a number of widely discussed welfare problems involving imperfect information and incomplete markets. Section III discusses some other important applications and extensions of the analysis. Finally, Section IV is a brief conclusion.

---

[1] The importance of these indirect effects was emphasized, for instance, by Harberger [1971b] in his classic paper.

I The Basic Model and Results

The agents in the model consist of households, firms, and a government with the following characteristics.

A Households

Households maximize a utility function,

$$u^h(x^h, z^h), h = 1, \ldots, H,$$

where

$x^h = (x_1^h, \bar{x}^h) \equiv$ consumption vector of household h, x_1^h is consumption of the numeraire good, $\bar{x}^h = (x_2^h, \ldots, x_N^h)$ is consumption of the $N - 1$ nonnumeraire goods,

$z^h \equiv$ vector of N^h other variables that affect the utility of household h (e.g., levels of pollution, average quality of a good consumed).

Households maximize u^h subject to a budget constraint of the form,

$$x_1^h + q \cdot \bar{x}^h \leqslant I^h + \sum_F a^{hf} \cdot \pi^f,$$

taking q, π^f, I^h, a^{hf}, and z^h as fixed, where

$q \equiv$ a vector of prices of the $N - 1$ nonnumeraire goods,

$\pi^f \equiv$ profits of firm f,

$a^{hf} \equiv$ fractional holding of household h in firm f, $\sum_H a^{hf} = 1$,

$I^h \equiv$ a lump sum government transfer to household h,

$I \equiv (I^1, \ldots, I^H)$.

We shall also use

$E^h(q, z^h, u^h) \equiv$ the expenditure function of household h that gives the minimum expenditure necessary to obtain a level of utility u^h, when prices are q and z^h is the level of "other" variables.

It is well-known that

$\hat{x}_k^h(q; z^h, u^h) \equiv$ the compensated demand for good k given z^h and u^h fixed

(where the caret is used to distinguish compensated from uncompensated demand functions)

$$\equiv \left. \frac{\partial E^h}{\partial q} \right|_{z^h, u^h}. \tag{1}$$

Finally,

$x^h(q, I, z^h) \equiv (x_1^h(q, I, z^h), \overline{x}^h(q, I, z^h)) \equiv$ the demand function (uncompensated) of household h.[2] We shall assume that this function is differentiable.[3]

B Firms

Firms maximize the profit function,

$$\pi^f = y_1^f + p \cdot \overline{y}^f,$$

where

$y^f = (y_1^f, \overline{y}^f) \equiv$ production vector[4] of firm f with y_1^f and $\overline{y}^f$ defined analogously to x_1^h and $\overline{x}^h$,

$p \equiv$ vector of producers' prices for the $N - 1$ nonnumeraire goods.

Firms maximize profits subject to the constraint that,

$$y_1^f - G^f(\overline{y}^f, z^f) \leqslant 0,$$

where

$G^f \equiv$ a production function of the usual sort,

$z^f \equiv$ vector of other N^f variables affecting firm f analogously defined to z^h.

---

[2] The household demand function depends on the entire vector of transfers since both z^h and $z^1, \ldots, z^F$ (which determine $\pi^1, \ldots, \pi^F$ and hence household income) may depend on the consumption choices of other households. In a pure exchange economy, $x^h(q, I^h; z^h(q, I)) = x^h(q, I)$. Also for the sake of expositional simplicity, household factor endowments have been arbitrarily set to zero. This has no substantive impact on the analysis.

[3] The problem of justifying this kind of differentiability assumption is examined in detail by Starrett [1980], who makes a similar assumption in a slightly different context. The difficulty here is that the usual convexity assumptions of preferences and production functions will not guarantee differentiability. The external effects may create discontinuities. The "excess demand" functions used here include the effect of prices on quantities both directly and indirectly via their impact on externality-generating activities (i.e., through their impact of z^f and z^h) which, in turn, affect consumption and production choices.

[4] $y_k^f < 0$ represents an input.

The firm's maximum profit function,

$$\pi_*^f(p, z^f),$$

has the property that

$$\left.\frac{\partial \pi_*^f}{\partial p_{k_1}}\right|_{z^f} = y_k^f, \quad k = 1, \ldots, N, \tag{2}$$

where y_k^f here denotes the profit-maximizing level of the production variable in question. Finally,

$$y^f(p, z^f) \equiv (y_1^f(p, z^f), \overline{y}^f(p, z^f)) \equiv \text{supply function of firm } f.$$

We shall assume that this function, like the demand function, is differentiable.

C Government

The government produces nothing, collects taxes, distributes the proceeds, and receives a net income,

$$R \equiv t \cdot \overline{x} - \sum_H I^h,$$

where the tax t is just the difference between consumer and producer prices,

$$t \equiv (q - p),$$

and

$$\overline{x} \equiv \sum_H \overline{x}^h \text{ (i.e., the sum of nonnumeraire consumption).}$$

D Equilibrium and Efficiency

An initial equilibrium with no taxes and $I^h = 0$ for all h, will be assumed to exist.[5] At this equilibrium, $p = q$, and[6]

$$\overline{x}(q, I, z) - \sum_F \overline{y}^f(p, z) = 0. \tag{3}$$

---

[5] As described so far, the model may not, of course, have an equilibrium price vector. However, having noted that possibility, it is still worth investigating the welfare implications of any equilibria that may exist. The case for this is made fully and compellingly by Starrett [1980]. We shall also ignore the problem of free goods. Accounting for them would merely complicate the analysis without altering any basic results.

[6] At the most general level,

$$z^h = z^h(x^1, \ldots x^h, y^1 \ldots y^f). \tag{3a}$$

We must solve simultaneously (3) and (3a) for the endogenous variables $\{x^h, z^h, x^f, z^f\}$ in terms of the exogenous variables $\{t, I\}$.

A simple test of the Pareto optimality of this equilibrium is to ask whether there exists a set of taxes, subsidies, and lump sum transfers that would (a) leave household utilities unchanged and (b) increase government revenues (assumed to be consumed in the numeraire good). This, in turn, implies that, if the original equilibrium is Pareto optimal, the problem,

$$\max_{t,I} R \equiv t \cdot \bar{x} - \sum_h I^h,\qquad(4)$$

subject to

$$I^h + \sum a^{hf} \pi^f = E^h(q, z^h; \bar{u}^h),\qquad(5)$$

where $\bar{u}^h$ = competitive equilibrium utility levels, and z^h, z^f, π^f, p, and q are functions of t and I, has a solution at $t = 0$.

This is, of course, *a necessary but not sufficient* condition for (constrained) Pareto optimality. Clearly, if we can find a set of tax-subsidy interventions that can make everyone better off, the economy is not Pareto efficient. But there might exist other forms of intervention, such as quotas, that might generate Pareto improvements even when no simple tax-subsidy scheme could do so.[7] To see when the solution to (4) entails $t = 0$, note that, along the constraint of equation (5),

$$\frac{dI^h}{dt} + \sum_F a^{hf}\left(\pi_z^f \frac{dz^f}{dt} + \pi_p^f \frac{dp}{dt}\right) = E_q^h \frac{dq}{dt} + E_z^h \frac{dz^h}{dt},\qquad(6)$$

where

$\dfrac{dI^h}{dt} \equiv$ change in lump sum income per unit change in tax[8] required to keep the individual at the given level of utility,

$\pi_z^f \equiv [\frac{\partial \pi_*^f}{\partial z^f}] = \frac{\partial G^f}{\partial z^f}$, an N^f element vector,

$E_z^h \equiv [\frac{\partial E^h}{\partial z^h}] = [\frac{\partial u^h}{\partial z^h}]$ (with u^h suitably normalized), an N^h element vector.

But, $dq/dt = I_{N-1} + dp/dt$ (here I_{N-1} is an identity matrix). Therefore, substitution into (5) and rearrangement of terms yields

$$E_q^h + \left(E_q^h - \sum_f a^{hf}\pi_p^f\right)\frac{dp}{dt} = \frac{dI^h}{dt} + \left\{\sum_F a^{hf}\pi_z^f \frac{dz^f}{dt} - E_z^h \frac{dz^h}{dt}\right\}.\qquad(7)$$

The left-hand side of (7) is the traditional pecuniary (or redistributive) effect of the tax, while the bracketed term on the righthand side is the externality effect. So far, the

---

[7] At the same time, it might be noted that we ignore any discussion of the political processes by which the tax-subsidy schemes described below might be effected. Critics may claim that as a result we have not really shown that a Pareto improvement is actually possible.

[8] All the derivatives of z (and p and q) with respect to t should be viewed as total derivatives, taking into account the associated changes in $I_1, \ldots, I_H$ (which, in principle, may affect z) as well as the direct effect of t.

derivation of equation (7) involves nothing more than keeping track of the impact on household h of a small change in taxes dt, where this impact includes the effects of any associated equilibrium price changes. Substitution of equations (1) and (2), summation over all households, and use of the fact that $\sum_h a^{hf} = 1$ help to simplify the distributive impact of the initial tax change. Thus,

$$\bar{x} + (\bar{x} - \bar{y})\frac{dp}{dt} = \sum_H \frac{dI^h}{dt} + \left(\sum_F \pi_z^f \frac{dz^f}{dt} - \sum_H E_z^h \frac{dz^h}{dt} \right).$$

It may be helpful here to recall how (1) and (2) are derived: an envelope theorem is used to eliminate the allocative effects of the tax-induced price changes. This is why no terms appear directly reflecting these allocative effects. Next, $\bar{y} \equiv \sum_F \bar{y}^f = \bar{x}$ in any market equilibrium. Therefore, the distributive effects, i.e., $(\bar{x} - \bar{y})dp/dt$, "net" out. And the total compensating payments that the government must make to satisfy the constraint (5) amount to

$$\sum_H \frac{dI^h}{dt} = \bar{x} - \left(\sum_F \pi_z^f \frac{dz^f}{dt} - \sum_H E_z^h \frac{dz^h}{dt} \right). \tag{8}$$

Now differentiating the objective function (4) with respect to t, we obtain

$$\frac{dR}{dt} = \bar{x} + \frac{d\bar{x}}{dt} \cdot t - \sum_H \frac{dI^h}{dt}. \tag{9}$$

Substitution from (8) into (9) yields

$$\frac{dR}{dt} = \frac{d\bar{x}}{dt} \cdot t + (\Pi^t - B^t), \tag{10}$$

where

$$\Pi^t \equiv \sum_F \pi_z^f \frac{dz^f}{dt}, \tag{11}$$

$$B^t \equiv \sum_H E_z^h \frac{dz^h}{dt}, \tag{12}$$

which is the derivative of R along directions in which the compensation constraint is satisfied. This can be used as a measure of the net change in welfare. The disappearance of the $\bar{x}$ term here is due to the elimination of one final distributive effect that is particular to the tax change. The total compensation to households is offset in part by the increase in tax revenue to the government embodied in the term $\bar{x} \cdot dt$. The remaining terms in equation (10) summarize the "pecuniary" effects of the tax change that cannot be ignored. These depend on existing distortion whether in the form of taxes (i.e., $d\bar{x}/dt \cdot t$) or technological externalities (i.e., Π^t and B^t).

For the initial equilibrium to be Pareto optimal, dR/dt must equal zero at $t = 0$, which implies that

$$\frac{dR}{dt} = (\Pi^t - B^t) = 0. \tag{13}$$

Thus, Pareto optimality depends on the absence of any z's that change with taxes and affect either profits or household utilities.[9]

The defining characteristics of externalities, which (in traditional language) are "nonpecuniary" and, therefore, justify some form of government intervention, is that they enter utility or profit functions in the form of the z-variables. The variables involved may, of course, be determined by the market interactions of agents (e.g., average product qualities, search times, average levels of unobservable effort or, with incomplete markets, future prices) and this will be the case in the examples analyzed below. Except in the special case (which is unlikely to hold generically) where Π^t and B^t exactly cancel each other out, the existence of these externalities will make the initial equilibrium inefficient and guarantee the existence of welfare-improving tax measures.

We should review here the important assumptions that underlie our analysis: (a) firms are competitive profit maximizers and individuals are competitive utility maximizers; this allows us to use the envelope theorem, to say that there is no welfare effect from the changes in actions induced by the changes in prices; (b) demand equals supply (and all profits accrue to individuals within the economy); this allows us to cancel out the distributive or *transfer effects*, the gains from price increases to sellers (owners of firms who are producers) being just offset by the losses to buyers.

E Optimal Taxes

Equation (10) not only allows us to ascertain whether an economy is a constrained Pareto optimum, but also provides a simple set of necessary conditions characterizing the optimal level of taxes in the presence of externalities. Since $dR/dt = 0$ is necessary for optimality, optimal tax levels have the property that

$$t \cdot \frac{d\bar{x}}{dt} = -(\Pi^t - B^t) \tag{14}$$

or

$$t = -(\Pi^t - B^t)\left(\frac{d\bar{x}}{dt}\right)^{-1}. \tag{14'}$$

---

[9] If the economy were Pareto optimal, dR/dt would equal zero, so we need not concern ourselves with how the government disposes of any excess revenues. For the same reason, (14) below characterizes the optimal tax structure for any rule for the disposition of net government revenues. (The simplest rule is for the government to spend all of its excess revenue on the numeraire good, in which case (3) is always satisfied in equilibrium.)

The left-hand side of (14) is the marginal deadweight loss from the distortion in consumption associated with an increase in the tax.[10] The right-hand side is the gain from reduction in the externalities. At the optimum, the marginal gain from the reduction in the externality should just equal the marginal deadweight loss from the (direct effect of the) tax.

A simple example may help clarify the implications of (14). Assume that a tax on alcohol reduces automobile accidents, and that individuals, in deciding on the level of care, do not fully take into account the social costs of their actions (e.g., because they are partially insured). Then a tax on alcohol will always be initially beneficial. However, successive tax increases will increase the deadweight loss: the marginal value of alcohol consumption to the individual will exceed (by increasing amounts) the producer cost. The tax should be increased until the marginal deadweight loss (the constant rate loss in tax revenue) exactly balances the marginal benefits of reductions in the accident costs that have not been internalized by the individual (the accident externalities).[11]

II Applications

The remainder of this paper is devoted to applying equation (13) to a variety of familiar situations, to ascertain conditions under which a small tax or subsidy will be welfare enhancing. One of the main virtues of our methodology is the ease with which it can be applied, in particular, to situations where information is imperfect and markets incomplete, to show that in such a situation there virtu-ally always exists a tax subsidy that is Pareto improving. But before applying our

---

[10] Heuristically, the marginal deadweight loss from an increase in the tax is just the difference between the increased income that would have to be given to an individual to keep him at the same level of utility and the extra revenue received by the government. In the simple case where producers' prices are fixed,

$$\frac{d(DWL)}{dt_i} = \sum_H \frac{dE^h(q, \bar{u})}{dq_i} - \frac{d(t \cdot \bar{x})}{dt_i}$$

$$= x_i - x_i + t \cdot \frac{d\bar{x}}{dt_i}$$

[11] The left-hand side is sometimes referred to as the "constant" rate loss in tax revenue, where constant rate changes in tax revenue are the changes in revenue that would have occurred at the existing tax rates.

Two further points about this optimal tax formula in the presence of externalities are worth making. First, because the impacts of t_i and t_j on externality distortions will not, in general, be equal, the standard equiproportionate reduction results do not obtain. Second, we have assumed that the government can adjust the I^h lump sum transfers to offset any distributional effects. If it cannot, and we ask what tax structure maximizes social welfare, then the formulae corresponding to (14) will employ distributional weights. See Atkinson and Stiglitz [1980].

methodology to these somewhat unfamiliar situations, it may be useful to see how it works in the more familiar context of some pre-existing (assumed to be fixed tax) distortions.

A Tax Distortions

For simplicity, we assume that there exists a single tax distortion, say on commodity 1, generating revenue $t_1 x_1$, the proceeds of which are redistributed back to households according to a fixed formula; i.e., the hth household gets a share β^h of the tax revenue from the first commodity. We then take the somewhat unnatural step in this case of rewriting the tax distortion as a traditional technological externality, defining

$$z^h = \beta^h t_1 x_1, \sum_H \beta^h = 1,$$

since tax proceed distributions are "externalities" to each household. Clearly now, the individual's utility (and his demands) are functions not only of all prices, but also of z^h. Directly applying (13), we obtain

$$\left. \frac{\partial R}{\partial t_i} \right|_{t_{i=0}} = t_1 \sum_H \beta^h \left(\frac{dx_1}{dt_i} \right)_{\bar{u}} = t_1 \left(\frac{dx_1}{dt_i} \right)_{\bar{u}} \gtrless 0 \quad \text{as} \quad \left(\frac{dx_1}{dt_i} \right)_{\bar{u}} \gtrless 0.$$

A small tax (subsidy) on any commodity that is a Hicks substitute (complement) to the first commodity is welfare enhancing.

B Adverse Selection

The simplest imperfect information case in which the analysis can be applied is to markets with asymmetrically distributed information and heterogeneous quality.[12] We shall assume that there is only a single commodity about which purchasers are uninformed and that there are no other externalities (or other distortions). Sellers know the quality of what they are selling. Buyers know only the average quality in the market as a whole. Buyers will be assumed to draw randomly from the market in which the commodity in question is offered for sale. We shall assume, in addition, that buyers are perfectly informed about and care only about the *average* quality of what they buy.[13] (Realistically, buyers may also care about the range of possible qualities, but taking this into account would change the analysis only in obvious ways and would greatly increase its complexity.)[14] The situation corresponding perhaps

[12] The basic model for these situations was developed by Akerlof [1970].
[13] As Stiglitz [1975f] noted earlier, ignorance (imperfect information) acts like a tax/subsidy, increasing the wage received by an individual above his marginal product for low-productivity workers, and decreasing it for high-productivity workers.
[14] This simple model applies equally well to a situation in which buyers purchase only a limited number of items and care about the individual qualities of each. In that case ex ante expected utility (the

most closely to this simple model is a labor market in which firms hire blindly from a pool of workers of heterogeneous quality.[15]

We let θ denote the quality of each unit of the heterogeneous commodity, and $\bar{\theta}$ denote the average quality in the marketplace. In terms of the model of this paper, the z^h (externality) vectors will consist of a single element that is equal to $\bar{\theta}$ (although households that do not purchase the commodity may have $du^h/dz^h = 0$). Similarly, z^f for all firms will have a single element equal to $\bar{\theta}$. Formally,

$$E^h = E^h(q; \bar{\theta}),$$

and

$$\pi^f = \pi^f(p; \bar{\theta}).$$

Under these circumstances, equation (13) for a small tax dt becomes

$$\frac{dR}{dt} = \left[\sum_F \pi^f_\theta - \sum_H E^h_\theta \right] \cdot \frac{d\bar{\theta}}{dt}. \tag{15}$$

If the commodity is an input into production supplied by households, since π^f increases and E^h is non-increasing $\bar{\theta}$, this means that any intervention which increases average quality in the marketplace is beneficial. Thus, *any small tax that increases the quality of the heterogeneous commodity is always beneficial.*

What is surprising about this result is its simplicity. The fact that an increase in $\bar{\theta}$ involves the sale of higher quality inputs by some households suggests the need for a careful balancing of the increased cost of these sales by owner households against the benefits to purchasers. Yet no such calculation is implied by equation (15). The necessary balancing of the costs and benefits of selling higher quality items is being done by owner households in the process of maximizing utility. This accounts for the simple form of the final policy prescription.

A typical example of tax changes leading to changes in average ability arises where different ability groups have different labor supply elasticities. If higher ability workers have greater supply elasticities than do low ability workers, a small proportionate wage subsidy will increase average quality.

Finally, it should be noted that there is, at least in principle, an observable basis for judging the effectiveness of government tax policy. Assuming that the *average "quality"* of labor entering a particular market can be monitored (short of determining the "quality" of each individual worker) by, for example, taking a

appropriate welfare measure) will depend on the mean and spread of the distribution of "quality" in the market pool.

[15] A question that might arise is whether agents, observing the dependence of quality on price, will behave in the manner described here. We assume here (following Akerlof) that the uninformed agents do not act strategically. This assumption seems reasonable, for instances when labor is engaged at a union hall, in which there are a large number of employers. Then the supply of laborers will essentially be unaffected by any single firm. Hence, a firm will have no incentive to pay a wage in excess of the market wage, and cannot obtain any workers at a lower wage. But there are other circumstances in which a single purchaser can obtain information about the characteristics of the particular good the seller is trying to sell by a variety of devices. See, e.g., Stiglitz [1992i] and Stiglitz and Weiss [1981].

statistical sample, any policy of "small" taxes that increases this quality is a beneficial one.

A question that naturally arises at this juncture is whether the compensations required by (5) can actually be carried out given the information available to the government. The answer depends, not unnaturally, on what the government knows and the extent to which lump sum taxes are available. If the government is restricted to commodity taxes and a uniform lump sum tax and knows the characteristics of each of the M classes of consumers (but not the class to which any particular individual belongs) then Pareto-improving commodity taxes will, in general, exist as long as the number of taxable commodities strictly exceeds M (i.e., $N > M$). Let the government restrict itself to tax changes that keep each class of consumers, except the first, at a given level of utility. As a rule, this will require $M - 1$ taxes (one for each group except the first). Then let the government change the tax on a further commodity making simultaneous changes in the $M - 1$ other taxes to keep the classes of consumers at all their given levels of utility. If the original equilibrium is not a Pareto optimum, then, in general, a composite tax change of this kind will exist that raises revenue.[16]

C Signaling-Screening

The previous section considered situations where there was no signal that a seller with a higher quality commodity (a more productive worker) could use to distinguish himself from lower quality workers. In many cases, such signals, like education, can be obtained, but at a cost. Though there has been considerable work describing the resulting equilibrium (and analyzing the conditions under which an equilibrium exists)[17] the welfare properties of these equilibria have received surprisingly little attention. This is perhaps because of the result, noted in Rothschild-Stiglitz, that the competitive equilibrium, when it exists, has the property that it maximizes the welfare of the better-off individual, subject to the self-selection constraint. This suggests, in turn, that if the government has no more information available to it than private firms (and thus in redistributing income, must rely on the same self-selection constraints) it cannot make a Pareto improvement. This conclusion, however, is wrong. Taxes on goods or wages, which firms and individuals take as given, may change the extent of signaling, the average quality of those obtaining each signal and the wages paid to each category of signaling workers. Many of the resulting transfer and allocation effects will indeed disappear from a calculation of the consequent change in welfare.

---

[16] In the subsequent analysis we shall ignore these issues. The questions are, however, of central importance: the failure to take account of what information is at the disposal of the government provides one of the most telling criticisms, both of the standard compensation criteria as well as the New Welfare Economics, which assumed that all lump sum transfers were feasible. The New New Welfare Economics and the Theory of Pareto Efficient Taxation [Stiglitz, 1982f, 1985d] focus explicitly on these issues. The empirical information required of the government to implement Pareto improvements is, of course, much greater when compensations must be done through the commodity tax system.

[17] See Spence [1973], Rothschild and Stiglitz [1976, and Wilson [1977] among others.

However, the average qualities of each signaling group are externalities just as average quality is in the adverse selection case. There remain, therefore, direct effects of any quality changes on purchasers, and these it can be shown will not in general net out: signaling market equilibria are essentially never constrained Pareto efficient.[18]

We develop here a simplified version of the signaling model, in which there is a single signal, which can be purchased at a cost; those who purchase the signal have mean quality $\bar{\theta}_1$, those who do not have mean quality, $\bar{\theta}_2$.[19] Since signals are costly and wages must, therefore, depend positively on signals, we shall assume that $\bar{\theta}_1 > \bar{\theta}_2$. For simplicity, we assume that only firms buy labor.

From application of equation (13), the net impact of a small tax dt is

$$\frac{dR}{dt} = \sum_i \sum_F \frac{\partial \pi^f}{\partial \bar{\theta}_i} \cdot \frac{d\bar{\theta}_i^f}{dt}. \tag{16}$$

If we assume that firms draw at random from the pools of workers with and without signals and that each firm hires a large number of workers, we can rewrite (16) as

$$\frac{dR}{dt} = \sum_i \frac{\partial \bar{\theta}_i}{\partial t} \left[\sum_F \frac{\partial \pi^f}{\partial \bar{\theta}_i} \right]. \tag{17}$$

Since $\partial \pi^f / \partial \bar{\theta}$ is positive (i.e., higher average worker quality leads to higher profits), it follows immediately that any tax which increases the average quality in both the signaling and nonsignaling pools is beneficial. This would be true of a tax that discouraged workers who are below the average of those in the signaling pool but above the average of those in the nonsignaling pools, from acquiring the signal. Again the simplicity of this result follows from the fact that the many complicated "pecuniary" transfer effects and the effects of quality on a firm's hiring decisions can be ignored. We now make several simplifying assumptions to sign the right-hand side of (17).

Assume that the value of higher quality to a firm is directly proportional to the number of workers of a particular type that it hires; for instance, if the production process is separable, so total output y_0^f is the sum of the outputs of each individual;[20] i.e.,

$$y_0^f = \sum_i n_i^f y_{0i}(\hat{y}_i^f, \bar{\theta}_i),$$

[18] Earlier analyses [Stiglitz, 1975f] showed that there might exist multiple equilibria, some of which Pareto dominated others. The analysis here, however, shows that in general, each of the equilibria themselves can be improved upon with a simple set of taxes.

[19] The version of the model presented here is considerably simpler than the standard formulation, where there are as many different signals (education levels) as there are types of individuals, and in which therefore there is an entire sequence of self-selection constraints. It is possible to apply the approach of this paper to equilibria of this sort. Externalities arise because the actions of one firm or individual affect the self-selection constraints of others. The essential insights are conveyed by the formulation presented. See Greenwald and Stiglitz [1985].

[20] The results stated below only require that the marginal effect of an improvement in quality be proportional to the number of workers.

where n_i^f is the number of workers of type i hired by firm f, and y_{0i} is the output of a worker of type i (given inputs per worker of $\hat{y}_i^f$). Then

$$\sum_F \frac{d\pi^f}{d\bar{\theta}_i} = n_i \sum_F \left[\frac{n_i^f}{n_i} \right] \left[\frac{\partial y_{0i}^f}{\partial \bar{\theta}_i} \right] \equiv n_i \frac{\partial \bar{y}_0}{\partial \bar{\theta}_i}, \bar{y}_0 = \sum \frac{n_i^f}{n_i} y_{0i},$$

where n_i is the total number of workers of type i. Thus,

$$\frac{dR}{dt} = n_1 \frac{\partial \bar{\theta}_1}{\partial t} \left[\frac{\partial \bar{y}_{01}}{\partial \bar{\theta}_1} \right] + n_2 \frac{\partial \bar{\theta}_2}{\partial t} \left[\frac{\partial \bar{y}_{02}}{\partial \bar{\theta}_2} \right]. \tag{18}$$

If we further assume that the overall average quality of the labor force is unaffected by the signal and is fixed (i.e., $n_1\bar{\theta}_1 + n_2\bar{\theta}_2$ is fixed), then

$$n_2 \frac{\partial \bar{\theta}_2}{\partial t} + n_1 \frac{\partial \bar{\theta}_1}{\partial t} + \frac{\partial n_1}{\partial t}(\bar{\theta}_1 - \bar{\theta}_2) = 0.$$

Substitution from this expression into (18) yields

$$\frac{dR}{dt} = \left[n_1 \frac{\partial \bar{\theta}_1}{\partial t} \right] \left[\frac{\partial \bar{y}_{01}}{\partial \bar{\theta}_1} - \frac{\partial \bar{y}_{02}}{\partial \bar{\theta}_2} \right] - \frac{\partial n_1}{\partial t} \left[\frac{\partial \bar{y}_{02}}{\partial \bar{\theta}_2} \right] (\bar{\theta}_1 - \bar{\theta}_2). \tag{19}$$

The first term in (19) captures the "sorting" value of the signal. It is the improvement in quality in the signaling pool (i.e., $\partial\bar{\theta}_1/\partial t$) multiplied by the differential value of "quality" for workers from the signaling compared with the nonsignaling pool. If "quality" is more important for signaling workers, then this term will be positive, and therefore a tax that increases the quality of the signaling pool will tend to be beneficial. If this increase in quality is achieved by reducing the number of workers who signal (i.e., $\partial n_1/\partial t < 0$), then the second term in (19) will also be positive (since $\bar{\theta}_1 - \bar{\theta}_2 > 0$ and $\partial \bar{y}_{02}/\partial\bar{\theta}_2 > 0$), and the tax will be unambiguously beneficial (remember that this applies to the case where overall average quality is constant).

Furthermore, if there is no "sorting" effect (pure hierarchical screening) (i.e., $\partial\bar{y}_{01}/\partial\bar{\theta}_1 = \partial\bar{y}_{02}/\partial\bar{\theta}_2$), then

$$\frac{dR}{dt} = -\frac{\partial n_1}{\partial t} \left[\frac{\partial \bar{y}_{02}}{\partial \bar{\theta}_2} \right] (\bar{\theta}_1 - \bar{\theta}_2), \tag{20}$$

and a small tax that reduces the amount of signaling is beneficial.

Finally, if the original equilibrium involves no signaling (i.e., $n_1 = 0$), then (20) again applies (with the reservation that $\partial n_1/dt$ now refers to the right-hand derivative at $n_1 = 0$).

D Moral Hazard

It has long been recognized that the provision of insurance attenuates incentives for accident avoidance. The insurance company knows this and takes this into account in designing the insurance contract that frequently has coinsurance and deductibility provisions. There is a tradeoff between the deadweight loss from the failure (with insurance) to take adequate accident avoidance precautions, and the welfare loss from risk bearing. But there is a widespread presumption that in competitive markets, the tradeoff is done in an efficient manner: indeed, the competitive equilibrium contract is generally described as that contract which maximizes individuals' expected utility, subject to the insurance company at least breaking even.[21] Hence, there has been a presumption that competitive economies, even with moral hazard, are constrained Pareto efficient. (Clearly, welfare would be higher if information were costless, so the insurance company could monitor the actions of the insured, in which case, the provision of the insurance would be contingent upon the individual taking certain accident prevention actions. But this is an irrelevant comparison.) This presumption is, unfortunately, wrong, and our framework provides an easy way of seeing this. The simplest way of doing so entails effectively embedding the zero-profit constraint on the insurance company into the utility function;[22] then the price an individual pays for insurance depends on the average level of accident avoidance of those who purchase insurance, which represents an externality to an individual purchaser. The government, by subsidizing complements of accident avoidance activities and taxing substitutes, encourages accident avoidance, reduces the externality, and improves welfare.

Assume for simplicity that the universe of insured agents consists of identical households and that a scalar level of effort that reduces the expected loss from accidents cannot be observed by insurers. Let households maximize,[23]

$$\xi[U^h(x^h, \mu^h, e^h)],$$

subject to the constraint that

$$q \cdot (x^h - w^h) + \gamma(\mu^h, \bar{e}) - I^h - \sum_F a^{hf} \pi^f \leqslant 0,$$

where ξ denotes an expectation across states of nature, μ^h is a vector of insurance payments across states of nature (i.e., μ_1^h, the first element of μ^h, is the insurance payment made to household h in state of nature 1), $\gamma(\mu^h, e)$ is the premium paid for insurance, e^h is the level of "care" exercised by household h, and $\bar{e}$ is the "average" level of care exercised by all households; i.e.,

$$\bar{e} = \frac{1}{H} \sum_H e^h$$

and w^h is the individual endowment vector.

[21] For a discussion of the nature of market equilibrium with moral hazard, see Pauly [1974], Shavell [1979a], and Arnott and Stiglitz [1990].
[22] This is not the only way of approaching the problem with our framework, but it provides the results most directly. We could, alternatively, treat purchasers of insurance as a heterogeneous pool (similar to adverse selection) with an average quality, which in this instance would be the level of care exercised in avoiding accidents.
[23] Accident losses are subsumed in this function. This formulation assumes that the individual commits himself to *all* nonnumeraire expenditures prior to knowing whether there will be an accident. Our results hold for more general formulations.

With constant returns to scale in the insurance industry and risk-neutral investors, equilibrium in the insurance industry implies that

$$\gamma(\mu^h, \bar{e}) = \mathcal{E}(\mu^h|\bar{e}).$$

This can be substituted into the household budget constraint so that (the competitive equilibrium is as if) households choose e^h, x^h, and μ^h in order to maximize $\mathcal{E}[U^{*h}]$ subject to the constraint,[24]

$$q \cdot (x^h - w^h) + \mathcal{E}(\mu^h|\bar{e}) - I^h - \sum_F a^{hf}\pi^f \leqslant 0,$$

where the function $U^* \equiv \mathcal{E}[U^h(x^h, \mu^h, e^h)]$ can be treated as a normal utility function. We derive an expenditure function, as before,

$$E^h = E^h(q, U^*, \mu^h, \gamma(\mu^h, \bar{e}))$$

where, for the moment, we take μ^h as given and $\bar{e}$ is our "z" (externality) variable. Application of equation (13) implies that the net impact per unit of tax dt is[25]

$$\frac{dR}{dt} = \sum_H \frac{d\mathcal{E}(\mu^h|\bar{e})}{d\bar{e}} \cdot \frac{d\bar{e}}{dt}. \tag{21}$$

Since $d\mathcal{E}(\mu^h|\bar{e})/d\bar{e}$ should be negative (more care reduces insurance payments), any small tax that increases household efforts at accident avoidance will improve welfare. Moreover, the net social value of the tax change is just equal to the reduction in the expected level of casualty insurance payments. Again this is an observable consequence against which the efficiency of a tax intervention can be measured. (It is obvious that in a one-good economy, commodity taxes cannot be used to effect a Pareto improvement; those who have studied insurance markets in isolation of other markets—taking other prices as fixed—have, not surprisingly, come to the misleading conclusions that competitive insurance markets ought not to be interfered with as long as a competitive equilibrium exists; see, for example, Shavell [1979a].)[26] The

---

[24] Note that, for each γ, individuals choose to maximize their expected utility; but they do not take into account the effect of e^h on $\bar{e}$ (which is negligible) and γ.

[25] Note that as t changes, the optimal policy μ^h, will change, but by the envelope theorem, this effect drops out. Also in this formulation, the change in the maximum expected utility of each household is the partial of the Lagrangian of the constrained household maximization problem.

[26] If we assume that insurance can be made to depend on the *complete* vector of household consumption, equilibrium in a competitive insurance industry will imply that

$$\gamma(\mu^h, x^h, \bar{e}) = \mathcal{E}(\mu^h|\bar{e}(x^h), x^h),$$

where the $\bar{e}$ in question is now that of households with consumption vector x^h, since these households constitute a separate insurance class. Under these conditions

$$\frac{dR}{dt} = \sum_H \frac{d\mathcal{E}(\mu|\bar{e}(x^h))}{d\bar{e}} \cdot \frac{d\bar{e}(x^h)}{dt},$$

where x^h is being held constant as taxes change. However, if taxes do not affect x^h, then they will not affect e^h and thus will have no impact on $\bar{e}$.

principle that emerges from (21) seems intuitive: commodities like fire extinguishers that decrease the frequency and size of insured against losses should be subsidized, while those, like alcohol, which increase the frequency and size of losses should be taxed. Arnott and Stiglitz [1986] have provided a general characterization of the set of optimal corrective taxes.

Note finally that because all individuals are identical, it is much easier to effect a Pareto improvement in this case than in the signaling and adverse selection models discussed earlier, where the government may face an informational problem concerning who should be compensated for any price change.

E Incomplete Markets

An economy without a full set of Arrow-Debreu contingent commodity markets is one in which many commodities (securities) are composites. When changes in demand change market prices, the nature of the composite product will often change. As a result, "quality" variable externalities will exist just as in the adverse selection case, and although the notion of "quality" is no longer unambiguous, small tax interventions will almost invariably exist that can improve an original market allocation. The initial allocation is not, therefore, a Pareto optimum.

A simple model of the phenomenon involved is one with two periods. Assume that, in period 2, the state of nature may take on one of k values. Assume further that there is a single store of value, denoted good zero, whose relative price in period 2 depends on the state of nature that materializes at that time.[27] Let an $(n+1)k$-dimensional vector $s = (s_1, \ldots, s_k)$ denote the vector of price vectors of n period-two nonnumeraire commodities with $s_{0k} \equiv 1$ for all k, in each of the period 2 states of nature. The value of this vector will depend upon market conditions in period 2, which depend, among other things, on taxes and the amount of the good zero available in period 2. If good zero is the only store of value, then a household's expected utility at the beginning of period 2 depends on its holdings W_0^h, of this good at that time and the vector of prices s. For each W_0^h and s, there is a function $V^h(W_0^h; s)$ which describes the maximum expected utility of household h in period 2.

Therefore, where insurance premiums are conditioned on *all* components x^h which affect $\bar{e}$, tax interventions will not be able to improve overall consumer welfare. (The original competitive equilibrium may still not be Pareto efficient, but commodity taxes will not help. See Arnott and Stiglitz [1990].) The ultimate policy question is whether insurance firms can monitor individual household consumption levels or whether it is easier for the government to control overall consumption levels via taxes. (A similar but slightly more complicated analysis can be applied to the adverse selection case presented earlier.)

[27] A more conventional approach would be to follow Diamond [1967] and Stiglitz [1972b, 1982b], who assume that the investment good yields a random return. If there are grounds for government intervention in the more restrictive model used here (in which the "real" return to the investment goods is fixed at zero), then there are certainly grounds for government intervention in the more general model.

For concreteness, V^h can be written as

$$V^h(W_0^h; s) = \sum_k u_{2k}^h(x_k^{h*}; W_0^h, s_k) b_k,$$

where b_k is the probability that state k materializes. The vector x_k^{h*} is the consumption that maximizes the utility of household h during period 2 in state k. It is selected to maximize $u_{2k}^h(x)$ subject to the constraint that

$$s_k \tilde{x}_k^h \leqslant 0,$$

where $\tilde{x}_k^h$ is the individual's (second period) net trade vector; for commodity zero,

$$\tilde{x}_{0k}^h = x_{0k}^{h*} - W_0^h,$$

while for the remaining commodities,

$$\tilde{x}_{jk}^h = x_{jk}^{h*} - W_{jk}^h,$$

where W_{jk}^h is the individual's second-period endowment vector in state k.

Looking forward from the beginning of period 1, we shall assume that a household's two-period expected utility is the sum of its expected utilities in period 1 and period 2 separately. Formally,

$$u^h(W_0^h; s) = u_1^h(\overline{W}^h - W_0^h) + V^h(W_0^h; s), \tag{22}$$

where $\overline{W}^h - W_0^h$ denotes consumption in period 1 of the store of value good, where $\overline{W}^h$ is his total initial endowment of that good. (We ignore first-period consumption other than of good zero.) Households choose W_0^h to maximize two-period utility.

Now consider the impact of a small change in period 2 prices. It will lead to changes in W_0^h purchased and, by this means, to changes in the vector s.[28] In equation (22), the vector s enters the overall utility function directly as a kind of externality. Like the quality variable in the adverse selection example, it describes the "composition" of a ticket in a lottery. In this instance, the lottery is a subsequent value lottery instead of a quality lottery (and the individual is concerned with more than the mean value). Thus, changes in the "prices" s have real welfare effects.

Application of equation (13) to this simple model implies that a small change in taxes dt will have a net impact per unit tax,

$$\frac{dR}{dt} = \sum_H \sum_k \frac{dE^h}{ds_k} \frac{ds_k}{dt} b_k = \sum_k \left[\sum_H \tilde{x}_k^h \cdot \frac{\lambda_k^h}{U_1^h} \right] \frac{ds_k}{dt} b_k,$$

---

[28] In addition, if there were a vector of consumption first period, it would lead to a readjustment of that vector, the effects of which net out.

where λ_k^h is the marginal utility of income to household h in state k.[29] Therefore, in general, there will exist taxes that can improve overall welfare.[30] Models that conclude otherwise typically impose conditions under which $ds_k/dt = 0$ for all k or in which the pattern of prices that occurs across states of nature has no welfare consequences (e.g., $\sum_H \bar{x}_k^h (\lambda_k^h / U_1^h) = 0$ for all k). For example, Diamond [1967] achieves this by having only a single good so that $s_k = 1$ for all k under all circumstances. The conditions involved are very special ones.[31]

In general, tax changes induce changes in the distribution of prices across the states of nature, and this affects the ability of the limited number of markets that are available to provide their important risk-transfer-risk-sharing functions. Each individual trader, however, takes the price distribution as given, and hence, in making his decisions, ignores these considerations. Our results thus provide a negative answer to what has become a long line of research, to find general conditions in which, though there is not a complete set of markets, the competitive economy is still constrained Pareto efficient, constrained, that is, by the limitations on the available risk market.[32]

F Queue Rationing

When information is imperfect and search (transactions) is costly, the benefits and costs of entering a market often depend on variables other than price. For instance,

[29] An increase in s_k reduces utility in the kth state by $x_k \lambda_k^h$. To compensate requires a first-period increase in income of $x_k \lambda_k^h / U_1^h$.

[30] It is worth noting that Pareto improvements can sometimes be effected by levying taxes or subsidies on variables that are not state contingent. (This may be important if, for instance, it is claimed that the reason that there is not a complete set of Arrow-Debreu securities is the unobservability by third parties, including the government, of the state.) Such is the case where the level of storage can be affected by taxes first period (which would arise if we had a vector of commodities the first period).

[31] Note that if all individuals are identical, $\bar{x}_k^h \equiv 0$, and the economy is constrained Pareto efficient (but then the risk markets serve no useful purpose, and no trade occurs on them). Note too that if individuals are risk neutral,

$$\lambda_k = U_1^h, \text{ so } \sum_H \bar{x}_k^h \frac{\lambda_k^h}{U_1^h} = \sum_H \bar{x}_k^h = 0 \text{ (by market clearing)}.$$

Again, the absence of risk markets causes no problems, since risk markets are really unnecessary. More general conditions under which risk markets are redundant (and the market equilibrium is constrained Pareto efficient) are derived in Stiglitz [1982b] and Newbery and Stiglitz [1981, 1982].

[32] Earlier studies [Stiglitz, 1972b; Drèze, 1974; Hart, 1975] showed that with an incomplete set of markets, there could be multiple equilibria, some of which Pareto dominated others. The results reported here show that in general every equilibrium is Pareto inefficient—that (to use the distinction introduced in Stiglitz [1972b]) there are marginal inefficiencies as well as (possibly) structural inefficiencies. Other studies identifying marginal inefficiencies include Stiglitz [1972b, 1975a, 1982b], Loong and Zeckhauser [1982], and Newbery and Stiglitz [1981, 1982, 1983, 1984].

Still other studies, in particular that of Grossman [1977a], have attempted to find a definition of constrained Pareto optimality such that the economy with limited risk markets is indeed constrained Pareto efficient. His Social Nash Optimality concept entails fixed transfers across individuals in the second period in different states. There appears to be no natural market interpretation of this constraint: the changes in prices induced by tax changes do entail changes in the relative magnitudes of the transfers.

the return to a worker entering the labor market depends on both the length of time that he has to search for a job as well as the wage he receives once he is employed. And the length of time that an individual has to search depends on the search activities of other individuals.

Similarly, in product markets, queues (and other nonprice mechanisms) may often be an integral part of the process of balancing supply and demand. The length of a queue and associated waiting costs may again depend on the actions of other firms and individuals.[33] In both cases, there is an externality. The question is whether these externalities result in markets being Pareto inefficient. We now show how these externalities can be analyzed using the framework of this paper. The example we investigate involves queue rationing. The reasons for looking at queues are threefold. First, they have not been investigated as thoroughly as search equilibria.[34] Second, the structure of the models is quite general. And third, queue rationing equilibria usefully illustrate the set of circumstances in which competitive equilibria are Pareto efficient (in ways that most conventional search models do not) even when nonprice mechanisms are an important part of the market-clearing process.

Again, to facilitate the exposition, we shall use a very simple model. Let there be a single good, subscript 1. The "good" is supplied in N separate markets indexed $i = 1, \ldots, N$, in each of which firms provide a different average waiting time. Consumers have rational expectations and know the probability distribution of waiting times for each type firm.[35] For simplicity, we assume that they are concerned only about the mean waiting time. An equilibrium set of prices equates supply and demand in each of these markets (as always, we ignore existence problems). Let

$q_i \equiv$ consumer price of the "good" in market $i = 1, \ldots, N$, $q = (q_1, q_N)$
$p_i \equiv$ producer price in market $i = 1, \ldots, N$,
$T_i \equiv$ average waiting time for consumers in market $i = 1, N, \ldots, T = (T_1, \ldots, T_N)$.

Each of the i markets are assumed to be competitive with both firms and consumers taking prices as given, and consumers taking waiting times as given.

---

[33] Similar externalities arise when firms must bear some part of the hiring and training costs of individuals, and individuals' quit rates depend on the actions of other firms. Still other search externalities that may be analyzed using our framework are those where the characteristics (quality) of individuals arriving at a firm are affected by the policies of other firms.

[34] An exception is Truman Bewley's unpublished paper, "Equilibrium Theory with Transactions Costs."

[35] Although this specification of "markets" may seem slightly unnatural, it is used to eliminate two obvious kinds of queuing inefficiency. First, having a separate price clear each waiting-time-defined market, we eliminate situations where time-on-queue substitutes for higher prices. Second, we eliminate situations, similar to the adverse selection or moral hazard cases analyzed above where consumers know the *average* waiting time (or processing rate) for a group of firms, but not the characteristics of individual firms. In our model it may be helpful to think of a firm's commitment to have an actual average waiting time equal to that of its waiting-time-defined market being enforced by a reputational mechanism.

Households will be assumed to divide up their purchase flows among the several markets. Let

$$x^h \equiv (x_1^h, \ldots, x_N^h) \equiv \text{vector of purchases by household } h,$$
$$x = \sum_H x^h.$$

Household utility will be assumed to depend on x^h and, also, implicitly on the waiting time associated with x^h.[36]

Each firm produces output using a single machine characterized by an output rate per unit time y^f. Machines break down in any given market period with a probability $(1 - r^f)$, where r^f is a machine's "reliability," and if they do so, we assume that they produce nothing for the period in question. The cost of a machine is a firm-specific function $c^f(r^f, y^f)$ of its output rate and reliability.

At the beginning of each period, consumers go to a particular market and select a firm. If the firm's machine is functioning, they look at the length of the queue and decide whether or not to wait (knowing the firm's processing rate). If the firm's machine has broken down, consumers select a new firm, and for simplicity, we assume that they do so costlessly until they join a queue.

Since firms in market i are committed to provide a waiting time T_i, their average process rates will have to be adjusted to meet this requirement, given the average rate of customer arrivals. That rate depends, in turn, on the reliabilities and processing rates of the machines of all firms in the ith market, since firms that have nonfunctioning or slow machines will tend to pass their customers on to others. The relationship even for this simple model will be a complex one, but, in general, it will take the form,

$$y^f = \Psi^f(\bar{y}_i, \bar{r}_i; T_i), \tag{23}$$

where $\bar{y}_i$ is an F_i-dimensional vector of the processing rates of the F_i firms in the ith market and $\bar{r}_i$ is an F_i-dimensional vector of reliabilities.

The average profit of an individual firm can, then, be written as

$$\Pi^f = p_i y^f r^f - c^f(r^f, y^f),$$

which is maximized subject to the constraint of equation (23). Substitution from (23) into the profit expression yields a reduced form profit function that now depends on the externality or z-variables $\bar{y}_i$ and $\bar{r}_i$. In general, the service rate required to attain a given mean service time depends on the actions of other firms in the market.

---

[36] For instance,

$$u^h \equiv u^h(x^h, w - p \cdot x^h, L - T \cdot x^h) \equiv \text{utility function of household } h,$$

where

$$w \equiv \text{total supply of labor} \equiv \text{labor income},$$
$$L \equiv \text{nonworker hours}.$$

Waiting times T will be assumed to be rates per units consumed which implies that there is a standard order quantity.

Notice that in this formulation, since individuals care only about mean service times, and these are "priced" by the market, externalities enter only through the profit function. Consequently, application of equation (13) yields

$$\frac{dR}{dt} = \sum_i \sum_{F_i} (p_i r^f - c_y^f) \left(\frac{\partial \Psi^f}{\partial \overline{y}_i} \cdot \frac{d\overline{y}_i}{dt} + \frac{\partial \Psi^f}{\partial \overline{r}_i} \cdot \frac{d\overline{r}_i}{dt} \right), \qquad (24)$$

where c_y^f is the marginal cost of additional processing capacity to firm f (note that $p_i r^s \neq c_y^f$ at the maximum profit, since firms must still meet a service time requirement).[37] Not only can, in general, a tax-subsidy scheme effect a Pareto improvement, but (24) shows that the appropriate direction of government policy can readily be determined by examining the impact of taxes on the service patterns facing firms and, in particular, on whether average extra processing capacity produces expected revenue below or in excess of its marginal cost.

We can also identify the special cases in which the market is Pareto efficient. Assume that firms could fix the arrival rates of consumers on their queues. This eliminates the spillover externalities from the actions of other firms. Then, assuming that consumers may search costlessly among firms to find a queue to which they will be admitted (we are not examining search externalities here), there are no externalities and the market is Pareto efficient.[38]

III FURTHER EXTENSIONS AND APPLICATIONS

Beyond the examples discussed in the previous section, the general approach that we have developed in this paper has a variety of other applications and easy extensions, providing insights in a variety of phenomena. In this section we briefly outline some of the more important of these.

---

[37] As usual, these are total derivatives. We consider here only small changes; note that for large changes, some firms may decide to change the market in which they enter; that is, firms must choose among all possible markets, the one that maximizes their profits. Though by the envelope theorem, the direct effects of these changes can be ignored, the discontinuities in the number of machines serving any particular market (which may result) imply that the relevant functions may not be continuous. We ignore these problems.

[38] Notice how restrictive these assumptions are. As both the search literature and these examples demonstrate, when nonprice processes play an important role in balancing supply and demand, the Pareto optimality of the "market" outcome will be unlikely.

A Self-Selection Constraints

Since the Rothschild-Stiglitz [1976], Wilson [1977], and Salop and Salop [1976] analyses of competitive equilibrium with self-selection constraints, the self-selection model has been used to investigate a variety of markets (insurance markets, labor markets, capital markets). Most of these studies were limited to a single market, taking all prices as given. The self-selection equilibrium, when it existed, was characterized as the allocation that maximized the welfare of the low-risk (high-ability, high-productivity) individual subject to the self-selection constraints being satisfied.[39] The equilibrium thus appeared to be (constrained) Pareto efficient. But as long as the self-selection constraints themselves can be affected by relative prices,[40] there exist taxes that can effect a Pareto improvement. Thus, in the education model if bright individuals use fewer pencils in going to school than do less bright individuals (they can do the necessary calculations in their head), then a tax on pencils has a differential effect on low- and high-ability individuals. Since the self-selection constraints represent a big wedge in the economy, it is not surprising that introducing a small wedge (in the pencil market) which reduces the magnitude of the big wedge (the self-selection constraint) may be desirable. (Formally, the effects of self-selection constraints can most easily be analyzed within our model by embedding them into a "derived" utility function, in a manner analogous to how we analyzed moral hazard.)

A special application of the self-selection model that has received considerable attention recently is that where workers are uninformed concerning the state of nature; self-selection constraints are used to induce firms to tell truthfully the state of nature. (See Grossman-Hart [1983], Azariadis and Stiglitz [1983], and Stiglitz [1985d] and the papers cited there.) The implicit contract equilibrium, with asymmetric information, is in general, not Pareto efficient.

B Moral Hazard and Incentives

The general set of issues discussed in subsection II.D arises not only in formal insurance markets, but also in a variety of other contexts in which there is implicit insurance, in which individuals do not bear the full costs of their actions. One well studied example arises in economies with sharecropping [Stiglitz, 1974b]. Braverman and Stiglitz [1982] have argued that in this context, the externalities across markets[41] may be so large and important that they are effectively internalized, through the interlinking of land, labor, and product markets. Similar effects arise in labor contracts in general, and managerial contracts in particular, when workers are not paid on a

---

[39] Also, implicitly, the highest risk (lowest ability) individuals obtain what they would have obtained were they the only individuals in the market.

[40] What is required is that the change in prices affect different types of individuals differently: there would almost always seem to be some commodity for which this is true.

[41] These arise from the effect of prices of credit or other commodities on effort exerted by the tenant; alternatively, the terms of the tenancy contract may affect default probabilities.

strictly piece rate basis. Moral hazard issues also arise in capital markets where both effort and risk-taking decisions may be affected [Stiglitz and Weiss, 1981].

C Unemployment Equilibria

Whenever the terms of a contractual arrangement affect the productivity of a worker (the riskiness of loan, etc.) either through selection or incentive effects, then there may exist equilibria that are not market clearing.[42] The informational problems imply that, in general, Pareto efficiency may entail unemployment; nonetheless, the market equilibrium is not, in general, a constrained Pareto optimum. It should be noted, however, that the approach developed here does not apply directly to this problem, since we have assumed here that markets clear (see Greenwald and Stiglitz [1985]).

D Rationing Equilibria

Again, it is easy to use our analysis to show that, in general, if there are distortions in the economy, caused by either commodity taxes, imperfect information, or incomplete markets, rationing may be desirable. Consider the effects, at a given set of prices, of a ration so large that only one individual (or a few) is affected adversely by it. The direct loss in welfare is negligible: at the margin, the individual is just indifferent to buying the last unit anyway. But the indirect effects, via prices, on the other distortions may be such as to make the rationing desirable. It might be argued that the resulting price changes are small and, thus, their consequences are negligible. However, as Appendix I demonstrates, this is not the case.

E Other Government Policies

Rationing is but one example of a government policy, other than uniform taxes, which may be used to effect Pareto-improving price and other changes in the presence of distortions. Price effects must be taken into account in designing other government policies as well. Thus, the optimal supply of public goods may no longer be described by the Samuelson condition of the sum of the marginal rates of substitution equaling the marginal rate of transformation: the effect of a marginal increase in the supply of the public good on all relative prices must be assessed.

Similarly, if the government has imposed an optimal income tax, whether differential commodity taxes will effect a Pareto improvement can be analyzed directly within our framework by embedding the self-selection constraints into the utility functions, and analyzing the effect of price changes on the associated implicit externalities. (Our analysis thus can be used to provide an interpretation of the Atkinson-Stiglitz [1976]

---

[42] For a survey of these theories see Stiglitz [1985d].

results, which give conditions under which no differential commodity taxation is desirable: see Stiglitz [1982f].)

F Prices Conveying Information

There have been several recent studies focusing on the role that prices play in conveying information, say about the state of nature. For instance, in the Grossman-Stiglitz model [1976, 1980a], as more individuals become informed, the price distribution changes and becomes more informative. Our analysis can again be used to show that the competitive equilibrium is not (constrained) Pareto efficient: not only do various tax policies affect the ability of the economy to share risks (as described earlier) but also affect the information available to each individual, and this too acts like a z-variable, except in the unusual case where essentially any set of equilibrium prices is fully informative.

G Large Welfare Consequences of Small Inefficiencies

Our analysis in Appendix I demonstrates how a small perturbation to the economy can have significant general equilibrium welfare effects, when there are already distortions in the economy. The perturbations we focused on in the body of the paper were government induced. But there is nothing in the mathematics that requires this. Thus, consider the consequences of one firm not adjusting some control variable in response to a disturbance to the economy. The welfare loss to the firm of this seemingly slight irrationality is negligible; however, with existing distortions, the welfare loss to the economy will, in general, not be. (See Akerlof and Yellen [1984].)

H Other Multipliers

This example illustrates that there may be "multiplier" effects in the presence of distortions. The total welfare loss may be a large multiple of the welfare loss to any individual. The analysis of this paper has focused on welfare effects, partly because the envelope theorem enables considerable simplification. Our model can, of course, be directly applied to illustrate other possible multiplers; any perturbation will not only have a direct effect, but also the standard indirect effect through prices (which, for stable systems, usually reduce the magnitude of the direct effect), and an externality (z-) effect; in a variety of situations the latter may reinforce, rather than dampen, the direct effect.

IV Concluding Remarks

We conclude with some general remarks concerning our approach to the study of externalities. In several of our examples we were able to relate the appropriate direction of government policy to some simple, in principle observable, parameters. On the other hand, we have considered relatively simple models, in which there is usually a single distortion (one kind of information imperfection, one kind of market failure). Though the basic qualitative proposition, that markets are not constrained Pareto efficient, would obviously remain in a more general formulation, the simplicity of the policy prescriptions would disappear. Does this make our analysis of little policy relevance? The same objection can, of course, be raised against standard optimal tax theory. (Some critics might say, so much the worse for both.) Though simple expositions of optimal tax theory often focus on the case of independent demand curves, in the general case, one needs to know all the cross elasticities of demand, and these are seldom available. What is worse, if one abandons the unrealistic assumption of the standard optimal commodity tax formulation (e.g., Diamond-Mirrlees [1971], with their assumption of 100 percent pure profits taxes, no restrictions on commodity taxation, and no (progressive) income tax), then the informational requirements on the government are even greater.

We believe, however, that in the case of the inefficiencies we have discussed here, there are some circumstances in which certain effects may be dominant, allowing the derivation of meaningful policy prescriptions, and there may be other circumstances in which all that is required is a reduced-form (general equilibrium) derivative, which it may be easier to obtain than to derive the underlying structural parameters. Thus, though there may be a complicated set of indirect effects from the imposition of a tax on alcohol, one might suspect that these indirect effects are outweighed by the direct effects associated with lower accident rates; and to assess whether taxation of alcohol is desirable, all that one needs to know is the net effect on accident rates.

It should be emphasized that none of the effects we have discussed depend on there being a finite number of individuals. It is sometimes thought that in "large" economies, pecuniary effects can be ignored, since the action of any individual has a very small effect on price. Although it is true that in large economies, the action of an individual has a very small effect on price, the change in the price affects a large number of individuals. The total welfare effect is the product of the magnitude of the change in the price, times the number of individuals who are affected. We show in Appendix I that this product does *not* go to zero as the size of the economy gets larger. Pecuniary effects do not matter in the standard competitive model simply because there are no distortions; if there are distortions—imperfect information, incomplete markets, etc.—they matter, regardless of the size of the economy.

Last, we had considerable difficulty in choosing a title for this paper. One suggested title was "Externalities in Imperfect Economies." This had one advantage over the title chosen: as should be clear from the analysis, our results apply to more than just the problems raised by imperfect information and incomplete markets. We rejected it, however, for two reasons. First, referring to economies with incomplete markets and imperfect information as "imperfect" seems to be wrong: we do not refer to economies in which inputs are required to produce outputs as "imperfect"; and the costs of obtaining information and running markets are no less real costs than other forms of production costs.

Second, the title seems to trivialize our results. It hardly seems surprising that there exist government interventions which can effect a Pareto improvement in an economy with externalities, and other imperfections. Nor should it come as much of a surprise that imperfect information and incomplete markets cause "problems." Our results do, however, run counter to much of (at least the older) folk-wisdom. This suggested that although an economy with, say, imperfect information would not do so well as one with perfect information, this was an irrelevant comparison. The relevant comparison had to take these costs of information into account; when this was done, it was suggested (though not proved) that the efficiency of the competitive economy would be re-established. We hope this paper will have laid to rest this heuristic argument.

The paper thus casts a new light on the First Fundamental Theorem of Welfare Economics asserting the Pareto efficiency of competitive equilibrium. The theorem is an achievement because it identifies what in retrospect has turned out to be the singular set of circumstances under which the economy is Pareto efficient. There is not a complete set of markets; information is imperfect; the commodities sold in any market are not homogeneous in all relevant respects; it is costly to ascertain differences among the items; individuals do not get paid on a piece rate basis; and there is an element of insurance (implicit or explicit) in almost all contractual arrangements, in labor, capital, and product markets. In virtually all markets there are important instances of signaling and screening. Individuals must search for the commodities that they wish to purchase, firms must search for the workers who they wish to hire, and workers must search for the firm for which they wish to work. We frequently arrive at a store only to find that it is out of inventory; or at other times we arrive, to find a queue waiting to be served. Each of these are "small" instances, but their cumulative effects may indeed be large.

We have constructed a general model which shows that in all of these circumstances, Pareto improvements can be effected through government policies, such as commodity taxes. Our methodology not only identifies the presence of inefficiencies, but also enables us to identify both the appropriate direction of policy intervention and observable measures of their successful application.

Appendix I

In order to investigate the nature of pecuniary externalities in the traditional sense, the natural starting point is to examine the impact of a small "balanced budget" shift in excess demand.[43]

[43] Only balanced budget shifts make sense if we are considering changes in equilibrium allocations. An unbalanced shift in excess demand would preclude the existence of a new equilibrium.

Let

$$d\bar{v}_0 \equiv (dv_1^0, dv^0),$$

where

$dv_1^0 \equiv -q \cdot dv^0 \equiv$ shift in demand for the numeraire good,
$dv^0 \equiv (N-1)$ vector of shifts in demand for the $N-1$ nonnumeraire goods.

The shift $d\bar{v}_0$ may be ascribed either to a shift in the demand of a single household or to entry of a new household. An analogous shift with $dv_1^0 = -p \cdot dv^0$ could be defined and ascribed to a change in behavior by the universe of firms.

If taxes are unchanged, the resulting change in market prices is

$$dp = dq = J^{-1} \cdot dv^0,$$

where

$J \equiv \left[\dfrac{dx_j}{dp_k} - \dfrac{dy_j}{dq_k} \right], j, k = 2, \ldots, N \equiv$ Jacobian[44] of the vector of nonnumeraire excess demands.

We assume that the excess demand functions are differentiable and that J is nonsingular at the initial equilibrium.

The change in income necessary to maintain the utility level of household h in the face of a change in price $dp = dq$ is

$$\frac{dI^h}{dp} = E_q^h + E_z^h \left(\frac{dz^h}{dp} + \frac{dz^h}{dq} \right) - \sum_F a^{hf} \left(\pi_p^f + \pi_z^f \left(\frac{dz^f}{dp} + \frac{dz^f}{dq} \right) \right).$$

Summation over all households and recognition that $\pi_p^f = y^f$, $E_q^h = x^h$, $\sum_H a^{hf} = 1$, and $\sum_F y^f = \sum_H x^h$ yields a total net change in government income compensation,

$$\sum_H \frac{dI^h}{dp} = \sum_H E_z^h \left(\frac{dz^h}{dp} + \frac{dz^h}{dq} \right) - \sum_F \pi_z^f \left(\frac{dz^f}{dp} + \frac{dz^f}{dq} \right).$$

The total change in the government surplus (once these compensations are paid) is

$$\frac{dR}{dp} = t \cdot \frac{dx}{dp} - \sum_H E_z^h \left(\frac{dz^h}{dp} + \frac{dz^h}{dq} \right) - \sum_F \pi_z^f \left(\frac{dz^f}{dp} + \frac{dz^f}{dq} \right).$$

At an initial tax level of zero this becomes

$$\frac{dR}{dp} = -\sum_H E_z^h \left(\frac{dz^h}{dp} + \frac{dz^h}{dq} \right) - \sum_F \pi_z^f \left(\frac{dz^f}{dp} + \frac{dz^f}{dq} \right).$$

---

[44] Since $dp_k = dq_k$ in the present instance, it makes sense to talk about this "Jacobian" without treating the p and q vectors separately.

As a function of the initial change in excess demand, the net change in the government surplus[45] is

$$\frac{dR}{dv^0} = \frac{dR}{dp} \cdot \frac{dp}{dv^0} = (\Pi^P - B^P) \cdot J^{-1}, \tag{A1}$$

where

$$\pi^P \equiv \sum_F \pi_z^f \left(\frac{dz^f}{dp} + \frac{dz^f}{dq} \right),$$

$$B^P \equiv \sum_H E_z^h \left(\frac{dz^h}{dp} + \frac{dz^h}{dq} \right),$$

This represents the net social impact of the initial change in price and, thus, the "pecuniary" externality[46] associated with original change in demand $d\bar{v}^0$.

It only remains to be shown that dR/dv^0 does not vanish as the number of households becomes large. To do this, let

$\eta_m \equiv$ fraction of households of type $m = 1, \dots, M$
(i.e., $\eta_m H =$ number of households of type m)
$\eta_\ell \equiv$ number of firms of type $l = 1, \dots, L$ per household
(i.e., $\eta_\ell H =$ number of firms of type l)

Since dz^f/dp and dz^f/dq ought not to be influenced by the number of households,[47]

$$\Pi^P \equiv \sum_L H \cdot \pi_z^l \left(\frac{dz^l}{dp} + \frac{dz^l}{dq} \right) = H \cdot \hat{\Pi}^P,$$

---

[45] The expression in equation (A-1) below ignores the externalities generated by changes in consumption that result from compensating government income transfers. This is not done because the changes in question are negligible; they are not negligible. Rather it is done to avoid keeping track of transfer-related externalities that add greatly to the notational burden without affecting the basic substance of the analysis. For rigor we could assume that (1) consumption and production of the numeraire good generates no externalities and (2) households are constrained to consume their compensating allotments of the numeraire good. Also we assume that the original shift affects no z-variables. Alternatively, the derivatives can be interpreted in the manner suggested in footnote 8.

[46] This effect differs from the tax effects of the body of the paper in that the dz/dp, dz/dq terms differ from the dz/dt terms. However, in both cases, externalities will not matter either when π_z^f and E_z^h are zero for all households and firms or when the z's are not affected by changes in market prices (other cases are fortuitous). If dz^f/dt and dz^h/dt are nonzero, then as a rule $(dz^f/dp + dz^f/dq)$ and $(dz^h/dp + dz^h/dq)$ will be nonzero. Thus (again in general), the conditions under which taxes can lead to Pareto-improving allocations are precisely circumstances under which "pecuniary" externalities do not net out.

[47] Clearly in some cases through crowding or other effects increases in the numbers of agents will themselves intensify the impact of a price change on particular externalities. Equally clearly we want to focus on cases where this does not happen. For instance, if z is the quality of air that is affected by the total level of consumption of some commodities, then replicating households but dividing the size of each household proportionately will, with homothetic preferences, lead to the appropriate limit for our purposes.

where

$$\hat{\Pi}^P \equiv \sum_L \pi_z^l \left(\frac{dz^l}{dp} + \frac{dz^l}{dp} \right),$$

$$\pi_z^l \equiv \pi_z^f \text{ for firms of type } l,$$

$$\frac{dz^l}{dp} \equiv \frac{dz^f}{dp}, \frac{dz^l}{dq} = \frac{dz^f}{dq} \text{ for firms of type } l.$$

The matrix $\hat{\Pi}^P$ will not change with the number of households H. Similarly,

$$B^P = H \cdot \hat{B}^P,$$

where

$$\hat{B}^P \equiv \sum_M E_z^m \left(\frac{dz^m}{dp} + \frac{dz^m}{dq} \right),$$

and $\hat{B}^P$ should be invariant to changes in H.

On the other hand, the Jacobian of the excess demands

$$J = \left[\frac{dx_i}{dq_j} - \frac{dy_i}{dp_j} \right] = \left[\sum_H \frac{dx_i^h}{dq_j} - \sum_F \frac{dy_i^f}{dp_j} \right]$$

$$= H \left[\sum_M \eta_m \frac{dx_i^m}{dq_j} - \sum_F \eta_l \frac{dy_i^l}{dp_j} \right] = H \cdot \hat{J},$$

where

$$\hat{J} \equiv \left[\sum_M \eta_m \frac{dx_i^m}{dq_j} - \sum_F \eta_l \frac{dy_i^l}{dp_j} \right],$$

which should be invariant to changes in H. The inverse of the Jacobian, J^{-1}, can now be written as

$$J^{-1} = 1/H \cdot \hat{J}^{-1},$$

which does go to zero as H increases. This reflects the fact that as the number of agents increases, the impact on prices of any single agent goes to zero.

However,

$$\frac{dR}{dv^0} = (\Pi^P - B^P) \cdot J^{-1} = H(\hat{\Pi}^P - \hat{B}^P) \cdot \frac{1}{H} \cdot \hat{J}^{-1}$$

$$= (\hat{\Pi}^P - \hat{B}^{-P}) \cdot \hat{J}^{-1},$$

which is invariant to the number of households. Thus, "pecuniary" externalities vanish in atomistic economies only when $\hat{\Pi}^P$ and $\hat{B}^P$ are zero, which occurs, in turn, only in the absence of nonpecuniary externalities.

MORAL HAZARD AND NONMARKET INSTITUTIONS: DYSFUNCTIONAL CROWDING OUT OR PEER MONITORING?*

We examine a situation in which insurance is characterized by moral hazard. When market insurance is provided, supplementary mutual assistance between family and friends (unobservable to market insurers) will occur. When nonmarket insurers have no better information than market insurers, the mutual assistance not only crowds out market insurance but is also harmful and therefore dysfunctional. Alternatively, when nonmarket insurers can observe each other's effort perfectly, mutual assistance is beneficial. These results point to the potential importance of peer-monitoring mechanisms in mitigating moral hazard.

THE economics literature over the past 15 years has directed attention to the ubiquity of moral-hazard and incentives problems. One way the market responds to moral hazard is to provide only partial insurance, since then individuals still have *some*

* Written with Richard Arnott. Financial support from the National Science Foundation, the Olin Foundation, and the Social Sciences and Humanities Research Council of Canada is gratefully acknowledged. We thank the referees and the seminar participants at Stanford University, in particular Ken Judd and Suzanne Scotchmer, for very helpful comments. Reprint with permission from the *American Economic Review*, 81(1), March (1991), pp. 179–90.

incentive to take care to avoid the accident. However, they must then bear more risk than they would like. A principal function of many nonmarket institutions, meanwhile, is to help those who have suffered some misfortune, which entails the provision of insurance: the marriage vows formalize and sanctify the mutual insurance aspects of the family; the acid test of a friend is his willingness to help in times of need; charity is regarded as meritorious and is subsidized by the government; and many government social assistance programs, such as unemployment insurance and workmen's compensation, have a strong insurance component. The importance of nonmarket insurance is illustrated by what happens if an individual catches pneumonia as a result of going on a hiking trip with inadequate rain gear. His employer gives him compensated sick leave; part or all of his medical expenses are reimbursed by his insurance policy or the state; uncovered medical expenses may be partially deductible from his income tax; and family and friends rally round to provide other forms of support. Such extensive support, while directly helpful, deleteriously affects individuals' care to avoid accidents. In terms of the example, had the individual borne all the costs of catching pneumonia himself, he might have taken the trouble to carry adequate rain gear. Thus, it is not obvious that the insurance provided by nonmarket institutions is always beneficial or, more specifically, whether nonmarket insurance institutions, when they supplement market insurance, improve the economy's ability to handle the moral-hazard trade-off between risk-bearing and incentives.

We address this issue by inquiring whether the reciprocal provision of insurance within families and between friends, which we term nonmarket insurance,[1] is welfare-improving when it supplements market insurance. We assume that a market insurer can observe his clients' market insurance purchases but not the nonmarket insurance they obtain through informal arrangements. We first show that nonmarket insurance will always be provided. Moral hazard causes fully insured individuals to expend too little effort. In response, the competitively determined market insurance contract rations the amount of insurance that can be obtained at the equilibrium price. The contract achieves this by specifying both a price and a quantity and by stipulating that it will pay in the event of accident only if the insured has no additional market insurance. Insured individuals would like to obtain additional insurance at the market price. Since they take the market insurance contract as given, they perceive that they can effectively do so by entering into informal insurance arrangements. They neglect that when everyone enters into such arrangements, the accident frequency will change, as will the market insurance contract.

After showing that nonmarket insurance will always be provided, we ask whether the level of expected utility is higher with such insurance than without it. The moral-hazard problem arises because of the inability of the insurance firm to monitor the actions of the insured. There are often other individuals, such as the members of the insured's family, who are in a better position to monitor the insured's action than the insurance firm. The welfare consequences of nonmarket insurance turn out

---

[1] The term "social insurance" is perhaps more appropriate but is used in some countries to refer to social security. The term "informal insurance" is appropriate for the example, but the phenomenon we identify arises in formal, nonmarket institutions as well.

to depend on whether these monitoring capabilities can be effectively harnessed to reduce the moral-hazard problem. If the members of the family (the providers of nonmarket insurance) do not monitor each other, we show that such nonmarket insurance always lowers welfare. The nonmarket insurance leads individuals to take less care; market insurance firms respond by providing less insurance; thus, in the new equilibrium, nonmarket insurance displaces market insurance. Since nonmarket insurance involves less risk-pooling, welfare is reduced; the less-effective insurance crowds out the more-effective insurance. The nonmarket insurance is dysfunctional.

If, alternatively, the members of the family do monitor each other, they will take greater care than they would without monitoring, which mitigates the moral-hazard problem. Thus, there appear to be two off-setting effects, the risk-pooling advantages of market insurance versus the monitoring advantages of nonmarket insurance. However, it turns out that, with perfect monitoring within the family, the latter effect dominates, and the nonmarket insurance is welfare-enhancing.

This is an example of what we call *peer monitoring*. Peer monitoring is an important mechanism for controlling moral hazard. It arises in credit markets. In less-developed countries, loans are often made to groups of individuals; the members of a group then have an incentive to monitor each other. In developed countries, one of the functions of co-signers on loans is to provide additional monitoring. Partnership arrangements also encourage monitoring. Peer monitoring is also important in labor markets; workers are often in a better position to monitor their co-workers than are employers, which may be one of the advantages of team production.

This raises an intriguing issue related to mechanism design with a principal and many agents when moral hazard is present. The principal can monitor his agents himself (direct monitoring), hire a supervisor to monitor his agents (supervision), or set up a mechanism to induce agents to monitor each other (indirect monitoring). While the literature has considered direct monitoring (e.g., Steven Shavell, 1979a; Bengt Holmstrom, 1979) and supervision (e.g., James Mirrlees, 1976; Stiglitz, 1975b; Jean Triole, 1988), it has largely ignored the design of indirect monitoring systems.[2] An indirect monitoring system will encourage peer monitoring through the creation of interdependence: the dependence of one agent's utility on others' effort. A good example is a university department. A faculty member's utility depends not only on his salary, performance, reputation, and working conditions, but also directly on his department's and university's reputation. Furthermore, his salary, performance, reputation, and working conditions all depend to some extent on the department's quality. For these reasons, faculty members have a strong incentive to monitor one another's performance, which they do through peer review, teaching evaluations, and so on. In other contexts, production may be physically organized to facilitate peer monitoring; the open office, the assembly line, and team production are examples. In this paper, we treat the peermonitoring system as exogenous and examine only the extreme cases in which there is either perfect monitoring or no monitoring.

[2] One exception is H. Lorne Carmichael (1988). He considers peer review in the university setting, which is a form of indirect monitoring system, and argues that the institution of tenure is needed to make peer review incentive-compatible.

I THE BASIC MODEL WITHOUT
NONMARKET INSURANCE

Moral hazard is an asymmetric-information phenomenon, and its defining characteristic is hidden action. In the context of insurance, the probability distribution of observable outcomes depends on the insured's unobservable actions. The insurer would like to write insurance contingent on the insured's actions but, since these are unobservable, must base his insurance on observable outcomes. Because of moral hazard, there is a trade-off between risk-bearing and incentives in the provision of insurance. At one extreme, if full insurance is provided,[3] the insured is equally well off whatever the outcome and therefore has no incentive to take care. At the other extreme, if no insurance is provided, the individual faces the appropriate incentives but is fully exposed to risk.

We first describe the canonical moralhazard model without nonmarket insurance (Arnott and Stiglitz, 1988a). There is a single, fixed-damage accident. The probability of its occurrence, p, depends on the individual's effort at accident avoidance, e. The probability-of-accident function is strictly convex: $p' < 0$, $p'' > 0$. The individual's wealth is w, and d is the damage caused by the accident.

If an accident occurs, the individual receives a (net of premium) payout of a, and his consumption is

$$y_1 = w - d + a. \tag{1a}$$

If an accident does not occur, he pays the premium β, and his consumption is

$$y_0 = w - \beta. \tag{1b}$$

For simplicity, we assume a separable, event-independent utility function.[4] Expected utility is then

$$EU = u(y_0)(1 - p) + u(y_1)p - e \tag{2}$$

with $u' > 0$, $u'' < 0$.

The individual chooses effort so as to maximize expected utility, taking a and β as given:[5]

$$e(a, \beta) = \underset{\{e\}}{\operatorname{argmax}} EU(a, \beta, e). \tag{3}$$

It is straightforward to show that, with the form of utility function assumed, $\partial e/\partial a < 0$ and $\partial e/\partial \beta < 0$; as more insurance is provided, the individual reduces

---

[3] Full insurance—equalization of the marginal utilities of income in all events—implies no incentive to take care when the utility function is event-independent, which we assume, but not generally otherwise.

[4] The general form of the utility function with event i is $U_t(y_i, e)$. Separability implies $U_t(y_t, e) = u_t(y_i) - e$. Event-independence implies that the utility-from-consumption function $u_t(y)$ is independent of the event; the accident causes neither pain nor pleasure and does not alter tastes.

[5] Throughout the paper, we ignore the complications that arise from the possibility that $e = 0$.

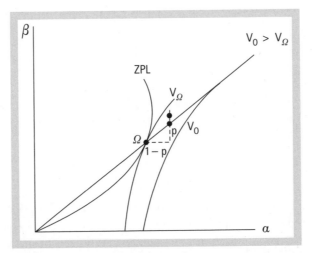

Fig. 1. The individual perceives that he can obtain additional insurance at the Market Price by entering into a Mutual Insurance Pact

effort. Substitution of (3) into (2) gives $V(a, \beta) \equiv EU(a, \beta, e(a, \beta))$, from which an individual's indifference curves in $a - \beta$ space can be plotted (see Fig. 1). The slope of an indifference curve is

$$\left.\frac{d\beta}{da}\right|_{\bar{V}} = \frac{u_1'p}{u_0'(1-p)} \qquad (4)$$

where $u_0 \equiv u(y_0)$ and $u_1 \equiv u(y_1)$. The locus of (a, β) for which there are zero profits, the zero-profit locus (ZPL), is $(1-p)\beta - pa = 0$. Substitution of (3) into this equation gives the ZPL as a function of a and β, which is plotted in Figure 1. Its slope is

$$\left.\frac{d\beta}{da}\right|_{ZPL} = \frac{p + (a+\beta)p'(\partial e/\partial a)}{(1-p) - (a+\beta)p'(\partial e/\partial\beta)}. \qquad (5)$$

In Figure 1, Ω is the point of optimal insurance, contingent on the unobservability of effort;[6] it occurs at the point of maximum utility on the zero-profit locus.

We now investigate competitive equilibrium for this model with insurance purchases observable (Arnott and Stiglitz, 1988a, 1987). Define $q \equiv \beta/a$ to be the price of insurance. Since Ω is on the ZPL, $q_\Omega \equiv (\beta/a)_\Omega = [p/(1-p)]_\Omega$. The precise shapes of the indifference curves and the ZPL are inessential for our analysis.[7] What is essential,

<hr>

[6] Ω is the optimal *deterministic* contract. The circumstances in which randomization is Pareto-improving are investigated in Arnott and Stiglitz (1988b).

[7] Indifference curves are positively sloped and can be nonconvex

$$\left(\left.\frac{d^2\beta}{da^2}\right|_{\bar{V}} > 0\right)$$

as can be seen from (4). As the amount of insurance provided increases, holding utility fixed, u_1'/u_0' falls, but since more insurance causes the probability of accidents to rise, $p/(1-p)$ increases. The zero-profit locus is positively sloped for small amounts of insurance but may bend backwards.

however, is that at Ω the slope of the ZPL exceeds the price of insurance. Since indifference curves are positively sloped and since Ω is at a point of tangency of an indifference curve and the ZPL, the ZPL must be positively sloped at Ω. Now consider increasing a by one unit. To maintain zero profits, β must be increased by more than the price of insurance, $q_\Omega = [p/(1-p)]_\Omega$. An increase in β of $[p/(1-p)]_\Omega$ causes zero profit to be made on the *marginal* unit of insurance; but the increase in a raises the probability of accident, and so β has to be increased further to offset losses on *inframarginal* units of insurance. Hence,

$$\left(\frac{d\beta}{da}\bigg|_{\overline{V}}\right)_\Omega = \left(\frac{d\beta}{da}\bigg|_{ZPL}\right)_\Omega > q_\Omega. \tag{6}$$

Since at Ω the slope of the indifference curve exceeds the price of insurance, individuals would like to acquire more insurance at the price q_Ω (see Pauly, 1974). Thus, competitive decentralization of Ω requires rationing of insurance at the price q_Ω.[8] The intuition for this result is that, because of moral hazard, at any price of insurance, the individual expends too little effort. Rationing induces him to increase his effort. The easiest[9] way for such rationing to be accomplished is for each insurer to offer the contract (a_Ω, β_Ω), conditional on its clients purchasing no additional insurance. This condition, which we term the exclusivity provision, is enforceable, since it is assumed that insurers are able to observe all insurance purchases.

To sum up, with moral hazard, when nonmarket insurance is absent and insurance purchases are observable, the social optimum conditional on the unobservability of effort is decentralizable. Competitive equilibrium entails each individual being restricted to purchase all his insurance from a single insurer and being rationed in the amount of insurance he can purchase at the equilibrium price.

II EFFORT UNOBSERVABLE BY THE NONMARKET INSURER

We now consider the simplest possible extension of this model that allows for the simultaneous provision of market and nonmarket insurance. We assume that,

[8] The point Ω can be decentralized by the insurer offering any locus of (a, β) such that Ω is the point of maximum utility on the locus and insisting that he be the sole insurer. One such possibility entails the insurer offering the zero-profit locus. This particular form of nonlinear pricing in this context was considered by Elhanan Helpman and Jean-Jacques Laffont (1975). The analysis of the paper carries through whatever form of pricing is employed to decentralize Ω.

[9] Insurers could alternatively agree to sell a client who has purchased a total amount of insurance from other insurers of (a', β') an insurance policy $(\hat{a}, \hat{\beta}) = (a_\Omega - a', \beta_\Omega - \beta')$, which would bring his total insurance up to (a_Ω, β_Ω). However, this is unnecessarily complicated. In fact, almost all insurance policies contain exclusivity provisions (life and air-flight accident insurance are the exceptions, but moral hazard is unimportant for both types of insurance).

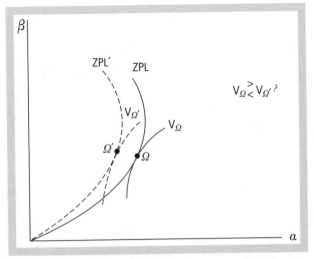

Fig. 2. The effect of nonmarket insurance when it reduces effort

although an insurer can observe his clients' insurance *purchases*, he cannot observe the nonmarket insurance they acquire.[10]

As described earlier, nonmarket insurance may be provided through many institutions. To simplify, we treat only nonmarket insurance provided reciprocally by pairs of symmetrical individuals. We label the two partners in a pair, H (husband) and W (wife). The two partners have the same tastes and probability-of-accident functions, and their accident probabilities are statistically independent.[11] The form of the nonmarket insurance is as follows: H and W agree that if one spouse has an accident and the other does not, the latter will transfer δ to the former.

The issues to be addressed can be posed in terms of Figure 2. The solid-lined ZPL and V_Ω are the zero-profit locus and equilibrium-indifference curve in the absence of nonmarket insurance (the same as in Fig. 1); the dashed-lined ZPL and $V_{\Omega'}$ are the corresponding curves with nonmarket insurance. Assume, for the sake of argument, that the provision of nonmarket insurance reduces effort. There are then two offsetting effects on equilibrium utility. On one hand, with α and β held fixed, the provision of nonmarket insurance increases utility; it shifts indifference curves to the left. On the other hand, since by assumption the provision of nonmarket insurance increases the probability of accident, the insurance firm must lower the payout for any level of the premium to continue making zero profits; as a result, the ZPL also shifts to the left. The analysis that follows examines which effect is dominant.

---

[10] If an insurer were able to observe the nonmarket insurance that his clients acquire, he could write the contract contingent on their nonmarket insurance. The resulting equilibrium would be efficient conditional on the information available (the efficiency result depends on there being only one commodity and one type of accident; see Arnott and Stiglitz, 1986, 1990).

[11] This assumption simplifies the analysis and does not affect the qualitative results. Depending on context, the accident probabilities of the partners may be positively correlated.

In this section, we characterize the equilibrium for the case in which an individual's accident-avoidance effort is observable by neither his partner nor market insurers. Equilibrium may entail a combination of market and nonmarket insurance. Subsequently, we shall investigate the efficiency properties of the equilibrium.

There are four events: 1) neither the individual nor his partner has an accident; 2) the individual has an accident, but his partner does not; 3) only the partner has an accident; 4) both have accidents. Let e denote the individual's effort and $\tilde{e}$ his partner's. Then, the probability that neither the individual nor his partner has an accident is $[1 - p(e)][1 - p(\tilde{e})]$ and similarly for the other events. We assume that the market insurer sells individual rather than group insurance policies[12] (i.e., he sells each partner a policy (a, β); if neither individual has an accident, each has to pay the market insurer the premium β, etc.).

Thus, an individual's expected utility is

$$
\begin{aligned}
EU = {} & u(w - \beta)[1 - p(e)][1 - p(\tilde{e})] + u(w - d + a)p(e)p(\tilde{e}) \\
& + u(w - \beta - \delta)[1 - p(e)]p(\tilde{e}) + u(w - d + a + \delta)p(e) \\
& \times [1 - p(\tilde{e})] - e
\end{aligned}
\tag{7}
$$

which may be written more succinctly as

$$
EU = u_0(1 - p)(1 - \tilde{p}) + u_1 p\tilde{p} + u_2(1 - p)\tilde{p} + u_3 p(1 - \tilde{p}) - e
\tag{7'}
$$

where $u_0 \equiv u(w - \beta)$, $u_1 \equiv u(w - d + a)$, $u_2 \equiv u(w - \beta - \delta)$, $u_3 \equiv u(w - d + a + \delta)$, and $\tilde{p} \equiv p(\tilde{e})$.

We assume that H and W are smart and take into account how the other will adjust effort in response to a change in δ.[13] Both assume that the market contract will be unaffected by their actions, which is perfectly reasonable in the atomistic environment we envisage.

We adopt the Nash assumption. W, in deciding on her level of effort, takes a, β, and δ as well as H's effort as fixed. W believes that H is rational and selfish and will accordingly choose the level of effort that maximizes his expected utility, given that W is acting similarly.[14] Then, from (7), the equation characterizing her level of precaution is

$$
[-u_0(1 - \tilde{p}) + u_1 \tilde{p} - u_2 \tilde{p} + u_3(1 - \tilde{p})] p' - 1 = 0
\tag{8}
$$

---

[12] Where the insurance company cannot identify the nonmarket insurance partners (friends, for example), this is the natural assumption. However, in other contexts, notably the family, the market typically provides group policies. We have run through the analysis when the market provides group rather than individual policies. Group policies are Pareto-superior, since they contain an extra policy parameter: an insurance policy specifies the group premium payable if neither has an accident, the net payout if only one has an accident, and the net payout if both have accidents. In other respects, the qualitative results are the same when the market provides group policies as when it provides individual policies.

[13] We would obtain the same qualitative results if we assumed instead that H and W ignore that the other will adjust effort in response to a change in δ.

[14] This is not an infinitely repeated game. If it were, the cooperative outcome might be obtained. We comment on this later.

which gives

$$e = \hat{e}(\alpha, \beta, \delta, \tilde{p}) \tag{9a}$$

and by symmetry

$$\tilde{e} = \hat{e}(\alpha, \beta, \delta, p). \tag{9b}$$

Combining (9a) and (9b) yields

$$e = e(\alpha, \beta, \delta) \tag{10a}$$

$$\tilde{e} = e(\alpha, \beta, \delta). \tag{10b}$$

From (7), the individual and his partner perceive expected utility to be related to δ in the following way:

$$\frac{\partial EU}{\partial \delta} = \left[-u_2'(1-p)\tilde{p} + u_3'p(1-\tilde{p}) \right] + \left\{ \left[-u_0(1-\tilde{p}) + u_1\tilde{p} - u_2\tilde{p} \right. \right.$$
$$+ u_3(1-\tilde{p}) \right] p' - 1 \right\} \frac{\partial e}{\partial \delta} + \left[-u_0(1-p) + u_1 p \right.$$
$$+ u_2(1-p) - u_3 p \right] \tilde{p}' \frac{\partial \tilde{e}}{\partial \delta}. \tag{11}$$

In so doing, they neglect that, since other couples too behave in this way, insurance companies adjust α and β in response to a change in δ. Combining (8), (10a), (10b), and (11), and noting that the equilibrium is symmetric, gives

$$\frac{\partial EU}{\partial \delta} = (-u_2' + u_3')(1-p)p + [1 + (u_2 - u_3)p'] \frac{\partial e}{\partial \delta}. \tag{12}$$

Furthermore, from (8),

$$\frac{\partial e}{\partial \delta} = -\frac{[u_2'p + u_3'(1-p)]p'}{(p''/p') + (p')^2(u_0 + u_1 - u_2 - u_3)} < 0. \tag{13}$$

At Ω (the competitive equilibrium in the absence of nonmarket insurance), $\delta = 0$, $1 + (u_2 - u_3)p' = 0$ [from (8) since $u_0 = u_2$ and $u_1 = u_3$], and $-u_2' + u_3' > 0$ (incomplete insurance). Hence, from (12),

$$\left. \frac{\partial EU}{\partial \delta} \right|_\Omega = (-u_2' + u_3')(1-p)p > 0. \tag{14}$$

Thus, at the competitive equilibrium in the absence of nonmarket insurance, the partners perceive a mutual insurance pact to be beneficial and would therefore provide one another with nonmarket insurance to supplement their market insurance. The intuition for this result is as follows. At Ω, the partners are rationed in the amount of insurance they can purchase at the price q_Ω. Each perceives that, by entering into a mutual insurance pact, he can acquire additional insurance at this price, which pays out when he, but not his partner, suffers an accident. More specifically, at Ω, since

$$\frac{\partial EU}{\partial a} = pu'_3 \quad \text{and} \quad \frac{\partial EU}{\partial \beta} = -(1-p)u'_2$$

from (12),

$$\frac{\partial EU}{\partial \delta} = (1-p)\frac{\partial EU}{\partial a} + p\frac{\partial EU}{\partial \beta}. \tag{15}$$

An individual regards a unit increase in δ as equivalent to a unit increase in a with probability $1 - p$ (the probability that his partner is not sick when he is) combined with a unit increase in β with probability p (the probability that his partner is sick when he is not), or equivalently, as an expected increase of $1 - p$ in the amount of insurance obtained at the price q (i.e., movement from Ω to ϕ in Fig. 1). As already noted, in reasoning in this way, individuals neglect that, when everyone enters into such a pact, which reduces effort [eq. (13)] and increases the probability of accident, market insurers are forced to offer a less attractive contract in order to maintain zero profits.

H and W choose δ to maximize their expected utilities, taking a and β as given. From $\partial EU/\partial \delta = 0$, $e = \tilde{e}$, and (8), one obtains $\delta = \delta(a, \beta)$. By observing how the probability of accident responds to changes in a and β, market insurers will implicitly take into account that δ responds to a and β according to $\delta = \delta(a, \beta)$. Competition, meanwhile, will continue to result in the equilibrium market contract maximizing expected utility subject to zero profits. Thus, in the presence of nonmarket insurance, the equilibrium market contract maximizes

$$EU = u(w - \beta)(1 - p)^2 + u(w - d + a)p^2 + u(w - \beta - \delta)(1 - p)p$$
$$+ u(w - d + a + \delta)p(1 - p) - e \tag{16}$$

subject to

(i) $\beta(1 - p) - ap = 0$
(ii) $e = e(a, \beta, \delta(a, \beta))$

where (ii) is obtained by combining (10a) and $\delta = \delta(a, \beta)$.

Given the assumed information technology, it can be shown that the nonmarket insurance is unambiguously harmful and dysfunctional. The line of proof is straightforward: welfare is at least as high if the market insurer chooses a, β, and δ as if he chooses just a and β, with δ being chosen by the nonmarket insurer; and if the market insurer chooses a, β, and δ, he will set $\delta = 0$.

The equilibrium without nonmarket insurance cannot be improved upon, and if it were possible, it would be desirable to outlaw the provision of nonmarket insurance. The intuitive rationale for this result is as follows. The provision of nonmarket insurance does not enhance the risk-sharing capabilities of the economy. Rather, such insurance crowds out market insurance. Not only is it less effective than market insurance since it randomizes an individual's event-contingent consumption and is provided by a risk-averse agent (see John M. Marshall, 1976), but also the simultaneous provision of market and nonmarket insurance violates exclusivity, which typically creates uninternalized externalities (see Arnott and Stiglitz, 1990).

The above analysis was predicated on the assumptions that a market which provides insurance against the accident in question exists and that there are no transaction costs associated with the provision of insurance. If market insurance against a given accident does not in fact exist, voluntary nonmarket insurance is unambiguously beneficial.[15] When transactions costs are present, non-market insurance may be beneficial if it is provided at lower transaction cost than market insurance.

III Effort Observable by the Nonmarket Insurer

This case is more interesting, since there appear to be two offsetting effects. On one hand, because individuals have information on their partner's effort, which an insurance company does not, the provision of nonmarket insurance has the potential of enhancing the risk-sharing capabilities of the economy. On the other hand, the provision of insurance by a risk-neutral agent is typically more efficient than provision by a risk-averse agent, if they have access to the same information. Furthermore, the simultaneous provision of market and nonmarket insurance violates exclusivity. This line of reasoning suggests that the provision of nonmarket insurance in this case may be beneficial in some circumstances and harmful in others.

We continue with the same model. When effort is observable within the family but not to the insurance firm, and when, as we have assumed, individuals are identical, family members will effectively choose the level of precaution to take cooperatively. Each will take α and β to be fixed and choose δ and e to maximize

$$EU = u_0(1 - p)^2 + u_1 p^2 + u_2(1 - p)p + u_3(1 - p)p - e. \tag{17}$$

This yields the following first-order conditions:

$$e: \ [-2(1 - p)u_0 + 2pu_1 + (1 - 2p)(u_2 + u_3)]p' = 1 \tag{18a}$$

$$\delta: \ (-u_2' + u_3')p(1 - p) = 0. \tag{18b}$$

Equation (18b) implies that

$$\delta = \frac{d - a - \beta}{2}. \tag{18b'}$$

---

[15] Market insurance is generally unavailable for the multitudinous small (but cumulatively substantial) risks faced in everyday life. How nonmarket institutions handle such risks is an important and interesting question.

Because the partners can observe each other's effort and treat α and β as fixed, they perceive there to be no moral-hazard problem associated with the insurance they provide and hence provide full insurance (or as full as possible). This stands in contrast to the previous section where, as a result of the inability of each partner to observe the other's effort, only partial nonmarket insurance was provided [see (12)].

The insurance firm effectively chooses α and β to maximize expected utility, subject to (18a), (18b), and the zero-profit constraint. The competitive equilibrium with nonmarket insurance is characterized by the constraints and first-order conditions of this program.

We now investigate the welfare properties of the equilibrium. To do this, we assume that the planner chooses α, β, and δ, knowing that individuals choose e according to (18a), which takes account of the fact that δ is chosen with effort observable, and subject to the break-even constraint on market insurance.

Substituting the zero-profit constraint into (17) gives

$$EU(\beta, \delta) = u(w - \beta)(1 - p)^2$$
$$+ u\left(w - d + \frac{\beta(1 - p)}{p}\right)p^2 + u(w - \beta - \delta)p(1 - p)$$
$$+ u\left(w - d + \frac{\beta(1 - p)}{p} + \delta\right)p(1 - p) - e. \tag{19}$$

The corresponding first-order condition for δ [using (18a)] is

$$\frac{\partial EU}{\partial \delta} = (-u_2' + u_3')p(1 - p) - \left(\beta u_1' p' + \frac{\beta(1 - p)}{p}u_3' p'\right)\frac{\partial e}{\partial \delta} = 0. \tag{20}$$

Using (18a) again,

$$\frac{\partial e}{\partial \delta} = \frac{(1 - 2p)(u_3' - u_2')}{\Delta} \tag{21}$$

where

$$\Delta = \frac{\beta p'}{p^2}[2pu_1' + (1 - 2p)u_3'] - 2p'(u_0 + u_1 - u_2 - u_3) - \frac{p''}{(p')^2}.$$

Substituting (21) into (20) gives

$$\frac{\partial EU}{\partial \delta} = \frac{(u_3' - u_2')}{\Delta}\left[\beta u_1' p' - 2p'p(1 - p)\right.$$
$$\left. \times (u_0 + u_1 - u_2 - u_3) - \frac{p''}{(p')^2}p(1 - p)\right]. \tag{20'}$$

Both Δ and the expression in brackets are unambiguously negative, and hence $\partial EU/\partial \delta = 0$ if and only if $u_3' = u_2'$ [i.e., iff $\delta = \delta^* \equiv (d - \alpha - \beta)/2$]. Furthermore, $u_3' > u_2'$ for $\delta < \delta^*$ and $u_3' < u_2'$ for $\delta > \delta^*$, and so δ^* is the utility-maximizing δ. Thus, when effort is observable by the nonmarket insurer, the equilibrium is constrained efficient.

Does the provision of nonmarket insurance in this case stimulate or discourage effort? To answer this, we hold α and β fixed and increase δ from 0 to $(d - \alpha - \beta)/2$. Though the increase in δ unambiguously reduces risk, it has an ambiguous effect on effort. The risk reduction, by itself, encourages a reduction in effort. However, as δ increases, individuals become less selfish in their choice of effort. From (21), the former effect dominates if $p < 1/2$, and the latter effect otherwise. In the normal case, $p < 1/2$, the trade-off illustrated in Figure 2 is present, but the direct utility-increasing effect of nonmarket insurance unambiguously dominates the effort-reducing effect.

We can draw together the results in the following inequalities:

$$EU^1 > EU^{NMO} > EU^M > EU^{NMU} \tag{22}$$

where EU^1 is expected utility in the first-best case (with effort observable to both market and nonmarket insurers), EU^{NMO} is expected utility with nonmarket insurance and with effort observable to the nonmarket insurer but not the market insurer, EU^M is expected utility with only market insurance and with effort unobservable to the market insurer, and EU^{NMU} is expected utility with nonmarket insurance and with effort unobservable to both market and nonmarket insurer.

IV Discussion

The above models were rather stark. Some discussion and interpretation will therefore be useful. The results of the two cases analyzed above lead naturally to the conjecture that, in intermediate situations in which nonmarket insurers observe their partners' effort imperfectly but better than the market insurer, an excessive amount of nonmarket insurance will be provided which may or may not be better than no nonmarket insurance at all. The analysis could be extended to compare the optimal and equilibrium numbers of members in a nonmarket insurance group; in a large group, there is greater diversification of risk but more imperfect observability.

We distinguished between the two cases treated on the basis of the observability of one partner's effort by the other. The essential difference between the two cases was, however, the severity of moral hazard within the partnership, and this depends on more than the observability of effort. Such factors as the duration of the partnership, the discount rate, the frequency of accidents, the severity of punishment for reneging on an agreement, the power of reputation and social pressure, and nonmonetary rewards from cooperation, are also important.[16]

---

[16] Altruism is also a factor in nonanonymous relationships. In terms of the model, let EU be an individual's expected utility and $\widetilde{EU}$ his partner's. The individual maximizes welfare $W = EU + \lambda\widetilde{EU}$, where $\lambda = 0$ corresponds to the selfish case, $\lambda = 1$ to balanced altruism, and $\lambda = \infty$ to selfless altruism. If both partners are equally altruistic and cooperate (the effort-observable case), the outcome is

We provided a rather narrow interpretation of our model. Other interpretations are possible. A market insurer and his clients can be replaced by a principal and his agents, and the partnerships (with some elaboration of the model) can be replaced by secondary markets.[17]

In the above analysis, we took the observability of one partner's accident-prevention effort by the other as exogenous and considered only the extreme cases of unobservability and perfect observability. As we noted earlier, the degree of observability depends on the indirect monitoring system—the means by which one partner observes the other's effort, as well as the incentives to do so. Furthermore, in a fuller analysis, the indirect monitoring system would be treated as endogenous. Indeed, how indirect monitoring systems develop in nonmarket insurance institutions is an exciting research topic, as is the more general issue of how principals should design indirect monitoring systems so as to mitigate the incentives problem.

There is widespread belief that when significant market failure occurs, there are strong incentives for nonmarket institutions to develop which go at least part of the way toward remedying the deficiency.[18] This paper has provided a counterexample[19] in which a nonmarket institution arises spontaneously (through the uncoordinated actions of atomistic agents), which is completely dysfunctional (has effects opposite to those intended).[20] In our stark model, though the market response to imperfect

independent of the degree of altruism. If both partners are equally altruistic and do not cooperate (the effort unobservable case), effort increases with the degree of altruism.

[17] One can develop a typology in terms of the primary and secondary insurance arrangements, each of which may be market or nonmarket. We have considered the case in which the primary insurance arrangement is a market and the secondary arrangement is a partnership. The case primary-market/secondary-market is an insurance market in which exclusivity cannot be enforced.

[18] In anthropology there is a functionalist tradition of long standing which attempts to explain social institutions (political, economic, sociological, cultural, and psychological) as functional adaptations to a society's environment or ecosystem. Functionalist theories differ in their degree of subtlety and sophistication and in their emphasis, but none seems to make a sharp distinction between equilibrium and optimum. In most theories, however, there seems to be a presumption that institutional adaptation to the environment is efficient. See Roger Keesing (1981) for an informative discussion of contemporary traditions in anthropology. .

[19] In our example, with effort unobservable to nonmarket insurers, the market by itself is constrained Pareto-efficient. However, there is *perceived* market failure, and the nonmarket institution (the provision of supplementary nonmarket insurance) arises in response to this perceived market failure.

In an expanded version of our model in which there are many kinds of accidents and many commodities, the market is not constrained Pareto-efficient; there is genuine potential market failure (Arnott and Stiglitz, 1990). Our result concerning the possible dysfunctionality of spontaneous nonmarket institutions carries over to this more realistic setting.

[20] In one sense, this result should come as no surprise, since it is by now well recognized that, even in large economies, Nash equilibria are Pareto-efficient only under special circumstances. One of the great achievements of modern economics was to identify a special set of assumptions under which competitive economies are Pareto-efficient.

George Akerlof (1980) has argued that inefficient social customs may persist as Nash equilibria and that there can be an arbitrarily large set of social customs sustainable as Nash equilibria. The point in our paper is related but different. Akerlof considers the possible *persistence* of inefficient institutions but does not investigate how the institutions came into being. We show not only that an inefficient institution can persist, but also that it can arise spontaneously. Furthermore, while in the Akerlof model there are multiple equilibria of which some may be efficient, in our model there is a unique equilibrium.

information (the rationing of insurance) did indeed give rise to a nonmarket response (nonmarket insurance), whether the nonmarket response was welfare-enhancing turned out to depend on whether the nonmarket institution was informationally advantaged relative to the market institution. Our example illustrates, in a vivid way, the functionalist fallacy: the fact that an institution (nonmarket insurance) has a clearly identifiable function (to improve risk-sharing by supplementing the rationed insurance provided by the market) does not mean, within a general equilibrium context, that it actually performs that function (indeed, in one case, the nonmarket insurance was completely dysfunctional). We speculate that the possible dysfunctionality of nonmarket institutions is a general phenomenon. This, too, is an interesting topic for future research.

V Conclusion

In this paper we developed a simple moral-hazard model in which individuals have an incentive to supplement market insurance with nonmarket insurance that is unobservable to the market insurer. Whether this nonmarket insurance is socially beneficial depends on whether the nonmarket insurance partners can monitor each other's accident-prevention effort better than the market. In the extreme case in which the partners have no more information than the market, the nonmarket insurance is unambiguously harmful. The nonmarket insurance crowds out the market insurance and results in less risk-spreading; it is therefore completely dysfunctional. In the other extreme case, in which the partners can observe each other's accident-prevention effort perfectly, the nonmarket insurance is ameliorative, and the equilibrium is constrained efficient. The peer monitoring by the nonmarket insurers is effectively utilized to mitigate the moral hazard and to improve the risk-sharing capabilities of the economy.

The simple model raises two broad questions which go beyond the context of moral hazard in insurance markets. In what other situations may nonmarket institutions be dysfunctional? And how may the economy utilize peer-monitoring systems to improve efficiency?

PART VI

....

INFORMATION
AND MACRO
ECONOMICS

....

INTRODUCTION TO PART VI

Modern macro economics attempts to relate aggregate behavior to micro economic foundations. Unemployment has long been attributed to wage rigidities, and efficiency wage theories help explain those wage rigidities.[1] Part of the cost of macro economic fluctuations arises from imperfections in capital markets, such as credit rationing and incomplete insurance, with individuals unable to smooth shocks to their income over time; and imperfect information (e.g. Stiglitz and Weiss 1981) help explain these market imperfections.

A key issue is why the economy sometimes responds so poorly to the shocks it experiences and why it isn't able to buffer these shocks, but sometimes actually amplifies them, with effects persisting for a number of periods. If markets enabled firms to divest themselves of risk—as good equity markets would—then firms would be better able to bear shocks. The first paper of this section (Chapter 25) helps explain "equity rationing," the limited use of equity. The argument is simple: insiders know more about the firm than outsiders, and when they attempt to sell shares of their firm, outsiders interpret this adversely, driving down the price. Thus, there may be a high "adverse selection effect" in issuing equity.

With limitations in issuing equity,[2] firms act in a risk adverse manner (Greenwald and Stiglitz 1990a); and this in turn explains much of their macro economic behavior. Most production involves some risk bearing, because most firms do not produce on order. A shock which diminishes their net worth will reduce production and investment,[3] adversely affecting both aggregate demand and supply. With firms' willingness to borrow also diminished, there may be a multiplier/accelerator effect,[4]

---

[1] Other imperfect information theories also helped explain wage and price nominal and real rigidities (see, for instance, Greenwald and Stiglitz 1989b; Stiglitz 1989b).

[2] Several others contemporaneously developed models of equity rationing, based on moral hazard, adverse selection, and costly state verification (see, e.g. Stiglitz 1982c; Ross 1973; Myers and Majluf 1984; Townsend 1982; Jensen 1976). Most of these can be viewed as straightforward application of the standard adverse selection (Rothschild-Stiglitz 1976) and moral hazard/principal agent (Stiglitz 1974e; Ross 1973) models. A large literature developed providing empirical verification of the predicted effects (see, e.g. Asquith and Mullins 1986).

[3] An important part of the analysis relates to the effect of shocks on firm balance sheets. Flexible prices and imperfectly indexed debt contracts mean that negative aggregate demand shocks that lead to lower prices diminish the real value of firm net wealth. Part of the dynamic effects here arise not from wage and price rigidities but from wage and price flexibilities.

[4] These effects have come to be called financial accelerator effects. Bernanke et al. (1996) have used a costly state verification model (which provides a less plausible basis of equity rationing) to explore the financial accelerator.

with supply and demand reduced by a multiple of the reduction in net worth. And because it may take several periods for net wealth to be restored, the effects may be persistent. The second paper of this section (Chapter 26) presents a simple general equilibrium model developing these ideas, which are explored further in Part IV.[5]

[5] For review essays on this literature, see Greenwald and Stiglitz (1987b, 1988a, 1993b) and Stiglitz (1988b, 1992b). See also Greenwald and Stiglitz (2003).

CHAPTER 25

INFORMATIONAL IMPERFECTIONS IN THE CAPITAL MARKET AND MACROECONOMIC FLUCTUATIONS*

TRADITIONAL neoclassical theory has one clear, unambiguous, and verifiable prediction: all factors which have a positive price are fully utilized. In recent years, there have been several responses to the apparent inconsistency between the predictions of neoclassical theory and what has in fact been observed. The first is to deny the empirical observations: the 25 percent of the population that were unemployed in the Great Depression, let alone the 10 percent of the population that were unemployed in the Reagan recession, were not involuntarily unemployed. This seems to us, at best, semantic quibbling, and we shall have nothing further to say here concerning that view. The second is to argue, without much justification, that there are two regimes; traditional neoclassical theory applies in "normal times." It seems more plausible to us that the market failures represented by the Great Depression are always present in the economy, but difficult to detect; it is only when they reach the proportions that they do periodically that we can no longer ignore them.

A third approach is to modify the standard theory, to assume that wages and prices are fixed. This approach has rightfully been criticized both for its *ad hocery* and its

* Written with Bruce Greenwald and Andrew Weiss. Financial support of the National Science Foundation is gratefully acknowledged. Reprinted with permission from the *American Economic Review*, 74(2), May (1984), pp. 194–9.

inconsistency—why should rational profit-maximizing firms, obeying all of the other neoclassical assumptions, not cut their prices in the face of excess demand?

This paper is part of an attempt to develop a consistent set of micro foundations for macroeconomics, based on imperfect information. We focus here on the capital market. Keynes argued that the sharp drop in investment and the failure of the interest rate to fall sufficiently to restore investment to a normal level was a central part of the description of any business cycle. Keynes' analysis of investment was, however, basically a neoclassical analysis: it was the failure of the real interest rate (the long-term bond rate) to fall sufficiently that was the source of the problem.

Three aspects of this analysis have always been troubling: first, Keynes' explanation of the failure of real interest rates to fall, the liquidity trap, is not persuasive. Second, surveys suggest that firms' investment behavior is not particularly sensitive to the interest rate that they pay. Third, it has always seemed difficult to account for the magnitude of the fluctuations in investment in terms of the observed magnitudes of variations in real interest rates, outputs, wages, and prices, unless firms are very risk averse; and it is hard to reconcile high degrees of risk aversion on the part of firms with well-functioning (neoclassical) capital markets.

This paper is based on the hypothesis that Keynes' judgment concerning the importance of fluctuations in investment is correct, but that he incorrectly analyzed the determinants of investment behavior. We argue that:

1) Many firms face credit constraints; thus it is the availability of credit, not the price which they have to pay, which restricts their investment, or when it is working capital which is curtailed, which limits their production.

2) Firms that are not credit constrained may still face an increase in the *effective* cost of capital, which induces them to reduce their investment. (The increase in the effective cost of capital has further effects, for example, on the pricing decisions of firms.)

I The Debt Market

The main informational problem facing banks is that they do not know how the money they lend is being invested. Stiglitz-Weiss (1981, 1983b) showed that an increase in the interest rate charged borrowers will, in general, increase the average riskiness of the projects a bank is financing. This is either because borrowers switch to riskier projects, or because safer projects become relatively less attractive and so investors with safe projects do not apply for loans. The effect on the riskiness of loans may outweigh the direct gain to the bank from increasing its interest rate. Thus, the bank's profit may be maximized at an interest rate at which there is an excess demand for loanable funds.

This kind of phenomenon (an interior price maximum and rationing, which may also occur in the labor market) helps to explain business cycles in three ways. First, and most obviously, it provides a rationale for the persistence of non-market-clearing. Second, it may account for variations in a firm's cost of capital which are unrelated to observed variations in interest rates. The likelihood and severity of credit rationing may well increase in a recession without necessarily any concurrent change in interest rates. An increase in credit rationing might be expected both because of greater uncertainty concerning the prospects of firms, and an increase in the deadweight loss associated with bankruptcy. Third, information-based rationing models can explain how stabilization policy is likely to work. For example, monetary policies which seek to increase investment by lowering interest rates will not have the desired effect: there is no shortage of willing borrowers. However, policies that increase the availability of loanable funds will increase investment, even though they may not affect the level of interest rates at all.

There are two objections to our credit rationing theory as an explanation of the cyclical fluctuations in investment. First, why don't firms that face credit constraints from banks attempt to raise capital by some other means, in particular, by issuing new equity. And second, many firms that do not appear to be credit constrained also seem to reduce their investment dramatically.

Thus, a necessary complement to the theory of credit rationing is a theory of informational imperfections in equity markets. This we present in the next two sections.

II Equity-Markets

A firm's ability to raise equity capital is limited by informational imperfections for two basic reasons. First, incentive problems may intensify when a firm is equity financed. Managers, who receive only a small fraction of any additional profit, are likely to put forth less-than-optimal amounts of effort. Imposing large bankruptcy costs on managers may act as a spur to added effort and the value of these incentives is reduced by additional equity finance. Debt financing also allows managers less flexibility in disposing of net income than equity does. Thus, equity funds may reduce the value of a firm by allowing more "profit" to be diverted to the private uses of the firm's managers. Finally, lenders have the power to discipline managers by withdrawing their funds. This is a sanction which can be imposed piecemeal, and may therefore be more effective than share voting to which majority rule applies.[1]

Second, signalling effects may restrict a firm's access to equity markets. Managers of firms, which they know to be "good," may be willing to assume greater debt burdens.

---

[1] There are well-known impediments, both theoretical and practical, to shareholder control whether mediated via takeovers or normal corporate governance.

Both the absolute level of bankruptcy risk and any incremental increase due to added debt will be smaller for good than for "bad" firms. Greater reliance on debt by good firms means that equity will predominantly be sold by inferior ones (see Stephen Ross, 1977). Thus, attempting to sell equity may convey a strong negative signal about a firm's quality and reduce its market value accordingly.

The model presented in this paper analyzes the cyclical cost of capital implications of the signalling process just described as an example of the macroeconomic impact of the many limitations on equity issue which are noted above. It provides an explanation for large, but not directly observable, variations in the marginal cost of capital (to be distinguished from the average cost of capital measured for example by Tobin's q) which can account for many of the variations in investment which are commonly associated with business cycles. The negative signal associated with issuing equity means that the cost of equity is prohibitive for many firms. Thus, the effective marginal cost of capital is the marginal cost of debt which consists of the monetary cost of interest plus the marginal increase in expected bankruptcy cost associated with additional debt. The latter bankruptcy cost will increase as a firm faces unexpectedly adverse economic conditions, and may do so dramatically. Moreover, it is likely that the adverse signal associated with issuing equity will intensify and place equity finance even further out of reach in just these circumstances.

III A SIMPLE MODEL

We construct a simple model that enables us explicitly to determine which investors will make use of the equity market and which of the debt market, and that enables us to calculate the effective marginal cost of capital. Because we wish to focus on the equity market, we assume bankers can perfectly discriminate among borrowers—indeed, the function of banks is to differentiate potential borrowers into their appropriate risk classes—but that the equity market treats all those seeking equity the same. (Thus, while Stiglitz-Weiss, 1981, were concerned with imperfect information in the credit market, we are concerned here with imperfect information in the equity market. In a sequel, we investigate a more general model incorporating both.) We make the following assumptions:

Assumption 1. *Each firm is characterized by a net cash flow, θ, from existing operations and a set of new investment opportunities whose return is $\epsilon Q(K)$, where ϵ is a random variable, $E(\epsilon) = 1$, $var(\epsilon) = \sigma_\epsilon^2$ and K is the level of investment.*[2]

---

[2] For simplicity, existing net cash flows are assumed to be certain. Making existing cash flows uncertain would merely complicate the analysis and reinforce the basic results.

For expositional reasons, although firms are assumed to have different levels of θ, $Q(\cdot)$ is assumed to be the same for all firms. The parameter θ describes the "quality" or "value" of a particular firm and has a distribution $N(\theta)$ across firms.[3]

At the beginning of the period, firms announce their equity sales intentions, and V_0, each firm's market value, adjusts accordingly. Firms then sell (or do not sell) equity, determine the level investment, and finance any uncovered balance with debt. At the end of the period, the results of new investment are determined, some firms go bankrupt, and the values of θ are revealed for the remaining firms. The terminal value of each firm's equity is determined based on its observed value of θ. Managers' compensation depends on current market value and the share of terminal market value held by original shareholders, if the firm does not go bankrupt. In the event of bankruptcy, managers bear a known fixed cost.

Assuming risk neutrality, the firm acts as if its maximizes,

$$T = mV_0 + (1 - m)(V_0/(V_0 + e))(\theta + Q(K) - b(1 + R)) - cP_B, \tag{1}$$

where $b = K - e \equiv$ level of new borrowing, $R \equiv$ expected return on debt, $c \equiv$ cost which "bankruptcy" imposes on a firm's managers, $P_B \equiv$ probability of bankruptcy, and $m \equiv$ factor describing the weight that firms place on their initial as opposed to their terminal market value.

Assumption 2. *Bankruptcy occurs if*

$$\theta + \epsilon Q(K) < (1 + R_0)b, \tag{2}$$

where $R_0 \equiv$ contractual rate of interest on a firm's debt $> R$.

Assumption 3. *Lenders are fully informed, risk neutral, and require an expected return R,*

$$(1 + R) = (1 + R_0)(1 - P_B) + \int_0^{\epsilon_0} [(\theta + \epsilon Q(K))/b]dF(\epsilon), \tag{3}$$

where $\epsilon_0 = [(1 + R_0)b - \theta]/Q(K) \equiv$ the value of ϵ below which bankruptcy occurs.

Assumption 4. *Equity investors are risk neutral and require an expected return R. They observe only the level of a firm's equity sales in determining V_0. Firms selling equity sell a common dollar amount e_0.*

The information structure of the model may appear restrictive, but is in fact quite general. Allowing equity investors to observe only the level of equity sales is a matter of interpreting the model as applying to a set of firms whose other observable

---

[3] The model as presented involves only a single period, but can be easily extended to a sequence of periods with independent θ draws in each period.

characteristics are identical. The analysis need only be replicated for each such class of firms to cover the full firm population.[4,5]

A firm's equity sale decision rule can be characterized by examining the function,

$$H(\theta) \equiv T^D(\theta) - T^E(\theta),$$

where

$$T^D \equiv mV_0^D + (1 - m)(\theta + Q(K^D) - K^D(1 + R)) - cP_B^D,$$

$V_0^D \equiv$ initial value of firms selling no equity, $K^D \equiv$ optimal level of investment for a nonequity selling firm of quality θ (the θ argument has been supressed), $P_B^D \equiv$ level of bankruptcy risk implied by the optimal investment decisions of a nonequity issuing firm (again the θ argument has been suppressed), and

$$T^E \equiv mV_0^E + (1 - m)\left(V_0^E / \left(V_0^E + e_0\right)\right)$$
$$\times \left(\theta + Q(K^E) - (K^E - e_0)(1 + R)\right) - cP_B^E,$$

where V_0^E, K^E, and P_B^E are defined analogously to V_0^D, K^D, and P_B^D. Assuming that ϵ_0 lies in the lower tail of a single peeked ϵ distribution, it is relatively straightforward to show that $dH(\theta)/d\theta > 0$. Thus, the optimal decision rule for individual firms on equity sales policy is the following,

$$e^* = \begin{cases} e_0 & \text{if } \theta \le \hat{\theta} \\ 0 & \text{if } \theta > \hat{\theta}, \end{cases} \tag{4}$$

where $\hat{\theta}$ is defined by $H(\hat{\theta}) = 0$. Given equation (4), *firms entering the equity market will be adversely selected.* And, although in this simple model an equilibrium always exists, it may be one with zero equity sales. However, if $\theta \ge 0$ for all firms and m is close to zero, then an equilibrium with positive equity sales will exist. In such an equilibrium, V_0^E is determined by the equation,

$$V_0^E = 1/N_E \int_0^{\hat{\theta}} ((\theta + Q(K^E))/(1 + R) - (K^E - e_0))N(\theta)d\theta - e_0,$$

where

$$N_E = \int_0^{\hat{\theta}} N(\theta)d\theta.$$

It is relatively easy to show that the resulting equilibrium level of V_0^E has the following properties, under suitable regularity conditions on F,

(i) $dV_0^E/dc \ge 0$,
(ii) $dV_0^E/dm \le 0$,

---

[4] The restriction to discrete levels of equity sales, though made primarily for expositional convenience, has certain important theoretical justifications and consequences.

[5] In order that each class include firms with more than a single value of θ, neither K nor b may be perfectly observable to equity investors. However, given current accounting conventions and the timing of debt reports, this is not implausible.

(iii) $dV_0^E/dR \geq 0$,

(iv) $dV_0^E/d\sigma_\varepsilon^2 \geq 0$.

In each instance an increase in V_0^E is associated with an increase in the number of firms issuing equity (a decrease in V_0^E is associated with a decrease in the number of firms issuing equity).

The optimal investment condition which characterizes nonequity issuing firms is[6]

$$Q_k = (1+R)[1 + (c/(1-m))(1/(f_0^D - P_B^D)Q) \tag{5}$$
$$\times (1 - (K \cdot Q_k/Q)(1 - \theta/K(1+R)))],$$

where f_0^D is the level of the ε density function at ε_0^D and ε_0^D is the level of the ε for a nonequity issuing firm at which, when K is optimally chosen, the firm defaults (ε_0^D depends of course on θ). The second bracketed term on the right-hand side of (5) represents the component of the cost of capital attributable to the marginal increase in the risk of bankruptcy. As θ falls (because a negative demand shock reduces the value of existing cash flows), this term may rise dramatically as f_0^D and P_B^D increase. Any such increase is limited ultimately by the possibility of issuing equity.

In practice, the "effective" cost of issuing equity may be so high as to be prohibitive, because any firm that issues equity obtains a "bad" label. Recent studies (for example, Paul Asquith and David Mullins, 1986) indicate that an equity issue announcement reduces the value of a firm by about 3 percent. And this may be a substantial underestimate since it is based on firms who actually issue equity and who are, as a result, likely to have the lowest cost of doing so. Thus, if $m = 1/2$ and a new equity issue amounts to 5 percent of a firm's outstanding stock, the signalling cost of equity will, by itself, amount to more than 30 percent. It is not surprising, therefore, that firms rarely issue equity. Moreover, if strong firms enjoy an enhanced advantage over weak ones in the face of adverse economic conditions, a negative economic surprise will increase the dispersion of $N(\theta)$ and increase the cost of issuing equity just when it is most needed.[7]

IV CONCLUDING REMARKS

Informational imperfections have a fundamental effect on the functioning of the capital market. In some circumstances, competitive markets will be characterized by credit rationing: it is the availability of capital and not its cost that determines the level of investment. Here we have provided an explanation for why firms whose credit is constrained do not avail themselves of the equity market. We have also shown that

[6] A similar condition would apply for equity issuing firms because they are limited to issuing only e_0 dollars of equity. This is an artifact of our assumptions.

[7] Under suitable regularity conditions on $N(\theta)$, an increase in the dispersion of $N(\theta)$ reduces V_0^F and increases the cost of issuing equity.

the effective marginal cost of capital for those who are not constrained is not simply related either to the real long-term interest rate (as Keynes' hypothesized), or to the price of equity (as more recent portfolio theories have argued); the effective marginal cost of capital may experience much larger cyclical fluctuations than either of these variables. These variations in the effective cost of capital in turn play an important role in explaining observed patterns of cyclical behavior regarding both investment and prices.

Although the former effect is obvious, the latter may not be. When current prices affect not only present but future demand (see Edmund Phelps and Sidney Winter, 1970), firms will maximize profits with a price at which short-run marginal costs lie above short-run marginal revenues. The gap is filled by the contribution of lower prices to future profits. Under these circumstances, an increase in the cost of capital reduces the present value of any future market position and will lead to an increase in current prices. Our cost of capital view leads to just such a conclusion; as a recession begins, this tendency toward higher prices might well counteract the effect of falling demand and account for some price stickiness. In this and other ways, informational imperfections may provide a consistent economic explanation for many hitherto unexplained aspects of macroeconomic behavior.

CHAPTER 26

....

FINANCIAL MARKET IMPERFECTIONS AND BUSINESS CYCLES*

....

Because of financial market imperfections, such as those generated by asymmetric information in financial markets, which lead to breakdowns in markets, like that for equity, in which risks are shared, firms act in a risk-averse manner. The resulting macroeconomic model accounts for many widely observed aspects of actual business cycles: (a) cyclical movements in real product wages, (b) cyclical patterns of output and investment including inventories, (c) sensitivity of the economy to small perturbations, and (d) persistence. More downward flexibility in wages and prices may exacerbate the plight of an economy that is in a deep recession.

THIS paper describes a simple model of macroeconomic fluctuations based upon the kinds of informational imperfections that are chiefly related to adverse selection and

* Written with Bruce Greenwald. Support from the Lynde and Harry Bradley Foundation, the National Science Foundation, and the Hoover Institution is gratefully acknowledged. The authors are indebted to participants in seminars at the Bank of Norway; the Federal Reserve Board, Washington; the Bank of Italy; the University of Arizona; the National Bureau of Economic Research; University of San Diego; Harvard Business School; Princeton University; Center for Economic Policy Research, London; Stanford University; the Far Eastern Meetings of the Econometric Society, Seoul, 1991; and the Symposium on Monetary Theory held at Taipei, Taiwan, at which earlier versions of this paper were presented. We are grateful for helpful comments from Michael Woodford, Lawrence Summers, and an anonymous referee. Research assistance from John Williams, Thomas Hellmann, and Marco Da Rin is gratefully acknowledged. © 1993 by the President and Fellows of Harvard College and the Massachusetts Institute of Technology (Reprinted with permission from *The Quarterly Journal of Economics*, 108(1), pp. 194–9 February 1993).

moral hazard and that have received substantial attention in the recent microeconomic literature. A major consequence of these informational imperfections already studied extensively in connection with insurance, labor, and financial markets is that they interfere with the proper distribution of risk among economic agents. In extreme cases, markets for sharing risk may break down completely.

The fact that firms can only partially diversify out of the risks that they face leads them to act in a risk-averse manner. This has two important implications. (1) In making all of their economic decisions—investment, production, and pricing—they take into account the risk consequences. (2) Firms' willingness to undertake risks is affected both by their total net worth and their stock of liquid assets, which can quickly be converted into cash. These asset balances can act as buffer stocks to absorb shocks.

The various decisions that the firm makes are obviously interrelated: a general theory requires a portfolio approach to firm decision making which takes the various correlations into account.[1] This paper is more modest in its ambition. We focus our attention on how risk considerations affect firms' production decisions. We argue that changes in firms' perceptions of the risks which they face and in their net worth position can have potentially large effects on their willingness to produce. The shifts in one firm's supply curve get translated into shifts in the demand curves facing other firms, and through this mechanism shocks to one agent in the economy get transmitted to others.

We derive a risk-based aggregate supply curve, which leads to the kind of persistence frequently observed in macroeconomic time series, and may even generate business fluctuations whose characteristics bear a striking resemblance to those observed.

In emphasizing problems of risk distribution, this paper can be thought of as continuing the line of research initiated by Kalecki [1939]. Our paper, however, is based on the microfoundations provided by recent work on financial markets with imperfect information, and attempts to integrate that approach into other, more recent macroeconomic traditions.[2]

The central role of information imperfections is to restrict a firm's ability to raise equity funds in external capital markets. The empirical evidence suggests that firms

---

[1] For a beginning of such a theory, see Greenwald and Stiglitz [1989b].

[2] This paper is thus in the same spirit as that of Bernanke and Gertler [1989], as well as both older [Kuh and Meyer, 1957] and more recent [Fazzari, Hubbard, and Peterson, 1988a; Hubbard, 1990] work emphasizing the importance of cash flow and balance sheet variables in determining investment. Also see Lindbeck [1963].

Within the macroeconomics literature Hicks [1988] (see Klamer [1989]) shortly before his death, recanted on the IS-LM framework that he had introduced and argued in favor of the kind of model that we have attempted to develop here. Other macroeconomists who have taken similar positions (without developing the kind of formal model presented here) include Leijonhufvud [1968] and Minsky [1975].

Our work differs from the Bernanke and Gertler analysis in the explanation of the source of the limitations on equity markets (they employ the costly state verification model; for a critique of that model, see Hart [1990]). The macroeconomic model that they construct appears heavily dependent on their specific formulation. The model presented here is constructed to illustrate the general properties of aggregate behavior in economies with risk-averse firms with limited recourse to equity (for whatever reason).

simply do not resort to equity markets for raising working capital; overall, new equity issues represent a small fraction of capital raised by firms. (In recent years, net equity issues have actually been negative both in the United States and United Kingdom [Mayer, 1990].) There is good reason for this: new equity issues normally have a large negative effect on the value of outstanding shares [Asquith and Mullins, 1986]. And these negative effects on market value have, in turn, been explained in terms of adverse selection, moral hazard, and signaling models.[3]

Because we are concerned in this paper with exploring the macroeconomic implications of these financial constraints, we simplify by assuming that firms cannot raise new equity, and that they always pay a fixed dividend on existing shares.[4] At the same time, in order to separate the risk distribution issues that are at the heart of the model from traditional credit restriction questions, we assume that there is a perfect loan market. The output decisions of firms are assumed to be made by managers who are averse to the possibility of bankruptcy.[5] Finally, we assume that futures markets do not exist and inputs must be paid for significantly before outputs are sold.[6] Thus, any decision to produce is inherently a risky investment decision.

---

[3] For formal models of this phenomenon see Greenwald, Stiglitz, and Weiss [1984] and Myers and Majluf [1984]. The basic argument is that if the managers of firms, who are better informed about a firm's future prospects than equity investors at large, are willing to issue stock at the current market price, then "outside" investors ought to be unwilling to buy at that price. Hence, an equity issue announcement ought to be associated with a decline in a firm's current stock price which should in turn inhibit equity issues. Agency considerations reinforce these arguments.

Shleifer [1986] has argued that, in addition, there is evidence that the market as a whole acts in a risk-averse manner; i.e., firms face downward sloping demand curves for their securities. For a theoretical model consistent with this observation, see Stiglitz [1972b, 1989c].

[4] The latter assumption, like the assumption of no (or limited) equity issues, can be justified as an approximation to a long-standing stylized fact: there is a large empirical literature, dating back at least to Lintner [1971] showing that firms adjust dividends relatively rarely. This behavior can also be related to information problems: reducing dividends is taken to be a very negative signal of the firm's prospects, having a correspondingly large negative effect on the firm's market value (see Bhattacharya [1979]).

In this paper the catastrophe facing the firm that we model is that it is not able to pay back its debts and accordingly it goes into bankruptcy. We could have, as well, modeled the catastrophe as that the firm is not able to maintain its dividends, and accordingly must reduce or eliminate them, with a correspondingly disastrous effect on market value. The analysis is the same, whatever the interpretation one takes.

[5] The justification for this kind of assumption is again informational. When a firm becomes financially distressed, it is usually impossible to tell whether this is due to bad luck with projects that were a priori properly undertaken or to bad management. Thus, managers will inevitably suffer a stigma associated with financial distress. Concepts like "financial distress" and "bankruptcy," while they have a clear intuitive meaning, are difficult to define precisely, at least in general terms. In the model presented below, they take on well-defined meanings. See, e.g., Eaton, Gersovitz, and Stiglitz [1986].

[6] Again, this assumption rests ultimately on informational failures, typically associated with product quality and terms of delivery, which inhibit the development and use of future markets. In practice, futures markets are far from complete.

A relatively small proportion of goods in our economy are "made to order," and even when they are, there remains a positive probability of default; that is, that the firm placing the order does not fulfill its contract. In most cases where goods are produced to order, a relatively small fraction of the payment is made by the purchaser up front. This, in turn, can be related to informational problems: the chance that the producer will default on his part of the bargain.

I The Basic Aggregate Supply Quandary and the Risk Resolution: Heuristics

Standard competitive economic theory argues that, in the absence of risk, firms produce up to the point where price P equals marginal costs. If we assume aggregate output q is a function of labor l alone, then

$$q = \Phi(l), \quad \Phi' > 0, \Phi'' < 0, \tag{1}$$

and we obtain

$$P = \omega/\Phi', \tag{2}$$

where ω is the (nominal) wage. If we divide both sides by P, define $\omega/P = w$ as the real wage, and note that w/Φ' = marginal cost of production (in real terms). Equation (2) can be rewritten as

$$1 = w/\Phi' = MC. \tag{2'}$$

Equation (2) implies that as the economy goes into a recession, l is reduced significantly, and accordingly real wages should rise significantly (see Figure Ia). The fact that they do not was an early objection raised to Keynes's use of the competitive supply model. Previous attempts to reconcile the data with the theory have taken three forms.

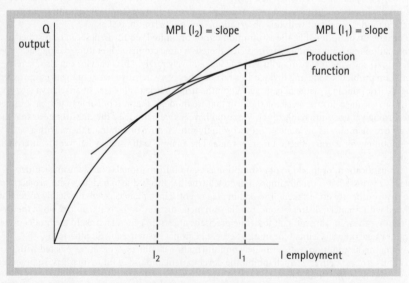

Fig. Ia. With a given technology a reduction in employment from l_1 to l_2 is associated with an increase in the marginal product of labor. In competitive labor and product markets this means that real wages should rise

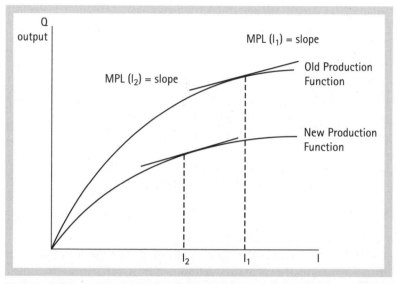

Fig. Ib. Real business cycle theory explains the apparent lack of variability in real product wages by assuming technological regress. The downward movement in the production function lowers the marginal product of labor, just offsetting the effect of the reduced employment

1. The production function is made a function of time, so that while l was reduced, there was technical regress which reduced the marginal productivity of labor (see Figure Ib). This view, popularized by the real business cycle literature, is both on its face implausible, and has a number of other counterfactual implications. See Mankiw [1989] or Greenwald and Stiglitz [1988a].

2. The data do not accurately reflect the real (product) wage that is relevant for the theory. This is the view taken by the implicit contract literature; but this literature argues that in a recession *observed* real wages are actually higher than "shadow" real wages, exacerbating the quandary. Moreover, much of the standard data refer to average wages, while what is relevant for the theory is marginal wages, i.e., taking into account overtime. Real marginal wages in booms exceed those in recessions by more than the conventional data suggest, again making the quandary more puzzling.

3. Most markets are imperfectly competitive, and so we must replace (2) with

$$P = \frac{\omega/\Phi'}{1 - (1/\eta)}, \qquad (2'')$$

where η is the elasticity of demand. If the elasticity of demand is lower in a recession, then firms' markups will increase.[7] But there is little evidence for the marked changes in demand elasticities over the cycle that would be required, and indeed, some have

---

[7] For a survey of alternative imperfect competition models, see Stiglitz [1984b]. For an econometric study arguing that price exceeds marginal costs, see Hall [1988]. He attributes the discrepancy to imperfect competition, but his empirical findings are equally consistent with the theory that we develop here.

argued that markets become even more competitive (elasticities become higher) in recessions, as collusive arrangements break down (see Rotemberg and Saloner [1987]).[8]

We argue that as firms produce more, they must bear more risk. We focus on a model with bankruptcy in which as firms produce more, the probability of bankruptcy increases. Bankruptcy is costly, and firms take these costs into account in their production decisions. Thus, we replace (1) by the equation,

$$P = \omega/\Phi' + MBC, \tag{3}$$

where MBC is the marginal bankruptcy cost.[9]

Alternatively, we can divide by P and thus replace (2') with

$$1 = w/\Phi' + \rho, \tag{3'}$$

where ρ equals real marginal bankruptcy costs.

Given ρ and w, (3') defines the equilibrium output of the firm. In Figure II we have drawn the marginal costs of production, ignoring bankruptcy, and then added to that the marginal bankruptcy cost. Production occurs at the level of output where price equals marginal cost of production (including bankruptcy costs). By plotting the value of output corresponding to different values of P, we can translate (3) into an aggregate supply schedule, as in Figure IIb. The problem posed earlier can be put: since real wages seem to vary so little over the business cycle, how can we account for the large changes in output? The real business cycle school claims that the aggregate supply schedule shifts to the left because of technological regress. We claim that the aggregate supply schedule shifts because the marginal bankruptcy risk increases. In the next section we show why this is so, by constructing a model that allows us to calculate explicitly this marginal bankruptcy cost.

II FIRM BEHAVIOR AND AGGREGATE SUPPLY

Firms, identified by an index $i = 1, \ldots, I$, will be assumed to make decisions at discrete intervals: $t = 1, \ldots, T$. At the beginning of each period a firm inherits both a nominal level of debt, B_{t-1}^i, and the previous period's output, q_{t-1}^i. We assume that there is a one-period lag between the use (and payment) of inputs and the availability of output. Thus, q_{t-1}^i results from production decisions made at the beginning of period $t - 1$, but becomes available for sale only at the beginning of

[8] Greenwald, Stiglitz, and Weiss [1984] explain why with a Phelps-Winter [1970] imperfect competition model and imperfect capital markets, we would expect cyclical movements in markups. For other models in which changes in the cost of capital have a direct effect on markups, see Stiglitz [1989a].
[9] Our theory works equally well with imperfect competition, in which case we replace (3) with

$$P(1 - 1/\eta) = \omega/\Phi' + MBC.$$

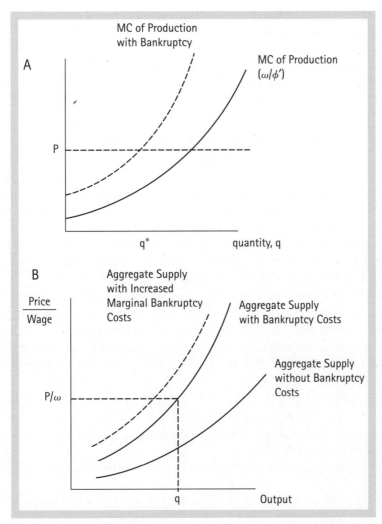

Fig. II. Panel A. Without bankruptcy firms produce up to the point where price equals marginal cost of production, ω/Φ'. With bankruptcy the marginal costs of bankruptcy must be taken into account.

Panel B. Without bankruptcy the aggregate supply curve is given by $q = \Phi(\Phi'^{-1}(\omega/P))$. Shifts in the supply curve must be related to shifts in Φ. With bankruptcy the aggregate supply curve is the solution to $1 = w/\Phi' + \rho$. Shifts in ρ, the marginal bankruptcy cost, give rise to shifts in the aggregate supply curve

period t. For simplicity, we assume also that output is perishable and q_{t-1}^i must all be sold at the beginning of period t. We assume that the nominal debt B_{t-1}^i was incurred at the beginning of period $t-1$ in order to pay for the inputs that were required for producing q_{t-1}^i. Associated with this debt is a nominal contractual rate of interest R_{t-1}^i determined at that time. Thus, nominal contractual repayments owed to debtholders by firm i on entering period t are $(1 + R_{t-1}^i)B_{t-1}^i$.

At the beginning of period t competitive goods markets open and clear. This determines the price P_t^i at which firm i sells its inherited output q_{t-1}^i. The price P_t^i also determines the nominal equity position of firm i at the beginning of period t since

$$A_t^i \equiv \text{Nominal Equity Position of firm } i \text{ at the beginning of period } t$$
$$\equiv P_t^i q_{t-1}^i - (1 + R_{t-1}^i)B_{t-1}^i. \tag{4}$$

The level of A_t^i then determines the solvency of firm i. For some level of A_t^i sufficiently low (or negative), firm i would presumably be declared bankrupt and reorganized with appropriately negative consequences for the managers (or owners, if owner-managed) of the firm. For simplicity, we shall assume that $A_t^i < 0$ implies bankruptcy, although a nonzero (either positive or negative) threshold could have been used without fundamentally altering the implications of the model.[10]

We assume that firms face a real wage w and at that wage, they can hire as much labor as they wish. We also assume that firms can borrow as much as they want, but at terms which must yield the lender an expected real return of r_t. The expected real return r_t then determines the terms at which loans will be made available to individual firms, typically a schedule relating R_t^i to q_t^i and A_t^i for a given expected real return and expected rate of inflation. Combined with expectations concerning future output prices and A_t^i, these factor prices lead managers to select a level of output, q_t^i, which, once workers have been paid, leads to a level of debt, B_t^i, and a contractual nominal return, R_t^i that firm i inherits at the beginning of period $t + 1$, when the entire process is repeated.

Within this temporal context we shall make the following assumptions.

A1. Firms produce output using only labor as an input with $l_t^i = \phi(q_t^i)$, where ϕ is a labor requirements function[11] with $\phi' > 0$ and $\phi'' \geq 0$.

A2. The price level P_t^i faced by an individual firm is determined by a sectoral random variable $\tilde{u}_t^i$, and the overall price level P_t, where

$$P_t^i = \tilde{u}_t^i P_t, \quad E(\tilde{u}_t^i) = 1 \tag{5}$$

and $\tilde{u}_t^i$, the relative price of the output of firm i, is i.i.d. with a distribution function $F(\cdot)$, and density $f(\cdot)$.

---

[10] The comparative static analysis of a bankruptcy threshold below zero is more complicated than that of a zero or positive threshold.

[11] ϕ could, of course, easily be made to vary across firms. However, doing this would merely complicate the notation without significantly altering the implications of the model. Note that ϕ^{-1} is a production function of the usual sort; i.e., $\phi^{-1} \equiv \Phi$.

A3. If $A_t^i < 0$, firms go "bankrupt," and the entire proceeds from the sale of q_{t-1}^i are distributed without further loss to debtholders (i.e., there are no reorganization or liquidation costs to debtholders).[12]

Firms borrow to supplement initial equity to pay production costs. Since the real wage is w_t, nominal wage payments are $P_t w_t \phi(q_t^i)$, and

$$B_t^i = P_t w_t \phi(q_t^i) - A_t^i. \tag{6}$$

Given A2 and A3, lenders to firm i at the beginning of period t earn returns that are a random variable whose value is resolved only when prices are revealed at the beginning of period $t + 1$. Firms go bankrupt if what they promise to pay exceeds their income; that is, when (using (4) and A3)

$$(1 + R_t^i)B_t^i \geq P_{t+1}^i q_t^i$$

or, using (5) and (6),

$$\tilde{u}_{t+1}^i \leq (1 + R_t^i)\left(\frac{P_t}{P_{t+1}}\right)\left(\frac{w_t \phi(q_t^i) - a_t^i}{q_t^i}\right) \equiv \overline{u}_{t+1}^i, \tag{7}$$

where

$a_t^i \equiv A_t^i/P_t \equiv$ real equity level of firm i at the beginning of period t

and

$\overline{u}_{t+1}^i$ is the level of relative price in period $t + 1$ at which firm i is just solvent.

If the firm i cannot meet its debt obligations, its total income $p_t^i q_t^i$ is divided equally among debtors. Thus, using (5) and (6), real returns to lenders are

$$(1 + \tilde{R}_t^i)\left(\frac{P_t}{P_{t+1}}\right) = \begin{cases} (1 + R_t^i)\left(\frac{P_t}{P_{t+1}}\right) & \text{if } \tilde{u}_{t+1}^i \geq \overline{u}_{t+1}^i \\ \dfrac{\tilde{u}_{t+1}^i \cdot q_t^i}{w_t \phi(q_t^i) - a_t^i} & \text{if } \tilde{u}_{t+1}^i < \overline{u}_{t+1}^i \end{cases}. \tag{8}$$

Strictly speaking, P_{t+1}, looking forward from the beginning of period t, is a random variable. However, in order to simplify the exposition, we assume for the moment that there is relatively little uncertainty about future price levels (as opposed to the relative sectoral prices P_{t+1}^i) and, thus, that[13]

$$P_{t+1} \cong P_{t+1}^e \equiv \text{Expected price level at the beginning of period}$$
$$t + 1 \text{ looking forward from the beginning of period } t. \tag{9}$$

[12] Introducing reorganization costs has an impact on the results similar, but not quite identical, to the effect of a negative bankruptcy threshold. Also with reorganization costs firms will have an additional incentive (beyond the managerial penalty) to avoid bankruptcy.

[13] This assumption may appear extreme. However, it can be relaxed without affecting the conclusions of the model in any fundamental way. Unfortunately, the price of such relaxation is considerable notational complexity since it requires definition of a bivariate price distribution covering both aggregate and sectoral prices; hence the use of the present assumption.

Given equation (9), the expected real return to lenders to firm i in period t is

$$E\left[(1 + \tilde{R}_t^i)\right]\left(\frac{P_t}{P_{t+1}^e}\right) = (1 + R_t^i)\left(\frac{P_t}{P_{t+1}^e}\right)$$

$$\times (1 - F(\overline{u}_{t+1}^i)) + \frac{q_t^i}{w_t\phi(q_t^i) - a_t^i}\int_0^{\overline{u}_{t+1}^i} x\, dF(x), \quad (10)$$

where P_{t+1}^e can now be substituted for P_{t+1} in the expression for $\overline{u}_{t+1}^i$. The first expression on the right-hand side of equation (10) represents the expected real return to lenders from those situations in which firm i is solvent in period $t + 1$. The second expression then represents the expected real return to lenders from situations in which firm i is insolvent in period $t + 1$. For determining the appropriate contractual rate of return, R_t^i, we next assume that

A4. Lenders are perfectly informed[14] and risk neutral, which implies that

$$E\left[1 + \tilde{R}_t^i\right]\left(\frac{P_t}{P_{t+1}^e}\right) = 1 + r_t, \quad (11)$$

where r_t is the tth period real interest rate.

Equations (7) and (11) can be solved for the equilibrium level of the contractual nominal interest rate R_t^i, and the solvency relative price, $\overline{u}_{t+1}^i$, as functions of q_t^i, a_t^i, w_t, r_t, and P_t/P_{t+1}^e.[15]

$$R_t^i = R_t^i(q_t^i, a_t^i, w_t, P_t/P_{t+1}^e, 1 + r_t),$$

$$\overline{u}_{t+1}^i = \overline{u}_{t+1}^i(q_t^i, a_t^i, w_t, P_t/P_{t+1}^e, 1 + r_t). \quad (12)$$

---

[14] Clearly, for the informational imperfections that interfere with the issue of equity to exist, lenders must not be able to use their information to purchase equity. The best way to interpret A4 is that lending is done through institutions that are legally enjoined from purchasing stock. In any event, imperfect information on the part of lenders would intensify rather than alleviate the problems embodied in the model.

[15] We can substitute (7) and (11) into (10) to obtain

$$1 + r_t = \frac{q_t^i}{w_t\phi(q_t^i) - a_t^i}\left\{(1 - F(\overline{u}_{t+1}^i))\overline{u}_{t+1}^i + \int_0^{\overline{u}_{t+1}^i} x\, dF\right\}.$$

The term in brackets is just a function of $\overline{u}_{t+1}^i$, $J(\overline{u}_{t+1}^i)$. Rearranging, we have

$$J(\overline{u}_{t+1}^i) = (1 + r_t)\left(\frac{w_t\phi(q_t^i) - a_t^i}{q_t^i}\right)$$

or

$$\overline{u}_{t+1}^i = J^{-1}\left(\frac{(1 + r_t)(w_t\phi(q_t^i) - a_t^i)}{q_t^i}\right)$$

and

$$1 + R_t^i = J^{-1}\left(\frac{(1 + r_t)(w_t\phi(q_t^i) - a_t^i)}{q_t^i}\right)\frac{P_{t+1}^e}{P_t}\frac{q_t^i}{w_t\phi(q_t^i) - a_t^i}.$$

Then, substitution from (12) into $F(u)$ yields

Probability of Bankruptcy $\equiv F[\bar{u}_{t+1}^i(q_t^i, a_t^i, w_t, P_t/P_{t+1}^e, 1 + r_t)]$

giving the probability of bankruptcy as a function of the decision variable q_t^i, the state variable a_t^i, and the parameters w_t (wages), P_t/P_{t+1}^e (the expected change in the price level), and r_t (the real interest rate).

In deciding upon a level of output, we shall assume that the objectives of a firm's managers are described by the assumption that

A5. Firms select q_t^i in order to maximize expected real profits (i.e., total sales revenues minus repayment to lenders) minus an expected real cost of bankruptcy; i.e.,

$$\max(1/P_{t+1}^e)E[P_{t+1}^i q_t^i - (1 + \tilde{R}_t^i)(P_t w_t \phi(q_t^i) - A_t^i)] - c_t^i F(\bar{u}_{t+1}^i), \qquad (13)$$

where c_t^i is the cost incurred by firms in the event of bankruptcy and $F(u_{t+1}^{-i})$ is the probability of bankruptcy.

Equation (13) is a simple way of capturing the hypothesis that firms act to avoid bankruptcy. As we shall see, this bankruptcy avoidance behavior induces a kind of risk aversion;[16] similar results obtain whether these bankruptcy costs are viewed as real (managerial) reorganization costs associated with bankruptcy or if we view firms as maximizing the expected utility of profits with the utility function characterized by a declining marginal utility of profits and decreasing absolute risk aversion (see Greenwald and Stiglitz [1987a]).

We assume further that

A6. Bankruptcy costs increase with the level of a firm's output:

$$c_t^i = cq_t^i. \qquad (14)$$

This assumption is made largely for analytic reasons; similar results hold for other bankruptcy cost functions as long as expected bankruptcy costs are convex in q_t^i. There are, however, three economic justifications which suggest that A6 represents a plausible simplification. First, as firms become larger, they presumably involve more managers whose loss of position, income, and power in the event of insolvency is likely to increase. Bankruptcy should, therefore, be a more serious matter for General Motors than for a local grocery store. Since q_t^i is the only scale variable in the model, having bankruptcy costs increase with q_t^i is the only way to capture these scale effects. Second, a significant role of managers is choosing a level of output (in the model this is their only role). Bankruptcy with high levels of output should reflect unfavorably on their ability to do this. Since bankruptcy in this model is due to low prices, a high level of output in the face of these low prices may, retrospectively at least, imply unusually bad judgment by managers and may thus be unusually costly to their future prospects. Third, having bankruptcy costs depend on q_t^i is necessary in order to ensure that the possibility of bankruptcy is never ignored. If there were a fixed cost of bankruptcy

---

[16] Strictly speaking, this is true only if $c_t^i F$ is appropriately convex in q_t^i and if a_t^i is not too small. See below and the appendix to Greenwald and Stiglitz [1988b].

independent of the level of output, then profits, which are increasing in output, may grow so large relative to bankruptcy costs that bankruptcy becomes a negligible consideration.[17] Since the purpose of this paper is to investigate the macroeconomic implications of conditions in which managers (or owners) are penalized for bad outcomes and are affected by the possibility of these penalties, Assumption A6 is a convenient way of ensuring that these conditions are met. Moreover, with the addition of fixed bankruptcy costs, there are reasonable circumstances under which the fundamental implications of the model continue to hold.[18]

Given A2 and A4, the objective function of A5 can be written as

$$\max_{q_t^i}[q_t^i - (1 + r_t)(w_t \phi(q_t^i) - a_t^i) - c_t^i F(\overline{u}_{t+1}^i)].$$ (15)

Under these assumptions, a firm's real output is, therefore, determined by real wages, real interest rates, real equity holdings, and relative price uncertainty. The first-order condition[19] for an interior maximum can now be written as

$$1 - (1 + r_t)w_t \phi' = \rho_t^i,$$ (16)

where ρ_t^i is the *marginal bankruptcy cost* of firm i in period t; i.e.,

$$\rho_t^i = \left(\frac{dc_t^i}{dq_t^i}\right) F + c_t^i f(\overline{u}_{t+1}^i)\frac{d\overline{u}_{t+1}^i}{dq_t^i}.$$ (17)

If ρ were zero, equation (16) would be the standard result that employment should be increased to the point where the marginal product $(1/\phi')$ equals the wage, taking into account the fact that the wage is paid the period before the output is received (and hence in present value terms, viewed at the time output is sold, wage costs are $w_t(1 + r_t)$). Equivalently, price (here, normalized at unity) is set equal to marginal costs $((1 + r_t)w_t\phi')$. Since ρ is positive, the impact of bankruptcy risks is to restrict output; these risks drive a wedge between expected prices and marginal costs in the traditional sense.

More importantly, the variables on the left-hand side of equation (16)—real interest rates, real wages, and technology—have historically shown substantial stability over time, changing only slowly at relatively predictable rates. In contrast, the variables that affect the right-hand side of equation (16)—such as the financial position of firms, a_t^i, and the degree of uncertainty concerning future prices (i.e., the distribution function F)—may change rapidly and unpredictably. It is these variables, many of which may be difficult to observe, that account for cyclical fluctuations in the model.

---

[17] In any case, we must assume that there is an upper limit on output (or that ϕ' increases sufficiently rapidly) and the bankruptcy costs coefficient c is sufficiently large that a maximum for the objective function in A5 exists. These technical assumptions are discussed in the appendix to Greenwald and Stiglitz [1988b].

[18] The implied restriction in A5 to a single-period horizon is a matter of expositional convenience. The multiperiod maximization problem as well as the consequences of fixed bankruptcy costs are examined in Greenwald and Stiglitz [1988b].

[19] There are several restrictions that have to be imposed to ensure that the second-order conditions are satisfied. These are discussed in the appendix to Greenwald and Stiglitz [1988b].

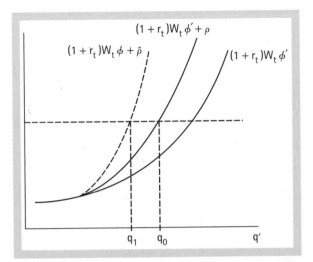

Fig. III. Determination of Equilibrium Output and Employment. A decrease in equity or an increase in perceived risk increases the marginal bankruptcy cost; ρ increases to $\hat{\rho}$, leading output to fall

Figure III depicts the solution to (16) graphically. Taking output as our numeraire, for small q, price is just equal to marginal cost, since $\rho = 0$. As q increases, so does ρ. Price exceeds marginal cost by the amount of the marginal bankruptcy costs.

A The Determinants of Marginal Bankruptcy Risk and Individual Firm Supply

An increase in the real wage or real interest rate has two effects: the direct effect on the left-hand side of (16), and the indirect effect of increasing the marginal bankruptcy cost, at each level of output. The higher real wage means that the firm must borrow more to produce any given level of output, and the higher real interest rate means that the firm must pay back more (on average) for any amount it borrows. Both effects lead to reduced equilibrium output. Thus, it is easy to derive the labor demand or the output supply curve.

The marginal bankruptcy cost ρ_t^i depends, of course, on the level of output. In addition, it is a function of the real wage, the real interest rate, the level of equity of the firm (a_t^i) as well as the subjective probability distribution of the random variable $\tilde{u}_{t+1}^i$. We can thus represent the supply function of a firm (the solution to (16)) and its demand curve for labor by equations of the form,

$$q_t^i = g^i(w_t, r_t, a_t^i, v_t^i)$$
$$l_t^i = \phi(q_t^i) = \phi(g^i(w_t, r_t, a_t^i, v_t^i)), \tag{18}$$

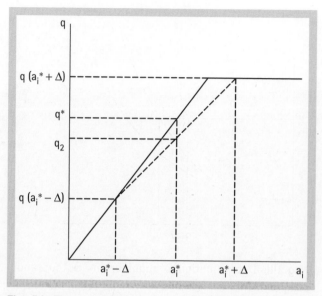

Fig. IV. Firm output increases with firm equity, up to capacity. The reduction in output from a reduction in equity by Δ exceeds that gain in output from an increase in equity by Δ

where v_t^i represents a measure of the riskiness of the distribution F.

$$g_w^i < 0: \text{ real wage increases depress supply;}$$

$$g_r^i < 0: \text{ real interest rate increases depress supply.}$$

Our main concern, however, is with the effect of equity levels and uncertainty (risk) on production. It is possible to verify

Proposition 1. *The higher the level of equity, the lower the marginal bankruptcy cost (risk premium) ρ_t^i, and hence the higher the level of production.*

Proposition 2. *Increases in the degree of uncertainty result in an increase in the marginal bankruptcy cost (risk premium) and hence in a lower level of investment.* [20]

Under the assumption that ϕ is linear, up to a capacity constraint, we can show that production, as a function of the equity level a_t^i, appears as in Figure IV. For the range within which the constant returns assumption holds, the elasticity of supply with respect to firm equity is unity. [21]

Accordingly,

---

[20] The precise meaning of increases in uncertainty and the conditions under which Proposition 2 is valid are discussed in the appendix to Greenwald and Stiglitz [1988b].

[21] More generally, with diminishing returns the elasticity of supply is less than or equal to unity. This is, of course, a partial-equilibrium result. To the extent that increases in a lead to increases in labor demand, and these increases lead to wage increases, the net effect on output will be smaller.

Proposition 3. *At least near the capacity level, output is a concave function of equity levels.*

These three propositions are the heart of the analysis. Proposition 1 implies that, if for some reason, a firm's equity is reduced (e.g., because the prices at which the firm is able to sell its goods are lower than anticipated) then, in subsequent periods, the firm's output will be reduced. Diagrammatically in Figure III a reduction of equity increases ρ, reducing output from q_0 to q_1.

Moreover, our analysis suggests that for high leverage economies, the output multipliers associated with equity injections may be substantial. For example, if, in equilibrium, equity represents one third of total capital (which in this circulating capital world is slightly less than output), then with constant returns to scale a \$1 increase in equity will yield \$3 of increased output. Note that there are a variety of ways that such equity injections may occur, most importantly larger than anticipated increases in prices, whether a result of monetary or fiscal policy, can result in substantial increases in the equity base of firms.[22]

Later, we shall show the not surprising result that losses in equity will not instantaneously be restored, and thus the model has the immediate implications of *persistence*; a loss of equity at time t results in lower output, not only at time t, but in subsequent periods as well.

Proposition 2 means that a sudden change in perception concerning the uncertainty of future prices will be translated directly into a contraction in production. In Figure III the marginal bankruptcy cost rises from ρ to $\hat{\rho}$, and output is accordingly reduced.

The fact that the output function is concave (Proposition 3) means that redistributions of wealth within the production sector may have deleterious consequences for production. Thus, unanticipated increases in prices (say oil) may have negative effects, and, at the same time, unanticipated decreases in prices of the same commodity may have negative effects. The oil price shocks increase the real equity of oil producers and decrease that of oil users. Figure IV illustrates that the reduction in output of the firm losing equity (equity goes from a^* to $a^* - \varDelta$) is greater than an increase in output of the firm with increased equity (equity goes from a^* to $a^* + \varDelta$). Average output of the two firms falls from q^* before the disturbance to q_2 afterwards. More generally, the magnitude of the fall in output is greater the greater is the disturbance and the greater is the curvature of g^i. Propositions 2 and 3 together imply that increased uncertainty, both ex ante (anticipated) and ex post, depresses production. This will be true whether the uncertainty is due to concerns about real shocks or to concerns regarding the instabilities of macroeconomic policy including monetary policy.

[22] In the model of this paper, sales at t are fixed, and thus the only source of variability in equity is prices (see equation (4)). If, on average, costs including interest payments represent 90 percent of the value of sales, a mere 5 percent reduction in sales price from the expected level translates into a 50 percent reduction in equity from its expected level, and a correspondingly large reduction in output. In a more general model, with firms selling out of inventory, and with prices possibly being chosen by firms, levels of demand have a direct effect on firms' financial positions.

B Aggregate Supply

An aggregate supply function can be derived straightforwardly by summing the supply functions of individual firms. For simplicity, we assume that all firms have the same production function (Φ) and face the same uncertainty (F). We can then write aggregate output as

$$q_t = \hat{g}(w_t, r_t, a_t^1, \ldots; v).$$

We can approximate the expression by taking a Taylor series expansion around the average level of firm equity holdings, a_t (under our symmetry assumptions), giving us an aggregate supply function of the form,

$$q_t = g(w_t, r_t, a_t; v, \sigma),$$

where σ^2 is the variance of firm equity levels. The comparative static properties of this aggregate supply function will, in general, mirror those of a representative firm's output (with the additional effect noted that an increase in the dispersion of equity ownership will generally lower output). Thus, Figure V shows the aggregate demand for labor (which can be directly translated into an aggregate supply of goods). The curve shifts with changes in a, v, or σ: decreases in average equity, increases in its dispersion, or increased perception of risk all shift the demand for labor curve or the output supply curve to the left.

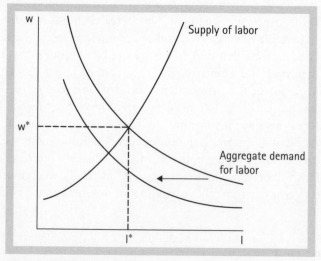

Fig. V. The aggregate demand for labor shifts down as a result of a reduction in a, an increase in perceived risk, and an increase in the dispersion of equity

III CLOSING THE MODEL:
COMPETITIVE EQUILIBRIUM

To explore the implications of this new aggregate supply curve, we need to embed it in a model of the economy. To highlight the central features of our theory of the risk-averse firm, we wish to model the rest of the economy in standard ways. In this section we present a competitive equilibrium model, in which the labor market always clears. In the next we present an efficiency wage model.

In order to embed the supply function of the previous section in a model which is as simple as possible, we assume that consumer behavior can be described by the behavior of a single, infinitely lived representative consumer. Furthermore, we shall assume that this representative consumer may borrow and lend freely at the competitive real rate of interest, r_t, and consequently faces a single lifetime budget constraint of the form,

$$\sum_{j=0}^{\infty} (z_{t+j} - w_{t+j} l_{t+j}) \pi_{t,j} = n_t,$$

where

$z_{t+j} \equiv$ real consumption in period $t + j$,

$l_{t+j} \equiv$ hours worked in period $t + j$,

$\pi_{t,j} \equiv \prod_{i=0}^{j} \left(\dfrac{1}{1 + r_{t+i-1}} \right)$ (and 1 for $j = 0$),

and

$n_t \equiv$ real wealth in period t.

Finally, we assume that the representative consumer has a utility function of the form,[23]

$$\sum_{j=0}^{\infty} \left(\frac{1}{1 + \delta} \right)^j (z_{t+j} - v(l_{t+j})),$$

where $v' > 0$ and $v'' > 0$.

Under these circumstances, equilibrium in the aggregate market for goods and services is characterized by the following conditions.[24]

---

[23] We are suppressing the role of product heterogeneity. There are several alternative specifications that might allow this to be brought in.

[24] That is, the utility function ensures that since the individual is willing to trade off a dollar of consumption at time $t + 1$ for $1 + \delta$ at t, regardless of the levels of consumption of goods or leisure, the market rate of interest must be δ.

(a) The real interest rate will always be equal to the individual's pure rate of time discount, δ:[25]

$$r_t = \delta.$$

(b) Consumption equals output:

$$z_t = q_{t-1}.$$

(c) The supply of labor, denoted by s, is an increasing function only of the wage in the current period, w_t.

Strictly speaking, the demand for labor is the sum of the demands of the individual firms. However, in order to simplify the notation, we write this as $\phi(q_t)$, where q_t is aggregate output and ϕ now represents an aggregate labor requirements function. The real wage is then determined by an equilibrium in the labor market of the form,

$$\phi(q_t) = s(w_t), \quad s' > 0. \tag{19}$$

The aggregate supply of output equation is equivalent to an aggregate demand for labor equation, and since the aggregate supply function depends on the value of equity, so does the aggregate demand for labor equation.

The equilibrium in the labor market is depicted in Figure V as the intersection of the labor demand and supply equations. Accordingly, the high sensitivity of the aggregate supply equation to variations in a (which itself depends on price shocks) means that employment and output can be highly variable. *Small shocks can lead to large aggregate consequences.*

More formally, we solve (19) for real wages as a function of aggregate output of the form,

$$w_t = \psi(q_t), \tag{20}$$

where $\psi' = (\phi'/s') > 0$. Finally, substitution from the labor and capital market equilibria into the aggregate supply function yields a relationship of the form,

$$q_t = g(\psi(q_t), \delta, a_t), \tag{21}$$

which can be solved to yield (recalling that δ is a constant)

$$q_t = H(a_t). \tag{22}$$

Thus, *in each period output is determined by the level of equity, and movements in output over time will be driven by movements in the level of equity* (see Figure VIa).

Note that

$$\frac{d \ln q}{d \ln a} = \frac{d \ln g/d \ln a}{1 - (d \ln g/d \ln w)(d \ln w/d \ln q)}.$$

[25] Though we do not wish to argue strongly for this assumption (other than on grounds of analytic simplicity, and its ability to allow us to focus on the central issues of concern in this paper), we note that for long periods of time, there has been relatively little variability in real interest rates.

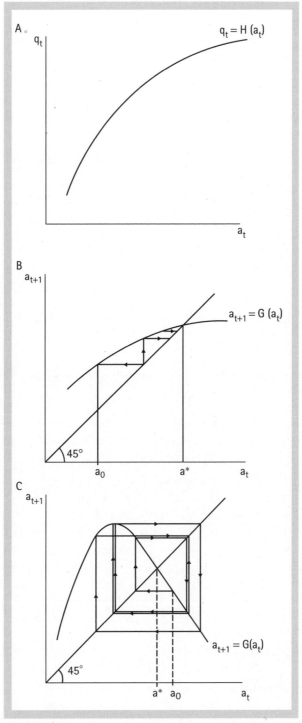

Fig. VI. Panel A. Aggregate output increases with aggregate equity.
Panel B. Aggregate equity at time $t + 1$ depends on aggregate equity at time t. a^*
is the steady state. If the economy gets perturbed, say to a_0, it takes several periods
to restore equilibrium.
Panel C. The model can also give rise to cycles

Thus, in general, the general-equilibrium volatility of output to changes in equity will be smaller than the partial-equilibrium volatility; wage adjustments help stabilize the economy.

A Dynamics

Equity in period $t + 1$ consists of equity in period t plus earning on that equity plus new equity sales less dividends paid.

In nominal terms,

$$\tilde{A}^i_{t+1} = \tilde{P}^i_{t+1} q^i_t - (1 + \tilde{R}^i_t)(P_t w_t \phi(q^i_t) - A^i_t) - \tilde{M}^i_{t+1},$$

where $\tilde{M}^i_{t+1}$ is a random variable representing the nominal value of dividends paid less new equity issued. Summation and averaging over firms and the taking of expected values, assuming that the law of large numbers applies, yields

$$A_{t+1} = E[\tilde{A}_{t+1}] = P_{t+1} q_t - (P^e_{t+1}) E\left[\frac{(1 + \tilde{R}^i_t) P_t}{P^e_{t+1}}\right](w_t \phi(q_t) - a_t) - M_{t+1}$$

$$= P_{t+1} q_t - (P^e_{t+1})(1 + \delta)(w_t \phi(q_t) - a_t) - M_{t+1},$$

where unsuperscripted variables now denote aggregate quantities. Division by P_{t+1} to convert to real terms yields an equation for real equity levels in period $t + 1$ of the form,

$$a_{t+1} = q_t - (P^e_{t+1}/P_{t+1})(1 + \delta)(w_t \phi(q_t) - a_t) - m_{t+1}, \tag{23}$$

where m_{t+1} now denotes the real value of dividends less equity sales, which we assume is simply a function of the state variable a_t.[26] Equations (22) and (23) together with whatever determine "price shocks" (i.e., the variable P^e_{t+1}/P_{t+1}) now completely determines the dynamic behavior of output in the model.

In order that this dynamic behavior be at least minimally interesting, the level of net equity outflows (i.e., m_{t+1}) must be sufficiently large—especially at high levels of a_t—so that the real equity level in the economy does not simply increase without bound. We assume that m is a function of a, such that when a_{t+1} is plotted as a function of a_t (see Figure VIb), the curve must at some point fall below the 45-degree line (it must also at some point obviously lie above that line). Formally, therefore, we shall assume that

$$a_{t+1} = q_t - (P^e_{t+1}/P_{t+1})(1 + \delta)(w_t \phi(q_t) - a_t) - m(a_t) \tag{24}$$

cuts the 45-degree line from above as shown in Figure VIb.[27]

---

[26] As noted earlier, adverse selection and signaling arguments similar to those used to argue that firms will not, in general, have recourse to equity markets have also been used to explain why dividend levels change so infrequently. For the short-run analysis on which this paper focuses, we can accordingly take these as related to the state variables of the system, in particular, to a_t.

[27] If we treat P_{t+1} as a random variable, equation (24), together with equation (22), defines a stochastic difference equation. The limiting properties of the stochastic process are studied elsewhere.

B Cycles

Cycles (in the sense of persistent fluctuations) may occur in this model for two reasons. First, even with $P_{t+1} = P^e_{t+1}$ in every period, deterministic cycles of multiple periodicity may occur if the slope of the curve,

$$a_{t+1} = q_t - (1 + \delta)(w_t \phi(q_t) - a_t) - m(a_t) \equiv G(a_t), \qquad (25)$$

is sufficiently highly negative when it crosses the 45-degree line (see Figure VIc).[28] Since

$$G' = (1 + \delta) - m' - ((1 + \delta)(\psi'\phi + \phi'w) - 1)H'$$

and $(1 + \delta)\phi'w < 1$ (from the first-order condition of firms), this requires that m' be large or that the impact of increased output on wages (i.e., $\psi'\phi$) be large. However, if these conditions are met, the resulting "real" cycles bear at least a casual resemblance to the "wage-shock" models that have been discussed, at least informally, in the empirical literature. Prosperity in the form of rising output and firm equity levels leads to both rising wages, which reduces profits and internal funds flows, and rising dividends. These in turn ultimately reduce equity levels and output, which both restores profitability (as wages fall) and reduces dividends, causing the cycle to begin again (see Figure VIc).

If G' is always greater than zero, then no such cycles are possible and convergence to the steady state is monotone. For future reference, we shall denote this steady-state level of equity by a^*, where

$$a^* = G(a^*). \qquad (26)$$

C Persistence

Second, random price shocks, which lead to unexpected fluctuations in the real value of debtor obligations and hence in real equity levels, will lead to output fluctuations that persist over several periods. Consider, for example, an unexpectedly low level of P_{t+1} (i.e., $P_{t+1} < P^e_{t+1}$). From equation (24) this will lead to an immediate and substantial drop in equity levels away from the steady-state level, a^* (assuming that the economy started at a^*), with an associated drop in output. The economy will return to a^* (and the associated "full-employment" level output) only slowly as a result of successive positive increments to a_t (see Figure VIb). Moreover, these increments (and the associated increments in wages) will be fully anticipated. They may not, however, be arbitraged away nor the process shortcut because doing so would involve levels of economic activity that require firms to bear unacceptably high levels

Here, we simply note that along each sample path, the property of persistence, to be described in the next subsection, will be observed.

[28] See Grandmont [1985] for a discussion of the mathematics of these cycles. We believe that the model formulated here provides a more satisfactory account of the structure of actual business cycles than the model of the Grandmont paper. Also see Woodford [1988].

of risk. Firms will do this only as they acquire equity funds which, for information (risk) reasons, they are assumed to do only slowly over time.

In the model presented in this section, while it generated volatility in the level of economic activity, there was (by assumption) no unemployment. In a sense, this model is very much in the spirit of the real business cycle literature, with one important distinction. Those models typically attribute economic variability to exogenous technology shocks. It has been difficult to identify changes in technology of the appropriate magnitudes to generate observed patterns of aggregate behavior; moreover, cross-country and intracountry correlations among industries make it clear that it is not changes in particular technologies that are driving economic behavior, but events within countries.

In our model the shifts in the supply functions are a result of changes in perceptions, e.g., of risk, and changes in equity. Small disturbances can have large macroeconomic effects.

IV Closing the Model: New Keynesian Models

Like the real business cycle models, the model of the previous section has the unattractive feature that there is (by assumption) no unemployment. However, the model may easily be extended to incorporate unemployment. We simply substitute for the labor supply equation a no-shirking equation (as in Shapiro and Stiglitz [1984]), which specifies the wages firms must pay to elicit effort from workers as a function of the employment level:[29]

$$w = \Omega(l). \tag{27}$$

Recognizing the dependence of l on q, we obtain an equation identical in form to (20). The rest of the analysis proceeds just as before.

In Figure VII we have drawn the no-shirking constraint, and the equilibrium is at the intersection of the labor demand curve and the no-shirking constraint. Shifts in the labor demand curve (caused by changes in equity levels or risk perceptions) now can cause marked changes in the level of unemployment, with relatively small changes in real wages.

A Aggregate Demand Effects

To traditional Keynesians the model of this paper may appear strange: it seems to attribute all the sources of output variability to the supply rather than the demand side.

---

[29] The no-shirking wage at time t will depend on expectations of wages and employment levels at future dates. For purposes of this analysis these expectations are being kept fixed.

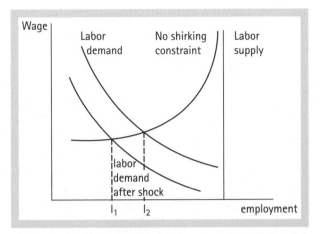

Fig. VII. Labor Market Equilibrium in a New Keynesian Model. Equilibrium occurs at the intersection of the labor demand curve and the no-shirking constraint. Shocks to the economy shift the demand curve for labor, leading to increased unemployment

In one sense, the paper can be thought of as attempting to establish the proposition that supply side effects, if appropriately modeled, may be able to explain a significant amount of the variability in economic activity, a proposition in accord with standard real business cycle doctrine.

On other hand, slight extensions of the model show how intimately demand and supply side considerations are interwoven, and that the dichotomy between "demand" and "supply" side shocks may be, at best, misleading.

In the model of this paper each firm only uses labor. But in fact, production of each commodity uses inputs from other sectors. Just as "equity" and "perception" shocks (whatever their sources) lead to decreased supply of output and decreased demand for labor, so too do they lead to decreased demand for the outputs of other firms. The demand curves these other firms face shift to the left, prices they receive fall, and hence, the effects of a shock to one sector have been transmitted to another sector, whence they can be retransmitted, amplified, back to the original sector. *Supply responses in one sector lead to demand disturbances in other sectors, which in turn lead to supply disturbances in those sectors.*

B Investment Behavior

Equally importantly, not only does a firm respond to equity and perception shocks by reducing output, labor, and inputs of other goods, it also reduces investment.

One widely observed characteristic of business cycles is that fluctuations are disproportionately severe in the investment goods sectors—fixed business investment and construction, residential construction, consumer durables—of a typical industrial economy. Peak-to-trough variations in activity in these sectors are greater than variations in the economy as whole. This presents a puzzle for traditional models since, in theory at least, investment projects should be less intensely subject to the pressures of cyclical variations than shorter term undertakings. If firms are risk neutral and on average forecast future output accurately (including a future recovery from the current recession), then even firms facing constraints on current demand should undertake some countercyclical investment (for plausible values of the relevant cost curves). The costs of installation and bringing plants on line should be lower in slack than in tight periods; long lead times for many investments argue against basing projections of demand at the time of plant completion on *current* capacity levels and relatively small reductions in investment goods prices should be sufficient to shift timing decisions. Thus, the fact that investment is so strongly procyclical suggests that more is involved than simply a passive response to fluctuations in aggregate demand. The paradoxical nature of these investment fluctuations is compounded by the observation that the fluctuations often appear largest in those sectors where traditional arguments for fixed prices (and wages) appear to be weakest, e.g., home construction.

There are at least two ways in which a simple extension of the model of this paper can account for these phenomena. First, investment goods sectors such as residential construction may for informational reasons (i.e., they produce highly complex goods with high private information content) have particularly restricted access to equity markets. At the same time firms in these industries operate with high degrees of leverage. Demand disturbances that reduce the equity bases of firms in these sectors will, thus, produce particularly large output responses.

Second, if fixed investment is thought of as current expenditures that yield output several periods in the future, the relative price uncertainty surrounding these expenditures is likely to be far greater than that associated with expenditures on next period's output. As depletion of a firm's equity base requires a reduction in the risk that management is willing to bear, this reduction should fall disproportionately on the firm's riskiest activities. Hence, the model predicts disproportionate cyclical variations in the demand for investment goods.

C Modeling Demand and Supply Effects Simultaneously

To see how these aggregate demand effects can easily be incorporated into our macro-model, we postulate that there are two sectors of the economy: an investment goods sector which produces to order, and for which, accordingly, there are no supply side effects; and the consumption goods sector, which we have previously modeled.

We postulate that the investment goods sector is competitive, and that its technology is described by the labor requirements function $\phi_I(I_t)$, with $\phi_I' > 0, \phi_I'' > 0$. There are (at least in the short run) diminishing returns in the investment goods sector. Let p_t be the price of capital goods at time t. Then, using an analysis parallel to that of the first part of the paper, it is easy to show that the demand for new capital

I_t^d, is given by

$$I_t^d = I^d(p_t, w_t, \delta; a_t; K_t; x), \tag{28}$$

where x is a vector describing firms' expectations of future values of the relevant variables, including p and w, and K is the inherited capital stock. The demand for new capital goods depends on the price of capital goods, the cost of capital δ, the cost of alternative inputs (labor), the current capital stock, and expectations. For simplicity, we take expectations as given.[30] Then equilibrium in the new capital goods market, which we assume is competitive, requires that price equal marginal cost, or

$$p_t = w_t \phi_I'(I_t), \tag{29}$$

and demand equal supply. Thus, substituting (28) into (29), we obtain

$$p_t = w_t \phi_I'(I_t^d(p_t, w_t, \delta; a_t; K_t; x)). \tag{30}$$

Equation (30) can, in turn, be solved for p_t as a function of w_t, a_t and the other variables:

$$p_t = y(w_t; a_t; \delta; K_t; x), \tag{31a}$$

and, substituting (31a) into (28), for investment,

$$I = I^*(w_t; a_t; \delta; K_t; x). \tag{31b}$$

If we assume that the labor market is competitive, we can now rewrite the labor market equilibrium condition (19) as

$$\phi(q_t) + \phi_I(I^*(w_t; a_t; \delta; K_t; x)) = s(w_t), \tag{32}$$

where, it will be remembered, q_t is now interpreted as the output of consumption goods, which depends on wages and a_t. This can be solved for w_t.

More relevant for our current purpose, with an efficiency wage model, we replace (32) with

$$\phi(q_t) + \phi_I(I^*(w_t', a_t; \delta; K_t; x)) = \Omega^{-1}(w_t). \tag{33}$$

The left-hand side of (33) is the aggregate demand curve for labor.

The amount firms are willing to supply, q, and I, the amount firms wish to invest, depend on the same factors. Shocks to a_t will depress both q_t and I_t, hence shifting the demand curve for labor to the left, and (in Figure VII) increasing the unemployment rate.

This section has shown how bankruptcy risk can depress economy activity in a way quite independent from that discussed in earlier sections: bankruptcy risk affects the demand for investment as well as the supply of output.

We now see more clearly why the dichotomy between demand and supply effects is somewhat misleading. Decisions to invest are at least partly related to decisions

---

[30] Though the analysis would be little affected if we made them dependent on the other exogenous or endogenous variables within the model.

concerning future supply. If similar factors affect current and future supply, similar factors will affect supply and investment demand.[31]

Separating out the demand and supply effects may be an empirically difficult matter. Consider commercial construction. Some of the decrease in production during a slump is due to builders who normally build speculatively, in anticipation of demand, decreasing their production.[32] Some of the decrease in production is due to a decrease in demand by firms for investment in plant. Restoration of the equity of builders (or increasing the availability of credit) will have a positive supply side effect; restoration of the equity of firms will have a positive demand side effect. Improved expectations about future economic conditions will have positive effects on both sides.

V Sources of Shocks

This paper has stressed how, in the absence of perfect risk markets, shocks to the economy can be amplified, and transmitted from one firm or sector to another. Given our claim that relatively small shocks can generate large effects, there is little necessity to search for the basic cause of economic fluctuations: one time it may be a monetary shock; another time an oil price shock; and another time a failed harvest.

There are two basic sources of shocks in our model: price shocks (resulting from unanticipated shifts in the demand curve) and "uncertainty" shocks.

A Sources of Price Shocks

There are innumerable possible ways to model the sources of these price shocks. The simplest is to assume that output is sold on a large international market and international prices vary in response to forces which are external to the economy in question.

A more traditional source of such "shocks" would be a monetary sector that determines the aggregate price level. From this perspective, an unexpectedly low level of P_{t+1} might be associated either with an unexpectedly low level of money supply or, for some money demand specifications, with an unexpectedly low level of

---

[31] The discussion of the preceding paragraph suggested several reasons why I might even be more sensitive to variations in a than is supply in the noninvestment goods sector.

By assuming that investment goods are produced to order, we have greatly simplified the analysis, but left out of it several of the considerations we noted in earlier paragraphs of this subsection. In this more general model, the price of investment goods would be determined to equate demand and supply in the investment goods sector. Shocks to a shift both the demand and supply curve for investment to the left. We may thus see large variations in employment in the investment goods sector, with relatively little change in the price.

[32] Part of this decrease is due to credit rationing effects, which we have ignored in this paper.

consumption demand. Explorations of these phenomena are contained in Greenwald and Stiglitz [1986c], but they add relatively little (at the cost of some complexity) to understanding the basic characteristics of the model in question.

In all cases, as in many monetary models with real effects, the source of the real effect is a redistribution of assets as a result of the "price shock." In most of these models (see, for example, Grossman [1985]), the redistribution involved is a redistribution of wealth among households, and it is difficult to believe that such a redistribution would have significant macroeconomic consequences. In contrast, the redistribution that occurs in the model of this paper is between the equity and debt of firms. It is for practical purposes a redistribution between managers or owners who make production decisions and passive investors or lenders. Given the important information asymmetries, this should more readily be expected to have a significant impact on output. In the model the effects of any associated redistributions of wealth among consumers are, given the underlying assumptions on consumer behavior, nonexistent.

B Uncertainty Shocks

The second variety of shock that might be expected to have persistent consequences is what might be referred to as an "uncertainty shock." An increase in the perceived uncertainty of future relative prices will, in general, lead to a reduction in the level of output (i.e., a downward shift in the function $H(a_t)$, the output supply equation (22)). If the increase in uncertainty is permanent, then the drop in output at each level of a will be permanent. However, if

$$1 - (1 + \delta)w_t\phi' - (1 + \delta)\psi'\phi < 0,$$

then the drop in output is associated with a simultaneous upward shift in the function G, the equity supply equation (25); assuming no change in the net dividend function $m(a_t)$, lower output raises profitability which increases the flow of new equity (see Figure VIII). As $G(a_t)$ shifts upward, a^* increases, and there is a gradual adjustment to the new higher steady-state level of equity. This is accompanied by a slow steady, but perhaps incomplete, recovery from the initial drop in output. The pattern is again one of slow, persistent, fully anticipated recovery.

VI APPLICATIONS AND EXTENSION

The formal model presented above is a model of "persistent" cycles in the sense that recovery from the trough of a recession follows an extended path involving a predictable sequence of positive increments to output. As noted in the introduction

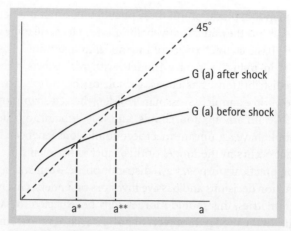

Fig. VIII. Effect of "Uncertainty" Shocks on the Equity "Supply" Equations. At each value of a_1, a_{t+1} is increased. Equilibrium a is increased

to this paper, simple extensions of the model can account for other widely noted cyclical phenomena. Several extensions are described in this section of the paper.

A Inventory Fluctuations and Interfirm Interactions

Traditional theory has found it particularly difficult to account for the cyclical pattern of inventory fluctuations (see Blinder [1986]). While firms typically accumulate excess inventories in the early part of a recession, they typically not only reduce inventories in later parts of recessions, but even reduce inventory-sales ratios. With traditional production models, inventories should serve as buffers, allowing firms to engage in production smoothing. Given the low levels of real interest rates, and their relative invariance over time, even if real wages (and other factor costs) did not vary much over the business cycle, one would expect inventories to move countercyclically; a fortiori, if shadow wages (reflecting labor hoarding) are lower in recessions, then inventory accumulation should be greater.

Although our model, as it stands, does not directly incorporate inventories, a simple extension of the model offers some insight into the problem. Inventory accumulation early in the business cycle may simply reflect the desire of firms to take advantage of the lower marginal costs accompanying a reduction in demand. They do this until their asset position (achieved by converting financial assets into real assets in the process of inventory accumulation) so increases their potential exposure to financial distress that the process stops and, in the face of continuing shortfalls in demand, is reversed. This may be augmented by the effect of transfers of risk as the initial shock is transmitted to other firms in a vertical chain.

B Unemployment

Earlier we suggested how the basic model could be extended to explain variations in unemployment, using the efficiency wage model. The model can also be used to explain why, in recessions, firms seem reluctant to hire new workers, even if there were no efficiency wage problems.

The existence of significant hiring and training costs may prevent the striking of mutually acceptable wage bargains between unemployed workers and potential employers. In making a wage offer in a recession (presumably involving an extended period of employment), a firm will count these costs highly since the associated outlays will carry a high "risk" premium at a time when the firm's equity base is severely depleted. In order to recoup this "risk" cost, the firm will require a substantial saving in future wages in order to justify countercyclical hiring. From the perspective of the worker, these wage sacrifices may not be justified. Unless his financial position is so impaired that immediate employment is a necessity, it may well pay the worker to attempt to outwait the recession. He knows that as the financial positions of firms improve, the effective cost to a firm of hiring and training will decline and wage offers will improve accordingly. Thus, the model provides a "waiting" motive for unemployment; in a recession a worker may rationally wait for an improvement in economic conditions (until his financial resources are depleted and he must accept a job). The worker could, of course, himself offer to bear hiring and training costs and to defer wages but there are some basic difficulties with this.

First, the commitments of the firm to pay higher wages in the future[33] may not be credible. Second, the individual in this position is, in effect, a supplier of a kind of equity capital: there is no fixed commitment to repay, even if the firm has the best of intentions. Thus, the usual moral hazard and adverse selection difficulties arise; it is precisely those firms that are in the worst financial position (e.g., Eastern Airlines) that will be most anxious to "borrow" from their employees, and offer seemingly the most attractive terms.

C Price Rigidities

Price rigidities may arise endogenously in the model whenever firms are imperfect competitors. Assume that these firms face demand curves that are inelastic in the short run but are characterized by sufficiently high long-run elasticities to restrain prices. Thus, raising prices increases current profits, but as customers are induced to search to find alternative suppliers, future profits are reduced. The restraint of this long-run elasticity depends on the rate at which future profits are discounted. As a firm's current equity base is depleted, the value of these uncertain future profits will fall relative to the immediate returns available from raising current prices. As a result,

---

[33] This is the flip side of the workers' inability to make commitments to accept low wages in the future. See Lindbeck and Snower [1989].

prices may increase despite low levels of current demand. And as all firms act in this way, the upward pressure on prices may be reinforced. In the context of empirical observation this may well look like downward price rigidity.[34]

D Wage Flexibility

Traditional theory has ascribed great importance to price and wage rigidities, without fully or even adequately explaining the sources of those rigidities.

We have already noted that sectors with more flexible prices are among the more volatile in the economy, which suggests that something beyond price and wage flexibility is at issue. Keynes too was skeptical about the importance of wage and price flexibility: he tried to argue that lowering wages might actually exacerbate the recession because of the induced aggregate demand effect.

Our paper has shown that the economy can exhibit high volatility even with flexible wages and prices. Indeed, as for Keynes, but for quite different reasons, downward wage and price flexibility may exacerbate an economic downturn. If prices and wages fall (or even rise less than anticipated), equity will be depleted, as firms have to pay back debt at real rates higher than anticipated. This paper has traced out the large negative effects that such equity depletion has on the whole economy.[35]

VII Concluding Comments

This paper has explored the consequences of three simple, but we believe plausible, characteristics of the economy: (a) firms act as if they are equity rationed; (b) firms act as if they are averse to risk, to increasing the likelihood of bankruptcy; and (c) there are imperfect futures markets, production takes time, and inputs have to be paid before goods are sold. Accordingly, every production decision is a risky decision.

Under these circumstances, the level and distribution of net worth among firms has real macroeconomic implications. The simple model we presented can generate cyclical behavior and can explain why a variety of shocks to the economy (such as price shocks) have persistent effects. Moreover, the theory provides a set of explanations for a variety of phenomena which, at best, are difficult to explain within

[34] It should finally be noted that all these phenomena may be intensified by expectations cycles (see Woodford [1988]) which may be added within the framework of the basic model.

[35] Elsewhere [Greenwald and Stiglitz 1990b] we model the banking sector, the effect of price declines on that sector, and the effect of that sector on the rest of the economy. Lower than anticipated prices represent a redistribution from firms to lenders, which, in many cases, are banks; at the same time higher rates of bankruptcy both increase their perception of risk and deplete bank's equity supply; both of these effects lead to reduced lending behavior.

the traditional neoclassical paradigm. Most notably, while in the traditional model, investment, particularly in inventories, should have a smoothing effect, dampening fluctuations in demand, the variability of investment seems to contribute to these fluctuations. Such fluctuations could only be consistent with plausible assumptions concerning technology (adjustment costs, etc.) if the cyclical movements were accompanied by greater variations in real interest rates and movements in (shadow) real wages than are in fact observed. While Keynes was willing to let Animal Spirits serve as the *deus ex machina* to retrieve an explanation of investment variability, our theory provides a more plausible explanation of variability in investment, or at least one that is more consistent with currently fashionable strictures on hypotheses concerning expectation formation.

We have noted too that traditional theory failed to provide a rationale for price (and wage) rigidity and, while ascribing considerable importance to these rigidities, failed to explain why output fluctuations were greater in the seemingly flexible price sectors. Our theory provides a rationale for price rigidities and an explanation for why sectors with flexible prices (e.g., residential construction) may suffer greater output variability.

Our model provides an explanation of another long-standing conundrum in economics. Keynes argued that firms should be on their supply functions, and that accordingly, when output was reduced, real wages should increase. Real wages do not increase to the extent that standard production function models would have predicted. The resolution provided by much of the recent (fixed-price) literature, that firms are demand constrained (just as in the labor market, workers are demand constrained), is not totally plausible: why in a competitive environment should firms that are able to solve the complex production problems which these models postulate that they can, not be able to discover that by lowering their prices, they could steal customers away from their rivals and hence increase their profits?

The explanation provided by our model is that firms may, indeed, be on their supply function; but that the supply function has shifted to the left, not because of the disappearance of capital, but because of increases in uncertainty and changes in the distribution of firm equity.

While our model suggests that wage and price flexibility may exacerbate the problems of an economy facing a downturn, it suggests that other government policies to stabilize the economy may be less effective than a partial-equilibrium model might suggest. Stabler environments induce firms to take more risks, making them and the economy more vulnerable to shocks. But the welfare gains from such stabilization measures are to be measured not just by the reduced volatility of the economy, but by the increased output (productivity, investment) which (at any level of firm equity) the firm undertakes.

Macroeconomic phenomena—unemployment, the variability in output and investment, the lack of variability in wages and prices—are complex. No single model, or even a simple set of explanations, is likely to inform us concerning all of its important aspects.

In this paper we have argued that understanding capital markets, the constraints that imperfect information imposes on the ability of individuals to divest themselves of risk, is essential to understanding certain aspects of macroeconomic behavior. Other informational problems and the constraints to which they give rise, including credit rationing, are, we would argue, essential to understanding other aspects of these phenomena.

BIBLIOGRAPHY

ABREU, D., 1983. "Repeated Games with Discounting: A General Theory and an Application to Oligopoly," PhD dissertation, Princeton University.

—— 1986. "Extremal Equilibria of Oligopolistic Supergames," *Journal of Economic Theory*, 39(1), pp. 191–225.

ADAMS, W. J. and J. YELLEN, 1976. "Commodity Bundling and the Burden of Monopoly," *Quarterly Journal of Economics*, 90(3), pp. 475–98.

AGHION, P. and O. BLANCHARD, 1996. "On Insider Privatization," *European Economic Review*, 40(3–5) (April), pp. 759–66.

AIGNER, D. and G. CAIN, 1977. "Statistical Theories of Discrimination in Labor Markets," *Industrial and Labor Relations Review*, 30(2), pp. 175–87.

AKERLOF, G., 1969. "Structural Unemployment in a Neoclassical Framework," *Journal of Political Economy*, 77(3), pp. 399–407.

—— 1970. "The Market for 'Lemons:' Qualitative Uncertainty and the Market Mechanism," *Quarterly Journal of Economics*, 84(3), pp. 488–500.

—— 1973. "A Theory of Information and Labor Markets," mimeo, University of California, Berkeley, presented at the NSF-NBER Conference on the Economics of Information, Princeton.

—— 1976. "The Economics of Caste and of the Rat Race and Other Woeful Tales," *Quarterly Journal of Economics*, 90(4), pp. 599–617.

—— 1980. "A Theory of Social Custom, of which Unemployment May Be One Consequence," *Quarterly Journal of Economics*, 94(4), pp. 749–75.

—— 1982. "Labor Contracts as Partial Gift Exchange," *Quarterly Journal of Economics*, 97(4), pp. 543–69.

—— 1984. "Gift Exchange and Efficiency-Wage Theory: Four Views," *American Economic Review*, 74(2), pp. 79–83.

—— 2001. "Behavioral Macroeconomics and Macroeconomic Behavior," Nobel Prize Lecture, Stockholm. Published in *American Economic Review*, 92(2), 2002, pp. 411–33.

—— J. E. STIGLITZ, 1969. "Capital, Wages and Structural Unemployment," *Economic Journal*, 79(314), pp. 269–81.

—— J. YELLEN, 1983. "The Macroeconomic Consequences of Near Rational Rule of Thumb Behavior," mimeo, University College, Berkeley.

—— —— 1985. "A Near-Rational Model of the Business Cycle, with Wage and Price Inertia," *Quarterly Journal of Economics*, 100(Supplement), pp. 823–38.

—— —— eds., 1986. *Efficiency Wage Models of the Labor Market*, New York: Cambridge University Press.

—— —— 1990. "The Fair Wage-Effort Hypothesis and Unemployment," *Quarterly Journal of Economics*, 105(2), pp. 255–83.

ALCHIAN, A. A., 1950. "Uncertainty, Evolution, and Economic Theory," *Journal of Political Economy*, 58(3), pp. 211–21.

—— and H. DEMSETZ, 1972. "Production, Information Costs, and Economic Organization," *American Economic Review*, 62(5), pp. 777–95.

ALEEM, I., 1990. "Imperfect Information, Screening, and the Costs of Informal Lending: A Study of a Rural Credit Market in Pakistan," *World Bank Economic Review*, 1990(4), pp. 329–49.

ALLEN, F, 1980a. "Loans, Bequests and Taxes Where Abilities Differ A Theoretical Analysis Using a Two-ability Model," DPhil thesis, Oxford University.

——1980b. "Capital, Sharecropping, Ability and Information," mimeo, Oxford University.

——1981. "The Prevention of Default," *Journal of Finance*, 36(2), pp. 271–6.

——1983. "Credit Rationing and Payment Incentives," *Review of Economic Studies*, 50(4), pp. 639–46.

——1984. "Reputation and Product Quality," *Rand Journal of Economics*, 15(3), pp. 311–27.

——1985. "On the Fixed Nature of Sharecropping Contrasts," *Economic Journal*, 95(377), pp. 30–48.

——1988. "A Theory of Price Rigidities When Quality Is Unobservable," *Review of Economic Studies*, 55(1), pp. 139–51.

American Law Institute, 1994. *Principles of Corporate Governance: Analysis and* Recommendations, St. Paul, MN: American Law Institute Publishers.

ANNABLE, J. E., 1977. "A Theory of Downward-Rigid Wages and Cyclical Unemployment," *Economic Inquiry*, 15(3), pp. 326–44.

——1980. "Money Wage Determination in Post Keynesian Economics," *Journal of Post Keynesian Economics*, 2(3), pp. 405–19.

——1988. "Another Auctioneer is Missing," *Journal of Macroeconomics*, 10(1), pp. 1–26.

AOKI, K. and M. FELDMAN, 1998. "Theoretical Aspects of the Evolution of Human Social Behaviour," Santa Fe Institute Working Paper No. 98-11-099.

ARNOTT, R. and J. E. STIGLITZ, 1979. "Aggregate Land Rents, Expenditure on Public Goods and Optimal City Size," *Quarterly Journal of Economics*, 93(4) (November), pp. 471–500.

——— 1981. "Aggregate Land Rents and Aggregate Transport Costs," *Economic Journal*, 91(362) (June), pp. 331–47.

——— 1985. "Labor Turnover, Wage Structure, and Moral Hazard: The Inefficiency of Competitive Markets," *Journal of Labor Economics*, 3(4), pp. 434–62.

——— 1986. "Moral Hazard and Optimal Commodity Taxation," *Journal of Public Economics*, 29(1), pp. 1–24.

——— 1987. "Equilibrium in Competitive Insurance Markets with Moral Hazard," Princeton University Discussion Paper 4 (also NBER Working Paper 3588, 1991).

——— 1988a. "The Basic Analytics of Moral Hazard," *Scandinavian Journal of Economics*, 90(3), pp. 383–413.

——— 1988b. "Randomization with Asymmetric Information," *Rand Journal of Economics*, 19(3), pp. 344–62.

——— 1990. "The Welfare Economics of Moral Hazard," in H. Louberge (ed.), *Risk, Information and Insurance: Essays in the Memory of Karl H. Borch*, Norwell: Kluwer Academic Publishers, pp. 91–122 (also NBER Working Paper 3316).

——— 1991a. "Moral Hazard and Nonmarket Institutions: Dysfunctional Crowding Out or Peer Monitoring?" *American Economic Review*, 81(1), pp. 179–90.

——— 1991b. "Price Equilibrium, Efficiency, and Decentralizability in Insurance Markets," NBER Working Paper 3642.

——A. HOSIOS, and J. E. STIGLITZ, 1988. "Implicit Contracts, Labor Mobility, and Unemployment," *The American Economic Review*, 78(5), pp. 1046–1066.

——B. GREENWALD, and J. E. STIGLITZ, 1994. "Information and Economic Efficiency," *Information Economics and Policy*, 6(1), pp. 77–88.

ARROW, K. J., 1951. "An Extension of the Basic Theorems of Classical Welfare Economics," in J. Neyman, (ed.), *Proceedings of the Second Berkeley Symposium on*

Mathematical Statistics and probability, Berkeley: University of California Press, pp. 507–32.

——1962a. "Economic Welfare and the Allocation of Resources of Invention", in R. Nelson (ed.), *The Rate and Direction of Inventive Activity: Economic and Social Factors*, Princeton, NJ: Princeton University Press.

——1962b. "The Economic Implications of Learning by Doing", *The Review of Economic Studies*, 29(3), pp. 155–73.

——1963. "Uncertainty and the Welfare Economics of Medical Care," *American Economic Review*, 53(5), pp. 941–73.

——1964. "The Role of Securities in the Optimal Allocation of Risk-Bearing," *The Review of Economic Studies*, 31(2), pp. 91–6.

——1965. *Aspects of the Theory of Risk-Bearing* (Yrjo Jahnsson Lectures), Helsinki, Finland: Yrjö Jahnsson Foundation.

——1971. *Essays in the Theory of Risk Bearing*, Chicago: Markham.

——1972a. "Models of Job Discrimination" and "Some Mathematic Models of Race in the Labor Markets," in M. H. Pascal (ed.), *Racial Discrimination in Economic Life*, Lanham, MD: Lexington Books.

——1972b. "The Value of and Demand for Information," in C. B. McGuire and R. Radner, (eds.), *Decision and Organization*, Amsterdam: North-Holland.

——1973a. "Higher Education as a Filter," *Journal of Public Economics*, 2(3), pp. 193–16.

——1973b. "The Theory of Discrimination," *Discrimination in Labor Markets*, in O. Ashenfelter and A. Rees (eds.), Princeton, NJ: Princeton University Press, pp. 3–33.

——1974a. "Limited Knowledge and Economic Analysis," *American Economic Review*, 64(1), pp. 1–10.

——1974b. "The Value of and Demand for Information," *Essays in the Theory of Risk-Bearing*, New York: North-Holland Publishing.

——1978. "Risk Allocation and Information: Some Theoretical Development," *Geneva Papers on Risk and Insurance*, 8.

——G. DEBREU, 1954. "Existence of an Equilibrium for a Competitive Economy," *Econometrica*, 22(3), pp. 265–90.

——F. H. HAHN, 1971. *General Competitive Analysis*, New York: North-Holland.

ARTHUR, W. B., J. H. HOLLAND, B. LeBARON, R. G. PALMER, and P. J. TAYLOR, 1996. "Asset Pricing under Endogenous Expectations in an Artificial Stock Market," *The Economy as an Evolving Complex System II, Santa Fe Institute Series in the Sciences of Complexity*, Santa Fe Institute Working Paper No. 96-12-093.

ASH, R. B., 1972. *Real Analysis and Probability*, New York: Academic Press.

ASQUITH, P. and D. W. MULLINS JR., 1986. "Equity Issues and Offering Dilution," *Journal of Financial Economics*, 15(1–2), pp. 61–89.

ATKINSON, A. B., 1970. "On the Measurement of Inequality," *Journal of Economic Theory*, 2(3), pp. 244–63.

——J. E. STIGLITZ, 1969. "A New View of Technological Change," *Economic Journal*, 79(315), pp. 573–78.

————1976. "The Design of Tax Structure: Direct Versus Indirect Taxation," *Journal of Public Economics*, 6(1–2), pp. 55–75.

————1980. *Lectures in Public Finance*, New York: McGraw-Hill.

AZARIADIS, C., 1983. "Employment with Asymmetric Information," *Quarterly Journal of Economics*, 98(Supplement), pp. 157–72.

——J. E. STIGLITZ, 1983. "Implicit Contracts and Fixed Price Equilibria," *Quarterly Journal of Economics*, 98(Supplement), pp. 1–22.

BALTENSPERGER, E. and H. MILDE, 1983. "Loan Rate Flexibility and Asymmetric Default Information," in H. Göppl and R. Henn (eds.), *Geld, Banken und Versicherungen II*, Karlsruhe, pp. 1165–78.

BANKS, J. and J. SOBEL, 1987. "Equilibrium Selection in Signaling Games," *Econometrica*, 55(3), pp. 647–61.

BARDHAN, P., 1973. "Size, Productivity and Returns to Scale: An Analysis of Farm Level Data in Indian Agriculture," *Journal of Political Economy*, 81(6), pp. 1370–86.

——— T. N. SRINIVASAN, 1971. "Crop-Sharing Tenancy in Agriculture: A Theoretical and Empirical Analysis," *American Economic Review*, 61(1), pp. 48–64.

BARRO, R., 1974. "Are Government Bonds Net Wealth?" *Journal of Political Economy*, 82(6), pp. 1095–117.

——— H. GROSSMAN, 1971. "A General Disequilibrium Model of Income and Employment," *American Economic Review*, 61(1), pp. 82–93.

BATOR, F. M., 1958. "The Anatomy of Market Failure," *Quarterly Journal of Economics*, 72(3), pp. 351–79.

BAUMOL, W. J., 1959. *Business Behavior, Value and Growth*, New York: The MacMillan Co. (revised edn, 1967).

——— J. C. PANZAR et al., 1982. *Contestable Markets and the Theory of Industry Structure*, New York: Harcourt Brace Jovanovich.

BECKER, G., 1964. *Human Capital*, New York.

——— 1971. *The Economics of Discrimination*, 2nd edn., Chicago: University of Chicago Press.

——— G. STIGLER, 1974. "Law Enforcement, Malfeasance, and Compensation of Enforcers," *Journal of Legal Studies*, 3(1), pp. 1–18.

BELL, C., 1990. "Interactions between Institutional and Informal Credit Agencies in Rural India," *World Bank Economic Review*, 1990(4), pp. 297–327.

BERLE JR, A. A., 1926. "Non-Voting Stock and 'Bankers' Control," *Harvard Law Review*, 39, pp. 673–93.

——— 1959. *Power Without Property: A New Development in American Political Economy*. New York: Harcourt, Brace.

——— G. C. MEANS, 1932. *The Modern Corporation and Private Property*, New York: Macmillan.

BERNANKE, B., 1993. "Credit in the Macro-Economy," *Federal Reserve Bank of New York Quarterly Review*, 18(1), pp. 50–70.

——— A. S. BLINDER, 1988. "Credit, Money, and Aggregate Demand," *American Economic Review*, 78(2), pp. 435–9.

——— M. GERTLER, 1989. "Agency Costs, Net Worth, and Business Fluctuations," *American Economic Review*, 79(1), pp. 14–31.

——— ——— 1995a. "Inside the Black Box: The Credit Channel of Monetary Policy Transmission," *Journal of Economic Perspectives*, 9(4), pp. 27–48.

——— ——— 1995b. "The Financial Accelerator and the Flight to Quality," *The Review of Economics and Statistics*, 78(1), pp. 1–15.

——— ——— S. GILCHRIST, 1996. "The Financial Accelerator and the Flight to Quality," *The Review of Economics and Statistics*, 78(1), pp. 1–15.

BERNHEIM, B. D. and M. D. WHINSTON, 1984. "Common Agency," *Econometrica*, 54(4), pp. 923–42.

BESANKO, D. and A. THAKOR, 1987. "Collateral and Rationing Sorting Equilibria in Monopolistic and Competitive Markets," *International Economic Review*, 28(3), pp. 671–89.

BESLEY, T. and S. COATE, 1991. "Group Lending, Repayment Incentives, and Social Collateral," R.P.D.S. Discussion Paper 152, Princeton University, Princeton.

BESTER, H., 1985. "Screening vs. Rationing in Credit Markets with Incomplete Information," *American Economic Review*, 75(4), pp. 850–5.

BHATTACHARYA, S., 1979. "Imperfect Information, Dividend Policy and the Bird-in-the-Hand Fallacy," *Bell Journal of Economics and Management Science*, 10(1), pp. 259–70.

—— 1980. "Nondissipative Signals and Dividend Policy." *Quarterly Journal of Economics*, 95(1), pp. 1–24.

—— 1985. "Tournaments, Termination Schemes and Forcing Contracts," mimeo, University of California, Berkeley (June).

BHIDÉ, A., 2001. "Taking Care: Ambiguity, Pooling and Error Control," Columbia Business School, Working Paper.

BLACK, B., R. KRAAKMAN, and A. TARASSOVA, 2000. "Russian Privatization and Corporate Governance: What Went Wrong?" *Stanford Law Review*, 52(6), pp. 1731–808.

BILS, M. and J. A. KAHN, 2000. "What Inventory Behavior Tells Us about Business Cycles," *American Economic Review*, 90(3), pp. 458–81.

BLANCHARD, O., F. LOPEZ-DE-SILANES, and A. SHLEIFER, 1994. "What Do Firms Do with Cash Windfalls?" *Journal of Financial Economics*, 36(3), pp. 337–60.

BLINDER, A. S., 1986. "Can the Production Smoothing Model of Inventory Behavior Be Saved?" *Quarterly Journal of Economics*, 101(3), pp. 431–54.

—— S. FISCHER, 1981. "Inventories, Rational Expectations, and the Business Cycle," *Journal of Monetary Economics*, 8(3), pp. 277–304.

—— L. MACCINI, 1991. "Taking Stock: A Critical Assessment of Recent Research on Inventories," *Journal of Economic Perspectives*, 5(1), pp. 73–96.

—— J. E. STIGLITZ, 1983. "Money, Credit Constraints and Economic Activity," *American Economic Review*, 73(2), pp. 297–302.

BLISS, C. J. and N. STERN, 1978. "Productivity, Wages and Nutrition," *Journal of Development Economics*, 5(4), pp. 331–97.

—— 1981. *Palanpur-Studies in the Economy of a North Indian Village*, New Delhi: Oxford University Press.

BORCH, K., 1968. *The Economics of Uncertainty*, Princeton: Princeton University Press.

BOSERUP, E., 1965. *The Conditions of Agricultural Growth: The Economics of Agrarian Change Under Population Pressure*, Chicago: Chicago University Press.

BOWLES, S., 1985. "The Production Process in a Competitive Economy Walrasian, Neo-Hobbesian, and Marxian *Models*", *American Economic Review*, 75(1), pp. 16–36.

—— H. GINTIS, 1976. *Schooling in Capitalist America*, New York: Basic Books.

BRADFORD, D. and H. KELEJIAN, 1977. "The Value of Information for Crop Forecasting in a Market System: Some Theoretical Issues," *The Review of Economic Studies*, 44(3), pp. 519–31.

BRAVERMAN, A., 1976. "Price Dispersion in Monopolistic Competition," PhD Dissertation, Stanford University.

—— K. HOFF, and J. E. STIGLITZ (eds.), 1993. *The Economics of Rural Organization: Theory, Practice, and Policy*, New York: Oxford University Press.

—— T. N. SRINIVASAN, 1981. "Credit and Sharecropping in Agrarian Societies," *Journal of Development Economics*, 9(3), pp. 289–312.

—— J. E. STIGLITZ, 1982. "Sharecropping and the Interlinking of Agrarcan Markets," *American Economic Review*, 72(4), pp. 695–715.

—— —— 1986a. "Cost Sharing Arrangement Under Sharecropping: Moral Hazard, Incentive Flexibility and Risk," *Journal of Agricultural Economics*, 68(3), pp. 642–52.

—— —— 1986b. "Landlords, Tenants and Technological Innovations," *Journal of Development Economics*, 23(2), pp. 313–32.

—— —— 1989. "Credit Rationing, Tenancy, Productivity and the Dynamics of Inequality," in P. Bardhan (ed.), *The Economic Theory of Agrarian Institutions*, Oxford: Clarendon Press, pp. 185–201.

BRAY, M. M., 1978. "Information in Futures Markets," PhD thesis, Oxford University.

Bray, M. M., 1981. "Futures Trading, Rational Expectations, and the Efficient Markets Hypothesis," *Econometrica*, May, 49(3), pp. 575–96.

Brito, D., J. H. Hamilton, S. M. Slutsky, and J. E. Stiglitz, 1990. "Pareto Efficient Tax Structures," *Oxford Economic Papers*, 42(1), pp. 61–77.

————————1991. "Dynamic Optimal Income Taxation With Government Commitment," *Journal of Public Economics*, 44(1), pp. 15–35.

————————1995, "Randomization in Optimal Income Tax Schedules," *Journal of Public Economics*, 56(2), pp. 189–223.

Brunnermeier, M., 2001. *Asset Pricing Under Asymmetric Information: Bubbles, Crashes, Technical Analysis, and Herding*, Oxford: Oxford University Press.

Bull, C., 1985. "Equilibrium Unemployment as a Worker Discipline Device: Comment," *American Economic Review*, 75(4), pp. 890–1.

Bulow, J. I. and L. H. Summers, 1985. "A Theory of Dual Labor Markets with Application to Industrial Policy, Discrimination and Keynesian Unemployment," NBER Working Paper No. 1666.

Burnside, C. and D. Dollar, 2000. "Aid, policies, and growth," *American Economic Review*, 90(4), pp. 847–68.

Butters, G. R., 1977. "Equilibrium Distributions of Sales and Advertising Prices," *Review of Economic Studies*, 44(3), pp. 465–91.

Cadbury Commission, 1992. "The Financial Aspects of Corporate Governance," London: Professional Publishing Ltd.

Calomiris, C. and R. G. Hubbard, 1989. "Price Flexibility, Credit Rationing, and Economic Fluctuations: Evidence from the US, 1894–1909," *Quarterly Journal of Economics*, 104(3), pp. 429–52.

————————1990. "Firm Heterogeneity, Internal Finance, and 'Credit Rationing,'" *The Economic Journal*, 100(399), pp. 90–104.

Calvo, G., 1979. "Quasi-Walrasian Theories of Unemployment," *American Economic Review*, 69(2), pp. 102–07.

————1981. "On the Inefficiency of Unemployment," Discussion paper, Columbia University.

————E. Phelps, 1977. "Indexation Issues: Appendix Employment Contingent Wage Contracts," in K. Brunner and A. H. Meltzer (eds.), *Stabilization of the Domestic and International Economy: Vol 5*, Carnegie-Rochester Conference Series on Public Policy, *Journal of Monetary Economics*, Supplementary Series 1977, 5, pp. 160–8.

————S. Wellisz, 1979. "Hierarchy, Ability and Income Distribution," *Journal of Political Economy*, Part 1, 87(5), pp. 991–1010.

Camerer, C. and R. H. Thaler, 1995. "Anomalies: Ultimatums, Dictators, and Manners," *Journal of Economic Perspectives*, 9(2), pp. 209–19.

Capen, E. C., R. Clapp, and W. Campbell, 1971. "Competitive Bidding in High Risk Situations," *Journal of Petroleum Technology*, 23(1), pp. 641–53.

Carmichael, H. L., 1985. "Equilibrium Unemployment: Comment," *American Economic Review*, 75(5), pp. 1213–14.

————1988. "Incentives in Academics: Why is There Tenure?" *Journal of Political Economy*, 96(3), pp. 453–72.

Carpenter, R., S. Fazzari, and B. Petersen., 1994. "Inventory Investment, Internal-Finance Fluctuations, and the Business Cycle," *Brookings Papers on Economic Activity*, 1994(2), pp. 75–138.

Card, D. and A. Krueger, 1994. "Minimum Wages and Employment: A Case Study of the Fast-Food Industry in New Jersey and Pennsylvania," *American Economic Review*, 84(4), pp. 772–93.

CARY, W., 1969. "Corporate Devices Used to Insulate Management from Attack," *Anti-Trust Law Journal*, 1, 318–24.

CASS, D. and K. SHELL, 1983. "Do Sunspots Matter?" *Journal of Political Economy*, 91(2), pp. 193–227.

CHADE, H. and E. SCHLEE, 2002. "Another Look at the Radner-Stiglitz Nonconcavity in the Value of Information," *Journal of Economic Theory*, (107)2, pp. 421–52.

CHAMBERLIN, E. H., 1933. *The Theory of Monopolistic Competition*, Cambridge, MA: Harvard University Press.

CHAMLEY, C., 2004. *Rational Herds: Economic Models of Social Learning*, Cambridge: Cambridge University Press.

CHEUNG, S., 1968. "Private Property Rights and Share-Cropping," *Journal of Political Economy*, 76(6), pp. 1107–22.

——1969a. *The Theory of Share Tenancy*, Chicago, IL: University of Chicago Press.

——1969b. "Transactions Costs, Risk Aversion and the Choice of Contractual Arrangements," *Journal of Law and Economics*, 12(1), pp. 23–42.

CHEVALIER, J. and D. SCHARFSTEIN, 1995. "Liquidity Constraints and the Cyclical Behavior of Markups," *American Economic Review*, 85(2), pp. 390–6.

——1996. "Capital-Market Imperfections and Countercyclical Markups: Theory and Evidence," *American Economic Review*, 86(4), pp. 703–25.

CHO, I.-K. and D. KREPS, 1987. "Signaling Games and Stable Equilibria," *Quarterly Journal of Economics*, 102(2), pp. 179–222.

CHRISTENSEN, M., and T. KNUDSEN, 2002. "The Architecture of Economic Organization: Toward a General Framework," Working Paper, University of Southern Denmark.

CHUMA, H., Y. HAYAMI, and K. OTSUKA, 1992. "Land and Labor Contracts in Agrarian Economies: Theories and Facts," *Journal of Economic Literature*, 30(4), pp. 1965–2018.

CLARK, G., 1986. "Productivity Growth without Technical Change in European Agriculture before 1850," *The Journal of Economic History*, 47(2), pp. 419–32.

CLARK, K. and L. SUMMERS, 1979. "Labor Market Dynamics and Unemployment A Reconsideration," *Brookings Paperps on Economic Activity*, 1, pp. 13–60.

CLEMENS, M., S. RADELET, and R. BHAVNANI, 2004. "Counting Chickens When they Hatch: the Short Term Effect of Aid on Growth," Center for Global Development Working Paper, No. 44.

CLEMENZ, G., 1984. "Credit Rationing in the Absence of Direct Observability of Efforts and Abilities of Borrowers," Institut für Wirtschaftswissenschaften der Universitat Wien, Working Paper No. 8405.

——1985. "Credit Markets with Asymmetric Information and the Role of Collateral," mimeo, University of Wien.

COASE, R., 1937. "The Nature of the Firm," *Economica*, 4(16), pp. 386–405.

——1988 [1960]. "The Problem of Social Cost," *The Firm, the Market, and the Law*, Chicago: University of Chicago Press, pp. 95–156. (Article previously published in *Journal of Law and Economics*, 1960, 3, pp. 1–44.)

COLLIER, P., 1986. "Economic Causes of Civil Conflict and Their Implications for Policy', in C. A. Crocker, F. O. Hampson and P. Aall (eds.), *Managing Global Chaos*, Washington, DC: US Institute of Peace.

——1998. "The Political Economy of Ethnicity," Working Papers Series 98-8, Centre for the Study of African Economies, University of Oxford.

——J. W. GUNNING, 1999. "Why has Africa Grown Slowly?" *Journal of Economic Perspectives*, 13(3), pp. 3–22.

COMPTE, O., 1991. "Self-Enforcing Mechanisms in Adverse Selection Models," manuscript, Stanford, University.

COOLEY, T. and E. PRESCOTT, 1973. "Varying Parameter Regression: A Theory and Some Applications," *The Annals of Economic and Social Measurement*, 2(4), pp. 463–73.

COTHREN, R., 1982. "On the Impossibility of Informationally Efficient Markets: Comment," *American Economic Review*, 72(4), pp. 873–4.

CUTLER, D., 1996. "Public Policy for Health Care," NBER Working Paper 5591.

DARWIN, C., 1859. "On the Origin of the Species by Means of Natural Selection, or the Preservation of Favoured Races in the Struggle for Life."

DASGUPTA, P. and E. MASKIN, 1986a. "The Existence of Equilibrium in Discontinuous Economic Games I: Theory," *Review of Economic Studies*, 53(1), pp. 1–26.

—— ——1986b. "The Existence of Equilibrium in Discontinuous Economic Games, II: Applications," *The Review of Economic Studies*, 53(2), pp. 27–42.

——D. RAY, 1986a. "Inequality as a Determinant of Malnutrition and Unemployment Theory," *Economic Journal*, 96(384), pp. 1011–34.

—— ——1986b. "Adapting to Undernourishment: The Clinical Evidence and Its Implications," WIDER Working Paper, Helsinki.

—— ——1987. "Inequality as a Determinant of Malnutrition and Unemployment Policy," *The Economic Journal*, 97(385), pp. 177–88.

——J. E. STIGLITZ, 1977. "Tariffs Versus Quotas As Revenue Raising Devices Under Uncertainty," *American Economic Review*, 67(5) (December), pp. 975–81.

—— ——1980a. "Industrial Structure and the Nature of Innovative Activity," *Economic Journal*, 90(358) (June), pp. 266–93 (reprinted in *The Economics of Technical Change*, Elgar Reference Collection, International Library of Critical Writings in Economics, Vol. 31, Edwin Mansfield and Elizabeth Mansfield (eds.), Aldershot, UK: Elgar, pp. 133–60).

—— ——1980b. "Uncertainty, Market Structure and the Speed of R&D," *Bell Journal of Economics*, 11(1), pp. 1–28.

—— ——1981. "Entry, Innovation, Exit: Toward a Dynamic Theory of Oligopolistic Industrial Structure," *European Economic Review*, 15(2), pp. 137–58.

—— ——1988a. "Learning by Doing, Market Structure, and Industrial and Trade Policies," *Oxford Economic Papers*, 40(2), pp. 246–68.

—— ——1988b. "Potential Competition, Actual Competition and Economic Welfare," *European Economic Review*, 32 (May), pp. 569–77.

——R. GILBERT, and J. E. STIGLITZ, 1982. "Invention and Innovation Under Alternative Market Structures: The Case of Natural Resources,' *Review of Economic Studies*, 49(4), pp. 567–82.

DAWES, R. M. and R. H. THALER, 1988. "Anomalies: Cooperation," *Journal of Economic Perspectives*, 2(3), pp. 187–97.

DE BONDT, W. F. M. and R. H. THALER, 1989. "Anomalies: A Mean-Reverting Walk Down Wall Street," *Journal of Economic Perspectives*, 3(1), pp. 189–202.

DEBREU, G., 1954. "Valuation Equilibrium and Pareto Optimum," *Proceedings of the National Academy of Sciences*, 40(7), pp. 588–92

——1959. *The Theory of Value*, New Haven: Yale University Press.

DEVINNEY, T. M., 1983. "Incentives and Multi-Period Rationing in Loan Contracts," in H. Göppl and R. Henn (eds.), *Geld, Banken und Versicherungen II*, Karlsruhe, pp. 629–46.

DEWATRIPONT, M. and P. BOLTON, 2005, *Contract Theory*, Cambridge: MIT Press.

DIAMOND, P. A., 1967. "The Role of a Stock Market in a General Equilibrium Model with Technological Uncertainty," *American Economic Review*, 57(4), pp. 759–76.

——1971. "A Model of Price Adjustment," *Journal of Economic Theory*, 3(2), pp. 156–68.

——1981. "Mobility Costs, Frictional Unemployment, and Efficiency," *Journal of Political Economy*, 89(4), pp. 798–812.

——J. A. MIRRLEES, 1971. "Optimal Taxation and Public Production: I," *American Economic Review*, 62(1/2), pp. 238.

——M. ROTHSCHILD (eds.), 1978. *Uncertainty in Economics: Readings and Exercises*, New York: Academic Press.

——J. E. STIGLITZ, 1974. "Increases in Risk and in Risk Aversion," *Journal of Economic Theory*, 8(3), pp. 337–60.

DIXIT, A., and J. E. STIGLITZ, 1977. "Monopolistic Competition and Optimal Product Diversity," *American Economic Review*, 67(3), pp. 297–308.

DRANDAKIS, E. M. and E. S. PHELPS., 1966. "A Model of Induced Invention, Growth and Distribution," *The Economic Journal*, 76(304), pp. 823–40.

DREZE, J. H., 1974. "Investment Under Private Ownership: Optimality, Equilibrium and Stability," in J. H. Dreze (ed.), *Allocation Under Uncertainty: Equilibrium and Optimality*, New York: Macmillan.

DYBVIG, P. H and G. JAYNES, 1980. "Output–Supply, Employment and Intra-Industry Wage Dispersion," Cowles Foundation Discussion Paper No. 546.

——C. S. SPATT, 1983. "Does It Pay to Maintain a Reputation? Consumer Information and Product Quality," mimeo, Yale University.

DYCK, A., 2001. "Privatization and Corporate Governance: Principles, Evidence, and Future Challenges," *World Bank Research Observer*, 16(1), pp. 59–84.

EASTERLY, W., R. LEVINE, and D. ROODMAN, 2004. "New Data, New Doubts: A Comment on Burnside and Dollar's 'Aid, policies, and growth,'" *American Economic Review*, 94(3), pp. 774–80.

EATON, B. C. and W. D. WHITE, 1982. "Agent Compensation and the Limits of Bonding," *Economic Inquiry*, 20(3), pp. 330–43.

EATON, J., 1986. "Lending with Costly Enforcement of Repayment and Potential Fraud," *Journal of Banking and Finance*, 10(2), pp. 281–93.

——M. GERSOVITZ, 1980. "LDC Participation in International Financial Markets Debt and Reserves," *Journal of Development Economics*, 7(1), pp. 3–21.

——1981a. "Debt with Potential Repudiation Theoretical and Empirical Analysis," *Review of Economic Studies*, 48(2), pp. 289–309.

——1981b. "Poor Country Borrowing and the Repudiation Issue," Princeton Studies in International Finance No. 47, Princeton.

——J. E. STIGLITZ, 1986. "The Pure Theory of Country Risk," *European Economic Review*, 30(3), pp. 481–513.

EDLIN, A. and J. E. STIGLITZ, 1995. "Discouraging Rivals: Managerial Rent-Seeking and Economic Inefficiencies," *American Economic Review*, 85(5), pp. 1301–12.

EMRAN, M. S. and J. E. STIGLITZ, 2006. "Financial Liberalization, Financial Restraint and Entrepreneurial Development," working paper (available at: wwwo.gsb.columbia.edu/ipd/pub/emran_financial_Restraint.pdf).

ENGERS, M. and FEMANDEZ, L., 1987. "Market Equilibrium with Hidden Knowledge and Self-Selection," *Econometrica*, 55(2), pp. 425–39.

European Corporate Governance Network, 1997. "The Separation of Ownership and Control: A Survey of 7 European Countries," Preliminary Report, Vol. 1, European Corporate Governance Network, Brussels.

FAMA, E., 1970. "Efficient Capital Markets: A Review of Theory and Empirical Work," *Journal of Finance*, 25(2), pp. 383–417.

——1991. "Efficient Capital Markets: II," *Journal of Finance*, 46(5), pp. 1575–617.

FAMA, E. and M. JENSEN, 1983. "Separation of Ownership and Control," *Journal of Law and Economics*, 26(2), pp. 301–25.

FARRELL, J., 1979. "Prices as Signals of Quality," MPhil dissertation, Oxford University.

—— 1980. "Repeat Sales, Quality and Prices," mimeo, MIT.

—— 1984. "Moral Hazard in Quality, Entry Barriers, and Introductory Offers," MIT Working Paper.

—— 1986. "Moral Hazard as an Entry Barrier," *Rand Journal of Economics*, 17(3), pp. 440–9.

—— 1987. "Information and the Coase Theorem," *Journal of Economic Perspectives*, 1(2), pp. 113–29.

FARRELL, M. J., 1970. "Some Elementary Selection Processes in Economies," *Review of Economic Studies*, 37(3), pp. 305–19.

FAZZARI, S., R. G. HUBBARD, and B. PETERSEN, 1988a. "Financing Constraints and Corporate Investment," *Brookings Papers on Economic Activity*, 1988(1), pp. 141–206.

—————— 1988b. "Investment, Financing Decisions, and Tax Policy," *American Economic Review*, 78(2), pp. 200–5.

FIELDS, G., 1972. "Private and Social Returns to Education to Labor Surplus Economies," *Eastern Africa Economic Review*, 4(1), pp. 41–62.

—— 1973. "Toward a Model of Education and Employment in Labor Surplus Economies," in K. Wohlmuth (ed.), *Employment Creation in Developing Countries*, Praeger.

—— 1975. "Rural–Urban Migration, Urban Unemployment and Underemployment, and Job-Search Activity in LDCs," *Journal of Development Economics*, 2(2), pp. 165–87.

FISHER, I., 1932. *Booms and Depressions: Some First Principles*, London: Allen and Unwin.

—— 1933. "The Debt Deflation Theory of Great Depressions," *Econometrica*, 1(4), pp. 337–57.

FITZROY, F, 1981. "Contests," mimeo, International Institute of Management, West Berlin.

FREIMER, M. and M. J. GORDON, 1965. "Why Bankers Ration Credit," *Quarterly Journal of Economics*, 79(3), pp. 397–416.

FRIEDMAN, B. M, 1983. "The Roles of Money and Credit in Macroeconomic Analysis," in J. Tobin (ed.), *Macroeconomics, Prices, and Quantities Essays in Memory of Arthur M. Okun*, Washington, DC:Brookings Institution, pp. 161–89.

FROOT, K. A. and R. H. THALER, 1990. "Anomalies: Foreign Exchange," *Journal of Economic Perspectives*, 4(3), pp. 179–92.

FUDENBERG, D. and D. LEVINE, 1998a. "Learning in Games," European Economic Review, 42(3–5), pp. 631–9.

—— —— 1998b. *The Theory of Learning in Games*, MIT Press Series on Economic Learning and Social Evolution, Vol. 2, Cambridge, MA: MIT Press.

—— J. TIROLE, 1991. *Game Theory*, Cambridge, MA: MIT Press.

—— —— 1983. "Sequential Bargaining with Incomplete Information," *Review of Economic Studies*, 50(2), pp. 221–48.

—— —— R. GILBERT, J. E. STIGLITZ, and J. TIROLE, 1983. "Preemption, Leapfrogging, and Competition in Patent Races," *European Economic Review*, 22(1) (June), pp. 3–31.

FUGLESANG, A. and D. CHANDLER, 1988. *Participation as a Process—What We Can Learn from Grameen Bank, Bangladesh*. Dhaka: Pearl Printing and Packaging.

FURMAN, J. and J. E. STIGLITZ, 1999. "Economic Crises: Evidence and Insights from East Asia," *Brookings Papers on Economic Activity*, 1999(2), pp. 1–135.

GABOR, A. and C. W. J. GRANGER, 1966. "Price as an Indicator of Quality Report of an Inquiry," *Economica*, NS(33), pp. 43–70.

GALBRAITH, J. K. 1967. *The New Industrial State*, Boston: Houghton Mifflin.

GALE, D., 1991. "Optimal Risk Sharing through Renegotiation of Simple Contracts," *Journal of Financial Intermediation*, 1(4), pp. 283–306

GALE, I. and J. E. STIGLITZ, 1986. "Multiple Stock Offerings and the Financing of New Firms," Financial Research Center, Research Memo #73, Princeton University.

———— 1989. "The Informational Content of Initial Public Offerings," *Journal of Finance*, 44(2), pp. 469–77.

GERTLER, M. and S. GILCHRIST, 1994. "Monetary Policy, Business Cycles, and the Behavior of Small Manufacturing Firms," *Quarterly Journal of Economics*, 109(2), pp. 309–40.

—— R. G. HUBBARD, 1988. "Financial Factors in Business Fluctuations," *Financial Market Volatility*, Kansas City: Federal Reserve Bank of Kansas City, pp. 33–71.

GIBBONS, R., 1998. "Incentives in Organizations," *Journal of Economic Perspectives*, 12(4), pp. 115–32.

GILBERT, R. J. and D. M. G. NEWBERY, 1982. "Preemptive Patenting and the Persistence of Monopoly," *The American Economic Review*, 72(3), pp. 514–26.

GILCHRIST, S., and E. ZAKRAJSEK, 1995. "The Importance of Credit for Macroeconomic Activity: Identification Through Heterogeneity," *Is Bank Lending Important for the Transmission of Monetary Policy?* Boston, MA: Federal Reserve Bank of Boston, pp. 129–58.

GINTIS, H. and T. ISHIKAWA, 1987. "Wages, Work Discipline, and Unemployment," *Journal of Japanese and International Economies*, 1(2), pp. 195–228.

———— 1985. "The Theory of Production and Price in Contingent Renewal Markets," mimeo, University of Massachusetts.

GOLDING, E., 1982. "Disclosure of Product Characteristics under Imperfect Information," doctoral dissertation, Princeton University.

GOULD, J. P., 1986. "Is the Rational Expectations Hypothesis Enough?" *The Journal of Business*, 59(4), pp. S371–S377.

GOULD, S. J., 1989. *Wonderful Life: The Burgess Shale and the Nature of History*, New York: W.W. Norton.

GRANDMONT, J. M., 1985. "On Endogenous Competitive Business Cycles," *Econometrica*, 53(5), pp. 995–1046.

GREEN, J. R., 1973. "Information, Efficiency and Equilibrium," Harvard Institute of Economic Research, Discussion Paper No. 284.

—— 1977. "The Non-Existence of Informational Equilibria," *Review of Economic Studies*, 44(3), pp. 451–63.

—— N. STOKEY, 1983. "A Comparison of Tournaments and Contracts," *Journal of Political Economy*, 91(3), pp. 349–64.

GREENWALD, B., 1979. *Adverse Selection in the Labor Market*, New York: Garland Press.

—— 1986. "Adverse Selection in the Labor Market," *Review of Economic Studies* 53(3), pp. 325–47.

—— M. KOHN, and J. E. STIGLITZ, 1990. "Financial Market Imperfections and Productivity Growth," *Journal of Economic Behavior and Organization*, 13(3), pp. 321–45.

—— M. SALINGER, and J. E. STIGLITZ, 1990. "Imperfect Capital Markets and Productivity Growth," Paper presented at NBER Conference in Vail, Colorado (April; revised March 1991 and April 1992).

—— J. E. STIGLITZ, 1985. "Externalities in Economies with Self-Selection Constraints," Unpublished paper, Princeton University.

———— 1986a. "Externalities in Economies with Imperfect Information and Incomplete Markets," *Quarterly Journal of Economics*, 101(2) (May), pp. 229–64 (reprinted in *Economic Theory and the Welfare State*, N. Barr (ed.), Cheltenham, UK: Edward Elgar, 2000).

———— 1986b. "The Inefficiency of Competitive Equilibria with Rationing," mimeo.

———— 1986c. "Information, Finance Constraints and Business Fluctuations," *Proceedings of the Taiwan Conference on Monetary Theory*, Taipei, Taiwan: Chung-Hua Institute.

GREENWALD, B. and J. E. STIGLITZ, 1987a. "Imperfect Information, Credit Markets and Unemployment," *European Economic Review*, 31(1–2), pp. 444–56.

———— 1987b. "Keynesian, New Keynesian and New Classical Economics," *Oxford Economic Papers*, 39(1), pp. 119–33.

———— 1988a. "Examining Alternative Macroeconomic Theories," *Brookings Papers on Economics Activity*, 1988(1), pp. 207–70.

———— 1988b. "Financial Market Imperfections and Business Cycles," NBER Working Paper No. 2494.

———— 1988c. "Imperfect Information, Finance Constraints and Business Fluctuations," in M. Kohn and S. C. Tsiang (eds.), *Finance Constraints, Expectations, and Macroeconomics*, Oxford: Oxford University Press, pp. 103–40.

———— 1988d. "Money, Imperfect Information and Economic Fluctuations," in M. Kohn and S. C. Tsiang(eds.), *Finance Constraints, Expectations and Macroeconomics*, Oxford: Oxford University Press, pp. 141–65.

———— 1988e. "Pareto Inefficiency of Market Economies: Search and Efficiency Wage Models," *American Economic Review*, 78(2), pp. 351–55.

———— 1989a. "Impact of the Changing Tax Environment on Investments and Productivity," *Journal of Accounting, Auditing and Finance*, 4(3), pp. 281–301.

———— 1989b. "Toward a Theory of Rigidities," *American Economic Review*, 79(2), pp. 364–9.

———— 1990a. "Asymmetric Information and the New Theory of the Firm: Financial Constraints and Risk Behavior," *American Economic Review*, 80(2), pp. 160–5.

———— 1990b. "Macroeconomic Models with Equity and Credit Rationing," in R. Glenn Hubbard (ed.), *Information, Capital Markets and Investments*, Chicago, IL: University of Chicago Press, pp. 15–42.

———— 1991. "Toward a Reformulation of Monetary Theory: Competitive Banking," *Economic and Social Review*, 23(1), pp. 1–34.

———— 1992. "Information, Finance and Markets: The Architecture of Allocative Mechanisms," *Industrial and Corporate Change*, 1(1), pp. 37–63.

———— 1993a. "Financial Market Imperfections and Business Cycles," *Quarterly Journal of Economics*, 108(1), pp. 77–114.

———— 1993b. "New and Old Keynesians," *Journal of Economic Perspectives*, 7(1), pp. 23–44.

———— 1995. "Labor Market Adjustments and the Persistence of Unemployment," *American Economic Review*, 85(2), pp. 219–25.

———— 2003. *Towards a New Paradigm for Monetary Policy*, London: Cambridge University Press.

———— 2006. "Helping Infant Economies Grow: Foundations of Trade Policies for Developing Countries," *American Economic Review*, 96(2), pp. 141–6.

———— A. M. WEISS, 1984. "Informational Imperfections in the Capital Market and Macroeconomic Fluctuations," *American Economic Review*, 74(2), pp. 194–9.

GROSSMAN, S. J., 1975. "Essays on Rational Expectations," Unpublished doctoral dissertation, University of Chicago.

—— 1976. "On the Efficiency of Competitive Stock Markets Where Trades have Diverse Information," *Journal of Finance*, 31(2), pp. 573–85.

—— 1977a. "A Characterization of the Optimality of Equilibrium in Incomplete Markets," *Journal of Economic Theory*, 15(1), pp. 1–15.

—— 1977b. "The Existence of Futures Markets, Noisy Rational Expectations and Informational Externalities," *The Review of Economic Studies*, 44(3), pp. 431–49.

—— 1978. "Further Results on the Informational Efficiency of Competitive Stock Markets," *Journal of Economic Theory*, 18(1), pp. 81–101.

——1981. "The Informational Role of Warranties and Private Disclosure about Product Quality," *Journal of Law and Economics*, 24(3), pp. 461–83.

——1985. "Money and Macroeconomic Fluctuations," Unpublished paper, Princeton University.

——O. HART, 1980. "Takeover Bids, the Free-rider Problem and the Theory of the Corporation," *Bell Journal of Economics*, 11(1), pp. 42–64.

——————1981a. "The Allocational Role of Takeover Bids in Situations of Asymmetric Information," *Journal of Finance*, 36(2), pp. 253–70.

——————1981b. "Implicit Contracts, Moral Hazard, and Unemployment," *American Economic Review*, 72(2), pp. 301–7.

——————1982. "Corporate Financial Structure and Managerial Incentives," in J. McCall (ed.), *Economics of Information and Uncertainty*, Chicago: University of Chicago Press, pp. 107–40.

——————1983. "Implicit Contracts under Asymmetric Information," *Quarterly Journal of Economics*, 98(Supplement), pp. 123–56.

——————1996. "Takeover Bids, the Free-rider Problem and the Theory of the Corporation," in M. Brennan (ed.), *The Theory of Corporate Finance Vol. 2*, Cheltenham, UK: Elgar, pp. 423–45.

——R. KIHLSTRON and L. MIRMAN, 1977. "A Bayesian Approach to the Production of Information and Learning by Doing," *Review of Economic Studies*, 44(3), pp. 533–47.

——J. E. STIGLITZ, 1976. "Information and Competitive Price Systems," *American Economic Review*, 66(2), pp. 246–53.

——————1977. "On Value Maximization and Alternative Objectives of the Firm," *Journal of Finance*, 32(2), pp. 389–402.

——————1980a. "On the Impossibility of Informationally Efficient Markets," *American Economic Review*, 70(3), pp. 393–408 (subsequently reprinted in S. Bhattacharya and G. Constantinides (eds.), *Financial Markets and Incomplete Information—Frontiers of Modern Financial Theory*, 2, Rowman and Littlefield, 1989, pp. 123–36.

——————1980b. "Stockholder Unanimity in the Making of Production and Financial Decisions," *Quarterly Journal of Economics*, 94(3), pp. 543–66.

GROVES, T. and J. LEDYARD, 1977. "Optimal Allocation of Public Goods: A Solution to the 'Free Rider' Problem," *Econometrica*, 45(4), pp. 783–809.

GUASCH, J. L. and A. WEISS, 1980a. "Adverse Selection by Markets and the Advantage of Being Late," *Quarterly Journal of Economics*, 94(3), pp. 453–66.

——————1980b. "Wages as Sorting Mechanisms in Markets with Asymmetric Information: A Theory of Testing," *Review of Economic Studies*, 47(4), pp. 653–64.

——————1981. "Self-Selection in the Labor Market," *American Economic Review*, 71(3), pp. 275–84.

——————1982. "An Equilibrium Analysis of Wage-Productivity Gaps," *Review of Economic Studies*, 49(4), pp. 485–97.

HAHN, F., 1966. "Equilibrium Dynamics with Heterogeneous Capital Goods," *Quarterly Journal of Economics*, 80(4), pp. 633–46.

——1973. "Notes on Rothschild-Stiglitz: Insurance Markets with Imperfect Information," mimeo, Cambridge University.

HALL, B. H., 1992. "Investment and Research and Development at the Firm Level: Does the Source of Financing Matter?" National Bureau of Economic Research Working Paper No. 4096.

HALL, B. J. and J. B. LIEBMAN, 1998. "Are CEO's Really Paid like Bureaucrats?" *Quarterly Journal of Economics*, 113(3), pp. 653–91.

HALL, R. E., 1975. "The Rigidity of Wages and the Persistence of Unemployment," *Brookings Papers on Economic Activity*, 2, pp. 301–49.

HALL, R. E., 1978. "Stochastic Implications of the Life Cycle-Permanent Income Hypothesis: Theory and Evidence," *Journal of Political Economy*, 86(6) (December), pp. 971–87.

——1980. "Employment Fluctuations and Wage Rigidity," *Brookings Papers on Economic Activity*, 1, pp. 91–123.

——1988. "The Relation Between Price and Marginal Cost in U.S. Industry," *Journal of Political Economy*, 96(5), pp. 921–47.

——D. W. JORGENSON, 1967. "Tax Policy and Investment Behavior," *American Economic Review*, 57(3), pp. 391–414.

HAMERMESH, D. S., 1975. "Interdependence in the Labour Market," *Economica*, 42(168), pp. 420–9.

HANNAWAY, J., 1992. "Higher Order Skills, Job Design, and Incentives: An Analysis and Proposal," *American Educational Research Journal*, 29(1), pp. 3–21.

HARBERGER, A. C., 1971a. "On Measuring the Social Opportunity Cost of Labor," *International Labor Review*, 103(6), pp. 559–79.

——1971b. "Three Postulates for Applied Welfare Economics: An Interpretative Essay," *Journal of Economic Literature*, 9(3), pp. 785–97.

HARRIS, J. and M. TODARO, 1970. "Migration, Unemployment and Development: A Two-Sector Analysis," *American Economic Review*, 60(1), pp. 126–42.

HART, O., 1975. "On the Optimality of Equilibrium When the Market Structure Is Incomplete," *Journal of Economic Theory*, 11(3), pp. 418–43.

——1983. "Optimal Labour Contracts under Asymmetric Information: An Introduction," *Review of Economic Studies*, 50(1), pp. 3–35.

——1990. "Comment on Costly State Verification Models," presented at Nobel Symposium, Saltsjöbaden/Stockholm.

——1995. *Firms, Contracts, and Financial Structure*, Oxford: Oxford University Press.

——B. HOLMSTROM, 1987. "The Theory of Contracts," in T. BEWLEY (ed.), *Advances of Economic Theory*, Cambridge. Cambridge University Press.

HAUBRICH, J., 1994. "Risk Aversion, Performance Pay and the Principal-Agent Problem," *Journal of Political Economy*, 102(2), pp. 258–76.

HAYEK, F. A., 1945. "The Use of Knowledge in Society," *American Economic Review*, 35(4), pp. 519–30.

HEAL, G. M., 1973. *The Theory of Economic Planning*, New York: North Holland.

——1976. "Do Bad Products Drive Out Good?" *Quarterly Journal of Economics*, 90(32), pp. 499–502.

HEAL, G., 1977. "Guarantees and Risk-Sharing," *The Review of Economic Studies* (44)3, pp. 549–60.

HELLMAN, T. F., 1998. "The Allocation of Control Rights in Venture Capital Contracts," *The Rand Journal of Economics*, 29(1), pp. 57–76.

——K. MURDOCK and J. E. STIGLITZ, 1996. "Deposit Mobilization Through Financial Restraint," in N. Hermes and R. Lensink (eds.), *Financial Development and Economic Growth*, Routledge, pp. 219–46.

——————2000. "Liberalization, Moral Hazard in Banking and Prudential Regulation: Are Capital Requirements Enough?" *American Economic Review*, 90(1), pp. 147–65.

——J. E. STIGLITZ, 2000. "Credit and Equity Rationing in Markets with Adverse Selection," *European Economic Review*, 44(2), pp. 281–304.

HELLWIG, M. F., 1977. "A Model of Borrowing and Lending with Bankruptcy," *Econometrica*, 45(8), pp. 1879–906.

——1983. "On Moral Hazard and Non-price Equilibrium in Competitive Insurance Markets," University of Bonn, Discussion Paper #109.

HELPMAN, E. and J. LAFFONT, 1975. "On Moral Hazard in General Equilibrium Theory," *Journal of Economic Theory*, 10(1), pp. 8–23.

HICKS, J. R., 1936. "Keynes' Theory of Employment", *Economic Journal*, 46(182), pp. 238–53.

——1975. *Value and Capital: An Inquiry Into Some Fundamental Principles of Economic Theory*, New York: Oxford University Press.

——1988. "Towards a More General Theory," in M. Kohn and S.-C. Tsiang (eds.), *Finance Constraints, Expectations, and Macroeconomics*, Oxford: Clarendon Press.

——1989. *A Market Theory of Money*, New York: Oxford University Press.

HILLAS, J. B., 1987. "Contributions to the Theory of Market Screening," PhD dissertation, Stanford University.

HINES, J. R. and R. H. THALER, 1995. "Anomalies: The Flypaper Effect," *Journal of Economic Perspectives*, 9(4), pp. 217–26.

HIRSHLEIFER, J., 1971. "The Private and Social Value of Information and the Reward to Inventive Activity," *American Economic Review*, 61(4), pp. 561–74.

——1995. "Mergers and Acquisitions: Strategic and Informational Issues," in R. A. Jarrow, V. Makismovic, and W. T. Ziemba (eds.), *Handbooks in Operations Research and Management Science*, Vol. 9, North-Holland.

——J. G. RILEY, 1992. *The Analytics of Uncertainty and Information*, Cambridge: Cambridge University Press.

HODGSON, G., 1982. "Theoretical and Political Implications of Variable Productivity," *Cambridge Journal of Economics*, 6(3), pp. 213–26.

HOEL, M. and B. VALE, 1986. "Effects of Reduced Working Time in an Economy Where Firms Set Wages," *European Economic Review*, 30(5), pp. 1097–104.

HOEL, P. G., 1962. *Introduction to Mathematical Statistics*, New York.

HOFF, K., 1994. "The Second Theorem of the Second Best," *Journal of Public Economics*, 54(2), pp. 223–42.

——A. BRAVERMAN and J. E. STIGLITZ (eds.), 1993. *The Economics of Rural Organization: Theory, Practice, and Policy*, New York: Oxford University Press.

——J. E. STIGLITZ, 1990. "Imperfect Information and Rural Credit Markets: Puzzles and Policy Perspectives," *World Bank Economic Review*, 4(3) (September), pp. 235–50.

——— 1997. "Moneylenders and Bankers: Price-increasing Subsidies in a Monopolistically Competitive Market," *Journal of Development Economics*, 52(2), pp. 429–62.

——— 2000. "Modern Economic Theory and Development," in G. Meier and J. E. Stiglitz (eds.), *Frontiers of Development Economics: The Future in Perspective*, Oxford University Press, pp. 389–485.

———, 2004a. "After the Big Bang? Obstacles to the Emergence of the Rule of Law in Post-Communist Societies," *American Economic Review*, 94(3), June 2004, pp. 753–63.

———, 2004b. "The Transition Process in Post-Communist Societies: Towards a Political Economy of Property Rights," in *Toward Pro-Poor Policies: Aid, Institutions and Globalization*, B. Tungodden, N. Stern, and I. Kolstad (eds.), World Bank/Oxford University Press, 2004, pp. 231–45. Published in Chinese: *Nanjing Business Review* 4 (2005), pp. 22–37 and in French: *Revue d'économie du développement*, 2003/2–3 (Vol. 17).

——— 2005. "The Creation of the Rule of Law and the Legitimacy of Property Rights: The Political and Economic Conseqences of a Corrupt Privatization," NBER Working Paper No. 11772. Published in *Economic Journal*, 118(531), pp. 1474–97.

HOLLAND, J. H., 1975. *Adaptation in Natural and Artificial Systems*, Cambridge: MIT Press.

HOLMSTROM, B., 1979. "Moral Hazard and Observability," *Bell Journal of Economics*, 10(1), pp. 74–91.

HOLMSTROM, B., 1983. "Equilibrium Long-Term Labor Contracts," *Quarterly Journal of Economics*, 98(5), pp. 23–54.

HONAHAN P. and J. E. STIGLITZ, 2001. "Robust Financial Restraint" in G. Caprio, P. Honohan, and J. E. Stiglitz (eds.), *Financial Liberalization: How Far, How Fast?*, Cambridge: Cambridge University Press.

HUBBARD, R. G. (ed.), 1990. *Asymmetric Information, Corporate Finance, and Investment*, Chicago, IL: University of Chicago Press.

——1998. "Capital-Market Imperfections and Investment," *Journal of Economic Literature*, 36(1), pp. 193–225.

HUDSON, K. L. et al., 1995. "Genetic Discrimination and Health Insurance: An Urgent Need for Reform," *Science*, 270(5235), pp. 391–3.

HULL, R. and L. PETERS, 1970. *The Peter Principle*, London: Bantam Books.

HURWICZ, L. 1960. "Optimality and Informational Efficiency in Resource Allocation Processes," in K. J. Arrow, S. Karlin, and P. Suppes (eds.), *Mathematical Methods in the Social Sciences*, Stanford, CA: Stanford University Press.

——1972. "On Informationally Decentralized Systems," in M. McGuire and R. Radner (eds.), *Decision and Organization*, North Holland.

HUSSEIN, A., N. STEM, and J. E. STIGLITZ, 2000. "Chinese Reforms from a Comparative Perspective" in P. J. Hammond and G. D. Myles (eds.), *Incentives, Organization, and Public Economics: Papers in Honour of Sir James Mirrlees*, Oxford: Oxford University Press, pp. 243–77.

JACKMAN, R., R. LAYARD, and C. PISSARIDES, 1986. "Policies for Reducing the Natural Rate of Unemployment," in J. L. Butkiewicz, K. J. Koford and J. B. Miller (eds.), *Keynes Economic Legacy*, Praeger, pp. 111–52.

——J. SUTTON, 1982. "Imperfect Capital Markets and the Monetarist Black-Box Liquidity Constraints, Inflation, and the Asymmetric Effects of Interest Rate Policy," *Economic Journal*, 92(365), pp. 108–28.

JAFFEE, D., 1971. *Credit Rationing and the Commercial Loan Market*, New York: John Wiley & Sons.

——T. RUSSELL, 1976. "Imperfect Information, Uncertainty, and Credit Rationing," *Quarterly Journal of Economics*, 90(4), pp. 651–66.

——J. E. STIGLITZ, 1990. "Credit Rationing," in B. Friedman and F. Hahn (eds.), *Handbook of Monetary Economics*, Amsterdam: Elsevier Science Publishers, pp. 837–88.

JENSEN, M. C., 1991. "Eclipse of the Public Corporation," in D. A. Oesterle (ed.), *The Law of Mergers, Acquisitions, and Reorganizations*, St Paul, MN: West.

——2000. *A Theory of the Firm: Governance, Residual Claims, and Organizational Forms*, Cambridge, MA: Harvard University Press.

——J. LONG, 1972. "Corporate Investment under Uncertainty and Pareto Optimality in Capital Markets," *The Bell Journal of Economics*, 3(1), pp. 151–74.

——W. H. MECKLING, 1976. "Theory of the Firm: Managerial Behavior, Agency Costs and Ownership Structure," *Journal of Financial Economics*, 3(4), pp. 305–60 (also in J. M. Brennan (ed.), *The Theory of Corporate Finance*, Vol. 1, Cheltenham, UK: Elgar, pp. 35–90).

——K. J. MURPHY, 1990. "Performance Pay and Top-Management Incentives," *Journal of Political Economy*, 98(2), pp. 225–64.

——R. S. RUBAC, 1983. "The Market for Corporate Control: The Scientific Evidence," *Journal of Financial Economics*, 11(1–4), pp. 5–55.

JOHNSON, D. G., 1950. "Resource Allocation Under Share Contracts," *Journal of Political Economy*, 58(2), pp. 111–23.

Journal of Law and Economics, 1983. "Corporations and Private Property," *Journal of Law and Economics*, 26 (special issue with papers by Thomas G. Moore; George J. Stigler; and Clare Friedland; Douglas C. North; R. Hessen; Nathan Rosenberg; Gardiner C. Means; Eugene Fama and Michael C. Jensen; Oliver E. Williamson; Burt Klein; Harold Demsetz; Rita Ricardo-Campbell; Frank Easterbrook and D. Fischel; Leonard W. Weiss; J. S. McGee; and C. Baldwin).

KAGEL, J. H. and D. LEVIN, 1986. "The Winner's Curse and Public Information in Common Value Auctions," *American Economic Review*, 76(5), pp. 894–920.

KAHN, J. A., 1987. "Inventories and the Volatility of Production," *American Economic Review*, 77(4), pp. 667–79.

KAHNEMAN, D., 2002. "Maps of Bounded Rationality," Stockholm: Nobel Prize Lecture.

——— J. L. KNETSCH, and R. H. THALER, 1991. "Anomalies: The Endowment Effect, Loss Aversion, and Status Quo Bias," *Journal of Economic Perspectives*, 5(1), pp. 193–206.

KALECKI, M., 1939. *Essays on the Theory of Economic Fluctuations*, New York: Russell and Russell.

KASHYAP, A., O. LAMONT, J., and STEIN, 1994. "Credit Conditions and the Cyclical Behavior of Inventories," *Quarterly Journal of Economics*, 109(3), pp. 565–92.

——— J. STEIN, 2000. "What Do A Million Observations on Banks Say About the Transmission of Monetary Policy?" *American Economic Review*, 90(3), pp. 407–28.

KATZ, M. L., 1984. "Price Discrimination and Monopolistic Competition," *Econometrica*, 52(6), pp. 1453–71.

KEESING, R. M., 1981. *Cultural Anthropology: A Contemporary Perspective*, 2nd Ed., New York: Holt, Rinehart, and Winston.

KEETON, W., 1979. *Equilibrium Credit Rationing*, New York: Garland Press.

KENNEDY, C., 1964. "Induced Bias in Innovation and the Theory of Distribution," *Economic Journal*, 74(295), pp. 541–7.

KESTER, C., 1993. "Banks in the Boardroom: Germany, Japan, and the United States," in S. Hayes III (ed.), *Financial Services: Perspectives and Challenges*, Boston: Harvard Business School Press.

KEYNES, J. M., 1936. *The General Theory of Employment, Interest and Money*, New York: Harcourt Brace.

KIHLSTROM, R. and L. MIRMAN, 1975. "Information and Market Equilibrium," *Bell Journal of Economics*, 6(1), pp. 357–76.

KINDLEBERGER, C. P., 1978. *Manias, Panics, and Crashes: A History of Financial Crises*, New York: Basic Books.

KING, R., and R. LEVINE, 1993. "Finance and Growth: Schumpeter Might Be Right," *Quarterly Journal of Economics*, 108(3), pp. 717–37.

KITCHER, P., 1996, *The Lives to Come*, New York: Simon and Schuster.

KLAMER, A., 1989. "An Accountant Among Economists: Conversations with Sir John Hicks," *Journal of Economic Perspectives*, 3(4), pp. 167–80.

KLEIN, B. and K. B. LEFFLER, 1981. "The Role of Market Forces in Assuring Contractual Performance," *Journal of Political Economy*, 89(4), pp. 615–41.

KLEMPERER, P., 1999. "Auction Theory: A Guide to the Literature," *Journal of Economic Surveys*, 13(3), pp. 227–86.

KLEVORICK, A. K. and R. E. ALCALY, 1970. "Judging Quality by Price, Snob Appeal, and the New Consumer Theory," *Zeitschrift für Nationalökonomie*, 30(1–2), pp. 53–64.

KNIESNER, T. and A. H. GOLDSMITH, 1985. "Does the Labor Market Clear? A Survey of the Evidence for the US," in R. G. Ehrenberg (ed.), *Research in Labor Economics*, Vol. 7, Greenwich, Conn: JAI Press, pp. 209–56.

KNIGHT, F. H., 1921. *Risk, Uncertainty and Profit*, Chicago: University of Chicago Press.

KOHLBERG, E. and J. MERTENS, 1986. "On the Strategic Stability of Equilibria," *Econometrica*, 54(5), pp. 1003–37.

KOHN, A., 1993. *Punished by Rewards*, New York: Houghton Mifflin.

KORNAI, J., 1986. "The Soft Budget Constraint," *Kyklos*, 39(1), pp. 3–30.

KREPS, D., P. MILGROM, J. ROBERTS, and R. WILSON, 1982. "Rational Cooperation in the Finitely Repeated Prisoner's Dilemma," *Journal of Economic Theory*, 27(2), pp. 245–52.

—— R. WILSON, 1982a. "Reputation and Imperfect Information," *Journal of Economic Theory*, 27(2), pp. 253–79.

—— —— 1982b. "Sequential Equilibrium," *Econometrica*, 50(4), pp. 863–94.

KRUEGER, A. O., 1974. "The Political Economy of the Rent-seeking Society," *American Economic Review*, 64(3), pp. 291–303.

KRUGMAN, P., 1998. *The Role of Geography in Development*, Annual World Bank Conference on Development Economics, Washington, DC: World Bank.

KUGLER, P, 1985. "Credit Rationing Evidence from Disequilibrium Interest Rate Equations," University of Basel, Working Paper No. 32.

KUH, E. and J. MEYER, 1957. *The Investment Decision: An Empirical Study*, Cambridge, MA: Harvard University Press.

KUHN, T. S., 1970. *The Structure of Scientific Revolutions*, Chicago: University of Chicago Press.

LA PORTA, R., F. LOPEZ-DE-SILANES, A. SHLEIFER, and R. VISHNY, 1998. "Law and Finance," *Journal of Political Economy*, 106(6), pp. 1113–55.

LAFFONT, J. J. and J. TIROLE, 1993. *A Theory of Incentives in Procurement and Regulation*, Cambridge, MA: MIT Press.

LAMONT, O., 1997. "Cash Flow and Investment: Evidence from Internal Capital Markets," *Journal of Finance*, 52(1), pp. 83–109.

LANGE, O. and F. M. TAYLOR, 1964. *On the Economic Theory of Socialism*, New York: McGraw-Hill.

LANE, D., 1993a. "Artificial Worlds and Economics, Part I," *Journal of Evolutionary Economics*, 3(2), pp. 89–107.

—— 1993b. "Artificial Worlds and Economics, Part II," *Journal of Evolutionary Economics*, 3(3), pp. 177–97.

LARSON, J., 1984. "Why Long Term Incentives Fail," paper presented to a Conference on the Economics of Incentive, Cooperation, and Risk Sharing, New York University.

LAZEAR, E. P., 1982. "Agency, Earnings Profiles, Productivity and Hours Restrictions," *American Economic Review*, 71(4), pp. 606–20.

—— S. ROSEN, 1981. "Rank-Order Tournaments as Optimum Labor Contracts," *Journal of Political Economy*, 89(5), pp. 841–64.

LEE, C. M. C., A. SHLIEFER, and R. H. THALER, 1990. "Anomalies: Closed-End Mutual Funds," *Journal of Economic Perspectives*, 4(4), pp. 217–26.

LEIBENSTEIN, H., 1957a. *Economic Backwardness and Economic Growth*, New York: Wiley.

—— 1957b. "The Theory of Underemployment in Backward Economies," *Journal of Political Economy*, 65(2), pp. 91–103.

—— 1966. "Allocative Efficiency vs. X-Efficiency", *American Economic Review*, 56(3), pp. 392–415.

LEIJONHUFVUD, A., 1968. *On Keynesian Economics and the Economics of Keynes*, New York: Oxford University Press.

LEITZINGER, J. and J. E. STIGLITZ, 1984. "Information Externalities in Oil and Gas Leasing," *Contemporary Policy Issues*, 1(5) (March), pp. 44–57.

LELAND, H. and D. PYLE, 1977. "Informational Asymmetries, Financial Structure, and Financial Intermediation," *Journal of Finance*, 32(2), pp. 371–87.

LINDBECK, A., 1963. *A Study in Monetary Analysis*, Stockholm: Almquist and Wiksell.

—— D. SNOWER, 1984a. "Involuntary Unemployment as an Insider-Outsider Dilemma" Seminar Paper No. 282, Institute for International Economic Studies, University of Stockholm (revised as "Wage Rigidity, Union Activity and Unemployment," in W. Beckerman (ed.), *Wage Rigidity and Unemployment*, Duckworth and Johns Hopkins University Press, 1986, ch. 5.

—————— 1984b. "Labor Turnover, Insider Morale and Involuntary Unemployment," Seminar Paper No. 310, Institute for International Economic Studies, University of Stockholm.

—————— 1986. "Explanations of Unemployment," *Oxford Review of Economic Policy*, 1(2), pp. 34–59.

—————— 1987. "Efficiency Wages Versus Insiders and Outsiders," *Eurpoean Economic Review*, 31(1–2), pp. 407–16.

—————— 1989. *The Insider–Outsider Theory of Employment and Unemployment*, Cambridge, MA: MIT Press.

LINTNER, J., 1971. "Corporate Finance: Risk and Investment," in R. Ferber (ed.), *Determinants of Investment Behavior*, New York: NBER.

LIPSEY, R. G. and K. LANCASTER, 1957. "The General Theory of Second Best," *The Review of Economic Studies*, 24(1), pp. 11–32.

LOEWENSTEIN, G. and R. H. THALER, 1989. "Anomalies: Intertemporal Choice," *Journal of Economic Perspectives*, 3(4), pp. 181–93.

LOONG, L., and R. ZECKHAUSER, 1982. "Pecuniary Externalities Matter When Contingent Claims Markets are Incomplete," *Quarterly Journal of Economics*, 97(1), pp. 171–9.

LUCAS JR., R. 1972. "Expectations and the Neutrality of Money," *Journal of Economic Theory*, 4(2), pp. 103–24.

—— 1973. "Some International Evidence on Output–Inflation Tradeoffs," *American Economic Review*, 63(3), pp. 326–34.

—— 1975. "An Equilibrium Model of the Business Cycle," *The Journal of Political Economy*, 83(6), pp. 1113–44.

—— 1987. *Models of Business Cycles*, New York: Basil Blackwell.

—— E. PRESCOTT, 1971. "Investment Under Uncertainty," *Econometrica*, 39(5), pp. 659–81.

LURIE, T., 1988. "Increasing Income and Employment in Bangladesh," *Ford Foundation Letter* 19(4), pp. 1–5.

MACEY, J., 1998. "Institutional Investors and Corporate Monitoring: A Demand-Side Perspective in a Comparative View," in Hopt et al. (eds.), *Comparative Corporate Governance: The State of the Art and Emerging Research*, Oxford: Clarendon Press.

MACHLUP, F., 1962. *The Production and Distribution of Knowledge in the United States*, Princeton: Princeton University Press.

MAILATH, G., 1992. "Introduction: Symposium on Evolutionary Game Theory," *Journal of Economic Theory*, 57(2), pp. 259–77.

MALCOLMSON, J., 1981. "Unemployment and the Efficiency Wage Hypothesis," *Economic Journal*, 92(364), pp. 848–66.

MANKIW, N. G., 1985. "Small Menu Costs and Large Business Cycles: A Macroeconomic Model of Monopoly," *Quarterly Journal of Economics*, 100(2), pp. 529–37.

—— 1989. "Real Business Cycles: A New Keynesian Perspective," *Journal of Economic Perspectives*, 3(3), 79–90.

MANNE, H., 1965. "Mergers and the Market for Corporate Control," *Journal of Political Economy*, 73(2), pp. 110–20.

MANOVE, M., 1986. "Job Responsibility, Pay, and Promotion," *The Economic Journal*, 107(440) (January), pp. 85–103.

MARCH, J. G. and H. A. SIMON, 1958. *Organizations*, London: John Wiley & Sons.

MARRIS R., 1964. *The Economic Theory of "Managerial" Capitalism*, London: Macmillan.

MARSCHAK, J., 1960. "Theory of an Efficient Several-Person Firm," *American Economic Review*, 50(2), pp. 541–8.

——1971. "Economics of Information Systems," *Journal of the American Statistical Association*, 66(333), pp. 192–219.

——R. RADNER, 1972. *Economic Theory of Teams*, New Haven: Yale University Press.

MARSHALL, A., 1890. *Principles of Economics*, New York: Macmillan and Co.

——1897. "The Old Generation of Economists and the New," *Quarterly Journal of Economics*, 11(2), pp. 115–35.

MARSHALL, J. M., 1976. "Moral Hazard," *American Economic Review*, 66(5), pp. 880–90.

MAS-COLELL, A., M. WHINSTON, and J. GREEN, 1995. *Microeconomic Theory*, Oxford: Oxford University Press.

MAYER, C., 1990. "Financial Systems, Corporate Finance, and Economic Development," in R. G. Hubbard (ed.), *Asymmetric Information, Corporate Finance, and Investment*, Chicago: University of Chicago Press, pp. 307–32.

MAYNARD SMITH, J. and G. R. PRICE, 1973. "The Logic of Animal Conflict," *Nature*, 246, pp. 15–18.

MCGUIRE, C. B., 1972. "Comparisons of Information Structures," in C. B. McGuire and R. Radner (eds.), *Decision and Organization* Amsterdam: North-Holland.

MEADE, J. E., 1955. *Trade and Welfare*, London: Oxford University Press.

MEDOFF, J. L. and K. ABRAHAM, 1981. "Are Those Paid More Really More Productive?" *Journal of Human Resources*, 26(2), pp. 186–216.

MELNIK, A and S. PLAUT, 1986. "Loan Commitment Contracts, Terms of Lending, and Credit Allocation," *Journal of Finance*, 41(2), pp. 425–35.

MEYER, J. and E. KUH, 1957. *The Investment Decision: An Empirical Study*, Cambridge, MA: Harvard University Press.

MIGOT-ADHOLLA, S., P. HAZELL, B. BLAREL and F. PLACE, 1991. "Indigenous Land Rights Systems in Sub-Saharan Africa: A Constraint on Productivity?" *The World Bank Economic Review*, 1991(1), pp. 155–75.

MILDE, H. and J. RILEY, 1988. "Signaling in Credit Markets," *Quarterly Journal of Economics*, 103(1), pp. 101–29.

MILGROM, P. and J. ROBERTS, 1982a. "Limit Pricing and Entry Under Incomplete Information: An Economic Analysis," *Econometrica*, 50(2), pp. 443–59.

—— ——1982b. "Predation Reputation and Entry Deterrence." *Journal of Economic Theory*, 27(2), pp. 280–312.

—— ——1992. *Economics, Organization, and Management*, Englewood Cliffs, NJ: Prentice-Hall.

MILL, J. S., 1848. *Principles of Political Economy*, London: J. P. Parker.

MILLER, M. and J. E. STIGLITZ, 1999. "Bankruptcy Protection Against Macro-economic Shocks: the Case for a 'Super Chapter 11'" Conference on Capital Flows, Financial Crises, and Policies, World Bank.

MINCER, J., 1974. *Schooling, Experience and Earnings*, New York: Columbia University Press.

MINSKY, H., 1975. *John Maynard Keynes*, Cambridge: Cambridge University Press.

MIROWSKI, P. and K. SOMEFUN, 2000. "Fecund, Cheap and Out of Control: Heterogeneous Agents as Flawed Computers vs. Markets as Evolving Computational Entities," in D. Delli Gatti, M. Gallegati, and A. Kirman (eds.), *Interaction and Market Structure Essays on*

Heterogeneity in Economics, Lecture Notes in Economics and Mathematical Systems, Berlin: Springer.

MIRRLEES, J. A., 1971. "An Exploration in the Theory of Optimum Income Taxation," *Review of Economic Studies*, 38(2), pp. 175–208.

——1974. "Notes on Welfare Economics, Information, and Uncertainty," in M. S. Balch, D. L. Mcfadden, and S. Y. Wu (eds.), *Contributions to Economic Analysis*, Amsterdam North-Holland.

——1975a. "Optimal Commodity Taxation in a Two-Class Economy," *Journal of Public Economics*, 4(1), pp. 27–33

——1975b. "A Pure Theory of Underdeveloped Economies," in L. A. Reynolds (ed.), *Agriculture in Development Theory*, New Haven: Yale University Press, pp. 84–106.

——1975c. "The Theory of Moral Hazard and Unobservable Behaviour I," mimeo, Nuffield College.

——1976. "The Optimal Structure of Incentives and Authority within an Organization," *Bell Journal of Economics and Management Science*, 7(1), pp. 105–31.

——1990. "Taxing Uncertain Incomes," *Oxford Economic Papers*, 42(1), pp. 34–45.

MIYAZAKI, H., 1977. "The Rate Race and Internal Labor Markets," *Bell Journal of Economics*. 8(2), pp. 394–418.

——1984. "Work Norms and Involuntary Unemployment," *Quarterly Journal of Economics*, 99(2), pp. 297–311.

MODIGLIANI, F. and M. MILLER, 1958. "The Cost of Capital, Corporation Finance, and the Theory of Investment," *American Economic Review*, 48(3), pp. 261–97.

————1961. "Dividend Policy, Growth, And The Valuation Of Shares," *Journal of Business*, 34(4), pp. 411–33.

MOENE, K. O., 1985. "A Note on Keynesian Unemployment as a Worker Discipline Device," *Economic Letters*, 18(1), pp. 17–19.

MOOKHERJEE, D., 1986. "Involuntary Unemployment and Worker Moral Hazard," *Review of Economic Studies*, 53(5), pp. 739–54.

MORCK, R., A. SHLEIFER and R. W. VISHNY, 1988. "Management Ownership and Market Valuation: An Empirical Analysis," *Journal of Financial Economics*, 20, pp. 293–315.

MORDUCH, J., 1999. "The Microfinance Promise," *Journal of Economic Literature*, 37(4) pp. 1569–614.

MORTENSEN, D. T., 1973. "Search Equilibrium in a Simple Multi-Market Economy," Center for Mathematical Studies, Discussion Paper No. 54, Northwestern University.

——1970. "A Theory of Wage and Employment Dynamics," in E. S. Phelps et al. (ed.), *Microeconomic Foundations of Employment and Inflation Theory*, New York: Norton.

MOSCARINI, G. and L. SMITH, 2002. "The Law of Large Demand for Information," *Econometrica*, 70(6), pp. 2351–66.

MOYNIHAN, P. D., 1998. *Secrecy: The American Experience*, New Haven, Conn: Yale University Press.

MURPHY, K. J., 1985. "Corporate Performance and Managerial Remuneration: An Empirical Analysis," *Journal of Accounting and Economics*, 7(1–3), pp. 11–42.

MUSGRAVE, R., 1959. *The Theory of Public Finance*, New York: McGraw-Hill.

MYERS, S. C. and N. S. MAJLUF, 1984. "Corporate Financing and Investment Decisions when Firms Have Information that Investors do not Have," *Journal of Financial Economics*, 13(2), pp. 187–222 (also in Michael J. Brennan (ed.), *The Theory of Corporate Finance Vol. 1*, Elgar Reference Collection, Cheltenham, UK: Elgar, pp. 207–41).

MYERSON, R., 1978. "Refinements of the Nash Equilibrium Concept," *International Journal of Game Theory*, 7(2), pp. 73–80.

MYERSON, R., 1979. "Incentive Compatibility and the Bargaining Problem," *Econometrica*, 47(1), pp. 61–73.

—— 1985. "Analysis of Two Bargaining Problems with Incomplete Information," in A. Roth (ed.), *Game-Theoretic Models of Bargaining*, Cambridge: Cambridge University Press.

NAKAMURA, L, 1985. "Customer Credit, Financial Intermediaries and Real Income Preliminary Evidence That Credit Matters," mimeo, Department of Economics, Rutgers University.

NALEBUFF, B., A. RODRIGUEZ, and J. E. STIGLITZ, 1993. "Equilibrium Unemployment as a Worker Screening Device," NBER Working Paper No. 4357.

—— J. E. STIGLITZ, 1982, "Quality and Prices," Princeton University Econometric Research Program Memorandum No. 297.

—— —— 1983a. "Information, Competition, and Markets," *American Economic Review*, 73(2), pp. 278–83.

—— —— 1983b. "Prizes and Incentives: Towards a General Theory of Compensation and Competition," *The Bell Journal of Economics*, 14(1), pp. 21–43.

—— —— 1985. "Unemployment as a Self-Selection Mechanism," mimeo, Princeton University.

NEARY, P. and J. E. STIGLITZ, 1983. "Toward a Reconstruction of Keynesian Economics: Expectations and Constrained Equilibria," *Quarterly Journal of Economics*, 98 (Supplement), pp. 199–228.

NELSON, P., 1970. "Information and Consumer Behavior," *Journal of Economic Theory*, 78(2), pp. 311–29.

NELSON, R. and S. WINTER, 1977. "Simulation of Schumpeterian Competition," *American Economic Review*, 67(1), pp. 271–6.

—— —— 1982. *An Evolutionary Theory of Economic Change*, Cambridge, MA: Belknap Press of Harvard University Press.

—— —— 1990. "Neoclassical vs. Evolutionary Theories of Economic Growth: Critique and Prospectus," in Christopher Freeman (ed.), *The Economics of Innovation*, International Library of Critical Writings in Economics, No. 2., Brookfield, VT: Elgar, pp. 3–22.

NEWBERY, D. and J. E. STIGLITZ, 1979. "Sharecropping: Risk Sharing and the Importance of Imperfect Information," in J. A. Roumasset et al. (eds.), *Risk Uncertainty and Development*, SEARCA, A/D/C, pp. 311–41.

—— —— 1981. *The Theory of Commodity Price Stabilization: A Study in the Economics of Risk*, Oxford: Clarendon Press.

—— —— 1982. "The Choice of Techniques and the Optimality of Market Equilibrium with Rational Expectations," *Journal of Political Economy*, 90(2), pp. 223–46.

—— —— 1983. "Risk and Trade Policy," World Bank Working Paper No. 53.

—— —— 1984. "Pareto Inferior Trade," *Review of Economic Studies*, 51(1), pp. 1–12.

NOLEDEKE, G. and E. VAN DAMME, 1990. "Signalling in a Dynamic Labor Market," *Review of Economic Studies*, 57(1), pp. 1–23.

NORDHAUS, W. D., 1969. "An Economic Theory of Technological Change," *The American Economic Review*, 59(2), pp. 18–28.

NORTH, D. C., 1990. *Institutions, Institutional Change and Economic Performance*, New York: Cambridge University Press.

OBSTFELD, M. and K. ROGOFF, 1995. "Exchange Rate Dynamics Redux", *Journal of Political Economy*, 103(3), pp. 624–60.

OLINER, S. and G. RUDEBUSCH, 1996. "Is There a Broad Credit Channel for Monetary Policy?" *Federal Reserve Bank of San Francisco Economic Review*, 1, pp. 3–13.

ORDOVER, J. and A. WEISS, 1981. "Information and the Law: Evaluating Legal Restrictions on Competitive Contracts," *American Economic Review*, 71(2), pp. 399–404.

OSTER, G., 1980. "Labour Relations and Demand Relations: A Case Study of the 'Unemployment Effect,'" *Cambridge Journal of Economics,* 4(4), pp. 337–48.

PAULY, M., 1974. "Overinsurance and Public Provision of Insurance: The Roles of Moral Hazard and Adverse Selection," *Quarterly Journal of Economics,* 88(1), pp. 44–62.

PENCAVEL, J. H., 1972. "Wages, Specific Training, and Labor Turnover in U.S. Manufacturing Industries," *International Economic Review,* 13(1), pp. 53–64.

—— 1977. "Industrial Morale," in O. Ashenfelter and W. E. Oates (eds.), *Essays in Labor Market Analysis in Memory of Yochanan Peter Comay,* New York: Wiley, pp. 129–46.

PENROSE, E. T., 1952. "Biological Analogies in the Theory of the Firm," *American Economic Review,* 42(5), pp. 804–19.

PHELPS, E. S., 1968. "Money–Wage Dynamics and Labor Market Equilibrium," *Journal of Political Economy,* 76(4), pp. 678–711.

—— 1969. "The New Microeconomics in Inflation and Employment Theory," *The American Economic Review,* 59(2), pp. 147–60.

—— (ed.), 1970. *Microeconomic Foundations of Employment and Inflation Theory,* New York: Norton.

—— 1972. "The Statistical Theory of Racism and Sexism," *American Economic Review,* 62(4), pp. 659–61.

—— S. G. WINTER, 1970. "Optimal Price Policy under Atomistic Competition," in E. S. Phelps (ed.), *Microeconomic Foundations of Employment and Inflation Theory,* New York: W. W. Norton and Co., pp. 309–37.

PHILLIPS, G., 1995. "Increased Debt and Industry Product Markets: An Empirical Analysis," *Journal of Financial Economics,* 37(2), pp. 189–238.

PIGOU, A. C., 1920. *The Economics of Welfare,* London: Macmillan and Co.

PITT, M. and S. KHANDKER., 1998a. "The Impact of Group-Based Credit Programs on Poor Households in Bangladesh: Does the Gender of Participants Matter?" *Journal of Political Economy,* 106(5), pp. 958–96.

—— —— 1998b. "Credit Programs for the Poor and Seasonality in Rural Bangladesh," draft paper, Brown University and World Bank.

Plato, 1968. *The Republic,* Oxford: Clarendon Press.

POPPER, K., 1950. *The Open Society and Its Enemies, Volume I—The Spell of Plato; Part II—The High Tide of Prophesy: Hegel, Marx and the Aftermath,* Princeton: Princeton University Press.

—— 1959. *The Logic of Scientific Discovery,* English edn., New York: Basic Books.

PRASAD, P. H., 1970. *Growth with Full Employment,* Bombay: Allied Publishers.

RABIN, M. and R. H. THALER, 2001. "Anomalies: Risk Aversion," *The Journal of Economic Perspectives,* 15(1), pp. 219–32.

RADNER, R., 1968. "Competitive Equilibrium Under Uncertainty," *Econometrica,* 36(1), pp. 31–58.

—— 1972. "Existence of Equilibrium of Plans, Prices, and Price Expectations in a Sequence of Markets," *Econometrica,* 40(2), pp. 289–303.

—— 1974. "A Note on Unanimity of Stockholders' Preferences Among Alternative Production Plans: A Reformulation of the Ekern-Wilson Model," *Bell Journal of Economics,* 5(1), pp. 181–4.

—— 1979. "Rational Expectations Equilibrium: Generic Existence and the Information Revealed by Prices," *Econometrica,* 47(3), pp. 655–78.

—— J. E. STIGLITZ, 1984. "A Nonconcavity in the Value of Information," in M. Boyer and R. Khilstrom (eds.), *Bayesian Models in Economic Theory,* Elsevier Science Publications, pp. 33–52.

RAIFFA, H. and R. SCHLAIFER, 1961. *Applied Statistical Decision Theory*, Boston: Harvard Business School.

RAMSEY, F. P., 1927. "A Contribution to the Theory of Taxation," *Economic Journal*, 37(1), pp. 47–61.

RAO, C., 1965. *Linear Statistical Inference and Its Applications*, New York: Wiley.

——1971. "Uncertainty, Entrepreneurship and Share Cropping in India," *Journal of Political Economy*, 79(3), pp. 578–95.

REBITZER, J. B., 1987. "Unemployment, Long-Term Employment Relations, and Productivity Growth," *Review of Economics and Statistics*, 69(4), pp. 627–35.

REPULLO, R., 1985. "A Simple Model of Interest Rate Deregulation," mimeo, London School of Economics and Bank of Spain.

REVESZ, P., 1960. *Laws of Large Numbers*, New York: Academic Press.

REY, P. and J. E. STIGLITZ, 1993, "Short-term Contracts as a Monitoring Device," NBER Working Paper No. 4514.

—— ——1996. "Moral Hazard and Unemployment in Competitive Equilibrium," unpublished Manuscript, University of Toulouse.

RILEY, J. G., 1975. "Competitive Signalling," *Journal of Economic Theory*, 10(2), pp. 174–86.

——1979. "Informational Equilibrium," *Econometrica*, 47(2), pp. 331–60.

——1987. "Credit Rationing, A Further Remark," *American Economics Review*, 77(1), pp. 224–7.

——2001. "Silver Signals: Twenty-five Years of Screening and Signaling," *Journal of Economic Literature*, 39(2), pp. 432–78.

——R. ZECKHAUSER, 1983. "Optimal Selling Strategies: When to Haggle, When to Hold Firm," *Quarterly Journal of Economics*, 98(2), pp. 267–89.

ROBERTSON, D. H., 1940. *Essays in Monetary Theory*, London: P. S. King & Son.

ROBINSON, J., 1933. *The Economics of Imperfect Competition*, London: Macmillan.

RODGERS, G. B., 1975. "Nutritionally Based Wage Determination in the Low Income Labour Market," *Oxford Economic Papers*, 27(1), pp. 61–81.

RODRIGUEZ, A., 1991. "Non-existence and Optimality of Equilibrium in a Model with Asymmetric Information and Market Screening," mimeo, Stanford University.

——J. E. STIGLITZ, 1991a. "Equilibrium Unemployment, Testing, and the Pure Theory of Selection," paper presented at NBER/CEPR Conference on Unemployment and Wage Determination, Boston.

—— ——1991b. "Unemployment and Efficiency Wages: The Adverse Selection Model," paper presented at NBER/CEPR Conference on Unemployment and Wage Determination, Boston.

RODRIK, D. and A. VELASCO, 1999. "Short-Term Capital Flows," NBER Working Paper No. 7364.

ROMER, P. M., 1986. "Increasing Returns and Long-Run Growth," *Journal of Political Economy*, 94(5), pp. 1002–37.

ROSEN, S., 1985. "Implicit Contracts: A Survey," *Journal of Economic Literature*, 23(3), pp. 1144–75.

ROSENSTEIN-RODAN, P., 1984. "Natura Facit Saltum: Analysis of the Disequilibrium Growth Process," in G. Meier and D. Seers (eds.), *Pioneers in Development*, New York: Oxford University Press for the World Bank.

ROSENTHAL, R. and A. WEISS, 1984. "Mixed Strategy Equilibrium in a Market with Asymmetric Information," *Review of Economic Studies*, 51(2), pp. 333–42.

ROSS, S., 1973. "The Economic Theory of Agency: The Principal's Problem," *American Economic Review*, 63(2), pp. 134–9.

—— 1977. "The Determination of Financial Structure: The Incentive-Signalling Approach," *Bell Journal of Economics*, 8(1), pp. 23–40.

ROTEMBERG, J. and G. SALONER, 1987. "The Relative Rigidity of Monopoly Pricing," *American Economic Review*, 77(5), pp. 917–26.

ROTHSCHILD, M., 1974. "A Two-Armed Bandit Theory of Market Pricing," *Journal of Economic Theory*, 9(2), pp. 185–202.

—— J. E. STIGLITZ, 1970. "Increasing Risk: I, A Definition," *Journal of Economic Theory*, 2(3), pp. 225–43.

—— —— 1973. "Some Further Results on the Measurement of Inequality," *Journal of Economic Theory*, 6(2), pp. 188–204.

—— —— 1975. "Equilibrium in Competitive Insurance Markets," Technical Report No. 170, IMSSS Stanford University.

—— —— 1976. "Equilibrium in Competitive Insurance Markets: An Essay on the Economics of Imperfect Information," *Quarterly Journal of Economics*, 90(4), pp. 629–49 (subsequently reprinted in O. E. Williamson (ed.), *Industrial Organization*, Edward Elgar, 1990, pp. 141–61; in G. Dionne and S. Harrington (eds.), *Foundations of Insurance Economics*, Kluwer Academic Publishers, 1992, pp. 355–75; and in Nicholas Barr (ed.), *Economic Theory and the Welfare State*, Cheltenham, UK: Edward Elgar, 2000).

—— —— 1982. "A Model of Employment Outcomes Illustrating the Effect of the Structure of Information on the Level and Distribution of Income," *Economic Letters*, 10(3–4), pp. 231–6.

—— —— 1997. "Competition and Insurance Twenty Years Later," *Geneva Papers on Risk and Insurance Theory* 22(2), pp. 73–9.

—— G. WERDEN, 1982. "Title VII and the Use of Employment Tests: An Illustration of the Limits of the Judicial Process," *Journal of Legal Studies*, 11(2), pp. 261–80.

RUBINSTEIN, A., 1979. "Strong Perfect Equilibrium in Supergames," *International Journal of Game Theory*, 9(1), pp. 1–12.

SAH, R. K., 1991. "Fallibility in Human Organizations and Political Systems," *Journal of Economic Perspectives*, 5(2), pp. 67–88.

—— J. E. STIGLITZ, 1985a. "Perpetuation and Self-Reproduction of Economic Systems: The Selection and Performance of Managers," presented at World Congress of Econometric Society, Cambridge.

—— —— 1985b. "Economics of Committees," Economic Growth Center Discussion Paper 486, Yale University.

—— —— 1985c. "Human Fallibility and Economic Organization," *American Economic Review*, 75(2), pp. 292–6.

—— —— 1985d. "The Social Cost of Labor and Project Evaluation: A General Approach," *Journal of Public Economics*, 28(2), pp. 135–63.

—— —— 1986. "The Architecture of Economic Systems: Hierarchies and Polyarchies," *American Economic Review*, 76(4), pp. 716–27.

—— —— 1987a. "The Invariance of Market Innovation to the Number of Firms," *Rand Journal of Economics*, 18(1) (Spring), pp. 98–108.

—— —— 1987b. "Taxation and Pricing of Agricultural and Industrial Goods" in D. Newbery and N. Stern (eds.), *The Theory of Taxation for Developing Countries*, Oxford: Oxford University Press, pp. 430–58.

—— —— 1988a. "Committees, Hierarchies and Polyarchies," *The Economic Journal*, 98(391) (June), pp. 451–70.

—— —— 1988b. "Qualitative Properties of Profit-Maximizing K-out-of-N Systems Subject to Two Kinds of Failure," *IEEE Transactions on Reliability*, 37(5), pp. 515–20.

SAH, R. K. and J. E. STIGLITZ, 1989a. "Sources of Technological Divergence between Developed and Less Developed Countries," in G. Calvo et al. (eds.), *Debt, Stabilizations and Development: Essays in Memory of Carlos Diaz-Alejandro*, London: Basil Blackwell, pp. 423–46.

————1989b. "Technological Learning, Social Learning and Technological Change," in S. Chakravarty (ed.), *The Balance between Industry and Agriculture in Economic Development*, London: MacMillan Press/International Economic Association, pp. 285–98.

————1991. "The Quality of Managers in Centralized Versus Decentralized Organizations," *Quarterly Journal of Economics*, 106(1), pp. 289–95. (abstracted from "Perpetuation and Self-Reproduction of Organizations: The Selection and Performance of Managers," presented at World Congress of Econometric Society, Cambridge, August 1985.)

————1992. *Peasants versus City-Dwellers: Taxation and the Burden of Economic Development*, Oxford: Clarendon Press.

SALANIE, B., 1997. *The Economics of Contracts*, Cambridge, MA: MIT Press.

SALOP, J. and S. SALOP, 1976. "Self-Selection and Turnover in the Labor Market," *The Quarterly Journal of Economics*, 90(4), pp. 619–27.

SALOP, S., 1973. "Wage Differentials in a Dynamic Theory of the Firm," *Journal of Economic Theory*, 6(4), pp. 321–44.

————1976. "On the Non-Existence of Competitive Equilibrium," Federal Reserve Board, St Louis.

————1977. "The Noisy Monopolist: Imperfect Information, Price Dispersion and Price Discrimination," *The Review of Economic Studies*, 44(3), pp. 393–406.

————1979a. "A Model of the Natural Rate of Unemployment," *American Economic Review*, 69(1), pp. 117–25.

————1979b. "Monopolistic Competition with Outside Goods," *Bell Journal of Economics*, 10(1), pp. 141–56.

————J. E. STIGLITZ, 1975. "A Framework for Analyzing Monopolistically Competitive Price Dispersion," Federal Reserve Board, St Louis.

————1977. "Bargains and Ripoffs: A Model of Monopolistically Competitive Price Dispersions," *Review of Economic Studies*, 44(3), pp. 493–510 (reprinted in S. A. Lippman and D. K. Levine (eds.), *The Economics of Information*, Edward Elgar, 1995, pp. 198–215).

————1982. "The Theory of Sales: A Simple Model of Equilibrium Price Dispersion with Identical Agents," *American Economic Review*, 72(5), pp. 1121–30.

————1987. "Information, Welfare and Product Diversity," in G. Feiwel (ed.), *Arrow and the Foundations of the Theory of Economic Policy*, London: MacMillan, pp. 328–40.

SAMUELSON, P., 1947. *Foundations of Economic Analysis*, Cambridge, Mass: Harvard University Press.

————1948. "International Trade and the Equalization of Factor Prices," *Economic Journal*, 58(230), pp. 163–84.

————1965. "A Theory of Induced Innovation on Kennedy-von Weisacker Lines," *Review of Economics and Statistics*, 47(4), pp. 343–56.

SANDERATNE, N., 1978. "An Analytical Approach to Small Farmer Loan Defaults," *Savings and Development*, 2(4), pp. 290–304.

SAPPINGTON, D. and J. E. STIGLITZ, 1987a. "Information and Regulation," in E. Bailey (ed.), *Public Regulation*, London: MIT Press, pp. 3–43.

————1987b. "Privatization, Information and Incentives," *Journal of Policy Analysis and Management*, 6(4), pp. 567–82.

SARGENT, T. J. and N. WALLACE, 1975. "'Rational' Expectations, the Optimal Monetary Instrument, and the Optimal Money Supply Rule," *Journal of Political Economy*, 83(2), pp. 241–54.

SAVAGE, L. J., (1954). *The Foundations of Statistics*. New York: Wiley.

SCHLICHT, E., 1978. "Labour Turnover, Wage Structure and Natural Unemployment," *Zeitschrift fur die gesamte Staatswissenschaft*, 134(2) (June), pp. 337–46.

——1981a. "Reference Group Behaviour and Economic Incentives: A Remark," *Zeitschrift fur die gesamte Staatswissenschaft*, 137(1), pp. 125–7.

——1981b. "Reference Group Behaviour and Economic Incentives: A Further Remark," *Zeitschrift fur die gesamte Staatswissenschaft*, 137(4), pp. 733–6.

——1985. "Dismissal vs. Fines as a Discipline Device: Comment on Shapiro-Stiglitz," mimeo, Institute for Advanced Study, Princeton.

——1986. "A Link Between Reservation Wage and Productivity," mimeo, Institute for Advanced Study, Princeton.

SCHULTZ, T. W., 1960. "Capital Formation by Education," *Journal of Political Economy*, 68(6), pp. 571–83.

SCHUMPETER, J. A., 1934. *The Theory of Economic Development*, Cambridge, MA: Harvard Economic Studies.

——1978 [1942]. *Capitalism, Socialism and Democracy*, New York: Harper & Row.

SCITOVSKY, T., 1945. "Some Consequences of the Habit of Judging Quality by Price," *Review of Economic Studies*, 12(2), pp. 100–5.

SELTEN, R., 1975. "Re-examination of the Perfectness Concept for Equilibrium Points in Extensive Games," *International Journal of Game Theory*, 4(1), pp. 25–55.

SHABAN, R. A., 1987. "Testing between Competing Models of Sharecropping," *Journal of Political Economy*, 95(5), pp. 893–920.

SHAKESPEARE, W., 2000. [1599]. *As You Like It*, (Act 2, Scene 7), New York: Cambridge University Press.

SHAPIRO, C., 1983. "Premiums for High Quality Products as Returns to Reputations," *Quarterly Journal of Economics*, 98(4), pp. 659–80.

——STIGLITZ, J. E., 1984. "Equilibrium Unemployment as a Worker Discipline Device," *American Economic Review*, 74(3), pp. 433–44.

————1985a. "Equilibrium Unemployment as a Worker Discipline Device: Reply," *American Economic Review*, 75(4), pp. 892–3.

————1985b. "Can Unemployment be Involuntary? Reply," *American Economic Review*, 75(5), pp. 1215–17.

SHAVELL, S., 1979a. "On Moral Hazard and Insurance," *Quarterly Journal of Economics*, 93(4), pp. 541–62.

——1979b. "Risk Sharing and Incentives in the Principal and Agent Problem," *Bell Journal of Economics*, 10(1), pp. 55–73.

SHELL, K., 1966. "Toward a Theory of Inventive Activity and Capital Accumulation," *The American Economic Review*, 56(1/2), pp. 62–8.

——(ed.), 1967. *Essays on the Theory of Optimal Economic Growth*, Cambridge MA: MIT Press.

——M. SIDRAUSKI, and J. E. STIGLITZ, 1969. "Capital Gains, Income and Saving," *Review of Economic Studies*, 36(105), pp. 15–26.

——J. E. STIGLITZ. 1967. "The Allocation of Investment in a Dynamic Economy," *Quarterly Journal of Economics*, 81(4), pp. 592–609.

SHILLER, R. J., 2000. *Irrational Exuberance*, Princeton University Press, Princeton.

SHILONY, Y., 1977. "Mixed Pricing in Locational Oligopoly," *Journal of Economic Theory*, 14(2), pp. 373–88.

SHLEIFER, A., 1986. "Do Demand Curves for Stock Slope Down?" *Journal of Finance*, 41(3), pp. 579–90.

——R. W. VISHNY, 1988. "Value Maximization and the Acquisition Process," *Journal of Economic Perspectives*, 2(1), pp. 7–20.

SHLEIFER, A. and R. W. VISHNY, 1989. "Management Entrenchment: The Case of Manager-Specific Investments," *Journal of Financial Economics*, 25(1), pp. 123–39.

——1997. "A Survey of Corporate Governance," *Journal of Finance*, 52(2), pp. 737–83.

——1998. *The Grabbing Hand: Government Pathologies and their Cures*, Cambridge, MA: Harvard University Press.

SIAMWALLA, A. et al., 1990. "The Thai Rural Credit System: Public Subsidies, Private Information, and Segmented Markets," *World Bank Economic Review*, 1990(4), pp. 271–95.

SIEGEL, J. J. and R. H. THALER, 1997. "Anomalies: The Equity Premium Puzzle," *Journal of Economic Perspectives*, 11(1), pp. 191–200.

SIMON H. A., 1991. "Organizations and Markets," *Journal of Economic Perspectives*, 5(2), pp. 25–44.

SIMONDE DE SISMONDI, J. C. L., 1966 [1814]. *Political Economy*, New York: Kelley.

SINGH, N., 1985. "Monitoring and Hierarchies: The Marginal Value of Information in a Principal-Agent Model," *The Journal of Political Economy*, 93(3), pp. 599–609.

SINGH, R., 1998. "Takeover Bidding with Toeholds: The Case of the Owners Curse," *Review of Financial Studies*, 11(4), pp. 679–704.

SLIGHTER, S. H., 1919. *The Turnover of Factory Labor*, New York: Appleton.

SMALLWOOD, D. and J. CONLISK, 1979. "Product Quality in Markets Where Consumers are Imperfectly Informed," *Quarterly Journal of Economics*, 93(1), pp. 1–23.

SMITH, A., 1904 [1776]. *An Inquiry into the Nature and Causes of the Wealth of Nations*, ed. E. Cannan, London: Methuen.

SMITH, B., 1983. "Limited Information, Credit Rationing, and Optimal Government Lending," *American Economic Review*, 73(3), pp. 305–18.

SOLOW, R. M., 1956. "A Contribution to the Theory of Economic Growth," *The Quarterly Journal of Economics*, 70(1), pp. 65–94.

——1979. "Another Possible Source of Wage Stickiness," *Journal of Macroeconomics*, 1(1), pp. 79–82.

——1980. "On Theories of Unemployment," *American Economic Review*, 70(1), pp. 1–11.

——1985. "Insiders and Outsiders in Wage Determination," *Scandinavian Journal of Economics*, 87(2), pp. 411–28.

——J. STIGLITZ, 1968. "Output, Employment and Wages in the Short Run," *Quarterly Journal of Economics*, 82(4), pp. 537–60.

SPENCE, M., 1973. "Job Market Signaling," *Quarterly Journal of Economics*, 87(3), pp. 355–74.

——1974a, "Competitive and Optimal Responses to Signals: An Analysis of Efficiency and Distribution," *Journal of Economic Theory*, 7(3), pp. 296–332.

——1974b. *Market Signalling: Information Transfer in Hiring and Related Processes*, Cambridge, MA: Harvard University Press.

——1976a. "Competition in Salaries, Credentials, and Signaling Prerequisites for Jobs," *The Quarterly Journal of Economics*, 90(1), pp. 51–74.

——1976b. "Informational Aspects of Market Structure: An Introduction," *The Quarterly Journal of Economics*, 90(4), pp. 591–97.

——1977a. "Consumer Misperceptions, Product Failure and Producer Liability," *The Review of Economic Studies*, 44(3), pp. 561–72.

——1977b. "Non-linear Prices and Welfare," *Journal of Public Economics*, 8(1), pp. 1–18.

STARRETT, D. A., 1980. "Measuring Externalities and Second Best Distortions in the Theory of Local Public Goods," *Econometrica*, 48(3), pp. 627–42.

STERN, N. and J. E. STIGLITZ, 1997. "A Framework for a Development Strategy in a Market Economy," in E. Malinvaued and A. K. Sen (eds.), *Development Strategy and the Management of the Market Economy*, Oxford: Clarendon Press, pp. 253–95.

STIGLER, G. J., 1961. "The Economics of Information," *Journal of Political Economy*, 69(3), pp. 213–25.

—— 1967. "Imperfections in the Capital Market," *Journal of Political Economy*, 75(3), pp. 287–92.

STIGLITZ, J. E., 1969a, "Distribution of Income and Wealth Among Individuals," *Econometrica*, 37(3), July, pp. 382–97 (presented at the December 1966 meetings of the Econometric Society, San Francisco).

—— 1969b. "A Re-Examination of the Modigliani-Miller Theorem," *American Economic Review*, 59(5), pp. 784–793.

—— 1969c. "Rural–Urban Migration, Surplus Labor and the Relationship Between Urban and Rural Wages," *East African Economic Review*, 1–2, pp. 1–27.

—— 1971a. "Notes on Education and Screening," Institute for Development Studies, Nairobi.

—— 1971b. "Perfect and Imperfect Capital Markets," paper presented to Econometric Society Meeting, New Orleans.

—— 1972a. "Education as a Screening Device and the Distribution of Income," mimeo, Yale University.

—— 1972b. "On the Optimality of the Stock Market Allocation of Investment," *Quarterly Journal of Economics*, 86(1), pp. 25–60.

—— 1972c. "Some Aspects of the Pure Theory of Corporate Finance Bankruptcies and Takeovers," *Bell Journal of Economics and Management Science*, 3(2), pp. 458–82.

—— 1973a. "Approaches to the Economics of Discrimination," *American Economic Review*, 63(2), pp. 287–95.

—— 1973b. "The Badly Behaved Economy with the Well Behaved Production Function," in J. Mirrless (ed.), *Models of Economic Growth*, MacMillan Publishing Company, pp. 118–37.

—— 1973c. "Conceptual Approaches to the Economics of Discrimination," *American Economic Review*, 63(2), 287–95.

—— 1973d. "Taxation, Corporate Financial Policy and the Cost of Capital," *Journal of Public Economics*, 2(1) (February), pp. 1–34.

—— 1974a. "Alternative Theories of Wage Determination and Unemployment in L.D.C.'s: the Labor Turnover Model," *Quarterly Journal of Economics*, 88(2), pp. 194–227.

—— 1974b. "Demand for Education in Public and Private School Systems," *Journal of Public Economics*, 3(4), pp. 349–85.

—— 1974c. "Equilibrium Wage Distributions," Technical Report No. 154, Economics Series, Institute for Mathematical Studies in the Social Science, Stanford University.

—— 1974d. "Information and Capital Markets," mimeo, Oxford University.

—— 1974e. "Incentives and Risk Sharing in Sharecropping," *Review of Economic Studies*, 41(2) pp. 219–55.

—— 1974f. "On the Irrelevance of Corporate Financial Policy," *American Economic Review*, 64(6), pp. 851–66.

—— 1974g. "Pure Theory of Local Public Goods," in M. Feldstein (ed.), *IEA Conference Volume*, Turin: IEA.

—— 1974h. "Theories of Discrimination and Economic Policy," in G. von Furstenberg et al. (eds.), *Patterns of Racial Discrimination, Volume II: Employment and Income*, London: D.C. Heath and Company, Lexington Books, pp. 5–26.

—— 1974i. "Wage Determination and Unemployment in LDCs: The Labor Turnover Model," *Quarterly Journal of Economics*, 88(2), pp. 194–227.

—— 1975a. "The Efficiency of Market Prices in Long-Run Allocations in the Oil Industry," in G. Brannon (ed.), *Studies in Energy Tax Policy*, Cambridge, MA: Ballinger, pp. 55–99, (report written for the Ford Foundation Energy Policy Project, August 1973).

STIGLITZ, J. E., 1975b. "Incentives, Risk and Information: Notes Towards a Theory of Hierarchy," *Bell Journal of Economics*, 6(2), pp. 552–79.

——1975c. "Information and Economic Analysis," in J. M. Parkin and A. R. Nobay (eds.), *Current Economic Problems*, Cambridge: Cambridge University Press, pp. 27–52.

——1975d. "Markets for Heterogeneous Labor with Imperfect Information," mimeo, Stanford University.

——1975e. "Monopolistic Competition and the Capital Market." IMSSS Technical Report No. 161, Stanford, Calif: Stanford University. Published as 1989e.

——1975f. "The Theory of Screening, Education and the Distribution of Income," *American Economic Review*, 65(3), pp. 283–300.

——1976a. "The Corporation Tax," *Journal of Public Economics*, 5(3–4), pp. 303–11.

——1976b. "The Efficiency Wage Hypothesis, Surplus Labour and the Distribution of Income in LDC's," *Oxford Economic Papers*, 28(2), pp. 185–207.

——1976c. "Prices and Queues in Screening Devices in Competitive Markets," IMSSS Technical Report No. 212, Stanford University, August.

——1977a. "Monopoly, Non-Linear Pricing and Imperfect Information: The Insurance Market," *Review of Economic Studies*, 44(3), pp. 407–30.

——1977b. "Symposium on the Economics of Information: Introduction," *Review of Economic Studies*, 44(138), pp. 389–91.

——1977c. "Theory of Local Public Goods," in M. S. Feldstein and R. P. Inman (eds.), *The Economics of Public Services*, Bath: MacMillan Press Ltd, pp. 274–333.

——1978. "Lectures in Macro-Economics," mimeo, Oxford University.

——1979a. "Equilibrium in Product Markets with Imperfect Information," *American Economic Review*, 69(2), pp. 339–45.

——1979b. "On Search and Equilibrium Price Distributions," in M. Boskin (ed.), *Economics and Human Welfare: Essays in Honor of Tibor Scitovsky*, York: Academic Press Inc, pp. 203–36.

——1980a. "Contests and Cooperation: Toward a General Theory of Compensation and Competition," presented at a Conference on the Internal Organization of Firms, International Institute of the Internal Organization of Firms, International Institute of Management, Berlin, July (and at a Conference on the Economics of Information, University of Pennsylvania, May 1981).

——1980b. "Information, Planning and Incentives," presented at the CSCCRP Sino-American Conference on Alternative Development Strategies in Wingspread, Racine, WI, November. (Chinese edition published 1982.)

——1981. "Pareto Optimality and Competition," *Journal of Finance*, 36(2), pp. 235–51.

——1982a. "Alternative Theories of Wage Determination and Unemployment the Efficiency Wage Model," in M. Gersovitz et al. (eds.), *The Theory and Experience of Economic Development's Essays in Honor of Sir W. Arthur Lewis*, London: Allen & Unwin, pp. 78–106.

——1982b. "The Inefficiency of the Stock Market Equilibrium," *Review of Economic Studies*, 49(2), pp. 241–61.

——1982c. "Information and Capital Markets," in W. F. Sharpe and C. Cootner (eds.), *Financial Economics: Essays in Honor of Paul Cootner*, New Jersey: Prentice Hall, pp. 118–58.

——1982d. "On the Relevance or Irrelevance of Public Financial Policy," paper presented to a conference at Rice University, NBER Working Paper No. 1057.

——1982e. "Ownership, Control, and Efficient Markets: Some Paradoxes in the Theory of Capital Markets," in K. D. Boyer and W. C. Shepherd (eds.), *Economic Regulation Essays in Honor of James R Nelson*, Ann Arbor, Mich: Michigan State University Press, pp. 311–41.

—— 1982f. "Self-Selection and Pareto Efficient Taxation," *Journal of Public Economics*, 17(2), pp. 213–40.

—— 1982g. "The Structure of Labor Markets and Shadow Prices in L.D.C.'s," in R. Sabot (ed.), *Migration and the Labor Market in Developing Countries*, Boulder, Col: Westview, pp. 13–64.

—— 1982h. "Utilitarianism and Horizontal Equity: The Case for Random Taxation," *Journal of Public Economics*, 18(1), pp. 1–33.

—— 1983a. "On the Relevance or Irrelevance of Public Financial Policy: Indexation, Price Rigidities and Optimal Monetary Policy," in R. Dornbusch and M. Simonsen (eds.), *Inflation, Debt and Indexation*, New York: MIT Press, pp. 183–222.

—— 1983b. "Risk, Incentives, and Insurance: The Pure Theory of Moral Hazard," *The Geneva Papers*, 8, pp. 4–32.

—— 1983c "The Theory of Local Public Goods Twenty-Five Years After Tiebout: A Perspective," in G. R. Zodrow (ed.), *Local Provision of Public Services: The Tiebout Model After Twenty-Five Years*, New York: Academic Press, pp. 17–53.

—— 1984a. "Information, Screening and Welfare," in M. Boyer and R. Khilstrom eds., *Bayesian Models in Economic Theory*, Elsevier Science Publications, pp. 209–39.

—— 1984b. "Price Rigidities and Market Structure," *American Economic Review*, 74(2), pp. 350–6.

—— 1985a. "Credit Markets and the Control of Capital," *Journal of Money, Banking, and Credit*, 17(2), pp. 133–52.

—— 1985b. "Economics of Information and the Theory of Economic Development," *Revista De Econometria*, 5(1), pp. 5–32.

—— 1985c. "Equilibrium Wage Distributions," *Economic Journal*, 95(379), pp. 595–618.

—— 1985d. "Information and Economic Analysis: A Perspective," *The Economic Journal*, 95(380a), pp. 21–41.

—— 1986a. "The New Development Economics," *World Development*, 14(2), pp. 257–65.

—— 1986b. "Theories of Wage Rigidities," in J. L. Butkiewicz et al. (eds.), *Keynes' Economic Legacy: Contemporary Economic Theories*, New York: Praeger Publishers, pp. 153–206.

—— 1986c. "Theory of Competition, Incentives and Risk," in J. E. Stiglitz and F. Mathewson (eds.), *New Developments in the Theory of Market Structure*, MacMillan/MIT Press, pp. 399–449.

—— 1986d. "Toward a More General Theory of Monopolistic Competition," in M. Peston and R. Quandt (eds.), *Prices, Competition, & Equilibrium*, Oxford: Philip Allan/Barnes & Noble Books, pp. 22–69.

—— 1987a. "The Causes and Consequences of the Dependence of Quality on Price," *Journal of Economic Literature*, 25(1), pp. 1–48.

—— 1987b. "Competition and the Number of Firms in a Market: Are Duopolies More Competitive Than Atomistic Markets?" *Journal of Political Economy*, 95(5), pp. 1041–61.

—— 1987c. "Design of Labor Contracts: Economics of Incentives and Risk-Sharing," in H. Nalbantian (ed.), *Incentives, Cooperation and Risk Sharing*, Totowa, NJ: Rowman & Allanheld, pp. 47–68.

—— 1987d "Efficient and Optimal Taxation and the New Welfare Economics," in A. Auerbach and M. Feldstein (eds.), *Handbook on Public Economics*, North Holland: Elsevier Science Publishers, pp. 991–1042.

—— 1987e. "Human Nature and Economic Organization," Jacob Marashak Lecture, presented at Far Eastern Meetings of the Econometric Society, October.

—— 1987f. "Learning to Learn, Localized Learning and Technological Progress," in P. Dasgupta and Stoneman (eds.), *Economic Policy and Technological Performance*, Cambridge University Press, pp. 125–53.

STIGLITZ, J. E., 1987g. "On the Microeconomics of Technical Progress," in Jorge M. Katz (ed.), Technology Generation in Latin American Manufacturing Industries, The Macmillan Press Ltd., pp. 56–77 (presented to IDB-Cepal Meetings, Buenos Aires, November 1978).

——1987h. "Sharecropping," The New Palgrave: A Dictionary of Economics, London: MacMillan Press.

——1987i. "Technological Change, Sunk Costs, and Competition," Brookings Papers on Economic Activity, 1987(3), pp. 883–947 (also in special issue of Microeconomics, M. N. Baily and C. Winston (eds.), 1988, pp. 883–947).

——1987j. "The Wage-Productivity Hypothesis: Its Economic Consequences and Policy Implications," in M. J. Boskin (ed.), Modern Developments in Public Finance, London: Basil Blackwell, pp. 130–65.

——1988a. "Economic Organization, Information, and Development," in H. Chenery and T. N. Srinivasan (eds.), Handbook of Development Economics, Amsterdam: Elsevier Science Publishers, pp. 185–201.

——1988b. "Money, Credit, and Business Fluctuations," Economic Record, 64(187) (December), pp. 62–72.

——1988c. "On the Relevance or Irrelevance of Public Financial Policy," The Economics of Public Debt (Proceedings of the 1986 International Economics Association Meeting), London: Macmillan Press, pp. 4–76.

——1988d. "Technological Change, Sunk Costs and Competition," Brookings Papers on Economic Activity, 1988, pp. 883–947.

——1988e. "Why Financial Structure Matters," Journal of Economic Perspectives, 2(4), pp. 121–6.

——1989a. "Financial Markets and Development," Oxford Review of Economic Policy, 5(4), pp. 55–68.

——1989b. "Imperfect Information in the Product Market," in R. Schmalensee and R. Willig (eds.), Handbook of Industrial Organization, Amsterdam: North-Holland, pp. 769–847.

——1989c. "Incentives, Information and Organizational Design," Empirica, 16(1), pp. 3–29.

——1989d. "Markets, Market Failures and Development," American Economic Review, 79(2) (May), pp. 197–203.

——1989e. "Monopolistic Competition and the Capital Market," in G. Feiwel (ed.), The Economics of Imperfect Competition and Employment-Joan Robinson and Beyond, New York: New York University Press, pp. 485–507.

——1989f. "Mutual Funds, Capital Structure, and Economic Efficiency," in S. Bhattacharya and G. Constantinides (eds.), Theory of Valuation–Frontiers of Modern Financial Theory, Vol. 1, Totowa, NJ: Rowman and Littlefield, pp. 342–56.

——1989g. "On the Economic Role of the State," in A. Heertje (ed.), The Economic Role of the State, London: Basil Blackwell and Bank Insinger de Beaufort NV, pp. 9–85.

——1989h. "Principal and Agent," in J. Eatwell et al. (eds.), The New Palgrave: Allocation, Information and Markets, London: MacMillan Press, pp. 241–53.

——1989i. "Rational Peasants, Efficient Institutions and the Theory of Rural Organization," in P. Bardhan (ed.), The Economic Theory of Agrarian Institutions, Oxford: Clarendon Press, pp. 18–29.

——1989j. "Reflections on the State of Economics: 1988," Economic Record, 65(188), pp. 66–72.

——1989k. "Using Tax Policy to Curb Speculative Short-Term Trading," Journal of Financial Services Research, 3(2–3), pp. 101–15.

——1990a. "Peer Monitoring and Credit Markets," World Bank Economic Review, 4(3), pp. 351–66.

—— 1990b. "Some Retrospective Views on Growth Theory Presented on the Occasion of the Celebration of Robert Solow's 65th Birthday," in P. Diamond (ed.), *Growth/ Productivity/ Unemployment*, Cambridge, Mass: MIT Press, pp. 50–68.

—— 1991a. "Another Century of Economic Science," *Economic Journal Anniversary Issue*, 101(404), pp. 134–41.

—— 1991b. "Development Strategies: The Roles of the State and the Private Sector," *Proceedings of the World Bank's Annual Conference on Development Economics 1990*, New York: World Bank, pp. 430–35.

—— 1991c. "The Economic Role of the State: Efficiency and Effectiveness" in T. P. Hardiman and M. Mulreany (eds.), *Efficiency and Effectiveness in the Public Domain. The Economic Role of the State*, New York: Institute of Public Administration, pp. 37–59.

—— 1991d. "Introduction to Symposium on Organizations and Economics," *Journal of Economic Perspectives* 5(2), pp. 15–24.

—— 1991e. "The Invisible Hand and Modem Welfare Economics," in D. Vines and A. Stevenson (eds.), *Information Strategy and Public Policy*, Oxford: Basil Blackwell, pp. 12–50.

—— 1991f. "Some Theoretical Aspects of the Privatization: Applications to Eastern Europe," *Revista di Politica Economica*, 81(158), pp. 179–204 (reprinted in M. Baldassarri, L. Paganetto and E. S. Phelps (eds.), *Privatization Processes in Eastern Europe*, Rome: St. Martin's Press, 1993, pp. 179–204).

—— 1992a. "Banks versus Markets as Mechanisms for Allocating and Coordinating Investment," in J. A. Roumasset and S. Barr (eds.), *The Economics of Cooperation: East Asian Development and the Case for Pro-Market Intervention*, Boulder, Co: Westview Press, pp. 15–38.

—— 1992b. "Capital Markets and Economic Fluctuations in Capitalist Economies," *European Economic Review*, 36(2–3), pp. 269–306.

—— 1992c. "Contract Theory and Macroeconomic Fluctuations," in L. Werin and H. Wijkander (eds.), *Contract Economics*, Oxford: Basil Blackwell, pp. 292–322.

—— 1992d. "The Design of Financial Systems for the Newly Emerging Democracies of Eastern Europe," in C. Clague and G. C. Rausser (eds.), *The Emergence of Market Economies in Eastern Europe*, Oxford: Basil Blackwell, pp. 161–184.

—— 1992e. "Explaining Growth: Competition and Finance," *Rivista di Politica Economica*, 82(169), pp. 227–343.

—— 1992f. "Introduction: S&L Bailout," in J. Barth and R. Brumbaugh Jr. (eds.), *The Reform of Federal Deposit Insurance: Disciplining the Government and Protecting Taxpayers*, London: HarperCollins Publishers, pp. 1–12.

—— 1992g. "The Meanings of Competition in Economic Analysis," *Rivista internazionale de scienze sociali*, 2 (April–June), pp. 191–212.

—— 1992h. "Methodological Issues and the New Keynesian Economics," in A. Vercelli and N. Dimitri (eds.), *Alternative Approaches to Macro-Economics*, Oxford: Oxford University Press, pp. 38–86.

—— 1992i. "Notes on Evolutionary Economics: Imperfect Capital Markets, Organizational Design, Long-Run Efficiency," paper presented at a conference at Osaka University, Osaka.

—— 1992j. "Prices and Queues as Screening Devices in Competitive Markets," in D. Gale and O. Hart (eds.), *Economic Analysis of Markets and Games: Essays in Honor of Frank Hahn*, Cambridge, Mass: MIT Press, pp. 128–66.

—— 1993a. "Consequences of Limited Risk Markets and Imperfect Information for the Design of Taxes and Transfers: An Overview," in K. Hoff, A. Braverman, and J. Stiglitz (eds.), *The Economics of Rural Organization: Theory, Practice, and Policy*, New York: Oxford University Press for the World Bank.

STIGLITZ, J. E., 1993b. "Perspectives on the Role of Government Risk-Bearing within the Financial Sector," in M. Sniderman (ed.), *Government Risk-bearing*, Norwell, Mass: Kluwer Academic Publishers, pp. 109–30.

——1993c. "The Role of the State in Financial Markets," *Proceeding of the World Bank Conference on Development Economics*, Washington, DC: World Bank, pp. 41–46.

——1993d. "Some Theoretical Aspects of the Privatization: Applications to Eastern Europe," in M. Baldassarri, L. Paganetto and E. S. Phelps (eds.), *Privatization Processes in Eastern Europe*, Rome: St. Martin's Press, pp. 179–204.

——1994a. "Economic Growth Revisited," *Industrial and Corporate Change*, 3(1), pp. 65–110.

——1994b. "Endogenous Growth and Cycles," in Y. Shionoya and M. Perlman (eds.), *Innovation in Technology, Industries, and Institutions*, Michigan: University of Michigan Press, pp. 121–56.

——1994c. "Reflections on Economics and on Being and Becoming an Economist," in Arnold Heertje (ed.), *The Markers of Modern Economics*, Vol. II, New York: Harvester Wheatsheaf (Simon & Schuster International Group) (May), pp. 140–83.

——1994d. "The Role of the State in Financial Markets," in M. Bruno and B. Pleskovic (eds.), *Proceeding of the World Bank Conference on Development Economics, 1993*, Washington, DC: World Bank, pp. 41–6.

——1994e. *Whither Socialism?* Cambridge, Mass: MIT Press.

——1995a "Interest Rate Puzzles, Competitive Theory and Capital Constraints," in J. P. Fitoussi (ed.), *Economics in a Changing World*, IEA Conference, Vol. 111, New York: St. Martin's Press: pp. 145–75.

——1995b. "Social Absorption Capability and Innovation," in B. H. Koo and D. H. Perkins (eds.), *Social Capability and Long-Term Economic Growth*, New York: St. Martin's Press, pp. 48–81.

——1996. "Some Lessons from the East Asian Miracle," *World Bank Research Observer* 11(2), pp. 151–77.

——1997a. "The Role of Government in Economic Development," in M. Bruno and B. Pleskovic (eds.), *Annual World Bank Conference on Development Economics 1996*, Washington, DC: World Bank, pp. 11–23.

——1997b. "The Role of Government in the Economies of Developing Countries," in E. Malinvaud and A. K. Sen (eds.), *Development Strategy and the Management of the Market Economy*, Oxford: Clarendon Press, pp. 61–109.

——1998a. "More Instruments and Broader Goals: Moving Toward the Post-Washington Consensus," The 1998 Wider Annual Lecture, Helsinki, January. Published as 1999c.

——1998b. "Pareto Efficient Taxation and Expenditure Policies, with Applications to the Taxation of Capital, Public Investment, and Externalities," presented at a conference in honor of Agnar Sandmo, Bergen.

——1998c. "Towards a New Paradigm for Development: Strategies, Policies and Processes," 9th Raul Prebisch Lecture delivered at the Palais des Nations, Geneva, UNCTAD, October 19. Subsequently published in *The Rebel Within*, Ha-Joon Chang (ed.), London: Wimbledon Publishing Company, 2001, pp. 57–93.

——1998d. "An Agenda for Development in the Twenty-First Century, in J. E. Stiglitz and B. Pleskovic (eds.), *Annual World Bank Conference on Development Economics 1997*, Washington, DC: World Bank, pp. 17–31.

——1999a. "Interest Rates, Risk, and Imperfect Markets: Puzzles and Policies," *Oxford Review of Economic Policy*, 15(2), pp. 59–76.

——1999b. "Knowledge as a Global Public Good," in I. Kaul, I. Grunberg, M. A. Stern (eds.), *Global Public Goods: International Cooperation in the 21st Century*, United Nations Development Programme, New York: Oxford University Press, pp. 308–25.

—— 1999c. "Knowledge for Development: Economic Science, Economic Policy, and Economic Advice," *Proceedings from the Annual Bank Conference on Development Economics 1998*, Keynote Address, Washington, DC: World Bank, pp. 9–58.

—— 1999d. "Public Policy for a Knowledge Economy," remarks at the Department for Trade and Industry and Center for Economic Policy Research, London, January 27, available at: http://web.worldbank.org/WBSITE/EXTERNAL/NEWS/0,,contentMDK:20025143~menuPK: 64255840~pagePK:34370~piPK:42770~theSitePK:4607,00.html

—— 1999e. "More Instruments and Broader Goals: Moving Toward the Post-Washington Consensus," *Revista de Economica Politica*, 19(1), pp. 94–120 (reprinted in H. J. Chang (ed.), *The Rebel Within: Joseph Stiglitz at the World Bank*, London: Anthem, 2001, pp. 19–56).

—— 1999f. "Responding to Economic Crises: Policy Alternatives for Equitable Recovery and Development," *The Manchester School*, 67(5), pp. 409–27.

—— 1999g. "Taxation, Public Policy and The Dynamics of Unemployment," *International Tax and Public Finance*, 6, pp. 239–62 (paper presented to the Institute of International Finance, Cordoba, Argentina, August 24, 1998).

—— 1999h. "Toward a General Theory of Wage and Price Rigidities and Economic Fluctuations," *American Economic Review*, 89(2), pp. 75–80.

—— 2000a. "Capital Market Liberalization, Economic Growth, and Instability," *World Development*, 8(6), pp. 1075–86.

—— 2000b. "The Contributions of the Economics of Information to Twentieth Century Economics," *Quarterly Journal of Economics*, 115(4), pp. 1441–77.

—— 2000c. "Democratic Development as the Fruits of Labor," *Perspectives on Work*, 4(1), pp. 31–8 (abbreviated version in 9 in H-J. Chang (ed.), *The Rebel Within*, London: Wimbledon Publishing Company, 2001, pp. 279–315).

—— 2000d. "Formal and Informal Institutions," in P. Dasgupta and I. Serageldin (eds.), *Social Capital: A Multifaceted Perspective*, Washington, DC: World Bank; pp. 59–68.

—— 2000e. "Quis custodiet ipsos custodes? Corporate Governance Failures in the Transition," in P-A. Muet and J. E. Stiglitz (eds.), *Governance, Equity and Global Markets, Proceedings from the Annual Bank Conference on Development Economics in Europe, June 1999*, Paris: Conseil d'Analyse economique, pp. 51–84.

—— 2000f. "Some Elementary Principles of Bankruptcy," in P-A. Muet and J. E. Stiglitz (eds.), *Governance, Equity and Global Markets: Proceedings from the Annual Bank Conference on Development Economics in Europe, June 1999*, Paris: Conseil d'analyse economique, pp. 605–20.

—— 2000g. "Whither Reform? Ten Years of the Transition," *Proceedings of the Annual Bank Conference on Development Economics 1999*, Washington, DC: World Bank: pp. 27–56.

—— 2001a. "Challenges in the Analysis of the Role of Institutions in Economic Development," in G. Kochendorfer-Lucius and B. Pleskovic (eds.), *Villa Borsig Workshop Series 2000: The Institutional Foundations of a Market Economy*, German Foundation for International Development (DSE), pp. 15–28.

—— 2001b. "Crisis y Restructuración Financiera: el Papel de la Banca Central," *Cuestiones Económicas*, 17(2), pp. 3–24.

—— 2001c. "From Miracle to Recovery: Lessons from Four Decades of East Asian Experience," in S. Yusuf (ed.), *Rethinking the East Asian Miracle*, Washington DC: World Bank.

—— 2001d. "On Liberty, the Right to Know and Public Discourse: The Role of Transparency in Public Life," in H. Chang (ed.), *The Rebel Within*, London: Wimbledon Publishing Company, pp. 250–78. Published as 2003a.

—— 2001e. "Principles of Financial Regulation: A Dynamic Approach," *The World Bank Observer*, 16(1), pp. 1–18.

STIGLITZ, J. E., 2001f. "Quis Custodiet Ipsos Custodes?" in J. E. Stiglitz and P. A. Muet (eds.), *Governance, equity, and global markets: the Annual Bank Conference on Development Economics, Europe,* New York: World Bank, Oxford University Press, pp. 22–54.

—— 2002a. "Employment, Social Justice, and Societal Well-Being," *International Labour Review,* 141(1–2), pp. 9–29 (also published in *Revista Internacional del Trabajo,* 121(1–2), pp. 9–31; and *Revue Internationale du Travail,* 141(1–2), pp. 9–31).

—— 2002b. "New Perspectives on Public Finance: Recent Achievements and Future Challenges," *Journal of Public Economics,* 86(3), pp. 341–60.

—— 2002c. "Nobel Memoirs," in T. Frangsmyr (ed.), *Les Prix Nobel; The Nobel Prizes 2001,* New York: The Nobel Foundation, pp. 447–71.

—— 2003a. "On Liberty, the Right to Know and Public Discourse: The Role of Transparency in Public Life," in M. Gibney (ed.), *Globalizing Rights,* Oxford: Oxford University Press, pp. 115–56.

—— 2003b. "Reflections on the State of the Theory of Monopolistic Competition," in S. Brakman and B. J. Hiejdra (eds.), *The Monopolistic Competition Revolution in Retrospect,* Cambridge: Cambridge University Press, pp. 134–48.

—— 2003c. *The Roaring Nineties,* New York: W. W. Norton.

—— 2004. "Capital-Market Liberalization, Globalization and the IMF," *Oxford Review of Economic Policy,* 20(1) (Spring), pp. 57–71.

—— 2005. "Retirement Savings—Games that Asset Managers, Distributors, and Investors Play," *Trends in Savings and Wealth,* Working Paper No. 4/05 (available online at: www.savingsandwealth.com/research_content/general_issues/stiglitz_games_paper.jhtml).

—— 2006. "Samuelson and the Factor Bias of Technological Change: Toward a Unified Theory of Growth and Unemployment," in M. Szenberg et al. (eds.), *Samuelsonian Economics and the Twenty-First Century,* Oxford: Oxford University Press, pp. 235–51.

—— A. ATKINSON, 1980. *Lectures on Public Economics,* New York: McGraw-Hill.

—— S. GROSSMAN, 1976. "Information and Competitive Price Systems," *American Economic Review,* 66(2), pp. 246–53.

—— R. RADNER, 1984. "A Non-Concavity in the Value of Information," in M. Boyer and R. Khilstrom (eds.), *Bayesian Models in Economic Theory,* New York: North-Holland, pp. 33–52.

—— A. WEISS, 1980. "Credit Rationing in Markets with Imperfect Information, Part II: A Theory of Contingency Contracts," mimeo, Bell Laboratories and Princeton University.

—— —— 1981. "Credit Rationing in Markets with Imperfect Information," *American Economic Review,* 71(3), pp. 393–411.

—— —— 1983a. "Alternative Approaches to the Analysis of Markets with Asymmetric Information," *American Economic Review,* 73(1), pp. 246–9.

—— —— 1983b. "Incentive Effects of Terminations: Applications to the Credit and Labor Markets," *American Economic Review,* 73(5), pp. 912–27.

—— —— 1986. "Credit Rationing and Collateral," in J. Edwards et al. (eds.), *Recent Developments in Corporate Finance,* New York: Cambridge University Press, pp. 101–35.

—— —— 1987a. "Credit Rationing: Reply," *American Economic Review,* 77(1), pp. 228–31.

—— —— 1987b. "Credit Rationing with Many Borrowers," *American Economic Review,* 77(3), pp. 228–31.

—— —— 1987c. "Macro-Economic Equilibrium and Credit Rationing," National Bureau of Economic Research Working Paper No. 2164, Cambridge, Mass.

—— —— 1990. "Banks as Social Accountants and Screening Devices for the Allocation of Credit," *Greek Economic Review,* 12(0) (Supplement), pp. 85–118.

—————— 1992. "Asymmetric Information in Credit Markets and Its Implications for Macro-Economics," *Oxford Economic Papers*, 44(4), pp. 694–724.

—————— 1994. "Sorting Out the Differences Between Screening and Signaling Models," in M. O. L. Bacharach, M. A. H. Dempster and J. L. Enos (eds.), *Mathematical Models in Economics*, Oxford: Oxford University Press.

—————— M. WOLFSON, 1988. "Taxation, Information, and Economic Organization," *Journal of the American Taxation Association*, 9(2), pp. 7–18.

—————— S. YUSUF, 2000. "Development Issues: Settled and Open" in G. M. Meier and J. E. Stiglitz (eds.), *Frontiers of Development Economic: The Future in Perspective*, Oxford: Oxford University Press, pp. 227–68.

STOFT, S., 1982. "Cheat Threat Theory An Explanation of Involuntary Unemployment," mimeo, Boston University.

—————— 1985. "Wages, Unemployment and Piece Rate Double Asymmetric Information," Boston University Discussion Paper No. 113.

STRAND, J., 1986. "Efficiency Wages, Implicit Contracts and Dual Labor Markets: A Theory of Work Habit Formation," mimeo, Department of Economics, University of Oslo.

STULZ, R., 1988. "Managerial Control of Voting Rights: Financing Policies and the Market for Corporate Control," *Journal of Financial Economics*, 20, pp. 25–54.

SUMMERS, L. H., 1981. "Taxation and Corporate Investment: A q-Theory Approach," *Brookings Papers on Economic Activity*, 1981(1), pp. 67–127.

SWEEZY, P., 1968. *The Theory of Capitalist Development*, New York: Monthly Review Press.

TAN, T. C. and S. R. DA COSTA WERLANG, 1985. "Life Cycle Credit Rationing," mimeo, University of Chicago.

TAYLOR, J. B., 1980. "Aggregate Dynamics and Staggered Contracts," *Journal of Political Economy*, 88(1), pp. 1–23.

THALER, R. H., 1987. "Anomalies: Seasonal Movements in Security Prices II: Weekend, Holiday, Turn of the Month, and Intraday Effects," *Journal of Economic Perspectives*, 1(2), pp. 169–77.

—————— 1988a. "Anomalies: The Ultimatum Game," *Journal of Economic Perspectives*, 2(4), pp. 195–206

—————— 1988b. "Anomalies: The Winner's Curse," *Journal of Economic Perspectives*, 2(1), pp. 191–202.

—————— 1989. "Anomalies: Interindustry Wage Differentials," *Journal of Economic Perspectives*, 3(2), pp. 181–93.

—————— 1990. "Anomalies: Saving, Fungibility, and Mental Accounts," *Journal of Economic Perspectives*, 4(1), pp. 193–205.

—————— W. T. ZIEMBA, 1988. "Anomalies: Parimutuel Betting Markets: Racetracks and Lotteries," *Journal of Economic Perspectives*, 2(2), pp. 161–74.

THUROW, L., 1972. "Education and Economic Equality," *Public Interest*, Summer, pp. 66–81.

TIEBOUT, C. M., 1956. "A Pure Theory of Local Expenditures," *Journal of Political Economy*, 64(5), pp. 416–24.

TINBERGEN, J., 1959. "On the Theory of Income Distribution," *J. Tinbergen Selected Papers*, Amsterdam: North-Holland.

TIROLE, J., 1988. "The Multicontract Organization," *Canadian Journal of Economics*, 21(3), pp. 459–66.

TODARO, M., 1968. "The Urban Employment Problem in Less Developed Countries An Analysis of Demand and Supply," *Yale Economic Essays*, 8(2), pp. 331–402.

—————— 1969. "A Model of Labor Migration and Urban Unemployment in Less Developed Countries," *American Economic Review*, 59(1), pp. 138–48.

TOWNSEND, R., 1979. "Optimal Contracts and Competitive Markets with Costly State Verification," *Journal of Economic Theory*, 21(2), pp. 265–93.

TVERSKY, A. and D. KAHNEMAN, 1974. "Judgment under Uncertainty: Heuristics and Biases," *Science*, 185(4157), pp. 1124–31.

—— R. H. THALER, 1990. "Anomalies: Preference Reversals," *Journal of Economic Perspectives*, 4(2), pp. 210–11.

UZAWA, H., 1965. "Optimum Technical Change in an Aggregative Model of Economic Growth," *International Economic Review*, 6(1), pp. 18–31.

—— J. E. STIGLITZ, 1969. *Readings in the Theory of Economic Growth*, Cambridge, MA: MIT Press.

VALE, B., 1986. "Effects of Bank Reserve Requirements with 'Grey' Credit Markets Under Asymmetric Information," mimeo No. 15, University of Oslo.

VAN DAMME, E., 1987. *Stability and Perfection of Nash Equilibria*, Berlin: Springer Verlag.

VARIAN, H., 1980. "A Model of Sales," *American Economic Review*, 70(4), pp. 651–9.

—— 1990. "Monitoring Agents with Other Agents," *Journal of Institutional and Theoretical Economics*, 146, pp. 153–74.

VICKREY, W., 1962 [1994]. "Auctions and Bidding Games," in R. Arnott et al. (eds). *Public Economics: Selected Papers by William Vickrey*, New York and Melbourne: Cambridge University Press, pp. 85–98 (reprinted from *Recent Advances in Game Theory*, Princeton, NJ: Princeton University Press, 1962).

—— 1995. "Counterspeculation, Auctions, and Competitive Sealed Tenders," *The Economics of Information*, D. Levine and S. Lippman, (eds.), Aldershot, UK: Elgar, pp. 15–44.

VISSER, B., 1998. "Binary Decision Structures and the Required Detail of Information," Working Paper No. 8911, Economic Department, European University Institute.

VON ZUR MUEHLEN, P., 1976. Sequential Search and Price Dispersion in Monopolistic Competition," Federal Reserve Board, St Louis.

WALDMAN M., 1984. "Job Assignments, Signaling and Efficiency," *Rand Journal of Economics*, 15(2), pp. 255–67.

WALLACE, N., 1981. "A Modigliani-Miller Theorem for Open Market Operations," *American Economic Review*, 71(3), pp. 267–74.

WEBER, M., 1925. *The Protestant Ethic and the Spirit of Capitalism*, New York: Scribner.

WEIBULL, J. W. 1996. *Evolutionary Game Theory*, Cambridge, MA: MIT Press.

WEISS, A., 1976. "A Theory of Limited Labor Markets," PhD dissertation, Stanford University.

—— 1980. "Job Queues and Layoffs in Labor Markets with Flexible Wages," *Journal of Political Economy*, 88(3), pp. 526–38.

—— 1985. "Education as a Test," *Economics of Education* Review, 4(2), pp. 123–8.

—— 1983. "A Sorting-cum-Learning Model of Education," *Journal of Political Economy*, 91(3), pp. 420–42.

—— 1990. *Efficiency Wages: Models of Unemployment, Layoffs and Wage Dispersion*, Princeton: Princeton University Press.

—— 1995. "Human Capital vs. Signaling Explanation of Wages and Sorting Models of Education and Training," *Journal of Economic Perspectives*, 9(4), pp. 133–54.

—— G. NIKITIN, 1998. "Performance of Czech Companies by Ownership Structure," Boston University Institute for Economic Development Discussion Paper Series No. 85.

—— J. E. STIGLITZ, 1981. "Credit Rationing in Markets with Imperfect Information," *American Economic Review*, 71(3), pp. 393–410.

—— 1983. "Incentive Effects of Terminations: Applications to the Credit and Labor Markets," American Economic Review, 73(5), pp. 912–27.

——1986. "Credit Rationing and Collateral," in J. Edwards et al. (eds.), *Recent Developments in Corporate Finance*, New York: Cambridge University Press, pp. 101–35.

WEISSKOPF, T. E., S. BOWLES, and D. M. GORDON, 1983. "Hearts and Minds: A Social Model of US Productivity Growth," *Brookings Papers on Economic Activity*, 2, pp. 381–441.

WEIZÄCKER, VON, C., 1966. "Tentative Notes on a Two-Sector Model with Induced Technical Progress," *Review of Economic Studies*, 33(3), pp. 245–51.

WERIN, L. and H. WIJKANDER (eds.), 1992. *Contract Economics*, Oxford: Blackwell Publishers.

WESSELS, W. J., 1979. "The Contribution by Firms to Unemployment: A Dynamic Model," *Southern Economic Journal*, 45(4), pp. 1130–50.

——1986. "The Uses and Limits of Unemployment as a Disciplining Device in the Efficiency Wage Model," mimeo, North Carolina State University.

WESTHOFF, F. H., 1974. "The Theory of Local Public Goods," PhD thesis, Yale University.

WETTE, H., 1983. "Collateral in Credit Rationing in Markets with Imperfect Information: Note," *American Economic Review*, 73(3), pp. 442–5.

WHITESIDE, H. D., 1974. "Wages: An Equity Approach," *Journal of Behavioral Economics*, 3(1), pp. 64–84.

WILLIAMSON, J. (ed.), 1990. "What Washington Means by Policy Reform," *Latin American Adjustment: How Much Has Happened?* Institute of International Economics, Washington, DC, April.

WILLIAMSON, O. E., 1979. "Transactions–Cost Economics: The Governance of Contractual Relations," *Journal of Law and Economics*, 22, pp. 233–61.

——1985. *The Economic Institutions of Capitalism*, New York: The Free Press.

——S. MASTEN (eds.), 1999. *The Economics of Transaction Costs*, Williston, VT: American International Distribution Corporation.

WILSON, C., 1973. "An Analysis of Simple Insurance Markets with Imperfect Differentiation of Consumers," mimeo, University of Rochester.

——1976. "Equilibrium in a Class of Self-Selection Models," PhD thesis, University of Rochester.

——1977. "A Model of Insurance Markets with Incomplete Information," *Journal of Economic Theory*, 16(2), pp. 167–207.

——1979. "Equilibrium and Adverse Selection," *American Economic Review*, 69(2), pp. 313–17.

——1980. "The Nature of Equilibrium in Markets with Adverse Selection," *Bell Journal of Economics*, 11(1), pp. 108–30.

WILSON, R., 1969. "Competitive Bidding with Disparate Information," *Management Science*, 15(7), pp. 446–8.

——1977. "A Bidding Model of Perfect Competition," *Review of Economic Studies*, 44(3), pp. 511–18.

WINTER, S. G., 1964. "Economic 'Natural Selection' and the Theory of the Firm," *Yale Economic Essays*, 4(1), pp. 225–72.

——1971. "Satisficing, Selection, and the Innovating Remnant," *Quarterly Journal of Economics*, 85(2), pp. 237–61.

WOJNILOWER, A., 1980. "The Central Role of Credit Crunches in Recent Financial History," *Brookings Papers on Economic Activity*, 2, pp. 277–326.

WOODFORD, M., 1988. "Expectations, Finance and Aggregate Instability," in M. Kohn and S, C. Tsiang (eds.), *Financial Constraints, Expectations, and Macroeconomics*, Oxford: Clarendon Press.

World Bank, 1993. *The East Asian Miracle*, Washington, DC: World Bank.

——1996. *World Development Report 1996: From Plan to Market*, Washington, DC: World Bank.

——1998. *Global Economic Prospects and the Developing Countries 1998/1999: Beyond Financial Crisis*, Washington, DC: World Bank.

——1999a. *Global Economic Prospects and the Developing Countries 2000*, Washington, DC: World Bank.

——1999b. *Knowledge for Development: 1998/99 World Development Report*, Washington, DC: World Bank.

——2002. *Building Institutions for Markets: 2001/02 World Development Report*, Washington, DC: World Bank.

YABUSHITA, S., 1983. "Theory of Screening and the Behavior of the Firm: Comment," *American Economic Review*, 73(1), pp. 242–245.

YELLEN, J., 1984. "Efficiency Wage Models of Unemployment," *American Economic Review*, 74(2), pp. 200–5.

YOON, C., 1984a. "A Reexamination of the Theory of Credit Rationing," mimeo, Stanford University.

——1984b. "On the Theory of Credit Rationing: Further Analysis," mimeo, Stanford University.

YOUNG, M., 1958. *The Rise of the Meritocracy*, Baltimore.

ZAMAN, H. 1998. "Who Benefits and to What Extent? An Evaluation of BRAC's Micro-Credit Program," DPhil thesis, University of Sussex.

ZINGALES, L., 1994. "The Value of the Voting Right: A Study of the Milan Stock Exchange Experience," *Review of Financial Studies*, 7(1), pp. 125–48.

Index of Names

Index of Subjects